기출하프 + 파생하프 + 복습모의고사

성정혜 기적사
하프 모의고사

— 퀵스타트편 —

Question

Miracle Routine

결국엔 성정혜 영어 하프모의고사 기적사

INTRO 들어가며

기적사는 수험생이 아닌 합격생을 만듭니다.
시험장에서의 확실한 출력을 위한 객관적 모의고사

- **합격생 추천 1위**

    수많은 합격생들이 엄지를 들어 올리며 추천하는 기적사의 본질은 교재나 강의가 아닙니다.
    합격으로 가는 시스템입니다.
    매일 10문항, 기적사는 개인의 의견이 아닌 객관적인 기출 DATA로 무장했습니다. 당신이
    노베이스에서 시작할지라도 매일 책상을 향해 몸을 당기게 하는, 나의 노력이 바로 다음날
    반영될 수 있도록 설계되었습니다.

- **주관이 아닌 객관을 담은 5일 반복 시스템**

    사실의 반대는 거짓이 아닌 의견입니다.
    기적사는 철저하게 개인의 의견을 배제하였습니다.
    기출문제의 객관적인 사실을 철저하게 분석하고 수치화해 설계한 문항이 수록되어있습니다.
    세상에 모의고사는 많습니다. 하지만 기적사는 무작위로 문항이 반복되지 않습니다.
    기출문제를 기반으로 출제 포인트가 주 5회 반복되도록 구성되어 실전 난도부터 시작해 점점
    난도가 높아지도록 설계되었습니다. 이는 시험장에서 어떠한 빈틈이나 매력적인 오답에도
    수험생이 흔들리지 않고 정답만을 마킹하게 하기 위함입니다.

- **기적사**

    기출을 적용해 합격으로 가는 길이 바로 '기적사'입니다.
    기적은 알아서 찾아오는 것이 아니라, 내가 끝내 찾아가는 것임을 지금 이 글을 마주하는
    당신은 알고 있습니다. 우리는 기적을 찾아 수많은 날을 책상 앞에서 잠과 사투할 것이고,
    피곤함을 이기고 책을 펼쳐낼 것입니다. 우리가 매일 함께하는 모든 하루의 끝에 바라는
    결과가 있음을 알기에 오늘도 기적사와 함께 성실한 하루를 보낼 당신께 경의를 표합니다.

    성정혜

System 기적사 시스템

• 회차별 구성

- Day 1: 핵심 기출 하프
- Day 2: 기출 파생 신출 하프 1
- Day 3: 기출 파생 신출 하프 2
- Day 4: 기출 파생 신출 하프 3
- Day 5: 기출 파생 신출 하프 4
- 동형: 복습 동형 모의고사

[Day별 구성]

어휘 3 + 생활영어 1 + 문법 3
+ 독해 3 = 10문항

[1세트]

핵심 기출 하프 1회
+ 기출 파생 신출 하프 4회
→ 총 12세트, 60회 구성
+ 동형 복습 모의고사 6회

• 회차별 특징

- **기출 하프 모의고사** : 방대한 기출 DATA에서 핵심 기출만 뽑아 구성된 하프 모의고사입니다.

- **기출 파생 하프 모의고사** : 기출 하프에서 학습한 핵심 출제포인트를 담아 파생 제작한 신출 하프 모의고사입니다. 기출 주요 포인트를 신출 문제로 반복 학습해 핵심 기출 포인트 반복 학습과 동시에 신규 문항에 포인트를 적용하는 훈련까지 할 수 있습니다.

- **동형 복습 모의고사** : 10회차의 하프 모의고사에서 오답률이 가장 높았던 문항과 꼭 다시 풀어봐야하는 문항을 20문항 선별해 동형 모의고사로 구성하였습니다. 무작위로 많은 양의 문제를 푸는 것이 아닌 출제포인트와 함께 최적의 문항들로 복습할 수 있도록 구성하였습니다.

결국엔 성정혜 영어 하프모의고사 기적사

Structure 교재 구성

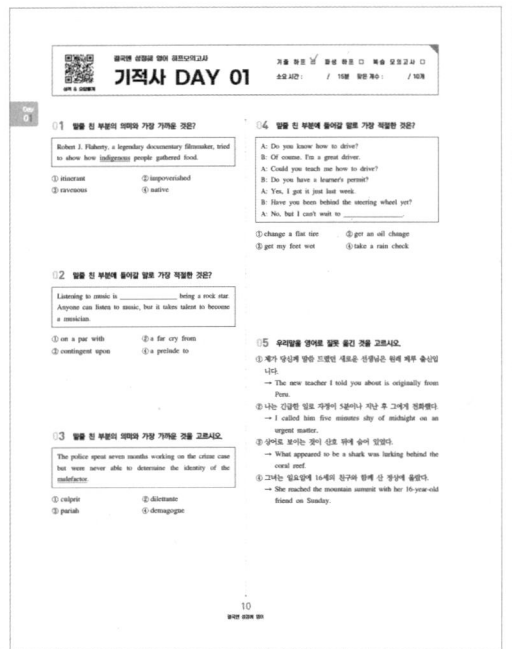
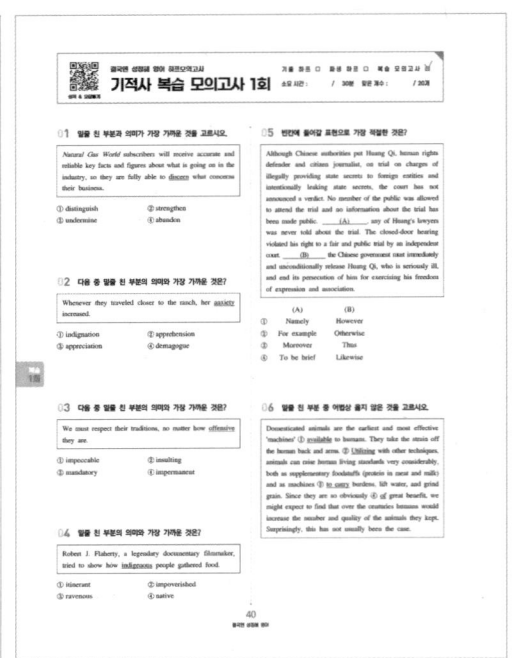

3·3·3·1 + 복습모의고사, 실전에 강한 균형 잡힌 학습

어휘 3문항, 생활영어 1문항, 문법 3문항, 독해 3문항으로 구성해 영어 전 영역을 균형 있게 학습할 수 있도록 배치하였습니다. 핵심 기출 문제, 핵심 기출 포인트를 반복 학습할 수 있는 기출 파생 문제, 그리고 실시간 성적&오답률 통계로 강점은 더욱 강화하고 약점은 확실하게 보완할 수 있습니다. 또한 10회차 단위로 구성된 복습 모의고사를 20문항으로 구성하여 실전 시험에서의 적응력을 높일 수 있도록 구성하였습니다.

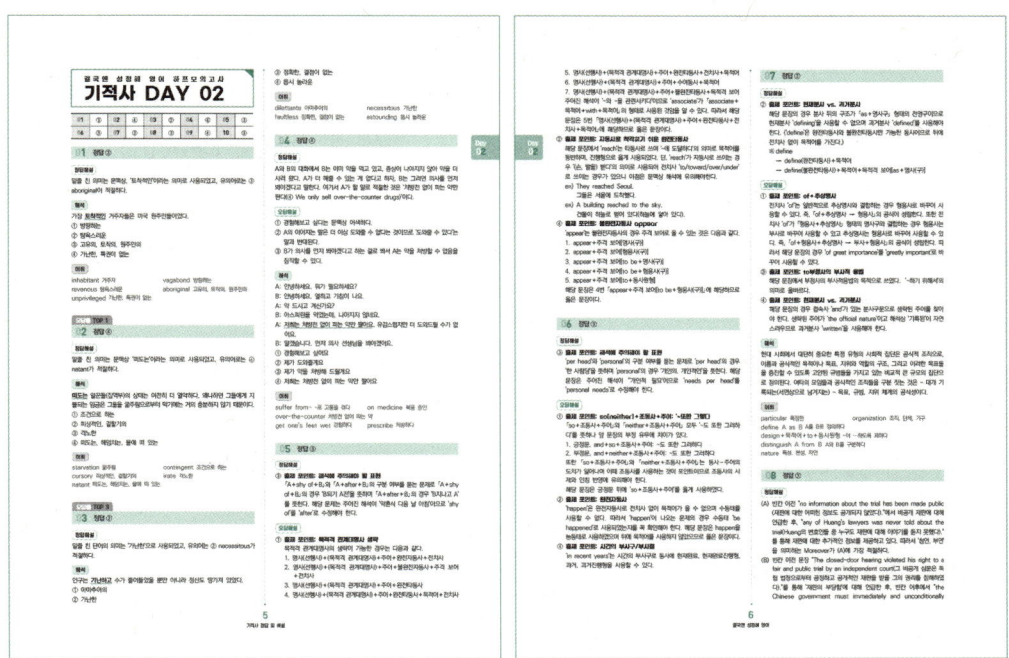

친절&꼼꼼한 해설 + 특별 부록 어휘 Handbook까지

효율적인 개인 학습을 위해 꼼꼼하고 상세한 해설을 담았습니다. 어휘와 생활영어는 핵심 어휘와 관용 표현을 함께 정리하였습니다. 문법은 출제포인트를 먼저 제시하여 학습 방향을 제시하고 정답해설 뿐만 아니라 오답해설까지 상세하고 꼼꼼하게 기재하여 읽는 것만으로도 학습이 될 수 있도록 구성하였습니다. 독해는 해석뿐만 아니라 정답을 찾아가는 과정과 근거를 명확히 제시하여 단순히 문제를 푸는 것이 아닌 논리적 사고력을 향상시킬 수 있도록 하였습니다. 또한 각 문항의 어휘는 특별 부록 Handbook으로 구성하여 어휘만 따로 정리하는 시간을 절약하고 효율적으로 학습할 수 있도록 구성하였습니다.

결국엔 성정혜 영어 하프모의고사 기적사

CONTENTS 목차

기출	기적사 DAY 01	10	기출	기적사 DAY 11	46
파생	기적사 DAY 02	13	파생	기적사 DAY 12	49
파생	기적사 DAY 03	16	파생	기적사 DAY 13	52
파생	기적사 DAY 04	19	파생	기적사 DAY 14	55
파생	기적사 DAY 05	22	파생	기적사 DAY 15	58
기출	기적사 DAY 06	25	기출	기적사 DAY 16	61
파생	기적사 DAY 07	28	파생	기적사 DAY 17	64
파생	기적사 DAY 08	31	파생	기적사 DAY 18	67
파생	기적사 DAY 09	34	파생	기적사 DAY 19	70
파생	기적사 DAY 10	37	파생	기적사 DAY 20	73
동형	복습 모의고사 1회	40	동형	복습 모의고사 2회	76

기출	기적사 DAY 21	82	기출	기적사 DAY 31	118
파생	기적사 DAY 22	85	파생	기적사 DAY 32	121
파생	기적사 DAY 23	88	파생	기적사 DAY 33	124
파생	기적사 DAY 24	91	파생	기적사 DAY 34	127
파생	기적사 DAY 25	94	파생	기적사 DAY 35	130
기출	기적사 DAY 26	97	기출	기적사 DAY 36	133
파생	기적사 DAY 27	100	파생	기적사 DAY 37	136
파생	기적사 DAY 28	103	파생	기적사 DAY 38	139
파생	기적사 DAY 29	106	파생	기적사 DAY 39	142
파생	기적사 DAY 30	109	파생	기적사 DAY 40	145
동형	복습 모의고사 3회	112	동형	복습 모의고사 4회	148

결국엔 성정혜 영어 하프모의고사 기적사

CONTENTS 목차

기출	기적사 DAY 41	154	기출	기적사 DAY 51	190
파생	기적사 DAY 42	157	파생	기적사 DAY 52	193
파생	기적사 DAY 43	160	파생	기적사 DAY 53	196
파생	기적사 DAY 44	163	파생	기적사 DAY 54	199
파생	기적사 DAY 45	166	파생	기적사 DAY 55	202
기출	기적사 DAY 46	169	기출	기적사 DAY 56	205
파생	기적사 DAY 47	172	파생	기적사 DAY 57	208
파생	기적사 DAY 48	175	파생	기적사 DAY 58	211
파생	기적사 DAY 49	178	파생	기적사 DAY 59	214
파생	기적사 DAY 50	181	파생	기적사 DAY 60	217
동형	복습 모의고사 5회	184	동형	복습 모의고사 6회	220

결국엔 성정혜 영어
하프모의고사 기적사

기적은 찾아오는 것이 아니라
내가 찾아가는 것입니다.

기적사 DAY 01

01 밑줄 친 부분의 의미와 가장 가까운 것은?

> Robert J. Flaherty, a legendary documentary filmmaker, tried to show how <u>indigenous</u> people gathered food.

① itinerant　　② impoverished
③ ravenous　　④ native

02 밑줄 친 부분에 들어갈 말로 가장 적절한 것은?

> Listening to music is _____ being a rock star. Anyone can listen to music, but it takes talent to become a musician.

① on a par with　　② a far cry from
③ contingent upon　　④ a prelude to

03 밑줄 친 부분의 의미와 가장 가까운 것을 고르시오.

> The police spent seven months working on the crime case but were never able to determine the identity of the <u>malefactor</u>.

① culprit　　② dilettante
③ pariah　　④ demagogue

04 밑줄 친 부분에 들어갈 말로 가장 적절한 것은?

> A: Do you know how to drive?
> B: Of course. I'm a great driver.
> A: Could you teach me how to drive?
> B: Do you have a learner's permit?
> A: Yes, I got it just last week.
> B: Have you been behind the steering wheel yet?
> A: No, but I can't wait to _____.

① change a flat tire　　② get an oil change
③ get my feet wet　　④ take a rain check

05 우리말을 영어로 잘못 옮긴 것을 고르시오.

① 제가 당신께 말씀 드렸던 새로운 선생님은 원래 페루 출신입니다.
　→ The new teacher I told you about is originally from Peru.
② 나는 긴급한 일로 자정이 5분이나 지난 후 그에게 전화했다.
　→ I called him five minutes shy of midnight on an urgent matter.
③ 상어로 보이는 것이 산호 뒤에 숨어 있었다.
　→ What appeared to be a shark was lurking behind the coral reef.
④ 그녀는 일요일에 16세의 친구와 함께 산 정상에 올랐다.
　→ She reached the mountain summit with her 16-year-old friend on Sunday.

06 우리말을 영어로 잘못 옮긴 것을 고르시오.

① 개인용 컴퓨터를 가장 많이 가지고 있는 나라는 종종 바뀐다.
→ The country with the most computers per person changes from time to time.

② 지난여름 나의 사랑스러운 손자에게 일어난 일은 놀라웠다.
→ What happened to my lovely grandson last summer was amazing.

③ 나무 숟가락은 아이들에게 매우 좋은 장난감이고 플라스틱병 또한 그렇다.
→ Wooden spoons are excellent toys for children, and so are plastic bottles.

④ 나는 은퇴 후부터 내내 이 일을 해 오고 있다.
→ I have been doing this work ever since I retired.

07 밑줄 친 부분 중 어법상 옳지 않은 것을 고르시오.

Domesticated animals are the earliest and most effective 'machines' ① available to humans. They take the strain off the human back and arms. ② Utilizing with other techniques, animals can raise human living standards very considerably, both as supplementary foodstuffs (protein in meat and milk) and as machines ③ to carry burdens, lift water, and grind grain. Since they are so obviously ④ of great benefit, we might expect to find that over the centuries humans would increase the number and quality of the animals they kept. Surprisingly, this has not usually been the case.

08 빈칸에 들어갈 표현으로 가장 적절한 것은?

HUANG QI, who has spent two decades documenting human rights abuses and corruption in China, is now enduring his third term in prison for his efforts. The Chinese penal system has a record of denying proper medical care to prisoners ___(A)___ they die, including Nobel Prize laureate Liu Xiaobo and others. Mr. Huang is now in ill health, and, ___(B)___ activists and his mother, his life is in danger. China should free him for medical care now and not add his name to the rolls of dissidents left to expire in a jail cell.

	(A)	(B)
①	though	without
②	while	with
③	until	according to
④	when	for

09 빈칸에 들어갈 표현으로 가장 적절한 것은?

Stereotypes are one way in which we "define" the world in order to see it. They classify the infinite variety of human beings into a convenient handful of "types" towards whom we learn to act in stereotyped fashion. Life would be a wearing process _____. Stereotypes economize on our mental effort by covering up the blooming, buzzing confusion with big recognizable cut-outs. They save us the "trouble" of finding out what the world is like—they give it its accustomed look.

① if we tried to stick to stereotypes
② if we learned to act in stereotyped fashion
③ if we prejudged people before we ever lay eyes on them
④ if we had to start from scratch with every human contact

10 다음 내용이 포함될 수 있는 글의 종류와 가장 가까운 것은?

Although Cathe did not have PhD students of her own, because she did not hold an academic position while at Haskins, there are many Haskins students who worked closely with her and were influenced by her. During her last, brief hospital stay in late June 2008, she was visited by a group of five current Haskins students and recent PhDs who had never had the opportunity of working with her. Since Cathe's caregivers were absent from the room at that moment, the other patient in the room asked: "So do you all work for her, too?" One of the group, not missing a beat, answered, "No. We are all her students."

① classified ad   ② ordinance
③ play   ④ obituary

01 다음 중 밑줄 친 부분의 의미와 가장 가까운 것은?

> The most indigenous inhabitants were the American Indians.

① vagabond ② ravenous
③ aboriginal ④ unprivileged

02 다음 중 밑줄 친 부분의 의미와 가장 가까운 것은?

> The condition of the itinerant labourers (peons) was still worse; the wages paid them being hardly sufficient to keep them from starvation.

① contingent ② cursory
③ irate ④ natant

03 다음 중 밑줄 친 부분의 의미와 가장 가까운 것은?

> The population was not only impoverished and reduced in numbers but broken in spirit.

① dilettante ② necessitous
③ faultless ④ astounding

04 다음 중 밑줄 친 부분에 들어갈 말로 가장 적절한 것을 고르시오.

> A: Hello, what do you need?
> B: Hello. I'm suffering from fever and coughing.
> A: Are you on medicine?
> B: Yes, I've taken some aspirin, but it didn't help.
> A: _____. I'm afraid I can't help you further.
> B: I see. I should go see a doctor first.

① I'll get my feet wet
② I can give you a hand
③ I'll prescribe you a medicine
④ We only sell over-the-counter drugs

05 우리말을 영어로 잘못 옮긴 것을 고르시오.

① 우리가 잘사는 것과 관련시키는 것들의 목록을 우리가 술술 말할 것이다.
  → We'll reel off a list of things we associate with living well.
② 모든 색들은 동등하게 당신의 눈에 도달하기 때문에 빛은 하얗게 보인다.
  → Light appears white because all colors are equally reaching your eyes.
③ 그의 차는 Tom의 약혼식 다음 날 아침 너희 집 밖에 있었다.
  → His car was outside your house the morning shy of Tom's engagement party.
④ 첫 자극이 되는 것만으로도 주관적 시간의 연장을 유도하기에 충분해 보인다.
  → Just being the first stimulus appears to be sufficient to induce subjective time expansion.

06 우리말을 영어로 잘못 옮긴 것을 고르시오.

① 당신은 테이블 위에 커피를 쏟았고 나 또한 그렇다.
→ You have spilled coffee on the table, and so have I.
② 미래는 아직 일어나지 않았고 단지 하나의 생각일 뿐이다.
→ The future has not happened yet and is only an idea.
③ 탄력근무제는 개인적 필요에 충족하도록 업무시간을 조정하는 것을 직원들에게 허락한다.
→ Flextime allows workers to adjust work hours to suit needs per head.
④ 최근에, 일부 미국인들은 그들의 아이들에게 두 개의 성을 주었다.
→ In recent years, some Americans have been giving their children two last names.

07 밑줄 친 부분 중 어법상 옳지 않은 것을 고르시오.

A particular kind of social group that is ① of great importance in modern society is the formal organization, which is ② defining as a relatively large-scale group having a name, some official purpose or goals, a structure of statuses and roles, and a set of rules designed ③ to promote these goals. What distinguishes formal organizations from other kinds of groups is the official — and usually ④ written — nature of the goals, rules, and status structure.

08 빈칸에 들어갈 표현으로 가장 적절한 것은?

Although Chinese authorities put Huang Qi, human rights defender and citizen journalist, on trial on charges of illegally providing state secrets to foreign entities and intentionally leaking state secrets, the court has not announced a verdict. No member of the public was allowed to attend the trial and no information about the trial has been made public. ____(A)____, any of Huang's lawyers was never told about the trial. The closed-door hearing violated his right to a fair and public trial by an independent court. ____(B)____ the Chinese government must immediately and unconditionally release Huang Qi, who is seriously ill, and end its persecution of him for exercising his freedom of expression and association.

	(A)	(B)
①	Namely	However
②	For example	Otherwise
③	Moreover	Thus
④	To be brief	Likewise

09 빈칸에 들어갈 표현으로 가장 적절한 것은?

Stereotypes are widely circulated oversimplifications of a group of people, whereas generalizations can not only be based on widely-accepted factors, but also on personal experience. In the U.S., certain racial groups have been linked to stereotypes such as being good at math or athletics. These are so well-known that the average American would not hesitate if asked to identify which racial group excels in basketball. That is, when one stereotypes something, one repeats the cultural mythology already present in society. On the other hand, a person can make a generalization that has not been perpetuated in society. For example, someone who meets a few individuals from a country and finds them to be friendly and cheerful may say all citizens of the country are friendly and cheerful. To be brief, _____.

① stereotypes are mostly rooted in personal experience unlike generalizations
② there is much debate over the roles stereotypes and generalizations play in society
③ generalizations as well as stereotypes enable people to respond rapidly to new situations
④ while all stereotypes are generalizations, not all generalizations are necessarily stereotypes

10 다음 내용이 포함될 수 있는 글의 종류와 가장 가까운 것은?

Peter graduated from Rootstown High School in 1974. He was always a hard worker with his first job at Beefy Cow's when he was fifteen years old. He worked for Schnell Scientific Services in Ravenna for many years and with Global Synthetic Rubber for the past twenty-three years. Peter is giving life with saving at least three others as an organ donor. He was always willing to help the others and his family whenever asked. He was very generous with his nieces and nephews and was niece Victoria's guardian. He was never mean or spiteful to anyone but he sure talked a big story! He loved camping with his friends and always had stories about each trip.

① reference letter   ② autobiography
③ obituary   ④ journal

01 다음 중 밑줄 친 부분의 의미와 가장 가까운 것은?

It was thick and slightly sweet in her mouth and made her ravenous.

① inadvertent ② allusive
③ insatiable   ④ uneven

02 다음 중 밑줄 친 부분의 의미와 가장 가까운 것은?

The native costumes is a far cry from ours.

① common   ② naive
③ indigenous   ④ candid

03 다음 중 밑줄 친 부분의 의미와 가장 가까운 것은?

The best of the New South Wales diamonds are harder and much whiter than the South African diamonds, and are classified as on a par with the best Brazilian gems, but any large specimens have not yet been found.

① far removed from   ② on equal terms with
③ on the spot   ④ being bombarded with

04 밑줄 친 부분에 들어갈 말로 적절한 것을 고르시오.

A: That faucet in my apartment is still dripping. I thought you said you were going to fix it.
B: Oh, you're right. The washer needs replacing.
A: Why don't you replace it then?
B: _____. I think you'd better call a plumber as soon as possible.

① It cuts corners
② I come to terms with it
③ You drop him a line about it
④ That is easier said than done

05 우리말을 영어로 잘못 옮긴 것을 고르시오.

① 우리가 받았던 제의는 한나절을 쉬는 것이었다.
→ The proposition we received was to take a half-day off.
② 몽골인들이 그들의 적들에게 더 무섭게 보인다.
→ The Mongols appeared more frightening to their enemies.
③ Marco Polo는 종이의 중요한 발명에 대해 언급하고 있지 않다.
→ Marco Polo does not mention about the important invention of paper.
④ 그녀는 자신의 20번째 생일 일주일 전에 결혼했다.
→ She was one week shy of her twentieth birthday when she got married.

06 우리말을 영어로 잘못 옮긴 것을 고르시오.

① 지난주 이후 그 문제를 곰곰이 생각하는 중이다.
→ I've been chewing the problem over since last week.

② 무엇이 발생했든지 간에, 그 경험은 그를 방해했다.
→ Whatever happened, the experience disturbed him.

③ Tom은 그녀가 했던 말을 믿지 않았고, 경찰들도 그러했다.
→ Tom didn't believe a word she said, and neither did the police.

④ 대학에는 개인적 문제를 가진 학생들을 돕기 위해 상담 전문가가 있다.
→ The college now has a counsellor to help students with problems per person.

07 밑줄 친 부분 중 어법상 옳지 않은 것을 고르시오.

Modern economies rely on the ability ① to move goods, people, and information safely and reliably. Adding to their importance is ② that many of the lifeline systems serve vital roles in disaster recovery. Consequently, it is ③ of equal importance to government, business, and the public at large that the flow of services ④ providing by a nation's infrastructure continues unimpeded in the face of a broad range of natural and technological hazards.

08 주어진 문장이 들어갈 위치로 가장 적절한 것은?

Although this social contract theory appears to be perfect in every respect yet he did not say anything about the legal sovereign.

John Locke seems to be the first philosopher to introduce a new element in the field of Political Science: the consent or the will of the people. (①) A government can remain in power and be strong so long as it enjoys the support of the people or governs in accordance with the will of the people. (②) In this way Locke gave the theory of limited sovereignty or constitutional government. (③) If the government fails to protect the life, liberty and property of the people, the people have the right to remove it and appoint a new government. (④) Besides, he failed to understand that revolution is desirable but it is also dangerous and under normal circumstances illegal.

09 주어진 문장 다음에 이어질 글의 순서로 가장 적절한 것은?

Empiricists have always claimed that sense experience is the ultimate starting point for all our knowledge.

(A) On the contrary, rationalists have claimed that the ultimate starting point for all knowledge is not the senses but reason.
(B) They maintain the senses give us all our raw data about the world, and without this raw material, there would be no knowledge at all. That is, perception starts a process, and from this process come all our beliefs.
(C) In its purest form, the theory holds that sense experience alone gives birth to all our beliefs and all our knowledge. A classic example of an empiricist is the British philosopher John Locke.

① (B) − (A) − (C)
② (B) − (C) − (A)
③ (A) − (B) − (C)
④ (A) − (C) − (B)

10 빈칸에 들어갈 표현으로 가장 적절한 것은?

According to Locke, land has the special character that when demand is high, supply is low, and vice versa. Demand for land is high when trade and manufacturing thrive, because profits are high and men are looking for alternative ways of investing their profits, but in that case, land being owned by that sort of industrial and thriving men, _____.
The assumption underlying Locke's analysis of the price of land is that land is not simply an alternative investment opportunity whose return will eventually equal the return on other investments.

① the price of land declines as a result
② restrictions on investments in land are needed
③ there will be more land thrown into the market
④ they have neither need nor will to sell their lands

01 다음 중 밑줄 친 부분의 의미와 가장 가까운 것은?

There are also extra charges under contingent regulations of great complexity, which are commonly added on to the bill.

① being subject to ② itinerant
③ juratory ④ vehement

02 다음 중 밑줄 친 부분의 의미와 가장 가까운 것은?

This victory was to be the prelude to new dangers.

① distress ② delegate
③ austerity ④ omen

03 다음 중 밑줄 친 부분의 의미와 가장 가까운 것은?

Dean tried hard to exclude Jennifer Radisson from consideration as a malefactor, although he reluctantly admitted his sole reason to pass on her as a suspect was his belief in her story.

① perpetrator ② deputy
③ anonymousness ④ principal

04 밑줄 친 부분에 들어갈 말로 가장 적절한 것을 고르시오.

A: I don't speak English very well.
B: What?
A: I said that I don't speak English very well.
B: I'm sorry. I'm having a hard time understanding you.
A: My English is not good.
B: Oh, I see. Yeah. I know.
A: _____
B: Sorry. What you said would be against the rules.

① So what about you?
② So do you get cold feet?
③ So can you give me a break?
④ So do you come out of your shell?

05 우리말을 영어로 잘못 옮긴 것을 고르시오.

① 당신이 지난주에 산 차를 보고 싶다.
   → I'd like to see the car you bought last week.
② 모든 원소 중에서 가장 찾기 힘든 원소는 프란슘인 것으로 보인다.
   → The most elusive element of all appears to be francium.
③ 멀리 떨어진 두 명의 독자가 동일한 책을 의논할 수 있게 되었다.
   → Two readers separated by distance could discuss identical books.
④ 눈물 없는 장례식은 오직 죽음 이후 2년이 될 때까지 의식을 연기하여야만 가능하다.
   → Tearless funeral is made possible only by postponing the rite until two years shy of the death.

06 우리말을 영어로 잘못 옮긴 것을 고르시오.

① John은 그 사고를 보지 못했고 Mary도 또한 그러했다.
→ John didn't see the accident and so did Mary.

② 유사성은 같은 집단의 일부가 되는 것으로 구성될 수 있다.
→ Similarity can consist of being part of the same group.

③ 개인적 경험상 네가 Tom을 신뢰할 수 없다는 것을 안다.
→ I know from personal experience that you can't trust Tom.

④ 그것은 세상에 알려진 이후로 사람들의 삶을 간소화 시키고 있다.
→ It has been simplifying the lives of people since its introduction to the world.

07 밑줄 친 부분 중 어법상 옳지 않은 것을 고르시오.

The American Academy of Pediatrics advises its members ① to reduce bad behavior by giving children timeouts, taking away privileges, or using discipline chairs. "Corporal punishment is of limited ② effective and has potentially deleterious side effects," reads its policy, set in 1998. The latest study on the effects of spanking, ③ released in September by the University of Michigan School of Social Work, found even "minimal amounts" of spanking ④ led to more antisocial behavior in children.

08 다음 글의 제목으로 가장 적절한 것은?

Though cookie files are quite small, they can still build up and slow down your system performance. By taking the time to delete the cookies, you can increase the speed and performance of your web browsing software. Doing so on a regular basis will also free space on your hard drive and prevent system crashes which often happen when your computer doesn't have sufficient space. While many cookies are harmless, moreover, others can be used to track your every move on the Internet. Businesses often use these tracking cookies to study consumer behavior, but many computer users consider them an invasion of privacy. By setting your web browser to delete cookies each time you close your browser, you can thwart these tracking attempts and reduce the risk of a security breach.

① Threats of Internet Cookies
② How Cookies Invade Privacy?
③ Benefits of Removing Cookies
④ Pros and Cons of Using Cookies

09 밑줄 친 부분 중 글의 흐름상 가장 어색한 것은?

Cookies are pieces of information generated by a web server or web hosting sites and stored in the user's computer, ready for future access. ① The first batch of cookies were originally cooked up as simple mechanism to help make it easier for users to access their favorite Web sites without having to go through a lengthy process of identifying themselves every time they visit. ② For example, upon your first visit to a given site, you may be asked to reveal your name and perhaps even some personal or financial information required to gain access to that site in the future. ③ Because cookies contain such information, the use of them on sites raises a number of privacy concerns. ④ The site will then place a cookie containing this information on your system. And when you return it will request information based on the cookie to determine who you are and whether you have authorization to access the site.

10 빈칸 (A), (B)에 들어갈 표현으로 가장 적절한 것은?

"Claims made by privacy activists over recent months that cookies have the potential to be used by website operators to spy on Internet users or to deliver harmful code to their computers are ____(A)____." the U.S. Department of Energy's Computer Incident Advisory Capability said in an information bulletin issued Friday. Web cookies are popularly seen as programs that can scan a hard drive and gather information about the computer's user, and such information allegedly includes passwords, credit card numbers, and a list of the software on your computer. According to the bulletin, none of these are close to the truth. Information gathered using cookies can also be recorded in Web servers' log files. Cookies just make it ____(B)____. A server cannot find out your name or e-mail address, or anything about your computer using cookies.

	(A)	(B)
①	incorrect	easier
②	inaccurate	further
③	proven	simpler
④	widespread	slower

기적사 DAY 05

01 다음 중 밑줄 친 부분의 의미와 가장 가까운 것은?

Betsy read a notice on the Internet a day later that the <u>culprit</u> was beaten and in serious condition, after allegedly resisting arrest.

① purgee ② fatality
③ criminal ④ fledgling

02 다음 중 밑줄 친 부분의 의미와 가장 가까운 것은?

Their continued existence as a <u>pariah</u> class after the Exile would be a perpetual reminder of the dangers and degradation of the most popular Syrian creed.

① refugee ② villain
③ casualty ④ par

03 다음 중 밑줄 친 부분의 의미와 가장 가까운 것은?

Whenever they traveled closer to the ranch, her <u>anxiety</u> increased.

① indignation ② apprehension
③ appreciation ④ demagogue

04 밑줄 친 부분에 들어갈 말로 가장 적절한 것은?

A: Can I speak to Mrs. TJ?
B: She is not here at the moment.
A: Is she gone for the day?
B: No. not yet _____.

① She's just stepped out
② She makes up with you
③ She always burns her bridges
④ She burns the candle at both ends

05 우리말을 영어로 잘못 옮긴 것을 고르시오.

① 그는 자신의 95번째 생일 이틀 전에 죽었다.
→ He died two days shy of his 95th birthday.
② 그보다 용감한 군인이 없다는 Jack 대장이 여기에 있다.
→ Here is Captain Jack than there is no braver soldier.
③ 소녀들은 다른 이들보다 나아 보이기 위해서 노력하는 또래들을 비난한다.
→ Girls criticize peers who try to appear better than others.
④ 과학자들이 인간 배아를 변형하였을 때 우리는 인종으로서 새로운 국면에 진입했다.
→ We entered a new phase as a species when scientists altered a human embryo.

06 우리말을 영어로 잘못 옮긴 것을 고르시오.

① 그녀는 감명받지 못했고, 나 또한 그러했다.
　→ She wasn't impressed, and neither was I.
② 우리는 2시 이후로 여기에서 기다리는 중이다.
　→ We've been waiting here since two o'clock.
③ 범죄의 대부분은 소매치기로 구성된다.
　→ The majority of the crimes are consisted of pick-pocketing.
④ 모든 개인 소지품은 소유주의 이름이 분명하게 표시되어 있어야 한다.
　→ All personal belongings should be clearly marked with the owner's name.

07 밑줄 친 부분 중 어법상 옳지 않은 것을 고르시오.

The modern borderline between childhood and adult life provided by education is of little ① help to us for much of the 19th century. Many young men in the schools for the rich were ② receiving full-time education at an age ③ which their poor contemporaries had been at work for ten years. Indeed, throughout these years, children at work were as common as they are today in poor countries and, for much of the period, working children were thought ④ to be economically important.

08 빈칸에 들어갈 표현으로 가장 적절한 것은?

What is known to us as metaphysics is what Aristotle called the "first philosophy." Metaphysics involves a study of the universal principles of being, the abstract qualities of existence itself. Perhaps the starting point of Aristotle's metaphysics is his _____ of Plato's Theory of Forms. In Plato's theory, material objects are changeable and not real in themselves; rather, they correspond to an ideal, eternal, and immutable Form by a common name, and this Form can be perceived only by the intellect. Thus a thing perceived to be beautiful in this world is in fact an imperfect manifestation of the Form of Beauty. Aristotle's arguments against this theory were numerous. Ultimately he denied Plato's ideas as poetic but empty language; as a scientist and empiricist he preferred to focus on the reality of the material world.

① rejection　　② detestation
③ admiration　　④ development

09 밑줄 친 부분 중 글의 흐름상 가장 어색한 것은?

The ancient Greeks such as Aristotle believed there were four elements that everything was made up of: earth, water, air, and fire. ① The idea that these four elements made up all matter was the cornerstone of philosophy, science, and medicine for long. ② The four elements were even used to describe the four temperaments a person could have, and Hippocrates used the four elements to describe the four "humors" found in the body. ③ These theories stated the temperaments and humors needed to be in balance with each other for a person to be well both mentally and physically. ④ Aristotle suggested there was a fifth element, aether, because it seemed strange that the stars would be made out of earthly elements. While now we know these previous theories are false, in a way the four elements do align with the four states of matter on which modern science has agreed: solid (earth), liquid (water), gas (air), and plasma (fire).

10 다음 글의 내용과 일치하는 것은?

The scientific revolution laid the foundations for the Age of Enlightenment and science came to play a leading role in Enlightenment discourse and thought. Many Enlightenment writers and thinkers had backgrounds in the sciences, and associated scientific advancement with the overthrow of religion and traditional authority, which had oppressed science, in favor of the development of free speech and thought. Broadly speaking, Enlightenment science greatly valued empiricism and rational thought, and was embedded with the Enlightenment ideal of advancement and progress. At the time, science was dominated by scientific societies and academies, which had largely replaced universities as centers of scientific research and development. Societies and academies were also the backbone of the maturation of the scientific profession. Another important development was the popularization of science among an increasingly literate population.

① The Enlightenment led the scientific revolution.
② Enlightenment thinkers highly regarded religious beliefs.
③ During the Age of Enlightenment, the freedom of speech and thought was curbed.
④ The Enlightenment caused traditional authority to lose its dominance over science.

01 밑줄 친 부분과 의미가 가장 가까운 것을 고르시오.

Natural Gas World subscribers will receive accurate and reliable key facts and figures about what is going on in the industry, so they are fully able to discern what concerns their business.

① distinguish   ② strengthen
③ undermine   ④ abandon

02 밑줄 친 부분과 의미가 가장 가까운 것을 고르시오.

Ms. West, the winner of the silver in the women's 1,500m event, stood out through the race.

① was overwhelmed   ② was impressive
③ was depressed   ④ was optimistic

03 밑줄 친 부분의 의미와 가장 가까운 것을 고르시오.

Schooling is compulsory for all children in the United States, but the age range for which school attendance is required varies from state to state.

① complementary   ② systematic
③ mandatory   ④ innovative

04 밑줄 친 부분에 들어갈 말로 가장 적절한 것은?

A: Would you like to try some dim sum?
B: Yes, thank you. They look delicious. What's inside?
A: These have pork and chopped vegetables, and those have shrimps.
B: And, um, _____?
A: You pick one up with your chopsticks like this and dip it into the sauce. It's easy.
B: Okay. I'll give it a try.

① how much are they   ② how do I eat them
③ how spicy are they   ④ how do you cook them

05 밑줄 친 부분 중 어법상 옳지 않은 것을 고르시오.

It would be difficult ① to imagine life without the beauty and richness of forests. But scientists warn we cannot take our forest for ② granted. By some estimates, deforestation ③ has been resulted in the loss of as much as eighty percent of the natural forests of the world. Currently, deforestation is a global problem, ④ affecting wilderness regions such as the temperate rainforests of the Pacific.

06 밑줄 친 부분 중 어법상 옳지 않은 것을 고르시오.

Focus means ① getting stuff done. A lot of people have great ideas but don't act on them. For me, the definition of an entrepreneur, for instance, is someone who can combine innovation and ingenuity with the ability to execute that new idea. Some people think that the central dichotomy in life is whether you're positive or negative about the issues ② that interest or concern you. There's a lot of attention ③ paying to this question of whether it's better to have an optimistic or pessimistic lens. I think the better question to ask is whether you are going to do something about it or just ④ let life pass you by.

07 우리말을 영어로 잘못 옮긴 것을 고르시오.

① 그 연사는 자기 생각을 청중에게 전달하는 데 능숙하지 않았다.
  → The speaker was not good at getting his ideas across to the audience.
② 서울의 교통체증은 세계 어느 도시보다 심각하다.
  → The traffic jams in Seoul are more serious than those in any other city in the world.
③ 네가 말하고 있는 사람과 시선을 마주치는 것은 서양 국가에서 중요하다.
  → Making eye contact with the person you are speaking to is important in western countries.
④ 그는 사람들이 생각했던 만큼 인색하지 않았다는 것이 드러났다.
  → It turns out that he was not so stingier as he was thought to be.

08 빈칸에 들어갈 문장으로 가장 적절한 것은?

Many people are risk-averse because they consider the negative consequences of failure to outweigh the reward of success. Our culture of looking down on failure makes us even less likely to risk our necks. _____. Progress and innovation are inextricably entwined with risk and failure.

① But we should not underestimate the importance of experimenting and taking risks, especially in these turbulent economic times
② But many organizations suffer from 'corporate anorexia nervosa' and have an unfavorable climate for enterprising people
③ That is why we need a paradigm shift marking a transition to a future
④ That is why combinatoric innovation is not an efficient process

09 빈칸에 들어갈 표현으로 가장 적절한 것은?

Human nature has many curious traits, but one of the most curious is _____. No one thinks it a fine thing to have a motor car that is perpetually going out of order: people do not boast that after a long run their car is completely useless for several weeks, or that it is perpetually developing strange troubles which even the most skillful mechanics cannot put right. Yet that is how people feel about their own bodies. To have a body that does its work satisfactorily is felt to be uninteresting and rather plebeian. A delicate digestion is almost indispensable in the equipment of a fine lady. I am aware in myself of the impulses to boast of illness: I have only been ill once, but I like people to know how very ill I was that once, and I feel vexed when I come across other people who have been more nearly dead without dying

① fear of diseases
② interests in motor cars
③ pride in illness
④ phobia of death

10 빈칸에 들어갈 표현으로 가장 적절한 것은?

In the huge, open lands of the American west, herding cattle is one way to make a living. The image of the cowboy on his horse is a familiar one, but in reality, women also participate in ranch work. This reality can be seen in the rodeo, where cowboys and cowgirls compete in roping young steers, and riding adult bulls. Throwing a rope around a steer is something ranchers must do in order to give the young animals medicine or to mark the steers as their property. _____, riding on the back of a large and angry bull is purely for sport - a brutal and dangerous sport. But that danger does not stop the men and women who love the rodeo.

① To take an example
② To be brief
③ On the other hand
④ By the same token

기적사 DAY 07

01 다음 중 밑줄 친 부분의 의미와 가장 가까운 것은?

Led by the great <u>demagogue</u> dictator, Jacob van Artevelde, they became the mainstay of the English party in the Netherlands.

① defector ② offender
③ agitator ④ subscriber

02 다음 중 밑줄 친 부분의 의미와 가장 가까운 것은?

Though I <u>detest</u> getting back to a city, I respond to business calls.

① discern ② estimate
③ allocate ④ abominate

03 다음 중 밑줄 친 부분의 의미와 가장 가까운 것은?

The project was <u>abandoned</u> when the Conservatives lost control of the County Council in 1993.

① despised ② unraveled
③ given up ④ conveyed

04 밑줄 친 부분에 들어갈 말로 가장 적절한 것을 고르시오.

A: What's happened to Anne? I've lost track of her lately.
B: I don't know, and I really don't care. Anne always makes fun of me.
A: Really? I thought you two were good friends.
B: We used to be. Not any more, though. I got tired of her remarks.
A: I'm sorry to hear that. Anne is really a nice girl. Why don't you call her? Come on. _____. I'm sure you will be good friends again.
B: I suppose you're right. I'll call her right now.

① Keep close tabs on it
② Let bygones be bygones
③ Shed light on this business
④ You come down with a cold

05 밑줄 친 부분 중 어법상 옳지 않은 것을 고르시오.

Even a journey through the stacks of a real library can be more fruitful than a trip through today's ① <u>distributed</u> virtual archives, because it seems difficult ② <u>to use</u> the available "search engines" to emulate ③ <u>efficiently</u> the mixture of predictable and surprising discoveries that typically ④ <u>are resulted from</u> a physical shelf-search of an extensive library collection.

06 밑줄 친 부분 중 어법상 옳지 않은 것을 고르시오.

Effective coaches focus on those things ① that need to get done and separate out everything else. Separating what's important from what's not important ② is prioritizing. Ineffective coaches fail to put the big tasks first. They either believe they have unlimited time, ③ thought that they will have more time tomorrow to ④ get something done, or they underestimate how much time they really do have.

07 우리말을 영어로 잘못 옮긴 것을 고르시오.

① 만약 당신이 무언가를 잘한다면, 당신은 그것을 하는 것에 능숙하고 성공한 것이다.
   → If you are good at something, you are skillful and successful at doing it.
② 많은 미디어에서 예술 작품들을 만들고 그것들에 반응하는 것은 사회적 행위이다.
   → Making and responding to works of art, in many media, are social practices.
③ 그 애플파이는 할머니께서 만들어주시곤 했던 것보다 훌륭하지 않다.
   → The apple pie was not so better as the one my grandmother used to make.
④ 경제학 원리들은 실험실 과학의 원리들보다 덜 확실하고 덜 정확하다.
   → Economic principles are less certain and less precise than those of laboratory sciences.

08 빈칸에 들어갈 문장으로 가장 적절한 것은?

Society does not reward defeat, and most of us avoid the prospect of failure. To many in our success-driven society, failure is not just considered a non-option — it is even deemed a deficiency or a sign of inferiority. _____ _____. We hardly attempt anything great at which we could possibly fail or succeed. Also, when we do make missteps while attempting something, we gloss over them, selectively editing out the miscalculations or mistakes in our life's 'résumé.' But, of all the things we are wrong about, this idea of error may top the list. It is our meta-mistake. We are wrong about what it means to be wrong. Far from being a sign of intellectual inferiority, the capacity to err and fail is crucial to human cognition and success. Failure can be our greatest teacher only if we embrace it with no fear.

① However, dealing with failure is one of the most difficult but important challenges we face in life
② In fact, all of us are already aware that failure is as powerful a tool as any in achieving great success
③ However, mistakes can be either stepping stones or stumbling blocks to our future growths and success
④ In fact, we are so focused on not failing that we do not aim for success, settling instead for a life of mediocrity

09 빈칸에 들어갈 표현으로 가장 적절한 것은?

We may not be so quick to admit it, but we have all felt that weird compulsion to nibble a cute baby's toes from time to time. As bizarre as it may sound, this is a typical human nature. Scientists believe there are at least a couple of factors at work here. When we see or smell a tiny, adorable, and huggable thing, it actually activates the same pleasure center of our brains that is turned on by looking at delicious food. So the desire might simply be a case of our brains having similar responses to similar stimuli. Another theory about this seemingly strange human behavior notes that "social biting" is a common occurrence among mammals. For instance, some other primates are known to gently bite each other in a non-threatening manner. Scientists believe that this may be _____ — demonstrating that even if you find one of your body parts in someone else's mouth, you will not get hurt.

① a way of building trust
② an instinct for survival
③ a method to protect their babies
④ a characteristic of animal society

10 빈칸에 들어갈 표현으로 가장 적절한 것은?

The rodeo has developed over time to turn into the attraction that draws so many to stadiums across the country each year. Today, it is a spectacle which we commonly enjoy and take for granted - rough and tough cowboys riding bulls or horses and competing in other events while fans look on. _____(A)_____, many of the things which are now considered rodeo events were simply tasks that needed to be completed on the ranch. Jobs like roping, riding, and herding were not competitions of any kind - they were just jobs. Now, cowboys take part in rodeo events which are based closely on those ranch tasks. _____(B)_____, if you have ever watched a professional cowboy compete in team roping or bronc riding, you are seeing something which has its history in legitimate ranch work.

	(A)	(B)
①	However	By contrast
②	For example	On the other hand
③	However	That is to say
④	For example	Therefore

기적사 DAY 08

01 다음 중 밑줄 친 부분의 의미와 가장 가까운 것은?

Betsy was hopeful she might be able to confirm where the people had lived.

① approve
② undermine
③ accelerate
④ renounce

02 다음 중 밑줄 친 부분의 의미와 가장 가까운 것은?

I particularly abhor the laziness that even literate people exhibit when writing an email message.

① overwhelm
② despise
③ revise
④ scan

03 다음 중 밑줄 친 부분의 의미와 가장 가까운 것은?

This wasn't compulsory and he wasn't going to defend or reprimand him.

① loathe
② deceive
③ protect
④ evade

04 밑줄 친 부분에 들어갈 말로 가장 적절한 것을 고르시오.

A: You don't look very well. What's the matter?
B: _____.
A: I'm not surprised.
B: Come on, man, we need to pig out once in a while. Besides, we are at a picnic.
A: As long as you feel alright. But look at you! You can hardly stand up. you look serious.
B: I know. I think I shouldn't have eaten that last pan cake.

① I have a stomachache
② I feel sometimes dizzy
③ I have butterflies in my stomach
④ I always have my shirt off because of my boss

05 밑줄 친 부분 중 어법상 옳지 않은 것을 고르시오.

People who can express themselves clearly are ① perceived as more intelligent and of higher status. Why do we stop doing what we spent most of our early years ② doing? The trouble is that we take our verbal abilities for ③ granting. Once we have mastered reading, writing and speaking we move on to other things. We have acquired the most important tool in our mental toolbox. We depend on it for all sorts of tasks but we rarely take time to sharpen it. It makes better sense ④ to maintain, enhance and extend the tool.

06 밑줄 친 부분 중 어법상 옳지 않은 것을 고르시오.

Even books that provide only pleasure will increase the confidence of students and ① encourage them to try to read more technical materials in school. Comics, magazines, audiobooks, and topics of interest on the Internet are sometimes not ② considered "real" reading materials. However, these materials ③ let students to enjoy the pleasure of reading and gain information, literacy skills, and more. This "light" reading is actually very beneficial because it is effortless reading, ④ which improves reading fluency.

07 우리말을 영어로 잘못 옮긴 것을 고르시오.

① 당신의 고객이 그 빚을 갚기 위해 노력해 온 사실을 알고 있다.
→ I'm cognizant of the fact that your client has tried to pay the debt.

② 그 사이클링은 훌륭했지만 우리가 했던 크로스컨트리 스키만큼 힘들지는 않았다.
→ The cycling was good but not so hard as the cross country skiing we did.

③ 후자의 용어들로 정의된 영화는 너무 다르고 따라서 너무 이상한 것으로 여겨졌다.
→ A film defined by the latter terms was seen as too different and hence too strange.

④ 뛰어난 청취자들은 대부분의 사람들보다 그들 주변에서 진행되는 것에 더 민감한 경향이 있다.
→ Good listeners tend to be sensitive to what is going on around them than most people.

08 주어진 문장 다음에 이어질 글의 순서로 가장 적절한 것은?

'Massacre in Korea' is a 1951 expressionistic painting by Pablo Picasso which is seen as a criticism of American intervention in the Korean War.

(A) Although the actual cause of the murders in Sinchon is in question, Massacre in Korea appears to depict them as civilians being killed by anti-Communist forces. The art critic Kirsten Hoving Keen says that it is "inspired by reports of American atrocities."

(B) She also considers it one of Picasso's communist works. This work of Picasso is drawn from Francisco Goya's painting 'The Third of May 1808', which shows Napoleon's soldiers executing Spanish civilians under the orders of Joachim Murat.

(C) It depicts the 1950 Sinchon Massacre, an act of mass killing carried out by North Koreans, South Koreans, and American forces in the town of Sinchon located in South Hwanghae Province, North Korea.

① (A) − (B) − (C) ② (A) − (C) − (B)
③ (B) − (A) − (C) ④ (C) − (A) − (B)

09 빈칸 (A), (B)에 들어갈 표현으로 가장 적절한 것은?

Probably Picasso's most famous work, Guernica, is certainly his most powerful political statement, painted as an immediate reaction to the Nazi's devastating bombing practice on the Basque town of Guernica during Spanish Civil War. Guernica shows the tragedies of war and the suffering it inflicts upon individuals, especially innocent civilians. This work has gained a ____(A)____ status, becoming a perpetual reminder of the tragedies of war, an anti-war symbol, and an embodiment of peace. Upon completion Guernica was displayed around the world in a brief tour, becoming famous and widely acclaimed. This tour helped bring the Spanish Civil War to the world's ____(B)____.

	(A)	(B)
①	monumental	apathy
②	paltry	reproach
③	monumental	attention
④	paltry	recognition

10 밑줄 친 인물(Pablo Picasso)에 대한 설명으로 옳은 것은?

Pablo Picasso's father José Ruiz y Blasco was a painter and art teacher who quickly picked up on the fact that his little son was special. So he himself began Picasso's art education when he was seven. He was a strict academic who believed that artists should learn by copying the great masters, as well as drawing plaster casts and live models. Picasso's early pencil drawings and oil paintings show how skilled he was as a child. His earliest oil painting, The Picador, was completed when he was just nine years old. And by thirteen he was admitted to the School of Fine Arts in Barcelona. Incredibly, he was able to complete the rigorous entrance exam, which typically took one month to complete, in just a week.

① His talent was discovered after the age of seven by his teacher.
② His father allowed him to reproduce paintings of earlier artists.
③ He only used pencil to draw until he became a teenager.
④ He painted *The Picador* while he was attending the School of Fine Arts.

01 다음 중 밑줄 친 부분의 의미와 가장 가까운 것은?

She has an uncanny way of sticking to pertinent details.

① impractical
② complementary
③ inerrant
④ odd

02 다음 중 밑줄 친 부분의 의미와 가장 가까운 것은?

He stopped to evaluate the gilded ornaments which were frail.

① compensate
② inflame
③ reckon
④ swear

03 다음 중 밑줄 친 부분의 의미와 가장 가까운 것은?

This action will culminate the editioning of this piece as an ongoing process, culminating when the entire edition is sold.

① incessant
② ponderous
③ chronic
④ imperious

04 밑줄 친 부분에 들어갈 말로 가장 적절한 것을 고르시오.

A: How do I know that I can trust you?
B: Just ask Janet, maybe she'll tell you.
A: How do I know that I can trust Janet?
B: Don't worry. _____.

① Get rid of her
② I'll vouch for her
③ She is a wet blanket
④ She is the tip of the iceberg

05 밑줄 친 부분 중 어법상 옳지 않은 것을 고르시오.

As you were informed by our staff last week, your short story will be published, in the December issue of *Novel Flash Fiction*. We thought hearing how you came up ① with your story would be meaningful to our readers. We would thus like ② to ask if you could give a speech about your writing process. This speech is expected ③ to last for about an hour, and it will ④ be taken place at Moon Bookstore downtown. You can choose a specific date and time depending on your schedule.

06 밑줄 친 부분 중 어법상 옳지 않은 것을 고르시오.

As Tom sat in his chair eating a biscuit that Dad ① had spread butter and homemade strawberry jam, Mom walked into the kitchen. She took one look at her little boy and started laughing; his little face and hands were ② covered with biscuit and jam. She thought how really cute he was. "Honey, what have you done? Look at him. I will never ③ get him clean again. I guess when he gets through eating you can take him out and dump him in the bathtub." Dad laughed. Tom giggled and tried to spit biscuit all over Dad. It didn't hit him because luckily he avoided the spray. That ④ made Mom laugh even more and soon the little cabin was full of love and laughter.

07 우리말을 영어로 잘못 옮긴 것을 고르시오.

① 나는 결코 그 시험만큼 어려운 기말고사를 경험한 적이 없었다.
   → I never went through a final exam that was as difficult as that one.
② 미국인들은 멕시코인들보다 훨씬 더 외향적인 것으로 밝혀졌다.
   → The Americans were found to be more extroverted than the Mexicans.
③ 소설은 독자들에게 전쟁 경험을 전달하는 것에 능숙하다.
   → The novel is good at getting the experience of war across to the reader.
④ 35-44세 사이의 노동자들 중 단지 대략 1/4의 노동자들만이 이 정도의 근무 기간을 가진다.
   → Only about one-quarter of workers between the ages of 35 and 44 has a tenure of this length.

08 다음 밑줄 친 단어가 가리키는 대상이 나머지 넷과 다른 것은?

Sharks don't have the jaws attached to the skull. Instead, they move as separate parts. The upper and the lower jaw can work independently without the other. This versatility provides sharks with a very powerful pull and latch onto what ① they want fiercely. Also, sharks have many rows of teeth. ② Their teeth are so sharp that they can rip through flesh and bones instantly without any struggle at all. Sharks lose their teeth all the time, and one from the row behind moves forward to replace it, so they are always geared with a full army of ③ them to attack. ④ They can lose their front row of teeth every couple of weeks to a month. Therefore, sharks will have around 30,000 teeth in their lifetime.

09 다음 글의 요지로 가장 적절한 것은?

Sharks are being plucked from the ocean and killed faster than they can reproduce due to the high demand for fins. As shark numbers decline, their prey species such as rays have increased, which in turn are taking more of their own prey like scallops. As a result, many species of mollusks are rapidly declining. Researchers are also seeing the ripple effects of dramatic shark declines in the Caribbean. Fish usually eaten by sharks are now increasing, such as groupers. There are too many groupers feeding on parrotfish that eat algae off coral reefs, which results in too much algae in water. This is changing the marine ecological system by limiting the resources available to all species that depend on coral reef habitats.

① Sharks must be protected by international law.
② Sharks are top predators in the marine eco-system.
③ If it were not for their fins, sharks could not survive.
④ Altering the numbers of sharks has a big impact on other species.

10 다음 글의 내용과 일치하지 않는 것은?

Due to the difficulties in determining precisely when a small species is sexually mature (i.e. an adult and fully grown), there are two, possibly three, contenders for the smallest species of shark. The most likely record holder is the dwarf lantern shark, males of which measure a total length of 16-17.5 cm, and mature females of which are typically 19-20 cm. Prior to the discovery of the dwarf lantern shark in 1964, the record holder was the spined pygmy shark, males of which measure over 15 cm, females 17-20 cm. A third rival species, the pygmy ribbontail catshark has males measuring 18-19 cm and females possibly mature at 15-16 cm.

① It is unclear which shark species is the world's smallest.
② The dwarf lantern shark had been unknown before the 1960s.
③ All mature female sharks are longer than mature male sharks.
④ The spined pygmy shark was once considered the tiniest shark in the world.

01 다음 중 밑줄 친 부분의 의미와 가장 가까운 것은?

As odd as it may seem, a wildlife expert says that this white fox is actually preying on the weasel.

① ostensible
② imperious
③ strange
④ adventitious

02 다음 중 밑줄 친 부분의 의미와 가장 가까운 것은?

It was obvious that he didn't want to talk about his depression.

① stealthy
② manifest
③ grudging
④ imprecise

03 다음 중 밑줄 친 부분의 의미와 가장 가까운 것은?

We must respect their traditions, no matter how offensive they are.

① impeccable
② insulting
③ mandatory
④ impermanent

04 다음 대화를 읽고, A의 말로 적절한 것을 고르시오.

A: You shouldn't vanish into thin air when I ask you to do an errand.
B: Mom, just let me watch this soccer game.
A: _____.
B: OK. I get the picture.

① Break a leg
② It's neck and neck
③ I hit the nail on the head
④ I'm at the end of my rope

05 밑줄 친 부분 중 어법상 옳지 않은 것을 고르시오.

Consider a chair. Before you can have an idea of a chair, you need ① to understand that there ② exist in the world certain functional objects. Some of these objects support human activity, in this case, sitting. Some of them are specialized for sitting at certain high places, like bar stools. If you ③ learning about a culture in which a certain type of chair was used only for the purpose of sitting while waiting for a bus, you might think this is odd but would have no difficulty ④ understanding it.

06 밑줄 친 부분 중 어법상 옳지 않은 것을 고르시오.

One of fear and doubt's chief aims is to ① make you feel alone, like you're the only one ② that feels a certain way. Fear wants to isolate you and put you on an island. As long as you keep your fear to yourself, no one can tell you the truth about it. No one can ③ help you see what is really going on. No one can encourage you. So if you're going to tell your voices, "Go away," you've got to share them with other people. You've got to tell your close friends or family or a counselor about your voices. The exact person will be different for everyone, but ④ never wastes time trying to battle a voice alone.

07 우리말을 영어로 잘못 옮긴 것을 고르시오.

① 같은 야구팀의 팬인 사람들은 내집단을 형성한다.
→ People who are fans of the same baseball team form an in-group.

② 이 새 신발은 내 오래된 신발만큼 대체로 편하진 않다.
→ These new shoes are not nearly as comfortable than my old ones.

③ 당신은 대중에게 말하는 것을 잘해야 하고 그리고 듣는 것을 훨씬 더 잘해야 한다.
→ You have to be good at talking to the public and even better at listening.

④ 유기농법을 사용하는 농부들은 전통적 재래 농법을 사용하는 농부들의 작물들 못지않게 해충에 시달리는 작물들을 재배한다.
→ Organic farmers grow crops that are no less plagued by pests than those of conventional farmers.

08 밑줄 친 (A), (B)에 들어갈 말로 가장 적절한 것은?

The debate over the relative contributions of inheritance and the environment generally referred to as the nature versus nurture debate is one of the oldest issues in both philosophy and psychology. Philosophers such as Plato and Descartes supported the idea that some ideas are inborn. _____(A)_____, thinkers such as John Locke argued for the concept of tabula rasa — a belief that the mind is a blank slate at birth, with experience determining our knowledge. Now, most psychologists believe that it is an interaction between these two forces that causes development. Some aspects of development are clearly biological, such as puberty. _____(B)_____, the onset of puberty can be affected by environmental factors such as diet and nutrition.

* tabula rasa: 백지상태

	(A)	(B)
①	On the other hand	However
②	On the contrary	As a result
③	Consequently	Nevertheless
④	For instance	In summary

09 글의 흐름상 빈칸에 들어갈 단어로 가장 옳지 않은 것은?

It is widely accepted now that heredity and the environment do not act _____. A perfect example of this nature and nurture interaction is perfect pitch which is the ability to detect the pitch of a musical tone without any reference. Researchers have found that this ability tends to run in families and believed that it might be tied to a single gene. However, they have also discovered that possessing the gene alone is not enough to develop this ability. Instead, proper musical training during early childhood is necessary to allow this inherited ability to manifest itself.

① comprehensively
② independently
③ separately
④ discretely

10 주어진 문장 다음에 이어질 글의 순서로 가장 적절한 것은?

Prior to David Reimer's case, it was felt that the social learning theory could be applied in the case of gender reassignment.

(A) Milton Diamond, professor of anatomy and reproductive biology at the University of Hawaii, for example, claimed that the application of the social learning theory was inadequate in gender reassignment, as behavioral differences in children are inherent and have little to do with the appearance of their genitals.

(B) Because of this belief, Dr. John Money suggested that David undergo gender reassignment surgery and be raised as a female.

(C) However, when he rebelled against his newly assigned gender, a number of individuals in the field of psychology began to question this decision.

① (A) − (C) − (B)
② (B) − (A) − (C)
③ (B) − (C) − (A)
④ (C) − (A) − (B)

01 밑줄 친 부분과 의미가 가장 가까운 것을 고르시오.

Natural Gas World subscribers will receive accurate and reliable key facts and figures about what is going on in the industry, so they are fully able to discern what concerns their business.

① distinguish   ② strengthen
③ undermine   ④ abandon

02 다음 중 밑줄 친 부분의 의미와 가장 가까운 것은?

Whenever they traveled closer to the ranch, her anxiety increased.

① indignation   ② apprehension
③ appreciation ④ demagogue

03 다음 중 밑줄 친 부분의 의미와 가장 가까운 것은?

We must respect their traditions, no matter how offensive they are.

① impeccable   ② insulting
③ mandatory   ④ impermanent

04 밑줄 친 부분의 의미와 가장 가까운 것은?

Robert J. Flaherty, a legendary documentary filmmaker, tried to show how indigenous people gathered food.

① itinerant   ② impoverished
③ ravenous   ④ native

05 빈칸에 들어갈 표현으로 가장 적절한 것은?

Although Chinese authorities put Huang Qi, human rights defender and citizen journalist, on trial on charges of illegally providing state secrets to foreign entities and intentionally leaking state secrets, the court has not announced a verdict. No member of the public was allowed to attend the trial and no information about the trial has been made public. ____(A)____, any of Huang's lawyers was never told about the trial. The closed-door hearing violated his right to a fair and public trial by an independent court. ____(B)____ the Chinese government must immediately and unconditionally release Huang Qi, who is seriously ill, and end its persecution of him for exercising his freedom of expression and association.

	(A)	(B)
①	Namely	However
②	For example	Otherwise
③	Moreover	Thus
④	To be brief	Likewise

06 밑줄 친 부분 중 어법상 옳지 않은 것을 고르시오.

Domesticated animals are the earliest and most effective 'machines' ① available to humans. They take the strain off the human back and arms. ② Utilizing with other techniques, animals can raise human living standards very considerably, both as supplementary foodstuffs (protein in meat and milk) and as machines ③ to carry burdens, lift water, and grind grain. Since they are so obviously ④ of great benefit, we might expect to find that over the centuries humans would increase the number and quality of the animals they kept. Surprisingly, this has not usually been the case.

07 다음 글의 제목으로 가장 적절한 것은?

Though cookie files are quite small, they can still build up and slow down your system performance. By taking the time to delete the cookies, you can increase the speed and performance of your web browsing software. Doing so on a regular basis will also free space on your hard drive and prevent system crashes which often happen when your computer doesn't have sufficient space. While many cookies are harmless, moreover, others can be used to track your every move on the Internet. Businesses often use these tracking cookies to study consumer behavior, but many computer users consider them an invasion of privacy. By setting your web browser to delete cookies each time you close your browser, you can thwart these tracking attempts and reduce the risk of a security breach.

① Threats of Internet Cookies
② How Cookies Invade Privacy?
③ Benefits of Removing Cookies
④ Pros and Cons of Using Cookies

08 밑줄 친 부분 중 어법상 옳지 않은 것을 고르시오.

As Tom sat in his chair eating a biscuit that Dad ① had spread butter and homemade strawberry jam, Mom walked into the kitchen. She took one look at her little boy and started laughing; his little face and hands were ② covered with biscuit and jam. She thought how really cute he was. "Honey, what have you done? Look at him. I will never ③ get him clean again. I guess when he gets through eating you can take him out and dump him in the bathtub." Dad laughed. Tom giggled and tried to spit biscuit all over Dad. It didn't hit him because luckily he avoided the spray. That ④ made Mom laugh even more and soon the little cabin was full of love and laughter.

09 빈칸에 들어갈 표현으로 가장 적절한 것은?

Human nature has many curious traits, but one of the most curious is _____. No one thinks it a fine thing to have a motor car that is perpetually going out of order: people do not boast that after a long run their car is completely useless for several weeks, or that it is perpetually developing strange troubles which even the most skillful mechanics cannot put right. Yet that is how people feel about their own bodies. To have a body that does its work satisfactorily is felt to be uninteresting and rather plebeian. A delicate digestion is almost indispensable in the equipment of a fine lady. I am aware in myself of the impulses to boast of illness: I have only been ill once, but I like people to know how very ill I was that once, and I feel vexed when I come across other people who have been more nearly dead without dying

① fear of diseases
② interests in motor cars
③ pride in illness
④ phobia of death

10 다음 글의 요지로 가장 적절한 것은?

Sharks are being plucked from the ocean and killed faster than they can reproduce due to the high demand for fins. As shark numbers decline, their prey species such as rays have increased, which in turn are taking more of their own prey like scallops. As a result, many species of mollusks are rapidly declining. Researchers are also seeing the ripple effects of dramatic shark declines in the Caribbean. Fish usually eaten by sharks are now increasing, such as groupers. There are too many groupers feeding on parrotfish that eat algae off coral reefs, which results in too much algae in water. This is changing the marine ecological system by limiting the resources available to all species that depend on coral reef habitats.

① Sharks must be protected by international law.
② Sharks are top predators in the marine eco-system.
③ If it were not for their fins, sharks could not survive.
④ Altering the numbers of sharks has a big impact on other species.

11 밑줄 친 부분에 들어갈 말로 가장 적절한 것을 고르시오.

A: You don't look very well. What's the matter?
B: _____.
A: I'm not surprised.
B: Come on, man, we need to pig out once in a while. Besides, we are at a picnic.
A: As long as you feel alright. But look at you! You can hardly stand up. you look serious.
B: I know. I think I shouldn't have eaten that last pan cake.

① I have a stomachache
② I feel sometimes dizzy
③ I have butterflies in my stomach
④ I always have my shirt off because of my boss

12 밑줄 친 부분에 들어갈 말로 적절한 것을 고르시오.

A: That faucet in my apartment is still dripping. I thought you said you were going to fix it.
B: Oh, you're right. The washer needs replacing.
A: Why don't you replace it then?
B: _____. I think you'd better call a plumber as soon as possible.

① It cuts corners
② I come to terms with it
③ You drop him a line about it
④ That is easier said than done

13 우리말을 영어로 잘못 옮긴 것을 고르시오.

① 만약 당신이 무언가를 잘한다면, 당신은 그것을 하는 것에 능숙하고 성공한 것이다.
  → If you are good at something, you are skillful and successful at doing it.
② 많은 미디어에서 예술 작품들을 만들고 그것들에 반응하는 것은 사회적 행위이다.
  → Making and responding to works of art, in many media, are social practices.
③ 그 애플파이는 할머니께서 만들어 주시곤 했던 것보다 훌륭하지 않다.
  → The apple pie was not so better as the one my grandmother used to make.
④ 경제학 원리들은 실험실 과학의 원리들보다 덜 확실하고 덜 정확하다.
  → Economic principles are less certain and less precise than those of laboratory sciences.

14 우리말을 영어로 잘못 옮긴 것을 고르시오.

① John은 그 사고를 보지 못했고 Mary도 또한 그러했다.
  → John didn't see the accident and so did Mary.
② 유사성은 같은 집단의 일부가 되는 것으로 구성될 수 있다.
  → Similarity can consist of being part of the same group.
③ 개인적 경험상 네가 Tom을 신뢰할 수 없다는 것을 안다.
  → I know from personal experience that you can't trust Tom.
④ 그것은 세상에 알려진 이후로 사람들의 삶을 간소화 시키고 있다.
  → It has been simplifying the lives of people since its introduction to the world.

15 다음 글의 내용과 일치하는 것은?

The scientific revolution laid the foundations for the Age of Enlightenment and science came to play a leading role in Enlightenment discourse and thought. Many Enlightenment writers and thinkers had backgrounds in the sciences, and associated scientific advancement with the overthrow of religion and traditional authority, which had oppressed science, in favor of the development of free speech and thought. Broadly speaking, Enlightenment science greatly valued empiricism and rational thought, and was embedded with the Enlightenment ideal of advancement and progress. At the time, science was dominated by scientific societies and academies, which had largely replaced universities as centers of scientific research and development. Societies and academies were also the backbone of the maturation of the scientific profession. Another important development was the popularization of science among an increasingly literate population.

① The Enlightenment led the scientific revolution.
② Enlightenment thinkers highly regarded religious beliefs.
③ During the Age of Enlightenment, the freedom of speech and thought was curbed.
④ The Enlightenment caused traditional authority to lose its dominance over science.

16 주어진 문장 다음에 이어질 글의 순서로 가장 적절한 것은?

'Massacre in Korea' is a 1951 expressionistic painting by Pablo Picasso which is seen as a criticism of American intervention in the Korean War.

(A) Although the actual cause of the murders in Sinchon is in question, Massacre in Korea appears to depict them as civilians being killed by anti-Communist forces. The art critic Kirsten Hoving Keen says that it is "inspired by reports of American atrocities."

(B) She also considers it one of Picasso's communist works. This work of Picasso is drawn from Francisco Goya's painting 'The Third of May 1808', which shows Napoleon's soldiers executing Spanish civilians under the orders of Joachim Murat.

(C) It depicts the 1950 Sinchon Massacre, an act of mass killing carried out by North Koreans, South Koreans, and American forces in the town of Sinchon located in South Hwanghae Province, North Korea.

① (A) − (B) − (C) ② (A) − (C) − (B)
③ (B) − (A) − (C) ④ (C) − (A) − (B)

17 밑줄 친 (A), (B)에 들어갈 말로 가장 적절한 것은?

The debate over the relative contributions of inheritance and the environment generally referred to as the nature versus nurture debate is one of the oldest issues in both philosophy and psychology. Philosophers such as Plato and Descartes supported the idea that some ideas are inborn. ___(A)___, thinkers such as John Locke argued for the concept of tabula rasa — a belief that the mind is a blank slate at birth, with experience determining our knowledge. Now, most psychologists believe that it is an interaction between these two forces that causes development. Some aspects of development are clearly biological, such as puberty. ___(B)___, the onset of puberty can be affected by environmental factors such as diet and nutrition.

* tabula rasa: 백지상태

	(A)	(B)
①	On the other hand	However
②	On the contrary	As a result
③	Consequently	Nevertheless
④	For instance	In summary

18 주어진 문장이 들어갈 위치로 가장 적절한 것은?

Although this social contract theory appears to be perfect in every respect yet he did not say anything about the legal sovereign.

John Locke seems to be the first philosopher to introduce a new element in the field of Political Science: the consent or the will of the people. (①) A government can remain in power and be strong so long as it enjoys the support of the people or governs in accordance with the will of the people. (②) In this way Locke gave the theory of limited sovereignty or constitutional government. (③) If the government fails to protect the life, liberty and property of the people, the people have the right to remove it and appoint a new government. (④) Besides, he failed to understand that revolution is desirable but it is also dangerous and under normal circumstances illegal.

19 밑줄 친 부분 중 글의 흐름상 가장 어색한 것은?

The ancient Greeks such as Aristotle believed there were four elements that everything was made up of: earth, water, air, and fire. ① The idea that these four elements made up all matter was the cornerstone of philosophy, science, and medicine for long. ② The four elements were even used to describe the four temperaments a person could have, and Hippocrates used the four elements to describe the four "humors" found in the body. ③ These theories stated the temperaments and humors needed to be in balance with each other for a person to be well both mentally and physically. ④ Aristotle suggested there was a fifth element, aether, because it seemed strange that the stars would be made out of earthly elements. While now we know these previous theories are false, in a way the four elements do align with the four states of matter on which modern science has agreed: solid (earth), liquid (water), gas (air), and plasma (fire).

20 빈칸에 들어갈 표현으로 가장 적절한 것은?

We may not be so quick to admit it, but we have all felt that weird compulsion to nibble a cute baby's toes from time to time. As bizarre as it may sound, this is a typical human nature. Scientists believe there are at least a couple of factors at work here. When we see or smell a tiny, adorable, and huggable thing, it actually activates the same pleasure center of our brains that is turned on by looking at delicious food. So the desire might simply be a case of our brains having similar responses to similar stimuli. Another theory about this seemingly strange human behavior notes that "social biting" is a common occurrence among mammals. For instance, some other primates are known to gently bite each other in a non-threatening manner. Scientists believe that this may be _____ _____ — demonstrating that even if you find one of your body parts in someone else's mouth, you will not get hurt.

① a way of building trust
② an instinct for survival
③ a method to protect their babies
④ a characteristic of animal society

MEMO

기적사 DAY 11

01 밑줄 친 부분의 의미와 가장 가까운 것을 고르시오.

Although the actress experienced much turmoil in her career, she never <u>disclosed</u> to anyone that she was unhappy.

① let on
② let off
③ let up
④ let down

02 밑줄 친 부분과 의미가 가장 가까운 것을 고르시오.

These days, Halloween has drifted far from its roots in pagan and Catholic festivals, and the spirits we <u>appease</u> are no longer those of the dead: needy ghosts have been replaced by costumed children demanding treats.

① assign
② apprehend
③ pacify
④ provoke

03 밑줄 친 부분과 의미가 가장 가까운 것을 고르시오.

I usually <u>make light of</u> my problems, and that makes me feel better.

① consider something as serious
② treat something as unimportant
③ make an effort to solve a problem
④ seek an acceptable solution

04 두 사람의 대화 중 가장 어색한 것은?

① A: I'm traveling abroad, but I'm not used to staying in another country.
  B: Don't worry. You'll get accustomed to it in no time.
② A: I want to get a prize in the photo contest.
  B: I'm sure you will. I'll keep my fingers crossed!
③ A: My best friend moved to Sejong City. I miss her so much.
  B: Yeah. I know how you feel.
④ A: Do you mind if I talk to you for a moment?
  B: Never mind. I'm very busy right now.

05 어법상 옳은 것은?

① They didn't believe his story, and neither did I.
② The sport in that I am most interested is soccer.
③ Jamie learned from the book that World War I had broken out in 1914.
④ Two factors have made scientists difficult to determine the number of species on Earth.

06 어법상 옳지 않은 것은?

① A few words caught in passing set me thinking.
② Hardly did she enter the house when someone turned on the light.
③ We drove on to the hotel, from whose balcony we could look down at the town.
④ The homeless usually have great difficulty getting a job, so they are losing their hope.

07 우리말을 영어로 잘못 옮긴 것을 고르시오.

① 그 회의 후에야 그는 금융 위기의 심각성을 알아차렸다.
→ Only after the meeting did he recognize the seriousness of the financial crisis.

② 장관은 교통 문제를 해결하기 위해 강 위에 다리를 건설해야 한다고 주장했다.
→ The minister insisted that a bridge be constructed over the river to solve the traffic problem.

③ 비록 그 일이 어려운 것이었지만, Linda는 그것을 끝내기 위해 최선을 다했다.
→ As difficult a task as it was, Linda did her best to complete it.

④ 그는 문자 메시지에 너무 정신이 팔려서 제한속도보다 빠르게 달리고 있다는 것을 몰랐다.
→ He was so distracted by a text message to know that he was going over the speed limit.

08 빈칸에 들어갈 표현으로 가장 적절한 것은?

What readers most commonly remember about John Stuart Mill's classic exploration of the liberty of thought and discussion concerns the danger of complacency. In the absence of challenge, one's opinions, even when they are correct, grow weak and flabby. Yet Mill had another reason for encouraging the liberty of thought and discussion. _____. Since one's opinions, even under the best circumstances, tend to embrace only a portion of the truth, and because opinions opposed to one's own rarely turn out to be completely erroneous, it is crucial to supplement one's opinions with alternative points of view.

① It is the replication of opinions
② It is the defense of individual liberties
③ It is the danger of partiality and incompleteness
④ It is the constraints on spreading opinions and information

09 글의 내용과 부합하지 않는 것은?

House prices have increased by 67 percent since 1990 and by 19 percent since 2006. However, interest rates have decreased during this period. The conventional mortgage rate fell from nearly 13 percent in 1990 to 7 percent in 2006 and is now below 4 percent.

The net result is that Canadians have the same average monthly housing costs they've had for decades. Mortgage payments relative to disposable income are in line with the average since 1990 and lower than the percentage through much of the 1990s.

However, these numbers do not reflect the real affordability problem in Toronto and Vancouver. To understand these markets, policy makers need to differentiate between condominiums and single-family housing. For condominiums in both markets, the monthly mortgage payments on the median house-price relative to median income have been flat since the early 2000s. However, it's in single-detached houses where we finally see rising monthly housing costs and thus a stronger case for unaffordability.

① House prices were inversely related with interest rates in the mid-2000s.
② Tenants had to make too high mortgage payments for condominiums in 2001.
③ Mortgage rate and interest rates showed a similar tendency in 2006.
④ It can be inferred that policy makers should focus more attention on single-detached houses than on condominiums in policy-making.

10 글의 흐름상 빈칸에 들어갈 가장 적절한 것은?

How are the new networks different? First, they are (㉠), meaning that all media-voice, audio, video, or data-are increasingly communicated over a single common network. This offers economies of scope and scale in both capital expenditures and operational costs, and also allows different media to be mixed within common applications. As a result, both technology suppliers and service providers are increasingly in the business of providing telecommunications in all media simultaneously rather than specializing in a (㉡) type such as voice, video, or data.

	㉠	㉡
①	expanded	specific
②	integrated	particular
③	scrutinized	elaborate
④	splitted	universal

기적사 DAY 12

01 다음 중 밑줄 친 부분의 의미와 가장 가까운 것은?

But no state could longer <u>tolerate</u> the affronts which English seamen offered Spain.

① concoct ② withstand
③ roam   ④ disclose

02 다음 중 밑줄 친 부분의 의미와 가장 가까운 것은?

He asked if he might <u>record</u> the interview in addition to taking notes.

① register ② examine
③ disclose ④ appease

03 다음 중 밑줄 친 부분의 의미와 가장 가까운 것은?

Reconsideration of the subject led him afterwards to <u>modify</u> his views to some extent, and he has since more fully discussed the question.

① seek   ② repress
③ rectify ④ provoke

04 다음 대화를 읽고, B의 말로 적절한 것을 고르시오.

A: Are you going to the swimming class this morning?
B: Of course, no sweat.
A: The advanced class is nonstop and hard.
B: Come on, it's going to be _____.

① a piece of cake
② wetting behind the ears
③ on the tip of my tongue
④ keeping my fingers crossed

05 어법상 옳은 것은?

① That was the meeting during which I kept falling asleep.
② They may not criticize the state, but neither praise they it.
③ Many things make women difficult to reach the top in US business.
④ Tom learned from the book that the eruption of Vesuvius had destroyed Pompeii.

06 어법상 옳지 않은 것?

① Hardly had a moment passed than the door creaked open.
② That was one of the few words that I had difficulty in spelling as a child.
③ Goods being offered at ultra-low prices should always set alarm bells ringing.
④ Kate, whose sister I used to share a house with, has gone to work in Australia.

07 우리말을 영어로 잘못 옮긴 것을 고르시오.

① 대통령이 인기 있을지라도, 언제나 자신의 생각대로 하지는 못했다.
→ As popular as he is, the president hasn't always managed to have his own way.
② 오직 사회 경제적 조건을 개선함으로써 건강이 성취될 수 있다.
→ Only by improving social and economic conditions can good health be achieved.
③ 경영진은 대신에 기사들이 고정된 월급을 받아야 한다고 주장하는 중이다.
→ The management is insisting that the drivers accept a fixed monthly salary instead.
④ 이것들은 너무 겁먹어서 자유롭게 말할 수 없는 사람들로부터 당신이 예상한 답들이 아니었다.
→ These are not the answers you would expect from people so frightened to speak freely.

08 빈칸에 들어갈 표현으로 가장 적절한 것은?

John Stuart Mill is recognized in modern philosophy chiefly for two reasons. He refined the Utilitarian tradition of philosophy established by Jeremy Bentham and he reemphasized the primacy of individual liberty and self-determination against the inroads of the majority in democratic societies. One part of Mill's contribution has been largely overlooked, however. It is his _____ _____. In his essay published in 1869, the subordination of others, he argued, was not only wrong in itself but one of the chief hindrances to human improvement. In addition, he attempted to substitute the word 'person' for 'man.' in the Reform Bill even though it was unsuccessful. In a nutshell, Mill advocated the liberation of females nearly 160 years ago, when they were subordinate to males by law and custom and living in the shadow of their "de facto masters."

① strong opposition to slavery of other races
② call for legal and social equality for women
③ great emphasis on the importance of democracy
④ being an influential advocate of freedom of speech

09 글의 내용과 일치하지 않는 것은?

With an urbanization rate of 54% and 20% of total population squatting in over 700 informal settlements, national and local authorities of Jamaica face a serious housing problem. Research undertaken for the National Housing Policy revealed that 15,000 new units are required annually up to 2030 to clear the backlog. However, between 1980 and 2012, the average annual production of housing stood at 4,456 in the formal sector. Meanwhile, low income households find it difficult to access loans and mortgages through the formal financial institutions, as many households are engaged in informal economy where they secure their livelihoods and incomes. Policies have not yet captured the role of micro-financing and flexible financing that could help increase access to formal housing for low income groups. As such, low income households resort to the informal sector and continue to undertake incremental housing development to house themselves. The land registration and development approval processes are also too expensive, rigid and cumbersome and thus; act as hindrances to low income households in accessing affordable formal housing.

① About one fifth of the population are living in unauthorized places.
② The gap between supply and demand of housing existed for more than 30 years.
③ People in the low income bracket rely heavily on unofficial income-generating activities.
④ The government encourages low income families to take advantage of microfinance services.

10 글의 흐름상 빈칸에 들어갈 가장 적절한 것은?

What is meant by the term telecommunications? It is simple: under telecommunications we imagine the whole complex of technical means that are intended to (㉠) information to any distance and its being successfully delivered and processed. This complex of technical equipment can contain: sounds, signals, text, other signs, images and much other stuff allowed by the local laws. All these are transferred through both wired and wireless channels, via optical fibers, radio and other electromagnetic systems. And the system of technical means by which telecommunications is (㉡) is called a telecommunication network.

	㉠	㉡
①	supplement	built up
②	transmit	carried out
③	facilitate	brought together
④	encrypt	dealt with

기적사 DAY 13

01 다음 중 밑줄 친 부분의 의미와 가장 가까운 것은?

Several futile attempts have been made to let on conclusions as to the intelligence of various birds.

① duteous ② vain
③ incandescent ④ clandestine

02 다음 중 밑줄 친 부분의 의미와 가장 가까운 것은?

What could be more enticing than sharing several, delectable dishes with your date?

① fortuitous ② provoking
③ scattered ④ seductive

03 다음 중 밑줄 친 부분의 의미와 가장 가까운 것은?

But Xander's enhanced eyesight was able to see one half of the interaction that we make light of.

① acquitted ② hoaxed
③ indisposed ④ consolidated

04 다음 대화를 읽고, A의 말로 적절한 것을 고르시오.

A: Guess what! I'm writing a letter to my boss because of asking for a raise.
B: Ah, at last! Good for you! You should have done it before.
A: I know _____.

① you get accustomed to it
② I always chicken out
③ you poke your nose into others
④ It seems that your head against the wall

05 어법상 옳은 것?

① Tom taught his pupils that water consisted of hydrogen and oxygen.
② The use of computers has made more people possible to work from home.
③ You should restrict yourself to words you are familiar and can use confidently.
④ The Cowboys won't be playing in the Superbowl this year, and neither will the Falcons.

06 어법상 옳지 않은 것은?

① His entry on his diagnosis of pancreatic cancer has set me thinking.
② It is a tragedy that such a splendid player has such difficult in running.
③ He had hardly collected the papers on his desk when the door burst open.
④ Tom, in whose house Jane has now lived, was described as a very curious gentleman.

07 우리말을 영어로 잘못 옮긴 것을 고르시오.

① 노력했을지 모르지만, 그녀는 자신의 걱정스러운 가족이 해체되는 것을 막을 수 없다.
→ Try as she might, she can't keep her troubled family from fragmenting.
② 그 대학은 학생들이 오로지 능력을 토대로 수용된다고 주장한다.
→ The university insists that students are accepted solely on the basis of ability.
③ 이 프로젝트는 너무 중요해서 자금 또는 자원 부족에 의해 방해받을 수 없다.
→ This project is too important to be hindered by a lack of funds or resources.
④ 나는 그제야 Tom이 직면했던 어려움을 평가하기 시작했다.
→ Only then I began to appreciate the difficulties that Tom had faced.

08 밑줄 친 부분 중 글의 흐름상 가장 어색한 것은?

Also known as Pastafarianism, the Church of the Flying Spaghetti Monster is a mock religion that was based on an open letter by Bobby Henderson to the Kansas School Board. ① He demanded in the letter that the theory of the Flying Spaghetti Monster should be taught along with theories of Evolution. ② Pastafarians, who worship the Flying Spaghetti Monster, have challenged laws that give particular privileges to religious ideas, practices, or bodies of worship in several countries and jurisdictions, frequently by seeking recognition as a religion, with varying degrees of success. ③ In 2011 a Pastafarian was allowed to wear a colander on his head in his driver's license photo in Austria, which permits religious headgear for official documents. ④ Pastafarianism is now legally recognized as a religion in the Netherlands and New Zealand. It was later recognized as religious headgear in the Czech Republic, New Zealand, and the U.S. states of Massachusetts and Utah.

09 빈칸에 들어갈 표현으로 가장 적절한 것은?

Indeed, few forces have historically been more powerful than religion in shaping people's existences. According to the latest poll by the Pew Research Center, 77 percent of Americans say that religion is at least somewhat important in their lives and 83 percent say they're fairly certain that God or a higher power exists. But _____. There has long been a debate among scholars about this issue, with some claiming that it facilitates well-being and others claiming that it leads to neurosis. In fact, there are few issues in the field of psychology as highly researched as this question.

① no one really knows whether God exists or not
② there are too many pseudo-religions around us
③ not everyone agrees that religion is good for us
④ it is obvious that religion plays a positive role in the society

10 다음 글의 제목으로 가장 적절한 것은?

Christianity is by far the largest religion in the United States; more than three-quarters of Americans identify as Christians. A little more than half of the Americans identify as Protestants, about 23 percent as Catholic and about 2 percent as Mormon. But what about the rest? In the Western U.S., Buddhists represent the next largest religious bloc in most states. In 20 states, mostly in the Midwest and South, Islam is the largest non-Christian faith tradition. And in 15 states, mostly in the Northeast, Judaism has the most followers after Christianity. Hindus come in second place in Arizona and Delaware, and there are more practitioners of the Baha'i faith in South Carolina than anyone else.

① Freedom of Religion in the U.S.
② The Biggest Religion within the U.S.
③ Various Types of Religions Existing in the U.S.
④ The Second Most Believed Religions around the U.S.

기적사 DAY 14

01 다음 중 밑줄 친 부분의 의미와 가장 가까운 것은?

There is an abundance of <u>fertile</u> soil and magnificent grazing land which never let down farmers.

① fructuous ② hollow
③ luxurious ④ rampant

02 다음 중 밑줄 친 부분의 의미와 가장 가까운 것은?

I'm sure you're in a hurry to get back out to Denton.

① comply ② apprehend
③ haste ④ adhere

03 다음 중 밑줄 친 부분의 의미와 가장 가까운 것은?

You may call or have friends over anytime you consider something as serious - as long as they don't <u>interfere</u> with your work.

① encumber ② seclude
③ mitigate ④ discern

04 밑줄 친 부분에 들어갈 가장 적절한 것을 고르시오.

W: What do you think about hiring some temporary staff for this season?
M: I think that's a good idea. We have enough money in our budget to pay for at least four more staff. Why don't you call Janet in human resources?
W: Okay. I know how you feel. I'll give her a call right away. With some extra staff, I'm sure we'll be able to handle all the customers. Otherwise, _____ _____.

① play it by ear
② turn a blind eye to
③ bite off more than one can chew
④ everyone has to start work overtime

05 어법상 옳은 것은?

① They found that Bill drank heavily every night.
② She doesn't find it easy to talk about her problems.
③ That's the place where she stays at when she's in London.
④ He hadn't done any homework, and neither he had brought any of his books to class.

06 어법상 옳지 않은 것은?

① Scarcely had they left before soldiers arrived armed with rifles.
② The idea is that you should want people whose opinions share to have an robust stance.
③ I regarded him as an honest witness and had no difficulty in believing what he told me.
④ It was what the soldiers at the airport said about their wives that set me thinking about this.

07 우리말을 영어로 잘못 옮긴 것을 고르시오.

① 데이터가 완료된 경우에만 이동이 발생한다.
→ Only when the data is complete does the transfer take place.
② 아무리 애써도, 나는 아직도 그 기억을 떨쳐 버릴 수 없다.
→ I still can't push that memory out of my mind, hard as I might try.
③ 루비 색깔은 너무 작아서 육안으로 볼 수 없는 아주 작은 금 입자 때문이다.
→ The ruby hue is due to tiny gold particles so small to see with the naked eye.
④ Gazette 기사에서 Tom씨는 우리가 사람들의 사적 그리고 공적인 삶을 구분해야 한다고 주장했다.
→ In the Gazette article Mr. Tom insisted we separate people's private and public lives.

08 다음 글의 주제로 가장 적절한 것은?

A referee is a person who officiates at athletic events such as football and basketball. Their responsibilities include imposing penalties if rules and regulations of the game are broken. Referees may work as the sole referee in sports such as boxing, or work in a group in sports such as football. Most officials need a minimum of a high school diploma or equivalent. Colleges that hire referees generally require you to be a graduate of a professional officiating school. To officiate minor or major league baseball games, you must have attended a professional umpire training school. To officiate major league games, umpires must possess 7 to 10 years experience in minor leagues. To become a referee for professional football, a minimum of ten years of experience is required, at least five of which occurred at the college level or higher.

① different kinds of referees
② the duties of referees in various games
③ the requirements to become a sports official
④ how to enter a professional officiating school

09 빈칸에 들어갈 표현으로 가장 적절한 것은?

Each season, MLB home plate umpires make tens of thousands of incorrect calls and _____. Right after the 2018 All-Star break, the Colorado Rockies and Arizona Diamondbacks met at Chase Field for an important National League game. The Rockies were up 6-5 in the ninth, but Arizona, with two outs and two on base, was threatening a comeback. Wade Davis, the Rockies closer, got ahead with a 1-2 count on slugger Nick Ahmed. The next pitch, a 90-mph cutter thrown toward the right-handed batter's box, landed significantly outside the strike zone. To the disbelief of Diamondback fans, umpire Paul Nauert called the stray ball a strike, ending the ballgame.

① they are seldom rectified after the game
② they are harshly berated for their mistakes
③ some of them significantly affect the result of a game
④ older, more experienced umpires make bad calls more often

10 주어진 문장이 들어갈 위치로 가장 적절한 것은?

Around the world, from France to Japan to Brazil, the naming of sports officials is clear, consistent, and straightforward.

Mention the 'referee' at a baseball game or the 'umpire' at a basketball game and it's clear you know nothing. (①) And that's perhaps a little unfair because the terminology for sports officials in English makes no sense and has no pattern — or if it does, it's so riddled with holes as to be pointless. (②) This is not the case in other languages. (③) In English-speaking countries sports officials have a dizzying array of names, without any kind of unifying structure as to the role each plays. (④) But it's more like a trap in English. The terms have slightly different base meanings and are not interchangeable, but their use in English does not follow any established pattern between sports. The lead official in an NBA game is a referee. In MLB, it's an umpire. Tennis, American football, and lacrosse all have both referees and a variety of judges.

기적사 DAY 15

01 다음 중 밑줄 친 부분의 의미와 가장 가까운 것은?

Since the Mall of America sees millions of visitors a year, they have direct contact with Homeland Security for not making turmoil and even have their own K-9 unit with dogs that sniff for bombs and drugs.

① stink
② snuff
③ convert
④ covert

02 다음 중 밑줄 친 부분의 의미와 가장 가까운 것은?

It was the sign it was time to resign, for her power assigned was nearly gone.

① step out
② flash on
③ hop off
④ take up

03 다음 중 밑줄 친 부분의 의미와 가장 가까운 것은?

Under a government which allowed to the people an unprecedented liberty of speech we make an effort to solve a problem.

① unsurpassed
② verbose
③ unadulterated
④ ordinary

04 다음 대화 중 어색한 것을 고르시오.

① A: What do you want for your birthday?
  B: It's up to you.
② A: Call me when you finish the class. I'll pick you up.
  B: Don't bother. Buses run until late.
③ A: The winter vacation is too short.
  B: Couldn't agree more. Speak for yourself.
④ A: I was very busy. I couldn't have finished the job without you.
  B: It was no big deal.

05 어법상 옳은 것은?

① We didn't see the castle, and neither saw we the cathedral.
② I think us important to agree on our position before the meeting.
③ He worked for the whole three months during which he lived there.
④ We more recently learned that the Normans had invaded England in 1066.

06 어법상 옳지 않은 것은?

① I have difficulty in walking, so getting to the top of town is virtually impossible.
② It hopes to give people whose opinions are rarely heard the chance to tell their story.
③ I had scarcely got up and put on my clothes than the messenger came into the yard.
④ These two events set me thinking why the two sports attract such different types of behaviour.

07 우리말을 영어로 잘못 옮긴 것을 고르시오.

① Tom의 묘사는, 그와 엘리자베스에게, 너무 생생해서 그는 그것을 지금까지 혼동할 수 없었다.
→ Tom's description, to him and Elizabeth, has been so vivid for him ever to confuse it.
② 그는 납세자에 의해 자금을 제공받으면서 제2의 집들로 이익을 얻은 하원 의원들이 그것을 갚아야 한다고 주장한다.
→ He has insisted MPs who make a profit on second homes funded by the taxpayer should repay it.
③ 캔자스주, 메디신 로지는, 비록 작지만, 지역 술꾼들의 편의를 위해 일곱 개의 술집들이 있었다.
→ Medicine Lodge, Kansas, small as it was, contained seven saloons for the comfort of local drinkers.
④ 의학적 도움은 저혈당증이 심각하고 환자가 의식이 없을 때만 요청될 가능성이 있다.
→ Medical help is likely to be sought only when hypoglycemia is severe and the patient is unconscious.

08 다음 글의 제목으로 가장 적절한 것은?

Inflation is a consistent increase in the prices of goods and services. During periods of inflation, a dollar loses some of its purchasing power and it takes more currency to buy the same amount of the goods or services. For example, if at the beginning of this year one widget is worth $1.00, but inflation is 5% over the year, it will take $1.05 to buy one widget one year later. Deflation is the opposite of inflation. It is a consistent decrease in the prices of goods and services. During deflationary periods, a dollar actually gains purchasing power and it takes less currency to buy the same amount of goods or services than it did before. For example, if at the beginning of this year one widget is worth $1.00, but deflation is 10% over the year, it will take only $0.90 to buy one widget one year later.

① We need Inflation, Not Deflation
② What Causes Inflation and Deflation?
③ The Difference between Inflation and Deflation
④ Inflation or Deflation: Which Is The Greater Risk?

09 다음 글에서 필자가 주장하는 것으로 가장 적절한 것은?

Many people view inflation as a bad thing: no one wants to spend more to buy the same amount of goods and services they paid for last year. However, inflation does have some upsides. The first example is when consumers anticipate it, which means they buy more now, knowing that their money will soon be worth less. Another example is when it prevents deflation. While deflation might sound great as it means you spend less to buy more, the problem is that the inverse of inflation happens: people now wait to see if prices are going to drop even more. Doing so means people buy less, so companies and manufacturers have to cut back on their workforces. Central banks usually try to avoid deflation at all costs.

① Deflation is not as good as it seems.
② Inflation has some positive effects on the economy.
③ Inflation and deflation should be prevented in advance.
④ Central banks play a critical role in stabilizing the economy.

10 밑줄 친 부분 중 글의 흐름상 가장 어색한 것은?

Imagine going to the store and finding that nothing has a price tag on it. Instead you take it to the cashier and they calculate the price. ① What you pay could be twice as much, or more, than an hour earlier. That's if there is even anything left in stock. ② This is the reality that underpins Venezuela's current "economic crisis" - though in truth that crisis has been going on for years. ③ The government headed by Nicolás Maduro, who has presided over Venezuela since 2013, declared a state of emergency in 2016. That year the inflation rate hit 800%. ④ About 3 million Venezuelans - a tenth of the population - have fled the country due to the Maduro regime's oppressive treatment of dissent. By 2018 the rate was an estimated 80,000%. It's difficult to say what the rate is now, but Bloomberg's Venezuelan Cafe Con Leche Index, based on the price of a cup of coffee, suggests it is now about 380,000%.

기적사 DAY 16

01 밑줄 친 부분과 의미가 가장 가까운 것을 고르시오.

A hamburger and French fries became the quintessential American meal in the 1950s, thanks to the promotional efforts of the fast food chains.

① healthiest ② affordable
③ typical   ④ informal

02 밑줄 친 부분에 공통으로 들어갈 말로 가장 적절한 것은?

- She's disappointed about their final decision, but she'll _____ it eventually.
- It took me a very long time to _____ the shock of her death.

① get away   ② get down
③ get ahead ④ get over

03 밑줄 친 부분에 들어갈 말로 가장 적절한 것을 고르시오.

As a middle-class Jew growing up in an ethnically mixed Chicago neighborhood, I was already in danger of being beaten up daily by rougher working-class boys. Becoming a bookworm would only have given them a decisive reason for beating me up. Reading and studying were more permissible for girls, but they, too, had to be careful not to get too _____, lest they acquire the stigma of being 'stuck up.'

① athletic   ② intellectual
③ hospitable   ④ inexperienced

04 다음 빈칸에 들어갈 말로 알맞은 것을 고르시오.

A: Wow! Look at the long line. I'm sure we have to wait at least 30 minutes.
B: You're right. _____.
A: That's a good idea. I want to ride the roller coaster.
B: It's not my cup of tea.
A: How about the Flume Ride then? It's fun and the line is not so long.
B: That sounds great! Let's go!

① Let's find seats for the magic show.
② Let's look for another ride.
③ Let's buy costumes for the parade.
④ Let's go to the lost and found.

05 우리말을 영어로 잘못 옮긴 것을 고르시오.

① 그 클럽은 입소문을 통해서 인기를 얻었다.
  → The club became popular by word of mouth.
② 무서운 영화를 좋아한다면 이것은 꼭 봐야 할 영화이다.
  → If you like scary movies, this is a must-see movie.
③ 뒤쪽은 너무 멀어요. 중간에 앉는 걸로 타협합시다.
  → The back is too far away. Let's promise and sit in the middle.
④ 제 예산이 빠듯합니다. 제가 쓸 수 있는 돈은 15달러뿐 입니다.
  → I am on a tight budget. I only have fifteen dollars to spend.

06 우리말을 영어로 잘못 옮긴 것을 고르시오.

① 식사가 준비됐을 때, 우리는 식당으로 이동했다.
→ The dinner being ready, we moved to the dining hall.
② 저쪽에 있는 사람이 누구인지 알겠니?
→ Can you tell who that is over there?
③ 이 질병이 목숨을 앗아가는 일은 좀처럼 없다.
→ It rarely happens that this disease proves fatal.
④ 과정을 관리하면서 발전시키는 것이 나의 목표였다.
→ To control the process and making improvement was my objectives.

07 어법상 옳은 것은?

① Undergraduates are not allowed to using equipments in the laboratory.
② The extent of Mary's knowledge on various subjects astound me.
③ If she had been at home yesterday, I would have visited her.
④ I regret to inform you that your loan application has not approved.

08 글의 흐름상 가장 불필요한 것은?

① Solving crimes is one of the most important jobs of law enforcement. Improvements in crime technology help detectives solve crimes faster, and more efficiently, today. ② For example, crime labs have new kinds of DNA testing, which can identify body fluids, such as blood, sweat, and saliva. There are also new kinds of fingerprint testing. ③ In the past, fingerprint testing was only helpful if the fingerprints from the crime scene could be matched with "prints" that were already on file. The fingerprints of convicted criminals are kept on file in police records permanently. ④ The fingerprints also reveal if the person takes medication. People whose fingerprints are not on file cannot be identified in this way, and as a result, many crimes have not been solved.

09 글의 내용과 일치하지 않는 것은?

The British juvenile justice system underwent significant philosophical changes in the early 20th century. Although there were many who clung to older ideas about the benefits of corporal punishment, the view that children who broke the law should be reclaimed and rehabilitated had become the orthodox view by the passing of the 1948 Children Act. This approach drew upon the views of social workers in the slums of British and American cities and of researchers in the new social and medical sciences. Delinquency was seen as part of a social matrix, as resulting from structural inequalities and deficient parenting styles. The solution to the problem of delinquency was seen as lying within the reformation of the structures which caused these inequities. For the more radical magistrates, the answer was not to overhaul society, but to reform the ways in which children were treated by the courts.

① The courts' better treatment of children could help curb delinquency in some judges' point of view.
② Social workers were among the proponents of the orthodox view.
③ Deficient parenting styles were considered as one cause of delinquency.
④ The 1948 Children Act accentuated the benefits of corporal punishment.

10 다음 글의 흐름상 가장 어색한 문장은?

The Renaissance kitchen had a definite hierarchy of help who worked together to produce the elaborate banquets. ① At the top, as we have seen, was the scalco, or steward, who was in charge of not only the kitchen, but also the dining room. ② The dining room was supervised by the butler, who was in charge of the silverware and linen and also served the dishes that began and ended the banquet— the cold dishes, salads, cheeses, and fruit at the beginning and the sweets and confections at the end of the meal. ③ This elaborate decoration and serving was what in restaurants is called "the front of the house." ④ The kitchen was supervised by the head cook, who directed the undercooks, pastry cooks, and kitchen help.

01 다음 중 밑줄 친 부분의 의미와 가장 가까운 것은?

In spite of being a mediocre athlete at best, Dean had thrived on sports.

① capable
② informal
③ bothersome
④ ordinary

02 다음 중 밑줄 친 부분의 의미와 가장 가까운 것은?

The most suggestive study of the pre-monarchical narratives is to get over the shock.

① outspoken
② principal
③ connotative
④ improvised

03 다음 중 밑줄 친 부분의 의미와 가장 가까운 것은?

Ozma was now greatly incensed by the kitten's conduct.

① abortive
② furious
③ intellectual
④ unparalleled

04 다음 중 밑줄 친 부분에 들어갈 속담으로 적절한 것은?

A: Here is your order.
B: Thanks. Um, excuse me, this is not the coffee I ordered.
A: Didn't you order latte?
B: No, I asked for caramel macchiato.
A: I'm sorry. I must have been confused.
B: _____. I've never seen you making a mistake.
A: I'll offer you the right one immediately.
B: Thanks.

① Let's go to the lost and found
② Still waters run deep
③ It never rains but it pours
④ Even Homer sometimes nods

05 우리말을 영어로 잘못 옮긴 것을 고르시오.

① 나는 결코 와인 한 잔 이상을 마시지 않을 것이다.
  → I will on no account drink more than one glass of wine.
② 그는 가까스로 비밀경찰로부터 달아났다.
  → He escaped from the secret police by the skin of his teeth.
③ 이 논쟁의 경쟁상대들은 타협하는 것을 아주 꺼린다.
  → The antagonists in this dispute are quite unwilling to promise.
④ 햇볕에 말린 야채들은 그것들을 태양 속에 둠으로써 건조되는 것이다.
  → Sun-dried vegetables have been dried by leaving them in the sun.

06 우리말을 영어로 잘못 옮긴 것을 고르시오.

① 혜성이 그 행성들 중 하나와 충돌할 것이라는 것은 예견되었다.
→ It was predicted that a comet would collide with one of the planets.

② 그 당시 그것이 유행이었기 때문에, 나는 내 청바지의 가장자리를 해어지게 했다.
→ That being the fashion in those days, I frayed the edges of my jeans.

③ 그들은 휴대전화로 통화하고, 음악을 다운로드하고 숙제를 한다.
→ They are talking on the cell phone, download music and doing homework.

④ Jane은 누가 그것을 했는지 궁금해했고 그들이 내년에 같은 것을 그녀에게 하도록 시킬지 궁금해했다.
→ Jane wondered who had done it and whether they would let her do the same next year.

07 어법상 옳은 것은?

① He was told us of his extraordinary childhood.
② The rewards that come from teaching is numerous.
③ The children are not allowed to watching violent TV programmes.
④ If they had done so, their careers would have been ruined for life.

08 주어진 문장이 들어갈 위치로 가장 적절한 것은?

The burden of proof clearly lies on the side of those who claim that welfare state programs are strangling productivity and growth.

Of course, many other factors besides social welfare spending have changed in the past 150 years. (①) However, welfare state spending is now very large relative to the total production of goods and services in all advanced industrialized nations. (②) If such expenditure had large adverse effects, it is doubtful that growth rates would have been so large in the last 30 years. (③) The crude historical relationship suggests, at a minimum, no great ill effects and, more likely, a positive effect. (④) If they are right, they need to explain not only why all rich nations have large welfare states, but more importantly why growth rates have grown in most rich nations as their welfare states have grown larger.

09 빈칸에 들어갈 표현으로 가장 적절한 것은?

During the last few years there has been a growing concern over the environment in the advanced countries of the world. This concern has provided ammunition for those who have questioned the desirability of further economic growth in these countries and even the feasibility or desirability of economic growth in the less developed countries. _____ have been expressed from time to time over the ages. For example, John Stuart Mill, writing in 1848, stated that "It is only in the backward countries of the world that increased production is still an important object; in those most advanced, what is economically needed is a better distribution."

① Responsibilities of advanced nations
② Doubts as to the wisdom of economic growth
③ Predictions regarding economic development in developing countries
④ Concerns about the environmental problems caused by economic growth

10 다음 글의 요지로 가장 적절한 것은?

In developing countries such as Indonesia, economic growth presents a contradiction. The "paradox of economic growth" is where the economy grows but so does income inequality. Indonesia's economy grew by 6.1% in 2012, 6.3% in 2013 and 6.4% in 2014. At the macro level, Indonesia's economic growth appeared to be good. But if we look closer, we see it was an illusion: behind the scenes Indonesia's Gini ratio was increasing. In 2012 it was 0.36, in 2013 0.39 and in 2014 0.41. As the national economy grew, so did the income gap. The benefits of economic growth - in Indonesia as well as in other developing counties - were reserved for the middle class and above; few benefits made it as far as the lower and working classes. The rich became richer and the poor poorer.

① Indonesia's income inequality can be solved with higher education.
② Indonesia needs to promote social welfare of the entire country by increasing Gini ratio.
③ Economic growth does not mean the equal financial improvement of all groups of population.
④ Economic growth benefits almost all citizens of a nation and therefore reduces poverty ultimately.

기적사 DAY 18

01 다음 중 밑줄 친 부분의 의미와 가장 가까운 것은?

In agility they are unsurpassed; in fact they are stated to be so swift in their movements as to be able to capture birds on the wing with their paws.

① enigmatic
② momentous
③ affordable
④ incomparable

02 다음 중 밑줄 친 부분의 의미와 가장 가까운 것은?

His aloof response made her get away.

① confident
② reserved
③ integrative
④ plentiful

03 다음 중 밑줄 친 부분의 의미와 가장 가까운 것은?

Maybe that was what she needed to do - tell the entire story to an unbiased audience.

① unprejudiced
② secluded
③ hospitable
④ unlabored

04 다음의 대화 중 이어질 A가 할 말로 적절한 것은?

A: When shall we have the meeting?
B: The sooner the better. We have to meet the deadline for the project.
A: That's why the whole team is working against the clock.
B: I can't count how many times we turned night into day.
A: There's one more to cross over. The vice president's approval to proceed.
B: The thing is, he's not in the office for the next two weeks.
A: _____
B: It's touch-and-go whether we will make it.

① It's not my cup of tea.
② We have to do it from scratch.
③ We have to call him on the carpet.
④ What are the odds of finishing the project?

05 우리말을 영어로 잘못 옮긴 것을 고르시오.

① 옷장 바닥에 당신의 것 중 오래된 신발 한 켤레가 놓여 있다.
→ There's an old pair of shoes of yours laying at the bottom of the wardrobe.
② 이러한 집중적인 개발들을 환영하지 않는 것은 편협한 것이고 편견이 아주 심한 것이다.
→ It would be narrow-minded and bigoted not to welcome these convergent developments.
③ 많은 소비자들은 덜 비싼 컴퓨터가 나타나길 기다리면서, 여전히 기회를 살핀다.
→ Many consumers are still on the fence, waiting for a less expensive computer to come along.
④ 오늘 행해진 시장성 테스트 없이 감으로 잡지를 시작했다.
→ We started a magazine by the seat of our pants, without the market testing that's done today.

06 우리말을 영어로 잘못 옮긴 것을 고르시오.

① 우리는 그것들을 흘러가게 하고 평화를 유지하는 선택권을 가지고 있다.
→ We have the choice to let them go and remain at peace.

② 내 무릎이 여전히 아팠기 때문에, 나는 선생님에게 축구 연습을 면제해 줄 수 있는지 여쭤보았다.
→ My knee still hurting, I asked the teacher if I could be excused from football practice.

③ 그가 그 상황에 대한 공개 성명을 하지 않고 떠났다는 것이 이상하다.
→ It's extraordinary that he left without making a public statement about the situation.

④ 의심할 여지 없이 우리가 도착할 때쯤 언론은 이 빛나는 신입 사원들 모두가 누구인지 궁금해할 것이다.
→ No doubt when we arrive the press will be wondering who are all these shiny new people.

07 어법상 옳은 것은?

① If you had stayed this would become more apparent.
② Hospitals are being forced to close departments because of lack of money.
③ The government didn't want to see to be making concessions to terrorists.
④ Seeing them succeed because of your tuition and guidance are a feeling without comparison.

08 Lobotomy에 관한 다음 글의 내용과 일치하지 않는 것은?

Lobotomy, which is now an obsolete treatment, won the Nobel Prize in Physiology and Medicine in 1949. It was designed to treat mental disorders by disrupting the circuits of the brain but came with serious risks. Popular during the 1940s and 1950s, lobotomies were always controversial and only prescribed in psychiatric cases deemed severe. It consisted of surgically cutting or removing the connections between the prefrontal cortex and frontal lobes of the brain. The procedure could be completed in five minutes. Some patients experienced improvement of symptoms; however, this was often at the cost of introducing other impairments. The procedure was largely discontinued after the mid-1950s with the introduction of the first psychiatric medications.

① It is one of the Nobel Prize-winning treatments.
② It was conducted for minor and serious mental diseases.
③ It is an operative procedure on the brain.
④ It seemed to be effective but had some side effects.

09 주어진 문장이 들어갈 위치로 가장 적절한 것은?

For instance, you may have too much, or not enough, activity of certain brain chemicals called "neurotransmitters" within those circuits.

Doctors don't know the exact cause of most mental illnesses. A combination of things, including your genes, biology, and your life experiences, seems to be involved. In fact, many mental illnesses run in families. (①) But that doesn't mean you will have one if your mother or father did. Some conditions involve circuits in your brain that are used in thinking, mood, and behavior. (②) Brain injuries are also linked to some mental conditions. (③) Some mental illnesses may be triggered or worsened by psychological trauma that happens when you're a child or teenager, such as severe emotional or physical abuse. (④) In addition, major sources of stress, such as a death or divorce, problems in family relationships, and job loss can trigger or aggravate some mental disorders in some people.

* neurotransmitter: 신경전달물질

10 다음 글의 밑줄 친 부분 중 문맥상 단어의 쓰임이 적절하지 않은 것은?

Evidence abounds of ① inhumane treatment of the mentally ill throughout history. For example, as the understanding of mental illness evolved, some practitioners came to believe seizures from such conditions as epilepsy and mental illness including schizophrenia could not exist together. So seizures were ② intentionally induced using medications like the stimulant metrazol in order to try to reduce mental illness. These seizures were not ③ effective, nor were the outcomes of the treatments. Researchers later realized that epilepsy and schizophrenia are not mutually ④ inclusive. This field of seizure-related therapies later led to the more effective study of electric shocks and electroconvulsive therapy(ECT).

01 다음 중 밑줄 친 부분의 의미와 가장 가까운 것은?

It is unpretentious enough to tolerate hiking clothed patrons.

① typical
② humble
③ subtle
④ delectable

02 다음 중 밑줄 친 부분의 의미와 가장 가까운 것은?

Its object is to distribute all the materials evenly throughout the mass, and it is performed in many different ways, both by hand and by machine.

① converse
② get down
③ refrain
④ assign

03 다음 중 밑줄 친 부분의 의미와 가장 가까운 것은?

While the restaurant's interior is small, it is meticulously decorated and the coziness adds to the romantic ambience by experienced owner.

① prudently
② inextricably
③ irrespectively
④ fastidiously

04 다음 대화 중 어색한 것은?

① A: Why didn't you answer his call?
   B: I thought he was crying wolf again.
② A: Could you put the package at Nora's door?
   B: I'm at your command.
③ A: Should I bring in the magazines stacked outside?
   B: No need. They are for the birds.
④ A: Go and see Jack. He's got cold feet for the contest.
   B: That sounds great! I should get him socks.

05 우리말을 영어로 잘못 옮긴 것을 고르시오.

① 오크 나무들을 베는 허가를 요청하는 것에 관한 복잡한 절차가 법적으로 도입되었다.
   → A complicated procedure for seeking permission to fall oak trees legally was introduced.
② 그들의 다리는 이것이 그것들을 치료할 것이라는 잘못 이해된 희망 속에 수년간 계속해서 묶여 있다.
   → Their legs are tied together for years on end in the misguided hope that this will heal them.
③ 나는 가격들이 오를 것이라고 생각하지 않지만, 마찬가지로, 나는 또한 그것들이 떨어진다고 보지 않는다.
   → I don't think that prices will go up but, by the same token, I don't see them going down either.
④ 고용 계층을 대표하는 사람들 사이에 너무 많은 편견이 심한 완고한 이기심이 있다.
   → There is too much bigoted pig-headed selfishness among those who represent the employing classes.

06 우리말을 영어로 잘못 옮긴 것을 고르시오.

① 그들이 코치로 성공했을 때, 그는 그들의 이름을 목록에 체크 표시했다.
→ They getting on the coach, he checked off their names on the list.

② 그가 그 법에 대한 주요 개혁이 있어야 한다고 주장할 것으로 예상된다.
→ It is expected that he will argue there must be major reform to the law.

③ 부모들에 관한 걱정은 그들의 아이들이 대학이 문을 닫을 때 어디에 갈지이다.
→ The concern for parents is where their children will go when the college closes.

④ 그것들이 수많은 어린 사람들이 그들의 잠재력을 실현하고 오늘날 성인들이 되도록 돕는다.
→ They have helped countless young people fulfill their potential and to become the adults today.

07 어법상 옳은 것은?

① His plane is expected to landing at about 7:30 this evening.
② We need to ensure that handwriting properly teach in our primary schools.
③ Had I known you were waiting outside, I would have invited you to come in.
④ The real potential for positive computing to make a difference in our lives are in the devices.

08 밑줄 친 (A), (B)에 들어갈 말로 가장 적절한 것은?

Have you ever wondered which evolved first, eyes or ears? The answer is the former, by at least 40 million years. The only invertebrates with ears are land arthropods and they did not emerge until about 480 million years ago. Older invertebrates had antennae that would have been able to sense vibrations in the water. _____(A)_____, that is not quite the same thing as hearing. Trilobites already had complex compound eyes about 521 million years ago. _____(B)_____ simple eyespots without a lens probably date back to 570 million years ago, when the first multicellular animals appeared.

* trilobite: 삼엽충

	(A)	(B)
①	Hence	On the other hand
②	However	Also
③	Namely	Otherwise
④	As a result	Additionally

09 주어진 문장 다음에 이어질 글의 순서로 가장 적절한 것은?

Although we depend on both vision and hearing to interact with our environment, we generally consider blindness a greater disability than deafness.

(A) However, Daniel Kish, who lost both eyes to retinal cancer before the age of two, doesn't think of his blindness as a great disability. Instead, he taught himself to see by using his ears.

(B) This is probably because, at least when we've lost our hearing, we can still see to navigate through the world and learn sign language or lip reading to communicate.

(C) Kish makes clicking sounds as he moves through the world, and his brain uses the echoes to create a three-dimensional image of his environment.

① (A) − (C) − (B)
② (A) − (B) − (C)
③ (B) − (A) − (C)
④ (B) − (C) − (A)

10 빈칸에 들어갈 표현으로 가장 적절한 것은?

Jennifer Groh at Duke University in Durham and her team have been using microphones inserted into people's ears to study _____ during saccades - the movement that occurs when we shift visual focus from one place to another. You won't notice it, but our eyes go through several saccades a second to take in our surroundings. Examining a number of people, the team detected changes in ear canal pressure that were probably caused by middle-ear muscles tugging on the eardrum. These pressure changes indicate that when we look left, for example, the drum of our left ear gets pulled further into the ear and that of our right ear pushed out, before they both swing back and forth a few times.

① how their eardrums change
② why their ears and eyes interact
③ how their eardrums perceive different sounds
④ how the way their ears move affects their eyes

기적사 DAY 20

01 다음 중 밑줄 친 부분의 의미와 가장 가까운 것은?

> Carefully she moved her feet into a position with better leverage.

① Deliberately ② Typically
③ Fleshly ④ Promptly

02 다음 중 밑줄 친 부분의 의미와 가장 가까운 것은?

> Dean hurriedly left the office before Ethel got ahead.

① termly ② minutely
③ permanently ④ promptly

03 다음 중 밑줄 친 부분의 의미와 가장 가까운 것은?

> Sandwiches and bagels are the staples here for athletic men, all of which are delightfully fresh and eco-friendly.

① precisely ② promptly
③ pleasantly ④ independently

04 다음 글의 밑줄 친 부분에 들어갈 가장 적절한 것은?

> A: You look depressed. What's wrong?
> B: I got fired yesterday. What can I do? I feel hopeless.
> A: Come on, _____. You'll have a good day to come.
> B: Thank you, you are right, but I still feel disheartened.

① it serves you right
② that's the way the cookie crumbles
③ every dog has its day
④ don't let the cat out of the bag

05 우리말을 영어로 잘못 옮긴 것을 고르시오.

① Jane은 짙고 흩날리는 눈을 통해 계속해서 운전하였다.
  → Jane drove on and on through the dense and blowing snow.
② 사장이 파업을 끝내기 위해 할 수 있는 것은 결코 분명하지 않다.
  → It is by no means clear what the president can do to end the strike.
③ 많은 운전자들은 겨울 동안에 짜증을 잘 내거나 성질을 낸다고 말했다.
  → Many drivers said they became irritable or short-tempered during the winter.
④ 그는 두 번의 심각한 부상을 입었고 그의 말들 중 두 마리가 그의 아래에서 총을 맞았다.
  → He was seriously wound twice and two of his horses were shot beneath him.

06 우리말을 영어로 잘못 옮긴 것을 고르시오.

① 북극곰은 두껍고, 기름기가 함유되었으며 방수가 되는 털을 가진다.
  → Polar bears have thick, oil, and water-repellent fur.
② 누구나 그녀를 죽이기를 원해야 한다는 것은 상상도 할 수 없었다.
  → It was unthinkable that anyone should want to kill her.
③ 우승자들이 메달을 받았을 때, 모든 사람들이 환호했다.
  → The winners receiving their medals, everyone cheered.
④ 그들이 그 작은 집에 들어갔을 때 물었던 첫 번째 것은 쓰레기통이 어디에 있는지였다.
  → The first thing they asked when entering the small house was where the dustbin was.

07 어법상 옳은 것은?

① Her body later found hidden in the bushes.
② Babies whose cries are responded to seems to become more self-confident.
③ You would be advised to have the appropriate vaccinations before you go abroad.
④ If the government did not raised food prices, there would not have been so many protests.

08 빈칸 (A), (B)에 들어갈 표현으로 가장 적절한 것은?

The Big Bang Theory is the leading explanation about how the universe began. At its simplest, it says that the universe started with a small singularity, and then inflated over the next 13.8 billion years to the cosmos that we know today. Unfortunately, current instruments do not allow astronomers to peer back at the universe's birth. _____(A)_____, much of what we understand about the Big Bang Theory comes from mathematical formulas and models. Astronomers can, _____(B)_____, see the "echo" of the expansion through a phenomenon known as the cosmic microwave background.

	(A)	(B)
①	Therefore	however
②	Therefore	similarly
③	In contrast	accordingly
④	Therefore	for example

09 주어진 문장이 들어갈 위치로 가장 적절한 것은?

If neither of these scenarios are correct, and the Universe continued to expand at an accelerating rate, the CMB will continue redshifting to the point where it is no longer detectable.

During the 1960s, astronomers became aware of microwave background radiation that was detectable in all directions. (①) Known as the Cosmic Microwave Background (CMB), the existence of this radiation has helped to inform our understanding of how the Universe began. (②) According to various cosmological theories, the Universe may at some point cease expanding and begin reversing, culminating in a collapse followed by another Big Bang - also known as the Big Crunch theory. (③) In another scenario, known as the Big Rip, the expansion of the Universe will eventually lead to all matter and space time itself being torn apart. (④) At this point, it will be overtaken by the first starlight created in the Universe, and then by background radiation fields produced by processes that are assumed will take place in the future of the Universe.

10 밑줄 친 인물(Georges Lemaître)에 대한 설명으로 가장 옳지 않은 것은?

A civil engineer, Georges Lemaître served as an artillery officer in the Belgian Army during World War I. After the war was over in 1918, he entered a seminary and in 1923 was ordained a priest. He studied at the University of Cambridge's solar physics laboratory and then at the Massachusetts Institute of Technology (MIT), where he became acquainted with the findings of the American astronomers Edwin P. Hubble and Harlow Shapley on the expanding universe. In 1927, the year when he became professor of astrophysics at the Catholic University of Leuven, he proposed his big bang theory, which explained the recession of the galaxies within the framework of Albert Einstein's theory of general relativity. Although expanding models of the universe had been considered earlier, notably by the Dutch astronomer Willem de Sitter, Lemaître's theory, as modified by George Gamow, has become the leading theory of cosmology.

① He was engaged in warfare.
② He became a clergyman about five years after World War I.
③ He met with Edwin P. Hubble and Harlow Shapley while attending MIT.
④ He suggested the big bang theory while he was teaching in university.

기적사 복습 모의고사 2회

01 밑줄 친 부분과 의미가 가장 가까운 것을 고르시오.

These days, Halloween has drifted far from its roots in pagan and Catholic festivals, and the spirits we appease are no longer those of the dead: needy ghosts have been replaced by costumed children demanding treats.

① assign ② apprehend
③ pacify ④ provoke

02 다음 중 밑줄 친 부분의 의미와 가장 가까운 것은?

You may call or have friends over anytime you consider something as serious - as long as they don't interfere with your work.

① encumber ② seclude
③ mitigate ④ discern

03 다음 중 밑줄 친 부분의 의미와 가장 가까운 것은?

His aloof response made her get away.

① confident ② reserved
③ integrative ④ plentiful

04 밑줄 친 부분에 들어갈 말로 가장 적절한 것을 고르시오.

As a middle-class Jew growing up in an ethnically mixed Chicago neighborhood, I was already in danger of being beaten up daily by rougher working-class boys. Becoming a bookworm would only have given them a decisive reason for beating me up. Reading and studying were more permissible for girls, but they, too, had to be careful not to get too _____, lest they acquire the stigma of being 'stuck up.'

① athletic ② intellectual
③ hospitable ④ inexperienced

05 어법상 옳은 것은?

① That was the meeting during which I kept falling asleep.
② They may not criticize the state, but neither praise they it.
③ Many things make women difficult to reach the top in US business.
④ Tom learned from the book that the eruption of Vesuvius had destroyed Pompeii.

06 어법상 옳은 것은?

① He was told us of his extraordinary childhood.
② The rewards that come from teaching is numerous.
③ The children are not allowed to watching violent TV programmes.
④ If they had done so, their careers would have been ruined for life.

07 우리말을 영어로 잘못 옮긴 것을 고르시오.

① 노력했을지 모르지만, 그녀는 자신의 걱정스러운 가족이 해체되는 것을 막을 수 없다.
  → Try as she might, she can't keep her troubled family from fragmenting.
② 그 대학은 학생들이 오로지 능력을 토대로 수용된다고 주장한다.
  → The university insists that students are accepted solely on the basis of ability.
③ 이 프로젝트는 너무 중요해서 자금 또는 자원 부족에 의해 방해받을 수 없다.
  → This project is too important to be hindered by a lack of funds or resources.
④ 나는 그제야 Tom이 직면했던 어려움을 평가하기 시작했다.
  → Only then I began to appreciate the difficulties that Tom had faced.

08 우리말을 영어로 잘못 옮긴 것을 고르시오.

① 북극곰은 두껍고, 기름기가 함유되었으며 방수가 되는 털을 가진다.
   → Polar bears have thick, oil, and water-repellent fur.
② 누구나 그녀를 죽이기를 원해야 한다는 것은 상상도 할 수 없었다.
   → It was unthinkable that anyone should want to kill her.
③ 우승자들이 메달을 받았을 때, 모든 사람들이 환호했다.
   → The winners receiving their medals, everyone cheered.
④ 그들이 그 작은 집에 들어갔을 때 물었던 첫 번째 것은 쓰레기통이 어디에 있는지였다.
   → The first thing they asked when entering the small house was where the dustbin was.

09 다음 대화 중 어색한 것을 고르시오.

① A: What do you want for your birthday?
   B: It's up to you.
② A: Call me when you finish the class. I'll pick you up.
   B: Don't bother. Buses run until late.
③ A: The winter vacation is too short.
   B: Couldn't agree more. Speak for yourself.
④ A: I was very busy. I couldn't have finished the job without you.
   B: It was no big deal.

10 다음의 대화 중 이어질 A가 할 말로 적절한 것은?

A: When shall we have the meeting?
B: The sooner the better. We have to meet the deadline for the project.
A: That's why the whole team is working against the clock.
B: I can't count how many times we turned night into day.
A: There's one more to cross over. The vice president's approval to proceed.
B: The thing is, he's not in the office for the next two weeks.
A: _____
B: It's touch-and-go whether we will make it.

① It's not my cup of tea.
② We have to do it from scratch.
③ We have to call him on the carpet.
④ What are the odds of finishing the project?

11 다음 글의 제목으로 가장 적절한 것은?

Inflation is a consistent increase in the prices of goods and services. During periods of inflation, a dollar loses some of its purchasing power and it takes more currency to buy the same amount of the goods or services. For example, if at the beginning of this year one widget is worth $1.00, but inflation is 5% over the year, it will take $1.05 to buy one widget one year later. Deflation is the opposite of inflation. It is a consistent decrease in the prices of goods and services. During deflationary periods, a dollar actually gains purchasing power and it takes less currency to buy the same amount of goods or services than it did before. For example, if at the beginning of this year one widget is worth $1.00, but deflation is 10% over the year, it will take only $0.90 to buy one widget one year later.

① We need Inflation, Not Deflation
② What Causes Inflation and Deflation?
③ The Difference between Inflation and Deflation
④ Inflation or Deflation: Which Is The Greater Risk?

12 빈칸에 들어갈 표현으로 가장 적절한 것은?

What readers most commonly remember about John Stuart Mill's classic exploration of the liberty of thought and discussion concerns the danger of complacency. In the absence of challenge, one's opinions, even when they are correct, grow weak and flabby. Yet Mill had another reason for encouraging the liberty of thought and discussion. _____. Since one's opinions, even under the best circumstances, tend to embrace only a portion of the truth, and because opinions opposed to one's own rarely turn out to be completely erroneous, it is crucial to supplement one's opinions with alternative points of view.

① It is the replication of opinions
② It is the defense of individual liberties
③ It is the danger of partiality and incompleteness
④ It is the constraints on spreading opinions and information

13 빈칸에 들어갈 표현으로 가장 적절한 것은?

Indeed, few forces have historically been more powerful than religion in shaping people's existences. According to the latest poll by the Pew Research Center, 77 percent of Americans say that religion is at least somewhat important in their lives and 83 percent say they're fairly certain that God or a higher power exists. But _____. There has long been a debate among scholars about this issue, with some claiming that it facilitates well-being and others claiming that it leads to neurosis. In fact, there are few issues in the field of psychology as highly researched as this question.

① no one really knows whether God exists or not
② there are too many pseudo-religions around us
③ not everyone agrees that religion is good for us
④ it is obvious that religion plays a positive role in the society

14 주어진 문장이 들어갈 위치로 가장 적절한 것은?

Around the world, from France to Japan to Brazil, the naming of sports officials is clear, consistent, and straightforward.

Mention the 'referee' at a baseball game or the 'umpire' at a basketball game and it's clear you know nothing. (①) And that's perhaps a little unfair because the terminology for sports officials in English makes no sense and has no pattern — or if it does, it's so riddled with holes as to be pointless. (②) This is not the case in other languages. (③) In English-speaking countries sports officials have a dizzying array of names, without any kind of unifying structure as to the role each plays. (④) But it's more like a trap in English. The terms have slightly different base meanings and are not interchangeable, but their use in English does not follow any established pattern between sports. The lead official in an NBA game is a referee. In MLB, it's an umpire. Tennis, American football, and lacrosse all have both referees and a variety of judges.

15 빈칸 (A), (B)에 들어갈 표현으로 가장 적절한 것은?

The Big Bang Theory is the leading explanation about how the universe began. At its simplest, it says that the universe started with a small singularity, and then inflated over the next 13.8 billion years to the cosmos that we know today. Unfortunately, current instruments do not allow astronomers to peer back at the universe's birth. ____(A)____, much of what we understand about the Big Bang Theory comes from mathematical formulas and models. Astronomers can, ____(B)____, see the "echo" of the expansion through a phenomenon known as the cosmic microwave background.

	(A)	(B)
①	Therefore	however
②	Therefore	similarly
③	In contrast	accordingly
④	Therefore	for example

16 다음 글의 흐름상 가장 어색한 문장은?

The Renaissance kitchen had a definite hierarchy of help who worked together to produce the elaborate banquets. ① At the top, as we have seen, was the scalco, or steward, who was in charge of not only the kitchen, but also the dining room. ② The dining room was supervised by the butler, who was in charge of the silverware and linen and also served the dishes that began and ended the banquet— the cold dishes, salads, cheeses, and fruit at the beginning and the sweets and confections at the end of the meal. ③ This elaborate decoration and serving was what in restaurants is called "the front of the house." ④ The kitchen was supervised by the head cook, who directed the undercooks, pastry cooks, and kitchen help.

17 주어진 문장 다음에 이어질 글의 순서로 가장 적절한 것은?

Although we depend on both vision and hearing to interact with our environment, we generally consider blindness a greater disability than deafness.

(A) However, Daniel Kish, who lost both eyes to retinal cancer before the age of two, doesn't think of his blindness as a great disability. Instead, he taught himself to see by using his ears.

(B) This is probably because, at least when we've lost our hearing, we can still see to navigate through the world and learn sign language or lip reading to communicate.

(C) Kish makes clicking sounds as he moves through the world, and his brain uses the echoes to create a three-dimensional image of his environment.

① (A) − (C) − (B)
② (A) − (B) − (C)
③ (B) − (A) − (C)
④ (B) − (C) − (A)

18 다음 글의 요지로 가장 적절한 것은?

In developing countries such as Indonesia, economic growth presents a contradiction. The "paradox of economic growth" is where the economy grows but so does income inequality. Indonesia's economy grew by 6.1% in 2012, 6.3% in 2013 and 6.4% in 2014. At the macro level, Indonesia's economic growth appeared to be good. But if we look closer, we see it was an illusion: behind the scenes Indonesia's Gini ratio was increasing. In 2012 it was 0.36, in 2013 0.39 and in 2014 0.41. As the national economy grew, so did the income gap. The benefits of economic growth − in Indonesia as well as in other developing counties − were reserved for the middle class and above; few benefits made it as far as the lower and working classes. The rich became richer and the poor poorer.

① Indonesia's income inequality can be solved with higher education.
② Indonesia needs to promote social welfare of the entire country by increasing Gini ratio.
③ Economic growth does not mean the equal financial improvement of all groups of population.
④ Economic growth benefits almost all citizens of a nation and therefore reduces poverty ultimately.

19 글의 내용과 일치하지 않는 것은?

The British juvenile justice system underwent significant philosophical changes in the early 20th century. Although there were many who clung to older ideas about the benefits of corporal punishment, the view that children who broke the law should be reclaimed and rehabilitated had become the orthodox view by the passing of the 1948 Children Act. This approach drew upon the views of social workers in the slums of British and American cities and of researchers in the new social and medical sciences. Delinquency was seen as part of a social matrix, as resulting from structural inequalities and deficient parenting styles. The solution to the problem of delinquency was seen as lying within the reformation of the structures which caused these inequities. For the more radical magistrates, the answer was not to overhaul society, but to reform the ways in which children were treated by the courts.

① The courts' better treatment of children could help curb delinquency in some judges' point of view.
② Social workers were among the proponents of the orthodox view.
③ Deficient parenting styles were considered as one cause of delinquency.
④ The 1948 Children Act accentuated the benefits of corporal punishment.

20 글의 내용과 일치하지 않는 것은?

With an urbanization rate of 54% and 20% of total population squatting in over 700 informal settlements, national and local authorities of Jamaica face a serious housing problem. Research undertaken for the National Housing Policy revealed that 15,000 new units are required annually up to 2030 to clear the backlog. However, between 1980 and 2012, the average annual production of housing stood at 4,456 in the formal sector. Meanwhile, low income households find it difficult to access loans and mortgages through the formal financial institutions, as many households are engaged in informal economy where they secure their livelihoods and incomes. Policies have not yet captured the role of micro-financing and flexible financing that could help increase access to formal housing for low income groups. As such, low income households resort to the informal sector and continue to undertake incremental housing development to house themselves. The land registration and development approval processes are also too expensive, rigid and cumbersome and thus; act as hindrances to low income households in accessing affordable formal housing.

① About one fifth of the population are living in unauthorized places.
② The gap between supply and demand of housing existed for more than 30 years.
③ People in the low income bracket rely heavily on unofficial income-generating activities.
④ The government encourages low income families to take advantage of microfinance services.

MEMO

기적사 DAY 21

01 밑줄 친 부분의 의미와 가장 가까운 것을 고르시오.

I came to see these documents as relics of a sensibility now dead and buried, which needed to be excavated.

① exhumed ② packed
③ erased   ④ celebrated

02 밑줄 친 부분의 의미와 가장 가까운 것을 고르시오.

Riding a roller coaster can be a joy ride of emotions: the nervous anticipation as you're strapped into your seat, the questioning and regret that comes as you go up, up, up, and the sheer adrenaline rush as the car takes that first dive.

① utter   ② scary
③ occasional ④ manageable

03 밑줄 친 부분의 의미와 가장 가까운 것을 고르시오.

Time does seem to slow to a trickle during a boring afternoon lecture and race when the brain is engrossed in something highly entertaining.

① enhanced by   ② apathetic to
③ stabilized by ④ preoccupied with

04 밑줄 친 부분에 들어갈 말로 가장 적절한 것은?

A: Hello. I need to exchange some money.
B: Okay. What currency do you need?
A: I need to convert dollars into pounds. What's the exchange rate?
B: The exchange rate is 0.73 pounds for every dollar.
A: Fine. Do you take a commission?
B: Yes, we take a small commission of 4 dollars.
A: _____?
B: We convert your currency back for free. Just bring your receipt with you.

① How much does this cost
② How should I pay for that
③ What's your buy-back policy
④ Do you take credit cards

05 밑줄 친 부분 중 어법상 옳지 않은 것은?

Each year, more than 270,000 pedestrians ① lose their lives on the world's roads. Many leave their homes as they would on any given day never ② to return. Globally, pedestrians constitute 22% of all road traffic fatalities, and in some countries this proportion is ③ as high as two thirds of all road traffic deaths. Millions of pedestrians are non-fatally ④ injuring — some of whom are left with permanent disabilities. These incidents cause much suffering and grief as well as economic hardship.

06 어법상 옳은 것은?

① The paper charged her with use the company's money for her own purposes.
② The investigation had to be handled with the utmost care lest suspicion be aroused.
③ Another way to speed up the process would be made the shift to a new system.
④ Burning fossil fuels is one of the lead cause of climate change.

07 우리말을 영어로 잘못 옮긴 것을 고르시오.

① 혹시 내게 전화하고 싶은 경우에 이게 내 번호야.
  → This is my number just in case you would like to call me.
② 나는 유럽 여행을 준비하느라 바쁘다.
  → I am busy preparing for a trip to Europe.
③ 그녀는 남편과 결혼한 지 20년 이상 되었다.
  → She has married to her husband for more than two decades.
④ 나는 내 아들이 읽을 책을 한 권 사야 한다.
  → I should buy a book for my son to read.

08 주어진 글 다음에 이어질 글의 순서로 가장 적절한 것은?

There is a thought that can haunt us: since everything probably affects everything else, how can we ever make sense of the social world? If we are weighed down by that worry, though, we won't ever make progress.

(A) Every discipline that I am familiar with draws caricatures of the world in order to make sense of it. The modern economist does this by building models, which are deliberately stripped down representations of the phenomena out there.

(B) The economist John Maynard Keynes described our subject thus: "Economics is a science of thinking in terms of models joined to the art of choosing models which are relevant to the contemporary world."

(C) When I say "stripped down," I really mean stripped down. It isn't uncommon among us economists to focus on one or two causal factors, exclude everything else, hoping that this will enable us to understand how just those aspects of reality work and interact.

① (A) − (B) − (C) ② (A) − (C) − (B)
③ (B) − (C) − (A) ④ (B) − (A) − (C)

09 다음 글의 내용과 일치하는 것은?

Prehistoric societies some half a million years ago did not distinguish sharply between mental and physical disorders. Abnormal behaviors, from simple headaches to convulsive attacks, were attributed to evil spirits that inhabited or controlled the afflicted person's body. According to historians, these ancient peoples attributed many forms of illness to demonic possession, sorcery, or the behest of an offended ancestral spirit. Within this system of belief, called *demonology*, the victim was usually held at least partly responsible for the misfortune. It has been suggested that Stone Age cave dwellers may have treated behavior disorders with a surgical method called *trephining*, in which part of the skull was chipped away to provide an opening through which the evil spirit could escape. People may have believed that when the evil spirit left, the person would return to his or her normal state. Surprisingly, trephined skulls have been found to have healed over, indicating that some patients survived this extremely crude operation.

※ convulsive: 경련의 ※ behest: 명령

① Mental disorders were clearly differentiated from physical disorders.
② Abnormal behaviors were believed to result from evil spirits affecting a person.
③ An opening was made in the skull for an evil spirit to enter a person's body.
④ No cave dwellers survived trephining.

10 다음 글의 주제로 가장 적절한 것은?

As the digital revolution upends newsrooms across the country, here's my advice for all the reporters. I've been a reporter for more than 25 years, so I have lived through a half dozen technological life cycles. The most dramatic transformations have come in the last half dozen years. That means I am, with increasing frequency, making stuff up as I go along. Much of the time in the news business, we have no idea what we are doing. We show up in the morning and someone says, "Can you write a story about(pick one) tax policy/immigration/climate change?" When newspapers had once-a-day deadlines, we said a reporter would learn in the morning and teach at night—write a story that could inform tomorrow's readers on a topic the reporter knew nothing about 24 hours earlier. Now it is more like learning at the top of the hour and teaching at the bottom of the same hour. I'm also running a political podcast, for example, and during the presidential conventions, we should be able to use it to do real-time interviews anywhere. I am just increasingly working without a script.

① a reporter as a teacher
② a reporter and improvisation
③ technology in politics
④ fields of journalism and technology

기적사 DAY 22

01 밑줄 친 부분의 의미와 가장 가까운 것을 고르시오.

It takes a long time to <u>excavate</u> a wall painting.

① expunge   ② shovel
③ reinforce   ④ immerse

02 밑줄 친 부분의 의미와 가장 가까운 것을 고르시오.

She earned her grades through <u>sheer</u> hard work.

① absolute   ② essential
③ bullish   ④ obligatory

03 밑줄 친 부분의 의미와 가장 가까운 것을 고르시오.

He <u>engrossed</u> himself in his writing for many months.

① loomed   ② immersed
③ ruined   ④ discriminated

04 다음 대화의 빈칸에 들어갈 가장 알맞은 표현을 고르시오.

A: Hey, how are you doing these days? I haven't seen you in a while.
B: Yeah, I had such a hard time last week, but I'm getting better these days.
A: Oh, I'm sorry for you. What happened to you last week?
B: Well, it's a long story. But to make it short, _____ and I was so stressed out that I couldn't even eat or sleep properly.

① I bit the bullet
② I gave a big hand
③ things got out of hand
④ I pulled the wool over my friend's eyes

05 밑줄 친 부분 중 어법상 옳지 않은 것은?

We find them by looking through the beliefs we already have. We are not ① <u>as concerned</u> with what we are ② <u>heard</u> as we are with finding what we already know that is relevant. Picture it in this way. As understanders, we have a list of beliefs, indexed by subject area. When a new story appears, we attempt to find a belief of ours that ③ <u>is related</u> to it. When we do, we find a story attached to that belief and ④ <u>compare</u> the story in our memory to the one we are processing.

06 어법상 옳은 것은?

① One of the girl you work with is getting married.
② Tom is too frightened to move, lest he disturb the infant.
③ The only logical solution is given the kid a split last name.
④ It displayed the possibility of conquer air itself to the world.

07 우리말을 영어로 잘못 옮긴 것을 고르시오.

① 그녀는 해외에 갈 예정인데, 먹고살 돈이 전혀 없다.
  → She's going abroad, and she has absolutely no money to live on.
② 느긋한 하루였고 모두가 그저 평화를 즐기느라 바빴다.
  → It was a lazy day and everyone was busy simply enjoying the peace.
③ 그것이 다시 발생해야 하는 경우에 그는 촬영되는 것을 원하지 않았다.
  → He did not want to be photographed in case it should happen again.
④ Jane이 Tom과 결혼한 단 하나의 이유는 그녀가 임신했기 때문이다.
  → The only reason Jane married to Tom was because she was pregnant.

08 다음 글의 밑줄 친 부분 중 문맥상 단어의 쓰임이 적절하지 않은 것은?

An economic model is a ① simplified description of reality, designed to yield hypotheses about the economy. Models generally consist of a set of mathematical equations that describe a theory of ② economical behavior. The aim of model builders is to ③ include enough equations to provide useful clues about how rational agents behave or how an economy works. An important feature of an economic model is that it is ④ necessarily subjective in design because there are no objective measures of economic outcomes. Each economist will make a different judgment about what is needed to explain their interpretations of reality.

09 밑줄 친 부분 중 글의 흐름상 가장 어색한 것은?

Prior to the discovery of ether anesthesia in 1846, all surgeries — from minor to major or absolutely radical — were performed on people who were wide-awake, oftentimes held down on the operating table by men whose only job was to ignore the patient's pleas, screams and sobs so that the surgeon could do his job. Anesthesia was discovered in a time before standardized medicine. ① There was no guaranteed quality when it came to medicine during this time period. ② When ether anesthesia was introduced, the surgical world was overjoyed and embraced this transformative innovation with widespread immediacy. ③ Surgeons also didn't fully trust the ether they were using. ④ Sometimes the mixture was too weak, and the patients wouldn't lose consciousness, or perhaps more horrifically, would regain consciousness mid-surgery. Other times, the mixture would be too strong, and the patient would die on the table from an overdose.

10 다음 글의 제목으로 가장 적절한 것은?

Many of these everyday voters will trust they're getting a neutral summary of what happened on debate night. Unfortunately, the reality is much more complicated. Traditional reporters want to be neutral, detached observers who deliver information about the political process without participating in it. But true neutrality and total detachment are basically impossible. In a primary debate, there's no higher authority or judge who will appear at the end of the night and declare a winner. Instead, journalists are forced to make their own determinations about who performed well, which moments mattered and what sections of the debate will be used for B-roll. Sometimes a consensus will organically form among mainstream news reporters. But there's no way to judge whether that consensus is right, because there's no objective standard for victory in this sort of forum.

* B-roll: 특징적인 소리가 빠진 영상, 리포터가 묘사와 해설을 할 때 쓰이는 영상

① The Importance of Primary Debates
② How Is Political News Content Created?
③ The Relationship Between Politics and Journalism
④ Being Neutral Is Impossible in Political Debate Coverage

01 밑줄 친 부분의 의미와 가장 가까운 것을 고르시오.

We pack each one in an oxygen-inflated plastic bag with enough water to keep the fish relaxed and comfortable.

① disclose ② ebb
③ bundle ④ preserve

02 밑줄 친 부분의 의미와 가장 가까운 것을 고르시오.

Apart from railing against the enforced inertia of train journeys, people utter no panegyrics about the scenery through which they pass; they only have hideous tales to tell about fellow passengers.

① extend ② daunt
③ dissatisfy ④ say

03 밑줄 친 부분의 의미와 가장 가까운 것을 고르시오.

Alcohol is a component of suicidal behavior. It leads to disinhibition, and it can enhance feelings of hopelessness and depression.

① slacken ② intensify
③ stow ④ unearth

04 다음 대화의 빈칸에 들어갈 가장 알맞은 표현을 고르시오.

A: What did you do last Monday?
B: I went to watch a musical with my family. I had such a great time.
A: I haven't seen any musical in a while. I'm jealous of you. What was the title?
B: It was 'Mamma Mia'. The actors and actresses on stage impressed me with their voice. I almost cried in the end.
A: Wow, who were the starring stars?
B: Oh, _____ I can't remember that now.

① you are a big mouth.
② it was a slip of the tongue.
③ I forgot on the tip of my tongue.
④ you took the words out of my mouth.

05 밑줄 친 부분 중 어법상 옳지 않은 것은?

Communicating the vision to organization members nearly always ① mean putting "where we are going and why" in writing, distributing the statement organizationwide, and ② having executives personally explain the vision and its justification to ③ as many people as possible. Ideally, executives should present their vision for the company in a manner that reaches out and grabs people's attention. An engaging and convincing strategic vision has enormous motivational value — for the same reason that a stone mason is ④ inspired by building a great cathedral for the ages.

06 어법상 옳은 것은?

① Listening to your baby cry is one of the hardest part of being a parent.
② She spent whole days in her room, wearing headphones lest she not disturb anyone.
③ In talking with other people, don't begin by discussing the things on which you differ.
④ The best way to deal with environmental problems is prevented them from happening.

07 우리말을 영어로 잘못 옮긴 것을 고르시오.

① 그녀는 자신의 딸들을 부자들과 결혼시키기로 결심했다.
→ She was determined to marry all of her daughters to rich men.
② 그 회사는 또한 콘텐츠 제작자들과의 합의에 대해 타결을 보느라 바쁘다.
→ The company is also busily hammering out deals with content producers.
③ 예술을 만들려는 한 개별 쪽의 의도는 의미 있을 것이다.
→ Any intention on the part of an individual to make art would be meaningful.
④ 어떤 일이 우리에게 벌어진 경우에 나는 경찰이 무엇이 일어났는지 알기를 원했다.
→ I wanted the police to know what was taking place in case something happened to us.

08 빈칸에 들어갈 표현으로 가장 적절한 것은?

Economic models are used for two main purposes: simulating and forecasting. They are great tools for simulations - given what we know about the behavioral workings of the economy, and taking these mostly as given, how might the economy respond to, say, an energy price spike? But models are much _____ at providing forecasts precisely not least because when making forecasts, very little can be taken as given. The further out the forecast, the larger the structural uncertainties, making model projections at best illustrative, especially when trying to forecast the impact of non-marginal impulses such as climate change impacts or the transformation of the global energy system.

① less vague
② less effective
③ more practical
④ less theoretical

09 다음 글의 내용과 일치하지 않는 것은?

Magic and religion were part of everyday life in ancient Egypt. Gods and demons were thought to be responsible for many ailments, so the treatments often involved some supernatural element. Often priests and magicians were called on to treat disease instead of, or in addition to a physician. Physicians themselves often used incantations and magical ingredients as part of their treatments. The impact of the emphasis on magic is seen in the selection of remedies, or the ingredients for those remedies. Ingredients were sometimes selected seemingly because they were derived from a substance, plant or animal that had characteristics which in some way corresponded to the symptoms of the patient. For instance, an ostrich egg was included in the treatment of a broken skull, and an amulet portraying a hedgehog was used against baldness.

① Ancient Egyptians believed that diseases were caused due to supernatural beings.
② In some cases, priests were asked to lead a treatment process.
③ It was not allowed for non-magicians to perform magic during treatments.
④ Magic greatly influenced the choices of remedy ingredients.

10 다음 글의 내용과 일치하지 않는 것은?

Consumers today receive news articles on their smart phones. Citizens now play a drastic role in journalism, and the usage of smart phones and social media allows citizens to partake in the news making process. Platforms such as Twitter, YouTube and WordPress allow ordinary citizens to produce their own news content and share it with larger news sources such as CNN. For some, this can create a problem. Who is a journalist? What defines a "journalist?" Social media is raising these questions and it is creating problems for jobs in the media. Social media, however, is now a required skill and tool for all journalists to use and gain expertise in. News organizations and media corporations want to see that journalists and prospective employees are savvy with social media, and can become powerful influencers online.

① The emergence of smartphones has changed the way news is generated and consumed.
② Large news companies sometimes use news content from social media users.
③ Social media has had positive effects only on the field of journalism.
④ Journalists today have no choice but to be engaged in social media.

기적사 DAY 24

01 밑줄 친 부분의 의미와 가장 가까운 것을 고르시오.

Minnie, a longtime client at my beauty salon, was about to celebrate her 100th birthday and I had promised her complimentary hair services when she reached the century mark.

① captivate ② differentiate
③ commemorate ④ discontinue

02 밑줄 친 부분의 의미와 가장 가까운 것을 고르시오.

The movie was great. I especially liked the scary part.

① ingenious ② frightening
③ splendid ④ efficient

03 밑줄 친 부분의 의미와 가장 가까운 것을 고르시오.

The first condition that a student can be successful in this apathetic world is that he should be sedulous.

① sporadic ② absolute
③ reciprocal ④ indifferent

04 다음 빈칸에 들어갈 가장 적절한 표현을 순서대로 나열한 것은?

A: Where are you headed to?
B: I am going to the cafeteria to grab something to eat. Did you have lunch?
A: Yes I did. But since I'm feeling hungry, can I join you?
B: Sure, I'm glad to have company. You don't look as you'll eat much. I thought you'd eat like a _____.
A: Oh, not at all. I eat like a _____ these days. I eat way too much.
B: Really? But you didn't gain any weight.

① cat-bird ② dog-horse
③ bird-horse ④ horse-bird

05 밑줄 친 부분 중 어법상 옳지 않은 것은?

In 2006, the percentage of women's ① waging non-agricultural employment in East Asia and Pacific countries was twice ② as high as that of South Asia. In that same year, the percentage of women's waged non-agricultural employment in the Middle East and North Africa ③ was less than that of Sub-Saharan Africa by ten percentage points. Between 1990 and 2006, the increase in the percentage of women's waged non-agricultural employment in Sub-Saharan Africa was larger than ④ that of the Middle East and North Africa.

06 어법상 옳은 것은?

① As to this it is necessary to avoid misapprehension lest the protection is too limited.
② One of the many strength of the African American community is an intrinsic support.
③ Some countries and some regions are more capable than others at address the problem.
④ The purpose of the positive comment might be to avoid a disagreement and support the friend.

07 우리말을 영어로 잘못 옮긴 것을 고르시오.

① 화자들은 그들이 말하고 싶은 바를 계획할 시간이 없다.
 → Speakers do not have the time to plan out what they want to say.
② Jane은 Tom에게 자신이 남편을 떠나 그와 결혼해서 미국으로 이사하기를 원했다고 말했다.
 → Jane told Tom she wanted to leave her husband, marry him, and move to America.
③ 내 동료는 폭풍우가 가게에서 물건 사는 것을 어렵게 하는 경우에 대비하여 내가 식량을 비축해야 한다고 말했다.
 → My colleagues said I should stock up on food in case of the storm made it difficult to shop.
④ 그들은 할리우드에서 영화 거래를 성사시키고 연극 각색에 대해 상담하느라 너무 바쁘다.
 → They are too busy negotiating film deals in Hollywood and consulting on theatrical adaptations.

08 다음 글의 내용과 일치하지 않는 것은?

During the Great Depression of the 1930s, the existing economic theory was unable either to explain the causes of the severe worldwide economic collapse or to provide an adequate public policy solution to jump-start production and employment. British economist John Maynard Keynes spearheaded a revolution in economic thinking that overturned the then-prevailing idea that free markets would automatically provide full employment — that is, that everyone who wanted a job would have one as long as workers were flexible in their wage demands. He asserted that free markets have no self-balancing mechanisms that lead to full employment. And, Keynesian economists, who follow economic theories developed by Keynes, justify government intervention through public policies that aim to achieve full employment and price stability.

① In the 1930s, there was a global recession.
② Up until the Great Depression, free market economy was the predominating economic theory.
③ According to the free market economy theory, the depression was due to low employment.
④ Keynes denied the free market economy theory.

09 빈칸에 들어갈 표현으로 가장 적절한 것은?

In the long process of discovering which plants were edible, humans in the Stone Age also identified many which seem to cure ailments or soothe a fever. The early physicians stumbled on herbal substances of real power, without understanding the manner of their working. Nonetheless, herbal medicine is the earliest scientific tradition in medical practice, and _____.

The snakeroot plant was traditionally used as a tonic in the east to calm patients; it is now used in orthodox medical practice to reduce blood pressure. Doctors in ancient India gave an extract of foxglove to patients with legs swollen by dropsy; digitalis, a constituent of foxglove, is now a standard stimulant for the heart.

① various herbs are now used for culinary purposes
② it remains an important part of medicine to this day
③ growing medicinal plants has become very popular today
④ a number of physicians in the west are practicing herbal medicine as well

10 주어진 문장이 들어갈 위치로 가장 적절한 것은?

Some bloggers have admitted changing their blog archives to make their previous incorrect predictions appear true.

Some bloggers have established a continuing presence on the Web and draw large daily audiences. Many political bloggers have sought legitimacy as news professionals and in recent years they have succeeded. (①) Bloggers were credentialed at the 2004 presidential conventions, and in 2009 President Obama called on a blogger at a White House press conference. (②) Traditional journalists are wary of these new entrants into the field. (③) Many reporters worry that without an institutional reputation at stake, bloggers are careless and prone to make false accusations or disseminate false information. (④) While professional journalists have deplored bloggers' casual attitude to truth and accuracy, bloggers point out that they are under constant scrutiny from their readers and the blogosphere.

기적사 DAY 25

01 다음 중 밑줄 친 부분의 의미와 가장 가까운 것은?

I'm sure he could read the <u>frustration</u> in my voice due to his sensibility.

① revival
② enlightenment
③ achievement
④ discouragement

02 밑줄 친 부분의 의미와 가장 가까운 것을 고르시오.

We saw <u>occasional</u> flashes of lightning in the northern sky.

① additional
② alarming
③ intermittent
④ feasible

03 밑줄 친 부분의 의미와 가장 가까운 것을 고르시오.

The short legs may have helped <u>stabilize</u> the huge body.

① sustain
② engulf
③ intensify
④ identify

04 두 사람의 대화 중 가장 어색한 것은?

① A: How should I make up for the mistake I made to my friend?
B: Well, I suggest you face the music and apologize.

② A: What's your comment on my presentation?
B: I'll give you thumbs up.

③ A: What do you think of the latest article I wrote on the political issue?
B: I thought you hit the nail on the head.

④ A: I donated half of my earnings this month to the charity.
B: You paid your debt to nature.

05 밑줄 친 부분 중 어법상 옳지 않은 것은?

Theories of all sorts promote the view that there are ways by which disagreement can be ① <u>processed</u> or managed so as ② <u>to make</u> it disappear. The assumption behind those theories is ③ <u>that</u> disagreement is wrong and consensus is the desirable state of things. In fact, consensus rarely comes without some forms of subtle coercion and the absence of fear in expressing a disagreement ④ <u>are</u> a source of genuine freedom.

06 어법상 옳은 것은?

① The community would not be ultimately enriched by cease to educate its children.
② Finding a cure for cancer is one of the biggest challenge facing medical researchers.
③ They usually prefer to keep their goals as vague as possible lest it does not count against them at the next election.
④ One way in which children can achieve better status among their peers is to be perceived as physically competent.

07 우리말을 영어로 잘못 옮긴 것을 고르시오.

① 그의 아내 Jane은 그가 자신이 만나본 가장 재미있는 남자였기 때문에 그와 결혼했다.
→ His wife, Jane married to him because he was the funniest man she had ever met.
② 어떤 사람은 분노를 배출하고 표현하라고 그 사람에게 독려할 것이다.
→ Someone would probably encourage the person to vent and express anger.
③ 그들은 젊고 유행에 밝지만 자신들의 일을 너무 즐기느라 휴일을 가질 수 없다.
→ They're young and hip but they're far too busy enjoying their jobs to take holidays.
④ 나는 무슨 일이 벌어질지 즐겁지만 일이 잘못될까 봐 여전히 초조하다.
→ I am chuffed about what is happening but still nervous in case anything goes wrong.

08 주어진 문장 다음에 이어질 글의 순서로 가장 적절한 것은?

There is a burning question in digital healthcare whether a well-managed smart home with health care technologies can be a substitute for hospital care.

(A) Nonetheless, connected home health is a vision that should be encouraged since it offers plenty of opportunities for patient empowerment and control, as well as lowering health expenses in many different situations.
(B) Connected smart homes might not yet be able to completely replace existing healthcare services, but they can add value to the healthcare continuum of care, improve the quality of care, and reduce the mounting pressures on a healthcare system that in many ways is over capacity.
(C) Experts in general agree that in many situations there will probably always be a need for hospitals and face-to-face health interventions.

① (A) − (C) − (B)   ② (B) − (A) − (C)
③ (B) − (C) − (A)   ④ (C) − (A) − (B)

09 글의 내용과 일치하는 것은?

When children are given the option of a super sweet food such as lollies or a mildly sweet food such as fruit, most will automatically choose the lolly. Young children are genetically programmed to have a preference for certain tastes and a dislike for others. From the very beginning babies are attracted to sweet flavor, which is what helps them to drink breast milk. They are also fond of salty tastes, and averse to sour and bitter. These are natural animal responses that would have helped humans survive during hunter-gatherer times. Since most poisonous or toxic plants have a sour or bitter taste, it makes sense that children are programmed to naturally avoid those flavors. A preference of familiar tastes over new tastes would have also prevented children from eating something potentially unsafe. This helps to explain why training toddlers' taste buds and introducing new foods to them can be ever so challenging.

① For genetic reasons, fruit is preferred over candy.
② Human breast milk is a naturally sweet food.
③ Young kids generally dislike salty, sour and bitter tastes.
④ In hunter-gatherer times, many children died from eating poisonous plants.

10 다음 글의 주제로 가장 적절한 것은?

Cholesterol travels through the blood on proteins called "lipoproteins." LDL(low-density lipoprotein), sometimes called "bad" cholesterol, makes up most of your body's cholesterol. High levels of LDL cholesterol raise your risk for heart disease and stroke. When your body has too much LDL cholesterol, the LDL cholesterol can build up on the walls of your blood vessels. This buildup is called "plaque." As your blood vessels build up plaque over time, the insides of the vessels narrow. This narrowing blocks blood flow to and from your heart and other organs. When blood flow to the heart is blocked, it can cause angina or a heart attack. HDL(high-density lipoprotein), or "good" cholesterol, absorbs cholesterol and carries it back to the liver. The liver then flushes it from the body. High levels of HDL cholesterol can lower your risk for heart disease and stroke.

* lipoprotein: 지질단백질, 리포 단백질
* angina: 협심증

① the ways to raise HDL levels
② the dangers of high cholesterol
③ the types of cholesterol we have
④ the main causes of heart disease

결국엔 성정혜 영어 하프모의고사

기적사 DAY 26

기출 하프 ☑ 파생 하프 ☐ 복습 모의고사 ☐

소요 시간 :   / 15분   맞은 개수 :   / 10개

01 밑줄 친 부분의 의미와 가장 가까운 것은?

Justifications are accounts in which one accepts responsibility for the act in question, but denies the pejorative quality associated with it.

① derogatory
② extrovert
③ mandatory
④ redundant

02 밑줄 친 부분에 들어갈 말로 가장 적절한 것은?

Tests ruled out dirt and poor sanitation as causes of yellow fever, and a mosquito was the _____ carrier.

① suspected
② uncivilized
③ cheerful
④ volunteered

03 밑줄 친 부분에 들어갈 말로 가장 적절한 것은?

To imagine that there are concrete patterns to past events, which can provide _____ for our lives and decisions, is to project on to history a hope for a certainty which it cannot fulfill.

① hallucinations
② templates
③ inquiries
④ commotion

04 대화 중 가장 어색한 것은?

① A: What was the movie like on Saturday?
   B: Great. I really enjoyed it.
② A: Hello. I'd like to have some shirts pressed.
   B: Yes, how soon will you need them?
③ A: Would you like a single or a double room?
   B: Oh, it's just for me, so a single is fine.
④ A: What time is the next flight to Boston?
   B: It will take about 45 minutes to get to Boston.

05 밑줄 친 부분 중 어법상 가장 옳지 않은 것은?

Inventor Elias Howe attributed the discovery of the sewing machine ① for a dream ② in which he was captured by cannibals. He noticed as they danced around him ③ that there were holes at the tips of spears, and he realized this was the design feature he needed ④ to solve his problem.

06 밑줄 친 부분 중 어법상 가장 옳지 않은 것은?

By 1955 Nikita Khrushchev ① had been emerged as Stalin's successor in the USSR, and he ② embarked on a policy of "peaceful coexistence" ③ whereby East and West ④ were to continue their competition, but in a less confrontational manner.

07 밑줄 친 부분 중 어법상 가장 옳지 않은 것은?

Squid, octopuses, and cuttlefish are all ① types of cephalopods. ② Each of these animals has special cells under its skin that ③ contains pigment, a colored liquid. A cephalopod can move these cells toward or away from its skin. This allows it ④ to change the pattern and color of its appearance.

08 글의 흐름상 가장 어색한 문장은?

Children's playgrounds throughout history were the wilderness, fields, streams, and hills of the country and the roads, streets, and vacant places of villages, towns, and cities. ① The term *playground* refers to all those places where children gather to play their free, spontaneous games. ② Only during the past few decades have children vacated these natural playgrounds for their growing love affair with video games, texting, and social networking. ③ Even in rural America few children are still roaming in a free-ranging manner, unaccompanied by adults. ④ When out of school, they are commonly found in neighborhoods digging in sand, building forts, playing traditional games, climbing, or playing ball games. They are rapidly disappearing from the natural terrain of creeks, hills, and fields, and like their urban counterparts, are turning to their indoor, sedentary cyber toys for entertainment.

09 다음 빈칸에 들어갈 말로 가장 알맞은 것을 고르시오.

In the 1840s, the island of Ireland suffered famine. Because Ireland could not produce enough food to feed its population, about a million people died of ____(A)____; they simply didn't have enough to eat to stay alive. The famine caused another 1.25 million people to ____(B)____; many left their island home for the United States; the rest went to Canada, Australia, Chile, and other countries. Before the famine, the population of Ireland was approximately 6 million. After the great food shortage, it was about 4 million.

	(A)	(B)
①	dehydration	be deported
②	trauma	immigrate
③	starvation	emigrate
④	fatigue	be detained

10 다음 빈칸에 들어갈 말로 가장 알맞은 것을 고르시오.

Today the technology to create the visual component of virtual-reality (VR) experiences is well on its way to becoming widely accessible and affordable. But to work powerfully, virtual reality needs to be about more than visuals. ____(A)____ what you are hearing convincingly matches the visuals, the virtual experience breaks apart. Take a basketball game. If the players, the coaches, the announcers, and the crowd all sound like they're sitting midcourt, you may as well watch the game on television — you'll get just as much of a sense that you are "there." ____(B)____, today's audio equipment and our widely used recording and reproduction formats are simply inadequate to the task of re-creating convincingly the sound of a battlefield on a distant planet, a basketball game at courtside, or a symphony as heard from the first row of a great concert hall.

	(A)	(B)
①	If	By contrast
②	Unless	Consequently
③	If	Similarly
④	Unless	Unfortunately

기적사 DAY 27

01 다음 중 밑줄 친 부분의 의미와 가장 가까운 것은?

But, although the union of the Roses ought to have extinguished controversy, a host of debatable questions and plausible pretexts for rebellion remained.

① pejorative ② pertinacious
③ controversial ④ guileless

02 다음 중 밑줄 친 부분의 의미와 가장 가까운 것은?

Vague and contradictory standards of liability threaten innocent companies for sanitation.

① drastic ② detrimental
③ impressionable ④ incongruous

03 다음 중 밑줄 친 부분의 의미와 가장 가까운 것은?

Nor is his theory of the weight essential to atoms as being due to an inner force impelling them to motion in any way reconcilable with his general doctrine of mechanical causes.

① corresponding ② avaricious
③ hallucinated ④ peremptory

04 밑줄 친 부분에 들어갈 표현으로 가장 적절한 것은?

Bob: Am I the last one to arrive? I am sorry for being late.
Amy: It's fine. You seem to _____(A)_____. Did you run here?
Bob: Yes, I planned on taking the bus, and then I heard about the traffic jam. So I decided to take the subway instead.
Amy: It must have been such a long trip for you to come here.
Bob: I can't say it was easy. But I managed to get off the subway _____(B)_____.
Amy: Oh, lucky you. So you ran here from the subway station _____(C)_____?
Bob: That's right. I feel too tired now.

	(A)	(B)	(C)
①	be around the clock	at full tilt	over the hill
②	feel at home	in hot water	under the counter
③	be short of breath	by the skin of my teeth	at full tilt
④	feel at home	in hot water	out of the frying pan into the fire

05 밑줄 친 부분 중 어법상 가장 옳지 않은 것은?

Tom said to John ① that in November 1971 he had lent a friend a copy of the book — a unique copy ② in what he had made notes on turning the British English ③ into American English for the publication of an American version — but his friend ④ had lost the copy in London.

06 밑줄 친 부분 중 어법상 가장 옳지 않은 것은?

In areas that ① are not especially relevant to our self-definition, we ② engage in reflection, ③ whereby we flatter ourselves by association with others' accomplishments. Suppose you care ④ very few about your own athletic skills.

07 밑줄 친 부분 중 어법상 가장 옳지 않은 것은?

"Research from cognitive science has shown," he explained, "that the sorts of ① skills that teachers want for their students — such as the ability ② to analyze and think critically — ③ require extensive factual knowledge." We have to know things, in other words, to think critically about ④ it.

08 다음 글의 내용과 일치하지 않는 것은?

According to the U.S. Consumer Product Safety Commission (USCPSC), emergency departments treat more than 200,000 children for playground-related injuries each year. Most playground injuries happen when a child falls from the equipment onto the ground. That's why the best way to prevent injuries is to make sure the surface underneath it can help absorb and soften the impact when children land on it. Steer clear of hard surfaces like concrete or asphalt. Although grass may look soft, it is not a shock absorbing surface. The USCPSC recommends a thick layer of one of the materials like wood chips, mulch, sand, and mats made of safety-tested rubber or rubber-like material, extending at least 6 feet in all directions, underneath play equipment.

① There are a great number of children who get injured in playgrounds.
② Injuries from falling from play equipment are most common.
③ Playgrounds built on asphalt are better avoided.
④ Surfaces made of grass are quite safe for children.

09 빈칸에 들어갈 표현으로 가장 적절한 것은?

The Irish Potato Famine was the most catastrophic event in Ireland's turbulent history. It is also regarded as being one of the worst Famines in history. ____(A)____, the use of the word 'Famine' in this context is controversial, for Ireland at the time was part of the richest Empire in the world (the British Empire). There was sufficient food in the country throughout the 'Famine' years, yet over a million people died from starvation and disease, and millions more were forced to flee. ____(B)____, some historians prefer to use the name 'Great Hunger' to describe this period of mass death from starvation and disease.

	(A)	(B)
①	Hence	Therefore
②	Accordingly	In contrast
③	However	Thus
④	Nevertheless	On the other hand

10 다음 글의 제목으로 가장 적절한 것은?

Augmented Reality (AR) is a variation of Virtual Environment (VE), or Virtual Reality (VR) as it is more commonly called. Virtual Reality technologies completely immerse a user inside a synthetic environment and while immersed, the user cannot see the real world around him. In contrast, Augmented Reality is taking digital or computer generated information, whether it be images, audio, video, and touch or haptic sensations and overlaying them over in a real-time environment. Augmented Reality technically can be used to enhance all five senses, but its most common present-day use is visual. Unlike Virtual Reality, Augmented Reality allows the user to see the real world, with virtual objects superimposed upon or composited with the real world.

① Which Is Better: VR or AR?
② VR vs. AR: What's the Difference?
③ Development of Augmented Reality
④ Augmented Reality and Its Applications

01 다음 중 밑줄 친 부분의 의미와 가장 가까운 것은?

Hypnosis is an augmentative intervention that should be used in conjunction with treatments determined by your physician.

① futile
② acute
③ redundant
④ increscent

02 다음 중 밑줄 친 부분의 의미와 가장 가까운 것은?

There grew up a mass of controversial matter which it is amusing to read now.

① suspected
② contentious
③ spiritous
④ corresponsive

03 다음 중 밑줄 친 부분의 의미와 가장 가까운 것은?

Regardless of what we suspect, it's still just conjecture of the templates.

① refine on
② at a charge of
③ pertaining to
④ notwithstanding

04 두 사람의 대화 중 가장 자연스러운 것은?

① A: How did you get the scholarship?
　B: I studied hard day and night.
② A: Did we cover all the materials last class?
　B: Congratulations. I feel happy for you.
③ A: I went to the groceries last Saturday but I forgot to buy milk.
　B: I've been thinking about making some investments. Are you in?
④ A: You've changed so much since the last time we met. What happened to you?
　B: I am not afraid to make changes anymore.

05 밑줄 친 부분 중 어법상 가장 옳지 않은 것은?

The very prospect of losing everything and having ① to start all over again would be overwhelming for anybody. That is the reason ② for which I want to provide you ③ for any assistance that I can. I have an extra bedroom ④ that you are welcome to use.

06 밑줄 친 부분 중 어법상 가장 옳지 않은 것은?

Traditional consumption ① was not particularly thrifty. The concept of thrift ② was emerged out of a more affluent money culture. ③ In traditional societies where resources ④ continued to be scarce, consumption was more seasonally and communally oriented.

07 밑줄 친 부분 중 어법상 가장 옳지 않은 것은?

Because the Internet is free space where anybody can post anything, ① it can be full of all sorts of ② the useless data. As a result, ③ organized knowledge could easily get corrupted or lost in a sea of junk data. For books, there are various filters that ④ help readers distinguish between reliable and unreliable information.

08 밑줄 친 (A), (B)에 들어갈 가장 적절한 것은?

In Asian countries like Japan, people are huge gift-givers. And across Asia - as with Europe - it's good manners to take a gift if you're invited to someone's home for a meal. But there are a couple of cultural differences to be mindful of. While in the west, popular gifts would be a bottle of wine or some flowers, this is not the case in Asia. There are a lot of people who don't drink alcohol so, depending on where you are, your hosts may not consider alcohol an _____(A)_____ gift. Similarly, flowers can be a minefield. In some Asian countries, different flower types, their color and even their arrangement may communicate specific messages you don't intend to convey. Basically, they're best _____(B)_____. Instead, it's a safe bet to find out what sweets are popular in the area you're visiting. Buy them from somewhere that comes highly recommended by locals, ensure they're attractively packaged, and you'll have a gift that's good in just about every context.

	(A)	(B)
①	appropriate	avoided
②	unsuitable	eschewed
③	appropriate	selected
④	unsuitable	presented

09 다음 글의 주제로 가장 적절한 것은?

The Great Famine, also called the Irish Potato Famine, proved to be a watershed in the demographic history of Ireland. As a direct consequence of the famine, Ireland's population of almost 8.4 million in 1844 had fallen to 6.6 million by 1851. The number of agricultural laborers and smallholders in the western and southwestern counties underwent an especially drastic decline. A further aftereffect of the famine was thus the clearing of many smallholders from the land and the concentration of landownership in fewer hands. Thereafter, more land than before was used for grazing sheep and cattle, providing animal foods for export to Britain.

① major causes of the Great Famine
② direct and indirect results of the Great Famine
③ effects of the Great Famine on Irish agriculture
④ demographic changes following the Great Famine

10 빈칸에 들어갈 표현으로 가장 적절한 것은?

Traveling through VR is a different kind of traveling. The immersive video allows you to experience your destinations before even packing your suitcase. With VR, you can _____. If you think you will feel claustrophobic in the cruise stateroom, then why not test the waters? Perhaps you will feel better in a suit. VR allows you to explore the cruise ship rooms as well as the rooms in a hotel prior to booking it. Aside from checking your room, you can also have a street view, check the venues, and restaurants nearby. With this virtual tour, you can decide whether the destination you have picked for yourself is good or not.

① travel wherever and whenever you want
② save your travel budget before you leave
③ relive your vacation after returning home
④ have the try－it－before－you－buy－it experience

기적사 DAY 29

01 다음 중 밑줄 친 부분의 의미와 가장 가까운 것은?

You both must agree to the terms you made, and I will agree on behalf of the Council for getting the justifications.

① in a person's stead ② in the matter of
③ in a class with ④ at a cost of

02 다음 중 밑줄 친 부분의 의미와 가장 가까운 것은?

High costs of complex server infrastructure can be unwieldy and expensive to manage in the civilized society.

① clonish ② callow
③ cumbersome ④ timid

03 다음 중 밑줄 친 부분의 의미와 가장 가까운 것은?

We need not, however, spend much time on the well-worn but inconclusive arguments of the older critics.

① inquiring ② offenseless
③ not in the least ④ not in conclusion

04 다음 대화의 빈칸에 들어갈 가장 알맞은 표현을 고르시오.

A: When does your mid-term exam start?
B: Next Wednesday. How about you?
A: Mine begins tomorrow, and I'm taking Mathematics. But it's _____.
B: It's not your fault, Mathematics isn't so easy. But you can ask me if you want. I got an A+ in Mathematics last semester.
A: Wow, seriously? How did you get such a good grade?
B: I actually felt the same as you at first. But I didn't give up.

① in body ② over my head
③ neck and neck ④ a pain in the neck

05 밑줄 친 부분 중 어법상 가장 옳지 않은 것은?

Competition becomes a zero sum game ① which one organization can only win at the expense of others. However, ② where the degree of competition is particularly intense a zero sum game can quickly become a negative sum game, in ③ that everyone in the market is faced ④ with additional costs.

06 밑줄 친 부분 중 어법상 가장 옳지 않은 것은?

Unless something ① <u>interferes</u>, the inferior competitor loses out and the competitively superior species ② <u>takes over</u>. When one species ③ <u>eliminate</u> another by outcompeting it, it ④ <u>is called</u> competitive exclusion.

07 밑줄 친 부분 중 어법상 가장 옳지 않은 것은?

All ① <u>smiled</u>, John, a cute three-year-old boy, was walking along the aisle of snacks, bars, and sweets. It was the aisle of all kinds of ② <u>temptation</u> for him. "Wow!" he exclaimed. Right in front of his eyes ③ <u>were</u> rows of delicious-looking chocolate bars waiting ④ <u>to be touched</u>.

08 빈칸 (A), (B)에 들어갈 표현으로 가장 적절한 것은?

Early playgrounds looked very different to what we've become used to today. The idea of creating a playground was first introduced in Germany, essentially as a platform to teach children the correct way to play. However, it wasn't until 1859 that the first children's playground was built in a park in Manchester, the Britain. The idea of building playgrounds for children spread to the United States and in 1886 America's first playgrounds started appearing in Boston. These early playgrounds were very _____(A)_____ by modern standards and definitely wouldn't comply with health and safety regulations today. When playgrounds first emerged, they usually consisted of roughly built structures, made from iron, with sharp edges that could do a lot of damage if they weren't used _____(B)_____.

	(A)	(B)
①	crude	properly
②	humble	exclusively
③	primitive	constantly
④	sophisticated	appropriately

09 주어진 문장 다음에 이어질 글의 순서로 가장 적절한 것은?

Scientists have long known that it was a strain of *Phytophthora infestans* that caused the widespread devastation of potato crops in Ireland beginning in 1845, leading to the Irish Potato Famine.

(A) After sequencing the genome of the 19th century samples and comparing them with modern blights, including US-1, the researchers concluded that it wasn't in fact US-1 that caused the blight, but a previously unknown strain, HERB-1, which had originated in the Americas sometime in the early 19th century before spreading to Europe in the 1840s.

(B) To solve the mystery, molecular biologists examined DNA extracted from nearly a dozen botanical specimens dating back as far as 1845.

(C) The most likely culprit, they believed, was a strain known as US-1.

* Phytophthora infestans 감자역병균

① (B) - (C) - (A)
② (B) - (A) - (C)
③ (C) - (A) - (B)
④ (C) - (B) - (A)

10 주어진 문장 다음에 이어질 글의 순서로 가장 적절한 것은?

Holoride, a start-up spun out of luxury carmaker Audi, has teamed up with Ford and Universal Pictures to showcase the world's first "in-car virtual reality experience".

(A) Then, Holoride takes data from the car — including GPS, navigation route, the steering angle and g-forces from acceleration — and translates them in real time into a virtual environment.

(B) The software company's technology enables gaming partners such as Disney to create virtual experiences that correspond to a car's real-time movements.

(C) Passengers wear a headset to immerse themselves in a virtual environment.

① (A) - (C) - (B)
② (B) - (A) - (C)
③ (B) - (C) - (A)
④ (C) - (A) - (B)

01 다음 중 밑줄 친 부분의 의미와 가장 가까운 것은?

And some offices remained the exclusive property of the doctors.

① monopolistic ② ingenuous
③ extrovert   ④ humdrum

02 다음 중 밑줄 친 부분의 의미와 가장 가까운 것은?

The preparations were made on an unprecedented scale.

① unreadable   ② unexampled
③ volunteered ④ unballasted

03 다음 중 밑줄 친 부분의 의미와 가장 가까운 것은?

Here he distinguished himself by his outspoken criticism of the Austrian government, leading the opposition of the duchy to the exactions of the central power.

① blunt   ② concrete
③ baffling   ④ numerous

04 다음 빈칸에 들어갈 가장 적절한 표현을 순서대로 적은 것은?

Peter: I'm excited to meet your friend at last. ___(A)___, she is noticeably tall.
Nancy: You already heard about her! Yes, she is very tall. But what makes her such a good person is that she is ___(B)___.
Peter: What a nice way to speak of a person! You two seem really close.
Nancy: Indeed, we are. We've been friends ever since we were born.
Peter: How surprising! So you guys were born in the same hospital?
Nancy: Yeah, and I hope we will be friends ___(C)___. I can't imagine life without her.

	(A)	(B)	(C)
①	Take it easy	bad blood	by a close call
②	Break a leg	a wild card	across the board
③	By a word of mouth	a heart of gold	for good
④	By a word of mouth	a skeleton in the closet	for good

05 밑줄 친 부분 중 어법상 가장 옳지 않은 것은?

Corporations add another layer of complication ① to the story of reduced personal responsibility in group settings because corporations are set up ② to assign legal responsibility to the corporation itself instead of to its members. There are other complex organizations ③ in which the individual members are often not sure ④ that their impact or power to bring about change.

06 밑줄 친 부분 중 어법상 가장 옳지 않은 것은?

In monkey colonies, ① where rigid dominance hierarchies exist, beneficial innovations do not spread quickly through the group unless they ② are taught first to a dominant animal. When a lower animal ③ is taught the new concept first, the rest of the colony ④ is remained mostly oblivious to its value.

07 밑줄 친 부분 중 어법상 가장 옳지 않은 것은?

We would like to ① know the rate of natural soil formation from solid rock ② to determine whether topsoil erosion from agriculture is too great. Likewise, understanding how climate has changed over millions of years ③ is vital to properly assess current global warming trends. Clues to past environmental change are well preserved in many different kinds of ④ the rocks.

08 다음 글에서 전체 흐름과 관계없는 문장은?

Have you ever heard someone described as "born to lead?" According to this point of view, great leaders are simply born with the necessary internal characteristics such as charisma, confidence, intelligence, and social skills that make them natural-born leaders. ① Great man theories assume that the capacity of great leaders is inherent - that great leaders are born, not made. ② These theories often portray great leaders as heroic, mythic and destined to rise to leadership when needed. ③ Rooted in behaviorism, these focus on the actions of leaders, not on natural mental qualities or internal states. ④ Such theories suggest that people cannot really learn how to become strong leaders. It is either something you are born with or born without. It is very much a nature (as opposed to nurture) approach to explaining leadership.

09 빈칸에 들어갈 표현으로 가장 적절한 것은?

Alzheimer's disease is the most common form of dementia. The risk for the disease increases with age and the causes are largely unknown. Seeking new treatments to slow the progression of Alzheimer's disease, researchers found the hypertension drug 'nilvadipine', a calcium channel blocker for patients with high blood pressure that leads to vascular relaxation and lowers blood pressure, increased blood flow to the brain's memory and learning center among people with Alzheimer's disease without affecting other parts of the brain, according to new research in the American Heart Association's journal *Hypertension*. These findings indicate that the known decrease in cerebral blood flow in patients with Alzheimer's can be _____ in some regions. However, an important question is whether this change translates to clinical benefits, the researchers noted.

① stimulated ② perceived
③ observed   ④ reversed

10 글의 흐름상 빈칸에 들어갈 가장 적절한 것은?

Many linguists predict that at least half of the world's 6,000 or so languages will be dead or dying by the year 2050. Languages are becoming extinct at twice the rate of endangered mammals and four times the rate of endangered birds. If this trend continues, the world of the future could be dominated by a dozen or fewer languages. Replacing a minor language with a more widespread one may even seem like a good thing, allowing people to communicate with each other more easily. But language diversity is not less important in its way than biological diversity. The extinction of a species causes some ecosystems to collapse. _____, when a language dies, a world dies with it, in the sense that a community's connection with its past, its traditions and its base of specific knowledge are all typically lost as the vehicle linking people to that knowledge is abandoned.

① Similarly   ② Outwardly
③ Conversely ④ Particularly

01 밑줄 친 부분의 의미와 가장 가까운 것은?

Justifications are accounts in which one accepts responsibility for the act in question, but denies the pejorative quality associated with it.

① derogatory ② extrovert
③ mandatory ④ redundant

02 밑줄 친 부분의 의미와 가장 가까운 것을 고르시오.

Minnie, a longtime client at my beauty salon, was about to celebrate her 100th birthday and I had promised her complimentary hair services when she reached the century mark.

① captivate ② differentiate
③ commemorate ④ discontinue

03 밑줄 친 부분에 들어갈 말로 가장 적절한 것은?

Tests ruled out dirt and poor sanitation as causes of yellow fever, and a mosquito was the _____ carrier.

① suspected ② uncivilized
③ cheerful ④ volunteered

04 밑줄 친 부분의 의미와 가장 가까운 것을 고르시오.

Time does seem to slow to a trickle during a boring afternoon lecture and race when the brain is engrossed in something highly entertaining.

① enhanced by ② apathetic to
③ stabilized by ④ preoccupied with

05 다음 글의 주제로 가장 적절한 것은?

The Great Famine, also called the Irish Potato Famine, proved to be a watershed in the demographic history of Ireland. As a direct consequence of the famine, Ireland's population of almost 8.4 million in 1844 had fallen to 6.6 million by 1851. The number of agricultural laborers and smallholders in the western and southwestern counties underwent an especially drastic decline. A further aftereffect of the famine was thus the clearing of many smallholders from the land and the concentration of landownership in fewer hands. Thereafter, more land than before was used for grazing sheep and cattle, providing animal foods for export to Britain.

① major causes of the Great Famine
② direct and indirect results of the Great Famine
③ effects of the Great Famine on Irish agriculture
④ demographic changes following the Great Famine

06 어법상 옳은 것은?

① Listening to your baby cry is one of the hardest part of being a parent.
② She spent whole days in her room, wearing headphones lest she not disturb anyone.
③ In talking with other people, don't begin by discussing the things on which you differ.
④ The best way to deal with environmental problems is prevented them from happening.

07 밑줄 친 부분 중 어법상 가장 옳지 않은 것은?

Competition becomes a zero sum game ① which one organization can only win at the expense of others. However, ② where the degree of competition is particularly intense a zero sum game can quickly become a negative sum game, in ③ that everyone in the market is faced ④ with additional costs.

08 다음 글의 제목으로 가장 적절한 것은?

Many of these everyday voters will trust they're getting a neutral summary of what happened on debate night. Unfortunately, the reality is much more complicated. Traditional reporters want to be neutral, detached observers who deliver information about the political process without participating in it. But true neutrality and total detachment are basically impossible. In a primary debate, there's no higher authority or judge who will appear at the end of the night and declare a winner. Instead, journalists are forced to make their own determinations about who performed well, which moments mattered and what sections of the debate will be used for B-roll. Sometimes a consensus will organically form among mainstream news reporters. But there's no way to judge whether that consensus is right, because there's no objective standard for victory in this sort of forum.

* B-roll: 특징적인 소리가 빠진 영상, 리포터가 묘사와 해설을 할 때 쓰이는 영상

① The Importance of Primary Debates
② How Is Political News Content Created?
③ The Relationship Between Politics and Journalism
④ Being Neutral Is Impossible in Political Debate Coverage

09 빈칸에 들어갈 표현으로 가장 적절한 것은?

In the long process of discovering which plants were edible, humans in the Stone Age also identified many which seem to cure ailments or soothe a fever. The early physicians stumbled on herbal substances of real power, without understanding the manner of their working. Nonetheless, herbal medicine is the earliest scientific tradition in medical practice, and _____. The snakeroot plant was traditionally used as a tonic in the east to calm patients; it is now used in orthodox medical practice to reduce blood pressure. Doctors in ancient India gave an extract of foxglove to patients with legs swollen by dropsy; digitalis, a constituent of foxglove, is now a standard stimulant for the heart.

① various herbs are now used for culinary purposes
② it remains an important part of medicine to this day
③ growing medicinal plants has become very popular today
④ a number of physicians in the west are practicing herbal medicine as well

10 빈칸에 들어갈 표현으로 가장 적절한 것은?

Economic models are used for two main purposes: simulating and forecasting. They are great tools for simulations - given what we know about the behavioral workings of the economy, and taking these mostly as given, how might the economy respond to, say, an energy price spike? But models are much _____ at providing forecasts precisely not least because when making forecasts, very little can be taken as given. The further out the forecast, the larger the structural uncertainties, making model projections at best illustrative, especially when trying to forecast the impact of non-marginal impulses such as climate change impacts or the transformation of the global energy system.

① less vague   ② less effective
③ more practical   ④ less theoretical

11 다음 대화의 빈칸에 들어갈 가장 알맞은 표현을 고르시오.

A: What did you do last Monday?
B: I went to watch a musical with my family. I had such a great time.
A: I haven't seen any musical in a while. I'm jealous of you. What was the title?
B: It was 'Mamma Mia'. The actors and actresses on stage impressed me with their voice. I almost cried in the end.
A: Wow, who were the starring stars?
B: Oh, _____ I can't remember that now.

① you are a big mouth.
② it was a slip of the tongue.
③ I forgot on the tip of my tongue.
④ you took the words out of my mouth.

12 두 사람의 대화 중 가장 어색한 것은?

① A: How should I make up for the mistake I made to my friend?
   B: Well, I suggest you face the music and apologize.
② A: What's your comment on my presentation?
   B: I'll give you thumbs up.
③ A: What do you think of the latest article I wrote on the political issue?
   B: I thought you hit the nail on the head.
④ A: I donated half of my earnings this month to the charity.
   B: You paid your debt to nature.

13 밑줄 친 부분 중 어법상 가장 옳지 않은 것은?

In areas that ① are not especially relevant to our self-definition, we ② engage in reflection, ③ whereby we flatter ourselves by association with others' accomplishments. Suppose you care ④ very few about your own athletic skills.

14 우리말을 영어로 잘못 옮긴 것을 고르시오.

① 화자들은 그들이 말하고 싶은 바를 계획할 시간이 없다.
   → Speakers do not have the time to plan out what they want to say.
② Jane은 Tom에게 자신이 남편을 떠나 그와 결혼해서 미국으로 이사하기를 원했다고 말했다.
   → Jane told Tom she wanted to leave her husband, marry him, and move to America.
③ 내 동료는 폭풍우가 가게에서 물건 사는 것을 어렵게 하는 경우에 대비하여 내가 식량을 비축해야 한다고 말했다.
   → My colleagues said I should stock up on food in case of the storm made it difficult to shop.
④ 그들은 할리우드에서 영화 거래를 성사시키고 연극 각색에 대해 상담하느라 너무 바쁘다.
   → They are too busy negotiating film deals in Hollywood and consulting on theatrical adaptations.

15 다음 글의 내용과 일치하지 않는 것은?

According to the U.S. Consumer Product Safety Commission (USCPSC), emergency departments treat more than 200,000 children for playground-related injuries each year. Most playground injuries happen when a child falls from the equipment onto the ground. That's why the best way to prevent injuries is to make sure the surface underneath it can help absorb and soften the impact when children land on it. Steer clear of hard surfaces like concrete or asphalt. Although grass may look soft, it is not a shock absorbing surface. The USCPSC recommends a thick layer of one of the materials like wood chips, mulch, sand, and mats made of safety-tested rubber or rubber-like material, extending at least 6 feet in all directions, underneath play equipment.

① There are a great number of children who get injured in playgrounds.
② Injuries from falling from play equipment are most common.
③ Playgrounds built on asphalt are better avoided.
④ Surfaces made of grass are quite safe for children.

16 다음 글의 내용과 일치하지 않는 것은?

Consumers today receive news articles on their smart phones. Citizens now play a drastic role in journalism, and the usage of smart phones and social media allows citizens to partake in the news making process. Platforms such as Twitter, YouTube and WordPress allow ordinary citizens to produce their own news content and share it with larger news sources such as CNN. For some, this can create a problem. Who is a journalist? What defines a "journalist?" Social media is raising these questions and it is creating problems for jobs in the media. Social media, however, is now a required skill and tool for all journalists to use and gain expertise in. News organizations and media corporations want to see that journalists and prospective employees are savvy with social media, and can become powerful influencers online.

① The emergence of smartphones has changed the way news is generated and consumed.
② Large news companies sometimes use news content from social media users.
③ Social media has had positive effects only on the field of journalism.
④ Journalists today have no choice but to be engaged in social media.

17 다음 빈칸에 들어갈 말로 가장 알맞은 것을 고르시오.

Today the technology to create the visual component of virtual-reality (VR) experiences is well on its way to becoming widely accessible and affordable. But to work powerfully, virtual reality needs to be about more than visuals. ___(A)___ what you are hearing convincingly matches the visuals, the virtual experience breaks apart. Take a basketball game. If the players, the coaches, the announcers, and the crowd all sound like they're sitting midcourt, you may as well watch the game on television — you'll get just as much of a sense that you are "there." ___(B)___, today's audio equipment and our widely used recording and reproduction formats are simply inadequate to the task of re-creating convincingly the sound of a battlefield on a distant planet, a basketball game at courtside, or a symphony as heard from the first row of a great concert hall.

	(A)	(B)
①	If	By contrast
②	Unless	Consequently
③	If	Similarly
④	Unless	Unfortunately

18 밑줄 친 부분 중 글의 흐름상 가장 어색한 것은?

Prior to the discovery of ether anesthesia in 1846, all surgeries — from minor to major or absolutely radical — were performed on people who were wide-awake, oftentimes held down on the operating table by men whose only job was to ignore the patient's pleas, screams and sobs so that the surgeon could do his job. Anesthesia was discovered in a time before standardized medicine. ① There was no guaranteed quality when it came to medicine during this time period. ② When ether anesthesia was introduced, the surgical world was overjoyed and embraced this transformative innovation with widespread immediacy. ③ Surgeons also didn't fully trust the ether they were using. ④ Sometimes the mixture was too weak, and the patients wouldn't lose consciousness, or perhaps more horrifically, would regain consciousness mid-surgery. Other times, the mixture would be too strong, and the patient would die on the table from an overdose.

19 주어진 문장이 들어갈 위치로 가장 적절한 것은?

Some bloggers have admitted changing their blog archives to make their previous incorrect predictions appear true.

Some bloggers have established a continuing presence on the Web and draw large daily audiences. Many political bloggers have sought legitimacy as news professionals and in recent years they have succeeded. (①) Bloggers were credentialed at the 2004 presidential conventions, and in 2009 President Obama called on a blogger at a White House press conference. (②) Traditional journalists are wary of these new entrants into the field. (③) Many reporters worry that without an institutional reputation at stake, bloggers are careless and prone to make false accusations or disseminate false information. (④) While professional journalists have deplored bloggers' casual attitude to truth and accuracy, bloggers point out that they are under constant scrutiny from their readers and the blogosphere.

20 주어진 문장 다음에 이어질 글의 순서로 가장 적절한 것은?

There is a burning question in digital healthcare whether a well-managed smart home with health care technologies can be a substitute for hospital care.

(A) Nonetheless, connected home health is a vision that should be encouraged since it offers plenty of opportunities for patient empowerment and control, as well as lowering health expenses in many different situations.

(B) Connected smart homes might not yet be able to completely replace existing healthcare services, but they can add value to the healthcare continuum of care, improve the quality of care, and reduce the mounting pressures on a healthcare system that in many ways is over capacity.

(C) Experts in general agree that in many situations there will probably always be a need for hospitals and face-to-face health interventions.

① (A) − (C) − (B) ② (B) − (A) − (C)
③ (B) − (C) − (A) ④ (C) − (A) − (B)

기적사 DAY 31

01 밑줄 친 부분의 의미와 가장 가까운 것을 고르시오.

The paramount duty of the physician is to do no harm. Everything else —even healing —must take second place.

① chief
② sworn
③ successful
④ mysterious

02 밑줄 친 부분의 의미와 가장 가까운 것을 고르시오.

It is not unusual that people get cold feet about taking a trip to the North Pole.

① become ambitious
② become afraid
③ feel exhausted
④ feel saddened

03 밑줄 친 부분의 의미와 가장 가까운 것은?

The student who finds the state-of-the-art approach intimidating learns less than he or she might have learned by the old methods.

① humorous
② friendly
③ convenient
④ frightening

04 밑줄 친 부분에 들어갈 말로 가장 적절한 것은?

A: My computer just shut down for no reason. I can't even turn it back on again.
B: Did you try charging it? It might just be out of battery.
A: Of course, I tried charging it.
B: _____
A: I should do that, but I'm so lazy.

① I don't know how to fix your computer.
② Try visiting the nearest service center then.
③ Well, stop thinking about your problems and go to sleep.
④ My brother will try to fix your computer because he's a technician.

05 밑줄 친 부분 중 어법상 옳지 않은 것은?

I am writing in response to your request for a reference for Mrs. Ferrer. She has worked as my secretary ① for the last three years and has been an excellent employee. I believe that she meets all the requirements ② mentioned in your job description and indeed exceeds them in many ways. I have never had reason ③ to doubt her complete integrity. I would, therefore, recommend Mrs. Ferrer for the post ④ what you advertise.

06 어법상 옳은 것은?

① Please contact to me at the email address I gave you last week.
② Were it not for water, all living creatures on earth would be extinct.
③ The laptop allows people who is away from their offices to continue to work.
④ The more they attempted to explain their mistakes, the worst their story sounded.

07 우리말을 영어로 옳게 옮긴 것은?

① 그녀는 며칠 전에 친구를 배웅하기 위해 역으로 갔다.
   → She went to the station a few days ago to see off her friend.
② 버릇없는 그 소년은 아버지가 부르는 것을 못 들은 체했다.
   → The spoiled boy made it believe he didn't hear his father calling.
③ 나는 버팔로에 가본 적이 없어서 그곳에 가기를 고대하고 있다.
   → I have never been to Buffalo, so I am looking forward to go there.
④ 나는 아직 오늘 신문을 못 읽었어. 뭐 재미있는 것 있니?
   → I have not read today's newspaper yet. Is there anything interested in it?

08 주어진 문장이 들어갈 위치로 가장 적절한 것은?

> The same thinking can be applied to any number of goals, like improving performance at work.

The happy brain tends to focus on the short term. (①) That being the case, it's a good idea to consider what short-term goals we can accomplish that will eventually lead to accomplishing long-term goals. (②) For instance, if you want to lose thirty pounds in six months, what short-term goals can you associate with losing the smaller increments of weight that will get you there? (③) Maybe it's something as simple as rewarding yourself each week that you lose two pounds. (④) By breaking the overall goal into smaller, shorter-term parts, we can focus on incremental accomplishments instead of being overwhelmed by the enormity of the goal in our profession.

09 다음 글의 내용과 일치하지 않는 것을 고르시오.

In the nineteenth century, the most respected health and medical experts all insisted that diseases were caused by "miasma," a fancy term for bad air. Western society's system of health was based on this assumption: to prevent diseases, windows were kept open or closed, depending on whether there was more miasma inside or outside the room; it was believed that doctors could not pass along disease because gentlemen did not inhabit quarters with bad air. Then the idea of germs came along. One day, everyone believed that bad air makes you sick. Then, almost overnight, people started realizing there were invisible things called microbes and bacteria that were the real cause of diseases. This new view of disease brought sweeping changes to medicine, as surgeons adopted antiseptics and scientists invented vaccines and antibiotics. But, just as momentously, the idea of germs gave ordinary people the power to influence their own lives. Now, if you wanted to stay healthy, you could wash your hands, boil your water, cook your food thoroughly, and clean cuts and scrapes with iodine.

① In the nineteenth century, opening windows was irrelevant to the density of miasma.
② In the nineteenth century, it was believed that gentlemen did not live in places with bad air.
③ Vaccines were invented after people realized that microbes and bacteria were the real cause of diseases.
④ Cleaning cuts and scrapes could help people to stay healthy.

10 다음 글의 내용과 일치하지 않는 것을 고르시오.

Followers are a critical part of the leadership equation, but their role has not always been appreciated. For a long time, in fact, "the common view of leadership was that leaders actively led and subordinates, later called followers, passively and obediently followed." Over time, especially in the last century, social change shaped people's views of followers, and leadership theories gradually recognized the active and important role that followers play in the leadership process. Today it seems natural to accept the important role followers play. One aspect of leadership is particularly worth noting in this regard: Leadership is a social influence process shared among all members of a group. Leadership is not restricted to the influence exerted by someone in a particular position or role; followers are part of the leadership process, too.

① For a length of time, it was understood that leaders actively led and followers passively followed.
② People's views of subordinates were influenced by social change.
③ The important role of followers is still denied today.
④ Both leaders and followers participate in the leadership process.

01 밑줄 친 부분의 의미와 가장 가까운 것을 고르시오.

The more advanced your training, the more successful your application as a police officer will be.

① overt ② fictitious
③ prosperous ④ arguable

02 다음 중 밑줄 친 부분의 의미와 가장 가까운 것은?

You've been so reserved lately.

① garrulous ② impromptu
③ taciturn ④ dubious

03 다음 중 밑줄 친 부분의 의미와 가장 가까운 것은?

Though his sentences themselves are not wordy, he is extremely diffuse in treatment, habitually repeating an idea in successive sentences of much the same import.

① enervate ② indifferent
③ talkative ④ ambitious

04 다음 대화의 빈칸에 들어갈 가장 알맞은 표현을 고르시오.

A: You look so tired today. Are you all right?
B: Not really, I only slept three hours studying for my exam today.
A: You should go to take some rest. I'm worried you are going to _____ on the test.
B: Well, let's just hope that I will not.

① shake a leg ② drop the ball
③ talk through my hat ④ call a spade a spade

05 밑줄 친 부분 중 어법상 옳지 않은 것은?

Internet entrepreneurs are creating job-search products and bringing them online regularly. Within the past few years, new Internet-based businesses ① have come online that help people find internships, complete online classes ② tailoring to individual employer job applications, or find volunteer work ③ that will lead to full-time employment. Job mastery will mean keeping up with the rapidly ④ evolving tools available on the Internet.

06 어법상 옳은 것은?

① Had Hitler invaded England in 1940, he would win the war.
② The sooner I get this piece of work done, sooner I can go home.
③ There are many aspects of this case that is directly relevant to church treasurers.
④ The cuckoo which resembles like a sparrow hawk in flight can be difficult to identify.

07 우리말을 영어로 옳게 옮긴 것은?

① 나는 사람들이 나를 우러러보게 하는 의상을 입어야 할 것이다.
→ I would have to wear a costume that would make people to look up to me.
② 흑색종이 그녀의 다리에서 발견된 이후 5년 전에 그녀는 그 질병을 물리쳤다.
→ She beat off the disease five years ago after a melanoma had been found on her leg.
③ 경기 회복을 다루는 것에 관한 한 그는 여전히 최고의 경제학자이다.
→ He is still the best economist when it comes to deal with the economic recovery.
④ 우리는 그들에게 흥미롭고 흥미진진하게 할 프로그램을 짜기 위해 노력하는 중이다.
→ We are trying to set up a programme which will be interested and excited for them.

08 밑줄 친 부분 중 글의 흐름상 가장 어색한 것은?

Once again, I'm not asking you to divide your large goal into small steps - I'm asking you to make a smaller goal. It doesn't even matter if they're unrelated to your big goal or dream - just start knocking down goals. The reasoning behind this is quite simple. ① You need momentum, and nothing builds momentum like getting a few wins under your belt. Don't get me wrong. ② I'm all about thinking big and having big dreams, but I also understand the need for momentum and confidence. ③ Once you come to a precise goal, you can work on breaking it up into manageable tasks. ④ Accomplishing a goal is a lot better than taking a step, especially for someone who has not been in business of large goal setting and achieving. The purpose of these smaller goals is not to get you closer to your goal, but to develop the skill of belief - the belief that you can accomplish goals - not steps.

09 다음 글의 내용과 일치하는 것은?

When Louis Pasteur theorized that "germs" caused disease in the 19th century, he and Florence Nightingale had a rigorous debate. The belief that bad air from pollution, exhalation from the lungs of the ill, and unhealthy vapors caused disease had held since the time of the Greeks. In fact, Nightingale's environmental theory was based on this same belief. Thus her hospital design included well-ventilated wards, lots of sunlight, and cleanliness of patient and their environment. When John Snow, the accepted founder of epidemiology, claimed that cholera was water borne, he supported the idea that microorganisms entering the body and going from person to person was the source of the epidemic. This argument was used by manufacturing companies that were being blamed for cholera because of the noxious-smelling exhaust coming from their factories.

① Nightingale was skeptical of Pasteur's point of view.
② Pasteur's idea was in line with the Greek's belief on the cause of disease.
③ Hospitals designed by Nightingale had poor ventilation systems.
④ Snow agreed with Nightingale's environmental theory.

10 빈칸에 들어갈 문장으로 가장 적절한 것은?

An authoritative leader will induce fear within the group and spur misunderstandings. We have exaggerated examples of authoritative leadership gone wrong in our history and we do not want to repeat that. Great leaders are those who know how to be great followers, and this is something that not many comprehend. Following someone requires carefully listening to instructions, conducting the necessary job that is being delegated, being inquisitive and making inquiries to guide the leader at every step of the way, and being the supporting body of the team to get the task done effectively. It is hence essential to understand that _____ _____. A leader is no one without followers and a follower is no one without a leader.

① we are all followers in some areas of our lives
② there are many qualities that leaders have to possess
③ leadership and followership is complementary to each other
④ good leaders are good at motivating their followers to change

01 밑줄 친 부분의 의미와 가장 가까운 것을 고르시오.

The process of journal-keeping through writing and drawing helped heal me from a mysterious illness which had defied the doctors and their medicines.

① sovereign
② bogus
③ enigmatic
④ pompous

02 다음 중 밑줄 친 부분의 의미와 가장 가까운 것은?

The retrospective exhibition of means of transport was unusual and interesting in view of the recent opening of the Simplon tunnel, the occasion of the exhibition.

① ecstatic
② material
③ systematic
④ reminiscent

03 다음 중 밑줄 친 부분의 의미와 가장 가까운 것은?

The owner was candid about the things that went wrong as well as the successes.

① frank
② down-to-earth
③ fave
④ intimidating

04 두 사람의 대화 중 가장 어색한 것은?

① A: What are you dressed up for?
   B: I have a family dinner out tonight.
② A: Where is the convenience store located?
   B: The map shows that it's right across the street.
③ A: I am thinking about taking a semester off next year.
   B: That's a good idea. Do you have plans in mind?
④ A: We should all make a New year's resolution before it turns twelve midnight.
   B: I am ready to leave right away once the bell ring.

05 밑줄 친 부분 중 어법상 옳지 않은 것은?

The most normal and competent child encounters ① what seem like insurmountable problems in living. But by playing them out, he may become able ② to cope with them in a step-by-step process. He often does so in symbolic ways that are hard for even him to understand, as he is reacting to inner processes whose origin may be ③ burying deep in his unconscious. This may result in play that makes ④ little sense to us at the moment, since we do not know the purposes it serves.

06 어법상 옳은 것은?

① She showed me round the towns, which were very kind of her.
② The more she thought about it, the more devastating it became.
③ It had not been for a seatbelt, he would have been killed in the accident.
④ It is important to emphasize on that dementia is a syndrome and not a disease.

07 우리말을 영어로 옳게 옮긴 것은?

① 도심지 주차 제한 규정이 지난달에 시행되었다.
→ Parking restrictions in the town centre come into force last month.
② 처음 몇 년 동안 괜찮은 것이 나타나는 것을 보는 것은 매우 놀랍지 않다.
→ It is not terribly surprised to see anything decent crop up in the first few years.
③ 그들은 그 근처 일대를 새롭게 하기 위하여 오래된 건물들을 허물었다.
→ They've torn down the old buildings with a view to renovating the whole neighborhood.
④ 그의 여동생은 1년 전에 심장마비로 죽었고 그의 아버지는 올해 3번 발병하셨다.
→ His sister has died of a heart attack a year ago and his father has had three attacks this year.

08 빈칸에 들어갈 표현으로 가장 적절한 것은?

In 1981, researchers Albert Bandura and Dale Schunk tested something interesting. Bandura and Schunk worked with 7 to 10-year-old children behind and with little interest in math. About half the children received the suggestion to set a goal of completing six pages of math problems per session, and the other half received the suggestion to set a distal goal of completing 42 pages of math problems over seven sessions. What happened? Smaller subgoals led to faster completion and more accurate answers than one large goal. It turned out that the proximal goal intervention _____ students' self-efficacy in math and their math learning.

① depleted
② eliminated
③ ameliorated
④ dispersed

09 주어진 문장이 들어갈 위치로 가장 적절한 것은?

By improving the housing, sanitation and general cleanliness of these existing areas, levels of disease were seen to fall, which lent weight to the theory.

In miasma theory, diseases were caused by the presence in the air of a miasma, a poisonous vapor in which were suspended particles of decaying matter that was characterized by its foul smell. (①) The theory originated in the Middle Ages and endured for several centuries. In 19th-century England the miasma theory made sense to the sanitary reformers. (②) Rapid industrialization and urbanization had created many poor, filthy and foul-smelling city neighborhoods that tended to be the focal points of disease and epidemics. (③) Although it had been disproved and rejected later, the miasma theory's existence was not without its merits. (④) By removing the causes of bad smells, reformers often inadvertently removed bacteria, the real cause of many diseases.

10 다음 글의 제목으로 가장 적절한 것은?

Leadership is a process that emerges from a relationship between leaders and followers who are bound together by their understanding that they are members of the same social group. People will be more effective leaders when their behaviors indicate that they are one of us, because they share our values, concerns and experiences, and are doing it for us, by looking to advance the interests of the group rather than own personal interests. This perspective identifies a major flaw in the usual advice for aspiring leaders. Instead of seeking to stand out from their peers, they may be better served by ensuring that they are seen to be a good follower — as someone who is willing to work within the group and on its behalf.

① Leaders Are Born Not Made
② Anyone Can Learn to Be a Leader
③ How to Be Seen as a Leader and Not a Follower
④ To Be a Good Leader, Start by Being a Good Follower

기적사 DAY 34

01 다음 중 밑줄 친 부분의 의미와 가장 가까운 것은?

He had the paramount courage to step forward and take chances, and the ability to persuade others to follow.

① conduct
② convince
③ plunge
④ oppress

02 다음 중 밑줄 친 부분의 의미와 가장 가까운 것은?

Exhausting people in this country, the new constitution, however, proved costly and unworkable, and failed to satisfy either section of the population.

① acquire
② assert
③ transfer
④ gratify

03 다음 중 밑줄 친 부분의 의미와 가장 가까운 것은?

And the whole thing has been unnatural because that cat and I are both able to talk your language, and to understand the words you say.

① tend
② daunt
③ comprehend
④ frighten

04 다음 대화의 빈칸에 들어갈 가장 알맞은 표현을 고르시오.

Jenny: Did I mention I will be moving next month?
Pat: Not at all. You live near the subway station, don't you?
Jenny: Yes I do. But the monthly rent is so expensive that I can barely afford it.
Pat: Oh, is that why you are moving?
Jenny: That's the only reason. I'll invite you to _____ once I move into my new house.
Pat: Thank you so much for the invitation.

① a big deal
② a blind date
③ the name of the game
④ a house-warming party

05 밑줄 친 부분 중 어법상 옳지 않은 것은?

During the last two decades many developing countries ① have joined the global tourism market as part of globalization processes and the fall of the Iron Curtain. These countries had suffered from negative public and media image ② of which made it challenging for them ③ to compete over tourists with countries with strong and familiar brands. In this global era, a problematic image is a major obstacle in ④ attracting tourists, high-quality residents and investors.

06 어법상 옳은 것은?

① Was it to rain this afternoon, the match would be cancelled.
② The more I learned, the much I found his theories to be flawed.
③ The situation is so serious that a police escort accompanies us off the plane.
④ That store on Milton Street which by the way are very nice is owned by Tom's brother.

07 우리말을 영어로 옳게 옮긴 것은?

① 그 강의가 지루하게 따분할 것이라고 확신하면서, 대부분의 사람들은 그것을 두려워하는 중이다.
→ Most people are dreading it, convincing that the lecture will be tediously boring.
② 아버지는 책임지는 것에 익숙했고 누군가로부터 명령을 받는 것은 그에겐 어려웠다.
→ Dad was used to be in charge and it was difficult for him to take orders from anyone.
③ 그것은 부동산 가격이 지난 3년에서 4년 내 요크에서 급등하기 시작한 이후로 첫 번째 상승이다.
→ It has been the first rise since property prices began spiraling in York in the last three to four years.
④ 그것은 불법 입국자들이 의료서비스와 다른 혜택들에 접근할 수 있어야 하는지에 대한 논쟁이다.
→ That is the debate over whether illegal aliens should have an access to health care and other benefits.

08 다음 글의 요지로 가장 적절한 것은?

Author and professional speaker Dorie Clark says setting smaller goals for shorter time periods makes you more flexible and quicker to adapt to new information or changing circumstances. Setting a year-long goal, for example, can leave you doing something that doesn't make sense six months later, after your circumstances or priorities have changed. Or you might give up on your year-long goal when it stops making sense, but be left goal-less until the new year rolls around. Clark, for example, set a goal to get fit by playing racquetball with a friend, but soon found the early-morning games left her sleep-deprived and unproductive. If that was a year-long goal, Clark might have been left without any fitness plan for the rest of her year when she gave up the morning racquetball games.

① Early-morning exercise is not good for everyone.
② Establishing a long-term goal can be sometimes inefficient.
③ Smaller goals are much easier to accomplish than larger goals.
④ Today we should be able to adapt to new circumstances quickly.

09 밑줄 친 (A), (B)에 들어갈 말로 가장 적절한 것은?

Today, we understand that infectious diseases like flu, chickenpox and pneumonia are caused by microscopic organisms - bacteria and viruses. Without this knowledge, we might have never developed ways to treat and prevent such infections. ____(A)____, this understanding - known as the 'germ theory' of disease - was a remarkably recent discovery. People have created theories to explain human disease for millennia: the Greek physician Hippocrates thought that 'bad air' from swampy areas was to blame. In the 19th century, improvements in microscope technology enabled a generation of microbiologists to investigate further the world of previously unseen disease - causing organisms. Many scientists carried out research that contributed towards the formation of the germ theory. ____(B)____, scientific proof of the theory was the achievement of only two European scientists: Louis Pasteur, a Frenchman, and Robert Koch, who was German.

	(A)	(B)
①	For example	Furthermore
②	Unfortunately	In the end
③	In fact	However
④	Otherwise	Nonetheless

10 다음 글의 요지로 가장 적절한 것은?

Anyone is capable of becoming a leader, but not everyone is cut out for leadership. That doesn't mean they're less capable of making an important contribution, just that they bring a different set of skills to the table. There's nothing wrong with being a follower - the world needs them as much as leaders. There's a balance to everything. The trick is knowing which role you're best qualified to fill. Both leaders and followers can be equally driven by their desire to make a difference. And it's not a clear distinction - most of them have elements of both sides, and one or the other may come to the forefront depending on the situation. You don't have to be in charge to be influential.

① There are people who are natural leaders.
② The roles of a leader and a follower are different.
③ It is leaders who make a great difference to the world.
④ Followers can contribute to the society as much as leaders.

기적사 DAY 35

01 다음 중 밑줄 친 부분의 의미와 가장 가까운 것은?

> They were wholly inadequate and unsuccessful, and the result of the attempt to <u>dominate</u> all Western Europe was the character of producing bankruptcy and exhaustion.

① govern ② settle
③ scrutinize ④ adulate

02 다음 중 밑줄 친 부분의 의미와 가장 가까운 것은?

> I did not have a chance to <u>finish</u> my letter yesterday, which made me feel saddened.

① dissolve ② triturate
③ complete ④ abridge

03 다음 중 밑줄 친 부분의 의미와 가장 가까운 것은?

> What would <u>emerge</u> when an equally good-looking woman tempted him?

① occur ② investigate
③ disjoint ④ remove

04 밑줄 친 부분에 들어갈 표현으로 가장 적절한 것은?

> A: Hey, I've been looking for you. Where have you been?
> B: Oh really? I've been in my office doing some paperwork. What can I help you with?
> A: It's not anything serious but I just need your advice. Do you have some spare time?
> B: Sure, go ahead.
> A: I want to go on a working holiday to Australia for a year or so.
> B: Then you should go. What's the issue with that?
> A: But I'm worried about being left alone. What if I encounter an unexpected problem while I'm all by myself?
> B: Don't be _____. You will be fine on your own.

① a fat cat ② a chicken
③ a copycat ④ a cold fish

05 밑줄 친 부분 중 어법상 옳지 않은 것은?

> The high school grounds were filled with ① <u>well-dressed</u> people, posing in fancy dresses and suits for cheerful photographers. Congratulations, hugs, and laughter were contagious. Jane looked at all the familiar faces ② <u>what</u> had been part of her life ③ <u>for the last few years</u>. Soon her mother would be joining them. She recalled the first day of school ④ <u>when</u> she had stood in that same place, in the middle of many anxious freshmen, some of whom had become her closest friends.

06 어법상 옳은 것은?

① She's got a green carpet with pink walls, which look all wrong to my mind.
② Has John been present at the meeting, he would have voted for the motion.
③ If you oppose ID cards, you now also oppose to measures to prevent electoral fraud.
④ The more confidence you build up in yourself, the greater are your chances of success.

07 우리말을 영어로 옳게 옮긴 것은?

① Jane, 이번 사업을 미루는 게 어때?
→ Jane, what would you say to leave this business behind?
② 숙제가 끝날 때 나는 Jane에게 전화할 것이다.
→ When I will have finished my homework, I'm going to phone Jane.
③ 십대 여학생 세 명은 닭고기 튀김과 감자튀김을 마음껏 먹는 중이었다.
→ Three teenage schoolgirls were feasting at deep-fried chicken and chips.
④ 기억은 오늘날 생각되는 것처럼 제한되고, 부서지기 쉽고, 지루한 것은 아니다.
→ Memory is not as limited, fragile and boring as it is thought to be today.

08 주어진 문장이 들어갈 가장 적절한 위치는?

In other words, the cooking, chopping, grinding, pounding and mixing entailed were done by women.

The role of meat sharing by men has dominated the discourse on food sharing, and the importance of foods gathered by women to the evolution of social organization and cultural kinship has been mostly overlooked. (①) The contributions made by women in gathering vegetal foods have merely been documented in terms of their caloric value or by weight. (②) However, it was the complementary array of foods acquired by men and women that allowed human populations to persist. (③) An important component of food sharing by women is the requirement to process many vegetal foods before consumption is possible. (④) In many cultures, women also kept the fire burning. And apportionment usually fell to the mother or grandmother after processing as well. This can represent a key role for women in the power dynamics of the group.

09 밑줄 친 인물(Émile Durkheim)에 대한 설명으로 가장 옳지 않은 것은?

The French sociologist Émile Durkheim is, with Max Weber, one of the two principal founders of modern sociology. He became interested in a scientific approach to society very early on in his career, which meant the first of many conflicts with the French academic system, which had no social science curriculum at the time. Durkheim found humanistic studies uninteresting, turning his attention from psychology and philosophy to ethics and eventually, sociology. He graduated with a degree in philosophy in 1882. Durkheim's views could not get him a major academic appointment in Paris, so he taught philosophy at several provincial schools. In 1885 he left for Germany, where he studied sociology for two years. Durkheim's period in Germany resulted in the publication of numerous articles on German social science and philosophy, which gained recognition in France, earning him a teaching appointment at the University of Bordeaux in 1887. From this position, Durkheim helped reform the French school system and introduced the study of social science in its curriculum.

① He has as much reputation as Max Weber.
② Having lost interest in philosophy, he dropped out of university.
③ He first started teaching outside of Paris.
④ His writings in Germany received attention by people of his own country.

10 Edward Burne-Jones에 관한 다음 글의 내용과 일치하지 않는 것은?

Edward Burne-Jones was educated at Exeter College, Oxford, where he met his future collaborator, the artist-poet William Morris. His meeting with the artist Dante Gabriel Rossetti in 1856 marked a turning point in his career, and he left Oxford without graduating. Morris and he then settled in London, working under Rossetti's guidance. Burne-Jones's vivid imagination delighted in the stories of medieval chivalry, as is seen in his "King Cophetua and the Beggar Maid" and "Merlin and Nimue". Stylistically, these works owe much to Rossetti's illustrations. Also his own dreamworld often drew inspiration from the melancholy, attenuated figures of the 15th-century Italian painters Filippino Lippi and Sandro Botticelli. His first big success came with an exhibition in 1877. From then until his death in 1898, he was increasingly considered to be among the great painters of England. After his death, Burne-Jones's influence was felt far less in painting than in the field of decorative design, particularly in that of ecclesiastical stained glass.

① Oxford에서 대학을 다녔으나, 졸업을 하지 않았다.
② Dante Gabriel Rossetti의 지도하에 런던에서 작업했다.
③ Merlin and Nimue는 Sandro Botticelli의 영향을 주로 받았다.
④ 1877년 열린 전시회에서 크게 성공했다.

01 밑줄 친 부분과 의미가 가장 가까운 것은?

He made a face when he saw the amount of homework he had to do.

① glanced
② rejoiced
③ grimaced
④ concentrated

02 밑줄 친 단어와 의미가 가장 가까운 것은?

Whether a guffaw at a joke or a reflective chuckle greeting a sarcastic remark, laughter is the audience's means of ratifying the performance.

① smirk
② tittle
③ giggle
④ belly laugh

03 밑줄 친 단어와 의미가 가장 가까운 것은?

The beauty of the pearl, winking and glimmering in the light of the little candle, cozened his brain with its beauty.

① deceived
② softened
③ connected
④ brightened

04 빈칸에 들어갈 표현으로 가장 적절한 것은?

A: What have you done for this project so far? Because it seems to me like you haven't done anything at all.
B: That's so rude! I do lots of work. It's you who is slacking off.
A: I don't see why you always have to fight with me.
B: _____. We wouldn't fight if you didn't initiate it!

① It takes two to tango
② More haste less speed
③ He who laughs last laughs longest
④ Keep your chin up

05 어법상 가장 옳은 것은?

① Had never flown in an airplane before, the little boy was surprised and a little frightened when his ears popped.
② Scarcely had we reached there when it began to snow.
③ Despite his name, Freddie Frankenstein has a good chance of electing to the local school board.
④ I would rather to be lying on a beach in India than sitting in class right now.

06 밑줄 친 부분 중 어법상 가장 옳은 것은?

Severe acute respiratory syndrome(SARS) is a serious form of pneumonia. It is caused by a virus that ① <u>identified</u> in 2003. Infection with the SARS virus causes acute respiratory distress and sometimes ② <u>dies</u>. SARS is caused by a member of the coronavirus family of viruses(the same family that can cause the common cold). It ③ <u>believes</u> the 2003 epidemic started when the virus ④ <u>spread</u> from small mammals in China.

07 빈칸에 들어갈 표현으로 가장 적절한 것은?

For every mystery, there is someone trying to figure out ____(A)____ happened. Scientists, detectives, and ordinary people search for evidence that will help to reveal the truth. They investigate prehistoric sites trying to understand how and why ancient people constructed pyramids or created strange artwork. They study the remains of long-extinct animals and they speculate about ____(B)____ the animals might have looked when they were alive. Anything ____(C)____ is unexplained is fascinating to people who love a mystery.

	(A)	(B)	(C)
①	what	what	that
②	what	how	that
③	that	what	what
④	that	how	which

08 밑줄 친 부분에 들어갈 말로 가장 적절한 것을 고르시오.

Language proper is itself double-layered. Single noises are only occasionally meaningful: mostly, the various speech sounds convey coherent messages only when combined into an overlapping chain, like different colors of ice-cream melting into one another. In birdsong also, _____ _____: the sequence is what matters. In both humans and birds, control of this specialized sound-system is exercised by one half of the brain, normally the left half, and the system is learned relatively early in life. And just as many human languages have dialects, so do some bird species: in California, the white-crowned sparrow has songs so different from area to area that Californians can supposedly tell where they are in the state by listening to these sparrows.

① individual notes are often of little value
② rhythmic sounds are important
③ dialects play a critical role
④ no sound-system exists

09 밑줄 친 부분에 들어갈 말로 가장 적절한 것을 고르시오.

Nobel Prize-winning psychologist Daniel Kahneman changed the way the world thinks about economics, upending the notion that human beings are rational decision-makers. Along the way, his discipline-crossing influence has altered the way physicians make medical decisions and investors evaluate risk on Wall Street. In a paper, Kahneman and his colleagues outline a process for making big strategic decisions. Their suggested approach, labeled as "Mediating Assessments Protocol," or MAP, has a simple goal: To put off gut-based decision-making until a choice can be informed by a number of separate factors. "One of the essential purposes of MAP is basically to _____ intuition," Kahneman said in a recent interview with The Post. The structured process calls for analyzing a decision based on six to seven previously chosen attributes, discussing each of them separately and assigning them a relative percentile score, and finally, using those scores to make a holistic judgment.

① improve
② delay
③ possess
④ facilitate

10 밑줄 친 부분에 들어갈 말로 가장 적절한 것을 고르시오.

Fear of loss is a basic part of being human. To the brain, loss is a threat and we naturally take measures to avoid it. We cannot, however, avoid it indefinitely. One way to face loss is with the perspective of a stock trader. Traders accept the possibility of loss as part of the game, not the end of the game. What guides this thinking is a portfolio approach; wins and losses will both happen, but it's the overall portfolio of outcomes that matters most. When you embrace a portfolio approach, you will be _____ because you know that they are small parts of a much bigger picture.

① more sensitive to fluctuations in the stock market
② more averse to the losses
③ less interested in your investments
④ less inclined to dwell on individual losses

기적사 DAY 37

01 다음 중 밑줄 친 부분의 의미와 가장 가까운 것은?

Howard had to pull out of the driveway slowly and gradually increase his speed.

① rejoice ② augment
③ occur ④ revise

02 다음 중 밑줄 친 부분의 의미와 가장 가까운 것은?

The insolvent debtor was withdrawn from the yoke of his sarcastic creditor.

① lethal ② unwonted
③ bankrupt ④ prevalent

03 다음 중 밑줄 친 부분의 의미와 가장 가까운 것은?

The guidelines were paramount in order to ensure that the academic standards of awards are maintained.

① occurrent ② glimmering
③ mischievous ④ superlative

04 밑줄 친 부분에 들어갈 표현으로 가장 적절한 것은?

A: Do you have a driver's license?
B: Yes, I got it last summer vacation. Why do you ask?
A: I'm planning to take the driver's license test next week.
B: It's _____. You'll pass it.
A: Thank you. It sounds like it's an easy job.

① in the dark
② a piece of cake
③ the call of nature
④ the name of the game

05 어법상 가장 옳은 것은?

① No sooner did he realize that he had made a mistake than the company went bankrupt.
② The shame means they would rather live homeless in a foreign country than returning home.
③ They used the threat of financing primary opponents, using the same techniques we saw in the past.
④ These finds are usually cleaned and identified in the field before packing for transport to the laboratory.

06 밑줄 친 부분 중 어법상 가장 옳은 것은?

① Given the methodologies of science, the law of gravity and the genome were bound to be discovered by somebody; the identity of the discoverer is incidental to the fact. But it ② is appeared that in the arts there are no second chances. We must assume that we had one chance each for The Divine Comedy and King Lear. If Dante and Shakespeare had ③ death before they wrote those works, nobody ever would have written ④ it.

07 빈칸에 들어갈 표현으로 가장 적절한 것은?

Good papers do not merely review literature and then say something like "there are many different points of view, all ___(A)___ have something useful to say." ___(B)___ you communicate via a paper, talk, or poster, be clear about ___(C)___ you want to show, and show it.

	(A)	(B)	(C)
①	of which	what	what
②	that	when	that
③	of which	when	what
④	that	what	that

08 다음 글의 주제로 가장 적절한 것은?

Language is a universal hallmark of humanity, but it sounds different in different parts of the world. On most Pacific islands and throughout Southeast Asia, words use more vowel sounds than consonants, and they're spoken in simple syllables, made up of a vowel sound and a consonant or two. Meanwhile, Georgian, a language of the Caucasus Mountains, is heavy with consonants, often strung together into clusters, creating syllables too complex for many foreigners to pronounce. The physical surroundings of Georgians and Southeast Asians are as varied as the words they use, and linguists say they've found a relationship between the types of sounds in a language and the climate and landscape where it evolved.

① languages and races
② languages and environments
③ learning a language as a foreigner
④ the usage of vowels and consonants

09 다음 글의 주제로 가장 적절한 것은?

Daniel Kahneman's most important work began in the 1960s. At this time he was attempting to figure out how people make economic decisions from a psychological perspective. Drawing on cognitive psychology, Kahneman managed to show the mental processes that appeared to be used to form judgments and make choices. Teaming up with Amos Tversky, the pair formulated a new branch of economics called prospect theory. Prospect theory is a behavioral model that shows how people decide between alternatives that involve risk and uncertainty. It demonstrates that people think in terms of expected utility relative to a reference point rather than absolute outcomes. Prospect theory was developed by framing risky choices and indicates that people are loss-averse; since individuals dislike losses more than equivalent gains, they are more willing to take risks to avoid a loss.

① Why do we hate losses?
② Who is Daniel Kahneman?
③ How do people make choices?
④ What did Daniel Kahneman do?

10 빈칸에 들어갈 표현으로 가장 적절한 것은?

Investors have to ensure their investments achieve their future needs. Irrespective of what the future financial goals are, a portfolio approach to investment decision making to create a diversified investment portfolio is important. The benefits of a diversified portfolio are best summarized by the anecdotal wisdom of "_____". If a portfolio is too heavily allocated to one individual security, and that security fails for some reason, an investment portfolio can be reduced to zero. Diversification allows investors to spread some of the downside risk associated with any one investment position without necessarily decreasing the expected rate of return.

① time is money
② look before you leap
③ step by step one goes a long way
④ don't put all your eggs in one basket

01 다음 중 밑줄 친 부분의 의미와 가장 가까운 것은?

Further, he extended the work of Maurolycus, and demonstrated the exact analogy between the eye and the camera and the arrangement by which an <u>inverted</u> image is produced on the retina.

① preeminent ② grimacing
③ mandatory ④ reversed

02 다음 중 밑줄 친 부분의 의미와 가장 가까운 것은?

The fear of crime <u>preoccupied</u> the community.

① disinterred ② subsided
③ occupied ④ rejoiced

03 다음 중 밑줄 친 부분의 의미와 가장 가까운 것은?

The library's 5,000 volumes made up a <u>manageable</u> collection.

① controllable ② insolvent
③ outright ④ convivial

04 밑줄 친 부분에 들어갈 가장 적절한 것은?

A: I used to live in England when I was young.
B: It must have been a valuable experience. How was it?
A: Back then was the best moment of my life. But I am sure I did have one of those days that made me feel depressed.
B: What caused you to feel so down?
A: Well, I don't remember now. I think it had something to do with language barriers.
B: Language problems make life so uneasy. Did you manage to _____ your classmates at school though?
A: Yes. In fact, I spent most of my time with them even after school.

① get away with ② get along with
③ keep away from ④ get through with

05 어법상 가장 옳은 것은?

① The individual film came to being described by the first term in each pair.
② I had rather heard it from Tom than hear some warped rumors off the street.
③ He had hardly sat down and received his fork before he had started to wolf down his breakfast.
④ They will test the limits of dive physiology, attempting deeper dives and dived for longer periods.

06 밑줄 친 부분 중 어법상 가장 옳은 것은?

The man who ① entered the room was young, well-groomed, and trimly dressed, with something of refinement and delicacy in his bearing. The streaming umbrella, which he held in his hand, and his long shining waterproof ② was told of the fierce weather through which he had come. He looked around ③ anxious in the glare of the lamp. Tom could see that his face was pale and his eyes heavy, like those of a man who ④ weighs down with some great anxiety.

07 빈칸에 들어갈 표현으로 가장 적절한 것은?

_____(A)_____ do we need to see our dentist twice a year? The simple answer to this question is preventative maintenance. _____(B)_____ many times have you heard of stories _____(C)_____ people ignored the warning signs and adverse situations seemed to present themselves overnight?

	(A)	(B)	(C)
①	Why	What	which
②	What	How	where
③	What	What	which
④	Why	How	where

08 밑줄 친 부분 중 글의 흐름상 가장 어색한 것은?

In a recent study, a group of linguists examined this relationship between sounds and words in a laboratory setting. Researchers asked students at the University of California Santa Cruz (UCSC) to create new words for 18 contrasting ideas: good, bad, smooth, rough, attractive, ugly, etc. ① In pairs, the students would guess the meaning of each word based only on their sounds. ② No bodily gestures or facial expressions could be used when delivering the word to the student who would guess the meaning. ③ The students were successful in guessing the meanings and improved with experience. ④ Instead of using higher pitches for positive ideas and lower pitches for negative ideas like the English-speaking students did, the Chinese-speaking students did the opposite. Analyzing the data, lead author of the study Marcus Perlman said the guessers were successful because the inventors consistently used certain types of vocalizations with certain words, linking ideas with acoustic labels.

09 다음 글의 밑줄 친 부분 중 문맥상 단어의 쓰임이 적절하지 않은 것은?

WYSIATI is the acronym for "What you see is all there is", a cognitive bias described by Daniel Kahneman, which explains how ① <u>rational</u> we are when making decisions. WYSIATI refers to the fact that we normally make our judgements and impressions according to the information we have ② <u>available</u>. In general we don't spend too much time thinking "Well, there are still many things I'm ③ <u>unaware</u> of". Simply, we assert what we do know. When we make decisions, our mind only takes into consideration the things it knows and, regardless of their quality and quantity the only thing it tries to do with them is to build a coherent story. That's enough. The story doesn't have to be ④ <u>accurate</u>, perfect or reliable; it only has to be coherent. It seems incredible, right? A small group of incomplete, non-representative information allows us to understand the world.

10 다음 글에서 필자가 주장하는 것으로 가장 적절한 것은?

You are in your favorite store, walking around simply to see what they have to offer. You have absolutely no intention to purchase anything while you are there. All you want to do is kill a little time window shopping before you leave the store and continue on with your day. However, out of the corner of your eye, you see a "FINAL DAY FOR SALE" sign in your favorite department of that store. One of the customer service representatives informs you that if you do not take advantage of this sale today, you will completely miss out because it is going to be over tomorrow. After an unspecified period of time has passed, you finally leave the store with several shopping bags in your hands. That is the power that is involved with fear of loss - being convinced that you are going to miss out on something if you do not take advantage of it today.

① Window shopping encourages impulsive buying.
② Fear of loss can cause you to spend more money.
③ The emotion of fear of loss can be triggered anytime.
④ Do not miss out on a good opportunity due to fear of loss.

결국엔 성정혜 영어 하프모의고사

기적사 DAY 39

기출 하프 □ 파생 하프 ☑ 복습 모의고사 □

소요 시간: / 15분   맞은 개수: / 10개

01 다음 중 밑줄 친 부분의 의미와 가장 가까운 것은?

Adept at leading a team or working as part of a team, I am also an enthusiastic self-starter able to work from home, while I sometimes grimace.

① imprecise
② pragmatic
③ hesitant
④ perfervid

02 다음 중 밑줄 친 부분의 의미와 가장 가까운 것은?

Developing countries are the most susceptible because eighty-four percent of all smokers currently live in middle to low income countries, where tobacco use has been increasing since 1970.

① irresolute
② vulnerable
③ impassioned
④ cozened

03 다음 중 밑줄 친 부분의 의미와 가장 가까운 것은?

Medical science could find no difference in the brains of the former primitives to account for their different behavior; colonists necessarily observed that yesterday's 'savage' might be today's shopkeeper, soldier, or servant.

① smirk
② intervene
③ expound
④ undertake

04 밑줄 친 부분에 들어갈 표현으로 가장 적절한 것은?

Waiter: Hello, sir. What would you like to order?
Man: We haven't decided yet. We'd like to have a few more minutes.
Waiter: No problem, _____(A)_____. You can call us whenever you are ready.
Man: Thank you. Oh, and could you please give us some _____(B)_____ for the menu?
Waiter: Apple pie and pumpkin soup are our best menus.
Man: Thanks a lot. We'll make our call once we are ready.

① (A) take your time   (B) recipes
② (A) feel free to speak (B) pictures
③ (A) feel free to speak (B) recipes
④ (A) take your time   (B) suggestions

05 어법상 가장 옳은 것은?

① It's the sensation of loving by other people that makes children laugh.
② The rush of air inflated the suit's three wings, allowed him to glide.
③ The guard had scarcely been out of sight than he heard a high shout from behind him.
④ They called it music and Tom felt we had better do something about understanding it.

06 밑줄 친 부분 중 어법상 가장 옳은 것은?

Whether such women are American or Iranian or whether they are Catholic or Protestant ① matter less than the fact that they are women. Similarly, when famine and civil war ② threat people in sub-Saharan Africa, many African-Americans ③ remind of their kinship with the continent in which their ancestors ④ originated centuries earlier, and they lobby their leaders to provide humanitarian relief.

07 빈칸에 들어갈 표현으로 가장 적절한 것은?

If you believe _____(A)_____ the obstacles are too great to overcome, you will prove yourself right even when you are wrong. Most seemingly impossible obstacles can be overcome by seeing possibilities, focusing on _____(B)_____ is within your control, taking the first step, and then focusing on the next step and the next step after that. If your commitment becomes weak, remember your dream and _____(C)_____ it is important to you, find simple joys in your daily pursuits, rejoice in the little victories or small steps forward, and embrace the process of ongoing learning.

	(A)	(B)	(C)
①	what	what	how
②	that	which	why
③	that	what	why
④	what	which	how

08 다음 글의 내용과 일치하지 않는 것은?

Just as our speech patterns vary regionally, the songs of many avian species also show geographic variation. Vocal dialects appear to be learned. Young birds hear the songs sung around their natal territories by their fathers and neighboring males, and acquire the peculiarities of these renditions. The "why" of dialects, their functional significance, has proven more elusive than the question of how they arise. Many ornithologists just assume that dialects serve as indicators of genetic adaptation to local conditions. The dialects thus enable females to choose males from their own birth area, who presumably are carrying genes closely adapted to the specific environment in which breeding occurs. In other words, dialects function to promote "positive assortative mating" – the breeding together of similar individuals.

① A bird species may sound differently depending on the region.
② Singing a dialect is the bird's innate ability.
③ The exact functions of vocal dialects of birds remain uncertain.
④ Female birds prefer to mate with males from their own region.

09 다음 글의 요지로 가장 적절한 것은?

Consider an investor is given a pitch for the same mutual fund by two separate financial advisors. One advisor presents the fund to the investor, highlighting that it has an average return of 12% over the past three years. The other advisor tells the investor that the fund has had above-average returns in the past 10 years, but in recent years it has been declining. The prospect theory assumes that though the investor was presented with the exact same mutual fund, he is likely to buy the fund from the first advisor, who expressed the fund's rate of return as an overall gain instead of the advisor presenting the fund as having high returns and losses.

① The riskier the investment, the more returns it brings.
② People prefer to invest in a mutual fund that has high returns.
③ It is important for an investor to choose a right financial advisor.
④ Investors are generally loss averse according to the prospect theory.

10 다음 글의 요지로 가장 적절한 것은?

The experiment showed that a neurotransmitter, or chemical messenger, called norepinephrine, is central to the response to losing money. Those with low levels of norepinephrine transporters had higher levels of the chemical in a crucial part of their brain – leading them to be less aroused by and less sensitive to the pain of losing money, the researchers found. People with higher levels of transporters and therefore lower levels of norepinephrine have what is known as "loss aversion," where they have a more pronounced emotional response to losses compared to gains. Loss aversion can vary widely between people, the researchers explained. While most people would only enter a two outcome gamble if it were possible to win more than they could lose, people with impaired decision making show reduced sensitivity to financial loss.

① Gambling addicts can be treated by training their brains.
② Loss aversion occurs when the odds of a game are not good.
③ Norepinephrine plays an important role in regulating fear-related responses.
④ People with higher levels of norepinephrine have lower fear of loss of money.

01 다음 중 밑줄 친 부분의 의미와 가장 가까운 것은?

In the eyes of most men his martyrdom had put the king so much in the wrong that the obstinacy and provocative conduct which had brought it about passed out of memory.

① confidential
② stimulating
③ overt
④ concentrating

02 다음 중 밑줄 친 부분의 의미와 가장 가까운 것은?

Carefully she moved her feet into a position with better leverage.

① Deliberately
② Lightly
③ Fleshly
④ Promptly

03 다음 중 밑줄 친 부분의 의미와 가장 가까운 것은?

The police announced that they ruled out suicide, but there was simply no evidence to begin an investigation.

① excluded
② redeemed
③ glimmered
④ scattered

04 밑줄 친 부분에 들어갈 가장 적절한 것은?

A: Why were you late for class today?
B: I watched the news in the morning and I completely forgot about the time.
A: Were there any interesting issue?
B: There was a political protest last Saturday and thankfully, it ended peacefully.
A: That's good to hear. Hearing from you, the demonstration reminds me of the nonviolent, nonresistant movement of Ghandi.
B: They do bear great similarity, except for their purposes.
A: What was the _____ for the protest this time?
B: It was about implementing affirmative actions to alleviate sex discrimination in the contemporary society.

① side effect
② dark horse
③ dead bargain
④ bone of contention

05 어법상 가장 옳은 것은?

① The clinic's report prevents you from cheating by mechanics.
② On their examining the log, the immediate cause of the error was instantly apparent.
③ Thrilling with the outing, Tom began climbing more and later took a trip to the Dolomites.
④ I think it is high time that elected political representatives will take a stand against this sort of behaviour.

06 밑줄 친 부분 중 어법상 가장 옳은 것은?

It well ① knows that first impressions are powerful, even when they ② base on faulty information. What may not be so obvious is the extent to which the ③ adaptive unconscious is doing the interpreting. When I saw Tom interrupt the principal I felt as though I were observing an objectively rude act. I had no idea that Tom's behavior was being interpreted by me and then ④ presenting to me as reality.

07 빈칸에 들어갈 표현으로 가장 적절한 것은?

When a principle is part of a person's moral code, that person is strongly motivated toward the conduct required by the principle, and against behavior ___(A)___ conflicts with that principle. The person will tend to feel guilty when his or her own conduct violates that principle and to disapprove of others ___(B)___ behavior conflicts with it. Likewise, the person will tend to hold in esteem those ___(C)___ conduct shows an abundance of the motivation required by the principle.

	(A)	(B)	(C)
①	whose	whose	that
②	whose	that	that
③	that	that	whose
④	that	whose	whose

08 글의 흐름상 빈칸에 들어갈 표현으로 가장 적절한 것은?

We develop perceptual schemas in order to organize impressions of people based on their appearance, social roles, interaction, or other traits; these schemas then influence our perceptions of other things in the world. These schemas are heuristics, or shortcuts that save time and effort on computation. For example, you might have a perceptual schema that the building where you go to work is symmetrical on the outside (sometimes called the "symmetry heuristic," or the tendency to remember things as being more symmetrical than they truly are). Even if it isn't, making that assumption saved your mind some time. This is the blessing and curse of perceptual schemas and heuristics: they are useful for making sense of a complex world, but _____.

① they can be inaccurate
② they might be insufficient
③ they can be more complicated
④ they are not easy to understand

09 다음 빈칸에 적절한 것을 고르시오.

While researchers have attempted to help people reduce the optimism bias, particularly to promote healthy behaviors and reduce risky behaviors, they have found that reducing or eliminating the bias is actually incredibly _____. In studies that involved attempts to reduce the optimism bias through actions such as educating participants about risk factors, encouraging volunteers to consider high-risk examples, and educating subjects on why they were at risk, researchers have found that these attempts led to little change and in some instances actually increased the optimism bias. For example, telling someone the risks of dying from a particular habit such as smoking can actually make them more likely to believe that they will not be negatively affected by the behavior.

① straightforward
② compulsory
③ paramount
④ tough

10 다음 중 빈칸에 가장 알맞은 것은?

The Ukrainian oligarchic system turned out _____. This system, i.e. a system based on links between the newly formed big business and the political class, emerged several years after Ukraine regained independence in 1991 and developed into its ultimate shape during Leonid Kuchma's second presidency. Although a similar phenomenon has also developed in other former Soviet republics, first of all in Russia, big business at present does not have so strong an influence on politics in any other Eastern European country as it does in Ukraine. Representatives of big business in Ukraine, as in Russia, are commonly referred to as oligarchs. The nature of close relations between the government and the oligarchs has not undergone any major changes either as a consequence of the Orange Revolution or following Victor Yanukovych's victory in the presidential election of 2010. Although reshuffles have taken place inside the political and business elites, nothing seems to be able to change this system, at least in the medium term.

① to need expanding
② to be very durable
③ to be more efficient
④ to have a dangerous flaw

01 밑줄 친 부분의 의미와 가장 가까운 것은?

The student who finds the state-of-the-art approach intimidating learns less than he or she might have learned by the old methods.

① humorous   ② friendly
③ convenient ④ frightening

02 밑줄 친 단어와 의미가 가장 가까운 것은?

The beauty of the pearl, winking and glimmering in the light of the little candle, cozened his brain with its beauty.

① deceived   ② softened
③ connected ④ brightened

03 다음 중 밑줄 친 부분의 의미와 가장 가까운 것은?

Exhausting people in this country, the new constitution, however, proved costly and unworkable, and failed to satisfy either section of the population.

① acquire   ② assert
③ transfer   ④ gratify

04 다음 중 밑줄 친 부분의 의미와 가장 가까운 것은?

Medical science could find no difference in the brains of the former primitives to account for their different behavior; colonists necessarily observed that yesterday's 'savage' might be today's shopkeeper, soldier, or servant.

① smirk   ② intervene
③ expound   ④ undertake

05 다음 중 밑줄 친 부분의 의미와 가장 가까운 것은?

Carefully she moved her feet into a position with better leverage.

① Deliberately ② Lightly
③ Fleshly   ④ Promptly

06 어법상 옳은 것은?

① Had Hitler invaded England in 1940, he would win the war.
② The sooner I get this piece of work done, sooner I can go home.
③ There are many aspects of this case that is directly relevant to church treasurers.
④ The cuckoo which resembles like a sparrow hawk in flight can be difficult to identify.

07 어법상 가장 옳은 것은?

① No sooner did he realize that he had made a mistake than the company went bankrupt.
② The shame means they would rather live homeless in a foreign country than returning home.
③ They used the threat of financing primary opponents, using the same techniques we saw in the past.
④ These finds are usually cleaned and identified in the field before packing for transport to the laboratory.

08 우리말을 영어로 옳게 옮긴 것은?

① Jane, 이번 사업을 미루는 게 어때?
→ Jane, what would you say to leave this business behind?

② 숙제가 끝날 때 나는 Jane에게 전화할 것이다.
→ When I will have finished my homework, I'm going to phone Jane.

③ 십대 여학생 세 명은 닭고기 튀김과 감자튀김을 마음껏 먹는 중이었다.
→ Three teenage schoolgirls were feasting at deep-fried chicken and chips.

④ 기억은 오늘날 생각되는 것처럼 제한되고, 부서지기 쉽고, 지루한 것은 아니다.
→ Memory is not as limited, fragile and boring as it is thought to be today.

09 다음 글의 요지로 가장 적절한 것은?

Anyone is capable of becoming a leader, but not everyone is cut out for leadership. That doesn't mean they're less capable of making an important contribution, just that they bring a different set of skills to the table. There's nothing wrong with being a follower - the world needs them as much as leaders. There's a balance to everything. The trick is knowing which role you're best qualified to fill. Both leaders and followers can be equally driven by their desire to make a difference. And it's not a clear distinction - most of them have elements of both sides, and one or the other may come to the forefront depending on the situation. You don't have to be in charge to be influential.

① There are people who are natural leaders.
② The roles of a leader and a follower are different.
③ It is leaders who make a great difference to the world.
④ Followers can contribute to the society as much as leaders.

10 다음 글의 주제로 가장 적절한 것은?

Language is a universal hallmark of humanity, but it sounds different in different parts of the world. On most Pacific islands and throughout Southeast Asia, words use more vowel sounds than consonants, and they're spoken in simple syllables, made up of a vowel sound and a consonant or two. Meanwhile, Georgian, a language of the Caucasus Mountains, is heavy with consonants, often strung together into clusters, creating syllables too complex for many foreigners to pronounce. The physical surroundings of Georgians and Southeast Asians are as varied as the words they use, and linguists say they've found a relationship between the types of sounds in a language and the climate and landscape where it evolved.

① languages and races
② languages and environments
③ learning a language as a foreigner
④ the usage of vowels and consonants

11 두 사람의 대화 중 가장 어색한 것은?

① A: What are you dressed up for?
B: I have a family dinner out tonight.

② A: Where is the convenience store located?
B: The map shows that it's right across the street.

③ A: I am thinking about taking a semester off next year.
B: That's a good idea. Do you have plans in mind?

④ A: We should all make a New year's resolution before it turns twelve midnight.
B: I am ready to leave right away once the bell ring.

12 밑줄 친 부분에 들어갈 표현으로 가장 적절한 것은?

A: Hey, I've been looking for you. Where have you been?
B: Oh really? I've been in my office doing some paperwork. What can I help you with?
A: It's not anything serious but I just need your advice. Do you have some spare time?
B: Sure, go ahead.
A: I want to go on a working holiday to Australia for a year or so.
B: Then you should go. What's the issue with that?
A: But I'm worried about being left alone. What if I encounter an unexpected problem while I'm all by myself?
B: Don't be _____. You will be fine on your own.

① a fat cat
② a chicken
③ a copycat
④ a cold fish

13 밑줄 친 부분 중 어법상 가장 옳은 것은?

Severe acute respiratory syndrome(SARS) is a serious form of pneumonia. It is caused by a virus that ① identified in 2003. Infection with the SARS virus causes acute respiratory distress and sometimes ② dies. SARS is caused by a member of the coronavirus family of viruses(the same family that can cause the common cold). It ③ believes the 2003 epidemic started when the virus ④ spread from small mammals in China.

14 주어진 문장이 들어갈 위치로 가장 적절한 것은?

By improving the housing, sanitation and general cleanliness of these existing areas, levels of disease were seen to fall, which lent weight to the theory.

In miasma theory, diseases were caused by the presence in the air of a miasma, a poisonous vapor in which were suspended particles of decaying matter that was characterized by its foul smell. (①) The theory originated in the Middle Ages and endured for several centuries. In 19th-century England the miasma theory made sense to the sanitary reformers. (②) Rapid industrialization and urbanization had created many poor, filthy and foul-smelling city neighborhoods that tended to be the focal points of disease and epidemics. (③) Although it had been disproved and rejected later, the miasma theory's existence was not without its merits. (④) By removing the causes of bad smells, reformers often inadvertently removed bacteria, the real cause of many diseases.

15 밑줄 친 부분 중 글의 흐름상 가장 어색한 것은?

In a recent study, a group of linguists examined this relationship between sounds and words in a laboratory setting. Researchers asked students at the University of California Santa Cruz (UCSC) to create new words for 18 contrasting ideas: good, bad, smooth, rough, attractive, ugly, etc. ① In pairs, the students would guess the meaning of each word based only on their sounds. ② No bodily gestures or facial expressions could be used when delivering the word to the student who would guess the meaning. ③ The students were successful in guessing the meanings and improved with experience. ④ Instead of using higher pitches for positive ideas and lower pitches for negative ideas like the English-speaking students did, the Chinese-speaking students did the opposite. Analyzing the data, lead author of the study Marcus Perlman said the guessers were successful because the inventors consistently used certain types of vocalizations with certain words, linking ideas with acoustic labels.

16 밑줄 친 (A), (B)에 들어갈 말로 가장 적절한 것은?

Today, we understand that infectious diseases like flu, chickenpox and pneumonia are caused by microscopic organisms – bacteria and viruses. Without this knowledge, we might have never developed ways to treat and prevent such infections. ____(A)____, this understanding – known as the 'germ theory' of disease – was a remarkably recent discovery. People have created theories to explain human disease for millennia: the Greek physician Hippocrates thought that 'bad air' from swampy areas was to blame. In the 19th century, improvements in microscope technology enabled a generation of microbiologists to investigate further the world of previously unseen disease-causing organisms. Many scientists carried out research that contributed towards the formation of the germ theory. ____(B)____, scientific proof of the theory was the achievement of two European scientists: Louis Pasteur, a Frenchman, and Robert Koch, who was German.

	(A)	(B)
①	For example	Furthermore
②	Unfortunately	In the end
③	In fact	However
④	Otherwise	Nonetheless

17 다음 중 빈칸에 가장 알맞은 것은?

The Ukrainian oligarchic system turned out _____. This system, i.e. a system based on links between the newly formed big business and the political class, emerged several years after Ukraine regained independence in 1991 and developed into its ultimate shape during Leonid Kuchma's second presidency. Although a similar phenomenon has also developed in other former Soviet republics, first of all in Russia, big business at present does not have so strong an influence on politics in any other Eastern European country as it does in Ukraine. Representatives of big business in Ukraine, as in Russia, are commonly referred to as oligarchs. The nature of close relations between the government and the oligarchs has not undergone any major changes either as a consequence of the Orange Revolution or following Victor Yanukovych's victory in the presidential election of 2010. Although reshuffles have taken place inside the political and business elites, nothing seems to be able to change this system, at least in the medium term.

① to need expanding
② to be very durable
③ to be more efficient
④ to have a dangerous flaw

18 빈칸에 들어갈 표현으로 가장 적절한 것은?

Investors have to ensure their investments achieve their future needs. Irrespective of what the future financial goals are, a portfolio approach to investment decision making to create a diversified investment portfolio is important. The benefits of a diversified portfolio are best summarized by the anecdotal wisdom of "_____". If a portfolio is too heavily allocated to one individual security, and that security fails for some reason, an investment portfolio can be reduced to zero. Diversification allows investors to spread some of the downside risk associated with any one investment position without necessarily decreasing the expected rate of return.

① time is money
② look before you leap
③ step by step one goes a long way
④ don't put all your eggs in one basket

19 다음 글의 내용과 일치하지 않는 것은?

Just as our speech patterns vary regionally, the songs of many avian species also show geographic variation. Vocal dialects appear to be learned. Young birds hear the songs sung around their natal territories by their fathers and neighboring males, and acquire the peculiarities of these renditions. The "why" of dialects, their functional significance, has proven more elusive than the question of how they arise. Many ornithologists just assume that dialects serve as indicators of genetic adaptation to local conditions. The dialects thus enable females to choose males from their own birth area, who presumably are carrying genes closely adapted to the specific environment in which breeding occurs. In other words, dialects function to promote "positive assortative mating" - the breeding together of similar individuals.

① A bird species may sound differently depending on the region.
② Singing a dialect is the bird's innate ability.
③ The exact functions of vocal dialects of birds remain uncertain.
④ Female birds prefer to mate with males from their own region.

20 Edward Burne-Jones에 관한 다음 글의 내용과 일치하지 않는 것은?

Edward Burne-Jones was educated at Exeter College, Oxford, where he met his future collaborator, the artist-poet William Morris. His meeting with the artist Dante Gabriel Rossetti in 1856 marked a turning point in his career, and he left Oxford without graduating. Morris and he then settled in London, working under Rossetti's guidance. Burne-Jones's vivid imagination delighted in the stories of medieval chivalry, as is seen in his "King Cophetua and the Beggar Maid" and "Merlin and Nimue". Stylistically, these works owe much to Rossetti's illustrations. Also his own dreamworld often drew inspiration from the melancholy, attenuated figures of the 15th-century Italian painters Filippino Lippi and Sandro Botticelli. His first big success came with an exhibition in 1877. From then until his death in 1898, he was increasingly considered to be among the great painters of England. After his death, Burne-Jones's influence was felt far less in painting than in the field of decorative design, particularly in that of ecclesiastical stained glass.

① Oxford에서 대학을 다녔으나, 졸업을 하지 않았다.
② Dante Gabriel Rossetti의 지도하에 런던에서 작업했다.
③ Merlin and Nimue는 Sandro Botticelli의 영향을 주로 받았다.
④ 1877년 열린 전시회에서 크게 성공했다.

MEMO

기적사 DAY 41

01 밑줄 친 부분에 들어갈 말로 가장 적절한 것은?

The campaign to eliminate pollution will prove _____ unless it has the understanding and full cooperation of the public.

① enticing
② enhanced
③ fertile
④ futile

02 밑줄 친 부분과 의미가 가장 가까운 것은?

Up to now, newspaper articles have only scratched the surface of this tremendously complex issue.

① superficially dealt with
② hit the nail on the head of
③ seized hold of
④ positively followed up on

03 밑줄 친 부분과 의미가 가장 가까운 것을 고르시오.

It was personal. Why did you have to stick your nose in?

① hurry
② interfere
③ sniff
④ resign

04 밑줄 친 부분에 들어갈 말로 가장 적절한 것을 고르시오.

A: I'd like to get a refund for this tablecloth I bought here yesterday.
B: Is there a problem with the tablecloth?
A: It doesn't fit our table and I would like to return it. Here is my receipt.
B: I'm sorry, but this tablecloth was a final sale item, and it cannot be refunded.
A: _____
B: It's written at the bottom of the receipt.

① Nobody mentioned that to me.
② Where is the price tag?
③ What's the problem with it?
④ I got a good deal on it.

05 우리말을 영어로 잘못 옮긴 것은?

① 나의 이모는 파티에서 그녀를 만난 것을 기억하지 못했다.
 → My aunt didn't remember meeting her at the party.
② 나의 첫 책을 쓰는 데 40년이 걸렸다.
 → It took me 40 years to write my first book.
③ 학교에서 집으로 걸어오고 있을 때 강풍에 내 우산이 뒤집혔다.
 → A strong wind blew my umbrella inside out as I was walking home from school.
④ 끝까지 생존하는 생물은 가장 강한 생물도, 가장 지적인 생물도 아니고, 변화에 가장 잘 반응하는 생물이다.
 → It is not the strongest of the species, nor the most intelligent, or the one most responsive to change that survives to the end.

06 어법상 옳은 것은?

① Jessica is a much careless person who makes little effort to improve her knowledge.
② But he will come or not is not certain.
③ The police demanded that she not leave the country for the time being.
④ The more a hotel is expensiver, the better its service is.

07 밑줄 친 부분 중 어법상 옳은 것은?

① <u>As the old saying go</u>, you are what you eat. The foods you eat ② <u>obvious affect your body's performance</u>. They may also influence how your brain handles tasks. If your brain handles them well, you think more clearly, and you are more emotionally stable. The right food can ③ <u>help you being concentrated</u>, keep you motivated, sharpen your memory, speed your reaction time, reduce stress, and perhaps ④ <u>even prevent your brain from aging</u>.

08 다음 글의 제목으로 가장 적절한 것은?

Mapping technologies are being used in many new applications. Biological researchers are exploring the molecular structure of DNA ("mapping the genome"), geophysicists are mapping the structure of the Earth's core, and oceanographers are mapping the ocean floor. Computer games have various imaginary "lands" or levels where rules, hazards, and rewards change. Computerization now challenges reality with "virtual reality," artificial environments that stimulate special situations, which may be useful in training and entertainment. Mapping techniques are being used also in the realm of ideas. For example, relationships between ideas can be shown using what are called concept maps. Starting from a general or "central" idea, related ideas can be connected, building a web around the main concept. This is not a map by any traditional definition, but the tools and techniques of cartography are employed to produce it, and in some ways it resembles a map.

① Computerized Maps vs. Traditional Maps
② Where Does Cartography Begin?
③ Finding Ways to DNA Secrets
④ Mapping New Frontiers

09 다음 글의 요지로 가장 적절한 것은?

When giving performance feedback, you should consider the recipient's past performance and your estimate of his or her future potential in designing its frequency, amount, and content. For high performers with potential for growth, feedback should be frequent enough to prod them into taking corrective action, but not so frequent that it is experienced as controlling and saps their initiative. For adequate performers who have settled into their jobs and have limited potential for advancement, very little feedback is needed because they have displayed reliable and steady behavior in the past, knowing their tasks and realizing what needs to be done. For poor performers—that is, people who will need to be removed from their jobs if their performance doesn't improve—feedback should be frequent and very specific, and the connection between acting on the feedback and negative sanctions such as being laid off or fired should be made explicit.

① Time your feedback well.
② Customize negative feedback.
③ Tailor feedback to the person.
④ Avoid goal-oriented feedback.

10 다음 글의 내용과 일치하지 않는 것은?

Langston Hughes was born in Joplin, Missouri, and graduated from Lincoln University, in which many African-American students have pursued their academic disciplines. At the age of eighteen, Hughes published one of his most well-known poems, "Negro Speaks of Rivers." Creative and experimental, Hughes incorporated authentic dialect in his work, adapted traditional poetic forms to embrace the cadences and moods of blues and jazz, and created characters and themes that reflected elements of lower-class black culture. With his ability to fuse serious content with humorous style, Hughes attacked racial prejudice in a way that was natural and witty.

① Hughes는 많은 미국 흑인들이 다녔던 대학교를 졸업하였다.
② Hughes는 실제 사투리를 그의 작품에 반영하였다.
③ Hughes는 하층 계급 흑인들의 문화적 요소를 반영한 인물을 만들었다.
④ Hughes는 인종편견을 엄숙한 문체로 공격하였다.

기적사 DAY 42

01 다음 빈칸에 들어갈 말로 가장 적절한 것을 고르시오.

If you say that someone is _____ about something, they seem to be uncertain whether they really want it, or whether they really approve of it.

① ambivalent
② itinerant
③ fertile
④ singular

02 다음 밑줄 친 어휘와 의미가 가장 먼 것을 고르시오.

Two casts of characters, although ostensibly cooperating to solve a crime of mutual interest, <u>detest</u> each other.

① seize
② abhor
③ loathe
④ dislike

03 다음 밑줄 친 어휘와 의미가 가장 가까운 것을 고르시오.

That changed suddenly in 2015, when authorities, citing security concerns, banned gay and trans-gender pride events chasing away shocked participants trying to <u>converge</u> on central Taksim Square with tear gas and water cannons.

① erode
② sniff
③ modify
④ assemble

04 다음 빈칸에 들어갈 가장 적절한 표현을 순서대로 지적한 것은?

A: Look at this poster! They are holding an audition.
B: Is it from the school dance club?
A: I don't think so. It's written on the bottom that a TV auditioning program is organizing the audition. Are you interested?
B: Well, I've been thinking about applying for an audition one day.
A: Then what's stopping you? I can lend a ___(A)___ if you want.
B: That's really nice of you. But the problem is that I don't know how to keep a straight ___(B)___ whenever I go on stage.
A: It's not easy, but take a couple of days to think it over and if you really audition for the program, I'll keep my ___(C)___ crossed for you.

① (A) hand   (B) face   (C) feet
② (A) body   (B) foot   (C) arms
③ (A) hat   (B) finger (C) hands
④ (A) hand   (B) face   (C) fingers

05 우리말을 영어로 잘못 옮긴 것은?

① 그녀의 눈이 어둠에 적응하는 데 시간이 좀 걸렸다.
→ It took a few minutes her eyes to adjust to the dark.

② 운전자는 도로표지를 읽기 위해 애쓰면서 그 거리를 자세히 들여다보는 중이었다.
→ The driver was peering into the distance trying to read the road sign.

③ 또 다른 산들바람이 그들을 지나서 불었는데 그것은 보통 일 년 중 이맘때 추웠다.
→ Another breeze of wind blew past them, usually cold for this time of the year.

④ 문제는 그들이 나무를 줄이는 것이 아니라 그것을 포식동물 같은 방식으로 한다는 것이다.
→ The problem is not that they are cutting down trees, but that they are doing it in a predatory way.

06 어법상 옳은 것은?

① The more I learn, the more I realize how much I don't know.
② The report recommends that more resources are devoted to teaching four-year-olds.
③ Emphasis on the omnipotence of God is even much pronounced in the writings of William.
④ He said what had surprised him was but many of those arrested had no previous convictions.

07 밑줄 친 부분 중 어법상 옳은 것은?

We are rather ① proudly of our ability to meet emergencies. So we do not plan and take precautions to prevent emergencies ② to arise. It is too easy to drift through school and college, taking the traditional, conventional studies that others take, following the lines of least resistance, ③ to elect "snap courses", and going with the crowd. It is too easy to take the attitude: "First I will get my education and develop myself, and then I will know better ④ what I am fitted to do for a life work."

08 주어진 문장 다음에 이어질 글의 순서로 가장 적절한 것은?

Among the main goals of the Human Genome Project (HGP) was to develop new, better and cheaper tools to identify new genes and to understand their function.

(A) Mapping also provides clues about which chromosome contains the gene and precisely where the gene lies on that chromosome.
(B) One of these tools is genetic mapping. Genetic mapping - also called linkage mapping - can offer firm evidence that a disease transmitted from parent to child is linked to one or more genes.
(C) Therefore, genetic maps have been used successfully to find the gene responsible for relatively rare, single-gene inherited disorders such as cystic fibrosis and Duchenne muscular dystrophy.

* cystic fibrosis: 낭포성 섬유증
* Duchenne muscular dystrophy: 듀시엔형 근이영양증

① (A) − (B) − (C)   ② (B) − (A) − (C)
③ (B) − (C) − (A)   ④ (C) − (A) − (B)

09 밑줄 친 (A), (B)에 들어갈 말로 가장 적절한 것은?

Depending on the way your team works, also your leadership style, and your direct relationships with your team members, performance feedback can take a number of forms. You might choose fortnightly or monthly one-on-one meetings. _____(A)_____, you might choose to provide your feedback through responding to your team members' daily or weekly reports. Or if your team is more project-based maybe it would make more sense to schedule a review meeting or report after each project milestone is reached. Whatever form you end up choosing, the most important thing is to make a regular commitment and stick to it. It's very easy in our busy work lives to let things slip and keep postponing meetings. Keeping a regular meeting, _____(B)_____, will not only keep you on track and providing useful feedback, but it will also send the message to your team that you're serious about helping to support their performance and development.

	(A)	(B)
①	Accordingly	moreover
②	Alternatively	however
③	Additionally	in a word
④	As a result	therefore

10 다음 글의 주제로 가장 적절한 것은?

While many slaves became tanned as they labored outdoors, the privileged had lighter complexions because they didn't. Thus, dark skin became associated with lower classes and light skin with the elite. Colorism didn't disappear after slavery ended in the U.S. In black America, those with light skin received employment opportunities off-limits to darker-skinned blacks. This is why upper-class families in black society were largely light-skinned. Soon, light skin and privilege were linked in the black community. Upper-crust blacks routinely administered the brown paper bag test to determine if fellow blacks were light enough to include in social circles. "The paper bag would be held against your skin. And if you were darker than the paper bag, you weren't admitted," explained Marita Golden, author of "Don't Play in the Sun: One Woman's Journey Through the Color Complex."

① History of slavery in the United States
② Privileges given to upper-class Americans
③ Discrimination from members of the same race
④ Conflicts between black people and white people

기적사 DAY 43

01 다음 빈칸에 들어갈 말로 가장 적절한 것을 고르시오.

She did, however, choose to _____ that "The nationality of the shooter, it sounds Hispanic, Latino," based on his name.

① interfere ② acquire
③ surmise ④ entice

02 다음 밑줄 친 어휘와 의미가 가장 먼 것을 고르시오.

The nearly half-decade movement to <u>repeal</u> and replace the medical device tax reached a crescendo on Tuesday.

① sniff ② revoke
③ abolish ④ annul

03 다음 밑줄 친 어휘와 의미가 가장 가까운 것을 고르시오.

But that did not stop Kennedy from delivering a joke that night that was nothing less than <u>audacious</u>.

① scornful ② valiant
③ hurry ④ terrifying

04 다음 대화의 빈칸에 들어갈 가장 알맞은 표현을 고르시오.

Amy: You seem to be full of anxiety. What's wrong?
Brian: I've got a lot on my mind. I have to decide whether to apply for the exchange student program or not.
Amy: I heard about the program too. People say it's a once-in-a-lifetime chance to live and attend school abroad.
Brian: Yeah, that's the greatest benefit. But there are some things I have to give up.
Amy: Decision making always accompanies responsibility. But don't think too much. I recommend you make a choice _____.
Brian: You're right. I think my path is made clear. I'll go for it.

① under the table
② out of the blue sky
③ to your heart's content
④ at the top of your lungs

05 우리말을 영어로 잘못 옮긴 것은?

① 그 캔은 폭발했는데 부엌과 욕실을 파괴하고 창문들을 날려버렸다.
→ The can exploded, wrecking the kitchen and bathroom and blowing out windows.

② 배심원들이 그가 유죄라고 판결하는 데 한 시간도 채 안 되었기 때문에 그의 항변은 무시되었다.
→ His pleas fell on deaf ears as the jury took less than an hour to find him guilty.

③ 그는 얼마 안 되는 장면들을 위해 재능 있는 배우들을 캐스팅하는 것은 쉽지도 않고 돈이 적게 드는 것도 아니라고 설명한다.
→ He explains that it's neither easy nor cheap to cast talented actors for just a small number of scenes.

④ 한 학생이 자신의 옷에서 총알을 발견했고, 고통스러워하는 몇몇의 학생들은 나중에 상담받는 것이 필요했다.
→ A student spotted the pistol in his clothes, and several distressed students needed to counsel afterwards.

06 어법상 옳은 것은?

① The more beautiful you are, the more he will need to be handsome.
② In the 1960s there was an even greater shift in emphasis to historical research.
③ You understand what there's no way to test this to see if the signal is actually going out.
④ In her speech she proposed that the UN sets up an emergency centre for the environment.

07 밑줄 친 부분 중 어법상 옳은 것은?

When I was in sixth grade, I noticed that many of my classmates carried paper lunch bags. I found out that from sandwich wrappers to ① <u>disposably</u> drink containers, the average school kid generates 65 pounds of lunch bag waste every year. To help kids ② <u>cut down</u> on lunch bag waste, I have invented a reusable lunch bag, which I am now selling on my website. It has ③ <u>handled</u> and a front pocket. And the fabric is partially made ④ <u>of</u> recycled plastic bottles.

08 다음 글의 주제로 가장 적절한 것은?

Concept maps are a visual illustration of concepts and ideas as a complex structure comprised of boxes or circles that are connected with linking words or phrases arranged around a central concept. Usually structured in a hierarchical relationship, the boxes and circles represent topics and sub-topics that are connected with descriptive expressions in order to define better the mutual relationships. Through the years, concept mapping has proved itself to be a highly applicable technique that allows people to acknowledge what they know and have learned for a specific discipline. Besides this, it has helped people orderly portray their thoughts and ideas, analyze what they know and don't know and, consequently, broaden their existing knowledge.

① definition and functions of concept maps
② history and development of concept mapping
③ advantages and disadvantages of concept maps
④ concept mapping skills and how to improve them

09 다음 글에서 필자가 주장하는 것으로 가장 적절한 것은?

A common misconception is that motivation in the workplace is primarily based on monetary rewards. It's not always possible to give your employees a raise every time they do well, and surprisingly it might not be the strongest incentive either. A study revealed that 83% of employees found recognition for contributions to be more fulfilling than rewards and gifts. Another 88% believed praise from managers was very - or even extremely motivating. Performance feedback lets your employees know they're valued and contributes to building confidence in newer employees. Also, let's not forget your top performers. Many managers tend to neglect their top performers when it comes to feedback, because they see it more as a tool for helping improve performance and consider top performers don't need any help. But they are working hard and their efforts shouldn't be taken for granted.

① Performance feedback should be given regularly.
② Performance feedback is necessary for every employee.
③ Managers should learn how to effectively give performance feedback.
④ Top performers need performance feedback more than any other employee.

10 빈칸에 들어갈 표현으로 가장 적절한 것은?

Although Hughes had trouble with both black and white critics, he was the first black American to earn his living solely from his writing and public lectures. Part of the reason he was able to do this was the phenomenal acceptance and love he received from average black people. A reviewer for *Black World* noted in 1970: "Those whose prerogative is to determine the rank of writers have never rated him highly, but if _____ _____, then Langston Hughes stands at the apex of literary relevance among black people. The poet occupies such a position in the memory of his people precisely because he recognized that 'we possess within ourselves a great reservoir of physical and spiritual strength,' and because he used his artistry to reflect this back to the people."

① his unpublished works are counted
② his private life is less controversial
③ he is living in the postmodern world
④ the weight of public response is any gauge

01 다음 밑줄 친 어휘와 의미가 가장 가까운 것을 고르시오.

Netanyahu, and even some innocent pundits, are bragging about how Israel and America have never been closer.

① enhanced
② ingenuous
③ problematic
④ sneering

02 다음 밑줄 친 어휘와 의미가 가장 먼 것을 고르시오.

Bieber tried to sneak out of the house, covering himself in a sheet, but vigilant photographers caught him in the act.

① cautious
② circumspect
③ tremendous
④ prudent

03 다음 밑줄 친 어휘와 의미가 가장 가까운 것을 고르시오.

As for Romney, Johnson describes the former Massachusetts governor as "terrific," " cordial," and "very gracious."

① personal
② methodical
③ genial
④ gutless

04 다음 대화의 빈칸에 들어갈 가장 알맞은 표현을 고르시오.

A: What are you looking at?
B: I'm looking at an internship notice.
A: Are you thinking of applying for an internship position?
B: Yeah, I want to gain some hands-on experience before I get my job and jump into the real task.
A: Are you sure? You seemed really busy these days. Don't _____. You will have no time for yourself.
B: I know it might be overwhelming, but it's on my bucket list.

① play it by ear
② bite the bullet
③ keep your nose clean
④ bite off more than you can chew

05 우리말을 영어로 잘못 옮긴 것은?

① 나는 학교에서 더 열심히 공부하지 않았던 것을 항상 후회한다.
→ I have always regretted not having studied harder at school.
② John은 팔을 비볐고 손가락을 따듯하게 하기 위해 입김을 불었다.
→ John rubbed his arms and blew on his fingers to warm them.
③ Tom이 눈으로 막힌 교통을 통해 3마일을 여행하는 데 3시간이 걸렸다.
→ It took Tom three hours traveling three miles through snow-blocked traffic.
④ 당신은 겨울에 따뜻하거나 여름에 차가운 초코 우유를 마실 수 있다.
→ You can drink chocolate milk either hot in the winter or cold in the summer.

06 어법상 옳은 것은?

① Her mother immediately commanded that Jane did not give the boy any money.
② William was wondering if Jane would like to come to the cinema with him this evening.
③ The cars come down this road quite more quickly and we have seen quite a few accidents.
④ The more generous you are towards others, the generously they are likely to be towards you.

07 밑줄 친 부분 중 어법상 옳은 것은?

The hunters, ① arming only with primitive weapons, were no real match for an angry mammoth. Many were probably killed or severely injured in the close ② encounter that were necessary to slay one of these gigantic animals. But the rewards were great when one was brought down. A single mammoth could feed, ③ cloth, and supply a band for a long time. The hunters had followed the mammoths and other large animals ④ eastward from Asia across what is now the Bering Sea.

08 밑줄 친 부분 중 글의 흐름상 가장 어색한 것은?

Cartography is the business of making maps. ① The terms 'mapmaking' and 'cartography' essentially mean the same thing: taking geographical information and transforming it into a map. ② Cartography has developed as allied occupations have evolved with new technology. ③ Land surveying, satellite remote sensing, aerial photography, geographical information systems, photogrammetry, hydrography, and geodesy as well as cartography are sometimes grouped together as 'geomatics' or the 'geosciences'. ④ The clear presentation of map data demands particular skills of design and creativity. However, although the boundaries and techniques of map making have moved, and it is integrated with other areas of applied geography, cartography remains essential to the successful visualization of spatial data, and the demand for skilled cartographers is still strong.

09 주어진 문장이 들어갈 위치로 가장 적절한 것은?

When providing this type of feedback, explain exactly what is that you're criticizing and the implications that come from it, and then create a plan to help the employee improve.

Constructive criticism is probably one of the most underused developmental tools. (①) Constructive criticism helps employees see where they need to improve and why making those improvements is important. (②) It's a well-rounded approach because it offers both a critique and a solution. (③) Imagine that you have an employee who consistently sends emails with typos and grammatical errors. (④) Instead of simply telling them that it's a problem and they need to stop doing it, explain the implications of the problem. Provide them with a clear example of why it's a problem and reiterate why it's important for them to rectify their behavior. Help them come up with ways to improve and set a timeframe that they should make the improvement by.

10 주어진 문장이 들어갈 위치로 가장 적절한 것은?

Moving away from the slave narrative tradition, authors began to explore issues that had evolved out of the social consequences of slavery.

The Harlem Renaissance was a period of U.S. history marked by a burst of creativity within the African American community in the areas of art, music and literature. (①) Centered within New York City's Harlem, the Harlem Renaissance began roughly with the end of World War I in 1918 and continued into the mid-1930s. (②) During this era Harlem became an inspiration and a destination point for African American artists from every discipline, especially writers. (③) Authors addressed the topics of racism, poverty, lack of identity and family structure. (④) Langston Hughes's *Simple* stories addressed poverty. Zora Neale Hurston celebrated African American heritage and culture. Dorothy West wrote about social and financial security. Richard Wright wrote powerfully about anger, frustration and violence.

기적사 DAY 45

01 다음 빈칸에 들어갈 말로 가장 적절한 것을 고르시오.

> He might make an _____ companion for Mubarak as they spend their sunset years reflecting on what might have been.

① agreeable ② uncanny
③ sanguinary ④ futile

02 다음 밑줄 친 어휘와 의미가 가장 먼 것을 고르시오.

> Like Socrates, Street Epistemologists are to understand themselves as <u>inquisitive</u> teachers, not combative lecturers.

① analytical ② nosy
③ meddlesome ④ superficial

03 다음 밑줄 친 어휘와 의미가 가장 가까운 것을 고르시오.

> Israel has destroyed 80% of the ones they have found, and needs only a few days to <u>obliterate</u> the rest.

① divulge ② let off
③ annihilate ④ stick

04 두 사람의 대화 중 가장 어색한 것은?

① A: Have you ever seen an aurora?
　B: Yes, I saw one last year when I traveled to Canada.
② A: Tomorrow is the day I've been looking forward to for several years.
　B: What's so special about tomorrow?
③ A: Do you know about the benefits of becoming a vegetarian?
　B: I know why people commonly suffer from chronic disease in the contemporary society.
④ A: I feel too exhausted today so I need some time-off from work.
　B: You've been working too hard. Go, get some rest.

05 우리말을 영어로 잘못 옮긴 것은?

① 누군가 내 의견을 받아들여 그것을 주요 논쟁으로 불어넣으려고 했다.
　→ Someone took my comment and tried to blow it into a major controversy.
② 마드리드로 가는 길에 있는 한 작은 마을에서 우리는 아이들을 위한 사탕 과자를 사기 위해 멈췄다.
　→ In a small village on the way to Madrid we stopped to buy sweets for the children.
③ 당신은 중요할 수 있는 다른 누군가에게 자기 의견을 말해보는데 딱 한두 시간 걸린다.
　→ You just take one or two hours to bounce ideas off somebody else that can be important.
④ 그 전쟁은 파괴와 죽음뿐만 아니라 두 사회 사이에 증오감의 형성을 야기했다.
　→ The war caused not only destruction and death but also generated hatred between the two communities.

06 어법상 옳은 것은?

① People are starting to ask if or not the warning was mishandled.
② It has been suggested that the new manager will resign if any more players leave.
③ There has been a even high degree of co-operation between everyone involved in this case.
④ The longer you have been in good shape in the past, the quick you will regain fitness in future.

07 밑줄 친 부분 중 어법상 옳은 것은?

Anyone who has ever rushed out of the house only to realize that their keys and wallet are sitting on the kitchen table ① knows this only too well. And it's not just our efficiency ② what is reduced. The quality of the experience suffers too, as we become less ③ awarer or 'mindful.' Have you ever eaten an entire meal without tasting any of it? Hurrying up doesn't just give us less time but it can also steal the pleasure and benefit ④ by the time that we do have.

08 다음 글의 제목으로 가장 적절한 것은?

It was found that sharks living in deep, cold waters tend to have very large fatty livers, sometimes making up over a quarter of their body. This adds to their buoyancy, allowing them to move through the water using little energy, but also going relatively slowly because of the added bulk. Fortunately, the deep-water animals that they eat, and that eat them, are also pretty slow. Sharks living in warmer and shallower waters, on the other hand, have comparatively smaller livers. This makes them negatively buoyant, meaning that they must move quickly in order for their wing-like pectoral fins to generate lift. While such a design might seem less energy-efficient than that of the blimp-like sharks, it actually makes sense for living in an ecosystem where everything else also moves faster.

① Why Do Sharks Need a Big Liver?
② Beware, There Are Sharks Everywhere!
③ How Do Sharks Use Their Energy Efficiently?
④ Different Shark Bodies for Different Environments

09 다음 글의 요지로 가장 적절한 것은?

Various studies stress the importance of listening as a communication skill. A typical study points out that people spend 70 to 80 percent of their waking hours in some form of communication. Of that time, 9 percent is writing, 16 percent reading, 30 percent speaking, and 45 percent listening. While the percentage of listening is highest, studies also confirm that a vast majority of people are poor and inefficient listeners. They have ears that hear very well, but seldom have they acquired the necessary skills to allow those ears to be used effectively for what is called listening. Research suggests that the majority of us only remember between 25 percent and 50 percent of what we hear. If this is accurate, it means that when talking to a boss, colleague, or spouse for 10 minutes, people pay attention to less than half of the conversation.

① Listening skills can be improved with practice.
② Every day we spend a large amount of time listening.
③ Listening well is sometimes more difficult than speaking well.
④ Listening is an important skill but people often lack the ability.

10 Macaulay Honors College에 관한 다음 글의 내용과 일치하는 것은?

All New York students who attend Macaulay Honors College may do so tuition-free. Students from outside of New York have the in-state portion of their tuition waived, but they must still pay the difference between the in-state and out-of-state portion of their tuition. Also, room and board are not included in the tuition waivers. As the room and board costs range from $13,000 to $25,000, many students live at home and commute. Students who earn combined degrees must also pay for their graduate study. Students who must pay over and above the scholarship to which all students are entitled can apply for financial aid.

① It only accepts students from New York.
② All of its students can study there free of cost.
③ Its scholarship is inclusive of accommodation fees.
④ It does not financially support postgraduate students.

기적사 DAY 46

01 밑줄 친 부분과 의미가 가장 가까운 것을 고르시오.

Newton made <u>unprecedented</u> contributions to mathematics, optics, and mechanical physics.

① mediocre ② suggestive
③ unsurpassed ④ provocative

02 밑줄 친 부분에 들어갈 말로 가장 적절한 것은?

The young knight was so _____ at being called a coward that he charged forward with his sword in hand.

① aloof ② incensed
③ unbiased ④ unpretentious

03 밑줄 친 부분에 들어갈 말로 가장 적절한 것은?

Back in the mid-1970s, an American computer scientist called John Holland _____ the idea of using the theory of evolution to solve notoriously difficult problems in science.

① took on ② got on
③ put upon ④ hit upon

04 밑줄 친 부분에 들어갈 말로 가장 적절한 것을 고르시오.

A: Hello? Hi, Stephanie. I'm on my way to the office. Do you need anything?
B: Hi, Luke. Can you please pick up extra paper for the printer?
A: What did you say? Did you say to pick up ink for the printer? Sorry, _____
B: Can you hear me now? I said I need more paper for the printer.
A: Can you repeat that, please?
B: Never mind. I'll text you.
A: Okay. Thanks, Stephanie. See you soon.

① My phone has really bad reception here.
② I couldn't pick up more paper.
③ I think I've dialed the wrong number.
④ I'll buy each item separately this time.

05 어법상 옳은 것은?

① China's imports of Russian oil skyrocketed by 36 percent in 2014.
② Sleeping has long been tied to improve memory among humans.
③ Last night, she nearly escaped from running over by a car.
④ The failure is reminiscent of the problems surrounded the causes of the fatal space shuttle disasters.

06 우리말을 영어로 잘못 옮긴 것을 고르시오.

① 가능한 모든 일자리를 알아보았음에도 불구하고, 그는 적당한 일자리를 찾지 못했다.
→ Despite searching for every job opening possible, he could not find a suitable job.

② 당신이 누군가를 믿을 수 있는지 알아보는 최선책은 그 사람을 믿는 것이다.
→ The best way to find out if you can trust somebody is to trust that person.

③ 미각의 민감성은 개인의 음식 섭취와 체중에 크게 영향을 미친다.
→ Taste sensitivity is largely influenced by food intake and body weight of individuals.

④ 부모는 그들의 자녀가 성장하고 학습하는 데 알맞은 환경을 제공할 책임이 있다.
→ Parents are responsible for providing the right environment for their children to grow and learn in.

07 우리말을 영어로 잘못 옮긴 것을 고르시오.

① 그는 자신의 정적들을 투옥시켰다.
→ He had his political enemies imprisoned.

② 경제적 자유가 없다면 진정한 자유가 있을 수 없다.
→ There can be no true liberty unless there is economic liberty.

③ 나는 가능하면 빨리 당신과 거래할 수 있기를 바란다.
→ I look forward to doing business with you as soon as possible.

④ 30년 전 고향을 떠날 때, 그는 다시는 고향을 못 볼 거라고 꿈에도 생각지 않았다.
→ When he left his hometown thirty years ago, little does he dream that he could never see it again.

08 밑줄 친 부분 중 글의 흐름상 가장 어색한 것은?

In 2007, our biggest concern was "too big to fail." Wall Street banks had grown to such staggering sizes, and had become so central to the health of the financial system, that no rational government could ever let them fail. ① Aware of their protected status, banks made excessively risky bets on housing markets and invented ever more complicated derivatives. ② New virtual currencies such as bitcoin and ethereum have radically changed our understanding of how money can and should work. ③ The result was the worst financial crisis since the breakdown of our economy in 1929. ④ In the years since 2007, we have made great progress in addressing the dilemma. Our banks are better capitalized than ever. Our regulators conduct regular stress tests of large institutions.

09 다음 글의 주제로 가장 적절한 것은?

Imagine that two people are starting work at a law firm on the same day. One person has a very simple name. The other person has a very complex name. We've got pretty good evidence that over the course of their next 16 plus years of their career, the person with the simpler name will rise up the legal hierarchy more quickly. They will attain partnership more quickly in the middle parts of their career. And by about the eighth or ninth year after graduating from law school the people with simpler names are about seven to ten percent more likely to be partners—which is a striking effect. We try to eliminate all sorts of other alternative explanations. For example, we try to show that it's not about foreignness because foreign names tend to be harder to pronounce. But even if you look at just white males with Anglo-American names—so really the true in-group, you find that among those white males with Anglo names they are more likely to rise up if their names happen to be simpler. So simplicity is one key feature in names that determines various outcomes.

① the development of legal names
② the concept of attractive names
③ the benefit of simple names
④ the roots of foreign names

10 밑줄 친 (A), (B)에 들어갈 말로 가장 적절한 것은?

Visionaries are the first people in their industry segment to see the potential of new technologies. Fundamentally, they see themselves as smarter than their opposite numbers in competitive companies—and, quite often, they are. Indeed, it is their ability to see things first that they want to leverage into a competitive advantage. That advantage can only come about if no one else has discovered it. They do not expect, ____(A)____, to be buying a well-tested product with an extensive list of industry references. Indeed, if such a reference base exists, it may actually turn them off, indicating that for this technology, at any rate, they are already too late. Pragmatists, ____(B)____, deeply value the experience of their colleagues in other companies. When they buy, they expect extensive references, and they want a good number to come from companies in their own industry segment.

	(A)	(B)
①	therefore	on the other hand
②	however	in addition
③	nonetheless	at the same time
④	furthermore	in conclusion

01 다음 빈칸에 들어갈 말로 가장 적절한 것을 고르시오.

One perspective that seems to have been ignored is what I regard as the _____ role of the Revolutionary Guards.

① contingent ② cardinal
③ suggestive ④ mandatory

02 다음 밑줄 친 어휘와 의미가 가장 먼 것을 고르시오.

If servants do not get their meat honestly and decently, they will neglect their master's business, or embezzle his goods.

① hit upon ② peculate
③ misappropriate ④ usurp

03 다음 밑줄 친 어휘와 의미가 가장 가까운 것을 고르시오.

Techies know they hold all the obscure and procrastinate cards on the grounds of engineering mysteries about notoriously difficult problems.

① peel ② meddle
③ distribute ④ dawdle

04 다음 대화의 빈칸에 들어갈 가장 알맞은 표현을 고르시오.

Sam: Mina, what are you doing right now?
Mina: Hi, Sam. I was just reading a book.
Sam: What's the book about?
Mina: It's about the Wright brothers. Have you ever heard of them?
Sam: Of course. They were the ones who made airplanes.
Mina: Yes. But during that period, people said that the Wright brothers were _____ because they believed flying the sky was an impossible idea.
Sam: It's amazing how they achieved success despite the hard times they had to go through.
Mina: I know. There's a lot to learn from their stories of life.

① a copycat ② under fire
③ blue blood ④ talking through their hats

05 어법상 옳은 것은?

① I went to get help and by the time I get back he had stopped breathing.
② He ripped out his old kitchen and looked forward to quickly installing the new units.
③ This is a strategy that has yielded huge profits so far and can continue to doing so.
④ Please include a stamped and addressing envelope with your letter requesting an application form.

06 우리말을 영어로 잘못 옮긴 것을 고르시오.

① 그 협력은 또한 노인들에게 범죄 예방 정보를 공급할 수 있다.
  → The partnership can also supply crime prevention information with the elderly.

② 나는 치료사로서 나에게 영향을 미쳤던 문화적인 차이를 완전히 탐구할 장소가 필요했다.
  → I needed a place to fully explore cultural differences that affected me as a therapist.

③ 기술적 결함 때문에 소수의 이메일 메시지를 분실하는 것은 짜증 나는 일이다.
  → The loss of a handful of email messages because of a technical glitch is an irritation.

④ 무장 강도 사건이 발생했던 약국의 주인은 그 사건에 대한 충격에 대해 말하는 중이었다.
  → The owner of the chemist's shop where the armed robbery took place was telling of his shock at the incident.

07 우리말을 영어로 잘못 옮긴 것을 고르시오.

① 우리는 그들이 양로원 같은 고위험 지역에서 오지 않는 한 사람들을 가려내지 않는다.
  → We don't screen people unless they come from a high risk area such as nursing homes.

② 우리는 날씨가 변하기 전 약 4주에서 6주 전에 그 일이 시작되기를 원했다.
  → We wanted to get the work started some four to six weeks ago before the weather turned.

③ 그 영향이 무엇인지는 말하는 것은 불가능하지만, 상상컨대 그것들은 세상을 변화시킬 것이다.
  → There is no to say what the effects might be, but they might conceivably transform the world.

④ 레코드처럼 완성된 제품을 소유하는 것은 누군가 당신에게 그것을 읽게 하는 대신 책을 갖는 것과 같다.
  → Owning a finished product like a record is like having a book instead of just having someone read it to you.

08 다음 글의 요지로 가장 적절한 것은?

At the end of the 1920s, the United States boasted the largest economy in the world. With the destruction wrought by World War I, Europeans struggled while Americans flourished. Upon succeeding to the Presidency, Herbert Hoover predicted that the United States would soon see the day when poverty was eliminated. Then, in a moment of apparent triumph, everything fell apart. The stock market crash of 1929 touched off a chain of events that plunged the United States into its longest, deepest economic crisis of its history. However, it is far too simplistic to view the stock market crash as the single cause of the Great Depression. A healthy economy can recover from such a contraction. Long-term underlying causes sent the nation into a downward spiral of despair.

① Multiple factors caused the Great Depression to occur.
② The Great Depression was solely due to the stock market crash.
③ It is important to keep the economy healthy to avoid a recession.
④ President Herbert Hoover failed to lift the country out of the depression.

09 빈칸에 들어갈 표현으로 가장 적절한 것은?

A 2009 study at Shippensburg University suggested that there's a relationship between _____. Researchers found that, regardless of race, young people with unusual names were more likely to engage in criminal activity. The findings obviously don't show that the unpopular names caused the behavior, but merely show a link between the two things. And the researchers have some theories about their findings. "Adolescents with unpopular names may be more prone to crime because they are treated differently by their peers, making it more difficult for them to form relationships," they explain. "Juveniles with unpopular names may also act out because they dislike their names."

① the popularity of one's first name and juvenile delinquency
② the popularity of one's first name and that of the person
③ one's personality and juvenile criminal behavior
④ one's popularity and juvenile criminal behavior

10 주어진 문장 다음에 이어질 글의 순서로 가장 적절한 것은?

Being pragmatic is to be concerned with factual data and real life occurrences.

(A) Meanwhile, being visionary is having utopian ideas. Visionary individuals are not much bothered about factual details and everyday occurrences.
(B) Pragmatists pay attention to the actual occurrences and deal with these situations in the best manner possible.
(C) They would attempt to choose the best path by analyzing and weighing the various advantages, disadvantages, obstacles, and opportunities in each path and arrive at a decision.

① (A) − (B) − (C)
② (C) − (A) − (B)
③ (B) − (A) − (C)
④ (B) − (C) − (A)

01 다음 밑줄 친 어휘와 의미가 가장 가까운 것을 고르시오.

If we encourage people to start dating earlier in their lives, maybe we can head off some of these unprecedented problems in the future.

① prevent ② review
③ correct ④ flatter

02 다음 빈칸에 들어갈 말로 가장 적절한 것을 고르시오.

U.S. President Donald Trump commented earlier in a tweet that it's hard to believe Seoul and Tokyo will _____ the North's provocations much longer and urged China to "put a heavy move" against the regime and "end this nonsense once and for all."

① charge with ② make over
③ come down with ④ put up with

03 다음 밑줄 친 어휘와 의미가 가장 먼 것을 고르시오.

As he did following the shootings in Arizona, Obama demonstrated his ability to move a crowd, to eulogize, and to capture the moment.

① venerate ② glorify
③ discard ④ idolize

04 다음 빈칸에 들어갈 가장 적절한 표현을 순서대로 나열한 것은?

Julie: I haven't gone to the movie theatre for quite a while.
Matt: Oh there are some good movies on screen these days.
Julie: Do you have any recommendations?
Matt: If you like horror movies, there's one coming out tomorrow.
Julie: Oh I'm ____(A)____ horror movies. I can spend a whole day watching horror films.
Matt: I'm not good with horror movies. I always get ____(B)____ when something scary pops up.

	(A)	(B)
①	nuts about	a wildcard
②	nuts about	goose bumps
③	in the wake of	sour grapes
④	in the heyday of	goose bumps

05 어법상 옳은 것은?

① We should not be afraid to testing these new data and concepts.
② For the past two weeks, the Western world seen something remarkable to occur in Ukraine.
③ The man staying next to me at the hotel had his travel bag stolen from the room yesterday.
④ He was not afraid of being competed with supermarkets but feared the effect on customer choice.

06 우리말을 영어로 잘못 옮긴 것을 고르시오.

① 다른 사람이 말했던 것임에도 불구하고, Jane은 정원사를 구하는 것이 좋은 생각이라는 것을 알고 있었다.
→ Jane had known it was a good idea to get a gardener, although what others said.

② 그는 돈과 재산 전부를 그 당시 자신과 동행했던 사람이라면 누구에게나 맡길 것이다.
→ He would entrust all his money and belongings to whoever was accompanying him at the time.

③ 실수하는 것 없이 읽거나 쓰는 것은 어렵다는 것을 알게 된 아이는 노래를 아주 잘 부르는 능력을 가진다.
→ A child who found it difficult to read or write without making mistakes has the ability to sing quite well.

④ 물고기의 몸은 집 지붕 위에 있는 지붕널처럼 서로 겹치는 비늘로 덮여 있다.
→ The fish's body is covered with scales that overlap each other like the shingles on the roof of a house.

07 우리말을 영어로 잘못 옮긴 것을 고르시오.

① 패딩은 통증을 예방하는 데 도움을 주고 당신이 안장 위에서 더 많은 시간을 보내도록 해준다.
→ The padding helps prevent soreness and lets you spending more time on the saddle.

② 이 게시물의 나머지 부분은 적어도 첫 시를 읽지 않으면 잘 이해할 수 없을 것이다.
→ The rest of this post won't make much sense unless you read at least the first poem.

③ 한 생존자는 폭발이 일어났을 때 위층 방에서 회의가 열리고 있었다고 말했다.
→ One survivor said a meeting was being held in an upstair room when the blast occurred.

④ 나는 앞으로 7일 이내에 570파운드의 총액에 대한 당신의 고객 수표를 받기를 기대한다.
→ I look forward to receiving your client's cheque for the sum of £570 within the next seven days.

08 주어진 문장 다음에 이어질 글의 순서로 가장 적절한 것은?

"Too big to fail" describes a concept in which the government will intervene in situations where a business has become so deeply ingrained in the functionality of an economy that its failure would be disastrous to the economy at large.

(A) If such a company fails, it would likely have a catastrophic ripple effect throughout the economy.

(B) Conceptually, in these situations, the government will consider the costs of a bailout in comparison to the costs of allowing economic failure in a decision to allocate funds for help.

(C) The failure may cause problems with companies that rely on the failing company's business as a customer as well as problems with unemployment as workers lose their jobs.

① (A) − (B) − (C)
② (A) − (C) − (B)
③ (B) − (C) − (A)
④ (C) − (A) − (B)

09 다음 글의 요지로 가장 적절한 것은?

The researchers gathered a few pairs of names from different regions around the world and asked participants to rate how reliable a person was based solely on their name. People with names like "Yevgeni Dherzhinsky" or "Shobha Bhattacharya" were thought to be more unreliable than those with more pronounceable names like "Putali Angami". In another experiment, the researchers paired true or false trivia statements like "Giraffes are the only mammals that cannot jump," with either difficult or easy to pronounce names. When participants thought that a statement had been made by someone with an easier name, they were more likely to consider it true than when the statement had been paired with a difficult name.

① Your name can greatly affect your success.
② It is undesirable to judge a person based on his or her name.
③ There is no relationship between one's personality and his or her name.
④ The harder your name is to pronounce, the more untrustworthy people will assume you are.

10 빈칸에 들어갈 표현으로 가장 적절한 것은?

It's the same with the Edison vs. Tesla debate. One of the major differences was that Edison would not entertain ideas that had no market viability. What's the point of an idea that would never get any traction with buyers? Who's paying the rent for the lab? This issue of pragmatism is a chief reason why Edison fired Tesla. JP Morgan decided to pick up the Serbian inventor and finance his lab, but when Morgan realized that none of Tesla's ideas could actually produce anything of direct value, he withdrew his funding. Tesla could no longer afford his lab and died destitute. His refusal or inability to be _____ cost him his ability to pursue his passion.

① creative
② sociable
③ practical
④ visionary

01 다음 밑줄 친 어휘와 의미가 가장 가까운 것을 고르시오.

Of course, most information about the undocumented is anecdotal, since this is a population that fears being counted.

① unsubstantiated ② unsurpassed
③ enraged ④ perplexed

02 다음 밑줄 친 어휘와 의미가 가장 먼 것을 고르시오.

The goals also include reforming the police, Ministry of Justice and its subordinate organizations, the National Intelligence Service and introducing a fairer tax system.

① aloof ② adjuvant
③ auxiliary ④ accessory

03 다음 빈칸에 들어갈 말로 가장 적절한 것을 고르시오.

I hit upon the hooks on the end of final strokes which indicate a(n) _____ mind that holds on to ideas and opinions as tight as a snapping turtle.

① augmentative ② tenacious
③ precise ④ supplementary

04 다음 대화의 빈칸에 들어갈 가장 알맞은 표현을 고르시오.

Student: Thank you for your time, Professor. I wanted to talk to you about a few things.
Professor: No problem at all. What can I help you with?
Student: As you know, I have an upcoming presentation next week.
Professor: Oh, I get it. You want some feedback on your topic, right?
Student: Um…. Not quite. Actually, I _____ whenever I stand in front of the crowd. Everything just blacks out.
Professor: You should be more confident and believe in yourself. Imagine that you are just talking to someone you feel comfortable.
Student: Thanks a lot for the advice. I was really worried about the presentation but I feel much better now.
Professor: I'm sure you'll do just fine. Don't be so nervous.

① roll out the red carpet
② keep an ear to the ground
③ have a chip on my shoulder
④ have butterflies in my stomach

05 어법상 옳은 것은?

① From the garden you walk down to discovering a large and beautiful lake.
② The noise of the blast has left him struggled to hear high frequency sounds.
③ We all worked long hours these days, but many men try to make up for it when they get home.
④ He said he would object to being relocated, arguing that he had lived in the area for more than 30 years.

06 우리말을 영어로 잘못 옮긴 것을 고르시오.

① 경찰은 그 침입(사건)을 그 지역의 다른 최근 절도(사건)와 관련짓고 있는 중이다.
→ The police are connecting the break-in with other recent thefts in the area.

② 제국, 국가, 기업의 힘은 그것을 지지하는 밑바닥 사람들로부터 온다.
→ The power of the empire, country or company comes from those at the bottom that support it.

③ 사람들은 아인슈타인이 일반 상대성 이론을 개발하는 동안 과학자로 성장했다고 주장한다.
→ People have argued that Einstein grew up as a scientist while he was developing the general theory of relativity.

④ 70개 이상의 토착어와 방언이 사용되는데, 그것들 중 가장 널리 사용되는 것은 Kikongo, Sangha, Bateke이다.
→ Over seventy local languages and dialects speak, the most widely used of which are Kikongo, Sangha, and Bateke.

07 우리말을 영어로 잘못 옮긴 것을 고르시오.

① 그것은 내가 다섯 살 때 나의 스코틀랜드 할머니께서 나에게 하라고 말씀하셨던 것이다.
→ That's what my Scottish grandmother told me I needed to do when I was five years old.

② 발연점을 지나 가열된 기름은 일반적으로 푸르스름한 연기를 내뿜고 음식이 탄 맛이 나도록 한다.
→ Oil heated past its smoke point usually emits a bluish smoke and makes food taste burnt.

③ 참석 중인 사람들은 분위기를 방해하지 않도록 패널리스트들을 똑바로 쳐다보지 말아 달라는 요청을 받는다.
→ Those in attendance are asked not to look directly at the panelists, lest you not disturb the mood.

④ 질병은 아닐지 모르지만, 곧 사라지지 않으면 의사에 의해 검진을 받을 가치가 있을지도 모른다.
→ It may not be a disease, but it might be worth getting checked out by a doctor if it does not go away soon.

08 빈칸에 들어갈 표현으로 가장 적절한 것은?

There are some 6,000 banks in the U.S. The biggest six have $10 trillion in assets, almost twice as much as the next 30 combined. The six biggest banks in the U.S. have increased their assets more than five-fold since 1997. That's a lot of money in a small number of hands. It might mean that _____, as governments decided in the panic of 2008. Anger soared over the disbursement of $700 billion to save banks, while many homeowners and businesses went under. Regulators have been working ever since to make it possible for even the biggest financial institutions to close without triggering a meltdown.

① failure is unpredictable
② failure is not an option
③ failure will be inevitable
④ failure is a great teacher

09 다음 글의 제목으로 가장 적절한 것은?

Students with stereotypically black-sounding names tend to be labeled as troublemakers by teachers. Job applicants with such names are less likely than their white-sounding counterparts to be called in for interviews. When residents with black-sounding names contact their local government for information about schools or libraries, they are less likely to get a response. Adding to this troubling compendium of results is a disturbing new study, published Thursday in the journal Evolution and Human Behavior. The study of mostly white participants shows that men with black-sounding names are more likely to be imagined as physically large, dangerous and violent than those with stereotypically white-sounding names.

① Names And Racial Bias
② Race And Social Status
③ Different Names in Different Races
④ Traditional Names and Trendy Names

10 다음 글의 밑줄 친 부분 중 문맥상 단어의 쓰임이 적절하지 않은 것은?

Here's the problem: we pay lip service to the concept, but in practice we ① dislike pragmatism. Because the pragmatist tries to take each situation on its own merits and figure out a sensible way forward, pragmatism tends to look ② hesitant, messy, and prone to error. The ideologue looks ③ indecisive in comparison. Ideology always offers a neat answer, whether through reference to Karl Marx, Milton Friedman or the latest corporate mission statement. The fact that the answer may simply be wrong is ④ irrelevant to the ideologue, as it needs no testing. The poor pragmatist, by contrast, must endure the rigmarole of figuring out whether his or her approach actually worked, and embarrassingly, many sensible seeming ideas fail.

01 다음 밑줄 친 어휘와 의미가 가장 먼 것을 고르시오.

The possibility of justice is more likely to deter a bloody tyrant than a travel ban on a few of his cronies.

① inhibit ② talk out of
③ obstruct ④ put upon

02 다음 밑줄 친 어휘와 의미가 가장 가까운 것을 고르시오.

But ill-considered personal choices and the accidents of history always seemed to conspire against Marrero.

① float over ② concede
③ collude ④ deal with

03 다음 빈칸에 들어갈 말로 가장 적절한 것을 고르시오.

We females believed that to be successful we had to "man up" and _____ masculine emotional restraint.

① impair ② emulate
③ brush up on ④ hit upon

04 다음 대화의 빈칸에 들어갈 가장 알맞은 표현을 고르시오.

A: I visited the hospital yesterday to get a regular check-up.
B: Good for you. What did the doctor say?
A: He said I have some minor problems in my backbone. It's not straight as it should be.
B: Maybe the cause is in your posture. Why don't you try exercising everyday?
A: Do you think exercising is effective in solving spinal issues?
B: Why not? Even stretching can help you stay _____.
A: You're right. I'll begin with a small step of stretching everyday.
B: Good luck on your progress!

① a big bug ② fit as a fiddle
③ on the water wagon ④ a needle in a haystack

05 어법상 옳은 것은?

① We bought our house known that it would be tight for the first four or five years.
② Since I was a child, there have been many wars which were supposed to impacting my life.
③ The judge said last night that he expected the terms of the new control orders to be very similar.
④ What's your best advice to others in your position when it comes to being built the proper security program?

06 우리말을 영어로 잘못 옮긴 것을 고르시오.

① 이번 사건의 결과로 경찰이 출동하고 탄약이 회수되었다.
→ The police were called as a result of this incident and ammunition was recovered.

② 검사는 그 소년이 자신의 나이에도 불구하고 마약 상용 습관에 드는 돈을 지불하기 위해 현금을 훔쳤다는 것을 시인했다고 말했다.
→ The prosecutor told that although his age the boy admitted stealing cash to pay for his drug habit.

③ 그것[편파적 발언]이 우리에게서 권리와 자유를 빼앗는다고 할 때 이러한 주권은 편파적 발언에서 기인한다.
→ This sovereign power is attributed to hate speech when it is said to deprive us of rights and liberties.

④ 그 소녀는 병이 나았고, 아마도 그녀가 필요로 했던 모든 것은 신체적인 접촉이었을 것이라고 믿게 만들었다.
→ The girl is cured of her sickness, leading one to believe that perhaps all she needed was some physical contact.

07 우리말을 영어로 잘못 옮긴 것을 고르시오.

① 나는 William이 어젯밤 말하는 것을 들었고 그 남자가 목소리를 잃고 있다는 것을 알아채지 않을 수 없었다.
→ I heard William speaking last night and couldn't help notice the man is losing his voice.

② 3년 전에 우리의 친구 중 한 명이 그의 미니카를 도둑맞았고, 이것은 그가 나에게 보낸 메일이다.
→ Three years ago a friend of ours had his minicar stolen, and this is the email he sent me.

③ 우리는 최근에 그가 죽기 직전 그 시기에 무슨 일이 일어날지에 대해 이야기했다.
→ We recently talked about what was going to happen in the period just before his death.

④ 그것들은 벌금이 지불될 때까지 그곳에 보관될 것이고 만약 벌금이 지불되지 않는다면 부서질 것이다.
→ They will be kept there until fines have been paid and if they are not they will be crushed.

08 밑줄 친 부분 중 글의 흐름상 가장 어색한 것은?

Dialect is used commonly in literature. An author may elect to use dialect if he or she wants to represent the characters well. In order to do so, the author will write dialogue specific to the region of the character. ① Authors want their characters to seem genuine; therefore, they must write dialogue between characters in such a way as they would speak it. George Bernard Shaw's Pygmalion does this well. ② Pygmalion was first presented on stage to the public in 1913. ③ A Cockney girl is "adopted" by a well-to-do gentleman who tries to change both her dialect and accent to Standard British English. ④ For many, this play is difficult to read because the Cockney is only specific to that region. However, if the play were not written with the Cockney dialect, it would not be effective at all.

09 다음 글의 주제로 가장 적절한 것은?

The British had an early interest in mapping as they wanted to expand their resources, riches, and power, and having good maps could help them achieve this goal. At this time in history, maps weren't just symbols of power — they conferred power. With a good map, a military had an advantage in battle and a king knew how much land could be taxed. So it makes sense that the British had taken an interest in this field and had a desire to map their territories. The British took mapping to the next level in the mid to late 1700s with the British Ordnance and The Great Trigonometrical Survey of India. This survey-based mapping marked a shift from a routing and descriptive-based process to a mathematical, grid-based technique using triangulation. It also introduced the notion of fixed reference points and scalability to the world of mapping.

① relationship between maps and power in the past
② changes of maps in the history of the British Empire
③ history of geography and cartography of Great Britain
④ influence of the British on advancements in mapping techniques

10 밑줄 친 (A), (B)에 들어갈 말로 가장 적절한 것은?

_____(A)_____ the HR industry has begun adopting more technological solutions into their processes, it is easier than ever to get started exchanging real-time performance feedback. Giving real-time feedback doesn't have to mean more emails, or potentially awkward chats. Tools such as Impraise help connect colleagues so they can share feedback easily, quickly, and even when they're on the go. At the push of a button, colleagues can request feedback, or send a praise when a job's done well, or a tip to help colleagues become a better professional. _____(B)_____, colleagues are instantly notified either via email or push notification whenever they receive feedback or feedback requests — that way everyone can get feedback right when it matters most.

	(A)	(B)
①	Even though	Nonetheless
②	Unless	Likewise
③	As	Otherwise
④	Now that	Meanwhile

01 다음 밑줄 친 어휘와 의미가 가장 가까운 것을 고르시오.

That changed suddenly in 2015, when authorities, citing security concerns, banned gay and trans-gender pride events chasing away shocked participants trying to converge on central Taksim Square with tear gas and water cannons.

① erode ② sniff
③ modify ④ assemble

02 다음 밑줄 친 어휘와 의미가 가장 가까운 것을 고르시오.

But that did not stop Kennedy from delivering a joke that night that was nothing less than audacious.

① scornful ② valiant
③ hurry ④ terrifying

03 다음 밑줄 친 어휘와 의미가 가장 가까운 것을 고르시오.

If we encourage people to start dating earlier in their lives, maybe we can head off some of these unprecedented problems in the future.

① prevent ② review
③ correct ④ flatter

04 밑줄 친 부분에 들어갈 말로 가장 적절한 것은?

The campaign to eliminate pollution will prove _____ unless it has the understanding and full cooperation of the public.

① enticing ② enhanced
③ fertile ④ futile

05 밑줄 친 부분에 들어갈 말로 가장 적절한 것은?

Back in the mid-1970s, an American computer scientist called John Holland _____ the idea of using the theory of evolution to solve notoriously difficult problems in science.

① took on ② got on
③ put upon ④ hit upon

06 어법상 옳은 것은?

① The more I learn, the more I realize how much I don't know.
② The report recommends that more resources are devoted to teaching four-year-olds.
③ Emphasis on the omnipotence of God is even much pronounced in the writings of William.
④ He said what had surprised him was but many of those arrested had no previous convictions.

07 어법상 옳은 것은?

① I went to get help and by the time I get back he had stopped breathing.
② He ripped out his old kitchen and looked forward to quickly installing the new units.
③ This is a strategy that has yielded huge profits so far and can continue to doing so.
④ Please include a stamped and addressing envelope with your letter requesting an application form.

08 주어진 문장이 들어갈 위치로 가장 적절한 것은?

When providing this type of feedback, explain exactly what is that you're criticizing and the implications that come from it, and then create a plan to help the employee improve.

Constructive criticism is probably one of the most underused developmental tools. (①) Constructive criticism helps employees see where they need to improve and why making those improvements is important. (②) It's a well-rounded approach because it offers both a critique and a solution. (③) Imagine that you have an employee who consistently sends emails with typos and grammatical errors. (④) Instead of simply telling them that it's a problem and they need to stop doing it, explain the implications of the problem. Provide them with a clear example of why it's a problem and reiterate why it's important for them to rectify their behavior. Help them come up with ways to improve and set a timeframe that they should make the improvement by.

09 주어진 문장 다음에 이어질 글의 순서로 가장 적절한 것은?

Among the main goals of the Human Genome Project (HGP) was to develop new, better and cheaper tools to identify new genes and to understand their function.

(A) Mapping also provides clues about which chromosome contains the gene and precisely where the gene lies on that chromosome.

(B) One of these tools is genetic mapping. Genetic mapping - also called linkage mapping - can offer firm evidence that a disease transmitted from parent to child is linked to one or more genes.

(C) Therefore, genetic maps have been used successfully to find the gene responsible for relatively rare, single-gene inherited disorders such as cystic fibrosis and Duchenne muscular dystrophy.

* cystic fibrosis: 낭포성 섬유증
* Duchenne muscular dystrophy: 듀시엔형 근이영양증

① (A) － (B) － (C) ② (B) － (A) － (C)
③ (B) － (C) － (A) ④ (C) － (A) － (B)

10 밑줄 친 부분 중 글의 흐름상 가장 어색한 것은?

Dialect is used commonly in literature. An author may elect to use dialect if he or she wants to represent the characters well. In order to do so, the author will write dialogue specific to the region of the character. ① Authors want their characters to seem genuine; therefore, they must write dialogue between characters in such a way as they would speak it. George Bernard Shaw's Pygmalion does this well. ② Pygmalion was first presented on stage to the public in 1913. ③ A Cockney girl is "adopted" by a well-to-do gentleman who tries to change both her dialect and accent to Standard British English. ④ For many, this play is difficult to read because the Cockney is only specific to that region. However, if the play were not written with the Cockney dialect, it would not be effective at all.

11 다음 대화의 빈칸에 들어갈 가장 알맞은 표현을 고르시오.

A: What are you looking at?
B: I'm looking at an internship notice.
A: Are you thinking of applying for an internship position?
B: Yeah, I want to gain some hands-on experience before I get my job and jump into the real task.
A: Are you sure? You seemed really busy these days. Don't _____. You will have no time for yourself.
B: I know it might be overwhelming, but it's on my bucket list.

① play it by ear
② bite the bullet
③ keep your nose clean
④ bite off more than you can chew

12 두 사람의 대화 중 가장 어색한 것은?

① A: Have you ever seen an aurora?
   B: Yes, I saw one last year when I traveled to Canada.
② A: Tomorrow is the day I've been looking forward to for several years.
   B: What's so special about tomorrow?
③ A: Do you know about the benefits of becoming a vegetarian?
   B: I know why people commonly suffer from chronic disease in the contemporary society.
④ A: I feel too exhausted today so I need some time-off from work.
   B: You've been working too hard. Go, get some rest.

13 우리말을 영어로 잘못 옮긴 것은?

① 나는 학교에서 더 열심히 공부하지 않았던 것을 항상 후회한다.
   → I have always regretted not having studied harder at school.
② John은 팔을 비볐고 손가락을 따뜻하게 하기 위해 입김을 불었다.
   → John rubbed his arms and blew on his fingers to warm them.
③ Tom이 눈으로 막힌 교통을 통해 3마일을 여행하는 데 3시간이 걸렸다.
   → It took Tom three hours traveling three miles through snow-blocked traffic.
④ 당신은 겨울에 따뜻하거나 여름에 차가운 초코 우유를 마실 수 있다.
   → You can drink chocolate milk either hot in the winter or cold in the summer.

14 우리말을 영어로 잘못 옮긴 것을 고르시오.

① 패딩은 통증을 예방하는 데 도움을 주고 당신이 안장 위에서 더 많은 시간을 보내도록 해준다.
   → The padding helps prevent soreness and lets you spending more time on the saddle.
② 이 게시물의 나머지 부분은 적어도 첫 시를 읽지 않으면 잘 이해할 수 없을 것이다.
   → The rest of this post won't make much sense unless you read at least the first poem.
③ 한 생존자는 폭발이 일어났을 때 위층 방에서 회의가 열리고 있었다고 말했다.
   → One survivor said a meeting was being held in an upstair room when the blast occurred.
④ 나는 앞으로 7일 이내에 570파운드의 총액에 대한 당신의 고객 수표를 받기를 기대한다.
   → I look forward to receiving your client's cheque for the sum of £570 within the next seven day.

15 다음 글의 제목으로 가장 적절한 것은?

It was found that sharks living in deep, cold waters tend to have very large fatty livers, sometimes making up over a quarter of their body. This adds to their buoyancy, allowing them to move through the water using little energy, but also going relatively slowly because of the added bulk. Fortunately, the deep-water animals that they eat, and that eat them, are also pretty slow. Sharks living in warmer and shallower waters, on the other hand, have comparatively smaller livers. This makes them negatively buoyant, meaning that they must move quickly in order for their wing-like pectoral fins to generate lift. While such a design might seem less energy-efficient than that of the blimp-like sharks, it actually makes sense for living in an ecosystem where everything else also moves faster.

① Why Do Sharks Need a Big Liver?
② Beware, There Are Sharks Everywhere!
③ How Do Sharks Use Their Energy Efficiently?
④ Different Shark Bodies for Different Environments

16 다음 글의 요지로 가장 적절한 것은?

At the end of the 1920s, the United States boasted the largest economy in the world. With the destruction wrought by World War I, Europeans struggled while Americans flourished. Upon succeeding to the Presidency, Herbert Hoover predicted that the United States would soon see the day when poverty was eliminated. Then, in a moment of apparent triumph, everything fell apart. The stock market crash of 1929 touched off a chain of events that plunged the United States into its longest, deepest economic crisis of its history. However, it is far too simplistic to view the stock market crash as the single cause of the Great Depression. A healthy economy can recover from such a contraction. Long-term underlying causes sent the nation into a downward spiral of despair.

① Multiple factors caused the Great Depression to occur.
② The Great Depression was solely due to the stock market crash.
③ It is important to keep the economy healthy to avoid a recession.
④ President Herbert Hoover failed to lift the country out of the depression.

17 Macaulay Honors College에 관한 다음 글의 내용과 일치하는 것은?

All New York students who attend Macaulay Honors College may do so tuition-free. Students from outside of New York have the in-state portion of their tuition waived, but they must still pay the difference between the in-state and out-of-state portion of their tuition. Also, room and board are not included in the tuition waivers. As the room and board costs range from $13,000 to $25,000, many students live at home and commute. Students who earn combined degrees must also pay for their graduate study. Students who must pay over and above the scholarship to which all students are entitled can apply for financial aid.

① It only accepts students from New York.
② All of its students can study there free of cost.
③ Its scholarship is inclusive of accommodation fees.
④ It does not financially support postgraduate students.

18 밑줄 친 (A), (B)에 들어갈 말로 가장 적절한 것은?

Depending on the way your team works, also your leadership style, and your direct relationships with your team members, performance feedback can take a number of forms. You might choose fortnightly or monthly one-on-one meetings. _____(A)_____, you might choose to provide your feedback through responding to your team members' daily or weekly reports. Or if your team is more project-based maybe it would make more sense to schedule a review meeting or report after each project milestone is reached. Whatever form you end up choosing, the most important thing is to make a regular commitment and stick to it. It's very easy in our busy work lives to let things slip and keep postponing meetings. Keeping a regular meeting, _____(B)_____, will not only keep you on track and providing useful feedback, but it will also send the message to your team that you're serious about helping to support their performance and development.

	(A)	(B)
①	Accordingly	moreover
②	Alternatively	however
③	Additionally	in a word
④	As a result	therefore

19 빈칸에 들어갈 표현으로 가장 적절한 것은?

It's the same with the Edison vs. Tesla debate. One of the major differences was that Edison would not entertain ideas that had no market viability. What's the point of an idea that would never get any traction with buyers? Who's paying the rent for the lab? This issue of pragmatism is a chief reason why Edison fired Tesla. JP Morgan decided to pick up the Serbian inventor and finance his lab, but when Morgan realized that none of Tesla's ideas could actually produce anything of direct value, he withdrew his funding. Tesla could no longer afford his lab and died destitute. His refusal or inability to be _____ cost him his ability to pursue his passion.

① creative
② sociable
③ practical
④ visionary

20 빈칸에 들어갈 표현으로 가장 적절한 것은?

Although Hughes had trouble with both black and white critics, he was the first black American to earn his living solely from his writing and public lectures. Part of the reason he was able to do this was the phenomenal acceptance and love he received from average black people. A reviewer for *Black World* noted in 1970: "Those whose prerogative is to determine the rank of writers have never rated him highly, but if _____, then Langston Hughes stands at the apex of literary relevance among black people. The poet occupies such a position in the memory of his people precisely because he recognized that 'we possess within ourselves a great reservoir of physical and spiritual strength,' and because he used his artistry to reflect this back to the people."

① his unpublished works are counted
② his private life is less controversial
③ he is living in the postmodern world
④ the weight of public response is any gauge

MEMO

기적사 DAY 51

01 밑줄 친 부분과 의미가 가장 가까운 것을 고르시오.

He took out a picture from his drawer and kissed it with deep reverence, folded it meticulously in a white silk kerchief, and placed it inside his shirt next to his heart.

① carefully
② hurriedly
③ decisively
④ delightfully

02 밑줄 친 부분과 의미가 가장 가까운 것을 고르시오.

The company cannot expect me to move my home and family at the drop of a hat.

① immediately
② punctually
③ hesitantly
④ periodically

03 밑줄 친 부분에 가장 적절한 것은?

Before she traveled to Mexico last winter, she needed to _____ her Spanish because she had not practiced it since college.

① make up to
② brush up on
③ shun away from
④ come down with

04 밑줄 친 부분에 가장 적절한 것을 고르시오.

A: What business is on your mind?
B: Do you think that owning a flower shop has good prospects nowadays?
A: It could. But have you prepared yourself mentally and financially?
B: _____.
A: Good! Then you should choose a strategic place and the right segment too. You must do a thorough research to have a good result.
B: I know that. It's much easier to start a business than to run it well.

① I plan to go to the hospital tomorrow
② I can't be like that! I must strive to get a job
③ I'm ready to start with what I have and take a chance
④ I don't want to think about starting my own business

05 우리말을 영어로 잘못 옮긴 것을 고르시오.

① 그녀는 등산은 말할 것도 없고, 야외에 나가는 것을 좋아하지 않는다.
→ She does not like going outdoor, not to mention mountain climbing.
② 그녀는 학급에서 가장 예쁜 소녀이다.
→ She is more beautiful than any other girl in the class.
③ 그 나라는 국토의 3/4이 바다로 둘러싸여 있는 소국이다.
→ The country is a small one with the three quarters of the land surrounding by the sea.
④ 많은 학생들이 졸업 후 취직을 위해 열심히 공부한다.
→ A number of students are studying very hard to get a job after their graduation.

06 어법상 옳은 것은?

① While worked at a hospital, she saw her first air show.
② However weary you may be, you must do the project.
③ One of the exciting games I saw were the World Cup final in 2010.
④ It was the main entrance for that she was looking.

07 밑줄 친 부분 중 어법상 옳은 것은?

Compared to newspapers, magazines are not necessarily up-to-the-minute, since they do not appear every day, but weekly, monthly, or even less frequently. Even externally they are different from newspapers, mainly because magazines ① resemble like a book. The paper is thicker, photos are more colorful, and most of the articles are relatively long. The reader experiences much more background information and greater detail. There are also weekly news magazines, ② which reports on a number of topics, but most of the magazines are specialized to attract various consumers. For example, there are ③ women's magazines cover fashion, cosmetics, and recipes as well as youth magazines about celebrities. Other magazines are directed toward, for example, computer users, sports fans, ④ those interested in the arts, and many other small groups.

08 주어진 문장이 들어갈 위치로 가장 적절한 것은?

Some of these ailments are short-lived; others may be long-lasting.

For centuries, humans have looked up at the sky and wondered what exists beyond the realm of our planet. (①) Ancient astronomers examined the night sky hoping to learn more about the universe. More recently, some movies explored the possibility of sustaining human life in outer space, while other films have questioned whether extraterrestrial life forms may have visited our planet. (②) Since astronaut Yuri Gagarin became the first man to travel in space in 1961, scientists have researched what conditions are like beyond the Earth's atmosphere, and what effects space travel has on the human body. (③) Although most astronauts do not spend more than a few months in space, many experience physiological and psychological problems when they return to the Earth. (④) More than two-thirds of all astronauts suffer from motion sickness while traveling in space. In the gravity-free environment, the body cannot differentiate up from down. The body's internal balance system sends confusing signals to the brain, which can result in nausea lasting as long as a few days.

09 밑줄 친 부분에 들어갈 말로 가장 적절한 것은?

Why bother with the history of everything? _____ _____. In literature classes you don't learn about genes; in physics classes you don't learn about human evolution. So you get a partial view of the world. That makes it hard to find meaning in education. The French sociologist Emile Durkheim called this sense of disorientation and meaninglessness anomie, and he argued that it could lead to despair and even suicide. The German sociologist Max Weber talked of the "disenchantment" of the world. In the past, people had a unified vision of their world, a vision usually provided by the origin stories of their own religious traditions. That unified vision gave a sense of purpose, of meaning, even of enchantment to the world and to life. Today, though, many writers have argued that a sense of meaninglessness is inevitable in a world of science and rationality. Modernity, it seems, means meaninglessness.

① In the past, the study of history required disenchantment from science
② Recently, science has given us lots of clever tricks and meanings
③ Today, we teach and learn about our world in fragments
④ Lately, history has been divided into several categories

10 다음 글의 내용과 일치하지 않는 것은?

The earliest government food service programs began around 1900 in Europe. Programs in the United States date from the Great Depression, when the need to use surplus agricultural commodities was joined to concern for feeding the children of poor families. During and after World War II, the explosion in the number of working women fueled the need for a broader program. What was once a function of the family—providing lunch—was shifted to the school food service system. The National School Lunch Program is the result of these efforts. The program is designed to provide federally assisted meals to children of school age. From the end of World War II to the early 1980s, funding for school food service expanded steadily. Today it helps to feed children in almost 100,000 schools across the United States. Its first function is to provide a nutritious lunch to all students; the second is to provide nutritious food at both breakfast and lunch to underprivileged children. If anything, the role of school food service as a replacement for what was once a family function has been expanded.

① The increase in the number of working women boosted the expansion of food service programs.
② The US government began to feed poor children during the Great Depression despite the food shortage.
③ The US school food service system presently helps to feed children of poor families.
④ The function of providing lunch has been shifted from the family to schools.

01 다음 밑줄 친 어휘와 의미가 가장 먼 것을 고르시오.

At this point, studio executives are still nervous that if they push too hard or hurriedly, theater chains might retaliate.

① make up to ② reciprocate
③ get even with ④ retort

02 다음 밑줄 친 어휘와 의미가 가장 가까운 것을 고르시오.

And yet, in his uncanny, intuitive way, he picked up whatever he needed to know, creating images that were knowing and sly.

① eerie ② retrospective
③ punctual ④ abrupt

03 다음 빈칸에 들어갈 말로 가장 적절한 것을 고르시오.

When times were good, _____ French and German banks were happy to loan money to the Greeks to make up to these countries, and overlooked the load of debt that Athens was amassing.

① candid ② egotistic
③ heedless ④ haphazard

04 두 사람의 대화 중 가장 어색한 것은?

① A: What did you dream of last night?
B: My dream is to become a flight attendant in the future.
② A: There is a scratch on your elbow.
B: No wonder it hurt so bad.
③ A: Have you ever been to the zoo?
B: I've been to one when I was really young.
④ A: Do you know where the nearest post office is located?
B: Go straight two blocks and turn left on the first corner.

05 우리말을 영어로 잘못 옮긴 것을 고르시오.

① Jane은 반에서 다른 아이들보다 훨씬 더 똑똑하다.
→ Jane is much brighter than all the other children in her class.
② 업무 관련 질병에 대해 법적 조치를 취하는 직원의 수가 증가하고 있다.
→ A number of employees taking legal action over work-related disease is increasing.
③ 이 나라를 휩쓸고 있는 그 정신 나간 문화는 우리를 돕기 전에 보험 비용을 올리는 중이다.
→ The crazy culture sweeping this country is driving up insurance costs before helping us.
④ 그 행사에서 작업자들은 그림을 전시하는 데 있어 어떤 위험이 관련되어 있건 간에 감수하기로 결정했다.
→ In the event the workers decided to take whatever risk might be involved in displaying the picture.

06 어법상 옳은 것은?

① It was Jane's car that got broken into last Friday night.
② She sees architects today designed intelligent and space-efficient buildings.
③ She is unlikely to succeed in getting the bill through Congress, however it is worthy.
④ Lack of investment, according to former employees, have been going on for many years.

07 밑줄 친 부분 중 어법상 옳은 것은?

A good deal of the information ① storing in working memory is encoded in an auditory form, especially when the information is based on language. For example, in an early study by Conrad, adults were shown six-letter sequences, with letters being presented visually, one at a time, at intervals of three-fourths of a second. As soon as the last letter of a sequence had been presented, participants in the study ② writing down all six of the letters they had seen, guessing at any letters they couldn't easily recall. When people recalled letters incorrectly, the letters they said ③ they had seen be more likely to ④ resemble the actual stimuli in terms of how the letters sounded than how they looked.

08 다음 글의 주제로 가장 적절한 것은?

The space shuttle *Challenger* disaster that occurred on January 28, 1986, marked one of the most devastating days in the history of space exploration. Just over a minute after the space shuttle lifted off, a malfunction in the spacecraft's O-rings — rubber seals that separated its rocket boosters — caused a fire to start that destabilized the boosters and spread up the rocket itself. The shuttle was moving faster than the speed of sound and quickly began to break apart. The disaster led to the deaths of all astronauts on board, including civilian Christa McAuliffe, a participant in NASA's Teacher in Space project who was to teach classes and perform experiments during the space voyage.

① The mission of the space shuttle Challenger
② The cause of the space shuttle Challenger accident
③ The fatalities of the space shuttle Challenger disaster
④ One of the most disastrous events in spaceflight history

09 다음 밑줄 친 단어가 가리키는 대상이 나머지 넷과 다른 것은?

Max Weber was born in Erfurt, Prussia (present-day Germany) on April 21, 1864. ① He was the eldest son of Max and Helene Weber. The sociologist's father was an aspiring liberal politician. ② His mother was raised in Calvinist orthodoxy. Though she gradually accepted a more tolerant theology, her Puritan morality never diminished. As a result, her husband's social activities distanced her from him, especially when he spurned her prolonged grief following the deaths of two of ③ his siblings. ④ He, in turn, adopted a traditionally authoritarian manner at home and demanded absolute obedience from wife and children. It is thought that this bleak home environment, marked by conflicts between Weber's parents, contributed to the inner agonies that haunted him in his adult life.

10 다음 글의 주제로 가장 적절한 것은?

Mayor Lyda Krewson announced this week the start of the City's summer food service program for youth, known as the Schools Out Café. Every summer, Schools Out Café provides free breakfast and lunch to daycare centers, recreation programs, churches, and other organizations which then serve those meals to young people. In St. Louis, an estimated 80-90% of students are enrolled in free or reduced lunch, which is a key indicator to a lack of regular access to nutritionally adequate food during the summer months. "Hunger doesn't take a break when schools close for the summer," Krewson said. "I am so thankful to all the groups and organizations that have volunteered to become food serving sites, but we are always looking for more. I encourage any organization that is willing to serve meals to young people to contact us. We will provide the food."

① a regular meal program
② the importance of school meals
③ places for youngsters in St. Louis
④ a problem of school lunch service

기적사 DAY 53

01 다음 밑줄 친 어휘와 의미가 가장 먼 것을 고르시오.

But what if the man, knowing that as a brutal tyrant he could not survive without his armor, was determined rather to suffocate people than to relax in the sun?

① asphyxiate ② smother
③ stifle ④ place

02 다음 밑줄 친 어휘와 의미가 가장 가까운 것을 고르시오.

But by 1953, with McCarthyism and the second Red Scare in full swing, the FBI moved from surreptitious research to direct and immediate contact.

① faultless ② clandestine
③ superb ④ interdependent

03 다음 밑줄 친 어휘와 의미가 가장 가까운 것을 고르시오.

Two of the events, nearly ten percent of this symposium, perpetuate the lie that Zionism is racism.

① make up to ② disentangle
③ eternize ④ reexamine

04 밑줄 친 부분에 들어갈 표현으로 가장 적절한 것은?

Tim: Is Matthew mad at me?
Linda: I'm not sure. But he looked really angry when I came across him during lunch time.
Tim: Where did you see him? What was he doing?
Linda: I met him in the coffee shop and he was looking at the menu. What happened between you two?
Tim: I _____. I regret saying that. Now I have no idea how to make up to him.
Linda: Try sincere apology. I'm sure he'll forgive you.

① held my tongue
② was caught red-handed
③ lived from hand to mouth
④ put my foot in his mouth

05 우리말을 영어로 잘못 옮긴 것을 고르시오.

① 사우디아라비아는 다른 어떤 국가보다 더 많은 석유를 생산한다.
  → Saudi Arabia produces more oil than any other countries.
② 현재 주가 변동에 영향을 미치는 많은 요인들이 있다.
  → There are a number of factors currently influencing stock-price fluctuations.
③ 그는 학교에서 아이들에게 스티커를 붙이자고 제안한 적이 없다고 부인했다.
  → He denied he had suggested to the children putting the stickers up in school.
④ 터치 패드를 사용하여 마우스 커서를 이동하기 위해서, 터치 패드의 표면을 따라 손가락을 단지 미끄러뜨리면 된다.
  → To move your mouse cursor using a touch pad, you simply glide your finger along the touch pad's surface.

06 어법상 옳은 것은?

① It was your husband to that John spoke on the phone.
② You have to sit the exam, however many you don't feel like doing it.
③ The persecution of Jews during the same period is established beyond all doubt.
④ She has reported one of the detained men after seeing him carried a bag containing letters.

07 밑줄 친 부분 중 어법상 옳은 것은?

In order to create interest in the product, companies will often launch pre-market advertising campaigns. In the nutrition industry, articles are often ① written discussing a new nutrient under investigation. Over a series of issues, you begin ② to see more articles to discuss this new nutrient and potential to enhance training and/or performance. Then, after 4-6 months, a new product is coincidentally launched that ③ contain the ingredient that has been discussed in previous issues. Books and supplement reviews have also been used as vehicles to promote the sale of fitness and nutrition products. This marketing technique ④ calls demand creation. It involves creating a buzz about a new potentially revolutionary nutrient or training technique through publishing articles and/or books that stimulate the reader's interest. Once this is done, a new product is launched.

08 다음 글의 내용과 일치하는 것은?

Gravity plays a major role in our spatial orientation. Changes in gravitational forces, such as the transition to weightlessness during a space voyage, influence our spatial orientation and require adaptation by many of the physiological processes in which our balance system plays a part. Unless this adaptation is complete, this can be coupled to motion sickness (nausea), visual illusions and disorientation. This 'space sickness' or Space Adaptation Syndrome (SAS), is experienced by over half of all astronauts during the first few days of their space voyage. Wubbo Ockels, the first Dutchman in space in 1986, also suffered from these symptoms. Interestingly, SAS symptoms can even be experienced after lengthy exposure to high gravitational forces in a human centrifuge, as is used for example for testing and training fighter pilots.

① Zero gravity affects an astronaut's weight.
② SAS symptoms include vision loss.
③ SAS symptoms usually present themselves at the beginning of an astronaut's time in space.
④ Wubbo Ockels was the first person who experienced SAS symptoms.

09 주어진 문장 다음에 이어질 글의 순서로 가장 적절한 것은?

Science has defined the modern era in many ways and is truly the reigning knowledge paradigm in the modern era.

(A) The key features of modernity, specialization and technology, were made possible primarily by the remarkable development of scientific techniques and knowledge over the last 400 years, since the time of Galileo and Kepler.

(B) This is the case because today's scientific worldview seems to deny the importance of many inquiries that humans have perennially found important, including questions about our place in the universe, the nature of consciousness, and questions about God, purpose, and many other deep topics.

(C) But while science has brought us the modern world, in a very real and direct way, it has also brought us to a point where man's perennial search for meaning is imperiled.

① (A) − (B) − (C)
② (A) − (C) − (B)
③ (B) − (A) − (C)
④ (B) − (C) − (A)

10 빈칸에 들어갈 표현으로 가장 적절한 것은?

California Gov. Gavin Newsom signed a law that mandates all students are entitled to a school lunch, whether or not they have the funds to pay. This is a strong step in the right direction. Unfortunately, we have seen a series of school districts recently take steps in the other direction, resulting in humiliation for their students. These practices have included stamping a child's hand with "I need lunch money," giving him or her a sunflower butter and jelly sandwich instead of a hot lunch, and even threatening to put children with outstanding school meal debt in foster care. Last month, a child had his lunch meal thrown in the trash on his birthday because he accrued $9 in unpaid school meals fees while the school district was still processing his free school meal application. Make no mistake._____ because of a lack of funds to pay for school lunch is unacceptable.

① Sending children to foster care
② Intimidating students into obedience
③ Subjecting students to embarrassment
④ Giving students food poor in nutrients

기적사 DAY 54

01 다음 밑줄 친 어휘와 의미가 가장 먼 것을 고르시오.

People are forever being unjustly and decisively persecuted, struggling with their conscience, risking all to do the right thing.

① compunction ② complacency
③ qualm ④ scruple

02 다음 빈칸에 들어갈 말로 가장 적절한 것을 고르시오.

Japan's district police _____ cartoon characters to alert people not to take calls from unknown phone numbers immediately.

① lets on ② makes up for
③ takes on ④ draws on

03 다음 밑줄 친 어휘와 의미가 가장 먼 것을 고르시오.

Paris had been cold and morose but in Spain with my parents I found this warm refuge of love to shun away from the cold.

① cranky ② dour
③ melancholy ④ enticing

04 다음 빈칸에 들어갈 가장 적절한 표현을 순서대로 지적한 것은?

Cindy: I am so frustrated. I just want to give up.
Dan: Why? Is anything wrong?
Cindy: I almost finished writing my report but the computer turned off. Now I have to start over.
Dan: Oh, no. So you're back to ____(A)____.
Cindy: Exactly. I spent the whole weekend writing my report. But now it's all useless.
Dan: I feel sorry for you. I know how much effort you put into it.
Cindy: Well, it just seems like I ____(B)____.
Dan: Think positively. Since you've written the report once, it'll take much less time for you to ____(C)____ in the second time.
Cindy: Thanks for cheering me up. I should get started on it now.

	(A)	(B)	(C)
①	square one	went on a wild goose chase	hit the bull's eye
②	bread and butter	went on a wild goose chase	hit the bull's eye
③	square one	had ants in my pants	teach an old dog new tricks
④	bread and butter	had ants in my pants	teach an old dog new tricks

05 우리말을 영어로 잘못 옮긴 것을 고르시오.

① 그것은 인터넷상의 다른 어떤 곳보다 더 적절한 콘텐츠를 제공한다.
→ It offers more relevant content than any other place on the Internet.

② 전체 취업자 수는 23만 4,000명 이상 증가하였다.
→ The total number of people in employment has increased by more than 234,000.

③ 내 앞의 낮은 책상 위에 놓인 책의 피지를 내려다보면서 나는 조금 더 오래 거기에 앉아 있었다.
→ I sat there a while longer, staring down at the vellum pages of the book on the low desk before me.

④ 미국 정부도 위원회가 노예 제도 문제를 철저하게 조사한다면 그 회담을 보이콧하겠다고 위협했다.
→ The US government has also threatened boycotting the conference if the committee delves into the issue of slavery.

06 어법상 옳은 것은?

① If Jane likes something she'll buy it however much does it cost.
② It is the commander who is the first to take the blame for accidents.
③ The joint intention of both these parties appear to me to be beyond all doubt.
④ Jane smiled and sat down at the foot of the bed watched her daughter open the brown bag.

07 밑줄 친 부분 중 어법상 옳은 것은?

Merely ① having goals clearly defined is not sufficient, for one must also know, moment by moment, ② what precisely needs to do. For instance, a salesperson's aim is to conclude a sale profitably. However, each sale requires a different approach: Should he be pushy or laid back, authoritative or friendly? And what aspect of ③ the product should he emphasize on? The answers to these questions depend on variables that cannot be predicted in advance. This ④ holds truly not only for sales but also for most human activities. One must select a particular strategy appropriate to the occasion and follow the chosen course of action. Doing so will ensure more lasting success in reaching one's goals.

08 빈칸 (A), (B)에 들어갈 표현으로 가장 적절한 것은?

Thankfully, most space motion sickness (SMS) sufferers gradually adapt to their new circumstances and the sickness subsides after a few days in space. One astronaut who suffered particularly badly was Jake Garn, a former US senator who is remembered not for his political achievements but for his _____(A)_____ contribution to the study of SMS. Senator Garn flew as a payload specialist on a 1985 Space Shuttle mission, when part of his role was to be subjected to tests designed to increase the understanding of space sickness. Unfortunately, his sickness was so _____(B)_____ that the Astronaut Corps adopted his experience as the standard for the maximum possible level of space sickness. They devised a scale on which being totally incapable was dubbed 1 Garn. Most astronauts apparently reach no more than 0.1 Garn.

	(A)	(B)
①	underestimated	extreme
②	unintentional	trivial
③	unwitting	severe
④	unconditional	abrupt

09 밑줄 친 부분에 들어갈 말로 가장 적절한 것은?

The paradoxical outcomes of the search for meaning in Western history have played a significant part in rendering modernity meaningless. It does not follow, however, that the concepts found in Weber's work, such as ideal interests and culture, no longer apply. Rather, Weber provides an understanding of modernity based on the continuing paradoxical outcomes found in modern searches for meaning. Without the unifying effect of enchanted, cosmic meaning the modern world is structured as a series of five competing, separate value-spheres: the economic, intellectual, political, aesthetic and erotic. It is through this theory of the value-spheres that Weber will try to understand the continuing search for meaning in modernity. Essentially, instead of a coherent life-conduct based on religion and set within the parameters of meaningful cosmos, different sections of the social whole – the value-spheres – offer a new, if _____, sense of meaning.

① ineffective and useless
② limited and conditional
③ empty and meaningless
④ restricted and old fashioned

10 다음 글의 내용과 일치하는 것은?

For the first time since 1959, we have made significant changes in our menu and prices. In lieu of a price increase for elementary students, we have removed one item from the menu and are using the dessert to meet the type A requirements. Previously in the majority of schools we have been providing more food than the average elementary child could eat, and much of the food was wasted. Our charge to the elementary student for the type A lunch, which includes milk, is 35 cents. In the junior high schools, we have eliminated the choice of vegetables and restricted a la carte service to ice cream and fresh fruit. A large number of students must go through the junior high cafeteria in a short period of time, and by simplifying the menu and limiting the a la carte items, we will be able to provide faster services. The price of the complete lunch in junior high schools is 40 cents.

① The price of the school lunch for elementary students has increased.
② The amount of wasted food in elementary schools is expected to decrease.
③ Milk is included in the lunch meals in all schools.
④ Junior high school students can no longer select ice cream or fresh fruit.

01 다음 밑줄 친 어휘와 의미가 가장 가까운 것을 고르시오.

"Humans are notorious for being lousy and hurried at estimating numbers of animals in large groups," Perryman explains.

① reconcilable ② disreputable
③ outlandish   ④ destitute

02 다음 빈칸에 들어갈 말로 가장 적절한 것을 고르시오.

"The outside forces that have been _____ in the slaughter in Syria speak in a Persian accent," concluded carefully Prosor.

① unreliable   ② impeccable
③ instrumental ④ innocent

03 다음 밑줄 친 어휘와 의미가 가장 먼 것을 고르시오.

The pursuit of equitable distribution of wealth must be replaced with the more realistic equitable distribution of opportunity for the college.

① provocative ② reasonable
③ impartial   ④ unbiased

04 밑줄 친 부분에 들어갈 표현으로 가장 적절한 것은?

A: What is the ultimate goal of your life?
B: That's a really difficult question. Give me some time to think. What is yours?
A: I want to get a job with a promising salary.
B: Then is money your first priority?
A: Yes, since _____(A)_____ in the capitalist society, I should get paid enough to enjoy my life.
B: That's a very realistic perspective. But I agree with you. If you're _____(B)_____, life can be devastating.

	(A)	(B)
①	money talks	dead broke
②	money talks	on the house
③	pigs may fly	dead broke
④	pigs may fly	a couch potato

05 우리말을 영어로 잘못 옮긴 것을 고르시오.

① 나는 그가 나에게 항상 무엇을 해야 할지를 말하는 것을 싫어한다.
  → I hate him telling me what to do all the time.
② 많은 연구원들이 매년 환경 프로젝트에 자원한다.
  → A great number of researchers volunteer each year for environmental projects.
③ 사용자는 압력에 반응하는 태블릿에 쓰는 장치처럼 펜을 사용하여 데이터를 입력할 것이다.
  → Users will input data using a pen like device writing on a pressure sensitive tablet.
④ 인디애나가 다른 어느 주보다 더 많이 만드는 강철조차도 가격이 비싸다.
  → Even steel, which Indiana makes much of than any other state, has been expensive.

06 어법상 옳은 것은?

① Stood up quickly, John went to his closet and took out his luggage bag.
② It was in 1939 which the Second World War started.
③ However hungry you are, you never seem to be able to finish off a whole pizza.
④ Apart from an engraving of the period all knowledge of the former structures were lost.

07 밑줄 친 부분 중 어법상 옳은 것은?

Chief among these advantages is the ability to control the first messages and how a story is first framed. That ① leaves others had to respond to you instead of the other way around. This approach is appropriately termed "stealing thunder." When an organization steals thunder, it breaks the news about its own crisis before the crisis is discovered by the media or other interested parties. In experimental research by Arpan and Roskos-Ewoldsen, stealing thunder in a crisis situation, ② as opposed to allow the information to be first disclosed by another party, ③ resulted in substantially higher credibility ratings. As significant, the authors found that "credibility ratings associated with stealing thunder ④ directly predicting perceptions of the crisis as less severe."

08 주어진 문장이 들어갈 위치로 가장 적절한 것은?

And often we find them in the realm of business, one of the rare places where mortal beings can actually create the future they're envisioning.

The pragmatists among us will say that peering into the future is impossible. (①) They'll say with a smirk that there are no crystal balls, no indelible lines on human palms that foretell our destinies. (②) The rest of us believe there are indeed some who can predict what will happen tomorrow. (③) We call them prophets, visionaries, or oracles. (④) Among the most remarkable of these prophets is British businessman James Dyson. Dyson's improbable bagless vacuum cleaners, impossible bladeless fans, and hyperspeed hair driers — all of which were figments of a *Jetsons*-like age before Dyson dreamed them up — have made his name a literal household brand in much of the world and turned the 72-year-old Briton into a billionaire.

09 빈칸에 들어갈 표현으로 가장 적절한 것은?

The mandate to feed poor children dramatically transformed the National School Lunch Program. The number of children eating at school increased sharply. But the federal subsidy paid only for food — not for equipment, labor, storage, or delivery. So local school districts had to scramble to find enough money to cover the costs of free meals. They turned to large foodservice corporations to deliver the meals. Since most schools did not have full kitchens, this meant that lunch consisted of pre-packaged and frozen foods. During the 1980s, the Reagan Administration, in its effort to cut federal funding for public programs, tried to restrict the cost of school lunch by declaring ketchup a vegetable. The public outcry was immediate and loud, which indicates _____.

① how high the food quality was
② how innutritious the school meals were
③ how popular the school lunch program was
④ how difficult it was for schools to provide free meals to children

10 다음 글의 내용과 일치하지 않는 것은?

In the 19th century, Manchester held the status of the international center of the cotton trade and textile industry. It was so well known for being a city of cotton that it was nicknamed 'Cottonopolis.' Back in 1782, when cotton mills were powered by water, Richard Arkwright opened the innovative - and the world's first - steam-driven textile mill in Manchester. As textile manufacturing moved from the home to large-scale factories, Manchester and its surrounding towns became by far the largest and most productive cotton spinning centers in the world. In 1871, 32 percent of global cotton production took place in Manchester. Over 200 years after Arkwright made that iconic mill, no working mills remain but Manchester is still a city shaped by cotton. There are still around 5,000 people in Greater Manchester employed in the textile industry. Manchester's cottonopolis past can be seen in its buildings: Converted mills have found new life as offices, hotels, and flats all alongside sparkling new glassy high-rises.

① Manchester was known for cotton in the 1800s.
② Arkwright established Manchester's first cotton mill driven by water.
③ Manchester once produced more than 30 percent of global output of cotton.
④ Today, no one living in Manchester is working in a cotton mill.

기적사 DAY 56

01 밑줄 친 부분과 의미가 가장 가까운 것은?

I was told to let Jim pore over computer printouts.

① examine
② distribute
③ discard
④ correct

02 밑줄 친 부분과 의미가 가장 가까운 것은?

Johannes Kepler believed that there would one day be "celestial ships with sails adapted to the winds of heaven" navigating the sky, filled with explorers "who would not fear the vastness" of space. And today those explorers, human and robot, employ as unerring guides on their voyages through the vastness of space the three laws of planetary motion that Kepler uncovered during a lifetime of personal travail and ecstatic discovery.

① faultless
② unreliable
③ gutless
④ unscientific

03 밑줄 친 부분에 들어갈 가장 적절한 것을 고르시오.

Visaokay assists the Australian travel industry, corporations and government, and individuals by _____ the entire visa advice and visa issuance process. Visaokay minimizes the complexity and time delays associated with applying for and obtaining travel visas.

① appreciating
② aggravating
③ meditating
④ facilitating

04 밑줄 친 부분에 가장 적절한 것을 고르시오.

M: What's that noise?
W: Noise? I don't hear anything.
M: Listen closely. I hear some noise. _____.
W: Oh, let's stop and see.
M: Look! A piece of glass is in the right front wheel.
W: Really? Umm... You're right. What are we going to do?
M: Don't worry. I got some experience in changing tires.

① I gave my customers sound advice
② Maybe air is escaping from the tire
③ I think the mechanic has an appointment
④ Oh! Your phone is ringing in vibration mode

05 어법상 옳은 것은?

① Few living things are linked together as intimately than bees and flowers.
② My father would not company us to the place where they were staying, but insisted on me going.
③ The situation in Iraq looked so serious that it seemed as if the Third World War might break out at any time.
④ According to a recent report, the number of sugar that Americans consume does not vary significantly from year to year.

06 밑줄 친 부분 중 어법상 옳지 않은 것은?

Noise pollution ① is different from other forms of pollution in ② a number of ways. Noise is transient: once the pollution stops, the environment is free of it. This is not the case with air pollution, for example. We can measure the amount of chemicals ③ introduced into the air, ④ whereas is extremely difficult to monitor cumulative exposure to noise.

07 우리말을 영어로 옮긴 것으로 가장 적절한 것은?

① 그들이 10년간 살았던 집이 폭풍에 심하게 손상되었다.
  → The house which they have lived for 10 years badly damaged by the storm.
② 수학 시험에 실패했을 때에서야 그는 공부를 열심히 하기로 결심했다.
  → It was not until when he failed the math test that he decided to study hard.
③ 냉장고에 먹을 것이 하나도 남아있지 않아서, 어젯밤에 우리는 외식을 해야 했다.
  → We had nothing to eat left in the refrigerator, we had to eat out last night.
④ 우리는 운이 좋게도 그랜드 캐니언을 방문했는데, 거기에는 경치가 아름다운 곳이 많다.
  → We were enough fortunate to visit the Grand Canyon, that has much beautiful landscape.

08 주어진 문장 다음에 이어질 글의 순서로 가장 적절한 것은?

South Korea boasts of being the most wired nation on earth.

(A) This addiction has become a national issue in Korea in recent years, as users started dropping dead from exhaustion after playing online games for days on end. A growing number of students have skipped school to stay online, shockingly self-destructive behavior in this intensely competitive society.

(B) In fact, perhaps no other country has so fully embraced the Internet.

(C) But such ready access to the Web has come at a price as legions of obsessed users find that they cannot tear themselves away from their computer screens.

① (A) − (B) − (C)   ② (A) − (C) − (B)
③ (B) − (A) − (C)   ④ (B) − (C) − (A)

09 빈칸 (A), (B)에 들어갈 표현으로 가장 적절한 것은?

The South Korean government on July 18, 2016 decided to ease regulations on the gaming industry, such as revising the online game "shutdown law," by leaving it to the choice of the gamers' parents. According to the plans drawn up as part of the government's strategy for boosting the game industry, the Ministry of Culture, Sports and Tourism decided to _____(A)_____ the curfew imposed on underage users from accessing online games late at night. Enacted in 2011 to _____(B)_____ video game addiction among youth, the shutdown law bans gamers aged 16 or under from playing online games between midnight and 6 a.m. Under the proposed change, parents can apply for a request to permit their adolescent gamers to play after midnight.

	(A)	(B)
①	lift	curb
②	loosen	aggravate
③	reinforce	tackle
④	implement	intensify

10 다음 글의 제목으로 가장 적절한 것은?

Over the last years of traveling, I've observed how much we humans live in the past. The past is around us constantly, considering that, the minute something is manifested, it is the past. Our surroundings, our homes, our environments, our architecture, our products are all past constructs. We should live with what is part of our time, part of our collective consciousness, those things that were produced during our lives. Of course, we do not have the choice or control to have everything around us relevant or conceived during our time, but what we do have control of should be a reflection of the time in which we exist and communicate the present. The present is all we have, and the more we are surrounded by it, the more we are aware of our own presence and participation.

① Travel: Tracing the Legacies of the Past
② Reflect on the Time That Surrounds You Now
③ Manifestation of a Hidden Life
④ Architecture of a Futuristic Life

01 다음 빈칸에 들어갈 말로 가장 적절한 것을 고르시오.

The N project by the company does not _____ at first glance, despite its sleek slogan of high-performance driving.

① ring a bell
② discard
③ divulge
④ dismay

02 다음 밑줄 친 어휘와 의미가 가장 가까운 것을 고르시오.

The plasma water treatment technology, which can convert water into plasma unscientifically, is being referred to as an alternative to chemicals that are conventionally used to remove the toxic algal blooms, which <u>proliferate</u> in warm conditions and can be detrimental to aquatic life.

① reproduce
② pore over
③ revise
④ resemble

03 다음 밑줄 친 어휘와 의미가 가장 먼 것을 고르시오.

But being perhaps more important in the longer run, robots also bring many <u>introverted</u> or disabled or nonconforming children into greater classroom participation.

① reserved
② introspective
③ mediating
④ restrained

04 다음 대화의 빈칸에 들어갈 가장 알맞은 표현을 고르시오.

A: I need to go shopping this weekend.
B: Do you need to buy something?
A: I was going through my closet yesterday, and I realized I don't have anything to wear to the homecoming party.
B: Oh, I forgot all about the homecoming party. I want to get selected as the best dresser.
A: So do I. Then we should definitely _____ on that day.
B: We should go shopping together.

① bury the hatchet
② blow our own trumpets
③ have a frog in our throats
④ be dressed up to the nines

05 어법상 옳은 것은?

① John sighed laying an arm gently over my shoulder.
② Music gives an enormous number of pleasure to many people.
③ There was no obvious reason why this could not be as a good film as the original.
④ Everything had happened too fast she barely was able to absorb all the information.

06 밑줄 친 부분 중 어법상 옳지 않은 것은?

The major effect comes from ① the fact that you hear yourself differently from the way ② others hear you. This is one of the main reasons why even the most accomplished singers have to listen to the opinion of coaches and voice teachers ③ so as to 'how they sound,' ④ whereas no concert violinist would have to do such a thing.

07 우리말을 영어로 옮긴 것으로 가장 적절한 것은?

① 다양한 물고기가 사는 작은 연못이 몇 개 있다.
→ There are several small ponds which a variety of fish lives.

② John은 아무 잘못도 하지 않아서 걱정할 것이 없었다.
→ John didn't do anything wrong he had nothing to be worried about.

③ Jane은 나에게 그것이 새것이라고 말했고 나는 그녀를 믿을 만큼 어리석었다.
→ Jane told me it was brand new and I was stupid enough to believe her.

④ 시가 한 쌍의 스피커에서 나오는 것을 듣고 나서야 당신은 시가 어떻게 들리는지 알 수 있다.
→ It is not until you hear it coming out of a pair of speakers which you can know how a poem sounds.

08 다음 글의 주제로 가장 적절한 것은?

Gaming addiction is a compulsive mental health disorder that can cause severe damage to one's life. It's common for a video game addict to spend over ten hours a day gaming, usually well into the night, and many suffer from sleep deprivation. Immersed in their experience, gamers are known to have poor diets comprised mainly of energy drinks full of caffeine and sugar. Many are dehydrated and malnourished. In more severe cases, gaming addicts report agoraphobia - a type of anxiety disorder in which they fear leaving the house - and others identify themselves with *hikikomori* — a term popularized in Japan as reclusive adolescents or adults who withdraw from social life.

① the causes of game addiction
② the characteristics of game addicts
③ the definition of the term hikikomori
④ the ways to overcome game addiction

09 밑줄 친 (A), (B)에 들어갈 말로 가장 적절한 것은?

Some degree of risk aversion in investing is perfectly rational. ____(A)____, if losing $10,000 in your investment account means you won't be able to make your monthly rent, while gaining an additional $10,000 means you can go on an extra vacation, it makes perfect sense for you to play it safe rather than risk the roof over your head. As such, it is also not irrational for investors to expect higher returns for taking on more risk. However, loss aversion holds that all else being equal, losses fundamentally loom larger than gains. This includes cases where, win or lose, the outcome will have little material effect on someone's life circumstances, and ____(B)____ suggests that people are too risk averse.

	(A)	(B)
①	Subsequently	on the other hand
②	In other words	otherwise
③	For example	thus
④	Nonetheless	moreover

10 주어진 문장이 들어갈 위치로 가장 적절한 것은?

Cultivating a nonjudgmental awareness of the present bestows a host of benefits.

We need to live more in the moment. Living in the moment — also called mindfulness — is a state of active, open, intentional attention on the present. (①) When you become mindful, you realize that you are not your thoughts; you become an observer of your thoughts from moment to moment without judging them. (②) Mindfulness involves being with your thoughts as they are, neither grasping at them nor pushing them away. (③) Mindfulness reduces stress, boosts immune functioning, reduces chronic pain, lowers blood pressure, and helps patients cope with cancer. (④) Mindful people are also happier, more exuberant, more empathetic, and more secure.

01 다음 빈칸에 들어갈 말로 가장 적절한 것을 고르시오.

There are many cases in which comments still leave many feelings insulting even if they don't have _____ words to examine something.

① unpretentious ② profane
③ eccentric ④ adventitious

02 다음 빈칸에 들어갈 말로 가장 적절한 것을 고르시오.

One of Barack Obama's _____ arguments in seeking the presidency was that his stance as an outsider uninvolved in past Washington battles would enable him to break through the capital's gutless partisanship.

① preliminary ② aberrant
③ contradictory ④ principal

03 다음 밑줄 친 어휘와 의미가 가장 먼 것을 고르시오.

Through a <u>clandestine</u> diplomatic avenue, dubbed "New York Channel," North Korea and the US have reportedly been engaging in a series of diplomatic talks, including facilitating negotiations over the release of US prisoners held in North Korea.

① covert ② furtive
③ surreptitious ④ condescending

04 두 사람의 대화 중 가장 어색한 것은?

① A: I had cereal and toast for breakfast.
   B: Did you prepare it yourself?
② A: The train will arrive in a few minutes.
   B: We should hurry up finding the platform.
③ A: Global warming is aggravating everyday.
   B: The weather is really warm today.
④ A: Watch out! There's a speed bump right in front of you.
   B: Oh, I didn't see that coming. I should slow down.

05 어법상 옳은 것은?

① Being a father isn't as bad than I thought at first.
② However carried away you get, don't rise your arms above your head.
③ On the Internet we had so many hits in the first hour that we were really struggling.
④ This is in total contrast to the number of walking or exercise involving the use of the legs.

06 밑줄 친 부분 중 어법상 옳지 않은 것은?

The audience receives a sound signal entirely through the vibrations ① generated in the air, ② whereas in a singer some of the auditory stimulus ③ is conducted to the ear through the singer's own bones. Since these two ways of transferring sound have quite different ④ from relative efficiencies at various frequencies, the overall quality of the sound will be quite different.

07 우리말을 영어로 옮긴 것으로 가장 적절한 것은?

① 두 번의 올림픽에서 권투를 한 22세의 Tom은 그의 친한 친구 John에 의해 관리받는다.
→ Tom, 22, who boxed in two Olympics, manages his close friend John.

② 가져갈 것이 없었기 때문에 아무것도 가져가지 않았다.
→ We didn't take anything because there was nothing for us to take it.

③ 요즘 밴드들은 단순히 수요를 충족시킬 만큼 충분한 음악을 생산하지 못하고 있다.
→ Bands these days are simply not producing music enough to satisfy demand.

④ 배관공이 마무리 짓고 나서야 우리는 새 카펫을 내려놓을 수 있었다.
→ It was not until the plumber had finished that we could put down the new carpet.

08 빈칸 (A), (B)에 들어갈 표현으로 가장 적절한 것은?

South Korea is famed for its skyscrapers and city lights, and the stereotype is true: 83% of its 53-million-person population currently resides in urban areas. While a similar ratio holds for the United States, consider that Korea essentially puts one seventh of the US population into an area equivalent to the space between Los Angeles and San Francisco. Population density isn't much fun if you're claustrophobic, but it makes fast internet a lot easier to get. With the high proportion of Koreans living in urban-area apartments, spreading connections between them is more like stitching a quilt than building a road. The ___(A)___ dramatically reduces the cost of infrastructure and "simplifies network development" as the International Telecommunication Union puts it. Fiber optic connections are expensive to build and DSL has steep performance loss over distances — but in South Korea physical gaps are ___(B)___ a problem.

	(A)	(B)
①	remoteness	seldom
②	proximity	barely
③	technology	frequently
④	closeness	absolutely

09 다음 글의 제목으로 가장 적절한 것은?

Negative news will normally cause individuals to sell stocks. Bad earnings reports, poor corporate governance, economic and political uncertainty, as well as unexpected, unfortunate occurrences will translate to selling pressure and a decrease in stock price. Positive news, on the other hand, will normally cause individuals to buy stocks. Good earnings reports, increased corporate governance, new products and acquisitions, as well as positive overall economic and political indicators, translate into buying pressure and an increase in stock price. For example, a hurricane making landfall may cause a drop in utility stocks. Meanwhile, depending on the severity of the storm, insurance stocks could also take a hit on the news or even climb higher if the expected damage is projected to be moderate.

① How to Succeed in Stock Investing
② Natural Disasters and Stock Market
③ How Does News Affect Stock Prices?
④ What Causes Stock Prices to Increase?

10 주어진 문장 다음에 이어질 글의 순서로 가장 적절한 것은?

The easiest way to explain living in the present is to start by explaining what it means not to be present, since this is the state we have become habitually used to.

(A) Of course, it's natural to spend moments thinking about the past or in daydreams of the future. Identifying impending dangers through associations with things that have happened in the past is important for self-preservation.

(B) But when our lives become dictated by thoughts and emotions attached to past events and potential future outcomes, standing peacefully rooted in the present becomes increasingly rare.

(C) When you aren't being present you become a victim of time. Your mind is pulled into the past or the future, or both.

① (A) − (B) − (C)
② (A) − (C) − (B)
③ (B) − (A) − (C)
④ (C) − (A) − (B)

01 다음 밑줄 친 어휘와 의미가 가장 가까운 것을 고르시오.

It was one of the very few effective methods out of some 60 ideas proposed so far to prevent air pollution.

① separate
② reinforce
③ head off
④ distribute

02 다음 빈칸에 들어갈 말로 가장 적절한 것을 고르시오.

The director says he takes mental notes of which points in the film _____ the collective sighs, gasps and laughter from the reliable audience.

① evoke
② shun away from
③ inspect
④ desert

03 다음 밑줄 친 어휘와 의미가 가장 먼 것을 고르시오.

The youthful actor captures the essence of a naive, young romanticist whose moral center - despite all that he has been through - remains strong and appreciated

① ingenuous
② innocent
③ childlike
④ inconclusive

04 밑줄 친 부분에 들어갈 가장 적절한 것은?

Shelly: What's your own way of relieving stress?
Trevor: I have several ways to deal with stress. One of them is to eat a tremendous amount of sweets.
Shelly: Oh, I heard about that. Whenever I eat sweets, it feels like all the tension in my body is alleviated.
Trevor: That's exactly why I tend to _____ when I start eating sugary food in stressful situations.
Shelly: I know what you're talking about. But you should be careful with the negative effects it can bring about on your health.
Trevor: Yeah, so I try to strain my desire for sweets.

① lose heart
② lose my head
③ paint the town red
④ beat my head against the wall

05 어법상 옳은 것은?

① Country life isn't always as peaceful as city-dwellers think.
② One of my neighbours was left in tears when the tree was fallen.
③ Sometimes Jane writes songs such slowly that she never gets around to recording them.
④ There is no denying that one of the major cause of obesity is the number of food that we eat.

06 밑줄 친 부분 중 어법상 옳지 않은 것은?

The children who listened to the radio produced more imaginative responses, ① <u>whereas the children</u> who watched the television ② <u>produced more words</u> that repeated the original story. Media scholars have used this study to illustrate the "visualization hypothesis," ③ <u>which states that</u> children's exposure to ready-made visual images ④ <u>restrict their ability</u> to generate novel images of their own.

07 우리말을 영어로 옮긴 것으로 가장 적절한 것은?

① 1850년에 완공된 이 집은 거대한 대리석 계단으로 유명했다.
→ The house, which completed in 1850, was famous for its huge marble staircase.
② 스스로를 살아가게 할 만큼 충분한 음식과 물을 가져오고 알맞은 방수복을 입어라.
→ Be sure to bring enough food and water to sustain you and wear suitable rainproof clothing.
③ 1880년대에 이르러서야 지방화를 뒷받침하는 지속적인 실험 결과가 있었다.
→ It was until the 1880s that there were consistent experimental findings to support localization.
④ Jane은 자신이 하는 일을 정말 좋아하므로, 그녀를 멈추도록 설득하는 것은 정말 놀라운 일이어야 할 것이다.
→ Jane loves what she does, so it would have to be something really amazing to persuade her to stop.

08 다음 글의 내용과 일치하는 것은?

North Korea boasts two versions of the world wide web: an exclusive, restriction-free model for high-ranking government officials and people in select industries, and a threadbare alternative for everyone else. The latter is heavily curated and mostly consists of state propaganda. To make matters worse, the dated service (dubbed "Kwangmyong") can only be accessed through a dial-up connection, not that dissimilar to AOL in the '90s. But its decrepit condition may not matter as most North Koreans likely can't afford it anyway. As a result, web adoption figures are shockingly low: the entirety of North Korea only has 1,024 IP addresses. South Korea has 112.32 million IPv4 addresses in use, and even the Pacific island of Palau, which has a population of 18,000, uses more IP addresses than North Korea.

① The network solely available to top government officials of North Korea is also highly restricted.
② North Korea uses the Internet as an instrument of conveying positive messages about the nation.
③ Every North Korean can access the Internet only via a dial-up connection.
④ Average North Koreans rarely use the Internet mainly because of its poor quality of service.

09 밑줄 친 부분에 들어갈 말로 가장 적절한 것을 고르시오.

One reason that stock fluctuations have limited direct effects is that _____.
According to a recent Gallup poll, only 55 percent of Americans say they or members of their household own stocks. Other surveys show even lower participation rates in the stock market. If you do not own any equities, there is little reason to change your spending, saving, or work plans because Wall Street suffers a major reverse. Gallup polls suggest stock ownership shrank over the past decade. Just before the Great Recession, more than 65 percent of Americans said they owned stocks. Evidently, the twin stock market crashes in 2000-2002 and 2008 reduced some savers' appetite for risk.

① a severe stock market crisis is in progress in the United States
② stocks are not an important form of saving for most households
③ government regulations on the stock market have become stricter
④ the number of people investing in the stock market has increased

10 다음 글의 요지로 가장 적절한 것은?

When you live in the here and now, you're living where life is occurring. There is no point dwelling on the past, full of guilt and regrets. When you live in the present, you identify the lessons you can learn from the past events and you implement what you have learned. Once you have learned from the past, it is time for you to let it go. It has served its purpose. Thank it and say goodbye to it. By constantly mulling over the past and clinging on to it, you are bringing with you the judgements of the past. This impacts your thinking, your ability to process what is happening in the here and now. The past is gone and cannot be undone. All you have is the here and now and it is the only place where you can make a difference.

① Accept the past as it is.
② Live in the present moment.
③ Learn lessons from the past.
④ Look at the future not the past.

결국엔 성정혜 영어 하프모의고사
기적사 DAY 60

기출 하프 □ 파생 하프 ☑ 복습 모의고사 □
소요 시간 :   / 15분   맞은 개수 :   / 10개

01 다음 밑줄 친 어휘와 의미가 가장 가까운 것을 고르시오.

The Chinese people suffer the most from coal combustion and <u>malevolent</u> industrial dumping practices.

① mediocre   ② malignant
③ correct   ④ forthright

02 다음 빈칸에 들어갈 말로 가장 적절한 것을 고르시오.

For the new film that he wrote and directed, he expanded his trademark on-screen world where law enforcement authorities _____ with crime organizations for their own gains to an international and faultless level.

① take over   ② collude
③ recognize   ④ swamp

03 다음 빈칸에 들어갈 말로 가장 적절한 것을 고르시오.

The exhibit, which has a hip-hop soundtrack, also features images of young people's turbulent inner worlds and their desire to _____ from existing norms.

① daunt   ② submerge
③ moderate   ④ deviate

04 다음 빈칸에 들어갈 가장 적절한 표현을 순서대로 나열한 것은?

A: I went to the Louvre Museum when I visited Paris two years ago.
B: Did you see the Mona Lisa?
A: Of course. It was way more gorgeous than I had imagined.
B: ____(A)____ me about it. There's a reason people stand in line to take pictures of it.
A: Now you're ____(B)____. If I have the chance to visit Paris again, I would head straight to the Louvre Museum, for Mona Lisa.
B: Good idea. It's doubtlessly worth seeing twice.

	(A)	(B)
①	Tell	saying
②	Say	talking
③	Tell	talking
④	Talk	telling

05 어법상 옳은 것은?

① The deal seems such attractively it would be ridiculous to say no.
② She cried out in pain and frustration, and remained in the place where she lay.
③ If you live in a built-up area, you have to expect a certainly amount of noise.
④ I don't think he's been watering these plants because the soil is as drier as a bone.

06 밑줄 친 부분 중 어법상 옳지 않은 것은?

In Holland, Ehret ① <u>became acquainted from</u> the Swedish naturalist Carl Linnaeus. Through his collaborations with Linnaeus and others, Ehret provided illustrations ② <u>for a number</u> of significant horticultural publications. Ehret's reputation for scientific accuracy ③ <u>gained him</u> many commissions from wealthy patrons, particularly in England, where ④ <u>he eventually settled</u>.

07 우리말을 영어로 옮긴 것으로 가장 적절한 것은?

① 그녀가 정확히 무엇을 하는지는 모르지만, 그것이 컴퓨터와 관련이 있다는 건 안다.
→ I don't know what she does exactly, I know it has something to do with computers.

② Tom은 지방 중등학교에서 교육을 받았고, 그 후에 캠브리지로 갔다.
→ Tom was educated at the local grammar school, after which he went on to Cambridge.

③ 그들이 교회를 떠나고 나서야 John은 그들이 뉴욕으로 2주 동안 간다는 것을 알았다.
→ It was not until they had just left the Church which John discovered they were going for two weeks to New York.

④ 만족할 만한 양의 격려를 제공할 만큼 충분한 가족들이 그 시골 지역 전역에 걸쳐 산재해 있다.
→ There were families around the countryside enough to provide a satisfying amount of encouragement.

08 주어진 문장 다음에 이어질 글의 순서로 가장 적절한 것은?

From time to time our worries are caused by procrastination or an inability to make a decision.

(A) However, in the long run, worry and anticipation can actually make you feel still more anxious than when you would just take care of your issue.
(B) If you are putting something off, worry can serve as a way to avoid facing the issue head-on.
(C) So, just face your worries. Stop worrying by taking the steps that you need to deal with the problem.

① (A) - (B) - (C)
② (A) - (C) - (B)
③ (B) - (A) - (C)
④ (B) - (C) - (A)

09 다음 글의 요지로 가장 적절한 것은?

Feel a twinge in your chest or take a nasty fall? One of the first responses of your body is to worry — and that's a good thing, according to Dr. Shelly Smith-Acuña. People who worry are more likely to seek preventative care like yearly check-ups, mammograms, colonoscopies, and even wear more sunscreen, she says. A little worry can also spur you to make a plan to help with current problems, like losing weight or cleaning up your diet. But there's a fine line between acting on your worries to prevent future problems and becoming a full-blown hypochondriac. "Don't constantly be checking 'Dr. Google,' and instead follow-up with people who can help you, like your doctor," she says. "And don't worry so much that it has the opposite effect, making you scared to see a doctor."

① You should not be afraid of seeing a doctor.
② Worrying can negatively affect the quality of life.
③ A modest amount of worry can be helpful for your health.
④ Worrying about things that have not happened is not necessary.

10 다음 글의 제목으로 가장 적절한 것은?

The housing market in the United States suffered greatly, as many homeowners who had taken out sub-prime loans found they were unable to meet their mortgage repayments. As the value of homes plummeted, a number of the borrowers found themselves with negative equity. With a large number of borrowers defaulting on loans, banks were faced with a situation where the repossessed house and land was worth less on the market than they had loaned out originally. The banks had a liquidity crisis on their hands, and giving and obtaining home loans became increasingly difficult as the sub-prime lending bubble burst. This is commonly referred to as the credit crunch of 2007-08, and the housing collapse in the United States is commonly considered as the trigger for the global financial crisis.

* negative equity: 역자산(담보를 잡힌 주택의 가격이 갚아야 할 대출금 액수보다 낮은 상황)

① How Does a Sub-Prime Loan Work?
② The Importance of Regulating the Housing Market
③ Global Financial Crisis: What May Have Caused It?
④ What Are the Aftereffects of the Global Financial Crisis?

기적사 복습 모의고사 6회

01 다음 밑줄 친 어휘와 의미가 가장 가까운 것을 고르시오.

"Humans are notorious for being lousy and hurried at estimating numbers of animals in large groups," Perryman explains.

① reconcilable ② disreputable
③ outlandish ④ destitute

02 다음 밑줄 친 어휘와 의미가 가장 가까운 것을 고르시오.

The Chinese people suffer the most from coal combustion and malevolent industrial dumping practices.

① mediocre ② malignant
③ correct ④ forthright

03 밑줄 친 부분과 의미가 가장 가까운 것을 고르시오.

The company cannot expect me to move my home and family at the drop of a hat.

① immediately ② punctually
③ hesitantly ④ periodically

04 다음 빈칸에 들어갈 말로 가장 적절한 것을 고르시오.

Japan's district police _____ cartoon characters to alert people not to take calls from unknown phone numbers immediately.

① lets on ② makes up for
③ takes on ④ draws on

05 어법상 옳은 것은?

① It was Jane's car that got broken into last Friday night.
② She sees architects today designed intelligent and space-efficient buildings.
③ She is unlikely to succeed in getting the bill through Congress, however it is worthy.
④ Lack of investment, according to former employees, have been going on for many years.

06 어법상 옳은 것은?

① John sighed laying an arm gently over my shoulder.
② Music gives an enormous number of pleasure to many people.
③ There was no obvious reason why this could not be as a good film as the original.
④ Everything had happened too fast she barely was able to absorb all the information.

07 우리말을 영어로 잘못 옮긴 것을 고르시오.

① 사우디아라비아는 다른 어떤 국가보다 더 많은 석유를 생산한다.
→ Saudi Arabia produces more oil than any other countries.
② 현재 주가 변동에 영향을 미치는 많은 요인들이 있다.
→ There are a number of factors currently influencing stock-price fluctuations.
③ 그는 학교에서 아이들에게 스티커를 붙이자고 제안한 적이 없다고 부인했다.
→ He denied he had suggested to the children putting the stickers up in school.
④ 터치 패드를 사용하여 마우스 커서를 이동하기 위해서, 터치 패드의 표면을 따라 손가락을 단지 미끄러뜨리면 된다.
→ To move your mouse cursor using a touch pad, you simply glide your finger along the touch pad's surface.

08 우리말을 영어로 옮긴 것으로 가장 적절한 것은?

① 그들이 10년간 살았던 집이 폭풍에 심하게 손상되었다.
→ The house which they have lived for 10 years badly damaged by the storm.

② 수학 시험에 실패했을 때에서야 그는 공부를 열심히 하기로 결심했다.
→ It was not until when he failed the math test that he decided to study hard.

③ 냉장고에 먹을 것이 하나도 남아있지 않아서, 어젯밤에 우리는 외식을 해야 했다.
→ We had nothing to eat left in the refrigerator, we had to eat out last night.

④ 우리는 운이 좋게도 그랜드 캐니언을 방문했는데, 거기에는 경치가 아름다운 곳이 많다.
→ We were enough fortunate to visit the Grand Canyon, that has much beautiful landscape.

09 두 사람의 대화 중 가장 어색한 것은?

① A: What did you dream of last night?
B: My dream is to become a flight attendant in the future.

② A: There is a scratch on your elbow.
B: No wonder it hurt so bad.

③ A: Have you ever been to the zoo?
B: I've been to one when I was really young.

④ A: Do you know where the nearest post office is located?
B: Go straight two blocks and turn left on the first corner.

10 다음 대화의 빈칸에 들어갈 가장 알맞은 표현을 고르시오.

A: I need to go shopping this weekend.
B: Do you need to buy something?
A: I was going through my closet yesterday, and I realized I don't have anything to wear to the homecoming party.
B: Oh, I forgot all about the homecoming party. I want to get selected as the best dresser.
A: So do I. Then we should definitely _____ _____ on that day.
B: We should go shopping together.

① bury the hatchet
② blow our own trumpets
③ have a frog in our throats
④ be dressed up to the nines

11 다음 글의 내용과 일치하지 않는 것은?

In the 19th century, Manchester held the status of the international center of the cotton trade and textile industry. It was so well known for being a city of cotton that it was nicknamed 'Cottonopolis.' Back in 1782, when cotton mills were powered by water, Richard Arkwright opened the innovative - and the world's first - steam-driven textile mill in Manchester. As textile manufacturing moved from the home to large-scale factories, Manchester and its surrounding towns became by far the largest and most productive cotton spinning centers in the world. In 1871, 32 percent of global cotton production took place in Manchester. Over 200 years after Arkwright made that iconic mill, no working mills remain but Manchester is still a city shaped by cotton. There are still around 5,000 people in Greater Manchester employed in the textile industry. Manchester's cottonopolis past can be seen in its buildings: Converted mills have found new life as offices, hotels, and flats all alongside sparkling new glassy high-rises.

① Manchester was known for cotton in the 1800s.
② Arkwright established Manchester's first cotton mill driven by water.
③ Manchester once produced more than 30 percent of global output of cotton.
④ Today, no one living in Manchester is working in a cotton mill.

12 다음 글의 주제로 가장 적절한 것은?

Mayor Lyda Krewson announced this week the start of the City's summer food service program for youth, known as the Schools Out Café. Every summer, Schools Out Café provides free breakfast and lunch to daycare centers, recreation programs, churches, and other organizations which then serve those meals to young people. In St. Louis, an estimated 80-90% of students are enrolled in free or reduced lunch, which is a key indicator to a lack of regular access to nutritionally adequate food during the summer months. "Hunger doesn't take a break when schools close for the summer," Krewson said. "I am so thankful to all the groups and organizations that have volunteered to become food serving sites, but we are always looking for more. I encourage any organization that is willing to serve meals to young people to contact us. We will provide the food."

① a regular meal program
② the importance of school meals
③ places for youngsters in St. Louis
④ a problem of school lunch service

13 주어진 문장 다음에 이어질 글의 순서로 가장 적절한 것은?

Science has defined the modern era in many ways and is truly the reigning knowledge paradigm in the modern era.

(A) The key features of modernity, specialization and technology, were made possible primarily by the remarkable development of scientific techniques and knowledge over the last 400 years, since the time of Galileo and Kepler.

(B) This is the case because today's scientific worldview seems to deny the importance of many inquiries that humans have perennially found important, including questions about our place in the universe, the nature of consciousness, and questions about God, purpose, and many other deep topics.

(C) But while science has brought us the modern world, in a very real and direct way, it has also brought us to a point where man's perennial search for meaning is imperiled.

① (A) − (B) − (C)   ② (A) − (C) − (B)
③ (B) − (A) − (C)   ④ (B) − (C) − (A)

14 주어진 문장이 들어갈 위치로 가장 적절한 것은?

And often we find them in the realm of business, one of the rare places where mortal beings can actually create the future they're envisioning.

The pragmatists among us will say that peering into the future is impossible. (①) They'll say with a smirk that there are no crystal balls, no indelible lines on human palms that foretell our destinies. (②) The rest of us believe there are indeed some who can predict what will happen tomorrow. (③) We call them prophets, visionaries, or oracles. (④) Among the most remarkable of these prophets is British businessman James Dyson. Dyson's improbable bagless vacuum cleaners, impossible bladeless fans, and hyperspeed hair driers — all of which were figments of a *Jetsons*-like age before Dyson dreamed them up — have made his name a literal household brand in much of the world and turned the 72-year-old Briton into a billionaire.

15 다음 글의 제목으로 가장 적절한 것은?

Negative news will normally cause individuals to sell stocks. Bad earnings reports, poor corporate governance, economic and political uncertainty, as well as unexpected, unfortunate occurrences will translate to selling pressure and a decrease in stock price. Positive news, on the other hand, will normally cause individuals to buy stocks. Good earnings reports, increased corporate governance, new products and acquisitions, as well as positive overall economic and political indicators, translate into buying pressure and an increase in stock price. For example, a hurricane making landfall may cause a drop in utility stocks. Meanwhile, depending on the severity of the storm, insurance stocks could also take a hit on the news or even climb higher if the expected damage is projected to be moderate.

① How to Succeed in Stock Investing
② Natural Disasters and Stock Market
③ How Does News Affect Stock Prices?
④ What Causes Stock Prices to Increase?

16 다음 글의 내용과 일치하는 것은?

For the first time since 1959, we have made significant changes in our menu and prices. In lieu of a price increase for elementary students, we have removed one item from the menu and are using the dessert to meet the type A requirements. Previously in the majority of schools we have been providing more food than the average elementary child could eat, and much of the food was wasted. Our charge to the elementary student for the type A lunch, which includes milk, is 35 cents. In the junior high schools, we have eliminated the choice of vegetables and restricted a la carte service to ice cream and fresh fruit. A large number of students must go through the junior high cafeteria in a short period of time, and by simplifying the menu and limiting the a la carte items, we will be able to provide faster services. The price of the complete lunch in junior high schools is 40 cents.

① The price of the school lunch for elementary students has increased.
② The amount of wasted food in elementary schools is expected to decrease.
③ Milk is included in the lunch meals in all schools.
④ Junior high school students can no longer select ice cream or fresh fruit.

17 밑줄 친 부분에 들어갈 말로 가장 적절한 것을 고르시오.

One reason that stock fluctuations have limited direct effects is that _____.
According to a recent Gallup poll, only 55 percent of Americans say they or members of their household own stocks. Other surveys show even lower participation rates in the stock market. If you do not own any equities, there is little reason to change your spending, saving, or work plans because Wall Street suffers a major reverse. Gallup polls suggest stock ownership shrank over the past decade. Just before the Great Recession, more than 65 percent of Americans said they owned stocks. Evidently, the twin stock market crashes in 2000-2002 and 2008 reduced some savers' appetite for risk.

① a severe stock market crisis is in progress in the United States
② stocks are not an important form of saving for most households
③ government regulations on the stock market have become stricter
④ the number of people investing in the stock market has increased

18 밑줄 친 부분에 들어갈 말로 가장 적절한 것은?

The paradoxical outcomes of the search for meaning in Western history have played a significant part in rendering modernity meaningless. It does not follow, however, that the concepts found in Weber's work, such as ideal interests and culture, no longer apply. Rather, Weber provides an understanding of modernity based on the continuing paradoxical outcomes found in modern searches for meaning. Without the unifying effect of enchanted, cosmic meaning the modern world is structured as a series of five competing, separate value-spheres: the economic, intellectual, political, aesthetic and erotic. It is through this theory of the value-spheres that Weber will try to understand the continuing search for meaning in modernity. Essentially, instead of a coherent life-conduct based on religion and set within the parameters of meaningful cosmos, different sections of the social whole – the value-spheres – offer a new, if _____, sense of meaning.

① ineffective and useless
② limited and conditional
③ empty and meaningless
④ restricted and old fashioned

19 밑줄 친 (A), (B)에 들어갈 말로 가장 적절한 것은?

Some degree of risk aversion in investing is perfectly rational. ____(A)____, if losing $10,000 in your investment account means you won't be able to make your monthly rent, while gaining an additional $10,000 means you can go on an extra vacation, it makes perfect sense for you to play it safe rather than risk the roof over your head. As such, it is also not irrational for investors to expect higher returns for taking on more risk. However, loss aversion holds that all else being equal, losses fundamentally loom larger than gains. This includes cases where, win or lose, the outcome will have little material effect on someone's life circumstances, and ____(B)____ suggests that people are too risk averse.

	(A)	(B)
①	Subsequently	on the other hand
②	In other words	otherwise
③	For example	thus
④	Nonetheless	moreover

20 다음 글의 내용과 일치하는 것은?

North Korea boasts two versions of the world wide web: an exclusive, restriction-free model for high-ranking government officials and people in select industries, and a threadbare alternative for everyone else. The latter is heavily curated and mostly consists of state propaganda. To make matters worse, the dated service (dubbed "Kwangmyong") can only be accessed through a dial-up connection, not that dissimilar to AOL in the '90s. But its decrepit condition may not matter as most North Koreans likely can't afford it anyway. As a result, web adoption figures are shockingly low: the entirety of North Korea only has 1,024 IP addresses. South Korea has 112.32 million IPv4 addresses in use, and even the Pacific island of Palau, which has a population of 18,000, uses more IP addresses than North Korea.

① The network solely available to top government officials of North Korea is also highly restricted.
② North Korea uses the Internet as an instrument of conveying positive messages about the nation.
③ Every North Korean can access the Internet only via a dial-up connection.
④ Average North Koreans rarely use the Internet mainly because of its poor quality of service.

기출하프 + 파생하프 + 복습모의고사

성정혜 기적사
하프 모의고사
퀵스타트편

Miracle Routine

결국엔 성정혜 영어 하프모의고사
기적사 DAY 01

| 01 | ④ | 02 | ② | 03 | ① | 04 | ③ | 05 | ② |
| 06 | ① | 07 | ② | 08 | ③ | 09 | ④ | 10 | ④ |

01 정답 ④
18 국가직

정답해설
'indigenous'는 '토종의, 토착민의'라는 뜻으로 선택지 ④의 'native'와 의미가 가장 가깝다.

해석
전설적인 다큐멘터리 제작자 Robert J. Flaherty는 어떻게 **토착**민들이 음식을 모았는지 보여주려 시도했다.
① 떠돌아다니는, 순회하는   ② 빈곤한, 결핍된
③ 배가 고파 죽을 지경인, 엄청난 ④ 토박이의

어휘
itinerant 떠돌아다니는, 순회하는   impoverished 빈곤한, 결핍된
ravenous 배가 고파 죽을 지경인, 엄청난
native 토박이의   legendary 전설적인
filmmaker 영화제작자, 감독   indigenous 토종의, 토착의
gather 모으다

02 정답 ②
18 국가직

정답해설
두 번째 문장에서 음악을 듣는 것과 뮤지션이 되는 것은 서로 다름을 대조하고 있으므로, 빈칸에 들어갈 것으로 적절한 것은 그 차이를 나타내는 ②이다.

해석
음악을 듣는 것은 록 스타가 되는 것과는 **거리가 멀**다. 누구나 음악을 들을 수 있지만, 뮤지션이 되기 위해서는 타고난 재능이 필요하다.
① ~와 동등한(같은)   ② ~와는 거리가 먼(전혀 다른)
③ ~여하에 달린   ④ ~의 서막

어휘
on a par with ~와 동등한(같은)
a far cry from ~와는 거리가 먼 (전혀 다른)
contingent upon ~여하에 달린   a prelude to ~의 서막
talent 재주, 재능, 장기

03 정답 ①
18 국가직

정답해설
'culprit'은 '범인, 미결수'라는 뜻으로 'malefactor'과 의미가 가장 가깝다. 어원 'mal'은 '악'을 나타내는 표현으로 'malaria(말라리아)' 'maleficent(악행을 저지르는)' 'malnutrition(영양실조)'의 어원이 되기도 한다.

해석
경찰은 그 범죄 사건에 일곱 달의 시간을 쏟았지만 그 **범죄자**의 신원을 결코 밝혀내지 못했다.
① 범인   ② 예술 애호가
③ (사회에서) 버림받은 사람   ④ 선동 정치가

어휘
crime 범죄   determine 알아내다, 밝히다
identity 신원   malefactor 범죄자
culprit 범인   dilettante 예술 애호가
pariah (사회에서) 버림받은 사람   demagogue 선동 정치가

04 정답 ③
18 국가직

정답해설
두 사람의 제시된 대화를 통해서 A가 B에게 운전을 가르쳐 달라고 요청하고 있는 상황을 제시하고 있다. A는 운전을 하고 싶은 의지가 있음을 알 수 있으므로 빈칸에 들어갈 것으로 가장 적절한 것은 ③ get my feet wet(참가하다, 시작하다)이다.

해석
A: 운전하는 법을 아세요?
B: 물론이죠, 저는 운전을 잘해요.
A: 제게 운전을 가르쳐 줄 수 있어요?
B: 임시운전면허증을 가지고 있으세요?
A: 네, 지난 주에 취득했어요.
B: 벌써 운전을 해보셨어요?
A: 아뇨, 그렇지만 **해보고 싶어서 참을 수가 없어요.**
① 펑크난 타이어를 교체하다   ② 오일을 교체하다
③ 참가하다, 시작하다   ④ 다음을 기약하다

어휘
learner's permit 임시운전면허증
be behind the steering wheel 운전하다
get my feet wet 참가하다, 시작하다
take a rain check 다음을 기약하다

05 정답 ②
19 국가직

정답해설
② 출제 포인트: 해석에 주의해야할 표현
'shy of'는 '~이 모자라는'이라는 뜻으로 문제에서는 '자정이 5분이나 지난 후'라고 하였으므로 영어로 옮긴 것이 적절하지 않다. 따라서 잘못 옮긴 문장은 ②이다. 올바른 문장은 "I called him five minutes after midnight on an urgent matter."이다.

오답해설
① 출제 포인트: 목적격 관계대명사
'제가 당신께 말씀드렸던 새로운 선생님'은 관계대명사를 사용하여 'The new teacher I told you about'으로 옮길 수 있다. 따라서 올바른 문장이다.

③ 출제 포인트: 불완전자동사 appear
'appear'는 '나타나다', '~처럼 보이다'라는 뜻의 불완전자동사로 '상어처럼 보이는 것'이라고 하였고 문장의 시제는 과거이므로 'What appeared to be a shark'는 알맞은 표현이다.

④ 출제 포인트: 자동사로 착각하기 쉬운 완전타동사
'reach'는 '도착하다, 도달하다'라는 뜻의 타동사이다. 따라서 다음에 전치사를 쓰지 않는다. 따라서 'She reached the mountain summit'는 올바른 표현이다. 또한 '16세의 친구'라고 나이가 명사 앞에서 수식하는 형용사가 되었을 때는 'years'가 아닌 'year'로 단수가 적절하다.

06 정답 ①
19 국가직

정답해설

① 출제 포인트: 해석에 주의해야할 표현
주어진 해석이 '개인용 컴퓨터를 가장 많이 가지고 있는'이므로 'with the most computers per person'을 'with the largest number of personal computers'로 수정해야 한다. 따라서 정답은 ①이고 올바른 문장은 "The country with the largest number of personal computers changes from time to time."이다.

오답해설

② 출제 포인트: 완전자동사
'happen'은 '일어나다'라는 자동사로 수동태로 쓸 수 없다. 따라서 'What happened to my lovely grandson'(나의 사랑스러운 손자에게 일어난 일)은 알맞은 표현이다.

③ 출제 포인트: so[neither]+조동사+주어: '~또한 그렇다'
'~ 또한 그렇다'라는 표현은 'so+동사+주어'로 표현할 수 있다. 따라서 'so are plastic bottles'(플라스틱 병 또한 그렇다)도 올바른 표현이다.

④ 출제 포인트: 시간의 부사구/부사절
과거에서부터 지금까지 진행되고 있는 동작이나 상태는 현재완료나 현재완료 진행형으로 쓸 수 있다. 은퇴이후부터 지금까지 일을 하고 있다고 하였으므로 'have been doing this work'는 적절한 표현이다.

07 정답 ②
19 국가직

정답해설

② 출제 포인트: 현재분사 vs. 과거분사
인간이 가축들을 어떻게 이용하여 왔는지 설명하고 있는 글이다. '② Utilizing with other techniques, animals can raise human living standards very considerably'에서 분사구문의 주어가 없으므로 주절의 주어와 같은 주어인 것을 알 수 있고 동사 'utilize'는 목적어를 수반하는 타동사인데 목적어가 없으므로 수동분사구문이 문법상 올바르다는 것을 알 수 있다. 따라서 어법상 틀린 부분은 ②이다.
'As animals are utilized with other techniques~'
→ Being utilized with other techniques
→ Utilized with other techniques

오답해설

① 출제 포인트: 주격 관계대명사
주격 관계대명사+be 동사가 생략된 구문이다. 'machines' that are available to humans'에서 'that are'가 생략된 표현이다. 따라서 어법상 적절하다.

③ 출제 포인트: to부정사의 형용사적 용법
형용사 용법의 to 부정사로 앞의 'machines'를 수식하는 용법이다.

④ 출제 포인트: of + 추상명사
'of+추상명사'는 추상명사의 형용사의 뜻을 갖는다. 따라서 'of great benefit'은 'greatly beneficial'이라는 의미이다.

해석

가축화된 동물들은 인간들에게 구할 수 있는 가장 이르고 가장 효과적인 '기계들'이었다. 그들은 인간의 등과 팔의 부담을 떨쳐내 준다. 다른 기술들과 함께 사용되면서, 동물들은 보충적인 음식재료들(고기와 우유의 단백질)과 짐을 실어 나르고 물을 끌어올리고 그리고 곡식을 가는 기계들 두 가지로 인간들의 삶의 기준을 매우 상당하게 올릴 수 있다. 그들이 명백하게 아주 이익이 되기 때문에, 우리는 아마 수세기를 지나 인간들은 그들이 소유하고 있는 동물들의 수와 질을 증가시킬 것이라는 것을 찾아낼 것이라고 예상할지 모른다. 놀랍게도, 이것은 보통에서 그렇지 않다.

어휘

domesticated 가축화된
strain 부담
considerably 상당하게
foodstuff 음식재료
obviously 명확하게
effective 효과적인
utilize 사용하다
supplementary 보충적인
burden 짐

오답률 TOP 3
08 정답 ③
19 서울시

정답해설

(A) 전에 'denying proper medical care to prisoners'(죄수들에 대한 적절한 의료를 거부)라는 표현으로 그들이 죽을 때까지 어느 의료 치료도 지원하지 않는다는 것을 알 수 있으므로 (A)에 적절한 표현은 'until'(~할 때까지)이다.

(B) Huang Qi가 지금 건강이 좋지 않다는 소식을 운동가들과 그의 어머니가 전해준 것이므로 '그들의 말에 따르면'이라는 표현이 가장 적절하다. 따라서 'according to'가 (B)에 적합하다.

오답해설

의료를 언제까지 거부했냐고 시간을 나타내는 접속사를 쓰는 것이 문맥상 (A)에 적절하다. 하지만 종결 시점을 나타내는 것이 아닌 'when'과 'while'은 (A)에 적절하지 않다.
(B)에도 문맥상 'with'나 'without' 그리고 'for'는 적절하지 않다.

해석

중국의 인권 유린과 부패를 기록하면서 20년을 보낸 HUANG QI는 이제 그의 노력으로 감옥에서 3번째 형기를 견뎌내고 있다. 중국 형벌제는 노벨상 수상자인 류샤오보 등을 포함한 그들이 죽을 (A) 때까지 죄수들에 대한 적절한 의료를 거부한 기록이 있다. Mr. Huang은 지금 건강이 좋지 않으며, 운동가와 그의 어머니에 (B) 따르면 그의 목숨이 위태롭다고 한다. 중국은 지금 치료를 위해 그를 석방해야 하며, 감옥에서 만기가 남은 반체제 인사들에 그의 이름을 덧붙이지 말아야 한다.

	(A)	(B)
①	~에도 불구하고	~없이
②	~하는 동안	~와 함께
③	~할 때까지	~에 따르면
④	~할 때	~을 위해, ~에 대해

어휘

document 기록하다, 서류로 만들다
corruption 부패
term 형기
proper 적절한, 알맞은
in danger 위험에 처한
roll 명단, 명부
expire 죽다, 기한이 다하다
abuse 유린, 학대, 남용
endure 견디다, 인내하다
penal 형벌의
laureate 수상자
free 풀어주다, 석방하다
dissident 반체제 인사
jail cell 감방

오답률 TOP 1
09 정답 ④
19 서울시

정답해설

정형화된 고정관념을 통해 세상을 쳐다봄으로써, 우리가 세상을 정의하는 것을 좀 더 쉽게 해준다고 본문에서 설명하고 있다. 빈칸 전에 'Life would be a wearing process'(인생은 과정을 닳아버리게 할 것이다)라고 하였으므로 고정관념이 아니라 매번 새롭게 세상을 받아들이게 되면 인생이 이렇게 된다는 것을 유추할 수 있다. 따라서 정답은 ④ if we had to start from scratch with every human contact(우리가 모든 인간의 접촉으로 처음부터 다시 시작해야 한다면)이다.

오답해설
① 인생의 과정을 닳아버리게 하는 것은 고정관념을 고수해서 그런 것이 아니므로 빈칸에 적절하지 않다.
② 이것 또한 빈칸 이전의 내용과 어울리지 않으므로 정답이 될 수 없다.
③ 미리 판단하는 것이 시간을 낭비하는 방법은 아니므로 빈칸에 어울리지 않는다.

해석
고정관념은 우리가 세상을 보기 위해 "정의"하는 한 가지 방법이다. 그들은 인간의 무한한 다양성을 우리가 정형화된 방식으로 행동하는 것을 배우는 편리한 소수의 "형식"으로 분류한다. 우리가 모든 인간의 접촉으로 처음부터 다시 시작해야 한다면 인생은 과정을 닳아 버리게 할 것이다. 고정관념은 피어나고 윙윙거리는 혼란을 크게 알아볼 수 있는 조각으로 덮음으로써 우리의 정신적 노력을 절약한다. 그들은 세상이 어떤 곳인지 알아내는 "곤란함"을 절약한다. 그들은 세상이 어떤 곳인지에 익숙해진 모습을 우리에게 준다.
① 만약 우리가 고정관념을 고수하려고 시도했다면
② 만약 우리가 진부한 방식 안에서 행동하는 것을 배웠다면
③ 만약 우리가 그들에게 우리의 눈을 두기 전에 사람들을 미리 판단했었다면
④ 우리가 모든 인간의 접촉으로 처음부터 다시 시작해야 한다면

어휘
stereotype 고정관념
classify 분류하다
handful 한 줌, 적은 수
fashion 방식
economize 절약하다, 아끼다
buzzing 웅성대는
trouble 수고
look 모습
prejudge 예단(속단)하다
lay eyes on ~을 보다[발견하다, 만나다]
from scratch 맨 처음부터
define 규정하다, 정의하다
infinite 무한한
stereotyped 판에 박은, 진부한
wearing 몹시 지치게 하는
blooming 만발한, 엄청난
cut-out 잘려진 것
accustomed 익숙한
stick to ~를 고수하다

오답률 TOP 2
10 정답 ④
19 서울시

정답해설
본문에서 'During her last, brief hospital stay in late June 2008, she was visited by a group of five current Haskins students and recent PhDs who had never had the opportunity of working with her.(2008년 6월 말에 있었던 그녀의 마지막 짧은 입원 기간 동안, 그녀는 그녀와 함께 일할 기회가 없었던 다섯 명의 현재 Haskins 학생들과 최근 박사들에 의해 방문을 받았다.)'라는 문장에서 그녀가 많이 아팠고 죽음을 준비했던 것을 알 수 있다. 따라서 이러한 글이 포함된 것은 ④ obituary(사망 기사)이다.

오답해설
나머지 보기들은 이 글의 종류가 될 수 없으므로 오답이다.

해석
비록 Cathe는 Haskins에 있을 때 학구적인 지위를 갖지 않기 때문에 그녀 자신의 박사학위 학생이 없었지만, 그녀와 가깝게 일하고 그녀에게 영향을 받은 Haskins의 많은 학생들이 있다. 2008년 6월 말에 있었던 그녀의 마지막 짧은 입원 기간 동안, 그녀는 그녀와 함께 일할 기회가 없었던 다섯 명의 현재 Haskins 학생들과 최근 박사들에 의해 방문을 받았다. 그 순간 Cathe의 간병인들이 그 방에 없었기 때문에, 그 방에 있던 다른 환자는 이렇게 물었다. "당신들도 모두 그녀를 위해 일하나요?" 그 그룹 구성원들 중 한 명이 주저하지 않고 "아니요, 우리는 모두 그녀의 제자들이에요."라고 대답했다.
① 안내 광고
② 법령, 조례
③ 연극
④ 사망기사

어휘
PhD 박사학위(학생)
closely 밀접하게, 면밀하게
caregiver 돌보미, 간호사
miss a beat 순간적으로 주저하다
classified ad (구인, 구직, 매매 등을 위한) 3행 광고, 안내광고
ordinance 법령, 조례
academic position 교수 자리
current 현재의
absent 부재 중인
obituary 부고, 사망기사

기적사 DAY 02

결국엔 성정혜 영어 하프모의고사

| 01 | ③ | 02 | ④ | 03 | ② | 04 | ④ | 05 | ③ |
| 06 | ③ | 07 | ② | 08 | ③ | 09 | ④ | 10 | ③ |

01 정답 ③

정답해설

밑줄 친 의미는 문맥상, '토착적인'이라는 의미로 사용되었고, 유의어로는 ③ aboriginal이 적절하다.

해석

가장 **토착적인** 거주자들은 미국 원주민들이었다.
① 방랑하는
② 탐욕스러운
③ 고유의, 토착의, 원주민의
④ 가난한, 특권이 없는

어휘

inhabitant 거주자
ravenous 탐욕스러운
unprivileged 가난한, 특권이 없는
vagabond 방랑하는
aboriginal 고유의, 토착의, 원주민의

오답률 TOP 1

02 정답 ④

정답해설

밑줄 친 의미는 문맥상 '떠도는'이라는 의미로 사용되었고, 유의어로는 ④ natant가 적절하다.

해석

떠도는 일꾼들(잡역부)의 상태는 여전히 더 열악하다, 왜냐하면 그들에게 지불되는 임금은 그들을 굶주림으로부터 막기에는 거의 충분하지 않기 때문이다.
① 조건으로 하는
② 피상적인, 겉핥기의
③ 격노한
④ 떠도는, 헤엄치는, 물에 떠 있는

어휘

starvation 굶주림
cursory 피상적인, 겉핥기의
natant 떠도는, 헤엄치는, 물에 떠 있는
contingent 조건으로 하는
irate 격노한

오답률 TOP 3

03 정답 ②

정답해설

밑줄 친 단어의 의미는 '가난한'으로 사용되었고, 유의어는 ② necessitous가 적절하다.

해석

인구는 **가난하고** 수가 줄어들었을 뿐만 아니라 정신도 망가져 있었다.
① 아마추어의
② 가난한
③ 정확한, 결점이 없는
④ 몹시 놀라운

어휘

dilettante 아마추어의
faultless 정확한, 결점이 없는
necessitous 가난한
astounding 몹시 놀라운

04 정답 ④

정답해설

A와 B의 대화에서 B는 이미 약을 먹고 있고, 증상이 나아지지 않아 약을 더 사러 왔다. A가 더 해줄 수 있는 게 없다고 하자, B는 그러면 의사를 먼저 봐야겠다고 말한다. 여기서 A가 할 말로 적절한 것은 '처방전 없이 파는 약만 판다(④ We only sell over-the-counter drugs)'이다.

오답해설

① 경험해보고 싶다는 문맥상 어색하다.
② A의 이어지는 말은 더 이상 도와줄 수 없다는 것이므로 '도와줄 수 있다'는 말과 반대된다.
③ B가 의사를 먼저 봐야겠다고 하는 걸로 봐서 A는 약을 처방할 수 없음을 짐작할 수 있다.

해석

A: 안녕하세요. 뭐가 필요하세요?
B: 안녕하세요. 열하고 기침이 나요.
A: 약 드시고 계신가요?
B: 아스피린을 먹었는데, 나아지지 않네요.
A: 저희는 처방전 없이 파는 약만 팔아요. 유감스럽지만 더 도와드릴 수가 없어요.
B: 알겠습니다. 먼저 의사 선생님을 봐야겠어요.
① 경험해보고 싶어요
② 제가 도와줄게요
③ 제가 약을 처방해 드릴게요
④ 저희는 처방전 없이 파는 약만 팔아요

어휘

suffer from~ ~로 고통을 겪다
over-the-counter 처방전 없이 파는 약
get one's feet wet 경험하다
on medicine 복용 중인
prescribe 처방하다

05 정답 ③

정답해설

③ **출제 포인트: 해석에 주의해야 할 표현**
「A+shy of+B」와 「A+after+B」의 구분 여부를 묻는 문제로 「A+shy of+B」의 경우 'B되기 A전'을 뜻하며 「A+after+B」의 경우 'B지나고 A'를 뜻한다. 해당 문제는 주어진 해석이 '약혼식 다음 날 아침'이므로 'shy of'를 'after'로 수정해야 한다.

오답해설

① **출제 포인트: 목적격 관계대명사 생략**
목적격 관계대명사의 생략이 가능한 경우는 다음과 같다.
1. 명사(선행사)+(목적격 관계대명사)+주어+완전자동사+전치사
2. 명사(선행사)+(목적격 관계대명사)+주어+불완전자동사+주격 보어+전치사
3. 명사(선행사)+(목적격 관계대명사)+주어+완전타동사
4. 명사(선행사)+(목적격 관계대명사)+주어+완전타동사+목적어+전치사

5. 명사(선행사)+(목적격 관계대명사)+주어+완전타동사+전치사+목적어
6. 명사(선행사)+(목적격 관계대명사)+주어+수여동사+목적어
7. 명사(선행사)+(목적격 관계대명사)+주어+불완전타동사+목적격 보어

주어진 해석이 '~와 ~을 관련시키다'이므로 'associate'가 「associate+목적어+with+목적어」의 형태로 사용된 것임을 알 수 있다. 따라서 해당 문장은 5번 「명사(선행사)+(목적격 관계대명사)+주어+완전타동사+전치사+목적어」에 해당하므로 옳은 문장이다.

② 출제 포인트: 자동사로 착각하기 쉬운 완전타동사

해당 문장에서 'reach'는 타동사로 쓰여 '~에 도달하다'의 의미로 목적어를 동반하며, 진행형으로 옳게 사용되었다. 단, 'reach'가 자동사로 쓰이는 경우 '(손, 발을) 뻗다'의 의미로 사용되어 전치사 'to/toward/over/under'로 쓰이는 경우가 있으니 이점은 문맥상 해석에 유의해야 한다.

ex) They reached Seoul.
그들은 서울에 도착했다.
ex) A building reached to the sky.
건물이 하늘로 뻗어 있다(하늘에 닿아 있다).

④ 출제 포인트: 불완전자동사 appear

'appear'는 불완전자동사의 경우 주격 보어로 올 수 있는 것은 다음과 같다.
1. appear+주격 보어[명사(구)]
2. appear+주격 보어[형용사(구)]
3. appear+주격 보어[to be+명사(구)]
4. appear+주격 보어[to be+형용사(구)]
5. appear+주격 보어[to+동사원형]

해당 문장은 4번 「appear+주격 보어[to be+형용사(구)]」에 해당하므로 옳은 문장이다.

06 정답 ③

정답해설

③ 출제 포인트: 해석에 주의해야 할 표현

'per head'와 'personal'의 구분 여부를 묻는 문제로 'per head'의 경우 '한 사람당'을 뜻하며 'personal'의 경우 '개인의, 개인적인'을 뜻한다. 해당 문장은 주어진 해석이 "개인적 필요'이므로 'needs per head'를 'personal needs'로 수정해야 한다.

오답해설

① 출제 포인트: so[neither]+조동사+주어: '~또한 그렇다'

「so+조동사+주어」와 「neither+조동사+주어」 모두 '~도 또한 그러하다'를 뜻하나 앞 문장의 부정 유무에 차이가 있다.
1. 긍정문, and+so+조동사+주어: ~도 또한 그러하다
2. 부정문, and+neither+조동사+주어: ~도 또한 그러하다

또한 「so+조동사+주어」와 「neither+조동사+주어」는 동사-주어의 도치가 일어나며 이때 조동사를 사용하는 것이 포인트이므로 조동사의 시제와 인칭 반영에 유의해야 한다.
해당 문장은 긍정문 뒤에 'so+조동사+주어'를 옳게 사용하였다.

② 출제 포인트: 완전자동사

'happen'은 완전자동사로 전치사 없이 목적어가 올 수 없으며 수동태를 사용할 수 없다. 따라서 'happen'이 나오는 문제의 경우 수동태 'be happened'로 사용되었는지를 꼭 확인해야 한다. 해당 문장은 happen을 능동태로 사용하였으며 뒤에 목적어를 사용하지 않았으므로 옳은 문장이다.

④ 출제 포인트: 시간의 부사구/부사절

'in recent years'는 시간의 부사구로 동사에 현재완료, 현재완료진행형, 과거, 과거진행형을 사용할 수 있다.

07 정답 ②

정답해설

② 출제 포인트: 현재분사 vs. 과거분사

해당 문장의 경우 분사 뒤의 구조가 「as+명사구」 형태의 전명구이므로 현재분사 'defining'을 사용할 수 없으며 과거분사 'defined'를 사용해야 한다. ('define'은 완전타동사와 불완전타동사만 가능한 동사이므로 뒤에 전치사 없이 목적어를 가진다.)

※ define
→ define(완전타동사)+목적어
→ define(불완전타동사)+목적어+목적격 보어[as+명사(구)]

오답해설

① 출제 포인트: of+추상명사

전치사 'of'는 일반적으로 추상명사와 결합하는 경우 형용사로 바꾸어 사용할 수 있다. 즉, 「of+추상명사 → 형용사」의 공식이 성립한다. 또한 전치사 'of'가 「형용사+추상명사」 형태의 명사구와 결합하는 경우 형용사는 부사로 바꾸어 사용할 수 있고 추상명사는 형용사로 바꾸어 사용할 수 있다. 즉, 「of+형용사+추상명사 → 부사+형용사」의 공식이 성립한다. 따라서 해당 문장의 경우 'of great importance'를 'greatly important'로 바꾸어 사용할 수 있다.

③ 출제 포인트: to부정사의 부사적 용법

해당 문장에서 부정사의 부사적용법의 목적으로 쓰였다. '~하기 위해서'의 의미로 올바르다.

④ 출제 포인트: 현재분사 vs. 과거분사

해당 문장의 경우 접속사 'and'가 있는 분사구문으로 생략된 주어를 찾아야 한다. 생략된 주어가 'the official nature'이고 해석상 '기록된'이 자연스러우므로 과거분사 'written'을 사용해야 한다.

해석

현대 사회에서 대단히 중요한 특정 유형의 사회적 집단은 공식적 조직으로, 이름과 공식적인 목적이나 목표, 지위와 역할의 구조, 그리고 이러한 목표들을 증진할 수 있도록 고안된 규범들을 가지고 있는 비교적 큰 규모의 집단으로 정의된다. 여타의 모임들과 공식적인 조직들을 구분 짓는 것은 – 대개 기록되는(서면상으로 남겨지는) – 목표, 규범, 지위 체계의 공식성이다.

어휘

particular 특정한
organization 조직, 단체, 기구
define A as B A를 B로 정의하다
design+목적어+to+동사원형 ~이 …하도록 꾀하다
distinguish A from B A와 B를 구분하다
nature 특성, 본성, 자연

08 정답 ③

정답해설

(A) 빈칸 이전 "no information about the trial has been made public (재판에 대한 어떠한 정보도 공개되지 않았다)."에서 비공개 재판에 대해 언급한 후, "any of Huang's lawyers was never told about the trial(Huang의 변호인들 중 누구도 재판에 대해 이야기를 듣지 못했다)."를 통해 재판에 대한 추가적인 정보를 제공하고 있다. 따라서 '첨언, 부언'을 의미하는 Moreover가 (A)에 가장 적절하다.

(B) 빈칸 이전 문장 "The closed-door hearing violated his right to a fair and public trial by an independent court(그 비공개 심문은 독립 법정으로부터 공정하고 공개적인 재판을 받을 그의 권리를 침해하였다)."를 통해 '재판의 부당함'에 대해 언급한 후, 빈칸 이후에서 "the Chinese government must immediately and unconditionally release Huang Qi(중국 정부는 즉각적이고 조건 없이 Huang Qi를 석방해야 한다)"라고 필자의 주장 및 글의 결론을 서술하고 있다. 따라서, 앞서 논의한 것의 '결론'을 나타내는 Thus가 (B)에 가장 적절하다.

오답해설

④ (A) 빈칸 이후 문장이 이전 내용을 요약하는 구조가 아니므로, 'To be brief(요컨대, 간단히 말해서)'는 (A)에 적절하지 않다. 또한 'Likewise(유사하게, 비슷하게)'는 앞서 언급한 내용과 유사한 내용을 서술할 때 사용되므로, 결론을 나타내는 (B)문장 앞에 위치하는 것은 적절하지 않다.

해석

중국 당국이 인권 운동가이자 시민 저널리스트인 Huang Qi를 국가 기밀을 해외 단체에 불법으로 제공하고 고의적으로 국가 기밀을 유출한 혐의로 재판에 회부했음에도 불구하고, 법원은 판결을 선고하지 않았다. 국민 중 누구도 재판에 참석하는 것이 허용되지 않았고, 재판에 대한 어떠한 정보도 공개되지 않았다. (A) 게다가, Huang의 변호인들 중 누구도 재판에 대해 이야기를 듣지 못했다. 그 비공개 심문은 독립 법정으로부터 공정하고 공개적인 재판을 받을 그의 권리를 침해하였다. (B) 따라서, 중국 정부는 즉각적이고 조건 없이 건강이 심각하게 안 좋은 Huang Qi를 석방하고, 표현과 결사의 자유 행사를 이유로 그를 박해하는 것을 멈추어야 한다.

① 즉 - 그러나
② 예를 들어 - 그렇지 않으면
③ 게다가 - 따라서
④ 요컨대 - 유사하게

어휘

authority 당국
human rights 인권
defender (주의, 사상 등의) 옹호자, 수호자
on charges of ~혐의로, ~죄로
entity 독립체, 실체
leak 유출하다
verdict 판결, 평결
attend 참석하다, 참가하다
closed-door 비공개의
violate 위배하다, 위반하다
independent 독립한
release 석방하다
exercise (권력·권리·역량 등을) 행사하다
association 결사, 연계, 유대
put ~ on trial ~를 재판에 회부하다
state 국가의
intentionally 고의적으로, 의도적으로
court 법원, 법정
allow 허락하다, 허용하다
make public 공표하다, 알리다
hearing 심문, 심리, 청문회
fair 공정한
unconditionally 무조건적으로
persecution 박해

오답률 TOP 2
09 정답 ④

정답해설

해당 지문은 고정관념과 일반화를 비교하고 있다. 빈칸 앞 "To be brief(간단히 말해)"로 보아 빈칸에는 앞 내용을 요약하는 문장이 들어가야 한다. 첫 문장에서 "Stereotypes are widely circulated oversimplifications ~, whereas generalizations can not only be based on ~(고정관념은 널리 퍼져 있는 한 집단의 사람들에 대한 지나친 단순화인 반면에, 일반화는 널리 받아들여지는 요인뿐만이 아니라 개인의 경험에도 기초할 수 있다)."라고 두 개념의 차이를 간단히 설명한 뒤, 구체적인 예를 차례대로 나열하고 있으므로, ④ while all stereotypes are generalizations, not all generalizations are necessarily stereotypes(모든 고정관념은 일반화이지만, 모든 일반화가 반드시 고정관념인 것은 아니다.)가 빈칸에 가장 적절하다.

오답해설

① "whereas generalizations can also be based on personal experience(반면에 일반화는 개인의 경험에도 기초할 수 있다)."를 통해 고정관념이 아니라 일반화가 개인의 경험에 뿌리를 둘 수 있다는 것을 알 수 있으므로 틀리다.
② 본문에 고정관념과 일반화의 사회적 역할(the roles stereotypes and generalizations play in society)이 언급되지 않았으므로 문맥상 빈칸에 적절하지 않다.
③ "These are so well-known that the average American would not hesitate ~(이것들은 너무나도 잘 알려져 있어서 만약 어떤 인종이 농구에 탁월한지 말해보라고 요청받는다면 평균적인 미국인은 망설이지 않을 것이다)."를 통해 고정관념에 따른 빠른 반응에 대한 언급을 하고는 있지만, 새로운 상황에 대한 예가 아니며, 전체적인 내용을 아우르지 못하고 있으므로 빈칸에 적절하지 않다.

해석

고정관념은 널리 퍼져 있는 한 집단의 사람들에 대한 지나친 단순화인 반면에, 일반화는 널리 받아들여지는 요인뿐만이 아니라 개인의 경험에도 기초할 수 있다. 미국에서, 특정한 인종 집단은 수학이나 체육을 잘한다는 것과 같은 고정관념에 연결되어 있다. 이것들은 너무나도 잘 알려져 있어서 만약 어떤 인종이 농구에 탁월한지 말해보라고 요청받는다면 평균적인 미국인은 망설이지 않을 것이다. 즉, 누군가가 고정관념을 형성할 때는, 사회에 이미 존재하고 있는 문화적인 믿음을 반복하는 것이다. 반면에, 개인은 사회에 영속되지 않은 일반화를 형성할 수 있다. 예를 들어, 한 국가 출신의 몇몇의 개인들을 만나고 그들이 친절하고 활기차다고 생각한 누군가는 그 국가의 모든 국민들이 친절하고 활기차다고 말할 수도 있다. 간단히 말해, 모든 고정관념은 일반화이지만, 모든 일반화가 반드시 고정관념인 것은 아니다.

① 일반화와 달리 고정관념은 주로 개인적인 경험에 기초를 두고 있다
② 고정관념과 일반화가 사회에서 수행하는 역할에 대한 많은 논쟁이 있다
③ 고정관념뿐만 아니라 일반화도 사람들이 새로운 상황에 빨리 대응할 수 있도록 해준다
④ 모든 고정관념은 일반화이지만, 모든 일반화가 반드시 고정관념인 것은 아니다

어휘

stereotype 고정관념; 고정관념을 형성하다
circulate 퍼뜨리다
whereas ~에 반하여
widely-accepted 널리[일반적으로] 받아들여지는[인정된]
factor 요인, 인자
well-known 잘 알려진, 유명한
hesitate 망설이다
excel 뛰어나다
repeat 되풀이하다
mythology (많은 사람들의) 근거 없는 믿음, 신화
perpetuate 영속시키다, 불멸하게 하다
to be brief 간단히 말해, 요컨대
unlike ~와 달리
A as well as B B뿐만 아니라 A도
enable ~할 수 있게 하다
rapidly 빨리
oversimplification 지나친 단순화
generalization 일반화
racial 인종의
average 평균의
identify 확인하다, 식별하다
that is 즉, 다시 말하면
be rooted in ~에 뿌리박고 있다
debate 논쟁, 논란
respond 대응하다, 응답하다
necessarily 반드시, 필연적으로

10 정답 ③

정답해설

본문에서 전체적으로 Peter라는 인물의 고등학교 입학, 취업 이후 장기 기증까지의 생애를 다루고 있으며, 이는 과거시제로 표현되고 있다. 또한, "Peter is giving life with saving at least three others as an organ donor(Peter는 장기 기증자로서 최소 3명을 구하며 새 생명을 줄 것이다)."를 통해 Peter가 사망하여 곧 장기 기증을 할 것이라는 것을 유추할 수 있다. 따라서 이러한 내용이 포함된 글의 종류는 ③ obituary(사망 기사)이다.

오답해설
① 글의 초반에 Peter의 경력에 대해 언급하고 있으나, 이후 내용은 사망에 따른 장기 기증을 언급하고 있다. 따라서 reference letter(추천서)와는 연관성이 없다.
② Peter 자신이 쓴 글이 아니므로 정답이 아니다.
④ 내용상 이 글의 종류가 아니므로 정답이 될 수 없다.

해석
Peter는 Rootstown 고등학교를 1974년에 졸업했다. 그는 15살 때 첫 번째 직장이었던 Beefy Cow's에서 항상 열심히 일하는 직원이었다. 그는 라벤나에 있는 Schnell Scientific Services에서 수년간 일했고, 지난 23년 동안 Global Synthetic Rubber에서 일했다. Peter는 장기 기증자로서 최소 3명을 구하며 새 생명을 줄 것이다. 그는 항상 요청받을 때마다 타인과 그의 가족을 기꺼이 도와주었다. 그는 조카들에게 매우 관대했으며, 조카 Victoria의 후견인이었다. 그는 결코 남에게 심술을 부리거나 악의를 품지 않았지만, 그는 정말 대단한 이야기꾼이었다. 그는 친구들과 캠핑하는 것을 매우 좋아했고 항상 여행에 대한 이야깃거리를 가지고 있었다.
① 추천서
② 자서전
③ 사망기사
④ 일기

어휘
synthetic rubber 합성 고무
organ donor 장기 기증자
guardian 후견인, 보호자
spiteful 악의에 찬, 앙심을 품은
autobiography 전기, 자서전
journal 일기, 일지
give life 살리다
be willing to 기꺼이 ~하다
mean 못된, 심술궂은
reference letter 추천서
obituary 부고, 사망 기사

결국엔 성정혜 영어 하프모의고사
기적사 DAY 03

| 01 | ③ | 02 | ③ | 03 | ② | 04 | ④ | 05 | ③ |
| 06 | ④ | 07 | ④ | 08 | ④ | 09 | ② | 10 | ④ |

01 정답 ③

정답해설
밑줄 친 단어의 의미는 문맥상 '탐욕스러운'으로, 유의어로는 ③ insatiable이 적절하다.

해석
그것은 그녀의 입안에서 두툼했고 달콤했으며 그녀를 더 **탐욕스럽게** 만들었다.
① 우연한, 우발적인, 예상 못한
② 암시하는, 냄새가 나는
③ 탐욕스러운, 만족할 줄 모르는
④ 울퉁불퉁한, 고르지 않은

어휘
inadvertent 우연한, 우발적인, 예상 못한
allusive 암시하는, 냄새가 나는
insatiable 탐욕스러운, 만족할 줄 모르는
uneven 이상한, 고르지 않은

02 정답 ③

정답해설
밑줄 친 단어의 의미는 문맥상 '원주민의'이고, 유의어로는 ③ indigenous가 적절하다.

해석
원주민의 의상은 우리의 것과는 거리가 멀다.
① 보통의, 공통의, 흔한
② 순진한, 생각이 얕은, 소박한
③ 고유의, 토착의
④ 솔직한, 공정한

어휘
a far cry from ~와는 거리가 먼
naive 순진한, 생각이 얕은, 소박한
candid 솔직한, 공정한
common 보통의, 공통의, 흔한
indigenous 고유의, 토착의

03 정답 ②

정답해설
밑줄 친 의미는 문맥상 '~와 대등하게'이며, 유의어로는 ② on equal terms with가 적절하다.

해석
뉴 사우스 웨일스 다이아몬드 중 최고는 남아프리카의 다이아몬드보다 더 단단하고 훨씬 더 휘황찬란하며, 브라질 최고의 보석과 **대등하게** 분류되지만, 아직 큰 표본은 발견되지 않았다.
① 아주 거리가 먼
② 동등하게, 완전히 부합하여

③ 당장
④ 폭격당하는

어휘

classify 분류하다　　　　　　　specimen 표본
far removed from 아주 거리가 먼
on equal terms with 동등하게, 완전히 부합하여
on the spot 당장　　　　　bombard with 비난을 받다

04 정답 ④

정답해설

스스로 하지 않고 고치라고 말만 하는 A에게 B는 일침을 가하고 있다. A에게 차라리 배관공을 부르는 게 낫다고 충고하고 있으므로 빈칸에는 이와 부합되는 말이 들어가는 것이 좋다. 즉 '말로만 하지 말고 행동으로 실천하라'고 하는 것을 설명하는 속담인 ④ That is easier said than done이 정답이다.

해석

A: 아파트 수도꼭지가 아직도 새는데. 네가 고친다고 했던 것 같은데.
B: 오, 그래. 와셔를 교체해야 해.
A: 그러면 왜 교체하지 않았니?
B: 말하기는 쉬우나 행하기는 어려운 거야. 난 네가 가능한 한 빨리 배관공한테 전화하는 게 낫다고 생각해.
① 그것은 절차를 무시한 거야
② 그것을 받아들이려고 애쓴다
③ 너는 그에게 그것에 대해 편지를 써봐
④ 말하기는 쉬우나 행하기는 어려운 거야

어휘

faucet 수도꼭지　　　　　　　drip 물이 떨어지다
washer 와셔　　　　　　　　replace 교체하다
had better ~하는 편이 낫다　　plumber 배관공
cut corners 절차를 무시하다　come to terms with it 합의를 보다
drop one a line 편지를 쓰다

오답률 TOP 3

05 정답 ③

정답해설

③ **출제 포인트: 자동사로 착각하기 쉬운 완전타동사**
'mention'은 완전타동사만 가능한 동사로 'mention'과 목적어 사이에 전치사를 사용하는 경우 비문이 된다. 해당 문장은 'mention'과 목적어 'the important invention' 사이에 전치사 'about'을 사용하였으므로 비문이다. 따라서 전치사 'about'을 삭제해야 한다.

오답해설

① **출제 포인트: 목적격 관계대명사 생략**
목적격 관계대명사의 생략이 가능한 경우는 다음과 같다.
1. 명사(선행사)+(목적격 관계대명사)+주어+완전자동사+전치사
2. 명사(선행사)+(목적격 관계대명사)+주어+불완전자동사+주격 보어+전치사
3. 명사(선행사)+(목적격 관계대명사)+주어+완전타동사
4. 명사(선행사)+(목적격 관계대명사)+주어+완전타동사+목적어+전치사
5. 명사(선행사)+(목적격 관계대명사)+주어+완전타동사+전치사+목적어
6. 명사(선행사)+(목적격 관계대명사)+주어+수여동사+목적어
7. 명사(선행사)+(목적격 관계대명사)+주어+불완전타동사+목적격 보어

해당 문장은 3번 「명사(선행사)+(목적격 관계대명사)+주어+완전타동사」에 해당하므로 옳은 문장이다.

② **출제 포인트: 불완전자동사 appear**
'appear'는 불완전자동사의 경우 주격 보어로 올 수 있는 것은 다음과 같다.
1. appear+주격 보어[명사(구)]
2. appear+주격 보어[형용사(구)]
3. appear+주격 보어[to be+명사(구)]
4. appear+주격 보어[to be+형용사(구)]
5. appear+주격 보어[to+동사원형]
해당 문장은 2번 「appear+주격 보어[형용사(구)]」에 해당하므로 옳은 문장이다.

④ **출제 포인트: 해석에 주의해야 할 표현**
「A+shy of+B」와 「A+after+B」의 구분 여부를 묻는 문제로 「A+shy of+B」의 경우 'B되기 A전'을 뜻하며 「A+after+B」의 경우 'B지나고 A'를 뜻한다. 해당 문제는 주어진 해석이 '자신의 20번째 생일 일주일 전'이므로 'shy of'를 사용하는 것이 옳다.

06 정답 ④

정답해설

④ **출제 포인트: 해석에 주의해야 할 표현**
'per person'과 'personal'의 해석을 구분할 수 있는 가를 묻는 문제로 'per person'의 경우 '한 사람당'을 뜻하며 'personal'의 경우 '개인의, 개인적인'을 뜻한다. 해당 문제는 주어진 해석이 주어진 해석이 '개인적'이므로 'problems per person'을 'personal problems'로 수정해야 한다.

오답해설

① **출제 포인트: 시간의 부사구/부사절**
'since+명사구'는 시간의 부사구로 동사에 현재완료, 현재완료진행형을 사용할 수 있다.

② **출제 포인트: 완전자동사**
'happen'은 완전자동사로 전치사 없이 목적어가 올 수 없으며 수동태를 사용할 수 없다. 따라서 'happen'이 나오는 문제의 경우 수동태 'be happened'로 사용되었는지를 꼭 확인해야 한다. 해당 문장은 'happen'을 능동태로 사용하였으며 뒤에 목적어를 사용하지 않았으므로 옳은 문장이다.

③ **출제 포인트: so[neither]+조동사+주어: '~또한 그렇다'**
「so+조동사+주어」와 「neither+조동사+주어」 모두 '~도 또한 그러하다'를 뜻하나 앞 문장의 부정 유무에 차이가 있다.
1. 긍정문, and+so+조동사+주어: ~도 또한 그러하다
2. 부정문, and+neither+조동사+주어: ~도 또한 그러하다
또한 「so+조동사+주어」와 「neither+조동사+주어」는 동사-주어의 도치가 일어나며 이때 조동사를 사용하는 것이 포인트이므로 조동사의 시제와 인칭 반영에 유의해야 한다.
해당 문장은 부정문 뒤에 'neither+조동사+주어'를 옳게 사용하였다.

07 정답 ④

정답해설

④ **출제 포인트: 현재분사 vs. 과거분사**
해당 문장의 경우 분사 뒤의 구조가 「by+명사구」 형태의 전명구이므로 현재분사 'providing'을 사용할 수 없으며 과거분사 'provided'를 사용해야 한다. ('provide'는 완전타동사만 가능한 동사이므로 뒤에 전치사 없이 목적어를 가진다.)
※ provide
→ provide(완전타동사)+목적어(사물)

→ provide(완전타동사)+목적어(사물)+for+목적어(대상)
→ provide(완전타동사)+목적어(대상)+with+목적어(사물)

오답해설

① **출제 포인트: to부정사의 형용사적 용법**
to부정사의 형용사적 용법은 수식어와 보어 역할로 나눌 수 있으며, 수식어 역할을 하는 경우 한정적 용법에 그리고 보어 역할을 하는 경우 서술적 용법에 해당한다. 한정적 용법의 경우 「명사+to+동사원형」의 형태로 사용되며 서술적 용법의 경우 다음과 같이 사용된다.
1. 불완전자동사+주격 보어[to+동사원형]
2. 불완전타동사+목적어+목적격 보어[to+동사원형]
3. be+과거분사[불완전타동사]+목적격 보어[to+동사원형]
4. 명사+과거분사+목적격 보어[to+동사원형]
따라서 해당 문장의 경우 「명사+to+동사원형」에 해당하므로 'to move'는 to부정사의 형용사적 용법 중 한정적 용법으로 사용되었다.

② **출제 포인트: 명사절을 이끄는 접속사 that**
해당 문장에서 'that'은 주격 보어 역할을 하는 「that+명사절」로 사용되었다.
※ 명사절을 이끄는 접속사 'that'의 역할은 다음과 같다.
  1. 주어 역할
    → 「that+명사절」이 주어 역할을 하는 경우 주로 문두에 가주어 'it'을 사용하며 「that+명사절」을 문미로 이동시킨다. 이때 'that'은 생략할 수 있다. 그러나 「that+명사절」이 문두에서 주어 역할을 하는 경우 'that'은 생략할 수 없다.
    ex) It's a pity (that) you don't know Russian.
    ex) That you don't know Russian is a pity.
  2. 목적어 역할
    → 「that+명사절」이 목적어 역할을 하는 경우 직접목적어로 사용하며 이때 'that'은 생략할 수 있다.
    ex) I can't believe (that) he's only 17.
  3. 보어 역할
    → 「that+명사절」이 보어 역할을 하는 경우 주격 보어로 사용하며 이때 'that'은 생략할 수 있다.
    ex) The problem is (that) Jane doesn't like me.
  4. 동격
    → 「that+명사절」이 동격으로 쓰이는 경우 추상명사가 'that'이전에 쓰이며 'that' 이후에는 완전한 문장이 와야 한다.
    ex) The fact that he is your brother-in-law should not affect your decision.

③ **출제 포인트: of+추상명사**
전치사 'of'는 일반적으로 추상명사와 결합하는 경우 형용사로 바꾸어 사용할 수 있다. 즉, 「of+추상명사 → 형용사」의 공식이 성립한다. 또한 전치사 'of'가 「형용사+추상명사」 형태의 명사구와 결합하는 경우 형용사는 부사로 바꾸어 사용할 수 있고 추상명사는 형용사로 바꾸어 사용할 수 있다. 즉, 「of+형용사+추상명사 → 부사+형용사」의 공식이 성립한다. 따라서 해당 문장의 경우 'of equal importance'를 'equally important'로 바꾸어 사용할 수 있다.

해석
현대 경제는 상품, 사람, 그리고 정보를 안전하고 믿을 만하게 이동시키는 능력에 의존한다. 그것들의 중요성을 더해 주고 있는 것은 생명선 시스템의 다수가 재난 복구에서 중대한 역할을 한다는 것이다. 결과적으로, 자연과 과학 기술의 광범위한 위험에 직면하여 한 국가의 기반 시설에 의해 제공되는 서비스의 흐름이 방해받지 않고 계속되는 것은 정부와 기업, 그리고 모든 대중에게 똑같이 중요하다.

어휘
goods 상품
lifeline 생명선
hazard 위험
reliably 확실하게, 믿음직하게
infrastructure 인프라, 기반 시설

오답률 TOP 2
08 정답 ④

정답해설
해당 지문은 John Locke의 '사회계약설(social contract theory)'에 대해 설명하고 있으며, 주어진 문장은 '사회계약설의 한계'에 대해 서술하고 있다. 마지막 문장 "Besides, he failed to understand that revolution is desirable but it is also dangerous and under normal circumstances illegal(게다가, 그는 혁명이 바람직하지만, 또한 위험하고 보통의 상황에서는 불법이라는 것을 이해하는 데 실패했다)."에서 '사회계약설의 한계'가 본문 최초로 언급되나, 'Besides'로 보아 이전에 언급된 내용에 대한 부가적인 내용을 서술하고 있다는 것을 알 수 있으므로, 마지막 문장 이전에 '사회계약설의 한계'에 대한 내용이 먼저 언급되어야 한다. 따라서 ④가 주어진 문장이 들어갈 위치로 가장 적절하다.

오답해설
③ 주어진 문장의 'this social contract theory(이러한 사회계약설)'가 ③이전의 'the theory of limited sovereignty or constitutional government(제한된 통치권 또는 입헌정치의 이론)'를 가리키고 있으나, ③이후에 해당 이론에 대한 예시를 구체적으로 이어서 언급하고 있으므로 ③은 주어진 문장의 위치로 부적절하다.

해석
John Locke는 정치학 분야에 국민의 동의 또는 의지라는 새로운 요소를 도입한 최초의 철학자인 것 같다. (①) 정부는 국민의 지지를 받거나 국민의 의지에 따라 통치하기만 한다면 정권을 유지하고 강해질 수 있다. (②) 이러한 방식으로 Locke는 제한된 통치권 또는 입헌정치의 이론을 제안했다. (③) 만일 정부가 국민의 생명, 자유, 재산을 보호하는 것에 실패한다면, 국민은 그것을 제거하고 새로운 정부를 임명할 권리를 가지고 있다. (④) **이러한 사회계약설은 모든 면에서 완벽한 것처럼 보이지만, 그는 법적인 통치자에 대해 아무 언급도 하지 않았다.**) 게다가, 그는 혁명이 바람직하지만, 또한 위험하고 보통의 상황에서는 불법이라는 것을 이해하는 데 실패했다.

어휘
social contract theory 사회계약설
in every respect 모든 면에서
consent 동의
so long as ~하는 한, ~이기만 하면
govern 통치하다, 다스리다
sovereignty 통치권
constitutional government 입헌정치
property 재산
besides 게다가, 뿐만 아니라
circumstance 상황
sovereign 통치자, 주권자
will 의지, (강한) 의견
in accordance with ~에 따라
appoint 임명하다, 정하다
desirable 바람직한

09 정답 ②

정답해설
주어진 문장은 '경험주의자'의 주장에 대해 언급하고 있다. (B)와 (C)에서 주어진 문장에서 서술한 '경험 감각'에 대해 서술하고 있으므로 '경험주의자'에 대한 서술임을 알 수 있다. 따라서 이후에는 경험주의자에 대해 설명하는 문장인 (B) 또는 (C)가 오는 것이 알맞다. (B)와 (C)이후에는 On the contrary

를 이용해 앞선 '경험주의자'에 대한 내용과 반대되는 '이성주의자'에 대한 내용을 이끄는 (A)가 이어지는 것이 자연스럽다. 따라서 '② (B) - (C) - (A)'가 정답이다.

오답해설
나머지 선지는 문맥상 어색하므로 오답이다.

해석
경험주의자들은 경험 감각이 우리의 모든 지식의 궁극적인 시작점이라고 항상 주장해왔다.
(B) 그들은 감각들이 우리에게 세상에 대한 모든 미가공 데이터를 제공하고, 이러한 원자재 없이, 지식은 전혀 존재하지 않을 것이라고 주장한다. 즉, 지각이 절차를 시작하고, 이러한 절차로부터 우리의 모든 신념이 온다.
(C) 가장 순수한 형태에서, 그 이론은 경험 감각만이 우리의 모든 신념과 지식을 탄생시킨다고 간주한다. 경험주의자의 대표적인 예에는 영국인 철학자 John Locke가 있다.
(A) 반대로 이성주의자들은 모든 지식의 궁극적인 시작점은 감각이 아니라 이성이라고 주장해왔다.

어휘
empiricist 경험주의자
ultimate 궁극적인, 최후의
raw 가공하지 않은, 원료 그대로의, 날것의
material 재료, 자료
process 절차, 과정
classic 대표적인, 전형적인
rationalist 이성주의자, 합리주의자
claim 주장하다
maintain 주장하다
perception 지각
hold 생각하다, 간주하다
on the contrary 반대로, 반면에
reason 이성

오답률 TOP 1
10 정답 ④

정답해설
해당 지문은 Locke가 분석한 토지 가격의 특성에 대해 서술하고 있다. 첫 문장에서 "land has the special character that when demand is high, supply is low, and vice versa(토지는 수요가 높을 때, 공급이 낮아지고 그 반대도 그러한 특수한 성질을 가지고 있다)"라고 서술하고 있으므로, 빈칸에는 경제가 호황이고 대안적인 투자처로서 토지의 수요가 높아질 경우에도 토지의 공급이 줄어드는 상황을 초래할 수 있는 경우가 들어가야 자연스럽다. 따라서 '토지 소유주들이 토지를 판매하지 않는다'라는 의미를 가진 '④ they have neither need nor will to sell their lands(그들은 자신들의 토지를 판매할 필요도 없고 의지도 없다)'가 빈칸에 가장 적절하다.

오답해설
① 토지의 공급이 줄어드는 것이며, 토지 가격이 하락하는 것은 아니다.
② 본문과는 관계없는 내용이므로 오답이다.
③ 토지 매물이 많아지면 공급이 증가하는 것이므로, 빈칸에 적절하지 않다.

해석
Locke에 따르면, 토지는 수요가 높을 때, 공급이 낮아지고 그 반대도 그러한 특수한 성질을 가지고 있다. 수익이 높아지고 사람들은 그들의 수익을 투자할 대안적인 방법을 찾기 때문에 무역과 제조가 번영할 때 토지 수요가 높아진다. 그러나 토지가 그러한 유형의 산업적이고 번창한 사람들에 의해 소유되는 그러한 경우에는 그들은 자신들의 토지를 판매할 필요도 없고 의지도 없다. Locke의 토지 가격에 대한 분석의 기저에 깔린 전제는 토지는 단순히 다른 투자에 대한 수익과 결국 동일한 수준의 수익을 창출하는 투자 기회가 아니라는 것이다.
① 결과적으로 토지의 가격이 하락한다
② 토지에 대한 투자의 제한이 필요하다
③ 더 많은 토지가 매물로 나올 것이다
④ 그들은 자신들의 토지를 판매할 필요도 없고 의지도 없다

어휘
vice versa 거꾸로, 역으로, 반대로; 역 또한 같다
thrive 번영하다
invest 투자하다
underlie 기저[기초]를 이루다
return 수익, 이윤
equal (수, 양, 가치 등이) 같다, 맞먹다, 필적하다
decline 감소하다, 줄다
neither A nor B A와 B 어느 것도 아닌
will 의지
alternative 대안의
assumption 전제, 가정, 추정
investment 투자
eventually 결국
restriction 제한

결국엔 성정혜 영어 하프모의고사
기적사 DAY 04

01	①	02	④	03	①	04	③	05	④
06	①	07	②	08	③	09	③	10	①

01 정답 ①

정답해설

밑줄 친 단어의 의미는 문맥상 '조건부의'로, 유의어로는 ① being subject to가 적절하다. 단, be subject to는 '~을 당하기 쉬운, 걸리기 쉬운'의 의미로도 문맥에 따라서 쓰일 수 있다.

해석

또한 매우 복잡한 **조건부** 규정 하에서 추가 요금이 있는데, 이 비용은 일반적으로 계산서에 포함된다.
① 조건으로 하는, 당하기 쉬운, 따라야 하는
② 떠돌아다니는
③ 선서한
④ 열정적인

어휘

be subject to 조건으로 하는, 당하기 쉬운, 따라야 하는
itinerant 떠돌아다니는   juratory 선서한
vehement 열정적인

오답률 TOP 1
02 정답 ④

정답해설

밑줄 친 의미는 문맥상 '전조'로 사용되었으며, 유의어로는 ④ omen이 적절하다.

해석

이번 승리는 새로운 위험들의 **전조**가 되었다.
① 고민
② 대리인, 대표자, 하원 의원
③ 근엄, 엄격
④ 전조, 예언, 징조

어휘

distress 고민   delegate 대리인, 대표자, 하원 의원
austerity 근엄, 엄격   omen 전조, 예언, 징조

03 정답 ①

정답해설

밑줄 친 단어의 의미가 문맥상 '악인'으로 쓰였기 때문에 유의어로는 ① perpetrator가 적절하다.

해석

그는 마지못해 그녀를 용의자로 넘겨야 할 유일한 이유가 그녀의 이야기에 대한 믿음이었음을 시인했을지라도, 딘은 재니퍼 래디슨을 **악인**이라는 생각에서 배제하려고 애썼다.
① 범인, 가해자, 하수인
② 대리인, 대표자
③ 익명, 개성(특색)이 없음
④ (단체의) 장, 주요한, 원금의

어휘

perpetrator 범인, 가해자, 하수인   deputy 대리인, 대표자
anonymousness 익명, 개성(특색)이 없음
principal (단체의) 장, 주요한, 원금의

오답률 TOP 2
04 정답 ③

정답해설

빈칸 다음에 따르는 대답이 규칙에 어긋나기 때문에 A가 말하는 것을 들어줄 수 없다는 내용이므로, 무언가 부탁을 하거나, 요구를 하는 질문이 적절하다. 따라서 정답은 휴식 시간을 달라는 ③ So can you give me a break?이다.

오답해설

문맥상 빈칸에 '무언가'를 요구해야 하므로, 가장 적절한 말은 ③ So can you give me a break?(잠시 쉬는 시간을 주시겠어요?)가 적절하다.

해석

A: 전 영어를 잘하지 못해요.
B: 네?
A: 영어를 잘하지 못한다고요.
B: 미안해요. 무슨 말인지 모르겠어요.
A: 제 영어 실력이 좋지 않다고요.
B: 아, 그렇군요. 이제 알겠어요.
A: 그래서 잠시 쉬는 시간을 주시겠어요?
B: 미안합니다만, 그건 규칙에 어긋나서요.
① 그래서 넌 어때?
② 그래서 당신은 무섭나요?
③ 그래서 잠시 쉬는 시간을 주시겠어요?
④ 그래서 너 너의 세계에서 나오는 건 어때?

어휘

give me a break 휴식 시간을 주다
understand 이해하다   get cold feet 무서워하다, 주눅 들다
come out of one's shell 소심함의 틀을 깨다 (너의 세상 밖으로 나오다)

05 정답 ④

정답해설

④ 출제 포인트: 해석에 주의해야 할 표현
「A+shy of+B」와 「A+after+B」의 구분 여부를 묻는 문제로 「A+shy of+B」의 경우 'B되기 A전'을 뜻하며 「A+after+B」의 경우 'B지나고 A'를 뜻한다. 해당 문제는 주어진 해석이 '죽음 이후 2년'이므로 'shy of'를 'after'로 수정해야 한다.

오답해설

① 출제 포인트: 목적격 관계대명사 생략
목적격 관계대명사의 생략이 가능한 경우는 다음과 같다.
1. 명사(선행사)+(목적격 관계대명사)+주어+완전자동사+전치사
2. 명사(선행사)+(목적격 관계대명사)+주어+불완전자동사+주격 보어+전치사

3. 명사(선행사)+(목적격 관계대명사)+주어+완전타동사
4. 명사(선행사)+(목적격 관계대명사)+주어+완전타동사+목적어+전치사
5. 명사(선행사)+(목적격 관계대명사)+주어+완전타동사+전치사+목적어
6. 명사(선행사)+(목적격 관계대명사)+주어+수여동사+목적어
7. 명사(선행사)+(목적격 관계대명사)+주어+불완전타동사+목적격 보어

해당 문장은 3번 「명사(선행사)+(목적격 관계대명사)+주어+완전타동사」에 해당하므로 옳은 문장이다.

② 출제 포인트: 불완전자동사 appear

'appear'는 불완전자동사의 경우 주격 보어로 올 수 있는 것은 다음과 같다.
1. appear+주격 보어[명사(구)]
2. appear+주격 보어[형용사(구)]
3. appear+주격 보어[to be+명사(구)]
4. appear+주격 보어[to be+형용사(구)]
5. appear+주격 보어[to+동사원형]

해당 문장은 3번 「appear+주격 보어[to be+명사(구)]」에 해당하므로 옳은 문장이다.

③ 출제 포인트: 자동사로 착각하기 쉬운 완전타동사

'discuss'는 완전타동사만 가능한 동사로 'discuss'와 목적어 사이에 전치사를 사용하는 경우 비문이 된다. 해당 문장은 'discuss'와 목적어 'identical books' 사이에 전치사를 사용하지 않았으므로 정문이다.

06 정답 ①

(정답해설)

① 출제 포인트: so[neither]+조동사+주어: '~또한 그렇다'

「so+조동사+주어」와 「neither+조동사+주어」 모두 '~도 또한 그렇다'를 뜻하나 앞 문장의 부정 유무에 차이가 있다.
1. 긍정문, and+so+조동사+주어: ~도 또한 그렇다
2. 부정문, and+neither+조동사+주어: ~도 또한 그렇다

또한 「so+조동사+주어」와 「neither+조동사+주어」는 주어-동사의 도치가 일어나며 이때 조동사를 사용하는 것이 포인트이므로 조동사의 시제와 인칭 반영에 유의해야 한다.

해당 문장은 부정문 뒤에 '~도 또한 그렇다'를 뜻하는 문장이 오는 경우이므로 'neither+조동사+주어'를 사용해야 한다. 따라서 'so'를 'neither'로 수정해야 한다.

(오답해설)

② 출제 포인트: 완전자동사

'consist'는 완전자동사로 전치사 'of' 없이 목적어가 올 수 없으며 수동태를 사용할 수 없다. 따라서 'consist'가 나오는 문제의 경우 수동태 'be consisted of'로 사용되었는지 꼭 확인해야 한다. 해당 문장은 완전자동사 'consist'가 능동태로 사용되었으며 뒤에 전치사 'of'를 사용하여 목적어를 가지므로 옳은 문장이다.

③ 출제 포인트: 해석에 주의해야 할 표현

'per person'과 'personal'의 구분 여부 묻는 문제로 'per person'의 경우 '한 사람당'을 뜻하며 'personal'의 경우 '개인의, 개인적인'을 뜻한다. 해당 문제는 주어진 해석이 주어진 해석이 '개인적'이므로 'personal'을 사용하는 것이 옳다.

④ 출제 포인트: 시간의 부사구/부사절

'since+명사구'는 시간의 부사구로 동사에 현재완료, 현재완료진행형을 사용할 수 있다.

07 정답 ②

(정답해설)

② 출제 포인트: of+추상명사

전치사 'of'는 일반적으로 추상명사와 결합하는 경우 형용사로 바꾸어 사용할 수 있다. 즉, 「of+추상명사 → 형용사」의 공식이 성립한다. 또한 전치사 'of'가 「과거분사+추상명사」 형태의 명사구와 결합하는 경우 과거분사는 부사로 바꾸어 사용할 수 있고 추상명사는 형용사로 바꾸어 사용할 수 있다. 즉, 「of+과거분사+추상명사 → 부사+형용사」의 공식이 성립한다. 해당 문장의 경우 「of+과거분사+추상명사」 대신 「of+과거분사+형용사」를 사용하였으므로 틀린 문장이다. 따라서 형용사 'effective'를 추상명사 'effectiveness'로 수정해야 한다.

(오답해설)

① 출제 포인트: to부정사의 형용사적 용법

to부정사의 형용사적 용법은 수식어와 보어 역할로 나눌 수 있으며, 수식어 역할을 하는 경우 한정적 용법에 그리고 보어 역할을 하는 경우 서술적 용법에 해당한다. 한정적 용법의 경우 「명사+to+동사원형」의 형태로 사용되며 서술적 용법의 경우 다음과 같이 사용된다.
1. 불완전자동사+주격 보어[to+동사원형]
2. 불완전타동사+목적어+목적격 보어[to+동사원형]
3. be+과거분사[불완전타동사]+목적격 보어[to+동사원형]
4. 명사+과거분사+목적격 보어[to+동사원형]

따라서 해당 문장은 2번 「불완전타동사+목적어+목적격 보어[to+동사원형]」에 해당하므로 'to reduce'는 to부정사의 형용사적 용법 중 서술적 용법으로 사용되었다.

③ 출제 포인트: 현재분사 vs. 과거분사

해당 문장의 경우 분사 뒤의 구조가 「in+명사」 형태의 전명구이므로 현재분사 'releasing'을 사용할 수 없으며 과거분사 'released'를 사용해야 한다. ('release'는 완전타동사만 가능한 동사이므로 뒤에 전치사 없이 목적어를 가진다.)

④ 출제 포인트: 동사의 자리 파악(동사 vs. 분사)

해당 문장의 경우 완전타동사 'find'의 과거형 'found'의 목적어로 접속사가 생략된 명사절이 사용되었으며 완전자동사 'lead'의 과거형 'led'는 명사절의 동사에 해당한다. 또한 완전자동사이므로 전치사 'to'와 결합하여 목적어 'more antisocial behavior'를 가지므로 옳은 문장이다.

(해석)

미 소아과 협회는 아이들에게 타임아웃을 주기, 특권을 박탈하기, 훈육용 의자에 앉히기 등으로 나쁜 행동을 줄이라고 회원들에게 충고한다. 1998년에 정해진 협회 정책에는 "체벌은 효과가 극히 제한적이고, 잠재적으로 해로운 부작용을 낳는다."라고 되어있다. (손바닥으로) 엉덩이를 때리는 것의 효과에 대한 가장 최근의 연구는, 미시간 대학 사회복지학과에서 9월에 발표되었는데, '최소한도로' 손바닥으로 때리는 것조차 아이들에게 반사회적인 행동을 하도록 유도한다는 것을 발견했다.

(어휘)

pediatrics 소아과
advise+목적어+to+동사원형 ~에게 ~하도록 권고하다
timeout 일시적 중단   discipline 훈육, 훈련, 징계, 징벌
corporal 육체의, 신체의   deleterious 해로운, 유독한

08 정답 ③

(정답해설)

해당 지문은 '쿠키 파일 삭제'에 대한 내용이며, 2, 3번째 문장 "By taking the time to delete the cookies, you can increase the speed and performance of your web browsing software(쿠키를 삭제하는 시간을 할애함으로써, 당신은 웹 브라우징 소프트웨어의 속도와 성능을 향상시킬 수 있다)," "Doing so on a regular basis will also free space on your hard drive and prevent system crashes(정기적으로 그렇게 하는 것은 또한 당신의 하드드라이브의 공간을 확보해 주고 시스템 충돌을 예방해줄 것이다)"와 마지막 문장 "By setting your web browser to delete cookies each time you close your browser, you can thwart these tracking attempts and reduce the risk of a security breach(브라우저를 종료할 때마다 쿠키를 삭제하도록 웹브라우저 설정을 해둠으로써, 당신은 이러한 추적 시도를 좌절시킬 수 있고, 보안 침해의 위험을 감소시킬 수 있다)."를 통해 '쿠키를 삭제하는 것의 이점'을 서술하고 있다. 따라서 '③ Benefits of Removing Cookies(쿠키 삭제의 이점)'가 글의 제목으로 가장 적절하다.

오답해설

① 쿠키가 시스템 성능을 저하시키고, 사생활 침해도 할 수 있다는 '쿠키의 위협'에 대해 일부 언급되지만, 주요 주제가 아니며, '쿠키 삭제를 통해 이러한 것들의 위험을 해소할 수 있다'는 것이 글의 요지이므로, 오답이다.
② 본문 후반에 '쿠키의 사생활 침해'에 대해 언급되지만, 전체 내용을 아우르는 것이 아니므로 제목으로 적절하지 않다.
④ 본문의 내용과는 관계없다.

해석

쿠키 파일은 꽤 작지만, 여전히 그것들은 축적될 수 있고 당신의 시스템 성능을 떨어뜨릴 수 있다. 쿠키를 삭제하는 시간을 할애함으로써, 당신은 웹 브라우징 소프트웨어의 속도와 성능을 향상시킬 수 있다. 정기적으로 그렇게 하는 것은 또한 당신의 하드드라이브의 공간을 확보해 주고 당신의 컴퓨터에 충분한 공간이 없을 때 종종 발생하는 시스템 충돌을 예방해줄 것이다. 게다가, 많은 쿠키들이 해롭지는 않지만, 일부는 인터넷상 당신의 모든 움직임을 추적하는 데 사용될 수도 있다. 사업체들은 소비자 행동을 연구하기 위해 종종 이러한 추적 쿠키를 사용하지만, 많은 컴퓨터 사용자들은 그것들을 사생활 침해로 여긴다. 브라우저를 종료할 때마다 쿠키를 삭제하도록 웹브라우저 설정을 해둠으로써, 당신은 이러한 추적 시도를 좌절시킬 수 있고, 보안 침해의 위험을 감소시킬 수 있다.

① 인터넷 쿠키의 위협
② 어떻게 쿠키가 사생활을 침해하는가?
③ 쿠키 삭제의 이점
④ 쿠키 사용의 장단점

어휘

performance 성능
on a regular basis 정기적으로, 규칙적으로
free 해방시키다, 석방하다
crash (시스템의) 고장, 충돌
invasion 침해, 침입
attempt 시도
threat 위협
pros and cons 장단점
prevent 예방하다, 막다
sufficient 충분한
thwart 좌절시키다, 방해하다
breach 침해, 위반
invade 침입하다, 침해하다

09 정답 ③

정답해설

해당 지문은 '쿠키의 정의와 작용 원리'에 대해 설명하고 있으며, ② 이하에서 'For example(예를 들어)'을 이용해 이에 대한 구체적인 예시를 서술하고 있다. 그러나 ③에서는 '쿠키를 사용하는 것이 사생활 침해의 우려를 불러일으킨다.'고 언급하고 있으므로, 쿠키의 '작용 원리'와는 거리가 먼 내용이다. 따라서 글의 흐름상 가장 어색한 것은 ③이다.

오답해설

③의 'such information(그러한 정보)'이 ②의 'some personal or financial information(개인정보 또는 결제 정보)'을 가리키는 것으로 혼동하지 않도록 주의한다.

해석

쿠키는 웹 서버 또는 웹호스팅 사이트에 의해 생성되고 사용자의 컴퓨터에 저장되는 미래의 접속을 위해 준비된 정보 조각이다. ① 최초의 쿠키는 사용자들이 좋아하는 웹사이트에 그들이 방문할 때마다 자신을 확인하는 긴 과정을 겪을 필요 없이 더 쉽게 접속하는 것을 돕기 위해 간단한 매커니즘으로 만들어졌다. ② 예를 들어, 특정한 사이트에 당신의 첫 번째 방문에서, 당신은 미래에 그 사이트에 접속하기 위해 요구되는 이름과 심지어 개인정보 또는 결제 정보를 밝히도록 요청받을 수도 있다. ③ <u>쿠키가 그러한 정보를 포함하고 있기 때문에, 사이트에서 그것들을 사용하는 것은 수많은 사생활 침해 우려를 불러일으킨다</u>. ④ 그리고 그 사이트는 이 정보를 포함하고 있는 쿠키를 당신의 시스템에 배치시킬 것이다. 그리고 당신이 재방문할 때, 그것은 당신이 누구이고 사이트에 접근 권한이 있는지 확인하기 위해 쿠키에 기반하여 정보를 요청할 것이다.

어휘

generate 생성하다, 발생시키다
access 접근, 접속; 접근하다, 접속하다
cook up 만들다
lengthy 긴, 지루한
identify 확인하다, 식별하다
reveal 밝히다, 드러내다
gain 얻다, 획득하다
place 위치[배치]시키다
authorization 권한
store 저장하다
batch 묶음, 무리, 다발
go through 겪다, 경험하다
process 과정, 절차
given 특정한, 정해진
require 요구하다, 필요하다
contain 포함하다
determine 결정하다, 알아내다

오답률 TOP 3

10 정답 ①

정답해설

해당 지문은 '쿠키에 대한 사생활 보호 운동가들의 주장'이 옳지 않다는 것을 밝히고 있다. 본문 초·중반에 걸쳐 이러한 주장에 대해 자세히 언급한 후, "According to the bulletin, none of this is close to the truth(이것들 중 진실에 가까운 것은 없다)."라고 서술하고 있으므로, 해당 주장이 사실이 아닌 것을 알 수 있다. 따라서 (A)에는 'incorrect(틀린)' 또는 'inaccurate(부정확한)'가 들어가는 것이 알맞다. 또한 이후 문장 "Information gathered using cookies can also be recorded in Web servers' log files(쿠키를 이용해 수집된 정보는 웹 서버의 로그 파일에서도 또한 기록될 수 있다)."를 통해 쿠키의 역할을 로그 파일도 동일하게 수행할 수 있음을 밝히고 있다. 그런데 쿠키가 이용되는 것은 그것이 '더 쉽고 편리하기' 때문이라는 것을 유추할 수 있으므로, (B)에는 easier(더 쉬운) 또는 simpler(더 간단한)가 들어가는 것이 자연스럽다. 따라서 정답은 '① incorrect(틀린)-easier(더 쉬운)'이다.

오답해설

② (A)에는 문맥상 '부정확한'이라는 의미의 'inaccurate'가 들어갈 수 있으나, (B)에는 far(먼)의 비교급인 'further(더 먼)'가 들어가는 것이 어색하므로 오답이다.
③ "none of this is close to the truth(이것들 중 진실에 가까운 것은 없다)."로 보아 사생활 보호 운동가들의 주장이 사실이 아니므로, (A)에 'proven(입증된)'이 들어가는 것은 문맥상 어색하다.
④ 웹 서버 로그 파일을 통해 할 수 있는 정보 수집을 쿠키를 통해서 하고 있는 것이므로, 쿠키가 그것을 더 느리게 한다는 것은 문맥상 어색하다. 따라서 (B)에 'slower(더 느린)'가 들어가는 것은 적절하지 않다.

해석

U.S. Department of Energy's Computer Incident Advisory Capability 가 금요일에 발행된 정보 회람을 통해 "쿠키가 웹사이트 운영자들에 의해 인터넷 사용자를 감시하거나 그들의 컴퓨터에 유해한 코드를 전달할 가능성이 있다는 사생활 보호 운동가들에 의한 최근의 주장은 (A) 틀리다"라고 말했다. 웹 쿠키는 일반적으로 하드 드라이브를 스캔하고 컴퓨터 사용자에 대한 정보를 수집할 수 있는 프로그램이라고 여겨지고, 그러한 정보는 이른바 비밀번호, 신용카드 번호, 그리고 당신의 컴퓨터의 소프트웨어 목록을 포함한다. 회람에 따르면, 이것들 중 진실에 가까운 것은 없다. 쿠키를 이용해 수집된 정보는 웹 서버의 로그 파일에서도 또한 기록될 수 있다. 쿠키는 단지 그것을 (B) 더 쉽게 만들어줄 뿐이다. 서버는 쿠키를 통해 당신의 이름이나 이메일 주소, 또는 당신의 컴퓨터에 대한 어떤 것도 알아낼 수 없다.

① 틀린 – 더 쉬운
② 부정확한 – 더 먼
③ 입증된 – 더 간단한
④ 널리 퍼진 – 더 느린

어휘

claim 주장
potential 가능성
spy on 염탐하다, 감시하다
issue 발행하다
allegedly 주장한[전해진, 알려진] 바에 의하면, 이른바
find out 알아내다
widespread 널리 퍼진
activist 운동가, 활동가
operator 운영자
bulletin 회람, 고시
inaccurate 부정확한

기적사 DAY 05

| 01 | ③ | 02 | ① | 03 | ② | 04 | ① | 05 | ② |
| 06 | ③ | 07 | ③ | 08 | ① | 09 | ④ | 10 | ④ |

01 정답 ③

정답해설

밑줄 친 단어의 의미는 문맥상 '범인'으로 사용되었고, 유의어로 ③ criminal 이 적절하다.

해석

벳시는 전하는 바에 의하면 체포에 저항한 후, **범인**이 구타당했고 심각한 상태라는 공지를 하루 후에 인터넷에서 읽었다.
① 망명자
② 사망자, 치사성, 숙명
③ 범인
④ 미숙한, 풋내기

어휘

allegedly 주장한(전해진) 바에 의하면, 이른바
purgee 망명자
criminal 범인
fatality 사망자, 치사성, 숙명
fledgling 미숙한, 풋내기

오답률 TOP 3
02 정답 ①

정답해설

밑줄 친 단어는 문맥상 '난민'이라는 의미로 사용되었으며, 유의어로는 ① refugee가 적절하다.

해석

그 망명 후에 **난민** 계급으로서의 그들의 지속적인 존재는 가장 유명한 시리아 신조의 위험과 타락상을 끊임없이 상기시켜 주는 것이었다.
① 난민, 이탈자, 망명자
② 악당, 악한, 악역
③ 사상자, 희생자, 피해자
④ 동등, 기준타수

어휘

existence 존재, 현존, 생존
villain 악당, 악한, 악역
par 동등, 기준타수
refugee 난민, 이탈자, 망명자
casualty 사상자, 희생자, 피해자

오답률 TOP 2
03 정답 ②

정답해설

밑줄 친 단어는 문맥상 '불안감'으로 사용되었고, 유의어로는 ② apprehension 이 적절하다.

해석

그들이 목장에 가까이 갈 때마다 그녀의 **불안감**은 더욱 커졌다.
① 분노, 분개
② 불안감
③ 이해, 감사, 상승, 강세
④ 선동 연설가

어휘

ranch 목장
apprehension 불안감
demagogue 선동 연설가
indignation 분노
appreciation 이해, 감사, 상승, 강세

04 정답 ①

정답해설

퇴근했냐는 말에 '아니오.'라고 대답했으므로 그에 상응하는 표현이 자연스럽다. 따라서 정답은 ① She's just stepped out(잠시 나가신 것 같습니다)이다.

오답해설

나머지 보기들은 퇴근한 것이 아니라 지금 현재 자리에 없다는 내용이 가장 적절한 빈칸에 문맥상 알맞지 않은 표현들이다.

해석

A: TJ와 통화할 수 있습니까?
B: 지금 안 계신데요.
A: 퇴근하셨나요?
B: 아니오. 잠시 나가신 것 같습니다.
① 그녀는 잠시 나갔다
② 그녀는 당신과 화해한다
③ 그녀는 항상 배수진을 친다
④ 그녀는 몹시 지쳐있다

어휘

yet 아직
make up with~ ~와 화해하다
burn the candle at both ends 몹시 지치다
step out 나가다
burn one's bridge 배수진을 치다

05 정답 ②

정답해설

② 출제 포인트: 목적격 관계대명사 생략

해당 문장의 경우 'than'의 품사를 구별하는 게 포인트이다. 해당 문장에서 'than'을 전치사로 보아야 하며 이 경우 접속사가 없는데 두 문장이 연결되어 있으므로 목적격 관계대명사가 누락되어 있다는 것을 유추할 수 있다. 선행사는 명사구 'Captain Jack'이며 전치사 'than'의 목적어 자리에 와야 하므로 목적격 관계대명사 whom을 사용해야 한다. 따라서 'than'을 'than whom'으로 수정해야 한다.

※ 관계대명사가 만들어지는 과정

Here is Captain Jack. + There is no braver soldier than Captain Jack.
(선행사가 사람을 뜻하는 명사구 'Captain Jack'이며 전치사 'than'의 목적어에 해당하므로 목적격 관계대명사 'whom'을 사용)

→ Here is Captain Jack whom there is no braver soldier than. (전치사 'than'을 목적격 관계대명사 'whom' 앞으로 이동)
→ Here is Captain Jack than whom there is no braver soldier.

오답해설

① 출제 포인트: 해석에 주의해야 할 표현

「A+shy of+B」와 「A+after+B」의 구분 여부를 묻는 문제로 「A+shy of+B」의 경우 'B되기 A전'을 뜻하며 「A+after+B」의 경우 'B지나고 A'를 뜻한다. 해당 문제는 주어진 해석이 '자신의 95번째 생일 이틀 전'이므로 'shy of'를 사용하는 것이 옳다.

③ 출제 포인트: 불완전자동사 appear

'appear'는 불완전자동사의 경우 주격 보어로 올 수 있는 것은 다음과 같다.
1. appear+주격 보어[명사(구)]
2. appear+주격 보어[형용사(구)]
3. appear+주격 보어[to be+명사(구)]
4. appear+주격 보어[to be+형용사(구)]
5. appear+주격 보어[to+동사원형]

해당 문장은 2번 「appear+주격 보어[형용사(구)]」에 해당하므로 옳은 문장이다.

④ 출제 포인트: 자동사로 착각하기 쉬운 완전타동사

'enter'가 '(활동·상황 등에) 진입하다'를 뜻하는 경우 완전타동사에 해당하며 이때 'enter'와 목적어 사이에 전치사를 사용하는 경우 비문이 된다. 해당 문장은 주어진 해석이 '국면에 진입했다'이므로 'entered'와 목적어 'a new phase' 사이에 전치사를 사용하지 않는 것이 옳다.

06 정답 ③

정답해설

③ 출제 포인트: 완전자동사

'consist'는 완전자동사로 전치사 'of' 없이 목적어가 올 수 없으며 수동태를 사용할 수 없다. 따라서 'consist'가 나오는 문제의 경우 수동태 'be consisted of'로 사용되었는지를 꼭 확인해야 한다. 해당 문장은 완전자동사 'consist'가 'be consisted of'로 사용되었으므로 틀린 문장이다. 따라서 'are consisted of'를 'consist of'로 수정해야 한다.

오답해설

① 출제 포인트: so[neither]+조동사/be동사+주어: '~또한 그렇다'

「so+조동사/be동사+주어」와 「neither+조동사/be동사+주어」 모두 '~도 또한 그러하다'를 뜻하나 앞 문장의 부정 유무에 차이가 있다.
1. 긍정문, and+so+조동사/be동사+주어: ~도 또한 그러하다
2. 부정문, and+neither+조동사/be동사+주어: ~도 또한 그러하다

또한 「so+조동사/be동사+주어」와 「neither+조동사/be동사+주어」는 주어-동사의 도치가 일어나며 이때 조동사/be동사를 사용하는 것이 포인트이므로 조동사의 시제와 인칭 반영에 유의해야 한다.

해당 문장은 부정문 뒤에 'neither+be동사+주어'를 옳게 사용하였다.

② 출제 포인트: 시간의 부사구/부사절

'since+명사구'는 시간의 부사구로 동사에 현재완료, 현재완료진행형을 사용할 수 있다.

④ 출제 포인트: 해석에 주의해야 할 표현

'per person'과 'personal'의 구분 여부를 묻는 문제로 'per person'의 경우 '한 사람당'을 뜻하며 'personal'의 경우 '개인의, 개인적인'을 뜻한다. 해당 문제는 주어진 해석이 '개인적'이므로 'personal'을 사용하는 것이 옳다.

07 정답 ③

정답해설

③ 출제 포인트: 관계대명사 vs. 관계부사

관계대명사와 관계부사를 구분하는 포인트는 뒤따라오는 문장구조의 완전성이다. 뒤따라오는 문장구조가 완전하면 관계부사를 사용해야 하고 뒤따

라오는 문장구조가 불완전하면 관계대명사를 사용해야 한다. 해당 문장의 경우 뒤따라오는 문장구조 「주어＋조동사＋서술어(완전자동사)＋수식어(부사구)＋수식어(부사구)」가 완전하므로 관계부사를 사용하는 것이 옳다. 따라서 선행사가 시간을 나타내는 명사구 'an age'이므로 관계대명사 'which'를 관계부사 'when'으로 수정해야 한다.

오답해설

① **출제 포인트: of＋추상명사**
전치사 'of'는 일반적으로 추상명사와 결합하는 경우 형용사로 바꾸어 사용할 수 있다. 즉, 「of＋추상명사 → 형용사」의 공식이 성립한다. 또한 전치사 'of'가 「형용사＋추상명사」 형태의 명사구와 결합하는 경우 형용사는 부사로 바꾸어 사용할 수 있고 추상명사는 형용사로 바꾸어 사용할 수 있다. 즉, 「of＋형용사＋추상명사 → 부사＋형용사」의 공식이 성립한다. 따라서 해당 문장의 경우 'of little help'를 'little helpful'로 바꾸어 사용할 수 있다. 또한 'little helpful'에서 'little'은 형용사인 'helpful'을 수식하는 부사로 형용사와 부사의 형태가 같음에 유의해야 한다.

② **출제 포인트: 현재분사 vs. 과거분사**
해당 문장의 경우 분사 뒤의 구조가 명사구 'full-time education'이므로 과거분사 'received'를 사용할 수 없으며 현재분사 'receiving'을 사용해야 한다.

④ **출제 포인트: to부정사의 형용사적 용법**
to부정사의 형용사적 용법은 수식어와 보어 역할로 나눌 수 있으며, 수식어 역할을 하는 경우 한정적 용법에 그리고 보어 역할을 하는 경우 서술적 용법에 해당한다. 한정적 용법의 경우 「명사＋to＋동사원형」의 형태로 사용되며 서술적 용법의 경우 다음과 같이 사용된다.
1. 불완전자동사＋주격 보어[to＋동사원형]
2. 불완전타동사＋목적어＋목적격 보어[to＋동사원형]
3. be＋과거분사[불완전타동사]＋목적격 보어[to＋동사원형]
4. 명사＋과거분사＋목적격 보어[to＋동사원형]
따라서 해당 문장은 3번 「be＋과거분사[불완전타동사]＋목적격 보어[to＋동사원형]」에 해당하므로 'to be'는 to부정사의 형용사적 용법 중 서술적 용법으로 사용되었다.

해석
교육에 의해 제공되는 아동기와 성년 사이의 현대적 경계선은 19세기 중 많은 부분에 대해서는 우리에게 거의 도움이 되지 못한다. 부유층 학교에 다니던 많은 아이들이 전 시간제로 교육을 받고 있는 그 나이에 당시의 가난한 아이들은 일을 한 지 10년이 되어있었다. 실제로 19세기라는 이 기간을 통틀어, 일하는 아이들은 오늘날 가난한 국가에서만큼 흔했으며, 19세기 대부분 동안, 일하는 아이들은 경제적으로 중요하다고 여겨졌다.

어휘
borderline 경계선
contemporary 현대의, 동시대의
receive 받다, 수용하다

08 정답 ①

정답해설
해당 지문은 '아리스토텔레스의 형이상학'에 대한 내용이다. 마지막 문장 "Ultimately he denied Plato's ideas as poetic but empty language; as a scientist and empiricist he preferred to focus on the reality of the material world(궁극적으로 그는 낭만적이지만 공허한 언어로서의 플라톤의 사상을 거부했다. 과학자이자 경험주의자로서 그는 물질세계의 실제에 집중하기를 선호했다)."를 통해 아리스토텔레스가 플라톤의 이론을 따르지 않았음을 알 수 있으므로, 빈칸에 가장 적절한 것은 '① rejection(거부)'이다.

오답해설
아리스토텔레스는 플라톤의 사상을 거부했으므로, '③ admiration(찬양)', '④ development(발전)'는 본문의 내용과 일치하지 않는 표현이다.

해석
형이상학이라고 우리에게 알려진 것은 아리스토텔레스가 "제1 철학"이라고 부르던 것이다. 형이상학은 존재에 대한 보편적 원리, 존재 자체의 추상적 특징에 대한 연구를 포함한다. 아리스토텔레스 형이상학의 출발점은 아마도 플라톤의 이데아론에 대한 그의 거부이다. 플라톤의 이론에서 사물은 변하기 쉽고 그것들 자체로 실제가 아니다. 오히려 그것들은 공통적인 명칭을 통해 이상적이고 영원하며 불변하는 이데아와 조화를 이루며, 이러한 이데아는 오직 지성을 통해서만 인식될 수 있다. 그러므로 현세에서 아름답다고 인식되는 것은 사실 미의 이데아의 불완전한 현시이다. 이 이론에 대한 아리스토텔레스의 논쟁은 다양하다. 궁극적으로 그는 낭만적이지만 공허한 언어로서의 플라톤의 사상을 거부했다. 과학자이자 경험주의자로서 그는 물질세계의 실제에 집중하기를 선호했다.
① 거부
② 혐오
③ 찬양
④ 발전

어휘
metaphysics 형이상학
principle 원리, 원칙
abstract 추상적인
Theory of Forms 이데아론
in oneself 그 자체로는, 본질적으로, 원래
rather 오히려, 차라리
correspond 조화하다, 일치하다, 부합하다
eternal 영원한
form [철학] 이데아; 형상(形相)
intellect 지성
manifestation 현시, (유령, 영혼 등이) 나타남
ultimately 궁극적으로
poetic 낭만적인, 시적인
rejection 거부, 거절
admiration 찬양, 감탄
involve 포함하다, 수반하다
being 존재, 생명체
existence 존재
material object 사물
immutable 불변의
perceive 인식하다, 지각하다, 이해하다
deny 거부하다, 부인하다
empiricist 경험주의자
detestation 혐오

09 정답 ④

정답해설
해당 지문은 고대 그리스인들이 믿었던 '4원소(earth, water, air, and fire (흙, 물, 공기, 불))'에 대해 서술하고 있으며, 마지막 문장에서는 4원소와 현대 과학에서의 물질의 4가지 상태에 대해 비교하고 있다. 그런데 ④에서 갑자기 아리스토텔레스가 주장했던 제5원소(aether, 에테르)에 대해 언급하는 것은 문맥상 어색하다. 따라서 글의 흐름상 가장 어색한 문장은 ④이다.

오답해설
나머지는 문맥상 자연스러우므로 오답이다.

해석
아리스토텔레스와 같은 고대 그리스인들은 모든 것을 구성하는 4원소, 즉 흙, 물, 공기 그리고 불이 있다고 믿었다. ① 이 4원소가 모든 물질을 구성하고 있다는 생각은 오랫동안 철학, 과학, 그리고 의학의 기초가 되었다. ② 4원소는 심지어 사람이 지닐 수 있는 4가지 기질을 묘사하기 위해 사용되기도 하였으며, 히포크라테스는 4원소를 신체에서 발견할 수 있는 4가지 "체액"을 묘사하기 위해 사용했다. ③ 이러한 이론들은 사람이 정신적으로, 신체적으로 모두 건강하기 위해서 기질과 체액이 서로 균형을 이루어야 한다고 말한다. ④ **별이 지구의**

원소로 구성되어있다는 것은 이상하게 보였기 때문에 아리스토텔레스는 에테르라고 하는 5번째 원소가 있다고 말했다. 이제 우리는 이러한 과거의 이론들이 틀렸다는 것을 알고 있지만, 어떤 면에서 4원소는 현대 과학이 동의하는 물질의 4가지 상태, 즉 고체(흙), 액체(물), 기체(공기), 그리고 플라스마(불)와 일치한다.

어휘

be made up of ~로 구성되다
describe 묘사하다
humor 체액(고대 생리에서 인간의 체질, 기질을 정한다고 생각되었던 4액)
aether 에테르, 하늘, 창공, (옛사람들이 상상한) 대기 밖의 정기(精氣), 영기(靈氣)
earthly 지구의, 이 세상의
plasma 플라스마 (고도로 이온화된 기체)
cornerstone 기초, 초석
temperament 기질
align 나란히 하다, 일렬로 서다, 일치하다

discourse 담화, 담론, 논설
associate A with B A를 B와 관련시켜 생각하다
overthrow 전복, 타도
in favor of …에 찬성[지지]하여
empiricism 경험주의
embed 깊숙이 박다
society -회, 단체, 협회
replace A as B A를 대신하여 B가 되다
backbone 중추, 근간
profession -계, 종사자들
literate 글을 읽고 쓸 줄 아는, 교양 있는
population 주민, 시민, 사람들
curb 억제하다, 억압하다
background 배경, 경력, 학력, 경험
authority 권위
broadly 대략적으로, 넓게
rational 합리적인, 이성적인
dominate 지배하다
academy 협회, 학회
maturation 성숙
popularization 대중화
regard 존중하다, 중요시하다
dominance 지배, 우세, 권세

오답률 TOP 1
10 정답 ④

정답해설

해당 지문은 '계몽주의 시대의 과학의 발전'에 대해 서술하고 있다. 해당 구 "associated scientific advancement with the overthrow of religion and traditional authority, which had oppressed science, in favor of the development of free speech and thought(자유로운 언론과 생각의 발전에 찬성하여 과학을 억압하던 종교와 전통적인 권위의 전복과 과학적 진보를 연결 지어 생각했다)."를 통해 '전통적인 권위가 전복되었음'을 알 수 있으며, 이후 "At the time, science became dominated by scientific societies and academies(그 당시 과학은 과학 단체와 학회들이 지배하고 있었다)."를 통해 '과학이 과학 단체와 학회에 의해 지배되었다'고 언급하고 있으므로, 계몽주의로 인해 기존의 전통적인 권위는 과학에 대한 지배력을 잃었다는 것을 유추할 수 있다. 따라서 글의 내용과 일치하는 것은 ④이다.

오답해설

① 첫 문장에서 과학적 혁명이 계몽주의의 토대를 쌓았다고 언급하고 있으므로 일치하지 않는다.
② 계몽주의 시대에는 종교와 전통적인 권위가 전복되었으므로 내용과 일치하지 않는다.
③ 두 번째 문장에서 '계몽주의 작가들과 사상가들은 자유로운 언론과 생각의 발전에 찬성하였다'고 언급하고 있으므로, 내용과 일치하지 않는다.

해석

과학적 혁명은 계몽주의 시대의 토대를 쌓았고 과학은 계몽 담론과 사상에 있어서 중요한 역할을 하게 되었다. 많은 계몽주의 작가들과 사상가들은 과학에 지식이 있었고, 자유로운 언론과 생각의 발전에 찬성하여 과학을 억압하던 종교와 전통적인 권위의 전복과 과학적 진보를 연결 지어 생각했다. 포괄적으로 말하자면 계몽주의 과학은 경험주의와 이성적인 사상을 대단히 중시했고, 진보와 발전에 대한 계몽주의적 이상이 깊숙이 내재되어 있었다. 그 당시 과학은 과학 단체와 학회들이 지배하고 있었으며, 이것이 대학을 대신하여 과학 연구 및 개발의 중심지가 되었다. 단체와 학회들은 또한 과학계 성숙의 중추였다. 또 하나의 중요한 발전은 점점 더 글을 읽고 쓸 줄 아는 사람들 사이에서의 과학의 대중화였다.
① 계몽주의가 과학적 혁명을 이끌었다.
② 계몽주의 사상가들은 종교적 신념을 매우 중요시했다.
③ 계몽주의 시대에 언론과 생각의 자유는 억제되었다.
④ 계몽주의는 과학에 대한 전통적인 권위의 지배력을 잃게 만들었다.

어휘

revolution 혁명
the Enlightenment 계몽주의 (시대)
come to ~하게 되다
foundation 토대, 근거, 기초
leading 가장 중요한, 선두적인

기적사 DAY 06

결국엔 성정혜 영어 하프모의고사

| 01 | ① | 02 | ② | 03 | ③ | 04 | ② | 05 | ③ |
| 06 | ③ | 07 | ④ | 08 | ① | 09 | ③ | 10 | ③ |

01 정답 ①
19 국가직

정답해설

'discern'은 '구별하다'라는 뜻을 가진 동사이다. 밑줄 친 단어 전에 내용으로 잡지 구독자들이 정확한 정보를 얻게 될 것이라고 하였으므로 무엇이 그들이 산업과 관계되는 것인지 정확하게 구별할 수 있다는 것으로 유추할 수 있다. 따라서 유의어 관계에 있는 보기는 ① distinguish이다.

해석

Natural Gas World 구독자들은 이 산업에서 어떤 일들이 일어나고 있는지에 대한 정확하고 믿을 수 있는 주요한 사실들과 수치들을 받게 될 것이다. 그래서 그들은 무엇이 그들의 사업과 관계되는 것인지 충분하게 **구별할** 수 있다.
① 구별하다, 식별하다
② 강화하다
③ 약화시키다
④ 버리다, 포기하다

어휘

subscriber 구독자
figure 수치
discern 구별하다
distinguish 구별하다
undermine 약화시키다
reliable 믿을 수 있는
industry 산업
concern 관계되다
strengthen 강화하다
abandon 버리다, 포기하다

02 정답 ②
19 국가직

정답해설

지문에서 Ms. West가 은메달리스트이므로 경기 내내 눈에 띄었다는 것이 알맞은 글의 내용이다. 따라서 'stood out(stand out)'은 '눈에 띄다, 돋보이다'라는 의미를 갖는 단어이다. 'stood out'과 비슷한 의미로는 ② was impressive(인상적이었다)이다.

오답해설

'overwhelmed'는 '압도당한'이라는 뜻이므로 반의어이다. 'depressed'도 은메달리스트에 관련된 내용에 적절하지 않다.

해석

여성 1,500m 대회의 은메달리스트인 Ms. West는 경기 내내 **돋보였다**.
① 압도되었다
② 인상적이었다
③ 우울했었다
④ 긍정적이었다

어휘

stand out 돋보이다
impressive 인상적인
optimistic 긍정적인
overwhelm 압도하다
depressed 우울한

03 정답 ③
19 국가직

정답해설

'compulsory'는 '강제적인, 의무적인'이란 뜻을 가진 형용사로 비슷한 뜻을 가진 단어는 ③ mandatory(의무적인)이다.

해석

학교 교육은 미국의 모든 아이들에게 **의무적**이지만, 학교 출석이 요구되어지는 나이대는 주마다 다양하다.
① 보완적인
② 체계적인
③ 의무적인
④ 혁신적인

어휘

schooling 학교 교육
vary 다르다, 다양하다
systematic 체계적인
innovative 혁신적인
compulsory 강제적인, 의무적인
complementary 보완적인
mandatory 의무적인

04 정답 ②
19 국가직

정답해설

밑줄 다음에 '젓가락으로 집어서 소스에 찍어 먹어라.'고 하였으므로 먹는 방법을 물어보는 것을 유추할 수 있다. 따라서 빈칸에 들어갈 말은 ② how do I eat them(제가 그것들을 어떻게 먹으면 되나요?)이다.

해석

A: 딤섬 약간 드셔 보시겠어요?
B: 네, 감사합니다. 맛있어 보여요. 안에 무엇이 들어있나요?
A: 이것들은 돼지고기와 다진 야채들이고 저것들은 새우가 들어 있어요.
B: 그리고 음, 전 그것들을 어떻게 먹으면 되나요?
A: 이렇게 젓가락으로 하나 집어서 소스에 찍으면 돼요. 아주 쉽습니다.
B: 네, 한번 해볼게요.
① 그것들은 얼마인가요?
② 전 그것들을 어떻게 먹으면 되나요?
③ 그것들은 얼마나 맵나요?
④ 당신은 그것들을 어떻게 요리하나요?

어휘

delicious 맛있는
vegetable 채소
chopped 다진
dip 찍다

05 정답 ③
18 국가직

정답해설

③ **출제 포인트: 완전자동사**
result in은 '결과를 낳다, 야기하다'라는 의미로 수동태로 사용하지 않는다. 따라서 has resulted in으로 고치는 것이 옳다.

오답해설

① **출제 포인트: to부정사의 명사적 용법**
to imagine은 가주어 It의 진주어로 알맞게 사용되었다.

② **출제 포인트: 동사 관용표현**
'take+목적어+for granted'는 '~을 당연한 것으로 여기다'라는 의미의 구문이다. 여기서 take 뒤의 목적어가 진목적어이므로 'take it for granted that S V' 구문과는 구별해서 사용해야 한다.

④ **출제 포인트: 현재분사 vs. 과거분사**
문장의 주어인 deforestation이 문맥상 능동적으로 영향을 미치는 것이므로 현재분사인 affecting이 적절하게 쓰였다. 즉, as the deforestation is affecting wilderness regions ~가 affecting wilderness regions ~의 분사구문으로 바뀐 문장이다.

해석

숲의 아름다움과 풍성함이 없는 삶을 상상하기란 어렵다. 그러나 과학자들은 우리가 숲을 당연한 것으로 여겨서는 안 된다고 경고한다. 몇몇 추정에 따르면, 삼림 벌채는 전 세계 숲의 80퍼센트에 달하는 손실을 가져 왔다. 최근, 삼림 벌채는 태평양의 온난한 열대 우림과 같은 황무지 지역에 영향을 미치며, 전 지구적인 문제가 되었다.

어휘

richness 풍부함, 풍성함
take ~ for granted ~을 당연한 것으로 여기다
deforestation 삼림 벌채   temperate 온난한
wilderness 황야, 황무지

Day 06

오답률 TOP 3

06 정답 ③
18 국가직

정답해설

③ **출제 포인트: 현재분사 vs. 과거분사**
attention과 pay는 서로 수동의 관계이다. 따라서 attention (which is) paid의 구조가 되도록 현재분사인 paying을 과거분사인 paid로 고쳐야 한다.

오답해설

① **출제 포인트: 준사역동사 get**
means의 목적어로 동명사 getting이 사용되었고, 「get+목적어(stuff)+목적격 보어(done)」의 구조도 올바르다.

② **출제 포인트: 주격 관계대명사**
the issues를 선행사로 하는 주격 관계대명사 that이 사용되었다.

④ **출제 포인트: 사역동사 let**
do와 동사원형인 let이 병렬 구조를 이루고 있다. 「let+목적어(life)+목적격 보어(pass)」의 쓰임도 알맞다.

해석

집중은 어떤 일들을 해내는 것을 의미한다. 많은 사람들이 좋은 아이디어를 가지고 있지만 그것들을 실행에 옮기지는 않는다. 내게 있어서, 예를 들어, 기업가의 정의는 혁신과 독창성을 그 새로운 아이디어를 실행하는 능력과 결합시키는 사람이다. 어떤 사람들은 삶의 중심이 되는 이분법은 당신에게 흥미를 주거나 심려를 끼치는 문제들에 대해 긍정적인 태도를 지니거나 부정적인 태도를 지니는 것이라고 생각한다. 낙관적인 시점을 가지는 것이 나은지 비관적인 시선을 가지는 것이 나은지에 대한 이 질문에 많은 관심을 가진다. 내 생각에 더 나은 질문은 당신이 그것에 대해 뭔가를 할 것인지 혹은 그저 시간이 지나가 버리도록 만들 것인지 묻는 것이다.

어휘

entrepreneur 기업가   ingenuity 독창성
execute 실행하다   dichotomy 양분, 이분

07 정답 ④
18 국가직

정답해설

④ **출제 포인트: 원급 비교**
우리말 의미 등으로 보아 '~만큼 …하지 않다'의 의미가 되도록 「not so+원급+as」의 원급비교 구문이 필요하다. 따라서 비교급 stingier를 stingy로 바꾸어야 한다.

오답해설

① **출제 포인트: 형용사 관용표현**
be good at은 '~을 잘한다'라는 관용표현으로 전치사 at 뒤의 동명사인 getting은 적절하다. 또한 get across는 '~을 이해시키다'라는 표현으로 적절하게 사용되었다.

② **출제 포인트: 비교급 비교**
주어는 The traffic jams로 복수형이다. 따라서 복수 동사 are가 사용되었다. '서울의 교통체증들'과 '다른 도시의 교통체증(들)'을 비교하고 있으므로 지시대명사 또한 복수형인 those가 적절하게 사용되었다. 비교 대상인 「any other+단수명사」도 알맞다.

③ **출제 포인트: 주어와 동사의 수일치**
주어는 동명사 형태인 Making ~ to이므로 동사는 3인칭 단수 동사인 is로 적절하게 사용되었다. the person과 you are speaking to 사이에는 목적격 관계대명사가 생략되었고 speak to의 목적어인 the person은 생략되어 관계대명사 이후에 불완전한 문장으로 옳게 사용되었다.

08 정답 ①
19 서울시

정답해설

빈칸 다음에 'Progress and innovation are inextricably entwined with risk and failure.'(진보와 혁신은 위험과 실패와 불가분의 관계에 있다.)고 하였으므로 실패를 두려워해서 도전을 하지 않는 것은 옳지 않다는 것을 알 수 있다. 따라서 빈칸에는 실패와 위험에 대해 두려워하지 않아야 한다는 표현이 와야 적절하다. 따라서 빈칸에 적절한 표현은 ① But we should not underestimate the importance of experimenting and taking risks, especially in these turbulent economic times(그러나 특히 이 격동적인 경제적인 시대에, 우리는 시도하는 것과 위험을 무릅쓰는 것의 중요성을 과소평가해서는 안 된다)이다.

오답해설

② But many organizations suffer from 'corporate anorexia nervosa' and have an unfavorable climate for enterprising people 하지만 많은 단체들이 집단 거식증을 겪고 있고 진취적인 사람들에 대해 우호적이지 않은 기운을 갖고 있다. – 본문에서 언급하고 있지 않으므로 빈칸에 적절하지 않다.

③ That is why we need a paradigm shift marking a transition to a future 저것은 우리가 미래로의 변천을 표시하면서 패러다임 전환을 필요로 하는 이유이다. – 본문에서 언급되고 있지 않은 내용이다.

④ That is why combinatoric innovation is not an efficient process 저것은 결합인 혁신이 효과적인 과정이 아니라는 이유이다. – 어떠한 혁신이 효과적인지 본문에서 서술하고 있지 않다.

해석

많은 사람들은 실패의 부정적인 결과를 성공의 보상보다 더 크게 여기기 때문에 위험을 회피한다. 실패를 경시하는 문화로 인해 우리는 더욱 위험을 무릅쓰지 않게 된다. <u>그러나 특히 이 격동적인 경제적인 시대에, 우리는 시도하는 것과 위험을 무릅쓰는 것의 중요성을 과소평가해서는 안 된다.</u> 진보와 혁신은 위험과 실패와 불가분의 관계에 있다.

① 그러나 특히 이 격동적인 경제적인 시대에, 우리는 시도하는 것과 위험을 무릅쓰는 것의 중요성을 과소평가해서는 안 된다.
② 하지만 많은 단체들이 집단 거식증을 겪고 있고 진취적인 사람들에 대해 우호적이지 않은 기운을 갖고 있다.
③ 저것은 우리가 미래로의 변천을 표시하면서 패러다임 전환을 필요로 하는 이유이다.
④ 저것은 결합적인 혁신이 효과적인 과정이 아니라는 이유이다.

어휘

risk-averse 위험을 회피하려는
outweigh ~보다 더 크다/대단하다
look down on ~을 경시하다/얕보다
risk one's neck 위험을 무릅쓰다
inextricably 불가분하게
underestimate 과소평가하다
turbulent 격동의, 격변의
anorexia (nervosa) 거식증
transition 과도, 이행, 이동
consequence 결과
reward 보상
likely 가능성 있는, 있음직한
progress 진보
entwine 얽히다
take risks 위험을 감수하다
suffer from ~로 고통스러워하다
enterprising 진취적인, 기획력 있는
combinatoric 결합의, 조합의

오답률 TOP 2
09 정답 ③
19 서울시

정답해설
본문의 후반부에 글쓴이 자신의 예를 들면서 인간의 본성은 자신이 얼마나 아팠고 많이 힘들었는지 알려지는 것을 좋아한다고 서술하고 있다. 따라서 빈칸에 가장 적절한 표현은 ③ pride in illness(질병에 대한 자부심)이다.

오답해설
다른 사람들에게 자신이 얼마나 아팠는지 알려주고 싶다고 본문에서 글쓴이가 언급하고 있으므로 죽음이나 병에 대한 공포에 관련된 언급은 빈칸에 적절하지 않다.

해석
인간의 본성은 호기심 많은 특징을 가지고 있지만, 가장 궁금한 것 중 하나는 질병에 대한 자부심이다. 아무도 끊임없이 고장 나는 자동차를 가지고 있는 것이 좋은 것이라고 생각하지 않는다. 사람들은 오래 달린 후에 차가 몇 주 동안 완전히 쓸모없게 되거나, 가장 능숙한 기계공들조차도 바로잡을 수 없는 이상한 문제를 끊임없이 발전시키고 있다고 자랑하지 않는다. 하지만 그것이 사람들이 자신의 몸에 대해 느끼는 방법이다. 만족스럽게 움직이는 몸을 갖는 것은 재미없고 오히려 평범한 것으로 여겨진다. 섬세한 소화는 아름다운 여인의 조건에 거의 필수 불가결한 것이다. 나는 나 스스로 병을 자랑하기 위한 충동을 알고 있다. 나는 단지 한번 병을 앓은 적이 있을 뿐이지만, 나는 사람들이 내가 그때 얼마나 많이 아팠는지 아는 것을 좋아하며, 죽지 않고 거의 죽은 다른 사람들을 만났을 때 나는 화가 난다.
① 질병에 대한 공포
② 자동차에 대한 흥미
③ 질병에 대한 자부심
④ 죽음의 공포

어휘

nature 본성, 천성
motor car 자동차
out of order 고장 난
skillful 숙련된, 능숙한
put right 고치다, 바로 잡다
plebeian 천한, 보통의
digestion 소화
indispensable 필수적인, 없어서는 안 되는
trait 특성, 특징
perpetually 영속적으로
boast 자랑(하다)
mechanic 정비공
uninteresting 재미없는, 시시한
delicate 허약한, 섬세한
equipment 갖추고 있어야 하는 것, 준비, 기술, 능력
impulse 충동, 자극
come across 우연히 만나다
vexed 화난
phobia 공포증

오답률 TOP 1
10 정답 ③
19 서울시

정답해설
본문 초반에 로데오에서 하는 것 두 가지를 설명하고 있다. 첫 번째가 roping young steers(어린 수소들을 올가미로 잡는 것)이고 두 번째가 riding adult bulls(성년의 황소들을 타는 것)이다. 그다음에 첫 번째를 하는 이유는 재산을 표시하고 동물들에게 약을 주기 위해 필요하다고 설명하고 있다. 그리고 빈칸 다음에 두 번째는 이러한 이유가 있는 것이 아니고 순수한 스포츠라고 서술하고 있으므로 앞의 것과 상반되는 내용이라는 것을 알 수 있다. 따라서 빈칸에 알맞은 표현은 'On the other hand'이다. 따라서 정답은 ③이다.

오답해설
나머지는 글의 문맥상 빈칸에 적절하지 않다.

해석
미국 서부의 넓고 탁 트인 땅에서, 소를 기르는 것이 생계를 유지하는 한 가지 방법이다. 그의 말에 올라탄 카우보이 이미지는 낯익은 것이지만, 실제로는 여자들도 목장 일에 참여한다. 이런 현실은 카우보이들과 카우걸들이 젊은 기수들이 어린 수소들을 올가미로 잡는 것과 성년의 황소들을 타는 것을 경쟁하는 로데오에서 볼 수 있다. 수소 주변에서 올가미를 던지는 것은 어린 동물들에게 약을 주거나 그들의 재산으로 수소들을 표시하기 위해 반드시 목장주들이 해야만 하는 것이다. 반면에, 크고 화가 난 소의 등에 타는 것은 순수한 스포츠이다. - 잔인하고 위험한 스포츠. 하지만 그러한 위험은 로데오를 사랑하는 남자들과 여자들을 막지 못한다.
① 예를 들면
② 간단히 말해서
③ 반면에
④ 같은 이유로

어휘

open land 평야
cattle 소 떼
ranch 목장
steer 거세한 수소
property 재산
brutal 잔인한
to take an example(=for example) 예를 들면
to be brief 간단히 말해서, 요컨대
on the other hand 반면에, 다른 한편으로는
by the same token 같은 이유로, 마찬가지로
herd 몰다, 모아서 몰다
make a living 생계를 꾸리다
rope 밧줄을 던져 잡다
rancher 목장에서 일하는 사람
sport 장난, 재미, 스포츠

기적사 DAY 07

결국엔 성정혜 영어 하프모의고사

| 01 | ③ | 02 | ④ | 03 | ③ | 04 | ② | 05 | ④ |
| 06 | ③ | 07 | ③ | 08 | ④ | 09 | ① | 10 | ③ |

01 정답 ③

정답해설

밑줄 친 단어는 문맥상 '민중 지도자'라는 의미로 사용되었으며, 유의어로는 ③ agitator가 적절하다.

해석

위대한 **민중 지도자** 제이콥 반 아르테벨데가 이끄는 그들은 네덜란드에서 영국 정당의 주역이 되었다.
① 탈주자, 망명자, 탈당자
② 범죄자, 위반자
③ 정치운동자, 선동자
④ 구독자

어휘

mainstay 주역
offender 범죄자, 위반자
subscriber 구독자
defector 탈주자, 망명자, 탈당자
agitator 정치운동자, 선동자

02 정답 ④

정답해설

밑줄 친 단어의 의미는 문맥상 '혐오하다'이며, 유의어로는 ④ abominate가 적절하다.

해석

비록 내가 도시로 돌아가는 것을 **혐오할지**라도, 나는 업무 전화에 응답한다.
① 구별하다
② 평가하다, 추정하다
③ 분배하다, 배치하다
④ 혐오하다

어휘

discern 구별하다
allocate 분배하다, 배치하다
estimate 평가하다, 추정하다
abominate 혐오하다

03 정답 ③

정답해설

밑줄 친 단어는 문맥상 '폐기된'으로 사용되었고, 유의어로는 ③ given up이 적절하다.

해석

그 계획은 보수당이 1993년도에 시의회에서 주도권을 잃었을 때 **폐기됐다**.
① 혐오하다, 멸시하다
② 해결하다, 해명하다
③ 포기하다
④ 양도하다, 운반하다, 전달하다

어휘

despise 혐오하다, 멸시하다
give up 포기하다
unravel 해결하다, 해명하다
convey 양도하다, 운반하다, 전달하다

오답률 TOP 1

04 정답 ②

정답해설

비록 안 좋은 일이 있긴 했어도 예전에 친하게 지냈던 친구에게 다시 연락할 것을 조언하는 내용이므로, 빈칸에는 '옛날 일은 잊어버리라'라는 의미의 ② Let bygones be bygones가 들어가는 것이 가장 적절하다.

해석

A: Anne에게 무슨 일 있니? 최근에는 소식을 못 들었어.
B: 나도 몰라. 그리고 사실은 신경 안 써. Anne은 항상 날 놀리거든.
A: 정말이야? 나는 너희 둘이 친한 친구 사이라고 생각했는데.
B: 전에는 그랬었지. 하지만 이젠 더 이상 아냐. 나는 걔가 하는 말들에 질려버렸어.
A: 유감이구나. 하지만 Anne은 정말 좋은 아이야. 전화 한번 하지 그래. 자아, 옛날 일은 잊어버려. 난 너희들이 다시 좋은 친구가 될 거라고 확신해.
B: 네가 맞는 거 같아. 당장 그 애한테 전화해 봐야겠다.
① 엄중히 감시하다
② 옛날 일은 잊어버려
③ 이 사업에 해결의 실마리를 던지다
④ 너는 감기에 걸린다

어휘

lose track of ~의 소식이 끊어지다, ~을 놓치다
remark 발언
bygone 과거의, 지나간
Let bygones be bygones. [속담] 과거사는 물에 흘려보내라, 과거는 잊어버려라
keep close tabs on ~을 엄중히 감시하다
shed light on~ ~에 빛을 비추다
come down with a cold 감기에 걸리다
make fun of~ ~을 놀리다
used to v ~하곤 했었다
suppose 가정하다

05 정답 ④

정답해설

④ **출제 포인트: 완전자동사**

'result'는 완전자동사로 전치사 'from'과 결합하는 경우 원인에 해당하는 명사(구)가 목적어로 오며, 전치사 'in'과 결합하는 경우 결과에 해당하는 명사(구)가 목적어로 온다. 또한 「result from+목적어」와 「result in+목적어」 모두 수동태로 사용할 수 없다. 따라서 'result'가 나오는 문제의 경우 수동태 'be resulted from/in'으로 사용되었는지를 꼭 확인해야 한다. 해당 문장은 'result from'을 수동태 'be resulted from'으로 사용하였으므로 틀린 문장이다. 따라서 'are resulted from'을 능동태 'result from'으로 수정해야 한다.

오답해설

① **출제 포인트: 현재분사 vs. 과거분사**

해당 문제는 한정적 용법으로 쓰인 현재분사와 과거분사의 구별을 묻는 문제로 수식하는 대상을 확인해야 한다. 해당 문장의 경우 분사가 수식하는 대상이 명사구 'virtual archives'이고 해석상 '배포된'이 자연스러우므로 과거분사 'distributed'를 사용해야 한다. 따라서 해당 문장은 옳은 문장이다.

② **출제 포인트: to부정사의 명사적 용법**
to부정사(구)가 긴 경우 문두에 가주어 'it'을 사용하고 to부정사(구)는 문미로 이동시킨다. 해당 문장은 to부정사(구) 'to use the available "search engines"'가 긴 경우에 해당하므로 문두에 가주어 'it'을 사용하였고 해당 to부정사(구)를 문미로 이동시켰으므로 옳은 문장이다.

③ **출제 포인트: 형용사 vs. 부사**
형용사와 부사를 구별을 묻는 문제는 수식하는 대상을 확인해야 한다. 해당 문장의 경우 수식하는 대상이 동사원형 'emulate'이므로 부사를 사용하는 것이 옳다. 따라서 해당 문장은 옳은 문장이다.

해석
심지어 실제 도서관의 서가를 훑고 다니는 것마저도 오늘 배포된 가상의 기록 보관소를 뒤지는 것보다 더 유익할 수 있는데, 왜냐하면 도서관의 방대한 장서가 있는 실제 서가에서 찾다가 흔히 달성할 수 있는 예측 가능한 발견과 놀라운 발견들이 섞여 있는 것을 효과적으로 따라 하기 위해 이용 가능한 '검색 엔진'을 사용하는 것이 어려워 보이기 때문이다.

어휘
fruitful 유익한, 열매가 많이 열리는
virtual 가상의
extensive 광범위한, 넓은
distribute 배포하다, 분배하다
emulate 모방하다

06 정답 ③

정답해설
③ **출제 포인트: 현재분사 vs. 과거분사**
'thought'는 완전타동사 'think'의 과거분사형태로 뒤에 목적어가 올 수 없으며 해석상 '~을 생각하면서'가 자연스러우므로 'thought'를 현재분사 'thinking'으로 수정해야 한다.

오답해설
① **출제 포인트: 주격 관계대명사**
선행사가 복수형태 'those things'이므로 주격 관계대명사절의 동사에 복수동사 'need'를 옳게 사용하였다.

② **출제 포인트: 주어와 동사 수일치**
동명사(구)와 to부정사(구)가 주어인 경우 단수로 취급하며 동사에 단수형태를 사용해야 한다. 해당 문장은 동명사구 'Separating ~ important'가 주어로 사용되었으므로 동사에 단수형태인 'is'를 사용하는 것이 옳다. 또한 밑줄 친 is prioritizing에서 prioritizing은 '우선순위를 결정하다'라는 자동사의 의미로 사용되었다.

④ **출제 포인트: 준사역동사 get**
준사역동사 'get'은 목적격 보어로 과거분사를 사용할 수 있다.

해석
유능한 코치는 해야 할 것들에 초점을 맞추고 다른 모든 것은 분리한다. 중요하지 않은 것으로부터 중요한 것을 분리하는 것이 우선순위를 결정하는 것이다. 무능한 코치는 중대한 과제를 제일 순위로 두지 않는다. 그들은 무언가를 할 시간이 내일 더 있을 거라고 생각하면서 자기들에게 무한한 시간이 있다고 믿거나 자기들이 실제로 얼마나 많은 시간을 가지고 있는지를 과소평가한다.

어휘
focus on ~에 초점을 맞추다, 주력하다
separate 분리하다, 나누다
task 과제, 일, 직무
prioritize 우선순위를 결정하다
underestimate 과소평가하다

07 정답 ③

정답해설
③ **출제 포인트: 원급 비교**
'not+so+원급+as'는 원급 비교 구문에 해당하며 원급이 올 자리에 비교급을 사용할 수 없다. 따라서 'better'를 'good'으로 수정해야 한다.

오답해설
① **출제 포인트: 형용사 관용표현**
'be good at+목적어'는 형용사 관용표현으로 '~을 잘하다'를 뜻한다.

② **출제 포인트: 주어와 동사의 수일치**
명사구와 명사구가 등위접속사를 통해 병렬구조를 이루고 있고 주어로 쓰인 경우 복수로 취급하며 동사에 복수형태를 사용한다. 해당 문장은 동명사 'making'과 'responding'이 등위접속사 'and'를 통해 병렬구조를 이루고 있고 주어로 사용되었으므로 동사에 복수동사 'are'를 사용하는 것이 옳다.

④ **출제 포인트: 비교급 비교**
비교급 비교 구문으로 비교 대상이 일치하여야 한다. 복수 주어 'economic principles'와 복수대명사 'those'가 일치하므로 옳게 사용되었다.

오답률 TOP 2

08 정답 ④

정답해설
빈칸 전과 후반에 나오는 "most of us avoid the prospect of failure(우리들 대부분은 실패할 가능성을 회피한다)"와 "We hardly attempt anything great(우리는 대단한 일을 거의 시도하지 않는다)"를 통해 '우리가 실패하기를 꺼려하여 성공을 위한 도전을 하지 않는다'라는 내용이 연이어 이어진다는 것을 알 수 있으며, 또한 유사한 맥락으로 이어지는 접속부사 in fact가 순접을 나타내므로 ④ In fact, we are so focused on not failing that we do not aim for success, settling instead for a life of mediocrity(사실, 우리는 실패하지 않는 것에 너무 집중하고 있어서 성공을 목표로 하지 않고, 대신에 평범한 삶에 만족한다)가 정답이라는 것을 알 수 있다.

오답해설
① 빈칸 이후의 내용인 "when we do make missteps while attempting something, we gloss over them(우리가 무엇을 시도하다가 실제로 실수를 할 때, 우리는 그것들을 얼버무리고 넘어간다)"을 통해 글의 맥락이 변하지 않았음을 유추할 수 있다. 따라서 'However(그러나)'가 이끄는 해당 문장은 문맥상 적절하지 않다.
② 본문에서 언급되지 않은 내용이므로 정답이 될 수 없다.
③ 실수가 우리의 성장(growths)이나 성공(success)에 미칠 수 있는 영향에 대해서는 지문 마지막에 간단히 언급하고 있으나 빈칸에 들어가기에는 위치상 어색하다.

해석
사회는 패배를 보상하지 않고 우리들 대부분은 실패할 가능성을 회피한다. 우리의 성공 지향적 사회에서 많은 사람들에게 실패는 단지 선택지가 아니라고 여겨지는 것만이 아니다 — 그것은 심지어 결함 또는 열등함의 신호라고 생각된다. 사실, 우리는 실패하지 않는 것에 너무 집중하고 있어서 성공을 목표로 하지 않고, 대신에 평범한 삶에 만족한다. 우리는 우리가 실패하거나 성공할 가능성이 있는 어떤 대단한 일을 거의 시도하지 않는다. 또한, 우리가 무엇을 시도하다가 실제로 실수를 할 때, 우리는 오판이나 실수를 선택적으로 우리 인생의 '이력서'에서 삭제해버리며 그것들을 얼버무리고 넘어가 버린다. 하지만 우리가 잘못 생각하고 있는 모든 것들 중 실수에 대한 생각이 가장 잘못된 것일지도 모른다. 이는 우리의 메타오류이다. 우리는 잘못된 것이 의미하는 바가 무엇인지에 대해 잘못 생각하고 있다. 실수하고 실패할 수 있는 능력은 지적인 열등함의 신호가 아닌 인간의 인지 능력과 성공 있어서 매우 중요한 것이다. 실패는 우리가 그것을 두려움 없이 받아들인다면 우리의 가장 좋은 선생님이 될 수 있다.

① 그러나, 실패를 극복하는 것은 우리가 인생에서 직면하는 가장 어렵지만 중요한 도전 과제 중 하나이다
② 사실, 우리 모두는 실패가 큰 성공을 이룩하는 데 있어서 가장 강력한 도구라는 것을 이미 알고 있다
③ 그러나, 실수는 우리의 장래의 발전과 성공에 있어서 디딤돌이 될 수도 있고 장애물이 될 수도 있다
④ 사실, 우리는 실패하지 않는 것에 너무 집중하고 있어서 성공을 목표로 하지 않고, 대신에 평범한 삶에 만족한다

어휘

reward 보상하다
prospect 가능성, 가망
non-option 비(非) 선택지
deficiency 결함, 부족
hardly 거의 ~않다
misstep 실수, 과실
gloss over 얼버무리고 넘어가다, 둘러대다
selectively 선택적으로
miscalculation 계산 착오, 오판
top the list 목록의 제일 위에 있다, 가장 위에 있다
meta- 자신과 관계되는, 복합의, 더 높은, 초월의
far from 전혀 ~이 아닌, ~이 아니라 오히려
as...as any 무엇에도 못지않게...한
capacity 능력
crucial 중대한
only if ~해야만, ~할 경우에 한해
challenge 도전, 도전 과제
be aware that 알다, 인식하다
either A or B A 이거나 B (둘 중 하나)
stepping stone 디딤돌, 발판
aim for ~를 겨냥하다, 목표로 하다
mediocrity 평범

defeat 패배
success-driven 성공 지향적인
deem 생각하다
inferiority 열등
attempt 시도하다

edit out 삭제하다, 잘라내다
resume 이력서

intellectual 지적인, 지성의
err 실수하다, 잘못하다
cognition 인지, 인식, 지식
embrace 기꺼이 받아들이다
face 직면하다
achieve 달성하다, 이루다

stumbling block 장애물
settle for ~로 만족하다, 받아들이다

오답률 TOP 3

09 정답 ①

정답해설

해당 지문은 귀여운 것을 입으로 깨물고 싶어 하는 인간의 본성에 대한 과학적 이론을 몇 가지 제시하고 있다. 그 중 빈칸 부분은 포유류 전체적으로 나타나는 "social biting"에 대해 언급하고 있는데, 빈칸 이전 문장 "some other primates are known to gently bite each other in a non-threatening manner(몇몇 다른 영장류들은 위협이 되지 않는 방식으로 서로를 부드럽게 깨무는 것으로 알려져 있다)."와 빈칸 바로 이후 "demonstrating that even if you find one of your body parts in someone else's mouth, you will not get hurt(너의 신체의 일부가 다른 사람의 입 속에 있더라도, 너는 다치지 않을 것이라는 것을 보여줌으로써)."로 보아, 서로를 깨무는 것은 '비위협적인 방식'을 통해 '해치지 않을 것이라는 믿음을 주기 위한 행동'이라는 것을 알 수 있으므로 빈칸에는 ① a way of building trust(신뢰를 쌓는 하나의 방식)가 가장 적절하다.

오답해설

④ "Another theory about this seemingly strange human behavior notes that "social biting" is a common occurrence among mammals(이 겉으로 보기에 이상한 인간 행동에 대한 또 다른 이론은

"사회적인 깨물기"가 포유동물 사이에 흔히 발생하는 일이라고 언급한다)."에서 포유류와 인간 사이에 공통으로 나타나는 현상이라고 언급하고 있으므로 틀리다. 포유류(mammal)를 동물(animal)로 확대해석하지 않도록 주의한다.
나머지 보기도 본문과 관련이 없으므로 정답이 아니다.

해석

우리가 그렇게 빨리 인정하지 않을지도 모르지만, 우리는 모두 때때로 아기의 발가락을 깨물고 싶은 이상한 충동을 느낀 적이 있다. 기괴하게 들리겠지만, 이것은 전형적인 인간의 특징이다. 과학자들은 여기에 작용하는 적어도 두어 개의 요인들이 있다고 생각한다. 우리가 자그마하고, 귀엽고, 껴안고 싶은 것을 보거나 냄새를 맡을 때, 그것은 실제로 맛있는 음식을 보는 것에 의해 활성화되는[켜지는] 우리 뇌의 동일한 쾌락 중추를 작동시킨다. 따라서 그 욕구는 단순히 우리의 뇌가 유사한 자극에 대해 유사한 반응을 보이는 경우라고 할 수 있다. 이 겉으로 보기에 이상한 인간 행동에 대한 또 다른 이론은 "사회적인 깨물기"가 포유동물 사이에 흔히 발생하는 일이라고 언급한다. 예를 들어, 몇몇 다른 영장류들은 위협이 되지 않는 방식으로 서로를 부드럽게 깨무는 것으로 알려져 있다. 과학자들은 이것이 너의 신체의 일부가 다른 사람의 입 속에 있더라도, 너는 다치지 않을 것이라는 것을 보여줌으로써 신뢰를 쌓는 하나의 방식일 것이라고 생각한다.

① 신뢰를 쌓는 하나의 방식
② 생존을 위한 본능
③ 자식을 지키기 위한 방법
④ 동물 사회의 특징

어휘

weird 이상한, 기묘한
nibble 조금씩 물어뜯다
bizarre 기괴한
nature 특징, 본성, 본질
at work 작용하여
huggable 껴안고 싶은
pleasure center 쾌락 중추
stimuli stimulus(자극)의 복수형
seemingly 겉으로 보기에
occurrence 발생
primate 영장류
demonstrate 보여주다, 입증하다
instinct 본능

compulsion 충동
from time to time 때때로
typical 전형적인
factor 요인
adorable 귀여운, 사랑스러운
activate 작동시키다, 활성화시키다
response 반응, 응답
theory 이론, 학설
note 언급하다, 주목하다
mammal 포유동물
non-threatening 위협적이지 않은
even if ~에도 불구하고
characteristic 특징

10 정답 ③

정답해설

해당 지문은 로데오의 역사에 대한 내용이며 (A), (B) 빈칸은 앞뒤 문맥을 연결하는 표현이 필요한 자리이다.
(A)의 앞에서 "it is a spectacle which we commonly enjoy and take for granted(그것은 우리가 흔히 즐기고 당연시 여기는 구경거리이다)"라고 언급하며 오늘날 로데오가 오락 경기로서 널리 퍼져 있다고 언급한 후, (A)의 뒤에서 "many of the things which are now considered rodeo events were simply tasks that needed to be completed on the ranch(현재 로데오 행사라고 여겨지는 많은 것들은 단순히 목장에서 완료되어야만 하는 일거리에 불과했다)"라고 말하며 오늘날 로데오 경기 종목들이 과거에는 단순한 일거리였던 사실을 밝혀주고 있으므로 현재와 과거의 차이점을 비교하여 말하고 있다고 볼 수 있다. 따라서 앞서 말한 내용과 대조되는 내용을 연결할 때 사용하는 However가 빈칸에 적절하다.
(B)의 앞에서는 "Now, cowboys take part in rodeo events which are based closely on those ranch tasks(현재, 카우보이들은 이러한 목장 일

에 밀접하게 기초한 로데오 행사들에 참여한다)"라고 로데오 행사 종목과 목장 일의 밀접한 관계를 설명한 후, (B)의 뒤에서 재차 "you are seeing something which has its history in legitimate ranch work(당신은 정통적인 목장 일에 역사를 둔 무언가를 보고 있는 것이다)"를 통해 로데오가 목장 일에 역사를 두고 있다고 앞서 등장한 내용과 유사한 내용을 재진술하고 있으므로 'That is to say'가 빈칸에 가장 적절하다.

오답해설

②, ④ (A)자리에 For example이 들어가는 것은 문맥상 어색하다.
① (A)자리의 However는 적절하나 (B)자리의 보기가 부적절하므로 오답이다.

해석

로데오는 시간이 지남에 따라 발전을 거듭하여 매년 전국에 있는 경기장에 매우 많은 사람들을 불러들이는 명물로 변모하였다. 오늘날, 그것은 우리가 흔히 즐기고 당연시 여기는 – 거칠고 강한 카우보이들이 팬들이 지켜보는 가운데 황소나 말을 타고 여러 행사에서 경쟁을 하는 그런 구경거리이다. (A) 그러나 현재 로데오 행사라고 여겨지는 많은 것들은 단순히 목장에서 완료되어야만 하는 일거리에 불과했다. 로프 던지기, 말 타기, 소몰이와 같은 일들은 어떠한 종류의 경기도 아니었다 – 그것들은 단지 일일 뿐이었다. 현재, 카우보이들은 이러한 목장 일에 밀접하게 기초한 로데오 행사에 참여한다. (B) 다시 말해, 만약 당신이 전문 카우보이가 단체 로프 던지기나 야생마 타기 등에서 경쟁하는 것을 본 적이 있다면, 당신은 정통적인 목장 일에 역사를 둔 무언가를 보고 있는 것이다.
① 그러나 – 그에 반해
② 예를 들어 – 반면에
③ 그러나 – 다시 말해
④ 예를 들어 – 그러므로

어휘

attraction 명물, 명소   draw (손님 등을) 끌다
spectacle 구경거리, 행사
take it for granted~ ~을 당연한 일로 여기다, 대수롭지 않게 여기다
compete 경쟁하다   ranch 목장, 농장
rope 밧줄을 던져 잡다   herd (짐승을) 몰다
take part in 참여하다   bronc 야생마
legitimate 정통의, 진짜의, 합법의

결국엔 성정혜 영어 하프모의고사
기적사 DAY 08

| 01 | ① | 02 | ② | 03 | ③ | 04 | ① | 05 | ③ |
| 06 | ③ | 07 | ④ | 08 | ④ | 09 | ③ | 10 | ② |

01 정답 ①

정답해설

밑줄 친 단어의 의미는 문맥상 '확인하다'로 사용되었고, 유의어로는 ① approve가 적절하다.

해석

벳시는 사람들이 어디에 살았었는지를 **확인할 수** 있게 될지 모른다는 것에 희망적이었다.
① 확인하다, 인정하다
② 약화시키다
③ 서두르다, 가속하다, 촉진시키다
④ 포기하다, 부인하다

어휘

approve 확인하다, 인정하다   undermine 약화시키다
accelerate 서두르다, 가속하다, 촉진시키다
renounce 포기하다, 부인하다

02 정답 ②

정답해설

밑줄 친 단어는 문맥상 '혐오하다'로 사용되었고, 유의어로는 ② despise가 적절하다.

해석

나는 특히 글을 잘 아는 사람들이 이메일 메시지를 쓸 때 보이는 게으름을 **혐오한다**.
① 압도하다
② 혐오하다, 경멸하다
③ 변경하다, 개정하다
④ 자세히 살펴보다, 조사하다, 훑어보다

어휘

laziness 게으름   overwhelm 압도하다
despise 경멸하다   revise 변경하다, 개정하다
scan 자세히 살펴보다, 조사하다, 훑어보다

03 정답 ③

정답해설

밑줄 친 단어의 의미는 문맥상 '변호하다'로 사용되었고, 유의어로는 ③ protect가 적절하다.

해석

이것은 의무는 아니었고, 그는 그를 **변호하거나** 질책하지 않을 것이다.
① 혐오하다, 싫어하다

② 속이다, 기만하다, 현혹시키다, 거짓말을 하다
③ 보호하다
④ 피하다, 빠져나가다, 얼버무려 넘기다

어휘

reprimand 질책하다, 비난하다   loathe 혐오하다, 싫어하다
deceive 속이다, 기만하다, 현혹시키다, 거짓말을 하다
protect 보호하다
evade 피하다, 빠져나가다, 얼버무려 넘기다

오답률 TOP 3

04 정답 ①

정답해설

뒤의 '팬케이크를 먹지 말아야 했다'라는 내용과 '가끔씩은 걸신들린 듯 먹는다'라는 내용을 통해 B가 과식을 했거나 음식을 잘못 먹었음을 알 수 있다. '안색이 안 좋아 보인다'라는 말과 연결해 생각하면, 빈칸에는 '배가 아프다'라는 내용이 들어가는 것이 가장 자연스럽다. 따라서 정답은 ① I have a stomachache이다.

해석

A: 너 안 좋아 보여. 무슨 일 있니?
B: 배가 아파.
A: 놀랄 일도 아니네.
B: 너무 그러지 마. 이따금씩은 걸신들리게 먹어야 한다고. 게다가, 우리는 소풍을 온 거잖아.
A: 네가 지장 없다고 느끼는 동안은 그래야겠지. 하지만 너 자신을 좀 봐! 겨우 서 있잖아. 너 심각해 보여.
B: 나도 알아. 그 마지막 팬케이크를 먹지 말았어야 했는데.
① 배가 아파
② 난 때때로 어지럼증을 느껴
③ 난 너무 긴장돼
④ 나는 사장님 때문에 항상 평정심을 잃어

어휘

stomachache 복통   dizzy 어지러운
pig out 게걸스럽게 먹다   hardly 거의 ~하지 않다
serious 심각한
have butterflies in one's stomach 긴장하다, 안달하다

05 정답 ③

정답해설

③ 출제 포인트: 동사 관용표현
'take+목적어+for granted'는 동사 관용표현으로 '~을 당연시하다'를 뜻한다. 따라서 'granting'을 'granted'로 수정해야 한다.

오답해설

① 출제 포인트: 현재분사 vs. 과거분사
'perceive'는 완전타동사이며 분사 뒤의 문장 구조가 「전명구+등위접속사+전명구」이고 해석상 '인식된'이 자연스러우므로 과거분사를 사용하는 것이 옳다. 따라서 과거분사 'perceived'를 사용하였으므로 해당 문장은 옳은 문장이다.
② 출제 포인트: 동사 관용표현
'spend+시간+-ing'은 동사 관용표현으로 '~하는 데 시간을 보내다'를 뜻한다.
④ 출제 포인트: to부정사의 명사적 용법

to부정사(구)가 긴 경우 문두에 가주어 'it'을 사용하고 to부정사(구)는 문미로 이동시킨다. 해당 문장은 to부정사(구) 'to maintain, enhance and extend the tool'이 긴 경우에 해당하므로 문두에 가주어 it을 사용하였고 해당 to부정사(구)를 문미로 이동시켰으므로 옳은 문장이다.

해석

자신을 명확하게 표현할 수 있는 사람들이 더 지적이고 더 지위가 높은 사람으로 인식된다. 우리는 왜 우리가 대부분의 어린 시절에 했던 것을 멈추는가? 문제는 우리가 우리의 언어능력을 당연하게 생각한다는 것이다. 일단 우리가 읽기, 쓰기, 말하기를 숙달하게 되면, 우리는 다른 것으로 나아가게 된다. 우리는 정신의 도구상자에서 가장 중요한 도구를 습득해 왔다. 우리는 모든 종류의 과업을 수행하는데 그것에 의존하지만, 우리는 그것을 연마하는 데 거의 시간을 보내지 않는다. 그 도구를 유지, 신장, 확장하는 것이 더 이치에 맞는 것이다.

어휘

perceive A as B A를 B로 인식하다
spend+시간+-ing ~하는 데 시간을 보내다
verbal 말의, 구두의
take+목적어+for granted ~을 당연시하다
toolbox 도구상자   enhance 강화하다, 향상시키다

06 정답 ③

정답해설

③ 출제 포인트: 사역동사 let의 목적격 보어
사역동사 'let'은 목적격 보어로 to부정사를 사용할 수 없다. 따라서 'to enjoy'를 'enjoy'로 수정해야 한다.

오답해설

① 출제 포인트: to부정사를 목적격 보어로 가지는 불완전타동사
'encourage'는 불완전타동사의 경우 목적격 보어로 to부정사를 사용한다.
② 출제 포인트: 현재분사 vs. 과거분사
'considered'는 불완전타동사 'consider'의 과거분사형태이며 수식하는 대상이 'Comics, magazines, audiobooks, and topics'이고 해석상 '간주된'이 자연스러우므로 옳게 사용되었다.
④ 출제 포인트: 주격 관계대명사
선행사가 단수형태 'this light reading'이므로 주격 관계대명사절의 동사에 단수동사 'improves'를 옳게 사용하였다.

해석

오로지 즐거움만을 제공하는 책조차도 학생들의 자신감을 증가시킬 것이고, 그들이 학교에서보다 전문적인 읽기 자료를 읽어 보도록 장려할 것이다. 만화, 잡지, 오디오북, 그리고 인터넷상의 흥미로운 화제들은 때때로 '진정한' 읽을 거리로 간주되지 않는다. 하지만 이러한 읽기 자료는 학생들에게 읽기의 즐거움을 만끽하고 정보, 글을 읽고 쓰는 기술 등을 얻게 해 준다. 이러한 '가벼운' 읽기는 노력이 필요 없는 읽기이기 때문에 실제로 매우 유익한데, 이것은 읽기의 능숙함을 향상시킨다.

어휘

encourage+목적어+to+동사원형 ~에게 ~하도록 격려하다
consider+목적어+(to be)+명사 ~을 …이라고 여기다, 생각하다
let+목적어+동사원형 ~에게 ~하도록 시키다
literacy 읽고 쓰는 능력   effortless 노력이 필요 없는, 쉬운
fluency 유창함

오답률 TOP 1
07 정답 ④

정답해설

④ 출제 포인트: 비교급 비교
주어진 해석이 '~보다 더 민감한'이므로 비교급이 사용된 문장임을 알 수 있다. 따라서 'sensitive'를 'more sensitive'로 수정해야 한다.

오답해설

① 출제 포인트: 형용사 관용표현
'be cognizant of+목적어'는 형용사 관용표현으로 '~을 알고 있다'를 뜻한다.

② 출제 포인트: 원급 비교
'not+so+원급+as'는 원급 비교 구문에 해당하며 원급자리에 형용사 원급 'hard'를 옳게 사용하였다.

③ 출제 포인트: 주어와 동사 수일치
주어가 단수형태 'a film'이므로 동사에 단수동사 'was'를 옳게 사용하였다. 또한 'defined by the latter terms'는 수식어에 해당하므로 'the latter terms'를 주어로 착각해서는 안 된다.

08 정답 ④

정답해설

해당 지문은 'Pablo Picasso(파블로 피카소)'의 작품 중 하나인 'Massacre in Korea(한국에서의 학살)'에 대해 설명하고 있다. 주어진 문장에서는 해당 작품에 대해 간략히 소개하고 있으므로, "It depicts the 1950 Sinchon Massacre(그것은 1950년 신천대학살을 묘사한다)"로 시작하여 해당 작품이 묘사하는 주제를 자세하게 서술하고 있는 (C)가 바로 이후에 이어지는 것이 적절하다. 이어 (A)에서 'the murders(학살)'를 이용해 (C)의 'an act of mass killing(대량학살 행위)'을 가리키며 작품에 대한 추가적인 설명을 하고 있다는 것을 알 수 있고, (A)의 두 번째 문장의 주어인 'The art critic Kirsten Hoving Keen'을 (B)의 대명사 'She'가 가리키고 있으므로, (B)가 (A) 이후에 이어지는 것이 자연스럽다. 따라서 정답은 '④ (C) - (A) - (B)'이다.

해석

'한국에서의 학살(Massacre in Korea)'은 미국의 한국전쟁 개입에 대한 비판으로 여겨지는 파블로 피카소의 1951년 작 표현주의적 그림이다.
(C) 그것은 북한인, 남한인, 그리고 미군에 의해 자행된 북한 황해도에 위치한 신천에서 발생한 대량학살 행위인 1950년 신천대학살을 묘사한다.
(A) 신천에서의 학살의 실질적인 원인은 미궁에 빠져있으나, 한국에서의 학살은 민간인이 반공산주의 세력에 의해 살해되고 있는 것으로 묘사하는 듯 하다. 예술 비평가 Kirsten Hoving Keen은 그것이 "미군의 잔학행위에 대한 보고서에서 영감을 받은"것이라고 말한다.
(B) 그녀는 또한 그것을 피카소의 공산주의적 작품 중 하나라고 여긴다. 피카소의 이 작품은 Francisco Goya의 그림 '1808년 5월 3일(The Third of May 1808)'에서 영감을 얻었으며, 그것은 Joachim Murat의 명령에 의해 나폴레옹 군대가 스페인 민간인을 처형하는 것을 묘사하고 있다.

어휘

massacre (대량)학살	expressionistic 표현주의적인
criticism 비판, 비난	intervention 개입
in question 문제의, 논의가 되고 있는	
depict 묘사하다	civilian 민간인
communist 공산주의자	force 세력, 집단, 군대
critic 비평가	inspire 영감을 주다
atrocity 잔학행위, 포악한 행위	
draw from (결론, 생각 등을) ~에서 끌어내다, 얻다	

execute 처형하다, 사형을 집행하다   mass 대량의, 집단의
province (행정 구역으로서의) 도(道), 주(州), 성(省)

오답률 TOP 2
09 정답 ③

정답해설

해당 지문은 피카소의 대표작인 게르니카(Geurnica)에 대해 서술하고 있다. (A) 빈칸 이후에서 "becoming a perpetual reminder of the tragedies of war, an anti-war symbol, and an embodiment of peace"을 통해 게르니카가 '전쟁의 비극을 끊임없이 상기시켜 주는 매개체, 반 전쟁의 상징, 그리고 평화의 실체'가 되었다고 언급하고 있으므로, '기념비적인(monumental)' 명성을 얻은 것이 문맥상 자연스럽다. 또한 (B) 빈칸 이전 문장에서 게르니카가 전 세계로 전시되며 'becoming famous and widely acclaimed(유명해지고 널리 극찬을 받게 되었다)'라고 언급하고 있으므로, 해당 작품으로 인해 스페인 내전에 대한 세계적인 관심(attention) 또는 인식(recognition)이 증가했음을 유추할 수 있다. 따라서 빈칸에 들어갈 표현이 알맞게 짝지어진 것은 '③ monumental(기념비적인) - attention(관심)'이다.

오답해설

④ (B)에는 '스페인 내전에 대한 세계의 인식을 불러일으켰다'라는 의미가 되는 'recognition(인식)'이 들어가는 것이 가능하나 (A)의 'paltry(하찮은)'는 문맥상 어색하므로 오답이다.

해석

아마도 피카소의 가장 유명한 작품인 게르니카(Guernica)는 분명히 그의 가장 강력한 정치적 표현이며, 그것은 스페인 내전 중 게르니카라는 바스크 마을에 행해진 엄청나게 파괴적인 나치의 폭탄 투하에 대한 즉각적인 반응으로서 그려졌다. 게르니카는 전쟁의 비극과 그것이 개인들 특히 무고한 민간인들에게 가하는 고통을 보여준다. 이 작품은 (A) 기념비적인 명성을 얻었고, 전쟁의 비극을 끊임없이 상기시켜 주는 매개체, 반 전쟁의 상징, 그리고 평화의 실체가 되었다. 완성되었을 때 게르니카는 짧은 투어에서 전 세계적으로 전시되며, 유명해지고 널리 극찬을 받게 되었다. 이 투어가 스페인 내전에 대한 세계의 (B) 관심을 불러일으키는 데 도움이 되었다.
① 기념비적인 - 무관심
② 하찮은 - 비난
③ 기념비적인 - 관심
④ 하찮은 - 인식

어휘

statement 표현	reaction 반응
devastating 엄청나게 파괴적인	practice 실행
tragedy 비극	suffering 고통
inflict 가하다, 주다	civilian 민간인, 일반 시민
status 신분, 지위, 신망	perpetual 끊임없는, 영속하는
embodiment 구현, 구체화, 실체	acclaimed 찬사를 받은, 호평을 받은
monumental 기념비적인, 역사적 의미가 있는	
apathy 무관심, 냉담	paltry 하찮은, 보잘것없는
reproach 비난	recognition 인식, 인지, 인정

10 정답 ②

정답해설

해당 지문은 파블로 피카소(Pablo Picasso)의 어린 시절에 관한 내용이다. 본문 두 번째 문장 "he himself began Picasso's art education when he was seven.(그는 피카소가 7살 때 직접 피카소의 미술 교육을 시작했다.)"에서 피카소의 아버지가 직접 그의 미술 지도를 했음을 알 수 있고, 세

번째 문장 "He was a strict academic who believed that artists should learn by copying the great masters, as well as drawing plaster casts and live models.(그는 예술가는 석고상과 실제 모델을 그리는 것뿐만 아니라 훌륭한 대가들의 작품을 모사하는 것을 통해서 배워야 한다고 믿는 엄격한 학자였다.)"을 통해 그의 교육 신조 중 하나가 '훌륭한 대가들의 작품을 모사하는 것을 통해서 배워야 한다'라는 것임을 알 수 있다. 따라서 본문의 내용과 일치하는 보기는 "② His father allowed him to reproduce paintings of earlier artists.(그의 아버지는 그가 과거 예술가들의 그림을 모사하는 것을 허용했다.)"이다.

오답해설

① 본문 초반에서 '피카소의 아버지가 어린 피카소의 재능을 발견해서 피카소가 7살일 때 미술 교육을 시작했다'라고 언급하고 있으므로 그의 재능이 7세 이후에 발견되었다는 것은 본문의 내용과 일치하지 않는다.
③ 피카소가 9살일 때 유화 The Picador를 완성하였다고 하였으므로 십대가 될 때까지 오직 연필만을 사용했다는 것은 본문의 내용과 일치하지 않는다.
④ 피카소는 School of Fine Arts에 13세 때 입학하였고 The Picador는 그 이전에 완성했으므로 오답이다.

해석

파블로 피카소(Pablo Picasso)의 아버지 José Ruiz y Blasco는 그의 어린 아들이 특별하다는 사실을 재빨리 알아챈 화가이자 미술 교사였다. 그래서 그는 피카소가 7살일 때 직접 피카소의 미술 교육을 시작했다. 그는 예술가는 석고상과 실제 모델을 그리는 것뿐만 아니라 훌륭한 대가들의 작품을 모사하는 것을 통해서 배워야 한다고 믿는 엄격한 학자였다. 피카소의 초기 연필화와 유화는 어린 시절 그가 얼마나 능숙했는지를 보여준다. 그의 가장 초기 유화 The Picador는 그가 겨우 9살일 때 완성됐다. 그리고 그는 13살에 바르셀로나에 있는 School of Fine Arts에 입학했다. 놀랍게도, 그는 보통 한 달이 걸리는 철저한 입학시험을 단 일주일 만에 끝낼 수 있었다.
① 그의 재능은 7세 이후 그의 교사에 의해 발견되었다.
② 그의 아버지는 그가 예전의 예술가들의 그림을 모사하는 것을 허용했다.
③ 그는 십대가 될 때까지 그림을 그리기 위해 오직 연필만을 사용했다.
④ 그는 The Picador를 School of Fine Arts 재학 당시 그렸다.

어휘

pick up on 알아차리다, 이해하다 academic 학자, 학구적인 사람, 교수
plaster cast 석고 모형
admit (단체·학교 등에서) 받아들이다, 가입[입학]을 허락하다
fine art 미술
rigorous 엄격한, 엄밀한   incredibly 믿기 힘들게도, 놀랍게도
entrance exam 입학시험   reproduce 모조하다, 복사하다

기적사 DAY 09

| 01 | ④ | 02 | ③ | 03 | ① | 04 | ② | 05 | ④ |
| 06 | ① | 07 | ④ | 08 | ③ | 09 | ④ | 10 | ③ |

01 정답 ④

정답해설

밑줄 친 단어는 문맥상 '기묘한'이라는 의미로 사용되었고, 유의어로는 ④ odd가 적절하다.

해석

그녀는 관련 세부 사항을 고수하는 **기묘한** 방법을 가지고 있다.
① 실용적이 아닌, 비현실적인
② 보완적인
③ 과오를 범하지 않는
④ 이상한, 특이한, 홀수의, 별난

어휘

uncanny 기묘한   complementary 보완적인
pertinent 적절한, 관계가 있는   impractical 비현실적인, 비실용적인
inerrant 과오를 범하지 않는   odd 이상한, 특이한, 홀수의, 별난

02 정답 ③

정답해설

밑줄 친 단어가 문맥상 '평가하다'로 사용되었고, 유의어로는 ③ reckon이 적절하다.

해석

그는 부서지기 쉬운 금박을 입힌 장식품을 **평가하기** 위해 멈추었다.
① 보상하다
② 자극하다, 타오르게 하다, 흥분시키다
③ 평가하다, 생각하다
④ 욕하다, 맹세하다, 단언하다

어휘

evaluate 평가하다   frail 약한
compensate 보상하다   inflame 악화시키다, 격분하게 하다
reckon 평가하다, 생각하다   swear 욕하다, 맹세하다, 단언하다

03 정답 ①

정답해설

밑줄 친 단어의 의미는 문맥상 '진행 중인'으로 사용되었으며, 유의어로는 ① incessant가 적절하다.

해석

이 조치는 이 작품의 판화를 **진행 중인** 과정으로 정점에 이르게 할 것이며, 전체 판이 판매될 때 절정에 이를 것이다.
① 진행 중인, 끊임없는
② 다루기 어려운, 크고 무거운, 장황한, 지루한

③ 상습적인, 만성의
④ 오만한

어휘

culminate 최고점에 달하다
ponderous 다루기 어려운, 크고 무거운, 장황한, 지루한
chronic 상습적인, 만성의
incessant 진행 중인, 끊임없는
imperious 오만한

오답률 TOP 3

04 정답 ②

정답해설

A가 계속 신뢰에 대한 의구심을 나타내고 있으므로, B가 Janet을 보장한다는 내용이 들어가야 한다. 따라서 정답은 ② I'll vouch for her이다.

해석

A: 당신을 믿을 수 있다는 것을 어떻게 알죠?
B: Janet에게 물어보세요, 그녀가 다 이야기해 줄 것입니다.
A: Janet을 믿을 수 있다는 것을 내가 어떻게 알죠?
B: 걱정하지 마세요. 내가 그녀를 보증합니다.
① 그녀를 없애요
② 내가 그녀를 보증합니다
③ 그녀는 흥을 깨는 사람이에요
④ 그녀는 빙산의 일각이에요

어휘

trust 믿다, 신뢰하다
vouch for 보증을 하다
tip of the iceberg 빙산의 일각
get rid of 없애다
wet blanket 흥을 깨는 사람

05 정답 ④

정답해설

④ 출제 포인트: 완전자동사
'take place'는 완전자동사로 수동태로 사용할 수 없다. 따라서 'take place'가 나오는 문제의 경우 수동태 'be taken place'로 사용되었는지를 꼭 확인해야 한다. 해당 문장은 'take place'를 수동태 'be taken place'로 사용하였으므로 틀린 문장이다. 따라서 'be taken place'를 능동태 'take place'로 수정해야 한다.

오답해설

① 출제 포인트: 동사 관용표현
'come up with'는 관용표현으로 '~을 생각해내다, 찾아내다'를 뜻한다. 따라서 전치사 'with'를 옳게 사용하였다.

② 출제 포인트: to부정사의 명사적 용법
'to ask'는 to부정사의 명사적 용법에 해당하며 'like'의 목적어로 옳게 사용되었다.

③ 출제 포인트: to부정사의 형용사적 용법
'to last'는 불완전타동사 'expect'의 목적격 보어에 해당하므로 to부정사의 형용사적 용법 중 서술적 용법으로 옳게 사용되었다.

해석

지난주에 저희 직원이 알려드린 것처럼 귀하의 단편소설은 Novel Flash Fiction의 12월 호에 게재될 것입니다. 저희는 귀하가 어떻게 귀하의 소설을 구상하게 되었는지 듣는 것이 저희 독자들에게 의미가 있을 것이라고 생각했습니다. 그래서 저희는 귀하가 창작 과정에 대해 강연을 해 주실 수 있는지 여쭤보고 싶습니다. 이 강연은 약 한 시간 동안 진행될 것으로 예상되고 시내에 있는 Moon 서점에서 열릴 것입니다. 귀하의 일정에 따라 특정한 날짜와 시간을 선택하실 수 있습니다.

어휘

short story 단편소설
come up with ~을 생각해내다
downtown 시내에
take place 발생하다
last 계속되다, 지속되다

오답률 TOP 1

06 정답 ①

정답해설

① 출제 포인트: 목적격 관계대명사
선행사가 'a biscuit'인 관계대명사 'that'이 쓰인 문장으로 뒤따라오는 문장은 불완전해야 하며 해석상 '버터와 집에서 만든 딸기잼을 발라놓은 비스킷'이 자연스러우므로 'spread butter'를 'spread with butter'로 수정해야 한다.

※ 관계대명사가 만들어지는 과정
Tom sat in his chair eating a biscuit. + Dad had spread it with butter and homemade strawberry jam. (선행사가 사물을 뜻하는 명사구 'a biscuit'이며 완전타동사 'spread'의 목적어에 해당하므로 목적격 관계대명사 'which' 또는 'that'을 사용)
→ Tom sat in his chair eating a biscuit that Dad had spread with butter and homemade strawberry jam.

오답해설

② 출제 포인트: 현재분사 vs. 과거분사
밑줄 친 'covered'는 완전타동사 'cover'의 과거분사형태로 뒤에 목적어가 올 수 없으나 해당 문장에서는 뒤에 수식어에 해당하는 전명구 'with biscuit'을 사용하였으므로 옳은 문장이다.

③ 출제 포인트: 불완전타동사 get
불완전타동사 'get'의 목적격 보어로 형용사를 사용할 수 있다.

④ 출제 포인트: 사역동사 make
사역동사 'make'의 목적격 보어로 원형부정사를 사용해야 한다.

해석

Tom이 자신의 의자에 앉아서 아빠가 버터와 집에서 만든 딸기잼을 발라놓은 비스킷을 먹고 있을 때 엄마가 주방으로 걸어 들어왔다. 그녀는 자신의 어린 아기를 한 번 보더니 웃기 시작했다. 그의 작은 얼굴과 손이 비스킷과 잼으로 덮여 있었다. 그녀는 그가 참으로 귀엽다고 생각했다. "여보, 무슨 짓을 한 거예요? 그를 보세요. 나는 그를 다시는 깨끗이 씻어줄 수 없을 거예요. 내 생각에 그가 먹는 것을 끝마치면 당신이 그를 데리고 가서 그를 욕조에 푹 담그면 되겠네요." 아빠는 웃었다. Tom은 낄낄 웃으며 비스킷을 몽땅 아빠를 향해 뿜어 버리려고 했다. 그가 운 좋게 뿜는 것을 피했기 때문에 그것은 그를 맞추지 못했다. 그것은 엄마를 더욱더 웃게 만들었으며 곧 작은 오두막집은 사랑과 웃음으로 가득 찼다.

어휘

spread A with B A에 B를 바르다
homemade 집에서 만든, 손으로 만든
little 어린, 작은, 거의 없는
giggle 낄낄 웃다
cover A with B A를 B로 덮다
cabin 오두막집

Day 09

07 정답 ④

정답해설

④ 출제 포인트: 주어와 동사 수일치
주어가 「부분 of 명사」의 형태이므로 동사 'has'는 복수명사 'workers'에 수일치 해야 한다. 따라서 'has'를 복수동사 'have'로 수정해야 한다.

오답해설

① 출제 포인트: 원급 비교
「as+원급+as」는 원급 비교 구문에 해당하며 원급자리에 형용사 원급 'difficult'를 옳게 사용하였다.

② 출제 포인트: 비교급 비교
비교급은 형용사와 부사 외에 분사에도 사용할 수 있다. 따라서 해당 문장은 「more+과거분사+than」 형태의 비교급 비교 구문이 쓰인 문장으로 옳은 문장이다.

③ 출제 포인트: 동명사 관용표현
'be good at+-ing'은 관용표현으로 '~에 능숙하다, ~을 잘하다'를 뜻한다. 또한 'get across+목적어[사물]+to+목적어[사람]'는 관용표현으로 '~을 ~에게 전달하다'를 뜻한다.

08 정답 ③

정답해설

③의 "Sharks lose their teeth all the time, and one from the row behind moves forward to replace it, so they are always geared with a full army of them to attack(상어는 항상 이빨이 빠지고, 뒷줄의 이빨이 그것을 대체하기 위해 앞으로 이동한다. 따라서 그들은 공격을 하기 위한 그것들로 항상 완전 무장을 하고 있다.)."에서 주어가 '상어'이고 밑줄 친 them은 상어가 공격을 위해 가지고 있는 '이빨'을 가리킨다는 것을 알 수 있다. ③은 상어가 지니고 있는 '이빨'을 가리키고 나머지 보기는 '상어'를 지칭하므로 ③이 정답이다.

오답해설

① "This versatility provides sharks with a very powerful pull and latch onto what they want fiercely."에서 밑줄 친 'they'가 문장의 목적어 'sharks'를 가리키고 있으므로 오답이다.

② 이전 문장에서 '상어의 이빨'에 관해 언급하고 있으므로 밑줄 친 'Their'는 '상어'를 가리킨다는 것을 알 수 있다.

④ 이빨이 빠지는 것의 주체는 '상어'이므로 밑줄 친 'They'는 '상어'를 가리킨다는 것을 알 수 있다.

해석

상어는 두개골에 부착된 턱이 없다. 대신 그것들은 별개의 부분으로 움직인다. 상부 그리고 하부 턱은 다른 하나 없이 개별적으로 기능할 수 있다. 이러한 융통성은 상어가 ①그들이 원하는 것을 사납게 끌어당기고 잡아둘 수 있는 매우 강력한 힘을 준다. 또한 상어는 많은 열의 이빨을 가지고 있다. ②그들의 이빨은 매우 강력하여 그들은 아무런 어려움 없이 뼈와 살을 즉각 찢어낼 수 있다. 상어는 항상 이빨이 빠지고, 뒷줄의 이빨이 그것을 대체하기 위해 앞으로 이동한다. 따라서 그들은 공격을 하기 위한 ③그것들로 항상 완전 무장을 하고 있다. ④그들은 앞줄의 이빨이 몇 주 내지 한 달 간격으로 빠질 수 있다. 따라서 그들은 그들의 일생동안 약 30,000개의 이빨을 가질 것이다.

어휘

attach 붙이다, 부착하다
skull 두개골
versatility 융통성, 다채, 다능
provide A with B A에게 B를 제공하다
pull 끌기, 끌어[잡아]당기기
latch 걸쇠, 잠금장치
fiercely 사납게
row 열, 줄
rip 찢다
flesh 살
struggle 투쟁, 몸부림
replace 대체하다, 대신하다
gear (장비 등을) 설치하다, 준비하다
army 집단, 무리

09 정답 ④

정답해설

해당 지문은 '상어 개체 수 변화에 따른 생태계 변화'를 먹이사슬의 측면에서 설명하고 있다. 첫 번째로, '상어 개체 수 감소로 인해 가오리 개체 수가 증가하고 가오리의 먹이가 되는 가리비는 감소한다'는 것, 두 번째로, '상어 개체 수 감소로 인해 그루퍼가 증가하고, 그루퍼의 먹이가 되는 비늘돔이 감소하였다. 산호초의 해조류를 먹이로 삼는 비늘돔의 감소로 인해, 산호초의 해조류가 증가하고 그에 따라 산호초를 서식지로 삼는 종에도 영향을 미친다'는 것을 예로 들고 있다. 따라서 전체 글의 요지로 가장 적절한 보기는 "④ Altering the numbers of sharks has a big impact on other species(상어의 개체 수를 변화시키는 것이 다른 종에 큰 영향을 미친다)."이다.

오답해설

① 상어 보호의 필요성에 관한 내용은 언급되지 않는다.
② 상위 포식자인 상어에 관해 언급하고 있으나, 글의 주된 요지는 아니므로 오답이다.
③ 본문과 관련 없는 내용이다.

해석

상어 지느러미의 높은 수요 때문에 상어는 그들이 번식할 수 있는 것보다 더 빠른 속도로 바다에서 잡혀 죽임을 당하고 있다. 상어의 개체 수가 감소함에 따라 가오리와 같은 그들의 먹이 종은 증가해왔다. 그리고 그 결과 그것들은 가리비와 같은 그들 자신의 먹이를 더 많이 섭취하고 있다. 결과적으로, 많은 연체동물종이 급격하게 감소하고 있다. 연구자들은 또한 카리브해의 급격한 상어의 감소에 따른 파급효과를 목격하고 있다. 상어에 의해 먹히는 그루퍼와 같은 물고기가 현재 증가하고 있다. 산호초에서 해조류를 먹어 치우는 비늘돔을 먹이로 삼는 그루퍼가 너무 많이 있고, 그것이 너무 많은 해조류가 수중에 존재하도록 야기한다. 이것이 산호초 서식지에 의존하는 모든 종에게 필요한 자원을 제한함으로써 해양 생태계를 변화시키고 있다.

① 상어는 국제법에 의해 보호되어야 한다.
② 상어는 해양 생태계에서 최상위 포식자이다.
③ 지느러미가 없다면 상어는 생존할 수 없을 것이다.
④ 상어의 개체 수를 변화시키는 것이 다른 종에 큰 영향을 미친다.

어휘

pluck (잡아당겨) 빼내다 [뽑아내다]
reproduce 번식하다
demand 수요
fin 지느러미
decline 감소하다
prey 먹이
species 종
ray 가오리
in turn 결국, 결과적으로
scallop 가리비
mollusk 연체동물
ripple effect 파급효과
dramatic 극적인, 급격한
grouper 그루퍼 (농엇과(科)의 식용어)
parrotfish 비늘돔
algae 조류, 해조
coral reef 산호초
result in (결과적으로) ~을 낳다[야기하다]
ecological system 생태계
resource 자원
habitat 서식지
predator 포식 동물
alter 변화시키다

오답률 TOP 2
10 정답 ③

정답해설

해당 지문은 '세계에서 가장 작은 상어'에 관한 내용이다. 본문에 언급된 세 종류의 상어 중 'dwarf lantern shark'와 'spined pygmy shark'는 성체 암컷 상어가 각각 19~20cm, 17~20cm로 성체 수컷 상어(각각 16-17.5cm, 15cm)보다 길다는 것을 알 수 있으나, 마지막에 언급된 'pygmy ribbontail catshark'는 성체 수컷이 18~19cm, 성체 암컷은 15~16cm로 수컷의 길이가 더 길다는 것을 알 수 있다. 따라서 암컷보다 수컷의 길이가 더 긴 상어 종이 존재하므로, "③ All mature female sharks are longer than mature male sharks(모든 성숙한 암컷 상어는 성숙한 수컷 상어보다 더 길다)."는 글의 내용과 일치하지 않는다.

오답해설

① 본문 첫 번째 문장에서 '세계에서 가장 작은 상어 종 경쟁자들이 둘 혹은 셋 있다'라고 언급하고 있으므로, 명확히 어느 종이 가장 작은지 알 수 없다는 것을 유추할 수 있다.
② "Prior to the discovery of the dwarf lantern shark in 1964(1964년에 dwarf lantern shark의 발견 이전의)"를 통해 1960년대 이전에는 'dwarf lantern shark'가 발견되지 않았다는 것을 알 수 있다.
④ 'dwarf lantern shark'의 발견 이전 '가장 작은 상어 기록 보유자'는 'spined pygmy shark'였다고 언급하고 있으므로 글의 내용과 일치한다.

해석

작은 종이 성적으로 성숙한 (즉, 성체이며 완전히 자란) 시기를 정확하게 알아내는 것의 어려움 때문에, 둘 어쩌면 세 종류의 가장 작은 상어 종 경쟁자들이 있다. 가장 가능성 있는 기록 보유자는 dwarf lantern shark로, 이것들 중 수컷은 총길이가 16-17.5cm이고, 성숙한 암컷은 보통 19~20cm이다. 1964년에 dwarf lantern shark의 발견 이전의 기록 보유자는 spined pygmy shark로, 이것들 중 수컷은 길이가 15cm 이상, 암컷은 17~20cm이다. 세 번째 경쟁자 종인 pygmy ribbontail catshark는 수컷이 18~19cm이고 암컷은 아마도 15~16cm에 이르면 성숙한다.
① 어느 상어 종이 세계에서 가장 작은지는 불분명하다.
② dwarf lantern shark는 1960년대 이전에는 알려지지 않았다.
③ 모든 성숙한 암컷 상어는 성숙한 수컷 상어보다 더 길다.
④ spined pygmy shark는 한때 세계에서 가장 작은 상어로 여겨졌다.

어휘

determine 결정하다 precisely 정확하게
species 종 mature 성숙한; 성숙하다
i.e. 즉 contender 경쟁자, 도전자
measure 길이(높이, 폭, 넓이 등)가 ~이다

결국엔 성정혜 영어 하프모의고사
기적사 DAY 10

01	③	02	②	03	②	04	④	05	③
06	④	07	②	08	①	09	①	10	③

01 정답 ③

정답해설

밑줄 친 단어는 문맥상 '이상한'으로 사용되었고, 유의어로는 ③ strange가 적절하다.

해석

이상하게 보일지 모르지만, 한 야생동물 전문가는 이 백여우가 실제로 족제비를 먹이로 하고 있다고 말한다.
① 표면상의
② 오만한, 긴급한
③ 이상한
④ 우연한

어휘

ostensible 표면상의 imperious 오만한, 긴급한
strange 이상한 adventitious 우연한

02 정답 ②

정답해설

밑줄 친 단어의 의미는 문맥상 '명확한'으로 쓰였고, 유의어로는 ② manifest가 적절하다.

해석

그가 그의 우울증에 대해 이야기하고 싶어 하지 않는다는 것은 **명확했다**.
① 은밀한
② 명백한, 분명한
③ 마지못해 하는
④ 모호한, 부정확한

어휘

depression 우울증 stealthy 은밀한
manifest 명백한, 분명한 grudging 마지못해 하는
imprecise 모호한, 부정확한

오답률 TOP 2
03 정답 ②

정답해설

밑줄 친 단어의 의미가 문맥상 '무례한, 모욕적인'으로 사용되었으므로 유의어로는 ② insulting이 적절하다.

해석

우리는 그들이 얼마나 **무례하든지** 간에, 그들의 전통들을 존중해야만 한다.
① 결점이 없는, 죄를 범하지 않는
② 무례한, 모욕적인

③ 의무적인
④ 순간적인, 덧없는

어휘
offensive 공격적인
impeccable 결점이 없는, 죄를 범하지 않는
insulting 무례한, 모욕적인   mandatory 의무적인
impermanent 순간적인, 덧없는

04 정답 ④

정답해설
심부름을 시킬 때마다 핑계를 대면서 없어지는 B에게 A가 할 수 있는 말은 '인내가 한계에 다다르다'라는 표현인 ④ I'm at the end of my rope이다.

해석
A: 내가 심부름을 시킬 때 사라지지 마라.
B: 엄마, 이 축구 경기만 보고요.
A: 난 이제 더 이상 못 참겠다.
B: 네, 알았어요.
① 행운을 빌어
② 그것은 막상막하야
③ 나는 맞는 말만 하네
④ 난 이제 더 이상 못 참겠다

어휘
vanish into thin air 완전히 사라지다, 흔적도 없어지다
get the picture 이해하다   break a leg 행운을 빌다
neck and neck 막상막하
hit the nail on the head 맞는 말만 하다
be at the end of one's rope 인내의 한계에 다다르다

Day 10

05 정답 ③

정답해설
③ 출제 포인트: 분사 vs. 동사
종속절에 'If'를 사용하였고 주절에 「조동사 과거형+동사원형」형태인 'might think'를 사용하였으므로 가정법 과거가 쓰인 문장임을 알 수 있다. 따라서 If절의 본동사 자리에 현재분사 'learning'을 사용하였으므로 과거시제 동사 'learned'로 수정해야 한다.

오답해설
① 출제 포인트: to부정사의 명사적 용법
'to understand'는 to부정사의 명사적 용법에 해당하며 완전타동사 'need'의 목적어로 옳게 사용되었다.
② 출제 포인트: 완전자동사/일치
'exist'는 완전자동사로 수동태를 사용할 수 없으며, 주어가 복수형태인 'certain functional objects'이므로 복수동사 'exist'를 사용하는 것이 옳다.
④ 출제 포인트: 동사 관용표현
'have no difficulty (in) -ing'는 관용표현으로 '~하는 데 어려움이 없다, ~하는 데 지장이 없다'를 뜻한다.

해석
의자를 생각해 보라. 여러분이 의자의 개념을 가질 수 있기 전에, 여러분은 기능적인 어떤 물체들이 세상에 존재한다는 것을 이해해야 한다. 이러한 물체들 중 일부는 인간 활동을 지원하는데, 이 경우에는 앉기이다. 그중에 어떤 것들은 술집의 의자와 같이 어떤 높은 장소에 앉기 위해 특화되어 있다. 여러분이 어떤 특정한 형태의 의자가 버스를 기다리는 동안에 앉는 목적으로만 사용되는 문화에 대해 알게 된다면, 여러분은 이것을 이상하다고 여길 수 있으나 그것을 이해하는 데는 전혀 어려움을 겪지 않을 것이다.

어휘
specialize 전문화하다, 특수화하다   stool 의자
have no difficulty (in) ~ing ~하는 데 어려움이 없다, ~하는 데 지장이 없다

06 정답 ④

정답해설
④ 출제 포인트: 등위접속사의 병렬구조
등위 접속사 뒤에 또 다른 절이 위치해야 옳은 문장이다. 해당 문장에서는 문맥상 '명령문'으로 '~하지 말아라'가 옳다. 따라서 부정명령문 형태의 never+동사원형이 옳다.

오답해설
① 출제 포인트: 사역동사의 목적격 보어
사역동사 'make'는 목적격 보어로 원형부정사를 사용해야 한다.
② 출제 포인트: 주격 관계대명사
선행사인 'the only one'이 단수이므로 주격 관계대명사 'that'과 주격 관계대명사절 동사에 단수동사 'feels'를 옳게 사용하였다.
③ 출제 포인트: 준사역동사의 목적격 보어
준사역동사 'help'의 목적격 보어로 원형부정사를 사용할 수 있다.

해석
두려움과 의구심의 주된 목표들 중 하나는 네가 특정 방식으로 느끼는 유일한 사람인 것처럼 너를 외롭게 느끼게 하는 것이다. 두려움은 너를 고립시키기를 그리고 너를 섬에 두기를 원한다. 네가 너의 두려움을 남에게 말하지 않는다면 아무도 너에게 그것에 관한 진실을 말할 수 없다. 아무도 정말 무슨 일이 일어나고 있는지 네가 보도록 도울 수 없다. 아무도 너를 격려할 수 없다. 그러므로 만약 네가 너의 목소리에게 "사라져"라고 말하려면 너는 그것들을 다른 사람들과 공유해야 한다. 너는 너의 가까운 친구나 가족 또는 상담사에게 너의 목소리에 관해 말해야만 한다.
바로 그 사람은 모두와는 다를 것이지만, 절대로 홀로 목소리와 싸우기 위해 노력하는 데 드는 시간을 낭비하지 마라.

어휘
isolate 고립시키다, 격리하다   go on 일어나다, 벌어지다
have got to+동사원형 ~해야 한다
share A with B A를 B와 공유하다
battle 싸우다

07 정답 ②

정답해설
② 출제 포인트: 원급 비교
「A+not nearly as+원급+as+B」는 원급 비교 형태의 관용 구문으로 'B는 A보다 훨씬 더 ~하다, A는 B보다 더 ~하진 않다'를 뜻한다. 따라서 'than'을 'as'로 수정해야 한다.

오답해설
① 출제 포인트: 주어와 동사의 수일치
주격 관계대명사절의 동사와 주절의 동사의 수일치 기준은 복수명사 'people'이므로 복수동사 'are'와 'form'을 사용하는 것이 옳다.
③ 출제 포인트: 동명사 관용표현
'be good at+-ing'은 관용표현으로 '~에 능숙하다, ~을 잘하다'를 뜻한다.

④ **출제 포인트: 비교급 비교**
비교급은 형용사와 부사 외에 분사에도 사용할 수 있다. 따라서 해당 문장은 「no+less+과거분사+than」 형태의 비교급 비교 구문이 쓰인 문장으로 옳은 문장이다.

오답률 TOP 1
08 정답 ①

정답해설
(A) 빈칸 전후 문장에서 '선천적 관념'을 주장한 'Plato and Descartes'와 '탄생 시에는 백지상태이고, 경험에 의해 지식을 획득한다'라고 주장한 'John Locke'의 상반된 의견을 제시하고 있으므로 '역접'을 나타내는 ① On the other hand가 빈칸에 알맞다.
(B) 빈칸 이전에는 '명백한 생물학적 발달 과정'인 '사춘기'에 대해 언급한 후, 빈칸 이후 사춘기에도 '식단, 영양과 같은 환경적 요인도 영향을 미친다'라고 이전과 반대되는 측면의 내용을 서술하고 있으므로, '역접'을 나타내는 ① However가 빈칸에 알맞다.

해석
보통 천성 대 양성 논쟁으로 칭해지는 유전과 환경의 상대적인 기여에 대한 논쟁은 철학과 심리학 모두에서 가장 오래된 쟁점 중 하나이다. 플라톤과 데카르트와 같은 철학자들은 일부 관념이 선천적이라는 생각을 지지했다. (A) 반면 존 로크와 같은 사상가들은 탄생 시에 마음은 비어있는 석판이며 경험이 우리의 지식을 결정한다는 백지상태 개념에 찬성했다. 오늘날 대부분의 심리학자들은 발달을 일으키는 것은 바로 이 두 가지 힘 사이의 상호작용이라고 믿는다. 사춘기와 같이 발달에 있어서 일부 측면은 명백히 생물학적이다. (B) 그러나 사춘기의 시작은 식단이나 영양과 같은 환경적인 요인에 의해 영향을 받을 수 있다.
① 반면 – 그러나
② 그와는 반대로 – 결과적으로
③ 그 결과 – 그럼에도 불구하고
④ 예를 들어 – 요컨대

어휘
debate 논쟁
contribution 기여
refer to 지칭하다
inborn 타고난, 선천적인
slate 석판
interaction 상호작용
puberty 사춘기
nutrition 영양
consequently 그 결과
in summary 요컨대, 요약하면
relative 상대적인
inheritance 유전(되는 것)
nurture 양성, 양육
argue for ~에 찬성 의견을 말하다
determine 결정하다
biological 생물학적인
onset (특히 불쾌한 일의) 시작, 발병
on the contrary 그와는 반대로
nevertheless 그럼에도 불구하고

09 정답 ①

정답해설
해당 지문은 '유전적 요인'과 '환경'의 상호작용에 대해 '절대음감'을 예로 들어 설명하고 있다. 빈칸에는 '유전적 요인'과 '환경'이 어떻게 작용하는지 설명하는 어휘가 들어가야 적절하다. 본동사에 부정어 not이 포함되어 있으므로, 빈칸에는 '독립적으로, 개별적으로, 따로따로'를 의미하는 어휘가 들어가 '독립적으로[개별적으로/따로따로] 작용하지 않는다는 것'이라는 의미의 절이 되는 것이 자연스럽다. 따라서 빈칸에 들어갈 단어로 가장 적절하지 않은 것은 '① comprehensively(포괄적으로)'이다.

오답해설
② independently(독립적으로), ③ separately(단독으로), ④ discretely(따로따로)는 모두 비슷하게 '개별적으로'라는 의미로 쓰일 수 있으므로 빈칸에 적절하다.

해석
유전적 형질과 환경이 독립적으로 작용하지 않는다는 것은 오늘날 널리 받아들여진다. 이러한 천성과 양성 상호작용의 완벽한 예시는 어떠한 참조도 없이 악음의 높이를 간파할 수 있는 능력인 절대음감이다. 연구자들은 이 능력이 유전인 경향이 있다는 것을 발견했고 단독 유전자와 관련이 있을 수도 있다고 생각해왔다. 그러나 그들은 또한 그 유전자를 보유하고 있는 것만으로는 이 능력을 발달시키기 충분하지 않다는 것을 알아냈다. 대신, 이러한 유전적인 능력이 발현하도록 하기 위해서는 조기의 적절한 음악 훈련이 필요하다.
① 포괄적으로
② 독립적으로
③ 단독으로
④ 따로따로

어휘
heredity 유전적 형질, 유전
interaction 상호작용
detect 간파하다, 감지하다
musical tone 악음
run in family 집안 내력이다, 유전되다
be tied to ~와 관련되다
possess 소유하다
inherit (육체적·정신적 성질 등을) 물려받다, 유전하다
manifest oneself 나타나다, 드러내다, 분명해지다
comprehensively 포괄적으로
separately 따로따로, 개별적으로, 단독으로
nurture 양성, 양육
perfect pitch 절대음감
pitch 음의 높이
reference 참조, 대조, 비교
gene 유전자
proper 적절한, 알맞은
discretely 따로따로, 별개로

오답률 TOP 3
10 정답 ③

정답해설
해당 지문은 'Dr. John Money'가 실시했던 David Reimer에 대한 실험과, 그에 따른 학계의 반응'에 대해 설명하고 있다. 주어진 문장에서는 'David Reimer의 사례' 이전의 학계의 정설에 대해 설명하고 있고, (B)에서 'this belief'를 이용해 해당 정설을 가리키고 있다. 또한 (B)에서 'David Reimer 사례'에 대해 자세히 언급하고 있으므로 (B)가 주어진 문장 바로 이후에 위치하는 것이 적절하다. 이후 (B)에서 언급된 '성전환 수술'에 이어진 'David의 행동'에 대해 (C)에서 언급하고 있으므로 다음에 위치해야 한다. 또한 (C)의 주절에서는 'a number of individuals in the field of psychology began to question this decision(심리학 분야의 수많은 사람들이 이 결정에 의문을 품기 시작했다)'를 통해 학계의 반응을 언급한 후, (A)에서 for example을 이용하여 해당 반응을 보인 대표적인 인물인 'Milton Diamond'를 소개하고 있으므로 (A)가 이어지는 것이 문맥상 자연스럽다. 따라서 가장 적절한 순서는 '③ (B) – (C) – (A)'이다.

해석
David Reimer 사례 이전에는 사회학습이론이 성전환의 경우에 적용될 수 있다고 생각되었다.
(B) 이러한 믿음 때문에 John Money박사는 David가 성전환 수술을 받고 여성으로 자라야 한다고 말했다.
(C) 그러나 그가 새로이 지정된 성에 저항했을 때, 심리학 분야의 수많은 사람들이 이 결정에 의문을 품기 시작했다.
(A) 예를 들어, University of Hawaii의 해부학 및 생식 생물학 교수인

Milton Diamond은 아이들의 행동적 차이는 선천적이며 성기의 외관과는 관련이 거의 없기 때문에 성전환에 있어서 사회학습이론을 적용한 것이 부적절했다고 주장했다.

어휘

prior to ~이전에
apply 적용시키다
rebel 저항하다, 반항하다
anatomy 해부학
application 적용
inherent 유전적인, 내재하는, 타고난
have little to do with ~와 거의 관련이 없다
appearance 외관
social learning theory 사회학습이론
gender reassignment 성전환
assign 할당하다, 지정하다
reproductive 생식의, 번식의
inadequate 부적당한
genital 성기, 생식기

결국엔 성정혜 영어 하프모의고사
기적사 복습 모의고사 1회

01	①	02	②	03	②	04	④	05	③
06	②	07	③	08	①	09	③	10	④
11	①	12	④	13	③	14	①	15	④
16	④	17	①	18	④	19	④	20	①

01 정답 ①   Day 06-01

정답해설

'discern'은 '구별하다'라는 뜻을 가진 동사이다. 밑줄 친 단어 전에 내용으로 잡지 구독자들이 정확한 정보를 얻게 될 것이라고 하였으므로 무엇이 그들이 산업과 관계되는 것인지 정확하게 구별할 수 있다는 것으로 유추할 수 있다. 따라서 유의어 관계에 있는 보기는 ① distinguish이다.

해석

Natural Gas World 구독자들은 이 산업에서 어떤 일들이 일어나고 있는지에 대한 정확하고 믿을 수 있는 주요한 사실들과 수치들을 받게 될 것이다. 그래서 그들은 무엇이 그들의 사업과 관계되는 것인지 충분하게 **구별할** 수 있다.
① 구별하다, 식별하다
② 강화하다
③ 약화시키다
④ 버리다, 포기하다

02 정답 ②   Day 05-03

정답해설

밑줄 친 단어는 문맥상 '불안감'으로 사용되었고, 유의어로는 ② apprehension가 적절하다.

해석

그들이 목장에 가까이 갈 때마다 그녀의 **불안감**은 더욱 커졌다.
① 분노, 분개
② 불안감
③ 이해, 감사, 상승, 강세
④ 선동 연설가

03 정답 ②   Day 10-03

정답해설

밑줄 친 단어의 의미가 문맥상 '무례한, 모욕적인'으로 사용되었으므로 유의어로는 ② insulting이 적절하다.

해석

우리는 그들이 얼마나 **무례하든지** 간에, 그들의 전통들을 존중해야만 한다.
① 결점이 없는, 죄를 범하지 않는
② 무례한, 모욕적인
③ 의무적인
④ 순간적인, 덧없는

04 정답 ④ Day 01-01

정답해설

'indigenous'는 '토종의, 토착민의'라는 뜻으로 선택지 ④의 'native'와 의미가 가장 가깝다.

해석

전설적인 다큐멘터리 제작자 Robert J. Flaherty는 어떻게 **토착**민들이 음식을 모았는지 보여주려 시도했다.
① 떠돌아다니는, 순회하는
② 빈곤한, 결핍된
③ 배가 고파 죽을 지경인, 엄청난
④ 토박이의

05 정답 ③ Day 02-08

정답해설

(A) 빈칸 이전 "no information about the trial has been made public (재판에 대한 어떠한 정보도 공개되지 않았다)."에서 비공개 재판에 대해 언급한 후, "any of Huang's lawyers was never told about the trial(Huang의 변호인들 중 누구도 재판에 대해 이야기를 듣지 못했다)."를 통해 재판에 대한 추가적인 정보를 제공하고 있다. 따라서 '첨언, 부연'을 의미하는 Moreover가 (A)에 가장 적절하다.

(B) 빈칸 이전 문장 "The closed-door hearing violated his right to a fair and public trial by an independent court(그 비공개 심문은 독립 법정으로부터 공정하고 공개적인 재판을 받을 그의 권리를 침해하였다)."를 통해 '재판의 부당함'에 대해 언급한 후, 빈칸 이후에서 "the Chinese government must immediately and unconditionally release Huang Qi(중국 정부는 즉각적이고 조건 없이 Huang Qi를 석방해야 한다)"라고 필자의 주장 및 글의 결론을 서술하고 있다. 따라서, 앞서 논의한 것의 '결론'을 나타내는 Thus가 (B)에 가장 적절하다.

해석

중국 당국이 인권 운동가이자 시민 저널리스트인 Huang Qi를 국가 기밀을 해외 단체에 불법으로 제공하고 고의적으로 국가 기밀을 유출한 혐의로 재판에 회부했음에도 불구하고, 법원은 판결을 선고하지 않았다. 국민 중 누구도 재판에 참석하는 것이 허용되지 않았고, 재판에 대한 어떠한 정보도 공개되지 않았다. (A) 게다가, Huang의 변호인들 중 누구도 재판에 대해 이야기를 듣지 못했다. 그 비공개 심문은 독립 법정으로부터 공정하고 공개적인 재판을 받을 그의 권리를 침해하였다. (B) 따라서, 중국 정부는 즉각적이고 조건 없이 건강이 심각하게 안 좋은 Huang Qi를 석방하고, 표현과 결사의 자유 행사를 이유로 그를 박해하는 것을 멈추어야 한다.
① 즉 - 그러나
② 예를 들어 - 그렇지 않으면
③ 게다가 - 따라서
④ 요컨대 - 유사하게

06 정답 ② Day 01-07

정답해설

② 출제 포인트: 현재분사 vs. 과거분사

인간이 가축들을 어떻게 이용하여 왔는지 설명하고 있는 글이다. '② Utilizing with other techniques, animals can raise human living standards very considerably'에서 분사구문의 주어가 없으므로 주절의 주어와 같은 주어인 것을 알 수 있고 동사 'utilize'는 목적어를 수반하는 타동사인데 목적어가 없으므로 수동분사구문이 문법상 올바르다는 것을 알 수 있다. 따라서 어법상 틀린 부분은 ②이다.
'As animals are utilized with other techniques~'
→ Being utilized with other techniques
→ Utilized with other techniques

해석

가축화된 동물들은 인간들에게 구할 수 있는 가장 이르고 가장 효과적인 '기계들'이었다. 그들은 인간의 등과 팔의 부담을 떨쳐내 준다. 다른 기술들과 함께 사용되면서, 동물들은 보충적인 음식재료들(고기와 우유의 단백질)과 짐을 실어 나르고 물을 끌어올리고 그리고 곡식을 가는 기계들 두 가지로 인간들의 삶의 기준을 매우 상당하게 올릴 수 있다. 그들이 명백하게 아주 이익이 되기 때문에, 우리는 아마 수세기를 지나 인간들은 그들이 소유하고 있는 동물들의 수와 질을 증가시킬 것이라는 것을 찾아낼 것이라고 예상할지 모른다. 놀랍게도, 이것은 보통에서 그렇지 않다.

07 정답 ③ Day 04-08

정답해설

해당 지문은 '쿠키 파일 삭제'에 대한 내용이며, 2, 3번째 문장 "By taking the time to delete the cookies, you can increase the speed and performance of your web browsing software(쿠키를 삭제하는 시간을 할애함으로써, 당신은 웹 브라우징 소프트웨어의 속도와 성능을 향상시킬 수 있다)," "Doing so on a regular basis will also free space on your hard drive and prevent system crashes(정기적으로 그렇게 하는 것은 또한 당신의 하드드라이브의 공간을 확보해 주고 시스템 충돌을 예방해줄 것이다)"와 마지막 문장 "By setting your web browser to delete cookies each time you close your browser, you can thwart these tracking attempts and reduce the risk of a security breach(브라우저를 종료할 때마다 쿠키를 삭제하도록 웹브라우저 설정을 해둠으로써, 당신은 이러한 추적 시도를 좌절시킬 수 있고, 보안 침해의 위험을 감소시킬 수 있다)."를 통해 '쿠키를 삭제하는 것의 이점'을 서술하고 있다. 따라서 '③ Benefits of Removing Cookies(쿠키 삭제의 이점)'가 글의 제목으로 가장 적절하다.

해석

쿠키 파일은 꽤 작지만, 여전히 그것들은 축적될 수 있고 당신의 시스템 성능을 떨어뜨릴 수 있다. 쿠키를 삭제하는 시간을 할애함으로써, 당신은 웹 브라우징 소프트웨어의 속도와 성능을 향상시킬 수 있다. 정기적으로 그렇게 하는 것은 또한 당신의 하드드라이브의 공간을 확보해 주고 당신의 컴퓨터에 충분한 공간이 없을 때 종종 발생하는 시스템 충돌을 예방해줄 것이다. 게다가, 많은 쿠키들이 해롭지는 않지만, 일부는 인터넷상의 당신의 모든 움직임을 추적하는 데 사용될 수도 있다. 사업체들은 소비자 행동을 연구하기 위해 종종 이러한 추적 쿠키를 사용하지만, 많은 컴퓨터 사용자들은 그것들을 사생활 침해로 여긴다. 브라우저를 종료할 때마다 쿠키를 삭제하도록 웹브라우저 설정을 해둠으로써, 당신은 이러한 추적 시도를 좌절시킬 수 있고, 보안 침해의 위험을 감소시킬 수 있다.
① 인터넷 쿠키의 위협
② 어떻게 쿠키가 사생활을 침해하는가?
③ 쿠키 삭제의 이점
④ 쿠키 사용의 장단점

08 정답 ① Day 09-06

정답해설

① 출제 포인트: 목적격 관계대명사

선행사가 'a biscuit'인 관계대명사 'that'이 쓰인 문장으로 뒤따라오는 문장은 불완전해야 하며 해석상 '버터와 집에서 만든 딸기잼을 발라놓은 비스킷'이 자연스러우므로 'spread butter'를 'spread with butter'로 수정해야 한다.

※ 관계대명사가 만들어지는 과정

Tom sat in his chair eating a biscuit. + Dad had spread it with butter and homemade strawberry jam. (선행사가 사물을 뜻하는 명사구 'a biscuit'이며 완전타동사 'spread'의 목적어에 해당하므로 목적격 관계대명사 'which' 또는 'that'을 사용)

→ Tom sat in his chair eating a biscuit that Dad had spread with butter and homemade strawberry jam.

해석

Tom이 자신의 의자에 앉아서 아빠가 버터와 집에서 만든 딸기잼을 발라놓은 비스킷을 먹고 있을 때 엄마가 주방으로 걸어 들어왔다. 그녀는 자신의 어린 아기를 한 번 보더니 웃기 시작했다. 그의 작은 얼굴과 손이 비스킷과 잼으로 덮여 있었다. 그녀는 그가 참으로 귀엽다고 생각했다. "여보, 무슨 짓을 한 거예요? 그를 보세요. 나는 그를 다시는 깨끗이 씻어줄 수 없을 거예요. 내 생각에 그가 먹는 것을 끝마치면 당신이 그를 데리고 가서 그를 욕조에 푹 담그면 되겠네요." 아빠는 웃었다. Tom은 킬킬 웃으며 비스킷을 몽땅 아빠를 향해 뿜어 버리려고 했다. 그가 운 좋게 뿜는 것을 피했기 때문에 그것은 그를 맞추지 못했다. 그것은 엄마를 더욱더 웃게 만들었으며 곧 작은 오두막집은 사랑과 웃음으로 가득 찼다.

09 정답 ③   Day 06-09

정답해설

본문의 후반부에 글쓴이 자신의 예를 들면서 인간의 본성은 자신이 얼마나 아팠고 많이 힘들었는지 알려지는 것을 좋아한다고 서술하고 있다. 따라서 빈칸에 가장 적절한 표현은 ③ pride in illness(질병에 대한 자부심)이다.

해석

인간의 본성은 호기심 많은 특징을 가지고 있지만, 가장 궁금한 것 중 하나는 질병에 대한 자부심이다. 아무도 끊임없이 고장 나는 자동차를 가지고 있는 것이 좋은 것이라고 생각하지 않는다. 사람들은 오래 달린 후에 차가 몇 주 동안 완전히 쓸모없게 되거나, 가장 능숙한 기계공들조차도 바로잡을 수 없는 이상한 문제를 끊임없이 발전시키고 있다고 자랑하지 않는다. 하지만 그것이 사람들이 자신의 몸에 대해 느끼는 방법이다. 만족스럽게 움직이는 몸을 갖는 것은 재미없고 오히려 평범한 것으로 여겨진다. 섬세한 소화는 아름다운 여인의 조건에 거의 필수불가결한 것이다. 나는 내 스스로 병을 자랑하기 위한 충동을 알고 있다. 나는 단지 한번 병을 앓은 적이 있을 뿐이지만, 나는 사람들이 내가 그때 얼마나 많이 아팠는지 아는 것을 좋아하며, 죽지 않고 거의 죽은 다른 사람들을 만났을 때 나는 화가 난다.

① 질병에 대한 공포
② 자동차에 대한 흥미
③ 질병에 대한 자부심
④ 죽음의 공포

10 정답 ④   Day 09-09

정답해설

해당 지문은 '상어 개체 수 변화에 따른 생태계 변화'를 먹이사슬의 측면에서 설명하고 있다. 첫 번째로, '상어 개체 수 감소로 인해 가오리 개체 수가 증가하고 가오리의 먹이가 되는 가리비는 감소한다'는 것, 두 번째로, '상어 개체 수 감소로 인해 그루퍼가 증가하고, 그루퍼의 먹이가 되는 비늘돔이 감소하였다. 산호초의 해조류를 먹이로 삼는 비늘돔의 감소로 인해, 산호초의 해조류가 증가하고 그에 따라 산호초를 서식지로 삼는 종에도 영향을 미친다'는 것을 예로 들고 있다. 따라서 전체 글의 요지로 가장 적절한 보기는 "④ Altering the numbers of sharks has a big impact on other species(상어의 개체 수를 변화시키는 것이 다른 종에 큰 영향을 미친다)."이다.

해석

상어 지느러미의 높은 수요 때문에 상어는 그들이 번식할 수 있는 것보다 더 빠른 속도로 바다에서 잡혀 죽임을 당하고 있다. 상어의 개체 수가 감소함에 따라 가오리와 같은 그들의 먹이 종은 증가해왔다. 그리고 그 결과 그것들은 가리비와 같은 그들 자신의 먹이를 더 많이 섭취하고 있다. 결과적으로, 많은 연체동물종이 급격하게 감소하고 있다. 연구자들은 또한 카리브해의 급격한 상어의 감소에 따른 파급효과를 목격하고 있다. 상어에 의해 먹히는 그루퍼와 같은 물고기가 현재 증가하고 있다. 산호초에서 해조류를 먹어치우는 비늘돔을 먹이로 삼는 그루퍼가 너무 많이 있고, 그것이 너무 많은 해조류가 수중에 존재하도록 야기한다. 이것이 산호초 서식지에 의존하는 모든 종에게 필요한 자원을 제한함으로써 해양 생태계를 변화시키고 있다.

① 상어는 국제법에 의해 보호되어야 한다.
② 상어는 해양 생태계에서 최상위 포식자이다.
③ 지느러미가 없다면 상어는 생존할 수 없을 것이다.
④ 상어의 개체 수를 변화시키는 것이 다른 종에 큰 영향을 미친다.

11 정답 ①   Day 08-04

정답해설

뒤의 '팬케이크를 먹지 말아야 했다'는 내용과 '가끔씩은 걸신들린 듯 먹는다'는 내용을 통해 B가 과식을 했거나 음식을 잘못 먹었음을 알 수 있다. '안색이 안 좋아 보인다'는 말과 연결해 생각하면, 빈칸에는 '배가 아프다'는 내용이 들어가는 것이 가장 자연스럽다. 따라서 정답은 ① I have a stomachache이다.

해석

A: 너 안 좋아 보여. 무슨 일 있니?
B: 배가 아파.
A: 놀랄 일도 아니네.
B: 너무 그러지 마. 이따금씩은 걸신들리게 먹어야 한다고. 게다가, 우리는 소풍을 온 거잖아.
A: 네가 지장 없다고 느끼는 동안은 그래야겠지. 하지만 너 자신을 좀 봐! 겨우 서 있잖아. 너 심각해 보여.
B: 나도 알아. 그 마지막 팬케이크를 먹지 말았어야 했는데.

① 배가 아파
② 난 때때로 어지럼증을 느껴
③ 난 너무 긴장 돼
④ 나는 사장님 때문에 항상 평정심을 잃어.

12 정답 ④   Day 03-04

정답해설

스스로 하지 않고 고치라고 말만하는 A에게 B는 일침을 가하고 있다. A에게 차라리 배관공을 부르는 게 낫다고 충고하고 있으므로 빈칸에는 이와 부합되는 말이 들어가는 것이 좋다. 즉 '말로만 하지 말고 행동으로 실천하라'고 하는 것을 설명하는 속담인 ④ That is easier said than done이 정답이다.

해석

A: 아파트 수도꼭지가 아직도 새는데. 네가 고친다고 했던 것 같은데.
B: 오, 그래. 와셔를 교체해야 해.
A: 그러면 왜 교체하지 않니?
B: 말하기는 쉬우나 행기기는 어려운 거야. 난 네가 가능한 빨리 배관공한테 전화하는 게 낫다고 생각해.

① 그것은 절차를 무시한 거야

② 그것을 받아들이려고 애쓴다
③ 너는 그에게 그것에 대해 편지를 써봐
④ 말하기는 쉬우나 행하기는 어려운 거야

13 정답 ③ Day 07-07

정답해설

③ 출제 포인트: 원급 비교
'not+so+원급+as'는 원급 비교 구문에 해당하며 원급이 올 자리에 비교급을 사용할 수 없다. 따라서 'better'를 'good'으로 수정해야 한다.

14 정답 ① Day 04-06

정답해설

① 출제 포인트: so[neither]+조동사+주어: '~또한 그렇다'
「so+조동사+주어」와 「neither+조동사+주어」 모두 '~도 또한 그러하다'를 뜻하나 앞 문장의 부정의 유무에 차이가 있다.
1. 긍정문, and+so+조동사+주어: ~도 또한 그러하다
2. 부정문, and+neither+조동사+주어: ~도 또한 그러하다
또한 「so+조동사+주어」와 「neither+조동사+주어」는 주어-동사의 도치가 일어나며 이때 조동사를 사용하는 것이 포인트이므로 조동사의 시제와 인칭 반영에 유의해야 한다.
해당 문장은 부정문 뒤에 '~도 또한 그러하다'를 뜻하는 문장이 오는 경우이므로 'neither+조동사+주어'를 사용해야 한다. 따라서 'so'를 'neither'로 수정해야 한다.

15 정답 ④ Day 05-10

정답해설

해당 지문은 '계몽주의 시대의 과학의 발전'에 대해 서술하고 있다. 해당 구 "associated scientific advancement with the overthrow of religion and traditional authority, which had oppressed science, in favor of the development of free speech and thought(자유로운 언론과 생각의 발전에 찬성하여 과학을 억압하던 종교와 전통적인 권위의 전복과 과학적 진보를 연결 지어 생각했다)."를 통해 '전통적인 권위가 전복되었음'을 알 수 있으며, 이후 "At the time, science became dominated by scientific societies and academies(그 당시 과학은 과학 단체와 학회들이 지배하고 있었다)."를 통해 '과학이 과학 단체와 학회에 의해 지배되었다'고 언급하고 있으므로, 계몽주의로 인해 기존의 전통적인 권위는 과학에 대한 지배력을 잃었다는 것을 유추할 수 있다. 따라서 글의 내용과 일치하는 것은 ④이다.

해석

과학적 혁명은 계몽주의 시대의 토대를 쌓았고 과학은 계몽 담론과 사상에 있어서 중요한 역할을 하게 되었다. 많은 계몽주의 작가들과 사상가들은 과학에 지식이 있었고, 자유로운 언론과 생각의 발전에 찬성하여 과학을 억압하던 종교와 전통적인 권위의 전복과 과학적 진보를 연결 지어 생각했다. 포괄적으로 말하자면 계몽주의 과학은 경험주의와 이성적인 사상을 대단히 중시했고, 진보와 발전에 대한 계몽주의적 이상이 깊숙이 내재되어 있었다. 그 당시 과학은 과학 단체와 학회들이 지배하고 있었으며, 이것이 대학을 대신하여 과학 연구 및 개발의 중심지가 되었다. 단체와 학회들은 또한 과학계 성숙의 중추였다. 또 하나의 중요한 발전은 점점 더 글을 읽고 쓸 줄 아는 사람들 사이에서의 과학의 대중화였다.

① 계몽주의가 과학적 혁명을 이끌었다.
② 계몽주의 사상가들은 종교적 신념을 매우 중요시했다.
③ 계몽주의 시대에 언론과 생각의 자유는 억제되었다.
④ 계몽주의는 과학에 대한 전통적인 권위의 지배력을 잃게 만들었다.

16 정답 ④ Day 08-08

정답해설

해당 지문은 'Pablo Picasso(파블로 피카소)'의 작품 중 하나인 'Massacre in Korea(한국에서의 학살)'에 대해 설명하고 있다. 주어진 문장에서는 해당 작품에 대해 간략히 소개하고 있으므로, "It depicts the 1950 Sinchon Massacre(그것은 1950년 신천대학살을 묘사한다)"로 시작하여 해당 작품이 묘사하는 주제를 자세하게 서술하고 있는 (C)가 바로 이후에 이어지는 것이 적절하다. 이어서 (A)에서 'the murders(학살)'를 이용해 (C)의 'an act of mass killing(대량학살 행위)'을 가리키며 작품에 대한 추가적인 설명을 하고 있다는 것을 알 수 있고, (A)의 두 번째 문장의 주어인 'The art critic Kirsten Hoving Keen'을 (B)의 대명사 'She'가 가리키고 있으므로, (B)가 (A) 이후에 이어지는 것이 자연스럽다. 따라서 정답은 '④ (C) - (A) - (B)'이다.

해석

'한국에서의 학살(Massacre in Korea)'은 미국의 한국전쟁 개입에 대한 비판으로 여겨지는 파블로 피카소의 1951년 작 표현주의적 그림이다.
(C) 그것은 북한인, 남한인, 그리고 미군에 의해 자행된 북한 황해도에 위치한 신천에서 발생한 대량학살 행위인 1950년 신천대학살을 묘사한다.
(A) 신천에서의 학살의 실질적인 원인은 미궁에 빠져있으나, 한국에서의 학살은 민간인이 반공산주의 세력에 의해 살해되고 있는 것으로 묘사하는 듯하다. 예술 비평가 Kirsten Hoving Keen은 그것이 "미군의 잔학행위에 대한 보고서에서 영감을 받은"것이라고 말한다.
(B) 그녀는 또한 그것을 피카소의 공산주의적 작품 중 하나라고 여긴다. 피카소의 이 작품은 Francisco Goya의 그림 '1808년 5월 3일(The Third of May 1808)'에서 영감을 얻었으며, 그것은 Joachim Murat의 명령에 의해 나폴레옹 군대가 스페인 민간인을 처형하는 것을 묘사하고 있다.

17 정답 ① Day 10-08

정답해설

(A) 빈칸 전후 문장에서 '선천적 관념'을 주장한 'Plato and Descartes'와 '탄생 시에는 백지상태이고, 경험에 의해 지식을 획득한다'고 주장한 'John Locke'의 상반된 의견을 제시하고 있으므로 '역접'을 나타내는 ① On the other hand가 빈칸에 알맞다.
(B) 빈칸 이전에는 '명백한 생물학적 발달 과정'인 '사춘기'에 대해 언급한 후, 빈칸 이후 사춘기에도 '식단, 영양과 같은 환경적 요인도 영향을 미친다'고 이전과 반대되는 측면의 내용을 서술하고 있으므로, '역접'을 나타내는 ① However가 빈칸에 알맞다.

해석

보통 천성 대 양성 논쟁으로 칭해지는 유전과 환경의 상대적인 기여에 대한 논쟁은 철학과 심리학 모두에서 가장 오래된 쟁점 중 하나이다. 플라톤과 데카르트와 같은 철학자들은 일부 관념이 선천적이라는 생각을 지지했다. (A) 반면 존 로크와 같은 사상가들은 탄생 시에 마음은 비어있는 석판이며 경험이 우리의 지식을 결정한다는 백지상태 개념에 찬성했다. 오늘날 대부분의 심리학자들은 발달을 일으키는 것은 바로 이 두 가지 힘 사이의 상호작용이라고 믿는다. 사춘기와 같이 발달에 있어서 일부 측면은 명백히 생물학적이다. (B) 그러나 사춘기의 시작은 식단이나 영양과 같은 환경적인 요인에 의해 영향을 받을 수 있다.

① 반면 – 그러나
② 그와는 반대로 – 결과적으로
③ 그 결과 – 그럼에도 불구하고
④ 예를 들어 – 요컨대

18 정답 ④   Day 03-08

정답해설

해당 지문은 John Locke의 '사회계약설(social contract theory)'에 대해 설명하고 있으며, 주어진 문장은 '사회계약설의 한계'에 대해 서술하고 있다. 마지막 문장 "Besides, he failed to understand that revolution is desirable but it is also dangerous and under normal circumstances illegal(게다가, 그는 혁명이 바람직하지만, 또한 위험하고 보통의 상황에서는 불법이라는 것을 이해하는 데 실패했다)."에서 '사회계약설의 한계'가 본문 최초로 언급되나, 'Besides'로 보아 이전에 언급된 내용에 대한 부가적인 내용을 서술하고 있다는 것을 알 수 있으므로, 마지막 문장 이전에 '사회계약설의 한계'에 대한 내용이 먼저 언급되어야 한다. 따라서 ④가 주어진 문장이 들어갈 위치로 가장 적절하다.

해석

John Locke는 정치학 분야에 국민의 동의 또는 의지라는 새로운 요소를 도입한 최초의 철학자인 것 같다. (①) 정부는 국민의 지지를 받거나 국민의 의지에 따라 통치하기만 한다면 정권을 유지하고 강해질 수 있다. (②) 이러한 방식으로 Locke는 제한된 통치권 또는 입헌정치의 이론을 제안했다. (③) 만일 정부가 국민의 생명, 자유, 재산을 보호하는 것에 실패한다면, 국민은 그것을 제거하고 새로운 정부를 임명할 권리를 가지고 있다. (④ <u>이러한 사회계약설은 모든 면에서 완벽한 것처럼 보이지만, 그는 법적인 통치자에 대해 아무 언급도 하지 않았다.</u>) 게다가, 그는 혁명이 바람직하지만, 또한 위험하고 보통의 상황에서는 불법이라는 것을 이해하는 데 실패했다.

19 정답 ④   Day 05-09

정답해설

해당 지문은 고대 그리스인들이 믿었던 '4원소(earth, water, air, and fire (흙, 물, 공기, 불))'에 대해 서술하고 있으며, 마지막 문장에서는 4원소와 현대 과학에서의 물질의 4가지 상태에 대해 비교하고 있다. 그런데 ④에서 갑자기 아리스토텔레스가 주장했던 제5원소(aether, 에테르)에 대해 언급하는 것은 문맥상 어색하다. 따라서 글의 흐름상 가장 어색한 문장은 ④이다.

해석

아리스토텔레스와 같은 고대 그리스인들은 모든 것을 구성하는 4원소, 즉 흙, 물, 공기 그리고 불이 있다고 믿었다. ① <u>이 4원소가 모든 물질을 구성하고 있다는 생각은 오랫동안 철학, 과학, 그리고 의학의 기초가 되었다.</u> ② <u>4원소는 심지어 사람이 지닐 수 있는 4가지 기질을 묘사하기 위해 사용되기도 하였으며, 히포크라테스는 4원소를 신체에서 발견할 수 있는 4가지 "체액"을 묘사하기 위해 사용했다.</u> ③ <u>이러한 이론들은 사람이 정신적으로, 신체적으로 모두 건강하기 위해서 기질과 체액이 서로 균형을 이루어야 한다고 말한다.</u> ④ <u>별이 지구의 원소로 구성되어있다는 것은 이상하게 보였기 때문에 아리스토텔레스는 에테르라고 하는 5번째 원소가 있다고 말했다.</u> 이제 우리는 이러한 과거의 이론들이 틀렸다는 것을 알고 있지만, 어떤 면에서 4원소는 현대 과학이 동의하는 물질의 4가지 상태, 즉 고체(흙), 액체(물), 기체(공기), 그리고 플라스마(불)와 일치한다.

20 정답 ①   Day 07-09

정답해설

해당 지문은 귀여운 것을 입으로 깨물고 싶어 하는 인간의 본성에 대한 과학적 이론을 몇 가지 제시하고 있다. 그 중 빈칸 부분은 포유류 전체적으로 나타나는 "social biting"에 대해 언급하고 있는데, 빈칸 이전 문장 "some other primates are known to gently bite each other in a non-threatening manner(몇몇 다른 영장류들은 위협이 되지 않는 방식으로 서로를 부드럽게 깨무는 것으로 알려져 있다)."와 빈칸 바로 이후 "demonstrating that even if you find one of your body parts in someone else's mouth, you will not get hurt(너의 신체의 일부가 다른 사람의 입 속에 있더라도, 너는 다치지 않을 것이라는 것을 보여줌으로써)."로 보아, 서로를 깨무는 것은 '비위협적인 방식'을 통해 '해치지 않을 것이라는 믿음을 주기 위한 행동'이라는 것을 알 수 있으므로 빈칸에는 ① a way of building trust(신뢰를 쌓는 하나의 방식)가 가장 적절하다.

해석

우리가 그렇게 빨리 인정하지 않을지도 모르지만, 우리는 모두 때때로 아기의 발가락을 깨물고 싶은 이상한 충동을 느낀 적이 있다. 기괴하게 들리겠지만, 이것은 전형적인 인간의 특징이다. 과학자들은 여기에 작용하는 적어도 두 개의 요인들이 있다고 생각한다. 우리가 자그마하고, 귀엽고, 껴안고 싶은 것을 보거나 냄새를 맡을 때, 그것은 실제로 맛있는 음식을 보는 것에 의해 활성화되는[켜지는] 우리 뇌의 동일한 쾌락 중추를 작동시킨다. 따라서 그 욕구는 단순히 우리의 뇌가 유사한 자극에 대해 유사한 반응을 보이는 경우라고 할 수 있다. 이 겉으로 보기에 이상한 인간 행동에 대한 또 다른 이론은 "사회적인 깨물기"가 포유동물 사이에 흔히 발생하는 일이라고 언급한다. 예를 들어, 몇몇 다른 영장류들은 위협이 되지 않는 방식으로 서로를 부드럽게 깨무는 것으로 알려져 있다. 과학자들은 이것이 너의 신체의 일부가 다른 사람의 입 속에 있더라도, 너는 다치지 않을 것이라는 것을 보여줌으로써 <u>신뢰를 쌓는 하나의 방식</u>일 것이라고 생각한다.

① 신뢰를 쌓는 하나의 방식
② 생존을 위한 본능
③ 자식을 지키기 위한 방법
④ 동물 사회의 특징

기적사 DAY 11

결국엔 성정혜 영어 하프모의고사

| 01 | ① | 02 | ③ | 03 | ② | 04 | ④ | 05 | ① |
| 06 | ② | 07 | ④ | 08 | ① | 09 | ② | 10 | ② |

01 정답 ①
19 국가직

정답해설

'disclose'는 '밝히다, 공개하다'라는 뜻을 가진 단어로 이와 비슷한 뜻을 가진 단어는 ① 'let on'이다.

해석

비록 그 여배우가 그녀의 경력에서 많은 혼란을 겪었지만, 그녀는 결코 어느 누구에게 자신이 불행하다고 **밝힌** 적이 없다.
① 말하다, 털어놓다
② 봐주다
③ 누그러지다
④ 실망시키다

어휘

turmoil 소란, 혼란   disclose 밝히다, 공개하다
let on 말하다, 털어놓다   let off 봐주다, 터뜨리다
let up 누그러지다, 약해지다   let down 실망시키다

오답률 TOP 3
02 정답 ③
17 국가직

정답해설

'appease'는 '~을 달래다'라는 뜻으로 선택지의 단어 중 가장 가까운 의미를 지닌 것은 ③ pacify이다.

해석

요즘, 핼러윈은 이교도와 가톨릭 축제의 기원으로부터 많이 변화해왔다, 그리고 우리가 **달래는** 영혼들은 더 이상 죽은 자들의 영혼이 아니다: 굶주린 영혼들은 분장을 하고 과자를 요구하는 아이들로 대체되었다.
① 할당하다, 배정하다
② 체포하다, 이해하다
③ 달래다, 진정시키다
④ 자극하다, 유발하다

어휘

drift 떠가다, 이동하다, ~하게 되다   root 근원, 기원, 뿌리
pagan 이교도   Catholic 가톨릭의
spirit 정신, 영혼   replace 교체하다, 대체하다

03 정답 ②
17 국가직

정답해설

'make light of'는 '~을 가볍게 여기다'의 뜻으로 선택지 ②와 의미가 가장 가깝다. 보통은 부정적인 의미로 주로 쓰이지만, 해당 문장과 같이 중립적인 의미로도 사용된다.

해석

나는 주로 내 문제들을 **가볍게 여긴다**, 그리고 그것은 내 기분을 한결 낫게 만든다.
① 어떤 것을 심각하게 여기다
② 어떤 것을 중요하지 않은 것으로 취급하다
③ 문제를 해결하기 위해 노력하다
④ 수용할 만한 해결책을 찾다

어휘

make light of ~을 가볍게 여기다, 얕보다, 경시하다
treat 취급하다, 대우하다   make an effort 노력하다
seek 찾다, 추구하다
acceptable 용인 가능한, 허용할 수 있는

04 정답 ④
19 국가직

정답해설

'mind'는 동사로 '꺼리다'라는 의미를 갖고 있고 무언가를 정중하게 부탁할 때 사용하는 단어이지만 부정적인 의미를 내포하고 있으므로 부정의 대답이 한국말로 긍정의 의미를 나타낸다는 것을 알아두어야 한다. A가 "제가 잠깐만 당신과 이야기를 해도 괜찮을까요?"라고 물어보았는데 B가 처음에는 'Never mind'(걱정하지 마, 신경 쓰지 마)라고 언급을 하고 바로 다음에 "전 지금 매우 바빠요."(I'm very busy right now.)라고 했으므로 대답으로 적절하지 않다. 따라서 정답은 ④이다.

오답해설

① 'be used to 명사'와 'get accustomed to 명사'는 '~에 익숙하다'라는 뜻으로 A가 다른 나라에서 머무르는 것이 익숙하지 않다고 하자 B가 곧 익숙해질 거라고 말하고 있으므로 적절한 대화이다.
② A가 사진 대회에서 상을 타고 싶다고 하자 B가 행운을 빈다고 했으므로 적절한 대화이다. 'keep one's fingers crossed'는 '행운을 빌다'라는 관용표현이다.
③ A가 가장 친한 친구가 이사를 갔고 그녀를 그리워한다고 하자 B가 그 기분이 어떤지 안다고 말하고 있으므로 적합한 대화이다.

해석

① A: 나는 해외여행 갈 거야. 하지만 나는 다른 나라에서 머무는 것에 익숙하지 않아.
   B: 걱정하지 마. 너는 금방 그것에 익숙해질 거야.
② A: 나는 사진 대회에서 상을 타고 싶어.
   B: 나는 네가 그럴 거라고 확신해. 행운을 빌어!
③ A: 나의 가장 친한 친구가 세종시로 이사를 갔어. 나는 그녀가 너무 그리워.
   B: 그래. 난 네가 어떤 기분인지 알아.
④ A: 제가 잠깐만 당신과 이야기를 해도 괜찮을까요?
   B: 그럼요. 전 지금 매우 바빠요.

어휘

be used to N ~에 익숙하다   get accustomed to N ~에 익숙하다
prize 상
keep one's fingers crossed 행운을 빌다
mind 꺼리다   never mind 걱정하지 마

05 정답 ①
17 국가직

정답해설

① 출제 포인트: so[neither] + 조동사 + 주어: '~또한 그렇다'
부정문이 앞에 있을 경우, 이에 대한 동의 표현은 「(and) neither + (대)동사 + 주어」의 형태이다. 부정문 They didn't believe his story 다음에 옳은 순서로 왔다.

오답해설

② 출제 포인트: 전치사 + 관계대명사
관계대명사 that은 그 앞에 전치사를 동반할 수 없으므로, 전치사를 동반할 수 있는 which로 고쳐 사용하는 것이 옳다.

③ 출제 포인트: 시제 예외 규칙
제 1차 세계대전이라는 역사적 사실은 단순 과거시제를 사용하는 원칙을 준수하는 것이 적절하다. 따라서 broke out으로 고쳐야 한다.

④ 출제 포인트: 가목적어 it
옳은 문장은 "Two factors have made it difficult for scientists to determine the number of species on Earth."이다. made의 진목적어는 to determine~ 이므로 가목적어인 it을 made 뒤에 위치시켜야 하며 scientists는 의미상 주어이므로 전치사 for와 함께 「for + 의미상 주어」로 사용한다.

해석

① 그들은 그의 이야기를 믿지 않았고, 나 역시도 믿지 않았다.
② 내가 가장 관심을 갖는 스포츠는 축구이다.
③ Jamie는 제1차 세계대전이 1914년에 발발했다고 책에서 배웠다.
④ 두 가지 요인이 과학자들로 하여금 지구상에 있는 종의 수를 결정하는 것을 어렵게 만들었다.

06 정답 ②
17 국가직

정답해설

② 출제 포인트: no sooner 구문
옳은 문장은 "Hardly had she entered the house when someone turned on the light."로 그녀가 그 집에 들어가고 난 후에 불이 켜진 것이므로, 과거시제보다 이전인 과거완료시제를 사용하여야 한다.

오답해설

① 출제 포인트: 불완전타동사 set
불완전타동사 set의 목적격 보어로 현재분사를 사용할 수 있다.

③ 출제 포인트: 소유격 관계대명사
whose는 hotel을 선행사로 하는 소유격 관계대명사로 사용되었다. 원문은 'We drove on to the hotel, and we could look down at the town from its balcony.'이다. 해당 문장에서 접속사와 'its balcony'는 관계사를 포함한 'whose balcony'로 변경되며 전치사를 포함한 전명구 'from whose balcony'는 선행사 뒤로 이동할 수 있다.

④ 출제 포인트: 동명사 관용표현
「have difficulty (in) -ing」는 관용표현으로 '~하는 데 어려움을 겪다'를 뜻한다.

해석

① 지나가면서 들은 몇몇 단어들이 나를 생각하게 만들었다.
② 그녀가 그 집에 들어가자마자 누군가 불을 켰다.
③ 우리는 호텔까지 차를 몰고 갔는데, 그곳의 발코니로부터 우리는 마을을 내려다 볼 수 있었다.
④ 대개 노숙자는 직업을 구하는 데에 큰 어려움을 겪기 때문에, 희망을 잃고 있다.

07 정답 ④
17 국가직

정답해설

④ 출제 포인트: too + 형용사/부사 + to + 동사원형 vs. so + 형용사/부사 + that + 절
'너무 ~해서 …할 수 없다'의 의미를 만들기 위해, 「too ~ to...」 구문이나 「so ~ that... can't」 구문으로 고쳐야 한다. 다음의 두 방법으로 고칠 수 있다.
1) He was <u>too</u> distracted by a text message <u>to</u> know that he was going over the speed limit.
2) He was <u>so</u> distracted by a text message <u>that</u> he <u>couldn't</u> know that he was going over the speed limit.

오답해설

① 출제 포인트: Only 부사구 도치
부정 부사구인 Only after가 문두로 와서 주절의 동사 주어가 도치되었다. 일반 동사는 대동사 do를 대신 도치시키며, 여기서는 시제가 과거이기 때문에 did로 변경하였다. Only가 들어간 또 다른 부정 부사구로는 Only in this way, Only then, Not only ~ but also 등이 있다.

② 출제 포인트: insist + that + 절
insist는 주장·요구 동사의 하나로 that절 동사에 should가 오거나 생략할 수 있다. 따라서 a bridge 다음에 동사원형인 be constructed의 형태가 오게 되었다. to solve ~ 이하는 to부정사의 부사적 용법(목적)으로 사용되었다.

③ 출제 포인트: as 양보 구문
양보절에 as를 사용할 시에 문장의 보어(형용사/명사)를 도치하여 사용할 수 있다. 맨 앞에 오는 as는 부사의 역할이니 참고하자.

오답률 TOP 1

08 정답 ③
19 서울시

정답해설

빈칸 다음에 빈칸의 내용을 다시 설명하는 내용이 나온다. 'to embrace only a portion of the truth'(진실의 일부만을 포용하는 것)에서 '편중성'(partiality)을 찾을 수 있다. 또한 'it is crucial to supplement one's opinions with alternative points of view.'(자신의 의견을 대체적인 시각으로 보완하는 것이 중요하다.)에서 모든 이의 '의견이 옳다 완전히 그르다'라고 확신할 수 없다는 것을 알 수 있다. 따라서 이 부분에서 의견의 '불완전성'(incompleteness)을 유추할 수 있다. 따라서 빈칸에 알맞은 표현은 ③ It is the danger of partiality and incompleteness(그것은 편중성과 불완전성의 위험이다.)이다.

오답해설

① 본문에서 언급하고 있지 않은 내용으로 글의 흐름상 적절하지 않다.
② 개인의 자유라기보다 토론의 자유를 글에서 서술하고 있다.
④ 본문에서 서술하고 있지 않은 내용이다.

해석

독자들이 존 스튜어트 밀의 생각과 토론의 자유에 대한 고전적인 탐험에 대해 가장 흔히 기억하는 것은 안일함의 위험성에 관한 것이다. 도전이 없을 때는, 설이 정확할 때에도, 자신의 의견이 약해지고 축 늘어진다. 그러나 밀은 생각과 토론의 자유를 장려하는 또 다른 이유가 있었다. <u>그것은 편중성과 불완전성의 위험이다.</u> 자신의 의견은 아무리 좋은 환경에서도 진실의 일부만을 포용하는 경향이 있기 때문에, 그리고 자신의 의견에 반대하는 의견이 완전히 그릇된 것으로 드러나는 경우는 드물기 때문에, 자신의 의견을 대체적인 시각으로 보완하는 것이 중요하다.

① 그것은 의견의 복제이다.
② 그것은 개인의 자유의 보호이다.
③ 그것은 편중성과 불완전성의 위험이다.
④ 그것은 의견과 정보가 퍼지는 것에 대한 제약이다.

어휘

commonly 흔히, 통상적으로
liberty of thought 생각의 자유
absence 부재
flabby 축 늘어진
rarely 거의 ~하지 않다
supplement 보완
replication 복제
partiality 편중성
constraint 제약
exploration 탐험
complacency 안일함
challenge 도전
oppose 반대하다
erroneous 잘못된
alternative 대안
defense 방어
incompleteness 불완전성

오답률 TOP 2

09 정답 ②
19 서울시

정답해설

② Tenants had to make too high mortgage payments for condominiums in 2001.(세입자들은 2001년에 콘도미니엄에 대해 너무 높은 담보대출을 해야 했다.)는 본문의 "For condominiums in both markets, the monthly mortgage payments on the median house-price relative to median income have been flat since the early 2000s."(두 시장의 콘도미니엄에 대해서는 2000년대 초반부터 중위소득 대비 중위 주택가격에 대한 월별 주택담보대출 지급액이 평준화돼 있다.)고 하였으므로 콘도미니엄은 지나치게 높은 지출이 필요가 없다는 것을 본문을 통해 알 수 있으므로 ②은 본문의 내용과 부합하지 않는다.

오답해설

① 본문 처음에 집값은 1990년 이후로 67% 그리고 2006년 이후 19%로 올랐고 그 기간 동안 금리는 내렸다고 하였으므로 집값과 금리는 반비례했다는 것은 알맞은 내용이다.
③ 금리도 내리고 주택담보대출 금리도 같이 하락하고 있으므로 본문과 일치하는 내용이다.
④ 본문 마지막에 "However, it's in single-detached houses where we finally see rising monthly housing costs and thus a stronger case for unaffordability."(그러나 그것은 우리가 마침내 월별 집값 상승과 그에 따라 비용을 감당할 수 없는 더 강력한 경우를 보게 되는 단독주택에 있다.)라고 하였으므로 콘도보다 단독주택이 큰 문제가 될 수 있다는 것을 알 수 있으므로 본문과 부합하는 내용이다.

해석

집값은 1990년 이후 67%, 2006년 이후 19% 올랐다. 하지만 이 기간 동안 금리가 내렸다. 기존 주택담보대출 금리는 1990년 13% 가까이에서 2006년 7%대로 떨어졌고 지금은 4%를 밑돌고 있다. 최종 결과는 캐나다인들이 그들이 수십 년 동안 가지고 있던 월평균 주택비용을 가지고 있다는 것이다. 가처분소득 대비 주택담보대출 지급액은 1990년대 이후 평균과 일치하며 1990년대 상당 부분을 통한 비율보다 낮다. 그러나 이 수치들은 토론토와 밴쿠버의 실제 비용 문제를 반영하지 못한다. 이런 시장을 이해하기 위해서는 정책 입안자들이 콘도미니엄과 단독주택을 구별할 필요가 있다. 두 시장의 콘도미니엄에 대해서는 2000년대 초반부터 중위소득 대비 중위 주택가격에 대한 월별 주택담보대출 지급액이 평준화돼 있다. 그러나 그것은 우리가 마침내 월별 집값 상승과 그에 따라 비용을 감당할 수 없는 더 강력한 경우를 보게 되는 단독주택에 있다.
① 2000년대 중반의 집값은 금리와 반비례했다.
② 세입자들은 2001년에 콘도미니엄에 대해 너무 높은 담보대출을 해야 했다.
③ 주택담보대출 금리와 금리는 2006년에도 비슷한 경향을 보였다.
④ 정책 입안자는 정책 결정의 콘도보다 단독주택에 더 많은 관심을 기울여야 한다는 추론을 할 수 있다.

어휘

conventional 기존의, 관습적인
net 최종의
affordability 비용
differentiate 구별하다
unaffordability 감당할 수 없는 비용
tendency 경향
tenant 세입자
mortgage 주택담보대출
disposable income 가처분 소득
policy maker 정책 입안자
median 중위
inversely 반비례하여
infer 추론하다

10 정답 ②
19 서울시

정답해설

㉠ 다음에 'meaning that all media—voice, audio, video, or data'(모든 미디어들—소리, 음성, 비디오, 혹은 데이터)가 하나의 공통된 네트워크로 소통된다고 하였으므로 모든 미디어를 하나로 묶는, 즉 '통합'과 관련된 표현이 빈칸에 적절하다. 따라서 'integrated'(통합된)이 적절하다.
㉡ 'all media simultaneously rather than specializing in a (㉡) type such as voice, video, or data.'에서 각각 미디어의 종류에 특화되기보다는 모든 미디어를 취급한다고 서술하고 있으므로 빈칸에 'particular'(특정한)이 적절하다.

오답해설

㉠에는 모든 미디어들을 통합하는 것이지 어떤 한 분야의 범위를 확장하는 것이 아니므로 'expanded'(확장된)는 빈칸에 적절하지 않다. ④ 'splitted'(분리된)도 문맥상 빈칸에 적절하지 않다.
㉡에는 '특정한' 종류라는 표현이 적절하므로 ④ 'universal'(일반적인)은 적합하지 않다.

해석

새로운 네트워크들은 어떻게 다른가? 우선 그것들은 ㉠(통합되어 있고,) 이는 모든 미디어들—소리, 음성, 비디오, 혹은 데이터—이 점점 더 하나의 공통 네트워크를 통해 소통된다는 것을 의미한다. 이것은 자본 지출과 업무비 모두에서 범위와 규모의 경제들을 제공하며, 또한 다른 미디어들이 공통의 적용들 내에서 섞일 수 있도록 허용해준다. 그 결과, 기술 제공업자들과 서비스 제공업자들 모두는 소리, 음성, 혹은 데이터와 같은 ㉡(특정한) 종류를 전문으로 하기보다는 점점 더 동시에 모든 미디어들에서의 전기통신을 제공하는 사업에 종사한다.

	㉠	㉡
①	확장된	특정한
②	통합된	특정한
③	검토된	정교한
④	분열된	보편적인

어휘

expenditure 지출, 소비, 경비
telecommunications 전기통신
specialize in ~를 전문으로 하다
specific 특정한, 구체적인
scrutinize 조사하다, 검토하다
split 분열시키다, 나누다
operational cost 업무비
rather than ~보다는 (오히려)
expand 확장하다
integrate 통합시키다
elaborate 정교한
universal 보편적인

기적사 DAY 12

결국엔 성정혜 영어 하프모의고사

01	②	02	①	03	③	04	①	05	①
06	①	07	④	08	④	09	④	10	②

01 정답 ②

정답해설

밑줄 친 단어가 문맥상 '견디다'로 사용되었고, 유의어로는 ② withstand가 적절하다.

해석

하지만 영국 뱃사람들이 스페인에게 제공하는 모욕을 어느 주도 더 이상 **견딜 수** 없었다.
① 만들어내다, 꾸며내다, 꾀하다
② 참다, 이겨내다
③ 돌아다니다
④ 밝히다, 공개하다

어휘

affront 모욕, 무례한 언동
withstand 참다, 이겨내다
disclose 밝히다, 공개하다
concoct 만들어내다, 꾸며내다, 꾀하다
roam 돌아다니다

02 정답 ①

정답해설

밑줄 친 단어가 문맥상 '녹음하다'로 사용되었으므로 유의어는 ① register가 적절하다.

해석

그는 메모를 하는 것에 더해 인터뷰를 **녹음**해도 되는지 물어보았다.
① 기록하다, 등록하다
② 살펴보다, 조사하다, 검토하다
③ 밝히다
④ 달래다

어휘

register 기록하다, 등록하다
disclose 밝히다
examine 살펴보다, 조사하다, 검토하다
appease 달래다

03 정답 ③

정답해설

밑줄 친 단어가 문맥상 '수정하다'로 사용되었으며, 유의어로는 ③ rectify가 적절하다.

해석

그 문제에 대한 재검토는 후에 그의 견해를 어느 정도 **수정하도록** 이끌었고, 그 이후로 그는 그 문제에 대해 좀 더 충분히 논의해 왔다.
① 추구하다
② 진압하다
③ 변경하다, 바로잡다
④ 자극하다, 도발하다

어휘

seek 추구하다
rectify 변경하다, 바로잡다
repress 진압하다
provoke 자극하다, 도발하다

04 정답 ①

정답해설

수업이 힘들까 봐 걱정스러워하는 A에게 격려하는 말로 쉽고 별거 아니라는 표현의 ① a piece of cake가 적절하다.

해석

A: 오늘 아침 너 수영 수업에 갈 거니?
B: 물론이지, 별거 아냐.
A: 고급반은 휴식도 없고 어려워.
B: 힘내, 그건 별거 아닐 거야.
① 별거 아니야
② 미숙하다
③ 생각이 날 듯 말 듯 하다
④ 행운을 빌 거야

어휘

no sweat 별거 아냐
a piece of cake 쉬운 일, 유쾌한 일
keep one's finger crossed 행운을 빌다
wet behind the ears 미숙한

오답률 TOP 1
05 정답 ①

정답해설

① **출제 포인트: 전치사 + 관계대명사**
「전치사+관계대명사」는 뒤따라오는 문장구조가 완전하다. 따라서 해당 문장은 during which 뒤에 오는 문장구조가 완전하므로 옳은 문장이다.

오답해설

② **출제 포인트: so[neither]+조동사+주어: '~또한 그렇다'**
「so+조동사+주어」와 「neither+조동사+주어」 모두 '~도 또한 그러하다'를 뜻하나 앞 문장의 부정 유무에 차이가 있다.
1. 긍정문, and+so+조동사+주어: ~도 또한 그러하다
2. 부정문, and+neither+조동사+주어: ~도 또한 그러하다
해당 문장은 부정문 뒤에 neither를 사용하였으나 뒤에 「조동사+주어」가 아닌 「동사+주어」를 사용하였으므로 틀린 문장이다. 따라서 praise they it을 may they praise it으로 수정해야 한다.

③ **출제 포인트: 가목적어 it**
해석상 불완전타동사 make의 목적어에 해당하는 부분이 '여성이 미국 사업에서 정상에 도달하는 것'이므로 해당 문장은 틀린 문장이다. 따라서 women difficult to reach the top in US business를 가목적어 it을 사용하여 it difficult for women to reach the top in US business로 수정해야 한다.

④ **출제 포인트: 시제 예외 규칙**
역사적 사실을 나타내는 경우 과거시제를 사용해야 한다. 해당 문장은 베수비오산의 분화가 폼페이를 파괴했다는 역사적 사실을 나타내므로 과거시제를 사용해야 하나 과거완료를 사용하였으므로 틀린 문장이다. 따라서 had destroyed를 destroyed로 수정해야 한다.

해석

① 그것은 내가 계속 잠들었던 그 미팅이었다.

② 그들은 그 상태를 비판하지 않을지도 모르지만, 그들은 또한 그것을 칭찬하지 않는다.
③ 많은 것들은 여성이 미국 사업에서 정상에 도달하는 것을 어렵게 만든다.
④ Tom은 베수비오산의 분화가 폼페이를 파괴했다고 책에서 배웠다.

오답률 TOP 3
06 정답 ①

정답해설

① **출제 포인트: no sooner 구문**
「Hardly+had+주어+과거분사 ~+before/when+주어+과거시제 동사 ~」는 no sooner 구문에 해당하며 '~하자마자 ~했다'를 뜻한다. 해당 문장은 before/when이 와야 할 자리에 than을 사용하였으므로 틀린 문장이다. 따라서 than을 before 또는 when으로 수정해야 한다.

오답해설

② **출제 포인트: 동명사 관용표현**
「have difficulty (in)+목적어(명사/동명사)」는 관용표현으로 '~하는 데 어려움을 겪다'를 뜻한다.

③ **출제 포인트: 불완전타동사 set**
set은 불완전타동사로 목적격 보어로 현재분사를 사용할 수 있다. 따라서 해당 문장은 현재분사 ringing을 목적격 보어로 사용하였으므로 옳은 문장이다.

④ **출제 포인트: 소유격 관계대명사**
소유격 관계대명사 whose는 「whose+명사+주어+동사」의 구조를 사용한다. 주어진 선지의 원문은 'Kate, and I used to share a house with her sister, has gone to work in Australia.'로 접속사와 'her sister'이 소유격 관계대명사 'whose sister'로 사용되었으며, 선행사인 'Kate' 바로 뒤에 위치하고 있다.

해석

① 한순간이 지나자마자 문이 삐걱거리며 열렸다.
② 그것은 내가 아이였을 때 철자를 쓰는 데 어려움을 겪었던 거의 없는 단어 중 하나였다.
③ 상품이 초자가로 제공된다는 것은 항상 경종이 울리는 상태로 만들어야 한다.
④ Kate는, 내가 집을 공유하곤 했던 그녀의 여자 형제, 오스트레일리아에서 일하기 위해 갔다.

07 정답 ④

정답해설

④ **출제 포인트: too+형용사/부사+to+동사원형 vs. so+형용사/부사+that+절(can't/couldn't 포함)**
「too+형용사/부사+to+동사원형」과 「so+형용사/부사+that+주어+절(can't/couldn't 포함)」은 모두 '너무 ~해서 ~할 수 없다'를 뜻한다. 해당 문장은 too가 와야 할 자리에 so를 사용하였으므로 틀린 문장이다. 따라서 so를 too로 수정해야 한다.

오답해설

① **출제 포인트: as 양보 구문**
해당 문장은 as 양보 구문이 쓰인 문장으로 주격 보어에 해당하는 형용사 popular가 양보의 접속사 as 밖으로 이동하였으며 이때 형용사 popular 앞에 부사 as를 사용할 수 있다.

② **출제 포인트: Only 부사구 도치**
「Only+부사구」가 문두에 오는 경우 뒤따라오는 문장구조는 「조동사+주어」로 도치가 발생한다.

③ **출제 포인트: insist+that+절**
insist의 목적어로 「that+절」이 오는 경우 당위성을 나타내면 「that+절」에 「(should)+동사원형」을 사용하며 당위성을 나타내지 않으면 「동사(시제 반영)」을 사용한다. 해당 문장은 주어진 해석이 당위성을 나타내는 '~해야 한다고 주장하다'이므로 「that+절」에 「(should)+동사원형」을 사용하였다. 따라서 옳은 문장이다.

08 정답 ②

정답해설

빈칸 이전에 '간과되어진 Mill의 기여'가 제시되고, 빈칸 이후에는 구체적인 사례가 언급되어있다. 따라서 빈칸에는 'Mill의 기여'내용 중 구체적인 사례를 일반화하는 표현이 적절함을 유추할 수 있다. 또한, "In a nutshell, Mill advocated the liberation of females nearly 160 years ago, when they were subordinate to males by law and custom and living in the shadow of their "de facto masters"(간단히 말해, Mill은 그들이 법과 관습에 의해 남성의 하위에 있었고 그들의 "사실상의 주인"의 그늘 아래에서 살고 있던 거의 160년 전에 여성의 해방을 옹호했다)."를 통해 앞서 말한 구체적인 예시가 여성 해방에 대한 내용이라는 것을 알 수 있으므로 정답은 ② call for legal and social equality for women(여성을 위한 법적 그리고 사회적인 평등에 대한 요구이다)이다.

오답해설

① "the subordination of others, he argued, was not only wrong in itself but one of the chief hindrances to human improvement(그는 타인의 종속은 그 자체로 잘못된 것일 뿐만 아니라 인류가 진보하는 데 있어서 최고의 방해물 중 하나라고 주장했다)" 때문에 혼동될 수 있으나, 그 이하의 내용은 주로 여성과 남성의 관계에 대해 서술하고 있으므로 노예제와는 거리가 먼 내용이라 볼 수 있다. 따라서 빈칸에 적절하지 않다.

③ "he reemphasized the primacy of individual liberty and self-determination against the inroads of the majority in democratic societies(그는 민주주의 사회에서의 다수가 행하는 침해에 대항하여 개인 자유와 자기 결정권이 최고라는 것을 다시 강조하였다)"로 보아, 보기는 Mill의 업적이라고 볼 수 없는 내용이므로 정답이 아니다.

④ 본문에 언급되지 않은 내용이므로 적절하지 않다.

해석

John Stuart Mill은 주로 두 가지 이유로 현대 철학에서 인정을 받는다. 그는 Jeremy Bentham이 정립한 철학의 공리주의 전통을 개선했으며, 그는 민주주의 사회에서의 다수가 행하는 침해에 대항하여 개인 자유와 자기 결정권이 최고라는 것을 다시 강조하였다. 그러나 Mill의 공헌 중 한 부분이 크게 간과되어왔다. 그것은 그의 여성을 위한 법적 그리고 사회적인 평등에 대한 요구이다. 1869년에 출판된 그의 에세이에서 그는 타인의 종속은 그 자체로 잘못된 것일 뿐만 아니라 인류가 진보하는 데 있어서 최고의 방해물 중 하나라고 주장했다. 게다가, 비록 실패로 돌아갔지만, 그는 개정 법안에서 '남자'를 '사람'이라는 단어로 대체하려고 시도하기도 했다. 간단히 말해, Mill은 그들이 법과 관습에 의해 남성의 하위에 있었고 그들의 "사실상의 주인"의 그늘 아래서 살고 있던 거의 160년 전에 여성의 해방을 옹호했다.

① 다른 인종을 노예로 삼는 것에 대한 강력한 반대이다
② 여성을 위한 법적 그리고 사회적인 평등에 대한 요구이다
③ 민주주의의 중요성에 대한 상당한 강조이다
④ 영향력 있는 언론의 자유 옹호자가 된 것이다

어휘

recognize 인정하다, 알아주다
chiefly 주로
Utilitarian 공리주의의
philosophy 철학
refine 개선하다, 세련되게 하다
establish 수립하다, 정립하다

reemphasize 다시 강조하다
liberty 자유
inroad 침해, 침략, 침입
democratic 민주주의의
equality 평등
in itself 그 자체로, 본질적으로
hindrance 방해물
in a nutshell 간단히 말해, 간결하게
advocate 옹호하다
subordinate 하위의, 지배된, 열등한
opposition 반대
race 인종
emphasis 강조
influential 영향력이 있는
primacy 최고, 제일
self-determination 자기 결정
majority 다수, 대부분
legal 법적인, 합법의
subordination 복종, 종속 관계
chief 최고의, 주요한
improvement 향상, 진보
liberation 해방
de facto 사실상의, 실제로
slavery 노예, 노예제
call for (~에 대한) 요구, 요청
democracy 민주주의
advocate 옹호자, 지지자

09 정답 ④

정답해설

본문에서 "Policies have not yet captured the role of micro-financing and flexible financing that could help increase access to formal housing for low income groups(정책은 저소득층의 정식 주택 입주 증가를 도울 수 있는 소액금융과 탄력적인 융자의 역할을 아직 확보하지 못했다)."를 통해 (정부의) 정책이 소액금융의 역할을 확보하지 못한 것을 주택문제를 심화시키는 하나의 원인으로 지적하고 있으며, 또한 저소득층이 주택 확보에 도움이 될 수도 있는 소액금융 서비스를 제대로 이용하지 못하고 있다는 것을 유추할 수 있다. 따라서 ④ The government encourages low income families to take advantage of microfinance services(정부는 저소득 가구들이 소액금융 서비스를 이용하도록 장려한다).는 본문의 내용과 부합하지 않는다.

오답해설

① 본문에 "20% of total population squatting in over 700 informal settlements(전체 인구의 20%가 700곳 이상의 임시 거주 구역에서 불법으로 거주하고 있는)"라고 언급되어 있으므로 본문의 내용과 일치한다. 20%를 5분의 1로 표현한 것에 주의한다.
② "15,000 new units are required annually up to 2030 to clear the backlog(부족분을 해결하기 위해서는 2030년까지 매년 15,000채의 신규 주택이 필요하다)"와 "However, between 1980 and 2012, the average annual production of housing stood at 4,456 in the formal sector(그러나 1980년과 2012년 사이에 공공 부문에서 연간 평균 주택 생산은 4,456채에 머물렀다)."를 통해 필요한 양 보다 공급되는 양이 매우 적다는 것을 알 수 있다. 따라서 본문의 내용과 일치한다.
③ "as many households are engaged in informal economy where they secure their livelihoods and incomes"를 통해 많은 가구가 비공식적인 업종에 종사하고 있다는 것을 알 수 있으므로, 본문의 내용과 일치한다.

해석

54%의 도시화율과 전체 인구의 20%가 700곳 이상의 임시 거주 구역에서 불법으로 거주하고 있는 가운데 자메이카 국가와 지역 당국은 심각한 주거 문제에 직면하고 있다. 국가 주거정책을 위해 실시된 연구는 부족분을 해결하기 위해서는 2030년까지 매년 15,000채의 신규 주택이 필요하다고 밝혔다. 그러나 1980년과 2012년 사이에 공공 부문에서 연간 평균 주택 생산은 4,456채에 머물렀다. 한편, 많은 가구가 그들의 생계와 소득을 확보하는 수단인 비공식 경제에 종사하고 있기 때문에, 저소득 가구는 공식 금융 기관을 통해 대출이나 융자를 받는 것을 어렵다고 생각한다. 정책은 저소득층의 정식 주택 입주 증가를 도울 수 있는 소액금융과 탄력적인 융자의 역할을 아직 확보하지 못했다. 그렇기 때문에 저소득 가구는 임시 거주지에 의존하며 거처를 마련하기 위해 계속해서 점진적 주택 개발을 하고 있는 것이다. 토지 등록과 개발 허가 절차 또한 너무 비용이 비싸고, 엄격하며 복잡하고 느리다. 그래서 저소득 가구가 알맞은 정식 주택을 확보하는 데 있어서 방해물로 작용한다.

① 인구의 약 5분의 1이 허가되지 않은 곳에서 살고 있다.
② 주택 수요와 공급의 격차는 30년 이상 지속됐다.
③ 저소득층의 사람들은 무허가 소득 창출 활동에 크게 의존한다.
④ 정부는 저소득 가구들이 소액금융 서비스를 이용하도록 장려한다.

어휘

urbanization 도시화
settlement 정착지, 거주지
face 직면하다
undertake 착수하다
reveal 드러내다, 밝히다
require 요구하다, 필요로 하다
up to ~까지
clear (재고 등을) 처분하다, (빚 등을) 청산하다
backlog 재고, 잔무, 밀린 일
stand (수준, 양 등이) ~이다
meanwhile 한편
household 가구, 가족
loan 대출, 대부
financial institution 금융 기관
secure 확보하다, 획득하다
capture 확보하다, 점유하다
flexible 탄력적인, 유연한
resort to ~에 의지하다, 기대다
house 거처를 제공하다, 살 곳을 주다
approval 허가, 승인
rigid 엄격한
thus 그래서, 그러므로
affordable (가격이) 알맞은, 감당할 수 있는
unauthorized 무허가의, 권한이 없는
supply and demand 수요와 공급
heavily 몹시, 크게
income-generating 소득을 창출하는
take advantage of (기회로 삼아) 이용하다
squat 불법 거주하다, 쪼그리고 앉다
authority 당국
housing problem 주거 문제
policy 정책
unit (한 개) 단위
annually 매년
average 평균의
sector 부문
low income 저소득
access 접근; 접근하다
mortgage 융자, 저당, 주택담보대출
be engaged in ~에 종사하다
livelihood 생계
micro-financing 소액금융
as such 그렇기 때문에, 그러함에 따라
incremental 점진적인
registration 등록
process 과정, 절차
cumbersome 복잡하고 느린, 번거로운
hindrance 방해물
gap 차이, 격차
bracket 계층
unofficial 무허가인, 비공식적인

오답률 TOP 2

10 정답 ②

정답해설

㉠ 두 번째 문장 "under telecommunications we imagine the whole complex of technical means that are intended to (㉠) information to any distance and its being successfully delivered and processed"에서 서술하듯이 우리가 기본적으로 통신 하에서 기술적 매체의 커다란 복합체를 통해 행하고자 하는 행위는 정보를 '전송'하고, 그것이 성공적으로 전달되고 처리되는 것을 기대하므로, ㉠에는 "transmit (전송하다)"이 가장 적절하다.
㉡ "the system of technical means by which telecommunications is (㉡) is called a telecommunication network."에서 통신이 이행되는 기술적 매체의 체계는 통신 네트워크라고 부른다고 서술하고 있으므로 빈 칸에는 "carried out(수행되는)"이 알맞다.

오답해설

㉠거리를 나타내는 표현이 있으므로 "encrypt(암호화하다)"는 문맥상 어색하다. ㉡는 '통신이 이행된다'는 의미가 되는 것이 맥락상 자연스러우므로 "brought together(결합되는)" 또는 "dealt with(다루어지는)"는 적절하지 않다.

해석

통신이라는 용어는 무엇을 의미하는가? 그것은 간단하다: 통신 하에 우리는 어느 거리로든지 정보를 ㉠ 전송하기 위한 기술적 매체의 커다란 복합체와 그것이 성공적으로 전달되고 처리되는 것을 상상한다. 이 기술적 매체는 소리, 신호, 문자, 다른 기호들, 이미지, 그리고 지역의 법이 허용하는 많은 여러 가지 것들을 포함할 수 있다. 이 모든 것들은 유선과 무선 경로, 즉 광섬유, 무선 통신, 그리고 다른 전자기 시스템을 통해 전송될 수 있다. 그리고 통신이 ㉡ 이행되는 기술적 매체의 체계는 통신 네트워크라고 부른다.

	㉠	㉡
①	보완하다	쌓인
②	전송하다	수행된
③	촉진하다	결합된
④	암호화하다	다뤄진

어휘

term 용어, 말
whole (정도에 대하여) 큰, 어마어마한
means 수단, 방법
distance 거리, 간격
equipment 장비
allow 허용하다, 허가하다
via 통하여
radio 무선 통신, 무전
supplement 보충하다
transmit 전송하다, 송신하다
facilitate 용이하게 하다
bring together ~을 합치다, 결합시키다
encrypt 암호화하다
telecommunications 통신
complex 복합체
be intended to ~할 의도이다
process 처리하다
contain 포함하다
transfer 옮기다, 전송하다
optical fiber 광섬유
electromagnetic 전자기의
build up 강화하다, 증진하다
carry out 수행하다

결국엔 성정혜 영어 하프모의고사
기적사 DAY 13

01	②	02	④	03	④	04	②	05	④
06	②	07	④	08	④	09	③	10	④

01 정답 ②

정답해설

밑줄 친 단어가 문맥상 '헛된'으로 쓰였으며, 유의어로는 ② vain이 적절하다.

해석

다양한 새의 지능에 대해 결론을 폭로하려는 **헛된** 시도가 몇 차례 있었다.
① 순종하는, 충실한
② 헛된, 시시한, 허영심이 강한
③ 열렬한, 백열광의, 훌륭한
④ 비밀의

어휘

let on 털어놓다
duteous 순종하는, 충실한
vain 헛된, 시시한, 허영심이 강한
incandescent 열렬한, 백열광의, 훌륭한
clandestine 비밀의

02 정답 ④

정답해설

밑줄 친 단어의 의미가 문맥상 '매력적인'이며, 유의어로는 ④ seductive가 적절하다.

해석

당신의 데이트 상대와 몇 가지 맛있는 요리를 나누는 것보다 더 **매력적인** 것은 무엇인가?
① 우연한, 우발성의
② 자극하는, 유발하는
③ 산발적인, 뿌려진
④ 매력적인, 유혹적인

어휘

fortuitous 우연한, 우발성의
provoking 자극하는, 유발하는
scattered 산발적인, 뿌려진
seductive 매력적인, 유혹적인

03 정답 ④

정답해설

밑줄 친 단어의 의미가 문맥상 '강화된'으로 사용되었고, 유의어로는 ④ consolidated가 적절하다.

해석

하지만 잰더의 **강화된** 시력은 우리가 가볍게 여기는 상호작용의 절반을 볼 수 있었다.
① 무죄인
② 속은
③ 마음이 내키지 않는, 불쾌한
④ 강화된, 통합된, 연결된

어휘

make light of 가볍게 여기다 acquitted 무죄인
hoaxed 속은 indisposed 마음이 내키지 않는, 불쾌한
consolidated 강화된, 통합된, 연결된

04 정답 ②

정답해설

A가 드디어 승진에 대한 편지를 썼다고 하자 B가 이미 예전에 그렇게 했어야 한다고 대답하고 있다. 그에 대해 A가 할 수 있는 가장 적절한 대답은 보기에서 '겁이 많다'라고 설명하는 ② I always chicken out이다.

해석

A: 있잖아! 난 사장님께 승진시켜달라는 편지를 쓰고 있어.
B: 아, 드디어! 좋아! 너는 몇 달 전에 그랬어야 했어.
A: 알지. 난 항상 겁이 많잖아.
① 넌 그것에 익숙해질 거야
② 난 항상 겁이 많잖아
③ 넌 다른 사람들에게 항상 참견한다
④ 쇠귀에 경 읽기 같아 보여

어휘

guess 추측하다 raise 올리다; 승급
should have p.p. 진작에 했어야 했다
get accustomed to~ ~에 익숙해지다
chicken out 겁이 많다 poke your nose into~ ~에 참견하다
your head against the wall 쇠귀에 경 읽기

05 정답 ④

정답해설

④ 출제 포인트: so[neither]+조동사+주어: '~또한 그렇다'
「so+조동사+주어」와 「neither+조동사+주어」 모두 '~도 또한 그러하다'를 뜻하나 앞 문장의 부정 유무에 차이가 있다.
1. 긍정문, and+so+조동사+주어: ~도 또한 그러하다
2. 부정문, and+neither+조동사+주어: ~도 또한 그러하다
또한 「so+조동사+주어」와 「neither+조동사+주어」는 주어-동사의 도치가 일어나며 이때 조동사를 사용하는 것이 포인트이므로 조동사의 시제와 인칭 반영에 유의해야 한다.
해당 문장은 부정문 뒤에 'neither+조동사+주어'를 옳게 사용하였다.

오답해설

① 출제 포인트: 시제 예외 규칙
진리를 나타내는 경우 현재시제를 사용해야 한다. 해당 문장은 물이 수소와 산소로 구성된다는 진리를 나타내므로 현재시제를 사용해야 하나 과거시제를 사용하였으므로 틀린 문장이다. 따라서 consisted를 consists로 수정해야 한다.

② 출제 포인트: 가목적어 it
해석상 불완전타동사 made의 목적어에 해당하는 부분이 '많은 사람들이 집에서 일하는 것'이므로 해당 문장은 틀린 문장이다. 따라서 more people possible to work from home을 가목적어 it을 사용하여 it possible for more people to work from home으로 수정해야 한다.

③ 출제 포인트: 전치사+관계대명사
해당 문장은 words를 선행사로 하는 목적격 관계대명사가 생략된 문장으로 뒤따라오는 문장구조는 불완전해야 하나 you are familiar의 경우 완전하므로 틀린 문장이다. 따라서 familiar 뒤에 전치사 with를 사용해야 한다.

해석

① Tom은 물은 수소와 산소로 구성된다는 것을 학생들에게 가르쳤다.
② 컴퓨터의 사용은 많은 사람들이 집에서 일하는 것을 가능하게 만든다.
③ 당신은 친숙하고 자신감 있게 사용할 수 있는 단어들로 자신을 한정해야 한다.
④ Cowboy들은 올해 슈퍼볼에서 공연하지 않을 것이며, Falcon들 또한 그러할 것이다.

06 정답 ②

정답해설

② 출제 포인트: 동명사 관용표현
「have difficulty (in)+목적어(명사/동명사)」는 관용표현으로 '~하는 데 어려움을 겪다'를 뜻한다. 해당 문장은 difficulty가 와야 할 자리에 difficult를 사용하였으므로 틀린 문장이다. 따라서 difficult를 difficulty로 수정해야 한다.

오답해설

① 출제 포인트: 불완전타동사 set
set은 불완전타동사로 목적격 보어로 현재분사를 사용할 수 있다. 따라서 해당 문장은 현재분사 thinking을 목적격 보어로 사용하였으므로 옳은 문장이다.

③ 출제 포인트: no sooner 구문
「주어+had+hardly+과거분사 ~+before/when+주어+과거시제 동사 ~.」는 no sooner 구문에 해당하며 '~하자마자 ~했다'를 뜻한다.

④ 출제 포인트: 소유격 관계대명사
소유격 관계대명사 whose는 「whose+명사+주어+동사」의 구조를 사용한다. 원문은 'Tom, and Jane has now lived in his house, was described as a very curious gentleman.'으로 접속사와 'his house'가 소유격 관계대명사 'whose house'로 사용되었으며 전치사 'in'을 포함한 전명구 'in whose house'가 선행사인 'Tom' 뒤로 이동한 경우이다.

해석

① 췌장암 진단에 대한 기재는 나를 생각하는 상태로 만들었다.
② 그러한 훌륭한 선수가 달리기에 있어 그러한 어려움을 겪는다는 것은 비극이다.
③ 그가 책상 위에 있는 종이를 모으자마자 문이 벌컥 열렸다.
④ Tom은, 그의 집에서 Jane이 지금 살고 있는, 호기심이 왕성한 신사로 묘사되었다.

오답률 TOP 2

07 정답 ④

정답해설

④ 출제 포인트: only 부사(구) 도치
「only+부사(구)」가 문두에 오는 경우 뒤따라오는 문장구조는 「조동사+주어」로 도치가 발생한다. 해당 문장은 「only+부사(구)」가 문두에 왔으나 뒤따라오는 문장구조가 「주어+동사」이므로 틀린 문장이다. 따라서 I began을 did I begin으로 수정해야 한다.

오답해설

① 출제 포인트: as 양보 구문
해당 문장은 as 양보 구문이 쓰인 문장으로 서술어에 해당하는 동사 try가 양보의 접속사 as 밖으로 이동하였다.

② 출제 포인트: insist+that+절
insist의 목적어로 「that+절」이 오는 경우 당위성을 나타내면 「that+절

」에 「(should)+동사원형」을 사용하며 당위성을 나타내지 않으면 「동사(시제 반영)」을 사용한다. 해당 문장은 주어진 해석이 당위성을 나타내지 않으므로 「that+절」에 「동사(시제 반영)」을 사용하였다. 따라서 옳은 문장이다.

③ **출제 포인트: too+형용사/부사+to+동사원형 vs. so+형용사/부사+that+절(can't/couldn't 포함)**
「too+형용사/부사+to+동사원형」은 '너무 ~해서 ~할 수 없다'를 뜻한다.

오답률 TOP 3
08 정답 ④

정답해설

해당 지문은 풍자 종교인 '날아다니는 스파게티 괴물교(Church of the Flying Spaghetti Monster, Pastafarianism)'에 대해 설명하고 있다. ④ 'Pastafarianism이 법적 종교로서 인정을 받는다'라는 내용이 해당 종교를 소개하고 있는 글의 내용과 부합한다고 볼 여지가 있으나, ③에서 '종교적 머리 장식(religious headgear)으로 여과기를 착용하는 것이 오스트리아에서 허용되었다'라고 언급한 후 후반부 '여과기'가 종교적 머리 장식(religious headgear)으로 인정되는 다른 국가들을 나열하고 있으므로, 두 문장이 바로 연결되는 것이 자연스럽다. 따라서 글의 흐름상 어색한 것은 '④ Pastafarianism is now legally recognized as a religion in the Netherlands and New Zealand(Pastafarianism은 현재 네덜란드와 뉴질랜드에서 법적으로 종교로서 인정받는다).'이다.

오답해설

나머지는 문맥상 자연스러우므로 오답이다.

해석

Pastafarianism으로도 알려진 날아다니는 스파게티 괴물교(Church of the Flying Spaghetti Monster)는 Bobby Henderson이 캔자스 교육위원회에 보낸 공개서한에 기반을 둔 풍자 종교이다. ① 그 서한에서 그는 날아다니는 스파게티 괴물 이론도 진화론과 함께 가르쳐야 한다고 요구했다. ② 날아다니는 스파게티 괴물을 숭배하는 Pastafarian들은 빈번하게 종교로서 인정을 받으려 노력함으로써 여러 국가에서 종교적 신념, 관습, 또는 예배의 주체들에게 특정한 특권을 주는 법률과 사법권에 도전해 왔으며 다양한 정도의 성공을 거두었다. ③ 2011년 공공 문서에서 종교적인 머리 장식물을 허용하는 오스트리아에서 한 Pastafarian이 운전면허증 사진에서 머리에 금속 여과기를 쓰는 것을 허가받았다. ④ *Pastafarianism은 현재 네덜란드와 뉴질랜드에서 법적으로 종교로서 인정받는다.* 그것은 후에 체코 공화국, 뉴질랜드, 그리고 미국의 매사추세츠주와 유타주에서 종교적인 머리 장식물로서 인정받았다.

어휘

Pastafarianism 파스타파리아니즘, 날아다니는 스파게티 괴물교
mock 가짜의, 조롱의, 풍자의   demand 요구하다
evolution 진화론
Pastafarian 파스타파리안, 날아다니는 스파게티 괴물 신도
worship 숭배하다   privilege 특권
jurisdiction 사법권, 관할권   seek 추구하다, 얻으려고 (노력)하다
recognition 인정   varying 다양한
colander (음식 재료의 물을 빼는 데 쓰는) 여과기, 체
permit 허가하다, 허락하다
headgear 머리 장식물, (머리에 쓰는 모자 등의) 쓸 것
recognize 인정하다, 인식하다

09 정답 ③

정답해설

빈칸 이전의 '역접'을 나타내는 접속사 'But(그러나)'으로 보아 빈칸 이전에 언급된 내용과 반대되는 내용이 들어가는 것이 적절하다는 것을 알 수 있다. 빈칸 이전에서 "77 percent of Americans say that religion is at least somewhat important in their lives and 83 percent say they're fairly certain that God or a higher power exists(미국인의 77%가 삶에 있어서 종교가 적어도 어느 정도 중요하다고 말했고, 83%가 신 또는 더 강한 권능이 존재한다는 것을 매우 확신한다고 말했다)."를 통해 '종교를 긍정적으로 판단하는 사람들의 의견'을 언급하고 있으므로, 빈칸에는 이에 대한 반대 의견을 서술하는 문장이 들어가는 것이 적절하다. 따라서 빈칸에는 '모든 사람들이 종교를 긍정적으로 보는 것이 아니다'라는 것을 의미하는 '③ not everyone agrees that religion is good for us(종교가 우리에게 유익하다는 것에 모든 사람이 동의하는 것은 아니다)'가 들어가는 것이 알맞다.

오답해설

① 빈칸 이전의 But으로 보아 앞서 언급된 '신의 존재'에 대해 부정적인 내용이 들어갈 수 있을 듯하나, 빈칸 이후 문장에서 '행복을 촉진시킨다'는 주장과 '신경증을 초래한다'라는 양측의 주장을 언급하고 있으므로, '신의 존재'여부와는 관련이 없는 내용이 이어진다는 것을 알 수 있다. 따라서 오답이다.
② 사이비종교에 대한 내용은 본문에 언급되지 않는다.
④ 빈칸 이전 내용과 유사하게 '종교의 긍정적 역할'에 대해 언급하고 있으므로 연결사 But 이후에 오는 것이 어색하다.

해석

사실 역사적으로 인간의 존재를 형성하는 데 있어서 종교보다 더 강력했던 힘은 거의 없다. Pew Research Center의 최신 여론 조사에 따르면 미국인의 77%가 삶에 있어서 종교가 적어도 어느 정도 중요하다고 말했고, 83%가 신 또는 더 강한 권능이 존재한다는 것을 매우 확신한다고 말했다. 그러나 종교가 우리에게 유익하다는 것에 모든 사람이 동의하는 것은 아니다. 일부는 그것이 행복을 촉진한다고 주장하고 다른 일부는 그것이 신경증을 초래한다고 주장하며, 학자들 사이에 이 쟁점에 대한 긴 논쟁이 있어왔다. 사실 심리학 분야에서 이 문제만큼 많이 연구되는 쟁점은 거의 없다.
① 신이 존재하는지 아닌지 정말로 아는 사람은 없다
② 우리 주변에 너무 많은 사이비종교가 있다
③ 종교가 우리에게 유익하다는 것에 모든 사람이 동의하는 것은 아니다
④ 종교가 사회에서 긍정적인 역할을 한다는 것은 분명하다

어휘

existence 존재   poll 여론 조사, 투표
somewhat 어느 정도, 다소   fairly 매우, 아주, 꽤
debate 논쟁   scholar 학자
claim 주장하다   facilitate 촉진하다, 용이하게 하다
well-being (건강과) 행복, 웰빙   lead to 초래하다, 일으키다, 이어지다
neurosis 신경증   pseudo-religion 사이비종교
obvious 명확한, 분명한

오답률 TOP 1
10 정답 ④

정답해설

본문 초반에서 '미국 최대의 종교'인 '기독교'에 대해 언급한 후, 미국 각 지역에서 기독교에 이어 두 번째로 많은 신자를 보유하고 있는 종교들을 각각 나열하고 있으므로 '④ The Second Most Believed Religions around the U.S.(미국에서 두 번째로 많이 믿는 종교들)'가 글의 제목으로 가장 적절하다.

오답해설

① 본문에 언급되지 않는 내용이므로 제목으로 적절하지 않다.
② 본문 초반에 언급되기는 하나, 두 번째로 큰 종교들을 설명하는 것이 본문의 주된 주제이므로 글의 제목으로는 부적절하다.
③ 다양한 종교가 나열되었으나, 단순히 종교의 종류를 설명하고 있는 글이 아니므로 제목으로 부적절하다.

해석

기독교는 미국에서 단연 가장 거대한 종교로, 미국인들의 4분의 3 이상이 기독교 신자라고 밝힌다. 미국인의 절반을 약간 웃도는 사람들이 개신교 신자라고 밝히고, 23%가 가톨릭 신자, 그리고 약 2%가 모르몬교 신자라고 밝힌다. 그렇다면 나머지는 어떠한가? 미국 서부에서는 대부분의 주에서 불교도들이 다음으로 가장 거대한 종교 진영을 대표한다. 주로 중서부와 남부에 위치한 20개의 주에서는 이슬람이 가장 거대한 비기독교 신앙 전통이다. 주로 북동부에 위치한 15개의 주에서는 유대교가 기독교를 이어 가장 많은 신봉자를 거느리고 있다. 힌두교도들은 애리조나와 델라웨어에서 2위이고, 사우스캐롤라이나에는 바하이교 신앙을 실천하는 사람이 다른 어떤 누구보다 더 많다.
① 미국의 종교의 자유
② 미국 내의 가장 거대한 종교
③ 미국에 존재하는 다양한 유형의 종교들
④ 미국에서 두 번째로 많이 믿는 종교들

어휘

identify as ~라고 밝히다
Mormon 모르몬교도
bloc 세력권, 진영, 연합
practitioner (특정 생활·종교 양식을) 실천하는 사람
Baha'i faith 바하이교 (신앙)
Protestant 개신교도
represent 대표하다
Judaism 유대교
various 다양한

결국엔 성정혜 영어 하프모의고사
기적사 DAY 14

| 01 | ① | 02 | ③ | 03 | ① | 04 | ④ | 05 | ② |
| 06 | ② | 07 | ③ | 08 | ③ | 09 | ③ | 10 | ④ |

오답률 TOP 2
01 정답 ①

정답해설

밑줄 친 단어가 문맥상 '비옥한'으로 사용되었고, 유의어로는 ① fructuous가 적절하다.

해석

비옥한 토양과 결코 농부들을 실망시키지 않는 훌륭한 방목지의 풍부함이 있다.
① 비옥한, 열매가 많은, 다산의
② 실속이 없는, 표면이 우묵한, 공허한
③ 낭비하는, 일류의, 화려한
④ (병, 범죄, 소문 등이)만연한, 무성한, 덤벼들 것 같은

어휘

magnificent 훌륭한, 멋진, 아름다운
let down 실망시키다
fructuous 비옥한, 열매가 많은, 다산의
hollow 실속이 없는, 표면이 우묵한, 공허한
luxurious 낭비하는, 일류의, 화려한
rampant (병, 범죄, 소문 등이)만연한, 무성한, 덤벼들 것 같은

02 정답 ③

정답해설

밑줄 친 단어의 의미가 문맥상 '서두르다'로 사용되었고, 유의어로는 ③ haste가 적절하다.

해석

나는 Denton으로 네가 나가서 돌아가기 위해 **서두르고** 있다고 확신한다.
① 준수하다
② 체포하다, 이해하다
③ 서두르다
④ 고집하다, 충실하다, 달라붙다

어휘

comply 준수하다
haste 서두르다
apprehend 체포하다, 이해하다
adhere 고집하다, 충실하다, 달라붙다

오답률 TOP 3
03 정답 ①

정답해설

밑줄 친 단어가 문맥상 '방해하다'로 사용되었고, 유의어로는 ① encumber가 적절하다.

해석

그들이 당신의 일을 **방해하지** 않는 한 당신은 당신이 중요한 무언가를 고려할 때마다, 언제든지 전화하거나 친구를 가질 수 있다.
① 간섭하다, (책임을) 지우다

② 고립시키다, 은퇴시키다
③ 완화하다, 경감하다
④ 구별하다, 알아보다

어휘

encumber 간섭하다, (책임을) 지우다 seclude 고립시키다, 은퇴시키다
mitigate 완화하다, 경감하다 discern 구별하다, 알아보다

04 정답 ④

정답해설

'otherwise'는 '그렇지 않으면'이라는 뜻을 가진 접속부사이다. 따라서 빈칸 전 문장에서 우리가 모든 고객들을 상대할 수 있다고 하였으므로 빈칸 다음에는 그와 반대되는 내용을 가진 초과 근무를 해야만 한다는 문장이 빈칸에 들어가는 것이 가장 적절하다. 따라서 정답은 ④ everyone has to start work overtime이다.

해석

W: 이번 기간에 임시 고용직원을 고용하는 것에 대해 당신은 어떻게 생각하나요?
M: 좋은 의견이에요. 우리는 우리의 예산 안에서 최소한 네 명 이상의 직원들에게 임금을 지불할 만큼 충분한 돈이 있어요. 인사부의 Janet에게 전화하지 않을래요?
W: 알았어요. 나도 당신 기분 알아요. 내가 당장 그녀에게 전화를 할게요. 추가 직원들과 함께, 나는 우리가 모든 고객들을 상대할 수 있을 거라 확신해요. 그렇지 않으면, 모든 사람들은 초과 근무를 시작해야만 해요.
① 임기응변하다
② 못 본 체하다
③ 분에 넘치는 일을 하려고 하다
④ 모든 사람들은 초과 근무를 시작해야 한다

어휘

hire 고용하다 temporary staff 임시직원
budget 예산 pay for 지불하다
human resources 인사부 right away 당장
handle 다루다, 처리하다 play it by ear 임기응변하다
turn a blind eye to 못 본 체하다
bite off more than one can chew 분에 넘치는 일을 하려고 하다
work overtime 초과 근무를 하다

05 정답 ②

정답해설

② 출제 포인트: 가목적어 it
해당 문장은 5형식 불완전 타동사 find가 쓰인 문장으로서 가목적어 it이 사용되었으며, 진목적어는 to talk about her problems에 해당된다. 가목적어를 취할 수 있는 동사는 find를 비롯하여 make, believe, consider, think 등이 있다. 해당 문장에서는 5형식 불완전타동사의 목적격 보어로 형용사 easy를 사용하여 'find + 가목적어 it + 목적격 보어 easy + 진목적어 to talk~'가 옳게 사용되었다.

오답해설

① 출제 포인트: 시제 예외 규칙
현재의 습관적 동작을 나타내는 경우 현재시제를 사용해야 한다. 해당 문장은 '매일 밤 술을 많이 마신다.'라는 현재의 습관적 동작을 나타내므로 현재시제를 사용해야 하나 과거시제를 사용하였으므로 틀린 문장이다. 따라서 drank를 drinks로 수정해야 한다.

③ 출제 포인트: 전치사 + 관계대명사
'the place'를 선행사로 하는 관계대명사 'which'나 관계부사 'where'이 올 수 있으나 뒤따라오는 문장에서 전치사 'at'의 목적어가 없으므로 목적격 관계대명사를 사용해야 한다. 따라서 'where'를 'which'로 수정해야 한다.

④ 출제 포인트: so[neither] + 조동사 + 주어: '~또한 그렇다'
「so + 조동사 + 주어」와 「neither + 조동사 + 주어」 모두 '~도 또한 그러하다'를 뜻하나 앞 문장의 부정 유무에 차이가 있다.
1. 긍정문, and + so + 조동사 + 주어: ~도 또한 그러하다
2. 부정문, and + neither + 조동사 + 주어: ~도 또한 그러하다
해당 문장은 부정문 뒤에 neither를 사용하였으나 뒤에 「조동사 + 주어」가 아닌 「주어 + 조동사」를 사용하였으므로 틀린 문장이다. 따라서 he had를 had he로 수정해야 한다.

해석

① 그들은 Bill이 매일 밤 술을 많이 마신다는 것을 알아차렸다.
② 그녀는 자신의 문제에 대해 말하는 것이 쉽다는 것을 알지 못한다.
③ 그곳은 그녀가 런던에 있을 때 머물렀던 장소이다.
④ 그는 어떤 숙제도 하지 않았으며, 또한 그는 수업에 어떤 책도 가져가지 않았다.

06 정답 ②

정답해설

② 출제 포인트: 소유격 관계대명사
'The idea is that you should want people and you share their opinion to have an robust stance.'에서 접속사와 their를 대신해서 소유격 관계대명사 whose를 사용한 경우이다. 소유격 관계사 이후에 you라는 주어가 빠졌으므로 share를 you share라고 해야 옳다. 주어진 문장은 소유격 관계대명사 절의 주어가 빠져있는 형태로 whose opinion을 주어로 보지 않도록 유의해야한다. whose opinion은 타동사로 사용된 share의 목적어로 사용되었으므로 해당 문장은 소유격 관계대명사 절의 주어가 빠진 옳지 않은 문장이다.

오답해설

① 출제 포인트: no sooner 구문
「Scarcely + had + 주어 + 과거분사 ~ + before/when + 주어 + 과거시제 동사 ~.」는 no sooner 구문에 해당하며 '~하자마자 ~했다'를 뜻한다.

③ 출제 포인트: 동명사 관용표현
「have no difficulty (in) + 목적어(명사/동명사)」는 관용표현으로 '~하는 데 어려움이 없다'를 뜻한다.

④ 출제 포인트: 불완전타동사 set
set은 불완전타동사로 목적격 보어로 현재분사를 사용할 수 있다. 따라서 해당 문장은 현재분사 thinking을 목적격 보어로 사용하였으므로 옳은 문장이다.

해석

① 그들이 떠나자마자 군인들이 총을 가지고 도착했다.
② 그 생각은 당신이 확고한 입장을 갖기 위해서 그들의 의견을 공유할 사람들을 원해야 한다는 것이다.
③ 나는 그를 정직한 증인이라고 여기며 그가 나에게 말한 것을 믿는 데 어려움이 없다.
④ 나를 이것에 대해 생각하는 상태로 만드는 것은 공항에서 군인들이 자신들의 아내에 대해 말했던 것이다.

07 정답 ③

정답해설

③ 출제 포인트: too+형용사/부사+to+동사원형 vs. so+형용사/부사+that+절(can't/couldn't 포함)

「too+형용사/부사+to+동사원형」과 「so+형용사/부사+that+주어+절(can't/couldn't 포함)」은 모두 '너무 ~해서 ~할 수 없다'를 뜻한다. 해당 문장은 too가 와야 할 자리에 so를 사용하였으므로 틀린 문장이다. 따라서 so를 too로 수정해야 한다.

오답해설

① 출제 포인트: only 부사(구/절) 도치

「only+부사절」이 문두에 오는 경우 뒤따라오는 문장구조는 「조동사+주어」로 도치가 발생한다.

② 출제 포인트: as 양보 구문

해당 문장은 as 양보 구문이 쓰인 문장으로 수식어에 해당하는 부사 hard가 양보의 접속사 as 밖으로 이동하였다.

④ 출제 포인트: insist+that+절

insist의 목적어로 「that+절」이 오는 경우 당위성을 나타내면 「that+절」에 「(should)+동사원형」을 사용하며 당위성을 나타내지 않으면 「동사(시제 반영)」을 사용한다. 해당 문장은 주어진 해석이 당위성을 나타내는 '~해야 한다고 주장하다'이므로 「that+절」에 「(should)+동사원형」을 사용하였다. 따라서 옳은 문장이다.

08 정답 ③

정답해설

본문 초반에서 '심판의 정의'에 대해 언급하고 심판으로서의 책임 및 업무 형태 등을 설명하고 있다. 이후에는 여러 가지 스포츠 경기의 심판이 될 수 있는 자격요건에 대해 각각 'need a minimum of a high school diploma(최소한 고등학교 졸업장 혹은 그에 준하는 학력이 필요하다)', 'require you to be a graduate of a professional officiating school(당신이 전문 심판 학교 졸업생일 것을 요구한다)', 'must have attended a professional umpire training school(전문 심판 훈련 학교를 다녔어야만 한다)', 'must possess 7 to 10 years experience in minor leagues(마이너리그에서의 7에서 10년의 경력을 보유하고 있어야 한다)', 'a minimum of ten years of experience is required(최소 10년의 경력이 필요하며)' 등을 통해 설명하고 있다. 따라서 글의 주제로 가장 적절한 것은 '③ the requirements to become a sports official(스포츠 심판이 되기 위한 요건)'이다.

오답해설

① 여러 경기의 심판에 대해 언급하기는 하지만, 구체적으로 각 경기의 자격요건이 주된 내용이므로 글의 주제로는 부적절하다.

② 두 번째 문장에서 일반적인 심판의 책임에 관해서 언급하기는 하나, 다양한 개별 스포츠 경기 심판의 책임은 구체적으로 언급되지 않으므로 글의 주제로 부적절하다.

④ 본문에 언급되지 않은 내용이다.

해석

심판은 축구와 농구 같은 체육 행사에서 심판을 보는 사람이다. 그들의 책임은 경기의 규칙과 규정이 위반되면 패널티를 부과하는 것을 포함한다. 심판들은 권투와 같은 스포츠에서 단독 심판으로 일하거나 축구와 같은 스포츠에서 단체로 일한다. 대부분의 심판은 최소한 고등학교 졸업장 혹은 그에 준하는 학력이 필요하다. 심판을 고용하는 대학교는 보통 당신이 전문 심판 학교 졸업생일 것을 요구한다. 마이너 또는 메이저리그 야구 경기를 심판하기 위해서 당신은 전문 심판 훈련 학교를 다녔어야만 한다. 메이저리그 경기를 심판하기 위해 심판들은 마이너리그에서의 7년에서 10년의 경력을 보유하고 있어야 한다. 프로 축구의 심판이 되기 위해 최소 10년의 경력이 필요하며, 그 중 적어도 5년은 대학교 또는 그 이상의 수준에서 발생해야 한다.

① 여러 종류의 심판들
② 다양한 경기에서의 심판의 책임
③ 스포츠 심판이 되기 위한 요건
④ 전문 심판 학교에 입학하는 법

어휘

referee 심판
athletic 운동(육상) 경기의
penalty 벌칙, 패널티
official (운동 경기의) 경기 임원 (심판원·기록원 등)
diploma 졸업 증서
umpire 심판
occur 생기다, 발생하다
officiate 심판을 맡아 보다
impose 부과하다
equivalent 동등한, 상당하는
possess 보유하다, 소유하다
requirement 요건, 필요조건

09 정답 ③

정답해설

해당 지문은 'MLB에서 발생하는 오심'에 대해 설명하고 있으며, 그에 대한 예시로 'Colorado Rockies와 Arizona Diamondbacks'의 경기를 소개하고 있다. 본문 중반 "Arizona, with two outs and two on base, was threatening a comeback(2아웃에 2명의 주자가 출루해있던 Arizona가 역전을 노리고 있었다)."과 마지막 문장 "umpire Paul Nauert called the stray ball a strike, ending the ballgame(Paul Nauert 심판은 벗어난 공을 스트라이크로 판정했고, 그것이 게임을 끝내버렸다)."을 통해 'Arizona는 역전의 기회가 있었으나 심판의 오심으로 인해 경기가 그대로 끝났다'라는 것을 알 수 있고, 해당 경기의 예시를 통해 말하고 싶은 주제가 빈칸에 들어가는 것이 적절하다. 따라서 "③ some of them significantly affect the result of a game(그들 중 일부는 경기 결과에 중대한 영향을 미친다)"이 가장 적절하다.

오답해설

① 빈칸 이후 예시가 오심 정정에 대한 것이 아니므로 빈칸에 적절하지 않다.
② 오심을 내린 심판에 대한 비난은 언급되지 않는다.
④ 오심을 내리는 심판의 연령대나 경력은 본문에 언급되지 않으므로 오답이다.

해석

매 시즌, MLB의 주심은 수많은 오심을 내리고 그들 중 일부는 경기 결과에 중대한 영향을 미친다. 2018년 올스타 휴식기 직후, Colorado Rookies와 Arizona Diamondbacks는 중요한 내셔널 리그 게임을 치르기 위해 Chase Field에서 만났다. 9회에 Rookies가 6대5로 앞서고 있었으나, 2아웃에 2명의 주자가 출루해있던 Arizona가 역전을 노리고 있었다. Rookies의 마무리 투수 Wade Davis는 강타자 Nick Ahmed에 1볼 2스트라이크 카운트로 앞선 상황이었다. 그 오른손 타자의 배터박스를 향해 던져진 시속 90마일의 다음 투구는 스트라이크존에서 상당히 떨어진 곳으로 떨어졌다. Diamondback의 팬들이 믿을 수 없게도, Paul Nauert 심판은 벗어난 공을 스트라이크로 판정했고, 그것이 게임을 끝내버렸다.

① 그것들은 경기 후 거의 정정되지 않는다
② 그들은 실수를 가혹하게 비난받는다
③ 그들 중 일부는 경기 결과에 중대한 영향을 미친다
④ 더 나이 들고 경력이 많은 심판들이 오심을 더 많이 내린다

어휘

home plate 본루, 홈베이스
call 판정
comeback 만회, 역전
umpire 심판
threat 위협하다
closer 마무리투수

slugger 강타자
mph 시속 …마일
batter's box 배터박스, 타자석
disbelief 불신
seldom 거의 ~않는
harshly 가혹하게, 심하게
pitch 투구
cutter 커터(컷패스트볼 (cut fastball))
significantly 상당히, 중대하게
stray 빗나간, 길 잃은
rectify 바로잡다, 정정하다
berate 비난하다, 몹시 꾸짖다

오답률 TOP 1
10 정답 ④

정답해설

주어진 문장에서 영어권 국가 외의 국가에서의 '심판 명칭은 분명하고 일관되며 간단하다'라고 언급하고 있으므로, 다른 국가를 언급한 ② "This is not the case in other languages(이것은 다른 언어에서는 사실이 아니다)." 이후의 자리에 주어진 문장이 들어가야 한다. ③에서 '영어권 국가에서의 심판 명칭의 복잡성'에 대해 언급한 후, ④에서 But을 이용해 재차 영어의 경우에 관해 언급하고 있으므로, 두 문장 사이인 ④ 자리에 영어와 비교하여 다른 언어권 국가에 대해 설명하는 주어진 문장이 들어가는 것이 적절하다. 따라서 정답은 ④이다.

오답해설

③ 다른 언어가 언급된 바로 이후인 ③자리에 주어진 문장이 위치하면 ③과 ④의 연결이 어색해지므로 주의한다.

해석

야구 경기에서 'referee'를 또는 농구 경기에서 'umpire'를 언급하면 당신이 아무것도 모른다는 것이 분명해진다. (①) 그리고 영어에서의 스포츠 심판 용어는 말이 되지 않고 규칙도 없기 때문에, 혹은 있다 하더라도 그것은 구명투성이라서 무의미하기 때문에 그것은 아마 조금 불공평할 것이다. (②) 이것은 다른 언어에서는 사실이 아니다. (③) 영어권 국가에서는 스포츠 심판은 각각이 하는 역할에 관한 어떠한 종류의 통일적인 구조도 없이 현기증을 불러일으킬 정도로 여러 종류의 명칭이 있다. (④ **프랑스에서부터 일본, 브라질까지 전 세계적으로는 스포츠 심판의 명칭이 분명하고 일관되며 간단하다.**) 그러나 영어에서 그것은 함정에 가깝다. 그 용어들은 약간의 차이가 나는 기본 의미가 있고, 바꾸어 쓸 수 없지만, 영어에서 그것들의 사용은 스포츠 간의 어떠한 확립된 규칙도 따르지 않는다. NBA 경기의 주심은 referee이다. MLB에서는 umpire이다. 테니스, 미식축구, 그리고 라크로스 전부 referee와 다양한 judge가 있다.

어휘

referee 심판
terminology 용어
be riddled with (특히 나쁜 것이) 가득하다[~투성이다]
case 사실, 실상
dizzying 어지럽게 만드는, 현기증을 일으키는
an array of 다수의, 다양한
structure 구조, 구성
trap (사람을 속이는) 함정 [덫]
established 확립된
lacrosse 라크로스(양 팀 10명씩 하는 하키 비슷한 구기)
a variety of 다양한
umpire 심판
sports official 스포츠 심판
unifying 통일[통합]하는, 통일적인
as to ~에 관한
interchangeable 교환할 수 있는
lead official 주심

결국엔 성정혜 영어 하프모의고사
기적사 DAY 15

| 01 | ② | 02 | ① | 03 | ① | 04 | ③ | 05 | ③ |
| 06 | ③ | 07 | ① | 08 | ③ | 09 | ② | 10 | ④ |

오답률 TOP 1
01 정답 ②

정답해설

밑줄 친 단어의 의미가 문맥상 '냄새를 맡다'로 사용되었고, 유의어로는 ② snuff가 적절하다.

해석

몰 오브 아메리카가 매년 수백만의 방문객들을 맞이한 이후로, 그들은 국토안보부와 소란을 만들지 않기 위해서 직통 연결을 갖고 있고 심지어 폭탄들과 마약에 대해 **냄새를 맡는** 개들과 같이하는 그들만의 K-9 유닛을 보유하고 있다.
① 악취가 나다, 평판이 나쁘다, 악취로 가득 차게 하다
② 킁킁 냄새 맡다
③ 전환하다, 바꾸다, 개조하다, 개종하다
④ 비밀의, 은밀한, 암암리의

어휘

turmoil 소란
stink 악취가 나다, 평판이 나쁘다, 악취로 가득 차게 하다
snuff 킁킁 냄새 맡다
convert 전환하다, 바꾸다, 개조하다, 개종하다
covert 비밀의, 은밀한, 암암리의

오답률 TOP 3
02 정답 ①

정답해설

밑줄 친 단어가 문맥상 '은퇴하다'로 사용되었고, 유의어로는 ① step out이 적절하다.

해석

그녀의 할당받은 힘이 거의 사라졌기 때문에, 그것은 **은퇴**를 할 때의 신호였다.
① 은퇴하다, 잠깐 떠나다
② 떠올리다
③ 이륙하다
④ 차지하다, 걸리다, 시작하다

어휘

assign 할당하다
flash on 떠올리다
take up 차지하다, 걸리다, 시작하다
step out 은퇴하다, 잠깐 떠나다
hop off 이륙하다

오답률 TOP 2
03 정답 ①

정답해설

밑줄 친 단어가 문맥상 '전례 없는'으로 사용되었으므로, 유의어로는 ① unsurpassed가 적절하다.

> **해석**

국민에게 **전례 없는** 언론의 자유를 허용한 정부 아래, 우리는 문제를 해결하기 위해서 노력했다.
① 전례 없는, 뛰어난, 비길 데 없는
② 말이 많은
③ 순수한, 완전한
④ 일상의, 평범한

> **어휘**

unsurpassed 전례 없는, 뛰어난, 비길 데 없는
verbose 말이 많은   unadulterated 순수한, 완전한
ordinary 일상의, 평범한

04 정답 ③

> **정답해설**

A는 겨울방학이 너무 짧다고 말하고 있다. B는 'Couldn't agree more(전적으로 동의해)'라고 했다가 뒷부분에는 'Speak for yourself(너나 그렇지)'라고 반대하고 있다. 상반된 문장을 동시에 말하고 있으므로 어색한 대화가 되었다.

> **오답해설**

① 'It's up to you'는 '너에게 달렸어' '네가 결정해'의 뜻이므로 적절한 답이다.
② 차로 데리러 가겠다는 말에 'Don't bother(내버려 둬요)'라고 말하고 있다.
④ A가 '너 없인 일을 끝내지 못했을 것'이라며 감사를 표하자, B가 'It was no big deal(별거 아니다)'이라고 말하고 있다.

> **해석**

① A: 생일날 뭐 받고 싶어?
   B: 네가 좋을 대로 해.
② A: 수업 끝나면 연락해. 데리러 올게.
   B: 신경 쓰지 마세요. 버스가 늦게까지 다녀요.
③ A: 겨울방학은 너무 짧아.
   B: 전적으로 동의해. 너에게나 그렇지.
④ A: 나는 너무 바빴어. 너 없인 이 일을 못 끝냈을 거야.
   B: 별거 아니었어.

> **어휘**

up to sb ~에게 달려있다
cannot agree more 전적으로 동의하다
Speak for yourself 너만 그렇다   It's no big deal 별거 아니다

05 정답 ③

> **정답해설**

③ **출제 포인트: 전치사 + 관계대명사**
「전치사 + 관계대명사」는 뒤따라오는 문장구조가 완전하다. 따라서 해당 문장은 'during which' 뒤에 오는 문장구조가 완전하므로 옳은 문장이다.

> **오답해설**

① **출제 포인트: so[neither] + 조동사 + 주어: '~또한 그렇다'**
「so + 조동사 + 주어」와 「neither + 조동사 + 주어」 모두 '~도 또한 그러하다'를 뜻하나 앞 문장의 부정 유무에 차이가 있다.
   1. 긍정문, and + so + 조동사 + 주어: ~도 또한 그러하다
   2. 부정문, and + neither + 조동사 + 주어: ~도 또한 그러하다
해당 문장은 부정문 뒤에 neither를 사용하였으나 뒤에 「조동사 + 주어」가 아닌 「동사 + 주어」를 사용하였으므로 틀린 문장이다. 따라서 saw we를 did we see로 수정해야 한다.

② **출제 포인트: 가목적어 it**
해석상 불완전타동사 think의 목적어에 해당하는 부분이 '우리가 회의 전에 우리의 지위에 동의하는 것'이므로 해당 문장은 틀린 문장이다. 따라서 us important to agree를 가목적어 it을 사용하여 it important for us to agree로 수정해야 한다.

④ **출제 포인트: 시제 예외 규칙**
역사적 사실을 나타내는 경우 과거시제를 사용해야 한다. 해당 문장은 '노르만족이 1066년에 영국을 침입했다'라는 역사적 사실을 나타내므로 과거시제를 사용해야 하나 과거완료를 사용하였으므로 틀린 문장이다. 따라서 'had invaded'를 'invaded'로 수정해야 한다.

> **해석**

① 우리는 성을 보지 못했고, 또한 대성당도 보지 못했다.
② 나는 우리가 회의 전에 우리의 지위에 동의하는 것이 중요하다고 생각한다.
③ 그는 전체 3달 동안 그곳에 살면서 일했다.
④ 우리는 최근 들어서 노르만족이 1066년에 영국을 침입했다는 것을 배웠다.

06 정답 ③

> **정답해설**

③ **출제 포인트: no sooner 구문**
「주어 + had + scarcely + 과거분사 ~ + before/when + 주어 + 과거시제 동사 ~」는 no sooner 구문에 해당하며 '~하자마자 ~했다'를 뜻한다. 해당 문장은 before/when이 와야 할 자리에 than을 사용하였으므로 틀린 문장이다. 따라서 than을 before 또는 when으로 수정해야 한다.

> **오답해설**

① **출제 포인트: 동명사 관용표현**
「have difficulty (in) + 목적어(명사/동명사)」는 관용표현으로 '~하는 데 어려움을 겪다'를 뜻한다.

② **출제 포인트: 소유격 관계대명사**
소유격 관계대명사 whose는 「whose + 명사 + 동사」의 구조를 사용할 수 있다.

④ **출제 포인트: 불완전타동사 set**
set은 불완전타동사로 목적격 보어로 현재분사를 사용할 수 있다. 따라서 해당 문장은 현재분사 thinking을 목적격 보어로 사용하였으므로 옳은 문장이다.

> **해석**

① 나는 걷는 데 어려움이 있어서, 도시 꼭대기에 도착하는 것은 사실상 불가능하다.
② 그것은 자신의 의견들이 거의 경청되지 않는 사람들에게 자신들의 이야기를 말할 기회를 주는 것을 희망한다.
③ 내가 일어나서 옷을 입자마자 메신저가 마당으로 들어왔다.
④ 이 두 사건들은 나를 왜 그 두 스포츠들이 그러한 다양한 종류의 행동을 불러일으키는지를 생각하는 상태로 만들었다.

07 정답 ①

> **정답해설**

① **출제 포인트: too + 형용사/부사 + to + 동사원형 vs. so + 형용사/부사 + that + 절(can't/couldn't 포함)**
「too + 형용사/부사 + to + 동사원형」과 「so + 형용사/부사 + that + 주어 + 절(can't/couldn't 포함)」은 모두 '너무 ~해서 ~할 수 없다'를 뜻한다. 해당 문장은 too가 와야 할 자리에 so를 사용하였으므로 틀린 문장이다. 따라서 so를 too로 수정해야 한다.

오답해설

② **출제 포인트: insist + that + 절**
insist의 목적어로 「that+절」이 오는 경우 당위성을 나타내면 「that+절」에 「(should)+동사원형」을 사용하며 당위성을 나타내지 않으면 「동사(시제 반영)」을 사용한다. 해당 문장은 주어진 해석이 당위성을 나타내는 '~해야 한다고 주장하다'이므로 「that+절」에 「(should)+동사원형」을 사용하였다. 따라서 옳은 문장이다.

③ **출제 포인트: as 양보 구문**
해당 문장은 as 양보 구문이 쓰인 문장으로 주격 보어에 해당하는 형용사 small이 양보의 접속사 as 밖으로 이동하였다.

④ **출제 포인트: only 부사(구/절) 도치**
「only+부사절」이 문두에 오는 경우 뒤따라오는 문장구조는 무조건도치의 일종으로 「조동사+주어」로 도치가 발생한다. 그러나 해당 문장에서는 「only+부사절」이 문두에 오지 않았으므로 도치가 발생하지 않는다. 따라서 옳은 문장이다.

08 정답 ③

정답해설

해당 지문은 '인플레이션'과 '디플레이션'에 관해 설명하고 있다. 본문 초반에서는 '인플레이션의 정의와 예시'에 대해 언급하고, "Deflation is the opposite of inflation(디플레이션은 인플레이션의 반대이다)."을 통해 앞서 언급된 인플레이션과 비교하여 디플레이션의 정의와 예시에 대해 본문 후반에서 서술하고 있다. 따라서 글의 제목으로 가장 적절한 것은 "③ The Difference between Inflation and Deflation(인플레이션과 디플레이션의 차이)"이다.

오답해설

① 본문은 두 가지를 단순 비교하는 내용이므로 적절하지 않다.
② 각각의 원인에 대해서는 언급되지 않는다.
④ 각각의 위험성과 그것을 비교하는 내용은 언급되지 않는다.

해석

인플레이션은 제품과 서비스 가격의 지속적인 증가이다. 인플레이션 기간에 달러는 구매력 일부를 상실하고 동일한 양의 제품 또는 서비스를 구매하는 데 더 많은 통화가 필요하다. 예를 들어 올해 초 하나의 제품이 1달러의 가치가 있으나 연중 인플레이션이 5%라면, 1년 후에 하나의 제품을 구매하는 데 1.05달러가 들 것이다. 디플레이션은 인플레이션의 반대이다. 그것은 제품과 서비스 가격의 지속적인 하락이다. 디플레이션 기간에 달러는 실제로 구매력을 얻고 동일한 양의 제품 또는 서비스를 구매하는 데 예전에 필요했던 것보다 더 적은 통화가 필요하다. 예를 들어 올해 초 하나의 제품이 1달러의 가치가 있으나 연중 디플레이션이 10%라면, 1년 후에 하나의 제품을 구매하는 데 오직 0.90달러가 들 것이다.
① 우리는 디플레이션이 아니라 인플레이션이 필요하다
② 무엇이 인플레이션과 디플레이션을 일으키는가?
③ 인플레이션과 디플레이션의 차이
④ 인플레이션과 디플레이션: 어느 것이 더 큰 위험인가?

어휘

inflation 인플레이션, 통화 팽창, 물가 상승
consistent 지속적인   currency 통화
widget (가공의 것으로써 말해지는) 이런저런 제품
worth …의 가치가 있는[되는]   opposite 반대
deflation 디플레이션, 통화 수축, 물가 하락
deflationary 디플레이션의

09 정답 ②

정답해설

첫 번째 문장에서 '인플레이션에 대한 일반적인 부정적 인식'에 대해 언급한 후, 두 번째 문장 "However, inflation does have some upsides(그러나 인플레이션의 좋은 면도 있다)."에서 필자의 주장을 나타내고 있다. 이어서 '인플레이션의 좋은 면'을 두 가지 예시를 들어 설명하고 있는데, 첫 번째로는 '소비자가 인플레이션을 예상하고 현재에 더 많은 소비를 하는 것'이며, 두 번째는 '디플레이션을 예방하는 것'이다. 따라서 글에서 필자가 주장하는 것으로 가장 적절한 것은 "② Inflation has some positive effects on the economy."이다.

오답해설

① 디플레이션의 부정적인 측면은 인플레이션의 긍정적인 측면을 설명하기 위한 예시로서 언급되었고, 필자의 주된 주장은 아니기 때문에 오답이다.

해석

많은 사람들은 인플레이션을 나쁜 것으로 본다. 동일한 양의 제품과 서비스를 구매하기 위해 작년에 지불했던 것보다 더 많이 소비하기를 원하는 사람은 없다. 그러나 인플레이션의 좋은 면도 있다. 첫 번째 예시는 소비자들이 그것을 예측하는 경우인데, 이것은 그들의 돈이 곧 가치가 떨어진다는 것을 알고 현재에 그들이 더 많이 구매를 한다는 것을 의미한다. 또 다른 예는 그것이 디플레이션을 예방하는 경우이다. 그것이 더 많이 구매하기 위해 더 적게 소비한다는 것을 의미하므로 디플레이션이 좋게 들릴 수 있지만, 문제는 인플레이션의 반대 상황이 발생한다는 것이다. 사람들은 가격이 훨씬 더 떨어질지 여부를 알아보기 위해 현재에는 기다린다. 그렇게 하는 것은 사람들이 구매를 덜 한다는 것을 의미하고, 그로 인해 기업들과 제조사들은 그들의 인력을 감축해야 한다. 중앙은행은 보통 어떻게 해서든지 디플레이션을 피하려고 노력한다.
① 디플레이션은 생각만큼 좋은 것은 아니다.
② 인플레이션은 경제에 일부 긍정적인 영향을 미친다.
③ 인플레이션과 디플레이션은 사전에 예방되어야 한다.
④ 중앙은행은 경제 안정화에 있어서 결정적인 역할을 한다.

어휘

inflation 인플레이션, 통화 팽창, 물가 상승
upside (나쁜 상황 속의) 좋은 면   anticipate 예상하다, 기대하다
worth …의 가치가 있는[되는]   prevent 예방하다, 막다
deflation 디플레이션, 통화 수축, 물가 하락
inverse 역의, 반대의   cut back 축소하다, 삭감하다
workforce 노동자, 노동력
at all costs 무슨 수를 써서라도, 어떻게 해서든, 반드시
critical 결정적인, 대단히 중요한   stabilize 안정시키다

10 정답 ④

정답해설

해당 지문은 '베네수엘라의 경제위기'에 대해 서술하고 있다. ④ 이전에서 '비상사태를 선포한 2016년 물가 상승률은 800%에 달했다'라는 내용을 언급한 후 ④ 이후 문장에서 2018년의 물가 상승률을 언급하고, 이후에서는 현재의 물가 상승률에 대해 추정하는 내용이 이어지고 있다. 물가 상승률에 대해 연속적으로 언급되는 가운데 ④에서 '베네수엘라의 국민들이 정권의 탄압을 피해 조국을 떠났다'라는 내용이 들어가는 것은 문맥상 자연스럽지 않다. 따라서 글의 흐름상 가장 어색한 문장은 "④ About 3 million Venezuelans – a tenth of the population – have fled the country due to the Maduro regime's oppressive treatment of dissent(인구의 10분의 1에 달하는 약 3백만 명의 베네수엘라인들이 반대 의견에 대한 Maduro 정권의 강압적인 대우 때문에 조국을 떠났다)."이다.

해석

상점에 가서 어느 것에도 가격표가 붙어있지 않은 것을 발견하는 것을 상상해보라. 대신 당신은 그것을 계산원에게 가져가고 그들이 가격을 계산한다. ① 당신이 지불하는 금액은 한 시간 전보다 두 배 또는 그 이상이 될 수도 있다. 심지어 그것은 어느 것이라도 재고가 있을 경우에 해당하는 일이다. ② 이것이 베네수엘라의 현 "경제위기"의 근거가 되는 현실이다. 그러나 사실 그 위기는 수년 동안 지속되어왔다. ③ 2013년부터 베네수엘라를 통치해 온 Nicolás Maduro가 이끄는 정부는 2016년에 비상사태를 선포했다. 그 해 물가 상승률은 800%로 치달았다. ④ <u>인구의 10분의 1에 달하는 약 3백만 명의 베네수엘라인들이 반대 의견에 대한 Maduro 정권의 강압적인 대우 때문에 조국을 떠났다</u>. 2018년 그 비율은 80,000%로 추정되었다. 현재의 비율이 어떠한지 판단하는 것은 어려우나, 커피 한 잔의 가격을 기준으로 하는 Bloomberg의 베네수엘라 Cafe Con Leche 지수는 그것이 현재 약 380,000%라는 것을 시사한다.

어휘

in stock 재고가 있는
head 이끌다
declare 선언하다
inflation rate 물가 상승률, 인플레이션율
flee(fled-fled) 떠나다, 벗어나다
oppressive 강압적인, 억압하는
estimated 추정의, 추측의
underpin 근거가 되다
preside 지배하다, 통솔하다
regime 정권
dissent 반대 의견, 반대

결국엔 성정혜 영어 하프모의고사
기적사 DAY 16

| 01 | ③ | 02 | ④ | 03 | ② | 04 | ② | 05 | ③ |
| 06 | ④ | 07 | ③ | 08 | ④ | 09 | ④ | 10 | ③ |

01 정답 ③ 17 국가직

정답해설

'quintessential'은 '전형적인'이라는 뜻으로 ③ 'typical'과 의미가 가장 가깝다.

해석

패스트푸드 체인의 홍보 노력 덕택에, 햄버거와 감자튀김은 1950년대에 <u>전형적인</u> 미국 식사가 되었다.
① 가장 건강한
② 입수 가능한, (가격 등이) 알맞은
③ 전형적인
④ 비공식적인, 격식 차리지 않는

어휘

promotional 선전용의, 홍보의

02 정답 ④ 17 국가직

정답해설

문맥상 빈칸에 공통으로 들어가기에 가장 자연스러운 것은 '극복하다'의 의미를 지닌 ④ 'get over'이다.

해석

• 그녀는 그들의 최종 결정에 실망을 했지만, 그녀는 결국 <u>극복할</u> 것이다.
• 그녀의 죽음으로 인한 충격을 <u>극복하기</u> 위해 내게 오랜 시간이 걸렸다.
① 도망치다, 벗어나다
② 내려가다, 엎드리다, 시작하다
③ 성공하다, 앞지르다
④ 극복하다, 이겨내다

어휘

disappoint 실망시키다
eventually 결국

오답률 TOP 2

03 정답 ② 17 국가직

정답해설

빈칸 앞에서 'Reading and studying were more permissible for girls'라고 제시하며 '독서와 공부는 여자아이들에게 더 허용'되었다고 언급하고 있다. 또한, 빈칸 뒤에서는 'lest they acquire the stigma of being 'stuck up'' 즉, '건방지다고 낙인찍히지 않기 위해'라고 하였다. 그러므로 인과관계를 고려하여 너무 '똑똑해지지' 않도록 주의해야 한다고 하는 것이 문맥상 자연스럽다. 따라서 정답은 ② 'intellectual'이다.

해석

민족적으로 뒤섞인 시카고 동네에서 자란 중산층 유대인으로서, 나는 이미 매일 더 거친 노동자 계급의 사내아이들로부터 맞을 위험에 처해있었다. 책벌레가 되는 것은 단지 그들에게 나를 때릴 결정적인 이유만 제공했을 것이다. 책을 읽고 공부를 하는 것은 여자아이들에게 조금 더 허용되는 것이었지만, 그들은 건방지다고 낙인찍히지 않기 위해 너무 **똑똑해지지** 않도록 주의를 기울여야만 했다.
① 운동의, 건강한   ② 지적인, 지성을 지닌
③ 친절한, 환대하는   ④ 미숙한

어휘

Jew 유대인
decisive 결정적인, 단호한
lest ~하지 않도록
stuck up 우쭐대는, 건방진
ethnically 민족적으로
permissible 허용되는, 무방한
stigma 치욕, 오명, 낙인

04 정답 ②
17 국가직

정답해설

빈칸을 듣고 A는 B의 생각에 동의하며 다른 놀이기구를 타고 싶다고 대답한다. 따라서 B가 다른 놀이기구를 타기를 제안했을 것으로 유추할 수 있다.

오답해설

①③④ 어떤 놀이기구를 탈지에 대해 논의하고 있는 본문 대화의 내용에 적절하지 않다.

해석

A: 우와! 저 긴 줄을 봐. 우린 적어도 30분은 기다려야 할 거야.
B: 네 말이 맞아. 다른 놀이기구를 찾아보자.
A: 그거 좋은 생각이다. 나는 롤러코스터를 타고 싶어.
B: 나는 그걸 별로 좋아하지 않아.
A: 그럼 후룸라이드는 어때? 재미도 있고 줄도 별로 안 길어.
B: 그거 괜찮네! 가자!
① 마술쇼 자리를 찾아보자.
② 다른 놀이기구를 찾아보자.
③ 퍼레이드 의상을 사자.
④ 분실물 보관소로 가보자.

어휘

cup of tea (보통 부정문에 사용) 기호에 맞는 사람(물건)
ride 놀이기구

오답률 TOP 3

05 정답 ③
17 국가직 (추)

정답해설

③ **출제 포인트: 혼동하기 쉬운 동사**
promise는 '~을 약속하다'라는 의미로 주로 타동사로 쓰인다. 우리말의 '타협하다'는 compromise로 쓴다.

오답해설

① **출제 포인트: 전치사 관용표현**
by word of mouth는 '입에서 입으로, 입소문을 통해서'라는 뜻으로 알맞게 사용되었다.

② **출제 포인트: 복합 형용사**
must-see는 '꼭 보아야 할[볼만한] 것'이라는 뜻으로 알맞게 사용되었다.

④ **출제 포인트: 전치사 관용표현/to부정사의 형용사적 용법**
on a tight budget은 '돈이 없는, 빈곤한'이라는 뜻의 관용구이고, 두 번째 문장에서 to spend는 명사 fifteen dollars를 수식하는 to부정사의 형용사적 용법으로 쓰였다.

06 정답 ④
17 국가직 (추)

정답해설

④ **출제 포인트: 등위접속사와 병렬구조**
해설이 3가지로 제시될 수 있다.
1) 주어에서 To control the process와 making improvement는 등위접속사 and에 의해 병렬 구조를 이루어야 한다. 따라서 To control the process and to make improvement 혹은 Controlling the process and making improvement로 바꿔야 한다. 또한 의미상, 이 두 개의 개념을 하나의 개념으로 간주하고 있으므로 단수 동사 was로 쓴 것은 적절하나 보어 역시도 일치하여 objective로 수정해야 한다. (단, 주어를 각각의 개념으로 볼 경우에는 were objectives가 옳다.)
2) 분사구문을 이용해서 To make improvement(부정사 주어), controlling the process(분사구문)로 주어를 우리말대로 표시하고 단수로 was로 나타낼 수 있다.
3) 주어진 문장의 어순을 그대로 활용한다면, 아래와 같은 경우도 가능하다. 분사구문을 활용해서 To control (Controlling) the process, making improvement를 주어로 우리말 동시 상황을 사용하여, '발전시키면서 과정을 관리하는 것'도 역시 가능하다.

오답해설

① **출제 포인트: 독립 분사구문**
부사절 When the dinner was ready를 분사구문으로 바꾼 것이다. 접속사 When은 생략하고, 주절과 종속절의 주어가 다르기 때문에 종속절의 주어 The dinner는 그대로 남아있다. was는 주절의 동사 moved와 시제가 일치하기 때문에 being이 된다.

② **출제 포인트: 간접의문문**
who that is over there은 동사 tell의 목적어 역할을 하고 있는 간접의문문에 해당한다. 따라서 「의문문+주어+동사」의 어순으로 왔다.

③ **출제 포인트: 명사절을 이끄는 접속사 that**
해당 문장에서 'that'은 주어 역할을 하는 「that+명사절」로 사용되었다.

07 정답 ③
17 국가직 (추)

정답해설

③ **출제 포인트: 가정법 과거완료**
가정법 과거완료 구문으로 과거 사실을 반대하여 가정할 때 쓰인다. 「If+주어+had p.p. ~, 주어+조동사 과거형+have p.p.」로 적절하다.

오답해설

① **출제 포인트: to부정사를 목적격 보어로 갖는 불완전 타동사의 수동태/불가산명사**
「be allowed to+동사원형」은 '~하는 것이 허용[허락]되다'라는 의미로 여기서 to는 전치사가 아니므로 using을 use로 바꿔야 한다. 또한 equipment는 불가산명사이므로 복수형이 불가능하다. 따라서 equipment로 고쳐야 한다.

② **출제 포인트: 주어와 동사 수일치**
주어는 The extent로 3인칭 단수이다. 따라서 동사는 주어에 수일치를 시켜 astounds가 되어야 한다.

④ **출제 포인트: 목적어의 형태에 따라 의미가 달라지는 동사/능동태 vs. 수동태**
regret은 '유감스럽게 생각하다'라는 의미의 동사로, 목적어로 동명사가 오면 이미 지난 일에 대한 후회를, to부정사가 오면 앞으로 일어날 일에 대한 유감을 나타내므로 regret to inform you는 옳게 사용되었다. 「inform+목적어+that+주어+동사」의 형태도 역시 옳다. 단, approve

는 타동사로 '~ 승인하다'의 뜻인데 여기서는 의미상 '승인되지 않다'라는 수동의 의미가 되도록 has not been approved가 되어야 옳다.

해석
① 학부생들은 실험실에서 장비를 사용하도록 허용되지 않는다.
② 다양한 주제들에 대한 Mary의 지식의 범위는 나를 놀라게 한다.
③ 만약 그녀가 어제 집에 있었다면, 나는 그녀를 방문했을 거야.
④ 당신의 대출 신청서가 승인되지 않았음을 알리게 되어 유감입니다.

08 정답 ④ 19 서울시

정답해설
본문은 수사 기술의 발전으로 범죄를 더 빠르게 해결할 수 있고 그러한 예로 새로운 DNA 테스트와 새로운 종류의 지문 테스트가 있다고 서술하고 있다. 하지만 "The fingerprints also reveal if the person takes medication." (지문들은 그 사람이 약물을 했는지 역시 밝혀낸다.)은 범죄 해결에 새로운 기술이 도움이 되고 있다는 본문의 내용과는 관련이 없는 내용이므로 정답은 ④이다.

오답해설
①은 지문의 주제이고 나머지는 글의 흐름에 적절하므로 정답이 될 수 없다.

해석
① 범죄를 해결하는 것은 법 집행의 가장 중요한 업무들 중 하나이다. 오늘날 범죄 기술의 발전은 수사관들이 범죄를 더 빨리, 그리고 더 효율적으로, 해결하는 것을 돕는다. ② 예를 들면, 범죄 수사 연구소는 새로운 종류의 DNA 테스트를 가지고 있는데, 혈액, 땀, 그리고 타액과 같은 체액을 확인할 수 있다. 새로운 종류의 지문 테스트 역시 있다. ③ 과거에, 지문 테스트는 범죄 현장에서 나온 지문들이 이미 파일에 있는 "지문들"과 일치될 수 있을 경우에만 도움이 됐다. 유죄 판결을 받은 범죄자들의 지문은 경찰 기록에 영구적으로 파일에 보관된다. ④ *지문들은 그 사람이 약물을 했는지 역시 밝혀낸다.* 파일에 지문이 없는 사람들은 이 방식으로 확인될 수 없고, 결과적으로, 많은 범죄들이 해결되지 않았다.

어휘
law enforcement 법 집행
crime lab 범죄 수사 연구소
saliva 타액, 침
match 일치하다
permanently 영구적으로
medication 약, 약물
as a result 결과적으로
detective 수사관
body fluid 체액
fingerprint 지문
convicted 유죄 판결을 받은
reveal 드러내다, 밝히다
identify 신분을 확인하다

오답률 TOP 1
09 정답 ④ 19 서울시

정답해설
본문에서 1948년에 채택된 아동법은 그 전의 견해인 'older ideas about the benefits of corporal punishment'(신체적 처벌의 혜택들에 대한 오래된 생각들)가 아동법의 통과로 'children who broke the law should be reclaimed and rehabilitated had become the orthodox view'(법을 어긴 아이들은 교정되고 갱생되어야 한다는 시각)가 정통적인 견해가 되었다는 것이므로 ④ The 1948 Children Act accentuated the benefits of corporal punishment.(1948년의 아동법은 신체적 처벌의 혜택들을 강조했다.)는 본문과 일치하지 않는 내용이다. 따라서 정답은 ④이다.

오답해설
① 본문 마지막 문장과 일치하는 내용이다.
② 본문의 'This approach drew upon the views of social workers in the slums of British and American cities'와 일치하는 내용이다.
③ 'Delinquency was seen as part of a social matrix, as resulting from structural inequalities and deficient parenting styles'와 일치하는 내용이다.

해석
영국의 청소년 사법제도는 20세기 초반에 상당한 철학적 변화들을 겪었다. 신체적 처벌의 혜택들에 대한 오래된 생각들을 고수하는 많은 이들이 있었지만, 법을 어긴 아이들은 교정되고 갱생되어야 한다는 시각이 1948년 아동법의 통과로 정통적인 견해가 되었다. 이 접근법은 영미의 빈민가의 사회복지사들과 새로운 사회과학과 의학 분야의 연구자들의 견해에 기대었다. 비행은 구조적 불평등과 부족한 육아 방식으로 인한 것으로, 사회적 매트릭스의 일부로 여겨졌다. 비행 문제에 대한 해결책은 이러한 불평등들을 발생시킨 구조들의 개혁 내에 놓여 있는 것으로 여겨졌다. 더 급진적인 치안 판사들에게는, 그 해답은 사회를 점검하는 것이 아니라, 아이들이 법정에 의해 다루어지는 방식들을 개혁하는 것이었다.
① 어떤 판사들의 견해에 따르면, 법정의 아이들에 대한 더 나은 취급이 비행을 억누르는 데 도움이 될 수 있다.
② 사회복지사들은 정통적인 견해의 지지자들 중 하나였다.
③ 부족한 육아 방식들은 비행의 한 원인으로 여겨졌다.
④ 1948년의 아동법은 신체적 처벌의 혜택들을 강조했다.

어휘
juvenile 청소년
cling to ~에 매달리다, ~을 고수하다
reclaim 갱생시키다, 교정하다
orthodox 정통의
draw upon[on] ~을 이용하다, ~에 의지하다
delinquency 비행, 범죄
reformation 개혁, 개선
overhaul 점검하다
proponent 옹호자, 지지자
undergo 겪다, 거치다
corporal 신체의
rehabilitate 재활시키다
passing (법안 등의) 통과
parenting 육아
magistrate 치안판사
curb 억누르다
accentuate 강조하다

10 정답 ③ 18 지방직

정답해설
주어진 본문은 도입부의 'The Renaissance kitchen had a definite hierarchy of help~'를 통해 '르네상스 시대의 명확했던 주방 계급에 대해 기술'할 것임을 짐작할 수 있다. ①에서 주방과 식당을 총괄하는 호텔종사원, ②에서 식당을 관리하는 집사, ④에서 최고 주방장에 의해 관리되는 주방에 대한 설명으로 이어진다. 그러나 ③에서 'This elaborate decoration and serving' 즉 '이러한 정교한 장식과 대접'은 이전의 내용에서 찾아볼 수 없을 뿐더러, 해당 문장은 글의 전체적인 내용의 흐름에서 벗어났다. 따라서 글의 흐름상 가장 어색한 문장은 ③이다.

해석
르네상스 시대의 주방은 정교한 만찬을 열기 위해 함께 일을 했던 일꾼들의 명확한 계급을 가지고 있었다. ① 제일 높은 곳에는, 우리가 봤듯이, 주방뿐 아니라 식당까지 총괄하는 scalco 혹은 호텔종사원이 있다. ② 식당은 은식기류와 린넨을 담당하는 집사에 의해 관리되었고 또한 연회를 시작하고 끝내는 음식을 제공했다 - 시작할 때에는 냉요리, 샐러드, 치즈, 과일이, 식사가 끝날 때에는 디저트와 제과류. ③ *이런 정교한 장식과 대접은 식당에서 "프런트 데스크"라고 불리는 것이다.* ④ 주방은 보조 주방장, 페이스트리 요리사, 주방 보조자들을 지시하는 최고 주방장에 의해 관리된다.

어휘

definite 분명한, 뚜렷한, 확실한, 확고한
hierarchy 계급, 계층
banquet 연회, 만찬
steward 호텔종사원
supervise 감독하다, 지휘하다, 지도하다
butler 집사(대저택의 남자 하인 중 책임자)
silverware 은식기류
undercook 요리사의 조수
elaborate 정교한, 정성을 들인
in charge of ~을 맡아서, 담당해서
confection 과자, 당과 제품

결국엔 성정혜 영어 하프모의고사
기적사 DAY 17

01	④	02	③	03	②	04	④	05	③
06	③	07	④	08	④	09	②	10	③

01 정답 ④

정답해설

밑줄 친 단어가 문맥상 '평범한'으로 사용되었고, 유의어로는 ④ ordinary가 적절하다.

해석

최선을 다해서 **평범한** 운동선수가 되었음에도 불구하고, Dean은 스포츠 분야에서 살아남았다.
① 유능한
② 비공식적인
③ 귀찮은, 성가신
④ 보통의, 일반적인, 평범한

어휘

capable 유능한
bothersome 귀찮은, 성가신
informal 비공식적인
ordinary 보통의, 일반적인, 평범한

오답률 TOP 3
02 정답 ③

정답해설

밑줄 친 단어가 문맥상 '암시적인'으로 사용되었고, 유의어로는 ③ connotative가 적절하다.

해석

군주제 이전 서사의 가장 **암시적인** 연구는 충격을 극복하는 것이다.
① 솔직한
② 주요한, 원금의, 우두머리, 장, 주연 배우
③ 암시하는
④ 즉흥적인

어휘

pre-monarchical 군주제 이전의
get over 극복하다
principal 주요한, 원금의, 우두머리, 장, 주연 배우
connotative 암시하는
narratives 이야기
outspoken 솔직한
improvised 즉흥적인

오답률 TOP 2
03 정답 ②

정답해설

밑줄 친 단어가 문맥상 '격분한'으로 쓰였고, 유의어로는 ② furious가 적절하다. 참고로 해당 문장에서 'now'는 문맥상 과거시제로 '이제(는)'라는 의미로 사용되었다.

해석

Ozma는 이제 새끼 고양이의 행동에 크게 **격분했다**.
① 쓸모없는, 실패한, 유산의

② 격노한, 격렬한
③ 지적인
④ 전례 없는, 비할 데 없는

어휘

abortive 쓸모없는
intellectual 지적인
furious 격노한, 격렬한
unparalleled 전례 없는

04 정답 ④

정답해설

A와 B의 대화에서 A는 B에게 주문한 커피를 잘못 주었음을 알 수 있다. 이어지는 대화를 통해서 '좀처럼 실수가 없는' A임을 알 수 있으므로 이어질 속담으로는 '④ Even Homer sometimes nods(원숭이도 나무에서 떨어질 때가 있다)'가 적절하다.

오답해설

① '분실물 보관소로 갑시다'는 문맥에 어울리지 않는다.
② '깊은 물은 조용히 흐른다'라는 뜻으로, 실력이 있거나 속이 깊을수록 말이 많지 않다는 의미이다.
③ '불행은 겹쳐서 온다'라는 뜻이다. 대화 속에는 커피를 잘못 만든 것 외에는 다른 나쁜 일이 언급되지 않았다.

해석

A: 주문하신 것 나왔습니다.
B: 고맙습니다. 음, 실례지만 이건 제가 주문한 커피가 아닌데요.
A: 라떼 시키지 않으셨나요?
B: 아니요, 캐러멜 마키아토 시켰어요.
A: 죄송해요. 제가 헷갈렸나 봐요.
B: 원숭이도 나무에서 떨어질 때가 있다더니. 실수하신 거 한 번도 본 적 없었는데.
A: 바로 제대로 된 걸로 해드릴게요.
B: 고마워요.
① 분실물 보관소로 갑시다
② 깊은 물은 조용히 흐른다 (빈 수레가 요란하다)
③ 불행은 겹쳐서 온다
④ 원숭이도 나무에서 떨어질 때가 있다

어휘

immediately 즉시, 바로   the lost and found 분실물 보관소
Even Homer sometimes nods. 원숭이도 나무에서 떨어질 때가 있다.

05 정답 ③

정답해설

③ **출제 포인트: 혼동하기 쉬운 동사**
주어진 해석이 '타협하다'이므로 compromise를 사용하여야 한다. 따라서 promise를 compromise로 수정해야 한다.

오답해설

① **출제 포인트: 전치사 관용표현**
on no account는 관용표현으로 '결코 ~않은'을 뜻한다.
② **출제 포인트: 전치사 관용표현**
by the skin of one's teeth는 관용표현으로 '간신히, 가까스로'를 뜻한다.
④ **출제 포인트: 복합 형용사**
sun-dried는 명사와 과거분사가 하이픈으로 이어진 복합 형용사이다.

06 정답 ③

정답해설

③ **출제 포인트: 등위접속사와 병렬구조**
등위접속사 and를 사용하여 현재분사가 「A, B, and C」의 구조를 이루고 있다. 따라서 download를 downloading으로 수정해야 한다.

오답해설

① **출제 포인트: 명사절을 이끄는 접속사 that**
해당 문장에서 'that'은 주어 역할을 하는 「that+명사절」로 사용되었다.
※ 명사절을 이끄는 접속사 'that'의 역할은 다음과 같다.
  1. 주어 역할
     「that+명사절」이 주어 역할을 하는 경우 주로 문두에 가주어 'it'을 사용하며 「that+명사절」을 문미로 이동시킨다. 이때 'that'은 생략할 수 있다. 그러나 「that+명사절」이 문두에서 주어 역할을 하는 경우 'that'은 생략할 수 없다.
     ex) It's a pity (that) you don't know Russian.
     ex) That you don't know Russian is a pity.
  2. 목적어 역할
     → 「that+명사절」이 목적어 역할을 하는 경우 직접목적어로 사용하며 이때 'that'은 생략할 수 있다.
     ex) I can't believe (that) he's only 17.
  3. 보어 역할
     → 「that+명사절」이 보어 역할을 하는 경우 주격 보어로 사용하며 이때 'that'은 생략할 수 있다.
     ex) The problem is (that) Jane doesn't like me.
  4. 동격
     → 「that+명사절」이 동격으로 쓰이는 경우 추상명사가 'that'이전에 쓰이며 'that' 이후에는 완전한 문장이 와야 한다.
     ex) The fact that he is your brother-in-law should not affect your decision.
② **출제 포인트: 독립 분사구문**
종속절의 주어와 주절의 주어가 다르므로 분사구문을 만들 때 종속절의 주어를 생략할 수 없다. 이때 해당 분사구문을 독립 분사구문이라 한다.
④ **출제 포인트: 간접의문문**
해당 문장은 의문문이 완전타동사 wondered의 목적어로 사용된 경우로 간접의문문에 해당하며 어순은 「의문사(주어)+동사」이다.

07 정답 ④

정답해설

④ **출제 포인트: 가정법 과거완료**
「If+주어+had+과거분사 ~, 주어+would/could/should/might +have+과거분사 ~.」는 가정법 과거완료에 해당한다.

오답해설

① **출제 포인트: 능동태 vs. 수동태**
수동태 was told 뒤에 목적어 us가 있으므로 틀린 문장이다. 따라서 was told를 told로 수정해야 한다.
② **출제 포인트: 주어와 동사 수일치**
주어가 명사구 The rewards이며 복수형태이므로 주절의 동사에 복수형태를 사용해야 한다. 따라서 is를 are로 수정해야 한다.
③ **출제 포인트: to부정사를 목적격 보어로 갖는 불완전타동사의 수동태**
불완전타동사 allow의 수동태는 「be allowed to+동사원형」이다. 따라서 watching을 watch로 수정해야 한다.

해석
① 그는 우리에게 자신의 기이한 어린 시절을 이야기해주었다.
② 가르치는 것으로부터 오는 보상들은 많다.
③ 아이들은 폭력적인 TV 프로그램들을 보는 것이 허락되지 않는다.
④ 그들이 그렇게 했다면, 그들의 경력은 평생 망치게 되었을 것이다.

08 정답 ④

정답해설
해당 지문의 필자는 '사회 복지 지출이 사회에 미치는 영향'을 전반적으로 긍정적으로 평가하고 있으며, 본문 후반에 '그에 반대하는 의견을 지닌 사람들이 그들의 주장을 뒷받칠 수 있는 설명을 해야 한다'고 주장한다. 주어진 문장의 'burden of proof(입증 책임)'에 대한 내용이 ④이후 문장 "they need to explain not only why all rich nations have large welfare states, but more importantly why growth rates have grown in most rich nations as their welfare states have grown larger(그들은 모든 부유한 국가들이 거대한 사회 복지를 유지하고 있는 이유뿐만 아니라, 더 중요한 것은 대부분의 부유한 국가에서 그들의 사회 복지가 더 거대해짐에 따라 성장률이 증가한 이유 또한 설명해야 한다)."에서 구체적으로 언급되고 있다는 것을 알 수 있다. 또한 ④ 이후 문장의 주어 'they'가 주어진 문장의 'those who ~'를 가리키고 있으므로, ④가 주어진 문장이 들어가기에 가장 적절한 위치이다.

오답해설
나머지 보기는 문맥상 부자연스러우므로 오답이다.

해석
물론, 사회 복지 외에도 많은 다른 요소들이 지난 150년 동안 변했다. (①) 그러나 오늘날 모든 발달된 산업 국가에서 사회 복지 지출은 재화와 서비스의 총생산에 비례하여 매우 높다. (②) 만일 그러한 지출이 큰 역효과를 낳았다면, 지난 30년 동안 성장률이 그렇게 높았을지 의문이 든다. (③) 있는 그대로의 역사상 관계가 최소한 커다란 부작용이 없고 오히려 긍정적인 영향을 미친다는 것을 암시한다. (④ **입증 책임은 명백히 사회 복지 프로그램이 생산성과 성장을 억제하고 있다고 주장하는 사람들의 편에 있다.**) 만약 그들이 옳다면, 그들은 모든 부유한 국가들이 거대한 사회 복지를 유지하고 있는 이유뿐만 아니라, 더 중요한 것은 대부분의 부유한 국가에서 그들의 사회 복지가 더 거대해짐에 따라 성장률이 증가한 이유 또한 설명해야 한다.

어휘
burden of proof 입증 책임
welfare state 사회 복지
productivity 생산성
social welfare 사회 복지
industrialized 산업화된
adverse effect 역효과
ill effect 부작용
claim 주장하다
strangle 억제하다, 억누르다
besides ~외에
relative to ~에 비례하여
expenditure 지출
crude 있는 그대로의, 날것의, 미가공의

오답률 TOP 1

09 정답 ②

정답해설
빈칸 이전에서 '경제 성장의 바람직함에 의문을 품은 사람들'에 대해 언급한 후, 빈칸 이후에서 그에 대한 예시로 John Stuart Mill의 글을 인용하고 있다. 인용구 "It is only in the backward countries of the world that increased production is still an important object; in those most advanced, what is economically needed is a better distribution.(오직 전 세계의 후진국에서만 증산이 여전히 중요한 목표이다. 대부분의 선진국에서 경제적으로 필요한 것은 더 나은 분배이다.)"을 통해 '성장보다 더 나은 분배가 필요하다'라고 언급하고 있으므로, 빈칸에는 경제 성장에 대해 부정적인 입장을 나타내는 내용이 들어가는 것이 글의 흐름상 자연스럽다. 따라서 빈칸에 가장 적절한 것은 "② Doubts as to the wisdom of economic growth(경제 성장의 타당성에 대한 의심)"이다.

오답해설
④ 경제 성장에 따른 환경 문제에 관해서는 빈칸 이후 예시에서 언급되지 않으므로 적절하지 않은 내용이다.
나머지 보기는 문맥상 부자연스러우므로 오답이다.

해석
지난 몇 년 동안 세계의 선진국들에서 환경에 대한 우려가 있어왔다. 이러한 우려는 이 국가들에서 더 이상의 경제 성장이 바람직한가와 심지어 덜 발전한 국가들의 경제 성장이 가능한가 또는 바람직한가에 대해 의문을 품은 사람들에게 명분을 제공했다. 경제 성장의 타당성에 대한 의심은 시간이 흐르며 이따금 표출되어왔다. 예를 들어 John Stuart Mill은 1848년 글에서 "오직 전 세계의 후진국에서만 증산이 여전히 중요한 목표이다. 대부분의 선진국에서 경제적으로 필요한 것은 더 나은 분배이다."라고 서술했다.
① 선진국들의 책임
② 경제 성장의 타당성에 대한 의심
③ 개발도상국의 경제 발전에 대한 예측
④ 경제 성장으로 인해 발생한 환경 문제에 대한 우려

어휘
ammunition 자신의 주장에 유리한 정보[조언], 공격[방어] 수단
desirability 바람직함
backward country 후진국
distribution 분배
prediction 예측, 예상
feasibility 가능성, 실행할 수 있음
object 목표, 목적
wisdom 타당성
regarding ~에 관한

10 정답 ③

정답해설
해당 지문은 '인도네시아'의 경우를 예로 들어 개발도상국의 경제 발전의 실상에 대해 서술하고 있다. 본문을 통해 인도네시아는 거시적으로는 6%대의 꾸준한 경제 성장을 이룩하며 발전해 나가고 있지만, 실제로는 소득 불평등 지수인 '지니계수'또한 함께 상승하고 있다는 것을 알 수 있다. 따라서 '경제가 성장하더라도 모든 계층이 재정적으로 혜택을 받는 것은 아니다'라는 것이 필자의 주장이므로, 글의 요지로 가장 적절한 것은 "③ Economic growth does not mean the equal financial improvement of all groups of population(경제 성장은 국민의 모든 집단의 동등한 재정적 발전을 의미하는 것은 아니다)."이다.

오답해설
① 소득격차에 대한 해결 방안은 본문에 언급되지 않으므로 오답이다.
② '지니계수'가 증가하면 '소득격차'가 증가하는 것이며, 이는 사회 복지를 저해시키는 요인이 되므로 문맥상 어색한 내용이다.
④ 본문에서 '소득격차'가 증가한 것의 예를 들고 있으므로, 본문의 주장과 반대되는 내용이다.

해석
인도네시아와 같은 개발도상국에서의 경제 성장은 모순을 보여준다. "경제 성장의 역설"은 경제가 성장하지만 소득 불평등 또한 성장하는 것이다. 인도네시아의 경제는 2012년에 6.1%, 2013년에 6.3%, 2014년에 6.4% 성장했다. 거시적인 측면에서 인도네시아의 경제 성장은 좋아 보였다. 그러나 우리가 더 가까이 들여다보면 우리는 그것이 환상이었다는 것을 알 수 있다. 그 이면에서 인도네시아의 지니계수는 증가하고 있었다. 2012년에 그것은 0.36

이었고, 2013년에는 0.39, 2014년에 0.41이었다. 국가의 경제가 성장함에 따라 소득격차도 증가한 것이다. 인도네시아를 비롯한 다른 개발도상국에서 경제 성장의 혜택은 중산층과 그 이상의 계층에게만 돌아갔고, 하층 그리고 노동자 계급에까지 도달한 혜택은 거의 없었다. 부유층은 더 부유해지고 빈곤층은 더 빈곤해졌다.
① 인도네시아의 소득 불평등은 더 높은 교육을 통해 해결될 수 있다.
② 인도네시아는 지니계수를 증가시킴으로써 전체 국가의 사회 복지를 촉진시켜야 한다.
　cf. Gini ratio(지니계수) : 소득 분포의 불평등도를 측정하기 위한 계수
③ 경제 성장은 국민의 모든 집단의 동등한 재정적 발전을 의미하는 것은 아니다.
④ 경제 성장은 한 국가의 거의 모든 시민에게 혜택을 주고, 따라서 궁극적으로 빈곤을 감소시킨다.

어휘

contradiction 모순 paradox 역설
income inequality 소득 불평등 macro 거시적인
illusion 환상, 환각
Gini ratio 지니계수(소득분배의 불균형 수치)
income gap 소득격차 reserve 확보하다
make it 가다, 도달하다 social welfare 사회 복지
poverty 빈곤 ultimately 궁극적으로

결국엔 성정혜 영어 하프모의고사
기적사 DAY 18

| 01 | ④ | 02 | ② | 03 | ① | 04 | ④ | 05 | ① |
| 06 | ④ | 07 | ② | 08 | ② | 09 | ② | 10 | ④ |

01 정답 ④

정답해설

밑줄 친 단어가 문맥상 '타의 추종을 불허하는, 비길 데 없는'으로 사용되었으므로, 유의어로는 ④ incomparable이 적절하다.

해석

민첩함에서 그들은 **타의 추종을 불허한다**; 사실 그들은 그들의 발로 하늘을 나는 새들을 잡을 수 있을 정도로 빠르다.
① 불가사의한, 수수께끼의
② 중요한
③ 입수 가능한, (가격 등이) 알맞은
④ 비길 데 없는, 비교할 수 없는

어휘

enigmatic 불가사의한, 수수께끼의　momentous 중요한
affordable 입수 가능한, (가격 등이) 알맞은
incomparable 비길 데 없는, 비교할 수 없는

오답률 TOP 1
02 정답 ②

정답해설

밑줄 친 단어의 의미가 문맥상 '냉담한'으로 사용되었으며, 유의어로는 ② reserved가 적절하다.

해석

그의 **냉담한** 반응에 그녀는 떠났다.
① 건방진, 확신 있는
② 냉담한, 남겨 둔, 예약되어있는
③ 불가결한, 통합적인
④ 풍부한

어휘

get away 도망가다 confident 건방진, 확신 있는
reserved 냉담한, 남겨 둔, 예약되어있는
integrative 불가결한, 통합적인 plentiful 풍부한

03 정답 ①

정답해설

밑줄 친 단어는 문맥상 '편파적이지 않은'으로 쓰였으며, 유의어로는 ① unprejudiced가 적절하다.

해석

아마도 그것이 그녀가 해야 할 일이었을 것이다. - **편파적이지 않은** 청중들에게 모든 이야기를 들려주는 것이다.
① 편견 없는
② 고독한, 격리된

③ 친절한, 환대하는; (기후, 환경이) 쾌적한
④ 자연스러운, 노력하지 않은, 불로 소득의

어휘

unprejudiced 편견 없는　　　secluded 고독한, 격리된
hospitable 친절한, 환대하는; (기후, 환경이) 쾌적한
unlabored 자연스러운, 노력하지 않은, 불로 소득의

오답률 TOP 2

04 정답 ④

정답해설

대화 속에서 '시간에 쫓기며 일'하고 있는 상황 말고도, '부사장의 결재'를 받아야 하는 상황임을 파악할 수 있다. 빈칸 이후 B는 이어지는 말에서 '아슬아슬하다(touch-and-go)'라고 말한다. 따라서 A가 했을 말로 '④ What are the odds of finishing the project?(프로젝트를 완료할 가능성은 얼마예요?)'가 적절하다.

오답해설

① 취향을 묻고 있지 않다.
② 처음부터 다시 할(do it from scratch) 이유는 제시되지 않았다
③ 'call him on the carpet'은 '그를 불러 혼내다'라는 뜻으로 적절하지 않다.

해석

A: 회의는 언제 할까요?
B: 빠를수록 좋아요. 프로젝트 마감 시한을 맞춰야 하니까요.
A: 팀 전체가 시간을 다퉈서 일하는 이유죠.
B: 얼마나 많은 날을 지새웠는지 셀 수도 없네요.
A: 넘어야 할 고비가 하나 더 있어요. 진행에 대한 부사장님의 결재죠.
B: 중요한 건 2주 동안 자리를 비우잖아요.
A: 프로젝트를 완료할 가능성은 얼마예요?
B: 완수할지는 아슬아슬해요.
① 나는 그걸 별로 좋아하지 않아.
② 우리는 처음부터 다시 해야 돼요.
③ 그를 불러 혼내야 돼요.
④ 프로젝트를 완료할 가능성은 얼마예요?

어휘

cup of tea (보통 부정문에 사용) 기호에 맞는 사람(물건)
The 비교급, the 비교급 ~할수록 ...하다
meet the deadline 마감 시한을 맞추다
work against the clock (마감을 맞추려) 시간을 다투며 일하다
turn night into day 밤늦게까지 일하거나 놀다
touch-and-go 아슬아슬한　　　odds 확률
from scratch 처음부터
call sb on the carpet ~을 불러 혼내다

05 정답 ①

정답해설

① **출제 포인트: 혼동하기 쉬운 동사**
laying은 완전타동사 lay의 현재분사로 뒤에 목적어가 있어야 한다. 따라서 laying을 lying 또는 laid로 수정해야 한다.

오답해설

② **출제 포인트: 복합 형용사**
narrow-minded는 형용사와 과거분사가 하이픈으로 연결된 복합 형용사이다.

③ **출제 포인트: 전치사 관용표현**
on the fence는 be와 결합하여 '기회를 살피다'를 뜻한다.

④ **출제 포인트: 전치사 관용표현**
by the seat of our pants는 관용표현으로 '감으로'를 뜻한다.

06 정답 ④

정답해설

④ **출제 포인트: 간접의문문**
해당 문장은 의문문이 현재분사 wondering의 목적어로 사용된 경우로 간접의문문에 해당하며 어순은 「의문사+주어+동사」를 사용해야 한다. 따라서 who are all these shiny new people을 who all these shiny new people are로 수정해야 한다.

오답해설

① **출제 포인트: 등위접속사와 병렬구조**
「to+동사원형」에서 동사원형에 해당하는 let과 remain이 등위접속사 and를 사용하여 병렬구조를 이루고 있다.

② **출제 포인트: 독립 분사구문**
종속절의 주어와 주절의 주어가 다르므로 분사구문을 만들 때 종속절의 주어를 생략할 수 없다. 이때 해당 분사구문을 독립 분사구문이라 한다.

③ **출제 포인트: 명사절을 이끄는 접속사 that**
해당 문장에서 'that'은 주어 역할을 하는 「that+명사절」로 사용되었다.
※ 명사절을 이끄는 접속사 'that'의 역할은 다음과 같다.
1. 주어 역할
   → 「that+명사절」이 주어 역할을 하는 경우 주로 문두에 가주어 'It'을 사용하며 「that+명사절」을 문미로 이동시킨다. 이때 'that'은 생략할 수 있다. 그러나 「that+명사절」이 문두에서 주어 역할을 하는 경우 'that'은 생략할 수 없다.
   ex) It's a pity (that) you don't know Russian.
   ex) That you don't know Russian is a pity.
2. 목적어 역할
   → 「that+명사절」이 목적어 역할을 하는 경우 직접목적어로 사용하며 이때 'that'은 생략할 수 있다.
   ex) I can't believe (that) he's only 17.
3. 보어 역할
   → 「that+명사절」이 보어 역할을 하는 경우 주격 보어로 사용하며 이때 'that'은 생략할 수 있다.
   ex) The problem is (that) Jane doesn't like me.
4. 동격
   → 「that+명사절」이 동격으로 쓰이는 경우 추상명사가 'that'이전에 쓰이며 'that' 이후에는 완전한 문장이 와야 한다.
   ex) The fact that he is your brother-in-law should not affect your decision.

07 정답 ②

정답해설

② **출제 포인트: to부정사를 목적격 보어로 갖는 불완전타동사의 수동태**
불완전타동사 force의 수동태는 「be forced to+동사원형」이다. 따라서 해당 문장은 옳은 문장이다.

오답해설

① **출제 포인트: 가정법 과거완료**
「If+주어+had+과거분사 ~, 주어+would/could/should/might +have+과거분사 ~.」는 가정법 과거완료에 해당한다. 따라서 would

become을 would have become으로 수정해야 한다.

③ 출제 포인트: 능동태 vs. 수동태
see 뒤에 to부정사구가 온 것으로 보아 see가 수동태로 사용된 것임을 알 수 있다. 따라서 to see를 to be seen으로 수정해야 한다.

④ 출제 포인트: 주어와 동사 수일치
주어가 명사구 Seeing them succeed이며 단수형태이므로 주절의 동사에 단수형태를 사용해야 한다. 따라서 are를 is로 수정해야 한다.

해석
① 만약 당신이 머물렀다면 이것은 더 명백해졌을 것이다.
② 병원들은 돈이 부족하기 때문에 부서들을 폐쇄하도록 강요당하는 중이다.
③ 정부는 테러리스트들에게 양보하도록 보여지는 것을 원하지 않는다.
④ 당신의 가르침과 지도로 그들이 성공하는 것을 보는 것은 비교할 수 없는 기분이다.

08 정답 ②

정답해설
해당 지문은 과거 시행되었던 정신 질환 치료의 일종인 '뇌엽절리술(Lobotomy)'에 대해 서술하고 있다. 본문의 세 번째 문장 "Popular during the 1940s and 1950s, lobotomies were always controversial and prescribed in psychiatric cases deemed severe(1940년대와 1950년대 성행했던 뇌엽절리술은 항상 논쟁거리였고 심각하다고 여겨지는 정신 의학적 사례에만 처방되었다)."를 통해 '뇌엽절리술은 심각한 정신 질환에만 처방되었음'을 알 수 있다. 따라서 "② It was conducted for minor and serious mental diseases.(이것은 경미한 정신 질환과 심각한 정신 질환에 시행되었다.)"는 글의 내용과 일치하지 않는다.

오답해설
① 첫 문장에서 '1949년 노벨생리의학상을 수상했다'라고 언급하고 있으므로 글의 내용과 일치한다.
③ 본문에서 '뇌의 전두엽 피질과 전두엽 사이의 연결을 외과적으로 자르거나 제거하는 것으로 구성되었다'라고 언급하고 있으므로 본문의 내용과 일치한다.
④ 본문 후반 "Some patients experienced improvement of symptoms; however, this was often at the cost of introducing other impairments(일부 환자들은 증상의 호전을 경험했다. 그러나 이것은 종종 다른 장애가 동반되는 희생에 따른 것이었다)."에서 '다른 장애'라는 부작용을 일으켰다는 것을 알 수 있으므로, 글의 내용과 일치한다.

해석
현재는 실시되지 않는 치료법인 뇌엽절리술은 1949년 노벨생리의학상을 수상했다. 그것은 뇌의 순환로를 절제함으로써 정신 질환을 치료하도록 설계되었으나 상당한 위험을 동반했다. 1940년대와 1950년대 성행했던 뇌엽절리술은 항상 논쟁거리였고 심각하다고 여겨지는 정신 의학적 사례에만 처방되었다. 그것은 뇌의 전두엽 피질과 전두엽 사이의 연결을 외과적으로 자르거나 제거하는 것으로 구성되었다. 수술은 5분 이내에 끝날 수 있었다. 일부 환자들은 증상의 호전을 경험했다. 그러나 이것은 종종 다른 장애가 동반되는 희생에 따른 것이었다. 그 수술은 최초의 정신 질환 약물의 도입과 함께 1950년대 중반 이후에 대체로 중단되었다.
① 이것은 노벨상을 수상한 치료법 중 하나이다.
② 이것은 경미한 정신 질환과 심각한 정신 질환에 시행되었다.
③ 이것은 뇌에 대한 수술적 방법이다.
④ 이것은 효과가 있는 것으로 보였으나 부작용이 있었다.

어휘
lobotomy 뇌엽절리술, 로보토미
physiology 생리학
disrupt 파열시키다, 잡아 찢다
controversial 논쟁을 불러일으키는
psychiatric 정신 의학의
surgically 외과적으로
frontal lobe 전두엽
symptom 증상
at the cost of ~라는 희생을 치르고 [대가로]
impairment 장애
discontinue 중단하다, 중지하다
operative 수술의
obsolete 쓸모없게 된, 구식의
disorder 장애, 이상
circuit 회로, 순환로
prescribe 처방하다
deem 간주하다, 여기다
prefrontal cortex 전두엽 피질
procedure 수술, 절차, 방식
largely 주로, 대부분
conduct 실시하다
side effect 부작용

09 정답 ②

정답해설
본문은 '정신 질환의 다양한 원인'에 대해 서술하고 있으며, 주어진 지문은 그 중 하나인 '뇌의 순환로(circuits)와 관련된 내용이다. 주어진 문장의 'those circuits(그러한 순환로)'로 보아 이전에서 먼저 'circuits(순환로)'에 대해 언급되어야 함을 알 수 있으며, ② 이전 문장 "Some conditions involve circuits in your brain that are used in thinking, mood, and behavior(어떤 질환은 사고, 기분, 행동에 사용되는 당신의 뇌의 순환로와 관련이 있다)."에서 최초로 '뇌의 순환로'에 대해 언급되므로, 주어진 문장이 들어갈 가장 적절한 곳은 ②이다.

오답해설
③ 이전 문장도 뇌와 관련된 정신 질환의 원인이나, 주어진 문장이 'Brain injuries(뇌의 손상)'에 관한 설명이 아니므로 오답이다.

해석
의사들은 대부분의 정신 질환의 정확한 원인을 알지 못한다. 당신의 유전자, 생활 현상, 그리고 당신의 인생 경험을 포함한 것들의 조합이 관련이 있는 것 같다. 사실, 많은 정신 질환은 유전이다. (①) 그러나 그것이 당신의 어머니 또는 아버지가 정신 질환을 앓았다고 해서 당신도 정신 질환을 앓을 것이라는 것을 의미하지는 않는다. 어떤 질환은 사고, 기분, 행동에 사용되는 당신의 뇌의 순환로와 관련이 있다. (② **예를 들어, 그러한 순환로 내에서 "신경전달물질"이라고 불리는 특정 뇌 화학물질이 너무 많이 또는 충분치 않게 활동하고 있는지도 모른다.**) 뇌의 손상은 또한 일부 정신 질환과 관련되어 있다. (③) 어떤 정신 질환은 심각한 감정적 또는 신체적 학대와 같은 당신이 어릴 때 또는 십대 때 발생하는 심리적인 트라우마에 의해 촉발되거나 악화될 수 있다. (④) 게다가, 죽음이나 이혼, 가족 관계상의 문제들, 그리고 실업과 같은 주요 스트레스 원인이 일부 사람들의 정신 질환을 촉발하거나 악화시킬 수 있다.

어휘
neurotransmitter 신경전달물질
biology (생물의 특유한) 생활 현상, 생활사
involve 관련시키다, 포함하다
trigger 촉발시키다
psychological 심리적인
divorce 이혼
circuit 순환(로), 순회(노선)
run in family 집안 내력이다, 유전되다
worsen 악화시키다
abuse 학대
aggravate 악화시키다

오답률 TOP 3

10 정답 ④

정답해설

해당 지문은 과거에 행해진 비인간적인 정신 질환 치료법 중 하나인 '경련'을 이용한 치료법을 소개하고 있다. 두 번째 문장 "some practitioners came to believe seizures from such conditions as epilepsy and mental illness including schizophrenia could not exist together(일부 의사들은 간질과 같은 질환에서 비롯된 경련과 조현병을 포함한 정신 질환이 함께 존재할 수 없다고 믿게 되었다)."에서 경련과 정신 질환이 함께 존재할 수 없다고 믿었다고 하였으므로, 당시 의사들은 두 질환이 서로 '배타적(exclusive)'이라고 생각했음을 알 수 있다. 그러나 여러 번의 시행 끝에 두 질환이 서로 동시에 존재할 수 없는 것, 즉 배타적인 것이 아님을 깨달았으므로, ④의 inclusive는 exclusive(배타적인)가 되어야 자연스럽다.

오답해설

① 본문에서 예시로 제시한 '경련' 요법은 의도적으로 환자들에게 경련 및 발작을 일으킨 것이므로 '비인간적(inhumane)'이라고 설명하는 것이 적절하다.
② 정신 질환 치료를 목적으로 경련 증상이 없는 환자들에게 고의로 경련을 일으키는 약물을 주입했으므로 'intentionally(의도적으로)'는 문맥상 적절하다.
③ 해당 치료법이 효과가 없었기 때문에 이후 연구자들이 두 질환 사이에 배타성이 존재하지 않음을 깨달을 수 있었다는 것을 유추할 수 있다. 부정어 not이 있으므로 ③에는 effective가 알맞다.

해석

역사 전반에 정신 질환 환자에 대한 ① 비인간적인 치료의 증거는 풍부하다. 예를 들어, 정신 질환에 대한 이해가 발전함에 따라 일부 의사들은 간질과 같은 질환에서 비롯된 경련과 조현병을 포함한 정신 질환이 함께 존재할 수 없다고 믿게 되었다. 따라서 정신 질환을 감소시키기 위해 중추신경 흥분제와 같은 약물을 이용해 경련이 ② 의도적으로 유도되었다. 이러한 경련은 ③ 효과도 없었고 치료의 결과도 아니었다. 이후 연구자들은 경련과 조현병이 상호적으로 ④ 포괄적인 (→ 배타적인) 것이 아니라는 점을 깨달았다. 경련 관련 치료 분야는 이후 전기충격과 전기 경련 요법(ECT)이라는 더욱 효과적인 연구로 이어졌다.

어휘

evidence 증거
inhumane 비인간적인, 비인도적인, 잔인한
evolve (서서히) 발전하다, 진화하다
seizure 발작, 경련
schizophrenia 조현병
induce 유도하다
stimulant 흥분제
effective 효과적인
realize 깨닫다, 알아차리다
inclusive 포괄적인, 포함하는
lead to ~로 이어지다, 초래하다
electroconvulsive therapy 전기 경련 요법
abound 풍부하다, 많이 있다
practitioner (개업) 의사
epilepsy 간질
intentionally 의도적으로, 고의적으로
medication 약물, 투약
metrazol 중추신경 흥분제, 메트라졸
outcome 결과
mutually 상호적으로, 서로
therapy 치료(법)
electric shock 전기충격

기적사 DAY 19

결국엔 성정혜 영어 하프모의고사

| 01 | ② | 02 | ④ | 03 | ④ | 04 | ④ | 05 | ① |
| 06 | ④ | 07 | ③ | 08 | ② | 09 | ③ | 10 | ① |

오답률 TOP 1

01 정답 ②

정답해설

밑줄 친 단어는 문맥상 '수수한'으로 사용되었고, 유의어로는 ② humble이 적절하다.

해석

등산복을 입은 손님들을 참을 만큼 충분히 **수수하다**.
① 전형적인
② 수수한
③ 근소한, 교묘한, 엷은
④ 맛있는, 기분 좋은

어휘

typical 전형적인   humble 수수한
subtle 미묘한   delectable 맛있는, 기분 좋은

02 정답 ④

정답해설

밑줄 친 단어는 문맥상 '분배하다'로 사용되었고, 유의어로는 ④ assign이 적절하다.

해석

그것의 목적은 모든 물질을 질량 전체에 고르게 **분배하는** 것이며, 그것은 손으로든 기계로든 여러 가지 다른 방법으로 수행된다.
① 이야기하다
② 내려가다, 엎드리다, 시작하다
③ 억제하다
④ 분배하다

어휘

converse 이야기하다   get down 내려가다
refrain 억제하다   assign 분배하다

오답률 TOP 3

03 정답 ④

정답해설

밑줄 친 단어는 문맥상 '꼼꼼하게'로 사용되었고, 유의어로는 ④ fastidiously가 적절하다.

해석

식당의 내부는 작지만 경험 있는 주인에 의해서 **꼼꼼하게** 꾸며져 있고 편안함이 낭만적인 분위기를 더한다.
① 신중하게
② 밀접하게

③ 관계없이
④ 꼼꼼하게, 세심하게, 까다롭게

> 어휘

interior 안의/내부
prudently 신중하게
irrespectively 관계없이
fastidiously 꼼꼼하게, 세심하게, 까다롭게
experienced 경험 있는
inextricably 밀접하게

04 정답 ④

> 정답해설

Jack이 대회로 인해 겁을 먹었다며(got cold feet) 가서 보라고 한다. 이에 대해 양말을 갖다준다는 것은 어색하다.

> 오답해설

① 'cry wolf'는 '(도와달라고) 거짓으로 소란을 피우다'라는 뜻이다. B는 진짜 도움이 필요해서 연락을 한 게 아니라는 생각에 전화를 안 받았다고 말하고 있다.
② 'be at your command'는 '시키는 대로 하겠다'라는 의미이다. 상대의 요구에 뭐든 응할 준비가 되었다는 표현이다.
③ 'for the birds'는 '필요 없는'이라는 뜻이다. 필요 없는 잡지들이므로 바깥에서 갖고 오지 않아도 된다고 말하고 있다.

> 해석

① A: 그의 전화를 왜 안 받았니?
   B: 또 별것도 아닌 걸로 소란 피우는 거 같아서.
② A: Nora의 집 앞에 이 택배 좀 놓고 올래?
   B: 시키는 대로 할게요.
③ A: 바깥에 쌓인 잡지들 갖고 올까요?
   B: 그럴 거 없어요. 필요 없는 것들이에요.
④ A: Jack한테 좀 가봐. 대회 때문에 겁먹었어.
   B: 잘 되었네! 양말 좀 갖다줘야겠네.

> 어휘

cry wolf (도와달라고) 거짓으로 소란 피우다
package 택배
I am at your command. 시키는 대로 하겠다.
stack 쌓다
for the birds 필요 없는
get cold feet 겁을 먹다

오답률 TOP 2
05 정답 ①

> 정답해설

① 출제 포인트: 혼동하기 쉬운 동사
fall은 완전자동사로 전치사 없이 목적어가 올 수 없으며 주어진 해석이 '~을 베다'이므로 fall을 fell로 수정해야 한다.

> 오답해설

② 출제 포인트: 전치사 관용표현
on end는 관용표현으로 '계속하여'를 뜻한다.
③ 출제 포인트: 전치사 관용표현
by the same token은 관용표현으로 '마찬가지로'를 뜻한다.
④ 출제 포인트: 복합 형용사
pig-headed는 명사와 과거분사가 하이픈으로 연결된 복합 형용사이다.

06 정답 ④

> 정답해설

④ 출제 포인트: 등위접속사와 병렬구조
준사역동사 help의 목적격 보어가 등위접속사 and를 사용하여 병렬구조를 이루고 있다. 따라서 fulfill을 to fulfill로 수정하거나 to become을 become으로 수정해야 한다.

> 오답해설

① 출제 포인트: 독립 분사구문
종속절의 주어와 주절의 주어가 다르므로 분사구문을 만들 때 종속절의 주어를 생략할 수 없다. 이때 해당 분사구문을 독립 분사구문이라 한다.
② 출제 포인트: 명사절을 이끄는 접속사 that
해당 문장에서 'that'은 주어 역할을 하는 「that+명사절」로 사용되었다.
※ 명사절을 이끄는 접속사 'that'의 역할은 다음과 같다.
  1. 주어 역할
     → 「that+명사절」이 주어 역할을 하는 경우 주로 문두에 가주어 'It'을 사용하며 「that+명사절」을 문미로 이동시킨다. 이때 'that'은 생략할 수 있다. 그러나 「that+명사절」이 문두에서 주어 역할을 하는 경우 'that'은 생략할 수 없다.
     ex) It's a pity (that) you don't know Russian.
     ex) That you don't know Russian is a pity.
  2. 목적어 역할
     → 「that+명사절」이 목적어 역할을 하는 경우 직접목적어로 사용하며 이때 'that'은 생략할 수 있다.
     ex) I can't believe (that) he's only 17.
  3. 보어 역할
     → 「that+명사절」이 보어 역할을 하는 경우 주격 보어로 사용하며 이때 'that'은 생략할 수 있다.
     ex) The problem is (that) Jane doesn't like me.
  4. 동격
     → 「that+명사절」이 동격으로 쓰이는 경우 추상명사가 'that'이전에 쓰이며 'that' 이후에는 완전한 문장이 와야 한다.
     ex) The fact that he is your brother-in-law should not affect your decision.
③ 출제 포인트: 간접의문문
해당 문장의 "where their children will go"는 의문문이 주격 보어로 사용된 경우로 간접의문문에 해당하며 어순은 「의문사+주어+동사」이다.

07 정답 ③

> 정답해설

③ 출제 포인트: 가정법 과거완료
「Had+주어+과거분사 ~, 주어+would/could/should/might+have+과거분사 ~.」는 가정법 과거완료에 해당한다.

> 오답해설

① 출제 포인트: to부정사를 목적격 보어로 갖는 불완전타동사의 수동태
불완전타동사 expect의 수동태는 「be expected to+동사원형」이다. 따라서 landing을 land로 수정해야 한다.
② 출제 포인트: 능동태 vs. 수동태
해석상 '필적이 적절하게 가르쳐진다'가 자연스러우므로 properly teach를 is properly taught로 수정해야 한다.
④ 출제 포인트: 주어와 동사 수일치
주어가 명사구 The real potential이며 단수형태이므로 주절의 동사에 단수형태를 사용해야 한다. 따라서 are를 is로 수정해야 한다.

해석

① 그의 비행기는 오늘 밤 약 7:30에 착륙할 것으로 예상된다.
② 우리는 필적이 초등학교에서 적절하게 가르쳐진다는 것을 확신할 필요가 있다.
③ 당신이 밖에서 기다리는 것을 알았더라면, 나는 당신을 들어오라고 초대했을 것이다.
④ 긍정적 컴퓨터 사용이 우리 삶에서 차이를 만드는 실제 잠재 능력은 그 기기에 있다.

08 정답 ②

정답해설

해당 지문은 '눈과 귀의 진화'에 대한 내용이다. (A) 빈칸 이전에서 "Older invertebrates had antennae that would have been able to sense vibrations in the water(그 이전의 무척추동물은 물속에서 진동을 느낄 수 있던 더듬이가 있었다)."라고 '진동을 느낄 수 있는 더듬이'에 관해 언급한 후, (A) 이후에서 "that is not quite the same thing as hearing."이라고 앞서 언급한 내용과 '청각'은 다르다는 이야기를 하고 있으므로, 빈칸에는 '역접'을 나타내는 'However(그러나)'가 들어가는 것이 가장 적절하다. (B) 이전 문장에서 "Trilobites already had complex compound eyes about 521 million years ago(삼엽충은 약 5억2천백만 년 전에 이미 복잡한 구조의 겹눈을 지니고 있었다)."라고 '복잡한 구조의 겹눈을 가진 삼엽충'에 대해 언급한 후, (B)에서 추가적으로 '수정체가 없는 단순한 안점(simple eyespots without a lens)을 가진 다세포 동물'에 대해 언급하고 있으므로, '추가, 부연'을 나타내는 'Also(또한)'가 빈칸에 가장 적절하다. 따라서 '② However(그러나) - Also(또한)'이 정답이다.

오답해설

④ (A) 이후 문장이 (A) 이전 문장의 결과가 아니기 때문에 'As a result(결과적으로)'는 (A)에 적절하지 않다.

해석

눈과 귀 중 어느 것이 먼저 진화했는지 궁금해한 적이 있는가? 최소 4천만 년의 차이로 정답은 전자이다. 귀가 있는 유일한 무척추동물은 육지 절지동물이고 그들은 4억8천만 년 이전까지는 등장하지 않았다. 그 이전의 무척추동물은 물속에서 진동을 느낄 수 있던 더듬이가 있었다. (A) 그러나 그것이 사실상 청각과 동일한 것은 아니다. 삼엽충은 약 5억2천백만 년 전에 이미 복잡한 구조의 겹눈을 지니고 있었다. (B) 또한, 수정체가 없는 단순한 안점은 아마도 다세포 동물이 처음 등장했던 5억7천만 년 이전까지 거슬러 올라간다.
① 그래서 - 반면에
② 그러나 - 또한
③ 즉 - 그렇지 않으면
④ 결과적으로 - 게다가

어휘

evolve 진화하다
invertebrate 무척추동물
emerge 나타나다, 등장하다, 나오다
trilobite 삼엽충
compound eye (곤충 등의) 겹눈, 복안
eyespot 안점 (하등 동물의 시각 기관)
multicellular 다세포의
former 전자
arthropod 절지동물
vibration 진동
lens 수정체

09 정답 ③

정답해설

주어진 문장 "we generally consider blindness a greater disability than deafness(우리는 보통 청각상실보다 시각상실을 더 큰 장애로 여긴다)"를 통해 '청각상실과 시각상실에 대한 일반적인 사람들의 견해'를 언급하고 있다. 이어서 앞 문장 전체를 가리키는 'This is probably because ~'를 이용해 이러한 견해가 보편화된 이유를 설명하는 (B)가 오는 것이 알맞다. 이후에는 'However(그러나)'를 이용해 앞서 언급된 보편된 견해와는 반대되는 행보를 보인 인물 'Daniel Kish'를 소개하는 (A)가 이어지고, (A)에서 언급된 '귀로 보는 것(see by using his ears)'에 대한 구체적인 방법을 언급하는 (C)가 이어지는 것이 자연스럽다. 따라서 '③ (B) - (A) - (C)'가 정답이다.

오답해설

④ 'Daniel Kish'가 (A)에서 최초로 언급되므로, (B) 이후 (A)가 위치해야 한다.

해석

비록 우리가 환경과 상호작용하기 위해 시각과 청각에 모두 의존하지만, 우리는 보통 청각상실보다 시각상실을 더 큰 장애로 여긴다.
(B) 이것은 아마 우리가 청각을 상실했을 때 적어도 우리는 세상을 헤쳐 나가기 위해 여전히 볼 수 있고 의사소통을 하기 위해 수화 또는 구화를 익힐 수 있기 때문일 것이다.
(A) 2세 전에 망막모세포종으로 양쪽 안구를 잃은 Daniel Kish는 그의 시각상실을 큰 장애로 생각하지 않는다. 대신에 그는 귀를 이용해 보는 법을 스스로 익혔다.
(C) Kish는 세상 속에서 그가 움직일 때 혀를 차는 소리를 내고, 그의 뇌는 주변 환경의 3차원 이미지를 생성하기 위해 그 반향음을 이용한다.

어휘

interact 상호작용하다
disability (신체) 장애
retinal cancer 망막모세포종
sign language 수화
clicking sound 혀 차는 소리, 흡착음, 딸각하는 소리
three-dimensional 3차원의
blindness 시각상실
deafness 청각상실
navigate 방향을 찾다, 돌아다니다
lip reading 구화, 독순술

10 정답 ①

정답해설

해당 지문은 '눈의 단속성 운동 중 고막의 변화에 대한 연구'에 대해 서술하고 있으며, 빈칸에는 연구의 주제를 구체적으로 언급하는 내용이 들어가야 한다. 마지막 문장 "These pressure changes indicate that when we look left, for example, the drum of our left ear gets pulled further into the ear and that of our right ear pushed out, before they both swing back and forth a few times(이러한 압력 변화는, 예를 들어 우리가 왼쪽을 볼 때, 양쪽 고막이 앞뒤로 여러 번 흔들리기 전에, 왼쪽 귀의 고막이 귓속으로 더 깊게 당겨지고 오른쪽 귀의 고막은 밀려난다는 것을 나타낸다)."를 통해 '시선의 변화에 따른 고막 움직임의 변화'에 대한 구체적인 설명을 하고 있고 해당 연구가 '피험자들의 고막이 어떻게 변화하는지'에 대한 연구임을 알 수 있다. 따라서 빈칸에 가장 적절한 것은 '① how their eardrums change(그들의 고막이 어떻게 변화하는지)'이다.

오답해설

② '귀와 눈이 같은 방향으로 움직인다'라는 내용이 언급되나, 그 이유에 대해서는 본문에 언급되지 않으므로 오답이다.
④ 본문의 내용은 '귀가 눈에 미치는 영향'이 아니라 '눈이 귀에 미치는 영향'에 대한 것이므로 오답이다.

해석

Durham에 위치한 Duke University의 Jennifer Groh와 그녀의 팀은 우리가 시각적 초점을 한 곳에서 다른 곳으로 이동시킬 때 발생하는 움직임인 단속성 운동 중에 그들의 고막이 어떻게 변화하는지 연구하기 위해 사람들의 귀에 삽입된 마이크를 이용한다. 당신은 알아차리지 못할 것이나, 우리의 눈은 주변 환경을 받아들이기 위해 1초 당 다수의 단속성 운동을 거친다. 수많은 사람들을 조사하면서 그 팀은 고막을 잡아당기는 중이근에 의해 발생한 것으로 보이는 외이도 압력의 변화를 탐지했다. 이러한 압력 변화는, 예를 들어 우리가 왼쪽을 볼 때, 양쪽 고막이 앞뒤로 여러 번 흔들리기 전에, 왼쪽 귀의 고막이 귓속으로 더 깊게 당겨지고 오른쪽 귀의 고막은 밀려난다는 것을 나타낸다.

① 그들의 고막이 어떻게 변화하는지
② 그들의 귀와 눈이 왜 상호작용하는지
③ 그들의 고막이 다른 소리를 어떻게 감지하는지
④ 그들의 귀가 움직이는 방식이 그들의 눈에 어떻게 영향을 미치는지

어휘

insert 삽입하다, 끼워 넣다
saccade 단속성 운동, 도약 안구 운동(안구가 한 응시점에서 다른 응시점으로 신속하게 이동하는 운동)
occur 발생하다, 일어나다
detect 탐지하다, 간파하다, 감지하다
middle-ear muscles 중이근
eardrum 고막
interact 상호작용하다
take in 받아들이다
ear canal 외이도
tug 잡아당기다, 끌어당기다
indicate 나타내다, 가리키다
perceive 지각하다, 감지하다

결국엔 성정혜 영어 하프모의고사
기적사 DAY 20

01	①	02	④	03	③	04	③	05	④
06	①	07	②	08	①	09	④	10	③

01 정답 ①

정답해설

밑줄 친 단어는 문맥상 '주의 깊게'로 사용되었고, 유의어로는 ① Deliberately가 적절하다.

해석

주의 깊게, 그녀는 더 나은 지렛대 쪽으로 발을 옮겼다.
① 신중하게, 의도적으로
② 전형적으로
③ 신체의, 속세의, 관능적인
④ 즉시, 급히, 신속히

어휘

leverage 지렛대
typically 전형적으로
promptly 즉시, 급히, 신속히
deliberately 신중하게, 의도적으로
fleshly 신체의, 속세의, 관능적인

02 정답 ④

정답해설

밑줄 친 단어의 의미가 문맥상 '서둘러'이므로, 유의어로는 ④ promptly가 적절하다.

해석

Dean은 Ethel이 성공하기 전에 **서둘러** 사무실을 떠났다.
① 정기적으로
② 세심하게
③ 영구적으로
④ 즉시, 급히, 신속히

어휘

get ahead 성공하다
minutely 세심하게
promptly 즉시, 급히, 신속히
termly 정기적으로
permanently 영구적으로

03 정답 ③

정답해설

밑줄 친 단어는 문맥상 '즐겁게'로 사용되었고, 유의어로는 ③ pleasantly가 적절하다.

해석

샌드위치와 베이글들은 여기에서 원기 왕성한 사람들을 위한 주식(主食)인데, 이것들은 **기분 좋게** 신선하고 친환경적이다.
① 세심하게, 정확하게
② 즉시
③ 매우 기쁘게
④ 관계없이

어휘

athletic 건강한, 운동선수의
precisely 세심하게, 정확하게
pleasantly 매우 기쁘게
eco-friendly 친환경적인
promptly 즉시
independently 관계없이

04 정답 ③

정답해설

A가 "You look depressed. What's wrong(너 우울해 보여. 무슨 일 있니)?"이라고 물어보았는데, B가 "I got fired yesterday."(나 어제 해고당했어.)라고 하면서 절망적(hopeless)이라고 기분을 말하고 있으므로 B에게 위로를 건네는 표현이 빈칸에 가장 적절하다. 따라서 정답은 ③ every dog has its day(쥐구멍에도 볕들 날이 온다)이다.

오답해설

① 위로를 해주는 말이 아니므로 정답으로 적절하지 않다.
② 위로의 표현이 아니라 그 상황을 받아들이라는 표현이므로 빈칸에 적절하지 않다.
④ 'let the cat out of the bag'이 '비밀을 누설하다'라는 뜻을 가진 관용표현이다. 따라서 대화의 흐름상 빈칸에 적절하지 않은 표현이다.

해석

A: 너 우울해 보여. 무슨 일 있니?
B: 어제 해고당했어. 내가 무엇을 할 수 있을까? 절망적이야.
A: 왜 이래, 쥐구멍에도 볕들 날이 있어. 곧 좋은 날이 다가올 거야.
B: 고마워, 네 말이 맞아, 하지만 난 여전히 마음이 좋지 않아.
① 꼴좋다
② 세상사가 다 그런 거야
③ 쥐구멍에도 볕들 날이 있어
④ 비밀을 말하지 마

어휘

depressed 우울한
disheartened 낙담한
hopeless 절망적인
it serves you right 꼴좋다
that's the way cookie crumbles 세상사가 그런 거야
every dog has its day 쥐구멍에도 볕들 날이 있다
let the cat out of the bag 비밀을 누설하다

오답률 TOP 3

05 정답 ④

정답해설

④ 출제 포인트: 혼동하기 쉬운 동사
해당 문장에서 wound는 완전자동사 wind의 과거분사로 수동태를 사용할 수 없다. 따라서 wound를 wounded로 수정해야 한다.

오답해설

① 출제 포인트: 전치사 관용표현/to부정사의 형용사적 용법
on and on은 관용표현으로 '계속하여'를 뜻한다.
② 출제 포인트: 전치사 관용표현
by no means는 관용표현으로 '결코 ~이 아닌'을 뜻한다.
③ 출제 포인트: 복합 형용사
short-tempered는 형용사와 과거분사가 하이픈으로 연결된 복합 형용사이다.

오답률 TOP 1

06 정답 ①

정답해설

① 출제 포인트: 등위접속사와 병렬구조
등위접속사 and를 사용하여 형용사가 「A, B, and C」의 병렬구조를 이루고 있다. 따라서 oil을 형용사 oily로 수정해야 한다.

오답해설

② 출제 포인트: 명사절을 이끄는 접속사 that
해당 문장에서 'that'은 주어 역할을 하는 「that+명사절」로 사용되었다.
※ 명사절을 이끄는 접속사 'that'의 역할은 다음과 같다.
  1. 주어 역할
     → 「that+명사절」이 주어 역할을 하는 경우 주로 문두에 가주어 'It'을 사용하며 「that+명사절」을 문미로 이동시킨다. 이때 'that'은 생략할 수 있다. 그러나 「that+명사절」이 문두에서 주어 역할을 하는 경우 'that'은 생략할 수 없다.
     ex) It's a pity (that) you don't know Russian.
     ex) That you don't know Russian is a pity.
  2. 목적어 역할
     → 「that+명사절」이 목적어 역할을 하는 경우 직접목적어로 사용하며 이때 'that'은 생략할 수 있다.
     ex) I can't believe (that) he's only 17.
  3. 보어 역할
     → 「that+명사절」이 보어 역할을 하는 경우 주격 보어로 사용하며 이때 'that'은 생략할 수 있다.
     ex) The problem is (that) Jane doesn't like me.
  4. 동격
     → 「that+명사절」이 동격으로 쓰이는 경우 추상명사가 'that' 이전에 쓰이며 'that' 이후에는 완전한 문장이 와야 한다.
     ex) The fact that he is your brother-in-law should not affect your decision.
③ 출제 포인트: 독립 분사구문
종속절의 주어와 주절의 주어가 다르므로 분사구문을 만들 때 종속절의 주어를 생략할 수 없다. 이때 해당 분사구문을 독립 분사구문이라 한다.
④ 출제 포인트: 간접의문문
해당 문장의 "where the dustbin was"는 의문문이 주격 보어로 사용된 경우로 간접의문문에 해당하며 어순은 「의문사+주어+동사」이다.

07 정답 ③

정답해설

③ 출제 포인트: to부정사를 목적격 보어로 갖는 불완전타동사의 수동태
불완전타동사 advise의 수동태는 「be advised to+동사원형」이다. 따라서 해당 문장은 옳은 문장이다.

오답해설

① 출제 포인트: 능동태 vs. 수동태
해석상 '그녀의 몸이 발견되었다'가 자연스러우므로 later found를 was later found로 수정해야 한다.
② 출제 포인트: 주어와 동사 수일치
주어가 명사 Babies이며 복수형태이므로 주절의 동사에 복수형태를 사용해야 한다. 따라서 seems를 seem으로 수정해야 한다.
④ 출제 포인트: 가정법 과거완료
「If+주어+had+과거분사 ~, 주어+would/could/should/might+have+과거분사 ~.」는 가정법 과거완료에 해당한다. 따라서 did를 had로 수정해야 한다.

해석

① 그녀의 몸은 덤불 속에 숨겨진 채 발견되었다.
② 그들의 울음이 응답되는 아기들은 좀 더 자신감 있게 되는 것으로 보인다.
③ 당신은 해외에 가기 전에 적절한 백신 접종을 하도록 충고받을 것이다.
④ 만약 정부가 음식 가격을 올리지 않았더라면, 그렇게 많은 항의가 있지 않았을 것이다.

오답률 TOP 2

08 정답 ①

정답해설

(A)가 포함된 문장에서 "much of what we understand about the Big Bang Theory comes from mathematical formulas and models(빅뱅이론에 대해 우리가 이해하고 있는 것들 중 많은 부분이 수학적인 공식과 모델로부터 기인한 것이다)."에 대한 이유가 (A) 이전 문장 "Unfortunately, current instruments do not allow astronomers to peer back at the universe's birth(안타깝게도 현재의 기구들로는 천문학자들이 우주의 탄생을 살펴볼 수 없다)."에서 드러난다. 따라서 빈칸에는 '인과관계'를 나타내는 접속부사인 'Therefore(따라서)'가 들어가는 것이 알맞다.

(B)가 포함된 문장에서 "Astronomers can ~ see the "echo" of the expansion through a phenomenon known as the cosmic microwave background(천문학자들은 우주배경복사라고 알려진 현상을 통해 확장의 "흔적"을 볼 수는 있다)"를 통해, 앞서 언급된 내용인 "current instruments do not allow astronomers to peer back at the universe's birth(현재의 기구들로는 천문학자들이 우주의 탄생을 살펴볼 수 없다)"와는 대조적으로 관측 가능한 것에 대해 언급하고 있으므로, '역접'을 나타내는 연결사인 however(그러나)가 빈칸에 가장 적절하다.

따라서 정답은 '① Therefore(따라서) – however(그러나)'이다.

오답해설

② (B) 이전과 이후가 유사한 내용이 아니므로 'similarly(유사하게)'는 빈칸에 적절하지 않다.
④ (B) 이후의 내용이 앞서 언급된 내용의 예시가 아니므로 'for example(예를 들어)'은 빈칸에 적절하지 않다.

해석

빅뱅이론은 우주가 어떻게 시작되었는지에 대한 대표적인 이론이다. 가장 간단히 말하면, 그것은 우주는 작은 특이점에서 시작했고, 이후 우리가 오늘날 알고 있는 우주로 138억 년 동안 팽창했다고 말한다. 안타깝게도 현재의 기구들로는 천문학자들이 우주의 탄생을 살펴볼 수 없다. (A) <u>따라서</u> 빅뱅이론에 대해 우리가 이해하고 있는 것들 중 많은 부분이 수학적인 공식과 모델로부터 기인한 것이다. (B) <u>그러나</u> 천문학자들은 우주배경복사라고 알려진 현상을 통해 확장의 "흔적"을 볼 수 있다.

① 따라서 – 그러나
② 따라서 – 유사하게
③ 반대로 – 그에 따라
④ 따라서 – 예를 들어

어휘

leading 대표적인, 선두적인
inflate 팽창하다
astronomer 천문학자
mathematical 수학적인
echo 흔적, 자취, 반향, 메아리
phenomenon 현상
cosmic microwave background 우주배경복사
singularity 특이점
instrument 기구, 장치
peer at ~을 응시하다, 살펴보다
formula 공식
expansion 확장

---

09 정답 ④

정답해설

해당 지문은 우주의 미래에 대한 이론에 관한 글이다. 주어진 문장에서 'neither of these scenarios'를 제시하고 있으므로, 이전에는 '이 시나리오들 중 둘 다 ~아니다'라는 표현에 걸맞게 '두 가지 시나리오'가 언급되어야 한다. ④ 이전 두 문장에서 각각 'Big Crunch(우주대붕괴)'와 'Big Rip(우주 대파열)'이라는 두 가지 이론을 각각 제시하고 있으므로, 뒤이어 'If neither of these scenarios are correct(만일 이 시나리오들이 둘 다 틀리고)'가 이어지는 것이 자연스럽다. 또한 ④이후의 'At this point(이 시점에서)'가 주어진 문장의 'the point(시점)'를 가리키고 있으므로, 주어진 문장이 들어갈 가장 적절한 위치는 ④이다.

오답해설

나머지 위치는 문맥상 자연스럽지 않기 때문에 오답이다.

해석

1960년대, 천문학자들은 모든 방향에서 감지가 가능한 마이크로파 배경복사에 대해 인지하게 되었다. (①) 우주배경복사(CMB)라고 알려진 이 방사선의 존재는 우주가 어떻게 시작했는지에 대해 우리의 이해력에 정보를 주도록 도왔다. (②) 다양한 우주 철학적 이론에 따르면 우주는 어떠한 시점에 팽창을 멈추고 그와 반대로의 진행을 시작하여, 결국 붕괴하여 또 다른 빅뱅이 이어질 것이다. 이것은 우주 대붕괴 이론으로도 알려져 있다. (③) 우주 대파열이라 알려진 또 다른 이론에서 우주의 팽창은 결국 모든 물질과 우주 시간 자체가 분열되는 것으로 이어질 것이다. (④ <u>만일 이 시나리오들이 둘 다 틀리고, 우주가 증가하는 속도로 계속해서 팽창한다면 CMB는 그것이 더 이상 감지될 수 없는 시점까지 계속 적색이동을 할 것이다.</u>) 이 시점에서 그것은 우주에서 생성된 최초의 별빛에 의해, 이후 우주의 미래에 발생할 것이라고 추정되는 과정에 의해 생성된 배경 복사영역에 의해 추월당할 것이다.

어휘

expand 확장하다
redshift 적색 이동하다
astronomer 천문학자
microwave background radiation 마이크로파 배경복사
existence 존재
cosmological 우주 철학의
reverse 거꾸로[반대로] 하다
collapse 붕괴, 무너짐
rip 찢어짐
lead to ~로 이어지다
overtake 추월하다, 따라잡다
accelerate 속도를 늘리다, 가속하다
detectable 찾아낼[탐지할] 수 있는
radiation 방사선
cease 중지하다, 멈추다
culminate in 드디어[결국] …이 되다
crunch 부서짐
eventually 결국, 마침내
tear apart 갈가리 찢어[뜯어] 버리다
take place 발생하다

---

10 정답 ③

정답해설

해당 지문은 빅뱅이론을 최초로 제안한 'Georges Lemaître(조르주 르메트르)'에 대한 내용이다. 본문 세 번째 문장 "He studied ~ at the Massachusetts Institute of Technology (MIT), where he became acquainted with the findings of the American astronomers Edwin P. Hubble and Harlow Shapley on the expanding universe(그는 University of Cambridge의 태양 물리학 연구실로, 이후에는 Massachusetts Institute of Technology (MIT)에서 연구를 했으며, 그곳에서 팽창하는 우주에 대한 미국인 천문학자 Edwin P. Hubble과 Harlow Shapley의 발견들에 대해 알게 되었다)."에서 'Lemaître가 MIT 재학 당시 Edwin P. Hubble과 Harlow Shapley의 발견들에 대해 알게 되었다'라는 내용이 언급되고 있으나, Lemaître가 Edwin P. Hubble과 Harlow Shapley를 만났다는 내용은 본문에 등장하지 않는다. 따라

서 정답은 '③ He met with Edwin P. Hubble and Harlow Shapley while attending MIT(그는 MIT에 다니는 동안 Edwin P. Hubble과 Harlow Shapley를 만났다).'이다.

오답해설
① 첫 번째 문장을 통해 포병 장교로 제1차 세계대전에 참전했음을 알 수 있다.
② 제1차 세계대전은 1918년에 끝났고, 5년 후인 1923년에 Lemaître가 사제로 임명되었으므로 내용과 일치한다.
④ Lemaître가 Catholic University of Leuven에서 교수직을 맡은 해에 빅뱅이론을 제시한 것이므로 내용과 일치한다.

해석
토목기사인 Georges Lemaître는 제1차 세계대전 중 벨기에 군대의 포병장교로 복무했다. 1918년 종전 후 그는 신학대학에 입학했고 1923년 사제로 임명되었다. 그는 University of Cambridge의 태양 물리학 연구실에서, 이후에는 Massachusetts Institute of Technology (MIT)에서 연구를 했으며, 그 곳에서 팽창하는 우주에 대한 미국인 천문학자 Edwin P. Hubble과 Harlow Shapley의 발견들에 대해 알게 되었다. 그가 Catholic University of Leuven에서 천체 물리학 교수가 된 해인 1927년에 그는 그의 빅뱅이론을 제시하였다. 그것은 Albert Einstein의 일반 상대성 이론의 틀 내에서 은하의 후퇴에 대해 설명했다. 비록 우주의 팽창 모델은, 특히 네덜란드 천문학자 Willem de Sitter에 의해 그 이전에도 고안되었으나, George Gamow에 의해 수정된 Lemaître의 이론은 우주론의 가장 중요한 이론이 되었다.
① 그는 참전했다.
② 그는 제1차 세계대전 종전 5년 뒤 성직자가 되었다.
③ 그는 MIT에 다니는 동안 Edwin P. Hubble과 Harlow Shapley를 만났다.
④ 그는 대학교에서 가르치는 동안 빅뱅이론을 제시했다.

어휘
civil engineer 토목기사
seminary (가톨릭의) 신학교[대학]
priest 신부, 사제
laboratory 연구실, 실험실
acquainted with ~를 알고 있는, ~을 알게 되어
finding 발견
expand 확장하다, 팽창하다
recession 후퇴, 침체
theory of general relativity 일반 상대성 이론
notably 특히
modify 수정하다, 변형하다
cosmology 우주론
warfare 전쟁
artillery officer 포병장교
ordain (성직자로) 임명하다
solar physics 태양 물리학
astronomer 천문학자
astrophysics 천체 물리학
framework 틀, 뼈대
Dutch 네덜란드의
leading 매우 중요한, 이끄는, 선두의
be engaged in ~에 종사하다
clergyman 성직자

결국엔 성정혜 영어 하프모의고사
기적사 복습 모의고사 2회

01	③	02	①	03	②	04	②	05	①
06	④	07	④	08	①	09	③	10	④
11	③	12	③	13	③	14	④	15	①
16	③	17	③	18	③	19	④	20	④

01 정답 ③
Day 11-02

정답해설
'appease'는 '~을 달래다'라는 뜻으로 선택지의 단어 중 가장 가까운 의미를 지닌 것은 ③ pacify이다.

해석
요즘, 핼러윈은 이교도와 가톨릭 축제의 기원으로부터 많이 변화해왔다, 그리고 우리가 **달래는** 영혼들은 더 이상 죽은 자들의 영혼이 아니다: 굶주린 영혼들은 분장을 하고 과자를 요구하는 아이들로 대체되었다.
① 할당하다, 배정하다
② 체포하다, 이해하다
③ 달래다, 진정시키다
④ 자극하다, 유발하다

02 정답 ①
Day 14-03

정답해설
밑줄 친 단어가 문맥상 '방해하다'로 사용되었고, 유의어로는 ① encumber가 적절하다.

해석
그들이 당신의 일을 **방해하지** 않는 한 당신은 당신이 중요한 무언가를 고려할 때마다, 언제든지 전화하거나 친구를 가질 수 있다.
① 간섭하다, (책임을) 지우다
② 고립시키다, 은퇴시키다
③ 완화하다, 경감하다
④ 구별하다, 알아보다

03 정답 ②
Day 18-02

정답해설
밑줄 친 단어의 의미가 문맥상 '냉담한'으로 사용되었으며, 유의어로는 ② reserved가 적절하다.

해석
그의 **냉담한** 반응에 그녀는 떠났다.
① 건방진, 확신 있는
② 냉담한, 남겨 둔, 예약되어있는
③ 불가결한, 통합적인
④ 풍부한

04 정답 ②
Day 16-03

정답해설
빈칸 앞에서 'Reading and studying were more permissible for girls'라고 제시하며 '독서와 공부는 여자아이들에게 더 허용'되었다고 언급하고 있다. 또한, 빈칸 뒤에서는 'lest they acquire the stigma of being 'stuck up''. 즉, '건방지다고 낙인찍히지 않기 위해'라고 하였다. 그러므로 인과관계를 고려하여 너무 '똑똑해지지' 않도록 주의해야 한다고 하는 것이 문맥상 자연스럽다. 따라서 정답은 ② 'intellectual'이다.

해석
민족적으로 뒤섞인 시카고 동네에서 자란 중산층 유대인으로서, 나는 이미 매일 더 거친 노동자 계급의 사내아이들로부터 맞을 위험에 처해있었다. 책벌레가 되는 것은 단지 그들에게 나를 때릴 결정적인 이유만 제공했을 것이다. 책을 읽고 공부를 하는 것은 여자아이들에게 조금 더 허용되는 것이었지만, 그들은 건방지다고 낙인찍히지 않기 위해 너무 **똑똑해지지** 않도록 주의를 기울여야만 했다.
① 운동의, 건강한
② 지적인, 지성을 지닌
③ 친절한, 환대하는
④ 미숙한

05 정답 ①
Day 12-05

정답해설
① 출제 포인트: 전치사 + 관계대명사
「전치사 + 관계대명사」는 뒤따라오는 문장구조가 완전하다. 따라서 해당 문장은 during which 뒤에 오는 문장구조가 완전하므로 옳은 문장이다.

해석
① 그것은 내가 계속 잠들었던 그 미팅이었다.
② 그들은 그 상태를 비판하지 않을지도 모르지만, 그들은 또한 그것을 칭찬하지 않는다.
③ 많은 것들이 여성이 미국 사업에서 정상에 도달하는 것을 어렵게 만든다.
④ Tom은 베수비오산의 분화가 폼페이를 파괴했다고 책에서 배웠다.

06 정답 ④
Day 17-07

정답해설
④ 출제 포인트: 가정법 과거완료
「If + 주어 + had + 과거분사 ~, 주어 + would/could/should/might + have + 과거분사 ~.」는 가정법 과거완료에 해당한다.

해석
① 그는 우리에게 자신의 기이한 어린 시절을 이야기해주었다.
② 가르치는 것으로부터 오는 보상들은 많다.
③ 아이들은 폭력적인 TV 프로그램들을 보는 것이 허락되지 않는다.
④ 그들이 그렇게 했다면, 그들의 경력은 평생 망치게 되었을 것이다.

07 정답 ④
Day 13-07

정답해설
④ 출제 포인트: only 부사(구) 도치
「only + 부사(구)」가 문두에 오는 경우 뒤따라오는 문장구조는 「조동사 + 주어」로 도치가 발생한다. 해당 문장은 「only + 부사(구)」가 문두에 왔으나 뒤따라오는 문장구조가 「주어 + 동사」이므로 틀린 문장이다. 따라서 I began을 did I begin으로 수정해야 한다.

08 정답 ①
Day 20-06

정답해설
① 출제 포인트: 등위접속사와 병렬구조
등위접속사 and를 사용하여 형용사가 「A, B, and C」의 병렬구조를 이루고 있다. 따라서 oil을 형용사 oily로 수정해야 한다.

09 정답 ③
Day 15-04

정답해설
A는 겨울방학이 너무 짧다고 말하고 있다. B는 'Couldn't agree more(전적으로 동의해)'라고 했다가 뒷부분에는 'Speak for yourself(너나 그렇지)'라고 반대하고 있다. 상반된 문장을 동시에 말하고 있으므로 어색한 대화가 되었다.

해석
① A: 생일날 뭐 받고 싶어?
   B: 네가 좋을 대로 해.
② A: 수업 끝나면 연락해. 데리러 올게.
   B: 신경 쓰지 마세요. 버스가 늦게까지 다녀요.
③ A: 겨울방학은 너무 짧아.
   B: 전적으로 동의해. 너에게나 그렇지.
④ A: 나는 너무 바빴어. 너 없인 이 일을 못 끝냈을 거야.
   B: 별거 아니었어.

10 정답 ④
Day 18-04

정답해설
대화 속에서 '시간에 쫓기며 일'하고 있는 상황 말고도, '부사장의 결재'를 받아야 하는 상황임을 파악할 수 있다. 빈칸 이후 B는 이어지는 말에서 '아슬아슬하다(touch-and-go)'라고 말한다. 따라서 A가 했을 말로 '④ What are the odds of finishing the project?(프로젝트를 완료할 가능성은 얼마예요?)'가 적절하다.

해석
A: 회의는 언제 할까요?
B: 빠를수록 좋아요. 프로젝트 마감 시한을 맞춰야 하니까요.
A: 팀 전체가 시간을 다퉈서 일하는 이유죠.
B: 얼마나 많은 날을 지새웠는지 셀 수도 없네요.
A: 넘어야 할 고비가 하나 더 있어요. 진행에 대한 부사장님의 결재요.
B: 중요한 건 2주 동안 자리를 비우시잖아요.
A: 프로젝트를 완료할 가능성은 얼마예요?
B: 완수할지는 아슬아슬해요.
① 나는 그걸 별로 좋아하지 않아.
② 우리는 처음부터 다시 해야 돼요.
③ 그를 불러 혼내야 돼요.
④ 프로젝트를 완료할 가능성은 얼마예요?

11 정답 ③
Day 15-08

정답해설
해당 지문은 '인플레이션'과 '디플레이션'에 관해 설명하고 있다. 본문 초반에서는 '인플레이션의 정의와 예시'에 대해 언급하고, "Deflation is the opposite of inflation(디플레이션은 인플레이션의 반대이다)."을 통해 앞서 언급된 인플레이션과 비교하여 디플레이션의 정의와 예시에 대해 본문 후반에서 서술하고 있다. 따라서 글의 제목으로 가장 적절한 것은 "③ The

Difference between Inflation and Deflation(인플레이션과 디플레이션의 차이)"이다.

> 해석

인플레이션은 제품과 서비스 가격의 지속적인 증가이다. 인플레이션 기간에 달러는 구매력 일부를 상실하고 동일한 양의 제품 또는 서비스를 구매하는 데 더 많은 통화가 필요하다. 예를 들어 올해 초 하나의 제품이 1달러의 가치가 있으나 연중 인플레이션이 5%라면, 1년 후에 하나의 제품을 구매하는 데 1.05달러가 들 것이다. 디플레이션은 인플레이션의 반대이다. 그것은 제품과 서비스 가격의 지속적인 하락이다. 디플레이션 기간에 달러는 실제로 구매력을 얻고 동일한 양의 제품 또는 서비스를 구매하는 데 예전에 필요했던 것보다 더 적은 통화가 필요하다. 예를 들어 올해 초 하나의 제품이 1달러의 가치가 있으나 연중 디플레이션이 10%라면, 1년 후 하나의 제품을 구매하는 데 오직 0.90달러가 들 것이다.
① 우리는 디플레이션이 아니라 인플레이션이 필요하다
② 무엇이 인플레이션과 디플레이션을 일으키는가?
③ 인플레이션과 디플레이션의 차이
④ 인플레이션과 디플레이션: 어느 것이 더 큰 위험인가?

12 정답 ③ — Day 11-08

> 정답해설

빈칸 다음에 빈칸의 내용을 다시 설명하는 내용이 나온다. 'to embrace only a portion of the truth'(진실의 일부만을 포용하는 것)에서 '편중성'(partiality)을 찾을 수 있다. 또한 'it is crucial to supplement one's opinions with alternative points of view.'(자신의 의견을 대체적인 시각으로 보완하는 것이 중요하다.)에서 모든 이의 '의견이 옳다 완전히 그르다'라고 확신할 수 없다는 것을 알 수 있다. 따라서 이 부분에서 의견의 '불완전성'(incompleteness)을 유추할 수 있다. 따라서 빈칸에 알맞은 표현은 ③ It is the danger of partiality and incompleteness(그것은 편중성과 불완전성의 위험이다.)이다.

> 해석

독자들이 존 스튜어트 밀의 생각과 토론의 자유에 대한 고전적인 탐험에 대해 가장 흔히 기억하는 것은 안일함의 위험성에 관한 것이다. 도전이 없을 때는, 설이 정확할 때에도, 자신의 의견이 약해지고 축 늘어진다. 그러나 밀은 생각과 토론의 자유를 장려하는 또 다른 이유가 있었다. 그것은 편중성과 불완전성의 위험이다. 자신의 의견은 아무리 좋은 환경에서도 진실의 일부만을 포용하는 경향이 있기 때문에, 그리고 자신의 의견에 반대하는 의견이 완전히 그릇된 것으로 드러나는 경우는 드물기 때문에, 자신의 의견을 대체적인 시각으로 보완하는 것이 중요하다.
① 그것은 의견의 복제이다.
② 그것은 개인의 자유의 보호이다.
③ 그것은 편중성과 불완전성의 위험이다.
④ 그것은 의견과 정보가 퍼지는 것에 대한 제약이다.

13 정답 ③ — Day 13-09

> 정답해설

빈칸 이전의 '역접'을 나타내는 접속사 'But(그러나)'로 보아 빈칸 이전에 언급된 내용과 반대되는 내용이 들어가는 것이 적절하다는 것을 알 수 있다. 빈칸 이전에서 "77 percent of Americans say that religion is at least somewhat important in their lives and 83 percent say they're fairly certain that God or a higher power exists(미국인의 77%가 삶에 있어서 종교가 적어도 어느 정도 중요하다고 말했고, 83%가 신 또는 더 강한 권능이 존재한다는 것을 매우 확신한다고 말했다)."를 통해 '종교를 긍정적으로 판단하는 사람들의 의견'을 언급하고 있으므로, 빈칸에는 이에 대한 반대 의견을 서술하는 문장이 들어가는 것이 적절하다. 따라서 빈칸에는 '모든 사람들이 종교를 긍정적으로 보는 것이 아니다'라는 것을 의미하는 '③ not everyone agrees that religion is good for us(종교가 우리에게 유익하다는 것에 모든 사람이 동의하는 것은 아니다)'가 들어가는 것이 알맞다.

> 해석

사실 역사적으로 인간의 존재를 형성하는 데 있어서 종교보다 더 강력했던 힘은 거의 없다. Pew Research Center의 최신 여론 조사에 따르면 미국인의 77%가 삶에 있어서 종교가 적어도 어느 정도 중요하다고 말했고, 83%가 신 또는 더 강한 권능이 존재한다는 것을 매우 확신한다고 말했다. 그러나 종교가 우리에게 유익하다는 것에 모든 사람이 동의하는 것은 아니다. 일부는 그것이 행복을 촉진한다고 주장하고 다른 일부는 그것이 신경증을 초래한다고 주장하며, 학자들 사이에 이 쟁점에 대한 긴 논쟁이 있어왔다. 사실 심리학 분야에서 이 문제만큼 많이 연구되는 쟁점은 거의 없다.
① 신이 존재하는지 아닌지 정말로 아는 사람은 없다
② 우리 주변에 너무 많은 사이비종교가 있다
③ 종교가 우리에게 유익하다는 것에 모든 사람이 동의하는 것은 아니다
④ 종교가 사회에서 긍정적인 역할을 한다는 것은 분명하다

14 정답 ④ — Day 14-10

> 정답해설

주어진 문장에서 영어권 국가 외의 국가에서의 '심판 명칭은 분명하고 일관되며 간단하다'라고 언급하고 있으므로, 다른 국가를 언급한 ② "This is not the case in other languages(이것은 다른 언어에서는 사실이 아니다)." 이후의 자리에 주어진 문장이 들어가야 한다. ③에서 '영어권 국가에서의 심판 명칭의 복잡성'에 대해 언급한 후, ④에서 But을 이용해 재차 영어의 경우에 관해 언급하고 있으므로, 두 문장 사이인 ④ 자리에 영어와 비교하여 다른 언어권 국가에 대해 설명하는 주어진 문장이 들어가는 것이 적절하다. 따라서 정답은 ④이다.

> 해석

야구 경기에서 'referee'를 또는 농구 경기에서 'umpire'를 언급하면 당신이 아무것도 모른다는 것이 분명해진다. (①) 그리고 영어에서의 스포츠 심판 용어는 말이 되지 않고 규칙도 없기 때문에, 혹은 있다 하더라도 그것은 구멍 투성이라서 무의미하기 때문에 그것은 아마 조금 불공평할 것이다. (②) 이것은 다른 언어에서는 사실이 아니다. (③) 영어권 국가에서는 스포츠 심판은 각각이 하는 역할에 관한 어떠한 종류의 통일적인 구조도 없이 현기증을 불러일으킬 정도로 여러 종류의 명칭이 있다. (④ **프랑스에서부터 일본, 브라질까지 전 세계적으로는 스포츠 심판의 명칭이 분명하고 일관되며 간단하다.**) 그러나 영어에서 그것은 함정에 가깝다. 그 용어들은 약간의 차이가 나는 기본 의미가 있고, 바꾸어 쓸 수 없지만, 영어에서 그것들의 사용은 스포츠 간의 어떠한 확립된 규칙도 따르지 않는다. NBA 경기의 주심은 referee이다. MLB에서는 umpire이다. 테니스, 미식축구, 그리고 라크로스 전부 referee와 다양한 judge가 있다.

15 정답 ① — Day 20-08

> 정답해설

(A)가 포함된 문장에서 "much of what we understand about the Big Bang Theory comes from mathematical formulas and models(빅뱅 이론에 대해 우리가 이해하고 있는 것들 중 많은 부분이 수학적인 공식과 모델로부터 기인한 것이다)."에 대한 이유가 (A) 이전 문장 "Unfortunately, current instruments do not allow astronomers to peer back at the universe's birth(안타깝게도 현재의 기구들로는 천문학자들이 우주의 탄생을 살펴볼 수 없다)."에서 드러난다. 따라서 빈칸에는 '인과관계'를 나타내는

접속부사인 'Therefore(따라서)'가 들어가는 것이 알맞다.
(B)가 포함된 문장에서 "Astronomers can ~ see the "echo" of the expansion through a phenomenon known as the cosmic microwave background(천문학자들은 우주배경복사라고 알려진 현상을 통해 확장의 "흔적"을 볼 수는 있다)"를 통해, 앞서 언급된 내용인 "current instruments do not allow astronomers to peer back at the universe's birth(현재의 기구들로는 천문학자들이 우주의 탄생을 살펴볼 수 없다)."와는 대조적으로 관측 가능한 것에 대해 언급하고 있으므로, '역접'을 나타내는 연결사인 however(그러나)가 빈칸에 가장 적절하다.
따라서 정답은 '① Therefore(따라서) – however(그러나)'이다.

해석

빅뱅이론은 우주가 어떻게 시작되었는지에 대한 대표적인 이론이다. 가장 간단히 말하면, 그것은 우주는 작은 특이점에서 시작했고, 이후 우리가 오늘날 알고 있는 우주로 138억 년 동안 팽창했다고 말한다. 안타깝게도 현재의 기구들로는 천문학자들이 우주의 탄생을 살펴볼 수 없다. (A) 따라서 빅뱅이론에 대해 우리가 이해하고 있는 것들 중 많은 부분이 수학적인 공식과 모델로부터 기인한 것이다. (B) 그러나 천문학자들은 우주배경복사라고 알려진 현상을 통해 확장의 "흔적"을 볼 수는 있다.
① 따라서 – 그러나
② 따라서 – 유사하게
③ 반대로 – 그에 따라
④ 따라서 – 예를 들어

16 정답 ③ — Day 16-10

정답해설

주어진 본문은 도입부의 'The Renaissance kitchen had a definite hierarchy of help~'를 통해 '르네상스 시대의 명확했던 주방 계급에 대해 기술'할 것임을 짐작할 수 있다. ①에서 주방과 식당을 총괄하는 호텔종사원, ②에서 식당을 관리하는 집사, ④에서 최고 주방장에 의해 관리되는 주방에 대한 설명으로 이어진다. 그러나 ③에서 'This elaborate decoration and serving' 즉 '이러한 정교한 장식과 대접'은 이전의 내용에서 찾아볼 수 없을 뿐더러, 해당 문장은 글의 전체적인 내용의 흐름에서 벗어났다. 따라서 글의 흐름상 가장 어색한 문장은 ③이다.

해석

르네상스 시대의 주방은 정교한 만찬을 열기 위해 함께 일을 했던 일꾼들의 명확한 계급을 가지고 있었다. ① 제일 높은 곳에는, 우리가 봐왔듯이, 주방뿐 아니라 식당까지 총괄하는 scalco 혹은 호텔종사원이 있다. ② 식당은 은식기류와 린넨을 담당하는 집사에 의해 관리되었고 또한 연회를 시작하고 끝내는 음식을 제공했다 – 시작할 때에는 냉요리, 샐러드, 치즈, 과일이, 식사가 끝날 때에는 디저트와 제과류. ③ *이런 정교한 장식과 대접은 식당에서 "프런트 데스크"라고 불리는 것이다.* ④ 주방은 보조 주방장, 페이스트리 요리사, 주방 보조자들을 지시하는 최고 주방장에 의해 관리된다.

17 정답 ③ — Day 19-09

정답해설

주어진 문장 "we generally consider blindness a greater disability than deafness(우리는 보통 청각상실보다 시각상실을 더 큰 장애로 여긴다)"를 통해 '청각상실과 시각상실에 대한 일반적인 사람들의 견해'를 언급하고 있다. 이어서 앞 문장 전체를 가리키는 'This is probably because ~'를 이용해 이러한 견해가 보편화된 이유를 설명하는 (B)가 오는 것이 알맞다. 이후에는 'However(그러나)'를 이용해 앞서 언급된 보편된 견해와는 반대되는 행보를 보인 인물 'Daniel Kish'를 소개하는 (A)가 이어지고, (A)에서 언급된 '귀로 보는 것(see by using his ears)'에 대한 구체적인 방법을 언급하는 (C)가 이어지는 것이 자연스럽다. 따라서 '③ (B) – (A) – (C)'가 정답이다.

해석

비록 우리가 환경과 상호작용하기 위해 시각과 청각에 모두 의존하지만, 우리는 보통 청각상실보다 시각상실을 더 큰 장애로 여긴다.
(B) 이것은 아마 우리가 청각을 상실했을 때 적어도 우리는 세상을 헤쳐 나가기 위해 여전히 볼 수 있고 의사소통을 하기 위해 수화 또는 구화를 익힐 수 있기 때문일 것이다.
(A) 2세 전에 망막모세포종으로 양쪽 안구를 잃은 Daniel Kish는 그의 시각 상실을 큰 장애로 생각하지 않는다. 대신에 그는 귀를 이용해 보는 법을 스스로 익혔다.
(C) Kish는 세상 속에서 그가 움직일 때 혀를 차는 소리를 내고, 그의 뇌는 주변 환경의 3차원 이미지를 생성하기 위해 그 반향음을 이용한다.

18 정답 ③ — Day 17-10

정답해설

해당 지문은 '인도네시아'의 경우를 예로 들어 개발도상국의 경제 발전의 실상에 대해 서술하고 있다. 본문을 통해 인도네시아는 거시적으로는 6%대의 꾸준한 경제 성장을 이룩하며 발전해 나가고 있지만, 실제로는 소득 불평등 지수인 '지니계수'또한 함께 상승하고 있다는 것을 알 수 있다. 따라서 '경제가 성장하더라도 모든 계층이 재정적으로 혜택을 받는 것은 아니다'라는 것이 필자의 주장이므로, 글의 요지로 가장 적절한 것은 "③ Economic growth does not mean the equal financial improvement of all groups of population(경제 성장은 국민의 모든 집단의 동등한 재정적 발전을 의미하는 것은 아니다)."이다.

해석

인도네시아와 같은 개발도상국에서의 경제 성장은 모순을 보여준다. "경제 성장의 역설"은 경제가 성장하지만 소득 불평등 또한 성장하는 것이다. 인도네시아의 경제는 2012년에 6.1%, 2013년에 6.3%, 2014년에 6.4% 성장했다. 거시적인 측면에서 인도네시아의 경제 성장은 좋아 보였다. 그러나 우리가 더 가까이 들여다보면 우리는 그것이 환상이었다는 것을 알 수 있다. 그 이면에서 인도네시아의 지니계수는 증가하고 있었다. 2012년에 그것은 0.36이었고, 2013년에는 0.39, 2014년에 0.41이었다. 국가의 경제가 성장함에 따라 소득격차도 증가한 것이다. 인도네시아를 비롯한 다른 개발도상국에서 경제 성장의 혜택은 중산층과 그 이상의 계층에게만 돌아갔고, 하층 그리고 노동자 계급에까지 도달한 혜택은 거의 없었다. 부유층은 더 부유해지고 빈곤층은 더 빈곤해졌다.
① 인도네시아의 소득 불평등은 더 높은 교육을 통해 해결될 수 있다.
② 인도네시아는 지니계수를 증가시킴으로써 전체 국가의 사회 복지를 촉진시켜야 한다.
 cf. Gini ratio(지니계수) : 소득 분포의 불평등도를 측정하기 위한 계수
③ 경제 성장은 국민의 모든 집단의 동등한 재정적 발전을 의미하는 것은 아니다.
④ 경제 성장은 한 국가의 거의 모든 시민에게 혜택을 주고, 따라서 궁극적으로 빈곤을 감소시킨다.

19 정답 ④ — Day 16-09

정답해설

본문에서 1948년에 채택된 아동법은 그 전의 견해인 'older ideas about the benefits of corporal punishment'(신체적 처벌의 혜택들에 대한 오래된 생각들)가 아동법의 통과로 'children who broke the law should be reclaimed and rehabilitated had become the orthodox view'(법을 어긴

아이들은 교정되고 갱생되어야 한다는 시각)가 정통적인 견해가 되었다는 것이므로 ④ The 1948 Children Act accentuated the benefits of corporal punishment.(1948년의 아동법은 신체적 처벌의 혜택들을 강조했다.)는 본문과 일치하지 않는 내용이다. 따라서 정답은 ④이다.

해석
영국의 청소년 사법제도는 20세기 초반에 상당한 철학적 변화들을 겪었다. 신체적 처벌의 혜택들에 대한 오래된 생각들을 고수하는 많은 이들이 있었지만, 법을 어긴 아이들은 교정되고 갱생되어야 한다는 시각이 1948년 아동법의 통과로 정통적인 견해가 되었다. 이 접근법은 영미의 빈민가의 사회복지사들과 새로운 사회과학과 의학 분야의 연구자들의 견해에 기대었다. 비행은 구조적 불평등과 부족한 육아 방식으로 인한 것으로, 사회적 매트릭스의 일부로 여겨졌다. 비행 문제에 대한 해결책은 이러한 불평등들을 발생시킨 구조들의 개혁 내에 놓여 있는 것으로 여겨졌다. 더 급진적인 치안 판사들에게는, 그 해답은 사회를 점검하는 것이 아니라, 아이들이 법정에 의해 다루어지는 방식들을 개혁하는 것이었다.
① 어떤 판사들의 견해에 따르면, 법정의 아이들에 대한 더 나은 취급이 비행을 억누르는 데 도움이 될 수 있다.
② 사회복지사들은 정통적인 견해의 지지자들 중 하나였다.
③ 부족한 육아 방식들은 비행의 한 원인으로 여겨졌다.
④ 1948년의 아동법은 신체적 처벌의 혜택들을 강조했다.

20 정답 ④ Day 12-09

정답해설
본문에서 "Policies have not yet captured the role of micro-financing and flexible financing that could help increase access to formal housing for low income groups(정책은 저소득층의 정식 주택 입주 증가를 도울 수 있는 소액금융과 탄력적인 융자의 역할을 아직 확보하지 못했다)."를 통해 (정부의) 정책이 소액금융의 역할을 확보하지 못한 것을 주택문제를 심화시키는 하나의 원인으로 지적하고 있으며, 또한 저소득층이 주택 확보에 도움이 될 수도 있는 소액금융 서비스를 제대로 이용하지 못하고 있다는 것을 유추할 수 있다. 따라서 ④ The government encourages low income families to take advantage of microfinance services(정부는 저소득 가구들이 소액금융 서비스를 이용하도록 장려한다).는 본문의 내용과 부합하지 않는다.

해석
54%의 도시화율과 전체 인구의 20%가 700곳 이상의 임시 거주 구역에서 불법으로 거주하고 있는 가운데 자메이카 국가와 지역 당국은 심각한 주거 문제에 직면하고 있다. 국가 주거정책을 위해 실시된 연구는 부족분을 해결하기 위해서는 2030년까지 매년 15,000채의 신규 주택이 필요하다고 밝혔다. 그러나 1980년과 2012년 사이에 공공 부문에서 연간 평균 주택 생산은 4,456채에 머물렀다. 한편, 많은 가구가 그들의 생계와 소득을 확보하는 수단인 비공식 경제에 종사하고 있기 때문에, 저소득 가구는 공식 금융 기관을 통해 대출이나 융자를 받는 것을 어렵다고 생각한다. 정책은 저소득층의 정식 주택 입주 증가를 도울 수 있는 소액금융과 탄력적인 융자의 역할을 아직 확보하지 못했다. 그렇기 때문에 저소득 가구는 임시 거주지에 의존하며 거처를 마련하기 위해 계속해서 점진적 주택 개발을 하고 있는 것이다. 토지 등록과 개발 허가 절차 또한 너무 비용이 비싸고, 엄격하며 복잡하고 느리다. 그래서 저소득 가구가 알맞은 정식 주택을 확보하는 데 있어서 방해물로 작용한다.
① 인구의 약 5분의 1이 허가되지 않은 곳에서 살고 있다.
② 주택 수요와 공급의 격차는 30년 이상 지속됐다.
③ 저소득층의 사람들은 무허가 소득 창출 활동에 크게 의존한다.
④ 정부는 저소득 가구들이 소액금융 서비스를 이용하도록 장려한다.

결국엔 성정혜 영어 하프모의고사
기적사 DAY 21

| 01 | ① | 02 | ① | 03 | ④ | 04 | ③ | 05 | ④ |
| 06 | ② | 07 | ③ | 08 | ② | 09 | ② | 10 | ② |

01 정답 ① 19 지방직

정답해설
'excavate'는 '발굴하다, 파내다'라는 뜻을 가진 단어로 밑줄 친 단어 전의 'dead and buried'를 통해 이것이 발굴되어져야 할 필요가 있다는 것을 유추할 수도 있다. 따라서 보기에서 유의어 관계에 있는 것은 ① exhumed이다.

해석
나는 현재 죽어서 매장된 감성이라는 유물들로서의 이 자료들을 보러 왔는데, 이것들은 **발굴되어야** 한다.
① 파내다
② 꾸려지다
③ 지워지다
④ 축하받다

어휘
relic 유물, 유적
bury 매장하다
exhume 파내다, 발굴하다
sensibility 감성, 감수성
excavate 발굴하다, 파내다
pack 짐을 싸다(꾸리다)

02 정답 ① 19 지방직

정답해설
'sheer'가 '완전한'이란 뜻을 가진 단어이므로 보기에서 유의어 관계인 단어는 ① utter이다. 해당 문제는 기출문제로 "the questioning and regret that comes as you go up~"에서 주격 관계대명사 "that"의 선행사인 "the questioning and regret"을 단일 개념으로 취급하였다.

해석
롤러코스터를 타는 것은 감정의 재미있는 드라이브일 수 있다: 당신이 좌석에 안전띠를 맬 때의 긴장되는 기대, 당신이 위로, 위로, 위로 올라갈 때 생기는 의문과 후회, 그리고 탈 것이 첫 다이빙을 할 때의 **완전한** 아드레날린의 급증
① 완전한
② 두려운
③ 가끔씩
④ 관리(감당)할 수 있는

어휘
joy ride 폭주 드라이브, 재미있는 드라이브
strap 끈으로 묶다
sheer 완전한, 순전한
utter 완전한
occasional 가끔의
questioning 의문, 의심
rush 급증
scary 무서운
manageable 관리(감당)할 수 있는

오답률 TOP 3

03 정답 ④
19 지방직

정답해설

'be engrossed in'은 '~에 열중해 있다'라는 뜻으로 본문 초반에 지루한 오후 수업 때는 느려진다고 설명하는 것과 대조적으로 재미있는 것을 할 때 밑줄 친 단어의 의미는 느려지는 것과 반의어 관계인 것을 유추할 수 있다. 따라서 'engrossed in'과 유의어 관계에 있는 것은 ④ preoccupied with이다.

해석

시간은 지루한 오후 수업 동안은 정말 느려지고, 뇌가 정말 재미있는 무언가에 **열중할** 때는 달려가는 것처럼 보인다.
① ~의해 강화되다
② ~에 무관심하다
③ ~의해 안정되다
④ ~에 사로잡히다

어휘

slow to a trickle 아주 느려지다, 아주 소량으로 줄다
race 급히 뛰다, 빨리 달리다
be engrossed in ~에 열중하다
apathetic 무관심한
stabilize 안정시키다
be preoccupied with ~에 사로잡히다

04 정답 ③
19 지방직

정답해설

빈칸 질문에 대한 답변으로 B가 무료로 외환을 다시 바꿔주며 영수증을 지참하라고 하는 것으로 보아, A는 환전한 돈을 다시 재환전할 때에 관한 질문을 했음을 알 수 있다. 따라서 빈칸에 적절한 표현은 ③ What's your buy-back policy(당신의 역 구매 정책은 무엇인가요?)이다.

오답해설

빈칸 다음에 비용이 얼마인지에 대한 언급은 없으므로 가격이나 비용에 대해 언급하는 질문들은 답이 될 수 없다.

해석

A: 안녕하세요. 돈을 좀 환전하고 싶은데요.
B: 네. 무슨 화폐가 필요하세요?
A: 달러를 파운드로 바꿔야 해요. 환율이 어떻게 되나요?
B: 환율은 1달러당 0.73 파운드입니다.
A: 좋아요. 수수료 받나요?
B: 네, 우리는 소액 수수료로 4달러를 받습니다.
A: 당신의 역 구매 정책은 무엇인가요?
B: 우리는 무료로 당신의 화폐를 다시 바꿔 드립니다. 영수증만 가지고 오세요.
① 이것은 비용이 얼마나 드나요?
② 내가 저것에 대해 얼마나 지불해야만 하나요?
③ 당신의 역 구매 정책은 무엇인가요?
④ 당신은 신용카드를 가져갈 건가요?

어휘

exchange 교환하다
convert 전환하다, 변환하다
commission 수수료
buy-back 역 구매, 되사기
currency 통화, 돈
exchange rate 환율
receipt 영수증

05 정답 ④
19 지방직

정답해설

④ **출제 포인트: 현재분사 vs. 과거분사**
동사 injure는 원칙적으로는 타동사(부상을 입히다)와 자동사(부상을 입다) 모두 가능하지만, 관용적으로 타동사 위주로 사용된다. 따라서 주어가 '수백만 명의 보행자들(Millions of pedestrians)'이므로 수동태 동사로 써야 '부상을 당하다(are (non-fatally) injured)'라는 의미가 된다. 관용적인 표현인 만큼 '부상당하다'라는 'be[get] injured'라고 숙지해두는 것이 좋다.

오답해설

① **출제 포인트: 주어와 동사 수일치**
'매년 벌어지는 일'(Each year)이므로 현재시제인 동사 'lose'(잃는다)가 어법상 적절하고 주어인 'more than 270,000 pedestrians'(27만 명이 넘는 보행자들)와 수일치도 된다. 따라서 적절한 어법이다.

② **출제 포인트: to부정사의 부사적 용법**
to부정사의 부사적 용법 중 (부정적) 결과로 부정어 never와 함께 사용되어 '~했으나 결국 ....지 못했다'라는 뜻으로 문맥에 적합한 어법이다.

③ **출제 포인트: 원급 비교**
원급비교로 'as ~ as...'의 구조이며 앞에 2형식 동사인 be 동사(is)가 있으므로 보어로 적합한 형용사 'high'(높은)가 원급비교 구문에 알맞게 쓰였다.

해석

매년, 27만 명이 넘는 보행자들이 세계의 도로에서 그들의 목숨을 ① 잃는다. 많은 사람들이 어느 주어진 날 그러하듯 집을 떠나지만 결코 ② 돌아오지 못한다. 세계적으로 보행자들은 모든 도로 교통 사망자들의 22%를 차지하며, 어떤 국가들에서 이 비율은 모든 도로 교통 사망자들의 2/3 ③ 만큼이나 높다. 수백만 명의 보행자들은 치명적이지 않은 ④ 부상을 당하는데 그들 중 일부는 영구적 장애를 계속 지니게 된다. 이러한 사건들은 경제적인 어려움뿐만 아니라 많은 고통과 슬픔을 야기한다.

어휘

pedestrian 보행자
constitute 구성하다
proportion 비율
be left with ~를 계속 지니다
disability 장애
grief 비탄
globally 전 세계적으로
fatality 사망자
injure 부상을 입히다
permanent 영구적인
suffering 고통
hardship 어려움, 곤란

오답률 TOP 2

06 정답 ②
19 지방직

정답해설

② **출제 포인트: lest + 주어 + (should) + 동사원형**
주어가 사물(The investigation)이므로 문맥상 동사는 수동태(조사가 다뤄지다)가 적합하게 쓰였다. 또한 접속사 'lest'(~하지 않기 위해서)가 이끄는 절은 조동사 'should'를 생략할 수 있으므로 종속절의 동사가 'be aroused'(생겨나다)로 올바르게 사용되었다.

오답해설

① **출제 포인트: 전치사 + 명사(구)**
전치사 'with' 이하에 동사원형(use)은 사용할 수 없으므로 명사 역할을 하는 동시에 목적어인 'the company's money'를 취할 수 있는 동명사 using이 사용되어야 한다.

③ **출제 포인트: 주격 보어(to부정사/동명사)**
문맥상 2형식 동사인 'would be' 뒤에 주격보어가 필요(또 다른 방법은

~일 것이다)하므로 과거분사 'made'가 아닌 to 부정사 또는 동명사인 'to make'나 'making'이 필요하다.

④ **출제 포인트: one of 목적어[복수형태]/분사**
'one of the' 다음에는 복수명사가 필요하며 또한 명사인 'causes'(원인들)를 수식할 수 있는 현재분사 'leading'(lead가 형용사로 '선도적인'의 의미가 있으나 문맥에 맞지 않음)이 어법상 적합하다. 즉, 'one of the leading causes'(잘 이끄는 원인들 중 하나)로 쓰여야 한다.

해석
① 그 신문은 자신의 목적을 위해 회사의 돈을 사용한 것으로 그녀를 비난했다.
② 의심이 생기지 않도록 그 조사는 최상의 주의를 기울여 다뤄져야만 했다.
③ 그 과정을 빠르게 할 수 있는 또 다른 방법은 새로운 시스템으로 바꾸는 것이다.
④ 화석 연료를 연소시키는 것이 기후 변화의 가장 중요한 원인들 중 하나이다.

07 정답 ③ 19 지방직

정답해설
③ **출제 포인트: 자동사로 착각하기 쉬운 완전타동사**
동사 'marry'(결혼하다)는 타동사로 뒤에 바로 목적어를 취해야 하는 동사이다. 또한, 관용표현으로 'get married to'는 결혼이라는 동작을 나타내고, 'be married to'는 결혼의 상태를 나타낸다. 따라서 해당 문장에서는 'for more than two decades'(20년 이상 동안)가 존재하므로 '결혼의 상태 지속임'을 알 수 있다. 즉, "She has married her husband.", "She has been married to her husband for more than two decades."로 바꿀 수 있다. 참고로, 'get married'는 '결혼하다'의 의미로 결혼 동작을 의미한다.

오답해설
① **출제 포인트: 부사절을 이끄는 접속사**
조건의 부사절 접속사 'in case (that)'이 문맥에 맞게 쓰였고, 'would like to부정사' 역시 알맞게 사용되었다.
② **출제 포인트: 동명사 관용표현**
동명사 관용표현 'be busy ~ing'(~하느라 바쁘다)가 적합하게 사용되었다.
④ **출제 포인트: to부정사의 형용사적 용법**
'to read'(읽을)가 to 부정사의 형용사적 용법으로 명사인 'a book'(책)을 수식하며 to부정사 앞의 'for my son'은 의미상의 주어로 'for + (대)명사[목적격]'의 형태로 알맞게 쓰였다.

오답률 TOP 1
08 정답 ② 19 지방직

정답해설
제시된 문장에서는 '우리가 세상을 이해하는 방법'(how can we ever make sense of the social world)이라는 글의 소재를 제시하고 있다. 다음에 주어진 3개의 보기 모두 '경제'(economics) 혹은 '경제학자들'(economists)을 다루는데 이것이 처음으로 언급되는 (A)가 보기 다음 문단으로 적합하다. (A)에서 경제학자들이 모델을 만들어서 세상을 이해하려고 한다고 했고 구체적으로 이 모델들은 '분해'(stripped down) 모델들이라고 하며(which are deliberately stripped down representations of the phenomena out there), (C)에서 이 '분해된'(stripped down)의 의미를 설명한다. 그리고 마지막으로 (B)에서 부연 설명 및 요약(경제학은 모델들을 선택하는 기술이다.) 한다. 따라서 글의 순서는 ② (A)-(C)-(B)이어야 문맥상 적절하다.

오답해설
(B)는 경제학이 무엇이라는 것을 요약하는 부분이므로 보기 지문 다음에 바로 나오는 것은 글의 문맥상 적절하지 않고 이와 비슷한 이유로 (A) 다음에 요약 부분인 (B)가 위치하는 것도 적절하지 않다.

해석
우리를 떠나지 않을 수도 있는 생각이 있다: 아마 모든 것이 다른 모든 것에 영향을 주기 때문에, 우리는 도대체 어떻게 사회적 세계를 이해할 수 있는가? 하지만, 만약 우리가 그 걱정에 짓눌리게 된다면, 우리는 결코 전진하지 못할 것이다.
(A) 내가 익숙한 모든 학문 분야는 세상을 이해하기 위해 그것의 캐리커처를 그린다. 현대 경제학자들은 모델들을 만들어서 이것을 하는데, 이것들은 밖에 있는 현상에 대한 의도적으로 분해된 묘사들이다.
(C) 내가 '분해된'이라고 말할 때, 나는 정말 분해된 것을 의미한다. 우리 경제학자들 사이에서는 현실의 그러한 측면들이 단지 어떻게 작동하고 상호 작용하는지를 우리가 이해할 수 있도록 해줄 것이라고 희망하며, 모든 것을 제외하고 한두 가지의 원인이 되는 요인들에 집중하는 것은 드물지 않다.
(B) 경제학자인 John Maynard Keynes는 우리의 주제를 이와 같이 설명했다: "경제학은 현대 세계와 관련된 모델들을 선택하는 기술과 이어진 모델들이라는 면에서 사고의 과학이다."

어휘
haunt 떠나지 않다, 계속 출몰하다 make sense of 이해하다
weigh down 짓누르다 make progress 전진하다, 진행하다
discipline 학문 분야, 훈련, 훈육 be familiar with ~에 익숙하다
deliberately 의도적으로, 고의적으로, 신중하게
strip down 분해하다, 분해되다, 벗겨내다, 벗겨지다
representation 묘사, 표현 phenomenon 현상
thus 이와 같이, 따라서 in terms of ~라는 면에서
join to ~로 잇다 relevant 관련된
contemporary 현대의, 동시대의 causal 원인이 되는, 원인의
enable 가능하게 해주다 aspect 측면, 양상
interact 상호작용하다

09 정답 ② 19 지방직

정답해설
본문에서 두 번째 문장인 "Abnormal behaviors, from simple headaches to convulsive attacks, were attributed to evil spirits that inhabited or controlled the afflicted person's body."(단순한 두통에서 발작 경련에 이르기까지, 비정상적인 행동들은 병에 걸린 사람의 신체에 살고 있거나 그것을 통제하는 악령의 탓으로 돌려졌다.)는 ② Abnormal behaviors were believed to result from evil spirits affecting a person.(비정상적인 행동은 사람에게 영향을 미치는 악령에서 비롯되었다고 믿어졌다.)과 일치하는 내용이므로 ②이 본문과 일치하는 보기이다. 따라서 정답은 ②이다.

오답해설
① 첫 번째 문장에서 이 '두 개를 명확하게 구별하지 않았다.'라고 하였으므로 본문과 일치하지 않는 내용이다.
③ 본문의 'part of the skull was chipped away to provide an opening through which the evil spirit could escape'(두개골의 일부가 깎여서 악령이 빠져나갈 수 있는 틈이 제공되었다)으로 본문과 반대되는 보기임을 알 수 있다.
④ 본문 마지막에 생존했음을 보여준다(some patients survived this extremely crude operation)고 하였으므로 본문과 일치하지 않는 내용이다.

해석

대략 50만 년 전 선사 시대의 사회들은 정신적 장애와 신체적 장애를 확실히 구별하지 않았다. 단순한 두통에서 발작 경련에 이르기까지, 비정상적인 행동들은 고통받는 사람의 신체에 깃들어 있거나 그것을 통제하는 악령의 탓으로 돌려졌다. 역사학자들에 따르면, 이러한 고대인들은 많은 형태의 질병들을 악령 빙의, 마법, 또는 화가 난 조상 영혼의 명령 탓으로 돌렸다. *귀신론*이라고 불리는 이러한 믿음 체계 내에서는, 피해자는 불운에 대해 적어도 부분적으로는 책임이 있었다. 석기시대 동굴 거주자들은 *두개골 수술*이라고 불리는 외과적 방법으로 행동 장애를 치료했을 수도 있음이 암시되었는데, 그 수술에서는 두개골의 일부가 깎여서 악령이 빠져나갈 수 있는 틈이 제공되었다. 악령이 떠나면, 그 사람은 그의 정상적인 상태로 돌아올 것이라고 사람들이 믿었을지도 모른다. 놀랍게도, 수술을 받은 두개골들이 아물었다고 발견되는데, 이는 일부 환자들이 이렇게 극히 조잡한 수술에도 생존했음을 보여준다.

① 정신적 장애는 신체적 장애와는 분명히 구분되었다.
② 비정상적인 행동은 사람에게 영향을 미치는 악령에서 비롯되었다고 믿어졌다.
③ 두개골에서 악령이 사람의 신체에 들어갈 수 있도록 틈이 만들어졌다.
④ 두개골 수술에서 생존한 동굴 거주자들은 없었다.

어휘

prehistoric 선사 시대의	distinguish 구별하다
physical 신체적인, 물리적인	disorder 장애
abnormal 비정상적인	convulsive 경련의
convulsive attack 경련 발작	
attribute A to B A를 B의 탓/덕분으로 돌리다	
evil spirit 악령	inhabit 거주하다
afflicted 병에 걸린	demonic possession 악령의 빙의
sorcery 마법	behest 명령, 간청
offended 화가 난	ancestral 조상의
demonology 귀신론	
be (held)responsible for ~에 책임이 있다	
partly 부분적으로	misfortune 불행(한 일), 불운
cave dweller 동굴 거주자	treat 치료하다
surgical 수술의, 외과의	skull 두개골
chip away 깎다, 쪼다	opening 구멍, 틈
escape 빠져나가다, 탈출하다	state 상태
heal over 아물다, 낫다	indicate 암시하다, 보여주다, 언급하다
patient 환자	crude 조잡한, 거친, 날것의
operation 수술	differentiate 구별하다
result from ~에서 비롯되다	

10 정답 ②   19 지방직

정답해설

본문 초반부에 글쓴이는 지난 25년간 많은 기술적 변화를 겪었다고 언급하며, 그로 인해 점점 더 기자로서 '이야기를 지어낸다'(making stuff up)라고 서술하고 있다. 그 이후 중반에서 그 예시들을 제시하며 글의 마지막에는 '점점 더 대본 없이 일한다.'(increasingly working without a script)라고 요약하고 있으므로, 현대의 기자로서 사전 준비의 비중이 계속 줄어들고 있는 상황에서 일하는 것을 묘사하고 있음을 알 수 있다. 따라서 'improvisation(즉흥적으로/즉석에서 하기)'이 글쓴이 직업의 특성을 가장 잘 나타내는 단어라는 것을 유추할 수 있다. 따라서 글의 주제로 가장 적절한 것은 ② a reporter and improvisation(기자와 즉흥성)이다.

오답해설

① 본문에서 기자의 역할 중 하나로 언급이 되었으나 지엽적인 내용이다.
③ 기자가 정치인들을 인터뷰하고 그들에 대해 기사를 쓰는 것이지 기자의 정치 생활에 대해 언급한 것이 아니므로 주제로 적절하지 않다.
④ 본문에서 언급하고 있지 않다.

해석

디지털 혁명이 전국적으로 뉴스룸에 충격을 주기 때문에, 여기 모든 기자들을 위한 나의 조언이 있다. 나는 25년 넘게 기자였기 때문에, 6번의 기술적 수명 주기를 거치며 살아왔다. 가장 급격한 변화는 지난 6년 동안 도래해왔다. 그것은 내가, 점점 더 높은 빈도로, 일을 진행하면서 이야기들을 만들어낸다는 것을 의미한다. 뉴스 업계에서의 많은 시간 동안, 우리는 우리가 무엇을 하는지 모른다. 우리가 아침에 출근하면 누군가 "세금 정책/이민/기후 변화에 관한 (하나를 선택하여) 이야기를 쓸 수 있어?"라고 말한다. 뉴스 기자들이 하루에 한 번 마감 시간이 있을 때, 우리는 기자가 아침에 배워서 밤에 가르친다-기자가 24시간 이전에는 전혀 몰랐던 주제에 관해 내일의 독자들에게 알려줄 수 있는 이야기를 쓴다는 것 -고 말했다. 지금은 매 정시에 배워서 매시 30분에 가르치는 것에 더 가깝다. 예를 들면, 나는 또한 정치 팟캐스트를 운영하고 있는데, 대선 후보 선정을 위한 전당대회 동안, 우리는 어디서든 실시간 인터뷰를 하기 위해 그것을 이용할 수 있어야 한다. 나는 그냥 점점 더 대본 없이 일하고 있다.

① 교사로서의 기자
② 기자와 즉흥성
③ 정치에서의 기술
④ 저널리즘과 기술 분야

어휘

upend 뒤집다, 충격을 주다	transformation 변신, 변형
frequency 빈도	make up 지어내다
go along 계속하다, 진행하다	show up 나타나다, 등장하다
immigration 이민	at the top of the hour 매 정시에
at the bottom of the hour 매시 30분에	
presidential convention 대선 후보 선정을 위한 전당대회	
script 대본	

결국엔 성정혜 영어 하프모의고사
기적사 DAY 22

| 01 | ② | 02 | ① | 03 | ② | 04 | ③ | 05 | ② |
| 06 | ② | 07 | ④ | 08 | ② | 09 | ② | 10 | ④ |

오답률 TOP 3

01 정답 ②

정답해설

밑줄 친 단어의 의미는 문맥상 '발굴하다'이고, 유의어로는 ② shovel이 적절하다.

해석

벽화 한 점을 **발굴하는** 데는 많은 시간이 걸린다.
① 지우다, 파괴하다, 멸종시키다
② ~을 파다, ~을 삽으로 뜨다
③ 강화하다
④ 몰두시키다

어휘

wall painting 벽화 expunge 지우다, 파괴하다, 멸종시키다
shovel ~을 파다, ~을 삽으로 뜨다. reinforce 강화하다
immerse 몰두시키다

02 정답 ①

정답해설

밑줄 친 단어는 문맥상 '순전한, 순수한'으로 사용되었고, 유의어로는 ① absolute가 적절하다.

해석

그녀는 **순전히** 열심히 노력하여 자기 성적을 땄다.
① 완전한, 순수한, 확고한
② 필수의, 본질적인
③ 낙관적인, 완고한, 어리석은
④ 강제적인, 필수의, 평소의

어휘

absolute 완전한, 순수한, 확고한 essential 필수의, 본질적인
bullish 낙관적인, 완고한, 어리석은 obligatory 강제적인, 필수의, 평소의

03 정답 ②

정답해설

밑줄 친 단어의 의미는 '몰두시키다'이고, 유의어로는 ② immersed가 적절하다.

해석

그는 몇 달 동안 집필에 **몰두했다**.
① 어렴풋이 나타났다, 솟아올랐다, 우뚝 섰다
② 몰두시켰다
③ 망가뜨렸다, 파산시켰다, ~을 타락시켰다
④ 식별했다, 차별했다

어휘

loom 어렴풋이 나타나다, 솟아오르다, 우뚝 서다
immerse 몰두시키다
ruin 망가뜨리다, 파산시키다, ~을 타락시키다
discriminate 식별하다, 차별하다

04 정답 ③

정답해설

A가 B의 안부를 묻자 B는 'I was so stressed out~eat or sleep properly(스트레스를 많이 받아 제대로 먹거나 잠을 이루지 못했다)'라고 답하고 있다. 따라서 B가 자신의 '③ 일들이 걷잡을 수 없게 되었다(things got out of hand)'라고 말하는 것이 적절하다.

오답해설

① "bite the bullet (어떻게든 견뎌내다)"은 긍정적인 의미를 나타내는 말로, B가 받은 스트레스의 원인으로 부적절하다.
② "give a big hand (힘찬 박수를 보내다)"는 문맥상 부적절하다.
④ "pull the wool over my friend's eyes (내 친구를 속이다)" 의 의미는 문맥상 어색하다.

해석

A: 안녕, 너 요새 뭐 하고 지내? 너 안 본 지 좀 된 것 같아.
B: 그러게 말이야. 저번 주에 좀 힘든 시간을 보냈는데 요새 나아지는 중이야.
A: 오, 안타깝다. 지난주에 무슨 일이 있었던 거야?
B: 말하자면 길어. 짧게 말하자면 일들이 걷잡을 수 없게 되었고 스트레스를 많이 받아서 먹지도, 잠을 제대로 자지도 못했어.
① 나는 어떻게든 견뎌냈어
② 나는 힘찬 박수를 보냈어
③ 일들을 걷잡을 수 없었어
④ 나는 내 친구를 속였어

어휘

in a while 최근에 get better 나아지다
stress out 스트레스를 받다 properly 제대로

오답률 TOP 2

05 정답 ②

정답해설

② 출제 포인트: 현재분사 vs. 과거분사

밑줄 친 과거분사 'heard'가 포함된 절을 이끄는 'what'은 선행사를 포함하는 관계대명사로 뒤에 오는 절은 불완전한 형태이어야 한다. 해당 문장에서 'we are heard'의 경우는 수동태로 불완전한 형태로 볼 수 없으므로, 해당 문장은 수동태 대신에 능동태인 'we are hearing'으로 수정하여 현재분사 hearing의 목적어가 빠져있는 상태로 보아야지만 불완전한 형태로 밑줄 이전에 선행사를 포함한 관계대명사 what이 사용될 수 있다. 밑줄 이후의 'with finding'의 목적어인 'what ~ relevant'는 주절인 'we already know의 종속절로서 'is relevant'가 온 경우이다. that은 접속사의 역할을 하고 있으며 is 앞에 주어가 없고 선행사도 없으므로 'with finding' 바로 뒤의 관계대명사 what은 옳게 사용되었다.

오답해설

① 출제 포인트: 원급 비교

'as+원급+as'는 원급 비교에 해당하며 이때 원급에는 형용사와 부사 외에 과거분사를 사용할 수 있다.

③ **출제 포인트: 주어와 동사 수일치**
주격 관계대명사의 동사의 수일치 기준은 선행사이다. 해당 문장은 선행사가 'a belief'이므로 동사에 단수형태인 'is'를 사용하였다. 또한 'relate'는 자동사와 타동사 모두 가능하며 해당 문장에서의 'be related to'는 '~와 연관되다'라는 뜻으로 쓰였다.

④ **출제 포인트: 등위접속사의 병렬구조**
동사 'find'와 'compare'이 등위접속사 'and'를 사용하여 병렬구조를 이루고 있다.

해석
우리는 우리가 이미 가지고 있는 신념들을 검토함으로써 이들을 발견한다. 우리는 연관된 우리가 이미 알고 있는 것을 발견하는 데에 관심을 갖는 것처럼 지금 듣고 있는 것에는 관심을 갖지 않는다. 이 상황을 다음과 같은 방식으로 생각해 보자. 이해하는 사람으로서, 우리는 주제에 따라 분류된 신념들의 목록을 가지고 있다. 새로운 이야기가 등장하면, 우리는 그것과 연관된 우리의 신념을 찾으려고 노력한다. 이러한 일을 할 때, 우리는 그 신념과 연관된 이야기를 찾고 우리의 기억 속에 있는 이야기를 우리가 지금 처리하고 있는 이야기와 비교한다.

어휘
look through ~을 자세히 살펴보다
appear 생기다, 나타나다
attach 붙이다, 첨부하다
relevant 관계가 있는
attempt 시도하다, 애써 해보다
compare 비교하다

06 정답 ②

정답해설

② **출제 포인트: lest + 주어 + (should) + 동사원형**
접속사 'lest'가 '~하면 안 되므로, ~하지 않도록'을 뜻하는 경우 뒤따라오는 절은 '(should)+동사원형'의 형태를 가지며 부정부사 'not' 또는 'never'를 사용하지 않는다. 해당 문장은 해석상 '~하면 안 되므로'가 자연스러우므로 'lest' 뒤에 오는 절에 '(should)+동사원형'을 사용하였고, 부정부사 'not' 또는 'never'를 사용하지 않았으므로 옳은 문장이다.

오답해설

① **출제 포인트: one of 목적어[복수형태]**
'one of 목적어'에서 목적어에 복수 형태를 사용해야 한다. 해당 문장은 'one of 목적어'가 쓰인 문장으로 목적어에 단수형태 'girl'을 사용하였으므로 틀린 문장이다. 따라서 'girl'을 복수 형태인 'girls'로 수정해야 한다.

③ **출제 포인트: 주격 보어(to부정사/동명사)**
해당 문장을 수동태로 볼 경우 간접목적어 'the kid'와 직접목적어 'a split last name'이 남아있으므로 틀린 문장이 된다. 따라서 해당 문장은 능동태로 보아야 하며 해석상 '유일한 논리적 해결책은 아이에게 분할된 성을 주는 것이다'가 자연스러우므로 과거분사 'given'을 to부정사 'to give' 또는 동명사 'giving'으로 수정해야 한다.

④ **출제 포인트: 전치사 + 명사(구)**
전치사 뒤에는 명사(구)가 와야 한다. 해당 문장은 전치사 'of' 뒤에 동사 'conquer'를 사용하였으므로 틀린 문장이다. 따라서 'conquer'를 동명사 'conquering'으로 수정해야 한다.

해석
① 너와 같이 일한 아가씨들 중 한 명이 결혼할 예정이다.
② Tom은 자신이 아기를 방해하면 안 되므로, 움직이기 너무 두렵다.
③ 유일한 논리적 해결책은 아이에게 분할된 성을 주는 것이다.
④ 그것은 공기 자체를 지배할 수 있는 가능성을 세계에 보여줬다.

07 정답 ④

정답해설

④ **출제 포인트: 자동사로 착각하기 쉬운 완전타동사**
'marry'는 완전타동사로 전치사 없이 목적어를 가진다. 해당 문장은 'marry'의 과거형인 'married'와 목적어 'Tom' 사이에 전치사 'to'를 사용하였으므로 틀린 문장이다. 따라서 'to'를 삭제해야 한다.

오답해설

① **출제 포인트: to부정사의 형용사적 용법**
'to live on'은 명사 'money'를 수식하므로 to부정사의 형용사적 용법에 해당한다. 또한 보어가 아닌 수식어로 사용되었으므로 한정적 용법에 해당한다.

② **출제 포인트: 동명사 관용표현**
'be busy -ing'는 동명사 관용표현으로 '~하느라 바쁘다'를 뜻한다.

③ **출제 포인트: 부사절을 이끄는 접속사**
'in case (that)'과 'in case of'를 혼동하지 않도록 유의해야 한다. 둘 다 '~할 경우에'를 뜻하지만 'in case (that)'은 부사절을 이끄는 접속사로 뒤에 절이 오며 'in case of'는 구전치사로 뒤에 명사(구)가 온다.

오답률 TOP 1

08 정답 ②

정답해설

해당 지문은 '경제 모델(economic model)의 정의와 특징'을 설명하고 있다. 첫 번째 문장 "An economic model is a simplified description of reality, designed to yield hypotheses about the economy(경제 모델은 경제에 대한 가설을 만들어 내도록 설계된 현실에 대한 단순화된 설명이다)."를 통해 경제 모델은 '경제'에 대한 가설을 만들기 위해 설계된다는 것을 알 수 있고, '경제 행위'에 대한 이론을 포함한다는 것을 알 수 있다. 그런데 ②의 'economical'은 '경제적인, 실속 있는, 절약하는'이라는 의미이므로 문맥상 적절하지 않으며, 'economic(경제의)'으로 교체되어야 한다. 따라서 문맥상 단어의 쓰임이 적절하지 않은 것은 '② economical(경제적인)'이다.

오답해설

① 경제 모델(economic model)은 현실 세계를 '단순화(simplified)'하여 가설을 만들어내는 것이므로 문맥상 자연스럽다.

③ 바로 이전 문장에서 '경제 모델은 방정식으로 이루어져 있다'라고 언급했으므로, 경제 모델 개발자들의 목적은 이러한 방정식을 충분히 '포함시키는(include)' 것이라고 할 수 있다.

④ 해당 문장 후반에서 '경제적 결과물에 대한 객관적인 기준(objective measures)'이 없다고 언급하였으므로, 경제 모델은 '필연적으로(necessarily)' 주관적이라 할 수 있다.

해석
경제 모델은 경제에 대한 가설을 만들어 내도록 설계된 현실에 대한 ① 단순화된 설명이다. 일반적으로 모델은 ② **경제적인(→ 경제의)** 행위 이론을 설명하는 일련의 수학 방정식으로 이루어져 있다. 모델을 개발하는 사람들의 목표는 합리적인 행위자가 어떻게 행동하는지 또는 한 경제가 어떻게 작동하는지에 대한 유용한 단서를 제공할 충분한 방정식을 ③ 포함시키는 것이다. 경제 모델의 중요한 특징은 경제적 결과물에 대한 객관적인 기준이 없기 때문에 설계에 있어서 그것이 ④ 필연적으로 주관적이라는 것이다. 각각의 경제학자들은 현실에 대한 그들의 해석을 설명하기 위해 무엇이 필요한지에 대해 다른 판단을 할 것이다.

어휘
simplify 단순화하다
description 설명, 묘사

yield 산출하다, 만들어내다
consist of ~로 구성되다
describe 설명하다, 묘사하다
rational 합리적인
feature 특징
subjective 주관적인
measure 기준, 척도
judgement 판단
interpretation 해석

hypothesis 가설 (pl. hypotheses)
equation 방정식
clue 단서, 실마리
agent 행위자
necessarily 필연적으로, 반드시
objective 객관적인
outcome 결과물
explain 설명하다

09 정답 ②

정답해설

해당 지문은 '에테르마취(ether anesthesia)가 처음 도입되었을 당시의 상황'을 설명하고 있다. "Anesthesia was discovered in a time before standardized medicine(마취는 표준화된 의학 이전의 시대에 발견되었다). ① There was no guaranteed quality when it came to medicine during this time period(이 시대에는 의학에 관한 한 보장된 품질은 없었다)."를 통해 마취의 발견 당시 의학이 완전히 안전성이 보증된 분야가 아니었으며, 이는 마취 자체도 안정적이지 않았다는 것을 의미한다. 또한 "③ Surgeons also didn't fully trust the ether they were using(의사들 또한 그들이 사용하는 에테르를 완전히 신뢰하지 않았다)."에서 의사들도 마취제를 신뢰하지 않았다고 언급하고 있고, 이후에 '마취가 제대로 이루어지지 않거나 너무 많은 용량이 투여되어 환자가 사망하는 경우까지 있었다'고 설명하고 있으므로, 초기에는 마취에 대한 신뢰도도 낮고 활용도도 적었다는 것을 유추할 수 있다. 따라서 "② When ether anesthesia was introduced, the surgical world was overjoyed and embraced this transformative innovation with widespread immediacy(에테르마취가 도입되었을 때, 외과계는 매우 기뻐했고 이 변혁적인 혁신을 널리 즉각적으로 받아들였다)."는 글의 전체 내용과 부합하지 않으므로, 정답은 ②이다.

오답해설

나머지 보기는 모두 마취제의 불안정성에 대해 언급하는 내용이며 문맥상 자연스러우므로 오답이다.

해석

1846년 에테르마취의 발견 이전에 간단한 것부터 주요한, 또는 매우 극단적인 것까지 모든 수술은 정신이 완전히 깨어 있는 사람들에게 행해졌고, 때로로 그들은 의사가 자신의 일을 할 수 있도록 환자의 간청, 비명 그리고 흐느낌을 무시하는 것을 담당하는 사람들에 의해 수술대에 제압된 상태였다. 마취는 표준화된 의학 이전의 시대에 발견되었다. ① 이 시대에는 의학에 관한 한 보장된 품질은 없었다. ② *에테르마취가 도입되었을 때, 외과계는 매우 기뻐했고 이 변혁적인 혁신을 널리 즉각적으로 받아들였다.* ③ 의사들 또한 그들이 사용하는 에테르를 완전히 신뢰하지 않았다. ④ 때때로 배합이 너무 약해 환자가 의식을 잃지 않거나, 아마 더 끔찍하게도 수술 중에 의식을 되찾곤 했다. 다른 때에는 배합이 너무 강해 수술대에서 환자가 과잉 투여로 사망하기도 했다.

어휘

prior to 이전에
anesthesia 마취
radical 극단적인, 과격한
oftentimes 종종, 자주(=often)
operating 수술의
sob 흐느낌, 흐느껴 울기
guarantee 보장하다, 보증하다
when it comes to …에 관한 한
embrace 수용하다, 받아들이다
transformative 변화시키는, 변화시키는 힘이 있는

ether 에테르
absolutely 극도로, 굉장히
wide-awake 완전히 깨어있는
hold down 억제하다, 제압하다
plea 간청
standardized 표준화된
quality 품질, 질
overjoy 매우 기쁘게 하다

innovation 혁신
surgeon (외과) 의사
horrifically 끔찍하게, 무시무시하게
overdose 과잉 투여, 과다 복용

immediacy 긴박, 즉시(성)
consciousness 의식
regain 회복하다, 되찾다

10 정답 ④

정답해설

해당 지문은 '저널리스트는 정치 과정에 대한 정보를 전달할 때 중립적이고 공정한 관찰자가 되길 원하지만 그것은 불가능하다'라고 설명하며, 그러한 이유를 '예비선거 토론회(primary debate)'를 취재하는 상황을 예시로 설명하고 있다. "But true neutrality and total detachment are basically impossible(그러나 진정한 중립성과 완전한 공정성은 근본적으로 불가능하다)."이라고 언급하여 글의 요지를 밝히고, 이후 '뉴스 소재를 선택하는 것이 저널리스트 자신이고 그것에 대해 옳고 그름을 판단하는 주체가 없기 때문에 기자 본인의 주관이 개입되는 것이 불가피하게 발생한다'라고 필자의 주장을 나타내고 있다. 따라서 글의 제목으로 가장 적절한 보기는 '④ Being Neutral Is Impossible in Political Debate Coverage(정치 토론 취재에서 중립적이 되는 것은 불가능하다)'이다.

오답해설

① 예비선거 토론회에 초점이 맞추어진 글이 아니며, 예비선거 토론회는 저널리스트의 정치 관련 취재 행위에 대해 설명하기 위해 예시로 언급된 것이므로 글의 제목으로 적절하지 않다.
② 글의 주요 내용과는 관련 없는 제목이므로 오답이다.
③ 본문에서 언급되지 않은 내용이므로 오답이다.

해석

이러한 평범한 투표자들은 토론의 밤에 무슨 일이 발생했는지에 대한 중립적인 요약을 보고 있다고 믿을 것이다. 안타깝게도, 현실은 훨씬 더 복잡하다. 전통적인 기자들은 정치적 과정에 참여하지 않고 정보만을 제공하는 중립적이고 공정한 관찰자가 되길 바란다. 그러나 진정한 중립성과 완전한 공정성은 근본적으로 불가능하다. 예비선거 토론회에서는 토론의 밤 마지막에 등장해 우승자를 선언하는 더 높은 지위의 권위자 또는 판정가가 없다. 대신에, 누가 잘했는지, 어떤 순간이 중요했는지, 그리고 토론의 어떤 부분이 B-roll로 사용될지에 대해 기자들이 스스로 결정을 하도록 강요된다. 때때로 주류 뉴스 기자들 사이에서 조직적으로 의견 일치가 이루어지기도 한다. 그러나 이러한 종류의 공개 토론에서 승리에 대한 객관적인 기준이 없기 때문에 그러한 의견 일치가 정확한 것인지를 판단할 방법이 없다.
① 예비선거 토론회의 중요성
② 정치 뉴스 콘텐츠는 어떻게 생성되는가?
③ 정치와 저널리즘의 관계
④ 정치 토론 취재에서 중립적이 되는 것은 불가능하다

어휘

neutral 중립적인
complicated 복잡한
detached 사심 없는, 공정한, 거리를 두는
observer 관찰자
participate in …에 참여하다
detachment 공정성, 분리
authority 권위자
determination 결정
B-roll 특징적인 소리가 빠진 영상, 리포터가 묘사와 해설을 할 때 쓰이는 영상
consensus (의견) 일치
mainstream 주류의
forum (공개) 토론

debate 토론
process 과정
neutrality 중립성
primary debate 예비선거 토론회
declare 선언하다
organically 조직적으로
objective 객관적인
coverage 보도, 취재

결국엔 성정혜 영어 하프모의고사
기적사 DAY 23

01	③	02	④	03	②	04	③	05	①
06	③	07	②	08	②	09	③	10	③

오답률 TOP 2

01 정답 ③

정답해설

밑줄 친 단어가 문맥상 '포장하다'로 사용되었으므로, 유의어로는 ③ bundle 이 적절하다.

해석

저희는 물고기를 느긋하고 편안하게 할 정도로 충분한 물을 담은, 산소가 충전된 비닐봉지 안에 각각의 물고기를 **포장합니다**.
① 공개하다, 폭로하다
② 쇠퇴하다
③ 싸다, 재촉하여 몰아내다
④ 보존하다

어휘

disclose 공개하다, 폭로하다
bundle 싸다, 재촉하여 몰아내다
ebb 쇠퇴하다
preserve 보존하다

02 정답 ④

정답해설

밑줄 친 단어는 동사로 쓰여 문맥상 '말하다'로 사용되었고, 유의어로는 ④ say가 적절하다.

해석

기차 여행의 강요된 무력감에 대한 욕설 이외에는, 사람들은 그들이 지나가는 풍경에 대한 어떠한 칭찬의 **말도 하지** 않는다; 그들은 대략 같은 처지에 있는 승객들에게 해줄 끔찍한 이야기들만 가지고 있을 뿐이다.
① 확장하다
② 기죽게 하다, ~을 위협하다
③ 언짢게 하다
④ 말하다

어휘

inertia 무력감
extend 확장하다
dissatisfy 언짢게 하다
railing 욕설
panegyric 칭찬, 찬사
hideous 끔찍한, 무시무시한
daunt 기죽게 하다, ~을 위협하다
say 말하다
rail 욕하다
fellow 같은 처지에 있는

03 정답 ②

정답해설

밑줄 친 단어는 문맥상 '강화시키다'로 사용되었고 유의어로는 ② intensify가 적절하다.

해석

술은 자살행위의 구성 요소다. 술은 탈억제로 이끌고(일시적으로 억제력을 잃게 만들고) 절망과 의기소침한 감정을 **강화시킨다**.
① 줄이다, 느슨하게 되다
② ~을 강하게 하다, ~을 증대하다
③ 채워 넣다, 수용할 수 있다
④ 발굴하다, 폭로하다, ~을 발견하다

어휘

component 구성 요소
disinhibition 탈억제
intensify ~을 강하게 하다, ~을 증대하다
stow 채워 넣다, 수용할 수 있다
unearth 발굴하다, 폭로하다, ~을 발견하다
suicidal 자살의
slacken 줄이다, 느슨하게 되다

04 정답 ③

정답해설

A와 B의 대화 속에서 A가 지난 월요일 일정을 묻고 있다. 이에 B가 "뮤지컬을 보았다"라는 대답에 A가 "뮤지컬 배우가 누구였냐?"라는 질문을 한다. 그 질문에 대한 답으로 B가 '지금 기억할 수가 없어'라고 답하고 있으므로 빈칸에는 "기억이 나려고 하는 찰나에 잊어버렸다"라고 답하는 문맥의 "I forgot on the tip of my tongue"가 가장 적절하다.

오답해설

① "you are a big mouth(너는 수다스러운 사람이야)."의 의미는 문맥상 어색하다.
② "it was a slip of the tongue(그건 말실수였어)."는 문맥상 빈칸에 적절하지 않다.
④ "you took the words out of a person's mouth(상대방이 의도한 말보다 먼저 말한다)."의 의미는 문맥상 부자연스럽다.

해석

A: 지난주 월요일에 뭐했어?
B: 가족들과 뮤지컬 보러 갔어. 진짜 좋은 시간 보냈어.
A: 난 최근에 뮤지컬 본 적이 없는데 부럽다. 뮤지컬 제목이 뭐였어?
B: '맘마미아'야. 무대 위 배우들 목소리를 듣고 감명받았어. 끝에는 거의 울었는걸.
A: 우와 주연 배우들이 누구였어?
B: 오, 말하려던 찰나에 잊어버렸어. 지금 기억할 수가 없어.
① 너는 수다스러운 사람이야.
② 그건 말실수였어.
③ 말하려던 찰나에 잊어버렸어.
④ 너는 내가 의도한 말을 먼저 말했어.

어휘

impress 감명을 주다
starring 주연의

05 정답 ①

정답해설

① **출제 포인트: 주어와 동사 수일치**
동명사(구)가 주어인 경우 단수로 취급하며 동사에 단수형태를 사용한다. 해당 문장은 주어가 동명사(구) 'Communicating the vision to organization members'이나 동사에 복수형태 'mean'을 사용하였으므로 틀린 문장이다. 따라서 'mean'을 단수형태인 'means'로 수정해야 한다.

오답해설

② 출제 포인트: 등위접속사의 병렬구조
동사 'mean'의 목적어로 동명사(구) 'putting ~', 'distributing ~', 'having ~'이 등위접속사 'and'를 사용하여 'A, B, and C'의 병렬구조를 이루고 있다.

③ 출제 포인트: 원급 비교
'as+원급+as possible'은 원급 비교에 해당하며 이때 원급 자리에 '원급 형용사+명사'의 형태를 사용할 수 있다.

④ 출제 포인트: 현재분사 vs. 과거분사
'inspired'는 완전타동사 'inspire'의 과거분사형태로 해석상 '고무되는'이 자연스러우며, 뒤에 전명구가 왔으므로 옳게 사용되었다.

해석

비전을 조직의 구성원들에게 전달하는 것은 거의 항상 '우리가 가는 곳과 이유'를 적어 두고, 그 진술을 조직 전체에 퍼뜨리고, 임원들로 하여금 가능한 한 많은 사람들에게 비전과 그것의 정당성을 개인적으로 설명하게 하는 것을 의미한다. 이상적으로는, 사람들의 관심에 도달해 그것을 붙잡는 방식으로 임원들이 회사를 위해 그들의 비전을 제시해야만 한다. 사람의 마음을 끌고 설득력 있는 전략적 비전은 엄청난 동기부여의 가치를 지니는데, 석공이 후세에 길이 남을 훌륭한 대성당을 건설하는 데에 고무되는 것과 동일한 이유로 그러하다.

어휘

communicate A to B A를 B에게 전달하다
organization 조직, 단체, 기구   organizationwide 조직 전체에
executive 간부, 임원   attention 관심, 주의, 주목
cathedral 대성당

오답률 TOP 1
06 정답 ③

정답해설

③ 출제 포인트: 전치사+명사(구)/자동사 differ
전치사 뒤에는 명사(구)가 와야 한다. 해당 문장은 전치사 'in'과 'by' 뒤에 동명사 'talking'과 'discussing'을 사용하였으므로 옳은 문장이다. 또한 'on which'는 '전치사+관계대명사'의 형태로 'which'의 선행사는 'the things'임에 유의해야 한다. 또한 해당 문장에서 differ는 자동사로 쓰였다. '~와 다르다'의 의미로 'differ from'을 사용하고 '~에 생각이 다르다, 의견이 맞지 않다'의 의미로는 'differ on/over/about'을 사용하므로 주의한다.

오답해설

① 출제 포인트: one of 목적어[복수형태]
'one of 목적어'에서 목적어에 복수 형태를 사용해야 한다. 해당 문장은 'one of 목적어'가 쓰인 문장으로 목적어에 단수형태 'part'를 사용하였으므로 틀린 문장이다. 따라서 'part'를 복수 형태인 'parts'로 수정해야 한다.

② 출제 포인트: lest+주어+(should)+동사원형/이중부정 주의
접속사 'lest'가 '~하면 안 되므로, ~하지 않도록'을 뜻하는 경우 뒤따라오는 절은 '(should)+동사원형'의 형태를 가지며 부정부사 'not' 또는 'never'를 사용하지 않는다. 해당 문장은 해석상 '~하지 않도록'이 자연스러우므로 'lest' 뒤에 오는 절에 '(should)+동사원형'을 사용하였으나, 부정부사 'not'을 사용하였으므로 틀린 문장이다. 따라서 'not'을 삭제해야 한다.

④ 출제 포인트: 주격 보어(to부정사/동명사)
해당 문장을 수동태로 볼 경우 목적어 'them'이 남아있으므로 틀린 문장이 된다. 따라서 해당 문장은 능동태로 보아야 하며 해석상 '환경적 문제들을 다루는 가장 좋은 방법은 애초에 그것들이 발생하는 것으로부터 예방하는 것이다'가 자연스러우므로 과거분사 'prevented'를 to부정사 'to prevent' 또는 동명사 'preventing'으로 수정해야 한다.

해석

① 당신의 아기의 울음소리를 듣는 것은 부모가 되는 것의 가장 힘든 부분 중 하나이다.
② 그녀는 아무도 방해하지 않도록 헤드폰을 쓰면서, 자신의 집에서 종일 보낸다.
③ 다른 사람들과 이야기할 때, 당신의 의견이 다르다는 것들을 논의함으로써 시작하지 말라.
④ 환경적 문제들을 다루는 가장 좋은 방법은 애초에 그것이 발생하지 않도록 예방하는 것이다.

07 정답 ②

정답해설

② 출제 포인트: 동명사 관용표현
'be busy -ing'는 동명사 관용표현으로 '~하느라 바쁘다'를 뜻한다. 해당 문장은 'be busily -ing'의 형태가 쓰인 문장으로 '바쁘게 ~하는 중이다'로 해석되나 주어진 해석이 '~하느라 바쁘다'이므로 틀린 문장이다. 따라서 'busily'를 'busy'로 수정해야 한다.

오답해설

① 출제 포인트: 자동사로 착각하기 쉬운 완전타동사
'marry'는 완전타동사로 전치사 없이 목적어를 가진다. 해당 문장은 동사원형 'marry'와 목적어 'all' 사이에 전치사가 없으므로 옳은 문장이다. 또한, 'marry A to B'는 'A를 B와 결혼시키다'의 의미로도 사용되므로 주의해야 한다.

③ 출제 포인트: to부정사의 형용사적 용법
to부정사(구) 'to make art'는 명사(구) 'an individual'을 수식하므로 to부정사의 형용사적 용법에 해당한다. 또한 보어가 아닌 수식어로 사용되었으므로 한정적 용법에 해당한다.

④ 출제 포인트: 부사절을 이끄는 접속사
'in case (that)'과 'in case of'를 혼동하지 않도록 유의해야 한다. 둘 다 '~할 경우에'를 뜻하지만 'in case (that)'은 부사절을 이끄는 접속사로 뒤에 절이 오며 'in case of'는 구전치사로 뒤에 명사(구)가 온다.

오답률 TOP 3
08 정답 ②

정답해설

해당 지문은 '경제 모델(economic model)'의 목적을 설명하는 글로, '경제 모델은 두 가지 목적으로 사용되는데, 첫째는 시뮬레이션(simulating), 둘째는 예측(forecasting)이다'라고 설명하고 있다. 빈칸 이전에서 경제 모델이 시뮬레이션을 위해 사용되는 예시를 설명하고, 빈칸에서는 이와 비교해 예측을 위해 사용될 때 경제 모델의 효과에 대해 설명하고 있다. 마지막 문장 "The further out the forecast, the larger the structural uncertainties, making model projections at best illustrative, ~(예측이 더 먼 미래에 대한 것일수록 구조적인 불확실성이 더 커지고, 모델의 예측을 기껏해야 설명적인 것으로 만들게 되는데~)"를 통해 경제 모델을 이용해 예측을 할 때는 불확실성이 동반된다는 것을 알 수 있다. 따라서 경제 모델은 시뮬레이션을 할 때보다 예측을 할 때 상대적으로 덜 효과적이라는 것을 유추할 수 있으므로, 빈칸에 가장 적절한 것은 '② less effective(덜 효과적인)'이다.

오답해설

③ '더 실용적인(more practical)'은 본문의 내용과 반대되는 표현이므로 오답이다.
나머지 보기는 문맥상 어색하므로 오답이다.

해석

경제 모델은 두 가지 주요 목적, 즉 시뮬레이션과 예측을 위해 사용된다. 그것들은 시뮬레이션을 위한 훌륭한 도구이다. 경제의 행동적인 작용에 대해 우리가 아는 것들을 고려해 볼 때, 그리고 이러한 것들을 대부분 기정사실이라고 생각할 때, 이를테면, 에너지 가격 급등에 경제가 어떻게 반응할 것인가? 그러나 모델은 정확하게 예측을 제공하는 것에 있어서 훨씬 덜 효과적인데, 특히 예측을 할 때, 기정사실로 생각할 수 있는 것들이 거의 없기 때문이다. 예측이 더 먼 미래에 대한 것일수록 구조적인 불확실성이 더 커지고, 모델의 예측을 기껏해야 설명적인 것으로 만들게 되는데, 이는 특히 기후 변화의 영향 또는 전 세계 에너지 시스템의 변화와 같은 거대한 충격의 영향을 예측하려고 시도할 때 그러하다.

① 덜 모호한
② 덜 효과적인
③ 더 실용적인
④ 덜 이론적인

어휘

simulate 시뮬레이션하다, 모의 실험하다
forecast 예측하다; 예측
behavioral 행동의, 행동에 관한
take ~ as given ~을 기정사실로 하다
respond to ~에 반응하다
effective 효과적인
not least 특히
uncertainty 불확실성
at best 기껏해야
marginal 미미한, 중요하지 않은, 주변부의
impulse 충격
vague 모호한, 애매한
given ~을 고려하면
working 작용
spike 급등, 급증
precisely 정확하게
structural 구조적인
projection 예상, 추정
illustrative 설명적인, 예증하는
transformation 변형, 변화
theoretical 이론적인

09 정답 ③

정답해설

해당 지문은 '고대 이집트의 의술'에 대해 설명하는 글이다. '고대 이집트에서는 질병은 신 또는 악령에 의해 발생한다고 믿었으며, 마술과 종교의 영향을 크게 받아 치료 절차에 마술사, 승려들이 참여하는 경우가 많았으며 치료약의 재료 선택 또한 마술의 영향을 받았다'라고 언급하고 있다. 본문 중반 "Physicians themselves often used incantations and magical ingredients as part of their treatments(때로는 의사들 스스로 그들의 치료의 일부로 주술 또는 마술적인 재료를 이용했다)."를 통해 마술사가 아닌 의사들도 주술과 마술 재료를 사용하여 치료를 실시하였다는 것을 언급하고 있으므로, '③ It was not allowed for non-magicians to perform magic during treatments(비마술사가 치료 중 마술을 행하는 것은 허용되지 않았다).'는 글의 내용과 일치하지 않는다.

오답해설

① "Gods and demons were thought to be responsible for many ailments(신과 악령은 많은 질병의 원인이라 생각되었고)"를 통해, '신 또는 악령과 같은 초현실적인 존재(supernatural beings)에게 질병의 원인이 있었다고 믿었음'을 알 수 있으므로, 글의 내용과 일치한다.
② "Often priests and magicians were called on to treat disease instead of, or in addition to a physician(의사 대신 또는 의사와 동반하여 승려와 마술사들에게 질병을 치료할 것이 종종 요청되었다)."을 통해 '의사를 대신해 승려가 질병 치료를 요청받았음을 알 수 있으므로, 글의 내용과 일치한다.
④ "The impact of the emphasis on magic is seen in the selection of remedies, or the ingredients for those remedies(마술을 강조하는 것의 영향은 치료약 또는 그러한 치료약의 재료를 선택하는 것에서 엿보인다)."를 통해 마술이 치료약 또는 치료약 재료 선택에 영향을 주었음을 알 수 있다.

해석

마술과 종교는 고대 이집트의 일상생활의 일부였다. 신과 악령은 많은 질병의 원인이라 생각되었고, 따라서 치료는 종종 초자연적인 요소를 포함했다. 의사 대신 또는 의사와 동반하여 승려와 마술사들에게 질병을 치료할 것이 종종 요청되었다. 때로는 의사들 스스로 그들의 치료의 일부로 주술 또는 마술적인 재료를 이용했다. 마술을 강조하는 것의 영향은 치료약 또는 그러한 치료약의 재료를 선택하는 것에서 엿보인다. 때때로 재료는 그것들이 환자의 증상과 어떤 점에서 일치하는 특징을 가진 물질, 식물 또는 동물로부터 나온 것이기 때문에 선택된 것으로 보인다. 예를 들어, 타조알은 금이 간 두개골 치료에 포함되었고, 고슴도치가 그려진 부적은 탈모를 치료하는 데 쓰였다.

① 고대 이집트인들은 질병이 초자연적인 존재 때문에 발생한다고 생각했다.
② 경우에 따라서 승려들은 치료 과정을 주도하도록 요청받았다.
③ 비 마술사가 치료 중 마술을 행하는 것은 허용되지 않았다.
④ 마술은 치료약 재료 선택에 크게 영향을 미쳤다.

어휘

ailment (그렇게 심각하지 않은) 질병
supernatural 초자연적인
priest 승려, 사제
physician (내과) 의사
ingredient 재료
remedy 치료(약)
derive 끌어내다, 얻다
in some way 어떤 점에서는
correspond to …에[와] 일치하다, 들어맞다
symptom 증상
amulet 부적
hedgehog 고슴도치
due to … 때문에
process 절차, 과정
involve 포함하다, 수반하다
element 요소
call on 요청하다, 요구하다
incantation 주문, 마법
emphasis 강조
seemingly 외견상으로, 겉보기에는
substance 물질
ostrich 타조
portray 그리다, 묘사하다
baldness 대머리, 탈모
being 존재
perform 행하다

10 정답 ③

정답해설

해당 지문은 '스마트폰과 소셜미디어의 등장으로 인한 저널리즘계의 변화'를 설명하는 글이다. 본문에서 '스마트폰과 소셜미디어 이용이 뉴스의 소비 행태 및 뉴스 생성 주체를 변화시켰고, 일반 시민도 뉴스 콘텐츠 개발에 참여할 수 있게 됨에 따라 진정한 저널리스트에 관한 의문이 등장하기 시작했다'라고 언급한다. '그러나 이미 저널리즘과 소셜미디어는 떼려야 뗄 수 없는 관계가 되었고, 저널리스트들은 소셜미디어 활동에 적극적으로 참여해야 한다'는 것이 글의 전체 내용이다. 본문 중반 "For some, this can create a problem. Who is a journalist? What defines a "journalist?" Social media is raising these questions and it is creating problems for jobs in the media(일부 사람들에게 이것은 문제를 야기할 수 있다. 누가 저널리스트인가? "저널리스트"를 정의하는 것은 무엇인가? 소셜미디어는 이러한 의문을 증가시키고, 미디어계 직종에 문제를 일으키고 있다)."를 통해 소셜미디어로 인해 발생한 문제, 즉 부정적 영향을 언급하고 있다. 따라서, '③ Social media has had positive effects only on the field of journalism(소셜미디어는 저널리즘 분야에 긍정적인 영향만을 미쳤다).'은 글의 내용과 일치하지 않는다.

오답해설

① "Consumers today receive news articles on their smart phones. Citizens now play a drastic role in journalism, and the usage of smart phones and social media allows citizens to partake in the news making process(오늘날의 소비자들은 스마트폰으로 뉴스 기사를 받아 본다. 이제 시민들은 저널리즘 분야에서 과감한 역할을 수행하고 있고 스마트폰과 소셜미디어 사용은 시민들이 뉴스 생산 과정에 참여할 수 있도록 한다)."를 통해 글의 내용과 일치하는 것을 알 수 있다.

② "Platforms such as Twitter, YouTube and WordPress allow ordinary citizens to produce their own news content and share it with larger news sources such as CNN(Twitter, YouTube, WordPress와 같은 플랫폼들은 평범한 시민들이 그들 자신의 뉴스 콘텐츠를 생산하고 CNN과 같은 거대한 뉴스 공급자와 그것을 공유할 수 있게 한다)."을 통해 '일반 시민이 만든 뉴스 콘텐츠를 CNN과 같은 거대 뉴스 기업과 공유한다'고 언급하고 있으므로, 글의 내용과 일치하는 것을 알 수 있다.

④ "Social media, however, is now a required skill and tool for all journalists to use and gain expertise in(그러나 소셜미디어는 이제 모든 저널리스트들이 사용하고 전문적 식견을 쌓아야 하는 필수 기술이며 도구이다)."을 통해 '모든 저널리스트들이 소셜미디어에 전문적 식견을 쌓아야 한다'고 언급하고 있으므로, 글의 내용과 일치한다.

해석

오늘날의 소비자들은 스마트폰으로 뉴스 기사를 받아 본다. 이제 시민들은 저널리즘 분야에서 과감한 역할을 수행하고 있고 스마트폰과 소셜미디어 사용은 시민들이 뉴스 생산 과정에 참여할 수 있도록 한다. Twitter, YouTube, WordPress와 같은 플랫폼들은 평범한 시민들이 그들 자신의 뉴스 콘텐츠를 생산하고 CNN과 같은 거대한 뉴스 공급자와 그것을 공유할 수 있게 한다. 일부 사람들에게 이것은 문제를 야기할 수 있다. 누가 저널리스트인가? "저널리스트"를 정의하는 것은 무엇인가? 소셜미디어는 이러한 의문을 증가시키고, 미디어계 직종에 문제를 일으키고 있다. 그러나 소셜미디어는 이제 모든 저널리스트들이 사용하고 전문적 식견을 쌓아야 하는 필수 기술이며 도구이다. 언론사와 방송국은 저널리스트들과 미래의 직원들이 소셜미디어에 정통하고, 온라인에서 힘 있는 인플루언서가 되는 것을 보길 원한다.
① 스마트폰의 등장은 뉴스가 생성되고 소비되는 방식을 변화시켰다.
② 대형 언론사는 때때로 소셜미디어 이용자가 만든 뉴스 콘텐츠를 이용한다.
③ 소셜미디어는 저널리즘 분야에 긍정적인 영향만을 미쳐왔다.
④ 오늘날의 저널리스트들은 소셜미디어를 이용할 수밖에 없다.

어휘

drastic 과감한, 강렬한
process 과정, 절차
source 공급자, 근원
required 필수의
gain expertise (in) 전문적 식견을 쌓다
prospective 장래의, 미래의
influencer 인플루언서(많은 SNS 팔로워를 보유한 유명인)
emergence 등장, 출현
positive 긍정적인
have no choice but to ~할 수밖에 없다
be engaged in …에 몰두하다, 종사하다
partake 참여하다
ordinary 평범한, 보통의
define 정의하다
savvy 소식에 밝은, (사정에) 정통해 있는
consume 소비하다

결국엔 성정혜 영어 하프모의고사
기적사 DAY 24

| 01 | ③ | 02 | ② | 03 | ④ | 04 | ③ | 05 | ① |
| 06 | ④ | 07 | ③ | 08 | ③ | 09 | ② | 10 | ④ |

01 정답 ③

정답해설

밑줄 친 단어는 문맥상 '축하하다'로 사용되었고, 유의어로는 ③ commemorate 가 적절하다.

해석

나의 미용실에서 오랜 고객인 Minnie는 그녀의 100번째 생일을 막 **축하하려던** 참이었고 100주년에 도달했을 때 나는 그녀에게 찬사(무료)의 머리 서비스를 약속했다.
① 마음을 사로잡다
② ~을 식별하다, 차이를 만들다, ~을 분화시키다
③ 축하하다, 기념하다
④ 그만두다, 포기하다, 중단되다

어휘

complimentary 찬사의, 무료의   captivate 마음을 사로잡다
differentiate ~을 식별하다, 차이를 만들다, ~을 분화시키다
commemorate 축하하다, 기념하다
discontinue 그만두다, 포기하다, 중단되다

02 정답 ②

정답해설

밑줄 친 단어는 '공포스러운, 무서운'으로 사용되었고, 유의어로는 ② frightening 이 적절하다.

해석

그 영화 대단했어. 특히 **공포스러운** 부분이 좋더라.
① 독창적인
② 무서운
③ 화려한, 훌륭한
④ 능률적인

어휘

ingenious 독창적인   frightening 무서운
splendid 화려한, 훌륭한   efficient 능률적인

03 정답 ④

정답해설

밑줄 친 단어의 의미는 '무관심한'으로 사용되었고, 유의어로는 ④ indifferent 가 적절하다.

해석

이 **무관심한** 세상에서 학생이 성공할 수 있는 첫 번째 조건은 그가 근면해야 한다는 것이다.
① 산발적인
② 완전한, 순수한, 확고한

③ 상호 간의, 보답의
④ 무관심한, 공평한

어휘

sedulous 근면한, 부지런한
sporadic 산발적인
absolute 완전한, 순수한, 확고한
reciprocal 상호 간의, 보답의
indifferent 무관심한, 공평한

04 정답 ③

정답해설

A와 B의 대화는 둘이 함께 식사를 하려는 상황이다. 첫 번째 빈칸의 경우, 대화 속에서 B가 A에게 "don't look as you'll eat much (많이 먹을 것처럼 보이진 않아)"라는 표현을 통해서 '적게 먹을 것'을 예상할 수 있다. 따라서 빈칸에 들어갈 표현은 'eat like a bird'가 적절하다. 두 번째 빈칸의 경우, "eat way too much (너무 많이 먹다)"를 통해서 '많이 먹는 것'을 유추할 수 있다. 따라서 빈칸에는 'eat like a horse (정말 많이 먹다)'가 적절하다.

오답해설

① 'eat like a cat (고양이처럼 먹는다)'은 관용표현으로써 존재하지 않는다. 또한, 'eat like a bird'가 두 번째 빈칸에 오게 되면 문맥을 해친다.
② 'eat like a dog (개처럼 먹는다)'는 문맥상 적절하지 않다.
④ 첫 번째 빈칸과 두 번째 빈칸이 바뀌어서 반대 표현이 되므로 부적절하다.

해석

A: 너 어디가?
B: 뭐 좀 먹으려고 구내식당에 가는 중이야. 점심 먹었어?
A: 응. 근데 배고프니까 너랑 같이 먹어도 될까?
B: 그럼, 같이 먹을 사람이 있다면 나야 좋지. 너 많이 안 먹게 생겼는데. 너 정말 (A) 조금 먹을 것 같다고 생각했어.
A: 오, 전혀 아니야. 나 요새 정말 (B) 많이 먹어. 지나칠 정도로 많이 먹어.
B: 정말? 근데 너 하나도 살 안 쪘어.
① 고양이 - 새
② 개 - 말
③ 새 - 말
④ 말 - 새

어휘

head to~ ~로 향하다, ~로 가다
be headed to ~로 향하다(상태에 초점)
be heading to ~로 향하다(진행에 초점)
cafeteria (기업, 학교의) 구내식당
have company 일행이 있다
gain weight 살이 찌다

05 정답 ①

정답해설

① **출제 포인트: 현재분사 vs. 과거분사**
'waging'은 'wage'의 현재분사형태로 수식하는 대상은 명사(구) 'non-agricultural employment'이다. 그러나 해석상 '임금을 주는 비 농업직'보다 '임금을 받는 비 농업직'이 자연스러우므로 'waging'을 과거분사 'waged'로 수정해야 한다.

오답해설

② **출제 포인트: 원급 비교**
'as+원급+as'는 원급 비교에 해당하며 이때 원급에는 형용사와 부사 외에 과거분사를 사용할 수 있다. 해당 문장은 원급 자리에 형용사 'high'를 사용하였다.

③ **출제 포인트: 주어와 동사 수일치**
주어가 단수형태인 'the percentage'이므로 동사에 단수형태인 'was'를 사용하였다.

④ **출제 포인트: 비교 대상 일치**
비교급이 쓰인 문장으로 해당 문장에서 'that'은 'the increase'를 가리키는 대명사이다.

해석

2006년에 동아시아와 태평양 연안 국가들에서 임금을 받는 비 농업직에 고용된 여성의 비율은 남아시아의 비율보다 두 배 높았다. 같은 해에 중동과 북아프리카에서 임금을 받는 비 농업직에 고용된 여성의 비율은 사하라 이남의 아프리카 지역 비율보다 10퍼센트 포인트 낮았다. 1990년과 2006년 사이에 사하라 이남의 아프리카 지역에서 임금을 받는 비 농업직에 고용된 여성의 비율 증가는 중동과 북아프리카의 비율 증가보다 더 컸다.

어휘

non-agricultural employment 비 농업직
Pacific 태평양의
percentage 비율

오답률 TOP 2

06 정답 ④

정답해설

④ **출제 포인트: 주격 보어(to부정사/동명사)**
to부정사(구) 'to avoid a disagreement and support the friend'를 주격보어로 사용하였으며 해석상 '긍정적인 말의 목적은 불일치를 피하고 친구를 지지하는 것일 수도 있다'가 자연스러우므로 옳은 문장이다.

오답해설

① **출제 포인트: lest + 주어 + (should) + 동사원형**
접속사 'lest'가 '~하면 안 되므로, ~하지 않도록'을 뜻하는 경우 뒤따라오는 절은 '(should)+동사원형'의 형태를 가지며 부정부사 'not' 또는 'never'를 사용하지 않는다. 해당 문장은 해석상 '~하지 않도록'이 자연스러우므로 'lest' 뒤에 오는 절에 '(should)+동사원형'을 사용해야 한다. 따라서 'is'를 'be'로 수정해야 한다.

② **출제 포인트: one of 목적어[복수형태]**
'one of 목적어'에서 목적어에 복수형태를 사용해야 한다. 해당 문장은 'one of 목적어'가 쓰인 문장으로 목적어에 단수형태 'strength'를 사용하였으므로 틀린 문장이다. 따라서 'strength'를 복수형태인 'strengths'로 수정해야 한다. 'strength'가 '강점'을 뜻하는 경우 가산명사로도 사용이 가능하다.

③ **출제 포인트: 전치사 + 명사(구)**
전치사 뒤에는 명사(구)가 와야 한다. 해당 문장은 전치사 'at' 뒤에 명사 'address'를 사용하였으나 뒤에 목적어 'the problem'이 있으므로 틀린 문장이다. 해석상 '문제를 다루는 데 있어'가 자연스러우므로 'address'를 동명사 'addressing'으로 수정해야 한다.

해석

① 이것에 관해서 보호가 너무 제한되지 않도록 오해를 피하는 것이 필요하다.
② 미국 흑인 사회의 많은 강점들 중 하나는 본질적인 지지이다.
③ 일부 국가들과 일부 지역들은 문제를 다루는 데 있어 다른 나라들보다 더 유능하다.
④ 긍정적인 말의 목적은 불일치를 피하고 친구를 지지하는 것일 수도 있다.

07 정답 ③

정답해설

③ 출제 포인트: 부사절을 이끄는 접속사
'in case (that)'과 'in case of'를 혼동하지 않도록 유의해야 한다. 둘 다 '~할 경우에'를 뜻하지만 'in case (that)'은 부사절을 이끄는 접속사로 뒤에 절이 오며 'in case of'는 구전치사로 뒤에 명사(구)가 온다. 해당 문장은 in case of 뒤에 절 'the storm made it difficult to shop'이 왔으므로 틀린 문장이다. 따라서 'of'를 'that'으로 수정하거나 'of'를 삭제해야 한다.

오답해설

① 출제 포인트: to부정사의 형용사적 용법
to부정사(구) 'to plan out what they want to say'는 명사(구) 'the time'을 수식하므로 to부정사의 형용사적 용법에 해당한다. 또한 보어가 아닌 수식어로 사용되었으므로 한정적 용법에 해당한다.

② 출제 포인트: 자동사로 착각하기 쉬운 완전타동사
'marry'는 완전타동사로 전치사 없이 목적어를 가진다. 해당 문장은 동사원형 'marry'와 목적어 'him' 사이에 전치사가 없으므로 옳은 문장이다.

④ 출제 포인트: 동명사 관용표현
'be busy –ing'는 동명사 관용표현으로 '~하느라 바쁘다'를 뜻한다.

오답률 TOP 1

08 정답 ③

정답해설

해당 지문은 '대공황 당시 경제 이론의 변화'에 대한 설명으로, '기존의 자유시장(free market)경제이론은 대공황의 원인을 설명할 수 없었고 적절한 대안을 제시하지도 못했다'라고 언급하고 있으며, 그에 따라 자유시장경제이론을 반박하는 Keynes의 이론이 등장했다'고 설명한다. 본문 중반의 "everyone who wanted a job would have one as long as workers were flexible in their wage demands(노동자들이 임금 요구에서 융통성이 있는 한 일자리를 원하는 모든 사람들은 일자리를 가질 것이다)."라고 주장하는 자유시장경제이론과 달리 경제는 스스로 회복하지 못하고 대공황으로 접어들었고, 자유시장경제이론은 공황의 원인을 규명하지 못했다고 언급하고 있으므로, '③ According to the free market economy theory, the depression was due to low employment(자유시장경제이론에 따르면 공황은 낮은 고용률 때문이었다).'은 글의 내용과 일치하지 않는다.

오답해설

① 첫 문장 "During the Great Depression of the 1930s(1930년대 대공황 당시)"을 통해 '1930년대 세계적인 불황이 있었음'을 알 수 있다.

② 두 번째 문장 "British economist John Maynard Keynes spearheaded a revolution in economic thinking that overturned the then-prevailing idea that free markets would automatically provide full employment(영국 경제학자 John Maynard Keynes는 자유시장이 자동적으로 완전 고용을 이룰 것이라는 그 당시 지배적이던 관념을 뒤집는 경제사상의 혁명의 선봉에 서 있었다)"을 통해 '당시에는 자유시장경제이론이 지배적이었음'을 알 수 있다.

④ 본문의 후반부의 "He asserted that free markets have no self-balancing mechanisms that lead to full employment(그는 자유시장은 완전 고용으로 이끄는 자기 균형 메커니즘을 가지고 있지 않다고 주장했다)."를 통해 'Keynes가 자유시장경제이론을 부정했음'을 알 수 있다.

해석

1930년대 대공황 당시 기존의 경제 이론은 극심한 전 세계적 경제 붕괴의 원인을 설명하거나, 생산과 고용을 활성화시킬 알맞은 공공 정책 해결책을 제공할 수 없었다. 영국 경제학자 John Maynard Keynes는 자유시장이 자동적으로 완전 고용을 이룰 것이라는, 즉, 노동자들이 임금 요구에서 융통성이 있는 한 일자리를 원하는 모든 사람들은 일자리를 가질 것이라는 그 당시 지배적이던 관념을 뒤집는 경제사상의 혁명의 선봉에 서 있었다. 그는 자유시장은 완전 고용으로 이끄는 자기 균형 메커니즘을 가지고 있지 않다고 주장했다. 그리고 Keynes에 의해 발전된 경제 이론을 따르는 Keynes 학파 경제학자들은 완전 고용과 물가 안정을 달성을 목표로 하는 공공 정책을 통한 정부 개입을 정당화한다.

① 1930년대 세계적인 불황이 있었다.
② 대공황이 발생할 때까지 자유시장경제가 우세한 경제 이론이었다.
③ 자유시장경제이론에 따르면 공황은 낮은 고용률 때문이었다.
④ Keynes는 자유시장경제이론을 부정했다.

어휘

existing 기존의
either A or B A 또는 B 둘 중 하나
explain 설명하다
severe 극심한, 심한
adequate 알맞은, 충분한
spearhead 선봉에 서다
overturn 뒤집다
as long as ~하는 한
demand 요구
lead to ~로 이어지다
intervention 개입
stability 안정
up until …까지
predominating 우세한, 주된, 지배적인
deny 부정하다, 거부하다
unable ~할 수 없는
cause 원인
collapse 붕괴, 무너짐
jump-start 활성화하다, 재생시키다
revolution 혁명
prevailing 우세한, 지배적인
flexible 융통성 있는
assert 주장하다, 단언하다
justify 정당화하다
achieve 달성하다, 도달하다
recession 불황, 침체

오답률 TOP 3

09 정답 ②

정답해설

해당 지문은 '약초학(herbal medicine)의 역사'에 대해 서술하고 있으며, '약초학은 의학의 역사상 가장 초기에 발달했고 현재까지도 시행되고 있다'라는 것이 본문의 주요 내용이다. 빈칸 이후 "The snakeroot plant was traditionally used as a tonic in the east to calm patients; it is now used in orthodox medical practice to reduce blood pressure(snakeroot 식물은 동양에서 전통적으로 환자를 진정시키기 위한 음료로 사용되었다. 현재 그것은 전통 의학에서 혈압을 낮추기 위해 사용된다)."와 "Doctors in ancient India gave an extract of foxglove to patients with legs swollen by dropsy; digitalis, a constituent of foxglove, is now a standard stimulant for the heart(고대 인도에서 의사들은 부종으로 인해 다리가 부은 환자들에게 foxglove 추출물을 주었다; 현재 foxglove의 성분인 digitalis는 심장을 위한 일반적인 각성제이다)."를 통해 과거에도 사용되었던 약초가 현재에도 의학에서 사용되고 있다는 점을 예시로 제시하고 있으므로, 빈칸에 가장 적절한 표현은 '② it remains an important part of medicine to this day(오늘날까지 의학의 중요한 부분을 차지하고 있다)'이다.

오답해설

① 요리용 약초에 대한 내용이 아니므로 오답이다.
③ 본문과 관련 없는 내용이므로 오답이다.
④ 서양에서의 약초 사용에 대해 강조하는 내용이 아니며, 또한 빈칸 이후에는 주로 동양에서 사용된 약초의 예시가 제시되고 있으므로 빈칸에 적절하지 않다.

해석

어떤 식물이 식용 가능한지 알아보는 긴 과정 중에, 석기시대 인간은 병을 치료하거나 열을 내리는 것처럼 보이는 많은 식물도 또한 식별했다. 초기 의사들은 그것들이 작용하는 방식을 이해하지 못한 채 실제 효익이 있는 약초를 우연히 발견했다. 그럼에도 불구하고 약초학은 의료 행위에 있어서 가장 초기의 과학적 전통이며, 오늘날까지 의학의 중요한 부분을 차지하고 있다. snakeroot 식물은 동양에서 전통적으로 환자를 진정시키기 위한 음료로 사용되었다; 현재 그것은 전통 의학에서 혈압을 낮추기 위해 사용된다. 고대 인도에서 의사들은 부종으로 인해 다리가 부은 환자들에게 foxglove 추출물을 주었다; 현재 foxglove의 성분인 digitalis는 심장을 위한 일반적인 각성제이다.
① 다양한 약초들은 현재 요리용으로 사용된다
② 오늘날까지 의학의 중요한 부분을 차지하고 있다
③ 약효가 있는 식물들을 재배하는 것이 오늘날 매우 인기 있다
④ 서양의 수많은 의사들 또한 약초학을 실행하고 있다

어휘

process 과정, 절차	edible 먹을 수 있는
identify 확인하다, 식별하다	ailment (그렇게 심각하지 않은) 질병
soothe 진정시키다	physician (내과) 의사
stumble on 우연히 발견하다	substance 물질
tonic 강장제[음료], 보약	orthodox medicine 전통 의학
extract 추출물	dropsy 수종, 부종
constituent 구성 성분[요소]	standard 일반적인, 보통의
stimulant 각성제, 흥분제	various 다양한
culinary 요리의	purpose 목적
practice 실행하다, 실천하다	as well 또한, 역시

10 정답 ④

정답해설

주어진 문장은 '블로거들이 자신들의 예측이 정확한 것처럼 보이기 위해 과거 게시글을 조작하기도 한다는 점을 인정했다'라는 내용이므로, 주어진 문장 이전에는 '진실 추구'에 대한 블로거들의 가벼운 태도에 대해 언급하는 내용이 등장하는 것이 자연스럽다. ④ 이전 문장에서 "Many reporters worry that without an institutional reputation at stake, bloggers are careless and prone to make false accusations or disseminate false information(많은 기자들은 제도상의 신망이 달려있지 않으면, 블로거들이 부주의하고 거짓 혐의를 제기하거나 거짓 정보를 퍼뜨릴 수도 있다고 우려한다)."라고 '블로거들이 잘못된 정보를 전달할 수도 있다는 것을 전통 기자들이 우려한다'라고 언급한 후, 실제로 블로거들이 진실을 왜곡하는 행위 중 하나인 게시글 조작을 하고 있다는 것이 이어지는 것으로 자연스러우므로, 주어진 글이 들어갈 가장 적합한 위치는 ④이다.

오답해설

나머지 위치는 문맥상 어색하므로 오답이다.

해석

일부 블로거들은 웹상에서 지속적인 존재감을 확립해왔고 많은 일일 독자들을 확보한다. 많은 정치 블로거들은 뉴스 종사자로서의 정당성을 추구했고, 최근 그들은 성공했다. (①) 블로거들은 2004년 대통령 후보 지명 전당대회에서 자격을 얻었고, 2009년 오바마 대통령은 백악관 기자회견에 한 블로거를 초청했다. (②) 전통적인 저널리스트들은 이 분야의 새로운 진입자들을 경계하고 있다. (③) 많은 기자들은 제도상의 신망이 달려있지 않으면, 블로거들이 부주의하고 거짓 혐의를 제기하거나 거짓 정보를 퍼뜨릴 수도 있다고 우려한다. (④ **일부 블로거들은 그들의 이전의 부정확한 예측들이 진실인 것처럼 보이도록 블로그 자료 보관소를 조작한 것을 인정했다.**) 전문 저널리스트들이 진실과 정확함에 대한 블로거들의 격의 없는 태도를 비탄해온 반면, 블로거들은 자신들이 독자들과 블로그 세상의 꾸준한 감시하에 있다는 것을 지적한다.

어휘

admit 인정하다, 시인하다	archive (데이터 등의) 보관(소)
previous 이전의	prediction 예측
establish 확립하다, 설립하다	continuing 지속적인
presence 존재(함), 있음	draw (사람의 마음을) 끌다, 끌어들이다
seek (sought-sought) 추구하다	legitimacy 정당성, 합법성, 타당성
credential 자격을 부여하다	presidential 대통령의
convention (전문직 종사자들이나 정당 등의 대규모) 대회[협의회]	press conference 기자회견
call on 초빙하다, 초청하다	entrant 갓 들어온[합류한] 사람
wary 경계하는, 조심하는	reputation 평판, 명성, 신망
institutional 제도상의, 규격화된	
at stake …에 달려있는, 위기에 처한	
prone to ~을 잘하는, ~하는 경향이 있다	
accusation 혐의 [제기], 고발, 비난	disseminate 퍼뜨리다
deplore 비탄하다	casual 격의 없는, 가벼운
accuracy 정확성	constant 꾸준한, 지속적인
scrutiny 감시	blogosphere 블로그 세상

결국엔 성정혜 영어 하프모의고사
기적사 DAY 25

| 01 | ④ | 02 | ③ | 03 | ① | 04 | ④ | 05 | ④ |
| 06 | ④ | 07 | ① | 08 | ④ | 09 | ② | 10 | ③ |

01 정답 ④

정답해설

밑줄 친 단어의 의미는 문맥상 '좌절'로 사용되었고, 유의어로는 ④ discouragement 가 적절하다.

해석

나는 그의 민감성 때문에 그가 내 목소리에서 **좌절**을 읽을 수 있었을 것이라고 확신한다.
① 부활, 재생, 회복, 신앙 부흥 운동
② 깨달음, 계발, 계몽
③ 업적, 성취
④ 좌절

어휘

sensibility 민감성 revival 부활, 재생, 회복, 신앙 부흥 운동
enlightenment 깨달음, 계발, 계몽 achievement 업적, 성취
discouragement 좌절

오답률 TOP 2

02 정답 ③

정답해설

밑줄 친 단어는 문맥상 '가끔, 때때로, 간헐적으로'로 사용되었고, 유의어로는 ③ intermittent가 적절하다.

해석

우리는 북쪽 하늘에서 **때때로** 섬광을 보았다.
① 부가된, 추가의
② 놀라운
③ 간헐적인, 주기적인
④ 편리한, 실현 가능한

어휘

additional 부가된, 추가의 alarming 놀라운
intermittent 간헐적인, 주기적인 feasible 편리한, 실현 가능한

03 정답 ①

정답해설

밑줄 친 단어는 문맥상 '안정화시키다, 고정시키다'로 사용되었고, 유의어로는 ① sustain이 적절하다.

해석

짧은 다리는 거대한 몸을 **안정화시키도록** 도울지도 모릅니다.
① 지지하다, 유지하다, 견디다
② 포로가 되다, 휩쓸리게 하다, ~을 침몰시키다
③ ~을 강하게 하다, ~을 증대하다
④ 식별하다, 동일시하다

어휘

sustain 지지하다, 유지하다, 견디다
engulf 포로가 되다, 휩쓸리게 하다, ~을 침몰시키다
intensify ~을 강하게 하다, ~을 증대하다
identify 식별하다, 동일시하다

04 정답 ④

정답해설

자선단체에 이번 달 자신의 월급의 절반을 기부했다는 말에 'You paid your debt to nature(너는 죽었네)'라는 대답은 문맥상 적절하지 않다.

오답해설

① 친구에게 저지른 실수를 어떻게 보상할지를 물어보는 질문에 'face the music and apologize(스스로 책임지고 사과하다)'는 대답은 알맞다.
② 자신의 발표가 어땠는지 의견을 묻는 말에 'I'll give you thumbs up(긍정의 표시)'이라는 답변은 발표에 대한 긍정적인 피드백을 주는 상황이므로 적합하다.
③ A가 최근에 쓴 정치적 문제에 관한 기사에 대한 B의 생각에 대해 질문하자, 'hit the nail on the head(못을 정확히 박았다=정수를 치다)'라는 표현은 A가 쓴 기사가 정확했다는 B의 생각을 나타내므로 적절한 답변이다.

해석

① A: 내가 친구에게 저지른 실수를 어떻게 보상해야 할까?
   B: 음, 나는 네가 **스스로 책임지고 사과하는** 것을 추천해.
② A: 내 발표에 대해 어떻게 생각해?
   B: 나는 엄지를 치켜세울게.
③ A: 내가 정치적 문제에 관해 쓴 최근의 기사에 대해 어떻게 생각해?
   B: 나는 네가 못을 정확히 박았다(정수를 쳤다)고 생각해.
④ A: 나는 이번 달에 내 월급의 절반을 자선단체에 기부했어.
   B: 너는 죽었네.

어휘

mistake 실수 suggest 제안하다, 추천하다
apologize 사과하다 political issue 정치적 문제
donate 기부하다, 기증하다 earnings 소득, 수입
charity 자선단체

05 정답 ④

정답해설

④ 출제 포인트: 주어와 동사 수일치
주어가 단수 형태인 'the absence'이므로 동사에 단수 형태를 사용해야 한다. 따라서 'are'를 단수형태인 'is'로 수정해야 한다.

오답해설

① 출제 포인트: 현재분사 vs. 과거분사
'processed'는 완전타동사 'process'의 과거분사형태로 해석상 '처리되는' 이 자연스러우며, 등위접속사 'or'를 통해 과거분사 'managed'와 병렬구조를 이루고 있으므로 옳게 사용되었다.
② 출제 포인트: to 부정사의 부사적 용법
'so as to+동사원형'은 '~하기 위해서'를 뜻하며 이때 'to+동사원형'은 to부정사의 부사적 용법에 해당한다.
③ 출제 포인트: 명사절을 이끄는 접속사 that
해당 문장에서 'that'은 명사절을 이끄는 접속사이며 명사절 'disagreement is wrong and consensus is the desirable state of things'와 결합하여 주격 보어로 사용되었다.

해석
온갖 종류의 이론이 의견 차이를 없애기 위하여 그것이 처리되거나 다뤄질 수 있는 방법들이 있다는 견해를 조장한다. 그런 이론들의 배경에 있는 전제는, 의견 차이는 잘못된 것이고 합의가 바람직한 상황이라는 것이다. 사실, 몇몇 형태의 교묘한 강압이 없이 합의가 이뤄지는 일은 드물며, 이견을 표현할 때 두려움이 없는 것이 진정한 자유의 원천이다.

어휘
promote 조장하다, 홍보하다, 승진시키다
disagreement 의견 차이, 다툼
consensus 의견 일치, 합의   coercion 강압, 강제

06 정답 ④

정답해설
④ 출제 포인트: 주격 보어(to부정사/동명사)
to부정사(구) 'to be perceived as physically competent'를 주격보어로 사용하였으며 해석상 '어린이들이 그들의 또래 사이에서 더 나은 지위를 얻을 수 있는 방법은 신체적으로 능숙한 것으로 여겨지는 것이다'가 자연스러우므로 옳은 문장이다. 또한 'to be perceived as physically competent'는 'to perceive 목적어 as physically competent'를 수동태로 고친 것으로 옳은 표현이다.

오답해설
① 출제 포인트: 전치사 + 명사(구)
전치사 뒤에는 명사(구)가 와야 한다. 해당 문장은 전치사 'by' 뒤에 동사 'cease'를 사용하였으므로 틀린 문장이다. 따라서 'cease'를 동명사 'ceasing'으로 수정해야 한다. 'cease'는 자동사와 타동사로 둘 다 사용 가능하며 격식체에서 명사의 의미로 종지라는 의미로도 사용하므로 'the cease of'로 사용해도 옳다.

② 출제 포인트: one of 목적어[복수형태]
'one of 목적어'에서 목적어에 복수형태를 사용해야 한다. 해당 문장은 'one of 목적어'가 쓰인 문장으로 목적어에 단수형태 'challenge'를 사용하였으므로 틀린 문장이다. 따라서 'challenge'를 복수형태인 'challenges'로 수정해야 한다.

③ 출제 포인트: lest + 주어 + (should) + 동사원형
접속사 'lest'가 '~하면 안 되므로, ~하지 않도록'을 뜻하는 경우 뒤따라오는 절은 '(should)+동사원형'의 형태를 가지며 부정부사 'not' 또는 'never'를 사용하지 않는다. 해당 문장은 lest 뒤에 오는 절에 'does not 동사원형'을 사용하였으나 해석상 '~하지 않도록'이 자연스러우므로 틀린 문장이다. 따라서 'does not count'를 '(should) count'로 수정해야 한다.

해석
① 지역사회는 그곳의 아이들을 교육시키는 것을 중단함으로써 궁극적으로 부유해지지는 않는다.
② 암에 대한 치료법을 발견하는 것은 의학 연구원들과 대면하는 가장 큰 난제들 중 하나이다.
③ 그것이 다음 선거에서 그들에게 불리하게 작용하지 않도록 그들은 자신의 목표를 애매한 상태로 두는 것을 일반적으로 선호한다.
④ 어린이들이 그들의 또래 사이에서 더 나은 지위를 얻을 수 있는 방법은 신체적으로 능숙한 것으로 여겨지는 것이다.

07 정답 ①

정답해설
① 출제 포인트: 자동사로 착각하기 쉬운 완전타동사
'marry'는 완전타동사로 전치사 없이 목적어를 가진다. 해당 문장은 'marry'의 과거형인 'married'와 목적어 'him' 사이에 전치사 'to'를 사용하였으므로 틀린 문장이다. 따라서 'to'를 삭제해야 한다.

오답해설
② 출제 포인트: encourage + 목적어 + 목적격 보어[to부정사(구)]
해당 문장에 쓰인 encourage는 5형식 동사로서 목적격 보어로 to부정사를 가진다. 또한 해당 문장에서는 to vent와 (to) express가 encourage의 목적격 보어로 병렬구조를 이루고 있다.

③ 출제 포인트: 동명사 관용표현
'be busy -ing'는 동명사 관용표현으로 '~하느라 바쁘다'를 뜻한다. 또한 해당 문장에서 'too busy ~ to take ~'는 'too+형용사+to+동사원형'의 형태로 '너무 ~해서 ~할 수 없다'를 뜻한다.

④ 출제 포인트: 부사절을 이끄는 접속사
'in case (that)'과 'in case of'를 혼동하지 않도록 유의해야 한다. 둘 다 '~할 경우에'를 뜻하지만 'in case (that)'은 부사절을 이끄는 접속사로 뒤에 절이 오며 'in case of'는 구 전치사로 뒤에 명사(구)가 온다.

오답률 TOP 1
08 정답 ④

정답해설
주어진 문장을 통해 '스마트 홈 케어가 병원 치료를 대체할 수 있는가'에 대한 문제가 소재인 것을 알 수 있다. (A)가 역접 의미의 접속부사인 'Nonetheless (그럼에도 불구하고)'로 시작하고 있는 것으로 보아 상반되는 내용이 (A) 이전에 등장하는 것이 자연스럽다. (B)는 (C)의 요지와 (A)의 요지를 등위접속사 but으로 연결하며 글 전체의 내용을 요약하고 있으므로 글의 마지막에 위치해야 한다. 또한, (C)는 '현존하는 의료 시스템의 필요성'이 계속하여 유지될 것이라는 전문가들의 대체적인 의견을 서술하고 있으므로, (A) 이전에 위치해야 한다. 따라서 이어질 글의 순서로 가장 적절한 것은 ④ (C) - (A) - (B) 이다.

오답해설
① Nonetheless로 보아 (A)는 주어진 문장 바로 뒤에 올 수 없다.
②, ③ (A), (C) 각각의 주장을 재차 서술하며 전체적인 글의 요지를 요약하는 (B)는 주어진 문장 바로 뒤에 올 수 없다.

해석
디지털 건강관리 분야에서 건강관리 기술이 탑재된 잘 관리되는 스마트 홈이 병원 치료의 대체가 될 수 있는지에 관해 의견이 분분한 문제가 있다.
(C) 전문가들은 대체로 많은 상황에서 병원과 면대면 보건 개입의 필요성은 아마도 항상 존재할 것이라는 것에 동의한다.
(A) 그럼에도 불구하고, 결합된 가정 보건은 여러 다른 상황에서 의료비용을 낮춰줄 뿐 아니라 환자에의 권한 부여와 조정을 위한 많은 기회를 제공하기 때문에 장려되어야 할 비전이다.
(B) 결합된 스마트 홈은 아직 현존하는 건강관리 서비스를 완전히 대신하지는 못할 것이다. 하지만 그것들은 돌봄의 의료 연속체에 가치를 더할 수 있고, 돌봄의 질을 향상시켜주며, 여러모로 과부하 상태인 의료 시스템의 증가하는 압력을 줄일 수 있다.

어휘
burning (문제 따위) 의견이 분분한   substitute 대체(물), 대용품
connected 결합된   encourage 장려하다

plenty of 많은
empowerment 권한[기능] 부여, 권한[기능] 분산
lower 낮추다
replace 대신하다, 대체하다
value 가치
mounting (흔히 우려스러울 정도로) 증가하는[커지는]
pressure 압력, 압박
capacity 수용력
intervention 개입, 간섭
expense 비용, 경비
existing 현존하는, 현재 있는
continuum 연속체, 군집 연속
in many ways 여러모로
face-to-face 마주 보는, 대면하는

prevent A from B A가 B하는 것을 막다[예방하다]
potentially 잠재적으로
taste bud 미뢰[맛봉오리]
challenging 도전적인, 힘든
explain 설명하다
ever so 매우, 몹시, 굉장히
genetic 유전의

오답률 TOP 3

09 정답 ②

정답해설

해당 지문은 '어린이들의 미각의 특징'에 대해 서술하고 있다. 세 번째 문장에서 "From the very beginning babies are attracted to sweet flavor, which is what helps them to drink breast milk."라고 언급하며, '단맛에 끌리는 아이들의 특성이 그들이 모유를 먹는 것을 돕는다'라고 언급하고 있으므로, '모유가 자연적으로 단맛이 나기 때문에 아이들이 거부감 없이 먹을 수 있다'는 사실을 유추할 수 있다. 따라서 "② Human breast milk is a naturally sweet food(인간의 모유는 자연적으로 달콤한 음식이다)."는 글의 내용과 일치한다.

오답해설

① 첫 문장 "When children are given the option of a super sweet food such as lollies or a mildly sweet food such as fruit, most will automatically choose the lolly(아이들이 사탕과 같은 매우 달콤한 음식과 과일과 같이 약간 달콤한 음식 중 고를 수 있는 선택권을 받는다면, 대부분이 자동적으로 사탕을 선택할 것이다)."를 통해 '사탕이 과일보다 더 선호된다'라는 것을 알 수 있다.
③ 본문 중반에서 "They are also fond of salty tastes, and averse to sour and bitter(그들은 또한 짠맛을 좋아하고, 신맛과 쓴맛은 싫어한다)."라고 언급했으므로 일치하지 않는다.
④ 본문에 언급되지 않는 내용이다.

해석

아이들이 사탕과 같은 매우 달콤한 음식과 과일과 같이 약간 달콤한 음식 중 고를 수 있는 선택권을 받는다면, 대부분이 자동적으로 사탕을 선택할 것이다. 어린아이들은 특정한 맛을 더 선호하고, 다른 맛은 싫어하도록 유전학적으로 설정되어 있다. 맨 처음부터 아기들은 단맛에 끌리는데, 이것이 모유를 그들이 먹도록 돕는다. 그들은 또한 짠맛을 좋아하고, 신맛과 쓴맛은 싫어한다. 이것들은 수렵-채집 시대에 인간들이 생존하도록 도왔던 자연적인 동물적 반응이다. 대부분의 독성 식물들은 시거나 쓴맛이 나기 때문에 아이들이 자연히 그러한 맛을 피하도록 설정되어 있다는 것은 이해가 된다. 새로운 맛보다 익숙한 맛을 더 선호하는 것도 또한 아이들이 어쩌면 위험할지도 모르는 어떤 것을 먹는 것을 방지했다. 이것이 유아의 미뢰[맛봉오리]를 훈련시키고 그들에게 새로운 음식을 소개해주는 것이 굉장히 어려울 수 있다는 것을 설명해준다.
① 유전적인 이유로 과일이 사탕보다 더 선호된다.
② 인간의 모유는 자연적으로 달콤한 음식이다.
③ 어린아이들은 보통 짠맛, 신맛 그리고 쓴맛을 싫어한다.
④ 수렵-채집 시대에 많은 아이들이 독성 식물을 먹고 죽었다.

어휘

lolly 사탕
genetically 유전적으로
response 반응, 응답
poisonous 유독한
make sense 이해하다, 타당하다
mildly 약간
averse 싫어하는
hunter-gatherer 수렵·채집인
toxic 유독한

10 정답 ③

정답해설

해당 지문의 첫 문장에서 "Cholesterol travels through the blood on proteins called "lipoproteins(콜레스테롤은 "지질단백질"이라 불리는 단백질 상에서 혈액을 통해 이동한다)."라고 콜레스테롤에 대해 전반적으로 설명한 후, 이어서 콜레스테롤의 종류인 'LDL'과 'HDL'에 대해 각각의 역할과 기능 등에 대한 세부적인 설명을 이어가고 있다. 따라서 전체적인 글의 주제로 가장 적절한 것은 "③ the types of cholesterol we have(우리가 가지고 있는 콜레스테롤의 종류)"이다.

오답해설

① 마지막 문장에서 "High levels of HDL cholesterol can lower your risk for heart disease and stroke(높은 수준의 HDL 콜레스테롤은 당신의 심장병과 뇌졸중 위험을 감소시킬 수 있다)."라고 '높은 수준의 HDL의 장점'에 대해 언급하고 있지만, HDL을 높이는 방법에 대해서는 언급되지 않는다.
② 네 번째 문장에서 "When your body has too much LDL cholesterol, the LDL cholesterol can build up on the walls of your blood vessels(당신의 몸에 너무 많은 LDL 콜레스테롤이 있으면, LDL 콜레스테롤은 당신의 혈관 벽에 축적될 수도 있다)."에서 '높은 LDL의 위험성'에 대해 언급하고는 있지만, 그 이전 문장에서는 '높은 HDL의 장점'에 대해 언급하고 있으므로, '고콜레스테롤의 위험성'은 글의 제목으로 적절하지 않다.
④ 세 번째 문장에서 "High levels of LDL cholesterol raise your risk for heart disease and stroke(높은 수준의 LDL 콜레스테롤은 당신의 심장병과 뇌졸중 위험을 증가시킨다)."라고 '높은 LDL이 심장병을 일으킬 수도 있다'고 언급하고 있으나, 본문 전체에 해당하는 주제가 아니므로 오답이다.

해석

콜레스테롤은 "지질단백질"이라 불리는 단백질 상에서 혈액을 통해 이동한다. 때때로 "나쁜" 콜레스테롤이라 불리는 LDL(저밀도지질단백질)은 당신의 신체의 콜레스테롤의 대부분을 구성한다. 높은 수준의 LDL 콜레스테롤은 당신의 심장병과 뇌졸중 위험을 증가시킨다. 당신의 몸에 너무 많은 LDL 콜레스테롤이 있으면, LDL 콜레스테롤은 당신의 혈관 벽에 축적될 수도 있다. 이렇게 축적된 것은 "플라크"라고 불린다. 시간이 경과하며 당신의 혈관이 플라크를 축적함에 따라, 혈관 내부가 좁아진다. 이렇게 좁아진 것이 심장과 다른 기관을 순환하는 혈류를 방해한다. 심장으로 가는 혈류가 막히면, 협심증이나 심장마비를 일으킬 수 있다. HDL(고밀도지질단백질), 또는 "좋은" 콜레스테롤은 콜레스테롤을 흡수하여 그것을 간으로 다시 운반한다. 그러면 간은 그것을 몸에서 배출시킨다. 높은 수준의 HDL 콜레스테롤은 당신의 심장병과 뇌졸중 위험을 감소시킬 수 있다.
① HDL 레벨을 증가시키는 방법
② 고 콜레스테롤의 위험성
③ 우리가 가지고 있는 콜레스테롤의 종류
④ 심장병의 주요 원인

어휘

density 밀도, 농도
stroke 뇌졸중
flush 내보내다, (물을) 내리다
blood vessel 혈관
make up 구성하다
absorb 흡수하다
lower 낮추다
plaque 플라크

narrow 좁아지다
organ 기관, 장기
heart attack 심장 발작, 심장마비, 심근경색

blood flow 혈류

결국엔 성정혜 영어 하프모의고사
기적사 DAY 26

| 01 | ① | 02 | ① | 03 | ② | 04 | ④ | 05 | ① |
| 06 | ① | 07 | ③ | 08 | ④ | 09 | ③ | 10 | ④ |

오답률 TOP 1

01 정답 ①   19 서울시

정답해설

밑줄 친 단어 'pejorative'는 '경멸적인'이란 뜻을 가진 단어로 유의어 관계에 있는 보기는 ① derogatory이다.

해석

정당화는 문제의 행위에 대한 책임을 인정하면서도 그것과 관련된 **경멸적인** 성질을 부정하는 설명이다.
① 경멸적인
② 외향적인
③ 의무적인
④ 여분의, 과다한, 불필요한

어휘

justification 정당화
deny 부정하다
derogatory 경멸적인
mandatory 의무적인
account 설명
pejorative 경멸적인
extrovert 외향적인
redundant 불필요한

02 정답 ①   19 서울시

정답해설

'yellow fever(황열병)'의 원인으로 'mosquito(모기)'가 'carrier(매개체)'로 명시되어서 매개체를 꾸미는 표현으로, 빈칸에 가장 적절한 표현은 '의심되는'이라는 뜻을 가진 ① suspected이다.

해석

테스트들은 먼지와 열악한 위생을 황열병의 원인으로 제외하였고, 모기가 **의심되는** 매개체였다.
① 의심되는
② 문명화되지 않은
③ 환호하는
④ 자진해서

어휘

rule out 제외하다
cause 원인
carrier 매개체
uncivilized 문명화되지 않은
sanitation 위생
yellow fever 황열병
suspected 의심되는
volunteered 자진해서

오답률 TOP 2

03 정답 ②   19 서울시

정답해설

빈칸 전의 'concrete patterns to past events(과거 사건들에 대한 구체적인 패턴들)'의 제공할 수 있는 것으로 '미래를 투사하기 위해서' 필요한 것을

고르는 문맥상 추론 문항이다. 오답 선지들을 통해서, 환각, 질문, 소동 등이 적절치 않음을 먼저 파악해야 한다. 과거의 '견본'을 통해서 미래를 투사한다는 표현이 가장 적절하여, ② templates(견본)가 적절하다.

해석
우리의 삶과 결정을 위한 **견본들**을 제공할 수 있는 과거의 사건들에 구체적인 패턴이 있다고 상상하는 것은 그것이 이행할 수 없는 확실성에 대한 희망을 역사에 투사하는 것이다.
① 환각
② 견본
③ 질문, 문의
④ 소동

어휘
concrete 구체적인   project 투사하다
certainty 확실성   fulfill 이행하다, 완수하다
hallucination 환각   template 견본
inquiry 질문, 문의   commotion 소동

04 정답 ④ 19 서울시

정답해설
보스턴으로 가는 다음 비행기가 몇 시인지를 물어보는(What time is the next flight to Boston?) 표현이 제시되고 있다. 이는 '보스턴까지 가는 데 시간이 얼마나 걸리는가(How much will it take to get to Boston)?'를 물어본 것이 아니므로 질문에 대한 대답으로 'It will take about 45 minutes to get to Boston.'(보스턴까지 약 45분 정도 걸릴 거 같아.)은 적절하지 않다. 따라서 어색한 대화는 ④이다.

오답해설
① 영화에 대해서 묻고 있고 그에 대한 대답으로 적절하다.
② 다림질을 부탁하고 있으며 그에 대해서 필요한 시기를 묻고 있으므로 적절하다.
③ 사용할 방의 종류를 묻고 있으며 그에 대해 사용할 방의 종류를 답하고 있으므로 적절하다.

해석
① A: 토요일에 봤던 영화는 어땠어?
   B: 훌륭했어. 난 정말 그것을 즐겼어.
② A: 안녕하세요. 전 셔츠 몇 장을 다림질을 하기를 원합니다.
   B: 네, 당신은 그것들이 얼마나 빨리 필요하십니까?
③ A: 싱글룸으로 하시겠습니까? 더블룸으로 하시겠습니까?
   B: 오, 저만 사용할 거라서 싱글룸이면 좋습니다.
④ A: 보스턴으로 가는 다음 비행기는 몇 시야?
   B: 보스턴까지 약 45분 정도 걸릴 거 같아.

어휘
pressed 다림질한   take 시간이 걸리다

05 정답 ① 19 서울시

정답해설
① **출제 포인트: 타동사구[완전자동사 + 목적어 + 전치사 + 목적어]**
해당 지문에 사용된 attribute는 동사로서 'attribute A to B'는 'A는 B의 덕분[탓]이다'라는 표현에 해당된다. 지문에서 'the discovery of the sewing machine(재봉틀의 발견)'이 'a dream(꿈)' 덕분임을 문맥을 통해서 알 수 있다. 따라서 'for'가 아니라 'to'가 되어야 어법상 적절하므로 정답은 ①이다.

오답해설
② **출제 포인트: 전치사 + 관계대명사**
꿈에서 식인종에게 붙잡힌 것이므로 'he was captured by cannibals in a dream'에서 'dream'이 선행사이므로 전치사+관계대명사 형태로 'in which he was captured by cannibals'는 어법상 알맞다.
③ **출제 포인트: 명사절을 이끄는 접속사 that**
동사 'notice'의 목적절 접속사 'that'이므로 어법상 적절하다.
④ **출제 포인트: to부정사의 부사적 용법**
'he need to solve'에서 '~하는 것을 필요로 하다'의 의미로 사용된 것이 아니라는 점에 주의하자. 문장에서 'need'의 목적어는 'the design feature'로 생략된 목적격 관계대명사 that으로 수식하고 있으므로, 'to solve'는 to부정사의 부사적 용법에 해당하며 '~하기 위해서'로 해석한다.

해석
발명가 Elias Howe는 재봉틀의 발견을 식인종에게 붙잡힌 꿈 덕분이라고 했다. 그는 그들이 그의 주위에서 춤을 추면서 창끝에 구멍이 있다는 것을 알아차렸고, 그는 이것이 그의 문제를 해결하는 데 필요한 디자인적 특징이라는 것을 깨달았다.

어휘
inventor 발명가   attribute A to B A는 B의 덕분이다
capture 잡다   cannibal 식인종
spear 창   sewing machine 재봉틀
feature 특징

06 정답 ① 19 서울시

정답해설
① **출제 포인트: 완전자동사**
'emerge'(드러나다, 알려지다)는 자동사로 수동태가 사용할 수 없는 완전 자동사다. 보통 emerge from으로 '~에서 나타나다'의 형태로 주로 사용된다. 따라서 'had been emerged'가 아니라 'had emerged'가 올바른 표현이다.

오답해설
② **출제 포인트: 동사 관용표현**
'embark on'은 관용표현으로 '~에 착수하다'를 뜻한다. 해당 문장은 밑줄 친 'embarked' 뒤에 전치사 'on'을 사용하였고 문맥상 '착수하다'가 자연스러우므로 옳은 문장이다.
③ **출제 포인트: 관계부사 vs. 관계대명사**
'whereby'는 '그로 인하여'라는 격식 표현으로 의미상 적절하며, 관계부사의 역할을 한다. 이때 뒤따라오는 절은 완전한 형태로 옳게 사용되었다.
④ **출제 포인트: 수일치**
주어가 'East and West'이므로 복수명사에 맞는 be 동사 'were'가 오는 것은 어법상 적절하다. 또한 be to 용법 중 '예정'에 해당되는 의미로 쓰였다.

해석
1955년까지 Nikita Khrushchev는 구소련에서 스탈린의 후계자로 드러났고, 그는 동서양이 그들의 경쟁은 계속하지만 덜 대립적인 방법으로 하는 "평화 공존" 정책에 착수했다.

어휘
emerge 드러나다   successor 후계자
embark 착수하다   policy 정책
peaceful coexistence 평화 공존   whereby ~하는
competition 경쟁   confrontational 대립하는
manner 방법

07 정답 ③
19 서울시

정답해설

③ 출제 포인트: 주어와 동사 수일치

문맥에 따른 주격관계대명사 선행사 수일치에 대한 문제이다. 관계대명사 'that'의 선행사가 'its skin'이라 생각하기 쉬운데 이후 문맥을 통해서 '피부'가 아니라 'special cells'가 색소를 가지고 있음을 반드시 파악해야한다. 따라서 선행사를 'cells'로 보아 복수명사에 맞는 동사 형태가 선행사절에 와야 한다. 따라서 'contains'가 아니라 'contain'이 되어야 한다. 따라서 정답은 ③이다.

오답해설

① 출제 포인트: sort/kind/type + of + 무관사 명사

주어가 복수명사이므로 '형태들'인 'types'가 오는 것이 적절하며, 밑줄 이후의 문장이 복수명사 cephalopods로 쓰이고 있다. 이는 sort, kind, type + of에 뒤따라오는 명사는 무관사 명사가 반드시 위치해야만 한다는 점에도 해당되므로 옳게 사용되었다.

② 출제 포인트: 대명사 each

'Each' 다음에 문장의 동사가 3인칭 단수형태인 'has'이므로 'Each'는 어법상 적절한 표현이다.

④ 출제 포인트: to부정사의 형용사적 용법

'allow + 목적어 + to부정사' 형태이다. '목적어가 ~하게 허용하다, 허락하다'라는 의미로 사용되어 적절하다.

해석

오징어, 문어, 갑오징어는 모두 두족류의 형태이다. 이 각각의 동물들은 피부 아래에 유색 액체, 즉 색소가 들어 있는 특별한 세포를 가지고 있다. 두족류는 이 세포들을 피부 쪽으로 또는 피부로부터 멀어지게 할 수 있다. 이것은 그것이 그것의 외모의 패턴과 색을 바꿀 수 있게 한다.

어휘

cuttlefish 갑오징어
contain 포함하다
appearance 외모, 외향
cephalopod 두족류
pigment 색소

오답률 TOP 3

08 정답 ④
19 서울시

정답해설

과거와 현대의 아이들의 놀이 장소의 차이를 설명하는 글이다. 초반의 설명에 따르면 과거에는 자연 속에서 아이들이 놀았던 반면, 중반 이후의 설명에 따르면 현대의 아이들은 자연을 떠나 인공적인 환경에서 주로 논다는 설명이다. ④ 문장은 방과 후 아이들이 집 근처에서 모래놀이 등을 한다는 묘사이므로 현대 아이들의 놀이에 대한 묘사로 부적합하다. 따라서 글의 흐름에 맞지 않는 문장은 ④이다.

오답해설

① 'playground'의 정의를 제시한 문장으로 전체 내용에 부합된다.
② 지난 몇십 년 동안 아이들의 놀이 장소가 자연에서 인공적인 것으로 변했음을 설명한다.
③ 현대 시골 지역에서도 자유롭게 돌아다니며 노는 아이들은 거의 없음을 설명한다.

해석

역사 전반에 걸쳐 아이들의 놀이터는 시골에서는 황무지, 들판, 개울, 그리고 언덕이었고, 마을, 시내, 도시에서는 도로, 거리, 그리고 비어있는 장소들이었다. ① *playground*라는 용어는 아이들이 그들의 자유롭고 즉흥적인 놀이를 하기 위해 모이는 곳들 모두를 의미한다. ② 오직 지난 몇십 년 동안 아이들은 비디오 게임, 문자 전송, 그리고 소셜 네트워크에 대한 커지는 애정 때문에 이 자연의 놀이터들을 떠나왔다. ③ 심지어 미국의 시골 지역에서도 여전히 어른의 동반 없이 자유롭게 돌아다니는 방식으로 돌아다니고 있는 아이들은 거의 없다. ④ **방과 후, 아이들은 모래를 파고, 요새를 짓고, 전통적인 놀이를 하고, 기어오르거나, 공놀이를 하며 집 근처에서 흔히 발견된다.** 그들은 개울, 언덕, 그리고 들판과 같은 자연 지형에서 빠르게 사라지고 있으며, 그들의 도시의 비교 대상들처럼, 오락으로 실내의, 움직임이 없는 사이버 장난감에 의지하고 있다.

어휘

throughout ~전반에 걸쳐, ~전역에, ~하는 내내
wilderness 황무지
term 용어
refer to ~를 의미하다
spontaneous 즉흥(자발)적인
texting 문자 전송
roam 돌아다니다, 배회하다
unaccompanied 동반되지 않는, 함께 하지 않는
fort 진지, 요새
creek 개울, 시내
counterpart 비교 대상, 상대방
sedentary 앉아서 지내는, 몸을 움직이지 않는
entertainment 오락
field 들판
vacant 비어 있는
gather 모이다, 모으다
vacate 비우다, 떠나다
rural 시골의
free-ranging 마음대로 돌아다니는
terrain 지형
urban 도시의
turn to ~에 의지하다

09 정답 ③
19 지방직

정답해설

(A) 빈칸 다음에 "살아남기 위해 먹을 것이 충분치 않았다"(they simply didn't have enough to eat to stay alive.)라는 것으로 보아 'starvation(기아)'이 적합하다.
(B) 빈칸 다음 "많은 사람들이 고국을 떠나 미국으로 갔다"(many left their island home for the United States)라는 것으로 보아 'emigrate(이주하다)'가 적합하다. 따라서 정답은 ③이다.

오답해설

나머지 보기들은 빈칸 다음에 나오는 설명에 적합하지 않으므로 정답이 될 수 없다.

해석

1840년대에, 아일랜드섬은 기근을 겪었다. 아일랜드는 그 인구를 먹일 만큼 충분한 식량을 생산할 수 없었기 때문에, 대략 100만 명이 (A) 기아로 사망했다; 그들은 단순히 생존하기 위한 먹을 것이 충분하지 않았다. 기근은 또 다른 125만 명의 사람들이 (B) 이주하도록 만들었다; 많은 이들은 그들의 고국 섬을 떠나 미국으로 갔다; 나머지는 캐나다, 호주, 칠레, 그리고 다른 국가들로 갔다. 기근 이전, 아일랜드의 인구는 대략 6백만이었다. 대기근 이후, 그것은 대략 4백만이었다.

	(A)	(B)
①	탈수	추방되다
②	트라우마	이민 들어오다
③	기근	이민가다
④	피로	억류되다

어휘

famine 기근
rest 나머지
dehydration 탈수
trauma 충격적 경험, 외상
die of ~로 죽다
shortage 부족
deport 강제 추방하다
immigrate 이주하다

starvation 기아
fatigue 피로
emigrate 이주하다
detain 억류하다

10 정답 ④
19 지방직

정답해설

(A)에서는 문맥상 부정어가 필요하다. (A) 빈칸 다음에 "what you are hearing convincingly matches the visuals, the virtual experience breaks apart(만약 당신이 듣고 있는 것이 시각적인 것들과 설득력 있게 일치하지 않는다면, 가상 체험은 부서진다)."라고 하였으므로 'Unless(그렇지 않다면)'가 적합하다.

(B) 다음의 내용이 '오늘날의 기술도 가상현실에 충분하지 않다'라는 것을 지적하고 있으므로 'Unfortunately'(안타깝게도)가 적합하다. 따라서 두 가지를 모두 충족시키는 정답은 ④이다.

오답해설

(A)는 문맥상 부정어가 들어가야 적절하므로 'If'(만약 ~라면)는 적절하지 않은 표현이다.

(B)다음의 내용에서 오늘날의 기술이 부적합하다고 하였으므로 'Similarly'(비슷하게)는 글의 흐름상 적합하지 않고 (B)를 사이에 두고 전후의 내용이 대조되는 것이 아니므로 'By contrast'(대조적으로) 또한 문맥상 올바른 표현이 아니다. (B) 다음이 본문의 결론을 서술하고 있는 것도 아니므로 'Consequently'(결과적으로)도 적절하지 않다.

해석

오늘날 가상현실(VR) 체험의 시각적 요소를 제작하는 기술은 널리 이용 가능하고 가격이 알맞게 되어 가는 도중에 있다. 그러나 강력하게 작동하기 위해서는, 가상현실은 시각적인 것 이상에 관한 것이어야 한다. (A) 만약 당신이 듣고 있는 것이 시각적인 것들과 설득력 있게 일치하지 않는다면, 가상 체험은 부서진다. 농구를 예로 들어보자. 만약 선수들, 코치들, 아나운서들, 그리고 관중들이 모두 코트 가운데 앉아 있는 것처럼 들린다면, 당신은 TV로 경기를 보는 것이 낫다 – 당신은 당신이 "거기" 있는 만큼만 감을 잡게 된다. (B) 안타깝게도, 오늘날의 오디오 기계와 우리의 널리 사용되는 녹화 및 재생 포맷은 먼 행성의 전쟁터, 코트 사이드에서의 농구 경기, 또는 훌륭한 콘서트홀의 첫 줄에서 들리는 것 같은 심포니의 소리를 설득력 있게 재현하는 일에는 단순히 부적합하다.

	(A)	(B)
①	만약 ~라면	대조적으로
②	그렇지 않다면	결과적으로
③	만약 ~라면	비슷하게
④	그렇지 않다면	안타깝게도

어휘

component 요소
on one's way to ~로 가는 도중에
accessible 이용(출입/접근) 가능한
convincingly 설득력 있게
midcourt 코트 가운데
get a sense 감을 잡다
battlefield 전장, 전쟁터
row 줄, 열
virtual-reality 가상현실
affordable (가격이) 알맞은
break apart 부서지다, 쪼개지다
may as well V ~하는 편이 낫다
inadequate 부적절한
distant 먼

결국엔 성정혜 영어 하프모의고사
기적사 DAY 27

| 01 | ③ | 02 | ④ | 03 | ① | 04 | ③ | 05 | ② |
| 06 | ④ | 07 | ④ | 08 | ④ | 09 | ③ | 10 | ② |

01 정답 ③

정답해설

밑줄 친 단어는 문맥상 '논쟁의 여지가 있는'으로 쓰였고, 유의어로는 ③ controversial이 적절하다.

해석

그러나, 장미 연합이 논란을 진화시켰어야 했지만, 많은 **논쟁의 여지가 있는** 질문들과 반란에 대한 그럴듯한 구실들이 남아있었다.
① 경멸적인, 비난하는 의미의
② 끈질긴, 집요한, 고수하는
③ 논란의 여지가 있는, 갈등을 빚고 있는
④ 순진한, 성실한

어휘

pejorative 경멸적인, 비난하는 의미의
pertinacious 끈질긴, 집요한, 고수하는
controversial 논란의 여지가 있는, 갈등을 빚고 있는
guileless 순진한, 성실한

오답률 TOP 3

02 정답 ④

정답해설

밑줄 친 단어는 문맥상 '모순된'으로 사용되었고, 유의어로는 ④ incongruous가 적절하다.

해석

모호하고 **모순된** 책임 기준들은 공중위생을 위한 무고한 기업들을 위협한다.
① 강렬한, 급격한
② 불리한, 해로운
③ 예민한
④ 앞뒤가 맞지 않는, 조화되지 않는

어휘

sanitation 공중위생
detrimental 불리한, 해로운
incongruous 앞뒤가 맞지 않는, 조화되지 않는
drastic 강렬한, 급격한
impressionable 예민한

03 정답 ①

정답해설

밑줄 친 단어의 의미가 문맥상 '일치할 수 있는'으로 사용되었고, 유의어로는 ① corresponding이 적절하다.

해석

그의 일반적인 기계적 원인들에 대한 학설과 어떤 식으로든 **일치할 수 있도록** 강요하는 내적인 힘 때문에 원자에 대한 필수적인 그의 무게 이론도 역시 아니다.

① 일치하는, 상응하는, 통신의
② 탐욕스러운, 갈망하는
③ 환각이 느껴진
④ 결정적인, 위압적인, 거만한

어휘

corresponding 상응하는, 통신의   avaricious 탐욕스러운, 갈망하는
hallucinated 환각이 느껴진
peremptory 결정적인, 위압적인, 거만한

04 정답 ③

정답해설

첫 번째 빈칸에서 지각에 대해 사과하는 Bob에게 Amy는 괜찮다고 이야기한 후, 뛰어왔냐고 묻는다. 따라서 뛰어오느라 숨이 차 보인다는 의미의 (A)'be short of breath(숨이 가쁘다)'가 적절하다. 두 번째 빈칸에서는 Bob이 약속 장소까지의 여정이 쉽지만은 않았다고 얘기하며, 지하철을 아슬아슬하게 하차했다는 맥락의 (B)'by the skin of one's teeth(아슬아슬하게)'가 자연스럽다. 또한, Bob이 피곤하다고 말한 상황을 고려해 봤을 때, Amy가 전력을 다해 뛰었냐고 묻는 (C)'at full tilt(전력을 다하여)'가 가장 적합하다.

오답해설

① (A)'be around the clock(24시간 내내, 항상)'은 지각한 상대에게 뛰어왔냐며 묻는 상황에 부적절하다. 지하철에서 전력을 다해 하차했다는 의미의 (B)'at full tilt(전력을 다하여)'는 어색하다. (C) 'over the hill(전성기가 끝난)'은 지하철역에서부터 약속 장소까지 뛰어온 문맥의 대화에서 부적합하다.
② (A)'feel at home(편안하게 느낀다)'은 지각한 상대에게 약속 장소까지 뛰어왔는지 묻는 상황에 적합하지 않다. 약속 장소까지 어렵게 도착한 Bob이 지하철에서 곤란에 빠져 하차했다는 내용의 (B)'in hot water(곤란에 빠져)'는 옳지 않다. (C) 'under the counter(불법으로)'는 지하철에서 내려 약속 장소까지 뛰어왔는지 묻는 맥락에서 어색하다.
④ 지하철역에서 약속 장소까지 뛰어왔다고 이야기하는 상황에서 (C)'설상가상으로(out of the frying pan into the fire' 뛰었다는 말은 부자연스럽다.

해석

Bob: 내가 마지막으로 도착한 거야? 늦어서 미안해.
Amy: 괜찮아. 너 (A) 숨이 가빠 보여. 여기 뛰어왔어?
Bob: 응, 버스를 타려고 했어. 그리고 그때 교통 체증에 대해 들었어. 그래서 대신 지하철을 타기로 한 거야.
Amy: 너 여기까지 긴 여정이었겠구나.
Bob: 쉽지만은 않았지. 근데 (B) 아슬아슬하게 지하철에서 가까스로 내릴 수 있었어.
Amy: 오, 행운이었네. 그래서 넌 지하철역에서 여기까지 (C) 전력을 다해 뛴 거야?
Bob: 맞아. 나 지금 너무 지쳤어.
① (A) 항상 (B) 전력을 다하여 (C) 전성기가 끝난
② (A) 편안하게 느끼다 (B) 곤란에 빠져 (C) 불법으로
③ (A) 숨이 가쁘다 (B) 아슬아슬하게 (C) 전력을 다하여
④ (A) 편안하게 느끼다 (B) 곤란에 빠져 (C) 설상가상으로

어휘

arrive 도착하다   plan on~ ~을 계획하다
traffic jam 교통 체증   decide 결정하다
trip 여행, 여정   manage to~ ~을 가까스로 해내다

05 정답 ②

정답해설

② 출제 포인트: 전치사 + 관계대명사
해당 문장은 'a unique copy'를 선행사로 사용하였으므로 선행사를 포함하는 관계대명사 'what'은 사용할 수 없다. 따라서 'what'을 'which'로 수정해야 한다. 해당 문장에서 'make notes on'은 '~에 메모를 하다'의 의미로 목적어 'turning ~ version'을 가지므로 완전한 문장에 해당된다. 따라서 뒤따라오는 문장은 완전하고 선행사는 'a unique copy'이므로 '전치사 + 관계대명사'인 'in which'로 수정하는 것이 옳다. 단, what 이후의 문장이 불완전하다고 분석할 경우 선행사를 포함한 관계대명사 'what'으로 잘못 분석할 수 있으니 주의해야 한다.

오답해설

① 출제 포인트: 명사절을 이끄는 접속사 that
해당 문장에서 'that'은 명사절을 이끄는 접속사로 완전타동사 'said'의 목적어로 사용되었다. 이때 'to John'은 완전타동사와 목적어 사이에 삽입된 전명구로 수식어에 해당한다.
③ 출제 포인트: 타동사구[완전타동사 + 목적어 + 전치사 + 목적어]
'turn A into B'는 'A를 B로 바꾸다'를 뜻한다. 해당 문장은 'turn A into B'를 동명사의 형태로 사용한 문장으로 옳은 문장이다.
④ 출제 포인트: 등위접속사의 병렬구조
과거완료 'had lent'와 'had lost'가 등위접속사 'but'을 통해 병렬구조를 이루고 있으므로 옳은 문장이다. 단, 주어진 문장에서 'a unique copy ~ for the publication of an American version'은 삽입절이기 때문에 삽입절 내 had made와 had lost가 병렬구조라고 볼 수 없다는 점에 주의해야 한다.

해석

Tom은 1971년 11월에 친구에게 그 책의 사본을 빌려주었고 - 그것은 미국판의 출판을 위해 영국식 영어를 미국식 영어로 바꾸는 것에 대한 메모를 해 두었던 특별한 사본이었는데 - 그 친구가 런던에서 그 사본을 잃어버렸다고 John에게 말했다.

어휘

lend A B A에게 B를 빌려주다   turn A into B A를 B로 바꾸다
publication 출판, 발행   version 판, 형태
copy 사본

오답률 TOP 1

06 정답 ④

정답해설

④ 출제 포인트: little vs. few
'little'은 부사로 사용할 수 있으나 'few'는 부사로 사용할 수 없다. 해당 문장은 완전자동사 'care'를 수식해야 하므로 부사를 사용해야 한다. 따라서 'few'를 'little'로 수정해야 한다.

오답해설

① 출제 포인트: 주어와 동사의 수일치
주격 관계대명사절 동사의 수일치 기준은 선행사이다. 해당 문장은 선행사 'areas'가 복수형태이므로 주격 관계대명사절 동사에 복수형태인 'are'를 옳게 사용하였다.
② 출제 포인트: 동사 관용표현
'engage in + 목적어'는 관용표현으로 '~에 관여하다, 참여하다'를 뜻한다.
③ 출제 포인트: 관계부사 vs. 관계대명사
'whereby'는 관계부사로 '(그것에 의하여) …하는'을 뜻하며 뒤따라오는

문장은 완전한 형태이다. 해당 문장은 관계부사 'whereby'가 쓰인 문장으로 뒤따라오는 문장이 완전한 형태이므로 옳은 문장이다.

해석

자기 인식과 특별히 관련되지 않은 분야에서는, 우리는 반영을 하고, 그럼으로써 다른 사람들이 성취한 것과 관련지어서 자기 자신을 치켜세운다. 여러분이 자신의 운동 기술에 신경을 거의 쓰지 않는다고 가정해 보자.

어휘

relevant 관련 있는, 적절한
engage in ~에 관여하다, 참여하다
whereby (그것에 의하여) …하는
self-definition 자기 인식
reflection 반영, 반사
accomplishment 성취, 업적, 공적

오답률 TOP 2

07 정답 ④

정답해설

④ 출제 포인트: 대명사의 수일치

대명사는 가리키는 대상과 수일치 한다. 해당 문장은 대명사 'it'이 복수명사 'things'를 가리키므로 틀린 문장이다. 따라서 'it'을 'them'으로 수정해야 한다. 이전 문장의 'knowledge'를 가리킨다고 생각하지 않도록 주의해야 한다.

오답해설

① 출제 포인트: sort/kind/type + of + 무관사 명사

'sort/kind/type + of' 뒤에 오는 명사(구)는 관사 없이 사용해야 한다. 해당 문장은 'sorts of' 뒤에 관사 없이 명사(구) 'skills'를 사용하였으므로 옳은 문장이다.

② 출제 포인트: to부정사의 형용사적 용법

'to analyze'는 to부정사의 형용사적 용법으로 사용되었으며, 명사(구) 'the ability'를 수식하는 수식어 역할을 하므로 한정적 용법에 해당한다.

③ 출제 포인트: 주어와 동사 수일치

주어 'the sorts'가 복수형태이므로 동사에 복수형태를 사용해야 한다. 따라서 'require'를 옳게 사용하였다.

해석

그는 "인지 과학의 연구는 – 비판적으로 분석하고 생각하는 능력과 같은 – 선생님이 학생이 갖추기를 원하는 종류의 능력이 광범위한 사실적 지식을 필요로 한다는 것을 보여주었다."라고 설명했다. 다른 말로 하면, 어떤 것에 관해 비판적으로 생각하려면 그것을 알고 있어야만 한다.

어휘

cognitive 인지의, 인식의
analyze 분석하다, 분해하다
factual 사실에 기반을 둔
sort 종류, 부류, 유형
extensive 아주 넓은, 광범위한

08 정답 ④

정답해설

해당 지문에서는 '놀이터에서 아이들의 부상은 놀이기구에서 추락하는 것에서 가장 많이 발생하므로, 안전한 놀이터 바닥 표면을 선택하는 것이 중요하다'라고 설명하고 있으며, 어떤 재질의 표면이 안전한 것인지 언급하고 있다. 본문 중반 "Although grass may look soft, it is not a shock absorbing surface(잔디는 부드러워 보이지만, 충격을 흡수하는 표면은 아니다)."로 보아, 잔디는 충격을 흡수하지 못한다는 것을 알 수 있으므로, 아이들에게 안전한 놀이터 바닥 재질이 아닌 것을 알 수 있다. 따라서 글의 내용과 일치하지 않는 것은 '④ Surfaces made of grass are quite safe for children(잔디로 만들어진 표면은 아이들에게 상당히 안전하다)'이다.

오답해설

① 매년 20만 명 이상의 아이들이 놀이터 관련된 부상으로 치료를 받는다고 언급되었으므로, 글의 내용과 일치한다.

② 두 번째 문장 "Most playground injuries happen when a child falls from the equipment onto the ground(대부분의 놀이터 부상은 아이가 기구에서 바닥으로 떨어질 때 발생한다)."를 통해 내용과 일치함을 알 수 있다.

③ 본문 중반 "Steer clear of hard surfaces like concrete or asphalt."를 통해 '콘크리트와 아스팔트와 같은 단단한 바닥 표면은 피하라'고 설명하고 있으므로, 글의 내용과 일치한다.

해석

미 소비자 제품 안전 위원회(USCPSC)에 따르면, 응급 병동은 매년 놀이터와 관련된 부상으로 20만 명 이상의 아이들을 치료한다. 대부분의 놀이터 부상은 아이가 기구에서 바닥으로 떨어질 때 발생한다. 이것이 부상을 예방하는 최상의 방법은 기구의 밑의 표면이 아이가 떨어질 때의 충격을 흡수하고 약화시킬 수 있도록 하는 것인 이유이다. 콘크리트나 아스팔트와 같은 단단한 표면은 피하라. 잔디는 부드러워 보이지만, 충격을 흡수하는 표면은 아니다. USCPSC는 우드칩, 피복, 모래, 안전 검사를 거친 고무 또는 고무 유사 재료로 만든 매트와 같은 재료들 중 하나로 만든 놀이기구 아래 사방으로 최소 6피트 넓이로 깔린 두꺼운 바닥을 추천한다.

① 놀이터에서 부상을 당하는 아이들이 매우 많다.
② 놀이기구에서의 낙상으로 인한 부상이 가장 흔하다.
③ 아스팔트 위에 지어진 놀이터는 이용하지 않는 것이 좋다.
④ 잔디로 만들어진 표면은 아이들에게 상당히 안전하다.

어휘

emergency 응급
equipment 기구, 설비
make sure 확실히 하다
underneath 아래에
soften 약화시키다, 부드럽게 하다
land (땅에) 떨어지다
steer clear of …에 가까이 가지 않다, …을 피하다
material 재료
wood chip 우드칩, 목재칩(목재를 잘게 끊은 목재 조각)
mulch 피복(포장 토양의 표면을 여러 가지 재료로 덮는 것)
extend (거리가 어떤 점까지) 달하다   avoid 피하다
treat 치료하다
prevent 예방하다
surface 표면
absorb 흡수하다
impact 충격

09 정답 ③

정답해설

(A) 빈칸 이전에서 '아일랜드 감자 기근(Irish Potato Famine)은 역사상 가장 극심했던 기근 중 하나라고 여겨진다.'라고 설명한 후, 그렇지만 '이 기간을 가리키는데 '기근(Famine)'이라는 용어를 사용하는 것에 대한 논란이 있다'라고 설명하고 있다. '가장 극심했던 기근이었지만, 엄밀한 의미의 기근은 아니므로 '기근'이라는 용어 사용에 이견이 있다'라는 내용이기 때문에, 전후 내용이 대조적이거나 양보를 나타낼 때 사용하는 'However(그러나)' 또는 'Nevertheless(그럼에도 불구하고)'가 빈칸에 들어갈 수 있다.

(B) 빈칸 이전에서 "There was sufficient food in the country throughout the 'Famine' years, yet over a million people died from starvation and disease, and millions more were forced to flee."를 통해 '기근(Famine) 동안 음식이 충분했지만, 굶주림과 질병에 의한 수많은 사망과 이주가 발생했다'라고 설명하며 '기근이라는 용어 사용의 논란 이유를 설명하고 있다. 이후에 빈칸 문장에서 이러한 이유로 '일부 역사학자들은 대기아(Great Hunger)라는 용어를 사용하는 것을 선호한다'고 서술하고

있으므로, 인과관계를 나타낼 때 사용하는 접속부사인 'Therefore(그러므로)' 또는 'Thus(따라서)'가 빈칸에 들어갈 수 있다. 따라서 가장 적합한 단어가 연결된 보기는 '③ However(그러나) – Thus(따라서)'이다.

> 오답해설

① (A) 전후의 내용이 인과관계를 나타내지 않기 때문에 'Hence(따라서)'는 빈칸에 부적절하므로 오답이다.
④ (B) 전후의 내용이 역접 관계를 나타내지 않기 때문에 'On the other hand(반면에)'는 빈칸에 부적절하므로 오답이다.
나머지 보기는 문맥상 부적절하므로 오답이다.

> 해석

아일랜드 감자 기근은 아일랜드 격변의 역사상 가장 비극적인 사건이었다. 그것은 또한 역사상 가장 극심했던 기근 중 하나라고 여겨진다. (A) 그러나 이러한 맥락에서 '기근'이라는 용어의 사용은 논란의 여지가 있다. 그 당시 아일랜드는 세계에서 가장 부유한 제국(대영 제국)의 일부였기 때문이다. '기근'이 발생한 해에 그 나라에는 충분한 식량이 있었으나, 백만 명 이상의 사람들이 기아와 질병으로 인해 숨졌고, 더 많은 수백만 명의 사람들이 피난을 가도록 만들었다. (B) 따라서 일부 역사학자들은 기아와 질병으로 인한 집단 사망의 이 기간을 설명하기 위해 '대기아'라는 이름을 사용하는 것을 선호한다.
① 그러므로 – 그러므로
② 그에 따라서 – 대조적으로
③ 그러나 – 따라서
④ 그럼에도 불구하고 – 반면에

> 어휘

famine 기근
turbulent 격동의
context 맥락, 상황
for 왜냐하면 …이므로, 그 까닭은
sufficient 충분한
flee 달아나다, 피난 가다, 도망치다
mass 대량의, 집단의
catastrophic 파멸의, 비극적인
regard 간주하다
controversial 논쟁의
empire 제국
starvation 기아, 굶주림
describe 설명하다, 묘사하다

10 정답 ②

> 정답해설

해당 지문은 '가상현실(Virtual Reality)과 증강현실(Augmented Reality)의 특징'을 서로 비교하여 설명하고 있다. 본문 초반에서 "Virtual Reality technologies completely immerse a user inside a synthetic environment and while immersed, the user cannot see the real world around him(가상현실 기술은 사용자를 합성환경에 완전히 몰입시키고, 몰입된 상태에서 사용자는 주변의 현실 세계를 볼 수 없다)."을 통해 가상현실의 특징을 설명한 후, "In contrast, Augmented Reality is taking digital or computer generated information, whether it be images, audio, video, and touch or haptic sensations and overlaying them over in a real-time environment(그에 반해, 가상현실은 그것이 이미지, 오디오, 비디오, 감촉, 또는 촉감이던지 간에 디지털 또는 컴퓨터로 생성된 정보를 가져와 실시간 환경에 덮어씌우는 것이다)."를 통해 가상현실과는 차이가 있는 증강현실에 대해 설명하고 있다. 또한 마지막 문장 "Unlike Virtual Reality, Augmented Reality allows the user to see the real world, with virtual objects superimposed upon or composited with the real world(가상현실과 달리 증강현실은 사용자가 가상 물체가 첨가되거나 합성된 상태로 현실 세계를 볼 수 있도록 해준다)."에서도 둘의 차이점을 언급하고 있으므로, 글의 제목으로 가장 적절한 것은 '② VR vs. AR: What's the Difference?(가상현실 대 증강현실: 차이는 무엇인가?)'이다.

> 오답해설

① 가상현실과 증강현실의 우열을 가리고 있지 않다.
③ 증강현실의 발달에 대해서 구체적으로 다루고 있지 않다.
④ 가상현실과 증강현실의 특징을 비교하여 설명하고 있는 글이지 증강현실과 응용에 관한 글이라고 볼 수 없다.

> 해석

증강현실(AR)은 가상환경(VE) 또는 더 흔하게 가상현실(VR)이라 불리는 것의 변형이다. 가상현실 기술은 사용자를 합성환경에 완전히 몰입시키고 몰입된 상태에서 사용자는 주변의 현실 세계를 볼 수 없다. 그에 반해, 증강현실은 그것이 이미지, 오디오, 비디오, 감촉, 또는 촉감이든지 간에 디지털 또는 컴퓨터로 생성된 정보를 가져와 실시간 환경에 덮어씌우는 것이다. 기술적으로 증강현실은 오감을 향상시키기 위해 사용될 수 있지만, 오늘날 가장 흔한 사용은 시각적인 것이다. 가상현실과 달리 증강현실은 사용자가 가상 물체가 첨가되거나 혼합된 상태로 현실 세계를 볼 수 있도록 해준다.
① 가상현실과 증강현실 중 무엇이 더 좋은가?
② 가상현실 vs. 증강현실: 차이는 무엇인가?
③ 증강현실의 발달
④ 증강현실과 응용

> 어휘

Augmented Reality (AR) 증강현실
Virtual Reality (VR) 가상현실
variation 다양성
immerse ~에 몰입시키다
whether it be~ ~이든지 아니든지 간에(성경이나 법조문에 주로 쓰이는 가정법 현재 표현, 현대영어에서는 주로 be 대신에 is를 사용함)
haptic 촉각에 관한, 촉각의
sensation 감각, 느낌, 감동
enhance ~을 강화하다
superimpose 첨가하다, 포개 놓다
composite 혼합하다
application 응용, 지원, 적용

결국엔 성정혜 영어 하프모의고사
기적사 DAY 28

01	④	02	②	03	④	04	①	05	③
06	②	07	②	08	①	09	②	10	④

오답률 TOP 1
01 정답 ④

정답해설

밑줄 친 단어는 문맥상 '증강적인'으로 사용되었고, 유의어로는 ④ increscent 가 적절하다.

해석

최면술은 당신의 의사가 결정한 치료와 함께 사용되어야 하는 **증강적** 개입이다.
① 무익한, 시시한
② 결정적인, 격렬한
③ 불필요한
④ 증가하는

어휘

conjunction 결합, 연결함
acute 결정적인, 격렬한
increscent 증가하는
futile 무익한, 시시한
redundant 불필요한

오답률 TOP 3
02 정답 ②

정답해설

밑줄 친 단어는 문맥상 '논쟁적인'으로 사용되었고, 유의어로는 ② contentious 가 적절하다.

해석

지금 읽기 재미있는 **논쟁적인** 문제의 덩어리로 자랐다.
① 의심되는
② 논쟁적인
③ 알코올성의, 순수한, 원기 있는, 정신적인
④ 상응하는, 노력에 반응하는

어휘

suspected 의심되는
spiritous 순수한, 알코올성의, 원기 있는, 정신적인
corresponsive 상응하는, 노력에 반응하는
contentious 논쟁적인

03 정답 ④

정답해설

밑줄 친 단어가 문맥상 '~과 관계없이'로 사용되었고, 유의어로는 ④ notwithstanding이 적절하다.

해석

우리가 의심하는 것**과 관계없이**, 그것은 여전히 단지 그 견본의 추측일 뿐이다.
① ~을 개량하다, ~을 갈고닦다, ~보다 우수하다
② ~의 비용으로
③ ~에 관하여
④ ~에도 불구하고

어휘

conjecture 추측, ~을 추측하다
refine on ~을 개량하다, ~을 갈고 닦다, ~보다 우수하다
at a charge of ~의 비용으로
pertaining to ~에 관하여
notwithstanding ~에도 불구하고

04 정답 ①

정답해설

장학금을 어떻게 받았는지 묻는 A의 질문인 "How did you get the scholarship? (너 장학금 어떻게 받았어?)"에 B는 자신이 장학금을 받은 방법에 관해 설명한다. B는 "I studied hard day and night. (난 밤낮으로 열심히 공부했어)"라고 대답한다. 이는 문맥상 자연스러운 대화의 흐름이다.

오답해설

② A가 '지난 수업에서 우리 모든 자료를 다루었어? (Did we cover all the materials last class?)'라고 묻자, B는 대화의 흐름에 적절하지 않은 '축하해. 내가 다 기뻐. (Congratulations. I feel happy for you)'라고 대답한다.
③ A는 B에게 지난주 토요일에 장 보러 갔지만, 우유 사는 것을 깜빡했다고 말한다. B는 투자하는 것에 대해 고민해보고 있었다고 답변하며 A에게 '너도 할래? (Are you in?)'라며 권유한다. 이는 문맥상 어색한 대화이다.
④ A가 B를 보고 많이 변했다고 이야기하며 너에게 무슨 일이 있었던 것인지 묻자, '더 이상 변화하는 것이 두렵지 않다. (not afraid to make changes anymore)' 맥락상 부적절한 답변을 한다. 무슨 일이 있었는지를 남겨야 한다.

해석

① A: 너 어떻게 장학금 받았어?
   B: 난 밤낮으로 열심히 공부했어.
② A: 우리가 지난 수업에 모든 자료를 다뤘나?
   B: 축하해, 내가 다 기쁘다.
③ A: 나는 지난주 토요일에 장 보러 갔는데 우유 사는 것을 까먹었어.
   B: 나는 투자하는 것에 대해 생각해 보고 있었어. 너도 할래?
④ A: 너 우리가 마지막으로 만났을 때와는 많이 달라졌다. 무슨 일이 있었던 거야?
   B: 난 더 이상 변화를 두려워하지 않아.

어휘

scholarship 장학금
grocery 식료품 잡화점, 식료품
materials 직물, 재료, 자료
investment 투자

05 정답 ③

정답해설

③ **출제 포인트: 타동사구[완전타동사 + 목적어 + 전치사 + 목적어]**
'provide A with B'는 'A에게 B를 제공하다'를 뜻하며 'provide B for/to A'로 바꾸어 사용할 수 있다. 이때 A에는 대상을 나타내는 목적어가 오며 B에는 사물을 나타내는 목적어가 온다. 해당 문장은 'provide + 대상 + 전치사 + 사물'의 형태이므로 전치사에 'with'를 사용해야 한다. 따라서 'for' 를 'with'로 수정해야 한다.

오답해설

① **출제 포인트: have to + 동사원형: ~해야 한다**
'~해야 한다'를 뜻하는 'have to + 동사원형'이 동명사 형태로 사용된 문장으로 옳은 문장이다.

② 출제 포인트: 전치사 + 관계대명사
'전치사 + 관계대명사'는 뒤따라오는 문장이 완전한 형태이다. 해당 문장은 'for which' 뒤에 오는 문장의 형태가 완전하므로 옳은 문장이다. 선행사는 the reason으로 for the reason이 for which가 된 경우이다.

④ 출제 포인트: what vs. that
'an extra bedroom'을 선행사로 하며 뒤따라오는 문장에서 'to use'의 목적어가 없으므로 목적격 관계대명사 'that'이 사용되었음을 알 수 있다.

[해석]
모든 것을 잃고 다시 모든 것을 처음부터 시작해야 한다는 예상은 누구에게나 압도적일 것입니다. 그런 이유로 저는 당신에게 제가 할 수 있는 어떤 도움이라도 제공하고자 합니다. 저에게 여분의 침실이 있는데 당신이 자유롭게 사용해도 됩니다.

[어휘]
prospect 가망, 예상, 전망 overwhelm 압도하다
provide A with B A에게 B를 제공하다
assistance 도움, 원조, 지원 extra 추가의, 가외의, 여분의

06 정답 ②

[정답해설]
② 출제 포인트: 수동태 불가동사
'emerge'는 완전자동사로 수동태로 사용할 수 없다. 해당 문장은 'emerge'의 수동태인 'was emerged'를 사용하였으므로 틀린 문장이다. 따라서 'was emerged'를 'emerged'로 수정해야 한다.

[오답해설]
① 출제 포인트: 수일치
주어 'Traditional consumption'은 단수 형태이므로 동사에 단수형태인 'was'를 옳게 사용하였다.

③ 출제 포인트: 관계부사 vs. 관계대명사
관계대명사는 뒤따라오는 문장이 불완전한 형태이며 관계부사는 뒤따라오는 문장이 완전한 형태이다. 해당 문장은 관계부사 'where'이 사용되었으며 뒤따라오는 문장이 완전한 형태이므로 옳은 문장이다.

④ 출제 포인트: to부정사의 명사적 용법
to부정사(구) 'to be scarce'는 to부정사의 명사적 용법에 해당하며 완전타동사 'continued'의 목적어로 사용되었다.

[해석]
전통적인 소비는 특별히 검소하지 않았다. 검소라는 개념은 좀 더 풍부한 화폐 문화에서 나타났다. 자원이 계속적으로 부족했던 전통 사회에서, 소비는 더욱 계절적이고 공동체 지향적이었다.

[어휘]
traditional 전통의 consumption 소비, 소모
thrift 절약, 검약, 검소 affluent 부유한
scarce 부족한, 드문 communally 공동으로

07 정답 ②

[정답해설]
② 출제 포인트: sort/kind/type + of + 무관사 명사
'sort/kind/type + of' 뒤에 오는 명사(구)는 관사 없이 사용해야 한다. 해당 문장은 'sorts of'와 명사(구) 'useless data' 사이에 정관사 'the'를 사용하였으므로 틀린 문장이다. 따라서 'the'를 삭제해야 한다.

[오답해설]
① 출제 포인트: 대명사 it
해당 문장에서 대명사 'it'은 단수명사(구) 'the Internet'을 가리키므로 옳게 사용되었다.

③ 출제 포인트: 현재분사 vs. 과거분사
수식하는 대상이 명사 'knowledge'이며 해석상 '체계화된 지식'이 자연스러우므로 과거분사 organized를 사용하는 것이 옳다.

④ 출제 포인트: 주격관계대명사 수일치
주격 관계대명사절 동사의 수일치 기준은 선행사이다. 해당 문장은 선행사 'various filters'가 복수형태이므로 주격 관계대명사절 동사에 복수형태인 'help'를 옳게 사용하였다.

[해석]
인터넷은 누구나 무언가를 게시할 수 있는 자유로운 공간이기 때문에 온갖 종류의 쓸모없는 자료로 가득 찰 수 있다. 그 결과, 허접한 자료의 바다에서 체계적인 지식이 쉽게 오염되거나 분실될 수 있다. 책의 경우에는, 독자들이 신뢰할 만한 정보와 신뢰할 수 없는 정보를 식별하도록 도와주는 다양한 여과장치들이 있다.

[어휘]
space 공간 post 게시하다, 발송하다
organize 체계화하다, 조직하다 corrupt 오염시키다, 타락시키다
junk 쓰레기, 폐물 filter 여과장치, 필터

08 정답 ①

[정답해설]
해당 지문은 '아시아에서 집으로 식사 초대를 받았을 때 가져갈 수 있는 적합한 선물'에 대해 설명하고 있다. (A)가 포함된 문장에서 "There are a lot of people who don't drink alcohol"이라고 '술을 마시지 않는 사람이 많다'라고 언급하고 있으므로, "your hosts may not consider alcohol an ___(A)___ gift"에서는 '초대자는 술을 적당한 선물로 여기지 않을 것이다'라는 내용이 들어가는 것이 적합하다. 따라서 (A)에는 'appropriate(적당한)'가 들어가야 한다. 또한, (B) 이전 문장에서 "In some Asian countries, different flower types, their color and even their arrangement may communicate specific messages you don't intend to convey."라고 '꽃이 의도하지 않은 메시지를 줄 수도 있다'라고 언급하고 있으므로, 꽃도 적당한 선물이 아님을 알 수 있다. 따라서 (B)에는 '꽃을 가져가지 않는 것이 좋다'는 내용이 들어가야 하므로 '피하다'라는 의미의 avoided 또는 eschewed가 적절하다. 따라서 정답은 '① appropriate(적당한) - avoided(피하다)'이다.

[오답해설]
② (B) eschewed는 문맥상 자연스러우나 (A) unsuitable이 흐름상 어색하므로 오답이다.
③ (A) appropriate은 문맥상 자연스러우나, (B) selected는 각각 글의 주장과는 반대되는 의미를 담고 있으므로, 오답이다.
④ (A), (B) 모두 글의 흐름과 어울리지 않는다.

[해석]
일본과 같은 아시아 국가에서 사람들은 엄청나게 선물을 준다. 그리고 유럽과 같이 아시아에서 만일 당신이 누군가의 집에 식사 초대를 받았다면 선물을 가지고 가는 것이 예의이다. 그러나 염두에 두어야 할 몇 가지 문화적 차이가 있다. 서양에서 인기 있는 선물은 와인 한 병이나 꽃인 반면, 아시아에서는 그렇지 않다. 많은 사람들이 술을 마시지 않으므로, 당신이 어디에 있는가에 따라 당신을 초대한 사람은 술을 (A) 적당한 선물로 여기지 않을 수도 있다. 유사하게, 꽃도 위험성이 많을 수 있다. 일부 아시아 국가에서, 다른 꽃의 종류, 색깔, 심지어 그것들의 배열은 당신이 전하려고 의도하지 않은 특정한 의

미를 전달할 수도 있다. 기본적으로, 그것들은 (B) 피하는 것이 가장 좋다. 대신에 당신이 방문하는 지역에서 어떤 달콤한 디저트가 인기 있는지 알아내는 것이 확실하다. 지역 사람들이 매우 많이 추천하는 곳에서 그것들을 사고, 그것들이 확실히 예쁘게 포장되도록 한다면 거의 모든 상황에서 좋은 선물을 갖게 될 것이다.
① 적당한 – 피하다
② 부적당한 – 피하다
③ 적당한 – 선택하다
④ 부적당한 – 선물하다

어휘

mindful 염두에 두는
depending on ~에 따라
minefield 지뢰밭(보이지 않는 위험들이 도사리는 곳)
arrangement 배열
communicate 전달하다, 의사를 소통하다
specific 특정한
convey 전하다, 전달하다
intend 의도하다
safe bet 확실한 것[일]
local (특정 지역에 사는) 주민, 현지인, 지역 사람
attractively 보기 좋게
just about 모든, 거의
context 상황

오답률 TOP 2

09 정답 ②

정답해설

해당 지문은 '아일랜드의 대기근의 영향'에 대해 설명하는 글이다. "As a direct consequence of the famine, Ireland's population of almost 8.4 million in 1844 had fallen to 6.6 million by 1851(기근의 직접적인 결과로서, 1844년 거의 8백 4십만이었던 아일랜드의 인구는 1851년 6백 6십만으로 감소했다)."에서 '기근의 직접적인 결과'를 설명한 후, "A further aftereffect of the famine was thus the clearing of many smallholders from the land and the concentration of landownership in fewer hands(그러므로 기근의 추가적 여파는 토지로부터의 소작농의 감소와 토지소유권이 더 적은 사람들에게로 집중되는 것이었다)."를 통해 '기근의 여파'를 설명하고 있으므로, 전체 글의 주제로 가장 적절한 보기는 '② direct and indirect results of the Great Famine(대기근의 직간접적 결과)'이다.

오답해설

① 기근의 원인은 본문에 언급되지 않는다.
③ 기근이 '농업/목축업'에 미친 영향은 언급되고 있으나, 글 전체를 아우르는 주요 주제가 아니므로 오답이다.
④ 기근으로 인한 인구 변화가 본문 초반에 언급되기는 하지만, 글 전체를 아우르는 주요 주제가 아니므로 오답이다.

해석

아일랜드 감자 기근이라고도 불리는 대기근은 아일랜드의 인구통계학적 역사상 분수령이라는 것이 입증되었다. 기근의 직접적인 결과로서, 1844년 거의 8백 4십만이었던 아일랜드의 인구는 1851년 6백 6십만으로 감소했다. 농장 서부 및 남서부 지방의 농장 노동자와 소작농의 수가 특히 급격한 감소를 겪었다. 그러므로 기근의 추가적 여파는 토지로부터의 소작농의 감소와 토지소유권이 더 적은 사람들에게로 집중되는 것이었다. 그에 따라, 영국 수출을 위한 육류를 공급하며, 이전보다 더 많은 토지가 양과 소의 방목을 위해 사용되었다.
① 대기근의 주요 원인
② 대기근의 직간접적 결과
③ 대기근이 아일랜드 농업에 미친 영향
④ 대기근에 이어진 인구통계학적 변화

어휘

famine 기근
watershed 분수령
demographic 인구(통계)학의
consequence 결과
agricultural 농업의
smallholder 소규모 자작농[소작농]
undergo 겪다, 경험하다
drastic 급격한
decline 감소
aftereffect 여파
clearing 제거, 청산
concentration 집중
landownership 토지소유권
thereafter 그에 따라, 그 후
graze 방목하다
export 수출
following 다음의, …에 이은

10 정답 ④

정답해설

해당 지문은 '가상현실(VR)을 통해 체험하는 여행'에 대한 글이며, 두 번째 문장 "The immersive video allows you to experience your destinations before even packing your suitcase(몰입형 영상은 당신이 여행 가방을 꾸리기도 전에 목적지를 경험할 수 있도록 해준다)."를 통해 '선택한 목적지를 미리 체험해 보는 것'에 대해 언급하고 있으며, 마지막 문장 "With this virtual tour, you can decide whether the destination you have picked for yourself is good or not(이러한 가상 여행을 통해 당신은 자신을 위해 선정한 목적지가 적합한지 아닌지 결정할 수 있다)."을 통해 다시 한 번 목적지를 체험해 볼 수 있다는 것을 언급해주고 있다. 따라서 VR을 이용해 할 수 있는 일을 설명하는 빈칸에는 '④ have the try-it-before-you-buy-it experience(구매 전 이용해보는 경험을 하다)'가 들어가는 것이 가장 적절하다.

오답해설

① 본문이 여행에 대해 언급하고 있으나, 구체적으로 '선택된 목적지를 미리 체험해보는 것'에 초점이 맞추어져 있으므로, 'travel wherever and whenever you want(당신이 원하는 어디든 그리고 언제든 여행하다)'는 본문의 내용보다 광범위한 내용에 관한 것임을 알 수 있다. 따라서 오답이다.
② 여행 경비에 대한 내용은 본문에서 언급되지 않는다.
③ 여행을 가기 전 체험하는 것에 대해 언급하고 있으므로, 여행을 다녀온 후에 대한 내용은 빈칸에 적절하지 않다.

해석

가상현실을 통해 여행하는 것은 다른 종류의 여행이다. 몰입형 영상은 당신이 여행 가방을 꾸리기도 전에 목적지를 경험할 수 있도록 해준다. 가상현실을 이용하여 당신은 구매 전 이용해보는 경험을 할 수 있다. 만일 당신이 크루즈의 특등실에서 밀실 공포증을 느낄 것이라고 생각한다면, 미리 알아보는 것이 어떤가? 슈트를 입으면 아마 당신은 기분이 나아질지도 모른다. 가상현실은 당신이 예약을 하기 전에 호텔 객실뿐만 아니라 유람선 객실도 답사할 수 있게 해준다. 객실을 확인하는 것 외에도, 당신은 또한 거리 경관을 보고 인근 건물들과 식당들을 확인할 수 있다. 이러한 가상 여행을 통해 당신은 자신을 위해 선정한 목적지가 적합한지 아닌지 결정할 수 있다.
① 당신이 원하는 어디든 그리고 언제든 여행하다
② 당신이 떠나기 전에 여행 경비를 절약하다
③ 집에 돌아온 후 휴가를 다시 체험하다
④ 구매 전 이용해보는 경험을 하다

어휘

immersive 몰입형의
destination 목적지
claustrophobic 밀실 공포증
stateroom 특등실, 특별실, 개인실
test the waters (행동하거나 결정을 내리기 전에) 미리 상황을 살피다[조심스럽게 알아보다]
explore 답사하다, 탐험하다
A as well as B B뿐만 아니라 A도

prior to …에 앞서, 먼저
aside from …외에
budget 예산, 경비

book 예약하다
venue 장소, 현장, 건물
relive 다시 체험하다

결국엔 성정혜 영어 하프모의고사
기적사 DAY 29

| 01 | ① | 02 | ③ | 03 | ④ | 04 | ② | 05 | ① |
| 06 | ③ | 07 | ① | 08 | ① | 09 | ④ | 10 | ③ |

01 정답 ①

정답해설

밑줄 친 단어가 문맥상 '~을 대신하여'로 사용되었으므로, 유의어로는 ① in a person's stead가 적절하다.

해석

당신 둘은 당신이 만든 용어들에 동의를 해야만 하고, 나는 의회를 **대신하여** 정당화를 확보하기 위해서 동의할 것이다.
① ~을 대신하여
② ~에 관하여
③ ~와 동등하게
④ ~의 비용으로

어휘

justification 정당화   on behalf of ~을 대신하여, 위해서
in a person's stead ~을 대신하여
in the matter of ~에 관하여   in a class with ~와 동등하게
at a cost of ~의 비용으로

02 정답 ③

정답해설

밑줄 친 단어가 문맥상 '다루기 힘든'의 의미로 사용되었고, 유의어로는 ③ cumbersome이 적절하다.

해석

고비용의 복잡한 서버 인프라는 문명화된 사회에서 관리하기가 **힘들고** 비용이 많이 들 수 있습니다.
① 독창성이 없는
② 미숙한
③ 다루기 어려운, 거추장스러운, 성가신
④ 내성적인, 겁이 많은

어휘

clonish 독창성이 없는   callow 미숙한
cumbersome 다루기 어려운, 거추장스러운, 성가신
timid 내성적인, 겁이 많은

03 정답 ④

정답해설

밑줄 친 단어가 문맥상 '결론 없는'의 의미로 쓰였고, 유의어로는 ④ not in conclusion이 적절하다.

해석

그러나 우리는 나이 든 비평가들의 진부하지만 **결론 없는** 주장에 많은 시간을 할애할 필요는 없다.
① 탐구심이 있는

② 거슬리지 않는, 악의가 없는
③ 조금도 ~가 아니다
④ 결론이 안 나는

어휘

well-worn 진부한, 오래 써서 낡은   inquiring 탐구심이 있는
offenseless 거슬리지 않는, 악의가 없는
not in the least 조금도 ~가 아니다
not in conclusion 결론이 안 나는

04 정답 ②

정답해설

A와 B는 중간고사 수학 과목에 관한 대화를 나눈다. A는 B에게 내일 중간고사에서 수학 과목을 치지만 내용을 ② '이해할 수 없다(over my head)'라고 이야기한다. B는 A의 말에 공감하며 수학 과목이 어렵다고 이야기한다. 하지만 지난 학기에 B는 수학 과목에서 A+라는 좋은 성적을 받았으므로 궁금한 것이 있으면 자기에게 물어보라고 말한다. A는 어떻게 그렇게 좋은 성적을 받았냐고 묻자, B는 처음에는 A와 마찬가지로 자기가 배운 모든 것들이 이해하기 어려웠지만 포기하지 않았다고 답변한다.

오답해설

① 'in body(스스로)'는 'over a person's head(이해되지 않는)'와 다른 의미를 지닌다.
③ 'neck and neck(비슷하게)'은 수학 과목이 이해하기 어렵다고 말하는 대화의 문맥상 어색하다.
④ 수학이 어렵다고 이야기하는 맥락의 대화에서 'a pain in the neck(불쾌한 것)'은 빈칸에 들어갈 마땅치 않다.

해석

A: 너 중간고사 시험 언제 시작해?
B: 다음 주 수요일. 너는 언제?
A: 나는 내일 시작하고 수학 과목을 봐. 근데 전혀 <u>이해할 수가 없어</u>.
B: 너의 잘못이 아니야, 수학이 쉽지만은 않지. 근데 원한다면 나한테 질문해도 돼. 나 지난 학기에 수학 과목 A+ 받았어.
A: 우와 진짜? 너 어떻게 그렇게 좋은 성적을 받았어?
B: 나 사실 처음엔 너랑 똑같이 느꼈어. 근데 난 포기하지 않았어.
① 스스로
② 이해되지 않는
③ 비슷하게
④ 불쾌한 것

어휘

mid-term 중간고사   Mathematics 수학
fault 잘못   semester 학기
grade 성적   actually 사실
give up 포기하다

오답률 TOP 1

05 정답 ①

정답해설

① **출제 포인트: 관계대명사 vs. 관계부사**
관계사 뒤에 오는 문장이 완전한 경우 관계부사 또는 '전치사+관계대명사'를 사용해야 한다. 해당 문장은 관계대명사 'which' 뒤에 오는 문장이 완전한 형태이므로 틀린 문장이다. 따라서 'which'를 'where' 또는 'in which'로 수정해야 한다.

오답해설

② **출제 포인트: 부사절을 이끄는 접속사 where**
해당 문장에서 'where'는 부사절을 이끄는 접속사로 '~한 경우'로 해석한다. 이때 'where'가 이끄는 절은 'the degree of competition is particularly intense'이다.
③ **출제 포인트: 명사절을 이끄는 접속사 that**
해당 문장에서 'that'은 명사절을 이끄는 접속사이며 전치사 'in'과 결합하여 '~라는 점에서'를 뜻한다.
④ **출제 포인트: 타동사구[완전타동사+목적어+전치사+목적어]**
'face A with B'는 'A를 B에 직면시키다'를 뜻하며 수동형은 'A be faced with B'이다. 따라서 해당 문장은 옳은 문장이다.

해석

경쟁은 한 조직이 다른 조직들을 희생해서만 승리할 수 있는 제로섬 게임이 된다. 하지만 경쟁의 정도가 특히 극심한 경우, 제로섬 게임은 시장 내의 모두가 추가적인 비용에 직면하므로, 급속하게 네거티브섬 게임이 될 수도 있다.

어휘

competition 경쟁, 대회, 시합   zero sum game 제로섬 게임
organization 조직, 기구   intense 극심한, 강렬한
face A with B A를 B에 직면시키다
cost 비용

06 정답 ③

정답해설

③ **출제 포인트: 수일치**
'species'는 단수와 복수형태가 같음에 유의해야 한다. 주어 'one species'에서 'species'를 수식하는 'one'이 있는 것으로 보아 해당 문장에서 species는 단수로 쓰였음을 알 수 있다. 따라서 단수 주어 'one species'에 수일치하여 동사 또한 단수 형태인 'eliminates'를 사용해야 한다. 따라서 'eliminate'를 'eliminates'로 수정해야 한다.

오답해설

① **출제 포인트: 수동태 불가동사**
'interfere'는 완전자동사로 전치사 없이 목적어를 가질 수 없으며 수동태로 사용할 수 없다. 해당 문장은 'interferes' 뒤에 목적어가 없으며 능동태로 사용하였으므로 옳은 문장이다.
② **출제 포인트: 동사 관용표현**
'take over'는 관용표현으로 '장악하다'를 뜻한다. 해당 문장에서는 'the inferior competitor loses out'과 'the competitively superior species takes over'가 등위접속사 'and'로 병렬구조를 이루고 있다. 대응되는 문장의 주어가 'the inferior competitor'로 단수이므로 'the competitively superior species'가 단수로 쓰였음을 알 수 있다. 따라서 'species'를 단수 취급하여 동사 또한 단수 동사인 'takes over'를 사용하는 것이 옳다.
④ **출제 포인트: 불완전타동사의 수동태**
불완전타동사 'call'의 수동태는 '목적어+be called+목적격 보어[명사(구)]'의 형태이다.

해석

만약 어떤 것도 방해하지 않는다면, 열등한 경쟁자는 지고 경쟁력이 있는 뛰어난 종들이 장악한다. 하나의 종이 다른 종과의 경쟁에서 이김으로써 그것을 몰아낼 때, 그것은 경쟁적 배제라고 불린다.

어휘

interfere 방해하다, 간섭하다   inferior 열등한
superior 우수한, 우월한   species 종
lose out 지다   take over 장악하다

07 정답 ①

정답해설

① **출제 포인트: 현재분사 vs. 과거분사**
생략된 주어 'John'과 'smile'의 관계가 능동이므로 현재분사 'smiling'을 사용하는 것이 옳다. 따라서 'smiled'를 'smiling'으로 수정해야 한다. 이때 'all'은 부사임에 유의하도록 한다.

오답해설

② **출제 포인트: sort/kind/type+of+무관사 명사**
'sort/kind/type+of' 뒤에 오는 명사(구)는 관사 없이 사용해야 한다. 해당 문장은 'kinds of' 뒤에 관사 없이 명사(구) 'temptation'을 사용하였으므로 옳은 문장이다.

③ **출제 포인트: 주어와 동사 수일치/장소 부사의 도치**
해당 문장은 장소 부사구가 문두로 이동하여 동사-주어의 도치가 일어난 문장으로 이때 주어는 복수명사 'rows'이다. 따라서 동사에 복수형태인 'were'를 옳게 사용하였다.

④ **출제 포인트: to부정사의 부사적 용법/to부정사의 태**
'to be touched'는 to부정사의 부사적 용법으로 목적을 나타낸다. 또한 해석상 '초코바 줄이 만져지기 위해 기다리는 중이었다'가 자연스러우므로 to부정사 내에 수동태를 사용하였다.

해석

귀여운 세 살짜리 남자아이 Tom은 환하게 웃으며 스낵류, (초콜릿)바류, 사탕류가 있는 통로를 따라 걷고 있었다. 그 아이에게 그것은 온갖 종류의 유혹이 있는 통로였다. "와!"하고 그는 외쳤다. 바로 그의 눈앞에 맛있게 보이는 초코바의 줄이 만져지기 위해 기다리는 중이었다.

어휘

aisle 통로
exclaim 소리치다, 외치다
temptation 유혹
row 줄, 열

08 정답 ①

정답해설

(A) 빈칸에는 초기 놀이터의 특징을 현재의 놀이터와 비교하여 설명하는 표현이 들어가는 것이 적절하다. 빈칸 이후에서 "definitely wouldn't comply with health and safety regulations today"라고 언급한 것으로 보아, 초기의 놀이터는 현재 놀이터보다 '위험했으며 질이 낮았다'는 것을 알 수 있다. 따라서 빈칸에 들어갈 수 있는 표현은 보기 중 'crude(조잡한)', 'primitive(원시적인)'이다.

(B) 빈칸에는 초기 놀이터에서 부상을 당할 수 있는 상황을 표현하는 단어가 들어가는 것이 적절하다. 초기 놀이터의 구조물들은 날카로운 모서리를 지니고 있었으므로, '주의하여 또는 제대로 사용되지 않으면 부상을 초래할 수 있다'라는 의미의 문장이 되는 것이 문맥상 자연스럽다. 그러므로 빈칸에 적절한 표현은 보기 중 'properly(올바르게)', 'appropriately(알맞게)'이다. 따라서 정답은 '① crude(조잡한)-properly(올바르게)'이다.

오답해설

② (B) 빈칸에 'exclusively(배타적으로)'는 문맥상 어색하므로 오답이다.
③ (B) 빈칸에 'constantly(지속적으로)'는 문맥상 어색하므로 오답이다.
④ (A) 빈칸에 'sophisticated(정교한)'는 문맥상 어색하므로 오답이다.

해석

초기의 놀이터는 우리가 오늘날 익숙해진 것과는 매우 다르게 생겼다. 놀이터를 만들려는 아이디어는 독일에서 최초로 도입되었으며, 기본적으로 아이들에게 올바르게 노는 방법을 가르치기 위한 기반으로서였다. 그러나 1859년이 되어서야 비로소 최초의 어린이 놀이터가 영국 Manchester의 한 공원에 설치되었다. 아이들을 위한 놀이터를 설치하자는 아이디어는 미국으로 퍼져 나갔고 1886년 미국 최초의 놀이터들이 보스턴에 나타나기 시작했다. 이러한 초기 놀이터들은 현대의 기준에 따르면 매우 (A) 조잡했고, 오늘날의 보건과 안전 기준에 명백히 맞지 않았다. 놀이터가 처음 생겼을 때, 그것들은 보통 만일 (B) 올바르게 사용되지 않으면 많은 해를 끼칠 수 있는 날카로운 모서리가 있는 대충 지은 철로 된 구조물들로 구성되어 있었다.

① 조잡한 - 올바르게
② 초라한, 겸손한 - 배타적으로
③ 원시적인 - 지속적으로
④ 정교한 - 알맞게

어휘

introduce 도입하다
platform 기반, 플랫폼
definitely 명확히
comply with ~을 따르다, 준수하다, 지키다
regulation 규정
consist of ~로 구성되다
structure 구조(물)
do damage 해를 끼치다
properly 제대로, 잘, 올바르게
exclusively 배타적으로, 독점적으로
constantly 지속적으로
sophisticated 정교한, 복잡한, 고도로 발달한
appropriately 알맞게, 적당하게
essentially 기본적으로, 본질적으로
standard 기준
emerge 나타나다, 생기다
roughly 대충
edge 모서리, 가장자리
crude 조잡한, 거친
humble 초라한, 보잘것없는
primitive 원시적인

오답률 TOP 2

09 정답 ④

정답해설

해당 지문은 '아일랜드 감자 기근(Irish Potato Famine)의 원인'이 규명되었다는 내용의 글이다. 주어진 문장에서는 "'아일랜드 감자 기근'이 *감자역병균(Phytophthora infestans)*의 한 종류에 의해 발생되었다"라는 것을 언급하고 있으므로, 이에 이어지는 내용으로는 과거 과학자들이 생각했던(they believed) 유력한 감자역병균의 종류를 밝히고 있는 (C)가 적절하다. 이후에는, 정확한 원인을 알아내기 위한 실험이 시작되었다는 내용의 (B)가 이어지고, 실험을 통해 '기존에 추정하고 있던 US-1이 아닌 HERB-1이 기근을 야기한 병충해의 원인이었다는 것을 알아냈다'는 내용인 (A)가 이어지는 것이 적절하다. 따라서 정답은 '④ (C) - (B) - (A)'이다.

오답해설

③ (B)는 실험의 착수에 대한 내용이고, (A)는 실험의 결과에 대한 내용이므로 (A)가 (B) 이전에 등장하는 것은 어색하다.
나머지 보기는 문맥상 어색하므로 오답이다.

해석

과학자들은 *감자역병균*의 한 종류가 아일랜드 감자 기근을 초래하면서 1845년 시작한 아일랜드의 광범위한 감자 작물의 황폐를 야기했다는 것을 오랫동안 알고 있었다.
(C) 그들은 가장 유력한 원인이 US-1이라고 알려진 종류라고 생각했다.
(B) 수수께끼를 풀기 위해 분자 생물학자들이 1845년 당시 거의 10여 개의 식물 표본에서 추출된 DNA를 검사했다.
(A) 19세기의 표본의 게놈의 유전자를 배열하고 그것들을 US-1을 포함한 현대의 병충해와 비교해 본 후 연구원들은 병충해를 유발한 것은 사실 US-1이 아니라, 이전에는 알려지지 않았던 종류인, 1840년대 유럽으로 전파되기 전 19세기 초 어느 시기에 미주에서 최초로 발생한 HERB-1이었다고 결론지었다.

어휘

strain (동,식물 질병 등의)종류[유형]
Phytophthora infestans 감자역병균
widespread 널리 퍼진, 광범위한
devastation 황폐, 폐허, 참해
lead to 초래하다, 일으키다
famine 기근
sequence (유전자 분자의) 배열 순서를 밝히다
genome 게놈
blight 병충해, 마름병
conclude ~을 결론짓다
previously 이전에
molecular biologist 분자 생물학자
extract ~에서 추출하다
botanical 식물의
specimen 견본, 표본
culprit 원인, 범인

오답률 TOP 3
10 정답 ③

정답해설

주어진 문장에서는 'Holoride'라는 신생 기업의 새로운 기술을 소개하고 있다. 이후 이어질 문장으로 가장 적절한 것은 'The software company's technology enables gaming partners such as Disney to create virtual experiences that correspond to a car's real-time movements (그 소프트웨어 회사의 기술은 Disney와 같은 게임 협력사들이 자동차의 실시간 움직임과 일치하는 가상 체험을 만들어낼 수 있게 했다)'를 통해 주어진 문장에서 언급한 "in-car virtual reality experience(자동차용 가상현실 체험)'를 보충하여 설명하고 있는 (B)이다. 이후에는 해당 기술이 이용되는 방식을 설명하는 내용이 이어지는 것이 자연스러운데, 우선 '해당 기술을 체험하기 위해 승객들이 헤드셋을 착용한다'라는 내용인 (C)가 이어지고, '그 이후(Then) 차량의 데이터를 실시간으로 전송한다'라는 내용인 (A)가 이어지는 것이 적절하다. 따라서 글의 순서로 가장 적절한 것은 '③ (B) – (C) – (A)'이다.

오답해설

①, ② (A)의 'Then(그 이후)'으로 보아, 이전에 기술 체험을 위한 절차를 설명하는 내용이 와야 하므로, (C) 이후에 (A)가 위치해야 한다. 따라서 오답이다.
나머지 보기는 문맥상 어색하므로 오답이다.

해석

고급 자동차 제조사 Audi가 설립한 신생 회사 Holoride는 세계 최초의 "자동차용 가상현실 체험"을 선보이기 위해 Ford와 Universal Pictures와 협력해왔다.
(B) 그 소프트웨어 회사의 기술은 Disney와 같은 게임 협력사들이 자동차의 실시간 움직임과 일치하는 가상 체험을 만들어낼 수 있게 했다.
(C) 승객은 가상환경에 몰입하기 위해 헤드셋을 착용한다.
(A) 그 이후 Holoride는 GPS, 주행 경로, 핸들의 각도, 가속도에서 오는 관성력을 포함한 데이터를 자동차로부터 수집하고 실시간으로 그것들을 가상환경으로 옮긴다.

어휘

start-up 신생 회사, 스타트업
spin out 만들다, 스핀아웃 (기업의 일부 사업부 또는 신규 사업을 분리하여 전문 회사를 만드는 것)
team up 협력하다
showcase 공개하다, 소개하다, 선보이다
navigation 운행, 조종
route 경로
steering (차량의) 조종 장치
g-force 관성력
acceleration 가속도
translate 옮기다
enable 가능하게 하다
correspond to …에[와] 일치하다, 들어맞다
real-time 실시간의
immerse 몰입시키다

결국엔 성정혜 영어 하프모의고사
기적사 DAY 30

| 01 | ① | 02 | ② | 03 | ① | 04 | ③ | 05 | ④ |
| 06 | ④ | 07 | ④ | 08 | ③ | 09 | ④ | 10 | ① |

오답률 TOP 3
01 정답 ①

정답해설

밑줄 친 단어는 문맥상 '전용의'를 뜻하며 유의어로는 ① monopolistic이 가장 적절하다.

해석

그리고 일부 사무실은 의사들의 **전용** 사유물로 남아있었다.
① 독점적인, 전매의
② 솔직한, 순진한
③ 외향적인
④ 평범한, 단조로운

어휘

monopolistic 독점적인
ingenuous 솔직한, 순진한
extrovert 외향적인
humdrum 평범한, 단조로운

02 정답 ②

정답해설

밑줄 친 단어는 문맥상 '전례 없는'으로 사용되었고, 유의어로는 ② unexampled가 적절하다.

해석

그 준비는 **전례 없는** 규모로 이루어졌다.
① 이해하기 어려운, 읽기 어려운
② 전례가 없는
③ 자진해서
④ 모호한, 불확실한

어휘

unreadable 이해하기 어려운, 읽기 어려운
unexampled 전례가 없는
volunteered 자진해서
unballasted 모호한, 불확실한

오답률 TOP 1
03 정답 ①

정답해설

밑줄 친 단어는 문맥상 '거침없는, 솔직한'으로 사용되었고, 유의어로는 ① blunt가 적절하다.

해석

여기서 그는 오스트리아 정부에 대한 **거침없는** 비판으로 두각을 나타내 공작 영지의 반대를 중앙 권력의 강제 징수로 이끌었다.
① 솔직한, 퉁명스러운, 둔화시키다
② 구체적인
③ 당황하게 만드는, 좌절시키는
④ 다양한, 수많은

어휘

distinguish oneself 두각을 나타내다
blunt 솔직한, 퉁명스러운, 둔화시키다
concrete 구체적인
baffling 당황하게 만드는, 좌절시키는
numerous 다양한, 수많은

04 정답 ③

정답해설

Peter는 Nancy의 친구를 드디어 만나게 되어 기쁘다며, (A)'By a word of mouth(소문에 의하면)' 그녀의 키는 눈에 띄게 크다고 말한다. Nancy는 친구의 키가 크다고 Peter의 말에 긍정하며 그녀가 (B)'a heart of gold(고운 마음씨)'를 지녔다고 한다. Nancy와 친구는 태어날 때부터 친구였으며 같은 병원에 태어났다고 말한다. 그리고 Nancy는 그녀와 (C)'for good(영영)' 친구로 지내고 싶다고 말하며 친구가 없는 삶은 상상할 수 없다고 덧붙인다.

오답해설

① (A) Nancy의 친구를 드디어 만나게 되어 기쁘다며 그녀의 '키가 눈에 띄게 크다(she is noticeably tall)'라고 말하는 상황에서 'Take it easy(마음을 편히 해)'는 부적절하다. (B) Nancy의 친구를 칭찬하는 맥락에서 'bad blood(원한)'는 어색하다. (C) Nancy가 그녀와 친구 하는 것을 'by a close call(조마조마하게)'이라고 하는 것은 문맥상 적절하지 않다.
② (A) Nancy의 친구를 만나는 상황에서 'Break a leg(행운을 빈다)'라는 말은 문맥상 적합하지 않다. (B) Nancy가 친구를 'a wild card(예측할 수 없는 사람 혹은 일, 만능의 패)'라고 묘사하는 것은 대화의 흐름을 해친다. (C) Nancy가 자신의 친구와 'across the board(전체적으로)' 친구 한다는 맥락의 대화는 부자연스럽다.
④ (B) 'a skeleton in the closet(비밀)'으로 친구를 묘사하는 것은 친구를 칭찬하는 상황에서 쓰이기에 어색하다.

해석

Peter: 난 드디어 네 친구를 만나게 되어 기뻐. (A) 소문에 의하면, 그녀는 눈에 띄게 키가 크다고 하던데.
Nancy: 너 이미 그 친구에 대해 들었구나! 맞아, 그녀는 아주 키가 커. 근데 그녀를 매우 좋은 사람으로 만들어 주는 것은 그녀가 (B) 고운 마음씨를 지녔다는 거야.
Peter: 사람에게 하는 정말 좋은 칭찬이야! 너희 둘이 되게 친해 보여.
Nancy: 맞아, 우리 친해. 우린 태어날 때부터 친구였어.
Peter: 정말 놀랍다! 그럼 너희들 같은 병원에서 태어난 거야?
Nancy: 맞아, 그리고 나는 우리가 (C) 영영 친구이길 바라. 그녀 없는 삶은 상상할 수 없어.

① (A) 마음 편히 해 (B) 원한 (C) 조마조마하게
② (A) 행운을 빌어 (B) 예측할 수 없는 사람 혹은 일, 만능의 패 (C) 전체적으로
③ (A) 소문에 의하면 (B) 고운 마음씨 (C) 영영
④ (A) 소문에 의하면 (B) 비밀 (C) 영영

어휘

noticeably 눈에 띄게
indeed (긍정적인 진술·대답을 강조하여) 정말
surprising 놀라운

05 정답 ④

정답해설

④ 출제 포인트: 접속사 vs. 전치사
'be sure of'는 목적어로 명사(구)가 오며 'be sure (that)'은 목적어로 명사절이 온다. 해당 문장은 'be sure (that)'을 사용하였으나 목적어가 명사구 'their impact or power'이므로 틀린 문장이다. 따라서 'that'을 'of'로 수정해야 한다.

오답해설

① 출제 포인트: 타동사구[완전타동사 + 목적어 + 전치사 + 목적어]
'add A to B'는 'A를 B에 더하다'를 뜻한다. 따라서 해당 문장은 옳은 문장이다.
② 출제 포인트: to부정사의 부사적 용법
'to assign'은 to부정사의 부사적 용법에 해당하며 목적을 나타낸다. 참고로 'instead of' 이후에는 'legal responsibility'가 생략되었으므로 'instead of to its members'는 옳은 표현이다.
③ 출제 포인트: 전치사 + 관계대명사
'전치사 + 관계대명사'는 뒤따라오는 문장이 완전한 형태이다. 해당 문장은 'in which' 뒤에 오는 문장의 형태가 완전하므로 옳은 문장이다.

해석

회사는 회사의 구성원 대신에 회사 자체에 법적인 책임을 부여하기 위해 설립되기 때문에 집단 환경에서 감소된 개인의 책임에 관한 이야기에 복잡성을 한층 더 더한다. 개별 구성원이 흔히 변화를 일으키는 자신의 영향력이나 능력을 확신하지 못하는 다른 복잡한 조직들이 있다.

어휘

corporation 회사, 기업
complication 복잡성, 복잡한 상태
set something up ~을 세우다
assign A to B A를 B에게 부여하다
bring about ~을 야기하다, 초래하다

06 정답 ④

정답해설

④ 출제 포인트: 수동태 불가동사
'remain'은 완전자동사와 불완전자동사만 가능하므로 수동태를 사용할 수 없다. 해당 문장은 'remain'을 수동태 'is remained'로 사용하였으므로 틀린 문장이다. 따라서 'is remained'를 'remains'로 수정해야 한다. 이때 주격 보어 'oblivious'가 있으므로 해당 문장에서 'remains'는 불완전자동사로 사용된 것임을 알 수 있다.

오답해설

① 출제 포인트: 관계부사 vs. 관계대명사
관계대명사는 뒤따라오는 문장이 불완전한 형태이며 관계부사는 뒤따라오는 문장이 완전한 형태이다. 해당 문장은 관계부사 'where'가 사용되었으며 뒤따라오는 문장이 완전한 형태이므로 옳은 문장이다.
② 출제 포인트: 능동태 vs. 수동태
대명사 'they'가 가리키는 대상은 명사(구) 'beneficial innovations'이며 문맥상 '유익한 혁신들이 가르쳐지다'가 자연스러우므로 수동태를 사용하는 것이 옳다. 이때 'are taught'는 완전타동사의 수동태임에 유의하자.
③ 출제 포인트: 수여동사의 수동태
문맥상 '낮은 동물이 새로운 개념을 배우다'가 자연스러우므로 수동태를 사용하는 것이 옳다. 이때 'is taught'는 수여동사의 수동태이며 능동태로 고치면 '주어 teaches a lower animal the new concept first'이다.

해석
엄격한 지배 위계질서가 존재하는 원숭이 집단에서 유익한 혁신은 만약 그것이 지배적인 원숭이에게 먼저 가르쳐지지 않는다면 집단 전체로 빠르게 퍼지지 않는다. 낮은 위계의 원숭이가 새로운 개념을 먼저 배우면 그 집단의 나머지는 그것의 가치를 거의 의식하지 못한 채로 남게 된다.

어휘
colony 식민지
dominance 지배, 우세
innovation 혁신
rigid 경직된, 엄격한
hierarchy 계급, 체계

07 정답 ④

정답해설
④ 출제 포인트: sort/kind/type + of + 무관사 명사
'sort/kind/type + of' 뒤에 오는 명사(구)는 관사 없이 사용해야 한다. 해당 문장은 'kinds of'와 명사(구) 'rocks' 사이에 정관사 'the'를 사용하였으므로 틀린 문장이다. 따라서 'the'를 삭제해야 한다.

오답해설
① 출제 포인트: to부정사 관용표현
'would like to + 동사원형'은 관용표현으로 '~하고 싶다'를 뜻한다. 따라서 해당 자리에 동사원형 'know'를 사용하는 것이 옳다.

② 출제 포인트: to부정사의 부사적 용법
'to determine whether topsoil erosion from agriculture is too great'은 to부정사의 부사적 용법으로 목적을 나타낸다.

③ 출제 포인트: 주어와 동사 수일치
주어가 동명사인 경우 단수로 취급하며 동사에 단수형태를 사용해야 한다. 해당 문장은 주어에 동명사 'understanding'을 사용하였으므로 동사에 단수형태 'is'를 사용하는 것이 옳다.

해석
농업으로 인한 표토의 부식이 매우 심한지 어떤지를 밝히기 위해 우리는 단단한 암석으로부터의 자연 발생적인 토양 생성의 속도를 알고 싶어 한다. 마찬가지로 수백만 년에 걸쳐 기후가 어떻게 변해 왔는지를 이해하는 것은 현재의 지구 온난화 추세를 제대로 가늠하는 데 매우 중요하다. 과거의 환경 변화에 대한 단서들은 서로 다른 많은 종류의 암석들에 잘 보존되어 있다.

어휘
would like to + 동사원형 ~하고 싶다
formation 형성
topsoil 표토, 표층토
clue 단서, 실마리
determine 알아내다, 밝히다
erosion 부식, 침식

08 정답 ③

정답해설
해당 지문에서는 'Great man theory'에 근거하여 '리더는 타고나는 것'이라고 설명하며, 리더의 '타고난 내적 자질'에 대해 서술하고 있다. 그러나 ③에서 "Rooted in behaviorism, these focus on the actions of leaders, not on mental qualities or internal states(행태 주의에 기반을 둔 이것들은 타고난 정신적 자질 또는 내적인 상태가 아닌 리더의 행동에 초점을 맞춘다)."라고 '리더의 타고난 자질보다는 행위에 더 초점을 맞춘다'라는 내용이 언급되는 것은 전체적인 글의 흐름에 부합하지 않는다. 따라서 ③이 정답이다.

오답해설
나머지는 문맥상 자연스러우므로 오답이다.

해석
당신은 "타고난 리더"라고 칭해지는 누군가에 대해 들어본 적이 있는가? 이 관점에 따르면 리더들은 그들을 천부적인 리더로 만드는 카리스마, 자신감, 지성, 그리고 사회적 기술과 같은 필수적인 내적 자질을 단순히 가지고 태어난다. ① 위인설은 리더십을 위한 능력은 타고난다고, 즉 훌륭한 리더들은 타고난 것이지 만들어진 것이 아니라고 생각한다. ② 이러한 이론들은 종종 훌륭한 리더를 영웅적이고 신화적이며 필요할 때 리더십 능력을 발휘할 운명이라고 묘사한다. ③ 행태 주의에 기반을 둔 이것들은 타고난 정신적 자질 또는 내적인 상태가 아닌 리더의 행동에 초점을 맞춘다. ④ 이러한 이론들은 사람들은 강력한 리더가 되는 방법을 진정으로 배울 수 없다고 말한다. 그것은 당신이 타고나거나 타고나지 않는 것이다. 이것은 리더십을 설명하는 매우 (양육과 반대의 의미로) 자연적인 접근이다.

어휘
describe 묘사하다
confidence 자신감
natural-born 타고난, 천부적인
assume 가정하다, 생각하다
inherent 고유의, 본래부터의
mythic 신화의
rooted ~에 뿌리[근원]를 둔
mental 정신의, 마음의
nurture 양성하다, 양육하다
explain 설명하다
internal 내적인, 내면의
intelligence 지능, 지성
great man theory 위인설
capacity 능력
portray 그리다, 묘사하다
destined …할 운명인
behaviorism 행동주의
opposed 반대된
approach 접근법, 접근

오답률 TOP 1

09 정답 ④

정답해설
해당 지문은 '고혈압 약이 알츠하이머 완화에 도움을 줄 수 있다'는 연구 결과를 소개하는 내용이다. 빈칸에는 해당 약이 알츠하이머 환자의 대뇌 혈류에 어떠한 변화를 발생시키는지 서술하는 내용이 들어가는 것이 알맞다. 빈칸 문장의 "the known decrease in cerebral blood flow in patients with Alzheimer's"를 통해 '알츠하이머를 앓는 사람들은 대뇌 혈류가 감소한다'라는 것을 알 수 있고, 본문 중반에서 "the hypertension drug 'nilvadipine' ~ increased blood flow to the brain's memory and learning center among people with Alzheimer's disease"라고 '고혈압 약인 'nilvadipine'이 뇌 일부분의 혈류를 증가시켰다'라는 사실을 밝히고 있다. 감소와 증가는 반대 관계이므로, 빈칸에는 '반대로 뒤바꾸다'라는 의미의 '④ reversed(반대로 뒤바꾸다)'가 오는 것이 가장 자연스럽다.

오답해설
① '감소가 활발하게 된다'라는 것은 본문의 요지에 반하는 의미가 되므로, 오답이다.
나머지 보기도 문맥상 어색하므로 틀리다.

해석
알츠하이머병은 치매의 가장 흔한 형태이다. 이 질환의 위험성은 나이가 들수록 증가하고 원인은 대체로 알려지지 않았다. American Heart Association의 학술지 *Hypertension*에 실린 새로운 연구에 따르면, 알츠하이머병의 진행을 늦추기 위한 새로운 치료제를 찾던 연구자들은 혈관을 이완시키고 혈압을 낮추는 고혈압 환자를 위한 칼슘채널차단제인 의약품 'nilvadipine'이 뇌의 다른 부분에 영향을 주지 않고 알츠하이머병을 앓고 있는 사람의 뇌의 기억과 학습 중추로 향하는 혈류를 증가시킨다는 것을 알아냈다. 이러한 발견은 알려져 있는 알츠하이머 환자들의 대뇌 혈류 감소가 일부 구역에서 반대로 뒤바뀔 수 있다는 것을 나타낸다. 그러나 중요한 문제는 이 변화가 의학적인 이점이 될 수 있는지 여부라고 연구자들은 언급했다.

① 활발하게 되다
② 지각되다
③ 관찰되다
④ 반대로 뒤바뀌다

어휘

dementia 치매
progression 진행
vascular (혈관 등의) 관의
journal 학술지
indicate 가리키다, 나타내다
translate 바뀌다
note (중요하거나 흥미로운 것을) 언급하다
treatment 치료, 치료법
hypertension 고혈압
affect 영향을 미치다
finding 발견
cerebral blood flow 대뇌 혈류

not less ~ than …못지않게 ~한
biological 생물학의
species 종(種: 생물 분류의 기초 단위)
cause 원인이 되다, 야기하다
ecosystem 생태계
in the sense that ~라는 점에서
community 공동 사회, 일반 사회, 공동체
typically 일반적으로, 전형적으로
abandon 버리다
in its way 그 나름대로
extinction 멸종, 사라짐

collapse 붕괴하다, 무너지다

vehicle 수단, 매개물

10 정답 ①

정답해설

해당 지문은 '언어 사멸(붕괴)'에 대해 서술하며 본문 중반의 "But language diversity is not less important in its way than biological diversity(그러나 언어 다양성은 그 나름대로 생물 다양성 못지않게 중요하다)."를 통해 'language diversity(언어 다양성)'의 중요성을 'biological diversity(생물 다양성)'의 중요성과 비교하고 있다. 이어지는 문장에서 "The extinction of a species causes some ecosystems to collapse."를 통해 '생물의 멸종 → 생태계 붕괴'라고 언급한 후, 빈칸 이후 문장에서 "when a language dies, a world dies with it(언어가 죽을 때, 한 사회는 그것과 함께 죽는다)"를 통해 '언어 사멸 → 한 사회의 소멸'이라고 비교 대상인 '생물학적 결과'와 유사한 논점으로 '언어 사멸의 결과'를 제시하고 있다. 빈칸을 기준으로 유사한 내용이 이어지고 있으므로, "① Similarly(유사하게)"가 들어가는 것이 가장 적절하다.

오답해설

②, ④ 문맥상 적절하지 않다.
③ 빈칸 전후가 대조적인 내용이 아니므로 오답이다.

해석

많은 언어학자들은 2050년까지 전 세계의 6,000개 언어의 절반 또는 그 이상이 사멸할 것이거나 사멸하는 중일 것이라고 예상한다. 언어는 멸종 위기에 있는 포유류보다 두 배의 비율로, 멸종 위기에 있는 조류보다 네 배의 비율로 사라지고 있다. 만약 이러한 추세가 계속된다면, 미래의 세계는 10여 개 또는 그 이하의 언어에 지배당할 수도 있다. 사람들이 서로 더 쉽게 의사소통할 수 있도록 소수인 언어를 더 널리 퍼져 있는 것으로 교체하는 것은 심지어 좋은 일인 것처럼 보일지도 모른다. 그러나 언어 다양성은 그 나름대로 생물 다양성 못지않게 중요하다. 한 종의 멸종은 어떤 생태계를 붕괴시킨다. 유사하게, 사람들을 그러한 지식으로 연결해 주는 수단이 버려짐에 따라 한 사회의 과거, 전통, 그리고 특정한 지식의 기초와의 연결이 모두 일반적으로 사라지게 된다는 점에서, 언어가 죽을 때, 한 사회는 그것과 함께 죽는다.

① 유사하게
② 겉으로 보기에
③ 반대로
④ 특히

어휘

linguist 언어학자
extinct 멸종된
mammal 포유동물
replace A with B A를 B로 교체[대체]하다
minor 소수의
allow 허용하다, 가능하게 하다
predict 예언하다, 예상하다
endangered 멸종 위기에 처한
dominate 지배하다
widespread 널리 퍼진
diversity 다양성

결국엔 성정혜 영어 하프모의고사
기적사 복습 모의고사 3회

01	①	02	③	03	①	04	④	05	②
06	③	07	①	08	④	09	②	10	②
11	③	12	④	13	④	14	③	15	④
16	③	17	④	18	②	19	④	20	④

01 정답 ①
Day 26-01

정답해설

밑줄 친 단어 'pejorative'는 '경멸적인'이란 뜻을 가진 단어로 유의어 관계에 있는 보기는 ① derogatory이다.

해석

정당화는 문제의 행위에 대한 책임을 인정하면서도 그것과 관련된 **경멸적인** 성질을 부정하는 설명이다.
① 경멸적인
② 외향적인
③ 의무적인
④ 여분의, 과다한, 불필요한

02 정답 ③
Day 24-01

정답해설

밑줄 친 단어는 문맥상 '축하하다'로 사용되었고, 유의어로는 ③ commemorate 가 적절하다.

해석

나의 미용실에서 오랜 고객인 Minnie는 그녀의 100번째 생일을 막 **축하하려던** 참이었고 100주년에 도달했을 때 나는 그녀에게 찬사(무료)의 머리 서비스를 약속했다.
① 마음을 사로잡다
② ~을 식별하다, 차이를 만들다, ~을 분화시키다
③ 축하하다, 기념하다
④ 그만두다, 포기하다, 중단되다

03 정답 ①
Day 26-02

정답해설

'yellow fever(황열병)'의 원인으로 'mosquito(모기)'가 'carrier(매개체)'로 명시되어서 매개체를 꾸미는 표현으로, 빈칸에 가장 적절한 표현은 '의심되는'이라는 뜻을 가진 ① suspected이다.

해석

테스트들은 먼지와 열악한 위생을 황열병의 원인으로 제외하였고, 모기가 **의심되는** 매개체였다.
① 의심되는
② 문명화되지 않은
③ 환호하는
④ 자진해서

04 정답 ④
Day 21-03

정답해설

'be engrossed in'은 '~에 열중해 있다'라는 뜻으로 본문 초반에 지루한 오후 수업 때는 느려진다고 설명하는 것과 대조적으로 재미있는 것을 할 때 밑줄 친 단어의 의미는 느려지는 것과 반의어 관계인 것을 유추할 수 있다. 따라서 'engrossed in'과 유의어 관계에 있는 것은 ④ preoccupied with이다.

해석

시간은 지루한 오후 수업 동안은 정말 느려지고, 뇌가 정말 재미있는 무언가에 **열중할** 때는 달려가는 것처럼 보인다.
① ~의해 강화되다
② ~에 무관심하다
③ ~의해 안정되다
④ ~에 사로잡히다

05 정답 ②
Day 28-09

정답해설

해당 지문은 '아일랜드의 대기근의 영향'에 대해 설명하는 글이다. "As a direct consequence of the famine, Ireland's population of almost 8.4 million in 1844 had fallen to 6.6 million by 1851(기근의 직접적인 결과로서, 1844년 거의 8백 4십만이었던 아일랜드의 인구는 1851년 6백 6십만으로 감소했다)."에서 '기근의 직접적인 결과'를 설명한 후, "A further aftereffect of the famine was thus the clearing of many smallholders from the land and the concentration of landownership in fewer hands(그러므로 기근의 추가적 여파는 토지로부터의 소작농의 감소와 토지 소유권이 더 적은 사람들에게로 집중되는 것이었다)."를 통해 '기근의 여파'를 설명하고 있으므로, 전체 글의 주제로 가장 적절한 보기는 '② direct and indirect results of the Great Famine(대기근의 직간접적 결과)'이다.

해석

아일랜드 감자 기근이라고도 불리는 대기근은 아일랜드의 인구통계학적 역사상 분수령이라는 것이 입증되었다. 기근의 직접적인 결과로서, 1844년 거의 8백 4십만이었던 아일랜드의 인구는 1851년 6백 6십만으로 감소했다. 농장 서부 및 남서부 지방의 농장 노동자와 소작농의 수가 특히 급격한 감소를 겪었다. 그러므로 기근의 추가적 여파는 토지로부터의 소작농의 감소와 토지소유권이 더 적은 사람들에게로 집중되는 것이었다. 그에 따라, 영국 수출을 위한 육류를 공급하며, 이전보다 더 많은 토지가 양과 소의 방목을 위해 사용되었다.
① 대기근의 주요 원인
② 대기근의 직간접적 결과
③ 대기근이 아일랜드 농업에 미친 영향
④ 대기근에 이어진 인구통계학적 변화

06 정답 ③
Day 23-06

정답해설

③ 출제 포인트: 전치사+명사(구)/자동사 differ

전치사 뒤에는 명사(구)가 와야 한다. 해당 문장은 전치사 'in'과 'by' 뒤에 동명사 'talking'과 'discussing'을 사용하였으므로 옳은 문장이다. 또한 'on which'는 '전치사+관계대명사'의 형태로 'which'의 선행사는 'the things'임에 유의해야 한다. 또한 해당 문장에서 differ는 자동사로 쓰였다. '~와 다르다'의 의미로 'differ from'을 사용하고 '~에 생각이 다르다, 의견이 맞지 않다'의 의미로는 'differ on/over/about'을 사용하므로 주의한다.

해석
① 당신의 아기의 울음소리를 듣는 것은 부모가 되는 것의 가장 힘든 부분 중 하나이다.
② 그녀는 아무도 방해하지 않도록 헤드폰을 쓰면서, 자신의 집에서 종일 보낸다.
③ 다른 사람들과 이야기할 때, 당신의 의견이 다르다는 것들을 논의함으로써 시작하지 말라.
④ 환경적 문제들을 다루는 가장 좋은 방법은 애초에 그것이 발생하지 않도록 예방하는 것이다.

07 정답 ①
Day 29-05

정답해설
① 출제 포인트: 관계대명사 vs. 관계부사
관계사 뒤에 오는 문장이 완전한 경우 관계부사 또는 '전치사+관계대명사'를 사용해야 한다. 해당 문장은 관계대명사 'which' 뒤에 오는 문장이 완전한 형태이므로 틀린 문장이다. 따라서 'which'를 'where' 또는 'in which'로 수정해야 한다.

해석
경쟁은 한 조직이 다른 조직들을 희생해서만 승리할 수 있는 제로섬 게임이 된다. 하지만 경쟁의 정도가 특히 극심한 경우, 제로섬 게임은 시장 내의 모두가 추가적인 비용에 직면하므로, 급속하게 네거티브섬 게임이 될 수도 있다.

08 정답 ④
Day 22-10

정답해설
해당 지문은 '저널리스트는 정치 과정에 대한 정보를 전달할 때 중립적이고 공정한 관찰자가 되길 원하지만 그것은 불가능하다'라고 설명하며, 그러한 이유를 '예비선거 토론회(primary debate)'를 취재하는 상황을 예시로 설명하고 있다. "But true neutrality and total detachment are basically impossible(그러나 진정한 중립성과 완전한 공정성은 근본적으로 불가능하다)."이라고 언급하여 글의 요지를 밝히고, 이후 '뉴스 소재를 선택하는 것이 저널리스트 자신이고 그것에 대해 옳고 그름을 판단하는 주체가 없기 때문에 기자 본인의 주관이 개입되는 것이 불가피하게 발생한다'라고 필자의 주장을 나타내고 있다. 따라서 글의 제목으로 가장 적절한 보기는 '④ Being Neutral Is Impossible in Political Debate Coverage(정치 토론 취재에서 중립적이 되는 것은 불가능하다)'이다.

해석
이러한 평범한 투표자들은 토론의 밤에 무슨 일이 발생했는지에 대한 중립적인 요약을 보고 있다고 믿을 것이다. 안타깝게도, 현실은 훨씬 더 복잡하다. 전통적인 기자들은 정치적 과정에 참여하지 않고 정보만을 제공하는 중립적이고 공정한 관찰자가 되길 바란다. 그러나 진정한 중립성과 완전한 공정성은 근본적으로 불가능하다. 예비선거 토론회에서는 토론의 밤 마지막에 등장해 우승자를 선언하는 더 높은 지위의 권위자 또는 판정가가 없다. 대신에, 누가 잘했는지, 어떤 순간이 중요했는지, 그리고 토론의 어떤 부분이 B-roll로 사용될지에 대해 기자들이 스스로 결정을 하도록 강요된다. 때때로 주류 뉴스 기자들 사이에서 조직적으로 의견 일치가 이루어지기도 한다. 그러나 이러한 종류의 공개 토론에서 승리에 대한 객관적인 기준이 없기 때문에 그러한 의견 일치가 정확한 것인지를 판단할 방법이 없다.
① 예비선거 토론회의 중요성
② 정치 뉴스 콘텐츠는 어떻게 생성되는가?
③ 정치와 저널리즘의 관계
④ 정치 토론 취재에서 중립적이 되는 것은 불가능하다

09 정답 ②
Day 24-09

정답해설
해당 지문은 '약초학(herbal medicine)의 역사'에 대해 서술하고 있으며, '약초학은 의학의 역사상 가장 초기에 발달했고 현재까지도 시행되고 있다'라는 것이 본문의 주요 내용이다. 빈칸 이후 "The snakeroot plant was traditionally used as a tonic in the east to calm patients; it is now used in orthodox medical practice to reduce blood pressure(snakeroot 식물은 동양에서 전통적으로 환자를 진정시키기 위한 음료로 사용되었다. 현재 그것은 전통 의학에서 혈압을 낮추기 위해 사용된다)."와 "Doctors in ancient India gave an extract of foxglove to patients with legs swollen by dropsy; digitalis, a constituent of foxglove, is now a standard stimulant for the heart(고대 인도에서 의사들은 부종으로 인해 다리가 부은 환자들에게 foxglove 추출물을 주었다; 현재 foxglove의 성분인 digitalis는 심장을 위한 일반적인 각성제이다)."를 통해 과거에도 사용되었던 약초가 현재에도 의학에서 사용되고 있다는 점을 예시로 제시하고 있으므로, 빈칸에 가장 적절한 표현은 '② it remains an important part of medicine to this day(오늘날까지 의학의 중요한 부분을 차지하고 있다)'이다.

해석
어떤 식물이 식용 가능한지 알아보는 긴 과정 중에, 석기시대의 인간은 병을 치료하거나 열을 내리는 것처럼 보이는 많은 식물도 또한 식별했다. 초기 의사들은 그것들이 작용하는 방식을 이해하지 못한 채 실제 효과가 있는 약초를 우연히 발견했다. 그럼에도 불구하고 약초학은 의료 행위에 있어서 가장 초기의 과학적 전통이며, 오늘날까지 의학의 중요한 부분을 차지하고 있다. snakeroot 식물은 동양에서 전통적으로 환자를 진정시키기 위한 음료로 사용되었다; 현재 그것은 전통 의학에서 혈압을 낮추기 위해 사용된다. 고대 인도에서 의사들은 부종으로 인해 다리가 부은 환자들에게 foxglove 추출물을 주었다; 현재 foxglove의 성분인 digitalis는 심장을 위한 일반적인 각성제이다.
① 다양한 약초들은 현재 요리용으로 사용된다
② 오늘날까지 의학의 중요한 부분을 차지하고 있다
③ 약효가 있는 식물들을 재배하는 것이 오늘날 매우 인기 있다
④ 서양의 수많은 의사들 또한 약초학을 실행하고 있다

10 정답 ②
Day 23-08

정답해설
해당 지문은 '경제 모델(economic model)'의 목적을 설명하는 글로, '경제 모델은 두 가지 목적으로 사용되는데, 첫째는 시뮬레이션(simulating), 둘째는 예측(forecasting)이다'라고 설명하고 있다. 빈칸 이전에서 경제 모델이 시뮬레이션을 위해 사용되는 예시를 설명하고, 빈칸에서는 이와 비교해 예측을 위해 사용될 때 경제 모델의 효과에 대해 설명하고 있다. 마지막 문장 "The further out the forecast, the larger the structural uncertainties, making model projections at best illustrative, ~(예측이 더 먼 미래에 대한 것일수록 구조적 불확실성이 더 커지고, 모델의 예측을 기껏해야 설명적인 것으로 만들게 되는데~)"를 통해 경제 모델을 이용해 예측을 할 때는 불확실성이 동반된다는 것을 알 수 있다. 따라서 경제 모델은 시뮬레이션을 할 때보다 예측을 할 때 상대적으로 덜 효과적이라는 것을 유추할 수 있으므로, 빈칸에 가장 적절한 것은 '② less effective(덜 효과적인)'이다.

해석
경제 모델은 두 가지 주요 목적, 즉 시뮬레이션과 예측을 위해 사용된다. 그것들은 시뮬레이션을 위한 훌륭한 도구이다. 경제의 행동적인 작용에 대해 우리가 아는 것들을 고려해 볼 때, 그리고 이러한 것들을 대부분 기정사실이라고 생각할 때, 이를테면, 에너지 가격 급등에 경제가 어떻게 반응할 것인가? 그러나 모델은 정확하게 예측을 제공하는 것에 있어서 훨씬 덜 효과적인데, 특히

예측을 할 때, 기정사실로 생각할 수 있는 것들이 거의 없기 때문이다. 예측이 더 먼 미래에 대한 것일수록 구조적인 불확실성이 더 커지고, 모델의 예측을 기껏해야 설명적인 것으로 만들게 되는데, 이는 특히 기후 변화의 영향 또는 전 세계 에너지 시스템의 변화와 같은 거대한 충격의 영향을 예측하려고 시도할 때 그러하다.
① 덜 모호한
② 덜 효과적인
③ 더 실용적인
④ 덜 이론적인

11 정답 ③   Day 23-04

정답해설

A와 B의 대화 속에서 A가 지난 월요일 일정을 묻고 있다. 이에 B가 "뮤지컬을 보았다"라는 대답에 A가 "뮤지컬 배우가 누구였냐?"라는 질문을 한다. 그 질문에 대한 답으로 B가 '지금 기억할 수가 없어'라고 답하고 있으므로 빈칸에는 "기억이 나려고 하는 찰나에 잊어버렸다"라고 답하는 문맥의 "I forgot on the tip of my tongue"가 가장 적절하다.

해석

A: 지난주 월요일에 뭐했어?
B: 가족들과 뮤지컬 보러 갔어. 진짜 좋은 시간 보냈어.
A: 난 최근에 뮤지컬 본 적이 없는데 부럽다. 뮤지컬 제목이 뭐였어?
B: '맘마미아'야. 무대 위 배우들 목소리를 듣고 감명받았어. 끝에는 거의 울었는걸.
A: 우와 주연 배우들이 누구였어?
B: 오, <u>말하려던 찰나에 잊어버렸어.</u> 지금 기억할 수가 없어.
① 너는 수다스러운 사람이야.
② 그건 말실수였어.
③ 말하려던 찰나에 잊어버렸어.
④ 너는 내가 의도한 말을 먼저 말했어.

12 정답 ④   Day 25-04

정답해설

자선단체에 이번 달 자신의 월급의 절반을 기부했다는 말에 'You paid your debt to nature(너는 죽었네)'라는 대답은 문맥상 적절하지 않다.

해석

① A: 내가 친구에게 저지른 실수를 어떻게 보상해야 할까?
    B: 음, 나는 네가 스스로 책임지고 사과하는 것을 추천해.
② A: 내 발표에 대해 어떻게 생각해?
    B: 나는 엄지를 치켜세울게.
③ A: 내가 정치적 문제에 관해 쓴 최근의 기사에 대해 어떻게 생각해?
    B: 나는 네가 못을 정확히 박았다(정수를 쳤다)고 생각해.
④ A: 나는 이번 달에 내 월급의 절반을 자선단체에 기부했어.
    B: 너는 죽었네.

13 정답 ④   Day 27-06

정답해설

④ **출제 포인트: little vs. few**
'little'은 부사로 사용할 수 있으나 'few'는 부사로 사용할 수 없다. 해당 문장은 완전자동사 'care'를 수식해야 하므로 부사를 사용해야 한다. 따라서 'few'를 'little'로 수정해야 한다.

해석

자기 인식과 특별히 관련되지 않은 분야에서는, 우리는 반영을 하고, 그럼으로써 다른 사람들이 성취한 것과 관련지어서 자기 자신을 치켜세운다. 여러분이 자신의 운동 기술에 신경을 거의 쓰지 않는다고 가정해 보자.

14 정답 ③   Day 24-07

정답해설

③ **출제 포인트: 부사절을 이끄는 접속사**
'in case (that)'과 'in case of'를 혼동하지 않도록 유의해야 한다. 둘 다 '~할 경우에'를 뜻하지만 'in case (that)'은 부사절을 이끄는 접속사로 뒤에 절이 오며 'in case of'는 구전치사로 뒤에 명사(구)가 온다. 해당 문장은 in case of 뒤에 절 'the storm made it difficult to shop'이 왔으므로 틀린 문장이다. 따라서 'of'를 'that'으로 수정하거나 'of'를 삭제해야 한다.

15 정답 ④   Day 27-08

정답해설

해당 지문에서는 '놀이터에서 아이들의 부상은 놀이기구에서 추락하는 것에서 가장 많이 발생하므로, 안전한 놀이터 바닥 표면을 선택하는 것이 중요하다'라고 설명하고 있으며, 어떤 재질의 표면이 안전한 것인지 언급하고 있다. 본문 중반 "Although grass may look soft, it is not a shock absorbing surface(잔디는 부드러워 보이지만, 충격을 흡수하는 표면은 아니다)."로 보아, 잔디는 충격을 흡수하지 못한다는 것을 알 수 있으므로, 아이들에게 안전한 놀이터 바닥 재질이 아닌 것을 알 수 있다. 따라서 글의 내용과 일치하지 않는 것은 '④ Surfaces made of grass are quite safe for children(잔디로 만들어진 표면은 아이들에게 상당히 안전하다).'이다.

해석

미 소비자 제품 안전 위원회(USCPSC)에 따르면, 응급 병동은 매년 놀이터와 관련된 부상으로 20만 명 이상의 아이들을 치료한다. 대부분의 놀이터 부상은 아이가 기구에서 바닥으로 떨어질 때 발생한다. 이것이 부상을 예방하는 최상의 방법은 기구의 밑의 표면이 아이가 떨어질 때의 충격을 흡수하고 약화시킬 수 있도록 하는 것인 이유이다. 콘크리트나 아스팔트와 같은 단단한 표면은 피하라. 잔디는 부드러워 보이지만, 충격을 흡수하는 표면은 아니다. USCPSC는 우드칩, 피복, 모래, 안전 검사를 거친 고무 또는 고무 유사 재료로 만든 매트와 같은 재료들 중 하나로 만든 놀이기구 아래 사방으로 최소 6피트 넓이로 깔린 두꺼운 바닥을 추천한다.
① 놀이터에서 부상을 당하는 아이들이 매우 많다.
② 놀이기구에서의 낙상으로 인한 부상이 가장 흔하다.
③ 아스팔트 위에 지어진 놀이터는 이용하지 않는 것이 좋다.
④ 잔디로 만들어진 표면은 아이들에게 상당히 안전하다.

16 정답 ③   Day 23-10

정답해설

해당 지문은 '스마트폰과 소셜미디어의 등장으로 인한 저널리즘계의 변화'를 설명하는 글이다. 본문에서 '스마트폰과 소셜미디어 이용이 뉴스의 소비 행태 및 뉴스 생성 주체를 변화시켰고, 일반 시민도 뉴스 콘텐츠 개발에 참여할 수 있게 됨에 따라 진정한 저널리스트에 관한 의문이 등장하기 시작했다'라고 언급한다. '그러나 이미 저널리즘과 소셜미디어는 떼려야 뗄 수 없는 관계가 되었고, 저널리스트들은 소셜미디어 활동에 적극적으로 참여해야 한다'는 것이 글의 전체 내용이다. 본문 중반 "For some, this can create a problem. Who is a journalist? What defines a "journalist?" Social media is raising these questions and it is creating problems for jobs in the media(일부 사람들에게 이것은 문제를 야기할 수 있다. 누가 저널리스트인가? "저널리스트"를 정의하는 것은 무엇인가? 소셜미디어는 이러한 의문을 증가시키고, 미디어계 직종에 문제를 일으키고 있다)."를 통해 소셜미디어로 인해 발생한 문제, 즉 부정적 영향을 언급하고 있다. 따라서, '③ Social media has had positive effects only on the field of journalism(소셜미디어는 저널리즘 분야에 긍정적인 영향만을 미쳐왔다).'은 글의 내용과 일치하지 않는다.

해석

오늘날의 소비자들은 스마트폰으로 뉴스 기사를 받아 본다. 이제 시민들은 저널리즘 분야에서 과감한 역할을 수행하고 있고 스마트폰과 소셜미디어 사용은 시민들이 뉴스 생산 과정에 참여할 수 있도록 한다. Twitter, YouTube, WordPress와 같은 플랫폼들은 평범한 시민들이 그들 자신의 뉴스 콘텐츠를 생산하고 CNN과 같은 거대한 뉴스 공급자와 그것을 공유할 수 있게 한다. 일부 사람들에게 이것은 문제를 야기할 수 있다. 누가 저널리스트인가? "저널리스트"를 정의하는 것은 무엇인가? 소셜미디어는 이러한 의문을 증가시키고, 미디어계 직종에 문제를 일으키고 있다. 그러나 소셜미디어는 이제 모든 저널리스트들이 사용하고 전문적 식견을 쌓아야 하는 필수 기술이며 도구이다. 언론사와 방송국은 저널리스트들과 미래의 직원들이 소셜미디어에 정통하고, 온라인에서 힘 있는 인플루언서가 되는 것을 보길 원한다.
① 스마트폰의 등장은 뉴스가 생성되고 소비되는 방식을 변화시켰다.
② 대형 언론사는 때때로 소셜미디어 이용자가 만든 뉴스 콘텐츠를 이용한다.
③ 소셜미디어는 저널리즘 분야에 긍정적인 영향만을 미쳐왔다.
④ 오늘날의 저널리스트들은 소셜미디어를 이용할 수밖에 없다.

17 정답 ④
Day 26-10

정답해설

(A)에서는 문맥상 부정어가 필요하다. (A) 빈칸 다음에 "what you are hearing convincingly matches the visuals, the virtual experience breaks apart(만약 당신이 듣고 있는 것이 시각적인 것들과 설득력 있게 일치하지 않는다면, 가상 체험은 부서진다)."라고 하였으므로 'Unless(그렇지 않다면)'가 적합하다.
(B) 다음의 내용이 '오늘날의 기술도 가상현실에 충분하지 않다'라는 것을 지적하고 있으므로 'Unfortunately'(안타깝게도)가 적합하다. 따라서 두 가지를 모두 충족시키는 정답은 ④이다.

해석

오늘날 가상현실(VR) 체험의 시각적 요소를 제작하는 기술은 널리 이용 가능하고 가격이 알맞게 되어 가는 도중에 있다. 그러나 강력하게 작동하기 위해서는, 가상현실은 시각적인 것 이상에 관한 것이어야 한다. (A) 만약 당신이 듣고 있는 것이 시각적인 것들과 설득력 있게 일치하지 않는다면, 가상 체험은 부서진다. 농구를 예로 들어보자. 만약 선수들, 코치들, 아나운서들, 그리고 관중들이 모두 코트 가운데 앉아 있는 것처럼 들린다면, 당신은 TV로 경기를 보는 것이 낫다 – 당신은 당신이 "거기" 있는 만큼만 감을 잡게 된다. (B) 안타깝게도, 오늘날의 오디오 기계와 우리의 널리 사용되는 녹화 및 재생 포맷은 먼 행성의 전쟁터, 코트 사이드에서의 농구 경기, 또는 훌륭한 콘서트홀의 첫 줄에서 들리는 것 같은 심포니의 소리를 설득력 있게 재현하는 일에는 단순히 부적합하다.

	(A)	(B)
①	만약 ~라면	대조적으로
②	그렇지 않다면	결과적으로
③	만약 ~라면	비슷하게
④	그렇지 않다면	안타깝게도

18 정답 ②
Day 22-09

정답해설

해당 지문은 '에테르마취(ether anesthesia)가 처음 도입되었을 당시의 상황'을 설명하고 있다. "Anesthesia was discovered in a time before standardized medicine(마취는 표준화된 의학 이전의 시대에 발견되었다). ① There was no guaranteed quality when it came to medicine during this time period(이 시대에는 의학에 관한 한 보장된 품질은 없었다)."를 통해 마취의 발견 당시 의학이 완전히 안전성이 보증된 분야가 아니었으며, 이는 마취 자체도 안정적이지 않았다는 것을 의미한다. 또한 "③ Surgeons also didn't fully trust the ether they were using(의사들 또한 그들이 사용하는 에테르를 완전히 신뢰하지 않았다)."에서 의사들도 마취제를 신뢰하지 않았다고 언급하고 있고, 이후에 '마취가 제대로 이루어지지 않거나 너무 많은 용량이 투여되어 환자가 사망하는 경우까지 있었다'고 설명하고 있으므로, 초기에는 마취에 대한 신뢰도도 낮고 활용도도 적었다는 것을 유추할 수 있다. 따라서 "② When ether anesthesia was introduced, the surgical world was overjoyed and embraced this transformative innovation with widespread immediacy(에테르마취가 도입되었을 때, 외과계는 매우 기뻐했고 이 변혁적인 혁신을 널리 즉각적으로 받아들였다)."는 글의 전체 내용과 부합하지 않으므로, 정답은 ②이다.

해석

1846년 에테르마취의 발견 이전에 간단한 것부터 주요한, 또는 매우 극단적인 것까지 모든 수술은 정신이 완전히 깨어 있는 사람들에게 행해졌고, 때때로 그들은 의사가 자신의 일을 할 수 있도록 환자의 간청, 비명 그리고 흐느낌을 무시하는 것을 담당하는 사람들에 의해 수술대에 제압된 상태였다. 마취는 표준화된 의학 이전의 시대에 발견되었다. ① 이 시대에는 의학에 관한 한 보장된 품질은 없었다. ② *에테르마취가 도입되었을 때, 외과계는 매우 기뻐했고 이 변혁적인 혁신을 널리 즉각적으로 받아들였다.* ③ 의사들 또한 그들이 사용하는 에테르를 완전히 신뢰하지 않았다. ④ 때때로 배합이 너무 약해 환자가 의식을 잃지 않거나, 아마 더 끔찍하게도 수술 중에 의식을 되찾곤 했다. 다른 때에는 배합이 너무 강해 수술대에서 환자가 과잉 투여로 사망하기도 했다.

19 정답 ④
Day 24-10

정답해설

주어진 문장은 '블로거들이 자신들의 예측이 정확한 것처럼 보이기 위해 과거 게시글을 조작하기도 한다는 점을 인정했다'라는 내용이므로, 주어진 문장 이전에는 '진실 추구'에 대한 블로거들의 가벼운 태도에 대해 언급하는 내용이 등장하는 것이 자연스럽다. ④ 이전 문장에서 "Many reporters worry that without an institutional reputation at stake, bloggers are careless and prone to make false accusations or disseminate false information(많은 기자들은 제도상의 신망이 달려있지 않으면, 블로거들이 부주의하고 거짓 혐의를 제기하거나 거짓 정보를 퍼뜨릴 수도 있다고 우려한다)."라고 '블로거들이 잘못된 정보를 전달할 수도 있다는 것을 전통 기자들이 우려한다'라고 언급한 후, 실제로 블로거들이 진실을 왜곡하는 행위 중 하나인 게시글 조작을 하고 있다는 것이 이어지는 것으로 자연스러우므로, 주어진 글이 들어갈 가장 적합한 위치는 ④이다.

해석

일부 블로거들은 웹상에서 지속적인 존재감을 확립해왔고 많은 일일 독자들을 확보한다. 많은 정치 블로거들은 뉴스 종사자로서의 정당성을 추구했고, 최근 그들은 성공했다. (①) 블로거들은 2004년 대통령 후보 지명 전당대회에서 자격을 얻었고, 2009년 오바마 대통령은 백악관 기자회견에 한 블로거를 초청했다. (②) 전통적인 저널리스트들은 이 분야의 새로운 진입자들을 경계하고 있다. (③) 많은 기자들은 제도상의 신망이 달려있지 않으면, 블로거들이 부주의하고 거짓 혐의를 제기하거나 거짓 정보를 퍼뜨릴 수도 있다고 우려한다. (④ 일부 블로거들은 그들의 이전의 부정확한 예측들이 진실인 것처럼 보이도록 블로그 자료 보관소를 조작한 것을 인정했다.) 전문 저널리스트들이 진실과 정확함에 대한 블로거들의 격의 없는 태도를 비탄해온 반면, 블로거들은 자신들이 독자들과 블로그 세상의 꾸준한 감시하에 있다는 것을 지적한다.

20 정답 ④
Day 25-08

정답해설
주어진 문장을 통해 '스마트 홈 케어가 병원 치료를 대체할 수 있는가'에 대한 문제가 소재인 것을 알 수 있다. (A)가 역접 의미의 접속부사인 'Nonetheless(그럼에도 불구하고)'로 시작하고 있는 것으로 보아 상반되는 내용이 (A) 이전에 등장하는 것이 자연스럽다. (B)는 (C)의 요지와 (A)의 요지를 등위접속사 but으로 연결하며 글 전체의 내용을 요약하고 있으므로 글의 마지막에 위치해야 한다. 또한, (C)는 '현존하는 의료 시스템의 필요성'이 계속하여 유지될 것이라는 전문가들의 대체적인 의견을 서술하고 있으므로, (A) 이전에 위치해야 한다. 따라서 이어질 글의 순서로 가장 적절한 것은 ④ (C) - (A) - (B) 이다.

해석
디지털 건강관리 분야에서 건강관리 기술이 탑재된 잘 관리되는 스마트 홈이 병원 치료의 대체가 될 수 있는지에 관해 의견이 분분한 문제가 있다.
(C) 전문가들은 대체로 많은 상황에서 병원과 면대면 보건 개입의 필요성은 아마도 항상 존재할 것이라는 것에 동의한다.
(A) 그럼에도 불구하고, 결합된 가정 보건은 여러 다른 상황에서 의료비용을 낮춰줄 뿐 아니라 환자에의 권한 부여와 조정을 위한 많은 기회를 제공하기 때문에 장려되어야 할 비전이다.
(B) 결합된 스마트 홈은 아직 현존하는 건강관리 서비스를 완전히 대신하지는 못할 것이다. 하지만 그것들은 돌봄의 의료 연속체에 가치를 더할 수 있고, 돌봄의 질을 향상시켜주며, 여러모로 과부하 상태인 의료 시스템의 증가하는 압력을 줄일 수 있다.

결국엔 성정혜 영어 하프모의고사
기적사 DAY 31

| 01 | ① | 02 | ② | 03 | ④ | 04 | ② | 05 | ④ |
| 06 | ② | 07 | ① | 08 | ④ | 09 | ① | 10 | ③ |

01 정답 ①
18 지방직

정답해설
① chief는 '주된, (계급, 직급상) 최고위자인, 중요한'의 뜻으로 밑줄 친 paramount(다른 무엇보다 중요한, 최고의)와 의미가 가장 가깝다.

해석
의사의 **다른 무엇보다 중요한** 의무는 해를 가하지 않는 것이다. 다른 모든 것 심지어 치유까지도 그 다음의 일이어야 한다.
① 가장 중요한, 주된, 최고의
② 맹세한, 선서한
③ 성공한, 성공적인
④ 불가사의한, 신비한

어휘
paramount 다른 무엇보다 중요한, 최고의
chief 가장 중요한, 주된, 최고의   sworn 맹세한, 선서한
successful 성공한, 성공적인   mysterious 불가사의한, 신비한

02 정답 ②
18 지방직

정답해설
get[have] cold feet은 '갑자기 초조해지다, 겁이 나다'의 뜻으로 ② become afraid와 의미가 가장 가깝다.

해석
사람들이 북극으로 가는 것에 대해 **겁이 나는** 것은 이상하지 않다.
① 포부에 차게 되다
② 겁을 먹게 되다
③ 지치다
④ 슬프다

어휘
unusual 특이한, 흔치 않은, 드문, 이상한
ambitious 야심 있는, 포부에 찬   exhausted 지친
saddened 슬픈

오답률 TOP 1
03 정답 ④
18 지방직

정답해설
밑줄 친 intimidating은 '겁을 주는, 위협하는'의 뜻으로 ④ frightening(무서운, 겁나게 하는)과 의미가 가장 가깝다.

해석
최첨단의 접근법이 **위협적**이라고 느끼는 학생은 그 혹은 그녀가 오래된 방법들로 배웠을 수도 있는 것보다 덜 배운다.
① 재미있는, 유머러스한
② 친근한

③ 편리한
④ 무서운, 겁나게 하는

어휘

state-of-the-art 최첨단의, 최신식의
intimidating 겁을 주는, 위협하는

04 정답 ②
18 지방직

정답해설

A의 컴퓨터가 고장이 난 상황이다. B의 빈칸 이후에 A가 '그렇게 해야 하지만, 나는 너무 게을러.'라고 한 것으로 미루어 보아, B는 A에게 무엇을 하라고 권유한 것으로 짐작할 수 있다. 그러므로 가장 적절한 것은 ② "Try visiting the nearest service center then(그럼 가장 가까운 서비스 센터에 가봐)." 이다.

오답해설

③ 가서 잠을 청하라고 한 상황에서 A가 그렇게 하기 너무 게으르다고 대답하는 것은 문맥과 전혀 관련이 없다.
나머지 보기는 문맥상 적절하지 않다.

해석

A: 내 컴퓨터가 아무 이유 없이 멈춰버렸어. 이걸 다시 켤 수도 없어.
B: 너 혹시 충전은 해봤어? 그냥 배터리가 나간 것일지도 몰라.
A: 물론이지, 충전을 해봤어.
B: 그럼 가장 가까운 서비스 센터에 가봐.
A: 그렇게 해야 하지만, 나는 너무 게을러.
① 나는 네 컴퓨터를 어떻게 고치는지 몰라.
② 그럼 가장 가까운 서비스 센터에 한번 가봐.
③ 음, 너의 문제는 그만 생각하고 가서 잠을 자.
④ 내 동생이 컴퓨터 기사이니까, 네 컴퓨터를 고쳐 볼 거야.

어휘

shut down 멈추다, 정지하다   charge 충전하다
technician 기술자, 기사

05 정답 ④
18 지방직

정답해설

④ **출제 포인트: what vs. that**
'what'은 선행사를 포함한 관계대명사로, 이전에 선행사를 동반할 수 없다. 그러나 문맥상 직전의 명사 'post'가 선행사의 역할을 하고 있으므로, 'what'을 'that' 혹은 'which'로 바꿔야 한다.

오답해설

① **출제 포인트: 시간의 부사구/부사절**
「for + 수사 명사」는 현재완료와 과거 시제 모두와 사용할 수 있다. 여기에서는 '지난 3년 동안'이라는 의미로 현재완료 시제와 결합해서 옳게 사용되었다.

② **출제 포인트: 현재분사 vs. 과거분사**
'requirements'를 후치 수식하는 분사로, 문맥상 수동의 의미이므로 과거분사가 옳게 사용되었다.

③ **출제 포인트: to부정사의 형용사적 용법**
to부정사의 형용사적 용법으로 앞의 명사 'reason'을 수식하고 있다.

해석

저는 Ferrer 부인의 추천서에 대한 당신의 요청에 응하여 이 글을 쓰고 있습니다. 그녀는 지난 3년간 제 비서로 근무했고, 뛰어난 직원이었습니다. 저는 그녀가 당신의 직무 기술서에 언급된 모든 요건에 부합하며, 여러 방면에서 그 이상이라고 생각합니다. 저는 그녀의 완전한 진실성을 의심할 이유가 있던 적이 한 번도 없습니다. 그러므로 당신이 게재한 공고에 대해 Ferrer 부인을 추천하고 싶습니다.

어휘

in response to ~에 응하여   reference 추천서
requirement 필요조건   job description 직무 기술서
indeed (강조하여) 정말   integrity 진실성, 무결함

오답률 TOP 3

06 정답 ②
18 지방직

정답해설

② **출제 포인트: If 생략 가정법**
현재 사실을 반대로 가정하는 가정법 과거의 「If it were not for ~((현재) ~이 없다면)」 구문에서 If가 생략되면 의문문의 어순으로 바뀐다. 즉, 종속절의 동사 'were'가 주어 앞으로 도치되면서 'Were it not for'의 형태로 쓰이게 된다.

오답해설

① **출제 포인트: 자동사로 착각하기 쉬운 완전타동사**
'contact'는 타동사로 전치사를 동반할 수 없다. 따라서 'contact to me'는 'contact me'로 바꾸는 것이 옳다. 또한 'the email address'와 'I gave you' 사이에는 목적격 관계대명사 'which' 혹은 'that'이 생략되어 있다.

③ **출제 포인트: 주어와 동사 수일치/주격관계대명사 수일치**
「allow + 목적어 + to부정사」는 '목적어가 ~하게끔 허락하다'의 뜻으로 여기서는 목적격 보어로 'to continue'가 알맞게 쓰였다. 다만 'who' 이하의 주격 관계대명사절의 동사는 선행사인 'people'과 수일치해야 하므로 'is'가 아닌, 'are'이 되어야 한다.

④ **출제 포인트: 'The + 비교급 ~, the + 비교급' 구문**
「The + 비교급 ~, the + 비교급 ~」은 '~할수록 더 ~하다'라는 뜻이다. 따라서 최상급인 'the worst'를 비교급인 'the worse'로 바꾸어야 한다.

해석

① 지난주 제가 드린 이메일 주소로 연락해주세요.
② 물이 없다면, 지구상 모든 살아있는 생명들은 멸종될 것이다.
③ 노트북은 사무실을 떠나있는 사람들이 일을 계속해서 할 수 있게끔 한다.
④ 그들이 그들의 실수에 대해 설명하려고 더 시도할 때마다, 그들의 이야기는 더 나쁘게 들렸다.

오답률 TOP 2

07 정답 ①
18 지방직

정답해설

① **출제 포인트: 시간의 부사구/부사절**
'a few days ago'는 시간의 부사구로 과거시제 동사와 함께 사용한다. 따라서 해당 문장의 동사에 'went'를 옳게 사용하였다.

오답해설

② **출제 포인트: 동사 관용표현**
'make believe (that)'은 '~인 체하다'라는 관용적 표현으로 'it'을 삭제해야 한다.

③ **출제 포인트: 동명사 관용표현**
'look forward to'는 '~하기를 고대하다'라는 뜻으로, 여기서 'to'는 전치사이다. 따라서 뒤의 'go'를 동명사 'going'으로 바꾸어야 한다.

④ **출제 포인트: 현재분사 vs. 과거분사**
'interested'는 감정형 분사 중 감정의 상태를 나타내는 의미로 쓰인다. 따라서 과거분사 'interested'를 감정의 제공을 나타내는 현재분사 'interesting (흥미로운, 흥미를 불러일으키는)'으로 바꾸는 것이 옳다.

08 정답 ④
18 지방직

정답해설

보기 문장의 'The same thinking'(동일한 사고방식)에 주목해야 한다. 보기 문장이 들어갈 위치 전에 생각에 대해 서술했으므로 그 부분을 찾으면 보기 문장이 위치할 곳을 자연스럽게 알 수 있다. 제시된 문장에서 '같은 사고방식이 적용될 수 있다'라고 했으므로 언급된 사고와 유사한 것이 다음에 전개될 것을 알 수 있다. 또한 본문 후반부에 '직장에서 실적을 향상하는 것'을 예시로 언급한 것 또한 힌트이다. ④의 전 문장까지는 몸무게 감량의 예시가 있고, ④ 다음의 문장에서는 '직장에서('in our profession')'의 목표 달성의 예시가 있다. 따라서 제시 문장은 ④에 위치하는 것이 가장 적합하다.

오답해설

동일한 사고방식과 직장에서의 실적을 향상시키는 것이 두 가지 모두를 충족시키는 곳은 ④밖에 없다. 따라서 나머지 자리에는 보기 문장이 위치할 수 없다.

해석

행복한 뇌는 단기적인 것에 집중하는 경향이 있다. (①) 그렇다면, 결국에는 장기 목표들을 달성하도록 해줄 어떤 단기 목표들을 우리가 성취할 수 있는지를 고려하는 것은 좋은 생각이다. (②) 예를 들면, 만약 당신이 6개월 후 30파운드를 감량하기를 원한다면, 당신은 어떤 단기 목표들을 당신 거기에 도달하게 해줄 더 적은 몸무게의 증가량을 감소시키는 것과 연관 지을 수 있는가? (③) 아마 당신이 2파운드를 감량하는 매주 당신 자신에게 보상을 해주는 것만큼 단순한 무언가일 것이다. (④ **동일한 사고방식이 직장에서 실적을 향상시키는 것과 같이 어떠한 수의 목표들에도 적용될 수 있다.**) 전체적 목표를 더 작고 더 단기적인 부분들로 나눔으로써, 우리는 우리 직장에서 목표의 엄청남에 압도되는 대신 서서히 증가하는 성취들에 집중할 수 있다.

어휘

apply to ~에 적용하다
tend to R ~하는 경향이 있다
that being the case 그렇다면, 사정이 그러하다면
eventually 결국, 끝내
increment 증가, 인상
incremental 서서히 증가하는
enormity 엄청남, 막대함
performance 실적, 수행능력
short term 단기
associate 연관 짓다
reward 보상해주다
overwhelm 압도하다
profession 직종, 분야

09 정답 ①
18 지방직

정답해설

본문 초반부에 'to prevent diseases, windows were kept open or closed, depending on whether there was more miasma inside or outside the room'(질병을 예방하기 위해서, 방의 내부 또는 외부에 더 많은 miasma가 있는지에 따라 창문들이 열린 채로 혹은 닫힌 채로 유지되었다)이라고 서술하고 있으므로 '① In the nineteenth century, opening windows was irrelevant to the density of miasma.(19세기에는, 창문을 여는 것은 나쁜 공기의 농도와는 무관했다.)'는 본문과 일치하지 않는 내용이다. 따라서 정답은 ①이다.

오답해설

② 본문의 'gentlemen did not inhabit quarters with bad air'(신사들은 나쁜 공기가 있는 주거지에서는 거주하지 않았다)와 일치하는 내용이다.
③ 'scientists invented vaccines and antibiotics.'(과학자들이 백신과 항생제를 발명했다.)에서 언급하고 있다.
④ 본문 마지막 부분에서 언급하고 있는 내용이다.

해석

19세기에는, 가장 존경받는 보건 의학 전문가들 모두가 질병들이 나쁜 공기를 위한 화려한 용어인 "miasma"에 의해 유발된다고 주장했다. 서양의 보건 시스템은 이 가정에 근거했다: 질병을 예방하기 위해서, 방의 내부 또는 외부에 더 많은 miasma가 있는지에 따라 창문들이 열린 채로 혹은 닫힌 채로 유지되었다; 신사들은 나쁜 공기가 있는 주거지에서는 거주하지 않았기 때문에 의사들은 질병을 옮길 수 없다고 믿어졌다. 그리고 나서, 균이라는 생각이 나타났다. 어느 날은, 나쁜 공기가 당신을 아프게 한다고 모두가 믿었다. 그러다가, 거의 하룻밤 새, 질병의 진짜 원인인 미생물과 박테리아라고 불리는 눈에 보이지 않는 것들이 있다고 사람들이 깨닫기 시작했다. 질병에 대한 이 새로운 시각은 의사들이 소독제를 채택하고 과학자들이 백신과 항생제를 발명하면서 의약에 대한 전면적인 변화를 가져왔다. 그러나, 그만큼 중요하게도, 세균에 대한 생각은 일반인들에게 그들 자신의 삶에 영향을 줄 수 있는 힘을 부여했다. 이제는, 만약 당신이 건강을 유지하기를 원한다면, 당신은 손을 씻고, 물을 끓이고, 음식을 완전히 익히며, 찰과상을 요오드로 소독할 수 있다.
① 19세기에는, 창문을 여는 것은 나쁜 공기의 농도와는 무관했다.
② 19세기에는, 신사들은 나쁜 공기가 있는 곳에서 살지 않았다고 믿어졌다.
③ 미생물과 박테리아가 질병의 진짜 원인임을 사람들이 깨달은 후 백신들이 발명되었다.
④ 찰과상을 소독하는 것은 사람들이 건강을 유지하는 것을 도울 수 있다.

어휘

expert 전문가
miasma 나쁜 공기(분위기)
term 용어
pass along 넘기다, 전달하다
quarter 처소, 숙소
come along 나타나다, 생기다
microbe 미생물
surgeon 외과 의사
antiseptic 소독약
momentously 중대하게
thoroughly 철저하게, 완전히
iodine 요오드
density 농도, 밀도
insist 주장하다
fancy 화려한
assumption 가정
inhabit 살다, 거주하다
germ 균
overnight 하룻밤 새
sweeping 전면적인, 광범위한
adopt 채택하다
antibiotic 항생제
ordinary 평범한
cuts and scrapes 찰과상
irrelevant 무관한

10 정답 ③
18 지방직

정답해설

본문 중반부 문장(the active and important role that followers play in the leadership process)에 따르면 오늘날에는 추종자들의 역할이 중요해 보인다고 진술하고 있다. 따라서 ③ 'The important role of followers is still denied today.'(추종자들의 역할은 오늘날 여전히 부인된다.)는 본문과 일치하지 않는 보기이다.

오답해설

① "the common view of leadership was that leaders actively led and subordinates, later called followers, passively and obediently followed."(리더십에 대한 흔한 견해는 리더들이 적극적으로 이끌고, 나중에 추종자들이라고 불린, 종속된 이들은 수동적이고 고분고분하게 따른다

는 것이었다.)라는 본문의 내용과 일치한다.
② "social change shaped people's views of followers"(사회 변화는 추종자들에 대한 사람들의 견해의 형태를 잡았다.)에 부합하는 보기이다.
④ "Leadership is a social influence process shared among all members of a group."(리더십은 그룹 내 모든 구성원들 사이에서 공유되는 사회적 영향 과정이다.)라는 본문의 내용과 일치하는 보기이다.

해석

추종자들은 리더십 방정식에서 중대한 부분이지만, 그들의 역할이 항상 인정받아온 것은 아니다. 사실 오랫동안, "리더십에 대한 흔한 견해는 리더들이 적극적으로 이끌고, 나중에 추종자들이라고 불린, 종속된 이들은 수동적이고 고분고분하게 따른다는 것이었다." 시간이 지남에 따라, 특히 지난 세기에, 사회 변화는 추종자들에 대한 사람들의 견해의 형태를 잡았고, 리더십에 관한 이론들은 리더십 과정에서 추종자들이 하는 능동적이고 중요한 역할을 점차 인정했다. 오늘날에는 추종자들이 하는 중요한 역할을 받아들이는 것이 자연스러워 보인다. 리더십의 한 측면은 이런 점에서 특히 주목할 가치가 있다: 리더십은 그룹 내 모든 구성원들 사이에서 공유되는 사회적 영향 과정이다. 리더십은 특정한 지위 또는 역할에 있는 누군가에 의해 행사되는 영향력에 국한되어 있지 않다; 추종자들 역시 리더십 과정의 일부이다.
① 상당 시간 동안, 리더들은 적극적으로 이끌고, 추종자들은 수동적으로 따른다고 이해되었다.
② 종속된 사람들에 대한 사람들의 견해는 사회 변화에 의해 영향을 받았다.
③ 추종자들의 역할은 오늘날 여전히 부인된다.
④ 리더들과 추종자들 모두 리더십 과정에 참여한다.

어휘

follower 추종자
equation 방정식, 상황
appreciate 감사하다, (진가를) 인정해주다
subordinate 하급자, 종속된 사람
obediently 고분고분하게
theory 이론
worth ~ing ~할 가치가 있는
regard 점, 사항
exert 가하다, 행사하다
deny 부인하다, 부정하다
critical 중대한, 비판적인
passively 수동적으로
over time 시간이 지남에 따라
gradually 점차
note 주목하다
restrict 제한하다
for a length of time 상당 시간 동안
participate in ~에 참여하다

기적사 DAY 32

| 01 | ③ | 02 | ③ | 03 | ③ | 04 | ② | 05 | ② |
| 06 | ③ | 07 | ② | 08 | ③ | 09 | ① | 10 | ③ |

01 정답 ③

정답해설

밑줄 친 단어는 '성공적인, 성공한'으로 사용되었고, 유의어로는 ③ prosperous가 적절하다.

해석

교육이 더 앞서갈수록, 경찰관으로서의 지원이 더 **성공적일** 것이다.
① 공공연한, 명백한
② 허구의, 가상의
③ 성공한, 번영한
④ 논란의 여지가 있는

어휘

overt 공공연한, 명백한
prosperous 성공한, 번영한
fictitious 허구의, 가상의
arguable 논란의 여지가 있는

오답률 TOP 2
02 정답 ③

정답해설

밑줄 친 단어가 문맥상 '말수가 적은'으로 사용되었고, 유의어로는 ③ taciturn이 적절하다.

해석

당신은 최근에 너무 **말수가 적었다**.
① 말이 많은
② 즉흥적인
③ 말수가 없는
④ 의지할 수 없는, 의심스러운

어휘

reserved [사람·기질이] 쌀쌀한, 마음을 털어놓지 않는; [언행이] 조심스러운, 주저하는, 말이 없는
garrulous 말이 많은
impromptu 즉흥적인
taciturn 말수가 없는
dubious 의지할 수 없는, 의심스러운

03 정답 ③

정답해설

밑줄 친 단어는 문맥상 '말이 많은'으로 사용되었고, 유의어로는 ③ talkative가 적절하다.

해석

비록 그의 문장 자체는 **말이 많지는** 않지만, 그는 치료에 있어서 극도로 번잡하며, 습관적으로 거의 같은 의미를 지닌 연속적인 문장에서 한 가지 생각을 반복한다.
① 무기력한
② 냉담한, 무관심한

③ 말이 많은
④ 야망의

어휘

enervate 무기력한
talkative 말이 많은
indifferent 냉담한, 무관심한
ambitious 야망의

04 정답 ②

정답해설

A는 B에게 피곤해 보인다며 괜찮냐고 묻자 B는 시험공부를 하느라 세 시간 밖에 자지 못해 괜찮지 않다고 답변한다. 그러자 A는 B에게 "가서 좀 쉬라"고 하며 "시험 볼 때 ②실수하게 될까(drop the ball) 봐 걱정된다."라고 말하자, B는 그저 자신이 "그러지 않기를 바라자"라고 한다.

오답해설

① 'shake a leg(서둘러 하다)'는 시험을 치를 때 실수하게 될까 봐 걱정하는 상황에 부적절한 표현이다.
③ 'talk through one's hat(비현실적인 이야기를 한다)'은 시험에서 실수하는 것에 대한 맥락의 대화에 어색하다.
④ 실수에 관해 이야기를 나누는 대화에서 'call a spade a spade(터놓고 이야기하다)'는 빈칸에 알맞지 않은 표현이다.

해석

A: 너 오늘 되게 피곤해 보인다. 괜찮아?
B: 아니 별로, 오늘 시험을 공부하느라 세 시간밖에 못 잤어.
A: 너 가서 좀 쉬어야겠다. 난 네가 시험에서 <u>실수할까</u> 걱정돼.
B: 글쎄, 그저 내가 그러지 않기를 바라자.
① 서두르다
② 실수하다
③ 비현실적인 이야기를 한다
④ 터놓고 이야기하다

어휘

shake a leg 서둘러 하다
drop the ball 실수하다
talk through one's hat 비현실적인 이야기를 하다
call a spade a spade 터놓고 이야기하다

05 정답 ②

정답해설

② **출제 포인트: 현재분사 vs. 과거분사**
'tailoring'은 완전타동사 'tailor'의 현재분사형태로 뒤에 전치사 없이 목적어를 가진다. 해당 문장은 'tailoring'과 목적어 'individual employer job applications' 사이에 전치사 'to'가 있으며 'tailoring'과 수식하는 대상 'online classes'와의 관계가 수동이므로 'tailoring'을 과거분사 'tailored'로 수정해야 한다.

오답해설

① **출제 포인트: 시간의 부사구/부사절**
'within the past few years'는 시간의 부사구로 현재완료와 함께 사용할 수 있다.
③ **출제 포인트: what vs. that**
'volunteer work'를 선행사로 하며 뒤따라오는 문장의 주어가 없으므로 주격 관계대명사 'that'을 옳게 사용하였다.
④ **출제 포인트: 현재분사 vs. 과거분사**

수식하는 대상이 도구를 나타내는 'tools'이므로 과거분사 'evolved'를 정답이라고 생각할 수 있으나 '발전하는 도구들'이므로 현재분사 'evolving'을 사용하는 것이 옳다.

해석

인터넷 사업가들은 구직 상품을 만들고 정기적으로 그것들을 온라인으로 가져온다. 지난 몇 년 이내에, 사람들이 인턴직을 발견하거나, 개별 고용주 구직 지원서에 맞춘 온라인 수업을 끝내거나, 혹은 정규직으로 이어질 자원봉사 일을 발견하도록 도와주는 인터넷에 기반을 둔 새로운 사업체들이 온라인으로 들어왔다. 일에 대한 숙달은 인터넷에서 이용 가능한 빠르게 발전하는 도구들을 계속 따라잡는 것을 의미할 것이다.

어휘

entrepreneur 사업가, 기업가
tailor 조정하다, 맞추다
keep up with ~을 따라잡다
internship 인턴직, 인턴사원 근무
mastery 숙달, 통달
evolving 발전하는

06 정답 ③

정답해설

③ **출제 포인트: 유도부사 수일치/주격관계대명사절 동사의 수일치**
'There'는 유도부사로 뒤에 오는 어순이 「동사+주어」의 도치된 어순이 온다. 따라서 복수동사 'are'의 주어는 복수형태의 명사구 'many aspects'이므로 옳게 사용되었다. 또한 해당 문장에서 'that'은 주격 관계대명사이며 선행사는 단수형태의 명사구 'this case'이므로 주격 관계대명사절의 동사에 단수형태인 'is'를 옳게 사용하였다.

오답해설

① **출제 포인트: If 생략 가정법**
과거 사실의 반대를 나타내므로 가정법 과거완료를 사용해야 한다. 가정법 과거완료는 종속절에 '주어+would/could/should/might+have+과거분사'를 사용해야 하므로 'would win'을 'would have won'으로 수정해야 한다. 또한 가정법 과거완료에서 'If'를 생략할 경우 'had'가 문두로 도치되어 'Had+주어+과거분사'의 어순이 되므로 주의해야 한다.
② **출제 포인트: 'The+비교급 ~, the+비교급' 구문**
해당 문장은 'The+비교급 ~, the+비교급' 구문에 해당하나 비교급 'sooner' 앞에 정관사 'the'를 사용하지 않았으므로 틀린 문장이다. 따라서 'sooner'를 'the sooner'로 수정해야 한다.
④ **출제 포인트: 자동사로 착각하기 쉬운 완전타동사**
'resemble'은 완전타동사이므로 전치사 없이 목적어를 가진다. 해당 문장은 'resembles'와 목적어 'a sparrow hawk' 사이에 전치사 'like'를 사용하였으므로 틀린 문장이다. 따라서 'like'를 삭제해야 한다.

해석

① 히틀러가 1940년에 영국을 침략했었다면 그는 그 전쟁에서 이겼을 것이다.
② 내가 이 작품을 더 빨리 끝낼수록, 나는 집에 더 빨리 갈 수 있다.
③ 교회 회계담당자들과 직접적으로 관련 있는 이 사건의 많은 측면들이 있다.
④ 비행 중인 새매를 닮은 뻐꾸기는 확인하기 어려울 수 있다.

07 정답 ②

정답해설

② **출제 포인트: 시간의 부사구/부사절**
해당 문장은 주절의 사건(그녀는 질병을 물리쳤다)이 종속절의 사건(흑색종이 그녀의 다리에서 발견되었다) 이후에 발생하였으며 주절의 사건이 과거시제이므로 종속절의 사건에는 과거완료시제를 사용해야 한다. 따라서 had been found로 적절하게 쓰였다. 단, 시간의 부사구와 함께 사용하

는 경우 대과거를 과거시제로 사용하여도 그 문맥상 의미를 파악할 수 있다는 점에 주의하자. 또한 'five years ago'는 시간의 부사구로 과거시제 동사와 함께 사용하므로 주절에 과거시제 동사 'beat'을 옳게 사용하였다.

오답해설

① **출제 포인트: 사역동사**
'look up to'는 관용표현으로 '~을 우러러보다'를 뜻한다. 또한 해당 문장에서 'make'는 사역동사이므로 목적격 보어로 원형부정사 'to look'을 look으로 수정해야 한다.

③ **출제 포인트: 동명사 관용표현**
'when it comes to+목적어'는 관용표현으로 '~에 관한 한'을 뜻하며 목적어에는 명사(구)가 온다. 해당 문장은 'when it comes to' 뒤에 동사원형 'deal'을 사용하였으므로 틀린 문장이다. 따라서 'deal'을 동명사 'dealing'으로 수정해야 한다.

④ **출제 포인트: 현재분사 vs. 과거분사**
감정 상태 형용사(과거분사) 'interested'와 'excited'가 수식하는 대상이 주격 관계대명사 'which'이므로 선행사를 찾아야 한다. 해당 문장에서 선행사는 'a programme'이며 감정을 제공하는 주체에 해당하므로 'interested'와 'excited'를 감정 제공 형용사(현재분사) 'interesting'과 'exciting'으로 수정해야 한다.

오답률 TOP 1

08 정답 ③

정답해설

해당 지문은 '작은 목표를 성취하는 것의 중요성'에 대해 설명하고 있다. 본문 첫 문장 "Once again, I'm not asking you to divide your large goal into small steps – I'm asking you to make a smaller goal."에서 '큰 목표를 작은 단계로 나누는 것이 아닌 작은 목표를 세우는 것'에 대해 언급하고 있으며, '작은 목표를 세워 성취해 나가면서 추진력과 확신을 얻을 수 있다'는 것이 필자의 주장이다. 그런데 '③ Once you come to a precise goal, you can work on breaking it up into manageable tasks.'에서는 하나의 목표를 세운 후, 해당 목표를 하위 단계로 나누는 것에 대한 내용이므로 글의 주제와는 반대되는 내용의 문장이다. 따라서 글의 흐름상 어색한 문장은 ③이다.

오답해설

① 작은 목표를 성취하는 것을 '승리를 거두는 것(getting a few wins under your belt)'에 비유하여 언급하고 있으므로 글의 흐름상 적절하다. 나머지 문장도 글의 흐름상 자연스러우므로 오답이다.

해석

다시 말하자면, 나는 당신의 큰 목표를 작은 단계로 세분화하라는 것이 아니다. 나는 당신에게 더 작은 목표를 세우라고 하는 것이다. 그것들이 당신의 큰 목표 또는 꿈과 관련이 없더라도 상관이 없다. 단지 목표를 쓰러뜨리는 것을 시작해 보라. 이것을 뒷받침하는 논거는 꽤 단순하다. ① 당신은 추진력이 필요하고, 몇 번의 승리를 거두는 것만큼 추진력을 형성해주는 것도 없다. 내 말을 오해하지 말라. ② 나는 크게 생각하고 큰 꿈을 지니는 것을 추구한다. 그러나 나는 또한 추진력과 자신감의 필요성을 이해한다. ③ <u>일단 명확한 목표를 설정하면, 당신은 그것을 처리할 수 있는 일들로 나눌 수 있다</u>. ④ 특히 큰 목표 설정과 성취를 요하는 비즈니스에 종사해보지 않은 사람에게 목표를 달성하는 것은 단계를 밟아 나가는 것보다 훨씬 더 낫다. 이러한 작은 목표의 목적은 당신의 목표에 더 가까이 다가가는 것이 아니라 확신, 즉 당신이 단계가 아니라 목표를 달성할 수 있다는 것을 확신하는 역량을 개발하는 것이다.

어휘

unrelated 관계가 없는 knock down 때려눕히다, 쓰러뜨리다
reasoning 논거, 추론 momentum 추진력, 탄력

get[have] under your belt …을 달성하다, 차지하다
come to 달하다, 다다르다, 이르다 precise 정확한, 명확한
manageable 처리할 수 있는, 감당할 수 있는
accomplish 달성하다, 이루다 achieve 이루다
skill 능력, 역량, 솜씨 belief 확신, 믿음

오답률 TOP 3

09 정답 ①

정답해설

해당 지문은 'Louis Pasteur가 세균 이론(germ theory)을 처음 제안하였을 때의 상황'에 대한 내용이다. 첫 문장 "When Louis Pasteur theorized that "germs" caused disease in the 19th century, he and Florence Nightingale had a rigorous debate."를 통해 'Nightingale'은 'Pasteur'의 이론에 동의하지 않았다는 것을 알 수 있고, 이후 설명에서 'Nightingale'은 '나쁜 공기(bad air)'가 질병을 유발한다고 믿었다는 것을 알 수 있다. 따라서 '① Nightingale was skeptical of Pasteur's point of view(Nightingale은 Pasteur의 관점을 의심했다).'는 글의 내용과 일치한다.

오답해설

② 2, 3번째 문장 "The belief that bad air from pollution, exhalation from the lungs of the ill, and unhealthy vapors caused disease had held since the time of the Greeks. In fact, Nightingale's environmental theory was based on this same belief(오염으로부터의 나쁜 공기, 환자의 폐에서 배출된 날숨, 그리고 해로운 증기가 질병을 유발한다는 믿음은 그리스 시대부터 이어져 왔다. 실제로, Nightingale의 환경 이론은 이와 동일한 믿음에 근거한 것이었다)."를 통해 그리스인들의 믿음과 일치하는 생각을 지닌 것은 'Nightingale'이라는 것을 알 수 있으므로 오답이다.

③ 본문 중반 "Thus her hospital design included well-ventilated wards, lots of sunlight, and cleanliness of patient and their environment(따라서 그녀의 병원 디자인은 환기가 잘되는 병동, 풍부한 햇빛, 그리고 환자와 환경의 청결을 포함했다)."를 통해 Nightingale의 병원 디자인에는 좋은 환기가 포함되어 있다는 것을 알 수 있으므로 오답이다.

④ 본문 후반 "When John Snow, the accepted founder of epidemiology, claimed that cholera was water borne, he supported the idea that microorganisms entering the body and going from person to person was the source of the epidemic(역학의 창시자로 알려진 John Snow가 콜레라가 수인성이라고 주장했을 때, 그는 체내에 유입되고 사람 간 전이되는 미생물이 유행성 전염병의 근원이라는 생각을 지지했다)."을 통해 'Snow'는 미생물(microorganism), 즉 세균(germ)이 질병을 유발한다는 생각을 지지했다는 것을 알 수 있으며, Pasteur의 의견에 동의한 것이므로 오답이다.

해석

19세기에 Louis Pasteur가 "세균"이 질병을 유발한다는 것을 이론화하였을 때, 그와 Florence Nightingale은 격렬한 논쟁을 벌였다. 오염으로부터의 나쁜 공기, 환자의 폐에서 배출된 날숨, 그리고 해로운 증기가 질병을 유발한다는 믿음은 그리스 시대부터 이어져 왔다. 실제로, Nightingale의 환경 이론은 이와 동일한 믿음에 근거한 것이었다. 따라서 그녀의 병원 디자인은 환기가 잘되는 병동, 풍부한 햇빛, 그리고 환자와 환경의 청결을 포함했다. 역학의 창시자로 알려진 John Snow가 콜레라가 수인성이라고 주장했을 때, 그는 체내에 유입되고 사람 간 전이되는 미생물이 유행성 전염병의 근원이라는 생각을 지지했다. 이 주장은 공장으로부터 배출되는 유독한 악취가 나는 배기가스로 인해 콜레라의 원인으로 비난받고 있던 제조회사들에 의해 이용되었다.
① Nightingale은 Pasteur의 관점을 의심했다.
② Pasteur의 아이디어는 질병의 원인에 대한 그리스인들의 믿음과 일치했다.

③ Nightingale이 디자인한 병원은 환기 시스템이 좋지 않았다.
④ Snow는 Nightingale의 환경 이론에 동의했다.

어휘

theorize 이론을 세우다
rigorous 혹독한, 가혹한
exhalation 날숨, 숨을 내쉼
hold 지속[계속]되다
ward 병동
founder 창시자, 창설자
claim 주장하다
water borne 수인성의, 물로 전파되는
microorganism 미생물
argument 주장, 논거
blame …을 탓하다, … 책임[때문]으로 보다
noxious 유독한, 유해한
skeptical 회의적인, 의심하는
in line with …와 비슷한, …에 따르는
ventilation 환기, 통풍
germ 세균
debate 논쟁
vapor (수)증기
well-ventilated 환기가 잘 되는
accepted 일반적으로 인정된
epidemiology 역학(疫學), 전염병학
cholera 콜레라
epidemic 유행병, (유행성) 전염병
manufacturing 제조의
exhaust 배기가스
point of view 관점, 견해

어휘

authoritative 권위의, 강압적인
spur …을 자극하다, 격려하다, 고무하다
misunderstanding 불화, 오해
comprehend 이해하다
instruction 지시, 명령, 설명
delegate 위임하다
make an inquiry 질문하다
body 주요부, 중심, 본체
hence 따라서
quality 자질, 자격
followership 추종, (지도자를) 따르는 것, (지도자에 대한) 지지, 충성
complementary 보완적인, 보충적인
induce 초래하다, 야기하다
exaggerated 과장된
require 필요로 하다, 요구하다
conduct 수행하다, 처리하다
inquisitive 탐구적인, 호기심 있는
supporting 지지하는
effectively 효율적으로
essential 중요한, 필수의
possess 보유하다, 소유하다

10 정답 ③

정답해설

해당 지문의 초반에 '권위적 리더(authoritative leader)'의 실패 사례에 대해 언급하며, 좋은 리더십은 단독으로 이루어지는 것이 아니라고 설명하고 있다. 세 번째 문장 "Great leaders are those who know how to be great followers, and this is something that not many comprehend(훌륭한 리더는 훌륭한 추종자가 되는 방법을 아는 사람들이고, 이것을 많은 사람들이 이해하는 것은 아니다)."에서 '리더십에 있어서 추종자 역할을 이해하는 것의 중요성'을 설명하고 있으며, 마지막 문장에서 "A leader is no one without followers and a follower is no one without a leader(추종자 없는 리더는 아무도 아니며, 리더 없는 추종자도 아무도 아니다)."를 통해 리더와 추종자의 관계는 서로 밀접하며 도움을 주는 관계라는 것을 언급하고 있다. 글의 전체 흐름으로 보아 빈칸에 가장 적절한 것은 '③ leadership and followership is complementary to each other(리더십과 추종은 서로 보완적인 것이다)'이다.

오답해설

① 글의 내용과는 무관한 문장이므로 오답이다.
② 빈칸 이전에서 리더가 아닌 추종자의 역할에 대해 자세히 설명하고 있으므로, 빈칸에 리더의 자질에 대해 설명하는 말이 들어가는 것은 어색하다.
④ 리더가 추종자에게 미치는 영향에 대해서는 언급되지 않으므로 오답이다.

해석

권위적 리더는 그룹 내 공포를 조성하고 불화를 야기할 것이다. 우리의 역사상 잘못된 권위적 리더십에 대한 과장된 예시들이 있고 우리는 그것을 반복하길 원하지 않는다. 훌륭한 리더는 훌륭한 추종자가 되는 방법을 아는 사람들이고, 이것을 많은 사람들이 이해하는 것은 아니다. 누군가를 추종하는 것은 지시 사항을 주의 깊게 듣고, 위임된 필수 업무를 수행하며, 모든 단계에서 리더를 가이드하기 위해 탐구하며 질문하고, 직무를 효율적으로 완수하기 위해 팀 내 원조의 중심이 될 것을 필요로 한다. 따라서 리더십과 추종은 서로 보완적인 것임을 이해하는 것이 중요하다. 추종자 없는 리더는 아무도 아니며, 리더 없는 추종자도 아무도 아니다.
① 우리는 모두 삶의 어느 영역에서는 추종자들이다
② 리더가 보유해야 하는 많은 자질이 있다
③ 리더십과 추종은 서로 보완적인 것이다
④ 훌륭한 리더는 그들의 추종자들이 변화하도록 동기를 부여하는 데 탁월하다

기적사 DAY 33

결국엔 성정혜 영어 하프모의고사

| 01 | ③ | 02 | ④ | 03 | ① | 04 | ④ | 05 | ③ |
| 06 | ② | 07 | ③ | 08 | ④ | 09 | ③ | 10 | ④ |

01 정답 ③

정답해설

밑줄 친 단어는 '불가사의한'으로 사용되었고, 유의어로는 ③ enigmatic이 적절하다.

해석

쓰기와 그리기를 통해서 일기를 적는 과정은 의사와 그들의 약을 거부했던 **불가사의한** 병으로부터 나를 치료하는 것을 도왔다.
① 최고의, 주권의
② 가짜의
③ 불가사의한, 수수께끼의
④ 자만하는, 화려한, 허풍 떠는

어휘

defy 거부하다
bogus 가짜의
pompous 자만하는, 화려한, 허풍 떠는
sovereign 최고의, 주권의
enigmatic 불가사의한, 수수께끼의

02 정답 ④

정답해설

밑줄 친 단어는 문맥상 '회고의'로 사용되었고, 유의어로는 ④ reminiscent가 적절하다.

해석

교통수단의 **회고전**은 최근 전시회의 개최지인 심플론 터널의 개장의 관점에서 특이하고 흥미로웠다.
① 무아지경의
② 물질의, 물질, 육체적인, 중요한
③ 조직적인, 체계적인
④ 회고의, 연상시키는

어휘

ecstatic 무아지경의
systematic 조직적인, 체계적인
material 물질의, 물질, 육체의, 중요한
reminiscent 회고의, 연상시키는

03 정답 ①

정답해설

밑줄 친 단어가 문맥상 '솔직한'으로 사용되었고, 유의어로는 ① frank가 적절하다.

해석

주인은 성공뿐만 아니라 잘못된 일들에 대해서도 **솔직했다**.
① 솔직한
② 현실적인, 견실한
③ 인기 있는
④ 위협적인

어휘

frank 솔직한
fave 인기 있는
down-to-earth 현실적인, 견실한
intimidating 위협적인

04 정답 ④

정답해설

A의 "We should all make~(우리는 모두 밤 열두 시가 되기 전에 새해 소원을 빌어야 한다)"는 말에 대한 답변으로 "I am ready to leave~(나는 종이 친 직후에 바로 떠날 준비가 됐어)"는 부자연스럽다.

오답해설

① A가 B에게 잘 차려입은 이유를 묻자 B는 오늘 저녁에 가족들과 외식을 하기로 했다고 답변하므로 자연스러운 맥락의 대화이다.
② 편의점의 위치를 묻는 A에게 B는 지도에는 길 건너면 바로 있다고 말하고 있으므로 적절한 답변이다.
③ 내년에 한 학기 동안 휴학할까 생각 중이라는 A에게 B는 좋은 생각이라며 계획을 묻는다. 이는 적합한 대화의 흐름이다

해석

① A: 너 뭘 위해 잘 차려입은 거야?
  B: 나 오늘 저녁에 가족들과 외식하기로 했어.
② A: 편의점이 어디에 있어?
  B: 지도에는 길 건너면 바로 있다고 나와.
③ A: 나는 내년에 한 학기 휴학할까 생각하고 있어.
  B: 좋은 생각이야. 너 생각해둔 계획 있어?
④ A: 우리는 모두 밤 열두 시가 되기 전에 새해 소원을 빌어야 해.
  B: 나는 종이 치면 바로 떠날 준비가 되어있어.

어휘

dress up 옷을 차려입다
convenience store 편의점
twelve midnight 밤 열두 시
dinner out 외식을 하다
take ~ off ~(동안)을 쉬다

05 정답 ③

정답해설

③ **출제 포인트: 현재분사 vs. 과거분사**
'burying'은 완전타동사 'bury'의 현재분사형태로 뒤에 전치사 없이 목적어를 가진다. 해당 문장은 'burying' 뒤에 부사 'deep'을 사용하였으며 문맥상 '기원이 깊이 숨겨져 있다'가 자연스러우므로 'burying'을 과거분사 'buried'로 수정해야 한다.

오답해설

① **출제 포인트: what vs. that**
선행사가 없으며 뒤따라오는 문장의 주어가 없으므로 '관계대명사 what (주격)'을 사용하는 것이 옳다.
② **출제 포인트: to부정사 관용표현**
'to cope'는 'be able to 동사원형(~할 수 있다)'의 관용표현과 함께 쓰였다.
④ **출제 포인트: little vs. few**
'~을 이해하다'를 뜻하는 'make sense'에서 'sense'는 불가산명사에 해당한다. 따라서 불가산명사를 수식하는 수량형용사 'little'을 옳게 사용하였다.

해석

가장 정상적이고 유능한 아이라도 살면서 극복할 수 없는 문제들처럼 보이는 것을 만난다. 하지만 그것들을 놀이로 해 봄으로써 아이는 단계적인 과정을 밟으며 그것들에 대처할 수 있게 될 수도 있다. 아이는 그 기원이 자신의 무의식 속에 깊이 숨겨져 있을 수도 있는 내부의 과정에 반응하고 있기 때문에, 자신도 이해하기 힘든 상징적인 방식으로 흔히 그렇게 한다. 이것은 그 순간에는 우리가 거의 이해하지 못하는 놀이라는 결과를 낳을 수 있는데, 우리가 그것이 기여하는 목적을 모르기 때문이다.

어휘

competent 능숙한
insurmountable 대처할 수 없는
step-by-step 단계적인, 점진적인
encounter 맞닥뜨리다, 마주치다
cope with ~에 대처하다, 대응하다
symbolic 상징적인, 상징하는

오답률 TOP 1

06 정답 ②

정답해설

② 출제 포인트: 'The+비교급 ~, the+비교급' 구문

해당 문장은 'The+비교급 ~, the+비교급' 구문이 옳게 사용된 문장으로 첫 번째 절의 'more'는 동사 'thought'를 수식하는 부사이며 두 번째 절의 'more'는 현재분사 'devastating'을 수식하는 부사이다.

오답해설

① 출제 포인트: 주어와 동사 수일치(주격 관계대명사)

해당 문장에서 주격 관계대명사 'which'의 선행사는 'the towns'가 아니라 앞 문장 전체이므로 'were'를 'was'로 수정해야 한다.

③ 출제 포인트: If 생략 가정법

해당 문장은 'If'가 생략된 가정법 과거완료가 쓰인 문장이므로 종속절에 'Had+주어+과거분사'의 어순을 사용해야 한다. 따라서 'It had'를 'Had it'으로 수정하거나 'It' 앞에 'If'를 추가하여 'If it had not been for~'로 수정해야 한다.

④ 출제 포인트: 자동사로 착각하기 쉬운 완전타동사

'emphasize'는 완전타동사로 전치사 없이 목적어를 가진다. 해당 문장은 'emphasize'와 목적어 'that dementia is a syndrome and not a disease' 사이에 전치사 'on'을 사용하였으므로 틀린 문장이다. 따라서 'on'을 삭제해야 한다.

해석

① 그녀는 나에게 도시들을 구경시켜주었는데, 매우 친절했다.
② 그녀가 그것에 대해 더 생각할수록, 그것은 더 충격적이었다.
③ 안전띠가 없었다면, 그는 그 사고로 죽었을 것이다.
④ 그 치매는 증후군이지 질병이 아니라고 주장하는 것은 중요하다.

오답률 TOP 3

07 정답 ③

정답해설

③ 출제 포인트: 동명사 관용표현

'with a view to+목적어'는 관용표현으로 '~할 목적으로'를 뜻하며 목적어에는 명사(구)를 사용해야 한다. 해당 문장은 'with a view to'의 목적어로 동명사 'renovating'을 사용하였으므로 옳은 문장이다.

오답해설

① 출제 포인트: 동사 관용표현/시간의 부사구, 부사절

'come into force'는 관용표현으로 '시행되다'를 뜻하며 'last month'는 시간의 부사구로 동사에 과거시제를 사용해야 한다. 해당 문장은 주어진 해석이 '지난달에 시행되었다'이므로 'came into force last month'를 사용하는 것이 옳다. 따라서 현재시제인 'come'을 과거시제인 'came'으로 수정해야 한다.

② 출제 포인트: 현재분사 vs. 과거분사

감정 상태 형용사(과거분사) 'surprised'가 수식하는 대상은 'It'이며 이때 'It'은 가주어에 해당하므로 진주어를 찾아야 한다. 진주어는 'to see anything decent crop up in the first few years'이며 감정을 제공하는 주체에 해당하므로 감정 상태 형용사(과거분사) 'surprised'를 감정 제공 형용사(현재분사) 'surprising'으로 수정해야 한다. 또한 해당 문장에서 'terribly'는 비격식체로 '매우'를 뜻하며, 지각동사 see의 목적격 보어 'crop up'도 비격식체로 '나타나다'의 의미로 사용되었다.

④ 출제 포인트: 시간의 부사구, 부사절

'a year ago'는 시간의 부사구로 과거시제와 함께 사용한다. 해당 문장은 'a year ago'를 현재완료 'has died'와 함께 사용하였으므로 틀린 문장이다. 따라서 'has died'를 'died'로 수정해야 한다. 또한 'this year'는 현재완료와 함께 사용할 수 있으므로 주의해야 한다.

---

08 정답 ③

정답해설

해당 지문은 '가까운 목표(proximal goal) 설정이 먼 목표(distal goal) 설정보다 더 효율적이다'라는 것을 '수학에 뒤처진 학생들을 대상으로 한 실험'을 통해 설명하고 있다. 본문 후반에서 "Smaller subgoals led to faster completion and more accurate answers than one large goal."이라고 실험 결과를 설명하며, '하나의 큰 목표를 세운 학생들보다 하위 목표를 세운 학생들이 더 빠르고 더 정확하게 문제를 해결했다'라고 밝히고 있다. 빈칸에는 '가까운 목표가 학생들에게 미친 영향'을 설명하는 표현이 들어가야 하므로, 빈칸에 가장 적절한 것은 '③ ameliorated(향상시켰다)'이다.

오답해설

나머지 보기는 각각 '① depleted(대폭 감소시켰다), ② eliminated(제거했다), ④ dispersed(분산시켰다)'라는 의미로, 본문의 내용과는 반대되는 문장을 만들게 되므로 오답이다.

해석

1981년 연구원 Albert Bandura와 Dale Schunk는 흥미로운 것을 실험했다. Bandura와 Shunk는 수학 과목에서 뒤처지고 관심이 거의 없는 7세에서 10세 사이의 아이들을 연구 대상으로 삼았다. 약 절반의 아이들은 각 세션마다 6페이지의 수학 문제를 푼다는 목표를 설정할 것을 제안받았고, 나머지 절반은 7개의 세션에 걸쳐 42페이지의 수학 문제를 푼다는 먼 목표를 설정하도록 제안받았다. 무엇이 발생했을까? 더 작은 하위 목표가 하나의 큰 목표보다 더 빠른 완수와 더 정확한 정답을 이끌었다. 가까운 목표 개입이 수학 과목과 수학 학습에 있어서 학생들의 자기효능감을 향상시킨 것으로 드러났다.

① 대폭 감소시켰다
② 제거했다
③ 향상시켰다
④ 분산시켰다

어휘

work with …을 연구[작업] 대상으로 하다
complete 완료하다
distal (중심에서) 먼
lead to ~로 이어지다, 이끌다
accurate 정확한
turn out …인 것으로 드러나다[밝혀지다]
session 세션, 회기, 기간
subgoal 하위 목표
completion 완수, 완료

proximal (중심에서) 가까운, 인접하는   intervention 개입
self-efficacy 자기효능감(자신이 어떤 일을 성공적으로 수행할 수 있는 능력이 있
                다고 믿는 기대와 신념)
deplete 대폭 감소시키다[격감시키다]   eliminate 제거하다, 없애다
ameliorate 향상시키다, 개선하다
disperse …을 흩어지게 하다, 분산시키다

오답률 TOP 2
09 정답 ③

정답해설

해당 지문은 '미아스마설(miasma theory)'에 관한 내용이며, 해당 이론이 당시 질병 예방에 어떠한 영향을 미쳤는지 설명하고 있다. 주어진 문장은 미아스마설이 지지를 받게 되는 과정을 설명하고 있고, "By improving the housing, sanitation and general cleanliness of these existing areas (이러한 기존 지역에서의 주거, 위생 그리고 일반 청결을 향상시킴으로써)"에서 'these existing areas(이러한 기존 지역)'가 가리키는 대상이 주어진 문장 이전에 등장해야 함을 알 수 있다. ③ 이전 문장 "Rapid industrialization and urbanization had created many poor, filthy and foul-smelling city neighborhoods that tended to be the focal points of disease and epidemics(급속한 산업화와 도시화는 질병과 전염병의 중심이 되는 경향이 있던 많은 빈곤하고 불결하고 악취가 나는 도시 지역을 만들어냈다)."에서 'city neighborhoods(도시 지역)'라는 지역을 나타내는 표현이 등장하므로, 주어진 문장은 ③에 들어가는 것이 가장 적절하다는 것을 알 수 있다.

오답해설

나머지 위치는 문맥상 어색하므로 오답이다.

해석

미아스마설에 따르면 질병은 악취로 특징지어진 부패하는 물질의 부유물인 독성 증기, 즉 미아스마가 공기 중에 존재하는 것에 의해 발생했다. (①) 그 이론은 중세 시대에 고안되었고 수 세기 동안 지속되었다. 19세기 영국의 위생 개혁가들에게 미아스마설은 타당했다. (②) 급속한 산업화와 도시화는 질병과 전염병의 중심이 되는 경향이 있던 많은 빈곤하고 불결하고 악취가 나는 도시 지역을 만들어냈다. (③ **이러한 기존 지역에서의 주거, 위생 그리고 일반 청결을 향상시킴으로써, 질병의 정도가 하락하는 것으로 보였고, 이는 그 이론을 뒷받침했다.**) 비록 그것이 향후 반박되고 거부되었지만, 미아스마설의 존재의 이점이 없는 것은 아니었다. (④) 악취의 원인을 제거함으로써 개혁가들은 종종 의도치 않게 많은 질병의 실제 원인인 박테리아도 제거했던 것이다.

어휘

sanitation 위생   existing 기존의, 현존의
lend weight to …을 뒷받침[입증]하다
miasma (지저분한·불쾌한) 공기[기운/냄새]
presence 존재, 있음   poisonous 유독한
vapor 증기
suspend 〈먼지·미립자 등을〉 (공중에·수중에) 떠 있게 하다, 부유(浮遊)시키다
particle 입자   decay 부식하다, 썩다
characterize 특징짓다   foul (냄새가) 더러운, 악취 나는
endure 오래가다[지속되다]   make sense 타당하다, 말이 되다
sanitary 위생의   reformer 개혁가
industrialization 산업화   urbanization 도시화
filthy 불결한, 지저분한   tend to ~하는 경향이 있다
focal point (관심·활동의) 초점[중심] epidemic 전염병, 유행병
disprove 틀렸음을 입증하다, 반박[반증]하다
reject 거부하다   merit 가치, 장점
inadvertently 우연히, 의도하지 않게

10 정답 ④

정답해설

해당 지문은 '리더십의 본질과 훌륭한 리더의 자질'에 대해 설명하고 있다. 본문의 마지막 문장 "Instead of seeking to stand out from their peers, they may be better served by ensuring that they are seen to be a good follower — as someone who is willing to work within the group and on its behalf(그들의 동료들 중 두드러지는 것을 추구하는 것 대신에, 그들은 그들이 좋은 추종자로 보임으로써, 즉 그룹 내에서 그룹의 이익을 위해 기꺼이 일하는 사람으로 보임으로써 더 나은 섬김을 받을 수 있을 것이다)."를 통해 '본인 단독으로 두드러지는 것보다 그룹 내에서 그룹의 일원이 되어 일하는 것이 더 나은 리더가 될 수 있는 길이다'라고 설명하고 있다. 따라서 글의 제목으로 가장 적절한 것은 '④ To Be a Good Leader, Start by Being a Good Follower(좋은 리더가 되기 위해서 좋은 추종자가 되는 것으로부터 시작하라)'이다.

오답해설

①, ② 리더의 자질이 타고나는 것인지, 학습되는 것인지에 대한 내용은 언급되지 않으므로 오답이다.
③ 글의 주장과는 반대되는 내용의 제목이므로 오답이다.

해석

리더십은 자신들이 동일한 사회적 그룹의 구성원이라는 것이라는 이해를 통해 서로 결속되어있는 리더와 추종자 사이의 관계로부터 발생하는 과정이다. 사람들은 그들의 행위가 그들이 우리들 중 하나라는 것을 나타낼 때 더 효율적인 리더가 될 것이다. 이는 그들이 우리의 가치, 관심사, 그리고 경험을 공유하고, 자신의 개인적인 이익보다 그룹의 이익을 증진시킬 것을 고려함으로써 우리를 위해 그것을 하고 있는 것이기 때문이다. 이러한 관점은 야심찬 리더를 위한 일반적인 조언에 커다란 결함이 있다는 것을 확인해준다. 그들의 동료들 중 두드러지는 것을 추구하는 것 대신에, 그들은 그들이 좋은 추종자로 보임으로써, 즉 그룹 내에서 그룹의 이익을 위해 기꺼이 일하는 사람으로 보임으로써 더 나은 섬김을 받을 수 있을 것이다.
① 리더는 만들어지는 것이 아니라 타고나는 것이다
② 누구나 리더가 되는 법을 배울 수 있다
③ 추종자가 아닌 리더로 보이는 법
④ 좋은 리더가 되기 위해서 좋은 추종자가 되는 것으로부터 시작하라

어휘

process 과정, 절차   emerge 생기다, 나타나다
bind (bound-bound) 결속시키다, 묶다
indicate 나타내다, 가리키다   look to ~을 생각해[고려해] 보다
advance 증진시키다, 개선하다   perspective 관점
identify 확인하다   flaw 결함, 흠
aspiring 포부[야심]를 가진   seek to ~하도록 시도[추구]하다
stand out from …중에 두드러지다
peer 동료, (법적·사회적으로) 동등한 사람
serve (사람을) 섬기다, 봉사하다, 모시다
ensure 확실히 하다   be willing to 기꺼이 ~하다
on one's behalf …의 이익을 위해, …을 대신하여

기적사 DAY 34

결국엔 성정혜 영어 하프모의고사

01	②	02	④	03	③	04	④	05	②
06	③	07	③	08	②	09	③	10	④

01 정답 ②

정답해설
밑줄 친 단어가 문맥상 '설득하다'로 사용되었고, 유의어로는 ② convince가 적절하다.

해석
그는 앞으로 나서서 모험을 할 수 있는 무엇보다 중요한 용기와 따르는 다른 사람들을 **설득할** 수 있는 능력이 있었다.
① 수행하다, 운영하다, 안내하다
② 납득시키다, 설득하다
③ 급격히 감소하다, 추락하다, (물, 구멍 등에) 뛰어들다
④ 억압하다, (권력 등으로) 압박하다

어휘
conduct 수행하다, 운영하다, 안내하다
convince 납득시키다, 설득하다
plunge 급격히 감소하다, 추락하다, (물, 구멍 등에) 뛰어들다
oppress 억압하다, (권력 등으로) 압박하다

02 정답 ④

정답해설
밑줄 친 단어가 문맥상 '만족시키다'로 사용되었고, 유의어로는 ④ gratify가 적절하다.

해석
그러나, 이 국가의 국민들을 지치게 하면서, 새로운 헌법은 비용이 많이 들고 실행이 불가능하다는 것이 입증되었고, 인구의 어느 한 부분을 **만족시키지** 못했다.
① 인수하다, 취득하다
② 주장하다
③ 양도하다, 옮기다, 바꾸다
④ 만족시키다

어휘
acquire 인수하다, 취득하다
transfer 양도하다, 옮기다, 바꾸다
assert 주장하다
gratify 만족시키다

03 정답 ③

정답해설
밑줄 친 단어는 문맥상 '이해하다'로 사용되었고, 유의어로는 ③ comprehend 가 적절하다.

해석
그리고 그 고양이와 나는 둘 다 당신의 언어를 말할 수 있고, 당신이 말하는 단어를 **이해할 수** 있기 때문에 모든 것이 부자연스러웠다.
① 돌보다, ~하는 경향이 있다
② (기력을) 꺾다
③ 이해하다, 포함하다
④ 놀라게 하다

어휘
tend 돌보다, ~하는 경향이 있다
comprehend 이해하다, 포함하다
daunt (기력을) 꺾다
frighten 놀라게 하다

04 정답 ④

정답해설
Jenny는 Pat에게 다음 달에 자신이 이사한다는 사실을 알고 있었냐고 묻자 Pat은 몰랐다며 Jenny가 현재 지하철역 근처에 살고 있지 않냐고 되묻는다. Jenny는 Pat의 말이 바르다고 긍정하며 월세가 너무 비싸 감당할 수 없어 이사하는 것이라고 언급한다. 그리고 이사하면 Pat을 ④ '집들이(a house-warming party)'에 초대하겠다고 말하고 Pat은 초대해줘서 고맙다고 답변한다.

오답해설
① '크거나 중요한 일(사람)(a big deal)'에 초대한다는 것은 대화의 흐름으로는 부자연스럽다.
② Jenny가 다음 달에 이사한다고 말하는 상황에서 '소개팅(a blind date)'에 Pat을 초대한다는 것은 적절하지 않다.
③ Pat에게 다음 달에 이사한다며 '문제의 본질(the name of the game)'에 초대한다고 말하는 것은 대화의 흐름을 해친다.

해석
Jenny: 나 다음 달에 이사한다고 말했었나?
Pat: 아니, 전혀. 너 지하철역 근처에 살지 않아?
Jenny: 맞아. 근데 월세가 너무 비싸서 감당할 수가 없어.
Pat: 아, 그래서 이사하는 거야?
Jenny: 그게 유일한 이유야. 나 새로운 집으로 이사하면 집들이에 초대할게.
Pat: 초대해줘서 정말 고마워.
① 크거나 중요한 일(사람)
② 소개팅
③ 문제의 본질
④ 집들이

어휘
mention 언급하다
monthly rent 월세
invitation 초대
subway station 지하철역
afford 감당하다

05 정답 ②

정답해설
② **출제 포인트: 주격 관계대명사 vs. 소유격 관계대명사**
'negative public and media image'를 선행사로 하며 뒤따라오는 문장의 주어가 없으므로 주격 관계대명사를 사용해야 한다. 따라서 'of which'를 주격 관계대명사 'which' 또는 'that'으로 수정해야 한다.

오답해설
① **출제 포인트: 시간의 부사구/부사절**
'during the last two decades'는 시간의 부사구로 현재완료와 함께 사용할 수 있다.
③ **출제 포인트: to부정사의 명사적 용법**
'to compete'는 불완전타동사 'made'의 진목적어이며 to부정사의 명사적 용법으로 사용되었다.

④ 출제 포인트: 전치사 + 명사(구)

전치사 'in'의 목적어로 동명사 'attracting'을 옳게 사용하였다.

해석

지난 20년 동안 많은 개발도상국들이 세계화 과정과 철의 장막 몰락의 일환으로 세계 관광 시장에 참여해 왔다. 이러한 나라들은 강력하고 친숙한 브랜드를 가진 나라들과 관광객을 놓고 경쟁하는 것을 어렵게 만든 대중과 미디어의 부정적 이미지 때문에 어려움을 겪었다. 이 세계화의 시대에, 문제가 있다는 이미지는 관광객과 수준 높은 거주자, 그리고 투자자들을 끌어들이는 데 주된 장애물이다.

어휘

developing country 개발도상국
the Iron Curtain 철의 장막
problematic 문제가 있는
globalization 세계화
compete 경쟁하다, 겨루다
obstacle 장애, 장애물

06 정답 ③

정답해설

③ 출제 포인트: 자동사로 착각하기 쉬운 완전타동사

'accompany'는 완전타동사로 전치사 없이 목적어를 가진다. 해당 문장은 'accompanies' 뒤에 목적어 'us'를 사용하였으므로 옳은 문장이다.

오답해설

① 출제 포인트: If 생략 가정법

가정법 과거에서 종속절에 be동사가 오는 경우 'were'를 사용해야 한다. 해당 문장은 'If'가 생략된 가정법 과거가 쓰인 문장으로 종속절에 'was'를 사용하였으므로 틀린 문장이다. 따라서 'was'를 'were'로 수정해야 한다.

② 출제 포인트: 'The + 비교급 ~, the + 비교급' 구문

해당 문장은 'The + 비교급 ~, the + 비교급' 구문에 해당하나 비교급 자리에 원급을 사용하였으므로 틀린 문장이다. 따라서 'much'를 'more'로 수정해야 한다.

④ 출제 포인트: 주어와 동사 수일치(주격 관계대명사)

선행사 'That store'가 단수 형태이므로 주격 관계대명사절 동사의 단수 형태를 사용해야 한다. 따라서 'are'를 'is'로 수정해야 한다.

해석

① 오늘 오후에 비가 온다면 시합은 취소될 것이다.
② 더 많이 배울수록 그의 이론에 흠이 있다는 것을 더 많이 알게 되었다.
③ 상황이 너무 심각해서 경찰 호송대가 비행기에서 우리와 동행한다.
④ 그런데 매우 멋진 밀턴 가에 있는 그 가게는 톰의 동생이 소유하고 있다.

오답률 TOP 2

07 정답 ③

정답해설

③ 출제 포인트: 시간의 부사구/부사절

'in the last + 숫자 + years'는 시간의 부사구로 과거시제와 함께 사용할 수 있다. 해당 문장은 'in the last three to four years'와 과거시제 동사 'began'을 함께 사용하였으므로 옳은 문장이다. 또한 since 종속절을 제외한 주절이 현재완료 have p.p.로 쓰여서 옳게 사용되었다.

오답해설

① 출제 포인트: 현재분사 vs. 과거분사

현재분사 'convincing'이 수식하는 대상은 생략된 주어 'most people'이며 주어진 해석(~라고 확신하면서)을 통해 둘의 관계가 수동임을 알 수 있다. 따라서 'convincing'을 과거분사 'convinced'로 수정해야 한다. 이때 'that + 절'은 목적어가 아니라 직접목적어임에 유의하도록 하자.

② 출제 포인트: 동명사 관용표현

'be used to + 목적어'는 관용표현으로 '~하는 것에 익숙하다'를 뜻한다. 해당 문장은 주어진 해석이 '~에 익숙하다'이므로 'was used to be'를 'was used to being'으로 수정해야 한다. 이때 'be used to + 동사원형'은 '~하기 위해 사용되다'를 뜻하므로 주의하도록 하자.

④ 출제 포인트: 동사 관용표현

'have access to + 목적어'는 관용표현으로 '~에 접근할 수 있다'를 뜻한다. 해당 문장은 주어진 해석이 '~에 접근할 수 있다'이므로 'have an access to'를 'have access to'로 수정해야 한다.

오답률 TOP 3

08 정답 ②

정답해설

해당 지문은 '장기적인 목표의 비효율성'에 대해 설명하고 있다. 첫 문장 "Author and professional speaker Dorie Clark says setting smaller goals for shorter time periods makes you more flexible and quicker to adapt to new information or changing circumstances(저자이자 전문 연사인 Dorie Clark는 짧은 기간 동안 작은 목표를 설정하는 것이 당신이 새로운 정보 또는 변화하는 상황에 더 융통성 있고 더 빠르게 적응할 수 있도록 만들어 준다고 말한다)."를 통해 '단기간의 작은 목표가 상황 변화 등에 더 유연하게 적응할 수 있도록 해준다'라고 설명하며, 이후 1년의 장기적인 목표가 비효율적으로 바뀌게 되는 상황을 아침 운동을 예시로 들어 설명하고 있다. 따라서 글의 요지로 가장 적절한 것은 '② Establishing a long-term goal can be sometimes inefficient(장기적인 목표를 세우는 것은 때때로 비효율적일 수도 있다).'이다.

오답해설

① 글의 요지를 설명하기 위해 '이른 아침 운동을 하는 것'에 대한 예시를 사용한 것이며, 글 전체를 아우르는 내용이 아니므로 오답이다.

③ 본문은 목표를 성취하는 것에 초점이 맞추어진 것이 아니며, 첫 문장 "setting smaller goals for shorter time periods makes you more flexible and quicker to adapt to new information or changing circumstances(짧은 기간 동안 작은 목표를 설정하는 것이 당신이 새로운 정보 또는 변화하는 상황에 더 융통성 있고 더 빠르게 적응할 수 있도록 만들어 준다)."를 통해 '작은 목표가 장기적인 목표보다 상황 또는 환경 변화에 적응하기 용이하다'라고 설명하고 있으므로, 글의 요지로 적절하지 않다.

④ 글의 내용과는 무관한 문장이므로 오답이다.

해석

저자이자 전문 연사인 Dorie Clark는 짧은 기간 동안 작은 목표를 설정하는 것이 당신이 새로운 정보 또는 변화하는 상황에 더 융통성 있고 더 빠르게 적응할 수 있도록 만들어 준다고 말한다. 예를 들어, 1년간의 목표를 세우는 것은 당신의 상황이나 우선순위가 바뀐 6개월 뒤에는 당신이 이치에 맞지 않는 일을 하고 있도록 만들 수 있다. 또는 1년간의 목표가 이치에 맞지 않게 되었을 때 그것을 포기하고 새로운 해가 다가올 때까지 목표 없이 지낼지도 모른다. 예를 들어, Clark는 친구와 라켓볼을 하는 것을 통해 건강을 유지할 목표를 세웠다. 그러나 곧 이른 아침의 경기가 그녀를 수면 부족과 비생산적이 되게 하였다. 만약 그것이 1년의 목표였다면, 그녀가 아침 라켓볼 경기를 포기했을 때 Clerk는 그 해의 남은 기간을 아무런 운동 계획 없이 지냈을 것이다.

① 이른 아침 운동이 모두에게 유익한 것은 아니다.
② 장기적인 목표를 세우는 것은 때때로 비효율적일 수도 있다.
③ 작은 목표가 큰 목표보다 훨씬 이루기 쉽다.
④ 오늘날 우리는 새로운 상황에 신속하게 적응할 수 있어야 한다.

어휘

- flexible 유연한, 융통성 있는
- circumstance 상황
- leave …을 (어떤 상태가) 되게 하다, …을 (어떤 상태) 그대로 두다
- make sense 이치에 맞다, 말이 되다, 타당하다
- priority 우선순위
- fit 건강한
- unproductive 비생산적인
- inefficient 비효율적인
- adapt to …에 적응하다
- roll around 다가오다
- sleep-deprived 수면 부족의
- establish 확립하다
- accomplish 달성하다, 이루다

오답률 TOP 1

09 정답 ③

정답해설

(A) 빈칸 이전에서 '세균이 질병을 야기한다는 지식'에 대해 설명하며 해당 지식이 우리에게 미친 주요 영향에 대해 강조한 후, 빈칸 이후에서 해당 지식에 대한 구체적인 추가 설명을 하고 있다. 따라서 빈칸에는 앞서 말한 내용에 자세한 내용을 덧붙일 때 사용하는 접속부사인 'In fact(사실은)'가 들어가는 것이 적절하다.

(B) 빈칸 이전에서 많은 과학자들이 세균 이론에 기여하는 연구를 수행했다고 언급한 후, 빈칸 이후에 그 많은 과학자들 중 오직 특정한 두 인물만이 이론 형성에 결정적인 기여를 했다고 설명하고 있으므로, 빈칸에는 '역접, 양보'를 나타내는 접속부사인 'However(그러나)'가 들어가는 것이 가장 적절하다. 따라서 정답은 '③ (A) In fact(사실) – (B) However(그러나)'이다.

오답해설

④ (A) 빈칸 이후의 내용이 이전 내용의 반대 상황을 가정하는 것이 아니기 때문에 'Otherwise(그렇지 않으면)'는 빈칸에 적절하지 않다.
나머지 보기는 문맥상 어색하므로 오답이다.

해석

오늘날 우리는 독감, 수두, 폐렴과 같은 전염병이 미생물, 즉 박테리아와 바이러스에 의해 발생한다는 것을 이해하고 있다. 이러한 지식이 없었다면, 우리는 이러한 감염을 치료하고 예방할 방법을 발전시키지 못했을 것이다. (A) 사실, 질병의 '세균이론'이라 알려진 이 지식은 상당히 근래의 발견이다. 사람들은 수천 년 동안 인간 질병을 설명하기 위해 이론들을 창시해 왔다. 그리스 내과 의사인 Hippocrates는 늪과 같은 곳에서 발생한 '나쁜 공기'가 원인이라고 생각했다. 19세기 현미경 기술의 발전은 미생물학자 세대가 이전에는 보지 못한 질병 유발 유기체의 세계를 더 깊게 연구할 수 있도록 해주었다. 많은 과학자들이 세균이론 형성에 기여하는 연구를 시행했다. (B) 그러나 그 이론의 과학적 증거는 오직 두 유럽 출신 과학자인 프랑스인 Louis Pasteur와 독일인이었던 Robert Koch의 성과였다.

① 예를 들어 – 게다가
② 안타깝게도 – 결국
③ 사실 – 그러나
④ 그렇지 않으면 – 그럼에도 불구하고

어휘

- infectious 전염성의
- pneumonia 폐렴
- prevent 예방하다
- remarkably 몹시, 매우
- millennium 천년(pl. millennia)
- swampy 늪 같은, 습지가 있는
- blame …을 탓하다, … 책임[때문으]로 보다
- microscope 현미경
- chickenpox 수두
- microscopic organism 미생물
- infection 감염
- discovery 발견
- physician 내과 의사
- enable 가능하게 하다
- generation 세대
- investigate 조사하다, 연구하다
- unseen 본 적이 없는, 미지의
- carry out 시행하다, 수행하다
- contribute towards …에 기여하다[공헌하다]
- formation 형성
- achievement 성과, 성취
- microbiologist 미생물학자
- previously 이전에
- organism 유기체
- proof 증거

10 정답 ④

정답해설

해당 지문은 '누구나 리더가 될 수는 있으나 모든 사람이 리더가 되어야 하는 것은 아니며, 추종자로서도 충분히 변화를 만들 수 있다'고 설명하고 있다. 두 번째 문장 "That doesn't mean they're less capable of making an important contribution, just that they bring a different set of skills to the table(그것이 그들이 중요한 기여를 할 수 있는 능력이 덜하다는 것을 의미하지 않는다. 단지 그들이 다른 종류의 능력을 제공한다는 것을 의미한다)."에서의 "they"는 첫 번째 문장에서 "누구나 리더가 될 수 있으나 모든 사람이 리더십에 적합한 것은 아니다"라고 하고 있으므로 "추종자(followers)"라는 것을 유추할 수 있으며, 추종자는 리더와 다른 종류지만 그만큼 중요한 기여를 할 수 있다고 언급하고 있다. 또한 마지막 문장 "You don't have to be in charge to be influential(영향력을 미치기 위해 당신이 책임자가 될 필요는 없는 것이다)."을 통해 리더 외의 사람도 영향력을 미칠 수 있다고 서술하고 있다. 따라서 글의 요지로 가장 적절한 것은 '④ Followers can contribute to the society as much as leaders(추종자도 리더만큼 사회에 많은 기여를 할 수 있다).'이다.

오답해설

① 본문과는 무관한 내용이므로 오답이다.
② 리더와 추종자의 역할이 다르다고 언급하고 있으나, 글의 주요 주제는 각각의 역할의 차이가 아니라 그러한 '다른 역할을 통해 사회에 영향을 미칠 수 있다'는 것이므로, 전체 글의 요지로는 부적절하다.
③ 본문에서 추종자 또한 차이를 만들고자 하며 영향을 미칠 수 있다고 언급하고 있으므로, 글의 요지로는 부적절하다.

해석

누구나 리더가 될 수 있다. 그러나 모든 사람이 리더십에 적합한 것은 아니다. 그것이 그들이 중요한 기여를 할 수 있는 능력이 덜하다는 것을 의미하지 않는다. 단지 그들이 다른 종류의 능력을 제공한다는 것을 의미한다. 추종자가 되는 것이 잘못된 일은 아니다. 세상은 그들을 리더만큼 필요로 한다. 모든 것에는 균형이 있다. 비결은 어떠한 역할이 당신이 수행하기에 가장 적합한지를 아는 것이다. 리더와 추종자 모두 똑같이 변화를 만들고자 하는 자신들의 욕망에 의해 움직일 수 있다. 그리고 이것은 분명한 차이가 아니다. 그들 대부분은 양쪽 측면의 요소를 지니고 있고, 하나 또는 다른 하나가 상황에 따라 선두로 나설 수 있다. 영향력을 미치기 위해 당신이 책임자가 될 필요는 없는 것이다.

① 타고난 리더인 사람들이 있다.
② 리더와 추종자의 역할은 다르다.
③ 세상의 변화를 이끄는 것은 리더이다.
④ 추종자도 리더만큼 사회에 많은 기여를 할 수 있다.

어휘

- be capable of ~할 수 있다
- contribution 기여, 공헌
- trick 비결, 요령
- fill (지위 등을) 차지하다, (직무를) 맡아 하다
- desire 욕망, 욕구
- cut out for 적합한, 알맞은
- bring … to the table …을 제공하다[기여하다]
- qualified 자격 있는, 적합한
- distinction 차이

element 요소
be in charge 담당하다, 책임지다
contribute 기여하다, 공헌하다
forefront 선두, 맨 앞
influential 영향력이 있는

결국엔 성정혜 영어 하프모의고사
기적사 DAY 35

| 01 | ① | 02 | ③ | 03 | ① | 04 | ② | 05 | ② |
| 06 | ④ | 07 | ④ | 08 | ④ | 09 | ② | 10 | ③ |

01 정답 ①

정답해설

밑줄 친 단어가 문맥상 '지배하다'로 사용되었고, 유의어로는 ① govern이 적절하다.

해석

그들은 완전히 적절하지 않고 비성공적이며, 모든 서유럽을 **지배하려는** 시도의 결과는 파산과 탈진을 생산하는 특징에 있었다.
① 지배하다, 관리하다
② 해결하다, 정착하다, 타협을 보다
③ 살펴보다, 조사하다, 검토하다
④ 아첨하다

어휘

govern 지배하다, 관리하다　　settle 해결하다, 정착하다, 타협을 보다
scrutinize 살펴보다, 조사하다, 검토하다
adulate 아첨하다

02 정답 ③

정답해설

밑줄 친 단어가 '끝마치다'로 사용되었고, 유의어로는 ③ complete가 적절하다.

해석

나는 어제 나의 편지를 **끝마칠** 기회를 가지지 못했고, 그것이 나를 슬프게 느끼도록 만들었다.
① 분해하다
② 갈다
③ 끝나다, 완성하다
④ 축소하다

어휘

dissolve 분해하다　　triturate 갈다
complete 끝나다, 완성하다　　abridge 축소하다

03 정답 ①

정답해설

밑줄 친 단어가 문맥상 '발생하다'로 사용되었고, 유의어로는 ① occur이 적절하다.

해석

똑같이 아름다운 여자가 그를 유혹하면 무슨 일이 **일어날까**?
① 일어나다
② 조사하다
③ 해체하다
④ 없애다

어휘

occur 일어나다
disjoint 해체하다
investigate 조사하다
remove 없애다

> 오답률 TOP 3
> **04 정답 ②**

정답해설

A는 조언을 구하기 위해 B를 찾아 시간이 있냐고 묻는다. B는 사무실에서 서류작업을 하다가 A의 고민을 듣는다. A가 일 년 정도의 기간 동안 호주로 워킹홀리데이를 다녀오고 싶다고 이야기하자 B는 그게 왜 문제냐며 가고 싶으면 가라고 답변한다. 그러자 A는 혼자 남겨지는 것이 걱정된다며 예상치 못한 문제에 직면하게 되면 어떡하냐고 묻는다. 걱정하는 A에게 B는 ②"겁쟁이처럼 굴지 마(Don't be a chicken)"라고 말하는 것이 가장 적절하다.

오답해설

① 부자(a fat cat)는 B가 A에게 조언하는 대화의 내용상 빈칸에 들어갈 말로 부자연스럽다.
③ 모방하는 인간(a copycat)은 대화의 흐름으로는 어색하다.
④ 냉혈한 사람(a cold fish)은 걱정하는 A에게 조언하는 말로 적절하지 않다.

해석

A: 안녕, 나 너 찾고 있었어. 너 어디에 있었어?
B: 아, 정말? 나 사무실에서 서류작업 좀 하고 있었어. 뭐 도와줄까?
A: 심각한 건 아닌데 난 그저 네 조언이 필요해. 너 시간 좀 남아?
B: 물론이지, 얘기해.
A: 나 일 년 정도 동안 호주로 워킹홀리데이를 가고 싶어.
B: 그럼 가야지. 그게 뭐가 문제야?
A: 나 혼자 남겨지는 것이 걱정돼. 만약 내가 완전히 홀로 있는 동안 예상치 못한 문제에 직면하면 어떡하지?
B: 겁쟁이처럼 굴지 마. 넌 혼자서도 잘 거야.
① 부자
② 겁쟁이
③ 모방하는 인간
④ 냉혈한 사람

어휘

paperwork 서류작업
spare time 여가
unexpected 예상치 못한
advice 조언
encounter 맞닥뜨리다

05 정답 ②

정답해설

② 출제 포인트: what vs. that
'all the familiar faces'를 선행사로 하며 뒤따라오는 문장의 주어가 없으므로 주격 관계대명사 'that'을 사용해야 한다. 따라서 'what'을 'that'으로 수정해야 한다.

오답해설

① 출제 포인트: 현재분사 vs. 과거분사
'well-dressed'는 부사와 과거분사가 결합한 복합형용사로 '(옷을) 잘 차려입은'을 뜻한다.
③ 출제 포인트: 시간의 부사구/부사절
'for the last few years'는 시간의 부사구로 과거완료와 함께 사용할 수 있다.

④ 출제 포인트: 관계부사 vs. 관계대명사
'the first day'를 선행사로 하며 뒤따라오는 문장이 완전하므로 관계부사 'when'을 사용하는 것이 옳다.

해석

고등학교 운동장은 화려한 드레스와 정장을 입고 즐거운 사진사들을 위해 포즈를 취하는, 옷을 잘 차려입은 사람들로 가득 찼다. 축하, 포옹, 그리고 웃음이 전파되었다. Jane은 지난 몇 년 동안 자신의 삶의 일부였던 모든 친숙한 얼굴들을 바라보았다. 곧 그녀의 어머니가 그들과 합류할 것이었다. 그녀는 자신이 불안해하는 많은 신입생들의 한가운데에서 그 똑같은 곳에 서 있었던 학교에서의 첫날을 기억해 냈는데, 그들 중 몇 명은 그녀의 가장 친한 친구들이 되었다.

어휘

well-dressed (옷을) 잘 차려입은
contagious 전염되는, 전염성의
freshman 신입생
fancy 화려한, 값비싼, 일류의
recall 상기하다, 생각나게 하다

> 오답률 TOP 1
> **06 정답 ④**

정답해설

④ 출제 포인트: 'The + 비교급 ~, the + 비교급' 구문
해당 문장은 'The + 비교급 ~, the + 비교급' 구문이 옳게 사용된 문장이다. 또한 두 번째 절의 경우 the + 비교급 'the greater'이 보어에 해당하므로 보어 도치가 일어났다.

오답해설

① 출제 포인트: 주어와 동사 수일치(주격 관계대명사)
주격 관계대명사 which의 선행사는 앞 문장 전체이므로 주격 관계대명사 절의 동사에 단수형태를 사용해야 한다. 따라서 look을 looks로 수정해야 한다. 또는 선행사를 a green carpet with pink walls로 보아도 선행사가 단수이므로 수일치가 수정되어야 한다.
② 출제 포인트: If 생략 가정법
해당 문장은 If가 생략된 가정법 과거완료가 쓰인 문장으로 종속절에 'Had + 주어 + 과거분사'를 사용해야 한다. 따라서 종속절의 'Has'를 'Had'로 수정해야 한다.
③ 출제 포인트: 자동사로 착각하기 쉬운 완전타동사
'oppose'는 완전타동사로 전치사 없이 목적어를 가진다. 해당 문장은 'oppose'와 목적어 'measures' 사이에 전치사 'to'를 사용하였으므로 틀린 문장이다. 따라서 'to'를 삭제해야 한다.

해석

① 그녀는 분홍색 벽에 초록색 카펫을 가지고 있는데, 그것이 내 마음속에는 모두 잘못된 것처럼 보인다.
② John이 그 모임에 있었다면, 그는 그 제안에 투표하였을 것이다.
③ 당신이 신분증에 반대한다면 당신은 지금 또한 부정 선거를 예방하는 수단에 반대하는 것이다.
④ 당신이 스스로에게 더 많은 신뢰를 쌓을수록, 당신의 성공 기회는 더 커진다.

> 오답률 TOP 2
> **07 정답 ④**

정답해설

④ 출제 포인트: 현재분사 vs. 과거분사
일반 과거분사는 수식하는 대상과 수동 관계인 경우 사용하며 감정 제공 형용사[현재분사]는 수식하는 대상과 능동 관계인 경우 사용한다. 해당 문

장은 일반 과거분사 'limited'와 감정 제공 형용사[현재분사] 'boring'을 사용하여 'memory'를 수식하고 있다. 이때 'memory'와 'limited'의 관계는 수동이며 'memory'와 'boring'의 관계는 능동임에 유의해야 한다.

(오답해설)

① **출제 포인트: 동명사 관용표현**
'what would you say to+목적어?'는 관용표현으로 '~하는 게 어때?'를 뜻하며 목적어에는 명사(구)가 온다. 해당 문장은 주어진 해석이 '~하는 게 어때?'이므로 전치사 'to' 뒤에 있는 동사원형 'leave'를 동명사 'leaving'으로 수정해야 한다.

② **출제 포인트: 시간의 부사구/부사절**
시간과 조건의 부사절에서 미래를 나타내는 경우 현재시제 또는 현재완료만 사용할 수 있다. 해당 문장은 시간의 부사절이 쓰인 문장으로 미래를 나타내므로 종속절의 'will'을 삭제해야 한다.

③ **출제 포인트: 동사 관용표현**
'feast on'은 관용표현으로 '~을 마음껏 먹다'를 뜻한다. 해당 문장은 주어진 해석이 '~을 마음껏 먹다'이므로 'feasting at'을 'feasting on'으로 수정해야 한다. 또한 feast는 완전자동사이므로 전치사 없이 목적어를 가질 수 없음에 유의해야한다.

08 정답 ④

(정답해설)

해당 지문에서는 '여성에 의한 식량 채집 및 공유의 역할'에 대해 설명하고 있다. 주어진 문장의 "In other words(다시 말해)"로 보아 앞서 말한 내용을 다시 한번 구체적으로 설명하고 있다는 것을 알 수 있다. 따라서 주어진 문장 이전에는 요리 및 식재료를 처리하는 것에 대한 내용이 언급되는 것이 자연스럽다. ④ 이전 문장에서 "An important component of food sharing by women is the requirement to process many vegetal foods before consumption is possible."이라며 "섭취 전 식물 식량 처리", 즉 "요리에 대한 필요성이 여성에 의한 식량 공유에 중요한 요소이다"라고 본문 최초로 '식재료 처리'에 대한 언급을 하고 있으므로, 이후에 구체적으로 처리하는 방식이 드러나는 것이 자연스럽다. 따라서 주어진 문장이 들어갈 가장 적절한 위치는 ④이다.

(오답해설)

나머지는 글의 흐름상 자연스럽지 않으므로 오답이다.

(해석)

남성에 의한 고기 공유의 역할이 식량 공유에 대한 담론을 지배해왔고, 사회적 조직과 문화적 공동체의 진화에 있어서 여성에 의해 채집된 식량의 중요성은 대부분 간과되어왔다. (①) 식물 식량을 채집하는 것에 있어서 여성에 의한 기여는 단지 그것들의 칼로리값과 관련하여 또는 중량에 의해서만 기록되어왔다. (②) 그러나 인류가 지속하는 것을 가능케 했던 것은 남성과 여성에 의해 획득된 식량의 상호 보완적인 집합체였다. (③) 여성에 의한 식량 공유에 있어서 하나의 중요한 요소는 많은 식물 식량을 섭취가 가능하기 전에 처리해야 할 필요성이다. (④ **다시 말해 요리하는 것, 자르는 것, 가는 것, 찧는 것, 섞는 것과 관련된 것들은 여성에 의해 이루어졌다.**) 많은 문화에서 여성은 또한 불씨가 계속 타도록 유지했다. 그리고 또한 처리 후에 분배도 보통 엄마 또는 할머니의 몫이었다. 이는 그 집단의 권력 역학관계에 있어서 여성의 중요한 역할을 대표할 수 있다.

(어휘)

dominate 지배하다	discourse 논설, 담론
evolution 진화, 발달	kinship 혈족 관계, 친족 관계
overlook 간과하다	contribution 기여
vegetal 식물의	merely 단지
in terms of ~측면에서	caloric 칼로리의
complementary 보완적인, 보충적인	array 집합체, 무리, 모음
acquire 획득하다	persist 지속하다
component 구성 요소	requirement 요건, 필요조건, 필요
process 가공하다, 처리하다	consumption 섭취, 소비
apportionment 배분, 할당	fall to ~에게 책임이 주어지다
represent 대표하다	dynamic 역학

09 정답 ②

(정답해설)

해당 지문은 '대표적인 프랑스 사회학자 Émile Durkheim의 학문 활동'에 대한 내용을 서술하고 있다. "② Having lost interest in philosophy, he dropped out of university(철학에 흥미를 잃었기 때문에, 그는 대학을 중퇴했다)."의 경우, 세 번째 문장 "Durkheim found humanistic studies uninteresting, turning his attention from psychology and philosophy to ethics and eventually, sociology(Durkheim은 인문학 연구를 재미가 없다고 생각했고, 그의 관심을 심리학 및 철학에서 윤리학으로, 그리고 마침내 사회학으로 옮겼다)."에서 분사구문의 내용은 본문과 일치하는 것을 알 수 있으나, 뒤이은 문장에서 "He graduated with a degree in philosophy in 1882(그는 1882년에 철학 학위를 취득하고 졸업했다)."라고 언급하고 있으므로 주절의 내용은 본문과 일치하지 않는다. 따라서 ②가 정답이다.

(오답해설)

① 첫 문장에서 "The French sociologist Émile Durkheim is, with Max Weber, one of the two principal founders of modern sociology."라고 서술하며, 'Durkheim은 Weber와 함께 현대 사회학의 주요 정립자 2인 중 1인'이라고 언급하고 있으므로, Max Weber만큼 명성이 있다는 것을 유추할 수 있다.

③ 본문 중반 "Durkheim's views could not get him a major academic appointment in Paris, so he taught philosophy at several provincial schools(Durkheim의 견해로 인해 파리에서 그는 주요 교수직을 맡을 수 없었고, 그래서 그는 몇몇 지방의 학교에서 철학을 가르쳤다)."를 통해 '파리에서는 교수직을 받지 못하고 지방에서 철학을 가르쳤다'라는 것을 알 수 있다.

④ 본문 말미의 "Durkheim's period in Germany resulted in the publication of numerous articles on German social science and philosophy, which gained recognition in France, earning him a teaching appointment at the University of Bordeaux in 1887(Durkheim이 독일에서 머문 기간에 독일의 사회과학과 철학에 대해 수많은 글을 발표하게 되었으며, 이것이 프랑스에서 인정을 받아 1887년 보르도 대학에서 교수직을 얻게 되었다)."를 통해 '독일에서의 저술 활동이 프랑스에서도 인정을 받았다'라고 언급하고 있으므로 내용과 일치한다.

(해석)

프랑스인 사회학자인 Émile Durkheim은 Max Weber와 함께 현대 사회학의 주요한 두 정립자 중 한 명이다. 그는 그의 커리어의 매우 초기에 사회에 대한 과학적인 접근에 관심을 갖게 되었다. 이것은 그 당시 사회과학 교육과정이 없었던 프랑스 교육 시스템과의 많은 갈등 중 최초의 갈등을 의미했다. Durkheim은 인문학 연구를 재미가 없다고 생각했고, 그의 관심을 심리학 및 철학에서 윤리학으로, 그리고 마침내 사회학으로 옮겼다. 그는 1882년에 철학 학위를 취득하고 졸업했다. Durkheim의 견해로 인해 파리에서 그는 주요 교수직을 맡을 수 없었고, 그래서 그는 몇몇 지방의 학교에서 철학을 가르쳤다. 1885년에 그는 독일로 떠났는데, 그곳에서 그는 2년 동안 사회학을 공부했다. Durkheim이 독일에서 머문 기간에 독일의 사회과학과 철학에 대해 수많은 글을 발표하게 되었으며, 이것이 프랑스에서 인정을 받아 1887년 보르도 대학에서 교수직을 얻게 되었다. 이 직책을 맡은 후부터, Durkheim은 프랑스 교육 시스템을 개혁하는 것을 도왔고 사회과학 연구를 교육과정에 도입했다.
① 그는 Max Weber만큼 많은 명성을 가지고 있다.
② 철학에 흥미를 잃었기 때문에, 그는 대학을 중퇴했다.
③ 그는 파리 외부에서 교사로 일하기 시작했다.
④ 그가 독일에서 쓴 글들은 그의 고국 사람들의 관심을 받았다.

어휘

sociologist 사회학자
founder 창설자
approach 접근
academic system 교육 제도
humanistic 인문학의, 인간성 연구의
psychology 심리학
ethics 윤리학
academic appointment 교수직
result in 야기하다
gain 얻다
earn 획득하다
position 위치, 직책
introduce 도입하다
principal 주요한
sociology 사회학
conflict 갈등
curriculum 교과 과정
attention 관심, 주의
philosophy 철학
eventually 결국
provincial 지방의
publication 출판, 발표
recognition 인식, 인정
teaching appointment 교사직
reform 개정하다

그때부터 1898년 사망할 때까지 그는 영국의 훌륭한 화가 중 하나라고 점점 더 여겨졌다. 사후에 Burne-Jones의 영향은 장식 디자인 분야, 특히 교회의 스테인드글라스 분야에서보다 미술계에 훨씬 적게 미쳐졌다고 느껴졌다.

어휘

collaborator 합작자, 협력자
guidance 지도, 안내
medieval 중세의
stylistically 양식상으로
melancholy 우울, 비애
exhibition 전시회
decorative 장식의
stained glass 스테인드글라스, 착색유리
settle 정착하다
vivid 선명한, 생생한
chivalry 기사도
inspiration 영감
attenuated 매우 마른, 야윈
influence 영향, 영향력
ecclesiastical 교회 조직의

10 정답 ③

정답해설

본문 중반에서 '중세 기사도에 대한 그의 대표작인 "King Cophetua and the Beggar Maid"와 "Merlin and Nimue"에 대해 언급이 되는데, 이후 문장에서 "Stylistically, these works owe much to Rossetti's illustrations."를 통해 '이 작품들은 양식상 Rossetti의 그림에 많은 영향을 받았다'라고 서술하고 있다. 따라서 "Merlin and Nimue"이 "Sandro Botticelli"의 영향을 받았다는 내용은 본문의 내용과 일치하지 않으므로 ③이 정답이다.

오답해설

① 첫 번째 문장을 통해 'Oxford의 Exeter College'에 다녔다는 것을 알 수 있으며, 두 번째 문장 말미에서 "he left Oxford without graduating(그는 졸업하지 않은 채 Oxford를 떠났다)"라고 언급하고 있으므로 본문과 일치한다.
② 세 번째 문장 "Morris and he then settled in London, working under Rossetti's guidance(Morris와 그는 이후 Rossetti의 지도하에 작업을 하며 London에 정착했다)."를 통해 내용과 일치한다는 것을 알 수 있다.
④ 본문 중반 이후에서 "His first big success came with an exhibition in 1877(그의 첫 번째 큰 성공은 1877년에 열린 전시회였다)."이라고 언급되고 있으므로 내용과 일치한다.

해석

Edward Burne-Jones는 Oxford에 있는 Exeter College에서 교육을 받았다. 그곳에서 그는 그의 미래 합작자인 예술가이자 시인인 William Morris를 처음 만났다. 그가 예술가 Dante Gabriel Rossetti와 1856년에 만난 것은 그의 커리어에 있어서 전환점이 되었고, 그는 졸업을 하지 않은 채 Oxford를 떠났다. Morris와 그는 이후 Rossetti의 지도하에 작업을 하며 London에 정착했다. 그의 "King Cophetua and the Beggar Maid"와 "Merlin and Nimue"에서 보이듯이, Burne-Jones의 생생한 상상력은 중세 기사도에 대한 이야기들을 기쁘게 받아들였다. 양식상으로, 이러한 작품들은 Rossetti의 그림으로부터 많은 영향을 받았다. 또한 그 자신의 꿈의 세계는 종종 15세기 이탈리아 화가 Filippino Lippi와 Sandro Botticelli의 우울하고 야윈 인물들로부터 영감을 얻었다. 그의 첫 번째 큰 성공은 1877년에 열린 전시회였다.

기적사 DAY 36

결국엔 성정혜 영어 하프모의고사

| 01 | ③ | 02 | ④ | 03 | ① | 04 | ① | 05 | ② |
| 06 | ④ | 07 | ② | 08 | ① | 09 | ② | 10 | ④ |

01 정답 ③
19 서울시

정답해설

'make a face'는 '얼굴을 찡그리다'라는 관용표현이고 보기 문장의 다음 부분에 '그가 해야 할 많은 양의 숙제를 보았다'라고 한 부분으로도 밑줄 친 부분의 의미를 유추할 수 있다. 따라서 정답은 ③ grimaced이다.

해석

그는 그가 해야 할 많은 양의 숙제를 보았을 때 **얼굴을 찡그렸다**.
① 흘끗 보았다
② 기뻐했다
③ 찡그렸다
④ 집중했다

어휘

make a face 얼굴을 찌푸리다, 침울한 표정을 짓다
glance 흘끗 보다
rejoice 크게 기뻐하다
grimace 얼굴을 찡그리다

오답률 TOP 2

02 정답 ④
19 서울시

정답해설

'guffaw'는 '크게 웃다; 큰 웃음'이라는 뜻을 가진 단어로 보기에서 이와 가장 비슷한 의미를 가진 단어는 ④ 'belly laugh'이다.

해석

농담에 **시끄럽게 웃는 것**이거나 냉소적인 표현을 맞이하는 사색적인 미소나, 웃음은 공연을 받아들이는 것에 대한 관객들의 수단이다.
① 히죽 웃음; 히죽거리며 웃다
② 작은 점; 조금도 ~않는
③ 낄낄 웃음; 낄낄거리다
④ 큰 웃음

어휘

guffaw 큰 웃음; 크게 웃다
chuckle 낄낄 웃음; 낄낄 웃다
sarcastic 빈정대는, 비꼬는
laughter 웃음
ratify 비준/인가하다, 승인하다
tittle 작은 점
belly laugh 큰 웃음
reflective 사색적인, 반영/반사하는
greet 반응을 보이다
remark 발언, 말, 언급
means 수단
smirk 히죽 웃음; 히죽거리며 웃다
giggle 낄낄 웃음; 낄낄거리다

오답률 TOP 3

03 정답 ①
19 서울시

정답해설

'cozen'은 '속이다'라는 뜻을 가진 단어로 보기에서 가장 비슷한 단어는 ① deceived이다.

해석

작은 촛불의 빛 속에서 반짝거리고 희미하게 빛나는 진주의 아름다움은 그 아름다움으로 그의 머리를 **속였다**.
① 속였다
② 부드럽게 했다
③ 연결했다
④ 밝혔다

어휘

pearl 진주
glimmer 희미하게 빛나다, 깜박이다
deceive 속이다, 기만하다
wink 깜박거리다, 반짝이다
cozen 속이다, 기만하다
brighten 밝히다

04 정답 ①
19 서울시

정답해설

밑줄 전에 A가 '왜 너는 항상 나랑 싸워야만 하는지 모르겠다.'라고 하자 B가 밑줄 다음에 '만약 네가 그것을 시작하지 않았다면 우리는 싸우지 않았을 거야.'라고 하고 있으므로 서로서로 상대방 때문에 싸움을 한다고 이야기하고 있으므로 빈칸에 가장 적절한 표현은 ① It takes two to tango(손바닥도 마주쳐야 소리가 난다)이다. 참고로 해당 문제는 기출문제로 본문의 'who is slacking off'는 선행사 'you'를 수식하는 관계사절로 'who are slacking off'가 더 적절하다.

오답해설

나머지 보기들은 글의 흐름상 빈칸에 적절하지 않다.

해석

A: 네가 지금까지 이 프로젝트를 위해 무엇을 해왔어? 왜냐하면 나한테 네가 아무것도 안 했던 것처럼 보여.
B: 정말 무례하네! 나는 많은 것을 하고 있어. 게으름을 부린 건 너야.
A: 왜 너는 항상 나랑 싸워야만 하는지 모르겠다.
B: **손바닥도 마주쳐야 소리가 나지**. 만약 네가 시작하지 않았다면 우리는 싸우지 않을 거야.
① 손바닥도 마주쳐야 소리가 난다
② 더 서두르면 더 느려진다
③ 마지막에 웃는 사람이 가장 오래 웃는다
④ 용기를 잃지 마

어휘

so far 지금까지
rude 무례한
initiate 시작하다
keep one's chin up 용기를 잃지 않다
at all 조금도, 전혀
slack off 빈둥대다
haste 서두름, 급함

05 정답 ②
19 서울시

정답해설

② 출제 포인트: '~하자마자 …했다' 구문
"A 하자마자 B했다"는 구문으로 "Hardly(Scarcely) had S1 p.p. ~ when[before] S2 + V2(과거) …"가 바르게 사용되었다. 따라서 정답은 ② Scarcely had we reached there when it began to snow.(우리가 거기에 도착하자마자 눈이 내리기 시작했다.)이다.

오답해설

① **출제 포인트: 분사구문**
"the little boys was surprised ~"가 주절이며, "Had never flown ~ before"는 종속절이거나 분사구문이 되어야 한다. 따라서 "Because he had never flown ~"이나 분사구문으로 "Having never flown ~"이 되어야 한다.

③ **출제 포인트: 동명사의 태**
'Despite'는 전치사로 다음에 명사나 명사구가 오는 것은 옳은 표현이다. 하지만 주어인 'Freddie Frankenstein'이 지역 학교 이사로 선출이 된 것이므로 능동이 아닌 수동의 와야 어법상 올바르다. 따라서 'electing'이 아니라 'being elected'가 되어야 한다.

④ **출제 포인트: 조동사 관용표현**
"B하는 것보다는 A하는 것이 낫다"라는 "would rather A than B"이며 A와 B는 모두 동사원형을 사용해야 한다. 따라서 "to be lying" 대신 "lie" 혹은 "be lying"이, "sitting" 대신 "sit" 혹은 "be sitting"이 쓰여야 한다. 즉, A와 B에 "lie"와 "sit"을 함께 쓰거나 "be lying"과 "be sitting"을 함께 사용해 병렬구조를 맞춰야 한다.

해석

① 예전에 한 번도 비행기를 타고 날아간 적이 없기 때문에, 그 어린 소년은 그의 귀가 뻥하고 뚫렸을 때 놀라면서도 약간 겁이 났다.
② 우리가 거기에 도착하자마자 눈이 내리기 시작했다.
③ 그의 평판에도 불구하고, Freddie Frankenstein은 지역 학교 이사회에 선출될 높은 가능성이 있다.
④ 나는 지금 수업에 앉아 있는 것보다 인도의 바닷가에 누워 있는 것이 낫겠다.

오답률 TOP 1

06 정답 ④   19 서울시

정답해설

④ **출제 포인트: 불규칙동사**
동사 'spread'는 과거형 동사와 과거분사 모두 동일한 형태이며, 이 문장에서는 문맥상 2003년이라는 과거 시점을 나타내는 과거 동사로 알맞게 쓰였다. 따라서 어법상 올바른 표현은 ④이다.

오답해설

① **출제 포인트: 능동태 vs. 수동태**
뒤에 목적어가 없으며 선행사가 "a virus"이므로 문맥상 수동의 의미가 적합하므로 "was identified"가 쓰여야 한다.

② **출제 포인트: 명사 vs. 동사**
문장의 주어가 "Infection"(감염)이므로 밑줄 친 부분에 동사 "dies"는 문맥상 어울리지 않으며, 동사인 "causes"의 두 번째 목적어(첫 번째 목적어는 "acute respiratory distress")로 명사 "death"가 적합하다.

③ **출제 포인트: 능동태 vs. 수동태**
앞의 "It"이 가주어이며 뒤에 명사절 접속사 that이 생략된 형태이므로 문맥상 "that 이하라고 믿어지다"라는 의미가 적합하므로 수동형 "is believed"가 알맞다.

해석

중증 급성 호흡 증후군(SARS)은 심각한 형태의 폐렴이다. 그것은 2003년에 확인되었던 한 바이러스에 의해 발생된다. SARS 바이러스에 대한 감염은 급성 호흡곤란과 때때로 사망을 발생시킨다. SARS는 바이러스들 중 코로나바이러스 일족의 하나(일반적 감기를 발생시킬 수 있는 것과 같은 일족)에 의해 발생된다. 2003년의 전염은 중국에서 작은 포유동물들로부터 그 바이러스가 퍼졌을 때 시작되었다고 믿어진다.

어휘

severe 극심한
respiratory 호흡(기)의
pneumonia 폐렴
infection 감염
respiratory distress 호흡곤란
epidemic 전염(병); 유행성의
acute 급성의
SARS 중급 급성 호흡 증후군
identify 확인하다
distress 고통
coronavirus 코로나바이러스
mammal 포유류

---

07 정답 ②   19 서울시

정답해설

② (A) **출제 포인트: what vs. that**
'happen'이라는 동사는 자동사로 목적어를 받을 수 없으므로 무슨 일이 일어났는지라고 설명할 때 무엇이라는 뜻을 가진 의문사 'what'을 사용하는 것이 가장 적절하다. 따라서 (A)에는 'what'이 들어가야 한다.

(B) **출제 포인트: what vs. how**
동물들이 보이는 것은 '어떻게'를 사용하는 것이 가장 알맞다. 따라서 (B)에는 'how'가 적절하다.

(C) **출제 포인트: what vs. that/which**
문장의 주어 부분은 'Anything ~ unexplained'이므로 관계대명사 절인 것을 알 수 있다. 따라서 관계대명사 'that'이나 'which'가 와야 한다. 따라서 정답은 ②이다.

오답해설

(A) 동사 'figure out' 다음에 목적어인 명사나 명사구 명사절이 와야 하고 빈칸 뒤의 문장이 불완전하므로 'that'이 (A)에 올 수 없다.
(B) 'look' 다음에 목적어가 바로 올 수 없으므로 'what'은 의문사로 (B)에 사용할 수 없다.
(C) 'what'은 선행사를 포함한 관계대명사이므로 'Anything'이라는 선행사 다음에 'what'은 사용할 수 없다.

해석

모든 미스터리에는 무슨 일이 일어났는지 알아내려는 누군가가 있다. 과학자, 형사, 일반인들은 진실을 밝히는 데 도움이 될 증거를 찾는다. 그들은 어떻게 그리고 왜 고대 사람들이 피라미드를 건설하거나 기묘한 예술 작품을 창조했는지 이해하려고 노력하며 선사 시대 유적들을 조사한다. 그들은 오래전에 멸종된 동물의 잔해를 연구하고, 그들이 살아있을 때 어떻게 보였을지에 대해 추측한다. 설명할 수 없는 것은 무엇이든 미스터리를 사랑하는 사람들에게 매혹적이다.

어휘

figure out 생각해내다, 이해하다
ordinary 평범한
reveal 드러내다, 밝히다
prehistoric 선사 시대의, 유사 이전의
long-extinct 멸종된
fascinating 흥미로운, 매력적인
detective 수사관
search for 찾다
investigate 조사하다
remain 잔해, 유물
speculate about 추측하다, 짐작하다

---

08 정답 ①   19 지방직

정답해설

빈칸 전의 부사인 'also'(또한)로 빈칸에는 전 문장과 유사한 내용이 적합함을 알 수 있다. 전 문장들에서 단일한 소리는 의미가 거의 없으며, 다양한 말소리들이 잘 결합되었을 때(when combined into an overlapping chain) 일관성 있는 메시지를 전달한다고 했으므로, 빈칸에서는 새들도 단일한 소리가 의미가 없고 잘 결합된 소리들이 메시지 전달에 필요하다는 내용이 적합하다.

따라서 보기들 중 ① individual notes are often of little value(개별적인 음은 종종 가치가 없다)가 정답이다.

오답해설

② 본문의 내용과 관계가 없다.
③ 본문 후반부에 언급되고 있지만 지엽적인 내용이고 방언이 메시지 전달에 역할을 한다는 의미로는 볼 수 없다.
④ 본문의 'In both humans and birds, control of this specialized sound-system is exercised'(인간과 새 모두에서, 이 전문된 소리 체계가 행사된다)로 소리 체계가 존재한다는 것을 알 수 있다.

해석

엄밀한 의미의 언어는 그 자체로 두 겹이다. 단일한 소리는 오직 이따금 의미가 있다: 대개는, 다양한 말소리들은, 서로 녹아드는 아이스크림의 다른 색들처럼, 오직 맞물리는 사슬로 합쳐질 때만 일관성 있는 메시지를 전달한다. 새 울음에서도 또한, 개별적인 음은 종종 거의 가치가 없다: 연속이 중요한 것이다. 인간과 새 모두에서, 이 전문화된 소리 체계의 조절은 뇌의 한쪽 절반, 보통은 왼쪽 절반에 의해 행사되며, 그 체계는 삶에서 상대적으로 일찍 학습된다. 그리고 많은 인간의 언어들이 방언을 가지는 것처럼, 일부 조류들도 마찬가지이다: 캘리포니아에서, 노랑턱멧새는 지역마다 상이해서 캘리포니아 사람들은 이 참새들을 들음으로써 그 주의 어디에 그들이 있는지를 아마 구별할 수 있는 울음소리들을 가지고 있다.

① 개별적인 음은 종종 거의 가치가 없다
② 리드미컬한 소리들이 중요하다
③ 방언들이 중대한 역할을 한다
④ 소리 체계는 존재하지 않는다

어휘

proper (명사 뒤에 사용되어) 엄밀한 의미의
double-layered 두 겹의   occasionally 이따금
convey 전달하다   coherent 조리 있는, 일관성 있는
one another 서로   sequence 연속, 순서
matter 중요하다   specialized 전문화된
exercise 행사하다, 발휘하다, 작용시키다
relatively 상대적으로   dialect 방언
species 종
white-crowned sparrow 노랑턱멧새
from area to area 지역마다   supposedly 아마, 추정상
tell 구별하다   note 음, 음표
critical 중대한, 비판적인   exist 존재하다

09 정답 ② 19 지방직

정답해설

주어진 글은 심리학자이자 경제학자인 Daniel Kahneman의 저서 중 "thinking fast and slow"의 일부를 인용하고 있다. 2002년 노벨상을 수상한 그는 책이 발표된 해에 행동경제학의 원년으로 불릴 만큼 그의 전망 이론(perspective theory)은 중요한 이론으로 자리 잡았다. 주어진 빈칸이 포함된 문장은 바로 직전 문장인 "To put off gut-based decision-making until a choice can be informed by a number of separate factors."(선택이 많은 개별적 요인들에 의해 정보를 제공받을 수 있을 때까지 감에 기반을 둔 의사 결정을 미루는 것이다.)의 부연 설명이다. 정보가 주어질 때까지 직감에 의존한 결정을 미루는 것이 목표라고 했으므로 빈칸에도 'put off'(미루다)와 같은 의미인 ② delay가 적합하다. 즉, 'put off'와 'delay'가 같은 의미이고, 'gut-based decision-making'(감에 기반을 둔 의사 결정)과 'intuition'(직감)도 같은 의미로 연결할 수 있다.

오답해설

빈칸이 포함된 문장이 빈칸 전의 문장을 부연 설명하는 것이므로 나머지 보기들은 글의 맥락상 정답이 될 수 없다.

해석

노벨상을 수상한 심리학자인 Daniel Kahneman은 인간이 이성적인 결정자라는 생각을 뒤집으며, 경제에 관해 세상이 생각하는 방식을 바꾸었다. 그 과정에서, 그의 여러 분야를 넘나드는 영향은 의사들이 의학적 결정을 내리고 투자자들이 월 스트리트의 위험성을 평가하는 방식을 바꾸어왔다. 한 논문에서, Kahneman과 그의 동료들은 중대한 전략적 결정을 내리기 위한 과정을 설명한다. "평가를 중재하는 규약", 즉 MAP이라고 불리는 그들의 제안된 접근법은 단순한 목표를 가지고 있다: 선택이 많은 개별적 요인들에 의해 정보를 제공받을 수 있을 때까지 감에 기반을 둔 의사 결정을 미루는 것이다. "MAP의 중대한 목표들 중 하나는 기본적으로 직감을 미루는 것이다."라고 The Post와의 최근 인터뷰에서 Kahneman이 말했다. 조직된 과정은 6개에서 7개의 이전에 선택된 특성들에 근거하여 결정을 분석하는 것을 필요로 하는데, 그것들 각각을 따로 논의하고, 그것들에 상대적 백분위의 점수를 할당하며, 마침내 그 점수들을 전체적 판단을 내리는 데 사용한다.

① 개선하다
② 미루다
③ 소유하다
④ 용이하게 하다

어휘

psychologist 심리학자   economics 경제(학)
upend 뒤집다   rational 이성적인
along the way 그 과정에서
discipline-crossing 여러 분야를 넘나드는, 여러 분야를 통합하는
alter 바꾸다   physician (내과) 의사
paper 논문   outline 개요를 설명하다[짜다]
strategic 전략적인, 전략상의   label 부르다, 분류하다, 식별하다
mediate 중재하다, 조정하다   assessment 평가
protocol 규약, 의례, 의식   put off 미루다, 연기하다
gut-based 감에 기반을 둔   a number of 많은
separate 분리된, 개별적인   intuition 직감, 직관력
structured 조직된   call for ~를 필요로 하다
analyze 분석하다   attribute 특성, 속성
assign 할당하다, 배정하다   relative 상대적인
holistic 전체론의   percentile 백분위의
possess 소지하다   facilitate 용이하게 만들어주다

10 정답 ④ 18 국가직

정답해설

본문에서 필자는 '손실을 영원히 피할 수 없으므로 그것에 대적하기 위해 주식 투자자의 관점을 가지라'고 말하고 있다. 또한 'wins and losses ~ matters most.'를 통해 수익과 손실은 모두 일어나지만, 그보다 중요한 것은 전체적인 포트폴리오의 결과라고 언급하고 있다. 이를 통하여 빈칸 뒤의 'because you know ~ bigger picture.' 문장에서 'a much bigger picture'는 전체적인 포트폴리오, 그리고 'small parts'는 개별적인 수익과 손실임을 유추할 수 있다. 즉 '포트폴리오 접근법을 수용하면 더 큰 그림을 위해 개별적인 손실에 덜 집착하게 된다'는 것을 유추할 수 있다. 따라서 빈칸에 들어갈 것으로 가장 적절한 것은 ④ less inclined to dwell on individual losses(개별적인 손실에 덜 연연해하게 될 것이다)이다.

오답해설
① 주식시장의 변동에 더 민감하다는 것은 손실의 두려움이 더 크다는 것과 같은 맥락으로 그러한 손실의 두려움을 받아들여야 한다고 조언하는 필자의 의도와 부합하지 않는다.
② 필자는 손실을 받아들이는 방법에 대해 제시하고 있다.
③ 화두는 '투자에 대한 관심'이 아니라 '손실의 두려움'이다.

해석
손실의 두려움은 인간의 기본적인 요소이다. 뇌에게 손실은 위협이며 우리는 자연적으로 그것을 피하기 위한 수단을 취한다. 그러나, 우리는 그것을 무한히 피할 수는 없다. 손실을 마주하는 한 가지 방법은 주식투자자의 관점을 가지는 것이다. 투자자들은 손실의 가능성을 게임의 끝이 아닌 게임의 한 부분으로서 받아들인다. 이러한 사고방식을 가이드하는 것은 포트폴리오 접근법이다; 수익과 손실은 모두 일어날 것이나, 가장 중요한 것은 전체적인 포트폴리오의 결과이다. 당신이 포트폴리오 접근법을 받아들일 때, 당신은 그것들이 더 큰 그림의 작은 부분들임을 알고 있기 때문에 당신은 <u>개별적인 손실에 덜 연연해하게 될 것이다</u>.
① 주식시장의 변동에 더 민감한
② 손실을 더 싫어하는
③ 당신의 투자에 관심을 덜 가지는
④ 개별적인 손실에 덜 연연해하게 되는

어휘
fear 두려움
measure 방법, 수단
stock trader 주식투자자
outcome 결과
threat 위협
perspective 관점
approach 접근
embrace 받아들이다

기적사 DAY 37

결국엔 성정혜 영어 하프모의고사

| 01 | ② | 02 | ③ | 03 | ④ | 04 | ② | 05 | ③ |
| 06 | ① | 07 | ③ | 08 | ② | 09 | ④ | 10 | ④ |

01 정답 ②

정답해설
밑줄 친 단어가 문맥상 '높이다'로 사용되었고, 유의어로는 ② augment가 적절하다.

해석
하워드는 천천히 차도를 빠져나와 점차 속도를 **높여야 했다**.
① 기뻐하다
② 증가시키다
③ 발생하다
④ 개정하다, 수정하다, 조정하다, 바꾸다

어휘
rejoice 기뻐하다
occur 발생하다
revise 개정하다, 수정하다, 조정하다, 바꾸다
augment 증가시키다

오답률 TOP 2
02 정답 ③

정답해설
밑줄 친 단어는 문맥상 '파산한'으로 사용되었고, 유의어로는 ③ bankrupt가 적절하다.

해석
파산한 채무자는 그의 빈정대는 채권자의 속박에서 빠져나왔다.
① 치명적인
② 드문
③ 파산한, 부도
④ 만연한, 유행하는

어휘
withdraw ~에서 ...을 빼다
sarcastic 빈정대는
unwonted 드문
prevalent 만연한, 유행하는
yoke 멍에, 속박
lethal 치명적인
bankrupt 파산한, 부도

03 정답 ④

정답해설
밑줄 친 단어는 문맥상 '가장 중요한'으로 사용되었고, 유의어로는 ④ superlative가 적절하다.

해석
이 지침들은 시상식의 학문적 기준을 유지하는 것을 확실하게 하기 위해 **가장 중요했다**.
① 우연한
② 희미하게 비치는

③ 말썽부리는
④ 최고의, 최상급의, 과장된

어휘

occurrent 우연한
mischievous 말썽부리는
glimmering 희미하게 비치는
superlative 최고의, 최상급의, 과장된

04 정답 ②

정답해설

A는 B에게 운전면허를 가지고 있냐고 물어보며 다음 주에 자신이 운전면허 시험을 볼 예정이라고 이야기한다. 그러자 B는 시험이 매우 쉽다며 A가 통과할 것이라고 이야기한다. B의 답변을 듣고 A는 시험이 쉬운 일처럼 들린다고 말하고 있기 때문에 빈칸에도 같은 맥락인 ② a piece of cake(아주 쉬운 일)가 들어가는 것이 옳다.

오답해설

① 운전면허 시험이 쉽다고 이야기하는 맥락의 대화에서 '알지 못하고(in the dark)' 있다는 것은 부자연스럽다.
③ 운전면허 시험이 '생리적인 욕구(the call of nature)'라는 것은 문맥상 어색하다.
④ 운전면허 시험이 쉽다고 이야기하는 맥락의 대화에서 운전면허 시험을 '문제의 본질(the name of the game)'이라고 하는 것은 부적절하다.

해석

A: 너 운전면허 있어?
B: 응, 나 지난 여름 방학에 땄어. 왜 물어봐?
A: 나 다음 주에 운전면허 시험 볼 계획이야.
B: 그거 아주 쉬운 일이야. 넌 통과할 거야.
A: 고마워. 그거 매우 쉬운 일 같이 들리네.
① 알지 못하고, 모르고, 비밀히
② 아주 쉬운 일
③ 생리적인 욕구
④ 문제의 본질

어휘

driver's license 운전면허
summer vacation 여름 방학

오답률 TOP 3

05 정답 ③

정답해설

③ **출제 포인트: 분사구문**
생략된 주어 'they'와 'use'의 관계가 능동이며 뒤에 목적어 'the same techniques'를 사용하였으므로 현재분사 'using'을 사용하는 것이 옳다.

오답해설

① **출제 포인트: '~하자마자 …했다' 구문**
'No sooner+had+주어+과거분사 ~ than 주어+과거시제 동사 ~.'는 '~하자마자 …했다' 구문에 해당한다. 해당 문장은 'No sooner' 뒤에 'had he realized'가 아닌 'did he realize'를 사용하였으므로 틀린 문장이다. 따라서 'did he realize'를 'had he realized'로 수정해야 한다.

② **출제 포인트: 조동사 관용표현**
'would rather A than B'는 관용표현으로 'B하느니 차라리 A하겠다'를 뜻한다. 이때 A와 B에 동사원형을 사용해야 한다. 해당 문장은 A에 동사원형 'live'를 사용하였으나 B에 동명사 'returning'을 사용하였으므로 틀린 문장이다. 따라서 'returning'을 'return'으로 수정해야 한다.

④ **출제 포인트: 동명사의 태/현재분사 vs. 과거분사**
'before'를 전치사로 보는 경우와 접속사로 보는 경우 두 가지로 해설할 수 있다. 먼저 'before'를 전치사로 보는 경우 목적어로 사용된 동명사 'packing'의 의미상 주어가 'these finds'이므로 능동태(이 발견물들이 포장하기 전)보다는 수동태(이 발견물들이 포장되기 전)가 문맥상 자연스럽다. 따라서 'packing'을 'being packed'로 수정해야 한다. 다음으로 'before'를 접속사로 보는 경우 현재분사 'packing'이 이끄는 분사구문의 주어는 'these finds'이다. 'these finds'와 'pack'의 관계는 수동이므로 'packing'을 과거분사 'packed' 또는 'being packed'로 수정해야 한다.

해석

① 그가 자신이 실수를 했다는 것을 깨닫자마자 그 회사는 파산했다.
② 그 수치심은 그들이 집으로 돌아가기보다는 차라리 외국에서 노숙자로 살겠다는 것을 의미한다.
③ 그들은 우리가 과거에 보았던 같은 기술들을 사용하면서, 자금을 조달하는 주요 상대들을 위협했다.
④ 이 발견물들은 보통 실험실로 운송되기 위해 포장되기 전 현장에서 세척되고 식별된다.

06 정답 ①

정답해설

① **출제 포인트: 혼동하기 쉬운 전치사**
해당 문장에서 'Given'은 전치사로 '~을 고려해 볼 때'를 뜻한다. 이때 'Given'을 과거분사로 보고 해당 문장을 비문으로 오해하지 않도록 주의해야 한다.

오답해설

② **출제 포인트: 수동태 불가동사**
'appear'는 완전자동사로 수동태로 사용할 수 없다. 해당 문장은 'appear'를 수동태로 사용하였으므로 틀린 문장이다. 따라서 'is appeared'를 'appears'로 수정해야 한다.

③ **출제 포인트: 명사 vs. 동사**
가정법 과거완료가 쓰인 문장이므로 종속절에는 과거완료 'had+과거분사'를 사용해야 한다. 따라서 명사 'death'를 과거분사 'died'로 수정해야 한다.

④ **출제 포인트: 대명사 수일치**
단수 대명사 'it'이 가리키는 대상이 복수형태인 'those works'이므로 복수 대명사 'them'을 사용하는 것이 옳다. 따라서 'it'을 'them'으로 수정해야 한다.

해석

과학의 방법론을 고려해 보면, 중력의 법칙과 게놈은 누군가에 의해 반드시 발견되게 되어있었고; 그 발견자의 신원은 그 사실에 부수적이다. 그러나 예술에서는 제2의 기회란 없는 것처럼 보인다. 우리는 The Divine Comedy (신곡)와 King Lear(리어왕)에 있어서 각각 한 번의 기회를 가졌다고 추정해야 한다. 단테와 셰익스피어가 그 작품들을 쓰기 전에 사망했더라면 결코 아무도 그것을 쓰지 않았을 것이다.

어휘

methodologies 방법론
genome 게놈
gravity 중력, 심각성, 중대성
incidental 부수적인

07 정답 ③

정답해설

③ (A) **출제 포인트: 소유격 관계대명사**
빈칸 뒤에 오는 절에서 주어가 없으므로 주격 관계대명사로 오해할 수 있으나 빈칸 앞에 'all'이 있으므로 'all'이 주어임을 알 수 있다. 따라서 'all'을 수식할 수 있어야 하므로 (A)에는 소유격 관계대명사 'of which'를 사용하는 것이 옳다.

(B) **출제 포인트: when vs. what**
빈칸 뒤에 오는 절이 부사절이므로 접속사 'when'을 사용하는 것이 옳다.

(C) **출제 포인트: what vs. that**
빈칸 뒤에 오는 절의 'show'의 목적어가 없으며 빈칸 앞에 선행사 없이 전치사 'about'만 있으므로 선행사를 포함한 '관계대명사 what(목적격)'을 사용하는 것이 옳다. 따라서 정답은 ③이다.

오답해설

(A) 'that'은 관계대명사의 경우 주격과 목적격으로 사용할 수 있으나 소유격으로는 사용할 수 없다.
(B) 'what'은 부사절을 이끌 수 없다.
(C) 'that'은 관계대명사의 경우 선행사를 포함하지 않으므로 앞에 선행사가 있어야 한다.

해석

좋은 논문은 단지 문헌을 검토하고 난 후 "많은 다른 관점들이 있고, 그 모든 관점들은 유용한 무언가를 말하고 있다."와 같은 말을 하지 않는다. 논문, 강연, 혹은 포스터를 통해서 의사소통할 때 여러분이 보여주고자 하는 것을 분명히 하고, 그것을 보여줘라.

어휘

paper 논문, 서류, 종이 review 검토하다
literature 문학 via ~을 통하여, ~을 거쳐

08 정답 ②

정답해설

해당 지문은 '환경의 차이에 따른 언어의 차이'에 대해 설명하고 있다. 태평양 일대 동남아시아 지역과 코카서스산맥 일대 그루지야의 언어에서의 모음과 자음 사용 차이를 예시로 들어 설명한 후, 마지막 문장에서 "The physical surroundings of Georgians and Southeast Asians are as varied as the words they use, and linguists say they've found a relationship between the types of sounds in a language and the climate and landscape where it evolved(그루지야인들과 동남아시아인들의 물리적인 환경은 그들이 사용하는 단어만큼 다양하고, 언어학자들은 언어의 소리 유형과 그것이 진화해온 기후 및 지형 사이의 관계를 발견했다고 말한다)."라고 결론짓고 있으므로, 글의 주제로 가장 적절한 것은 '② languages and environments(언어와 환경)'이다.

오답해설

① 인종(race)에 대해서는 언급되지 않고, 환경적인 차이에 따른 언어의 차이에 대해 서술하고 있으므로 글의 주제로 적절하지 않다.
③ 본문과 관련 없는 내용이므로 오답이다.
④ 그루지야와 동남아시아 일대 언어의 차이를 모음과 자음 용례를 이용해 설명하고 있으나, 글 전체를 아우르는 내용은 아니므로 오답이다.

해석

언어는 인류의 보편적인 특징이지만, 세계의 다른 곳에서 다르게 들린다. 대부분의 태평양 섬과 동남아시아 지역에서 단어는 자음보다 모음 소리를 더 많이 사용하고, 하나의 모음과 한 두 개의 자음으로 이루어진 단순한 음절로 사용된다. 한편 코카서스산맥의 언어인 그루지야어는 많은 자음을 포함하고, 때때로 자음군으로 결합되어 많은 외국인들이 발음하기 너무 복잡한 음절을 만들어내기도 한다. 그루지야인들과 동남아시아인들의 물리적인 환경은 그들이 사용하는 단어만큼 다양하고, 언어학자들은 언어의 소리 유형과 그것이 진화해온 기후 및 지형 사이의 관계를 발견했다고 말한다.

① 언어와 인종
② 언어와 환경
③ 외국인으로서의 언어 학습
④ 모음과 자음 사용법

어휘

universal 보편적인 hallmark 특징
humanity 인류 vowel 모음
consonant 자음 syllable 음절
string together 연결하다, 결합시키다
cluster 자음군(string에서의 str처럼 연이어 나타나는 자음들)
surrounding 환경, 주변 varied 다양한
linguist 언어학자 landscape 지형, 풍경
evolve 진화하다 race 인종

오답률 TOP 1

09 정답 ④

정답해설

해당 지문은 'Daniel Kahneman의 전망 이론(prospect theory)'에 대해 설명하는 글이다. 첫 문장 "Daniel Kahneman's most important work began in the 1960s(Daniel Kahneman의 가장 중요한 작업은 1960년대에 시작되었다)."를 통해 그의 연구의 시초를 언급한 후, 'Amos Tversky'와 협력하여 '인지 심리학(cognitive psychology)'에 기초한 '전망 이론'을 제시했다는 것을 언급하고 있다. 이후 "Prospect theory is a behavioral model that shows how people decide between alternatives that involve risk and uncertainty(전망 이론은 사람들이 위험성과 불확실성을 동반하는 대안들 사이에서 어떻게 결정을 내리는지 보여주는 행동학적 모델이다)."를 통해 본문 후반에서 '전망 이론'이 무엇인지 구체적으로 설명하고 있다. 전체적인 글의 내용으로 보아 'Daniel Kahneman의 중요 업적'에 대해 개괄적으로 설명하고 있다는 것을 알 수 있으므로, 글의 주제로 가장 적절한 것은 '④ What did Daniel Kahneman do?(Daniel Kahneman이 무엇을 하였는가?)'이다.

오답해설

① 사람들이 손실을 싫어하는 이유는 본문에 언급되지 않는다.
② Daniel Kahneman이라는 인물을 구체적으로 소개하는 글이 아니므로 오답이다.
③ '전망 이론'이 사람들의 의사 결정에 대해 설명하는 이론이며, 본문 후반 '사람들은 손실을 싫어한다'라고 언급하고 있으나, 전체 글이 '사람들의 의사 결정 방식'에 초점이 맞추어진 것이 아니므로 오답이다.

해석

Daniel Kahneman의 가장 중요한 작업은 1960년대에 시작되었다. 그때 그는 사람들이 어떻게 경제적인 결정을 하는지를 심리학적인 관점으로 파악하려고 시도하고 있었다. 인지 심리학에 기초하여 그는 판단을 형성하고 선택을 하기 위해 사용되는 것처럼 보이는 정신적 과정을 보여주는 데 성공했다. Amos Tversky와 협력하여, 두 사람은 전망 이론이라 불리는 새로운 경제학 분야를 창조했다. 전망 이론은 사람들이 위험성과 불확실성을 동반하는 대안들 사이에서 어떻게 결정을 내리는지 보여주는 행동학적 모델이다. 그것은 사

람들은 절대적인 결과물보다 참고 기준에 비례하는 예상 효용의 측면에서 생각을 한다고 설명한다. 전망 이론은 위험성 있는 선택을 표현하는 것으로부터 발전했고, 사람들은 손실 회피 성향이 있다는 것을 나타낸다; 개인은 동일한 수익보다 손실을 더 싫어하기 때문에, 그들은 손실을 피하기 위해 더 기꺼이 위험을 감수한다.
① 우리는 왜 손실을 싫어하는가?
② Daniel Kahneman은 누구인가?
③ 사람들은 어떻게 선택을 하는가?
④ Daniel Kahneman이 무엇을 하였는가?

어휘

attempt 시도하다	figure out 알아내다, 파악하다
psychological 심리학의	perspective 관점
draw on 의지하다	cognitive psychology 인지 심리학
manage to ~해내다	team up 협력하다
formulate 만들다	prospect theory 전망 이론
alternative 대안	involve 포함하다, 수반하다
in terms of …에 관하여, … 면에서	
utility 효용, 실리, 유익	
relative to …에 비례하여, …에 관하여	
reference point (판단, 비교용) (참고) 기준	
absolute 절대적인	outcome 결과
frame 표현하다, 말하다	indicate 나타내다, 가리키다
loss-averse 손실을 회피하려 하는	equivalent 동등한, 상당하는
be willing to 기꺼이 ~하다	

① 시간은 돈이다
② 뛰기 전에 보라(돌다리도 두드려보고 건너라)
③ 한 걸음 한 걸음 가는 사람이 멀리 간다(천 리 길도 한 걸음부터)
④ 모든 계란을 한 바구니에 담지 말라 (한 가지 일에 모든 것을 걸지 마라)

어휘

achieve 달성하다, 성취하다	irrespective of …와 관계[상관]없이
diversify 분산시키다	anecdotal 일화적인
wisdom 명언	allocate 할당하다
security (증권·회사채 등의) 유가증권	diversification 분산
downside risk (투자 예측시의) 가능 손실액, 가격 하락 리스크	
necessarily 반드시, 필연적으로	return 수익
leap 도약하다, 껑충 뛰다	

10 정답 ④

정답해설
해당 지문은 '미래의 재정적 목표와 관계없이 위험 분산형 투자를 하는 것이 중요하다'라고 설명하고 있다. 빈칸에는 위험 분산형 포트폴리오를 설명할 수 있는 명언이 들어가야 한다. 빈칸 이후에서 "If a portfolio is too heavily allocated to one individual security, and that security fails for some reason, an investment portfolio can be reduced to zero(만약 포트폴리오가 단일한 개별 유가증권에 과도하게 집중되어 할당되어 있고, 어떠한 이유로 그 유가증권이 폭락한다면, 투자 포트폴리오는 완전히 무용지물이 될 수도 있다)."라고 설명하며, '한 곳에 집중적으로 투자할 경우 손실의 위험도 커진다'라고 언급하고 있으므로, 다양한 곳에 분산하여 투자하는 것이 바람직하다는 것을 유추할 수 있다. 따라서 빈칸에 가장 적절한 표현은 '④ don't put all your eggs in one basket(모든 계란을 한 바구니에 담지 말라 (한 가지 일에 몽땅 다 걸지 말라))'이다.

오답해설
① 시간에 관련된 내용은 언급되지 않는다.
② 투자 시 신중하게 결정해야 한다(돌다리도 두드려보고 건너라)는 내용의 글이 아니므로 오답이다.
③ 본문과 관련 없는 내용이다.

해석
투자자들은 그들의 투자가 확실히 자신들의 미래의 요구를 충족시키도록 해야 한다. 미래의 재정적 목표가 무엇인지에 관계없이, 위험 분산형 투자 포트폴리오를 만들기 위해 투자 결정에 대한 포트폴리오 접근법은 중요하다. 위험 분산형 포트폴리오의 이점은 "모든 계란을 한 바구니에 담지 말라"는 일화적인 명언으로 가장 잘 요약된다. 만약 포트폴리오가 단일한 개별 유가증권에 과도하게 집중되어 할당되어 있고, 어떠한 이유로 그 유가증권이 폭락한다면, 투자 포트폴리오는 완전히 무용지물이 될 수도 있다. 투자의 분산은 투자자들이 예상 수익을 반드시 감소시키지 않고 어떠한 하나의 투자포지션과 관련된 가능 손실액을 분산시킬 수 있게 한다.

결국엔 성정혜 영어 하프모의고사
기적사 DAY 38

| 01 | ④ | 02 | ③ | 03 | ① | 04 | ② | 05 | ① |
| 06 | ① | 07 | ④ | 08 | ④ | 09 | ① | 10 | ② |

01 정답 ④

정답해설

밑줄 친 단어가 문맥상 '반전된'으로 사용되었고, 유의어로는 ④ reversed가 적절하다.

해석

또한, 그는 Maurolycus의 작업을 확장하였고, 눈과 카메라 그리고 망막에서 **반전된** 영상이 생성되는 배열 사이의 정확한 유사성을 보여주었다.
① 우세한, 출중한
② 얼굴을 찡그리는
③ 필수의, 의무적인
④ 거꾸로의, 파기된

어휘

preeminent 우세한, 출중한
mandatory 필수의, 의무적인
grimacing 얼굴을 찡그리는
reversed 거꾸로의, 파기된

02 정답 ③

정답해설

밑줄 친 단어는 문맥상 '선점하다'로 사용되었고, 가장 가까운 유의어로는 ③ occupied가 적절하다.

해석

범죄에 대한 공포가 그 지역사회를 **점령했다**.
① 발굴했다, 세상에 내놓았다, 빛을 보게 했다
② 진정됐다, 가라앉았다, 드러누웠다
③ 점령했다
④ 기뻐했다

어휘

disinter 발굴하다, 세상에 내놓다, 빛을 보게 하다
subside 진정되다, 가라앉다, 드러눕다
occupy 점령하다
rejoice 기뻐하다

03 정답 ①

정답해설

밑줄 친 단어는 문맥상 '관리할 수 있는, 지배할 수 있는'으로 사용되었고, 유의어로는 ① controllable이 적절하다.

해석

도서관에 소장된 5,000권은 **관리할 만한** 규모였다.
① 지배할 수 있는
② 파산한
③ 완전한, 솔직한, 무조건의
④ 친목적인, 우호적인

어휘

controllable 지배할 수 있는
outright 완전한, 솔직한, 무조건의
insolvent 파산한
convivial 친목적인, 우호적인

04 정답 ②

정답해설

A는 어렸을 때 영국에 살았다고 말한다. B는 값진 경험이었을 것이라며 어땠냐고 묻자 A는 그때 당시가 생애 최고의 순간이었으나 힘든 날들도 물론 있었다고 한다. B는 힘들었던 이유에 대해 되묻고 A는 잘 기억나지 않지만, 언어장벽과 연관된 것이라고 말한다. B는 이에 대해 그런데도 학급 친구들과 ② '관계를 잘 유지했냐(get along with)'고 묻는다. 그리고 A는 그들과 관계가 좋았다며 대부분 시간을 친구들과 보냈다고 말한다.

오답해설

① 학급 친구들과의 관계를 '피하다(get away with)'는 어색한 표현이다.
③ 영국에 살던 때가 생에 최고의 순간이었다고 말하는 A에게 학급 친구들로부터 '멀어졌다(keep away with)'라는 표현은 문맥상 어색하다.
④ 학급 친구들을 '꾸짖다 (get through with)' 표현은 대화의 흐름으로는 부적절하다.

해석

A: 나 어렸을 때 영국 살았었어.
B: 정말 귀중한 경험이었겠다. 어땠어?
A: 그때가 내 생애 최고의 순간이었어. 근데 물론 나를 우울하게 했던 힘든 날들도 있었어.
B: 뭐가 널 그렇게 우울하게 했어?
A: 글쎄, 이젠 기억이 안 나. 언어장벽과 관련 있었던 것으로 기억해.
B: 언어 문제는 삶을 불편하게 해. 그렇지만 학교에서 너의 반 친구들이랑 좋은 관계를 유지할 수 있었어?
A: 응. 사실 방과 후에도 대부분 시간을 그 친구들과 보냈어.
① ~을 피하다, 모면하다
② ~와 좋은 관계를 유지하다
③ ~로부터 멀어지다
④ ~을 끝내다, 꾸짖다

어휘

valuable 귀중한
depressed 우울한
uneasy 불편한
classmate 학급 친구
moment 순간
language barrier 언어장벽
manage to ~간신히 ~하다

오답률 TOP 2

05 정답 ①

정답해설

① **출제 포인트: 동명사의 태**

'come to+목적어'는 관용표현으로 '~이 되다'를 뜻하며 목적어에 명사(구)가 온다. came to는 come to의 과거형이다. 해당 문장은 'came to'의 목적어로 동명사를 사용하였으며 동명사의 의미상 주어가 'The individual film'이므로 수동관계가 성립한다. 따라서 수동형 동명사 'being described'를 사용하는 것이 옳다.

오답해설

② **출제 포인트: 조동사 관용표현**

'had rather A than B'는 관용표현으로 'B하느니 차라리 A하겠다'를 뜻

한다. 이때 A와 B에 동사원형을 사용해야 한다. 해당 문장은 B에 동사원형 'hear'를 사용하였으나 A에 과거분사 'heard'를 사용하였으므로 틀린 문장이다. 따라서 'heard'를 'hear'로 수정해야 한다.

③ **출제 포인트: '~하자마자 …했다' 구문**
'주어+had+hardly+과거분사 ~ when[before] 주어+과거시제 동사 ~.'는 '~하자마자 …했다' 구문에 해당한다. 해당 문장은 'before' 뒤에 'he started'가 아닌 'he had started'를 사용하였으므로 틀린 문장이다. 따라서 'had started'를 'started'로 수정해야 한다.

④ **출제 포인트: 분사구문**
해당 문장은 현재분사구문과 과거분사구문이 등위접속사 'and'를 통해 병렬구조를 이루고 있으며 생략된 주어는 'they'이다. 과거분사구문(dived for longer periods)의 경우 'they'와 'dive'의 관계가 능동이므로 현재분사를 사용해야 한다. 따라서 'dived'를 현재분사 'diving'으로 수정해야 한다.

해석

① 개별 영화가 각 짝의 첫 번째 용어에 의해 묘사되는 것이 된다.
② 길거리의 몇몇 비뚤어진 소문들을 들을 바에야 차라리 Tom으로부터 그것을 듣겠다.
③ 그는 자리에 앉아 포크를 받자마자 아침을 급하게 먹기 시작했다.
④ 그들은 더 깊은 잠수를 시도하고 오랜 기간 잠수하면서, 잠수 생리의 한계를 시험할 것이다.

오답률 TOP 3

06 정답 ①

정답해설

① **출제 포인트: 자동사로 착각하기 쉬운 완전타동사**
해당 문장에서 'entered'는 완전타동사 'enter'의 과거시제로 목적어 'the room'을 가진다. 따라서 옳은 문장이다.

오답해설

② **출제 포인트: 능동태 vs. 수동태**
'주어+tell of+목적어'와 '주어+be told of+목적어'를 구분할 수 있어야 한다. '주어+tell of+목적어'에서 주어는 알리는 주체에 해당하며 '주어+be told of+목적어'에서 주어는 알림을 받는 대상에 해당한다. 해당 문장에서 주어는 the streaming umbrella and his long shining waterproof이며 알림을 받는 대상이 아니라 알리는 주체에 해당하므로 '주어+tell of+목적어'의 형태를 사용해야 한다. 따라서 'was told'를 'told'로 수정해야 한다.

③ **출제 포인트: 형용사 vs. 부사**
'looked around'는 '완전자동사+부사'의 형태이므로 뒤에 형용사가 올 수 없다. 따라서 'anxious'를 부사 'anxiously'로 수정해야 한다.

④ **출제 포인트: 능동태 vs. 수동태**
'weigh+목적어+down'은 '~을 짓누르다'를 뜻하며 '완전타동사+목적어+부사'의 형태이다. 해당 문장은 주격 관계대명사절의 동사에 'weighs down'을 사용하였으나 목적어가 없으므로 틀린 문장이다. 따라서 'weighs down'을 'is weighed down'으로 수정해야 한다.

해석

그 방으로 들어온 남자는 젊고, 말쑥하고, 깔끔하게 옷을 입고 있었으며, 그의 거동에서 무언가 세련됨과 우아함이 배어났다. 그가 손에 들고 있는 물이 뚝뚝 떨어지는 우산과 그의 길고 (빗물에 젖어) 반짝이는 우비는 그가 뚫고 온 사나운 날씨를 말해주었다. 그는 전등 불빛 속에서 초조하게 주변을 둘러보았다. Tom은 그의 얼굴이 창백하고 그의 눈이 엄청난 불안에 짓눌린 남자의 눈처럼 지쳐 있음을 알 수 있었다.

어휘

well-groomed 단정한, 말쑥한　　trimly 정돈하여, 손질하여
refinement 세련, 고상함, 개선, 정제
delicacy 섬세함, 사려 깊음, 연약함　　bearing 태도, 자세, 영향, 관련
fierce 사나운, 격렬한, 맹렬한

07 정답 ④

정답해설

④ (A) **출제 포인트: what vs. why**
뒤따라오는 문장이 완전하고, 문맥상 '왜 우리는 일 년에 두 번 치과 의사를 만나는 것이 필요할까?'가 자연스러우므로 의문부사 'Why'를 사용하는 것이 옳다.
(B) **출제 포인트: what vs. how**
빈칸 뒤에 오는 것이 형용사 'many'이므로 의문부사 'How'를 사용하는 것이 옳다.
(C) **출제 포인트: 관계대명사 vs. 관계부사**
빈칸 뒤에 오는 절이 완전한 형태이므로 관계부사 'where'를 사용하는 것이 옳다. 따라서 정답은 ④이다.

오답해설

(A) 질문에 대한 답변이 'preventative maintenance(예방 관리)'이므로 'what'을 사용한 의문문(일 년에 두 번 치과 의사를 만나기 위해 무엇을 필요로 하는가?)의 답변으로 적절하지 않다.
(B) 'what'은 의문부사로 사용할 수 없다.
(C) 관계대명사 'which'는 뒤따라오는 문장이 불완전하다.

해석

왜 우리는 일 년에 두 번 치과 진료를 받을 필요가 있는가? 이러한 질문에 대한 간단한 답은 예방 관리이다. 여러분은 사람들이 경고 신호를 무시해서 불운한 상황이 하룻밤 사이에 나타난 듯한 이야기를 얼마나 많이 들어봤는가?

어휘

dentist 치과 의사, 치과
preventative maintenance 예방 관리
hear of ~에 대해 듣다　　ignore 무시하다

08 정답 ④

정답해설

해당 지문은 '단어의 소리와 의미 간 관계에 대한 언어학자들의 연구'에 대해 소개하는 글이다. '대조되는 의미를 나타내는 단어를 표현하는 새로운 단어를 만들어 의미를 유추하도록 했을 때, 전혀 새로운 단어임에도 불구하고 청각적 표식만을 통해 단어의 의미를 올바르게 유추하는 것에 성공했다'라는 것이 실험의 주된 내용이다. 그런데 ④에서는 서로 다른 언어권의 학생들 간의 차이점을 설명하고 있으며, 본문의 실험에서는 언어 별 차이를 언급하고 있지 않으므로 글 전체의 내용과 어울리지 않는다. 따라서 글의 흐름상 가장 어색한 문장은 '④ Instead of using higher pitches for positive ideas and lower pitches for negative ideas like the English-speaking students did, the Chinese-speaking students did the opposite(영어권 학생들이 그랬던 것처럼 긍정적인 개념에는 고음을 쓰고 부정적인 개념에는 저음을 쓰는 것 대신, 중국어권 학생들은 그 반대로 했다).'이다.

오답해설

나머지 보기는 문맥상 자연스러우므로 오답이다.

해석

최근 한 연구에서 한 그룹의 언어학자들이 실험에서 소리와 단어 사이의 이 관계를 조사했다. 연구원들은 University of California Santa Cruz (UCSC)의 학생들에게 좋은, 나쁜, 부드러운, 거친, 매력적인, 추한 등 18가지의 대조적인 개념을 나타내는 새로운 단어를 만들도록 요청했다. ① 학생들은 짝을 이루어 오직 소리에만 근거해 각각의 단어의 의미를 추측해야 했다. ② 의미를 추측하는 학생에게 단어를 전달할 때 몸짓이나 얼굴 표정이 사용될 수 없었다. ③ 학생들은 의미를 추측하는 데 성공했고 경험을 쌓을수록 더 나아졌다. ④ 영어권 학생들이 그랬던 것처럼 긍정적인 개념에는 고음을 쓰고 부정적인 개념에는 저음을 쓰는 것 대신, 중국어권 학생들은 그 반대로 했다. 데이터를 분석한 후 연구의 주 저자인 Marcus Perlman은 단어를 만든 사람들이 일관성 있게 특정 단어에 특정 유형의 발성을 이용하며, 청각적인 표식을 개념과 연결시켰기 때문에 추측하는 사람들이 성공했다고 말했다.

어휘

linguist 언어학자
laboratory 실험실
contrasting 대조적인
analyze 분석하다
vocalization 발성
label 표식, 표시
examine 조사하다
setting 환경
deliver 전하다, 전달하다
consistently 일관하여, 지속적으로
acoustic 청각의, 음향의

오답률 TOP 1

09 정답 ①

정답해설

해당 지문은 'Daniel Kahneman'이 제시한 'WYSIATI'의 의미를 설명하며, '우리는 불완전한 정보에 기초하여 판단하고 의사 결정을 한다'는 것을 서술하고 있다. 본문 중반 "Simply, we assert what we do know. When we make decisions, our mind only takes into consideration the things it knows and, regardless of their quality and quantity the only thing it tries to do with them is to build a coherent story(단순히 우리는 우리가 알고 있는 것을 주장한다. 우리가 결정을 할 때, 우리의 정신은 오직 그것이 알고 있는 것들만 고려하고, 정신이 그것들을 이용하려고 하는 것은 정보의 질과 양에 관계없이 단지 앞뒤가 맞는 이야기를 만들어내는 것이다)."를 통해 '우리는 정보의 질이나 양에 관계없이 우리가 알고 있는 것만 고려한다'라는 것을 알 수 있고, 이후 마지막 문장에서 '비 대표적인 정보를 통해 세상을 이해한다'라고 설명하고 있으므로, 우리는 '비합리적으로' 의사 결정을 하고 있다는 것을 알 수 있다. 따라서 '① rational(합리적인)'이 irrational(비합리적인)로 바뀌어야 글의 흐름상 적절하다.

오답해설

② 본문 중반에서 "When we make decisions, our mind only takes into consideration the things it knows(우리가 결정을 할 때, 우리의 정신은 오직 그것이 알고 있는 것들만 고려한다)"라고 언급하고 있으므로, 우리가 '이용 가능한(available) 정보'에 따라 판단을 내린다는 내용은 문맥상 적합하다.
③ 본문 중반 "Simply, we assert what we do know."를 통해 '우리가 알고 있는 것만 주장한다'라는 것을 알 수 있으므로, '우리가 알지 못하는(unaware) 것에 대해서 생각하는 데 시간을 많이 소비하지 않는다'는 내용이 오는 것은 자연스럽다.
④ 보기 이전 문장에서 'regardless of their quality and quantity the only thing it tries to do with them is to build a coherent story(양과 질에 관계없이 앞뒤가 맞는 이야기를 만들어 내기만 하면 된다)'고 언급하고 있으므로, 이야기는 '정확하거나(accurate), 완벽하거나 신뢰가 갈 필요가 없다'라는 내용이 오는 것은 자연스럽다.

해석

WYSIATI는 Daniel Kahneman이 설명한 인지적 편향인 "보이는 것이 전부다"의 약자이며, 이것은 우리가 결정을 할 때 얼마나 ① **합리적인(→ 비합리적인)**지를 설명한다. WYSIATI는 우리는 보통 우리가 ② 이용 가능한 정보에 따라 판단과 감상을 한다는 사실을 표현한다. 일반적으로 우리는 "내가 ③ 알지 못하는 것들이 여전히 많이 있어"라고 생각하는 데 매우 많은 시간을 소비하지 않는다. 단순히 우리는 우리가 알고 있는 것을 주장한다. 우리가 결정을 할 때, 우리의 정신은 오직 그것이 알고 있는 것들만 고려하고, 정신이 그것들을 이용하려고 하는 것은 정보의 질과 양에 관계없이 단지 앞뒤가 맞는 이야기를 만들어내는 것이다. 그것이면 충분하다. 이야기는 ④ 정확하거나 완벽하거나 또는 신뢰성이 높을 필요가 없다; 그것은 오직 앞뒤가 맞기만 하면 된다. 놀랍지 않은가? 불완전한 비 대표적인 정보의 작은 집단이 우리가 세상을 이해하도록 하는 것이다.

어휘

acronym 두문자어, 약어, 줄임말
bias 편향, 편견
rational 합리적인
assert 주장하다
take into consideration 고려하다, 참작하다
regardless of …에 관계없이
coherent 앞뒤가 맞는, 조리 있는, 일관성 있는
accurate 정확한
incomplete 불완전한
non-representative 대표적이지 않은
cognitive 인지적인
describe 묘사하다, 설명하다
refer to 표현하다, 말하다, 언급하다
reliable 신뢰할 수 있는

10 정답 ②

정답해설

해당 지문은 '쇼핑을 할 계획이 없이 시간을 보내려 아이쇼핑을 하던 중 '세일 마지막 날'이라는 기회를 잃고 싶지 않아 계획에 없던 소비를 하게 된다'라는 예시를 들며, "That is the power that is involved with fear of loss - being convinced that you are going to miss out on something if you do not take advantage of it today(그것이 손실의 두려움과 연관된 힘이다 - 즉, 당신이 만일 오늘 그 기회를 이용하지 않는다면 당신이 어떤 것을 놓칠 것이라고 확신하는 것이다)."라고 언급하며, '어떠한 기회를 놓치게 될 수도 있다는 두려움' 또한 '손실의 두려움(fear of loss)'에 해당한다고 주장한다. 따라서 '손실의 두려움'으로 인해 계획에 없던 쇼핑을 하게 되는 상황을 보여주고 있으므로, 필자의 주장으로 가장 적절한 것은 '② Fear of loss can cause you to spend more money(손실의 두려움은 당신이 더 많은 돈을 소비하도록 할 수 있다).'이다.

오답해설

① 본문에서 '아이쇼핑을 하던 중 계획에 없던 소비를 하는 상황'을 예시로 들어 '손실의 두려움'에 대해 설명하고 있으나, 아이쇼핑을 하는 것만으로 충동구매를 하게 된다는 내용은 아니므로 필자의 주장으로 적합하지 않다.
③ 본문의 주요 내용은 손실의 두려움이 생기는 시기에 대한 것이 아니므로 오답이다.
④ 본문의 내용에 따르면 '마지막 기회를 놓칠 수도 있다는 것을 두려워하는 것 또한 손실의 두려움에 해당'하는 것이고, 손실의 두려움으로 인해 기회를 놓치는 것이 아니라, 필요 없는 기회도 잡게 된다는 내용이므로, 본문의 주장과는 반대되는 문장이다.

해석

당신은 가장 좋아하는 상점에서 단순히 그들이 무엇을 제공하는지 보기 위해 돌아다니고 있다. 당신은 그곳에 있는 동안 물건을 구매할 의도가 전혀 없다. 당신이 원하는 것은 당신이 상점을 떠나고 당신의 하루를 계속해서 이어 나가

기 전까지 아이쇼핑을 하며 약간의 시간을 보내는 것이다. 그러나, 곁눈질로 당신은 그 상점 내 당신이 가장 좋아하는 매장에서 "세일 마지막 날"이라는 표지판을 보게 된다. 고객 서비스 담당자 중 한 명이 당신에게 할인이 내일은 끝날 것이기 때문에 만약 오늘 이 할인의 기회를 이용하지 않는다면, 당신은 기회를 완전히 놓칠 것이라고 말한다. 불특정 시간이 지나고 난 후, 결국 당신은 양손에 쇼핑백 여러 개를 들고 상점을 떠난다. 그것이 손실의 두려움과 연관된 힘이다. 즉, 당신이 만일 오늘 그 기회를 이용하지 않는다면 당신이 어떤 것을 놓칠 것이라고 확신하는 것이다.

① 아이쇼핑은 충동구매를 조장한다.
② 손실의 두려움은 당신이 더 많은 돈을 소비하도록 할 수 있다.
③ 손실의 두려움의 감정은 언제든지 촉발될 수 있다.
④ 손실의 두려움 때문에 좋은 기회를 놓치지 말라.

어휘

absolutely 전혀
intention 의도
window(-)shop 쇼윈도 속을 보며 걷다
out of the corner of one's eye 곁눈질로, 흘낏 보고
customer service representative 고객 서비스 담당자
take advantage of …을 이용하다, …을 기회로 활용하다
miss out (on something) (참석하지 않음으로써 유익하거나 즐거운 것을) 놓치다
unspecified 불특정한, 명시되지 않은
involved with …와 연관된
be convinced 확신하다
encourage 조장하다, 부추기다
impulsive 충동적인
trigger 촉발하다

기적사 DAY 39

| 01 | ④ | 02 | ② | 03 | ③ | 04 | ④ | 05 | ④ |
| 06 | ④ | 07 | ③ | 08 | ② | 09 | ④ | 10 | ④ |

01 정답 ④

정답해설

밑줄 친 단어는 문맥상 '열정적인'으로 쓰였고, 유의어로는 ④ perfervid가 적절하다.

해석

팀을 이끌거나 팀의 일원으로 활동하는 것에 능숙하면서 또한 나는 가끔 얼굴을 찡그리지만, 집에서까지 일을 할 수 있는 **열정적인** 자발적 사람이다.
① 모호한, 부정확한
② 실용적인, 분주한
③ 우유부단한, 주저하는
④ 열정적인

어휘

adept 능숙한
imprecise 모호한, 부정확한
pragmatic 실용적인, 분주한
hesitant 우유부단한, 주저하는
perfervid 열정적인

02 정답 ②

정답해설

밑줄 친 단어는 문맥상 '취약한, 예민한'으로 사용되었고, 유의어로는 ② vulnerable이 적절하다.

해석

개발도상국들은 가장 **취약하다**, 왜냐하면 현재 모든 흡연자들 중 84퍼센트가 소득이 낮은 나라들 가운데 살고 있기 때문이다. 그곳의 담배 사용은 1970년 이후로 증가하고 있다.
① 우유부단한
② 취약한, 민감한
③ 열정적인
④ 속은

어휘

irresolute 우유부단한
vulnerable 취약한, 민감한
impassioned 열정적인, 인상적인
cozen 속이다, 기만하다

03 정답 ③

정답해설

밑줄 친 단어는 '설명하다'의 의미로 사용되었고, 유의어로는 ③ expound가 적절하다.

해석

의학에서는 이전 원시인들의 두뇌에서 그들의 다른 행동을 **설명해줄** 만한 차이를 발견할 수 없었으며; 개척자들은 지난날의 야만인이 오늘날의 상점 주인, 군인, 또는 고용인이 될 수 있음을 필연적으로 알게 되었다.

① 히죽거리며 웃다
② 간섭하다, 화해시키다, 사이에 있다
③ 설명하다, 해석하다
④ 떠맡다, 착수하다

어휘

smirk 히죽거리며 웃다
intervene 간섭하다, 화해시키다, 사이에 있다
expound 설명하다, 해석하다   undertake 떠맡다, 착수하다

04 정답 ④

정답해설

레스토랑의 웨이터와 남자 손님이 주문하려는 상황에서의 대화이다. 웨이터가 남자 손님에게 무엇을 주문하겠냐며 묻자 남자 손님은 아직 결정하지 못해 몇 분 더 기다려 달라고 답변한다. 웨이터는 '천천히 결정하라(take your time)'라고 하며 준비되면 불러 달라고 이야기한다. 남자 손님은 '추천(suggestions)' 메뉴를 물어보고 웨이터는 사과파이와 호박 수프를 추천한다.

오답해설

① (B) 남자 손님이 웨이터에게 추천 메뉴를 묻는 상황에서 '조리법(recipes)'을 알려달라고 요청하는 것은 부적절하다.
② (A) 주문할 준비가 되면 웨이터를 불러 달라고 말하며 '거리낌 없이 말해 달라(feel free to speak)'는 것은 의미상 부자연스럽다. (B) 사과파이와 호박 수프가 최고의 메뉴들이라고 한 웨이터의 답변을 참고했을 때, 메뉴 '사진들(pictures)'을 달라고 요청하는 것은 적합하지 않다.
③ (A) 주문할 준비가 되면 웨이터를 불러 달라고 말하며 '거리낌 없이 말해 달라(feel free to speak)'는 것은 의미상 부자연스럽다. (B) 남자 손님이 웨이터에게 추천 메뉴를 묻는 상황에서 '조리법(recipes)'을 알려달라고 요청하는 것은 부적절하다.

해석

Waiter: 안녕하세요 손님. 무엇을 주문하시겠습니까?
Man: 우린 아직 결정하지 못했어요. 몇 분만 더 기다려 주세요.
Waiter: 물론이죠, (A) 천천히 하세요. 언제든 준비되면 저희를 불러주세요.
Man: 감사합니다. 아, 메뉴 (B) 추천 좀 해주시겠습니까?
Waiter: 사과파이와 호박 수프가 저희의 최고 메뉴들입니다.
Man: 정말 고맙습니다. 준비되면 주문하겠습니다.
① (A) 천천히 하다 (B) 조리법
② (A) 거리낌 없이 말하다 (B) 사진들
③ (A) 거리낌 없이 말하다 (B) 조리법
④ (A) 천천히 하다 (B) 추천

어휘

order 주문하다   decide 결정하다
suggestion 추천

05 정답 ④

정답해설

④ 출제 포인트: 조동사 관용표현
'had better+동사원형'은 관용표현으로 '~하는 편이 낫다'를 뜻한다. 해당 문장은 'had better' 뒤에 동사원형 'do'를 사용하였으므로 옳은 문장이다.

오답해설

① 출제 포인트: 동명사의 태
전치사의 목적어에 동명사 'loving'을 사용한 문장으로 동명사의 의미상 주어는 'children'이며 'by other people'로 수식받고 있다. 이때 동명사와 의미상 주어가 수동관계이므로 'loving'을 수동형 동명사 'being loved'로 수정해야 한다.
② 출제 포인트: 분사구문
생략된 주어 'the rush'와 'allow'의 관계가 능동이며 뒤에 '목적어+목적격 보어'의 구조가 따라오므로 현재분사를 사용하는 것이 옳다. 따라서 'allowed'를 'allowing'으로 수정해야 한다.
③ 출제 포인트: '~하자마자 …했다' 구문
'주어+had scarcely+과거분사 ~ when[before] 주어+과거시제 동사 ~.'는 '~하자마자 …했다' 구문에 해당한다. 해당 문장은 'when/before' 자리에 'than'을 사용하였으므로 틀린 문장이다. 따라서 'than'을 'when' 또는 'before'로 수정해야 한다.

해석

① 아이들을 웃게 만드는 것은 다른 사람들에게 사랑받을 때의 그 감각이다.
② 공기가 세차게 들어오는 것은 그를 활공하도록 하면서, 그 슈트의 세 날개를 부풀렸다.
③ 그 경호원이 시야에서 멀어지자마자 그는 자신의 뒤에서부터 고함을 들었다.
④ 그들은 그것을 음악이라고 불렀고 Tom은 우리가 그것을 이해하는 것에 대한 어떤 것을 해야 한다고 느꼈다.

오답률 TOP 1

06 정답 ④

정답해설

④ 출제 포인트: 수동태 불가동사
'originate'는 완전자동사로 수동태로 사용할 수 없다. 따라서 해당 문장은 옳은 문장이다.

오답해설

① 출제 포인트: 주어와 동사 수일치
주어가 'A or B'의 형태인 경우 동사의 수일치 기준은 'B'이다. 해당 문장은 'whether+절'과 'whether+절'이 등위접속사 'or'를 통해 'A or B'의 병렬구조를 이루고 있다. 이때 B에 해당하는 것이 명사절이므로 동사에 단수형태를 사용하는 것이 옳다. 따라서 'matter'를 'matters'로 수정해야 한다.
② 출제 포인트: 명사 vs. 동사
해당 문장은 접속사 'when'이 이끄는 부사절의 동사 자리에 명사를 사용하였으므로 틀린 문장이다. 따라서 'threat'을 'threaten'으로 수정해야 한다.
③ 출제 포인트: 능동태 vs. 수동태
'remind'는 뒤에 'of+목적어'가 올 수 없으며 수동태 'be reminded'의 경우에만 뒤에 'of+목적어'가 올 수 있다. 해당 문장은 'remind' 뒤에 'of+목적어'를 사용하였으므로 틀린 문장이다. 따라서 'remind'를 'are reminded'로 수정해야 한다.

해석

그런 여성들이 미국인인지 이란인인지, 혹은 그들이 가톨릭 신자인지 개신교도인지의 여부는 그들이 여성이라는 사실보다 덜 중요하다. 마찬가지로 기근과 내전이 사하라 사막 이남의 아프리카 사람들을 위태롭게 하는 경우, 많은 아프리카계 미국인들은 수 세기 이전에 자기 조상들이 기원했던 대륙과의 혈족 관계가 생각나서 자신들의 지도자들에게 인도주의적 구호를 제공하라는 압력을 가한다.

어휘

Iranian 이란 사람
civil war 내전
lobby 영향력을 행사하다, 로비를 하다
matter 중요하다
kinship 친족
humanitarian 인도주의적인

07 정답 ③

정답해설

③ (A) 출제 포인트: what vs. that
빈칸 뒤에 오는 절이 완전하므로 접속사 'that'을 사용하는 것이 옳다.

(B) 출제 포인트: what vs. which
빈칸 뒤에 오는 절의 주어가 없으며 빈칸 앞에 선행사 없이 전치사 'on'만 있으므로 선행사를 포함한 '관계대명사 what(주격)'을 사용하는 것이 옳다.

(C) 출제 포인트: why vs. how
문맥상 '왜 그것이 너에게 중요한지'가 자연스러우므로 의문부사 'why'를 사용하는 것이 옳다. 따라서 정답은 ③이다.

오답해설

(A) 'what'은 관계대명사의 경우 선행사를 포함하며 뒤따라오는 절은 불완전하다.
(B) 'which'는 관계대명사의 경우 선행사를 포함하지 않으므로 앞에 선행사가 있어야 한다.
(C) 'how'를 사용할 경우 'how important it is'의 어순이 되어야 한다. 다만, 'how it is important'의 경우 '어떻게 그것이 중요하냐'의 의미로 문맥상 어색하다.

해석

만일 당신이 장애물이 너무 커서 극복할 수 없다는 것을 믿는다면, 심지어 당신이 틀렸을 때도 자신이 옳다는 것을 증명하게 될 것이다. 당신이 통제할 수 있는 것에 집중하고, 첫발을 내딛고, 그다음 단계와 이후에 그 사람 다음 단계에 집중하면서, 가능성을 봄으로써 대부분의 겉보기에 불가능해 보이는 장애물들은 극복될 수 있다. 만일 당신의 전념이 약해진다면, 당신의 꿈과 그리고 왜 그것이 당신에게 중요한지 기억하고, 당신이 일상에서 추구하는 것들에서 단순한 기쁨을 찾고, 작은 승리 혹은 약간의 발전을 기뻐하고, 그리고 계속 진행되는 배움의 과정을 받아들여라.

어휘

obstacle 장애, 장애물
commitment 전념, 약속
embrace 받아들이다, 수용하다, 포옹하다
overcome 극복하다
rejoice 크게 기뻐하다

08 정답 ②

정답해설

해당 지문은 '조류 방언(dialect)의 특징 및 기능'에 대해 서술하고 있다. 본문 2, 3번째 문장에서 "Vocal dialects appear to be learned. Young birds hear the songs sung around their natal territories by their fathers and neighboring males, and acquire the peculiarities of these renditions(음성 방언은 학습되는 것으로 보인다. 어린 새들은 그들의 출생 구역 주변에서 아버지와 이웃의 수컷들에 의해 불리는 노래를 듣고, 이러한 연주의 특색을 습득한다)."라고 설명하며 '방언의 후천적 습득'에 대해 밝히고 있으므로, '방언은 선천적 능력이다'라고 서술하고 있는 보기 '② Singing a dialect is the bird's innate ability(방언으로 노래하는 것은 조류의 타고난 능력이다).'는 글의 내용과 일치하지 않는다.

오답해설

① 첫 번째 문장 "Just as our speech patterns vary regionally, the songs of many avian species also show geographic variation(우리의 말하기 유형이 지역적으로 다른 것과 마찬가지로 많은 조류 종의 노래 또한 지리적인 차이를 보인다)."을 통해 '같은 종이 지역에 따라 다른 소리를 낼 수도 있다'라는 것을 유추할 수 있다.

③ "The "why" of dialects, their functional significance, has proven more elusive than the question of how they arise(방언의 "이유", 즉 그것들의 기능적인 중요성은 그것들이 어떻게 생기는가라는 질문보다 더 파악하기 어려운 것으로 판명되었다)."라고 언급하며, 이후 조류학자들은 방언의 기능을 단지 '추정(assume)'한다고 설명하고 있으므로, 새의 방언의 정확한 기능이 알려지지 않았음을 유추할 수 있다. 따라서 ③은 글의 내용과 일치한다.

④ 본문 후반 "The dialects thus enable females to choose males from their own birth area, who presumably are carrying genes closely adapted to the specific environment in which breeding occurs(따라서 방언은 암컷들이 번식이 이루어지는 특정 환경에 밀접하게 적응된 유전자를 아마 보유하고 있을 그들 고유의 출생 지역 출신의 수컷을 선택하는 것을 가능하게 한다는 것이다)."를 통해 '암컷 새들이 방언을 통해 자신의 출생 지역 출신의 수컷을 선택할 수 있다'라고 언급하고 있으므로, '번식이 이루어지는 환경에 적응한 유전자를 가진 동일 지역 출신의 수컷을 선택하는 것이 암컷의 본능'임을 유추할 수 있다. 따라서 ④는 글의 내용과 일치한다.

해석

우리의 말하기 유형이 지역적으로 다른 것과 마찬가지로 많은 조류 종의 노래 또한 지리적인 차이를 보인다. 음성 방언은 학습되는 것으로 보인다. 어린 새들은 그들의 출생 구역 주변에서 아버지와 이웃의 수컷들에 의해 불리는 노래를 듣고, 이러한 연주의 특색을 습득한다. 방언의 "이유", 즉 그것들의 기능적인 중요성은 그것들이 어떻게 생기는가라는 질문보다 더 파악하기 어려운 것으로 판명되었다. 많은 조류학자들은 방언이 지역 환경에 대한 유전적인 적응을 나타내는 지표로서 역할을 한다고 단지 추정한다. 따라서 방언은 암컷들이 번식이 이루어지는 특정 환경에 밀접하게 적응된 유전자를 아마 보유하고 있을 그들 고유의 출생 지역 출신의 수컷을 선택하는 것을 가능하게 한다는 것이다. 다시 말해, 방언은 "동종 교배", 즉 유사 개체 간 번식을 활성화시키는 역할을 한다.

① 하나의 조류종이 지역에 따라 다른 소리를 낼 수도 있다.
② 방언으로 노래하는 것은 조류의 타고난 능력이다.
③ 음성 방언의 정확한 기능은 불확실하다.
④ 암컷 조류는 자신의 지역 출신의 수컷과 교배하는 것을 선호한다.

어휘

vary 다르다
avian 조류의, 새의
geographic 지리적인
vocal 음성의, 목소리의, 발성의
natal 출생의
acquire 습득하다, 얻다
rendition (노래·음악의) 연주[공연]
significance 중요성, 의의, 의미
elusive 붙잡기[파악하기] 어려운, 이해하기 어려운
arise 생기다, 발생하다
assume 추정하다
genetic 유전적인
condition 환경
presumably 아마
gene 유전자
breeding 번식
regionally 지역적으로
species 종
variation 차이, 변화
dialect 방언
territory 구역
peculiarity 특색
functional 기능적인
ornithologist 조류학자
indicator 지표, 나타내는 것
adaptation 적응
enable 가능하게 하다
carry (특질·특징을) 지니다
adapt 적응시키다, 조정하다, 맞추다
occur 발생하다

function 기능하다 promote 촉진시키다, 활성화하다
positive assortative mating 동종 교배
innate 타고난, 선천적인

오답률 TOP 2
09 정답 ④

정답해설

해당 지문은 투자자의 성향을 '전망 이론(prospect theory)'에 기초하여 설명하는 글이다. 두 명의 재정 자문가로부터 동일한 뮤추얼 펀드를 권유받았을 때, "The prospect theory assumes that though the investor was presented with the exact same mutual fund, he is likely to buy the fund from the first advisor, who expressed the fund's rate of return as an overall gain instead of the advisor presenting the fund as having high returns and losses."라고 설명하며 '투자자는 높은 수익률과 손실을 함께 언급한 자문가보다는, 손실을 언급하지 않은 투자자를 선택할 가능성이 높다'라고 언급하고 있다. 즉, 투자자는 손실회피성향이 있다는 것을 유추할 수 있으므로, 글의 요지로 가장 적절한 것은 '④ Investors are generally loss averse according to the prospect theory(전망 이론에 따르면 투자자들은 일반적으로 손실을 싫어한다).'이다.

오답해설

① 투자의 위험성과 수익성의 관계에 대해 설명하는 글이 아니다.
② 마지막 문장에서 '수익률이 높지만 손실률도 함께 존재하는 경우에는 투자자들이 선택하지 않는 경향이 있다'라고 언급하고 있으므로 사람들이 단순히 높은 수익률만을 선호하는 것은 아님을 알 수 있다.
③ 본문에 언급되지 않는 내용이다.

해석

한 투자자가 두 명의 다른 재정 자문가로부터 동일한 뮤추얼펀드를 권유받았다고 생각해보자. 한 자문가는 그 펀드가 지난 3년 동안 평균적으로 12%의 수익을 달성했다는 것을 강조하며 투자자에게 펀드를 소개한다. 다른 자문가는 그 펀드는 지난 10년 동안 평균 이상의 수익을 달성했지만, 최근에는 하락하는 추세라고 투자자에게 말한다. 전망 이론은 비록 투자자가 완전히 동일한 뮤추얼펀드를 소개받았음에도 불구하고 그는 그 펀드가 높은 수익과 손실을 가지고 있다고 설명한 자문가 대신에, 펀드의 수익률을 전반적인 수익으로 표현한 첫 번째 자문가로부터 펀드를 구입할 가능성이 더 높다고 추측한다.
① 투자가 위험성이 클수록 더 많은 수익을 낸다.
② 사람들은 높은 수익을 내는 뮤추얼펀드에 투자하는 것을 선호한다.
③ 투자는 알맞은 재정 자문가를 선택하는 것이 중요하다.
④ 전망 이론에 따르면 투자자들은 일반적으로 손실을 싫어한다.

어휘

investor 투자자
pitch (물건을 팔거나 사람을 설득하기 위해 하는) 권유[주장], 홍보
present (특히 손윗사람에게 …을 정식으로) 소개하다
highlight 강조하다 return 수익
decline 하락하다, 감소하다 prospect theory 전망 이론
assume 추측하다, 가정하다 gain 수익
loss 손실 averse 싫어하는, 꺼리는

오답률 TOP 3
10 정답 ④

정답해설

해당 지문은 '재정적 손실에 대한 두려움이 생기는 이유와 개개인 간 두려움의 정도가 전부 다른 이유'를 생물학적인 측면에서 밝히고 있다. 첫 번째 문장 "The experiment showed that a neurotransmitter, or chemical messenger, called norepinephrine, is central to the response to losing money."를 통해 'norepinephrine'이라는 화학물질이 재정적 손실에 대한 반응을 조절한다는 것을 언급한 후, 두 번째 문장 "Those with low levels of norepinephrine transporters had higher levels of the chemical in a crucial part of their brain – leading them to be less aroused by and less sensitive to the pain of losing money"를 통해 '높은 수치의 norepinephrine을 지닌 사람들은 돈을 잃는 고통에 덜 자극받고 덜 민감하다'라고 설명하고, 이어서 낮은 수치의 'norepinephrine'을 지닌 사람들은 '손실회피성향(loss aversion)'이 있다는 것을 밝히고 있다. 따라서 전체 글의 요지로 가장 적절한 보기는 '④ People with higher levels of norepinephrine have lower fear of loss of money(높은 수치의 norepinephrine을 지닌 사람들은 돈을 잃는 것에 대한 두려움이 더 낮다).'이다.

오답해설

① 본문과 관계없는 내용이므로 오답이다.
② '손실회피성향'은 승률이 낮을 때만 발생하는 것이 아니라, 낮은 수치의 norepinephrine을 보유한 사람들의 기본 특성이며, 승률이 높다고 해서 해당 성향이 사라지는 것은 아니므로, 본문의 요지와는 거리가 멀다.
③ 본문에서는 모든 '두려움과 관련된 반응'이 아닌, 특정한 두려움, 즉 재정적 손실에 대한 두려움에 관해 집중적으로 다루고 있으며, 해당 보기는 본문보다 더 광범위한 내용을 아우르는 문장이므로 해당 지문의 요지로는 적절하지 않다.

해석

그 실험은 norepinephrine이라 불리는 신경 전달 물질, 또는 화학 전달 물질이 돈을 잃는 것에 대한 반응의 중심이 된다는 것을 보여주었다. 연구원들은 낮은 수치의 norepinephrine 운반체를 지닌 사람들은 그들의 뇌 중추에 높은 수치의 그 화학물질을 지니고 있었고, 이것이 그들을 돈을 잃는 고통에 덜 자극받고, 덜 민감하게 만든다는 것을 발견했다. 높은 수치의 운반체를 지니고, 그에 따라 낮은 수치의 norepinephrine을 지닌 사람들은 수익과 비교해 손실에 좀 더 명백한 감정적인 반응을 하는 소위 "손실회피성향"이라고 알려진 것을 가지고 있었다. 연구원들은 손실회피성향은 사람에 따라 크게 다를 수 있다고 설명했다. 대부분의 사람들이 그들이 패할 가능성보다 승리할 가능성이 높을 경우에만 승패가 있는 도박을 하는 반면, 손상된 의사결정능력을 지닌 사람들은 재정적인 손실에 낮은 민감성을 보인다.
① 도박 중독자들은 뇌 훈련을 통해 치료될 수 있다.
② 손실회피성향은 게임의 승률이 좋지 않을 때 발생한다.
③ Norepinephrine은 두려움과 관련된 반응을 조절하는 데 있어서 중요한 역할을 한다.
④ 높은 수치의 norepinephrine을 지닌 사람들은 돈을 잃는 것에 대한 두려움이 더 낮다.

어휘

neurotransmitter 신경 전달 물질 norepinephrine 노르에피네프린
response 반응 transporter 운반체
crucial 주요한 arouse 자극하다, 각성하다
loss aversion 손실회피성향 pronounced 명백한, 단호한
compared to …와 비교하여 vary 다양하다, 각기 다르다
outcome 결과 impaired 손상된, 제 기능을 못 하는
addict 중독자 occur 발생하다
odds (노름에서) 승률, 배당률 regulate 조절하다, 규제하다

기적사 DAY 40

결국엔 성정혜 영어 하프모의고사

01	②	02	①	03	①	04	④	05	②
06	③	07	④	08	①	09	④	10	②

01 정답 ②

정답해설

밑줄 친 단어가 문맥상 '도발적인'으로 사용되었으며, 유의어로는 ② stimulating 이 적절하다.

해석

대부분의 사람들의 눈에는 그의 순교가 왕을 너무나 잘못으로 몰아넣어서 그것을 불러온 고집과 **도발적인** 행동이 기억에서 지워졌다.
① 은밀한, 신용 있는
② 도발적인, 자극적인, 격려되는
③ 명백한
④ 집중시키는

어휘

martyrdom 순교, 고난
confidential 은밀한, 신용 있는
stimulating 도발적인, 자극적인, 격려되는
overt 명백한
obstinacy 완고함, 고집셈, 집요한 끈기
concentrate 집중시키다, 전념하다

02 정답 ①

정답해설

밑줄 친 단어는 문맥상 '주의 깊게'로 사용되었고, 유의어로는 ① Deliberately 가 적절하다.

해석

주의 깊게, 그녀는 더 나은 지렛대 쪽으로 발을 옮겼다.
① 신중하게, 의도적으로
② 가볍게
③ 신체의, 속세의, 관능적인
④ 즉시

어휘

leverage 지렛대
lightly 가볍게
promptly 즉시
deliberately 신중하게, 의도적으로
fleshly 신체의, 속세의, 관능적인

03 정답 ①

정답해설

밑줄 친 단어는 문맥상 '제외하다, 배제하다'로 사용되었고, 유의어로는 ① excluded가 적절하다.

해석

경찰은 자살의 가능성을 **배제했지만**, 조사를 시작할 증거가 전혀 없다고 발표했습니다.
① 배제했다, 불가능하게 했다
② 보상했다, 상환했다
③ 희미하게 빛났다
④ 분배했다, 뿌렸다, 쫓아 버렸다

어휘

suicide 자살
exclude 배제하다, 불가능하게 하다
glimmer 희미하게 빛나다
evidence 증거
redeem 보상하다, 상환하다
scatter 분배하다, 뿌리다, 쫓아 버리다

04 정답 ④

정답해설

오늘 아침 뉴스를 보다가 수업에 늦었다는 B에게 A는 뉴스에서 다룬 내용에 대해 질문한다. B는 지난주 토요일의 정치적 시위를 다룬 흥미로운 뉴스에 관해 이야기하며 시위가 평화롭게 끝났다고 말한다. A는 시위가 간디의 비폭력 무저항 시위를 연상시킨다고 하자 B는 두 정치적 운동의 목적을 제외하고는 큰 유사성을 지닌다며 A의 말에 동의한다. 그리고 이번 시위의 ④'분쟁의 원인(bone of contention)'에 관해 물어보자, B는 현대 사회의 성차별을 완화하기 위해 차별 철폐 조처법을 시행하는 것이었다고 답변한다.

오답해설

① 시위가 현대 사회의 성차별을 완화 시키기 위한 차별 철폐 조처법을 시행시키는 것에 관련되어 있었다고 말한 B의 답변을 고려했을 때 이번 시위의 '부작용(side effect)'에 대해 질문하는 것은 적합하지 않다.
② 이번 시위의 '의외의 능력을 가진 사람(dark horse)'에 대해 질문하는 것은 문맥상 어색하다.
③ 대화의 흐름으로는 A가 이번 시위의 '헐값에 산 물건(dead bargain)'이 무엇이었는지 묻는 것은 부적절하다.

해석

A: 너 오늘 수업에 왜 늦었어?
B: 아침에 뉴스를 보다가 시간을 아예 잊어버렸어.
A: 재미있는 쟁점이 있었어?
B: 지난 토요일에 정치적 시위가 있었는데 다행히도 평화적으로 끝났어.
A: 반가운 소리네. 너에게 듣다 보니 그 시위는 간디의 비폭력 무저항 운동을 연상시킨다.
B: 그 두 시위의 목적을 제외하고는 유사성이 꽤 크지.
A: 이번 시위의 분쟁의 원인은 뭐였어?
B: 현대 사회에서 성차별을 완화하기 위한 차별 철폐 조처법을 시행하는 것에 대한 거였어.
① 부작용
② 숨겨진 인물, 의외의 능력을 가진 사람
③ 싸게 산 물건
④ 분쟁의 원인

어휘

interesting 흥미로운
demonstration 시위
nonviolent 비폭력의
movement 운동
purpose 목적
affirmative action 차별 철폐 조처
sex discrimination 성차별
political protest 정치적 시위
peacefully 평화롭게
nonresistant 무저항의
similarity 유사성
implement 시행하다
alleviate 완화하다
contemporary society 현대 사회

오답률 TOP 1

05 정답 ②

정답해설

② **출제 포인트: '~하자마자 …했다' 구문**
'On + -ing, 주어 + 과거시제 동사'는 '~하자마자 …했다' 구문에 해당한다.

오답해설

① **출제 포인트: 동명사의 태**
전치사의 목적어에 동명사 'cheating'을 사용한 문장으로 동명사의 의미상 주어는 'you'이다. 이때 동명사와 의미상 주어가 수동관계이므로 'cheating'을 수동형 동명사 'being cheated'로 수정해야 한다.

③ **출제 포인트: 분사구문**
생략된 주어 'Tom'은 감정을 제공하는 주체가 아닌 감정을 제공받는 대상이므로 'thrill'과 수동관계가 성립한다. 따라서 감정 제공 형용사(현재분사) 'Thrilling'을 감정 상태 형용사(과거분사) 'Thrilled'로 수정해야 한다.

④ **출제 포인트: 조동사 관용표현**
'It is high time that + 절'은 관용표현으로 '~할 시간이다'를 뜻하며 절에는 과거시제 동사 또는 'should + 동사원형'을 사용해야 한다. 해당 문장은 'It is high time that' 뒤에 오는 절에 'will take'를 사용하였으므로 틀린 문장이다. 따라서 'will take'를 'took' 또는 'should take'로 수정해야 한다.

해석

① 클리닉의 보고서는 당신이 정비공에게 사기당하는 것을 막아준다.
② 그들이 그 기록을 검사하자마자, 오류의 직접적인 원인이 즉시 명백해졌다.
③ 그 여행에 흥분하면서, Tom은 더 많이 등반하기 시작했고 나중에 돌로미티산맥을 여행했다.
④ 나는 선출된 정치적인 대표자들이 이러한 종류의 행동에 반대할 시간이라고 생각한다.

06 정답 ③

정답해설

③ **출제 포인트: 형용사 vs. 부사**
형용사 'adaptive'가 명사 'unconscious'를 수식하고 있으므로 옳은 문장이다. 이때 해당 문장에서 'unconscious'가 명사로 사용되었다는 점에 유의해야 한다.

오답해설

① **출제 포인트: 능동태 vs. 수동태**
해당 문장에서 'knows'의 주어인 'It'은 가주어이므로 진주어를 찾아야 한다. 진주어는 접속사 'that'이 이끄는 명사절이므로 'knows'와 수동관계가 성립한다. 따라서 'well knows'를 'is well known'으로 수정해야 한다.

② **출제 포인트: 능동태 vs. 수동태**
'base'는 주로 타동사로 쓰여 이후에 'on + 목적어'가 올 수 없으며 수동태 'be based'의 경우에만 뒤에 'on + 목적어'가 올 수 있다. 해당 문장은 'base' 뒤에 'on + 목적어'를 사용하였으므로 틀린 문장이다. 따라서 'base'를 'are based'로 수정해야 한다.

④ **출제 포인트: 현재분사 vs. 과거분사**
'present'는 타동사이므로 뒤에 목적어가 온다. 해당 문장은 현재분사 'presenting' 뒤에 목적어가 아닌 전명구 'to me'가 왔으므로 틀린 문장이다. 따라서 'presenting'을 과거분사 'presented'로 수정해야 한다. 또는 동사 'was being interpreted'와 등위접속사 'and'를 사용하여 병렬구조를 이루고 있으므로 'was being presented'로 수정해야 한다. 단 'was being'은 문맥상 중복되므로 생략할 수 있다.

해석

잘못된 정보에 기초하고 있을 때조차도 첫인상의 힘은 강하다는 것은 잘 알려진 사실이다. 눈에 별로 잘 띄지 않는 것은, 적응 무의식이 그 해석 행위를 하는 정도이다. Tom이 교장 선생님의 말씀에 끼어드는 것을 보았을 때, 나는 객관적으로 무례한 행동을 보고 있는 것처럼 느꼈다. 나에 의해서 Tom의 행동을 해석하여 나에게 현실로서 제시하고 있다는 것을 몰랐다.

어휘

first impression 첫인상
faulty 결함이 있는, 불완전한
unconscious 무의식; 의식이 없는
have no idea 전혀 모르다
principal 교장; 주요한

07 정답 ④

정답해설

④ (A) **출제 포인트: that vs. whose**
'behavior'를 선행사로 하며 뒤따라오는 절의 주어가 없으므로 주격 관계대명사 'that'을 사용하는 것이 옳다.

(B) **출제 포인트: that vs. whose**
'others'를 선행사로 하며 뒤따라오는 절의 주어가 'behavior'이므로 소유격 관계대명사 'whose'를 사용하는 것이 옳다.

(C) **출제 포인트: that vs. whose**
'those'를 선행사로 하며 뒤따라오는 절의 주어가 'conduct'이므로 소유격 관계대명사 'whose'를 사용하는 것이 옳다. 이때 해당 문장에서 'conduct'를 동사로 오해하지 않도록 주의해야 한다. 'hold + 목적어 + in esteem'에서 목적어가 esteem 뒤로 이동해서 whose절에 의해 수식받는 형태에 해당된다. 따라서 정답은 ④이다.

오답해설

(A) 'whose'는 소유격 관계대명사이므로 주어 자리에 사용할 수 없다.
(B) 관계대명사 'that'은 뒤따라오는 절의 주어를 수식할 수 없다.
(C) 관계대명사 'that'을 사용하게 되면 'conduct'를 동사로 보고 'shows'를 목적어로 보아야 한다. 그러나 'shows' 뒤에 명사구 'an abundance'가 있으므로 'shows'는 동사이며 따라서 'conduct'는 주어이므로 'that'을 사용할 수 없다.

해석

어떤 원칙이 어떤 사람의 도덕적 규범의 일부일 때, 그 사람은 그 원칙에 의해 요구되는 행동을 하도록, 그리고 그 원칙과 충돌하는 행동은 하지 않도록 강하게 동기를 부여받는다. 그 사람은 자기 자신의 행동이 그 원칙에 위배될 때 죄책감을 느끼는 경향이 있을 것이며, 행동이 그것과 충돌하는 다른 사람을 못마땅해하는 경향이 있을 것이다. 마찬가지로, 그 사람은 그 원칙이 요구하는, 풍부한 동기부여를 보여주는 행동을 하는 사람을 존경하는 경향이 있을 것이다.

어휘

moral 도덕적인
code 규칙, 암호
conduct 행동, 처리
disapprove of ~을 못마땅해하다
conflict with ~와 충돌하다, 상충하다
hold 목적어 in esteem ~을 존경하다

08 정답 ①

정답해설

해당 지문은 '지각적 도식이 우리의 인식에 어떻게 영향을 미치는가'에 대한 내용이며, 빈칸이 포함되어있는 문장에서 "This is the blessing and curse of perceptual schemas and heuristics(이것은 지각적 도식과 경험적 접근법의 축복인 동시에 저주이다)."를 통해, 이후에 '축복'과 '저주'에 해당하는 내용이 구체적으로 드러나야 한다는 것을 알 수 있다. 빈칸 바로 이전 "they are useful for making sense of a complex world(그것들은 복잡한 세상을 이해하는 데 도움이 되지만,)"에서 긍정적인 내용이 나왔으므로, 역접의 의미인 'but'으로 연결된 빈칸에는 부정적인 내용이 들어가야 한다. 또한 빈칸 이전 문장 "Even if it isn't, making that assumption saved your mind some time."을 통해 '그것이 사실이 아닐 수도 있더라도, 정신의 시간을 절약해줄 수 있다'고 언급하고 있으므로, 빈칸에는 이 중 부정적인 내용인 "① they can be inaccurate(그것들은 부정확할 수도 있다)"가 들어가는 것이 가장 적절하다.

오답해설

나머지 보기는 본문의 주장과는 문맥상 관련이 없으므로 오답이다.

해석

우리는 사람들에 대한 인상을 그들의 외모, 사회적 역할, 상호작용 또는 다른 특성들에 기초해 체계화하기 위해 지각적 도식을 발달시킨다; 이러한 도식들은 세계의 다른 것들에 대한 우리의 인식에 영향을 미친다. 이러한 도식들은 경험적 접근법, 또는 평가에 소요되는 시간과 노력을 줄여주는 지름길이다. 예를 들어 당신이 일하기 위해 가는 건물이 외관상 대칭적이라는 (때때로 "symmetry heuristic" 또는 어떠한 것들을 실제보다 더 대칭적으로 기억하려는 경향이라 불리는) 지각적 도식을 가지고 있을지도 모른다. 설사 그렇지 않다 하더라도, 그러한 생각을 하는 것이 당신의 정신이 시간을 절약하도록 해주었다. 이것은 지각적 도식과 경험적 접근법의 축복인 동시에 저주이다. 그것들은 복잡한 세상을 이해하는 데 도움이 되지만, <u>그것들은 부정확할 수도 있다</u>.

① 그것들은 부정확할 수도 있다
② 그것들은 불충분할지도 모른다
③ 그것들이 더 복잡할 수도 있다
④ 그것들은 이해하기 쉽지 않다

어휘

perceptual 지각의, 지각에 의한	schema 스키마, 도식, 개요
impression 인상	appearance 외모
interaction 상호작용	trait 특징, 특성
perception 지각, 인식	heuristic 휴리스틱, 발견적[경험적] 방법
shortcut 지름길	computation 계산
symmetrical 대칭적인	symmetry 대칭
tendency 경향	assumption 추정, 생각
blessing 축복	curse 저주
make sense 이해하다	complex 복잡한
inaccurate 부정확한	insufficient 부족한, 불충분한
complicated 복잡한	

오답률 TOP 3

09 정답 ④

정답해설

해당 지문은 '낙관주의 편향을 줄이거나 없애기 위한 시도가 실제로는 그러한 편향을 줄이는 데 거의 영향을 미치지 않거나 오히려 더 증가하게 만들었다'라는 내용을 서술하고 있다. 빈칸 이후 문장에서 "In studies that involved attempts to reduce the optimism bias through actions such as educating participants about risk factors, encouraging volunteers to consider high-risk examples, and educating subjects on why they were at risk, researchers have found that these attempts led to little change and in some instances actually increased the optimism bias(위험 요인에 대해 참가자를 교육하고, 지원자들이 위험성이 큰 예시들을 염두에 두도록 장려하고, 그들이 왜 위험에 처했는지 대상을 교육하는 등의 조치를 통해 낙관주의 편향을 줄이려는 시도가 포함된 연구에서, 연구원들은 이러한 시도들이 변화를 거의 낳지 않았고, 일부 사례에서는 실제로 낙관주의 편향을 증가시켰다는 것을 알았다)."라고 서술하며 '낙관주의 편향을 줄이거나 없애려는 시도가 변화를 거의 일으키지 않거나 오히려 편향을 증가시켰다'라는 내용을 구체적으로 언급하고 있으므로, 빈칸에 가장 알맞은 단어는 "④ tough(어려운)"이다.

오답해설

① 본문의 주장과 상반되는 어휘이므로 오답이다.
②, ③ 문맥상 자연스럽지 않으므로 오답이다.

해석

연구원들은 특히 건강한 행위를 촉진시키고 위험성이 있는 행위를 줄이기 위해 사람들이 낙관주의 편향을 줄이도록 돕는 것을 시도하는 동안 그들은 그러한 편향을 줄이거나 없애는 것이 실제로 엄청나게 어렵다는 것을 깨달았다. 위험 요인에 대해 참가자를 교육하고, 지원자들이 위험성이 큰 예시들을 염두에 두도록 장려하고, 그들이 왜 위험에 처했는지 대상을 교육하는 등의 조치를 통해 낙관주의 편향을 줄이려는 시도가 포함된 연구에서, 연구원들은 이러한 시도들이 변화를 거의 낳지 않았고, 일부 사례에서는 실제로 낙관주의 편향을 증가시켰다는 것을 알았다. 예를 들어, 누군가에게 흡연과 같은 특정한 습관으로 인해 사망할 위험성에 대해 말하는 것은 실제로는 그들이 더욱더 자신들은 그러한 행동에 의해 부정적인 영향을 받지 않을 것이라고 믿도록 만들었다.

① 간단한, 확실한, 솔직한
② 의무적인
③ 가장 중요한
④ 어려운

어휘

attempt 시도하다	reduce 줄이다, 감소시키다
optimism bias 낙관주의 편향	particularly 특히
promote 촉진시키다	risky 위험한
eliminate 제거하다, 없애다	
incredibly 믿을 수 없을 정도로, 엄청나게	
involve 포함하다, 수반하다	participant 참가자
risk factor 위험 요소	encourage 장려하다
subject 연구[실험] 대상, 피험자	lead to ~로 이어지다
instance 사례, 경우	negatively 부정적으로
affect 영향을 미치다	

오답률 TOP 2

10 정답 ②

정답해설

해당 지문은 '우크라이나의 과두정치 체제'에 대한 설명이며, 빈칸에는 해당 체제의 특징에 관한 내용이 들어가는 것이 적합하다. 본문 후반에서 "The nature of close relations between the government and the oligarchs has not undergone any major changes(정부와 과두제 집권층 간의 밀접한 관계의 본질은 어떠한 주요 변화도 겪지 않았다)"라고 언급하며, '과두정치 체제가 거의 변하지 않았다'라는 것을 알 수 있으며, 마지막 문장 "Although reshuffles have taken place inside the political and business elites, nothing seems to be able to change this system, at least in the medium term(정치계와 재계 엘리트 내부에서 개편이 일긴 했지만, 적어도 중기적으로 이 체제를 변화시킬 수 있는 것은 아무것도 없는 것으로 보인다)."을 통해 해당 체제가 매우 견고하다는 주장을 펼치고 있음을 알 수 있다. 따라서 빈칸에 가장 적절한 것은 "② to be very durable(매우 견고한 것)"이다.

> 오답해설

① 문맥상 어색하므로 오답이다.
③ 해당 체제가 변화하지 않았다는 내용만 있을 뿐, 효율적인지는 서술되지 않았다.
④ 본문에 언급되지 않는 내용이다.

> 해석

우크라이나의 과두정치 체제는 <u>매우 견고한 것</u>으로 드러났다. 이 체제, 즉 새로이 형성된 대기업과 정치 계층의 유대를 기반으로 한 체제는 우크라이나가 1991년 독립을 쟁취한 몇 년 후에 생겨났고 Leonid Kuchma 대통령의 재임 중에 최종 형태로 발전했다. 다른 구소련국가들, 특히 러시아에서도 또한 유사한 현상이 발달했음에도 불구하고, 다른 동유럽 국가에서 현재의 대기업이 정치에 우크라이나에서처럼 그렇게 강력한 영향을 미치지는 않는다. 우크라이나 대기업의 대표자들은 러시아에서와 같이 보통 과두제 집권층이라고 일컬어진다. 정부와 과두제 집권층 간의 밀접한 관계의 본질은 오렌지혁명의 결과 또는 Victor Yanukovych의 2010년 대선 승리 이후에도 어떠한 주요 변화도 겪지 않았다. 정치계와 재계 엘리트 내부에서 조직개편이 일긴 했지만, 적어도 중기적으로 이 체제를 변화시킬 수 있는 것은 아무것도 없는 것으로 보인다.
① 확대될 필요가 있는 것
② 매우 견고한 것
③ 더욱 효율적인 것
④ 위험한 결함을 가지고 있는 것

> 어휘

oligarchic 과두정치의, 소수 독재 정치의
i.e. 즉
regain 되찾다, 회복하다
presidency 대통령의 지위[임기]
representative 대표자
oligarch 과두제 집권층의 일원
as a consequence 그 결과, 결과적으로
presidential election 대선, 대통령 선거
reshuffle 조직개혁
expand 확장하다
efficient 효율적인
emerge 나타나다, 생기다
ultimate 최후의, 궁극적인
phenomenon 현상
refer to 칭하다, 언급하다
undergo 겪다
take place 발생하다
durable 견고한, 영속성 있는
flaw 결점, 결함

결국엔 성정혜 영어 하프모의고사
기적사 복습 모의고사 4회

01	④	02	①	03	④	04	③	05	①
06	③	07	③	08	④	09	④	10	②
11	④	12	②	13	④	14	③	15	④
16	③	17	②	18	④	19	②	20	③

01 정답 ④
Day 31-03

> 정답해설

밑줄 친 intimidating은 '겁을 주는, 위협하는'의 뜻으로 ④ frightening(무서운, 겁나게 하는)과 의미가 가장 가깝다.

> 해석

최첨단의 접근법이 **위협적**이라고 느끼는 학생은 그 혹은 그녀가 오래된 방법들로 배웠을 수도 있는 것보다 덜 배운다.
① 재미있는, 유머러스한
② 친근한
③ 편리한
④ 무서운, 겁나게 하는

02 정답 ①
Day 36-03

> 정답해설

'cozen'은 '속이다'라는 뜻을 가진 단어로 보기에서 가장 비슷한 단어는 ① deceived이다.

> 해석

작은 촛불의 빛 속에서 반짝거리고 희미하게 빛나는 진주의 아름다움은 그 아름다움으로 그의 머리를 **속였다**.
① 속였다
② 부드럽게 했다
③ 연결했다
④ 밝혔다

03 정답 ④
Day 34-02

> 정답해설

밑줄 친 단어가 문맥상 '만족시키다'로 사용되었고, 유의어로는 ④ gratify가 적절하다.

> 해석

그러나, 이 국가의 국민들을 지치게 하면서, 새로운 헌법은 비용이 많이 들고 실행이 불가능하다는 것이 입증되었고, 인구의 어느 한 부분을 **만족시키지** 못했다.
① 인수하다, 취득하다
② 주장하다
③ 양도하다, 옮기다, 바꾸다
④ 만족시키다

04 정답 ③   Day 39-03

정답해설

밑줄 친 단어는 '설명하다'의 의미로 사용되었고, 유의어로는 ③ expound가 적절하다.

해석

의학에서는 이전 원시인들의 두뇌에서 그들의 다른 행동을 **설명해줄** 만한 차이를 발견할 수 없었으며; 개척자들은 지난날의 야만인이 오늘날의 상점 주인, 군인, 또는 고용인이 될 수 있음을 필연적으로 알게 되었다.
① 히죽거리며 웃다
② 간섭하다, 화해시키다, 사이에 있다
③ 설명하다, 해석하다
④ 떠맡다, 착수하다

05 정답 ①   Day 40-02

정답해설

밑줄 친 단어는 문맥상 '주의 깊게'로 사용되었고, 유의어로는 ① Deliberately가 적절하다.

해석

주의 깊게, 그녀는 더 나은 지렛대 쪽으로 발을 옮겼다.
① 신중하게, 의도적으로
② 가볍게
③ 신체의, 속세의, 관능적인
④ 즉시

06 정답 ③   Day 32-06

정답해설

③ **출제 포인트: 유도부사 수일치/주격관계대명사절 동사의 수일치**
'There'는 유도부사로 뒤에 오는 어순은 「동사+주어」의 도치된 어순이 온다. 따라서 복수동사 'are'의 주어는 복수형태의 명사구 'many aspects'이므로 옳게 사용되었다. 또한 해당 문장에서 'that'은 주격 관계대명사이며 선행사는 단수형태의 명사구 'this case'이므로 주격 관계대명사절의 동사에 단수형태인 'is'를 옳게 사용하였다.

해석

① 히틀러가 1940년에 영국을 침략했었다면 그는 그 전쟁에서 이겼을 것이다.
② 내가 이 작품을 더 빨리 끝낼수록, 나는 집에 더 빨리 갈 수 있다.
③ 교회 회계담당자들과 직접적으로 관련 있는 이 사건의 많은 측면들이 있다.
④ 비행 중인 새매를 닮은 뻐꾸기는 확인하기 어려울 수 있다.

07 정답 ③   Day 37-05

정답해설

③ **출제 포인트: 분사구문**
생략된 주어 'they'와 'use'의 관계가 능동이며 뒤에 목적어 'the same techniques'를 사용하였으므로 현재분사 'using'을 사용하는 것이 옳다.

해석

① 그가 자신이 실수를 했다는 것을 깨닫자마자 그 회사는 파산했다.
② 그 수치심은 그들이 집으로 돌아가기보다는 차라리 외국에서 노숙자로 살겠다는 것을 의미한다.
③ 그들은 우리가 과거에 보았던 같은 기술들을 사용하면서, 자금을 조달하는

주요 상대들을 위협했다.
④ 이 발견물들은 보통 실험실로 운송되기 위해 포장되기 전 현장에서 세척되고 식별된다.

08 정답 ④   Day 35-07

정답해설

④ **출제 포인트: 현재분사 vs. 과거분사**
일반 과거분사는 수식하는 대상과 수동 관계인 경우 사용하며 감정 제공 형용사[현재분사]는 수식하는 대상과 능동 관계인 경우 사용한다. 해당 문장은 일반 과거분사 'limited'와 감정 제공 형용사[현재분사] 'boring'을 사용하여 'memory'를 수식하고 있다. 이때 'memory'와 'limited'의 관계는 수동이며 'memory'와 'boring'의 관계는 능동임에 유의해야 한다.

09 정답 ④   Day 34-10

정답해설

해당 지문은 '누구나 리더가 될 수는 있으나 모든 사람이 리더가 되어야 하는 것은 아니며, 추종자로서도 충분히 변화를 만들 수 있다'고 설명하고 있다. 두 번째 문장 "That doesn't mean they're less capable of making an important contribution, just that they bring a different set of skills to the table(그것이 그들이 중요한 기여를 할 수 있는 능력이 덜하다는 것을 의미하지 않는다. 단지 그들이 다른 종류의 능력을 제공한다는 것을 의미한다)."에서의 "they"는 첫 번째 문장에서 "누구나 리더가 될 수 있으나 모든 사람이 리더십에 적합한 것은 아니다"라고 하고 있으므로 "추종자(followers)"라는 것을 유추할 수 있으며, 추종자는 리더와 다른 종류지만 그만큼 중요한 기여를 할 수 있다고 언급하고 있다. 또한 마지막 문장 "You don't have to be in charge to be influential(영향력을 미치기 위해 당신이 책임자가 될 필요는 없는 것이다)."을 통해 리더 외의 사람도 영향력을 미칠 수 있다고 서술하고 있다. 따라서 글의 요지로 가장 적절한 것은 '④ Followers can contribute to the society as much as leaders(추종자도 리더만큼 사회에 많은 기여를 할 수 있다).'이다.

해석

누구나 리더가 될 수 있다. 그러나 모든 사람이 리더십에 적합한 것은 아니다. 그것이 그들이 중요한 기여를 할 수 있는 능력이 덜하다는 것을 의미하지 않는다. 단지 그들이 다른 종류의 능력을 제공한다는 것을 의미한다. 추종자가 되는 것이 잘못된 일은 아니다. 세상은 그들을 리더만큼 필요로 한다. 모든 것에는 균형이 있다. 비결은 어떠한 역할이 당신이 수행하기에 가장 적합한지를 아는 것이다. 리더와 추종자 모두 똑같이 변화를 만들고자 하는 자신들의 욕망에 의해 움직일 수 있다. 그리고 이것은 분명한 차이가 아니다. 그들 대부분은 양쪽 측면의 요소를 지니고 있고, 하나 또는 다른 하나가 상황에 따라 선두로 나설 수 있다. 영향력을 미치기 위해 당신이 책임자가 될 필요는 없는 것이다.
① 타고난 리더인 사람들이 있다.
② 리더와 추종자의 역할은 다르다.
③ 세상의 변화를 이끄는 것은 리더이다.
④ 추종자도 리더만큼 사회에 많은 기여를 할 수 있다.

10 정답 ②   Day 37-08

정답해설

해당 지문은 '환경의 차이에 따른 언어의 차이'에 대해 설명하고 있다. 태평양 일대 동남아시아 지역과 코카서스산맥 일대 그루지야의 언어에서의 모음과 자음 사용 차이를 예시로 들어 설명한 후, 마지막 문장에서 "The physical surroundings of Georgians and Southeast Asians are as varied as the words they use, and linguists say they've found a relationship between the types of sounds in a language and the climate and landscape where it evolved(그루지야인들과 동남아시아인들의 물리적인 환경은 그들이 사용하는 단어만큼 다양하고, 언어학자들은 언어의 소리 유형과 그것이 진화해온 기후 및 지형 사이의 관계를 발견했다고 말한다)."라고 결론짓고 있으므로, 글의 주제로 가장 적절한 것은 '② languages and environments(언어와 환경)'이다.

해석

언어는 인류의 보편적인 특징이지만, 세계의 다른 곳에서 다르게 들린다. 대부분의 태평양 섬과 동남아시아 지역에서 단어는 자음보다 모음 소리를 더 많이 사용하고, 하나의 모음과 한 두 개의 자음으로 이루어진 단순한 음절로 사용된다. 한편 코카서스산맥의 언어인 그루지야어는 많은 자음을 포함하고, 때때로 자음군으로 결합되어 많은 외국인들이 발음하기 너무 복잡한 음절을 만들어내기도 한다. 그루지야인들과 동남아시아인들의 물리적인 환경은 그들이 사용하는 단어만큼 다양하고, 언어학자들은 언어의 소리 유형과 그것이 진화해온 기후 및 지형 사이의 관계를 발견했다고 말한다.
① 언어와 인종
② 언어와 환경
③ 외국인으로서의 언어 학습
④ 모음과 자음 사용법

11 정답 ④   Day 33-04

정답해설

A의 "We should all make~(우리는 모두 밤 열두 시가 되기 전에 새해 소원을 빌어야 한다)"는 말에 대한 답변으로 "I am ready to leave~(나는 종이 친 직후에 바로 떠날 준비가 됐어)"는 부자연스럽다.

해석

① A: 너 뭘 위해 잘 차려입은 거야?
   B: 나 오늘 저녁에 가족들과 외식하기로 했어.
② A: 편의점이 어디에 있어?
   B: 지도에는 길 건너면 바로 있다고 나와.
③ A: 나는 내년에 한 학기 휴학할까 생각하고 있어.
   B: 좋은 생각이야. 너 생각해둔 계획 있어?
④ A: 우리는 모두 밤 열두 시가 되기 전에 새해 소원을 빌어야 해.
   B: 나는 종이 치면 바로 떠날 준비가 되어있어.

12 정답 ②   Day 35-04

정답해설

A는 조언을 구하기 위해 B를 찾아 시간이 있냐고 묻는다. B는 사무실에서 서류작업을 하다가 A의 고민을 듣는다. A가 일 년 정도의 기간 동안 호주로 워킹홀리데이를 다녀오고 싶다고 이야기하자 B는 그게 왜 문제냐며 가고 싶으면 가라고 답변한다. 그러자 A는 혼자 남겨지는 것이 걱정된다며 예상치 못한 문제에 직면하게 되면 어떡하냐고 묻는다. 걱정하는 A에게 B는 ②"겁쟁이처럼 굴지 마(Don't be a chicken)"라고 말하는 것이 가장 적절하다.

해석

A: 안녕, 나 너 찾고 있었어. 너 어디에 있었어?
B: 아, 정말? 나 사무실에서 서류작업 좀 하고 있었어. 뭐 도와줄까?
A: 심각한 건 아닌데 난 그저 네 조언이 필요해. 너 시간 좀 남아?
B: 물론이지, 얘기해.
A: 나 일 년 정도 동안 호주로 워킹홀리데이를 가고 싶어.
B: 그럼 가야지. 그게 뭐가 문제야?
A: 나 혼자 남겨지는 것이 걱정돼. 만약 내가 완전히 홀로 있는 동안 예상치 못한 문제에 직면하면 어떡하지?
B: 겁쟁이처럼 굴지 마. 넌 혼자서도 잘 할 거야.
① 부자
② 겁쟁이
③ 모방하는 인간
④ 냉혈한 사람

13 정답 ④   Day 36-06

정답해설

④ **출제 포인트: 불규칙동사**
동사 'spread'는 과거형 동사와 과거분사 모두 동일한 형태이며, 이 문장에서는 문맥상 2003년이라는 과거 시점을 나타내는 과거 동사로 알맞게 쓰였다. 따라서 어법상 올바른 표현은 ④이다.

해석

중증 급성 호흡 증후군(SARS)은 심각한 형태의 폐렴이다. 그것은 2003년에 확인되었던 한 바이러스에 의해 발생된다. SARS 바이러스에 대한 감염은 급성 호흡곤란과 때때로 사망을 발생시킨다. SARS는 바이러스들 중 코로나바이러스 일족의 하나(일반적 감기를 발생시킬 수 있는 것과 같은 일족)에 의해 발생된다. 2003년의 전염은 중국에서 작은 포유동물들로부터 그 바이러스가 퍼졌을 때 시작되었다고 믿어진다.

14 정답 ③   Day 33-09

정답해설

해당 지문은 '미아스마설(miasma theory)'에 관한 내용이며, 해당 이론이 당시 질병 예방에 어떠한 영향을 미쳤는지 설명하고 있다. 주어진 문장은 미아스마설이 지지를 받게 되는 과정을 설명하고 있고, "By improving the housing, sanitation and general cleanliness of these existing areas(이러한 기존 지역에서의 주거, 위생 그리고 일반 청결을 향상시킴으로써)"에서 'these existing areas(이러한 기존 지역)'가 가리키는 대상이 주어진 문장 이전에 등장해야 함을 알 수 있다. ③ 이전 문장 "Rapid industrialization and urbanization had created many poor, filthy and foul-smelling city neighborhoods that tended to be the focal points of disease and epidemics(급속한 산업화와 도시화는 질병과 전염병의 중심이 되는 경향이 있던 많은 빈곤하고 불결하고 악취가 나는 도시 지역을 만들어냈다)."에서 'city neighborhoods(도시 지역)'라는 지역을 나타내는 표현이 등장하므로, 주어진 문장은 ③에 들어가는 것이 가장 적절하다는 것을 알 수 있다.

해석

미아스마설에 따르면 질병은 악취로 특징지어진 부패하는 물질의 부유물인 독성 증기, 즉 미아스마가 공기 중에 존재하는 것에 의해 발생했다. (①) 그 이론은 중세 시대에 고안되었고 수 세기 동안 지속되었다. 19세기 영국의 위생 개혁가들에게 미아스마설은 타당했다. (②) 급속한 산업화와 도시화는 질병과 전염병의 중심이 되는 경향이 있던 많은 빈곤하고 불결하고 악취가 나는 도시 지역을 만들어냈다. (③ **이러한 기존 지역에서의 주거, 위생 그리고 일반 청결을 향상시킴으로써, 질병의 정도가 하락하는 것으로 보였고, 이는 그 이론을 뒷받침했다.**) 비록 그것이 향후 반박되고 거부되었지만, 미아스마설의 존재의 이점이 없는 것은 아니었다. (④) 악취의 원인을 제거함으로써 개혁가들은 종종 의도치 않게 많은 질병의 실제 원인인 박테리아도 제거했던 것이다.

15 정답 ④
Day 38-08

정답해설

해당 지문은 '단어의 소리와 의미 간 관계에 대한 언어학자들의 연구'에 대해 소개하는 글이다. '대조되는 의미를 나타내는 단어를 표현하는 새로운 단어를 만들어 의미를 유추하도록 했을 때, 전혀 새로운 단어임에도 불구하고 청각적 표식만을 통해 단어의 의미를 올바르게 유추하는 것에 성공했다'라는 것이 실험의 주된 내용이다. 그런데 ④에서는 서로 다른 언어권의 학생들 간의 차이점을 설명하고 있으며, 본문의 실험에서는 언어 별 차이를 언급하고 있지 않으므로 글 전체의 내용과 어울리지 않는다. 따라서 글의 흐름상 가장 어색한 문장은 '④ Instead of using higher pitches for positive ideas and lower pitches for negative ideas like the English-speaking students did, the Chinese-speaking students did the opposite(영어권 학생들이 그랬던 것처럼 긍정적인 개념에는 고음을 쓰고 부정적인 개념에는 저음을 쓰는 것 대신, 중국어권 학생들은 그 반대로 했다).'이다.

해석

최근 한 연구에서 한 그룹의 언어학자들이 실험에서 소리와 단어 사이의 이 관계를 조사했다. 연구원들은 University of California Santa Cruz (UCSC)의 학생들에게 좋은, 나쁜, 부드러운, 거친, 매력적인, 추한 등 18가지의 대조되는 개념을 나타내는 새로운 단어를 만들도록 요청했다. ① 학생들은 짝을 이루어 오직 소리에만 근거해 각각의 단어의 의미를 추측해야 했다. ② 의미를 추측하는 학생에게 단어를 전달할 때 몸짓이나 얼굴 표정이 사용될 수 없었다. ③ 학생들은 의미를 추측하는 데 성공했고 경험을 쌓을수록 더 나아졌다. ④ *영어권 학생들이 그랬던 것처럼 긍정적인 개념에는 고음을 쓰고 부정적인 개념에는 저음을 쓰는 것 대신, 중국어권 학생들은 그 반대로 했다.* 데이터를 분석한 후 연구의 주 저자인 Marcus Perlman은 단어를 만든 사람들이 일관성 있게 특정 단어에 특정 유형의 발성을 이용하며, 청각적인 표식을 개념과 연결시켰기 때문에 추측하는 사람들이 성공했다고 말했다.

16 정답 ③
Day 34-09

정답해설

(A) 빈칸 이전에서 '세균이 질병을 야기한다는 지식'에 대해 설명하며 해당 지식이 우리에게 미친 주요 영향에 대해 강조한 후, 빈칸 이후에서 해당 지식에 대한 구체적인 추가 설명을 하고 있다. 따라서 빈칸에는 앞서 말한 내용에 자세한 내용을 덧붙일 때 사용하는 접속부사인 'In fact(사실은)'가 들어가는 것이 적절하다.

(B) 빈칸 이전에서 많은 과학자들이 세균 이론에 기여하는 연구를 수행했다고 언급한 후, 빈칸 이후에 그 많은 과학자들 중 오직 특정 두 인물만이 이론 형성에 결정적인 기여를 했다고 설명하고 있으므로, 빈칸에는 '역접, 양보'를 나타내는 접속부사인 'However(그러나)'가 들어가는 것이 가장 적절하다. 따라서 정답은 '③ (A) In fact(사실) - (B) However(그러나)'이다.

해석

오늘날 우리는 독감, 수두, 폐렴과 같은 전염병이 미생물, 즉 박테리아와 바이러스에 의해 발생한다는 것을 이해하고 있다. 이러한 지식이 없었다면, 우리는 이러한 감염을 치료하고 예방할 방법을 발전시키지 못했을 것이다. (A) 사실, 질병의 '세균이론'이라 알려진 이 지식은 상당히 근래의 발견이다. 사람들은 수천 년 동안 인간 질병을 설명하기 위해 이론들을 창시해 왔다. 그리스 내과 의사인 Hippocrates는 늪과 같은 곳에서 발생한 '나쁜 공기'가 원인이라고 생각했다. 19세기 현미경 기술의 발전은 미생물학자 세대가 이전에는 보지 못한 질병 유발 유기체의 세계를 더 깊게 연구할 수 있도록 해주었다. 많은 과학자들이 세균이론 형성에 기여하는 연구를 시행했다. (B) 그러나 그 이론의 과학적 증거는 두 유럽 출신 과학자인 프랑스인 Louis Pasteur와 독일인이었던 Robert Koch의 성과였다.

① 예를 들어 - 게다가
② 안타깝게도 - 결국
③ 사실 - 그러나
④ 그렇지 않으면 - 그럼에도 불구하고

17 정답 ②
Day 40-10

정답해설

해당 지문은 '우크라이나의 과두정치 체제'에 대한 설명이며, 빈칸에는 해당 체제의 특징에 관한 내용이 들어가는 것이 적합하다. 본문 후반에서 "The nature of close relations between the government and the oligarchs has not undergone any major changes(정부와 과두제 집권층 간의 밀접한 관계의 본질은 어떠한 주요 변화도 겪지 않았다)"라고 언급하며, '과두정치 체제가 거의 변하지 않았다'라는 것을 알 수 있으며, 마지막 문장 "Although reshuffles have taken place inside the political and business elites, nothing seems to be able to change this system, at least in the medium term(정치계와 재계 엘리트 내부에서 개편이 일긴 했지만, 적어도 중기적으로 이 체제를 변화시킬 수 있는 것은 아무것도 없는 것으로 보인다)."을 통해 해당 체제가 매우 견고하다는 주장을 펼치고 있음을 알 수 있다. 따라서 빈칸에 가장 적절한 것은 "② to be very durable(매우 견고한 것)"이다.

해석

우크라이나의 과두정치 체제는 매우 견고한 것으로 드러났다. 이 체제, 즉 새로이 형성된 대기업과 정치 계층의 유대를 기반으로 한 체제는 우크라이나가 1991년 독립을 쟁취한 몇 년 후에 생겨났고 Leonid Kuchma 대통령의 재임 중에 최종 형태로 발전했다. 다른 구소련국가들, 특히 러시아에서도 또한 유사한 현상이 발달했음에도 불구하고, 다른 동유럽 국가에서 현재의 대기업이 정치에 우크라이나에서처럼 그렇게 강력한 영향을 미치지는 않는다. 우크라이나 대기업의 대표자들은 러시아에서와 같이 보통 과두제 집권층이라고 일컬어진다. 정부와 과두제 집권층 간의 밀접한 관계의 본질은 오렌지혁명의 결과 또는 Victor Yanukovych의 2010년 대선 승리 이후에도 어떠한 주요 변화도 겪지 않았다. 정치계와 재계 엘리트 내부에서 조직개편이 일긴 했지만, 적어도 중기적으로 이 체제를 변화시킬 수 있는 것은 아무것도 없는 것으로 보인다.

① 확대될 필요가 있는 것
② 매우 견고한 것
③ 더욱 효율적인 것
④ 위험한 결함을 가지고 있는 것

18 정답 ④
Day 37-10

정답해설

해당 지문은 '미래의 재정적 목표와 관계없이 위험 분산형 투자를 하는 것이 중요하다'라고 설명하고 있다. 빈칸에는 위험 분산형 포트폴리오를 설명할 수 있는 명언이 들어가야 한다. 빈칸 이후에서 "If a portfolio is too heavily allocated to one individual security, and that security fails for some reason, an investment portfolio can be reduced to zero(만약 포트폴리오가 단일한 개별 유가증권에 과도하게 집중되어 할당되어 있고, 어떠한 이유로 그 유가증권이 폭락한다면, 투자 포트폴리오는 완전히 무용지물이 될 수도 있다)."라고 설명하며, '한 곳에 집중적으로 투자할 경우 손실의 위험도 커진다'라고 언급하고 있으므로, 다양한 곳에 분산하여 투자하는 것이 바람직하다는 것을 유추할 수 있다. 따라서 빈칸에 가장 적절한 표현은 '④ don't put all your eggs in one basket(모든 계란을 한 바구니에 담지 말라 (한 가지 일에 몽땅 다 걸지 말라))'이다.

해석

투자자들은 그들의 투자가 확실히 자신들의 미래의 요구를 충족시키도록 해야 한다. 미래의 재정적 목표가 무엇인지에 관계없이, 위험 분산형 투자 포트폴리오를 만들기 위해 투자 결정에 대한 포트폴리오 접근법은 중요하다. 위험 분산형 포트폴리오의 이점은 "모든 계란을 한 바구니에 담지 말라"는 일화적인 명언으로 가장 잘 요약된다. 만약 포트폴리오가 단일한 개별 유가증권에 과도하게 집중되어 할당되어 있고, 어떠한 이유로 그 유가증권이 폭락한다면, 투자 포트폴리오는 완전히 무용지물이 될 수도 있다. 투자의 분산은 투자자들이 예상 수익을 반드시 감소시키지 않고 어떠한 하나의 투자포지션과 관련된 가능 손실액을 분산시킬 수 있게 한다.

① 시간은 돈이다
② 뛰기 전에 보라(돌다리도 두드려보고 건너라)
③ 한 걸음 한 걸음 가는 사람이 멀리 간다(천 리 길도 한 걸음부터)
④ 모든 계란을 한 바구니에 담지 말라 (한 가지 일에 모든 것을 걸지 마라)

19 정답 ② Day 39-08

정답해설

해당 지문은 '조류 방언(dialect)의 특징 및 기능'에 대해 서술하고 있다. 본문 2, 3번째 문장에서 "Vocal dialects appear to be learned. Young birds hear the songs sung around their natal territories by their fathers and neighboring males, and acquire the peculiarities of these renditions(음성 방언은 학습되는 것으로 보인다. 어린 새들은 그들의 출생 구역 주변에서 아버지와 이웃의 수컷들에 의해 불리는 노래를 듣고, 이러한 연주의 특색을 습득한다)."라고 설명하며 '방언의 후천적 습득'에 대해 밝히고 있으므로, '방언은 선천적 능력이다'라고 서술하고 있는 보기 '② Singing a dialect is the bird's innate ability(방언으로 노래하는 것은 조류의 타고난 능력이다).'는 글의 내용과 일치하지 않는다.

해석

우리의 말하기 유형이 지역적으로 다른 것과 마찬가지로 많은 조류 종의 노래 또한 지리적인 차이를 보인다. 음성 방언은 학습되는 것으로 보인다. 어린 새들은 그들의 출생 구역 주변에서 아버지와 이웃의 수컷들에 의해 불리는 노래를 듣고, 이러한 연주의 특색을 습득한다. 방언의 "이유", 즉 그것들의 기능적인 중요성은 그것들이 어떻게 생기는 가라는 질문보다 더 파악하기 어려운 것으로 판명되었다. 많은 조류학자들은 방언이 지역 환경에 대한 유전적인 적응을 나타내는 지표로서 역할을 한다고 단지 추정한다. 따라서 방언은 암컷들이 번식이 이루어지는 특정 환경에 밀접하게 적응된 유전자를 아마 보유하고 있을 그들 고유의 출생 지역 출신의 수컷을 선택하는 것을 가능하게 한다는 것이다. 다시 말해, 방언은 "동종 교배", 즉 유사 개체 간 번식을 활성화시키는 역할을 한다.

① 하나의 조류종이 지역에 따라 다른 소리를 낼 수도 있다.
② 방언으로 노래하는 것은 조류의 타고난 능력이다.
③ 음성 방언의 정확한 기능은 불확실하다.
④ 암컷 조류는 자신의 지역 출신의 수컷과 교배하는 것을 선호한다.

20 정답 ③ Day 35-10

정답해설

본문 중반에서 '중세 기사도에 대한 그의 대표작인 "King Cophetua and the Beggar Maid"와 "Merlin and Nimue"에 대해 언급이 되는데, 이후 문장에서 "Stylistically, these works owe much to Rossetti's illustrations."를 통해 '이 작품들은 양식상 Rossetti의 그림에 많은 영향을 받았다'라고 서술하고 있다. 따라서 "Merlin and Nimue"이 "Sandro Botticelli"의 영향을 받았다는 내용은 본문의 내용과 일치하지 않으므로 ③이 정답이다.

해석

Edward Burne-Jones는 Oxford에 있는 Exeter College에서 교육을 받았다. 그곳에서 그는 그의 미래 합작자인 예술가이자 시인인 William Morris를 처음 만났다. 그가 예술가 Dante Gabriel Rossetti와 1856년에 만난 것은 그의 커리어에 있어서 전환점이 되었고, 그는 졸업을 하지 않은 채 Oxford를 떠났다. Morris와 그는 이후 Rossetti의 지도하에 작업을 하며 London에 정착했다. 그의 "King Cophetua and the Beggar Maid"와 "Merlin and Nimue"에서 보이듯이, Burne-Jones의 생생한 상상력은 중세 기사도에 대한 이야기들을 기쁘게 받아들였다. 양식상으로, 이러한 작품들은 Rossetti의 그림으로부터 많은 영향을 받았다. 또한 그 자신의 꿈의 세계는 종종 15세기 이탈리아 화가 Filippino Lippi와 Sandro Botticelli의 우울하고 야윈 인물들로부터 영감을 얻었다. 그의 첫 번째 큰 성공은 1877년에 열린 전시회였다. 그때부터 1898년 사망할 때까지 그는 영국의 훌륭한 화가 중 하나라고 점점 더 여겨졌다. 사후에 Burne-Jones의 영향은 장식 디자인 분야, 특히 교회의 스테인드글라스 분야에서보다 미술계에 훨씬 적게 미쳤다고 느껴졌다.

기적사 DAY 41

결국엔 성정혜 영어 하프모의고사

| 01 | ④ | 02 | ① | 03 | ② | 04 | ① | 05 | ④ |
| 06 | ③ | 07 | ④ | 08 | ① | 09 | ③ | 10 | ④ |

오답률 TOP 1

01 정답 ④
16 국가직

정답해설

공해를 없애자는 캠페인이 대중의 협조를 얻지 못한다면 의미가 없어질 것이므로, ④ futile이 정답이다.

해석

공해를 없애자는 캠페인은 대중의 이해와 온전한 협조를 얻지 못한다면 **무용지물**로 판명될 것이다.
① 유혹적인, 마음을 홀리는
② 향상된, 강화한
③ 풍부한, 비옥한
④ 무용지물인, 무효인

어휘

eliminate 제거하다, 없애다
cooperation 협조
enticing 유혹적인, 마음을 홀리는
enhanced 향상된, 강화한
fertile 풍부한, 비옥한
futile 무용지물인, 무효인

오답률 TOP 2

02 정답 ①
16 국가직

정답해설

'scratched the surface of'는 '~을 수박 겉핥기식으로 다뤘다'의 의미이며, 'superficially dealt with'와 동일한 의미를 가진다.

해석

지금까지, 신문 기사들은 이 엄청나게 복잡한 문제를 **수박 겉핥기식으로 다뤄 왔다**.
① ~을 피상적[표면적]으로 다뤘다
② 적절한 말을 했다, 요점을 찔렀다
③ ~을 붙잡았다, 잡았다
④ ~을 긍정적으로 끝까지 했다, ~을 긍정적으로 추적보도 했다

어휘

scratch the surface of ~을 수박 겉핥기식으로 다루다
superficially deal with ~을 피상적[표면적]으로 다루다
hit the nail on the head of ~에 대해 적절한 말을 하다, 요점을 찌르다
seize hold of ~을 붙잡다, 잡다
positively follow up on ~을 긍정적으로 끝까지 하다, ~을 긍정적으로 추적보도 하다

03 정답 ②
16 국가직

정답해설

'stick one's nose in(~에 참견하다)'은 ② interfere과 유사한 의미를 가지고 있다.

해석

그건 개인적인 것이었어. 왜 너는 **참견을 해야**만 했니?
① 서두르다
② 참견하다, 간섭하다
③ 코를 훌쩍거리다
④ 물러나다

어휘

personal 개인적인
stick 내밀다, 붙이다, 찔리다
hurry 서두르다
interfere 참견하다, 간섭하다
sniff 코를 훌쩍거리다
resign 물러나다

04 정답 ①
16 국가직

정답해설

환불이 안 된다는 B의 말에 A는 어떤 반박을 하였을 것이다. B의 마지막 말인 'It's written at the bottom of the receipt(그것이 영수증 아래쪽에 쓰여 있다).'로 보아 A는 그것(환불 불가 안내)에 대해 모르고 있었음을 알 수 있다. 따라서 정답은 ①이다.

오답해설

②③④ 나머지 보기는 환불에 대해 이야기하는 문맥상 적절하지 않다.

해석

A: 제가 어제 여기서 산 식탁보를 환불받고 싶은데요.
B: 식탁보에 문제가 있나요?
A: 저희 식탁에 맞지 않아서 반품하고 싶어요. 여기 영수증이요.
B: 죄송하지만 이 식탁보는 마지막 세일 품목이어서 환불이 안 됩니다.
A: 아무도 저에게 그걸 말해주지 않았어요.
B: 그건 영수증 아래쪽에 쓰여 있어요.
① 아무도 저에게 그걸 말해주지 않았어요.
② 가격표는 어디 있나요?
③ 그것에 무슨 문제가 있나요?
④ 나는 그것을 좋은 가격에 샀어요.

어휘

tablecloth 식탁보
fit 맞다, 적합하다, 어울리다

오답률 TOP 3

05 정답 ④
16 국가직

정답해설

④ **출제 포인트: 등위접속사의 병렬구조**
의미상 「not A nor B but C」(A도 B도 아닌 C)의 구조가 되어야 하므로 'or'를 'but'으로 변경하는 것이 옳다. 즉, '끝까지 생존하는 생물은 가장 강한 생물(A)도, 가장 지적인 생물(B)도 아니고, 변화에 가장 잘 반응하는 생물(C)이다.'의 구조이다.

오답해설

① **출제 포인트: 완전타동사+목적어[to부정사 vs. 동명사]**
「remember + -ing」는 '과거에 ~했던 것을 기억하다'의 의미로 영작이 올바르게 되었다. 참고로 「remember + to부정사」는 '미래에 ~할 것을 기억하다'의 의미를 지닌다.

② **출제 포인트: take의 관용표현(It takes+목적어+시간+to부정사)**
「It takes + 목적어 + 시간 + to부정사 ~」는 '목적어가 to부정사 하는 데 ~만큼의 시간이 걸리다'라는 의미로 올바르게 사용되었다.

③ 출제 포인트: blow의 문장구조

해당 문장에서 'blew'는 완전타동사 'blow'의 과거시제로 뒤에 전치사 없이 목적어를 사용하였으므로 옳은 문장이다. 또한 'inside out'은 부사구로 동사 'blew'를 수식한다.

06 정답 ③
16 국가직

정답해설

③ 출제 포인트: 완전타동사[주장 / 요구 / 명령 / 제안] + 목적어[that + 주어 + (should) + 동사원형]

'demand'는 요구 동사로 that절의 동사에 「(should) + 동사원형」이 필요하다. 이때 'should'는 생략이 가능하므로 'should'를 생략하면 'not leave'만 남게 된다. 따라서 옳은 문장은 ③이다.

오답해설

① 출제 포인트: 강조 부사

'much'는 비교급을 강조할 때 사용한다. 원급인 'careless'를 꾸미는 부사는 'very'가 더 적절하다.

② 출제 포인트: 명사절을 이끄는 접속사

주어는 명사만이 가능하며, 절을 사용할 경우 명사절로 바꾸어 줄 접속사가 필요하다. 'But'은 명사절을 이끌 수 없으므로 틀리다. 여기서는 뒤의 'or not'으로 보아 'Whether'로 고치는 것이 적절하다.

④ 출제 포인트: The + 비교급, the + 비교급

「The + 비교급, the + 비교급」 구문이다. 'more'와 형용사는 붙어 있어야 하며, 'more'가 있으므로 그 형용사는 '-er'를 쓰지 않고 원형 그대로 사용하여야 한다. 즉, 'The more a hotel is expensiver, ~'는 'The more expensive a hotel is, ~'가 되어야 한다.

해석

① Jessica는 자신의 지식 향상을 위해 거의 노력을 하지 않는 아주 부주의한 사람이다.
② 그가 올지 안 올지 확실치 않다.
③ 그 경찰은 그녀가 당분간은 그 나라를 떠나지 말라고 요구했다.
④ 호텔이 더 비쌀수록, 호텔 서비스는 더 좋다.

07 정답 ④
16 국가직

정답해설

④ 출제 포인트: 타동사구[완전타동사+목적어+전치사+목적어]

「prevent + 목적어 + from + -ing」 구문을 묻는 문제이다. '목적어가 ~하는 것을 예방[방해]하다'의 의미로, 출제 포인트는 'prevent'와 어울리는 전치사 및 동명사의 사용이다. 해당 문장에서는 전치사 'from'을 사용하였고 자동사로 쓰인 'age'의 동명사 형태인 'aging'을 사용하였으므로 옳게 사용되었다. 또한 해당 문장의 동사인 help와 이후에 동사 keep, sharpen, speed, reduce, prevent가 연이어 병렬구조를 이루고 있다.

오답해설

① 출제 포인트: 주어와 동사의 수일치

밑줄 친 부분은 관용적으로 사용되는 표현으로, '옛말에'라는 뜻이다. 'the old saying'은 단수 주어이므로 'go'가 'goes'로 변경되어야 한다.

② 출제 포인트: 부사 vs. 형용사

문장 주어는 'The foods'이며 문장 동사는 'affect'이다. 'obvious'는 동사 'affect'를 수식하는 부사 형태여야 하므로 'obviously'로 변경하여야 한다.

③ 출제 포인트: help+목적어+목적격 보어[to부정사/원형부정사]

'help'는 준사역동사로 목적어와 목적격 보어의 관계가 능동일 때는 원형 또는 to부정사를 목적격 보어로 사용한다. 또한 목적어와 목적격 보어의 관계가 수동일 때는 과거분사를 사용한다. 이 문장에서는 목적어와 목적격 보어의 관계가 능동이므로 '(to) be concentrated'를 사용해야 한다. 또한, 자동사로 'concentrate'나 'to concentrate'로 변경해주어서 '집중하다'의 의미로 사용할 수도 있다.

해석

옛말에, 당신이 먹는 것이 곧 당신이라고 했다. 당신이 섭취하는 음식은 분명하게 당신의 신체 활동에 영향을 미친다. 그것들은 또한 당신의 뇌가 업무를 처리하는 방법에 영향을 끼칠지도 모른다. 만약 당신의 뇌가 그것들을 잘 처리한다면, 당신은 좀 더 명확하게 사고할 것이며, 당신은 정신적으로 더욱 안정될 것이다. 적절한 음식은 당신이 집중할 수 있게 도움을 주며, 동기부여가 되도록 유지해주며, 기억이 선명해지도록 해주며, 당신의 반응 속도를 빠르게 해주며, 스트레스를 줄여주며, 아마도 심지어는 당신의 뇌가 나이 들지 않도록 예방해줄 것이다.

어휘

saying 속담, 격언
handle 다루다
prevent A from B A가 B하는 것을 막다
affect 영향을 미치다
stable 안정된, 안정적인

08 정답 ④
19 국가직

정답해설

과거의 지도 제작 기술들이 과거의 분야가 아니라 'the realm of ideas'(생각들의 영역)에서 사용된다고 서술하면서 전통적인 개념의 지도가 아니라고 본문에서 설명하고 있으므로 글의 주제로 알맞은 것은 ④ Mapping New Frontiers(새로운 분야들을 지도 제작하는 것)이다.

오답해설

① 이 글은 전산화된 지도와 전통적인 지도를 비교하고 있는 것은 아니므로 글의 주제로 적절하지 않다.
② 본문에서 언급하고 있지 않다.
③ 본문에서 DNA는 하나의 예로 언급하고 있지 주제는 아니다.

해석

지도 제작 기술들은 많은 새로운 응용 분야에서 사용되고 있다. 생물학적 연구원들은 DNA("게놈을 지도 제작")의 분자적 구조를 탐험하고 있는 중이고, 지구 물리학자들은 지구의 핵의 구조를 지도화하고 있고 해양학자들은 해저를 지도화하고 있는 중이다. 컴퓨터 게임들도 규칙들, 위험 요소, 그리고 보상들이 변하는 다양한 가상의 "지역들" 혹은 단계들을 가지고 있다. 전산화는 지금 "가상현실", 즉 특별한 상황들을 자극하는 인공적인 환경들과 함께 현실에 도전하고 있고, 그것들은 훈련과 오락에 유용할지 모른다. 지도 제작 기술들은 생각들의 영역에서 또한 사용될 수 있다. 예를 들면, 생각들 사이에서 관계들은 콘셉트 지도들이라고 불리는 것을 사용하면서 보일 수 있다. 일반적이거나 "중심적인" 생각들로부터 시작하여, 연관된 생각들은 주요 콘셉트 주변에 그물망을 지으면서, 연결될 수 있다. 이것은 어떤 전통적인 개념에 의한 지도가 아니다. 하지만 지도 제작의 도구들과 기술들은 그것을 생산하기 위해 이용된다. 그리고 어떤 방법에서 그것은 지도와 닮았다.

① 전산화된 지도들 vs. 전통적인 지도들
② 지도 제작은 어디에서 시작하는가?
③ DNA 비밀들에 대한 방법들을 발견하는 것
④ 새로운 분야들을 지도 제작하는 것

어휘

mapping 지도 제작
molecular 분자의
core 핵
ocean floor 대양저, 해저
application 응용(분야)
geophysicist 지구물리학자
oceanographer 해양학자
imaginary 상상의, 허구의

hazard 위험(요소)
virtual reality 가상현실
stimulate 자극하다
realm 영역
related 관련된
cartography 지도 제작
resemble 닮다

computerization 전산화
artificial 인공의
entertainment 오락
general 전반적인, 일반적인
definition 정의, 규정
employ 이용하다, 고용하다
frontier 경계, 새로운 분야

09 정답 ③
19 국가직

정답해설
글의 내용이 가치가 큰 수행자, 적절한 수행자 그리고 실력이 부족한 수행자에 대한 피드백이 어때야 하는지 각각의 경우에 따라 피드백을 설명하고 있으므로 글의 요지로 적절한 것은 ③ Tailor feedback to the person.(사람마다 피드백을 조정해라.)이다.

오답해설
① 시간을 맞추라기보다는 대상에 대해 피드백을 맞추라는 것이 본문의 내용이므로 정답이 될 수 없다.
② 본문의 소재는 '부정적인 피드백'에 한정되어 있지 않다.
④ 어떤 피드백을 피해야 한다는 내용은 언급하고 있지 않다.

해석
수행 피드백을 할 때, 당신은 그것의 빈도, 양, 그리고 내용을 설계하는 데 있어서 받는 사람의 과거 수행과 그 또는 그녀의 미래 잠재력에 대한 당신의 예상을 고려해야만 한다. 성장에 대한 잠재력을 갖고 있는 가치가 큰 수행자에 대해, 피드백이 충분히 빈번하여 시정 조치를 취하도록 유도해야 하지만, 너무 빈번해서 이를 통제하고 진취성을 약화하는 것으로 경험되면 안 된다. 자신의 직업에 정착하여 발전 가능성이 제한되어있는 적절한 수행자들에게는, 그들의 일을 알고 무엇을 해야 할 필요가 있는지를 인식하면서, 과거에 신뢰할 수 있고 안정된 행동을 보여 왔기 때문에, 피드백은 거의 필요하지 않다. 실력이 부족한 수행자의 경우, 즉 성과가 개선되지 않으면 직장에서 퇴출될 필요가 있는 사람들은 피드백이 빈번하고 매우 구체적이어야 하며, 피드백에 따라 행동하는 것과 해고되거나 해고되는 것과 같은 부정적인 제재 사이의 연관성을 분명히 해야 한다.
① 당신의 피드백을 시간을 잘 조절해라.
② 부정적인 피드백을 (상황에 따라) 조정해 만들어야 한다.
③ 사람마다 피드백을 조정해라.
④ 목적 지향적인 피드백을 피해라.

어휘
performance 수행(능력)
past 지나간, 과거의
frequency 빈도
prod 자극하다, 찌르다
sap 약화시키다
adequate 적절한, 중간의
advancement 발전, 진전
sanction 제재; 승인
explicit 분명한
customize 맞춰주다, 주문 제작하다
avoid 피하다

recipient 수신자
estimate 추정(치)
content 내용(물)
corrective 교정의
initiative 진취성, 계획
settle into ~에 자리 잡다
specific 구체적인
lay off 해고하다
time 시간을 맞추다[조절하다]
tailor 맞추다, 조정하다
goal-oriented 목표 지향적인

10 정답 ④
19 국가직

정답해설
본문 마지막에 "With his ability to fuse serious content with humorous style, Hughes attacked racial prejudice in a way that was natural and witty."(진지한 내용과 재미있는 스타일을 융합시키는 능력으로 Hughes는 자연스럽고 재치 있는 방법으로 인종적 편견을 공격했다.)로 인종 편견을 엄숙한 문체로 공격한 것은 본문의 내용과 일치하지 않는 보기이다. 따라서 정답은 ④이다.

오답해설
① 'graduated from Lincoln University, in which many African-American students have pursued their academic disciplines(많은 아프리카계 미국 학생들이 학업을 추구한 Lincoln 대학교를 졸업했다).'를 통해 많은 흑인들이 졸업한 Lincoln University를 졸업하였으므로 본문과 일치하는 내용이다.
② 'Hughes incorporated authentic dialect in his work(Hughes는 작품에 진정한 사투리를 접목했다).'에서 알 수 있는 내용이다.
③ 'created characters and themes that reflected elements of lower-class black culture(하류 흑인 문화의 요소를 반영하는 캐릭터와 테마를 창조했다).'에서 본문과 일치하는 것을 알 수 있다.

해석
Langston Hughes는 미주리주 Joplin에서 태어나 많은 아프리카계 미국 학생들이 학업을 추구한 Lincoln 대학교를 졸업했다. Hughes는 열여덟 살 때 가장 잘 알려진 시 중 하나인 'Negro Speaks of Rivers'를 출간했다. 창의적이고 실험적인 Hughes는 작품에 진정한 사투리를 접목시켰고, 블루스와 재즈의 리듬과 분위기를 수용하기 위해 전통적인 시적 형식을 채택했으며, 하류 흑인 문화의 요소를 반영하는 캐릭터와 테마를 창조했다. 진지한 내용과 재미있는 스타일을 융합시키는 능력으로 Hughes는 자연스럽고 재치 있는 방법으로 인종적 편견을 공격했다.

어휘
pursue 추구하다
poem 시
incorporate 통합시키다
dialect 지역 언어
embrace 수용하다
fuse 결합(융합)시키다
witty 재치 있는

discipline 교육, 훈련, 훈육
experimental 실험적인
authentic 진짜의
adapt 변형시키다, 적응시키다
cadence 리듬, 억양
prejudice 편견

기적사 DAY 42

결국엔 성정혜 영어 하프모의고사

| 01 | ① | 02 | ① | 03 | ④ | 04 | ④ | 05 | ① |
| 06 | ① | 07 | ④ | 08 | ② | 09 | ② | 10 | ③ |

01 정답 ①

정답해설

주어진 빈칸에는 문맥상 '애증이 엇갈리다'가 적절하므로 ① ambivalent가 정답이다.

해석

만약 당신이 누군가가 무엇에 대해 **애증이 엇갈린다고** 말한다면, 그들은 그들이 그것을 정말로 원하는지, 혹은 그들이 정말로 그것을 승인하는 것인지 불확실해 보이는 것이다.
① 상반하는 감정을 품은, 애증이 엇갈리는
② 순회하는, 떠도는; 순회자, 편력자
③ 풍부한, 비옥한
④ 전례 없는, 뛰어난, 유일한

어휘

ambivalent 상반하는 감정을 품은, 애증이 엇갈리는
itinerant 순회하는, 떠도는, 순회자, 편력자
fertile 풍부한, 비옥한   singular 전례 없는, 뛰어난, 유일한

02 정답 ①

정답해설

밑줄 친 단어는 문맥상 '싫어하다, 혐오하다'로 사용되었고, 유의어가 아닌 것은 ① seize이다.

해석

상호 간의 이익이 얽힌 범죄를 해결하기 위해 표면상으로 협력함에도 불구하고, 등장인물 중 두 배역은 서로를 **싫어한다**.
① ~을 붙잡다, 잡다
② 혐오하다
③ 혐오하다
④ 싫어하다

어휘

ostensibly 표면상으로   seize ~을 붙잡다, 잡다
abhor 혐오하다   loathe 혐오하다
dislike 싫어하다

오답률 TOP 2

03 정답 ④

정답해설

밑줄 친 단어는 문맥상 '모이다'로 사용되었고, 유의어로는 ④ assemble이 가장 적절하다.

해석

그것은 정부가 안전 문제를 언급하면서 중앙 Taksim 광장에 **모이려던** 겁에 질린 참가자들을 최루탄과 물대포로 쫓아내 동성연애자와 트랜스젠더의 프라이드 이벤트를 금지했던 2015년에 갑작스럽게 바뀌었다.
① 손상시키다, 침식하다, 부식하다
② 코를 훌쩍거리다
③ 변경하다
④ 모이다

어휘

erode 손상시키다, 침식하다, 부식하다   sniff 코를 훌쩍거리다
modify 변경하다   assemble 모이다
(the) authorities 정부 당국

04 정답 ④

정답해설

A와 B는 한 TV 프로그램에서 개최하는 오디션 포스터를 보며 대화를 나눈다. B는 "언제 한 번 오디션을 볼까 생각했었다"라고 하자 A는 망설이는 이유에 관해 물으며 "자신이 (A) 도와줄(lend a hand) 수 있다"고 한다. B는 "무대에 오를 때마다 어떻게 (B) 웃음을 참고 표정 관리를 해야 할지(keep a straight face) 모르겠다"라고 답변한다. 그러자 A는 B에게 "며칠 더 고민해보라"라고 말하며 "만약 진짜로 오디션을 보게 되면 (C) 행운을 빌어주겠다(keep my fingers crossed)"라고 한다.

오답해설

① (C) B가 오디션을 진짜 본다면 '행운을 빌어주겠다(keep one's fingers crossed)'라고 하는 맥락에서 발을 꼬겠다고 하는 것은 어색하다.
② (A) A가 B에게 도움을 권하는 상황에서 '몸(body)'을 빌려주겠다고 하는 것은 부적절하다. (B) 웃음을 참고 표정 관리가 되지 않는 것이 고민인 B에게 올곧은 '발(foot)'을 유지하라는 것은 옳지 않다. (C) B가 오디션에 참가하면 행운을 빈다고 하는 내용상 '팔짱(arms)'을 끼고 있겠다는 것은 문맥상 부자연스럽다.
③ (A) A가 오디션을 '도와주겠다(lend a hand)'라고 발화하는 맥락에서 '모자(hat)'를 빌려주겠다는 것은 대화의 흐름상 어색한 표현이다. (B) 무대에 서면 '웃음을 참고 표정 관리하는 (keep a straight face)'것이 힘들다는 B가 '손가락(finger)'을 올곧게 유지하는 것이 어렵다는 표현은 옳지 않다. (C) 약속을 하다라는 표현으로 'keep my hands'는 적절하지 않다.

해석

A: 저 포스터 봐봐! 오디션을 연대.
B: 이 포스터가 학교 춤 동아리에서 온 거야?
A: 아닌 것 같아. 밑에 어떤 TV 오디션 프로그램이 오디션을 개최한다고 쓰여 있어. 관심 있어?
B: 글쎄, 언젠가 오디션을 지원해볼까 생각 중이었어.
A: 그럼 뭐가 널 멈추게 하는 거야? 네가 원한다면 (A) 도와줄 수 있어.
B: 너 정말 친절하다. 근데 문제는 내가 무대에만 올라가면 어떻게 (B) 웃음을 참고 표정 관리를 해야 할지 모르겠어.
A: 그건 쉽진 않아, 그러나 며칠 동안 곰곰이 더 생각해보고 만약 네가 진짜 프로그램 오디션을 본다면 너를 위해 (C) 행운을 빌어줄게.

① (A) 손   (B) 얼굴   (C) 발
② (A) 몸   (B) 발   (C) 팔
③ (A) 모자 (B) 손가락 (C) 손
④ (A) 손   (B) 얼굴   (C) 손가락

어휘

audition 오디션; 춤, 연기, 노래 등을 테스트 하다(받다)
organize 개최하다   apply 지원하다
lend a hand 도움을 주다   cross 꼬다
keep a straight face 웃음을 참고 무표정한 얼굴을 하다
keep one's fingers crossed 행운을 빌다

05 정답 ①

정답해설

① 출제 포인트: take의 관용표현(It takes+목적어+시간+to부정사)

「It takes+목적어+시간+to+동사원형」은 '~가 ~하는 데 시간이 걸리다'를 뜻하며 이때 시간을 나타내는 명사(구)가 목적어 앞으로 이동하는 경우 「It takes+시간+for+목적어+to+동사원형」이 된다. 해당 문장은 「It takes+시간+for+목적어+to+동사원형」을 사용하였으나 'for+목적어' 자리에 목적어 'her eyes'만 사용하였으므로 틀린 문장이다. 따라서 'her eyes'를 'for her eyes'로 수정해야 한다. 또한 「It takes+목적어+시간+to+동사원형」을 사용한다면 'It took her eyes a few minutes to adjust to the dark.'도 가능하다.

오답해설

② 출제 포인트: 완전타동사+목적어[to부정사 vs. 동명사]

'try'는 완전타동사로 전치사 없이 목적어를 가지며 '~을 노력하다'의 의미로 목적어로 to부정사를 목적어로 갖는다.

③ 출제 포인트: blow의 문장구조

해당 문장에서 'blow'의 과거시제인 'blew'는 완전자동사이므로 뒤에 부사 역할을 하는 전치사구 'past them'이 올바르다. 또한 "usually cold for this time of the year"는 'being'이 생략된 분사구문으로 분사구문의 의미상 주어는 'another breeze of wind'로서 생략되어있다.

④ 출제 포인트: 등위접속사의 병렬구조

보어 역할을 하는 'that+절'이 'not A but B'를 통해 병렬구조를 이루고 있는 문장으로 옳은 문장이다.

06 정답 ①

정답해설

① 출제 포인트: The+비교급, the+비교급 / 간접의문

'The+비교급 ~, the+비교급 ~'이 '~하면 할수록 점점 더 ~하다'의 의미로 쓰인 문장으로 옳은 문장이다. 또한 'realize'의 목적어 절로 온 'how much I don't know'는 간접의문문으로 적절하게 쓰였다.

오답해설

② 출제 포인트: 완전타동사[주장/요구/명령/제안] + 목적어[that+주어+(should)+동사원형]

'recommend'의 목적어로 'that+절'이 오는 경우 「that+주어+(should)+동사원형 ~」의 구조를 가진다. 해당 문장은 'recommend'의 목적어로 'that+절'을 사용하였으나 현재시제동사 'are'를 사용하였으므로 틀린 문장이다. 따라서 'are'를 'be' 또는 'should be'로 수정해야 한다.

③ 출제 포인트: 강조 부사

비교급 강조 부사 'even'이 원급 부사 'much'를 수식하고 있으므로 틀린 문장이다. 따라서 'much'를 비교급 'more'로 수정해야 한다. 또한 'even'을 삭제하거나 'very'로 수정하여도 옳은 문장이 된다.

④ 출제 포인트: 명사절을 이끄는 접속사

등위접속사 'but'이 이끄는 절은 등위절이므로 주격 보어로 사용할 수 없다. 해당 문장은 주격 보어로 'but'이 이끄는 등위절을 사용하였으므로 틀린 문장이다. 따라서 'but'을 종속접속사 'that'으로 수정해야 한다.

해석

① 더 많이 배울수록, 내가 얼마나 많이 알지 못하는지 더 많이 깨닫는다.
② 그 보고서는 많은 자원이 4살짜리 아이들을 가르치는 데에 쏟아져야 한다고 권한다.
③ 신의 전능함에 대한 강조는 윌리엄의 글에서 훨씬 더 많이 표명된다.
④ 자신을 놀라게 했던 것은 체포된 사람들 중 많은 이들이 전과가 없다는 것이었다고 그가 말했다.

07 정답 ④

정답해설

④ 출제 포인트: 관계대명사 what vs. that

해당 문장에서 관계대명사 'what'은 'to do'의 목적어에 해당하며 앞에 선행사가 없으므로 옳게 사용되었다.

오답해설

① 출제 포인트: 부사 vs. 형용사

해당 문장에서 'are'는 불완전자동사이므로 주격 보어가 필요하다. 따라서 부사 'proudly'를 형용사 'proud'로 수정해야 한다.

② 출제 포인트: 타동사구[완전타동사+목적어+전치사+목적어]

'prevent'는 완전타동사로 「prevent+목적어[명사]」와 「prevent+목적어[명사]+from+목적어[명사/동명사]」의 구조를 가진다. 해당 문장은 「prevent+목적어[명사]+to+동사원형」을 사용하였으므로 틀린 문장이다. 따라서 'to arise'를 'from arising'으로 수정해야 한다.

③ 출제 포인트: 등위접속사의 병렬구조

해당 문장은 등위접속사 'and'를 통해 'A, B, C, and D'의 병렬구조를 이루고 있으며 A, B, D는 모두 「현재분사+목적어」이다. 따라서 C의 형태인 'to elect "snap course"'를 'electing "snap courses"'로 수정해야 한다.

해석

우리는 비상사태에 대응하는 우리의 능력을 다소 자랑스러워한다. 그래서 비상사태가 생기는 것을 막기 위해 계획을 세우거나 예방조치를 취하지 않는다. 다른 사람들이 수강하는 전통적이고 관례적인 과목들을 택하고, 가장 저항이 적은 방향을 따라가고, '쉬운 과정들'을 선택하고, 그리고 대세에 따르면서 학창 시절을 빈둥거리며 보내기가 너무 쉽다. "나는 먼저 교육을 받고 스스로를 발전시킬 것이고, 그런 후에 나는 평생의 일로 하기에 딱 맞는 것을 더 잘 알게 될 거야."라는 태도를 가지기가 너무 쉽다.

어휘

be proud of ~을 자랑스러워하다
conventional 관습적인, 관례적인
life work 평생의 일
precaution 예방조치
snap 쉬운, 수월한

오답률 TOP 3
08 정답 ②

정답해설

주어진 문장에서 언급된 'new, better and cheaper tools(새롭고 더 나은 더 저렴한 수단들)'를 (B)의 'One of these tools(이러한 수단들 중 하나)'가 가리키고 있으므로, 주어진 문장 이후에 (B)가 연결되는 것이 알맞다. (B)에서는 "~ can offer firm evidence that a disease transmitted from parent to child is linked to one or more genes(부모로부터 아이에게 전달된 질병은 하나 또는 그 이상의 유전자와 연결되어 있다는 확실한 증거를 제공할 수 있다)."라고 '유전자 지도 분석의 기능'에 대해 설명하고 있으므로, 이후에는 'also(또한)'를 이용해 유전자 지도의 다른 기능을 추가적으로 설명하고 있는 (A)가 이어져야 한다. 이후에는 인과관계를 나타내는 'Therefore'를 활용해 '(B) – (A)'에서 서술한 유전자 분석에 따른 활용되는 분야를 서술하고 있는 (C)가 이어지는 것이 자연스럽다. 따라서 정답은 '② (B) – (A) – (C)'이다.

오답해설

①, ④ (A), (B), (C) 중 '유전자 지도'에 대해 최초로 언급되는 문장이 (B)에 존재하므로, 주어진 문장 이후에는 (B)가 이어지는 것이 자연스럽다.

해석

Human Genome Project(HGP)의 주요 목표들 중에 새로운 유전자를 발견하고 그것들의 기능을 이해할 수 있는 새롭고 더 나은 그리고 더 저렴한 수단을 개발하는 것이 있었다.

(B) 이러한 수단들 중 하나가 유전자 지도 분석이다. 연결 지도 분석이라고도 불리는 유전자 지도 분석은 부모로부터 아이에게 전달된 질병이 하나 또는 그 이상의 유전자와 연결되어 있다는 확실한 증거를 제공할 수 있다.

(A) 지도 분석은 또한 어느 염색체가 그 유전자를 포함하고 있는지, 그리고 정확히 그 염색체의 어느 곳에 그 유전자가 있는지에 대한 단서를 제공한다.

(C) 그러므로, 유전자 지도는 낭포성 섬유증과 듀시엔형 근이영양증과 같은 상대적으로 희귀한 단일 유전자 유전병들을 유발하는 유전자를 알아내기 위해 성공적으로 사용되어왔다.

어휘

identify 발견하다, 확인하다
chromosome 염색체
transmit 전송하다, 전달하다, 전염시키다
relatively 상대적으로
inherited 유전의

오답률 TOP 1

09 정답 ②

정답해설

(A) 본문 첫 문장 "performance feedback can take a number of forms(수행 피드백은 수많은 형태를 띨 수 있다)"를 통해 '수행 피드백의 다양한 형태'에 대해 설명할 것이라는 것을 유추할 수 있고, 이후 '2주 또는 1달 간격의 1대1 미팅', '일간 또는 주간 보고서', 또는 '프로젝트 일정에 기반을 둔 피드백' 등 여러 가지 피드백 유형에 대해 언급하고 있다. 다양한 유형 중 한 가지를 선택한다는 의미가 되어야 하므로, (A)에 가장 적절한 것은 '선택, 대안'을 나타낼 수 있는 'Alternatively(그 대신에)'이다.

(B) 이전 문장 "It's very easy in our busy work lives to let things slip and keep postponing meetings(우리의 바쁜 업무 생활에서 일정이 슬며시 지나가게 하고 계속해서 미팅을 미루는 것은 매우 쉽다)."에서는 '미팅을 거르거나 미루는 것'에 대해 언급하고 있으며, (B) 문장에서는 'Keeping a regular meeting, ~'을 통해 '규칙적으로 미팅을 하는 것'에 대해 언급하고 있으므로, 전후 관계가 '역접' 관계임을 알 수 있다. 따라서 (B)에 가장 적절한 것은 '역접, 대조'를 나타내는 'however(그러나)'이다.

따라서 정답은 '② Alternatively(그 대신에) - however(그러나)'이다.

오답해설

③ (A) 'Additionally(게다가)'는 앞서 언급된 내용에 대한 '부가적인 정보를 첨가'할 때 사용되며, (A) 이후 문장이 '추가'가 아닌 '선택'을 나타내는 'Or(또는)'로 연결되는 것으로 보아, (A)에는 'Additionally'보다 'Alternatively'가 문맥상 더 자연스럽다는 것을 알 수 있다. 또한 (B)의 'in a word(한 마디로)'는 앞서 언급된 내용을 '재서술, 요약'할 때 사용되므로 빈칸에 적절하지 않다.

나머지 보기는 문맥상 어색하므로 오답이다.

해석

당신의 팀이 일을 하는 방식과 당신의 리더십 스타일, 당신의 팀 구성원들과의 직접적인 관계에 따라, 수행 피드백은 수많은 형태를 띨 수 있다. 당신은 2주 또는 한 달 간격의 1대1 미팅을 선택할 수도 있다. (A) 그 대신에 당신은 팀 구성원들의 일간 또는 주간 보고서에 응답을 하는 것을 통해 피드백을 제공하도록 선택할 수도 있다. 또는, 만약 당신의 팀이 프로젝트에 기반을 두고 있다면, 각각의 프로젝트 건이 달성되고 난 후 평가 미팅 또는 보고서 일정을 잡는 것이 아마 더 타당할 것이다. 당신이 어떠한 형태를 선택하든 가장 중요한 것은 정기적인 일정을 세우고 그것을 고수하는 것이다. 우리의 바쁜 업무 생활에서 일정이 슬며시 지나가게 하고 계속해서 미팅을 미루는 것은 매우 쉽다. (B) 그러나 정기적인 미팅을 유지하는 것은 당신이 순조롭게 나아가도록 할 것이며, 당신이 계속 유용한 피드백을 제공하도록 할 뿐만 아니라, 당신이 그들의 성과와 발전을 지원하는 것에 도움이 되는 것을 진지하게 생각한다는 메시지를 당신의 팀에게 전할 것이다.

① 그에 따라 - 게다가
② 그 대신에 - 그러나
③ 게다가 - 한 마디로
④ 결과적으로 - 따라서

어휘

fortnightly 2주일마다, 격주로
milestone 중요한 시점[단계]
postpone 미루다, 연기하다
make sense 타당하다, 말이 되다
commitment 약속, 의무, 책임

---

10 정답 ③

정답해설

해당 지문은 '색 차별주의(Colorism)'에 대한 내용이다. 본문 초반에서 '노예제가 있을 당시, 흑인들 중 야외에서 노동을 하는 어두운 피부를 지닌 흑인들은 하층 계급으로 여겨졌고, 그렇지 않은 상대적으로 밝은 피부를 지닌 흑인들은 엘리트 계급으로 여겨졌다'라고 언급하며, 노예제가 유효할 당시에도 흑인들 사이에 피부색에 따른 계층 분리가 이루어졌다고 설명하고 있다. '흑인'이라는 특정 인종은 뒤에서 언급되어 유추할 수 있을 뿐 본문의 이 부분에서는 '노예'라고만 서술하며 계급제 사회에 대한 일반론을 이야기하고 있다. 이후, 노예제 폐지 이후에도 '밝은 피부를 가진 흑인들이 상류층을 구성했으며, 어두운 피부를 가진 흑인들이 얻을 수 없는 특혜를 누렸다'라는 것을 제시한 뒤, 심지어 '갈색 종이봉투' 테스트를 거쳐 '종이봉투보다 어두운 피부를 지닌 흑인들은 사교계에 받아들여지지 않았다'라는 것을 언급하며 같은 흑인들 사이에서도 피부색에 따른 차별이 존재했다는 것을 설명하고 있다. 따라서 글의 주제로 가장 적절한 것은 '③ Discrimination from members of the same race(동일 인종 구성원들에게 받는 차별)'이다.

오답해설

① 본문에서 언급되지 않는 내용이므로 오답이다.
② 본문에서 언급되는 '상류층'은 '흑인 사회의 상류층'을 의미하며, 전체 미국인의 상류층에 대한 내용은 아니므로 오답이다.
④ 본문은 '흑인들 간 피부색에 따른 차별'에 대해 설명하고 있으며, 백인과 흑인의 갈등은 언급되지 않으므로 오답이다.

해석

많은 노예들이 야외에서 노동을 함에 따라 햇볕에 타게 되었던 반면, 특혜를 받은 사람들은 야외 노동을 하지 않았기 때문에 더 밝은 피부색을 지니게 되었다. 따라서 어두운 피부는 하층 계급과 관련되고 밝은 피부는 엘리트층과 관련된 것이 되었다. 색 차별주의는 미국에서 노예제가 종식된 후에도 사라지지 않았다. 미국 흑인 사회에서 밝은 피부를 지닌 사람들은 더 어두운 피부색을 지닌 흑인들에게는 금지되었던 고용 기회가 주어졌다. 이것이 흑인 사회에서 상류층 가족이 대부분 밝은 피부였던 이유이다. 머지않아 밝은 피부와 특혜가 흑인 공동체에서 연관을 가지게 되었다. 상류층의 흑인들은 동료 흑인들이 사교계에 포함될 정도로 피부색이 밝은지 알아보기 위해 일상적으로 갈색 종이봉투 테스트를 실시했다. "종이봉투를 당신의 피부 가까이에 들고 있을 것이다. 그리고 만약 당신이 종이봉투보다 더 어둡다면, 당신은 받아들여지지 않을 것이다"라고 "Don't Play in the Sun: One Woman's Journey Through the Color Complex."의 저자 Marita Golden이 설명했다.

① 미국 노예제의 역사
② 상류층 미국인에게 주어진 특혜들
③ 동일 인종 구성원들에게 받는 차별
④ 흑인과 백인 사이의 갈등

어휘

privileged 특권[특전]을 가진
colorism 색 차별주의
upper-crust 상류층의
administer 시행하다, 실시하다
admit 받아들이다, 가입[입학]을 허락하다
complexion 피부색, 안색
off-limits 출입[사용] 금지의
routinely 일상적으로
social circle 사교계

결국엔 성정혜 영어 하프모의고사
기적사 DAY 43

| 01 | ③ | 02 | ① | 03 | ② | 04 | ③ | 05 | ④ |
| 06 | ② | 07 | ② | 08 | ① | 09 | ② | 10 | ④ |

오답률 TOP 2

01 정답 ③

정답해설

주어진 빈칸은 문맥상 '추측하다'가 적절하므로 ③ surmise가 정답이다.

해석

그러나, 그녀는 그의 이름에 근거하여 "발포자의 국적이 스페인계 라틴 사람처럼 보인다[들린다]"라고 **추측하는** 것을 선택했다.
① 간섭하다, 방해하다, 지장을 주다
② 인수하다
③ 추측하다, 짐작하다
④ 유혹하다

어휘

interfere 간섭하다, 방해하다, 지장을 주다
acquire 인수하다
surmise 추측하다, 짐작하다
entice 유혹하다

02 정답 ①

정답해설

밑줄 친 단어는 문맥상 '폐지하다'로 사용되었고, 유의어가 아닌 것은 ① sniff다.

해석

거의 5년간 의료 장비 세금을 **폐지하고** 교체하려는 운동은 화요일에 최고조에 달했다.
① 코를 킁킁거리다
② 폐지하다
③ 폐지하다
④ 무효로 하다

어휘

sniff 코를 킁킁거리다.
revoke 폐지하다
abolish 폐지하다
annul 무효로 하다

오답률 TOP 3

03 정답 ②

정답해설

밑줄 친 단어는 문맥상 '대담한, 용맹한'의 의미로 사용되었고, 유의어로는 ② valiant가 적절하다.

해석

하지만 저것은 그날 밤 Kennedy가 그야말로 **대담했던** 농담을 하는 것을 막지 않았다.
① 경멸하는
② 용맹한

③ 서두르는
④ 무서운

어휘

scornful 경멸하는
hurry 서두르는
valiant 용맹한
terrifying 무서운

04 정답 ③

정답해설

Brian은 교환학생 프로그램에 지원할지에 대한 고민을 Amy에게 이야기한다. Amy는 교환학생 프로그램이 일생일대의 기회라고 하는 사람들의 말을 들었다고 말해 준다. Brian은 교환학생 프로그램의 장점의 이면에는 포기해야 할 것들도 있다며 답변한다. Amy는 선택에는 항상 책임이 따른다며 너무 많이 생각하지 말고 '원하는 대로(to one's heart's content)' 결정하라고 조언한다. Brian은 수긍하며 교환학생 프로그램에 지원해보겠다고 한다.

오답해설

① Amy가 고민하는 Brian에게 교환학생 프로그램에 참여할지를 '남몰래(under the table)' 결정하라고 추천하는 것은 문맥상 어색하다.
② 교환학생 프로그램 지원 여부를 고민하는 Brian에게 Amy가 '예기치 못하게(out of the blue sky)' 결정하라고 하는 것은 적절하지 않다.
④ Brian이 교환학생 프로그램에 지원할지 말지를 고민하는 상황에서 '목소리를 높여(at the top of one's lungs)' 결정하는 것을 추천한다는 말은 대화의 흐름상 부자연스럽다.

해석

Amy: 너 근심이 가득해 보여. 무슨 일이야?
Brian: 나 머리가 복잡해. 교환학생 프로그램에 지원할지 말지 결정해야 해.
Amy: 나도 프로그램에 대해 들어봤어. 사람들이 해외에 살면서 학교에 다녀 보는 것이 일생일대의 기회라고 하던데.
Brian: 응, 그게 가장 큰 장점이지. 근데 내가 포기해야 할 것들도 있어.
Amy: 결정을 내리는 데에는 항상 책임이 따라. 근데 너무 많은 생각하지 마. 난 네가 원하는 대로 결정하는 것을 추천해.
Brian: 네 말이 맞아. 내 길이 분명해진 것 같아. 도전해 봐야겠다.
① 남몰래
② 예기치 못하게
③ 원하는 대로
④ 목소리를 높여

어휘

anxiety 근심
once-in-a-lifetime 일생일대의
abroad 해외에
responsibility 책임
path 길
exchange student 교환학생
attend 다니다
accompany 수반하다
recommend 추천하다
under the table 남몰래
out of the blue sky 예기치 못하게
to one's heart's content 원하는 대로, 흡족하게
at the top of one's lungs 목소리를 높여

오답률 TOP 1

05 정답 ④

정답해설

④ 출제 포인트: 완전타동사+목적어[to부정사 vs. 동명사]/to부정사의 태
'need'는 완전타동사의 경우 목적어로 to부정사를 가지며 이때 to부정사가 수동태인 경우 동명사로 바꾸어 사용할 수 있다. 해당 문장은 'need'의 과거시제인 'needed'를 사용하였고 목적어로 능동형 to부정사를 사용하였으나 주어진 해석 '상담받는 것'과 일치하지 않으므로 수동형 to부정사 또는 동명사로 수정해야 한다. 따라서 'to counsel'을 'to be counselled' 또는 'counselling'으로 수정하는 것이 옳다. 또한 주어진 우리말 표현에 따라 'his'대신 'his own'으로 표현할 수 있다.

오답해설

① 출제 포인트: blow의 문장구조
해당 문장에서 'blowing'은 완전타동사 'blow'의 현재분사이며 「blow+부사+목적어」의 구조를 가진다. 이때 「blow+목적어+부사」로 바꾸어 사용할 수 있다.

② 출제 포인트: take의 관용표현(It+takes+목적어+시간+to부정사)
「It takes+목적어+시간+to+동사원형」은 '~가 ~하는 데 시간이 걸리다'를 뜻하며 이때 목적어가 주어 자리로 이동할 경우 「주어[목적어] + take[수일치/시제반영] + 시간 + to + 동사원형」의 구조를 가진다. 해당 문장은 「주어[목적어]+take[수일치/시제반영] + 시간 + to + 동사원형」을 사용하였으므로 옳은 문장이다. 또한 'fall on deaf ear'는 '무시당하다'의 의미로 사용되었다.
※ fall on deaf ears
1. 무시하다
2. 무시당하다
3. 들은 체 만 체하다

③ 출제 포인트: 등위접속사의 병렬구조
주격 보어로 쓰인 형용사 'easy'와 'cheap'이 'neither A nor B'를 통해 병렬구조를 이루고 있다.

06 정답 ②

정답해설

② 출제 포인트: 강조 부사
해당 문장에서 'even'은 비교급 강조 부사로 비교급 형용사 'greater'를 수식하고 있다.

오답해설

① 출제 포인트: The+비교급, the+비교급
'The+비교급 ~, the+비교급 ~'은 수식하는 대상과 분리해서 사용할 수 없다. 해당 문장은 'The+비교급 ~, the+비교급 ~'을 사용하였으나 'the more he will need to be handsome'에서 'the more'와 수식하는 대상 'handsome'을 분리해서 사용하였으므로 틀린 문장이다. 따라서 'the more he will need to be handsome'을 'the more handsome he will need to be'로 수정해야 한다.

③ 출제 포인트: 명사절을 이끄는 접속사
완전타동사 'understand'의 목적어로 쓰인 절의 형태가 완전하므로 관계대명사 'what'을 접속사 'that'으로 수정해야 한다.

④ 출제 포인트: 완전타동사[주장/요구/명령/제안] + 목적어[that+주어+(should)+동사원형]
'propose'의 목적어로 'that+절'이 오는 경우 「that+주어+(should)+동사원형 ~」의 구조를 가진다. 해당 문장은 'propose'의 목적어로 'that+절'을 사용하였으나 현재시제동사 'sets'를 사용하였으므로 틀린 문장이다. 따라서 'sets'를 'set' 또는 'should set'으로 수정해야 한다.

해석

① 당신이 더 아름다워질수록, 그는 더 잘생겨질 필요가 있을 것이다.
② 1960년대에 역사 연구에 대한 강조에 있어 훨씬 더 큰 변화가 있었다.
③ 당신은 그 신호가 실제로 나가는지를 보기 위해 이것을 시험할 방법이 없다는 것을 이해한다.
④ 연설에서 그녀는 유엔이 환경을 위해 비상센터를 설립해야 한다고 제안했다.

07 정답 ②

정답해설

② 출제 포인트: help+목적어+목적격 보어[to부정사/원형부정사]
준사역동사 'help'의 목적격 보어로 동사원형 'cut'을 옳게 사용하였다. 또한 'cut down on'은 관용표현으로 '~을 줄이다'를 뜻한다.

오답해설

① 출제 포인트: 부사 vs. 형용사
'from A to B'의 구조이므로 'drink'는 동사가 아니며 'containers'와 결합하여 명사구를 이루는 명사이다. 따라서 명사구 'drink containers'를 수식해야 하므로 부사 'disposably'를 형용사 'disposable'로 수정해야 한다.

③ 출제 포인트: 등위접속사의 병렬구조
'has'의 목적어가 등위접속사 'and'를 통해 병렬구조를 이루고 있으므로 과거분사 'handled'를 명사 'a handle' 또는 'handles'로 수정해야 한다.

④ 출제 포인트: 수동태 관용표현(be made from vs. be made of)
'be made of'는 '~로부터 만들어지다(성분 변화 없음)'을 뜻하며 'be made from'은 '~로부터 만들어지다(성분 변화 있음)'을 뜻한다. 해당 문장의 경우 재활용된 플라스틱병에서 천이 만들어지는 것이므로 성분 변화가 있음을 알 수 있다. 따라서 전치사 'of'를 'from'으로 수정해야 한다.

해석

6학년 때, 저는 많은 급우들이 종이로 된 점심 도시락 가방을 가지고 다닌다는 것을 알게 되었습니다. 저는 샌드위치 포장지에서 일회용 음료 용기에 이르기까지, 보통의 학생들이 매년 65파운드의 점심 도시락 가방 쓰레기를 만들어 낸다는 것을 발견했습니다. 아이들이 점심 도시락 가방 쓰레기를 줄이는 것을 돕기 위해, 저는 재사용할 수 있는 점심 도시락 가방을 발명했는데, 지금 그 가방을 제 웹 사이트에서 판매하고 있습니다. 그것에는 손잡이와 앞주머니가 달려 있습니다. 그리고 그 가방의 천은 부분적으로 재활용된 플라스틱병으로 만들어집니다.

어휘

wrapper 포장지
drink container 음료 용기
cut down on ~을 줄이다
disposable 일회용의
generate 만들어내다, 발생시키다
reusable 재사용할 수 있는

08 정답 ①

정답해설

본문 첫 문장에서 "Concept maps are a visual illustration of concepts and ideas as a complex structure comprised of boxes or circles that are connected with linking words or phrases arranged around a central concept(개념 지도는 중심 개념 주변에 배치된 연결 단어 또는 구절들로 이어져 있는 사각형 또는 원형 칸으로 구성된 복합적 구조의 개념과 생각의 시각적 도해이다)."라고 '개념 지도의 정의'에 대해 언급한 후, 일반적인 개념 지도의 구조에 대해 설명하고 있으며, 본문 중후반에서는 개념 지도가 '알고 있는 것과 배운 것들을 확인하는 적절한 기법'이며, 그 외에도 '질서 정연한 생각과 아이디어 묘사, 아는 것과 모르는 것을 분석, 지식 확장' 등에서 도움이 된다고 언급하고 있으므로, '개념 지도의 기능'에 대해 설명하고 있다는 것을 알 수 있다. 따라서 글의 주제로 가장 적절한 것은 '① definition and functions of concept maps(개념 지도의 정의와 기능)'이다.

오답해설

② 본문에 언급되지 않는 내용이므로 오답이다.
③ 개념 지도의 단점은 본문에서 다루지 않는다.
④ 개념 지도 제작 기술을 향상시키는 법은 본문에 언급되지 않는다.

해석

개념 지도는 중심 개념 주변에 배치된 연결 단어 또는 구절들로 이어져 있는 사각형 또는 원형 칸으로 구성된 복합적 구조의 개념과 생각의 시각적 도해이다. 보통 계층적인 구조로 이루어진 사각형과 원은 상호 관계를 더 잘 정의하기 위해 서술적인 표현들로 연결된 주제와 하위 주제를 나타낸다. 수년간 개념도 제작은 사람들이 특정 분야에 대해 그들이 무엇을 알고 있고 무엇을 배웠는지 확인하도록 해주는 매우 적절한 기법이라는 것을 스스로 증명했다. 이 외에도, 그것은 사람들이 자신들의 생각과 아이디어를 질서 정연하게 묘사하고, 그들이 아는 것과 모르는 것을 분석하고, 결과적으로 그들의 현재 지식을 확장시키는 데 도움을 주었다.
① 개념 지도의 정의와 기능
② 개념 지도 제작의 역사와 발전
③ 개념 지도의 장점과 단점
④ 개념 지도 제작 기술과 그것들을 향상시키는 법

어휘

illustration 도해, 삽화
hierarchical 계층적인
descriptive 기술적인, 서술적인
mutual 상호의, 서로의
acknowledge 인지하다, 확인하다, 인정하다
discipline 지식 분야, 학과목
consequently 결과적으로
existing 기존의
arrange 배열시키다
represent 표현하다, 나타내다
define 정의하다
applicable 적절한
portray 묘사하다
broaden 넓히다, 확장시키다

09 정답 ②

정답해설

본문에서 필자는 '수행 피드백(performance feedback)'이 금전적 보상 또는 선물보다 더 동기부여가 될 수 있다고 설명하며 '수행 피드백의 중요성'에 대해 언급한 후, "Performance feedback lets your employees know they're valued and contributes to building confidence in newer employees(수행 피드백은 당신의 직원들이 존중받고 있다는 것을 알게 해주고, 신입직원들이 자신감을 쌓는데 기여한다)."를 통해 '새로운 직원들에게 수행 피드백이 미치는 긍정적 영향'을 제시하고 있다. 이후에는 '최우수 직원들(top performer)'에 대해 언급하며, 마지막 문장에서 "But they are working hard and their efforts shouldn't be taken for granted(그러나 그들은 열심히 일하고 있고 그들의 노력이 당연시되어서는 안 된다)."를 통해 '최우수 직원들 또한 수행 피드백이 필요하다'라는 점을 시사하고 있다. 따라서 어떠한 직원이든 수행 피드백이 필요하다는 점을 나타내고 있으므로 필자의 주장으로 가장 적절한 것은 '② Performance feedback is necessary for every employee(수행 피드백은 모든 직원들에게 필요하다).'이다.

오답해설

① 본문에 언급되지 않는 내용이므로 오답이다.
③ 본문에 언급되지 않는 내용이므로 오답이다.
④ '최우수 직원들은 수행 피드백이 필요하다'라는 내용이 본문 후반에 언급되나, 본문에서는 어떠한 직원에게 수행 피드백이 가장 필요한지 제시하고 있지 않으므로, 필자의 주장으로 적절하지 않다.

해석

흔한 오해는 직장에서의 동기부여가 주로 금전적 보상에 기초한다는 것이다. 직원이 잘할 때마다 급여를 인상해주는 것이 항상 가능한 것은 아니며, 놀랍게도 그것이 가장 강력한 인센티브가 아닐 수도 있다. 한 연구는 직원들의 83%가 기여에 대한 인정이 보상과 선물보다 더 만족스럽다고 생각한다는 것을 밝혔다. 다른 88%는 상사로부터의 칭찬이 매우, 또는 극도로 동기부여가 된다고 생각했다. 수행 피드백은 당신의 직원들이 존중받고 있다는 것을 알게 해주고, 신입직원들이 자신감을 쌓는데 기여한다. 또한, 최우수 직원들을 잊지 말자. 많은 관리자들이 피드백을 성과를 향상시키는 것을 도와주는 도구로 생각하고 최우수 직원들은 도움이 필요하지 않다고 생각하기 때문에, 피드백에 관하여 최우수 직원들을 등한시하는 경향이 있다. 그러나 그들은 열심히 일하고 있고 그들의 노력이 당연시되어서는 안 된다.
① 수행 피드백은 규칙적으로 제공되어야 한다.
② 수행 피드백은 모든 직원들에게 필요하다.
③ 관리자들은 효과적으로 수행 피드백을 제공하는 방법을 배워야 한다.
④ 최우수 직원들은 다른 어떤 직원보다 더 수행 피드백이 필요하다.

어휘

misconception 오해
reveal 밝히다
contribution 기여, 공헌
contribute to …에 기여하다, 공헌하다
neglect 등한시하다, 무시하다
when it comes to …에 관한 한
give a raise 급여를 인상하다
recognition 인정, 표창
fulfilling 성취감을 주는
take A for granted A를 당연시하다

10 정답 ④

정답해설

해당 지문은 미국의 흑인 시인 'Langston Hughes'에 관한 글이다. 빈칸 이후 문장 "then Langston Hughes stands at the apex of literary relevance among black people(그렇다면 Langston Hughes는 흑인 가운데 문학 관련 분야의 정점에 서게 된다)."로 보아, 빈칸에는 그의 문학적 지위를 평가하는 평가 기준에 대해 설명하는 내용이 들어가는 것이 적절하다. 본문 초반에서 '비평가들로부터 좋은 평가를 받지 못했음에도 불구하고, 글쓰기와 강연만으로도 생계를 유지할 수 있었다'고 언급하며 그 이유로 "Part of the reason he was able to do this was the phenomenal acceptance and love he received from average black people(그가 그렇게 할 수 있었던 이유 중 일부는 평범한 흑인들로부터 받았던 놀랄만한 수용과 사랑이었다)."을 제시하며 '일반 대중들 사이에서의 높은 인기'에 대해 설명한다. 즉, '비평가들의 평가가 기준이 아니라, 일반 대중들의 반응이 기준이라면 그의 문학적 지위는 정점에 서게 된다'라는 내용이 되어야 문맥상 자연스러우므로, 빈칸에 가장 적절한 보기는 '④ the weight of public response is any gauge(대중의 반응의 무게가 기준이다)'이다.

오답해설

① 그의 미발표 작품에 대해서는 본문에 언급되지 않는다.
② 그의 사생활에 대한 평가는 본문에서 다루지 않는 부분이다.
③ 그가 살았던 시대에도 그는 '대중들에게는' 높이 평가를 받고 있었으며, 본문 어디에도 그가 활동한 시기로 인해 문학적 지위가 낮았다고 언급되지 않고 있으므로 빈칸에 부적절하다.

해석

비록 Hughes가 흑인 비평가와 백인 비평가 모두와 문제가 있었지만, 그는 글쓰기와 공공 강연을 통해서만 생계를 유지했던 최초의 흑인계 미국인이었다. 그가 그렇게 할 수 있었던 이유 중 일부는 평범한 흑인들로부터 받았던 놀랄만한 수용과 사랑이었다. 1970년 *Black World*의 평론가는 "작가의 순위를 결정하는 특권을 가진 사람들은 그를 결코 높게 평가한 적이 없으나, 만일 <u>대중의 반응의 무게가 기준이라면</u>, Langston Hughes는 흑인 가운데 문학 관련 분야의 정점에 서게 된다. 그가 '우리는 내면에 신체적 정신적 강인함을 지닌 거대한 저장소를 지니고 있다'라는 것을 인식했고, 이를 사람들에게 보여주기 위해 그의 예술적 재능을 사용했기 때문에 정확하게 그 시인은 그의 사람들의 기억 속에서 그러한 지위를 지니고 있는 것이다"라고 언급했다.
① 그의 미발표 작품이 포함된다
② 그의 사생활이 덜 논란을 일으킨다
③ 그가 포스트모던 세계에 살고 있다
④ 대중의 반응의 무게가 기준이다

어휘

earn one's living 생계를 꾸리다
acceptance 수용, 받아들임
apex 꼭대기, 정점
precisely 바로, 꼭, 정확히
artistry 예술적 재능
count 넣어 생각하다, 포함시키다
gauge (평가, 판단 등의) 기준
phenomenal 놀라운, 경이로운
prerogative 특권
relevance 관련(성)
reservoir 저장소
reflect 반영하다
controversial 논란을 일으키는

기적사 DAY 44

| 01 | ② | 02 | ③ | 03 | ③ | 04 | ④ | 05 | ③ |
| 06 | ② | 07 | ④ | 08 | ④ | 09 | ③ | 10 | ③ |

01 정답 ②

정답해설

'innocent'는 '순진한'을 뜻한다. 따라서 가장 가까운 표현은 ② ingenuous이다.

해석

Netanyahu, 그리고 심지어 몇몇 **순진한** 전문가들(학자들)은, 어떻게 이스라엘과 미국이 더 가까운 적이 없었는지에 대해 떠벌리고 있다.
① 향상된, 강화한
② 순진한, 천진난만한
③ 논란의 여지가 있는, 미해결된
④ 조롱하는, 비웃는

어휘

pundit 권위자, 전문가 brag 자랑하다
enhanced 향상된, 강화한
ingenuous 순진한, 천진난만한
problematic 논란의 여지가 있는, 미해결된
sneering 조롱하는, 비웃는

02 정답 ③

정답해설

밑줄 친 단어는 문맥상 '조심성 있는'으로 사용되었고, ③ tremendous가 의미가 가장 먼 단어이다.

해석

Bieber은 요를 덮고 그 집을 몰래 빠져나가려고 시도했지만, **조심성 있는** 사진사들은 현장에서 그를 잡았다.
① 조심하는, 신중한
② 신중한
③ 거대한
④ 신중한, 검약하는

어휘

sneak out 몰래 빠져나가다
vigilant 조금도 방심하지 않는, 조심성 있는
cautious 조심하는, 신중한   circumspect 신중한
tremendous 거대한   prudent 신중한, 검약하는

오답률 TOP 3

03 정답 ③

정답해설

밑줄 친 단어는 문맥상 '다정한'으로 사용되었고, 유의어로는 ③ genial이 적절하다.

해석

Romney에 대해 말하자면, Johnson은 이전 메사추세츠의 주지사를 "훌륭한", "**다정한**" 그리고 "굉장히 자비롭다"라고 묘사한다.

① 개인적인
② 조직적인, 꼼꼼한, 공들인
③ 상냥한, 다정한
④ 무기력한

어휘

cordial 다정한   personal 개인적인
methodical 조직적인, 꼼꼼한, 공들인
genial 상냥한, 다정한   gutless 무기력한

04 정답 ④

정답해설

A와 B는 인턴직 공지를 보며 대화를 나눈다. B는 A에게 취직해서 실무에 뛰어들기 전에 실전 경험을 쌓고 싶어 인턴직에 지원할지 고민 중이라고 이야기한다. A는 최근에 B가 아주 바빠 보였다며 "너무 과욕을 보이지(bite off more than one can chew)말라"고 말한다.

오답해설

① 인턴직에 지원할까 고민하는 B에게 A는 너무 바빠 보인다고 말하는 상황에서 "임기응변으로 대처하지(play it by ear) 마"라고 답변하는 것은 부적절하다.
② A가 B에게 최근에 바빠 보였다며 자신을 위한 시간이 없을 거라고 얘기하는 대화에서 "어떻게든 견뎌내지(bite the bullet) 마"라고 하는 것은 맥락상 부자연스럽다.
③ 인턴직을 해보고 싶다는 B에게 A가 "나쁜 일에서부터 멀어지지(keep your nose clean) 마"라고 답변하는 것은 문맥상 어색하다.

해석

A: 너 뭐 보고 있어?
B: 나 인턴십 공지를 보고 있어.
A: 인턴직에 지원할 생각이야?
B: 응, 취직하기 전에 실전 경험을 쌓고 진짜 일에 뛰어들고 싶어.
A: 진짜? 너 요새 되게 바빠 보이던데. <u>과욕을 보이지</u> 마. 너 자신을 위한 시간이 없을 거야.
B: 이게 벅찰 수도 있다는 걸 아는데 내 버킷리스트에 있어.
① 임기응변으로 대처하다
② 어떻게든 견뎌내다
③ 나쁜 일에서부터 멀어지다
④ 과욕을 보인다

어휘

apply 지원하다   hands-on experience 실전 경험
overwhelming 압도적인, 대항할 수 없는
play it by ear 임기응변으로 대처하다
bite the bullet 어떻게든 견뎌내다
keep one's nose clean 나쁜 일에서부터 멀어지다
bite off more than one can chew 과욕을 보인다

05 정답 ③

정답해설

③ **출제 포인트: take의 관용표현(It+takes+목적어+시간+to부정사)**

「It takes+목적어+시간+to+동사원형」은 '~가 ~하는 데 시간이 걸리다'를 뜻한다. 해당 문장은 「It takes+목적어+시간+to+동사원형」을 사용하였으나 'to+동사원형' 자리에 -ing 형태인 'traveling'을 사용하였으므로 틀린 문장이다. 따라서 'traveling'을 'to travel'로 수정해야 한다.

오답해설

① **출제 포인트: 완전타동사+목적어[to부정사 vs. 동명사]**
'regret'은 완전타동사이며 목적어로 동명사가 오는 경우 '~했던 것을 후회하다'를 뜻하며, 목적어로 to부정사가 오는 경우 '~하게 되어 유감이다'를 뜻한다. 해당 문장은 'regret'의 목적어로 동명사를 사용하였으며 주어진 해석 '~했던 것을 후회하다'와 일치하므로 옳은 문장이다.

② **출제 포인트: blow의 문장구조**
해당 문장에서 'blow'의 과거시제인 'blew'는 완전자동사이므로 뒤에 부사 역할을 하는 전치사구 'on his fingers'가 올 수 있다.

④ **출제 포인트: 등위접속사의 병렬구조/주격 관계대명사+be동사 생략**
'형용사+부사구'가 'either A or B'를 통해 병렬구조를 이루고 있다. 이때 'milk' 뒤에는 '주격 관계대명사+be동사'가 생략되어있다.

06 정답 ②

정답해설

② **출제 포인트: 명사절을 이끄는 접속사**
해당 문장에서 'if'는 명사절을 이끄는 접속사로 '~인지'를 뜻하며 해당 명사절은 'wondering'의 목적어 역할을 한다.

오답해설

① **출제 포인트: 완전타동사[주장/요구/명령/제안] + 목적어[that+주어+(should)+동사원형]**
'command'의 목적어로 'that+'절이 오는 경우 「that+주어+(should)+동사원형 ~」의 구조를 가진다. 해당 문장은 'command'의 목적어로 'that+'절을 사용하였으나 과거시제 조동사 'did'를 사용하였으므로 틀린 문장이다. 따라서 'did'를 삭제하거나 'should'로 수정해야 한다.

③ **출제 포인트: 강조 부사**
원급 강조 부사 'quite'가 비교급 부사 'more quickly'를 수식하고 있으므로 틀린 문장이다. 따라서 'quite more quickly'를 'even/much/(by) far/a lot/still more quickly'로 수정해야 한다.

④ **출제 포인트: The+비교급, the+비교급**
'The+비교급 ~, the+비교급 ~'은 양쪽 절에 'the+비교급'을 사용해야 하며 비교급의 품사는 뒤에 오는 절의 구조에 의해 결정된다. 해당 문장은 첫 번째 절에는 'the+비교급'을 사용하였으나 두 번째 절에는 'the+원급'을 사용하였으므로 틀린 문장이다. 따라서 'the generously'를 'the more generously'로 수정해야 하는데 뒤에 오는 절의 구조상 be동사의 주격 보어가 필요하므로 비교급 부사가 아닌 비교급 형용사가 사용되어야 함을 알 수 있다. 그러므로 'the generously'를 'the more generous'로 수정해야 한다.

해석

① 그녀의 어머니는 Jane이 그 소년에게 어떤 돈도 주지 말 것을 즉시 명령했다.
② William은 Jane이 오늘 밤 그와 함께 영화관에 가고 싶어 할까 생각하던 중이었다.
③ 차들이 이 길을 매우 빠르게 내려오고 우리는 꽤 많은 사고들을 보았다.
④ 당신이 다른 사람들에게 더 관대해질수록, 그들은 당신에게 더 관대해지기 쉽다.

오답률 TOP 1

07 정답 ④

정답해설

④ **출제 포인트: 부사 vs. 형용사**
해당 문장에서 'eastward'는 동사 'had followed'를 수식하는 부사로 사용되었다. 'eastward'는 형용사와 부사 둘 다 사용되지만, 형용사로 사용될 때는 한정적 용법으로만 쓰여 주로 명사 앞에서 수식하는 반면 'eastwards'는 부사로만 사용된다.

오답해설

① **출제 포인트: 현재분사 vs. 과거분사**
"arming only with primitive weapons"는 분사구문으로 'arm'은 완전타동사로 쓰여 현재분사인 'arming'을 사용하였으나 뒤에 목적어가 없으며 생략된 주어 'the hunters'와 수동관계이므로 틀린 문장이다. 따라서 'arming'을 과거분사 'armed'로 수정해야 한다.

② **출제 포인트: 주어와 동사의 수일치**
주격 관계대명사절의 동사가 복수형태인 'were'이므로 선행사도 복수형태이어야 한다. 해당 문장에서 'encounter'는 '마주침'의 의미인 명사로 쓰였으므로 선행사 'encounter'를 복수형태인 'encounters'로 수정해야 한다.

③ **출제 포인트: 등위접속사의 병렬구조**
해당 문장은 등위접속사 'and'를 통해 'A, B, and C'의 병렬구조를 이루고 있으며 A와 C는 동사원형이다. 따라서 C의 명사 'cloth'를 동사원형인 'clothe'로 수정해야 한다.

해석

원시적인 무기로만 무장한 사냥꾼들은 화난 매머드의 실제 적수가 되지 못했다. 많은 사람이 이 거대한 동물 중 한 마리를 잡기 위해 필요했던 (그것과의) 마주침에서 아마도 죽거나 심각한 상처를 입었을 것이다. 하지만 한 마리가 쓰러졌을 때 보상은 엄청났다. 한 마리의 매머드만으로도 긴 시간 동안 무리를 먹이고, 입히며, 지탱할 수 있었다. 그 사냥꾼들은 아시아에서부터 지금의 베링해를 가로질러 동쪽으로 매머드와 다른 큰 동물들을 쫓아 이동했다.

어휘

primitive 원시적인, 원초적인
encounter 만남, 직면
bring+목적어+down ~을 쓰러뜨리다
clothe ~에게 옷을 입히다
match 맞수, 호적수
slay 죽이다, 살해하다

08 정답 ④

정답해설

본문은 직업적 영역에서의 '작도(cartography)'에 대해 설명하는 글이다. 본문 초반에서 작도의 정의에 대해 서술한 후, ②에서 타 분야와 연계된 작도의 발전을 언급하고 ③에서는 구체적으로 작도와 관련이 있는 분야를 제시하며 해당 분야들이 통합적으로 분류된다는 것을 설명한 뒤, 마지막으로 '앞서 언급된 통합에도 불구하고 작도는 여전히 중요하고 지도 제작자는 수요가 높다'라고 결론짓는 것이 자연스럽다. ④는 작도에서 필요한 기술을 언급하고 있는데, 작도와 연계된 분야를 설명하고 있는 중간에 해당 내용이 위치하는 것은 문맥상 어색하다. 따라서 정답은 '④ The clear presentation of map data demands particular skills of design and creativity(지도 자료를 분명히 표현해내는 것은 디자인적이고 창의적인 특별한 기술을 요한다).'이다.

오답해설

나머지 보기는 문맥상 자연스러우므로 오답이다.

해석

작도는 지도를 만드는 일이다. ① '지도 제작'과 '작도'라는 용어는 본질적으로 같은 것을 의미한다: 지리학적 정보를 획득하고 그것을 지도로 변환시키는 것. ② 관련된 직종이 새로운 기술과 함께 진화함에 따라 작도도 발전했다. ③ 작도뿐만 아니라 토지 측량, 위성 원격 탐사, 항공 사진술, 지리정보 시스템, 사진 측량, 수로 측량, 그리고 측지학은 때때로 '지리정보학' 또는 '지구과학'으로 분류되기도 한다. ④ **지도 자료를 분명히 표현해내는 것은 디자인적이고 창의적인 특별한 기술을 요한다.** 그러나 지도 제작의 경계와 기술이 변화하고 그것이 응용 지리학의 다른 분야와 통합되었지만, 작도는 공간 데이터의 성공적인 시각화에 있어서 필수적이며, 숙련된 지도 제작자에 대한 수요는 여전히 높다.

어휘

cartography 작도, 지도 제작
geographical 지리학의
occupation 직업
surveying 측량
remote 원격의, 먼
aerial 공중의, 항공의
photogrammetry (항공사진에 의한) 사진 측량[제도]법
hydrography 수로 측량
geomatics 지리정보학[연구]
boundary 경계, 한계
applied 응용의
essential 필수적인, 극히 중요한
spatial 공간의
essentially 본질적으로
allied 관련된, 동종의
evolve 진화하다
satellite 인공위성
sensing 감지, 탐지
geodesy 측지학
geoscience 지구 과학, 지학
integrate 통합시키다
geography 지리학
visualization 시각화, 구체화

오답률 TOP 2
09 정답 ③

정답해설

해당 지문은 피드백 유형 중 하나인 '건설적 비판(Constructive criticism)'에 대해 설명하는 글이다. 주어진 문장은 'When providing this type of feedback, explain exactly what is that you're criticizing and the implications that come from it, and then create a plan to help the employee improve(이러한 유형의 피드백을 제공할 때, 당신이 비판하는 것이 무엇인지, 그것으로 인해 예상되는 결과가 무엇인지 정확히 설명한 후, 그 직원이 개선하도록 도울 수 있는 계획을 세워라).'라고 설명하며 '실제로 건설적 비판을 활용할 경우 유념할 점을 제시하고 있다. 본문의 첫 세 문장은 '건설적 비판의 특징'에 대해 설명하고 있으므로, 구체적인 활용 방법을 설명하는 주어진 문장 이전에 등장하는 것이 문맥상 자연스럽다. 그리고 ③ 이후에서는 주어진 문장에서 언급된 것과 같이 건설적 비판을 활용하는 상황을 구체적인 예시를 들어 설명하고 있으므로, '활용 방법'에 대해 언급한 주어진 문장 이후에 등장하는 것이 자연스럽다. 따라서 주어진 문장이 들어갈 위치로 가장 적절한 것은 ③이다.

오답해설

② 이후 문장에서 "because it offers both a critique and a solution(비판과 해결책을 모두 제시하기 때문에)"이라고 설명하고 있는데, 이에 대해 좀 더 구체적으로 설명하는 내용이 주어진 문장 "explain exactly what is that you're criticizing and the implications that come from it, and then create a plan to help the employee improve(당신이 비판하는 것이 무엇인지, 그것으로 인해 예상되는 결과가 무엇인지 정확히 설명한 후, 그 직원이 개선하도록 도울 수 있는 계획을 세워라)."에서 언급되므로, 주어진 문장이 ②에 들어가는 것은 문맥상 어색하다. 또한 관사 a 사용 후 지시 형용사 this가 오는 게 자연스럽다(a well-rounded approach=this type of feedback). 주장의 요지가 담긴 청유문/명령문

은 아예 문두에 오거나 연속되지 않는 이상 보통 구체적인 예시/사례 바로 앞에 위치한다.
나머지 위치는 문맥상 어색하므로 오답이다.

해석

건설적 비판은 아마도 가장 충분히 활용되지 못하는 개발 수단 중 하나일 것이다. (①) 건설적 비판은 직원들이 개선될 필요가 있는 분야와 그렇게 개선을 하는 것이 중요한 이유를 알 수 있게 도와준다. (②) 그것은 비판과 해결책을 모두 제시하기 때문에 균형 잡힌 접근이다. (③ **이러한 유형의 피드백을 제공할 때, 당신이 비판하는 것이 무엇인지, 그것으로 인해 예상되는 결과가 무엇인지 정확히 설명한 후, 그 직원이 개선하도록 도울 수 있는 계획을 세워라.**) 지속적으로 오타와 문법적 오류가 있는 이메일을 보내는 직원이 있다고 상상해보라. (④) 단순히 그들에게 그것이 문제이고 그것을 그만해야 한다고 말하는 것 대신에, 그 문제의 예상 결과를 설명하라. 그들에게 그것이 문제가 되는 이유에 대한 명확한 예시를 제시하고, 그들의 행동을 교정해야 하는 것이 중요한 이유를 반복하여 말하라. 그들이 개선할 수 있는 방법을 생각해 내도록 도와주고 그들이 개선할 기간을 정해주어라.

어휘

constructive 건설적인
well-rounded (문제·프로그램 따위가) 균형이 잡힌
implication (행동·결정이 초래할 수 있는) 영향/결과
consistently 지속적으로
reiterate 반복하여 말하다, 반복하다
come up with (해답·아이디어 등을) 찾아내다[내놓다]
timeframe (어떤 일에 쓰이는) 시간[기간]
underused 충분히 이용[활용]되지 않는
typo 오타
rectify (잘못된 것을) 바로잡다

10 정답 ③

정답해설

해당 지문은 뉴욕의 할렘에서 일어난 민족적 각성과 흑인 예술 문화의 부흥 시기인 '할렘 르네상스(Harlem Renaissance)'에 대한 내용으로, 주어진 문장은 특히 '문학' 분야에서 당시 작가들이 어떻게 목소리를 내었는지 설명하고 있다. 주어진 문장의 "issues that had evolved out of the social consequences of slavery(노예제의 사회적 결과로 인해 생겨난 문제들)"를 구체적으로 나타내는 표현이 ③이후 문장 "~ the topics of racism, poverty, lack of identity and family structure(인종차별, 빈곤, 정체성 결핍 그리고 가족구조에 대한 주제들)"에서 언급되고 있으므로, 주어진 문장이 들어갈 위치로 가장 알맞은 것은 ③이다.

오답해설

④ 이전의 문장에서 언급되는 '주제(topics)'들이 주어진 문장에서 설명한 '문제(issues)'를 구체적으로 제시하고 있는 구조이므로, 주어진 문장이 ④에 들어가는 것은 문맥상 어색하다.

해석

Harlem Renaissance는 아프리카계 미국인들 공동체 내에서 발생한 예술, 음악, 문학 영역에서의 창의성의 분출로 특징지어지는 미국 역사의 한 기간이다. (①) 뉴욕시의 할렘 내에 집중되었던 Harlem Renaissance는 대략 1918년 제1차 세계대전 종전과 함께 시작되었으며 1930년대 중반까지 지속되었다. (②) 이 시대 동안 할렘은 모든 분야의 아프리카계 미국인 예술가들, 특히 작가들의 영감이자 목표 지점이 되었다. (③ **노예에 대한 서술의 전통에서 나아가, 작가들은 노예제의 사회적 결과로 인해 생겨난 문제들을 탐구하기 시작했다.**) 작가들은 인종차별, 빈곤, 정체성 결핍 그리고 가족구조에 대한 주제들을 다루었다. (④) Langston Hughes의 *Simple* 이야기들은 빈곤을 다루었다. Zora Neale Hurston은 아프리카계 미국인들의 유산과 문화를 찬양했다. Dorothy West는 사회적, 재정적 안전에 대해 서술했다. Richard Wright는 분노, 좌절, 그리고 폭력에 대해 강력하게 서술했다.

어휘

narrative 서술, 기술
consequence 결과
inspiration 영감, 고취
discipline (지식, 학문 등) 분야
address (문제·상황 등에 대해) 고심하다[다루다]
heritage (국가·사회의) 유산
evolve (점진적으로) 발달[진전]하다
era 시대
destination point 목표[목적] 지점

결국엔 성정혜 영어 하프모의고사
기적사 DAY 45

| 01 | ① | 02 | ④ | 03 | ③ | 04 | ③ | 05 | ④ |
| 06 | ② | 07 | ① | 08 | ④ | 09 | ④ | 10 | ④ |

오답률 TOP 3

01 정답 ①

정답해설

주어진 빈칸에는 문맥상 '알맞은'의 의미가 적절하다. 따라서 ① agreeable이 정답이다.

해석

그들은 어떤 일이 일어날 수도 있었는지 회고하면서 황혼기를 보내며 그는 아마 Mubarak에게 **알맞은** 친구가 될 수도 있다.
① 알맞은, 동의할 만한, 상냥한
② 불가사의한, 신비로운
③ 피를 흘리는, 포악한
④ 무용지물인, 무효인

어휘

sunset years 황혼기
uncanny 불가사의한, 신비로운
futile 무용지물인, 무효인
agreeable 알맞은, 동의할 만한, 상냥한
sanguinary 피를 흘리는, 포악한

02 정답 ④

정답해설

밑줄 친 단어는 문맥상 '탐구적인, 캐묻기 좋아하는'으로 사용되었고, 유의어가 아닌 것은 ④ superficial이다.

해석

소크라테스처럼, 거리의 인식론자들은 그들 자신을 전투적인 강연자들이 아니라 **탐구적인** 선생님으로서 이해하려고 한다.
① 분석적인
② 꼬치꼬치 캐묻는, 참견하기 좋아하는, 코가 큰
③ 참견하기 좋아하는
④ 피상적인

어휘

Epistemologist 인식론자
combative 전투적인
nosy 꼬치꼬치 캐묻는
superficial 피상적인
inquisitive 탐구적인, 캐묻기 좋아하는
analytical 분석적인
meddlesome 참견하기 좋아하는

오답률 TOP 2

03 정답 ③

정답해설

밑줄 친 단어는 문맥상 '없애다, 전멸시키다'의 의미이고, 유의어로는 ③ annihilate가 적절하다.

해석

이스라엘은 그들이 발견해온 것의 80%를 파괴해왔고, 나머지를 **없애는** 데에는 단지 며칠이 필요할 뿐이다.
① 폭로하다, 파헤치다
② 발사하다, 내리게 하다
③ 전멸시키다
④ 고수하다

어휘

obliterate 없애다
let off 발사하다, 내리게 하다
stick 고수하다
divulge 폭로하다, 파헤치다
annihilate 전멸시키다

04 정답 ③

정답해설

A는 채식주의자가 되는 것의 이점들에 대해 알고 있는지 질문한다. B는 현대 사회의 사람들이 왜 만성 질환을 흔히 앓는지 알고 있다고 답변한다. 이는 채식주의자가 되는 것의 이점들에 알고 있는지를 묻는 A의 질문에 적절한 답변이 아니다. 또한 의문사가 없는 의문문의 경우 긍정, 부정 여부를 먼저 제시하여야 한다.

오답해설

① A는 B에게 오로라를 본 경험이 있는지 묻자 B는 작년에 캐나다로 여행 갔을 때 본 적이 있다고 답변한다. 이는 자연스러운 흐름의 대화이다.
② A가 내일이 자신이 수년 동안 기대해왔던 날이라고 하자 B는 내일이 뭐가 그렇게 특별한지 묻는 맥락은 적절하다.
④ A는 오늘 너무 피곤해 일을 좀 쉬어야겠다고 하자 B는 너무 열심히 일했다며 가서 쉬라고 답변한다. B의 답변은 문맥상 적합하다.

해석

① A: 너 오로라 본 적 있어?
  B: 응, 작년에 캐나다 갔을 때 한 번 봤어.
② A: 내일이 내가 수년 동안 기대해왔던 날이야.
  B: 내일이 뭐가 그렇게 특별해?
③ A: 너 채식주의자가 되는 것의 이점들에 대해 알아?
  B: 나는 왜 현대 사회의 사람들이 왜 흔히 만성 질병을 앓는지 알아.
④ A: 나 오늘 너무 피곤해서 좀 쉬어야겠어.
  B: 너 너무 열심히 일했어. 가서 좀 쉬어.

어휘

aurora 오로라
vegetarian 채식주의자
chronic disease 만성 질병
exhausted 피곤한, 지친
look forward to ~를 기대하다
suffer from ~을(를) 앓다
contemporary society 현대 사회
time-off 일을 쉰 시간(수)

05 정답 ④

정답해설

④ **출제 포인트: 등위접속사의 병렬구조**

'caused'의 목적어가 'not only A but also B'를 통해 병렬구조를 이루고 있으므로 'generated'를 명사 'generation'으로 수정해야 한다. 또한 'generation'의 목적어 'hatred'가 있으므로 'generation' 뒤에 전치사 'of'를 사용해야 한다. 즉, 'generated'를 'generation of'로 수정하는 것이 옳다.

오답해설

① **출제 포인트: blow의 문장구조**

해당 문장에서 'blow'는 완전타동사로 뒤에 목적어 'it'을 사용하였으며 이때 'into a major controversy'는 부사구로 'blow'를 수식한다. 또한 'try+목적어[to+동사원형]'는 '~하려고 하다, ~하기 위해 애쓰다'를 뜻한다.

② **출제 포인트: 완전타동사+목적어[to부정사 vs. 동명사]**

해당 문장에서 'stop'은 완전자동사로 사용되었으며 뒤에 오는 'to buy sweets for the children'은 'stop'의 목적어가 아닌 'stop'을 수식하는 부사의 역할을 한다.

③ **출제 포인트: take의 관용표현(It+takes+목적어+시간+to부정사)**

「It takes+목적어+시간+to+동사원형」은 '~가 ~하는 데 시간이 걸리다'를 뜻하며 이때 목적어가 주어 자리로 이동할 경우 「주어[목적어]+take[수일치/시제반영]+시간+to+동사원형」의 구조를 가진다. 해당 문장은 「주어[목적어]+take[수일치/시제반영]+시간+to+동사원형」을 사용하였으므로 옳은 문장이다. 또한 'bounce ~ off somebody'는 관용표현으로 '누군가에게 ~을 제시해 보이다'의 의미로 옳게 사용되었다.

오답률 TOP 1

06 정답 ②

정답해설

② **출제 포인트: 완전타동사[주장/요구/명령/제안] + 목적어[that+주어+(should)+동사원형]**

'suggest'가 '말하다, 암시하다'를 뜻하는 경우 목적어로 쓰인 'that+'절은 「that+주어+동사[수일치/시제반영] ~」의 구조를 가진다. 해당 문장은 문맥상 'suggest'가 '말하다, 암시하다'를 뜻하며 진주어로 쓰인 'that+절'에 'will resign'을 사용하였으므로 옳은 문장이다.

오답해설

① **출제 포인트: 명사절을 이끄는 접속사**

해당 문장에서 'if'는 'ask'의 목적어 역할을 하는 명사절을 이끌고 있으나 'if' 바로 뒤에 'or not'을 사용할 수 없으므로 틀린 문장이다. 따라서 'if'를 'whether'로 수정하거나 'or not'을 문미로 이동시켜야 한다.

③ **출제 포인트: 강조 부사**

비교급 강조 부사 'even'이 원급 형용사 'high'를 수식하고 있으므로 틀린 문장이다. 따라서 'even'을 원급 강조 부사 'very'로 수정해야 한다. 또는 'even'을 삭제해도 옳은 문장이 된다.

④ **출제 포인트: The+비교급, the+비교급**

'The+비교급 ~, the+비교급 ~'은 양쪽 절에 'the+비교급'을 사용해야 한다. 해당 문장은 첫 번째 절에는 'the+비교급'을 사용하였으나 두 번째 절에는 'the+원급'을 사용하였으므로 틀린 문장이다. 또한, 문맥상 'regain'을 수식하므로 형용사가 아닌 부사의 의미로 'quickly'의 비교급인 'more quickly'를 사용해야 옳다. 따라서 'the quick'을 'the more quickly'로 수정해야 한다. 단, 'quick'의 부사의 의미가 있으나 격식체로는 부사의 경우 'quick'보다는 'quickly'를 더욱 선호한다.

해석

① 사람들은 그 경고가 잘못 처리된 것인지 아닌지 묻기 시작했다.
② 더 이상의 선수들이 떠난다면, 새 관리자는 사임할 것이라는 의견이 암시되어왔다.
③ 이 사건에 연루된 모든 사람들 사이에 매우 높은 수준의 협업이 있어왔다.
④ 과거에 건강한 상태를 더 오래 유지할수록, 미래에 체력을 더 빠르게 회복할 것이다.

07 정답 ①

정답해설

① **출제 포인트: 주어와 동사 수일치**

밑줄 친 'knows'는 동사 'know'의 단수형태이며 주어는 단수형태인 'Anyone'이므로 옳게 사용되었다. "who has ever rushed ~ the house"는 주격관계대명사절, "only to realize ~ on the kitchen table"은 to부정사의 부사적 용법이므로 수식어에 해당한다. 이처럼 주어와 본동사의 위치가 떨어져 있는 경우 수일치에 주의해야 한다.

오답해설

② **출제 포인트: It ~ that 강조구문**

해당 문장은 「It ~ that」 강조 구문으로 'that'의 자리에 관계대명사 'what'을 사용하였으므로 틀린 문장이다. 따라서 'what'을 'that' 또는 'which'로 바꾸어야 한다.

③ **출제 포인트: 혼동하기 쉬운 형용사**

'awarer'를 'aware'의 비교급으로 오해할 수 있으나 'aware'는 서술적 형용사이므로 'more aware' 또는 'less aware'로 쓰여야만 한다. 따라서 해당 문장에서는 열등 비교로 이미 쓰이고 있으므로 'awarer'를 'aware'로 수정해야 한다.

④ **출제 포인트: 타동사구[완전타동사+목적어+전치사+목적어]**

'steal'은 완전타동사로 「steal+목적어[사물]」과 「steal+목적어[사물]+from+목적어[대상]」의 구조를 가진다. 따라서 전치사 'by'를 'from'으로 수정해야 한다. 단, 주어진 by the time의 경우 시간의 접속사로 이후에 완전한 문장을 불러와야 하는데 불완전한 상태이므로 접속사로 볼 수는 없다.

해석

급하게 집을 나가다가 결국 열쇠와 지갑을 식탁에 두고 온 것을 깨닫게 된 적이 있는 사람이라면 누구나 이러한 것을 너무도 잘 알고 있다. 그리고 줄어드는 것은 비단 효율성만이 아니다. 우리가 의식을 덜 하거나 '유념'을 덜 하게 되어 경험의 질 또한 악화된다. 아무것도 맛을 느끼지 못한 채 식사 전체를 끝내 본 적이 있는가? 서두르는 것은 우리에게 더 적은 시간을 제공할 뿐만 아니라 우리가 진짜로 가지고 있는 그 시간으로부터 즐거움과 혜택을 또한 빼앗아 갈 수 있다.

어휘

rush 급히 움직이다, 서두르다
efficiency 효율성, 능률성
suffer 악화되다, 고통받다, 시달리다, 겪다
mindful ~을 의식하는, ~에 유념하는
steal+목적어[사물]+from+목적어[대상] ~을 ~에게서 빼앗다

08 정답 ④

정답해설

해당 지문은 '상어의 신체적 특징'에 관해 설명하는 글이다. 첫 문장 "It was found that sharks living in deep, cold waters tend to have very large fatty livers, sometimes making up over a quarter of their body(깊고 차가운 물에 서식하는 상어는, 때때로 몸의 4분의 1 이상을 구성하기도 하는, 매우 거대한 지방질의 간을 가지고 있는 경향이 있다는 것이 발견되었다)."를 통해 '심해에 사는 상어의 신체적 특징'에 대해 언급한 후, 본문 중반 "Sharks living in warmer and shallower waters, on the other hand, have comparatively smaller livers(반면, 따뜻하고 얕은 물에 서식하는 상어는 비교적 더 작은 간을 가지고 있다)."를 통해 '연안에 서식하는 상어는 심해에 사는 상어와 비교해 간의 크기가 비교적 작다'라고 언급하고 있다. '심해'와 '연안'이라는 지리적 서식 환경과, '찬물'과 '따뜻한 물'이라는 물리적 서식 환경의 차이에 따른 상어의 신체적 차이에 대해 설명하고 있으므로, 글의 제목으로 가장 적절한 것은 '④ Different Shark Bodies for Different Environments(다른 환경에서의 다른 상어의 신체)'이다.

오답해설

① 서식지에 따른 상어의 간 크기 차이에 대해 언급하고, '심해에 사는 상어는 큰 간으로 인해 몸의 부피가 커지고, 부력이 상승한다'라고 설명하고 있으나, 이후 '연안에 사는 상어들은 오히려 빠르게 움직이기 위해 간의 크기가 비교적 작다'고 언급하고 있으므로, 모든 상어가 큰 간이 필요한 것은 아님을 알 수 있다.

② 상어의 위험성에 대한 내용이 아니므로 글의 제목으로 부적절하다.

③ 본문 초반에서 '심해에 사는 상어는 큰 간으로 부력을 증가시켜 적은 에너지로 움직인다고 설명하지만, 반대로 얕은 물에 사는 상어는 작은 간 때문에 더 빠르게 움직여야 해서 비효율적으로 보일 수 있다고 설명하므로 글 전체를 포괄하지 못한다.

해석

깊고 차가운 물에 서식하는 상어는, 때때로 몸의 4분의 1 이상을 구성하기도 하는, 매우 거대한 지방질의 간을 가지고 있는 경향이 있다는 것이 발견되었다. 이것은 그들의 부력을 증가시키고, 적은 에너지를 이용해, 그러나 동시에 부가적인 부피로 인한 상대적으로 느린 속도로 수중에서 이동하는 것을 가능하게 해준다. 다행히도 그들이 먹이로 삼는, 그리고 그들을 먹이로 삼는 심해 동물들 또한 상당히 느리다. 반면, 따뜻하고 얕은 물에 서식하는 상어는 비교적 더 작은 간을 가지고 있다. 이것이 그들의 부력을 저해하는데, 그것은 부력을 발생시키기 위해 날개와 같은 가슴지느러미가 빠르게 움직여야만 한다는 것을 의미한다. 이러한 구조는 비행선처럼 생긴 상어의 구조보다 덜 에너지 효율적인 것처럼 보일 수 있으나, 다른 모든 것들이 또한 더 빠르게 움직이는 생태계에서 서식하는 것에 있어서는 사실 이치에 맞는 일이다.

① 상어는 왜 큰 간이 필요한가?
② 조심하라, 상어는 모든 곳에 존재한다!
③ 상어는 어떻게 에너지를 효율적으로 사용하는가?
④ 다른 환경에서의 다른 상어의 신체

어휘

add to …을 늘리다[증가시키다]
buoyancy 부력
relatively 상대적으로
bulk 부피, 크기
shallow 얕은
comparatively 비교적
negatively 반대 방향으로, 부정적으로
buoyant 부력이 있는, 물에 뜨는
pectoral fin 가슴지느러미
lift 상승력, 양력
energy-efficient 에너지 효율적인, 연비가 좋은
blimp 비행선
make sense 이치에 맞다
ecosystem 생태계
beware 조심하다
efficiently 효율적으로

09 정답 ④

정답해설

해당 지문은 '경청(listening)'에 대한 내용으로, 본문 첫 문장 "Various studies stress the importance of listening as a communication skill (다양한 연구가 의사소통 기술로서의 듣기의 중요성을 강조한다)."에서 '경청의 중요성'에 대해 언급한 후, 경청이 중요한 이유로 '사람들이 깨어있는 시간 중 듣기에 가장 많은 시간을 소비한다'라고 설명한다. 본문 중반 "While the percentage of listening is highest, studies also confirm that a vast majority of people are poor and inefficient listeners(듣기의 비율이 가장 높은 반면, 연구들은 또한 다수의 사람들이 형편없고 비효율적인 청자라는 것을 확인해준다)."를 통해 '대부분의 사람들이 좋은 청자'가 아님을 언급하고 이후 문장에서 사람들의 '경청 기술'이 부족한 것을 지적하며 구체적인 수치로

그 근거를 제시하고 있다. 따라서 본문 전체의 내용으로 보아 글의 요지로 가장 적절한 것은 '④ Listening is an important skill but people often lack the ability(경청은 중요한 기술이지만 사람들은 종종 그 능력이 결여되어 있다).'이다.

오답해설
① 듣기 기술 향상 방법에 대한 내용은 본문에 언급되지 않으므로 오답이다.
② 본문 초반에서 언급되는 내용이지만, 글 전체를 아우르는 내용은 아니므로 글의 요지로 적절하지 않다.
③ 듣기와 말하기를 비교하는 내용이 아니므로 오답이다.

해석
다양한 연구가 의사소통 기술로서의 듣기의 중요성을 강조한다. 한 대표적인 연구는 사람들은 깨어있는 시간 중 70에서 80퍼센트를 일종의 의사소통을 하면서 보낸다고 지적한다. 그 시간 중 9퍼센트는 쓰기, 16퍼센트는 읽기, 30퍼센트는 말하기, 그리고 45퍼센트는 듣기이다. 듣기의 비율이 가장 높은 반면, 연구들은 또한 다수의 사람들이 형편없고 비효율적인 청자라는 것을 확인해준다. 그들은 매우 잘 들리는 귀를 가지고 있지만, 그러한 귀가 소위 경청이라 불리는 것을 위해 효과적으로 사용되도록 해주는 필수 기술을 좀처럼 습득하지 못했다. 연구는 우리 대부분이 우리가 듣는 것의 25퍼센트에서 50퍼센트만을 기억한다고 말한다. 만약 이것이 정확하다면, 그것은 상사, 동료 또는 배우자와 10분 동안 대화를 할 때, 사람들은 대화의 절반 이하에만 집중을 한다는 것이다.
① 듣기 기술은 연습을 통해 향상될 수 있다.
② 우리는 매일 듣는 데 많은 시간을 소비한다.
③ 잘 듣는 것은 때때로 잘 말하는 것보다 더 어렵다.
④ 경청은 중요한 기술이지만 사람들은 종종 그 능력이 결여되어 있다.

어휘
various 다양한
inefficient 비효율적인
acquire 습득하다, 획득하다
accurate 정확한
lack …이 없다[부족하다]
vast 거대한
seldom 좀처럼[거의] ~않는
what is called 소위, 이른바
spouse 배우자

10 정답 ④

정답해설
해당 지문은 'Macaulay Honors College'의 학비 정책에 대한 내용이다. 본문 내용에 따르면, Macaulay Honors College는 뉴욕 출신의 학생들에게는 학비를 전액 면제해주고, 뉴욕 이외의 주 학생들에게는 장학금을 제공하기는 하지만 전액 장학금은 아니며, 해당 주 이외의 주에서 부과하는 비용과의 차액은 학생들이 지불해야 한다고 언급하고 있다. 또한 숙식은 별도로 비용을 지불해야 하며, 복합 학위를 취득하는 학생들도 대학원 과정에서 발생하는 비용은 자비로 충당해야 한다고 명시한다. 따라서 글의 내용과 일치하는 보기는 '④ It does not financially support postgraduate students(대학원생을 금전적으로 지원하지 않는다).'이다.

오답해설
① 본문에서 '뉴욕 외부 출신의 학생'에 대해 언급하고 있으므로, '뉴욕 출신의 학생들만 받는다'라는 것은 내용과 일치하지 않는다.
② '뉴욕 출신 학생들은 수업료가 무료이나, 뉴욕 이외 출신 학생들과 대학원 과정 학생들은 비용을 지불해야 한다'고 설명하고 있으므로, 글의 내용과 일치하지 않는다.
③ 본문 중반 '숙식(room and board)은 학비 면제에 포함되지 않는다.'라고 언급하고 있으므로, 글의 내용과 일치하지 않는다.

해석
Macaulay Honors College에 다니는 모든 뉴욕 학생들은 학비를 면제받고 학교를 다닌다. 뉴욕 외부 출신의 학생들은 그들의 학비 중 주내 해당액을 면제받지만, 그들은 여전히 학비의 주내와 주외 해당액의 차액을 지불해야 한다. 또한 숙식은 학비 면제에 포함되지 않는다. 숙식이 13,000달러에서 25,000달러의 비용이 들기 때문에 많은 학생들은 자택에 거주하며 통학한다. 복합 학위를 받는 학생들은 또한 그들의 대학원 과정을 위해 비용을 지불해야 한다. 모든 학생에게 자격이 주어진 장학금 이상의 비용을 지불해야 하는 학생들은 학자금 융자를 신청할 수 있다.
① 뉴욕 출신의 학생들만 받는다.
② 모든 학생들은 그곳에서 무료로 공부할 수 있다.
③ 장학금은 숙박비를 포함한다.
④ 대학원생을 금전적으로 지원하지 않는다.

어휘
tuition 학비, 등록금
portion 부분
out-of-state 주외(州外)의, 다른 주의
room and board 식사비를 포함한 숙박 요금, 식사를 제공하는 하숙
waiver 면제
graduate study 대학원 과정
be entitled to …를 받을 자격이 있다
apply for 신청하다
inclusive of …를 포함한
in-state 주내(州內)의
waive [규칙 등을] 적용하지 않다
commute 통학하다, 통근하다
scholarship 장학금
financial aid 학자금 융자
postgraduate student 대학원생

기적사 DAY 46

결국엔 성정혜 영어 하프모의고사

| 01 | ③ | 02 | ② | 03 | ④ | 04 | ① | 05 | ① |
| 06 | ③ | 07 | ④ | 08 | ② | 09 | ③ | 10 | ① |

01 정답 ③
16 국가직

정답해설

'unprecedented'는 '전례 없는, 엄청난'을 의미하며, ③ unsurpassed와 유의어 관계이다.

해석

Newton은 수학, 광학, 역학 물리학에 **전례 없는** 공헌을 하였다.
① 보통의
② 시사하는, 암시적인, 도발적인
③ 유례없는, 매우 뛰어난
④ 도발적인, 자극하는

오답률 TOP 2

02 정답 ②
15 국가직

정답해설

'겁쟁이'라고 불린 것에 대해 빈칸의 반응이 와서 검을 들고 돌진했다면, 그 반응은 '화가 난'일 것이다. 따라서 정답은 ② incensed이다.

해석

그 젊은 기사는 겁쟁이라 불린 것에 너무 **격노하여** 손에 검을 들고 돌진했다.
① 초연한, 냉담한
② 분개한, 격노한
③ 공정한, 편견 없는
④ 순수한, 겉을 꾸미지 않는

어휘

charge forward 돌진하다 aloof 초연한, 냉담한
incensed 분개한, 격노한 unbiased 공정한, 편견 없는
unpretentious 순수한, 겉을 꾸미지 않는

오답률 TOP 3

03 정답 ④
15 국가직

정답해설

난제를 해결하기 위한 '아이디어'(생각)를 목적어로 가질 수 있는 동사는 ④ hit upon이다. 'hit upon'은 '떠올리다'라는 뜻으로, 목적어인 '아이디어'와의 연관성을 확인할 수 있다.

해석

1970년대 중반으로 돌아가, John Holland라는 미국의 한 컴퓨터 과학자는 과학 분야의 악명 높은 난제들을 해결하기 위해 진화 이론을 이용하는 생각을 **불현듯 떠올렸다**.
① 고용했다, 떠맡았다
② 탔다, 올랐다
③ 속였다, 부당하게 이용했다
④ 불현듯 떠올렸다[생각했다]

어휘

take on 고용하다, 떠맡다 get on 타다, 오르다
put upon 속이다, 부당하게 이용하다 hit upon 불현듯 떠올리다[생각하다]

04 정답 ①
16 국가직

정답해설

A가 "What did you say(뭐라고 했어?)"라고 언급한 후, B의 대답을 통해 A가 한 말을 잘 못 알아들었다는 것을 알 수 있다. B는 A의 말을 듣고 "Can you hear me now(지금은 들려?)"라고 말하며 A에게 수신 상태를 재확인하고 있다. 따라서 빈칸에 들어갈 말로 적절한 것은 A의 수신 상태가 좋지 않음을 나타낼 수 있는 "① My phone has really bad reception here(내 핸드폰이 여기에서 수신이 잘 안돼)."이다.

오답해설

②③④ 나머지 보기는 수신이 잘되지 않는 A의 상황을 나타내기에 문맥상 적절하지 않다.

해석

A: 여보세요? 안녕, Stephanie. 나는 사무실로 가는 길이야. 뭐 필요한 거라도 있니?
B: 안녕, Luke. 프린터 여분 종이 좀 가져다줄래?
A: 뭐라고 했어? 프린터 잉크 가져다 달라고? 미안, 내 핸드폰이 여기에서 수신이 잘 안돼.
B: 지금은 들려? 프린터에 넣을 종이가 더 필요하다고 말했어.
A: 다시 말해줄래?
B: 됐어. 문자할게.
A: 그래. 고맙다, Stephanie. 이따 보자.
① 내 핸드폰이 여기서 수신이 잘 안돼.
② 나는 종이를 더 가져올 수 없었어.
③ 전화를 잘못 건 것 같아.
④ 이번엔 각 품목을 따로따로 살 거야.

오답률 TOP 1

05 정답 ①
15 국가직

정답해설

① **출제 포인트: 헷갈리기 쉬운 자동사와 타동사 / 시간의 부사구**

'skyrocket'은 자동사로 쓰일 수 있기 때문에 뒤에 목적어 없이 적절하게 사용되었다. 또한「in + 특정 연도」와 함께 쓰인 과거시제 'skyrocketed'도 알맞다.

오답해설

② **출제 포인트: to+[동사원형 vs. 동명사]**

'be tied to'는 '~와 연관되다'를 뜻한다. 해당 표현에서 to는 전치사이므로 뒤에는 (동)명사가 와야 하며 'memory'라는 목적어가 있으므로 명사가 아닌 동명사를 사용해야 한다. 따라서 'to improve'를 'to improving'으로 수정해야 한다.

③ **출제 포인트: 동명사의 태**

의미상 그녀가 '차에 치인' 것이니 수동으로 표현되어야 한다. 따라서 'running over'가 아닌 'being run over'가 되어야 한다.

④ **출제 포인트: 현재분사 vs. 과거분사**

문맥상 problems(문제)를 '둘러싸진'의 수동의 의미가 아니라 '둘러싼'의 능동의 의미가 되어야 한다. 또한 목적어 'the causes ~ disasters'가 있으므로 surrounded를 surrounding으로 변경하는 것이 옳다.

해석

① 중국의 러시아 석유 수입이 2014년에 36%까지 급등했다.
② 수면은 인간의 기억 향상에 오랜 관련이 있어왔다.
③ 지난밤, 그녀는 차에 치이는 것을 가까스로 면했다.
④ 그 실패는 치명적인 우주 왕복선 참사의 원인을 둘러싼 문제들을 연상시킨다.

06 정답 ③ 15 국가직

정답해설

③ 출제 포인트: 능동태 vs. 수동태
영문 자체는 문법적으로 이상이 없지만, 한글 해석과 상이하기에 틀렸다. 한글 해석은 미각의 민감성이 개인의 음식 섭취와 체중에 '~에 크게 영향을 미친다'(largely influences)인데, 영문은 그 반대로 '~에 의해 크게 영향을 받는다'(is largely influenced by)의 의미이다. 따라서 'is largely influenced by'를 'largely influences'로 바꿔야 한다.

오답해설

① 출제 포인트: 전치사 vs. 접속사
'Despite'는 양보 전치사로 뒤에 (동)명사를 취할 수 있으며 해당 문장에서 쓰인 'search for'는 '~를 찾다'의 의미로 사용되었다. 또한 'every' 다음에 단수 명사가 수반되는 것도 적절하게 사용되었다.

② 출제 포인트: 주어와 동사 수일치
동사 'is'의 주어는 'The best way ~ somebody'에 해당된다. 'if'는 명사절을 이끌 수 있기 때문에 'if you can trust somebody'를 'find out'의 목적어 절로 사용하는 것이 가능하다. 또한 to부정사인 'to find out'은 형용사적 용법으로 명사 'way'를 후치 수식하며, 또 다른 to부정사인 'to trust'는 'is'의 보어로 사용되었다.

④ 출제 포인트: to부정사의 한정적 용법/provide+목적어[사물]+for+목적어[대상] vs. provide+목적어+수식어[for+목적어+to+동사원형]
'to grow and learn in'의 의미상의 주어를 'for their children'으로 적절히 표시하였으며, 'to grow and learn in'은 형용사적 용법으로 명사 'the right environment'를 수식한다. 이때 해당 문장은 「provide+목적어[사물]+for+목적어[대상]」의 구조가 아니라 「provide+목적어+수식어[for+목적어+to+동사원형]」의 구조이므로 주의해야 한다.

07 정답 ④ 15 국가직

정답해설

④ 출제 포인트: 시간의 부사구, 부사절
부사절의 시점과 주절의 시점이 동일하기에 시제를 일치시켜 주어야 한다. 부사절의 시제가 과거(left)이므로, 주절의 시제도 does가 아닌 did로 변경하여야 한다. 또한 부정어 little로 인해 주어와 동사가 도치된 것에 주의해야 한다.

오답해설

① 출제 포인트: 사역동사
사역동사 'have'의 목적격 보어로 과거분사 'imprisoned'가 왔다. 목적어인 'his political enemies'와의 관계가 수동관계이므로 적절하다. 직역하면 '그는 자신의 정적들을 투옥되게 하였다.'이다.

② 출제 포인트: 부사절의 접속사/유도부사 수일치
'unless'는 부정의 의미를 포함하고 있으므로 부사절에 따로 부정을 포함할 필요가 없다. 또한 유도부사 'There'를 사용하였는데, 주절의 주어는 'no true liberty'로, 조동사가 아닌 일반동사였다면 수일치까지 확인해 보아야 한다. 'unless' 이후의 부사절에서는 there 구문의 주어가 'economic liberty'이므로 단수 동사인 'is'가 알맞게 사용되었다.

③ 출제 포인트: 동명사 관용표현
「look forward to + -ing」(~하는 것을 기대하다)에서 'to'가 전치사임을 명심해야 한다. 해당 문장에서는 전치사 'to' 뒤에 동명사 'doing'이 적절하게 사용되었다.

08 정답 ② 19 국가직

정답해설

'2007년 월스트리트의 금융 시스템 붕괴'에 대해 설명하고 있는 글이다. ①, ③, ④에서는 '금융 붕괴 및 위기'에 대해 서술하고 있지만 ②에서는 '금융 붕괴 및 위기'와 관련이 없는 '가상통화들(New virtual currencies)'에 대해 서술하고 있다. 따라서 정답은 ②이다.

오답해설

①③④ 나머지 문장은 '금융 시스템 붕괴'를 서술하는 글의 흐름과 부합하는 내용이다.

해석

2007년에 우리의 가장 큰 걱정은 "실패하기에는 너무 크다"라는 것이었다. 월스트리트의 은행들은 그렇게 엄청난 규모로 성장했고, 금융 시스템의 건전성에 매우 중요한 역할을 했기 때문에, 어떤 합리적인 정부도 그들을 실패하게 내버려 둘 수 없었다. ① 은행들은 그들의 보호되어진 상태를 알고, 주택 시장에 지나치게 위험한 내기를 했고, 그 어느 때보다 더 많은 복잡한 파생상품들을 만들었다. ② _bitcoin과 ethereum 같은 새로운 가상통화들은 근본적으로 어떻게 돈이 작동할 수 있고 작동해야 하는지에 대한 우리의 생각을 변화시켰다._ ③ 그 결과는 1929년 우리 경제가 붕괴된 이후 최악의 금융위기였다. ④ _2007년 이후 몇 년 동안, 우리는 그 딜레마를 다루는 데 큰 진전을 이루었다._ 우리 은행들은 그 어느 때보다도 자본화가 잘되어 있다. 우리의 규제 기관은 대형 기관의 정기적인 부하 테스트를 수행한다.

어휘

staggering 충격적인, 믿기 힘든
rational 이성적인
status 지위, 상태
make a bet on ~에 돈을 걸다
derivative 파생상품
currency 통화
crisis 위기
progress 진전, 진척, 진행
capitalize 자본화하다
conduct 수행하다

financial 금융의, 재정의
aware of ~을 인식하는
excessively 과도하게
complicated 복잡한
virtual 가상의
radically 근본적으로, 극단적으로
breakdown 붕괴
address 다루다
regulator 규제 기관
stress test 부하 검사

09 정답 ③ 19 국가직

정답해설

본문 마지막 문장이 주제 문장이다. "So simplicity is one key feature in names that determines various outcomes."(따라서 단순성은 여러 가지 결과를 결정하는 이름에서 하나의 핵심적 특징이다.)에서 단순한 이름이 그렇지 않은 이름보다 승진이나 성공을 더 많이 한다는 것을 본문에서 서술하고 있으므로 글의 주제는 ③ the benefit of simple names(단순한 이름들의 혜택)이다.

오답해설

① 본문에서 언급하고 있지 않은 내용이다.
② 본문에서 설명하고 있지 않다.
④ 복잡한 외국 이름들과 그렇지 않은 단순한 이름들에 대한 비교를 하고 있지 그것의 뿌리들은 언급하고 있지 않다.

해석

두 사람이 같은 날 로펌에서 일을 시작한다고 상상해 보라. 한 사람은 아주 간단한 이름을 가지고 있다. 상대방은 아주 복잡한 이름을 가지고 있다. 우리는 그들의 다음 16년 이상의 경력 동안 더 단순한 이름을 가진 사람이 더 빨리 법적 계층을 오를 것이라는 꽤 좋은 증거를 가지고 있다. 그들은 경력 중간에 더 빨리 파트너십을 획득할 것이다. 그리고 로스쿨을 졸업한 지 8년 내지 9년쯤 되었을 때, 더 단순한 이름을 가진 사람들이 파트너가 될 가능성이 약 7~10% 더 높아지는데, 이것은 놀라운 효과이다. 우리는 모든 종류의 다른 설명들을 없애려고 노력한다. 예를 들어, 우리는 외국 이름이 발음하기가 더 어려운 경향이 있기 때문에 이질성에 관한 것이 아니라는 것을 보여주려고 노력한다. 하지만 여러분이 영미인 이름을 가진 백인 남성 - 그러니까 정말 진정한 집단 내에서 본다면 - 여러분은 영미인 이름을 가진 백인 남성들 중에서, 만약 그들의 이름이 더 단순해진다면, 그들이 성공할 가능성이 더 높다는 것을 알게 될 것이다. 따라서 단순성은 여러 가지 결과를 결정하는 이름에서 하나의 핵심적 특징이다.

① 법적 이름들의 발전
② 매력적인 이름들의 개념
③ 단순한 이름들의 혜택
④ 외국 이름들의 뿌리들

어휘

complex 복잡한
rise up 올라가다
attain 얻다, 달성하다
striking 눈에 띄는, 현저한
alternative 대안(의)
outcome 결과
over the course of ~동안
hierarchy 계층, 계급
partnership 동업자 관계
eliminate 제거하다
in-group 내집단

---

10 정답 ①   19 국가직

정답해설

(A) 전에 선지자들이 무언가를 최초로 발견하는 것에 초점을 두는 사람들이라는 내용이다. 빈칸 뒤는 선지자들은 검증된(이미 많은 사람들이 쓰는) 제품은 사지 않는다는 내용이다. 따라서 (A) 전은 이유(최초 발견을 중시)이고 빈칸 뒤는 결과(최초가 아닌 제품은 사지 않음)이므로 인과의 접속사인 'therefore(그러므로)'가 적합하다.

(B) 전까지는 선지자들의 특성을 설명하고, (B) 다음부터 실용주의자들에 대해 서술하고 있다. 따라서 대조를 나타내는 접속사 'on the other hand (반면에)'가 적합하다. 따라서 정답은 ①이다.

오답해설

(A) 선지자들에 대한 설명을 계속하고 있으므로 (A)에 역접의 접속사 'however(그러나)'나 'nonetheless(그럼에도 불구하고)'가 오는 것은 적절하지 않다.

(B) 빈칸 다음으로 실용주의자들에 대한 내용이 나오므로 부연 설명에 대한 접속사 'in addition(게다가)'과 결과를 나타내는 접속사 'in conclusion (결론적으로, 끝으로)' 또한 적절하지 않다. 'at the same time'은 '동시에'라는 의미로 문맥상 적합하지 않다.

해석

선지자들은 그들의 업계에서 새로운 기술들의 잠재력을 볼 수 있는 첫 번째 사람이다. 근본적으로, 그들은 자신들은 경쟁사들에 있는 그들의 상대방들보다 더 똑똑하다고 여긴다. - 그리고 꽤 자주, 그들은 그렇다. 실제로, 그들이 경쟁 우위를 향해 지렛대로 이용하기를 원하는 것들을 먼저 알아보는 것이 그들의 능력이다. 그 우위는 다른 누구도 그것을 발견하지 않았을 때만 발생할 수 있다. (A) 그러므로, 그들은 광범위한 업계 참조의 목록을 가진 검증된 제품을 사는 것을 기대하지 않는다. 정말로, 만약 그러한 참조의 근거가 존재한다면, 이것은 이 기술에 대해서는, 아무튼, 그들은 이미 너무 늦었다는 것을 암시하기 때문에 그것은 실제로 그들이 신경을 쓰지 않도록 만들 수도 있다. (B) 반면에, 실용주의자들은 다른 기업에 있는 그들의 동료들의 경험을 크게 가치 있게 여긴다. 그들이 구매를 할 때는, 그들은 광범위한 언급들을 기대하며, 그들은 그들 자신의 업계 내의 기업들에서 좋은 숫자가 나오기를 원한다.

(A)	(B)
① 그러므로	반면에
② 그러나	게다가
③ 그럼에도 불구하고	동시에
④ 게다가	결과적으로

어휘

visionary 선지자
fundamentally 근본적으로
leverage ~에게 영향을 주다; ~에 지레를 사용하다
competitive advantage 경쟁 상의 우위
come about 발생하다, 생기다
extensive 광범위한
indicate 암시하다
pragmatist 실용주의자
segment 분야, 부분
opposite number 상대방
well-tested 입증된
reference 참조, 언급
at any rate 아무튼
value 가치 있게 여기다

결국엔 성정혜 영어 하프모의고사
기적사 DAY 47

01	②	02	①	03	④	04	④	05	②
06	①	07	③	08	①	09	①	10	④

01 정답 ②

정답해설

주어진 밑줄에는 문맥상 '중요한'이 적절하므로 ② cardinal이 정답이다.

해석

무시되어온 듯 보이는 한 가지 관점은 내가 혁명수비대의 가장 **중요한** 역할로 여기는 것이다.
① 의존적인, 일어나기 쉬운, 우발적인, 조건으로 하는
② 가장 중요한, 진홍색의; 추기경
③ 시사하는, 암시적인, 도발적인
④ 강제적인, 명령을 받은

어휘

perspective 관점
contingent 의존적인, 일어나기 쉬운, 우발적인, 조건으로 하는
cardinal 가장 중요한, 진홍색의; 추기경
suggestive 시사하는, 암시적인, 도발적인
mandatory 강제적인, 명령을 받은

02 정답 ①

정답해설

밑줄 친 단어는 '횡령하다'로 사용되었다. 유의어가 아닌 것은 '불현듯 떠올리다[생각하다]'의 의미인 ① hit upon이다.

해석

만약에 하인들이 그들의 고기를 정직하고 관대하게 받지 못한다면, 그들은 주인의 사업을 방치하거나, 그의 재산을 **횡령할** 것이다.
① 불현듯 떠올리다[생각하다]
② 횡령하다
③ (남의 돈, 재산을) 유용하다
④ 빼앗다

어휘

decently 깔끔하게, 상당히
peculate 횡령하다
misappropriate (남의 돈, 재산을) 유용하다
usurp 빼앗다
hit upon 불현듯 떠올리다[생각하다]

오답률 TOP 3

03 정답 ④

정답해설

밑줄 친 단어는 문맥상 '연기시키다'로 사용되었다. 따라서 유의어로는 ④ dawdle이 적절하다.

해석

기술 전문가들은 악명 높게 어려운 문제들에 대해 공학 기술의 신비를 구실로 그들이 모든 모호함을 가지고 결정적 수단을 **지연시키는** 것을 안다.
① 벗기다
② 간섭하다
③ 분배하다
④ 꾸물거리다

어휘

on the ground of ~라는 까닭으로
card 결정적 수단, 카드, 표, 명함
meddle 간섭하다
dawdle 꾸물거리다
procrastinate 미루다, 연기하다
peel 벗기다
distribute 분배하다

04 정답 ④

정답해설

Sam이 Mina에게 무엇을 하고 있는지 질문하자 Mina는 라이트 형제에 대한 책을 읽고 있었다고 답한다. Mina는 라이트 형제가 살던 당시에 사람들은 하늘을 나는 것이 불가능하다고 믿었다고 말한다. 따라서 문맥상 빈칸에 들어갈 말은 '사람들은 라이트 형제가 비현실적인 이야기를 한다고 했다'라는 의미가 되어야 하므로 ④ talking through their hats(비현실적인 이야기를 하다)'가 정답이다.

오답해설

① 사람들은 하늘을 나는 것이 불가능한 생각이라고 믿었기에 라이트 형제가 '모방하는 인간(a copy cat)'이라고 했다는 것은 문맥상 어색하다.
② 라이트 형제가 '공격을 받았다(under fire)'라는 것은 하늘을 나는 것이 불가능하다고 믿었다는 사람들에 관해 얘기하는 대화의 흐름에 알맞지 않다.
③ 하늘을 나는 것이 불가능하다고 믿었던 당시의 사람들이 라이트 형제를 '귀족 가문(blue blood)'이라고 했다는 것은 맥락상 부적절하다.

해석

Sam: Mina, 너 지금 뭐 하고 있어?
Mina: 안녕, Sam. 나 그냥 책 읽고 있었어.
Sam: 책이 뭐에 대한 거야?
Mina: 라이트 형제에 관한 것이야. 그들에 대해 들어본 적 있어?
Sam: 물론이지. 그들이 비행기를 제작한 사람들이잖아.
Mina: 응. 근데 그 당시에는 사람들이 하늘을 나는 것이 불가능하다고 믿어서 라이트 형제가 비현실적인 이야기를 한다고 말했어.
Sam: 그들이 겪어야 했던 힘든 시간에도 불구하고 그들이 성공을 이뤄낸 것이 대단해.
Mina: 그러니까. 그들의 인생 이야기에서 배울 점들이 참 많아.
① 모방하는 인간
② 공격을 받다
③ 명문, 귀족 가문
④ 비현실적인 이야기를 하다

어휘

impossible 불가능한
a copycat 모방하는 인간
blue blood 명문, 귀족 가문
talk through one's hat 비현실적인 이야기를 하다
despite ~에도 불구하고
under fire 공격을 받다

05 정답 ②

정답해설

② 출제 포인트: 동명사 관용표현/동명사의 태
'look forward to'는 '~하기를 고대하다'를 뜻하며 뒤에 명사와 동명사가 목적어로 올 수 있다. 해당 문장은 'look forward to' 뒤에 동명사 'installing'을 사용하였으며 동명사의 목적어 'the new units'가 있으므로 능동형 동명사를 사용하는 것이 옳다.

오답해설

① 출제 포인트: 시간의 부사절 시제 일치
'by the time+주어+동사'는 시간의 부사절로 동사에 과거시제를 사용할 때 주절의 동사에 과거시제와 과거완료를 사용할 수 있다. 해당 문장은 'by the time+주어+동사'가 쓰인 문장으로 동사에 현재시제 'get'을 사용하였으나 주절의 동사에 과거완료 'had stopped'를 사용하였으므로 틀린 문장이다. 따라서 현재시제 'get'을 과거시제 'got'으로 수정해야 한다.

③ 출제 포인트: to+[동사원형 vs. 동명사]/시간의 부사구
'continue'는 to부정사나 동명사를 목적어로 사용한다. 해당 문장은 'continue'의 목적어로 'to+~ing'를 사용하였으므로 틀린 문장이다. 따라서 'doing'을 동사원형 'do'로 수정하거나 to를 삭제해야 한다. 또한 해당 문장에서 'so far'는 시간의 부사구로 현재완료와 함께 사용한다.

④ 출제 포인트: 현재분사 vs. 과거분사
완전타동사 'address'의 현재분사인 'addressing'이 사용되었으나 해석상 '주소가 적힌 봉투'의 의미로 수식하는 대상 'envelope'와 수동관계이므로 틀린 문장이다. 따라서 현재분사 'addressing'을 과거분사 'addressed'로 수정해야 한다.

해석

① 나는 도움을 얻기 위해 나갔고 내가 돌아왔을 때쯤 그는 숨 쉬는 것을 멈췄다.
② 그는 낡은 부엌을 뜯어내고 새로운 세트들로 빨리 설치하기를 고대했다.
③ 이것은 지금까지 거대한 이익을 창출해왔고 계속해서 그렇게 할 수 있는 전략이다.
④ 신청서를 요청하는 편지와 함께 우표가 붙여진 그리고 주소가 적힌 봉투를 포함하십시오.

오답률 TOP 2

06 정답 ①

정답해설

① 출제 포인트: 타동사구[완전타동사+목적어+전치사+목적어]
「supply+목적어[사물]+to/for+목적어[대상]」는 '~에게 ~을 공급하다'를 뜻하며, 대상을 나타내는 목적어와 사물을 나타내는 목적어의 위치를 바꾸는 경우 「supply+목적어[대상]+with+목적어[사물]」을 사용한다. 해당 문장은 「supply+목적어[사물]+with+목적어[대상]」을 사용하였으므로 틀린 문장이다. 따라서 'with'를 'for' 또는 'to'로 수정해야 한다.

오답해설

② 출제 포인트: 능동태 vs. 수동태 / 관계대명사
능동태로 쓰인 'needed'와 'affected'는 각각 목적어 'a place'와 'me'를 가지므로 옳은 문장이다. 또한 해당 문장에서 'that'은 선행사 'cultural differences'를 수식하는 주격관계대명사로 쓰였다.

③ 출제 포인트: 전치사 vs. 접속사
'because of'는 전치사로 뒤에 명사(구)와 동명사(구)를 사용한다. 해당 문장은 'because of' 뒤에 명사(구) 'a technical glitch'를 사용하였으므로 옳은 문장이다. 이때 해당 문장에서 'is'의 주어는 'The loss'임에 유의하도록 하며 'a technical glitch'를 주어로 착각하지 않도록 주의해야 한다.

④ 출제 포인트: 주어와 동사 수일치 / 관계부사
주어가 단수형태인 'The owner'이므로 동사에 단수형태인 'was'를 옳게 사용하였다. 또한 'where'는 관계부사로 장소를 나타내는 선행사를 가지며 뒤따라오는 문장은 완전한 형태이다. 해당 문장에서 'where'는 선행사 'the chemist's shop'을 가지며 뒤따라오는 문장인 'the armed ~ took place'는 완전한 문장이다.

오답률 TOP 1

07 정답 ③

정답해설

③ 출제 포인트: 동명사 관용표현
「There is no+(in)+동명사」는 관용표현으로 '~하는 것은 불가능하다'를 뜻한다. 해당 문장은 동명사 자리에 to부정사 'to say'를 사용하였으므로 틀린 문장이다. 따라서 'to say'를 'saying'으로 수정해야 한다.

오답해설

① 출제 포인트: 부사절의 접속사
'unless'는 부사절을 이끄는 접속사이다. 또한 부정의 의미를 내포하므로 뒤에 오는 부사절에는 부정부사를 사용하지 않는다. 해당 문장은 'unless'가 쓰인 문장으로 뒤에 오는 부사절에 부정부사를 사용하지 않았으며 주어진 해석과 일치하므로 옳은 문장이다.

② 출제 포인트: 시간의 부사구, 부사절 / 준사역동사 get / 현재분사 vs. 과거분사
'some four to six weeks ago'는 시간의 부사구로 과거시제 동사와 함께 사용한다. 이때 'before the weather turned'는 부사구 'some four to six weeks ago'를 수식하므로 부사 역할을 하는 부사절임을 알 수 있다. 또한 준사역동사 'get'의 목적격 보어로 과거분사 'started'를 옳게 사용하였다.

④ 출제 포인트: 사역동사의 목적격 보어 / 주어-동사 수일치
'having someone read it to you'에서 'having'은 사역동사의 성격을 가진 동명사로 「have+목적어+목적격 보어[원형부정사]」의 구조를 가진다. 또한 해당 문장에서 주어는 'Owning ~ record'로 동명사 주어가 사용되었으며 동명사 주어는 단수 취급한다. 따라서 단수 주어에 따라 단수 형태의 동사인 'is'를 옳게 사용하였다.

08 정답 ①

정답해설

해당 지문은 '1920년대 강력했던 미국 경제가 1929년 주식시장 붕괴 이후 한순간에 대공황에 접어들었다'라고 설명하고 있다. 본문 후반 "However, it is far too simplistic to view the stock market crash as the single cause of the Great Depression(그러나 주식시장 붕괴를 대공황의 단일 원인으로 보는 것은 너무나 지나친 단순화이다)."을 통해, '주식시장 붕괴가 대공황을 촉발시킨 것은 사실이나 그것을 대공황의 유일한 원인으로 보는 것은 무리가 있음'을 설명한 후, 본문 마지막 문장 "Long-term underlying causes sent the nation into a downward spiral of despair(장기적인 근본적 원인들이 그 국가를 절망의 하향곡선으로 떨어뜨린 것이다)."에서 '장기적인 근본적 원인들이 혼합되어 대공황을 초래했다'라고 설명하고 있다. 따라서 글의 요지로 가장 적절한 것은 '① Multiple factors caused the Great Depression to occur(복수의 요인들이 대공황을 발생시켰다).'이다.

오답해설

② 본문 후반 "However, it is far too simplistic to view the stock market crash as the single cause of the Great Depression(그러나 주식시장 붕괴를 대공황의 단일 원인으로 보는 것은 너무나 지나친 단순화

이다)."이라고 언급하며 '주식시장 붕괴가 대공황을 일으킨 단일 원인이라고 할 수 없다'라고 설명하며, 마지막 문장 "Long-term underlying causes sent the nation into a downward spiral of despair(장기적인 근본적 원인들이 그 국가를 절망의 하향곡선으로 떨어뜨린 것이다)."에서 '장기적인 근본적 원인들'이 있었다고 언급하고 있으므로, 본문의 내용과 반대되는 문장이다. 따라서 오답이다.
③ 본문과 관련 없는 내용이다.
④ Herbert Hoover 대통령의 정책에 대한 내용은 구체적으로 제시되지 않는다.

해석
1920년대 말, 미국은 세계에서 가장 거대한 경제를 자랑했다. 제1차 세계대전으로 인해 발생한 파괴로 인해 미국이 번성하는 동안 유럽인들은 분투했다. 대통령직을 이어받은 뒤 Herbert Hoover는 미국이 곧 빈곤이 퇴치된 날을 보게 될 것이라 예측했다. 그리고 겉으로 보이는 승리 속에서 모든 것이 허물어졌다. 1929년 주식시장 붕괴는 미국을 역사상 가장 길고 가장 깊은 경제 위기로 몰아넣은 일련의 사건들을 촉발했다. 그러나 주식시장 붕괴를 대공황의 단일 원인으로 보는 것은 너무나 지나친 단순화이다. 건강한 경제는 그러한 침체에서 회복할 수 있다. 장기적인 근본적 원인들이 그 국가를 절망의 소용돌이로 떨어뜨린 것이다.
① 복수의 요인들이 대공황을 발생시켰다.
② 대공황은 오직 주식시장 붕괴 때문이었다.
③ 불황을 피하기 위해 경제를 건강하게 유지하는 것이 중요하다.
④ Herbert Hoover 대통령은 국가를 공황에서 빠져나오게 하는 데 실패했다.

어휘
boast 자랑하다, 뽐내다
wrought 만들어진, 초래된
succeed to …를 잇다, 계승하다
apparent 외견상의, 겉보기의
plunge 밀어 넣다, 쑤셔 박다
contraction 침체, 불황
spiral 소용돌이, 나선형
multiple 복수의, 다수의
destruction 파괴
flourish 번영하다
eliminate 없애다, 제거하다
touch off 촉발하다, 야기하다
simplistic 지나치게 단순화된
underlying 근본적인, 기저의
despair 절망
recession 불황, 침체

09 정답 ①

정답해설
빈칸에는 연구에 대한 결과를 설명하는 표현이 들어가야 한다. 빈칸 이후 "Researchers found that, regardless of race, young people with unusual names were more likely to engage in criminal activity(연구원들은 인종에 관계없이 특이한 이름을 지닌 젊은이들이 범죄 활동에 연루될 가능성이 더 높다는 점을 발견했다)."를 통해 '특이한 이름을 지닌 젊은이들이 범죄를 더 많이 저지를 가능성이 있다'라고 설명하고 있으며, 그러한 현상이 발생하는 원인으로 '이름으로 인한 또래 집단에서의 차별과 그에 따른 관계 형성 능력 결여', 그리고 '자기 자신의 이름 혐오' 등을 들고 있다. 이름과 청소년 범죄 사이의 관계에 대해 설명하고 있는 글이므로, 빈칸에 가장 적절한 것은 ① the popularity of one's first name and juvenile delinquency(한 사람의 이름의 인기도와 청소년 비행)'이다.

오답해설
② '이름의 인기도가 낮으면 범죄에 연루될 가능성이 높다'라는 것이 본문의 요지이며, 인물 자체의 인기도에 대해서는 언급하고 있지 않으므로 오답이다.
③ 성격에 대해서는 본문에 언급되지 않는다.
④ 사람 자체의 인기도에 대해서는 본문에 언급되지 않는다.

해석
Shippensburg University에서 실시된 2009년 연구는 한 사람의 이름의 인기도와 청소년 비행 사이에 관계가 있다고 말했다. 연구원들은 인종에 관계없이 특이한 이름을 지닌 젊은이들이 범죄 활동에 연루될 가능성이 더 높다는 점을 발견했다. 연구 결과는 인기 없는 이름이 행위를 야기했다는 점을 명확하게 보여주는 것은 아니며, 단지 둘 간의 연관성만을 보여준다. 그리고 연구원들은 연구 결과에 대한 이론을 가지고 있다. "인기 없는 이름을 지닌 청소년들은 그들이 또래들에게 다르게 대우를 받고, 이것이 그들로 하여금 관계를 형성하는 것을 더 어렵게 만들기 때문에 범죄를 일으키기 더 쉽다."라고 그들은 설명한다. "인기 없는 이름을 지닌 청소년들은 또한 자신들의 이름을 싫어하기 때문에 반항을 할 수도 있다."
① 한 사람의 이름의 인기도와 청소년 비행
② 한 사람의 이름의 인기도와 그 사람의 인기도
③ 한 사람의 성격과 청소년 범죄 행위
④ 한 사람의 인기도와 청소년 범죄 행위

어휘
juvenile 청소년의; 청소년
finding 결과, 결론
prone to …하기 쉬운
delinquency 비행, 범죄
engage in …에 관여하다
adolescent 청소년
peer 또래

10 정답 ④

정답해설
본문의 내용상 (A)는 '선지적인' 사람에 대한 내용이고, (B), (C)는 '실용적인' 사람에 대한 내용이라는 것을 알 수 있다. 주어진 문장에서는 '실용주의'에 대해 언급하고 있으므로, (B) 또는 (C)가 이어져야 하는데, (C)의 'They'가 (B)의 'Pragmatists'를 가리킨다는 것을 알 수 있으므로, (B) - (C)의 순서가 자연스럽다. 이후에는 화제를 전환할 때 사용하는 접속부사인 'Meanwhile(한편)'을 이용하여 '선지적인 사람'들에 대해 설명하는 것으로 내용이 전환되는 것이 자연스러우므로 (A)가 이어져야 한다. 따라서 정답은 '④ (B) - (C) - (A)'이다.

오답해설
③ (B) 이후에 '실용주의자'의 특징에 대해 설명하고 있는 (C)가 이어지는 것이 자연스러우므로 오답이다.
나머지 선지는 문맥상 부자연스러우므로 오답이다.

해석
실용적인 것은 사실적 데이터와 실생활 사건에 관심을 가지는 것이다.
(B) 실용주의자들은 실제 사건에 관심을 가지고 이러한 상황에 가능한 최선의 방식으로 대처한다.
(C) 그들은 각각의 방향의 다양한 장점, 단점, 장애물, 그리고 기회를 분석하고 따져 가장 최선의 방향을 선택하려고 시도하고 결론에 도달할 것이다.
(A) 한편, 선지적인 것은 이상향적인 아이디어를 갖는 것이다. 선지적인 사람들은 사실적 사항과 일상의 사건을 별로 개의치 않는다.

어휘
pragmatic 실용적인
occurrence 사건, 일어난 일
utopian 이상향의
path (목표에 이르는) 길, 방향
weigh (결정을 내리기 전에) 따져 보다, 저울질하다
obstacle 장애물
factual 사실의
visionary 선지적인, 예언적인
manner 방식

결국엔 성정혜 영어 하프모의고사
기적사 DAY 48

01	①	02	④	03	③	04	②	05	③
06	①	07	①	08	②	09	④	10	③

01 정답 ①

정답해설

밑줄 친 단어는 문맥상 '막다'로 사용되었고, 유의어로는 ① prevent가 적절하다.

해석

사람들이 그들의 삶에 좀 더 이른 시기에 연애를 시작하도록 격려한다면, 아마도 우리는 미래의 이러한 전례 없는 문제들을 일부 **막을** 수 있을 것이다.
① 막다
② 평가하다, 재검하다
③ 수정하다
④ 아첨하다

어휘

head off 막다, 회피하다 prevent 막다
review 평가하다, 재검하다 correct 수정하다
flatter 아첨하다

02 정답 ④

정답해설

주어진 빈칸은 문맥상 '참다'의 의미가 적절하다. 따라서 ④ put up with가 정답이다.

해석

미국 대통령 도널드 트럼프는 이전에 트위터에서 서울과 도쿄가 북한의 도발을 더 이상 **참을 것**이라고 믿기 힘들다고 언급했고, 중국에 그 정권에 대항하여 "적극적인 조치를 취하고", "이런 말도 안 되는 상황을 완전하게 끝내 달라"고 촉구했다.
① ~으로 가득 채우다
② ~을 양도하다; ~을 고치다
③ ~에 걸리다
④ ~을 참다

어휘

provocation 도발, 자극 regime 정권
charge with ~으로 가득 채우다 make over 양도하다, ~을 고치다
come down with ~ (병 등에) 걸리다
put up with ~을 참다

03 정답 ③

정답해설

밑줄 친 단어는 문맥상 '칭송하다'로 사용되었고, 유의어가 아닌 것은 ③ discard이다.

해석

애리조나주에서 있었던 총격에 이어 그가 했던 것처럼, 오바마는 대중을 감동시키고, **칭송하고**, 그 순간을 포착하는 그의 능력을 입증했다.
① 숭배하다
② 찬미하다
③ 버리다
④ 숭배하다

어휘

eulogize 칭송하다, ~을 칭송하다 venerate 숭배하다
glorify 찬미하다 discard 버리다
idolize 숭배하다

04 정답 ②

정답해설

Julie와 Matt는 영화에 관해 대화한다. Julie가 영화관에 가지 않은 지 오래됐다고 하자, Matt는 요즘 상영하는 좋은 영화들이 몇 개 있다고 한다. Julie가 추천할 만한 것이 있냐고 묻자 Matt는 Julie가 공포 영화를 좋아한다면 내일 개봉하는 영화가 있다고 한다. Julie는 공포 영화에 (A) '빠져 있다(nuts about)'라며 온종일 공포 영화를 보며 보낼 수 있다고 답변한다. 반면에 Matt는 공포 영화를 잘 못 본다며 무서운 것이 튀어나올 때마다 (B) '소름(goose bumps)'이 돋는다고 한다.

오답해설

① (B) 공포 영화에 빠져 있다는 Julie의 말에 Matt는 공포 영화를 잘 못 본다며 무서운 것이 튀어나올 때마다 '만능의 패(a wild card)'를 갖는다고 하는 것은 문맥상 어색하다.
③ (A) 공포 영화를 좋아하는지 이야기하는 Julie의 말에 공포 영화의 '영향을 받아(in the wake of)' 공포 영화를 온종일 볼 수 있다고 말하는 것은 부자연스럽다. (B) 공포 영화를 잘 보지 못한다는 Matt는 무서운 것이 튀어나올 때마다 '오기(sour grapes)'를 부린다고 하는 것은 적합하지 않다.
④ (A) Julie가 공포 영화의 '한창 시절(in the heyday of)'에 있다고 말하는 것은 맥락의 흐름으로는 부적절하다.

해석

Julie: 나 꽤 오랫동안 영화관에 가지 않았어.
Matt: 오, 요즘 상영하는 좋은 영화들이 몇 가지 있어.
Julie: 추천할 만한 것들이 있어?
Matt: 네가 공포 영화를 좋아한다면 내일 개봉하는 게 하나 있어.
Julie: 오, 나 공포 영화에 (A) 빠져 있어. 나는 종일 공포 영화를 보면서 보낼 수 있어.
Matt: 나는 공포 영화를 잘 못 봐. 무서운 것이 튀어나올 때마다 나는 (B) 소름이 돋아.

	(A)	(B)
①	~에 빠지다	만능의 패
②	~에 빠지다	소름
③	~의 영향을 받아	지기 싫어함, 오기
④	한창 시절에	소름

어휘

movie theatre 영화관 on screen 상영하는
recommendation 추천 pop up 튀어나오다
nuts about ~에 빠지다 a wildcard 만능의 패
goose bumps 소름 in the wake of ~의 영향을 받아
sour grapes 지기 싫어함, 오기 in the heyday of 한창 시절에

오답률 TOP 2
05 정답 ③

정답해설

③ 출제 포인트: 현재분사 vs. 과거분사
해당 문장은 완전자동사 'stay'의 현재분사인 'staying'이 'the man'을 수식하며, 완전타동사 'steal'의 과거분사인 'stolen'이 수식하는 대상 'his travel bag'와 수동관계이므로 '사역동사 have+목적어+과거분사 구문'으로 옳은 문장이다.

오답해설

① 출제 포인트: to+[동사원형 vs. 동명사]
'be afraid to 동사원형'은 관용표현으로 '~하는 것을 두려워하다'를 뜻한다. 여기에서 to는 전치사가 아닌 to부정사의 to임에 유의해야한다. 따라서 해당 문장은 'afraid' 뒤에 'to'가 왔으나 동명사 'testing'을 사용하였으므로 틀린 문장이다. 따라서 'testing'을 동사원형 'test'로 수정해야 한다.

② 출제 포인트: 동사 vs. 준동사 / 시간의 부사구
해당 문장은 본동사 역할을 하는 동사가 없으며 동사 자리에 과거분사 'seen'을 사용하였으므로 틀린 문장이다. 따라서 'seen'을 수정해야 하며, 이때 'For the past two weeks'는 시간의 부사구로 현재완료와 함께 사용하므로 'has seen'으로 수정해야 한다.

④ 출제 포인트: 동명사의 태
'afraid' 뒤에 'of'가 오는 경우 명사 또는 동명사를 사용한다. 해당 문장은 'afraid' 뒤에 'of'가 왔으며 수동형 동명사 'being competed'를 사용하였으나 'compete'는 완전자동사이므로 수동형 동명사를 사용할 수 없다. 따라서 'being competed'를 능동형 동명사 'competing'으로 수정해야 한다. 또한 'but'은 등위접속사로 'was'와 'feared'는 병렬구조를 이루고 있다.

해석

① 우리는 이 새로운 자료와 개념들을 테스트하는 것을 두려워하지 말아야 한다.
② 지난 2주 동안, 서방세계는 우크라이나에서 놀라운 일이 발생한 것을 보았다.
③ 호텔에서 내 옆에 머무른 그 남자는 어제 방에서 자신의 여행 가방을 도둑 맞았다.
④ 그는 슈퍼마켓들과 경쟁하는 것을 두려워하지 않았지만 고객의 선택에 미치는 영향을 두려워했다.

오답률 TOP 1
06 정답 ①

정답해설

① 출제 포인트: 전치사 vs. 접속사
양보를 나타내는 접속사 although는 절을 이끄는 연결사의 일종이다. 해당 문장에서는 '주어+동사~' 형태의 완전한 절을 이끌지 않으므로 옳지 않은 문장이다. 'what others said'는 단순히 '다른 사람들이 말한 것'이라는 의미이므로, 'although'를 유사한 의미의 '양보(~에도 불구하고)'를 나타내는 전치사(구)인 'in spite of' 또는 'despite'로 수정해야 한다. 또한 주절의 'had known'은 종속절의 시제와 동일하게 과거시제 'knew'로 수정하는 것이 옳다.

오답해설

② 출제 포인트: 타동사구[완전타동사+목적어+전치사+목적어]
「entrust+목적어[사물]+to+목적어[대상]」는 '~에게 ~을 맡기다'를 뜻하며, 대상을 나타내는 목적어와 사물을 나타내는 목적어의 위치를 바꾸는 경우「entrust+목적어[대상]+with+목적어[사물]」을 사용한다. 해당 문장은「entrust+목적어[사물]+to+목적어[대상]」을 사용하였으며 주어진 해석과 일치하므로 옳은 문장이다. 문장에서 쓰인 whoever는 복합관계대명사 주격으로 뒤따라오는 문장의 주어가 없는 불완전한 문장이 와야 한다. 단, 복합관계대명사는 선행사를 이미 포함하고 있음에 주의해야 한다.
※ He would entrust all his money and belongings to **anyone who(=whoever)** was accompanying him at the time.

③ 출제 포인트: 주어와 동사 수일치
단수형태 주어 'A child'와 단수형태 동사 'has'가 수일치하므로 옳은 문장이다. 또한 'who found it difficult to read of write'는 주어 'A child'를 수식하는 주격관계대명사절이다.

④ 출제 포인트: 능동태 vs. 수동태
해당 문장은 'cover A with B'의 수동태인 'A be covered with B'가 쓰인 문장으로 주어진 해석과 일치하므로 옳은 문장이다. 또한 'that'은 'scales'를 선행사로 가지는 주격관계대명사이다.

07 정답 ①

정답해설

① 출제 포인트: 사역동사
'let'은 사역동사로 목적어와 능동 관계인 경우 목적격 보어에 동사원형을 사용하며 수동 관계인 경우 목적격 보어에 'be+과거분사'를 사용한다. 해당 문장은 사역동사 'let'을 사용하였으나 목적격 보어에 현재분사 'spending'을 사용하였으므로 틀린 문장이다. 따라서 목적어 'you'와 능동 관계이므로 'spending'을 동사원형 'spend'로 수정해야 한다.

오답해설

② 출제 포인트: 부사절의 접속사
'unless'는 부사절을 이끄는 접속사이다. 또한 부정의 의미를 내포하므로 뒤에 오는 부사절에는 부정부사를 사용하지 않는다. 해당 문장은 'unless'가 쓰인 문장으로 뒤에 오는 부사절에 부정부사를 사용하지 않았으며 주어진 해석과 일치하므로 옳은 문장이다.

③ 출제 포인트: 시간의 부사구, 부사절 / 수동태 불가동사
「when+주어+동사」는 시간의 부사절로 동사에 과거시제를 사용하는 경우 주절의 동사에도 과거시제를 사용한다. 따라서 과거시제로 쓰인 'said', 'occurred'는 옳게 사용되었다. 또한 'occur'는 완전자동사이므로 수동태로 사용할 수 없다.

④ 출제 포인트: 동명사 관용표현
'look froward to'는 동명사 관용표현으로 '~하기를 고대하다, 기대하다'를 뜻하며 뒤에 목적어로 명사와 동명사가 온다. 해당 관용표현에서의 'to'는 'to부정사'의 'to'가 아니라 전치사로 쓰인 'to'임에 유의해야한다.

08 정답 ②

정답해설

주어진 문장에서는 "Too big to fail"의 개념을 "한 사업체가 경제의 기능에 매우 깊이 관련되어 그것의 도산이 경제에 전반적으로 막심한 피해를 주게 될 상황에 정부가 개입하겠다는 발상"이라고 소개하고 있다. 주어진 문장의 'a business'를 (A)의 'such a company'가 가리키고 있으므로, (A)가 주어진 문장에 이어지는 것이 적절하며, (A)의 "a catastrophic ripple effect throughout the economy(경제 전체에 비극적인 파급효과)"에 해당하는 구체적인 예시를 (C)에서 '실업 문제(problems with unemployment), 타 사업체에의 영향(problems with companies ~)' 등으로 설명하고 있으므로, (A)에 (C)가 이어져야 한다. 마지막으로 이러한 상황이 발생할 경우 '정부'의 대처에 대해 언급하고 있는 (B)가 이어지는 것이 자연스럽다. 따라서 정답은 '② (A) - (C) - (B)'이다.

오답해설

① (A)에서 설명한 파급효과에 대한 예시를 나타내는 (C)가 바로 이어지는 것이 자연스러우므로, (A)에 (B)가 이어지는 것이 부적절하다.
③, ④ 나머지는 문맥상 어색하므로 오답이다.

해석

"Too big to fail"은 한 사업체가 경제의 기능에 매우 깊이 관련되어 그것의 도산이 경제에 전반적으로 막심한 피해를 주게 될 상황에 정부가 개입하겠다는 발상을 묘사한다.
(A) 만일 그러한 기업이 도산한다면, 그것은 경제 전체에 비극적인 파급효과를 미칠 것이다.
(C) 도산은 직원들이 실직함에 따라 실업 문제를 일으킬 뿐만 아니라, 고객으로서 도산한 회사의 사업에 의지하는 회사들에게도 문제를 일으킬 것이다.
(B) 개념적으로, 이러한 상황에서, 정부는 지원을 위한 자금 할당을 결정할 때 경제 실패를 허용하는 비용과 비교하여 긴급 구제의 비용을 고려할 것이다.

어휘

intervene 개입하다, 끼어들다
disastrous 처참한
catastrophic 비극적인, 파멸의
conceptually 개념적으로
in comparison to …와 비교하여
ingrained 깊이 배어든, 뿌리 깊은
at large 전반적으로
ripple effect 파급효과
bailout 긴급 구제
allocate 할당하다

09 정답 ④

정답해설

본문 초반에서 'People with names like "Yevgeni Dherzhinsky" or "Shobha Bhattacharya" were thought to be more unreliable than those with more pronounceable names like "Putali Angami".(Yevgeni Dherzhinsky 또는 Shobha Bhattacharya와 같은 이름을 지닌 사람들이 "Putali Angami"와 같이 더 발음하기 쉬운 이름을 지닌 사람들보다 더 신뢰할 수 없다고 생각되었다.)'라고 하며 사람들은 발음하기 어려운 이름을 가진 사람들을 더 신뢰할 수 없다고 생각했다'라고 언급하고 있으며, 본문 후반에서는 'When participants thought that a statement had been made by someone with an easier name, they were more likely to consider it true than when the statement had been paired with a difficult name(그 문제가 어려운 이름과 짝지어져 있을 때 보다 참여자가 그 문제가 쉬운 이름을 가진 사람에 의해 만들어졌다고 생각했을 때 그들이 그것을 참이라고 생각할 가능성이 더 높았다).'라고 하며 '문제가 쉬운 이름과 짝지어져 있을 때 그것을 참이라고 생각할 가능성이 더 높았다'라고 언급하고 있다. 즉, 발음하기 어려운 이름을 지닌 사람들을 '덜 신뢰한다'라는 것이 연구의 결과이다. 따라서 글의 요지로 가장 적절한 문장은 '④ The harder your name is to pronounce, the more untrustworthy people will assume you are(당신의 이름이 발음하기 더 어려울수록 사람들은 당신을 더 신뢰할 수 없다고 생각할 것이다).'이다.

오답해설

① 이름과 성공의 관계는 본문에 언급되지 않는다.
② 본문에 등장한 연구에서는 '이름에 기반을 둔 판단'을 조사하고 있으며, 그러한 행위가 부적절한지 여부에 대해서는 언급하고 있지 않다.
③ 본문에 언급되지 않는 내용이므로 오답이다.

해석

연구원들은 전 세계의 여러 지역에서 사용되는 이름들 몇 쌍을 모아, 참여자들에게 오직 이름에만 기초해 그 사람을 얼마나 신뢰할 수 있는지 평가해 달라고 요청했다. "Yevgeni Dherzhinsky" 또는 "Shobha Bhattacharya"와 같은 이름을 지닌 사람들이 "Putali Angami"와 같이 더 발음하기 쉬운 이름을 지닌 사람들보다 더 신뢰할 수 없다고 생각되었다. 또 다른 실험에서, 연구원들은 "기린은 점프를 할 수 없는 유일한 포유류이다"와 같은 참, 거짓 퀴즈 문제를 발음하기 어렵거나 쉬운 이름들 중 하나와 함께 짝을 지었다. 그 문제가 어려운 이름과 짝지어져 있을 때 보다 참여자가 그 문제가 쉬운 이름을 가진 사람에 의해 만들어졌다고 생각했을 때 그들이 그것을 참이라고 생각할 가능성이 더 높았다.

① 당신의 이름이 당신의 성공에 큰 영향을 미칠 수 있다.
② 사람을 이름으로 판단하는 것은 바람직하지 않다.
③ 한 사람의 성격과 그 또는 그녀의 이름 사이에는 아무 관계가 없다.
④ 당신의 이름이 발음하기 더 어려울수록 사람들은 당신을 더 신뢰할 수 없다고 생각할 것이다.

어휘

pronounceable 발음할 수 있는
trivia 퀴즈, 상식
untrustworthy 믿을 수 없는, 신뢰할 수 없는
unreliable 믿을 수 없는, 신뢰할 수 없는
undesirable 바람직하지 않은

오답률 TOP 3
10 정답 ③

정답해설

본문 중반 "This issue of pragmatism is a chief reason why Edison fired Tesla(이러한 실용주의 문제는 Edison이 Tesla를 해고한 주요 이유이다)."를 통해 'Tesla는 실용주의자가 아니었음'을 유추할 수 있으며, "JP Morgan decided to pick up the Serbian inventor and finance his lab, but when Morgan realized that none of Tesla's ideas could actually produce anything of direct value, he withdrew his funding(JP Morgan이 이 Serbia인 발명가를 발탁하여 그의 실험실에 자금을 지원해주기로 결정했지만, Morgan이 Tesla의 아이디어 중 아무것도 직접적인 수익을 낼 수 있는 어떠한 것을 실제로 생산해낼 수 없다는 것을 깨달았을 때, 그는 그의 자금지원을 중단했)."을 통해 'Tesla의 아이디어는 즉각적인 수익을 낼 수 있는 실용적인 것들이 아니었음'을 알 수 있다. 이러한 'Tesla의 실용적이지 못함' 때문에 그는 빈곤 속에서 죽어갔으므로, 빈칸에 가장 적절한 표현은 '③ practical(실용적인)'이다.

오답해설

① Tesla의 창의성에 대한 내용은 본문에 언급되지 않는다.
② Tesla의 사교성에 대한 내용은 본문에 언급되지 않는다.
④ 본문의 내용과 반대되는 표현으로, 본문 내용을 통해 Tesla는 '실용적'이기보다는 '이상적'이었음을 알 수 있으므로 빈칸에 적절하지 않다.

해석

그것은 Edison 대 Tesla 논쟁에서도 동일하다. 주요한 차이점 중 하나는 Edison이 시장성이 없는 아이디어는 생각하지 않았다는 것이다. 구매자의 주목을 받지 못할 아이디어가 무슨 의미가 있는가? 누가 실험실 임대료를 지불할 것인가? 이러한 실용주의 문제는 Edison이 Tesla를 해고한 주요 이유이다. JP Morgan이 이 Serbia인 발명가를 발탁하여 그의 실험실에 자금을 지원해주기로 결정했지만, Morgan이 Tesla의 아이디어 중 아무것도 직접적인 수익을 낼 수 있는 어떠한 것을 실제로 생산해낼 수 없다는 것을 깨달았을 때, 그는 그의 자금지원을 중단했다. Tesla는 더 이상 실험실 비용을 감당할 수 없었고 빈곤하게 죽었다. 그가 <u>실용적</u>이 되길 거부한 것 또는 <u>실용적</u>이 될 수 없었던 것이 그의 열정을 추구할 그의 능력을 희생시켰다.

① 창의적인
② 사교적인
③ 실용적인
④ 공상적인

어휘

debate 논쟁
viability 생존 능력, 실행 가능성
pragmatism 실용주의
withdraw 중단[취소/철회]하다
cost 희생하게 하다, 잃게 하다
entertain (생각·희망·감정 등을) 품다
traction 끄는 힘, 매력
fire 해고하다
destitute 빈곤한, 결핍한
pursue 추구하다

결국엔 성정혜 영어 하프모의고사
기적사 DAY 49

| 01 | ① | 02 | ① | 03 | ② | 04 | ④ | 05 | ④ |
| 06 | ④ | 07 | ③ | 08 | ② | 09 | ① | 10 | ③ |

오답률 TOP 2

01 정답 ①

정답해설

밑줄 친 단어는 문맥상 '입증되지 않은'의 의미이고, 유의어로는 ① unsubstantiated가 적절하다.

해석

물론, 이들은 고려되기를 우려하는 인구이기 때문에, 증거자료가 없는 것에 대한 대부분의 정보는 **입증되지 않은** 것이다.
① 입증되지 않은
② 유례없는, 매우 뛰어난
③ 격노한
④ 이해하기 어려운, 당혹한, 복잡한

어휘

undocumented 증거가 없는, 증명서를 가지지 않은
anecdotal 일화의, 일화적인, 입증되지 않은
unsubstantiated 입증되지 않은   unsurpassed 유례없는, 매우 뛰어난
enraged 격노한
perplexed 이해하기 어려운, 당혹한, 복잡한

02 정답 ①

정답해설

밑줄 친 단어는 문맥상 '종속된, 보조의'로 사용되었고, 유의어가 아닌 ① aloof가 정답이다.

해석

그 목표들은 또한 경찰, 법무부와 그것에 **종속된** 기관들, 국가정보원을 개혁하고, 더 공정한 조세 제도 도입하는 것을 포함한다.
① 초연한, 냉담한
② 보조의
③ 보조의
④ 부수적인

어휘

Ministry of Justice 법무부
National Intelligence Service 국가정보원
aloof 초연한, 냉담한   adjuvant 보조의
auxiliary 보조의   accessory 부수적인

오답률 TOP 3

03 정답 ②

정답해설

주어진 빈칸은 문맥상 '강인한'이 적절하다. 따라서 정답은 ② tenacious이다.

해석
마지막 스트로크들의 끝에서 그 혹은 자라[악어거북]만큼이나 단호한 생각과 의견들을 고수하는 **강인한** 정신 상태를 나타낸다는 것이 불현듯 떠올랐다.
① 증가적인, 증대하는
② 강인한, 완강한
③ 정확한, 꼼꼼한
④ 보충의, 임시의

어휘
hit upon 불현듯 떠오르다
snapping turtle 무는 힘이 강해 한번 물면 잘 떨어지지 않는 거북류의 동물을 총칭. 한국식으로는 자라, 미국식으로는 악어거북
augmentative 증가적인, 증대하는   tenacious 강인한, 완강한
precise 정확한, 꼼꼼한   supplementary 보충의, 임시의

04 정답 ④

정답해설
학생은 교수님에게 몇 가지 말씀드리고 싶은 것이 있다고 하자 교수님은 무엇을 도와줄지 묻는다. 학생은 다음 주에 있을 발표에 관해 말을 꺼내자 교수님은 주제에 대한 피드백이 필요하냐고 묻지만, 학생은 사실 군중 앞에 서 있을 때 '가슴이 벌렁거리는(have butterflies in my stomach)' 자신의 고민을 털어놓는다. 학생의 고민을 듣고 교수님은 좀 더 자신감을 가지고 자기 자신을 믿으라고 조언해준다. 학생이 편하다고 생각하는 사람과 대화한다고 생각해보라고 말해주자 학생은 기분이 한결 나아졌다며 감사의 말씀을 드린다.

오답해설
① 학생이 교수님에게 발표에 관한 고민을 털어놓으며 군중 앞에 서 있을 때 '각별히 환영한다(roll out the red carpet)'라는 것은 문맥상 어색하다.
② 발표에 관해 이야기하며 군중 앞에 설 때 '새로운 것을 주의 깊게 지켜보는(keep an ear to the ground)' 것이 고민이라는 것은 대화의 흐름상 적합하지 않다.
③ 학생은 발표할 때 군중 앞에 서면 모든 것이 깜깜해진다며 '안 좋은 감정을 가진다(have a chip on my shoulder)'라고 하는 것은 맥락의 흐름을 해친다.

해석
학생: 시간 내주셔서 감사합니다, 교수님. 저 몇 가지 사항들에 대해 말씀드리고 싶었어요.
교수님: 전혀 문제없어. 무엇을 도와줄까?
학생: 아시다시피 제가 다음 주에 발표를 해요.
교수님: 오, 알겠다. 네 주제에 대해서 피드백이 필요하구나, 맞지?
학생: 음…. 아니요. 사실 제가 군중 앞에 설 때마다 <u>가슴이 철렁철렁해요</u>. 모든 것이 그저 깜깜해져요.
교수님: 네가 좀 더 자신감을 가지고 너 자신을 믿어봐. 그저 네가 편한 사람과 대화한다고 상상해봐.
학생: 조언해주셔서 감사합니다. 발표에 대해서 정말 걱정했는데 지금은 훨씬 나아졌어요.
교수님: 잘 될 거야. 너무 긴장하지 마.
① 각별히 환영하다
② 새로운 것을 주의 깊게 지켜보다
③ 안 좋은 감정을 갖다
④ 가슴이 철렁철렁하다, 걱정을 하다

어휘
upcoming 다가오는   feedback 피드백
crowd 군중   black out 깜깜해지다
confident 자신감 있는   comfortable 편안한
advice 조언
roll out the red carpet 각별히 환영하다
keep an ear to the ground 새로운 것을 주의 깊게 지켜보다
have a chip on one's shoulder 안 좋은 감정을 갖다
have butterflies in one's stomach 가슴이 철렁철렁하다, 걱정을 하다

05 정답 ④

정답해설
④ 출제 포인트: 동명사의 태
'object to'는 '~에 반대하다'를 뜻하며 목적어로 명사와 동명사를 사용한다. 해당 문장은 'object to'의 목적어로 동명사를 사용하였으며 동명사의 목적어가 없으므로 수동형 동명사 'being relocated'를 사용하는 것이 옳다.

오답해설
① 출제 포인트: to+[동사원형 vs. 동명사]
해당 문장에서 'to'는 전치사가 아닌 부정사이므로 뒤에 동사원형을 사용해야 한다. 따라서 'discovering'을 'discover'로 수정해야 한다. 여기에서 to부정사는 부사적 용법에 목적으로 '~하기 위해서'의 의미로 해석된다. 단, 'walk down to + 장소'는 '~(장소)로 걸어 내려오다'를 뜻하는 숙어이므로 혼동하지 않도록 유의해야한다.
② 출제 포인트: 현재분사 vs. 과거분사
과거분사 'struggled'가 목적격 보어로 사용되었으나 'struggle'은 완전자동사이므로 완료시제를 제외하고는 과거분사를 사용할 수 없다. 따라서 'struggle'을 'struggling'으로 수정해야 한다.
③ 출제 포인트: 시간의 부사구
'these days'는 시간의 부사구로 현재시제와 함께 사용한다. 해당 문장은 시간의 부사구로 'these days'를 사용하였으나 동사에 과거시제인 'worked'를 사용하였으므로 틀린 문장이다. 따라서 'worked'를 현재시제 'work'로 수정해야 한다.

해석
① 당신은 크고 아름다운 호수를 발견하기 위해 정원에서 걸어 내려온다.
② 폭발음은 그가 고주파 소리를 듣기 위해 애쓰는 상태로 두었다. (= 그 폭발음 때문에 그는 고주파 소리를 듣는 데 어려움을 겪었다.)
③ 우리 모두는 오늘날 오랜 시간 일하지만, 많은 사람들은 귀가하면 그것을 보충하려고 애쓴다.
④ 그는 자신이 30년 이상 그 지역에서 살아왔다고 주장하면서, 이전되는 것에 반대할 것이라고 말했다.

06 정답 ④

정답해설
④ 출제 포인트: 능동태 vs. 수동태
'speak'가 능동태로 사용되었으나 'Over seventy local languages and dialects'는 'speak'의 행위자가 될 수 없으며 주어진 해석과 일치하지 않으므로 틀린 문장이다. 따라서 'speak'을 수동태 'are spoken'으로 수정해야 한다.

오답해설
① 출제 포인트: 타동사구[완전타동사+목적어+전치사+목적어]
「connect+A[목적어]+with+B[목적어]」는 'A를 B와 연결하다'를 뜻한다. 또한 'police'는 집합명사로 정관사 the와 함께 쓰이며 반드시 복수 동사로 수일치한다.
② 출제 포인트: 주어와 동사 수일치
단수형태 주어 'The power'와 단수형태 동사 'comes'가 수일치하므로

옳은 문장이다. 또한 해당 문장에서의 'that'은 'those'를 선행사로 가지는 주격관계대명사이다.

③ **출제 포인트: 전치사 vs. 접속사**
해당 문장에서 'that'과 'while'은 접속사이므로 뒤에 절이 온다. 'that'은 동사 'have argued'의 목적어절을 이끄는 접속사로 사용되었으며, 'while'은 부사절을 이끄는 접속사로 옳게 사용되었다.

07 정답 ③

정답해설

③ **출제 포인트: 부사절의 접속사**
'lest'는 부사절을 이끄는 접속사이다. 또한 부정의 의미를 내포하므로 뒤에 오는 부사절에는 부정부사를 사용하지 않는다. 해당 문장은 'lest'가 쓰인 문장으로 뒤에 오는 부사절에 부정부사 'not'을 사용하였으므로 틀린 문장이다. 따라서 'not disturb'를 'disturb'로 수정해야 한다.

오답해설

① **출제 포인트: 시간의 부사구, 부사절 / what vs. that**
「when+주어+동사」는 시간의 부사절로 동사에 과거시제를 사용하는 경우 주절의 동사에도 과거시제를 사용한다. 또한 해당 문장에서 'what'은 관계대명사로 'to do'의 목적어 역할을 하며 관계대명사절이 만들어지는 과정은 다음과 같다.

That's the thing. + My Scottish grandmother told me I needed to do the thing when I was five years old. (the thing을 선행사)
That's the thing which my Scottish grandmother told me I needed to do when I was five years old. (목적격 관계대명사 which를 사용)
That's what my Scottish grandmother told me I needed to do when I was five years old. (목적격 관계대명사 what을 사용)

② **출제 포인트: 사역동사**
해당 문장에서 'make'는 사역동사이므로 목적격 보어에 원형부정사 'taste'를 사용하는 것이 옳다. 해당 문장에서 원형부정사로 쓰인 'taste'는 불완전자동사이므로 'taste'의 주격 보어로 과거분사 'burnt'를 사용하였다.

④ **출제 포인트: 동명사 관용표현**
「be worth+동명사」는 관용표현으로 '~할 가치가 있다'를 뜻한다. 또한 동명사 'getting'은 불완전자동사의 성격을 가지고 있으므로 주격 보어로 과거분사 'checked'를 사용하였다.

오답률 TOP 1

08 정답 ②

정답해설

해당 지문은 '미국의 금융 경제 구조'에 대해 설명하고 있다. 본문 초반에서 "The biggest six have $10 trillion in assets, almost twice as much as the next 30 combined(가장 거대한 6곳의 은행이 10조 달러의 자산을 보유하고 있으며, 이는 다음으로 거대한 30곳의 은행을 합한 것의 거의 두 배에 달한다)."를 통해 '6곳의 거대한 은행에 막대한 자금이 몰려 있음'을 설명하며, "That's a lot of money in a small number of hands(그것은 소수의 손아귀 안의 수많은 액수이다)."라고 언급하고 있다. 빈칸 이후에서 '정부는 2008년 경제 위기 당시, 수많은 주택 보유자와 사업가들의 분노에도 불구하고, 은행의 도산을 막기 위해 엄청난 액수의 자금을 투입했다'라는 것을 설명하며, 마지막 문장 "Regulators have been working ever since to make it possible for even the biggest financial institutions to close without triggering a meltdown(규제 기관들은 그때 이후로 가장 거대한 금융 기관조차도 붕괴를 초래하지 않고 폐업하는 것을 가능하게 만들기 위해 노력해오고 있다)."을 통해, 그러한 거대 기업의 도산이 경제 붕괴를 일으킬 수도 있음을 암시하고 있다. 현재에도 소수의 은행에 자금이 몰려 있는 상황이므로, 정부로서는 해당 은행의 도산은 경제 안정을 위해 '있어서는 안 되는 시나리오'인 셈이다. 따라서 빈칸에 가장 적절한 표현은 '② failure is not an option(실패는 선택지가 아니다)'이다.

오답해설

① '실패를 예측'하는 것에 대한 내용은 본문에 언급되지 않는다.
③ 본문에서 '실패를 막은 정부의 개입'에 대해 언급하고 있으므로, '실패는 불가피하다'라는 표현은 빈칸에 적절하지 않다.
④ 본문의 내용에 따르면 '실패'는 경제에 부정적인 영향을 미치는 요소인데, '실패는 훌륭한 교사이다'라는 표현은 실패를 긍정적으로 묘사하고 있으므로, 본문의 내용에 부합하지 않는다.

해석

미국에는 약 6,000곳의 은행이 있다. 가장 거대한 6곳의 은행이 10조 달러의 자산을 보유하고 있으며, 이는 다음으로 거대한 30곳의 은행을 합한 것의 거의 두 배에 달한다. 미국의 가장 거대한 6곳의 은행은 1997년 이래로 5배 이상의 자산을 증식시켜왔다. 그것은 소수의 손아귀 안의 수많은 액수이다. 이것은 정부가 2008년의 공황 중에 결정했던 것과 같이 <u>실패는 선택지가 아니라는 것</u>을 의미할지도 모른다. 많은 주택 보유자와 사업가들이 파산하는 가운데 은행을 살리기 위해 7,000억 달러를 지출한 것에 대한 분노가 치솟았다. 규제 기관들은 그때 이후로 가장 거대한 금융 기관조차도 붕괴를 초래하지 않고 폐업하는 것을 가능하게 만들기 위해 노력해오고 있다.

① 실패는 예측할 수 없다
② 실패는 선택지가 아니다
③ 실패는 불가피할 것이다
④ 실패는 훌륭한 교사이다

어휘

asset 자산
soar 급증하다, 치솟다
go under 도산하다, 파산하다
meltdown 붕괴, 폭락
inevitable 불가피한
five-fold 5배의
disbursement 지출, 지불
trigger 촉발시키다
unpredictable 예측할 수 없는

09 정답 ①

정답해설

본문에서는 '흑인처럼 들리는 이름(black-sounding name)'과 '백인처럼 들리는 이름(white-sounding name)'이 각각 받는 평가에 대해 비교하며, 전자가 후자보다 더 열등한 평가 및 대우를 받는 경향이 있다고 설명하고 있다. 즉, 전형적인 흑인 이름을 가진 사람들에 대한 편견이 존재한다고 설명하는 글이므로, 본문의 제목으로 가장 적절한 것은 '① Names And Racial Bias (이름과 인종적 편견)'이다.

오답해설

② 본문에서는 '흑인처럼 들리는 이름(black-sounding name)'과 '백인처럼 들리는 이름(white-sounding name)'에 대해 언급하고 있으며, 그러한 이름을 가진 사람들에 대한 실제 '인종(race)'에 대해서는 언급하지 않는다. 즉, '흑인처럼 들리는 이름을 가진 백인'은 실제 인종에 관계없이 이름 때문에 '몸집이 크고, 위험하며 폭력적으로 생각될 가능성'이 있는 것이다. 또한 본문에서는 '인종적인 이름에 대한 사람들의 인식'에 대해 언급하고 있고, 인종에 따른 실제 '사회적 지위(Social Status)'의 차이에 대해서는 언급하지 않는다. 따라서 글의 제목으로 부적절하다.
③, ④ 본문에서 언급되지 않은 내용이므로 오답이다.

적 공론가에게는 ④ <u>상관이 없다</u>, 왜냐하면 그것은 검증될 필요가 없기 때문이다. 반면, 불쌍한 실용주의자는 그 또는 그녀의 접근이 실제로 작동을 하는지 아닌지를 알아보기 위한 복잡한 절차를 감내해야 하고, 당황스럽게도 합리적으로 보이는 많은 아이디어들이 실패한다.

어휘

pragmatism 실용주의
on one's (own) merits 시비곡직에 따라
hesitant 주저하는, 망설이는
prone to …을 잘하는
indecisive 결단력 없는, 우유부단한
reference 인용, 언급
irrelevant 관계없는, 무의미한
rigmarole 복잡한 절차

pragmatist 실용주의자
messy 골치 아픈, 성가신, 지저분한
ideologue 이론적 공론가
decisive 결단력 있는
mission statement 강령
endure 참다, 견디다
seeming …하게 보이는

해석

전형적으로 "흑인"처럼 들리는 이름을 가진 학생들은 선생님들에 의해 문제아로 분류되는 경향이 있다. 그러한 이름을 가진 일자리 지원자들은 백인처럼 들리는 상대보다 면접을 제안받을 가능성이 더 낮다. "흑인"처럼 들리는 이름을 가진 주민이 학교 또는 도서관에 대한 정보를 얻기 위해 지역 정부에 연락을 할 때, 그들은 응답을 받을 가능성이 더 낮다. 학술지 Evolution and Human Behavior에 목요일에 게재된 충격적인 새로운 연구가 이러한 불편한 결과의 목록을 더 추가한다. 대부분 백인 참가자로 이루어진 그 연구는 흑인처럼 들리는 이름을 가진 사람이 전형적으로 백인처럼 들리는 이름을 가진 사람들보다 몸집이 크고, 위험하며 폭력적으로 생각될 가능성이 더 높다는 것을 보여준다.

① 이름과 인종적 편견
② 인종과 사회적 지위
③ 다른 인종에서의 다른 이름
④ 전통 이름과 최신 유행 이름

어휘

stereotypically 전형적으로, 진부하게
be labeled as …로 분류되다
counterpart 상대방
compendium 목록, 개론, 개요
bias 편견
applicant 지원자
call in 부르다, 요구하다
disturbing 충격적인

10 정답 ③

정답해설

본문에서 '사람들은 실용주의를 찬양하지만, 실제로는 실용주의를 싫어한다'라고 언급하며, 그 이유로 '실용주의는 합리적인 방향을 찾기 위해 모든 것을 검증하고 확인하는 절차를 거쳐야 하고, 이로 인해 실용주의는 '망설이는 (hesitant)' 것처럼 보이며 해당 아이디어의 옳고 그름에 대한 판단이 가능해지게 된다'라고 설명한다. 이에 반해 '이론적 공론가(The ideologue)'는 '옳고 그름을 확인할 필요 없이, 이론적인 해답을 내놓으면 되기 때문에 실용주의자와는 반대로 "결단력이 있어" 보인다'라는 내용이 되어야 한다. 따라서 ③의 'indecisive(결단력이 없는)'는 'decisive(결단력이 있는)'로 바뀌어야 한다.

오답해설

① 문장 초반에서 "we pay lip service to the concept(우리는 그 개념에 대해 입에 바른 소리를 한다)"라고 언급한 후, 'but(그러나)'으로 연결하고 있으므로 '좋은 이야기를 해주는 것'과 반대되는 내용인 'dislike(싫어하다)'가 들어가는 것이 적절하다.
② '실용주의는 각각의 상황의 시시비비를 따지며 앞으로 나아갈 합리적인 방향을 찾아내려고 노력한다(the pragmatist tries to take each situation on its own merits and figure out a sensible way forward,~)'라고 언급하고 있으므로, 신중한 태도임을 알 수 있다. 이러한 신중함이 실용주의를 '망설이는(hesitant)' 것처럼 보이게 할 수 있으므로 문맥에 적절하다.
④ 이론적 공론가의 해답은 '검증될 필요가 없다(~ it needs no testing.)'라고 언급하고 있으므로, 해답이 틀렸는지 여부는 이론적 공론가에게는 '상관이 없음(irrelevant)'을 알 수 있다.

해석

여기 문제가 있다: 우리는 그 개념에 대해 입에 바른 소리를 하지만, 실제로 우리는 실용주의를 ① <u>싫어한다</u>. 실용주의자는 각각의 상황의 시시비비를 따지며 앞으로 나아갈 합리적인 방향을 찾아내려고 노력하기 때문에, 실용주의는 ② <u>망설이고</u> 성가시며 오류가 나기 쉽게 보이는 경향이 있다. 그에 비해 이론적 공론가는 ③ **결단력이 없어(→ 결단력이 있어)** 보인다. 이데올로기는 Karl Marx와 Milton Friedman 또는 최신 기업 강령을 인용하여 항상 깔끔한 해답을 내놓는다. 그 해답이 단순히 잘못된 것일 수도 있다는 사실은 이론

결국엔 성정혜 영어 하프모의고사
기적사 DAY 50

01	④	02	③	03	②	04	②	05	③
06	②	07	①	08	②	09	④	10	④

01 정답 ④

정답해설

밑줄 친 단어는 문맥상 '저지하다, 막다'로 사용되었다. 따라서 의미가 가장 먼 ④ put upon이 정답이다.

해석

정의의 가능성은 그의 몇몇 측근들의 여행 규제보다는 잔인한 폭군을 **저지할** 가능성이 더 높다.
① 억제하다
② 설득해서 그만두게 하다
③ 막다
④ 속이다, 부당하게 이용하다

어휘

tyrant 독재자, 폭군 inhibit 억제하다
talk out of 설득해서 그만두게 하다 obstruct 막다
put upon 속이다, 부당하게 이용하다 crony 친구, 측근자

오답률 TOP 2
02 정답 ③

정답해설

밑줄 친 단어는 문맥상 '공모하다'로 사용되었고, 유의어로는 ③ collude가 적절하다.

해석

하지만 신중하지 못한 개인의 선택들과 역사의 우연들은 항상 Marrero를 향해 **음모를 꾸몄던** 것처럼 보였다.
① 떠다니다
② 인정하다, 허용하다
③ 공모하다
④ 대하다, 처리하다

어휘

float over 떠다니다 concede 인정하다, 허용하다
collude 공모하다 deal with 대하다, 처리하다

03 정답 ②

정답해설

주어진 빈칸은 문맥상 '따라 하다'가 적절하므로 ② emulate가 정답이다.

해석

우리 여성들은 성공하기 위해서는 우리가 "남성처럼 행동"하고 남성의 감정적 억제를 **따라야**만 했다고 믿었다.
① 손상시키다
② 따라 하다, 모방하다
③ 복습하다
④ 불현듯 떠올리다[생각하다]

어휘

masculine 남자다운 restraint 억제, 규제
impair 손상시키다 emulate 따라 하다, 모방하다
brush up on 복습하다 hit upon 불현듯 떠올리다[생각하다]

04 정답 ②

정답해설

A는 어제 정기 건강검진을 받기 위해 병원에 다녀온 이야기를 B에게 한다. 의사께서 A에게 척추가 올곧지 않다고 말씀하셨다는 이야기를 했다. 이를 들은 B는 A의 자세에 문제가 있는 것 아니냐며 매일 운동을 해보라고 권유한다. 운동이 척추 문제를 해결하는 데 효과적인지 묻는 A에게 B는 스트레칭조차도 ② '건강하게(fit as a fiddle)' 지낼 수 있도록 도움을 줄 수 있다고 답변한다. 그러자 A는 B의 말에 수긍하며 매일 스트레칭하는 것으로 시작해보겠다고 다짐한다.

오답해설

① 운동이 척추 문제를 해결하는 데 효과적인지 묻는 A에게 B는 스트레칭조차도 '대단한 인물(a big bug)'이라고 말하는 것은 문맥상 부자연스럽다.
③ 스트레칭은 건강하게 지낼 수 있도록 해준다고 말하는 맥락의 대화에서 스트레칭이 '금주하고 있을(on the water wagon)' 수 있도록 해준다는 것은 부적절하다.
④ 운동이 척추 문제를 해결하는 데 효과적이며 스트레칭조차도 '발견하기 힘든 것(a needle in a haystack)'이라고 말하는 것은 부적절하다.

해석

A: 나는 어제 정기 건강검진을 받으러 병원을 방문했어.
B: 잘했어. 의사께서 뭐라고 하셨어?
A: 내 척추에 사소한 문제들이 있다고 하셨어. 올곧아야 하는 만큼 그렇지 않다고 하셔.
B: 아마 네 자세에 문제가 있나 봐. 매일 운동을 해 보는 건 어때?
A: 운동이 척추 문제를 해결하는 데 효과적이라고 생각해?
B: 왜 아니야? 스트레칭조차도 네가 건강하게 지낼 수 있도록 도울 수 있어.
A: 네 말이 맞아. 매일 스트레칭을 하는 작은 행동으로 시작해볼게.
B: 앞으로 잘 되길 바라!
① 대단한 인물
② 건강한
③ 금주하고 있는
④ 발견하기 힘든 것

어휘

check-up 건강검진 regular 정기적인
backbone 척추 posture 자세
exercise 운동하다 effective 효과적인
spinal issues 척추 문제 progress 진전, 성과
a big bug 대단한 인물 fit as a fiddle 건강한
on the water wagon 금주하고 있는
a needle in a haystack 발견하기 힘든 것

오답률 TOP 1
05 정답 ③

정답해설

③ 출제 포인트: 시간의 부사구

'last night'은 시간의 부사구로 과거시제 동사와 함께 사용한다. 해당 문장은 시간의 부사구로 'last night'을 사용하였으며 동사에 'say'의 과거시제인 'said'를 사용하였으므로 옳은 문장이다. 또한 that절 이하의 동사 'expected'는 목적격 보어로 to부정사를 가지는 동사 'expect'의 과거형으로 목적격 보어 자리에 'to be'가 옳게 사용되었다.

오답해설

① 출제 포인트: 현재분사 vs. 과거분사

완전타동사 'know'의 과거분사인 'known'이 사용되었으나 뒤에 목적어 'that ~ five years'가 있으며 수식하는 대상인 생략된 주어 'we'와 능동관계이므로 틀린 문장이다. 따라서 과거분사 'known'을 현재분사 'knowing'으로 수정해야 한다.

② 출제 포인트: to+[동사원형] vs. 동명사

'be supposed to'는 '~인 것으로 여겨지다, ~해야 한다'를 뜻하며 뒤에 동사원형이 온다. 해당 문장은 'be supposed to'가 사용되었으나 뒤에 동명사 'impacting'을 사용하였으므로 틀린 문장이다. 따라서 동명사 'impacting'을 동사원형 'impact'로 수정해야 한다. 'be supposed to'에서 'to'는 전치사가 아닌 to부정사의 'to'라는 사실에 주의해야 한다.

④ 출제 포인트: 동명사의 태

'when it comes to'는 관용표현으로 '~에 관한 한'을 뜻하며 해당 표현에서의 'to'는 전치사로서 뒤에 명사와 동명사를 사용한다. 해당 문장은 'when it comes to'가 쓰인 문장으로 뒤에 수동형 동명사를 사용하였으나 동명사의 목적어 'the proper security program'이 있으므로 틀린 문장이다. 따라서 'being built'를 능동형 동명사 'building'으로 수정해야 한다.

해석

① 우리는 처음 4, 5년간 빠듯할 것이라는 것을 알면서 집을 샀다.
② 내가 아이였을 때 이후로, 내 삶에 영향을 미친 것으로 여겨지는 많은 전쟁들이 있었다.
③ 판사는 새로운 통제 명령 조건이 매우 비슷할 것으로 예상한다고 지난밤에 말했다.
④ 적절한 보안 프로그램을 만드는 것에 관해 당신의 위치에서 다른 사람들에게 해줄 수 있는 최고의 조언은 무엇입니까?

06 정답 ②

정답해설

② 출제 포인트: 전치사 vs. 접속사

접속사 'although' 뒤에 명사(구) 'his age'를 사용하였으므로 틀린 문장이다. 따라서 절을 이끄는 접속사 'although'를 전치사 'in spite of' 또는 'despite'로 수정해야 한다. 이때 'the boy ~ his drug habit'은 접속사 'that'이 이끄는 절이므로 'although'가 이끄는 절로 오해하지 않도록 주의해야 한다. 또한 주절의 동사 'told'가 과거 시점임을 밝히고 있으므로 정확하게는 'admitted'를 'the boy'가 인정한 것은 대과거(과거완료)임을 나타내는 'had admitted'로 사용할 수 있다.

오답해설

① 출제 포인트: 주어와 동사 수일치

'The police'는 복수로 취급하므로 동사에 복수형태인 'were'를 사용하는 것이 옳다.

③ 출제 포인트: 능동태 vs. 수동태 / 타동사구[완전타동사+목적어+전치사+목적어]

해당 문장은 'attribute A to B'의 수동태인 'A be attributed to B'가 쓰인 문장으로 주어진 해석과 일치하므로 옳은 문장이다. 또한 'deprive'는 '빼앗다'의 의미로 'deprive+목적어[대상]+of+목적어[사물]'의 형태로 쓰이므로 해당 문장에서 옳게 사용되었다.

④ 출제 포인트: 타동사구[완전타동사+목적어+전치사+목적어]/능동태 vs. 수동태

해당 문장은 「cure+목적어[대상]+of+목적어[사물]」의 수동태인 「목적어[대상]+be cured of+목적어[사물]」이 쓰인 문장으로 주어진 해석과 일치하므로 옳은 문장이다. 또한 분사구문으로 사용된 현재분사 'leading'은 불완전타동사로 「lead+목적어+목적격 보어[to+동사원형]」의 구조를 가진다.

07 정답 ①

정답해설

① 출제 포인트: 동명사 관용표현

「cannot help+-ing」는 관용표현으로 '~하지 않을 수 없다'를 뜻한다. 해당 문장은 「cannot help+-ing」의 과거형인 「could not help+-ing」를 사용하였으나 -ing 자리에 동사원형 'notice'를 사용하였으므로 틀린 문장이다. 따라서 'notice'를 'noticing'으로 수정해야 한다.

오답해설

② 출제 포인트: 사역동사

해당 문장에서 'had'는 사역동사로 목적어 'his minicar'와 수동관계이므로 목적격 보어에 과거분사 'stolen'을 사용하는 것이 옳다. 또한 'and this is the email he sent me'에서 수여동사 'send'의 과거형인 'sent'의 직접목적어가 빠졌으므로 'the email'과 'he' 사이에 목적격관계대명사가 생략되었다는 것을 알 수 있다.

③ 출제 포인트: 시간의 부사구, 부사절

'recently'는 시간의 부사구로 이때 동사에는 현재완료와 과거시제를 둘 다 사용할 수 있다. 해당 문장은 'recently'가 쓰인 문장으로 과거시제 동사 'talked'를 사용하였으므로 옳은 문장이다.

④ 출제 포인트: 부사절의 접속사

시간의 부사절 접속사 'until' 그리고 조건의 부사절 접속사 'if'가 쓰인 문장으로써 옳게 사용되었다. 특히, 시간 조건의 부사절의 시제의 경우 미래(완료)가 현재(완료)로 쓰이고 있어서 시제 표현도 올바르다. 단, 'if'절에 'they are not'은 문맥상 'paid'가 생략되어 원래의 의미는 'they are not paid'로 보아야 함에 주의해야 한다.

08 정답 ②

정답해설

해당 지문의 첫 번째 문장 "Dialect is used commonly in literature(방언은 문학에서 흔히 사용된다)."를 통해 방언이 문학에 자주 사용된다고 서술하며, 이후 방언이 사용되는 이유는 '캐릭터를 진짜처럼 보이게 하기 위함'이라는 것을 언급하고 있다. 그리고 George Bernard Shaw의 작품 Pygmalion을 예시로 들어 문학 작품에서 어떻게 방언이 효과적으로 사용될 수 있는지 보여주고 있다. 그런데 ②에서는 '방언'과는 관계가 없는, 'Pygmalion의 최초 공연 시기'에 대해 언급하고 있으므로 글의 전체 흐름에 부합하지 않는다. 따라서 글의 흐름상 가장 어색한 것은 '② Pygmalion was first presented on stage to the public in 1913(Pygmalion은 1913년 최초로 무대에서 대중들을 상대로 공연되었다).'이다.

오답해설

나머지는 글의 흐름상 자연스러우므로 오답이다.

해석

방언은 문학에서 흔히 사용된다. 작가가 캐릭터를 잘 표현하길 원한다면 방언을 사용하는 것을 택할 수도 있다. 그렇게 하기 위해 작가는 캐릭터의 지역 고유의 방언을 쓸 것이다. ① 작가들은 그들의 캐릭터가 진짜인 것처럼 보이길 원한다. 따라서 그들은 캐릭터 간의 대화를 그들이 실제로 말하는 방식으로 써야만 한다. George Bernard Shaw의 Pygmalion에서 이것이 잘 나타난다. ② *Pygmalion은 1912년 최초로 무대에서 대중들을 상대로 공연되었다.* ③ 런던 토박이 소녀가 그녀의 사투리와 억양을 표준 영국 영어로 바꾸려고 시도하는 부유한 신사에게 "입양"된다. ④ 런던 사투리가 그 지역에만 한정되어 있기 때문에 많은 사람들에게 이 희곡은 읽기 어렵다. 그러나 만일 그 희곡이 런던 고유의 사투리로 쓰여 있지 않다면, 그것은 전혀 효과적이지 않을 것이다.

어휘

represent 보여주다, 기술하다, 표현하다
specific to …에 한정된, … 고유의   genuine 진짜의
Cockney 런던 토박이, 런던 내기; 런던 사투리; 런던 사투리의
well-to-do 부유한   effective 효과적인

오답률 TOP 3

09 정답 ④

정답해설

해당 지문은 '영국인들의 지도에 대한 이른 관심(The British had an early interest in mapping)'에 대해 언급하며, 그에 대한 관심이 '지도 제작을 한 단계 업그레이드 시켰다(The British took mapping to the next level in the mid to late 1700s)'고 설명하고 있다. 본문 후반 "This survey-based mapping marked a shift from a routing and descriptive-based process to a mathematical, grid-based technique using triangulation (측량에 기초한 지도 제작은 항로 설정과 도형 묘사에 기초한 과정으로부터 삼각측량을 이용한 수학적인 격자 기반 기술로의 변화를 남겼다)."을 통해, 새로운 지도 제작 기술이 도입되었다는 것을 알 수 있고, 마지막 문장 "It also introduced the notion of fixed reference points and scalability to the world of mapping(그것은 또한 지도 제작의 세계에 고정된 기준점과 확장성이라는 개념을 도입시켰다)."을 통해, 새로운 지도 제작 기법으로 인해 지도 제작 분야에 새로운 개념이 도입되었다'고 설명하고 있다. 따라서 글의 주제로 가장 적절한 보기는 '④ influence of the British on advancements in mapping techniques(지도 제작 기술의 발전에 미친 영국인들의 영향)'이다.

오답해설

① 본문 초반 지도와 권력의 관계가 언급되기는 하지만, 본문 전체를 아우르는 내용이 아니므로 오답이다.
② 지도 '제작 기법'의 변화에 대해 본문 후반에 언급되기는 하지만, 대영제국의 '역사상' 지도의 변화에 대해서는 언급되지 않는다.
③ 본문은 '지도 제작'에 관한 내용이며, '지리학'에 관한 내용은 언급되지 않으므로 오답이다.

해석

영국인들은 그들의 자원, 부, 그리고 권력을 확장하길 원했고, 좋은 지도를 보유하는 것이 그들이 이 목표를 달성하는 데 도움이 될 것이기 때문에 지도 제작에 일찍부터 관심을 가지게 되었다. 역사상 이 시기에 지도는 단지 권력의 상징이 아니었다. 그것들은 권력을 부여했다. 훌륭한 지도를 가진 군대는 전투에서 이점이 있었고, 왕은 얼마나 많은 토지에 세금을 부과할 수 있는지 알 수 있었다. 그러므로 영국인들이 이 분야에 관심을 가지게 되었고 그들의 영토의 지도를 제작하고자 하는 열망을 가졌던 것은 이해가 된다. 영국인들은 1700년대 중후반 British Ordnance와 The Great Trigonometrical Survey of India를 통해 지도 제작을 한 단계 더 발전시켰다. 측량에 기초한 지도 제작은 항로 설정과 도형 묘사에 기초한 과정으로부터 삼각측량을 이용한 수학적인 격자 기반 기술로의 변화를 남겼다. 그것은 또한 지도 제작의 세계에 고정된 기준점과 확장성이라는 개념을 도입시켰다.

① 과거 지도와 권력의 관계
② 대영제국의 역사에서 지도의 변화
③ 영국 지리학과 지도 제작의 역사
④ 지도 제작 기술들의 발전에 미친 영국인들의 영향

어휘

confer 부여[수여]하다
make sense 이해가 되다, 의미가 통하다, 타당하다
territory 영토   ordnance 군수품, 육지 측량
trigonometrical 삼각법의   survey 측량
shift 변화   routing 여정의 설정
descriptive 도형 묘사의   grid 격자, (지도의) 경선·위선
triangulation 삼각측량   notion 개념
reference point 기준   scalability 확장성
cartography 지도 제작   advancement 발전

10 정답 ④

정답해설

(A) 문맥상 빈칸이 이끄는 절 "the HR industry has begun adopting more technological solutions into their processes(인사계가 그들의 절차에 더욱더 기술적인 해법을 도입해왔다)"가, 주절 "it is easier than ever to get started exchanging real-time performance feedback(실시간 수행 피드백을 주고받는 것이 그 어느 때보다 더 수월해졌다)"의 원인이므로, '원인, 이유'를 나타내는 접속사 'As(…에 따라)' 또는 'Now that(…이므로, …이기 때문에)'이 빈칸에 적절하다.

(B) 빈칸 이전 "At the push of a button, colleagues can request feedback, send a praise when a job's done well, or a tip to help colleagues become a better professional(버튼을 누르면 동료들은 피드백을 요청하거나, 업무가 잘 처리되었을 때 칭찬 또는 동료가 더 나은 전문가가 되도록 도울 수 있는 조언을 보낼 수도 있다)."의 상황과 빈칸 이후 "colleagues are instantly notified either via email or push notification whenever they receive feedback or feedback requests(동료들은 그들이 피드백 또는 피드백 요청을 받을 때마다 이메일 또는 푸시 알람을 통해 즉시 통보를 받는다)"가 거의 동시에 발생하는 상황이므로, 빈칸에는 'Meanwhile(한편, 그동안에)'이 들어가는 것이 가장 적절하다. 따라서 정답은 ④이다.

오답해설

③ (B) 'Otherwise(그렇지 않으면)'는 '반대 상황을 가정'할 때 사용하는 접속부사이므로, (B)에 적절하지 않다.
나머지 보기는 문맥상 자연스럽지 않으므로 오답이다.

해석

인사계가 그들의 절차에 더욱더 기술적인 해법을 채택해왔기 (A) 때문에 실시간 수행 피드백을 주고받는 것이 그 어느 때보다 더 수월해졌다. 실시간 피드백을 제공한다는 것이 반드시 더 많은 이메일 또는 어쩌면 어색할 수도 있는 채팅을 의미할 필요는 없다. Impraise와 같은 도구는 동료들을 연결하는 것을 도와서 그들이 쉽고 빠르게, 또 심지어 진행 중에 있을 때도 피드백을 공유할 수 있다. 버튼을 누르면 동료들은 피드백을 요청하거나, 업무가 잘 처리되었을 때 칭찬 또는 동료가 더 나은 전문가가 되도록 도울 수 있는 조언을 보낼 수도 있다. (B) 한편, 동료들은 그들이 피드백 또는 피드백 요청을 받을 때마다 이메일 또는 푸시 알람을 통해 즉시 통보를 받는다. 그러한 방식으로 모든

사람들이 그것을 가장 필요한 바로 그때 피드백을 받을 수 있다.
① …에도 불구하고 – 그럼에도 불구하고
② …이 아닌 한 – 마찬가지로
③ …에 따라 – 그렇지 않으면
④ …이므로,…이기 때문에 – 한편, 그 동안에

> **어휘**

adopt 채택하다, 택하다　　　　process 과정, 절차
performance 성과, 수행, 업무
potentially 어쩌면, 잠재적으로, 가능성 있게
awkward 어색한
on the go 끊임없이 일하는, 계속 일하는
praise 칭찬　　　　　　　　　matter 중요하다, 문제되다

결국엔 성정혜 영어 하프모의고사
기적사 복습 모의고사 5회

01	④	02	②	03	①	04	④	05	④
06	①	07	②	08	③	09	②	10	②
11	④	12	③	13	③	14	①	15	④
16	①	17	④	18	②	19	③	20	④

01 정답 ④
Day 42-03

> **정답해설**

밑줄 친 단어는 문맥상 '모이다'로 사용되었고, 유의어로는 ④ assemble이 가장 적절하다.

> **해석**

그것은 정부가 안전 문제를 언급하면서 중앙 Taksim 광장에 **모이려던** 겁에 질린 참가자들을 최루탄과 물대포로 쫓아내 동성연애자와 트랜스젠더의 프라이드 이벤트를 금지했던 2015년에 갑작스럽게 바뀌었다.
① 손상시키다, 침식하다, 부식하다
② 코를 훌쩍거리다
③ 변경하다
④ 모이다

02 정답 ②
Day 43-03

> **정답해설**

밑줄 친 단어는 문맥상 '대담한, 용맹한'의 의미로 사용되었고, 유의어로는 ② valiant가 적절하다.

> **해석**

하지만 저것은 그날 밤 Kennedy가 그야말로 **대담했던** 농담을 하는 것을 막지 않았다.
① 경멸하는
② 용맹한
③ 서두르는
④ 무서운

03 정답 ①
Day 48-01

> **정답해설**

밑줄 친 단어는 문맥상 '막다'로 사용되었고, 유의어로는 ① prevent가 적절하다.

> **해석**

사람들이 그들의 삶에 좀 더 이른 시기에 연애를 시작하도록 격려한다면, 아마도 우리는 미래의 이러한 전례 없는 문제들을 일부 **막을** 수 있을 것이다.
① 막다
② 평가하다, 재검하다
③ 수정하다
④ 아첨하다

04 정답 ④ — Day 41-01

정답해설

공해를 없애자는 캠페인이 대중의 협조를 얻지 못한다면 의미가 없어질 것이므로, ④ futile이 정답이다.

해석

공해를 없애자는 캠페인은 대중의 이해와 온전한 협조를 얻지 못한다면 **무용지물**로 판명될 것이다.
① 유혹적인, 마음을 홀리는
② 향상된, 강화한
③ 풍부한, 비옥한
④ 무용지물인, 무효인

05 정답 ④ — Day 46-03

정답해설

난제를 해결하기 위한 '아이디어'(생각)를 목적어로 가질 수 있는 동사는 ④ hit upon이다. 'hit upon'은 '떠올리다'라는 뜻으로, 목적어인 '아이디어'와의 연관성을 확인할 수 있다.

해석

1970년대 중반으로 돌아가, John Holland라는 미국의 한 컴퓨터 과학자는 과학 분야의 악명 높은 난제들을 해결하기 위해 진화 이론을 이용하는 생각을 **불현듯 떠올렸다**.
① 고용했다, 떠맡았다
② 탔다, 올랐다
③ 속였다, 부당하게 이용했다
④ 불현듯 떠올렸다[생각했다]

06 정답 ① — Day 42-06

정답해설

① **출제 포인트: The+비교급, the+비교급 / 간접의문문**

'The+비교급 ~, the+비교급 ~'이 '~하면 할수록 점점 더 ~하다'의 의미로 쓰인 문장으로 옳은 문장이다. 또한 'realize'의 목적어 절로 온 'how much I don't know'는 간접의문문으로 적절하게 쓰였다.

해석

① 더 많이 배울수록, 내가 얼마나 많이 알지 못하는지 더 많이 깨닫는다.
② 그 보고서는 많은 자원이 4살짜리 아이들을 가르치는 데에 쏟아져야 한다고 권한다.
③ 신의 전능함에 대한 강조는 윌리엄의 글에서 훨씬 더 많이 표명된다.
④ 자신을 놀라게 했었던 것은 체포된 사람들 중 많은 이들이 전과가 없다는 것이었다고 그가 말했다.

07 정답 ② — Day 47-05

정답해설

② **출제 포인트: 동명사 관용표현/동명사의 태**

'look forward to'는 '~하기를 고대하다'를 뜻하며 뒤에 명사와 동명사가 목적어로 올 수 있다. 해당 문장은 'look forward to' 뒤에 동명사 'installing'을 사용하였으며 동명사의 목적어 'the new units'가 있으므로 능동형 동명사를 사용하는 것이 옳다.

해석

① 나는 도움을 얻기 위해 나갔고 내가 돌아왔을 때쯤 그는 숨 쉬는 것을 멈췄다.
② 그는 낡은 부엌을 뜯어내고 새로운 세트들로 빨리 설치하기를 고대했다.
③ 이것은 지금까지 거대한 이익을 창출해왔고 계속해서 그렇게 할 수 있는 전략이다.
④ 신청서를 요청하는 편지와 함께 우표가 붙여진 그리고 주소가 적힌 봉투를 포함하십시오.

08 정답 ③ — Day 44-09

정답해설

해당 지문은 피드백 유형 중 하나인 '건설적 비판(Constructive criticism)'에 대해 설명하는 글이다. 주어진 문장은 'When providing this type of feedback, explain exactly what is that you're criticizing and the implications that come from it, and then create a plan to help the employee improve(이러한 유형의 피드백을 제공할 때, 당신이 비판하는 것이 무엇인지, 그것으로 인해 예상되는 결과가 무엇인지 정확히 설명한 후, 그 직원이 개선하도록 도울 수 있는 계획을 세워라).'라고 설명하며 '실제로 건설적 비판을 활용할 경우 유념할 점을 제시하고 있다. 본문의 첫 세 문장은 '건설적 비판의 특징'에 대해 설명하고 있으므로, 구체적인 활용 방법을 설명하는 주어진 문장 이전에 등장하는 것이 문맥상 자연스럽다. 그리고 ③ 이후에서는 주어진 문장에서 언급된 것과 같이 건설적 비판을 활용하는 상황을 구체적인 예시를 들어 설명하고 있으므로, '활용 방법'에 대해 언급한 주어진 문장 이후에 등장하는 것이 자연스럽다. 따라서 주어진 문장이 들어갈 위치로 가장 적절한 것은 ③이다.

해석

건설적 비판은 아마도 가장 충분히 활용되지 못하는 개발 수단 중 하나일 것이다. (①) 건설적 비판은 직원들이 개선될 필요가 있는 분야와 그렇게 개선을 하는 것이 중요한 이유를 알 수 있게 도와준다. (②) 그것은 비판과 해결책을 모두 제시하기 때문에 균형 잡힌 접근법이다. (③ **이러한 유형의 피드백을 제공할 때, 당신이 비판하는 것이 무엇인지, 그것으로 인해 예상되는 결과가 무엇인지 정확히 설명한 후, 그 직원이 개선하도록 도울 수 있는 계획을 세워라.**) 지속적으로 오타와 문법적 오류가 있는 이메일을 보내는 직원이 있다고 상상해보라. (④) 단순히 그들에게 그것이 문제이고 그것을 그만해야 한다고 말하는 것 대신에, 그 문제의 예상 결과를 설명하라. 그들에게 그것이 문제가 되는 이유에 대한 명확한 예시를 제시하고, 그들의 행동을 교정해야 하는 것이 중요한 이유를 반복하여 말하라. 그들이 개선할 수 있는 방법을 생각해 내도록 도와주고 그들이 개선할 기간을 정해주어라.

09 정답 ② — Day 42-08

정답해설

주어진 문장에서 언급된 'new, better and cheaper tools(새롭고 더 나은 더 저렴한 수단들)'를 (B)의 'One of these tools(이러한 수단들 중 하나)'가 가리키고 있으므로, 주어진 문장 이후에 (B)가 연결되는 것이 알맞다. (B)에서는 "~ can offer firm evidence that a disease transmitted from parent to child is linked to one or more genes(부모로부터 아이에게 전달된 질병은 하나 또는 그 이상의 유전자와 연결되어 있다는 확실한 증거를 제공할 수 있다)."라고 '유전자 지도 분석의 기능'에 대해 설명하고 있으므로, 이후에는 'also(또한)'를 이용해 유전자 지도의 다른 기능을 추가적으로 설명하고 있는 (A)가 이어져야 한다. 이후에는 인과관계를 나타내는 'Therefore'를 활용해 '(B) - (A)'에서 서술한 유전자 분석에 따른 활용되는 분야를 서술하고 있는 (C)가 이어지는 것이 자연스럽다. 따라서 정답은 '② (B) - (A) - (C)'이다.

해석

Human Genome Project(HGP)의 주요 목표들 중에 새로운 유전자를 발견하고 그것들의 기능을 이해할 수 있는 새롭고 더 나은 그리고 더 저렴한 수단을 개발하는 것이 있었다.
(B) 이러한 수단들 중 하나가 유전자 지도 분석이다. 연결 지도 분석이라고도 불리는 유전자 지도 분석은 부모로부터 아이에게 전달된 질병은 하나 또는 그 이상의 유전자와 연결되어 있다는 확실한 증거를 제공할 수 있다.
(A) 지도 분석은 또한 어느 염색체가 그 유전자를 포함하고 있는지, 그리고 정확히 그 염색체의 어느 곳에 그 유전자가 있는지에 대한 단서를 제공한다.
(C) 그러므로, 유전자 지도는 낭포성 섬유증과 듀시엔형 근이영양증과 같은 상대적으로 희귀한 단일 유전자 유전병들을 유발하는 유전자를 알아내기 위해 성공적으로 사용되어왔다.

10 정답 ②   Day 50-08

정답해설

해당 지문의 첫 번째 문장 "Dialect is used commonly in literature(방언은 문학에서 흔히 사용된다)."를 통해 방언이 문학에 자주 사용된다고 서술하며, 이후 방언이 사용되는 이유가 '캐릭터를 진짜처럼 보이게 하기 위함'이라는 것을 언급하고 있다. 그리고 George Bernard Shaw의 작품 Pygmalion을 예시로 들어 문학 작품에서 어떻게 방언이 효과적으로 사용될 수 있는지 보여주고 있다. 그런데 ②에서는 '방언'과는 관계가 없는, 'Pygmalion의 최초 공연 시기'에 대해 언급하고 있으므로 글의 전체 흐름에 부합하지 않는다. 따라서 글의 흐름상 가장 어색한 것은 '② Pygmalion was first presented on stage to the public in 1913(Pygmalion은 1913년 최초로 무대에서 대중들을 상대로 공연되었다).'이다.

해석

방언은 문학에서 흔히 사용된다. 작가가 캐릭터를 잘 표현하길 원한다면 방언을 사용하는 것을 택할 수도 있다. 그렇게 하기 위해 작가는 캐릭터의 지역 고유의 방언을 쓸 것이다. ① 작가들은 그들의 캐릭터가 진짜인 것처럼 보이길 원한다. 따라서 그들은 캐릭터 간의 대화를 그들이 실제로 말하는 방식으로 써야만 한다. George Bernard Shaw의 Pygmalion에서 이것이 잘 나타난다. ② <u>Pygmalion은 1912년 최초로 무대에서 대중들을 상대로 공연되었다.</u> ③ 런던 토박이 소녀가 그녀의 사투리와 억양을 표준 영국 영어로 바꾸려고 시도하는 부유한 신사에게 "입양"된다. ④ 런던 사투리가 그 지역에만 한정되어 있기 때문에 많은 사람들에게 이 희곡은 읽기 어렵다. 그러나 만일 그 희곡이 런던 고유의 사투리로 쓰여 있지 않다면, 그것은 전혀 효과적이지 않을 것이다.

11 정답 ④   Day 44-04

정답해설

A와 B는 인턴직 공지를 보며 대화를 나눈다. B는 A에게 취직해서 실무에 뛰어들기 전에 실전 경험을 쌓고 싶어 인턴직에 지원할지 고민 중이라고 이야기한다. A는 최근에 B가 아주 바빠 보였다며 "너무 과욕을 보이지(bite off more than one can chew)말라"고 말한다.

해석

A: 너 뭐 보고 있어?
B: 나 인턴십 공지를 보고 있어.
A: 인턴직에 지원할 생각이야?
B: 응, 취직하기 전에 실전 경험을 쌓고 진짜 일에 뛰어들고 싶어.
A: 진짜? 너 요새 되게 바빠 보이던데. <u>과욕을 보이지 마.</u> 너 자신을 위한 시간이 없을 거야.
B: 이게 벅찰 수도 있다는 걸 아는데 내 버킷리스트에 있어.
① 임기응변으로 대처하다
② 어떻게든 견뎌내다
③ 나쁜 일에서부터 멀어지다
④ 과욕을 보인다

12 정답 ③   Day 45-04

정답해설

A는 채식주의자가 되는 것의 이점들에 대해 알고 있는지 질문한다. B는 현대 사회의 사람들이 왜 만성 질환을 흔히 앓는지 알고 있다고 답변한다. 이는 채식주의자가 되는 것의 이점들에 알고 있는지를 묻는 A의 질문에 적절한 답변이 아니다. 또한 의문사가 없는 의문문의 경우 긍정, 부정 여부를 먼저 제시하여야 한다.

해석

① A: 너 오로라 본 적 있어?
  B: 응, 작년에 캐나다 갔을 때 한 번 봤어.
② A: 내일이 내가 수년 동안 기대해왔던 날이야.
  B: 내일이 뭐가 그렇게 특별해?
③ A: 너 채식주의자가 되는 것의 이점들에 대해 알아?
  B: 나는 왜 현대 사회의 사람들이 왜 만성 질병을 앓는지 알아.
④ A: 나 오늘 너무 피곤해서 좀 쉬어야겠어.
  B: 너 너무 열심히 일했어. 가서 좀 쉬어.

13 정답 ③   Day 44-05

정답해설

③ **출제 포인트: take의 관용표현(It+takes+목적어+시간+to부정사)**
「It takes+목적어+시간+to+동사원형」은 '~가 ~하는 데 시간이 걸리다'를 뜻한다. 해당 문장은 「It takes+목적어+시간+to+동사원형」을 사용하였으나 'to+동사원형' 자리에 -ing 형태인 'traveling'을 사용하였으므로 틀린 문장이다. 따라서 'traveling'을 'to travel'로 수정해야 한다.

14 정답 ①   Day 48-07

정답해설

① **출제 포인트: 사역동사**
'let'은 사역동사로 목적어와 능동 관계인 경우 목적격 보어에 동사원형을 사용하며 수동 관계인 경우 목적격 보어에 'be+과거분사'를 사용한다. 해당 문장은 사역동사 'let'을 사용하였으나 목적격 보어에 현재분사 'spending'을 사용하였으므로 틀린 문장이다. 따라서 목적어 'you'와 능동 관계이므로 'spending'을 동사원형 'spend'로 수정해야 한다.

15 정답 ④   Day 45-08

정답해설

해당 지문은 '상어의 신체적 특징'에 관해 설명하는 글이다. 첫 문장 "It was found that sharks living in deep, cold waters tend to have very large fatty livers, sometimes making up over a quarter of their body(깊고 차가운 물에 서식하는 상어는, 때때로 몸의 4분의 1 이상을 구성하기도 하는, 매우 거대한 지방질의 간을 가지고 있는 경향이 있다는 것이 발견되었다)."를 통해 '심해에 사는 상어의 신체적 특징'에 대해 언급한 후, 본문 중반 "Sharks living in warmer and shallower waters, on the other hand, have comparatively smaller livers(반면, 따뜻하고 얕은 물에 서식

하는 상어는 비교적 더 작은 간을 가지고 있다).'를 통해 '연안에 서식하는 상어는 심해에 사는 상어와 비교해 간의 크기가 비교적 작다'라고 언급하고 있다. '심해'와 '연안'이라는 지리적 서식 환경과, '찬물'과 '따뜻한 물'이라는 물리적 서식 환경의 차이에 따른 상어의 신체적 차이에 대해 설명하고 있으므로, 글의 제목으로 가장 적절한 것은 '④ Different Shark Bodies for Different Environments(다른 환경에서의 다른 상어의 신체)'이다.

해석

깊고 차가운 물에 서식하는 상어는, 때때로 몸의 4분의 1 이상을 구성하기도 하는, 매우 거대한 지방질의 간을 가지고 있는 경향이 있다는 것이 발견되었다. 이것은 그들의 부력을 증가시키고, 적은 에너지를 이용해, 그러나 동시에 부가적인 부피로 인한 상대적으로 느린 속도로 수중에서 이동하는 것을 가능하게 해준다. 다행히 그들이 먹이로 삼는, 그리고 그들을 먹이로 삼는 심해 동물들 또한 상당히 느리다. 반면, 따뜻하고 얕은 물에 서식하는 상어는 비교적 더 작은 간을 가지고 있다. 이것이 그들의 부력을 저해하는데, 그것은 부력을 발생시키기 위해 날개와 같은 가슴지느러미가 빠르게 움직여야만 한다는 것을 의미한다. 이러한 구조는 비행선처럼 생긴 상어의 구조보다 덜 에너지 효율적인 것처럼 보일 수 있으나, 다른 모든 것들이 또한 더 빠르게 움직이는 생태계에서 서식하는 것에 있어서는 사실 이치에 맞는 일이다.
① 상어는 왜 큰 간이 필요한가?
② 조심하라, 상어는 모든 곳에 존재한다!
③ 상어는 어떻게 에너지를 효율적으로 사용하는가?
④ 다른 환경에서의 다른 상어의 신체

16 정답 ① Day 47-08

정답해설

해당 지문은 '1920년대 강력했던 미국 경제가 1929년 주식시장 붕괴 이후 한순간에 대공황에 접어들었다'라고 설명하고 있다. 본문 후반 "However, it is far too simplistic to view the stock market crash as the single cause of the Great Depression(그러나 주식시장 붕괴를 대공황의 단일 원인으로 보는 것은 너무나 지나친 단순화이다)."을 통해, '주식시장 붕괴가 대공황을 촉발시킨 것은 사실이나 그것을 대공황의 유일한 원인으로 보는 것은 무리가 있음'을 설명한 후, 본문 마지막 문장 "Long-term underlying causes sent the nation into a downward spiral of despair(장기적인 근본적 원인들이 그 국가를 절망의 하향곡선으로 떨어뜨린 것이다)."에서 '장기적인 근본적 원인들이 혼합되어 대공황을 초래했다'라고 설명하고 있다. 따라서 글의 요지로 가장 적절한 것은 '① Multiple factors caused the Great Depression to occur(복수의 요인들이 대공황을 발생시켰다).'이다.

해석

1920년대 말, 미국은 세계에서 가장 거대한 경제를 자랑했다. 제1차 세계대전으로 인해 발생한 파괴로 인해 미국이 번성하는 동안 유럽인들은 분투했다. 대통령직을 이어받은 뒤 Herbert Hoover는 미국이 곧 빈곤이 퇴치된 날을 보게 될 것이라 예측했다. 그리고 겉으로 보이는 승리 속에서 모든 것이 허물어졌다. 1929년 주식시장 붕괴는 미국을 역사상 가장 길고 가장 깊은 경제 위기로 몰아넣은 일련의 사건들을 촉발했다. 그러나 주식시장 붕괴를 대공황의 단일 원인으로 보는 것은 너무나 지나친 단순화이다. 건강한 경제는 그러한 침체에서 회복할 수 있다. 장기적인 근본적 원인들이 그 국가를 절망의 소용돌이로 떨어뜨린 것이다.
① 복수의 요인들이 대공황을 발생시켰다.
② 대공황은 오직 주식시장 붕괴 때문이었다.
③ 불황을 피하기 위해 경제를 건강하게 유지하는 것이 중요하다.
④ Herbert Hoover 대통령은 국가를 공황에서 빠져나오게 하는 데 실패했다.

17 정답 ④ Day 45-10

정답해설

해당 지문은 'Macaulay Honors College'의 학비 정책에 대한 내용이다. 본문 내용에 따르면, Macaulay Honors College는 뉴욕 출신의 학생들에게는 학비를 전액 면제해주고, 뉴욕 이외의 주 학생들에게는 장학금을 제공하기는 하지만 전액 장학금은 아니며, 해당 주 이외의 주에서 부과하는 비용과의 차액은 학생들이 지불해야 한다고 언급하고 있다. 또한 숙식은 별도로 비용을 지불해야 하며, 복합 학위를 취득하는 학생들도 대학원 과정에서 발생하는 비용은 자비로 충당해야 한다고 명시한다. 따라서 글의 내용과 일치하는 보기는 '④ It does not financially support postgraduate students(대학원생을 금전적으로 지원하지 않는다).'이다.

해석

Macaulay Honors College에 다니는 모든 뉴욕 학생들은 학비를 면제받고 학교를 다닌다. 뉴욕 외부 출신의 학생들은 그들의 학비 중 주내 해당액을 면제받지만, 그들은 여전히 학비의 주내와 주외 해당액의 차액을 지불해야 한다. 또한 숙식은 학비 면제에 포함되지 않는다. 숙식이 13,000달러에서 25,000달러의 비용이 들기 때문에 많은 학생들은 자택에 거주하며 통학한다. 복합 학위를 받는 학생들은 또한 그들의 대학원 과정을 위해 비용을 지불해야 한다. 모든 학생에게 자격이 주어진 장학금 이상의 비용을 지불해야 하는 학생들은 학자금 융자를 신청할 수 있다.
① 뉴욕 출신의 학생들만 받는다.
② 모든 학생들은 그곳에서 무료로 공부할 수 있다.
③ 장학금은 숙박비를 포함한다.
④ 대학원생을 금전적으로 지원하지 않는다.

18 정답 ② Day 42-09

정답해설

(A) 본문 첫 문장 "performance feedback can take a number of forms(수행 피드백은 수많은 형태를 띨 수 있다)"를 통해 '수행 피드백의 다양한 형태'에 대해 설명할 것이라는 것을 유추할 수 있고, 이후 '2주 또는 1달 간격의 1대1 미팅', '일간 또는 주간 보고서', 또는 '프로젝트 일정에 기반을 둔 피드백' 등 여러 가지 피드백 유형에 대해 언급하고 있다. 다양한 유형 중 한 가지를 선택한다는 의미가 되어야 하므로, (A)에 가장 적절한 것은 '선택, 대안'을 나타낼 수 있는 'Alternatively(그 대신에)'이다.

(B) 이전 문장 "It's very easy in our busy work lives to let things slip and keep postponing meetings(우리의 바쁜 업무 생활에서 일정이 슬며시 지나가게 하고 계속해서 미팅을 미루는 것은 매우 쉽다)."에서는 '미팅을 거르거나 미루는 것'에 대해 언급하고 있으며, (B) 문장에서는 'Keeping a regular meeting, ~'을 통해 '규칙적으로 미팅을 하는 것'에 대해 언급하고 있으므로, 전후 관계가 '역접' 관계임을 알 수 있다. 따라서 (B)에 가장 적절한 것은 '역접, 대조'를 나타내는 'however(그러나)'이다. 따라서 정답은 '② Alternatively(그 대신에) - however(그러나)'이다.

해석

당신의 팀이 일을 하는 방식과 당신의 리더십 스타일, 당신의 팀 구성원들과의 직접적인 관계에 따라, 수행 피드백은 수많은 형태를 띨 수 있다. 당신은 2주 또는 한 달 간격의 1대1 미팅을 선택할 수도 있다. (A) 그 대신에 당신은 팀 구성원들의 일간 또는 주간 보고서에 응답을 하는 것을 통해 피드백을 제공하도록 선택할 수도 있다. 또는, 만일 당신의 팀이 프로젝트에 기반을 두고 있다면, 각각의 프로젝트 건이 달성되고 난 후 평가 미팅 또는 보고서 일정을 잡는 것이 아마 더 타당할 것이다. 당신이 어떠한 형태를 선택하든 가장 중요한 것은 정기적인 일정을 세우고 그것을 고수하는 것이다. 우리의 바쁜 업무 생활에서 일정이 슬며시 지나가게 하고 계속해서 미팅을 미루는 것은 매우 쉽다. (B) 그러나 정기적인 미팅을 유지하는 것은 당신이 순조롭게 나아가도록 할 것이며, 당신이 계속 유용한 피드백을 제공하도록 할 뿐만 아니라, 당신이 그들의 성과와 발전을 지원하는 것에 도움이 되는 것을 진지하게 생각한다는 메시지를 당신의 팀에게 전할 것이다.
① 그에 따라 - 게다가
② 그 대신에 - 그러나
③ 게다가 - 한 마디로
④ 결과적으로 - 따라서

19 정답 ③   Day 48-10

정답해설

본문 중반 "This issue of pragmatism is a chief reason why Edison fired Tesla(이러한 실용주의 문제는 Edison이 Tesla를 해고한 주요 이유이다)."를 통해 'Tesla는 실용주의자가 아니었음'을 유추할 수 있으며, "JP Morgan decided to pick up the Serbian inventor and finance his lab, but when Morgan realized that none of Tesla's ideas could actually produce anything of direct value, he withdrew his funding(JP Morgan이 이 Serbia인 발명가를 발탁하여 그의 실험실에 자금을 지원해주기로 결정했지만, Morgan이 Tesla의 아이디어 중 아무것도 직접적인 수익을 낼 수 있는 어떠한 것을 실제로 생산해낼 수 없다는 것을 깨달았을 때, 그는 그의 자금지원을 중단했다)."을 통해 'Tesla의 아이디어는 즉각적인 수익을 낼 수 있는 실용적인 것들이 아니었음'을 알 수 있다. 이러한 'Tesla의 실용적이지 못함' 때문에 그는 빈곤 속에서 죽어갔으므로, 빈칸에 가장 적절한 표현은 '③ practical(실용적인)'이다.

해석

그것은 Edison 대 Tesla 논쟁에서도 동일하다. 주요한 차이점 중 하나는 Edison이 시장성이 없는 아이디어는 생각하지 않았다는 것이다. 구매자의 주목을 받지 못할 아이디어가 무슨 의미가 있는가? 누가 실험실 임대료를 지불할 것인가? 이러한 실용주의 문제는 Edison이 Tesla를 해고한 주요 이유이다. JP Morgan이 이 Serbia인 발명가를 발탁하여 그의 실험실에 자금을 지원해주기로 결정했지만, Morgan이 Tesla의 아이디어 중 아무것도 직접적인 수익을 낼 수 있는 어떠한 것을 실제로 생산해낼 수 없다는 것을 깨달았을 때, 그는 그의 자금지원을 중단했다. Tesla는 더 이상 실험실 비용을 감당할 수 없었고 빈곤하게 죽었다. 그가 실용적이 되길 거부한 것 또는 실용적이 될 수 없었던 것이 그의 열정을 추구할 그의 능력을 희생시켰다.
① 창의적인
② 사교적인
③ 실용적인
④ 공상적인

20 정답 ④   Day 43-10

정답해설

해당 지문은 미국의 흑인 시인 'Langston Hughes'에 관한 글이다. 빈칸 이후 문장 "then Langston Hughes stands at the apex of literary relevance among black people(그렇다면 Langston Hughes는 흑인 가운데 문학 관련 분야의 정점에 서게 된다)."로 보아, 빈칸에는 그의 문학적 지위를 평가하는 평가 기준에 대해 설명하는 내용이 들어가는 것이 적절하다. 본문 초반에서 '비평가들로부터 좋은 평가를 받지 못했음에도 불구하고, 글쓰기와 강연만으로도 생계를 유지할 수 있었다'고 언급하며 그 이유로 "Part of the reason he was able to do this was the phenomenal acceptance and love he received from average black people(그가 그렇게 할 수 있었던 이유 중 일부는 평범한 흑인들로부터 받았던 놀랄만한 수용과 사랑이었다)."을 제시하며 '일반 대중들 사이에서의 높은 인기'에 대해 설명한다. 즉, '비평가들의 평가가 기준이 아니라, 일반 대중들의 반응이 기준이라면 그의 문학적 지위는 정점에 서게 된다'라는 내용이 되어야 문맥상 자연스러우므로, 빈칸에 가장 적절한 보기는 '④ the weight of public response is any gauge(대중의 반응의 무게가 기준이다)'이다.

해석

비록 Hughes가 흑인 비평가와 백인 비평가 모두와 문제가 있었지만, 그는 글쓰기와 공공 강연을 통해서만 생계를 유지했던 최초의 흑인계 미국인이었다. 그가 그렇게 할 수 있었던 이유 중 일부는 평범한 흑인들로부터 받았던 놀랄만한 수용과 사랑이었다. 1970년 Black World의 평론가는 "작가의 순위를 결정하는 특권을 가진 사람들은 그를 결코 높게 평가한 적이 없으나, 만일 대중의 반응의 무게가 기준이라면, Langston Hughes는 흑인 가운데 문학 관련 분야의 정점에 서게 된다. 그가 '우리는 내면에 신체적 정신적 강인함을 지닌 거대한 저장소를 지니고 있다'라는 것을 인식했고, 이를 사람들에게 보여주기 위해 그의 예술적 재능을 사용했기 때문에 정확하게 그 시인은 그의 사람들의 기억 속에서 그러한 지위를 지니고 있는 것이다"라고 언급했다.
① 그의 미발표 작품이 포함된다
② 그의 사생활이 덜 논란을 일으킨다
③ 그가 포스트모던 세계에 살고 있다
④ 대중의 반응의 무게가 기준이다

결국엔 성정혜 영어 하프모의고사
기적사 DAY 51

01	①	02	①	03	②	04	③	05	③,①
06	②	07	④	08	④	09	③	10	②

01 정답 ①
15 국가직

정답해설

'meticulously'는 '조심스럽게'라는 뜻을 가지며 이와 유사한 의미를 가지는 것은 ① carefully이다.

해석

그는 서랍에서 사진을 꺼내고 진심으로 우러난 존경심을 갖고 입을 맞추고 그것을 **조심스럽게** 흰 실크 스카프 안에 접어서 그의 셔츠 안 심장 가까이에 넣어 두었다.
① 조심스럽게
② 급히
③ 결정적으로
④ 즐겁게, 유쾌하게

어휘

reverence 존경심 kerchief 스카프
meticulously 조심스럽게 carefully 조심스럽게
hurriedly 급히 decisively 결정적으로
delightfully 즐겁게, 유쾌하게

02 정답 ①
15 국가직

정답해설

'at the drop of a hat'은 '즉시'라는 뜻을 가지며, 이와 유사한 의미를 가지는 것은 ① immediately이다.

해석

그 회사는 내가 집과 가족을 **즉시** 이사시키는 것을 기대할 수 없다.
① 즉시
② 시간대로, 늦지 않게
③ 주저하면서, 말을 더듬으며
④ 정기적으로

어휘

at the drop of a hat 즉시 immediately 즉시
punctually 시간대로, 늦지 않게 hesitantly 주저하면서, 말을 더듬으며
periodically 정기적으로

03 정답 ②

정답해설

Mexico는 스페인어를 사용하는 나라이기 때문에 대학 시절 이후로 공부해오지 않았다면, 여행 전 'brush up on(복습하다)'할 필요가 있을 것이다. 따라서 정답은 ② brush up on이다.

해석

그녀가 지난겨울 Mexico를 여행하기 전에, 그녀는 스페인어를 **복습할** 필요를 느꼈는데 왜냐하면 대학 시절 이후로 공부해오지 않았기 때문이다.

① 아첨하다, 친해지려고 하다
② 복습하다
③ ~로부터 떠나다
④ (병에) 걸리다, 몸져눕다

어휘

make up to 아첨하다, 친해지려고 하다
brush up on 복습하다 shun away from ~로부터 떠나다
come down with (병에) 걸리다, 몸져눕다

04 정답 ③
15 국가직

정답해설

A가 B에게 정신적, 재정적으로 준비가 되었느냐고 질문을 했는데 B의 대답을 듣고는 A가 "Good!"이라고 하면서 일의 진행에 대해 설명해 주고 있다. 따라서 문맥상 B가 '③ I'm ready to start with what I have and take a chance(저는 제가 가진 것으로 시작하고, 해볼 준비가 되어 있어요)'라고 말했음을 유추할 수 있다.

해석

A: 어떤 사업을 구상 중에 있으신가요?
B: 요즘 꽃 가게를 운영하는 건 전망이 좋다고 생각하세요?
A: 그럴 수 있죠. 그런데, 정신적으로나 재정적으로 준비가 되어 있으신가요?
B: 저는 제가 가진 것으로 시작하고, 해볼 준비가 되어 있어요.
A: 좋아요! 그렇다면 당신은 전략적인 장소와 알맞은 부문을 선택해야 해요. 좋은 결과를 위해 철저한 조사를 꼭 하도록 해요.
B: 알고 있어요. 사업을 잘 운영하는 것보다 시작하는 게 훨씬 쉽다는 걸.
① 내일 병원에 갈 계획이에요
② 전 그렇게는 못 해요! 취직하기 위해서 노력해야겠어요
③ 저는 제가 가진 것으로 시작하고, 해볼 준비가 되어 있어요
④ 전 제 사업을 시작하는 것에 대해 생각하고 싶지 않아요

어휘

mentally 정신적으로 financially 재정적으로
strategic 전략적인, 중요한 segment 부문, 부분, 영역

05 정답 ③, ①
14 국가직

정답해설

③ **출제 포인트: 현재분사 vs. 과거분사**
'surround(둘러싸다)'는 타동사이며 목적어를 수반한다. 현재분사로 사용되려면 뒤에 목적어를 수반하여야 하나 그렇지 않으며 의미상으로도 '~로 둘러싸여 있는'이 되어야 하므로 과거분사형으로 사용해야 한다. 따라서 과거분사 'surrounded'가 되어야 한다. 'surrounded'는 명사인 'the land'를 후치 수식한다.

① **출제 포인트: 완전타동사+목적어[to부정사 vs. 동명사]**
'like'는 목적어로 동명사와 to부정사를 모두 취할 수 있다. 'not to mention'은 '~은 말할 것도 없이'라는 의미의 독립부정사이다. 그러나 'outdoor'는 형용사로 문맥상 동명사 'going'을 수식할 수 없다. 따라서 형용사 'outdoor'을 부사 'outdoors'로 수정해야 한다. 기출 당시 해당 선지도 잘못된 문장으로 인정되어 이중정답이 인정되었던 문항이다.

오답해설

② **출제 포인트: 최상급 대용표현**
비교 대상인 'She'와 'any other girl'은 품사(명사)와 성분(주어)이 일치한다. 또한 「비교급 + than any other」 뒤에는 단수 명사가 수반되며, 최상급의 의미를 갖는다.

④ 출제 포인트: 주어[a number of 목적어 vs. the number of 목적어]와 동사의 수일치

'A number of(많은 ~)'는 복수명사를 수반한다. 단수 동사만이 용인되는 'The number of(~의 수)'와 의미도, 수일치도 다르다. 'students'가 그 복수명사 역할을 하고 있으며, 'are'가 복수 동사로 알맞게 쓰였다. 'to get a job'은 to부정사의 부사적 용법으로 사용되어 '~하기 위해서'의 의미를 가진다.

오답률 TOP 2

06 정답 ②
14 국가직

정답해설

② 출제 포인트: 복합관계부사

여기서 'However(아무리 ~일지라도)'는 복합관계부사로, 부사절을 이끌 수 있으며, 그 어순은 「However + 형용사/부사 + 주어 + 동사 ~」이다. 해당 문장에서는 'you may be weary'에서 be동사의 보어로 온 형용사 'weary'가 'However' 뒤로 이동한 것으로 'However'가 수식하는 단어의 품사에 유의해야한다.

오답해설

① 출제 포인트: 현재분사 vs. 과거분사

분사구문과 주절이 어우러져 있는 문장이다. 분사구문에서 주어가 생략되었다는 것은 주절의 주어와 일치한다는 의미이다. 즉, 주어인 'she'는 'work'를 하는 주체이기 때문에 과거분사 'worked'가 아닌 현재분사 'working'이 되어야 옳다.

③ 출제 포인트: 주어[one of 복수명사]와 동사의 수일치 / 목적격 관계대명사

「one of + 복수명사」(복수 명사들 중 하나)의 주어는 'one'이므로 단수 동사를 수반하게 된다. 따라서 'were'를 'was'로 변경하는 것이 적절하다. 해당 문장에서 'I saw'는 선행사 'games'를 수식하는 관계대명사절로 'games'와 'I saw'사이에 목적격 관계대명사가 생략되었다.

④ 출제 포인트: It ~ that 강조 용법

해당 문장은 「It ~ that」 강조 구문과 목적격 관계대명사절 두 가지 경우로 볼 수 있다.

1. 「It ~ that」 강조 구문
   She was looking for <u>the main entrance</u>. (the main entrance를 강조)
   It was the main entrance that she was looking for. (O/이때 that은 which로 바꾸어 사용할 수 있다.)
   It was the main entrance for which she was looking. (O/이때 해당 문장은 「It ~ that」 강조 구문으로 볼 수 없으며 목적격 관계대명사절로 보아야 한다.)
   It was the main entrance for that she was looking. (X/'It~that 강조구문'에서는 'that'을 목적격 관계대명사로 볼 수 있으며 목적격 관계대명사 'that'은 앞에 전치사를 사용할 수 없다.)

2. 목적격 관계대명사절
   It was <u>the main entrance</u>. + She was looking for <u>the main entrance</u>. (the main entrance를 선행사)
   It was the main entrance that she was looking for. (O/이때 that은 which로 바꾸어 사용할 수 있다.)
   It was the main entrance for that she was looking. (X/목적격 관계대명사 that은 앞에 전치사를 사용할 수 없다.)
   It was the main entrance for which she was looking. (O/목적격 관계대명사 which는 앞에 전치사를 사용할 수 있다.)

따라서 해당 문장은 「It ~ that」 강조 구문으로 보아도 틀린 문장이고 목적격 관계대명사절로 보아도 틀린 문장이다. 옳은 문장으로 고치기 위해서는 두 가지 방법이 있다. 첫 번째 방법은 'for'를 'looking' 뒤로 이동하는 것이며 이때 'It was the main entrance that she was looking for.'는 「It ~ that」 강조 구문과 목적격 관계대명사절 두 가지 모두로 볼 수 있다. 두 번째 방법은 'that'을 'which'로 수정하는 것이며 이때 'It was the main entrance for which she was looking.'은 목적격 관계대명사절로 보아야 한다.

해석

① 병원에서 일하는 동안에, 그녀는 그녀의 첫 번째 에어쇼를 보았다.
② 네가 아무리 피곤해도, 그 프로젝트는 해야 한다.
③ 내가 본 경기 중에 흥미진진한 것은, 2010년 월드컵 결승전이었다.
④ 그녀가 찾고 있었던 것은 다름 아닌 정문이었다.

07 정답 ④
14 국가직

정답해설

④ 출제 포인트: 현재분사 vs. 과거분사

'interest'는 '관심을 끌다'로, '~에 관심을 가지다'는 'be interested in'이 된다. '~에 관심을 갖는 사람들'의 표현으로 만들기 위해서는 과거분사형으로 'those(사람들)'를 수식해야 한다. 따라서 'those (who are) interested in ~(~에 관심을 갖는 사람들)'은 적절히 표현되었다.

오답해설

① 출제 포인트: 자동사로 착각하기 쉬운 완전타동사

'resemble(~와 닮다, 비슷하다)'은 타동사이므로 전치사를 취하지 않으므로, 'like'를 삭제한 'resemble a book'이 되어야 한다. 또한 'resemble'은 일반적으로 '~와 닮다'의 의미로는 수동형과 진행형으로 사용하는 것도 불가하다는 점에 유의해야한다.

② 출제 포인트: 주격 관계대명사절 동사의 수일치

주격 관계대명사 다음에 동사가 올 경우에는 선행사가 동사의 수를 결정한다. 선행사 'weekly news magazines'는 복수 명사이기 때문에, 복수 동사가 수반되어야 한다. 따라서 단수 동사 'reports'는 복수 동사 'report'가 되어야 한다.

③ 출제 포인트: 동사 vs. 준동사

문장의 동사는 'are'이다. 따라서 'cover'는 앞의 명사 'women's magazines'를 수식하는 형용사의 역할을 하는 분사가 와야 하는데, 수식 받는 명사와 분사와의 관계가 능동이므로 현재분사가 와야 한다. 따라서 'cover'는 현재분사 'covering'이 되어야 한다.

해석

신문과 비교해서 잡지는 반드시 최신 정보를 가진 것만은 아니다. 잡지는 매일 나오는 것이 아니라, 매주, 매월 혹은 그보다도 덜 빈번하게 나오기 때문이다. 심지어 외적으로도 잡지는 신문과 다르다. 주로 잡지는 책과 비슷하기 때문이다. 종이는 더 두껍고, 사진은 더욱 색채가 풍부하며, 대부분의 기사는 상대적으로 길다. 독자는 훨씬 더 많은 배경지식과 더 상세한 사항을 경험한다. 또한, 여러 토픽들을 보도하는 주간 뉴스 잡지들이 있지만, 대부분의 잡지는 다양한 고객들을 끌기 위해 전문화되어 있다. 예를 들어, 연예인에 관한 청소년 잡지뿐만 아니라 패션, 화장품, 그리고 요리법을 다루는 여성 잡지도 있다. 또 다른 잡지들은 예를 들면, 컴퓨터 사용자들, 스포츠팬들, 예술에 관심을 갖는 사람들, 그리고 많은 기타 소수 그룹을 대상으로 하고 있다.

어휘

up-to-the-minute 가장 최근의, 최첨단의
externally 외적으로, 외부에서
attract 마음을 끌다, 끌어들이다, 불러일으키다
cover 다루다, 덮다, 걸치다   celebrity 유명 인사, 연예인

08 정답 ④
19 국가직

정답해설

보기 문장에서 '질병들 중 일부는 오래가지 않지만 다른 것들은 오래 갈 수도 있다.'라고 서술하고 있으므로 보기 문장 전후로 질병에 관련된 내용이 언급되는 것이 글의 흐름상 적절하다. 본문에서 'many experience physiological and psychological problems when they return to the Earth(많은 이들이 지구에 복귀할 때는 생리적 그리고 심리적 문제들을 겪는다.)'고 서술하였고 그다음에 '멀미(motion sickness)'를 예로 들면서 그것이 최대 며칠 동안 지속될 수 있다고 설명하고 있으므로 이 두 문장 사이에 보기 문장이 들어가는 것이 가장 적절하다. 따라서 정답은 ④이다.

오답해설

질병과 관련된 내용이 서술된 곳에 보기 문장이 들어가는 것이 글의 흐름에 부합된다. 따라서 나머지 보기들은 문맥상 알맞지 않다.

해석

수 세기 동안, 인간들은 하늘을 올려다보며 우리 행성의 영역 바깥에 무엇이 존재하는지를 궁금해했다. (①) 고대 천문학자들은 우주에 관해 더 많이 배우기를 희망하며 밤하늘을 조사했다. 더 최근에, 다른 영화들은 외계 생명체의 형태들이 우리 행성을 방문했을 수도 있는지를 궁금해했던 반면, 어떤 영화들은 우주 공간에서 인간의 삶을 지속시킬 가능성을 탐구했다. (②) 우주 비행사인 Yuri Gagarin이 1961년에 우주에서 여행한 최초의 인간이 된 이래로, 과학자들은 지구의 대기권 너머에 어떤 환경이 존재할지, 그리고 우주여행이 인간 신체에 어떤 영향을 주는지를 연구해왔다. (③) 대부분의 우주 비행사들은 수개월 넘게는 우주에서 시간을 보내지 않음에도 불구하고, 많은 이들이 지구에 복귀할 때는 생리적 그리고 심리적 문제들을 겪는다. (④ <u>이 질병들 중 일부는 오래 가지 않는다; 다른 것들은 오래 지속될 수도 있다.</u>) 모든 우주 비행사들 중 2/3 넘게는 우주에서 여행을 하는 동안 멀미로 고통을 받는다. 무중력 환경에서, 신체는 위와 아래를 구분할 수 없다. 신체의 내부 균형 시스템이 뇌에 혼란스러운 신호를 전달하고, 이는 최대 며칠 동안 지속되는 메스꺼움을 초래할 수 있다.

어휘

ailment 질병
long-lasting 오래 지속되는
realm 영역
astronomer 천문학자
sustain 지속시키다, 유지하다
physiological 생리학적인
suffer from ~로 고통을 겪다
gravity 중력
internal 내부의
result in ~를 초래하다
short-lived 오래가지 못하는
exist 존재하다
ancient 고대의
examine 조사하다, 점검하다
extraterrestrial 외계의
psychological 심리적인
motion sickness 멀미
differentiate 구별하다
confusing 혼란스러운
nausea 매스꺼움

오답률 TOP 1

09 정답 ③
19 국가직

정답해설

빈칸 다음에 'In literature classes you don't learn about genes; in physics classes you don't learn about human evolution.'을 통해서 '문학 수업에서 생물학을 배우지 않고 물리 수업에서 진화를 배우지 않는다.'라고 하면서 그다음에 'So you get a partial view of the world(따라서 당신은 세상에 대한 부분적 견해를 얻는다).'라고 하였으므로 이와 관련된 내용이 빈칸에 들어가야 적절하다. 따라서 정답은 '③ Today, we teach and learn about our world in fragments(오늘날, 우리는 세상을 단편적으로 가르치고 배운다).'이다.

오답해설

① 과거에는 각성이 아니라 통합된 시각을 지녔다고 서술하고 있으므로 빈칸에 적절하지 않다.
② 본문 마지막에 '현대성은 무의미함을 의미한다(Modernity, it seems, means meaninglessness).'라고 하였으므로 정답이 될 수 없는 문장이다.
④ 본문에서 설명하고 있지 않은 내용이다.

해석

왜 모든 것의 역사로 괴롭히는가? 오늘날, 우리는 <u>단편적으로 세상에 대해 가르치고 배운다</u>. 문학 수업에서 당신은 유전자에 관해 배우지 않는다. 물리 수업에서 당신은 인간 진화에 관해 배우지 않는다. 따라서 당신은 세상에 대한 부분적 견해를 얻는다. 그것은 교육에서 의미를 찾는 것을 어렵게 만든다. 프랑스 사회학자인 Emile Durkheim은 이 혼란과 무의미함의 느낌을 사회적 무질서라고 불렀고, 그는 그것이 절망과 심지어 자살로 이끌 수도 있다고 주장했다. 독일 사회학자인 Max Weber는 세상의 "각성"에 관해 이야기했다. 과거에, 사람들은 그들의 세상에 대한 통합된 시각을 지녔고, 이는 보통 그들 자신의 종교적 전통의 기원 설화에 의해 제공되는 시각이었다. 그 통합된 시각은 목적에 대한, 의미에 대한, 심지어 세상에 현혹됨에 대한, 그리고 삶에 대한 감각을 제공했다. 그러나 오늘날, 많은 작가들은 무의미함의 느낌은 과학과 이성의 세상에서 필연적이라고 주장해왔다. 현대성은 무의미하는 것처럼 보인다.

① 과거에, 역사 연구는 과학으로부터의 각성을 요구했다
② 최근에, 과학은 우리에게 영리한 속임수들과 의미들을 제공해왔다
③ 오늘날, 우리는 세상을 단편적으로 가르치고 배운다
④ 최근에, 역사는 몇 가지 항목으로 나뉘어졌다

어휘

bother 애쓰다, 괴롭히다
gene 유전자
disorientation 혼미, 혼란, 방향 감각 상실
anomie 사회적 무질서
disenchantment 각성, 환멸
origin story 기원 설화
argue 주장하다
rationality 이성, 합리성
fragment 조각, 파편
literature 문학
physics 물리학
despair 절망
unified 통합된
enchantment 황홀감, 현혹
inevitable 불가피한, 필연적인
modernity 현대성

오답률 TOP 3

10 정답 ②
19 국가직

정답해설

본문에서 'Programs in the United States date from the Great Depression, when the need to use surplus agricultural commodities was joined to concern for feeding the children of poor families(정부 급식 프로그램은 대공황 때 잉여 농작물의 사용의 필요와 빈곤층의 아이들을 먹이는 것의 필요가 합쳐졌을 때 시작되었다).'고 설명하고 있으므로 '② The US government began to feed poor children during the Great Depression despite the food shortage(미국 정부는 식량 부족에도 불구하고 대공황 동안 가난한 아이들에게 급식을 하기 시작했다).'는 본문과 일치하지 않는 내용이다. 따라서 정답은 ②이다.

오답해설

① 본문에서 'the explosion in the number of working women fueled the need for a broader program(근로 여성의 수의 폭발이 프로그램의 확대의 필요성을 자극했다).'고 하였으므로 본문과 일치하는 문장이다.
③ 본문 후반부에 'to provide nutritious food at both breakfast and lunch to underprivileged children(소외계층의 아이들에게 아침과 점

을 제공하는 것).'이 현재 미국의 급식 프로그램의 기능이라고 설명하고 있으므로 본문과 부합한다.

④ 본문 중반부에 'What was once a function of the family—providing lunch—was shifted to the school food service system(가정의 기능에서 학교의 급식 시스템으로 점심을 제공하는 기능이 이동되었다).'고 하였으므로 본문과 일치하는 내용이다.

해석

가장 초기의 정부 급식 프로그램은 유럽에서 1900년경에 시작되었다. 잉여 농산물들을 사용해야 할 필요가 빈곤가정 아이들을 먹이는 것에 대한 걱정에 합쳐졌을 때, 미국의 프로그램은 대공황부터 시작되었다. 2차 세계대전 동안과 그 이후에는, 근로 여성들의 수의 폭발이 더 폭넓은 프로그램에 대한 필요를 자극했다. 한때 가정의 기능이었던 것 – 점심을 제공하는 것 – 이 학교의 급식 시스템으로 이동되었다. National School Lunch Program은 이 노력들의 결과이다. 그 프로그램은 연방정부의 지원을 받는 식사를 학령 아동들에게 제공하기 위해 만들어졌다. 2차 세계대전의 종결에서 1980년대 초까지, 학교 급식을 위한 자금지원은 꾸준히 확대되었다. 오늘날 그것은 미국 전역에서 거의 10만 개의 학교의 아이들에게 급식을 제공하는 것을 돕는다. 그것의 첫 번째 기능은 영양가 높은 점심을 모든 학생들에게 제공하는 것이다; 두 번째는 아침과 점심 모두 영양가 높은 음식을 소외계층 아이들에게 제공하는 것이다. 말하자면, 한때 가정의 기능이었던 것에 대한 대체물로서 학교 급식의 역할이 확대되어왔다.

① 일하는 여성의 수의 증가가 급식 프로그램의 확대를 신장시켰다.
② 미국 정부는 식량 부족에도 불구하고 대공황 동안 가난한 아이들에게 급식을 하기 시작했다.
③ 미국 학교의 급식 시스템은 현재 빈곤가정의 아이들에게 급식하는 것을 돕는다.
④ 점심을 제공하는 기능은 가정에서 학교로 이동되었다.

어휘

date from ~부터 시작되다 Great Depression 대공황
surplus 잉여의 agricultural 농업의
commodity 상품 explosion 폭발
fuel 연료를 공급하다, 자극하다 shift 이동시키다
federally 연방 차원에서 fund 자금을 지원하다
steadily 꾸준히 nutritious 영양가 높은
underprivileged 혜택을 받지 못한, 소외계층의
if anything 말하자면 boost 신장시키다
shortage 부족

결국엔 성정혜 영어 하프모의고사
기적사 DAY 52

| 01 | ① | 02 | ① | 03 | ③ | 04 | ① | 05 | ② |
| 06 | ① | 07 | ④ | 08 | ④ | 09 | ④ | 10 | ① |

01 정답 ①

정답해설

밑줄 친 단어는 '보복하다'로 사용되었고, 유의어가 아닌 것은 ① make up to이다.

해석

이 시점에서, 스튜디오 경영진들은 만약에 그들이 너무 강하게 또는 서둘러서 밀어붙이면, 영화관 체인들이 **보복을 할까 봐** 여전히 긴장한다.
① ~에게 아첨하다
② 앙갚음하다, 보답하다
③ 복수하다, 되갚음하다
④ 응수하다

어휘

executive 경영자, 행정부의 make up to ~에게 아첨하다
reciprocate 앙갚음하다, 보답하다 get even with 복수하다
retort 응수하다

02 정답 ①

정답해설

밑줄 친 단어는 문맥상 '이상한'으로 사용되었고, 유의어로는 ① eerie가 적절하다.

해석

그렇다 하더라도, 그의 **이상한**, 직관적인 방식으로, 그는 빈틈없고 교활한 이미지들을 만들어 내면서, 그가 알아야 할 필요가 있는 것들은 무엇이든 익혔다.
① 괴상한
② 회고의
③ 시간을 잘 지키는
④ 가파른, 갑작스러운, 퉁명스러운

어휘

intuitive 직관력 있는, 통찰력 있는 knowing 빈틈없는, 박식한 체하는
sly 교활한, 은밀한 eerie 괴상한
retrospective 회고의 punctual 시간을 잘 지키는
abrupt 가파른, 갑작스러운, 퉁명스러운

오답률 TOP 2
03 정답 ③

정답해설

주어진 빈칸은 문맥상 '경솔한'이 적절하므로 ③ heedless가 정답이다.

해석

시기가 좋았을 때, **경솔한** 프랑스와 독일 은행들은 이런 나라들에게 대출해주는 것에 기뻐했고, 아테네가 쌓아가는 중이었던 빚의 양을 간과했다.

① 솔직한
② 자기중심인, 독선적인
③ 부주의한, 경솔한
④ 우연의, 우연히

어휘

make up to 아첨하다, 친해지려고 하다
candid 솔직한
egotistic 자기중심인, 독선적인
heedless 부주의한, 경솔한
haphazard 우연의, 우연히

04 정답 ①

정답해설

A는 B에게 어젯밤에 무슨 꿈을 꾸었는지 묻는다. B는 A의 질문에 자기의 꿈은 승무원이 되는 것이었다고 답변한다. B가 말한 '꿈(dream)'은 장래희망의 의미로 사용한 것이므로 A가 한 질문 의도에 어긋난다.

오답해설

② A는 B에게 팔꿈치에 상처가 난 사실을 말해주자 B는 "어쩐지 많이 아팠다(No wonder it hurt so bad)"라고 답한다. 이는 문맥상 자연스러운 대화의 흐름이다.
③ A가 B에게 동물원에 간 적 있는지 묻자 B는 어렸을 적에 한 번 가본 적이 있다고 답변한다. B의 말은 A의 질문에 대한 적절한 답변이다.
④ A가 가장 가까운 우체국의 위치에 관해 묻자 B는 우체국에 가는 경로를 알려준다. A와 B의 대화는 맥락상 적합하다.

해석

① A: 너 어젯밤에 무슨 꿈 꿨어?
　 B: 내 꿈은 미래에 승무원이 되는 것이야.
② A: 네 팔꿈치에 상처 났어.
　 B: 어쩐지 많이 아프더라.
③ A: 너 동물원 가본 적 있어?
　 B: 나 되게 어렸을 적에 가봤어.
④ A: 가장 가까운 우체국이 어디 있는지 알아?
　 B: 두 구역 직진하고 첫 번째 모퉁이에서 왼쪽으로 가.

어휘

flight attendant 승무원
elbow 팔꿈치
zoo 동물원
post office 우체국

05 정답 ②

정답해설

② 출제 포인트: 주어[a number of 목적어 vs. the number of 목적어]
주어진 우리말 '직원의 수'라고 표현하기 위해서는 'A number of~'가 아닌 'The number of~'라고 표현해야 하며, 'The number of~'가 주어로 오는 경우 동사는 반드시 단수동사로 나타내야 한다. 따라서 'A'를 'The'로 고쳐야 하며 동사 'is'는 단수동사로 옳게 사용되었다. 단, 'taking legal action over work-related disease'는 현재분사의 형태로 employees를 올바르게 꾸미고 있다.

오답해설

① 출제 포인트: 최상급 대용표현
「비교급+than+the other 복수명사」는 최상급 대용표현으로 해당 문장의 경우 'Jane is the brightest child in her class.'로 바꾸어 사용할 수 있다. 또한 'much'는 비교급 'brighter'를 수식하는 비교급 강조 부사로 옳게 사용되었다.

③ 출제 포인트: 현재분사 vs. 과거분사
'sweeping'은 'sweep'의 현재분사로 수식하는 대상 'The crazy culture'와 능동 관계이고 주어진 해석 '휩쓸고 있는'과 일치하므로 옳게 사용되었다.

④ 출제 포인트: 완전타동사+목적어[to부정사 vs. 동명사]
'decide'는 완전타동사로 전치사 없이 목적어를 가지며 이때 to부정사를 목적어로 사용할 수 있으나 동명사는 목적어로 사용할 수 없다. 또한 'whatever risk ~ picture'는 간접의문문으로 'take'의 목적어절로 옳게 사용되었다.

오답률 TOP 1

06 정답 ①

정답해설

① 출제 포인트: It ~ that 강조용법
해당 문장은 「It ~ that」 강조 구문과 주격 관계대명사절 두 가지 경우로 볼 수 있다.
1. 「It ~ that」 강조 구문
　Jane's car got broken into last Friday night. (Jane's car를 강조)
　It was Jane's car that got broken into last Friday night. (이때 that은 which로 바꾸어 사용할 수 있다.)
2. 주격 관계대명사절
　It was Jane's car. + Jane's car got broken into last Friday night. (Jane's car를 선행사)
　It was Jane's car that got broken into last Friday night. (이때 that은 which로 바꾸어 사용할 수 있다.)
따라서 해당 문장은 「It ~ that」 강조 구문으로 보아도 옳은 문장이고 주격 관계대명사절로 보아도 옳은 문장이다.

오답해설

② 출제 포인트: 현재분사 vs. 과거분사 / 지각동사의 목적격 보어
해당 문장은 지각동사 'sees('see'의 3인칭 단수 현재시제)'의 목적격 보어로 과거분사 'designed'를 사용하였으나 뒤에 목적어 'intelligent and space-efficient buildings'가 있으며 수식하는 대상 'architects'와의 관계가 능동이므로 틀린 문장이다. 따라서 과거분사 'designed'를 현재분사 'designing' 또는 원형 부정사 'design'으로 수정해야 한다.

③ 출제 포인트: 복합관계부사
해당 문장에서 'however'는 복합관계부사로 '아무리 ~해도'를 뜻하며 「however+형용사/부사+주어+동사」의 형태로 사용된다. 따라서 'however it is worthy'를 'however worthy it is'로 수정해야 한다.

④ 출제 포인트: 주어와 동사의 수일치
주어가 단수형태인 'Lack'이므로 동사에 단수형태를 사용해야 한다. 따라서 복수 동사 'have'를 단수 동사 'has'로 수정해야 한다.

해석

① 지난 금요일 밤에 망가진 것은 Jane의 차이다.
② 그녀는 오늘날 건축가들이 지적이고 공간 효율적인 건물을 설계하는 것을 본다.
③ 그것이 아무리 가치가 있다고 해도 그녀가 그 법안을 의회에서 통과시키는 데 성공할 것 같지 않다.
④ 이전 종업원들에 따르면, 투자 부족은 여러 해 동안 계속되고 있다.

07 정답 ④

정답해설

④ 출제 포인트: 자동사로 착각하기 쉬운 완전타동사 / to부정사 관용표현
'resemble'은 완전타동사이므로 전치사 없이 목적어를 가진다. 또한 'be likely to'는 '~하는 경향이 있다'라는 뜻으로 해당 표현에서의 'to'는 전치사가 아닌 to부정사의 'to'임에 유의해야한다. 따라서 'be likely to' 뒤에 동사원형 'resemble'을 옳게 사용하였다.

오답해설

① 출제 포인트: 현재분사 vs. 과거분사
완전타동사 'store'의 현재분사인 'storing'이 사용되었으나 뒤에 목적어가 없으며 수식하는 대상 'the information'과 수동관계이므로 틀린 문장이다. 따라서 현재분사 'storing'을 과거분사 'stored'로 수정해야 한다. 또한 해당 문장의 주어는 'the information'으로 불가산명사에 해당하기 때문에 동사는 단수동사 'is'가 옳게 사용되었다.

② 출제 포인트: 동사 vs. 준동사
'writing'이 쓰인 위치를 준동사의 자릿값으로 인식한다면 'participants'를 주어로 하는 절의 동사가 없게 된다. 따라서 'writing'이 쓰인 위치는 동사의 자릿값으로 보아야 하며 'writing'은 시제를 적용하여 과거시제 동사 'wrote'로 수정해야 한다.

③ 출제 포인트: 동사 vs. 준동사/주어와 동사의 수일치
'be'가 쓰인 위치를 'seen'의 목적격 보어인 준동사의 자릿값으로 인식한다면 'the letters'를 주어로 하는 절의 동사가 없게 된다. 따라서 'be'가 쓰인 위치는 동사의 자릿값으로 보아야 하며 'be'는 시제와 수일치를 적용하여 과거시제 복수동사 'were'로 수정해야 한다.

해석

작동 기억 내에 저장된 많은 정보는, 특히 그 정보가 언어를 기반으로 할 때, 청각 형태로 암호화된다. 예를 들어 Conrad의 초창기 한 연구에서, 성인들에게 한 번에 하나씩 3/4초의 간격으로 글자가 시각적으로 제시된 여섯 개의 글자를 연속으로 보여 줬다. 연속된 글자들의 마지막 글자가 제시되자마자, 그 연구 참가자들은 그들이 쉽게 기억해 낼 수 없는 글자들을 짐작해 보면서, 자신들이 봤던 여섯 개의 글자들 모두를 적었다. 사람들이 글자들을 부정확하게 기억해 냈을 때, 그들이 봤다고 말한 그 글자들은 그것들이 어떻게 보였는가 보다는 어떻게 들렸는가의 관점에서 실제 자극과 유사한 경향이 더 컸다.

어휘

a good deal of 다량의, 많은
auditory 청각의
recall 기억해 내다, 상기하다
encode 암호화하다, 부호화하다
interval 간격, 사이, 중간 휴식 시간

08 정답 ④

정답해설

본문은 우주 왕복선 Challenger호의 참사에 대해서 언급하고 있다. 따라서 해당 참사를 모두 아우르는 정답은 '④ One of the most disastrous events in spaceflight history(우주 비행 역사상 가장 끔찍한 사건 중 하나)'가 가장 적절하다.

오답해설

① 우주 왕복선 Challenger호의 임무는 본문에 언급되지 않은 내용이다.
② 사고의 원인이 구체적으로 언급되지 않았으므로 적절하지 않다.
③ 참사로 인한 사망자들에 대한 언급은 본문 후반에만 언급될 뿐 글의 전체적인 주제라고 볼 수 없다.

해석

1986년 1월 28일에 발생한 우주 왕복선 Challenger호 참사는 우주 탐사의 역사상 가장 충격적인 날들 중 하나로 기록되었다. 우주 왕복선이 이륙하고 약 1분여가 흐른 뒤 우주선의 원형 링 – 로켓 부스터를 분리시키는 고무마개 – 의 기능 불량이 부스터를 불안정하게 만들고 로켓 자체로 확산된 화재를 발생시켰다. 우주선은 음속보다 더 빠르게 움직이고 있었고 빠르게 파손되기 시작했다. 참사는 우주에서의 여정 동안 수업을 가르치고 실험을 진행할 예정이었던 NASA의 Teacher in Space 프로젝트의 참가자인 민간인 Christa McAuliffe를 포함한 탑승해 있던 모든 우주 비행사의 사망으로 이어졌다.
① 우주 왕복선 Challenger호의 임무
② 우주 왕복선 Challenger호 사고의 원인
③ 우주 왕복선 Challenger호 참사로 인한 사망자들
④ 우주 비행 역사상 가장 끔찍한 사건 중 하나

어휘

devastating 엄청나게 충격적인
seal 밀봉[밀폐] 부분[물질]
astronaut 우주 비행사
fatality 사망자
malfunction 기능 불량, 고장
destabilize 불안정하게 만들다
civilian 민간인, 일반 시민

오답률 TOP 3

09 정답 ④

정답해설

본문은 '독일인 사회학자 Max Weber의 부모와의 관계와 그것이 Max Weber의 삶에 미친 영향'을 서술하고 있다. ① 'Max와 Helene Weber의 장자'가 가리키는 것은 'Max Weber'이고, ② 본문에서 'Max Weber'의 어머니에 대해 언급하고 있으므로 'His'는 'Max Weber'를 가리킨다는 것을 알 수 있다. 또한 ③ '그의 형제 중 두 사람'의 사망에 의해 Max Weber의 어머니가 오래된 슬픔을 겪었다고 언급한 것으로 보아, Max Weber의 형제, 즉, 그녀의 자녀가 사망했음을 알 수 있다. 따라서 'his'는 'Max Weber'를 가리킨다. 그런데 ④의 'He'는 '가정에서 권위주의적인 방식을 채택해 아내와 아이들에게 절대적 복종을 요구했다는 것으로 보아 'Max Weber의 아버지'에 대한 설명이라는 것을 알 수 있으므로, ④가 가리키는 대상은 나머지와 일치하지 않는다.

오답해설

①, ②, ③은 모두 Max Weber를 가리키므로 오답이다.

해석

Max Weber는 1864년 4월 21일 (현재의 독일인) 프로이센의 Erfurt에서 태어났다. ① 그는 Max와 Helene Weber의 장자였다. 그 사회학자의 아버지는 출세 지향적인 진보적 정치가였다. ② 그의 어머니는 매우 엄격한 정교적 신앙의 영향을 받고 자랐다. 비록 그녀가 더 관대한 신학을 점차 수용하기는 했으나, 그녀의 청교도적 도덕성은 결코 줄어들지 않았다. 결과적으로, 그녀의 남편의 사회적 활동이, 특히 ③ 그의 형제 중 두 사람의 사망에 따른 그녀의 오래된 슬픔을 그가 냉대하였을 때, 그녀를 그로부터 멀어지게 했다. 그 결과 ④ 그는 가정에서 전통적으로 권위주의적인 방식을 채택했고, 아내와 아이들의 절대적 복종을 요구했다. Weber 부모 사이의 갈등으로 나타난 이러한 암울한 가정환경이 그의 성인기에 그를 계속 괴롭힌 내면의 고통들의 원인이 되었다고 여겨진다.

어휘

sociologist 사회학자
liberal 진보의
orthodoxy 정통[정교] 신앙
theology 신학
aspiring 출세 지향적인
Calvinist 아주 엄격한, 칼뱅파의
tolerant 관대한, 너그러운
Puritan 청교도의

morality 도덕
distance 멀어지게[거리를 두게] 하다
prolonged 오래 끄는, 장기의
in turn 결국, 그 결과
obedience 복종
mark 상처를 남기다, 자국을 남기다, 오점을 남기다
contribute to …의 원인이 되다
haunt (오랫동안) 계속 문제가 되다[괴롭히다]
diminish 줄어들다, 감소하다
spurn 냉대하다, 퇴짜 놓다, 일축하다
grief 슬픔
authoritarian 권위주의적인
bleak 암울한, 어두운, 황량한
agony 고통, 고뇌

10 정답 ①

정답해설

본문은 'St. Louis에서 매년 여름 실시하는 무료 급식 프로그램인 Schools Out Café'에 대해 소개하고 있다. 두 번째 문장 "Every summer, Schools Out Café provides free breakfast and lunch to daycare centers, recreation programs, churches, and other organizations which then serve those meals to young people(매년 여름 Schools Out Café는 음식을 젊은이들에게 배식할 어린이집, 레크리에이션 프로그램, 교회, 그리고 기타 기관들에 무료 아침과 점심을 제공한다)."에서 해당 프로그램이 '매년 여름(Every summer)'에 실시된다고 언급하고 있으므로, '정기적인(regular) 행사'라는 것을 유추할 수 있다. 따라서 글의 주제로 가장 적절한 것은 '① a regular meal program(정기 급식 프로그램)'이다.

오답해설

② 학교 급식이 제공되지 않는 여름 동안에 실시하는 프로그램이므로, '학교 급식의 중요성'은 주제로 적합하지 않다.
③ 본문에서 언급되는 장소는 '무료 배급'이 이루어지는 곳이며, St. Louis 모든 젊은이들을 위한 곳을 소개하는 내용이 아니므로 오답이다.
④ 본문에 언급되지 않는 내용이다.

해석

이번 주 Lyda Krewson 시장은 Schools Out Café라고 알려진 청소년을 위한 시의 여름 급식 프로그램의 시작을 발표했다. 매년 여름 Schools Out Café는 음식을 젊은이들에게 배식할 어린이집, 레크리에이션 프로그램, 교회, 그리고 기타 기관들에 무료 아침과 점심을 제공한다. St. Louis의 학생들 중 약 80~90%가 무료 또는 할인 급식에 등록되어 있는데, 이는 여름 동안 영양이 충분한 음식에의 규칙적인 접근 기회가 부족하다는 주요 지표이다. "배고픔은 학교들이 여름 동안 문을 닫을 때도 쉬지 않습니다."라고 Krewson은 말했다. "저는 또한 음식 배급 장소가 되길 자원한 모든 단체와 기관에 매우 감사드립니다. 그러나 우리는 항상 더 많은 곳을 찾고 있습니다. 젊은이들에게 식사를 기꺼이 배급할 어느 기관이든지 우리에게 연락주시길 바랍니다. 우리가 음식을 제공할 것입니다."
① 정기 급식 프로그램
② 학교 급식의 중요성
③ St. Louis의 젊은이들을 위한 장소
④ 학교 급식 서비스의 문제점

어휘

estimated 추측의, 예상의
indicator 지표, 표시
nutritionally 영양적으로
be enrolled in …에 등록하다
access 접근, 접촉[접근] 기회
adequate 충분한, 적절한

결국엔 성정혜 영어 하프모의고사
기적사 DAY 53

| 01 | ④ | 02 | ② | 03 | ③ | 04 | ④ | 05 | ① |
| 06 | ③ | 07 | ① | 08 | ③ | 09 | ② | 10 | ③ |

01 정답 ④

정답해설

밑줄 친 단어는 '억압하다'로 사용되었고, 의미가 가장 먼 것은 ④ place이다.

해석

하지만 만약에 잔인한 독재자로서 그가 무기 없이 살아남을 수 없다는 것을 아는 사람이 양지에서 휴식을 취하기보다 오히려 사람들을 **숨차게 하기로[억압하기로]** 마음을 먹었다면 어떨까?
① 질식시키다
② 질식시켜 죽이다
③ 질식시키다
④ ~에 두다

어휘

suffocate 숨차다, 억압하다
smother 질식시켜 죽이다
place ~에 두다
asphyxiate 질식시키다
stifle 질식시키다

오답률 TOP 3

02 정답 ②

정답해설

밑줄 친 단어는 '은밀한'으로 사용되었고, 유의어로는 ② clandestine이 적절하다.

해석

그러나 1953년까지, 매카시즘과 2차 적색공포의 대활약으로, FBI는 **은밀한** 조사에서 직접적이고 즉각적인 접촉으로 이동했다.
① 결점이 없는
② 비밀리에 하는, 은밀한
③ 훌륭한, 웅장한
④ 상호 의존의

어휘

surreptitious 비밀의
clandestine 비밀리에 하는, 은밀한
interdependent 상호 의존의
faultless 결점이 없는
superb 훌륭한, 웅장한

03 정답 ③

정답해설

밑줄 친 단어는 문맥상 '영구화하다'로 사용되었고, 유의어로는 ③ eternize가 적절하다.

해석

이번 심포지엄의 거의 10%에 달하는, 사건들 중 두 가지는, 시오니즘은 인종차별이라는 거짓말을 **영구화한다**.
① 아첨하다, 친해지려고 하다

② 얽힘을 풀다, 해방되다
③ 영원성을 부여하다
④ 재시험하다, 재검토하다, 재심문하다

어휘

perpetuate 영속하게 하다　　　make up to 아첨하다, 친해지려고 하다
disentangle 얽힘을 풀다, 해방되다　eternize 영원성을 부여하다
reexamine 재시험하다, 재검토하다, 재심문하다

04 정답 ④

정답해설

Matthew가 Tim에게 화난 상황에서 Linda가 Matthew를 점심시간에 마주친다. Tim은 Linda에게 그를 어디에서 보았는지, 무엇을 하고 있었는지 묻자 Linda는 커피숍에서 마주쳤다며 Matthew가 메뉴판을 보고 있었다고 알려준다. 그리고 둘 사이에 무슨 일이 있었던 것인지 질문한다. Tim은 자신이 '④ 실언했다(put my foot in his mouth)'라고 얘기하며 그런 말을 한 것을 후회한다고 한다. 그러자 Linda는 그에게 진실한 사과를 하면 용서해줄 것이라고 조언한다.

오답해설

① Matthew와 Tim 사이에 무슨 일이 있었냐는 Linda의 질문에 Tim이 '묵묵부답했다(held my tongue)'라고 답변하는 것은 이어지는 "나는 그 말을 한 것을 후회해(I regret saying that)"라는 발언과 모순된다.
② Matthew와 Tim 사이가 틀어진 이유에 관해 묻는 Linda의 질문에 Tim이 '현장에서 발각됐다(was caught red-handed)'라고 말하는 것은 문맥상 부적절하다.
④ Tim은 Matthew와 자신의 관계가 틀어진 이유에 대한 답변으로 '겨우 삶을 연명했다(lived from hand to mouth)'라고 대답한 것은 맥락상 부자연스럽다.

해석

Tim: Matthew가 나한테 화났어?
Linda: 확실히는 모르겠어. 근데 내가 점심시간에 우연히 마주쳤을 때는 되게 화나 보였어.
Tim: 그를 어디서 봤어? 뭐 하고 있었어?
Linda: 커피숍에서 마주쳤는데 메뉴판을 보고 있었어. 둘 사이에 무슨 일이 있었던 거야?
Tim: 나는 그에게 실언했어. 그 말을 한 것을 후회해. 이젠 그와 어떻게 친해져야 할지 모르겠어.
Linda: 진심으로 사과해 봐. 그는 틀림없이 너를 용서해 줄 거야.
① 묵묵부답했다
② 현장에서 발각됐다
③ 겨우 삶을 연명했다
④ 실언했다

어휘

come across~ ~을 우연히 마주치다　sincere 진실된
apology 사과　　　　　　　　　forgive 용서하다
hold one's tongue 묵묵부답하다
be caught red-handed 현장에서 발각되다
live from hand to mouth 겨우 삶을 연명하다
put one's foot in one's mouth 실언하다

05 정답 ①

정답해설

① **출제 포인트: 최상급 대용표현**

「비교급+than+any other 단수 가산명사」는 최상급 대용표현에 해당한다. 해당 문장은 최상급 대용표현을 사용하였으나 'any other' 뒤에 복수 가산명사 'countries'를 사용하였으므로 틀린 문장이다. 따라서 'countries'를 단수형태 'country'로 수정해야 한다. 또한 'any other countries'를 'the other countries'로 사용하는 것도 옳다.

오답해설

② **출제 포인트: 주어[a number of 목적어 vs. the number of 목적어]와 동사의 수일치**

'a number of'는 뒤에 복수 가산명사가 목적어로 오며 주어인 경우 동사에 복수형태를 사용한다. 해당 문장은 유도부사구문으로 'a number of 목적어'가 주어인 경우에 해당하며 이때 목적어에 복수 가산명사 'factors'를 사용하였고 동사에 복수형태인 'are'를 사용하였으므로 옳은 문장이다.

③ **출제 포인트: 완전타동사+목적어[to부정사 vs. 동명사]**

'suggest'는 완전타동사로 전치사 없이 목적어를 가지며 이때 동명사를 목적어로 사용할 수 있으나 의문사 없는 to부정사를 목적어로 사용할 수 없다. 해당 문장은 'suggest'의 목적어로 동명사 'putting'이 사용되었으므로 옳은 문장이다.
※ suggest의 목적어 종류: ① 명사 ② 동명사 ②that절 ③의문사절 ④ 의문사+to부정사

④ **출제 포인트: 현재분사 vs. 과거분사**

'using'은 'use'의 현재분사로 수식하는 대상 'you'와 능동 관계이며 주어진 해석 '사용하여'와 일치하므로 옳게 사용되었다. 이때 'using'의 수식 대상을 'your mouse cursor'로 오해해서는 안 되며 문맥을 통해 수식 대상을 파악해야 한다.

06 정답 ③

정답해설

③ **출제 포인트: 주어와 동사의 수일치**

주어가 단수형태인 'The persecution'이므로 동사에 단수형태인 'is'를 옳게 사용하였다.

오답해설

① **출제 포인트: It ~ that 강조용법**

해당 문장은 「It ~ that」 강조 구문과 목적격 관계대명사절 두 가지 경우로 볼 수 있다.

1. 「It ~ that」 강조 구문
   John spoke to your husband on the phone. (your husband를 강조)
   It was your husband that John spoke to on the phone. (O/이때 that은 whom으로 바꾸어 사용할 수 있다.)
   It was your husband to that John spoke on the phone. (X/'It~that 강조 구문'에서는 'that'을 목적격 관계대명사로 볼 수 있으며 목적격 관계대명사 that은 앞에 전치사를 사용할 수 없다.)
   It was your husband to whom John spoke on the phone. (이때 해당 문장은 「It ~ that」 강조 구문으로 볼 수 없으며 목적격 관계대명사절로 보아야 한다.)

2. 목적격 관계대명사절
   It was your husband. + John spoke to your husband on the phone. (your husband를 선행사)
   It was your husband that John spoke to on the phone. (O/이

때 that은 whom으로 바꾸어 사용할 수 있다.)
It was your husband to that John spoke on the phone. (X/목적격 관계대명사 that은 앞에 전치사를 사용할 수 없다.)
It was your husband to whom John spoke on the phone. (O/목적격 관계대명사 whom은 앞에 전치사를 사용할 수 있다.)
따라서 해당 문장은 「It ~ that」 강조 구문으로 보아도 틀린 문장이고 목적격 관계대명사절로 보아도 틀린 문장이다. 옳은 문장으로 고치기 위해서는 두 가지 방법이 있다. 첫 번째 방법은 'to'를 'spoke' 뒤로 이동하는 것이며 이때 'It was your husband that John spoke to on the phone.'은 「It ~ that」 강조 구문과 목적격 관계대명사절 두 가지 모두로 볼 수 있다. 두 번째 방법은 'that'을 'whom'으로 수정하는 것이며 이때 'It was your husband to whom John spoke on the phone.'은 목적격 관계대명사절로 보아야 한다.

② 출제 포인트: 복합관계부사 / 형용사 vs. 부사
해당 문장에서 'however'는 복합관계부사로 '아무리 ~해도'를 뜻하며 「however+형용사/부사+주어+동사」의 형태로 사용된다. 또한 'however' 뒤에 오는 품사는 뒤에 오는 문장구조에 의해 결정되며 해당 문장의 경우 타동사구 'feel like'를 수식해야 하므로 부사가 와야 한다. 따라서 'many'를 'much'로 수정해야 한다.

④ 출제 포인트: 현재분사 vs. 과거분사 / 지각동사의 목적격 보어
해당 문장에서 'carry'의 과거분사인 'carried'가 'seeing(지각동사 see의 현재분사)'의 목적격 보어로 사용되었으나 뒤에 목적어 'a bag'이 있으며 수식하는 대상 'him'과 능동 관계이므로 틀린 문장이다. 따라서 'carried'를 현재분사 'carrying' 또는 원형부정사 'carry'로 수정해야 한다.

해석
① John이 전화로 통화한 사람은 네 남편이다.
② 아무리 시험을 치르고 싶지 않더라도 당신은 시험을 치러야 한다.
③ 같은 시기에 유대인 박해는 의심할 여지 없이 성립된다.
④ 그녀는 구금된 사람들 중 한 명이 편지가 들어 있는 가방을 옮기는 것을 본 후에 그를 신고했다.

오답률 TOP 2

07 정답 ①

정답해설

① 출제 포인트: 현재분사 vs. 과거분사
완전타동사 'write'의 과거분사인 'written'이 사용된 문장으로 뒤에 목적어가 없으며 수식하는 대상 'articles'와 수동관계이므로 옳은 문장이다. 이때 해당 문장에서 'discussing'은 동명사가 아닌 현재분사로 분사구문을 이끌고 있다는 점에 유의해야 한다.

오답해설

② 출제 포인트: 지각동사의 목적격 보어
지각동사는 목적격 보어로 능동 관계인 경우 원형부정사와 현재분사를 사용하며 수동관계인 경우 과거분사를 사용한다. 해당 문장은 지각동사 'see'의 목적격 보어에 to부정사 'to discuss'를 사용하였으므로 틀린 문장이다. 따라서 'to discuss'를 수정해야 하며 목적격 보어와 목적어가 능동 관계이므로 'discuss' 또는 'discussing'으로 수정해야 한다.

③ 출제 포인트: 주격 관계대명사절 동사의 수일치
주격 관계대명사절 동사의 수일치의 기준은 선행사이다. 해당 문장은 주격 관계대명사절 동사에 복수형태인 'contain'을 사용하였으나 선행사가 단수형태인 'a new product'이므로 틀린 문장이다. 따라서 'contain'을 단수형태의 동사인 'contains'로 수정해야 한다.

④ 출제 포인트: 능동태 vs. 수동태
'calls' 뒤에 목적어가 있으므로 'calls'를 완전타동사로 오해할 수 있으나 'This marketing technique'은 'calls'의 행위자가 될 수 없다. 따라서 'calls'를 수동태인 'is called'로 수정해야 한다. 이때 'call'은 불완전타동사로 사용되었으며 'demand creation'은 복합명사로 쓰여 하나의 의미로 '수요 창출'을 뜻한다. 이는 불완전타동사 'call'의 목적격 보어로 사용되었다.

해석
그 제품에 대한 관심을 창출하기 위해 회사들은 흔히 출시 전 광고 캠페인에 착수하곤 한다. 영양제 업계에서는 연구 중인 새로운 영양분에 대해 논의하는 기사가 흔히 작성된다. 일련의 간행물에 걸쳐 당신은 이 새로운 영양분과 훈련 그리고/또는 경기력을 향상시킬 수 있는 잠재력에 대해 논의하는 더 많은 기사를 보기 시작한다. 그런 다음 4~6개월 후에, 이전의 간행물에서 논의되던 성분을 함유한 신제품이 우연의 일치처럼 출시된다. 책과 영양 보충제 논평 기사도 건강 및 영양 제품의 판매를 촉진하기 위한 도구로 이용되어왔다. 이런 마케팅 기술을 수요 창출이라고 부른다. 그것은 독자의 관심을 자극하는 기사 그리고/또는 책의 출간을 통해, 어쩌면 혁명적일 수도 있는 새로운 영양분이나 훈련 기법에 관한 소문을 만들어 내는 것을 포함한다. 일단 이것이 이루어지고 나면 신제품이 출시된다.

어휘
launch 착수하다, 출시하다   article 기사
investigation 조사, 연구   enhance 높이다, 향상시키다
coincidentally (우연히) 일치하여, 동시적으로
supplement 부록, 보충

08 정답 ③

정답해설
본문은 '우주의 무중력상태에 제대로 적응하지 못했을 때 발생하는 Space Adaptation Syndrome (SAS) 증상'에 대해 설명하고 있다. 본문 중반 "This 'space sickness' or Space Adaptation Syndrome (SAS), is experienced by over half of all astronauts during the first few days of their space voyage(이러한 '우주병' 또는 우주적응증후군(SAS)은 모든 우주 비행사들 중 절반 이상이 그들의 우주 여정의 초반 며칠 동안 경험한다)."에서 'SAS는 보통 우주여행의 초반 며칠 동안 경험된다.'라고 설명하고 있으므로 '③ SAS symptoms usually present themselves at the beginning of an astronaut's time in space(SAS 증상은 보통 우주 비행사가 우주에서 보내는 시간의 초기에 나타난다).'는 글의 내용과 일치한다. 따라서 정답은 ③이다.

오답해설
① 본문에서는 무중력이 우주 비행사의 '공간적 방위(spatial orientation)'에 미치는 영향에 대해 설명하고 있으며, 체중에 관한 언급은 없으므로 글의 내용과 일치하지 않는다.
② "Unless this adaptation is complete, this can be coupled to motion sickness (nausea), visual illusions and disorientation(이러한 적응이 완료되지 않는다면, 이것은 멀미(메스꺼움), 시각적 환각, 그리고 방향 감각 상실로 연결될 수 있다)."을 통해 SAS 증상에 '시각적 환각(visual illusions)'이 포함되기는 하지만, '시력 상실(vision loss)'은 포함되지 않는 것을 알 수 있다. 따라서 오답이다.
④ Wubbo Ockels은 최초의 네덜란드인 우주 비행사이지 최초로 SAS 증상을 겪은 사람은 아니다.

해석
중력은 우리의 공간적 방위에 있어서 주요한 역할을 한다. 우주여행 중 무중력상태로 진입하는 것과 같은 중력의 변화는 우리의 공간적 방위에 영향을 미치고, 우리의 균형 시스템이 작용하는 여러 생리적 과정을 통한 적응을 필요로 하게 된다. 이러한 적응이 완료되지 않는다면, 이것은 멀미(메스꺼움), 시

각적 환각, 그리고 방향 감각 상실로 연결될 수 있다. 이러한 '우주병' 또는 우주적응증후군(SAS)은 모든 우주 비행사들 중 절반 이상이 그들의 우주 여정의 초반 며칠 동안 경험한다. 1986년 우주에 간 최초의 네덜란드인 Wubbo Ockels 또한 이러한 증상들을 겪었다. 흥미롭게도 SAS 증상은 예를 들어 전투기 조종사를 테스트하고 훈련시키는 데 사용되는 경우와 같이 인간 원심분리기의 고중력 상태에 오랜 시간 노출된 후에도 심지어 경험될 수 있다.

① 무중력은 우주 비행사의 체중에 영향을 미친다.
② SAS 증상은 시력 상실을 포함한다.
③ SAS 증상은 보통 우주 비행사가 우주에서 보내는 시간의 초기에 나타난다.
④ Wubbo Ockels는 SAS 증상을 겪은 최초의 사람이다.

어휘

orientation 방향
transition 변환, 이동
adaptation 적응
couple to …에 연결하다
nausea 메스꺼움
disorientation 방향 감각 상실, 혼미
exposure 노출
gravitational force 중력
voyage 여정, 여행
physiological 생리학적인
motion sickness 멀미
illusion 환상, 환각
astronaut 우주 비행사
centrifuge 원심 분리기

09 정답 ②

정답해설

주어진 문장 "Science has defined the modern era in many ways ~(과학은 여러 방식으로 현대 시대를 정의했고)"를 통해 '현대 시대에서의 과학의 역할'에 대해 언급하고 있다. 이어서 이어질 문장으로는 '과학에 의해 정의된 현대성의 특징(The key features of modernity, specialization and technology ~)'에 대해 언급하는 (A)가 이어지는 것이 적절하며, 이후 'But(그러나)'을 이용해 앞서 언급된 내용과는 대조되는 논점을 제시하며, '과학이 현대 세계를 이끈 반면, 인간의 의미 추구를 위태롭게 만들기도 했다'라고 서술하는 (C)가 이어지는 것이 자연스럽다. 마지막으로 (B)의 "This is the case because ~"를 이용해, (C)에서 언급된 내용의 근거를 설명하고 있으므로 (C)에 (B)가 이어지는 것이 적절하다. 따라서 정답은 '② (A) – (C) – (B)'이다.

오답해설

① (B)와 (C)에서 동일한 논점을 가지고 글을 서술하고 있으므로, (B)에 이어서 '역접'을 나타내는 'But'을 이용해 (C)가 이어지는 것은 어색하다.
③, ④ (B)의 'This'가 가리키는 것이 주어진 문장에 언급되지 않으므로 오답이다.

해석

과학은 여러 방식으로 현대 시대를 정의했고, 현대 시대에서 진정으로 우세한 지식 패러다임이다.
(A) 과학에 의해 정의된 현대성의 주요 특징인 전문화와 기술은 Galileo와 Kepler 시대 이래로 지난 400년 동안의 과학 기술과 지식의 놀라운 발전에 의해 가능해졌다.
(C) 그러나 과학이 매우 실제적이고 직접적인 방식으로 우리를 현대 세계로 데려다준 반면, 그것은 또한 우리를 인간의 끊임없는 의미 추구가 위태로워진 지점까지 데려왔다.
(B) 오늘날의 과학적 세계관이 우주에서 우리의 공간에 대한 질문, 의식의 본질, 그리고 신, 목적, 및 여러 다른 심오한 주제에 관한 질문들을 포함해 인간이 지속적으로 중요하다고 생각했던 많은 탐구들의 중요성을 부인하는 것처럼 보이기 때문에 이것은 사실이다.

어휘

define 정의하다
primarily 주로
case 사실, 실정
perennially 지속적으로, 영속적으로
reigning 단연 우세한, 지배적인
remarkable 놀라운
consciousness 의식, 자각
imperil 위태롭게 하다, 위험에 빠뜨리다

오답률 TOP 1

10 정답 ③

정답해설

본문은 '급식비를 지불하지 못하는 학생들에게 바람직하지 못한 행위를 자행하고 있는 일부 학교들'에 대해 서술하고 있다. 세 번째 문장 "Unfortunately, we have seen a series of school districts recently take steps in the other direction, resulting in humiliation for their students(안타깝게도, 우리는 다른 방향으로의 조치를 취하여 그 결과 학생들이 수치심을 느끼게 하는 일련의 교구들을 최근 목격해 왔다)."에서, 일부 교구들에서 이루어지는 일들이 '학생들이 수치심을 느끼게' 만들고 있다고 언급하며, 이후에 구체적인 예시로 '손에 도장 찍기', '다른 아이들과 다른 음식 제공', '위탁 시설로 보낸다는 위협', '점심식사 버리기'를 제시하고 있다. 이후 "Make no mistake(실수를 하지 말라)."를 통해 이러한 행위들이 올바르지 않다는 것을 지적하며, 빈 칸의 행위는 용납할 수 없다고 말한다. 따라서 빈칸에는 앞서 언급된 행위들을 통틀어 설명할 수 있는 '③ Subjecting students to embarrassment (학생들에게 창피를 주는 것)'이 들어가는 것이 가장 적절하다.

오답해설

① 아이들을 위탁 시설로 보내겠다고 위협하는 행위에 대해 언급되기는 하지만, 본문의 주제를 뒷받침하는 하나의 예시일 뿐이므로 빈칸에 적절하지 않다.
② 본문과 관련이 없는 내용이므로 오답이다.
④ "giving him or her a sunflower butter and jelly sandwich instead of a hot lunch(그 또는 그녀에게 따뜻한 점심 대신에 해바라기 버터와 젤리 샌드위치를 주고)"에서 영양이 부족한 점심을 제공하는 것의 예시가 제시되긴 하지만, 지엽적인 내용이므로 빈칸에는 적절하지 않다.

해석

California 주지사 Gavin Newsom은 지불할 자금을 가지고 있든 아니든 모든 학생들이 학교 급식을 먹을 자격이 있다는 것을 명령하는 법안에 서명했다. 이것은 옳은 방향으로의 강력한 조치이다. 안타깝게도, 우리는 다른 방향으로의 조치를 취하여 그 결과 학생들이 수치심을 느끼게 하는 일련의 교구들을 최근 목격해 왔다. 이러한 행위들은 아이의 손에 "저는 점심값이 필요해요"라는 도장을 찍고, 그 또는 그녀에게 따뜻한 점심 대신에 해바라기 버터와 젤리 샌드위치를 주고, 심지어 미지불 학교 급식 대금이 있는 아이들을 위탁 시설로 보내겠다고 위협하는 것을 포함한다. 지난달 한 아이가 해당 교구가 그의 무료 급식 신청서를 처리하고 있는 동안, 그의 미지급 급식비가 9달러 누적되었다는 이유로 그의 생일에 그의 점심식사가 쓰레기통에 버려지게 되었다. 실수를 하지 말라. 학교 급식비를 지불할 자금 부족 때문에 학생들에게 창피를 주는 것은 용인될 수 없다.

① 아이들을 위탁 시설로 보내는 것
② 학생들이 복종하도록 위협하는 것
③ 학생들에게 창피를 주는 것
④ 학생들에게 영양이 부실한 음식을 주는 것

어휘

mandate 명령하다
be entitled to ~할 자격이 있다, 권리가 주어지다
district 구역
outstanding 아직 처리되지 않은, 미지불된
humiliation 수치심, 창피함, 굴욕

debt 빚
accrue 모으다, 축적하다
embarrassment 무안함, 당혹감
subject 받게 하다

forster care 위탁 가정[시설]
intimidate 위협하다, 겁을 주다
obedience 복종
nutrient 영양분

결국엔 성정혜 영어 하프모의고사
기적사 DAY 54

| 01 | ② | 02 | ④ | 03 | ④ | 04 | ① | 05 | ④ |
| 06 | ② | 07 | ① | 08 | ③ | 09 | ② | 10 | ② |

오답률 TOP 1

01 정답 ②

정답해설

밑줄 친 단어는 문맥상 '양심'으로 사용되었으므로 가장 먼 것은 ② complacency가 정답이다.

해석

사람들은 영원히 부당하고 결정적으로 박해를 받고, 그들의 **양심**과 고군분투하며, 모든 위험을 무릅쓰고 옳은 일을 하고 있다.
① 양심의 가책, 뉘우침, 회한
② 자기만족
③ 꺼림직함, 양심의 가책, 불안
④ 양심

어휘

persecute 박해하다, 처벌하다
compunction 죄책감, 거리낌
qualm 꺼림직함, 양심의 가책, 불안
conscience 양심의 가책, 뉘우침, 회한
complacency 자기만족
scruple 양심

02 정답 ④

정답해설

주어진 빈칸에는 문맥상 '이용하다'가 적절하다. 따라서 정답은 ④ draws on 이다.

해석

일본의 구 관할 경찰서는 사람들에게 모르는 번호로 걸려 오는 전화를 즉시 받지 말라고 주의를 주기 위해 만화 캐릭터들을 **이용한다**.
① 폭로하다, 자백하다, ~인 체하다
② 보상하다
③ 고용하다, 떠맡다
④ 이용하다

어휘

let on 폭로하다, 자백하다, ~인 체하다
make up for 보상하다
draw on 이용하다
take on 고용하다, 떠맡다

03 정답 ④

정답해설

밑줄 친 단어는 문맥상 '우울한'으로 사용되었고, 유의어가 아닌 단어는 ④ enticing이다.

해석

파리는 차갑고 **우울한** 곳이었지만 스페인에서 부모님과 함께 나는 추위를 피하기 위해서 이 따뜻한 사랑의 쉼터를 발견했다.
① 짜증을 내는

② 시무룩한, 음침한
③ 구슬픈
④ 유혹적인

어휘

morose 우울한
cranky 짜증을 내는
melancholy 구슬픈
refuge 쉼터, 피난처
dour 시무룩한, 음침한
enticing 유혹적인

04 정답 ①

정답해설

Cindy와 Dan은 Cindy가 처한 상황에 관한 대화를 나눈다. Cindy는 보고서를 다 썼는데 컴퓨터가 꺼져서 처음부터 새로 시작해야 하는 상황에 처해있다. 짜증이 난 Cindy의 상황을 보며 Dan은 (A) '원점(square one)'으로 되돌아왔다고 말한다. Cindy는 주말 내내 보고서를 썼지만 이제 모두 소용이 없다면서 자신이 (B) '헛된 노력을 한(went on a wild goose chase)' 것 같다고 한다. 그러자 Dan은 Cindy에게 긍정적으로 생각하라고 하면서, 보고서를 한 번 써봤으니 두 번째 (C) '목표를 달성할(hit the bull's eye)' 때에는 훨씬 더 적은 시간이 소요될 것이라고 말한다.

오답해설

② (A) 보고서를 다 썼지만, 컴퓨터가 꺼져 처음부터 시작해야 한다는 Cindy의 상황을 '생계 수단(bread and butter)'으로 묘사하는 것은 문맥상 부자연스럽다.
③ (B) Cindy는 보고서를 두 번째로 처음부터 다시 써야 하는 상황을 '초조해(had ants in my pants)' 보인다고 말하는 것은 적절하지 않다. (C) Dan은 Cindy에게 보고서를 한번 써보았으니 두 번째로 '노인에게 새로운 것을 가르쳐 줄(teach an old dog new tricks)' 때에는 적은 시간이 걸리리라는 것은 대화의 흐름상 어색하다.
④ (A) 보고서를 다 썼지만, 컴퓨터가 꺼져 처음부터 시작해야 한다는 Cindy의 상황을 '생계 수단(bread and butter)'으로 묘사하는 것은 문맥상 자연스럽지 않다. (B) Cindy는 보고서를 두 번째로 처음부터 다시 써야 하는 상황을 '초조해(had ants in my pants)' 보인다고 말하는 것은 부적합하다. (C) Dan은 Cindy에게 보고서를 한번 써보았으니 두 번째로 '노인에게 새로운 것을 가르쳐 줄(teach an old dog new tricks)' 때에는 적은 시간이 걸리리라는 것은 알맞지 않다.

해석

Cindy: 나는 지금 아주 짜증 나. 그냥 포기하고 싶어.
Dan: 왜? 안 좋은 일 있어?
Cindy: 보고서 쓰는 것을 거의 다 끝냈는데 컴퓨터가 꺼졌어. 이제 다시 시작해야 해.
Dan: 어쩌지. 그럼 너 (A) 원점으로 되돌아왔네.
Cindy: 맞아. 나는 주말 내내 보고서를 썼어. 하지만 이제 모두 쓸모없네.
Dan: 안타깝다. 난 네가 얼마나 노력했는지 알아.
Cindy: 글쎄, 내가 그냥 (B) 헛된 노력을 한 것으로 보여.
Dan: 긍정적으로 생각해. 네가 보고서를 한번 써봤으니까 두 번째에는 네가 (C) 목표를 달성하는 데 훨씬 적은 시간이 걸릴 거야.
Cindy: 위로해줘서 고마워. 이제 시작해야겠어.

① (A) 원점 (B) 헛된 노력을 했다 (C) 목표를 달성하다
② (A) 생계 수단 (B) 헛된 노력을 했다 (C) 목표를 달성하다
③ (A) 원점 (B) 초조했다 (C) 노인에게 새로운 것을 가르쳐 주다
④ (A) 생계 수단 (B) 초조했다 (C) 노인에게 새로운 것을 가르쳐 주다

어휘

frustrated 짜증 난
report 보고서
useless 소용없는, 쓸모없는
square one 원점
bread and butter 생계 수단
go on a wild goose chase 헛된 노력을 하다
have ants in one's pants 초조하다
hit the bull's eye 목표를 달성하다
teach an old dog new tricks 노인에게 새로운 것을 가르쳐 주다(오래된 사고 방식은 고치게 하기 힘들다)

05 정답 ④

정답해설

④ **출제 포인트: 완전타동사+목적어[to부정사 vs. 동명사]**
'threaten'은 완전타동사로 전치사 없이 목적어를 가지며 이때 to부정사를 목적어로 사용할 수 있으나 동명사를 목적어로 사용할 수 없다. 해당 문장은 'threaten'의 목적어로 동명사 'boycotting'을 사용하였으므로 틀린 문장이다. 따라서 'boycotting'을 to부정사 'to boycott'으로 수정해야 한다.

오답해설

① **출제 포인트: 최상급 대용표현**
「비교급+than+any other 단수 가산명사」는 최상급 대용표현으로 해당 문장의 경우 'any other' 뒤에 단수 가산명사 'place'를 사용하였으므로 옳은 문장이다.
② **출제 포인트: 주어[a number of 목적어 vs. the number of 목적어]와 동사의 수일치**
'The number of'는 뒤에 복수 가산명사가 목적어로 오며 주어인 경우 동사에 단수형태를 사용한다. 해당 문장은 'The number of 목적어'가 주어인 경우에 해당하며 이때 목적어에 복수 가산명사 'people'을 사용하였고 동사에 단수형태인 'has increased'를 사용하였으므로 옳은 문장이다.
③ **출제 포인트: 현재분사 vs. 과거분사**
'staring'은 'stare'의 현재분사이며 수식하는 대상은 생략된 주어 'I'이다. 따라서 해당 문장은 'I'와 'staring'이 능동 관계이며 주어진 해석 '내려다보면서'와 일치하므로 옳은 문장이다.

06 정답 ②

정답해설

② **출제 포인트: It ~ that 강조용법**
해당 문장은 「It ~ that」 강조 구문과 주격 관계대명사절 두 가지 경우로 볼 수 있다.
1. 「It ~ that」 강조 구문
   The commander is the first to take the blame for accidents. (The commander를 강조)
   It is the commander that is the first to take the blame for accidents. (이때 that은 who로 바꾸어 사용할 수 있다.)
2. 주격 관계대명사절
   It is the commander. + The commander is the first to take the blame for accidents. (the commander를 선행사)
   It is the commander that is the first to take the blame for accidents. (이때 that은 who로 바꾸어 사용할 수 있다.)
따라서 해당 문장은 「It ~ that」 강조 구문으로 보아도 옳은 문장이고 주격 관계대명사절로 보아도 옳은 문장이다.

오답해설

① **출제 포인트: 복합관계부사**
해당 문장에서 'however'는 복합관계부사로 '아무리 ~해도'를 뜻하며 「however+형용사/부사+주어+동사」의 형태로 사용된다. 따라서 'however much does it cost'를 'however much it costs'로 수정해야 한다.

③ 출제 포인트: 주어와 동사의 수일치
주어가 단수형태인 'The joint intention'이므로 동사에 단수형태를 사용해야 한다. 따라서 'appear'를 단수형태의 동사 'appears'로 수정해야 한다.

④ 출제 포인트: 현재분사 vs. 과거분사
해당 문장에서 'watched'는 분사구문을 이끄는 과거분사로 사용되었으나 뒤에 목적어 'her daughter'이 있고 수식하는 대상 'Jane'과 능동 관계이므로 틀린 문장이다. 따라서 과거분사 'watched'를 현재분사 'watching'으로 수정해야 한다. 또한 현재분사로 쓰인 'watching'은 지각동사에 해당하므로 목적격보어 자리에 온 원형부정사 'open'은 옳게 사용되었다.

해석
① 어떤 것을 좋아한다면 Jane은 그것이 아무리 비싸다 하더라도 살 것이다.
② 사고의 책임을 가장 먼저 지는 사람은 바로 지휘관이다.
③ 이 두 당사자의 공동 목적은 나에게 전혀 의심의 여지가 없는 것으로 보인다.
④ Jane은 딸이 갈색 가방을 여는 것을 지켜보면서 웃으며 침대 발치에 앉았다.

07 정답 ①

정답해설
① 출제 포인트: 현재분사 vs. 과거분사 / 주어-동사의 수일치
완전타동사 'define'의 과거분사인 'defined'가 사용된 문장으로 뒤에 목적어가 없으며 수식하는 대상 'goals'와 수동관계이므로 옳은 문장이다. 또한 주어는 'Merely having ~ defined'로 동명사 주어이다. 동명사 주어는 단수 취급하므로 단수 형태의 동사 'is'는 옳게 사용되었다.

오답해설
② 출제 포인트: 부정사의 태
문맥상 관계대명사 'what'은 'needs'의 주어에 해당하나, 'to do'의 목적어마저 없는 상황이므로 틀린 문장이다. 따라서 'to do'를 수동태 'to be done'으로 수정해서 목적어가 필요하지 않도록 만들면 성립할 수 있다.

③ 출제 포인트: 자동사로 착각하기 쉬운 완전타동사
'emphasize'는 완전타동사이므로 전치사 없이 목적어를 가진다. 해당 문장은 'emphasize'를 사용하였으나 뒤에 전치사 'on'을 사용하였으므로 틀린 문장이다. 따라서 'on'을 삭제해야 한다. 또한 해당 문장에서 'what'은 'emphasize'의 목적어에 해당한다.

④ 출제 포인트: 불완전자동사 hold / not only A but also B
해당 문장에서 'holds'는 불완전자동사이나 주격 보어에 부사 'truly'를 사용하였으므로 틀린 문장이다. 따라서 'truly'를 형용사 'true'로 수정해야 한다. 또한 'for+명사(구)'가 등위상관접속사 'not only ~ but also ~'를 사용하여 병렬구조를 이루고 있다.

해석
명확하게 정의를 내린 목표를 갖는 것만으로는 충분하지 않는데, 왜냐하면 사람들은 또한 정확하게 무엇이 행해질 필요가 있는지를 시시각각으로 알아야 하기 때문이다. 예를 들어, 한 판매원의 목표는 수익성 있게 판매를 끝내는 것이다. 그러나 각각의 판매는 다른 접근 방법을 필요로 한다. 그가 강력히 밀어붙여야 하는가 아니면 느긋해야 하는가? 위압적이어야 하는가 아니면 다정해야 하는가? 그리고 그가 제품의 어떤 면을 강조해야 하는가? 이런 질문들에 대한 답은 사전에 예측될 수 없는 변수에 달려 있다. 이것은 판매뿐만 아니라 대부분의 인간 활동에도 딱 들어맞는다. 사람들은 그 경우에 알맞은 특별한 전략을 선택해야 하고 선택된 행동 방침을 따라야 한다. 그렇게 하는 것이 목표를 달성하는 것에서 더 지속적인 성공을 보장할 것이다.

어휘
sufficient 충분한
authoritative 권위적인, 권위 있는
lasting 지속적인, 영속적인
conclude 끝내다, 결론을 내리다
variable 변수; 가변적인, 변동이 심한

08 정답 ③

정답해설
본문은 '우주 멀미(space motion sickness) 연구에 대한 Jake Garn의 공헌'에 대해 설명하고 있다. (A) 빈칸에는 그의 공헌의 '성격'을 표현할 수 있는 어휘가 들어가야 하고 (B) 빈칸에는 그가 경험한 우주 멀미의 '특징'을 표현할 수 있는 어휘가 들어가야 한다. 본문의 내용에 따르면, 'Jake Garn은 우주 멀미에 대한 이해를 강화하기 위한 테스트를 받기 위해 우주선에 탑승하였는데, 그가 경험한 우주 멀미가 예상 밖으로 너무 심했기 때문에 그의 경험이 최고 수준의 우주 멀미의 기준으로 채택되었다'라는 것을 알 수 있다. 따라서 그의 우주 멀미 연구에 대한 그의 공헌은 의도된 것이 아니며 우연히 발생한 것임을 알 수 있다. 따라서 (A)에는 'unintentional(의도하지 않은)' 또는 'unwitting(자신도 모르는)'이 적절하다. 또한, 그가 경험한 증상이 '최고 수준(the maximum possible level of space sickness).'으로 기록된 것으로 보아, 당시 Jake Garn이 매우 심한 멀미를 경험했음을 알 수 있다. 따라서 (B)에는 'extreme(극심한)' 또는 'severe(심각한)'가 적절하다. 그러므로 알맞은 어휘가 짝지어진 보기는 '③ unwitting(자신도 모르는) - severe(심각한)'이다.

오답해설
① Jake Garn의 경험을 기준으로 우주 멀미의 등급이 정해지게 되었으므로, 그의 공헌이 '과소평가'된 것은 아니다. 따라서 (A)에 'underestimated(과소평가되는)'가 들어가는 것은 부적절하다.
② 본문의 내용을 통해 Jake Garn의 멀미 수준이 매우 심각했음을 알 수 있으므로 (B)에 'trivial(하찮은)'이 들어가는 것은 부적절하다.
④ 문맥상 어색한 어휘이므로 오답이다.

해석
다행스럽게도 대부분의 우주 멀미(SMS)를 겪는 사람들은 점진적으로 새로운 환경에 적응하게 되고 메스꺼움은 우주에서의 며칠이 지난 후에 가라앉는다. 특히 심하게 멀미를 겪은 한 우주 비행사는 그의 정치적 업적이 아니라 SMS 연구에 대한 (A) 자신도 모르는 공헌으로 기억되는 전 미국 상원의원인 Jake Garn이다. Garn 상원의원은 1985 우주 왕복선 임무에 탑승 과학 기술자로서 참여했고, 그의 역할의 일부는 우주 멀미에 대한 이해를 강화하기 위해 설계된 테스트를 받는 것이었다. 안타깝게도 그의 멀미는 너무 (B) 심각해서 Astronaut Corps는 그의 경험을 우주 멀미의 최대 가능 수준의 기준으로 채택했다. 그들은 완전히 몸을 가눌 수 없는 것이 1 Garn으로 불리는 등급을 고안했다. 듣자 하니 대부분의 우주 비행사들은 겨우 0.1 Garn에 도달한다.
① 과소평가되는 - 극심한
② 의도하지 않은 - 하찮은
③ 자신도 모르는 - 심각한
④ 무조건적인 - 갑작스러운

어휘
adapt to …에 적응하다
astronaut 우주 비행사
payload specialist (우주선에 탑승하여 실험하는) 탑승 과학 기술자
be subjected to …을 받다[당하다]
devise 창안[고안]하다
incapable 몸을 제대로 가누지[정신을 차리지] 못하는
be dubbed …로 불리다
no more than 고작, 겨우
unintentional 의도하지 않은, 고의가 아닌
trivial 사소한, 하찮은
abrupt 갑작스러운, 돌연한
subside 가라앉다, 진정되다
contribution 공헌, 기여
adopt 채택하다
scale 척도, 등급
apparently 보기에, 외견상으로
underestimated 과소평가되는
unwitting 자신도 모르는, 본의 아닌

오답률 TOP 1
09 정답 ②

정답해설

본문은 '현대에서의 의미 추구'에 관한 글이며, 빈칸에는 '현대 세계에서 추구되는 의미의 특성'을 묘사할 수 있는 표현이 들어가야 한다. 과거에는 "a coherent life-conduct based on religion and set within the parameters of meaningful cosmos(종교와 의미가 가득한 우주의 범위 내의 사회에 기반을 둔 일관성 있는 생활 방식)"에 근거하여 '통합적인 의미 추구'를 했지만, '현대 세계에서는 5가지의 독립된 가치 영역 내에서 개별적인 의미 추구가 이루어진다(the modern world is structured as a series of five competing, separate value-spheres).'라고 설명한다. 즉, 각 영역 내에서만 유효한 의미이기 때문에, 현대 세계에서의 의미는 '제한적이고 조건적인 것'이라고 볼 수 있다. 따라서 빈칸에 가장 적절한 표현은 '② limited and conditional(제한적이고 조건적인)'이다.

오답해설

① 문맥상 어색한 표현이므로 오답이다.
③ 본문에서는 현대성이 '무의미한(meaningless)' 것만은 아니며, 분리된 영역 내에서 각자의 의미가 존재한다고 설명하고 있으므로, 'empty and meaningless(텅 비어있고 무의미한)'는 빈칸에 적절하지 않다.
④ 개별적인 의미 추구는 현대 세계에 들어서 나타난 현상이므로 'old fashioned(구식의)'라는 표현은 빈칸에 부적절하다.

해석

서양 역사상에서 의미 추구의 모순적인 결과는 현대성을 무의미하게 만드는 데 커다란 역할을 해왔다. 그러나 이상적인 이해관계와 문화와 같은 Weber의 연구에서 발견된 개념들이 더 이상 적용되지 않는 것은 아니다. 오히려 Weber는 현대적인 의미 추구에서 발견되는 지속적인 모순적 결과에 기초한 현대성의 이해를 제공해준다. 매혹적이고 장대한 의미의 통합 효과 없이 현대 세계는 5가지의 경쟁적이고 독립된 가치 영역으로서 구성되어 있다: 경제, 지성, 정치, 미학, 그리고 성애. 바로 이 가치 영역 이론을 통해 Weber는 현대에서 지속적인 의미 추구를 이해하려고 노력할 것이다. 본질적으로, 종교와 의미가 가득한 질서 내의 사회에 기반을 둔 일관성 있는 생활 방식 대신에, 사회 전체의 다른 분야, 즉 가치 영역은, 제한적이고 조건적이긴 하지만, 새로운 의미를 제공해 준다.
① 효과적이지 못하고 쓸모없는
② 제한적이고 조건적인
③ 텅 비어 있고 무의미한
④ 한정되고 구식의

어휘

paradoxical 모순적인, 역설적인
significant 커다란, 주요한
rather 오히려
enchanted 매혹된, 황홀한
aesthetic 미의, 심미의
conduct 경영, 운영, 처리
parameter 한계, 제한(범위)
whole 전체, 완전체
old fashioned 구식의
outcome 결과
render (어떤 상태가 되게) 만들다
unify 통합시키다
cosmic 장대한, 우주의
coherent 일관적인
set (특수) 사회, 집단
cosmos 질서, 우주
if …더라도[…이긴 하지만]

오답률 TOP 3
10 정답 ②

정답해설

본문은 어느 교구의 급식 정책의 변화에 대해 설명하는 글이다. 세 번째 문장 "Previously in the majority of schools we have been providing more food than the average elementary child could eat, and much of the food was wasted(과거에 대부분의 학교에서 우리는 보통의 초등학생이 먹을 수 있는 것보다 더 많은 음식을 제공해왔고, 많은 음식이 낭비되었다)."에서 '기존의 급식 체제에서는 필요보다 많은 음식을 제공하여 낭비되는 음식이 많았다'라고 설명하고 있다. 그리고 두 번째 문장 "In lieu of a price increase for elementary students, we have removed one item from the menu and are using the dessert to meet the type A requirements(초등학생들을 대상으로 한 가격 인상 대신에 우리는 메뉴에서 한 가지 품목을 제외시켰고 A유형의 요건에 맞추기 위해 디저트를 이용하고 있다)."에서 '기존의 메뉴에서 한 가지 품목이 제외되었으며', 기존보다 적은 양의 음식이 제공될 것임을 유추할 수 있다. 따라서 변화된 정책에 따라 낭비되는 음식이 줄어들 것을 기대할 수 있으므로, 글의 내용과 일치하는 보기는 '② The amount of wasted food in elementary schools is expected to decrease(초등학교에서 낭비되는 음식의 양이 줄어들 것이라 기대된다).'이다.

오답해설

① 두 번째 문장 "In lieu of a price increase for elementary students, we have removed one item from the menu and are using the dessert to meet the type A requirements(초등학생들을 대상으로 한 가격 인상 대신에 우리는 메뉴에서 한 가지 품목을 제외시켰고 A유형의 요건에 맞추기 위해 디저트를 이용하고 있다)."를 통해, 가격은 인상되지 않았으며 메뉴에서 하나의 품목이 제외되었음을 알 수 있다. 따라서 글의 내용과 일치하지 않는다.
③ "Our charge to the elementary student for the type A lunch, which includes milk, is 35 cents(우유를 포함하는 A유형의 초등학생 점심의 가격은 35센트이다)."를 통해 초등학생의 급식에는 우유가 포함된 것을 알 수 있으나, 본문 어디에도 중학생의 급식에 우유가 포함되었다는 내용이 언급되지 않으므로, '모든 학교에서의 급식에 우유가 포함된다'라는 것은 글의 내용과 일치하지 않는다.
④ "In the junior high schools, we have eliminated the choice of vegetables and restricted a la carte service to ice cream and fresh fruit(중학교에서 우리는 채소의 선택을 제외시켰고, 특별 주문 서비스를 아이스크림과 신선한 과일로 제한시켰다)."에서, '특별 주문 서비스를 아이스크림과 신선한 과일로 제한했다'라고 언급하고 있으므로, 아이스크림과 신선한 과일을 제외한 다른 메뉴를 주문할 수 없다는 것을 알 수 있다. 따라서 글의 내용과 일치하지 않는다.

해석

1959년 이래 최초로 우리는 메뉴와 가격을 크게 변화시켰다. 초등학생들을 대상으로 한 가격 인상 대신에 우리는 메뉴에서 한 가지 품목을 제외시켰고 A유형의 요건에 맞추기 위해 디저트를 이용하고 있다. 과거에, 대부분의 학교에서 우리는 보통의 초등학생이 먹을 수 있는 것보다 더 많은 음식을 제공해왔고, 많은 음식이 낭비되었다. 우유를 포함하는 A유형의 초등학생 점심의 가격은 35센트이다. 중학교에서 우리는 채소의 선택을 제외시켰고, 특별 주문 서비스를 아이스크림과 신선한 과일로 제한시켰다. 수많은 학생들이 짧은 시간에 중학교 급식실을 이용해야 하며, 메뉴를 간소화하고 특별 주문 품목을 제한함으로써 우리는 더 빠른 서비스를 제공할 수 있을 것이다. 중학교의 완전한 점심 식사의 가격은 40센트이다.
① 초등학생을 위한 학교 급식의 가격은 증가해왔다.
② 초등학교에서 낭비되는 음식의 양이 줄어들 것이라 기대된다.

③ 우유는 모든 학교의 점심 급식에 포함되어 있다.
④ 중학생들은 아이스크림 또는 신선한 과일을 더 이상 선택할 수 없다.

어휘

significant 커다란, 주요한
meet (필요, 요구 등을) 충족시키다
restrict 제한하다
in lieu of … 대신에
eliminate 제거하다, 없애다
a la carte 특별 주문의, 따로따로 시키는

결국엔 성정혜 영어 하프모의고사
기적사 DAY 55

| 01 | ② | 02 | ③ | 03 | ① | 04 | ① | 05 | ④ |
| 06 | ③ | 07 | ③ | 08 | ④ | 09 | ③ | 10 | ② |

01 정답 ②

정답해설

밑줄 친 단어는 '악명이 높은'의 의미로 사용되었고, 유의어로는 ② disreputable이 적절하다.

해석

"인간은 큰 수로 모여 있는 동물의 수를 추정하는 것에 형편없고 서두르기로 **악명이 높다**," Perryman은 설명한다.
① 조화시킬 수 있는
② 평판이 안 좋은
③ 기이한, 이국풍의
④ 가난한, 가지지 않은

어휘

notorious 악명이 높은
reconcilable 조화시킬 수 있는
outlandish 기이한, 이국풍의
lousy 형편없는, 볼품없는
disreputable 평판이 안 좋은
destitute 가난한, 가지지 않은

오답률 TOP 2

02 정답 ③

정답해설

주어진 빈칸은 문맥상 '중요한'의 의미의 단어가 필요하다. 따라서 정답은 ③ instrumental이다.

해석

"시리아 대량학살에서 **중요한** 역할을 해왔던 외부의 세력들은 페르시안 악센트로 말한다," Prosor는 조심스럽게 결론지었다.
① 의지할 수 없는
② 결점이 없는, 죄를 범하지 않는
③ 주된 역할을 하는, 악기로 연주되는
④ 결백한

어휘

unreliable 의지할 수 없는
impeccable 결점이 없는, 죄를 범하지 않는
instrumental 주된 역할을 하는, 악기로 연주되는
innocent 결백한

03 정답 ①

정답해설

밑줄 친 단어는 문맥상 '공정한'으로 사용되었다. 따라서 의미가 가장 먼 것은 ① provocative이다.

해석

공정한 부의 분배에 대한 추구는 반드시 더 현실적이고 공정한 대학에 대한 기회의 분배로 대체되어야만 한다.

① 도발적인
② 합리적인
③ 공정한
④ 편견에 치우치지 않은

어휘

equitable 공정한, 정당한
reasonable 합리적인
unbiased 편견에 치우치지 않은
provocative 도발적인
impartial 공정한

04 정답 ①

정답해설

A는 B에게 인생의 최종 목표가 무엇인지 묻는다. B는 어려운 질문이라며 생각할 시간을 달라고 말한 후, A의 최종 목표는 무엇인지 되묻는다. A는 급여가 유망한 직업을 가지고 싶다고 답변한다. B는 돈이 A에게 최우선 사항인지 묻자, A는 맞다고 한다. 자본주의 사회에서는 (A) '돈으로 다 되기(money talks)' 때문에 인생을 즐기기 위해서는 충분한 보수를 받아야 한다고 덧붙인다. B는 A에게 매우 현실적인 관점이지만 자신도 동의한다고 말하며, (B) '완전히 파산(dead broke)'하면 삶이 비탄스러울 수 있다고 한다.

오답해설

② (B) A가 자신의 최우선 사항이 돈이라는 말에 B가 동의하며 '무료(on the house)'이면 삶이 비탄스러울 수 있다는 것은 문맥상 부자연스럽다.
③ (A) A에게 돈이 최우선 사항이냐고 묻는 B의 말에 A는 맞다고 말하며, 자본주의 사회에서 '말도 안 되는 일(pigs may fly)'이기 때문에 인생을 즐기려면 충분한 급여를 받아야 한다는 것은 맥락상 알맞지 않다.
④ (A) A에게 돈이 최우선 사항이냐고 묻는 B의 말에 A는 맞다고 말하며, 자본주의 사회에서 '말도 안 되는 일(pigs may fly)'이기 때문에 인생을 즐기려면 충분한 급여를 받아야 한다는 것은 흐름상 어색하다. (B) 돈을 최우선 사항으로 여기는 A의 관점을 현실적이라고 말하며, 'TV를 보며 소파에 앉아 감자를 먹는 게으른 유형의 사람(a couch potato)'이면 삶이 비탄스러울 수 있다고 말하는 것은 빈칸에 들어갈 말로 옳지 않다.

해석

A: 네 인생의 최종 목표는 뭐야?
B: 그건 매우 어려운 질문이다. 나에게 생각할 시간 좀 줘. 네 것은 뭐야?
A: 나는 급여가 유망한 직업을 갖고 싶어.
B: 그럼 돈이 네 최우선 사항이야?
A: 응, 자본주의 사회에서 (A) 돈으로 다 되기 때문에 인생을 즐기기 위해서는 충분한 보수를 받아야 해.
B: 그건 매우 현실적인 관점이다. 하지만 난 너의 말에 동의해. 만약 (B) 완전히 파산하면 삶은 비탄스러울 수 있어.

	(A)	(B)
①	돈으로 다 된다	완전히 파산하여
②	돈으로 다 된다	무료로
③	말도 안 되는 일	완전히 파산하여
④	말도 안 되는 일	TV를 보며 소파에 앉아 감자를 먹는 게으른 유형의 사람

어휘

ultimate 최종적인
salary 월급, 급여
capitalist society 자본주의 사회
perspective 관점
money talks 돈으로 다 된다
dead broke 완전히 파산하여
a couch potato TV를 보며 소파에 앉아 감자를 먹는 게으른 유형의 사람
promising 유망한
first priority 최우선
realistic 현실적인
devastating 파괴적인, 비탄스러운
pigs may fly 말도 안 되는 일
on the house 무료로

05 정답 ④

정답해설

④ **출제 포인트: 최상급 대용표현**

「비교급+than+any other 단수 가산명사」는 최상급 대용표현으로 해당 문장의 경우 'any other' 뒤에 단수 가산명사 'state'를 사용하였으나 비교급 자리에 원급 'much'를 사용하였으므로 틀린 문장이다. 따라서 'much'를 비교급 'more'로 수정해야 한다. 또한 'which'는 목적격 관계대명사로 전치사 'of'의 목적어이며 선행사는 'steel'이다. 즉, 다음과 같다.

Even steel has been expensive. + Indiana makes more of steel than any other state.
→ Even steel, steel Indiana makes more of than any other state, has been expensive.
→ Even steel, which Indiana makes more of than any other state, has been expensive.

오답해설

① **출제 포인트: 불완전타동사+목적어+[to부정사 vs. 동명사]**

'hate'는 불완전타동사로 전치사 없이 목적어를 가지며 이때 to부정사와 동명사 모두 목적격 보어로 사용할 수 있다. 또한 'hate'가 완전타동사로 쓰는 경우 to부정사와 동명사를 목적어로 가질 수 있음에 주의해야 한다.

② **출제 포인트: 주어[a number of 목적어 vs. the number of 목적어]와 동사의 수일치**

'a number of'는 뒤에 복수 가산명사가 목적어로 오며 주어인 경우 동사에 복수형태를 사용한다. 해당 문장은 'A number of 목적어'가 주어인 경우에 해당하며 이때 목적어에 복수 가산명사 'researchers'를 사용하였고 동사에 복수형태인 'volunteer'를 사용하였으므로 옳은 문장이다. 또한 해당 문장에서 'great'은 명사 'number'를 수식하는 형용사이다.

③ **출제 포인트: 현재분사 vs. 과거분사**

'using'은 'use'의 현재분사이며 수식하는 대상은 주어 'Users'이다. 따라서 해당 문장은 'Users'와 'using'이 능동 관계이며 주어진 해석 '사용하여'와 일치하므로 옳은 문장이다. 또한 'writing'은 수식하는 대상 'device'와 능동 관계이며 주어진 해석 '쓰는'과 일치하므로 옳게 사용되었다.

06 정답 ③

정답해설

③ **출제 포인트: 복합관계부사**

해당 문장에서 'However'는 복합관계부사로 '아무리 ~해도'를 뜻하며 「however+형용사/부사+주어+동사」의 형태로 사용된다. 또한 'however' 뒤에 오는 품사는 뒤에 오는 문장구조에 의해 결정되며, 해당 문장의 경우 'you are hungry'에서 보어에 해당되는 형용사 'hungry'가 'However' 뒤로 이동한 경우로 'hungry'가 옳게 사용되었다.

오답해설

① **출제 포인트: 현재분사 vs. 과거분사**

해당 문장에서 'Stood'는 분사구문을 이끄는 과거분사로 사용되었으나 'stand'는 완전자동사이므로 완료시제를 제외하고는 과거분사를 사용할 수 없다. 또한 생략된 주어 'John'과 능동 관계이므로 과거분사 'Stood'를 현재분사 'Standing'으로 수정해야 한다.

② **출제 포인트: It ~ that 강조용법**

해당 문장은 「It ~ that」 강조 구문과 관계부사절 두 가지 경우로 볼 수 있다.

1. 「It ~ that」 강조 구문
   The Second World War started in 1939. (in 1939를 강조)
   It was in 1939 that the Second World War started. (이때 that

은 when으로 바꾸어 사용할 수 있다.)
2. 관계부사절
It was in 1939. + The Second World War started in 1939. (1939를 선행사)
It was in 1939 when the Second World War started. (이때 when은 that으로 바꾸어 사용할 수 있다.)
따라서 옳은 문장으로 고치기 위해서는 'which'를 'that' 또는 'when'으로 수정해야 한다. 또한 해당 문장에서의 'started'는 완전자동사로 목적어 없이 옳게 사용되었다.

④ 출제 포인트: 주어와 동사의 수일치
해당 문장에서는 주어가 단수형태인 'all knowledge'이므로 동사에 단수 형태를 사용해야 한다. 따라서 'were'를 'was'로 수정해야 한다.

해석
① 빠르게 일어서면서, John은 그의 옷장에 가서 그의 짐 가방을 꺼냈다.
② 제 2차 세계대전이 시작된 것은 바로 1939년이다.
③ 네가 아무리 배가 고파도 결코 피자 한 판을 다 먹을 수 있을 것 같지 않다.
④ 그 시대의 판화를 제외하고 이전의 구조들에 대한 모든 지식은 사라졌다.

오답률 TOP 3
07 정답 ③

정답해설
③ 출제 포인트: 동사 vs. 준동사
'resulted'는 과거시제 동사로 적절하게 사용되었으며 주어는 'stealing thunder'이다. 이때 'resulted'의 자릿값을 분사로 오해하고 현재분사 'resulting'으로 수정하지 않도록 유의해야 한다. 또한 'result'는 일반적으로 수동형과 진행형으로 사용할 수 없음에 주의해야 한다.

오답해설
① 출제 포인트: 현재분사 vs. 과거분사/동사 vs. 준동사
해당 문장에서 주어는 'That'이고 동사는 'leaves'이므로 목적어인 'others'를 꾸며주는 목적격 보어로서 'had'는 옳지 않다. 현재분사인 'having'으로 써서 'leave + 목적어 + 현재분사(~을 …한 상태로 두다)'로 사용해야 옳다. 단, 'That leaves'를 주어로 보는 경우 'leaves'가 명사로 쓰이면 수식하는 지시 형용사는 'That'이 아닌 'Those'로 수일치한 형용사가 수식해야만 한다. 따라서 'That leaves'는 주어라고 할 수 없다.

② 출제 포인트: to+[동사원형 vs. 동명사]
'as opposed to'는 '~와는 정반대로'를 뜻하며 전치사 'to' 뒤에 명사 또는 동명사 목적어가 온다. 해당 문장은 'as opposed to' 뒤에 동사원형 'allow'를 사용하였으므로 틀린 문장이다. 따라서 'allow'를 동명사 'allowing'으로 수정해야 한다. 해당 표현에서 'to'는 전치사이므로 to부정사의 'to'로 생각하지 않도록 유의해야한다.

④ 출제 포인트: 동사 vs. 준동사
'predicting'이 쓰인 위치를 준동사의 자릿값으로 인식한다면 'credibility ratings'를 주어로 하는 that절의 동사가 없게 된다. 따라서 'predicting'이 쓰인 위치는 동사의 자릿값으로 보아야 하며 'predicting'은 시제를 적용하여 과거시제 동사 'predicted'로 수정해야 한다.

해석
이러한 장점들 중에서 주된 것은 최초의 메시지와 이야기가 처음 표현되는 방식을 조절하는 능력이다. 그것은 다른 사람들이 정반대로 하는 대신에 여러분에게 반응을 해야만 하게 만든다. 이런 접근법은 '선수를 치는 것'으로 적절하게 일컬어진다. 어떤 조직체가 선수를 칠 때, 그것은 자신의 위기가 매체나 다른 이해 관계자들에 의해 발견되기 전에 그것에 대한 소식을 알린다. Arpan과 Roskos-Ewoldsen에 의한 실험적인 연구에서 위기 상황에서 선수를 치는 것은, 정보가 다른 당사자에 의해 먼저 폭로되도록 허용하는 것과는 정반대로, 대체로 더 높은 신뢰성 평가라는 결과를 초래했다. 마찬가지로 중요하게 그 저자들은 '선수를 치는 것과 관련된 신뢰성 평가는 곧장 위기에 대한 인식을 덜 심각한 것으로 예측했다'라는 것을 발견했다.

어휘
frame 표현하다, 틀에 넣다
leave+목적어+목적격 보어 ~을 ~한 상태가 되게 하다
appropriately 적절하게
as opposed to ~와는 정반대로, ~와는 대조적으로
disclose 밝히다, 폭로하다, 드러내다
associate A with B A를 B와 연관 짓다

08 정답 ④

정답해설
해당 지문은 '선지자들은 비즈니스 분야에서 종종 찾아볼 수 있다'라고 주장하며, 그러한 선지자의 대표적인 예로 영국 사업가 James Dyson을 제시하고 있다. 주어진 문장의 'them'이 가리키는 대상을 ④ 이전 문장 "We call them prophets, visionaries, or oracles(우리는 그들은 예언자, 선지자 또는 현인이라 부른다)."에서 찾을 수 있으며, 또한 주어진 문장에서 'in the realm of business(비즈니스계에서)'에서 '선지자(them)'를 찾을 수 있다고 언급하고 있는데, 이에 해당하는 인물의 예(James Dyson)를 ④ 이후 문장에서 최초로 언급하고 있다. 따라서 주어진 문장이 들어가기에 가장 적절한 곳은 ④이다.

오답해설
③ 주어진 문장의 'them'이 ③이전의 'some'을 가리킨다고 생각할 수도 있으나, 주어진 문장에서 business에 대한 언급이 등장하므로, 주어진 문장 이후에는 비즈니스계와 관련된 내용이 연달아 등장하는 것이 자연스러우며, 중간에 '예언하는 사람들'에 대한 명칭을 설명하는 문장이 들어가는 것은 어색하다. 따라서 오답이다.
나머지 위치는 문맥상 어색하므로 오답이다.

해석
우리들 중 실용주의자들은 미래를 들여다보는 것을 불가능하다고 말할 것이다. (①) 그들은 능글맞게 웃으며 수정 구슬과 우리의 운명을 예언하는 인간의 손바닥의 지워지지 않는 선은 없다고 말할 것이다. (②) 우리들 중 나머지는 실제로 내일 무엇이 일어날지를 예언할 수 있는 사람들이 있다고 믿는다. (③) 우리는 그들은 예언자, 선지자 또는 현인이라 부른다. (④ **그리고 우리는 종종 인간이 실제로 그들이 상상하는 미래를 창조해 낼 수 있는 얼마 되지 않는 분야 중 하나인 비즈니스계에서 그들을 발견한다.**) 이러한 예언자들 중 가장 놀라운 사람 중 하나는 영국인 사업가 James Dyson이다. Dyson이 그것들을 생각해내기 이전에는 모두 *Jetsons*과 같은 시대의 허구였던 Dyson의 기발한 먼지봉투 없는 청소기, 불가능한 것 같은 날 없는 선풍기, 그리고 초고속 헤어드라이어는 대부분의 국가에서 그의 이름을 문자 그대로 가정용 브랜드로 만들었고, 72세 영국인을 억만장자로 변화시켰다.

어휘
realm 영역, 분야
mortal being 인간, 죽는 존재
pragmatist 실용주의자
smirk 능글맞은 웃음
destiny 운명
visionary 선지자
remarkable 놀라운, 주목할 만한
improbable 일어나지 않을 듯한, 기발한
figment 허구, 꾸며낸 것
rare 드문
envision 상상하다, 마음에 그리다
peer into 자세히 들여다보다
indelible 지워지지 않는
prophet 예언자
oracle 현인

Jetsons 젯슨 가족(우주의 자동화된 주택에 사는 젯슨 가족을 중심으로 벌어지는 일상 이야기를 담은 애니메이션)
dream up 생각해 내다

restrict 제한하다
outcry 강력한 항의
innutritious 영양 불량의, 영양분이 없는
declare 선언하다, 공표하다
indicate 나타내다, 보여주다, 가리키다

오답률 TOP 1

09 정답 ③

정답해설

해당 지문은 "National School Lunch Program(학교 급식 프로그램)"에 대한 내용으로, 첫 문장 "The mandate to feed poor children dramatically transformed the National School Lunch Program(빈곤층 아이들에게 급식을 제공하라는 명령은 National School Lunch Program을 대폭 변화시켰다). The number of children eating at school increased sharply(학교에서 급식을 먹는 학생들의 숫자는 급격히 증가하였다)."에서 언급했듯이, 학교에서 급식을 먹는 학생들이 급격히 증가했다는 것은, 학교 급식 프로그램의 인기가 높았다는 반증이며, 본문 중반에서 언급했듯이 비록 학교 급식의 질은 좋지 않았으나, 많은 학생들이 급식 프로그램에 참여했다는 것을 알 수 있다. 이후, 본문 후반의 내용을 통해 이미 질이 좋지 않은 학교 급식에 들어가는 비용을 더 낮추려는 행정부의 시도로 인해, 대중의 즉각적이고 강력한 항의가 발생했다'라는 것을 알 수 있으며, 항의가 거셌다는 것은 학교 급식 프로그램에 대한 대중의 관심과 인기가 높았다는 것을 시사하므로, 빈칸에 가장 적절한 표현은 '③ how popular the school lunch program was(학교 급식 프로그램이 얼마나 인기가 있었는지)'이다.

오답해설

① 본문에서 음식의 질이 낮았다고 설명하고 있으므로 본문의 내용과 일치하지 않는 표현이다.
② 본문에서 '사전 포장된 냉동식품'이 급식에 사용되었다고 언급하고 있으나, 급식의 질에 대해 설명하기 위한 사실일 뿐이며, 기존 음식의 영양 부족으로 인해 대중의 항의가 발생한 것이 아니므로 오답이다.
④ 무상 급식 비용 충당의 어려움이 언급되기는 하지만, 글의 흐름상 빈칸에는 적절하지 않다.

해석

빈곤층 아이들에게 급식을 제공하라는 명령은 National School Lunch Program을 대폭 변화시켰다. 학교에서 급식을 먹는 학생들의 숫자는 급격히 증가하였다. 그러나 연방 보조금은 오직 음식에 대해서만 지급되었고, 장비, 노동, 보관 또는 배송에 대해서는 지급되지 않았다. 따라서 지역 교구는 무상 급식의 비용을 충당할 수 있는 충분한 자금을 확보하기 위해 애써야 했다. 그들은 급식을 배달하기 위해 대형 급식 업체들에 의지했다. 대부분의 학교들이 완전한 주방을 가지고 있지 않았기 때문에, 이것은 점심이 사전 포장되고 냉동된 식품으로 구성되어 있다는 것을 의미했다. 1980년대, Reagan 행정부는 공공 프로그램을 위한 연방 기금을 삭감하기 위한 노력으로 케첩을 채소라고 선언함으로써 학교 급식의 비용을 제한하려는 시도를 했다. 대중의 항의는 즉각적이고 강력했는데, 이는 <u>학교 급식 프로그램이 얼마나 인기가 있었는지</u>를 나타낸다.
① 음식의 질이 얼마나 높았는지
② 학교 급식이 얼마나 영양 불량이었는지
③ 학교 급식 프로그램이 얼마나 인기가 있었는지
④ 학교들이 학생들에게 무료 급식을 제공하는 것이 얼마나 힘들었는지

어휘

mandate 명령, 칙령, 지령
subsidy 보조금
scramble to R (앞을 다투어) ~하려고 애쓰다
cover (무엇을 하기에 충분한 돈을[이]) 대다[되다]
turn to 의지하다, 의존하다
federal 연방의
district 구역, 지구
consist of …로 구성되다

10 정답 ②

정답해설

본문에서 세 번째 문장 "Back in 1782, when cotton mills were powered by water, Richard Arkwright opened the innovative – and the world's first – steam-driven textile mill in Manchester(면직 공장이 물로부터 동력을 얻던 시절인 1782년 Richard Arkwright가 혁신적이고 세계 최초의 증기로 동력을 얻는 직물 공장을 Manchester에 열었다)."를 통해 '물로 동력을 얻는 면직 공장은 1782년 이전에도 있었고, Arkwright가 Manchester에 최초로 세운 공장은 증기 동력 직물 공장인 것을 알 수 있으므로, 글의 내용과 일치하지 않는 것은 "② Arkwright established Manchester's first cotton mill driven by water(Arkwright는 Manchester 최초의 물로 움직이는 면직 공장을 설립했다)."이다.

오답해설

① 첫 문장에서 "In the 19th century, Manchester held the status of the international center of the cotton trade and textile industry(19세기 Manchester는 면 무역 및 직물 산업의 국제 중심이라는 지위를 지녔다)."라고 언급하고 있으므로 내용과 일치한다.
③ 본문 중반의 "In 1871, 32 percent of global cotton production took place in Manchester(1871년 전 세계 면 생산의 32%가 Manchester에서 이루어졌다)."를 통해 내용과 일치하는 것을 알 수 있다.
④ "no working mills remain but Manchester(여전히 작동하는 공장은 없지만)"라고 언급하고 있으므로, 현재 운영되고 있는 면직 공장은 없다는 것을 알 수 있다. 이후에 "There are still around 5,000 people in Greater Manchester employed in the textile industry(Great Manchester에는 여전히 면직 산업에 종사하는 약 5,000명의 사람들이 있다)."라고 서술하기는 하지만, '직물 산업에 종사한다'라는 것을 '직물 공장에서 일한다'라는 것과 혼동하지 않도록 주의한다.

해석

19세기 Manchester는 면 무역과 직물 산업의 국제 중심이라는 지위를 지녔다. 그곳은 면의 도시라는 것이 매우 잘 알려져 있어서 'Cottonopolis'라는 별칭이 붙었다. 면직 공장이 물로부터 동력을 얻던 시절인 1782년 Richard Arkwright가 혁신적이고 세계 최초의 증기로 동력을 얻는 직물 공장을 Manchester에 열었다. 직물 제조업이 가정으로부터 대규모의 공장으로 옮겨감에 따라 Manchester와 주변 도시들은 세계에서 단연 가장 크고 가장 생산적인 면방적의 중심지가 되었다. 1871년 전 세계 면 생산의 32%가 Manchester에서 이루어졌다. Arkwright가 상징적인 공장을 세운지 200년 이상이 지난 후, 여전히 작동하는 공장은 없지만 Manchester는 여전히 면에 의해 형성된 도시이다. Great Manchester에는 여전히 면직 산업에 종사하는 약 5,000명의 사람들이 있다. Manchester의 방적의 도시로서의 과거는 건물에서 찾아볼 수 있다: 개조된 공장이 사무실, 호텔, 그리고 아파트로서 새 유리 같이 반짝거리는 고층 건물들과 나란히 하며 새 삶을 찾았다.
① Manchester는 1800년대에 면으로 알려져 있었다.
② Arkwright는 Manchester 최초의 물로 움직이는 면직 공장을 설립했다.
③ Manchester는 한때 세계 면 생산량의 30% 이상을 생산했다.
④ 오늘날 Manchester에 사는 사람들은 면직 공장에서 일하지 않는다.

어휘

textile 직물, 섬유
nickname ~에게 별명을 붙이다
innovative 혁신적인
industry 산업
cottonopolis 방적의 도시
steam-driven 증기로 움직이는

manufacturing 제조
surrounding 주변의
cotton spinning 면방적
iconic 상징이 되는
flat (연립주택, 다세대 주택 등을 포함하는) 아파트식 주거지
sparkling 반짝이는, 생기 넘치는
high-rise 고층 건물

large-scale 대규모의
productive 생산적인
take place 발생하다
convert 변하게 하다, 개조하다
glassy 유리 같은

Day 55

결국엔 성정혜 영어 하프모의고사
기적사 DAY 56

| 01 | ① | 02 | ① | 03 | ④ | 04 | ② | 05 | ③ |
| 06 | ④ | 07 | ② | 08 | ④ | 09 | ① | 10 | ② |

01 정답 ①
14 국가직

정답해설

'pore over(살펴보다, 세세히 보다)'와 유사한 의미를 갖는 것은 ① examine 이다.

해석

나는 Jim이 컴퓨터 인쇄물을 **살펴보게** 하도록 지시받았다.
① 살펴보다, 조사하다, 검토하다
② 나눠주다, 배포하다
③ 버리다
④ 수정하다

어휘

pore over 살펴보다, 세세히 보다
distribute 나눠주다, 배포하다
correct 수정하다
examine 살펴보다, 조사하다, 검토하다
discard 버리다

02 정답 ①
14 국가직

정답해설

'unerring(정확한)'은 ① faultless와 유사한 의미를 가지고 있다.

해석

Johannes Kepler는 우주의 "광대함을 두려워하지 않는" 탐험가들로 가득 찬 하늘을 항해하는 "하늘 바람에 적합한 돛 달린 하늘의 배"가 언젠가 나올 것이라고 믿었다. 그리고 오늘날, 그러한 탐험가들인 인간과 로봇은 그들의 광대한 우주 항해의 **정확한** 가이드로, Kepler가 일생의 개인적 노고와 열광적인 발견으로 알아낸, 행성 운동의 세 가지 법칙을 사용한다.
① 정확한, 결점 없는
② 의지할 수 없는
③ 무기력한
④ 비과학적인

어휘

celestial 하늘의, 천체의
employ 이용하다, 고용하다
voyage 항해, 여행, 탐험
travail 노고, 진통; 산고를 겪다
unreliable 의지할 수 없는
unscientific 비과학적인
vastness 광대함
unerring 정확한
planetary 행성의, 지구의
faultless 정확한, 결점 없는
gutless 무기력한

03 정답 ④
13 국가직

정답해설

Visaokay라는 것이 여행 산업, 기업, 그리고 개인을 도우려면 비자 정보와 발급 과정을 '쉽게 할' 것이다. 여행 비자의 신청 및 발급에 관련된 복잡함과 시간 지연을 최소화한다는 뒤의 설명 자체가 'facilitate(쉽게 하다)'를 말하는 것이므로 정답은 ④ facilitating이다.

해석

Visaokay는 모든 비자 정보와 비자 발급 과정을 **쉽게 함**으로써, 호주 여행 산업, 기업들과 정부, 그리고 개인들을 돕는다. Visaokay는 여행 비자를 신청하고 발급받는 것과 관련된 복잡함과 시간 지연을 최소화한다.
① (가치를) 정당하게 평가하기
② 악화시키기
③ 숙고하기
④ 쉽게 하기, 용이하게 하기

어휘

issuance 발급, 발행, 배포 minimize 최소화하다, 과소평가하다
appreciating (가치를) 정당하게 평가하기
aggravating 악화시키기 meditating 숙고하기
facilitating 쉽게 하기, 용이하게 하기

04 정답 ②
15 국가직

정답해설

남자가 소리가 났다고 하자, 여자는 처음에 소리를 듣지 못했다고 말한다. 또 다시 남자가 소리가 들린다고 말한 뒤 여자가 잠깐 멈춰서 살폈고 다시 남자가 오른쪽 앞바퀴에 유리 조각이 박힌 것을 발견했으므로 밑줄에는 '② Maybe air is escaping from the tire(아마 타이어에서 바람이 새고 있는 것 같아)'라고 하는 것이 문맥상 가장 적절하다.

해석

남: 무슨 소리야?
여: 소리? 난 아무것도 안 들리는데.
남: 잘 들어봐. 난 소리가 들리는데. <u>아마 타이어에서 바람이 새고 있는 것 같아.</u>
여: 오, 세우고 보자.
남: 봐! 오른쪽 앞바퀴에 유리 조각이 있네.
여: 정말? 음... 맞네. 이제 어떻게 하지?
남: 걱정하지 마. 내가 타이어를 바꿔 본 경험이 있어.
① 나는 고객에게 적절한 조언을 해줬어
② 아마 타이어에서 바람이 새고 있는 것 같아
③ 내 생각에 수리공이 다른 약속이 있는 것 같아
④ 이런! 네 핸드폰이 진동 모드로 울리고 있어

어휘

sound 적절한, 건강한 mechanic 수리공, 정비사
appointment 약속, 임명, 예약

오답률 TOP 3

05 정답 ③
13 국가직

정답해설

③ **출제 포인트: 불완전자동사의 주격 보어/부사절의 접속사 that**
불완전자동사인 'look' 다음에 주격 보어로 형용사 'serious'가 수반되었다. 또한 「so ~ that …」 (너무~해서 …하다)의 표현도 알맞다.

오답해설

① **출제 포인트: 원급 비교**
한글 해석으로는 이상이 없어 마치 옳은 문장 같지만, 'than' 대신 'as'로 써야 한다. 「as+원급+as」의 구조가 되도록 'as intimately than'을 'as intimately as'로 변경해야 옳다.

② **출제 포인트: 혼동하기 쉬운 동사**
동사 자리에는 명사 'company(회사, 친구)'가 아닌 동사 'accompany(동행하다)'가 와야 한다. 즉, 'company'는 'accompany'로 바뀌어야 한다. 참고로, 'company'가 동사의 쓰임이 아예 없는 것은 아니지만, 2013년도 국가직 9급에서는 'company'를 명사의 뜻만 있는 것으로 간주했다.

④ **출제 포인트: number of vs. amount of**
'sugar(설탕)'는 셀 수 없는 명사이기 때문에 수가 아니라 양으로 표시해야 한다. 즉, 'the number'를 'the amount'로 변경해야 한다.

해석

① 꿀벌과 꽃만큼 친밀하게 연결되어 있는 생물체는 거의 없다.
② 나의 아버지는 그들이 머무는 곳까지 우리와 동행하려 하지 않으셨지만 내가 가기를 요구했다.
③ 이라크의 상황은 너무나 심각해 보여서, 언제라도 제3차 세계대전이 일어날 것 같았다.
④ 최근 한 보고에 따르면, 미국인들이 소비하는 설탕의 양은 매년 크게 바뀌지 않는다고 한다.

06 정답 ④
13 국가직

정답해설

④ **출제 포인트: 접속사의 역할**
부사절 접속사 'whereas' 다음에는 「주어 + 동사」의 완전한 문장이 수반되어야 한다. 밑줄 친 부분에서는 가주어 'it'이 빠져 있으므로 'whereas is'를 'whereas it is'로 변경해야 옳다. 진주어는 'to monitor cumulative exposure to noise.'이다.

오답해설

① **출제 포인트: 형용사 관용표현**
'be different from(~와 다르다)'의 구조가 올바르게 사용되었다.

② **출제 포인트: a number of vs. an amount of**
'a number of ~'는 '많은~'의 뜻으로 목적어로 복수명사를 취한다. 밑줄 친 부분에서는 'a number of'에 이어 복수 형태의 명사 'ways'가 왔으므로 올바르게 사용되었다.

③ **출제 포인트: 현재분사 vs. 과거분사**
동사 'introduce(도입하다, 유입하다)'가 명사 'chemicals'를 수식하려면 분사의 형태를 취해야 한다. 문맥상 'chemicals'와 'introduce'의 관계가 서로 수동이므로, 과거분사 'introduced'가 알맞게 쓰였다.

해석

소음 공해는 많은 면에서 다른 형태의 공해와 다르다. 소음은 일시적이다. 즉, 일단 멈추면, 환경은 그것에 자유로워진다. 예를 들면, 대기 오염의 경우는 그렇지 않다. 우리는 공기로 유입된 화학물질의 양을 측정할 수 있지만, 소음에 누적되는 노출을 측정하는 것은 매우 어렵다.

어휘

transient 일시적인, 순간적인 be free of ~에서 자유롭다
whereas ~이지만, ~임에 반하여 monitor 측정하다, 감시하다, 관찰하다
cumulative 누적되는

오답률 TOP 2
07 정답 ②
13 국가직

정답해설

② 출제 포인트: not A until B/It ~ that 강조용법
「It is ~ that」 강조 구문의 형태로, 'not until ~ math test'를 강조한 구문이다. 원래 문장은 'He did not decide to study hard until when he failed the math test.'이다.

오답해설

① 출제 포인트: 관계대명사 vs. 관계부사 / 시제일치 / 능동태 vs. 수동태
관계대명사 'which' 이하에는 불완전한 문장이 수반되어야 하는데 완전한 문장이 왔으므로 틀리다. 따라서 뒤따라오는 문장이 완전하고 선행사가 장소(The house)이므로 관계대명사 'which'를 관계부사 'where'로 고쳐야 올바르다. 또한 현재까지 그 집에 살고 있는 것이 아니므로 시제 'have lived'를 'had lived'의 과거분사로 고쳐야 한다. 그리고 의미상 '집이 손상된' 것이므로 'damaged'를 수동태의 'was damaged'로 고쳐야 올바르다. 이 문장에서는 관계대명사, 시제, 동사의 태 모두 틀렸다.

③ 출제 포인트: 접속사의 역할/-thing류 대명사 수식
문장이 두 개인데, 이를 연결하는 접속사가 없으므로 틀린 문장이다. 한글 해석에 따라 콤마 뒤에 접속사 'so(그래서)'를 추가해야 한다. 또한 '-ing'으로 끝나는 명사를 to부정사가 수식하는 경우, 위치는 반드시 뒤에 위치하여 후치수식임에 주의해야 한다.

④ 출제 포인트: enough의 위치 / 관계대명사의 계속적 용법
'enough'는 형용사 뒤에서 수식하기 때문에, 'fortunate enough to'의 어순이 와야 한다. 또한 'that'은 계속적 용법으로 쓰이지 않으므로 'that'을 선행사 'the Grand Canyon'에 맞는 계속적 용법의 관계대명사 'which'로 고쳐야 올바르다.

08 정답 ④
19 국가직

정답해설

제시 문장에서 남한이 인터넷 보급이 가장 잘 되어 있음을 언급한다. (B)에서는 'In fact'로 부연 설명을 제시하고 다른 국가들과의 비교를 언급하여 한국의 인터넷 보급이 최상임을 강조한다. 따라서 (B)가 제시 문장 다음으로 적합하다. (C)에서는 'But'으로 시작하여 훌륭한 인터넷 보급이 '대가가 따른다(has come at a price)'고 언급하며 부정적 측면이 있음을 지적한다. 특히 '강박적 사용자들(obsessed users)'이 컴퓨터 사용을 멈출 수 없음을 언급한다. 이것이 (A)에서 'This addiction(이 중독)'으로 연결되므로 정답은 '④ (B) - (C) - (A)'이다.

오답해설

나머지는 문맥상 흐름에 부합하지 않는 보기들이다.

해석

남한은 지구상에서 가장 인터넷 연결이 가장 잘 되어 있는 국가임을 자랑한다.
(B) 사실, 아마도 그 어떤 국가도 인터넷을 그렇게 완전히 수용한 적은 없을 것이다.
(C) 그러나 웹에 대한 그렇게 손쉬운 접근은 많은 수의 강박적인 사용자들이 그들 자신을 그들의 컴퓨터 스크린에서 떼어 놓을 수 없음을 발견하듯 대가가 따랐다.
(A) 사용자들이 여러 날 동안 계속해서 온라인 게임을 한 후 탈진하여 급사하기 시작하면서 이 중독은 최근 몇 년간 한국에서 국가적 이슈가 되었다. 점점 더 많은 학생들이 온라인에 머물기 위해 학교를 가지 않았고, 이것은 이 강렬하게 경쟁적인 사회에서 충격적일 정도로 자기 파괴적인 행동이다.

어휘

boast of 자랑하다, 뽐내다
addiction 중독
exhaustion 탈진
self-destructive 자기 파괴적인
embrace 수용하다
come at a price 상당한 대가를 치르다
wired 컴퓨터 시스템에 연결된
drop dead 급사하다
skip 건너뛰다
intensely 강렬하게
ready 손쉬운, 준비된

오답률 TOP 1
09 정답 ①
19 국가직 응용

정답해설

해당 지문은 '2011년 제정되었던 셧다운제에 관한 규제를 완화하기로 결정한 2016년 정부의 결정'에 대한 내용이다. 본문 초반에서 "The South Korean government on July 18, 2016 decided to ease regulations on the gaming industry, such as revising the online game "shutdown law," by leaving it to the choice of the gamers' parents(2016년 7월 18일 대한민국 정부는 결정권을 게임 이용자의 부모에게 부여함으로써 온라인 게임 "셧다운제"를 개정하는 등 게임 산업에 대한 규제를 완화하기로 결정했다)."를 통해, '부모의 재량에 결정을 맡기고, 규제를 완화하기로 했다'라는 것을 알 수 있으므로 (A)에 가장 적절한 표현은 'lift(해제하다)' 또는 'loosen(완화하다)'이다. 또한 (B)는 2011년 해당 규정이 제정된 목적을 설명하고 있으므로, '비디오게임 중독(video game addiction)'을 '막다, 억제하다'라는 표현이 들어가는 것이 자연스럽다. 따라서 문맥상으로는 'curb(억제하다)', 'tackle(다루다, (해결을 위해)부딪치다)'이 적절하다. 따라서 알맞은 단어가 짝지어진 보기는 '① lift(해제하다)-curb(억제하다)'이다.

오답해설

② (B)의 'aggravate'는 '악화시키다'라는 뜻으로, '비디오 게임 중독을 악화시킨다'라는 의미가 된다. 따라서 본문의 내용과 반대되는 표현이기 때문에 오답이다.
③ (A)의 'reinforce'는 '강화하다'라는 의미로, 본문의 내용과 반대되는 표현이므로 빈칸에 적절하지 않다.
④ (A)의 'implement'는 '시행하다'라는 뜻으로, 이미 규제가 시행되고 있으므로 문맥상 어색하다. 또한 (B)의 'intensify'는 '심화시키다'라는 의미로, '비디오 게임 중독을 심화시킨다'라는 의미가 되기 때문에 오답이다.

해석

2016년 7월 18일 대한민국 정부는 결정권을 게임 이용자의 부모에게 부여함으로써 온라인 게임 "셧다운제"를 개정하는 등 게임 산업에 대한 규제를 완화하기로 결정했다. 게임 산업을 부양하기 위한 정부 전략의 일환으로 만들어진 계획에 따르면 문화체육관광부는 미성년 사용자들이 밤늦은 시간에 온라인 게임에 접속하는 것에 적용된 금지 시간을 (A) 해제하기로 결정했다. 청소년의 비디오 게임 중독을 (B) 억제하기 위해 2011년 제정된 셧다운제는 16세 이하 게임 사용자들이 자정과 오전 6시 사이에 온라인 게임을 하는 것을 금지한다. 제안된 변화에 입각하여 부모들은 청소년 게임 사용자들이 자정 이후에도 게임을 할 수 있도록 허용할 것을 신청할 수 있다.
① 해제하다 - 억제하다
② 완화하다 - 악화시키다
③ 강화하다 - 다루다
④ 시행하다 - 심화시키다

어휘

ease 완화하다
revise 개정하다, 수정하다
strategy 전략
impose 적용하다, 부과하다
regulation 규제
draw up 만들다, 작성하다
curfew 출입제한 시간
access 접속하다, 접근하다

enact 제정하다
permit 허가하다, 허용하다
lift 해제하다, 폐지하다
loosen 약화시키다, 느슨하게 하다
reinforce 강화하다
tackle (힘든 문제 상황과[을]) 씨름하다, 부딪치다, 다루다
implement 시행하다, 실시하다
addiction 중독
adolescent 청소년
curb (특히 좋지 않은 것을) 억제하다
aggravate 악화시키다
intensify 심화시키다, 강화하다

10 정답 ②

18 국가직

정답해설
글의 도입부에서 필자는 '여행을 통해 과거 속에서 살고 있는 인간들을 본 경험'을 언급하며 글을 시작하고 있다. 이에 대하여 필자는 글의 중반부에서 주제문인 'We should live with what is part of our time, part of our collective consciousness, those things that were produced during our lives.'를 통해서 '우리 인간들은 과거의 것이 아닌 현재 우리를 둘러싼 것들과 더불어 살아야 한다'고 역설하고 있다. 마지막으로 글의 후반부에서 'the 비교급, the 비교급' 구문을 포함하여 의미를 강조하고 있다. 'The present is all we have, and the more we are surrounded by it, the more we are aware of our own presence and participation.'은 '현재가 우리가 가진 모든 것이며, 그것에 더 많이 둘러싸일수록 우리 고유의 존재에 더 자각하게 된다'고 말하며 글을 마무리하고 있다. 따라서 본문 전체의 내용을 아우를 제목으로 가장 적절한 것은 '② Reflect on the Time That Surrounds You Now(현재 당신을 에워싸는 시간을 반영하라)'이다.

오답해설
① 과거가 아닌 현재의 중요성에 대해 설명하고 있는 글이다.
③ 본문에서 언급되지 않은 내용이다.
④ 본문의 중심 소재와 거리가 있다.

해석
지난 수년간의 여행을 통하여, 나는 우리 인간들이 얼마나 과거에 살고 있는지를 관찰해왔다. 과거는 우리 주변에 끊임없이 존재함을 고려하면, 무언가가 명백해지자마자, 그것은 과거이다. 우리를 둘러싼 것들, 우리의 집, 우리의 환경, 우리의 건축물, 우리의 물건들 모두 과거의 구조물이다. 우리는 우리의 시간과 집단의 의식을 구성하는 것, 우리가 사는 시간 동안에 창조된 것들과 더불어 살아야 한다. 물론, 우리는 우리가 사는 시간 동안 우리 주변의 모든 것을 적절하거나 계획대로 할 수 있는 선택이나 통제 능력은 가지고 있지 않지만, 우리가 통제할 수 있는 것은 우리가 존재하고 현재와 소통하는 시간을 반영하는 것이다. 현재는 우리가 가진 모든 것이고, 우리가 그것에 더 많이 둘러싸여 있을수록, 우리는 우리 고유의 존재와 참여에 더 자각하게 된다.
① 여행: 과거의 유적을 쫓는 것
② 현재 당신을 에워싸는 시간을 반영하라
③ 숨겨진 삶의 표명
④ 초현대적인 삶의 건축

어휘
observe 관찰하다
the minute …하자마자
surrounding 인근 환경, 주변 환경
architecture 건축, 건축물
collective 집단의, 공동의
relevant 관련 있는, 적절한
reflection 반영
presence 존재
legacy 유산
futuristic 초현대적인
constantly 끊임없이, 거듭
manifested 명시된, 분명한
environment 환경
construct 건설, 구성
consciousness 자각, 의식
conceive 계획하다
surround 둘러싸다, 에워싸다
participation 참여
manifestation 징후, 표명

기적사 DAY 57

결국엔 성정혜 영어 하프모의고사

| 01 | ① | 02 | ① | 03 | ③ | 04 | ④ | 05 | ① |
| 06 | ③ | 07 | ③ | 08 | ② | 09 | ③ | 10 | ① |

01 정답 ①

정답해설
주어진 빈칸은 문맥상 '반응을 불러일으키다'로 사용되었고, 유의어로는 ① ring a bell이 적절하다.

해석
그 회사에 의한 N 프로젝트는 그것의 높은 성능의 운전을 자랑하는 날렵한 슬로건에도 불구하고, 처음에는 **반응을 불러일으키지** 않는다.
① 반응을 불러일으키다, 생각나게 하다
② 버리다
③ 폭로하다, 파헤치다
④ 겁먹게 하다, 당황하게 하다

어휘
sleek 매끈한, 유선형의
ring a bell 반응을 불러일으키다, 생각나게 하다
discard 버리다
divulge 폭로하다, 파헤치다
dismay 겁먹게 하다, 당황하게 하다

02 정답 ①

정답해설
밑줄 친 단어는 문맥상 '급증하다'로 사용되었고, 유의어로는 ① reproduce가 적절하다.

해석
물을 비과학적으로 플라스마로 변형시킬 수 있는, 플라스마 물 트리트먼트 기술은, 따뜻한 환경에서 **급증하고** 수중 생물에 해로울 수 있는 독성을 지닌 조류 대증식을 통상적으로 제거해오던 화학물질의 대안으로 일컬어지고 있다.
① 번식하다
② 탐독하다, 살펴보다
③ 복습하다, 개정하다, 변경하다
④ 닮다, 같다

어휘
convert ~을 변하게 하다, 변형시키다
reproduce 번식하다
revise 복습하다, 개정하다, 변경하다
proliferate 증식하다, 급증하다
pore over 탐독하다, 살펴보다
resemble 닮다, 같다

오답률 TOP 1

03 정답 ③

정답해설
밑줄 친 단어는 문맥상 '내향적인'으로 사용되었고, 가장 먼 것은 ③ mediating이다.

해석

하지만 아마도 장기적으로 더 중요한 것은, 로봇들은 또한 **내향적이거나** 장애가 있거나 혹은 잘 적응하지 못하는 수많은 아이들이 학교 수업에 훨씬 많이 참여하도록 만든다.
① 말을 잘 하지 않는
② 자기 성찰적인
③ 조정하는
④ 자제하는, 차분한

어휘

reserved 말을 잘 하지 않는
introspective 자기 성찰적인
mediating 조정하는
restrained 자제하는, 차분한

04 정답 ④

정답해설

A는 B에게 쇼핑을 가야 한다며 대화를 시작한다. B는 A에게 살 것이 있는지 묻는다. A는 자신이 어제 옷장을 살펴보다가 '귀향 파티(homecoming party)'에 입고 갈 것이 없다는 것을 깨달았다고 한다. B는 귀향 파티에 대해 완전히 잊고 있었다며, 베스트 드레서로 선정되고 싶다고 한다. 그러자 A는 자신도 마찬가지라고 B의 말에 동의하면서, 그러면 둘은 그날 ④ '최상의 옷을 차려입어야(be dressed up to the nines)' 한다고 말한다.

오답해설

① B가 귀향 파티에서 베스트 드레서로 선정되고 싶다고 한 말에 A는 동의하며 그렇다면 둘은 '평화를 구해야(무기를 거두어야, 화해해야)(bury the hatchet)' 한다고 말하는 것은 문맥상 어색하다.
② A와 B가 귀향 파티에서 베스트 드레서로 선정되려면 둘은 '허풍을 떨어야(blow our own trumpet)' 한다는 말은 옳지 않다.
③ A와 B의 바람대로 귀향 파티에서 베스트 드레서가 되려면 둘은 '목이 쉬어야(have a frog in our throat)' 한다는 것은 대화의 흐름에 부적절하다.

해석

A: 나는 이번 주말에 쇼핑을 가야 해.
B: 너 뭐 좀 사야 해?
A: 내가 어제 내 옷장을 살펴봤는데, 내가 귀향 파티에 입고 갈 옷이 아무것도 없다는 것을 깨달았어.
B: 오, 나는 귀향 파티에 대해 완전히 잊고 있었어. 나는 베스트 드레서로 선정되고 싶어.
A: 나도. 그러면 우린 그날 <u>최상의 옷을 차려입어야 해.</u>
B: 우리 같이 쇼핑가야겠다.
① 평화를 구하다, 무기를 거두다, 화해하다
② 허풍을 떨다
③ 목이 쉬다
④ 최상의 옷을 차려입다

어휘

go through 뒤지다
homecoming party 귀향 파티
closet 옷장
select 선정하다
bury the hatchet 평화를 구하다, 무기를 거두다, 화해하다
blow one's own trumpets 허풍을 떨다
have a frog in one's throats 목이 쉬다
be dressed up to the nines 최상의 옷을 차려입다

오답률 TOP 3
05 정답 ①

정답해설

① **출제 포인트: 혼동하기 쉬운 동사**
'laying'은 완전타동사 'lay(~을 놓다)'의 현재분사이며 뒤에 목적어 'an arm'을 사용하였으므로 옳은 문장이다. 또한 'sighed'는 'sigh'의 과거형으로 '한숨 쉬다'의 의미를 가지고 있으며 해당 문장에서는 완전자동사로 쓰였다.

오답해설

② **출제 포인트: number of vs. amount of**
'a number of'의 경우 목적어로 복수가산명사가 오며 'an amount of'의 경우 목적어로 불가산명사가 온다. 해당 문장은 'an enormous number of' 뒤에 불가산명사 'pleasure'를 목적어로 사용하였으므로 틀린 문장이다. 따라서 'number'를 'amount'로 수정해야 한다.

③ **출제 포인트: 원급 비교/관사의 위치**
「as+원급+as」는 원급 비교 구문으로 원급자리에 형용사 원급과 단수 가산명사가 결합한 형태의 명사구가 올 경우 「형용사 원급+부정관사+단수 가산명사」의 형태를 사용해야 한다. 따라서 'a good film'을 'good a film'으로 수정해야 한다.

④ **출제 포인트: so 원인 that 결과 부사절 접속사**
해당 문장은 'she'앞에 부사절을 이끄는 접속사 'that'이 생략되어 있다. 「so+형용사/부사 ~ that+주어+동사」는 '너무 ~해서 ~하다'를 뜻하며 「too+형용사/부사 ~ to+동사원형」은 '너무 ~해서 ~할 수 없다'를 뜻한다. 해당 문장은 부사 'fast' 앞에 'too'를 사용하였으나 뒤에 'that'이 생략된 부사절이 왔으므로 틀린 문장이다. 따라서 'too'를 'so'로 수정해야 한다. 또한 'barely'는 빈도를 나타내는 '빈도부사'로 쓰일 때, be동사 뒤에 위치하는 것이 더욱 일반적이다.

해석

① John은 내 어깨에 팔을 살며시 올려놓고 한숨을 쉬었다.
② 음악은 많은 사람들에게 엄청난 양의 즐거움을 준다.
③ 왜 이것이 오리지널만큼 좋은 영화일 수 없는지 분명한 이유가 없다.
④ 모든 것이 너무 빠르게 발생해서 그녀는 모든 정보를 좀처럼 받아들일 수 없었다.

06 정답 ③

정답해설

③ **출제 포인트: as to+목적어 vs. so as to+동사원형**
'so as to'는 뒤에 동사원형이 오며 '~하기 위해서'를 뜻한다. 'as to'는 뒤에 명사(구) 또는 명사절이 오며 '~에 관해'를 뜻한다. 해당 문장은 'so as to' 뒤에 명사절 'how they sound'가 왔으므로 틀린 문장이다. 이때 해석상 '자신의 목소리가 어떻게 들리는지에 관해'가 자연스러우므로 'so as to'를 'as to'로 수정해야 한다.

오답해설

① **출제 포인트: 명사절의 접속사 that**
해당 문장에서 'that'은 명사절을 이끄는 접속사로 추상명사 'fact'의 동격 역할을 한다.

② **출제 포인트: other vs. others/관계부사 how**
'others'는 '다른 사람들'을 뜻하는 복수 대명사이므로 동사에 복수형태인 'hear'를 옳게 사용하였다. 또한 'the way'와 'others'사이에 선행사 'the way'를 수식하는 관계부사 'how'가 생략되어있다.

④ 출제 포인트: 접속사의 역할

'whereas'는 접속사이므로 뒤에 완전한 형태의 절이 온다.

해석

그 주된 효과는 여러분이 자신의 목소리를 다른 사람들이 듣는 방식과 다른 방식으로 듣는다는 사실 때문에 생긴다. 이는 가장 뛰어난 기량을 지닌 가수들조차도 '자신의 목소리가 어떻게 들리는지'에 관해 성악 지도자나 발성 지도 교사의 의견을 들어야 하지만, 콘서트 바이올린 연주자들은 전혀 그런 일을 할 필요가 없는 주된 이유들 중 하나이다.

어휘

effect 효과, 영향, 결과　　　others 다른 사람들
accomplished 기량이 뛰어난, 재주가 많은
so as to+동사원형 ~하기 위해서　　as to+목적어 ~에 관해

07 정답 ③

정답해설

③ 출제 포인트: enough의 위치 / tell

'enough'는 부사로 형용사 'stupid'를 뒤에서 수식하므로 'stupid enough'는 옳게 사용되었다. 또한 'told'는 'tell'의 과거형으로 해당 문장에서는 4형식 동사로 사용되었으며 'me'와 'it' 사이에는 직접목적어절을 이끄는 접속사 'that'이 생략되어있다.

오답해설

① 출제 포인트: 관계대명사 vs. 관계부사/주어와 동사 수일치

관계대명사가 이끄는 절은 불완전한 형태이며 관계부사가 이끄는 절은 완전한 형태여야 한다. 해당 문장은 which가 이끄는 절이 완전한 형태이므로 옳지 않은 문장이다. 또한 「a variety of 복수 가산명사」가 주어인 경우 동사의 수일치 기준은 복수 가산명사가 되어 동사에 복수형태를 사용해야 한다. 주어인 'a variety of fish'가 복수명사인 데 반해 동사가 단수동사 lives이므로 수일치하지 않아 틀린 문장이다. 따라서 which 대신에 선행사를 'ponds'로 하는 관계부사인 'where'로 수정하고 동사 'lives'를 'live'로 수정해야 한다. 해당 문장에서는 주어 'fish'가 복수로 쓰인 'fish'임에 유의해야 한다.

② 출제 포인트: 접속사의 역할 / -thing류 대명사 수식 / to부정사의 한정적 용법

두 문장 'John didn't do anything wrong'과 'he had nothing to be worried about'이 접속사 없이 연결되어 있으므로 틀린 문장이다. 따라서 주어진 해석을 통해 'he' 앞에 접속사 'so'를 사용해야 한다. 또한 to부정사구 'to be worried about'이 부정대명사 'nothing'을 수식하고 있으며 이때 'nothing'은 to부정사구의 의미상 목적어에 해당한다.

④ 출제 포인트: not A until B / It ~ that 강조용법

해당 문장은 'You can know how a poem sounds not until you hear it coming out of a pair of speakers.'에서 부사절에 해당되는 'not until you hear it coming out of a pair of speakers'를 강조하기 위해 'It ~ that 강조용법'을 사용하고 있다. 따라서 'which'를 'that'으로 수정해야 한다. 'It ~ that 강조 용법'의 경우 'that'이 문장에서 관계사를 대신하는 경우이기 때문에 부사절인 'not until 주어+동사~'를 강조하는 경우에는 'that'대신에 관계부사 'when'을 사용할 수도 있는 점에 유의하자.

08 정답 ②

정답해설

본문 첫 문장에서 '게임 중독의 심각성'에 대해 언급한 후, 이어서 '게임 중독자들의 특징'에 대해 나열하고 있다. '게임 중독자들은 10시간 이상 게임을 하며, 수면 부족에 시달리고, 나쁜 식습관을 지니고 있기 때문에 영양이 부족하고 탈수 증세를 보이기도 한다'고 일반적인 게임 중독자의 특징에 대해 언급한 후, 이어서 '광장 공포증'을 겪거나 '은둔형 외톨이인 히키코모리'가 되는 등 좀 더 심각한 정도의 게임 중독자의 특징에 대해 설명하고 있다. 따라서 전체 글의 주제로 가장 적절한 것은 '② the characteristics of game addicts (게임 중독자들의 특징들)'이다.

오답해설

① 게임 중독의 원인에 대해서는 본문에 언급되지 않는다.
③ 히키코모리 용어에 대한 설명이 본문 마지막 문장에 언급되지만, '심각한 정도의 게임 중독자'에 대한 설명으로 제시된 것이며 전체 글을 아우르는 내용이 아니므로, 글의 주제로 적절하지 않다.
④ 본문에 언급되지 않는 내용이다.

해석

게임 중독은 한 사람의 인생에 심각한 피해를 야기하는 강박적인 정신 질환이다. 비디오 게임 중독자가 하루에 10시간 이상을, 보통 밤까지 줄곧 게임을 하며 보내는 것은 흔한 일이며, 많은 사람들이 수면 부족을 겪는다. 그들의 경험에 몰두한 게임 이용자들은 카페인과 당 함량이 높은 에너지음료로 주로 이루어진 나쁜 식습관을 가지고 있는 것으로 알려져 있다. 많은 사람들은 탈수 증세를 보이고 영양이 부족하다. 더욱더 심각한 경우에, 게임 중독자들은 광장 공포증 – 집을 떠나는 것에 대한 공포를 느끼는 불안장애의 한 유형 – 을 겪는다고 보고하며, 다른 사람들은 자신들을 히키코모리 – 일본에서 은둔형 청소년 또는 사회생활을 포기한 성인으로 알려진 용어 – 라고 생각한다.

① 게임 중독의 원인들
② 게임 중독자들의 특징들
③ 히키코모리라는 용어의 정의
④ 게임 중독을 극복하는 방법들

어휘

compulsive 강박적인, 강제적인　　addict 중독자
deprivation 부족, 결핍　　immerse 몰두하게 하다, 몰입시키다
comprised of …로 구성된　　dehydrated 탈수 상태의
malnourished 영양 부족의　　agoraphobia 광장 공포증
identify A with B A를 B와 동일시하다
popularize 대중화하다　　reclusive 은둔한, 세상을 버린
adolescent 청소년
withdraw from …에서 철수하다, 끊다, 중단하다

09 정답 ③

정답해설

(A) 빈칸 이전에서 'Some degree of risk aversion in investing is perfectly rational(투자에 있어서 어느 정도의 위험 회피는 매우 합리적이다).'라고 언급한 후, 빈칸 이후에서 '위험을 회피하는 상황'에 대해 예를 들어 설명하고 있으므로, 빈칸에는 '예시'를 나타내는 'For example(예를 들어)' 또는 '재서술'을 나타내는 'In other words(다시 말해)'가 들어갈 수 있다.

(B) 본문 초중반에서는 '사람들이 투자를 할 때 어느 정도 위험 회피적(risk averse) 또는 위험 지향적(to expect higher returns for taking on more risk)이 되는 것은 모두 합리적인 성향이다'라고 설명하고 있다. 이후에는 '손실 회피(loss aversion)'의 경우에 대해 언급하며 'loss aversion holds that all else being equal, losses fundamentally loom larger than gains(위험 회피는 모든 상황이 동일할 때에도 수익보다는 손실을 더 크게 받아들인다).'라고 설명한다. "This includes cases where, win or lose, the outcome will have little material effect on someone's life circumstances(이것은 이기든 지든 그 결

과가 누군가의 생활 환경에 물질적 영향을 거의 미치지 않는 경우를 포함하며)"의 상황, 즉 수익과 손실이 인생에 큰 영향을 미치지 않는 경우에도 위험 회피적이라는 것은 '사람들이 과도하게 위험 회피적'이라는 것을 보여주는 근거이므로, 빈칸에는 '인과관계'를 나타내는 'thus(따라서)' 또는 'therefore(그러므로)'가 들어가는 것이 적절하다. 따라서 정답은 ③이다.

오답해설

① (A) 전후의 관계가 '인과관계'를 나타내지 않으므로 'Subsequently(결과적으로)'는 빈칸에 적절하지 않으며, (B) 전후의 관계가 '역접'이 아니기 때문에 'on the other hand(반면에)'는 빈칸에 적절하지 않다.
② (B) 전후 문장의 관계가 '반대의 상황'을 가정하는 것이 아니므로, 'otherwise(그렇지 않으면)'는 빈칸에 적절하지 않다.
④ 문맥상 어색하므로 빈칸에 적절하지 않다.

해석

투자에 있어서 어느 정도의 위험 회피는 매우 합리적이다. (A) 예를 들어, 만일 당신의 투자 계좌에서 1만 달러를 잃는 것이 당신이 월세를 마련하지 못할 것이라는 것을 의미하고, 반면 추가적인 1만 달러를 획득하는 것이 당신이 추가 휴가를 보낼 수 있다는 것을 의미한다면, 당신의 거처를 잃을 위험을 무릅쓰기보다 안전책을 강구하는 것이 완전히 합리적이다. 이와 같이, 투자자들이 더 많은 위험을 무릅쓰는 것에 대해 더 높은 수익을 기대하는 것 또한 비합리적이지 않다. 그러나 손실 회피는 모든 상황이 동일할 때, 수익보다 손실이 근본적으로 더 크게 다가온다고 간주한다. 이것은 이기든 지든 그 결과가 누군가의 생활 환경에 물질적 영향을 거의 미치지 않는 경우를 포함하며, (B) 따라서 사람들이 과도하게 위험 회피적이라는 것을 암시한다.
① 결과적으로 - 반면에
② 다시 말해 - 그렇지 않으면
③ 예를 들어 - 따라서
④ 그럼에도 불구하고 - 게다가

어휘

aversion 싫어함, 혐오
roof over one's head 거처
irrational 비합리적인
hold 간주하다, 생각하다
loom large (걱정·위기 등이) 크게 다가오다
averse 싫어하는
rational 합리적인
as such 이와 같이, 그러한 것처럼
return 수익
fundamentally 근본적으로

오답률 TOP 2

10 정답 ③

정답해설

본문은 '현재 순간을 있는 그대로 수용적인 태도로 자각하는 것'인 "마음 챙김(mindfulness)"을 통해 '있는 그대로의 현재를 사는 것'에 대해 설명하고 있다. 주어진 문장의 'Cultivating a nonjudgmental awareness of the present(현재에 대한 개인적 판단을 하지 않는 인식을 배양하는 것)'가 가리키는 내용이 ③ 이전 문장 'being with your thoughts as they are(있는 그대로의 생각과 함께 하는 것)'에 등장하고 있으며, 또한 주어진 문장의 'a host of benefits(수많은 이점)'의 구체적인 내용이 ③ 이후 두 문장에서 나열되고 있으므로, 주어진 문장이 들어갈 가장 적절한 위치는 ③이다.

오답해설

② 주어진 문장의 'a host of benefits(수많은 이점)'로 보아, 주어진 문장 이후에는 'mindfulness(마음 챙김)'의 이점이 언급되어야 하는데, ② 이후 문장에서는 '이점'이 언급되지 않으므로 주어진 문장이 들어가기에 적절하지 않다.
나머지 보기는 문맥상 어색하므로 오답이다.

해석

우리는 더욱더 현재에 살아야 한다. 현재를 사는 것은 - 마음 챙김이라고도 불리는 - 활동적이고, 개방적이며 의도적인 현재에의 집중 상태이다. (①) 당신이 집중할 때, 당신은 당신의 생각이 아니라는 것을 깨닫는다; 당신은 그것들을 판단하지 않고 순간순간 당신의 생각의 관찰자가 된다. (②) 마음 챙김은 생각을 붙들고 있거나 밀어내지 않고, 있는 그대로의 생각과 함께 하는 것을 포함한다. (③ <u>현재에 대한 개인적 판단을 하지 않는 인식을 배양하는 것은 수많은 이점을 제공한다.</u>) 마음 챙김은 스트레스를 감소시키고, 면역 기능을 신장시키며, 만성적인 고통을 줄여주고, 혈압을 낮추고, 환자들이 암을 극복하도록 도와준다. (④) 집중하는 사람들은 또한 더 행복하고, 원기가 더 왕성하며, 더 공감적이고 더욱 안정되어 있다.

어휘

cultivate 배양하다, 양성하다, 계발하다
bestow 주다, 부여하다
a host of 많은
mindfulness 마음 챙김(현재 순간을 있는 그대로 수용적인 태도로 자각하는 것)
intentional 의도적인
mindful 집중하는, 유념하는, 마음에 새기는
involve 포함하다, 수반하다
grasp 쥐다, 잡다
immune functioning 면역 기능
cope with 대항하다, 대처하다, 극복하다
exuberant 원기 왕성한
empathetic 공감적인
secure 불안이 없는, 안정된

결국엔 성정혜 영어 하프모의고사
기적사 DAY 58

01	②	02	④	03	④	04	③	05	③
06	④	07	④	08	②	09	③	10	④

오답률 TOP 2
01 정답 ②

정답해설

주어진 빈칸에는 빈칸 이전에 'insulting'을 통해서 문맥상 '모독적인'이 적절하기 때문에 ② profane이 정답이다.

해석

무언가를 조사하기 위해서 **모독적인** 단어들을 포함하지 않더라도 많은 지적들이 여전히 수많은 모욕적인 기분을 남기는 상황들이 많다.
① 수수한
② 모독적인, 불경한
③ 비정상적인
④ 우발적인, 부정의, 외래의

어휘

unpretentious 수수한
eccentric 비정상적인
profane 모독적인, 불경한
adventitious 우발적인, 부정의, 외래의

02 정답 ④

정답해설

주어진 밑줄에는 문맥상 '주요한'이 적절하므로 ④ principal이 정답이다.

해석

대권을 추구함에 있어 버락 오바마의 **주요한** 주장들 중 하나는 과거의 워싱턴 전투에 관련되지 않은 외부인으로서 그의 입장이 그가 그 수도의 무기력한 당파심을 돌파할 수 있도록 만들 것이라는 점이었다.
① 서두의, 준비의, 예비의
② 비정상인, 엉뚱한
③ 모순되는
④ 주요한

어휘

gutless 무기력한
preliminary 서두의, 준비의, 예비의
contradictory 모순되는
partisanship 당파심
aberrant 비정상인, 엉뚱한
principal 주요한

오답률 TOP 3
03 정답 ④

정답해설

밑줄 친 단어는 문맥상 '은밀한, 비밀의'로 사용되었으므로, 의미가 가장 먼 것은 ④ condescending이다.

해석

"New York Channel,"이라고 이름 붙여진 **은밀한** 외교적 방안을 통해, 소문에 따르면 북한과 미국은 북한에 있는 미국의 수감자들을 석방시키는 협상을 용이하게 하는 것을 포함하는, 일련의 정상 회담을 진행해오고 있다고 전해진다.

① 비밀의, 은밀한
② 은밀한
③ 비밀리의
④ 생색내는 듯한, 잘난척하는

어휘

clandestine 비밀의, 은밀한
avenue 방법, 수단
facilitating 용이하게 하는
furtive 은밀한
condescending 생색내는 듯한, 잘난척하는
diplomatic 외교적인
dub ~이라고 부르다, 찌르다
covert 비밀의, 은밀한
surreptitious 비밀리의

04 정답 ③

정답해설

A는 "지구 온난화는 매일 악화하고 있어 (Global warming is aggravating everyday)"라고 말한다. 그러자 B는 "오늘 날씨가 매우 따뜻해 (The weather is really warm today)"라고 대답한다. A의 말에 대한 B의 답변은 흐름상 부자연스럽다.

오답해설

① A가 아침으로 시리얼과 토스트를 먹었다고 하자, B는 스스로 준비한 것인지 묻는다. 이는 자연스러운 대화이다.
② 기차가 몇 분 후에 도착할 것이라는 A의 말에 B는 서둘러 타는 곳을 찾아야 한다고 말한다. A의 말에 대한 B의 답변은 적절하다.
④ A는 B에게 바로 앞에 방지턱이 있으니 조심하라고 말해준다. B는 보지 못했다며 속도를 줄여야겠다고 대답한다. B의 반응은 적합하다.

해석

① A: 나는 아침으로 시리얼과 토스트를 먹었어.
B: 너 스스로 준비한 거야?
② A: 기차는 몇 분 후에 도착할 거야.
B: 우리는 서둘러 타는 곳을 찾아야 해.
③ A: 지구 온난화는 매일 악화하고 있어.
B: 오늘 날씨가 매우 따뜻해.
④ A: 조심해! 너 바로 앞에 방지턱이 있어.
B: 오, 그게 있는 줄 몰랐어. 속도를 줄여야겠다.

어휘

prepare 준비하다
global warming 지구 온난화
speed bump 방지턱
platform 타는 곳, 승강장
aggravate 악화하다

05 정답 ③

정답해설

③ **출제 포인트: so 원인 that 결과 부사절 접속사 / 혼동하기 쉬운 동사**
「so+형용사/부사 ~ that+주어+동사」는 '너무 ~해서 ~하다'를 뜻한다. 해당 문장은 「so+형용사/부사 ~ that+주어+동사」가 옳게 사용되었으며 이때 'struggle'은 완전자동사이므로 'that'을 목적격 관계대명사로 착각해서는 안 된다.

오답해설

① **출제 포인트: 원급 비교**
원급 형용사 'bad' 앞에 부사 'as'가 있으므로 「as+원급+as」 형태의 원급 비교 구문이 쓰인 문장임을 알 수 있다. 따라서 'than'을 'as'로 수정해야 한다.

② **출제 포인트: 혼동하기 쉬운 동사 / 복합관계부사**
'rise'는 완전자동사이므로 전치사 없이 목적어를 가질 수 없다. 해당 문장은 'rise' 뒤에 목적어 'your arms'를 사용하였으므로 틀린 문장이다. 따라서 'rise'를 완전타동사 'raise'로 수정해야 한다. 또한 'However(아무리 ~일지라도)'는 복합관계부사로, 부사절을 이끌 수 있으며, 그 어순은 「However + 형용사/부사~ + 주어 + 동사 ~」이다. 해당 문장에서는 'you get carried away'에서 'get'의 보어로 온 과거분사 'carried away'가 'However' 뒤로 이동해 'However carried away you get, ~'으로 옳게 사용되었다. 'However'가 수식하는 단어의 품사에 유의해야한다.

④ **출제 포인트: number of vs. amount of**
'the number of'는 뒤에 가산명사가 목적어로 오며 'the amount of'는 뒤에 불가산명사가 목적어로 온다. 해당 문장은 'the number of' 뒤에 불가산명사 'walking'을 사용하였으므로 'number'를 'amount'로 수정해야 한다. 또한 'walking'과 병렬구조를 이루는 'exercise'도 불가산명사로 사용되었다.

해석

① 아버지가 된다는 것은 내가 처음에 생각했던 것만큼 나쁘지 않다.
② 아무리 흥분하더라도, 팔을 머리 위로 올리지 마라.
③ 우리는 처음 한 시간 동안 인터넷에서 너무 많은 히트를 쳐서 정말로 어려움을 겪고 있는 중이었다.
④ 이것은 걷기 또는 다리를 사용하는 것과 관련된 운동의 양과는 완전히 대조적이다.

오답률 TOP 1

06 정답 ④

정답해설

④ **자릿값[목적어 vs. 수식어]**
완전자동사 'have'가 쓰인 문장으로 뒤에 목적어에 해당하는 명사구가 없으므로 틀린 문장이다. 따라서 해당 문장은 전치사 'from'을 삭제해「부사+형용사+형용사+명사」형태의 명사구 'quite different relative efficiencies'로 수정하는 것이 옳다. 명사를 수식하는 형용사가 이어지는 표현 역시 가능하다.

오답해설

① **출제 포인트: 현재분사 vs. 과거분사**
'generated'는 완전타동사 'generate'의 과거분사로 뒤에 목적어가 없으며 수식하는 대상 'the vibrations'와 수동관계이므로 옳게 사용되었다.

② **출제 포인트: 접속사의 역할**
'whereas'는 접속사이므로 뒤에 완전한 형태의 절이 온다. 해당 문장은 'whereas' 뒤에「수식어(in a singer)+주어(some of the auditory stimulus)+서술어(is conducted)+수식어(to the ear)+수식어(through the singer's own bones)」로 된 완전한 형태의 절이 왔으므로 옳은 문장이다.

③ **출제 포인트: 주어와 동사의 수일치 / 능동태 vs. 수동태**
주어가 'some of+명사(구)'인 경우 동사의 수일치 기준은 명사(구)이다. 해당 문장은 'some of' 뒤에 단수형태의 명사(구) 'the auditory stimulus'가 왔으므로 동사에 단수형태를 사용해야 하며 문맥상 '자극의 일부가 전달된다'가 자연스러우므로 수동태 'is conducted'를 사용하는 것이 옳다.

해석

청중은 전적으로 공기 중에서 생성된 진동을 통해서 소리 신호를 수용하는 반면에, 가수의 경우에는 청각적 자극의 일부가 가수 자신의 뼈를 통해서 귀로 전달된다. 소리를 전달하는 이 두 가지 방식은 다양한 소리의 주파수에서 상당히 다른 상대적인 효율성을 지니고 있으므로, 전반적인 소리의 질이 상당히 다를 것이다.

어휘

entirely 전적으로, 완전히, 전부
auditory 청각의
transfer 전하다, 옮기다, 바꾸다
vibration 진동, 흔들림
stimulus 자극
overall 전반적인, 전체의

07 정답 ④

정답해설

④ **출제 포인트: not A until B / It ~ that 강조용법**
해당 문장은 'We could put down the new carpet not until the plumber had finished.'에서 'not until the plumber had finished'를 강조하기 위해 'It ~ that 강조용법'을 사용한 문장으로 옳은 문장이다.

오답해설

① **출제 포인트: 주격 관계대명사 / 능동태 vs. 수동태**
영어 문장만 보면 옳은 문장이나 주어진 해석이 '친구 John에 의해 관리 받는다.'이므로 'manages'를 수동태 'is managed by'로 수정해야 한다. 또한 'who'는 주격 관계대명사로 선행사는 'Tom'이다.

② **출제 포인트: 접속사의 역할/-thing류 명사 수식/to부정사의 한정적 용법**
접속사 because를 사용하여 두 개의 절을 옳게 연결하였고 부정대명사 nothing을 to부정사구가 옳게 수식하고 있으나 nothing은 to take의 의미상 목적어이므로 take 뒤에 있는 대명사 it을 삭제해야 한다.

③ **출제 포인트: enough의 위치**
해당 문장에서 'enough'는 형용사이므로 명사 'music'을 앞에서 수식해야 한다. 따라서 'music enough'를 'enough music'으로 수정해야 한다.

08 정답 ②

정답해설

본문은 '대한민국의 인터넷이 발달한 이유'로 '인구 밀집(Population density)'을 제시하고 있다. 본문 중반 "With the high proportion of Koreans living in urban-area apartments, spreading connections between them is more like stitching a quilt than building a road(한국인 중 높은 비율이 도시 지역의 아파트에 거주함에 따라 그들 사이에 연결선을 퍼뜨리는 것은 도로를 건설하는 것보다 퀄트를 꿰매는 것에 더 가깝다)."에서 '도시 지역에 많은 한국인들이 거주하는 것'에 대해 언급한 후 (A)에서 이러한 특징이 '인터넷 보급'을 용이하게 만들었다고 설명하고 있으므로, (A)에 들어갈 알맞은 표현은 'proximity(근접성)' 또는 'closeness(가까움)'이다. 이러한 맥락에서, 미국과 비교해 대한민국에서 물리적 간격을 그다지 크지 않다는 것을 알 수 있으므로, (B)에는 'physical gaps(물리적 간격)'는 '문제가 되지 않는다'라는 의미의 표현이 들어가는 것이 적절하다. 따라서 부정의 의미를 지닌 'seldom(좀처럼 ~않는)', 'barely(거의 ~않는)'가 (B)에 적절하다. 그러므로 적절한 표현이 연결된 보기는 ②이다.

오답해설

① 'remoteness'는 '인구 밀집'에 대한 설명과 반대되는 표현이므로 (A)에 적절하지 않다.
③ 본문에서는 '인터넷 기술력'의 차이에 대해 언급하고 있지 않으므로, (A)에 'technology'가 들어가는 것은 어색하다. 또한 'frequently'가 (B)에 들어가면 '자주 문제가 된다'라는 의미가 되므로 본문의 주장과는 반대되는 내용이 된다. 따라서 (B)에 적절하지 않다.
④ 'absolutely'가 (B)에 들어가면 '틀림없이 문제가 된다'라는 의미가 되므로 본문의 주장과는 반대되는 내용이 된다. 따라서 (B)에 적절하지 않다.

해석

대한민국은 고층 건물과 도시의 불빛으로 유명하며, 그 고정관념은 사실이다. 5천3백만 명의 인구 중 83퍼센트가 도시 지역에 거주한다. 유사한 비율이 미국에도 적용되지만, 대한민국이 근본적으로 로스앤젤레스와 샌프란시스코 사이의 공간과 맞먹는 지역에 미국 인구의 7분의 1을 집어넣은 것이라고 생각해 보라. 만일 당신에게 폐쇄공포증이 있다면 인구 밀집은 별로 유쾌하지 않을 것이다. 그러나 그것은 인터넷을 얻는 것을 훨씬 쉽게 만든다. 한국인 중 높은 비율이 도시 지역의 아파트에 거주함에 따라 그들 사이에 연결선을 퍼뜨리는 것은 도로를 건설하는 것보다 퀼트를 꿰매는 것에 더 가깝다. (A) 근접성은 기반 시설의 비용을 극적으로 감소시키고, International Telecommunication Union의 말처럼 "네트워크 개발을 단순화시킨다". 광섬유 연결선은 설치에 비용이 많이 들고 DSL은 거리에 따라 급격한 성능 저하를 일으킨다 - 그러나 대한민국의 물리적 간격은 (B) 거의 문제가 되지 않는다.

① 멀리 떨어짐 - 좀처럼 ~않는
② 근접성 - 거의 ~않는
③ 기술 - 자주
④ 가까움 - 절대적으로

어휘

famed 아주 유명한
reside 거주하다
ratio 비율
essentially 근본적으로, 본질적으로
density 밀도, 밀집
infrastructure 기반 시설
fiber optic 광섬유
remoteness 멀리 떨어짐
proximity 근접, 가까움
skyscraper 고층 건물, 마천루
urban 도시의
hold 유효하다, 적용되다, 들어맞다
equivalent 맞먹는, 동등한, 상당하는
claustrophobic 폐쇄 공포증의
put it 말하다
steep 급격한, 가파른
seldom 좀처럼 ~않는
barely 거의 ~않는

09 정답 ③

정답해설

본문 첫 문장 "Negative news will normally cause individuals to sell stocks(부정적인 뉴스는 보통 개인이 주식을 매각하도록 만들 것이다)."에서 '부정적인 뉴스가 주식 투자자들에게 미치는 영향'에 대해 언급한 후 '부정적인 뉴스가 주식 가격 하락으로 이어질 것이다'라고 설명하고 있다. 이어서 "Positive news, on the other hand, will normally cause individuals to buy stocks(반면, 긍정적인 뉴스는 보통 개인이 주식을 구매하도록 만들 것이다)."를 통해 '긍정적인 뉴스가 주식 투자자들에게 미치는 영향'에 대해 언급한 후, '긍정적인 뉴스가 주식 가격 상승으로 이어질 것이다'라고 설명하고 있다. 이후, 실제로 '자연재해'라는 부정적인 뉴스가 주가에 미치는 영향을 예로 들어 '뉴스가 주식 가격에 미치는 영향'에 대해 설명하고 있으므로, 글의 제목으로 가장 적절한 것은 '③ How Does News Affect Stock Prices?(뉴스가 주가에 어떻게 영향을 미치는가?)'이다.

오답해설

① 본문과 관련 없는 내용이므로 오답이다.
② 본문 마지막에 제시된 예시는 '자연재해에 관한 뉴스'가 주가에 미치는 영향을 언급한 것이며, '자연재해' 자체와 주식시장에 대해서는 본문에 언급되지 않는다.
④ 본문에서는 '주식 가격이 하락하는 경우(부정적인 뉴스의 영향)'와 '주식 가격이 상승하는 경우(긍정적인 뉴스의 영향)'를 모두 언급하고 있으므로, 주가 상승에 대한 제목은 본문에 적절하지 않다.

해석

부정적인 뉴스는 보통 개인이 주식을 매각하도록 만들 것이다. 예상치 못한 불행한 사건들뿐만 아니라 좋지 않은 수익 보고서, 빈약한 기업 지배구조, 경제적 그리고 정치적 불확실성이 매각 압박과 주식 가격 하락으로 이어질 것이다. 반면 긍정적인 뉴스는 보통 개인이 주식을 구매하도록 만들 것이다. 긍정적인 경제 그리고 정치의 전반적 지표뿐만 아니라 좋은 수익 보고서, 발전된 기업 지배구조, 신제품 및 인수는 구매 압력과 주식 가격 상승으로 이어질 것이다. 예를 들어, 산사태를 일으키는 허리케인은 공공사업의 주가의 하락을 야기할 것이다. 한편, 폭풍의 강도에 따라 뉴스에 의해 보험사의 주가 또한 타격을 입거나, 또는 예상된 피해가 크지 않을 것이라고 추정된다면 주가가 더 높게 올라갈 것이다.

① 주식 투자 성공법
② 자연재해들과 주식시장
③ 뉴스가 주가에 어떻게 영향을 미치는가?
④ 주가 상승을 야기하는 것은 무엇인가?

어휘

corporate governance 기업 지배구조
as well as …뿐만 아니라 ~도
translate (다른 형태로) 바뀌다
indicator 지표
utility 공익[공공]사업
project 예상[추정]하다
occurrence 사건, 일어난 일
acquisition 인수
landfall 산사태
take a hit 타격을 입다
moderate 보통의, 중간의, 적당한

10 정답 ④

정답해설

주어진 문장의 "The easiest way to explain living in the present is to start by explaining what it means not to be present(현재에 사는 것을 설명하는 가장 쉬운 방법은 현재에 있지 않은 것이 무엇을 의미하는지 설명하는 것으로 시작하는 것이다)"를 통해, 이어질 문장에서는 '현재에 살고 있지 않은 것'에 대해 언급되어야 한다는 것을 유추할 수 있다. 따라서 "When you aren't being present ~(당신이 현재에 있지 않을 때)"로 시작하는 (C)가 주어진 문장에 이어지는 것이 자연스럽다. 이후 (A)의 "to spend moments thinking about the past or in daydreams of the future(과거를 생각하며 또는 미래에 대한 공상을 하며 시간을 보내는 것)."이 (C)의 'Your mind is pulled into the past or the future, or both(당신의 정신은 과거 또는 미래에, 혹은 두 곳 모두로 끌려가게 된다).'를 가리키고 있으므로, (A)가 이어진 후, 마지막으로 'But ~(그러나)'을 통해 '현재에 살고 있지 않은 것이 미치는 부정적 영향'에 대해 설명하며 글을 마무리 짓는 (B)가 이어지는 것이 적절하다. 따라서 정답은 '④ (C) - (A) - (B)'이다.

오답해설

나머지 보기는 문맥상 어색하므로 오답이다.

해석

현재에 사는 것을 설명하는 가장 쉬운 방법은 현재에 있지 않은 것이 무엇을 의미하는지 설명하는 것으로 시작하는 것이다. 왜냐하면 이것이 우리가 습관적으로 익숙해지는 상태이기 때문이다.
(C) 당신이 현재에 있지 않을 때, 당신은 시간의 희생양이 된다. 당신의 정신은 과거 또는 미래에, 혹은 두 곳 모두로 끌려가게 된다.
(A) 물론 과거를 생각하며 또는 미래에 대한 공상을 하며 시간을 보내는 것은 자연스럽다. 과거에 발생한 것들을 연상하는 것을 통해 다가오는 위험을 감지하는 것은 자기 보호를 위해 중요하다.
(B) 그러나 과거의 사건과 잠재적인 미래의 결과와 관련된 생각과 감정에 의해 우리의 삶이 좌우될 때, 평화롭게 현재에 뿌리를 두고 서 있는 것이 점점 더 드물게 된다.

어휘

habitually 습관적으로
become[be] used to …에 익숙해지다
daydream 공상, 백일몽
identify 확인하다
impending 다가오는
association 관련, 연관, 연상
self-preservation 자기 보호
dictate …을 좌우하다, …에 영향을 주다
attached to …에 소속된, …에 연관된
outcome 결과

결국엔 성정혜 영어 하프모의고사
기적사 DAY 59

| 01 | ③ | 02 | ① | 03 | ④ | 04 | ② | 05 | ① |
| 06 | ④ | 07 | ④ | 08 | ② | 09 | ② | 10 | ② |

01 정답 ③

정답해설

밑줄 친 단어는 문맥상 '예방하다, 막다'로 사용되었고, 유의어로는 ③ head off가 적절하다.

해석

이것은 대기 오염을 **예방하기** 위해 지금까지 제안된 60여 개의 의견들 중에서 효율성이 있는 몇 안 되는 방안 중 하나였다.
① 구별하다
② 강화하다
③ ~을 피하다, ~의 앞을 가로막아 진로를 방해하다
④ 나눠주다, 배포하다

어휘

separate 구별하다 reinforce 강화하다
head off ~을 피하다, ~의 앞을 가로막아 진로를 방해하다
distribute 나눠주다, 배포하다

02 정답 ①

정답해설

주어진 빈칸은 문맥상 '일으키다'가 적절하므로 ① evoke가 정답이다.

해석

그 감독은 영화의 어떤 포인트들이 신뢰성 있는 관중으로부터 집단적인 한숨을 내쉬게 하고, 숨을 차게 하고 웃음을 **일으키는지** 마음에 되새긴다고 말한다.
① 불러일으키다
② 피하다
③ 자세히 살펴보다, 조사하다
④ 버리다, 탈주하다

어휘

gasp 숨이 차다, 헐떡거리다 evoke 불러일으키다
shun away from 피하다 inspect 자세히 살펴보다, 조사하다
desert 버리다, 탈주하다

03 정답 ④

정답해설

밑줄 친 단어는 '순진한'으로 사용되었으므로, 의미가 가장 먼 ④ inconclusive가 정답이다.

해석

어린 배우들은 **순진무구한** 영혼, - 그가 겪어온 그 모든 것들에도 불구하고 - 그들의 도덕성이 강하고 정당하게 평가받은 채로 남아있는 어린 낭만주의자들의 본질을 잘 담아낸다.
① 솔직한, 순진한
② 순진한, 결백한

③ 순진한
④ 결론에 이르지 못하는

어휘

ingenuous 솔직한, 순진한
childlike 순진한
innocent 순진한, 결백한
inconclusive 결론에 이르지 못하는

04 정답 ②

정답해설

Shelly는 Trevor에게 그만의 스트레스 해소 방식이 무엇인지 묻는다. Trevor는 여러 가지 방법 중 하나는 엄청난 양의 단 음식을 먹는 것이라고 답변한다. Shelly는 그러한 방법에 대해 들어봤다며, 단것을 먹을 때마다 자기 몸 안의 긴장이 완화되는듯하다고 동의한다. 그러자 Trevor는 긴장이 완화되는 것이 바로 자신이 스트레스받는 환경에서 단 음식을 먹기 시작하면 ② 자제심을 잃게 되는(lose my head) 이유라고 설명한다.

오답해설

① 단것을 먹으면 몸 안의 모든 긴장이 완화되는 것이 Trevor가 스트레스받는 상황에서 단 음식을 먹기 시작하면 '실망하게(lose heart)' 되는 이유라는 것은 맥락상 적합하지 않다.
③ Trevor는 단 음식을 먹으면 몸 안의 모든 긴장이 완화되기 때문에 스트레스가 많은 상황에서 단것을 먹으면 '신명 나게 노는(paint the town red)' 이유라고 말하는 것은 문맥상 어색하다.
④ 스트레스받는 환경에서 단 음식을 먹기 시작하면 '달걀로 바위 치는(beat my head against the wall)' 경향이 있다는 말은 옳지 않다.

해석

Shelly: 스트레스를 해소하는 너만의 방식이 뭐야?
Trevor: 나는 스트레스를 극복하는 여러 가지 방법이 있어. 그중 하나는 어마어마한 양의 단 음식을 먹는 거야.
Shelly: 오, 나 그것에 대해 들어봤어. 내가 단것을 먹을 때마다 내 몸 안의 모든 긴장감이 완화되는 것처럼 느껴져.
Trevor: 그게 바로 내가 스트레스를 받는 환경에서 단 음식을 먹게 되면 자제심을 잃는 경향이 있는 이유야.
Shelly: 네가 무슨 말 하는지 알아. 그렇지만 그것이 네 건강에 끼칠 수 있는 부정적인 영향을 조심해야 해.
Trevor: 맞아, 그래서 단 것에 대한 내 욕망을 짓누르려고 노력해.
① 실망하다
② 자제심을 잃다
③ 신명 나게 놀다
④ 달걀로 바위 치다

어휘

relieve 해소하다, 완화하다
sweets 단 음식들
alleviate 완화하다
desire 욕망
lose one's head 자제심을 잃다
beat one's head against the wall 달걀로 바위 치다
tremendous 어마어마한, 엄청난
tension 긴장
strain 짓누르다
lose heart 실망하다
paint the town red 신명 나게 놀다

05 정답 ①

정답해설

① **출제 포인트: 원급 비교**

해당 문장은 불완전 자동사 'is'의 보어로 형용사 'peaceful'을 사용한 경우로 이를 다시 원급 비교로 수식해주고 있다. always는 빈도 부사로 be 동사 뒤에 있으며, be동사는 다시 부사 not과 결합해서 isn't always로 옳게 사용된 경우이다.

Counrty life isn't always **as peaceful as** city-dwellers think
　　　　　　　　　　　　　　원급비교
that country life is peaceful.
　　문맥상 생략

오답해설

② **출제 포인트: 혼동하기 쉬운 동사**

'fallen'은 'fall'의 과거분사이며 'fall'은 완전자동사이므로 수동태로 사용할 수 없다. 또한 문맥상 '나무가 쓰러졌을 때'가 자연스러우므로 'was fallen'을 'fell'로 수정하기보다는 완전타동사 'fell(~을 베어 넘어뜨리다, 쓰러뜨리다)'의 수동태인 'was felled'로 수정해야 한다.

③ **출제 포인트: so원인 that결과 부사절 접속사/such vs. so**

'so'는 부사이므로 형용사와 부사를 수식하며 'such'는 형용사이므로 명사를 수식한다. 해당 문장은 「so+형용사/부사 ~ that+주어+동사」가 쓰인 문장으로 부사 'so'자리에 형용사 'such'를 사용하여 부사 'slowly'를 수식하고 있다. 따라서 'such'를 'so'로 수정해야 한다. 'get around to'는 '~까지 해내다'라는 의미의 관용 표현이다.

④ **출제 포인트: number of vs. amount of/one of 복수가산명사**

'one of'의 경우 목적어로 복수가산명사가 오며 또한 'the number of'도 목적어로 복수가산명사가 온다. 해당 문장은 'one of' 뒤에 단수가산명사 'cause'를 사용하였고 'the number of' 뒤에 불가산명사 'food'를 사용하였으므로 틀린 문장이다. 따라서 'cause'를 복수형태인 'causes'로 수정하고 'number'를 'amount'로 수정해야 한다.

해석

① 전원생활은 도시 거주자가 생각하는 것만큼 항상 평화로운 것은 아니다.
② 그 나무가 쓰러졌을 때 내 이웃 중 한 명은 눈물을 흘렸다.
③ 때때로 Jane은 노래를 너무 천천히 작곡해서 노래를 녹음할 시간을 결코 낼 수 없다.
④ 비만의 주요 원인 중 하나가 우리가 먹는 음식의 양이라는 것을 부인할 수 없다.

06 정답 ④

정답해설

④ **출제 포인트: 주어와 동사 수일치**

'restrict'는 'that'이 이끄는 명사절의 동사로 수일치 기준은 단수형태의 명사구 'children's exposure'이다. 따라서 'restrict'를 단수형태의 동사인 'restricts'로 수정해야 한다.

오답해설

① **출제 포인트: 접속사의 역할**

'whereas'는 접속사이므로 뒤에 완전한 형태의 절이 온다. 'whereas' 이하의 절에서 주어는 'the children', 동사는 'produced'이며 목적어는 'words'이므로 완전한 형태의 절이 왔다. 따라서 접속사 'whereas'는 옳게 사용되었다.

② **출제 포인트: 동사 vs. 준동사**

해당 문장에서 'produced'는 'produce'의 과거분사가 아니라 과거시제이며 whereas 절의 동사로 사용되었다.

③ **출제 포인트: 관계대명사의 계속적 용법/주어와 동사의 수일치**

'which'는 주격 관계대명사로 선행사는 the "visualization hypothesis'"이며 단수형태이다. 따라서 주격 관계대명사절의 동사에 단수형태인 'states'를 옳게 사용하였다.

해석

라디오를 들었던 어린이들은 더 상상력이 풍부한 응답을 한 반면에, 텔레비전을 시청했던 어린이들은 원작 이야기를 반복하는 말을 더 많이 했다. 미디어 학자들은 '시각화 가설'을 설명하기 위해 이 연구를 이용해 왔는데, 이것은 이미 만들어진 시각적 이미지에 대한 어린이들의 노출이 그들 자신의 새로운 이미지를 만들어 내는 그들의 능력을 제한한다고 진술한다.

어휘

response 응답, 반응
hypothesis 가설
restrict 제한하다, 방해하다
visualization 시각화, 구상화
state 진술하다, 말하다

오답률 TOP 2
07 정답 ④

정답해설

④ 출제 포인트: 접속사의 역할/-thing류 명사 수식/to부정사의 명사적 용법
관계대명사 'what'과 접속사 'so'를 사용하여 3개의 절을 연결하고 있고, 감정 제공 형용사(현재분사) 'amazing'이 부정대명사 'something'을 뒤에서 수식하고 있으므로 옳은 문장이다. 또한 to부정사구 'to persuade her to stop'은 가주어 'it'의 진주어로 사용된 to부정사의 명사적 용법에 해당한다.

오답해설

① 출제 포인트: 주격 관계대명사/능동태 vs. 수동태
'complete'는 완전타동사이므로 목적어를 가진다. 해당 문장은 'complete'의 과거시제인 'completed' 뒤에 목적어가 없으며 주어진 해석이 '1850년에 완공된'이므로 능동태가 아니라 수동태임을 알 수 있다. 따라서 'completed'를 'was completed'로 수정해야 한다. 또한 'which'는 주격 관계대명사로 선행사는 'The house'이다.

② 출제 포인트: enough의 위치 / 재귀대명사의 역할
해당 문장은 명령문으로 'to sustain'의 의미상 주어는 'you'임을 유추할 수 있다. 따라서 'sustain'의 목적어에 'you'를 사용할 수 없다. 생략된 명령문의 대상이 '당신' 또는 '당신들'이 될 가능성이 모두 존재하므로, 단수 주어 you인 경우라고 가정한다면, 'yourself' 또는 복수 주어 'you'라고 가정한다면, 'yourselves'로 수정해야 한다. 단, 해당 문장에서 'enough'는 형용사이므로 명사 'food'를 앞에서 수식해야 하며 'enough food'는 옳게 사용되었다.

③ 출제 포인트: not A until B/It ~ that 강조용법
주어진 해석이 'A하고 나서야 B했다'이므로 'A not until B'가 사용되었고, 'not until B'를 강조하기 위해 'It ~ that 강조용법'도 쓰인 문장임을 알 수 있다. 그러나 'not until'의 자리에 'until'만 사용하였으므로 'until' 앞에 'not'을 사용해야 한다.

오답률 TOP 1
08 정답 ②

정답해설

본문은 '북한의 인터넷 시스템'에 관한 글로써, 북한에는 두 가지 버전의 통신망이 있는데 '첫 번째는 고위층을 위한 상대적으로 자유로운 통신망이며, 두 번째는 일반 대중이 이용할 수 있는 다이얼 접속 방식의 구식 통신망'이라고 설명한다. 그 중 '광명'이라 불리는 두 번째 통신망은 "The latter is heavily curated and mostly consists of state propaganda(후자는 과도하게 관리되며 대부분 국가에 대한 선전으로 구성되어 있다)."라고 언급하고 있다. 즉, 일반 대중이 접속할 수 있는 인터넷망을 대부분 '국가 선전(state propaganda)'을 위해 이용하고 있다는 것을 알 수 있으므로, 글의 내용과 일치하는 것은 '② North Korea uses the Internet as an instrument of conveying positive messages about the nation(북한은 국가에 대한 긍정적인 메시지를 전달하는 수단으로 인터넷을 이용한다).'이다.

오답해설

① 첫 문장 "an exclusive, restriction-free model for high-ranking government officials(고위 관료들과 상류 산업에 종사하는 사람들을 위한 배타적이고 통제가 없는 모델)"를 통해 '고위 간부들이 이용하는 통신망은 통제가 없다'라는 것을 알 수 있다.

③ 본문에서 '북한에는 두 가지 버전의 인터넷이 있고, 일반 대중이 이용하는 인터넷은 다이얼 접속을 통해 접근할 수 있다'고 설명하지만, '고위 간부들이 사용하는 인터넷'의 접속 방식에 대해서는 언급하지 않고 있다. 따라서 '모든 북한 사람들은 다이얼 접속을 통해서만 인터넷에 접근할 수 있다.'는 본문과 일치하지 않는 내용이다.

④ "But its decrepit condition may not matter as most North Koreans likely can't afford it anyway(그러나 어쨌든 대부분의 북한 사람들이 그것의 비용을 감당할 수 없을 가능성이 있으므로 그것의 노후한 환경은 별로 중요하지 않을 수도 있다)."를 통해, 많은 북한인들이 인터넷을 사용하지 않는 것은 인터넷의 질이 낮기 때문이 아니라 형편 때문이라는 것을 알 수 있다. 따라서 글의 내용과 일치하지 않는다.

해석

북한은 두 가지 버전의 월드 와이드 웹을 자랑한다: 고위 관료들과 상류 산업에 종사하는 사람들을 위한 배타적이고 통제가 없는 모델과 나머지 모든 사람들을 위한 빈약한 대안이다. 후자는 과도하게 관리되며 대부분 국가에 대한 선전으로 구성되어 있다. 설상가상으로, ("광명"이라 불리는) 구식의 서비스는 90년대의 AOL과 별반 다르지 않은 다이얼 접속을 통해서만 접근이 가능하다. 그러나 어쨌든 대부분의 북한 사람들이 그것의 비용을 감당할 수 없을 가능성이 있기 때문에 그것의 노후한 환경은 별로 중요하지 않을 수도 있다. 결과적으로, 웹 사용 수치는 깜짝 놀랄 만큼 낮다: 북한 전체가 단지 1,024개의 IP주소를 보유하고 있다. 남한에서는 1억 1,232만 개의 IPv4 주소가 사용 중이며, 심지어 인구가 18,000명인 태평양의 팔라우섬에서 북한보다 더 많은 IP주소를 사용한다.

① 북한의 고위 관료만이 사용할 수 있는 통신망 또한 극심히 통제가 된다.
② 북한은 국가에 대한 긍정적인 메시지를 전달하는 수단으로 인터넷을 이용한다.
③ 모든 북한 사람들은 다이얼 접속을 통해서만 인터넷에 접근할 수 있다.
④ 일반 북한 사람들은 주로 질이 낮은 서비스 때문에 인터넷을 거의 이용하지 않는다.

어휘

boast 자랑하다, 뽐내다
restriction-free 통제가 없는
threadbare 빈약한, 초라한, 케케묵은
latter 후자
propaganda 선전
dub 별명을 붙이다
afford (금전적) 여유가 되다
entirety 전체
instrument 수단, 도구
exclusive 배타적인, 독점적인
select 상류 사회의, 고급의
alternative 대안
curate 관리하다, 조직하다
dated 구식의
decrepit 노후한, 낡은
figure 수치
restrict 제한하다, 통제하다
convey 전달하다, 전하다

오답률 TOP 3

09 정답 ②

정답해설

빈칸에는 '주가 변동(stock fluctuations)'의 영향이 제한적인 이유를 설명하는 내용이 들어가야 한다. 빈칸 이후에서 '대공황 이전 65% 이상의 미국인들이 주식을 보유하였으나, 몇 차례의 주식시장 붕괴를 경험한 후인 현재는 55%만이 주식을 보유하고 있고, 일부 조사에서는 그보다 더 낮은 주식 보유 비율을 나타내고 있다'라는 내용을 설명하고 있으므로, '과거에 비해 주식을 보유한 인구의 비율이 낮으므로 주가 변동이 직접적인 영향을 미치는 대상도 상대적으로 축소되었다'라는 것을 유추할 수 있다. 따라서 빈칸에는 '② stocks are not an important form of saving for most households (대부분의 가정에서 주식은 주요한 저축 형태가 아니다)'가 들어가는 것이 가장 자연스럽다.

오답해설

① 본문에서 언급된 주식시장 붕괴는 과거에 발생한 것이며, 현재 진행 중이 아니므로 오답이다.
③ 주식시장에 대한 규제에 대해서는 본문에 언급되지 않는다.
④ 본문의 설문 조사 결과에 따르면 과거보다 더 적은 사람들이 주식에 투자하고 있으므로, 본문의 내용과 반대되는 문장이다.

해석

주가 변동이 제한된 직접적 영향을 미치는 한 가지 이유는 <u>대부분의 가정에서 주식은 주요한 저축 형태가 아니기 때문이다</u>. 최근 갤럽 여론 조사에 따르면 미국인 중 오직 55퍼센트만이 그들 또는 가정의 구성원들이 주식을 보유하고 있다고 말한다. 다른 설문 조사들은 훨씬 더 낮은 주식시장 참여율을 보여준다. 만일 당신이 주식을 보유하고 있지 않다면, 월스트리트가 심각한 실패를 겪는다는 이유로 당신의 소비, 저축 또는 업무 계획을 변경할 이유가 거의 없다. 갤럽 여론 조사는 지난 10년간 주식 보유가 줄어들었다는 것을 나타낸다. 대공황 직전, 미국인 중 65퍼센트 이상이 주식을 보유하고 있다고 답했다. 분명, 2000~2002년 그리고 2008년의 두 번의 주식시장 붕괴가 위험성에 대한 저축자들의 기호를 위축시킨 것이다.
① 미국에서 극심한 주식시장 위기가 현재 진행 중이다
② 대부분의 가정에서 주식은 주요한 저축 형태가 아니다
③ 주식시장에 대한 정부의 규제가 더 엄격해졌다
④ 주식시장에 투자하는 사람들의 수가 증가했다

어휘

fluctuation 변동, 오르내림
reverse 실패, 좌절, 후퇴
appetite 기호, 좋아함
equity 주식
shrink 줄다, 감소하다

10 정답 ②

정답해설

본문의 마지막 두 문장 "The past is gone and cannot be undone. All you have is the here and now and it is the only place where you can make a difference(과거는 지나갔고 되돌릴 수 없다. 당신이 가지고 있는 것은 현재이며, 이것이 당신이 차이를 만들 수 있는 유일한 곳이다)."를 통해 '과거는 이미 지나갔고 바꿀 수 없으며, 오직 현재만이 변화를 만들 수 있는 유일한 때이다'라고 설명하며 '현재를 사는 것의 중요성'에 대해 언급하고 있다. 따라서 글의 요지로 가장 적절한 것은 "② Live in the present moment(현재의 순간을 살아라)."이다.

오답해설

① 본문은 '과거에 매달리지 말고, 과거로부터 얻은 교훈을 통해 현재를 사는 것에 집중하라'라고 서술하고 있으므로, '과거를 있는 그대로 받아들여라'라는 문장은 글의 전체 요지로 적절하지 않다.
③ 본문에서 '과거로부터 교훈을 얻으라'는 내용이 언급되지만, 본문의 요점이 교훈을 얻는 것에 초점이 맞추어진 것이 아니며 '교훈을 얻은 후 과거를 잊으라(Once you have learned from the past, it is time to let it go.)'고 서술하고 있으므로 글의 요지로 적절하지 않다.
④ 미래에 대한 내용은 본문에 언급되지 않으므로 오답이다.

해석

현재를 살아갈 때, 당신은 삶이 이루어지는 곳에 살고 있다. 죄책감과 후회로 가득한 채로 과거에 대해 깊이 생각할 의미가 없다. 당신이 현재를 살 때, 당신은 과거의 사건으로부터 얻을 수 있는 교훈을 발견하고, 당신이 배운 것을 실행한다. 일단 과거로부터 교훈을 얻었다면, 이제 당신이 그것을 보내 줄 때이다. 그것은 목적을 다 한 것이다. 그것에 감사하고 이별을 고하라. 과거에 대해 지속적으로 생각하고 그것에 매달림으로써, 당신은 과거의 판단을 당신에게 가져오게 된다. 이것은 당신의 사고와 현재 발생하고 있는 것을 처리하는 당신의 능력에 영향을 끼친다. 과거는 지나갔고 되돌릴 수 없다. 당신이 가지고 있는 것은 현재이며, 이것이 당신이 차이를 만들 수 있는 유일한 곳이다.
① 과거를 있는 그대로 받아들여라.
② 현재의 순간을 살아라.
③ 과거로부터 교훈을 얻어라.
④ 과거가 아닌 미래를 바라보라.

어휘

the here and now 현시점, 현재
dwell on …을 곱씹다[깊게 생각하다]
implement 실행하다
cling on to …에 매달리다, 달라붙다
occur 일어나다, 발생하다
identify 확인하다, 발견하다
mull over …에 대해 곰곰이 생각하다

결국엔 성정혜 영어 하프모의고사
기적사 DAY 60

01	②	02	②	03	④	04	③	05	②
06	①	07	②	08	③	09	③	10	③

01 정답 ②

정답해설

밑줄 친 단어는 '악의적인'의 의미이고, 유의어로는 ② malignant가 적절하다.

해석

그 중국인들은 대부분 석탄 연소와 **악의적인** 산업의 덤핑 관행으로부터 고통 받는다.
① 보통의
② 악의가 있는
③ 옳은
④ 솔직한, 똑바른

어휘

mediocre 보통의
correct 옳은
malignant 악의가 있는
forthright 솔직한, 똑바른

02 정답 ②

정답해설

주어진 빈칸에는 문맥상 '공모하다'가 적절하므로 ② collude가 정답이다.

해석

그가 쓰고 감독한 새로운 영화로, 그는 사법당국이 그들의 사익을 위해 국제적이고 정확한 범위에 걸쳐 범죄 조직과 **공모하는**, 그의 특징적인 영화 세계를 확장시켰다.
① 인수하다
② 공모하다
③ 분간하다, 인정하다
④ 물에 잠기게 하다, 압도하다, 쇄도하다

어휘

take over 인수하다
collude 공모하다
recognize 분간하다, 인정하다
swamp 물에 잠기게 하다, 압도하다, 쇄도하다

03 정답 ④

정답해설

주어진 빈칸에는 문맥상 '벗어나다'가 적절하므로 ④ deviate가 정답이다.

해석

힙합 사운드트랙을 가진 그 전시회는 또한 젊은 사람들의 요동치는 내부 세계와 존재하는 규범들을 **벗어나고자** 하는 그들의 욕망의 이미지를 특징으로 삼는다.
① 기가 죽다
② 물에 잠기다
③ 누그러지다, 완화되다
④ 벗어나다, 일탈하다

어휘

turbulent 사나운, 동요한
submerge 물에 잠기게 하다, 매몰시키다
moderate 누그러지다, 완화되다
daunt 기가 죽다
deviate 벗어나다, 일탈하다

04 정답 ③

정답해설

A는 B와 모나리자에 관해 이야기한다. 2년 전에 파리를 방문해 루브르 박물관을 갔다는 A에게 B는 모나리자를 본 경험이 있는지 질문한다. A는 본 적이 있다며 상상했던 것보다 훨씬 아름다웠다고 한다. B는 (A) '그런 말은 듣지 않아도 알 수 있다(Tell me about it)'이라고 말하며 사람들이 사진 찍으려고 줄을 서는 이유가 있다고 얘기한다. A는 B의 말에 동의하며, (B) '이제야 이야기가 된다(Now you're talking)'라고 하면서 파리를 다시 방문할 기회가 있다면 모나리자를 보기 위해 루브르 박물관으로 직행할 것이라고 말한다.

오답해설

① (B) 사람들이 모나리자 사진을 찍기 위해 줄을 서는 이유가 있다는 A의 말에 B는 동의하면서 '이제야 말이 된다(Now you're talking)'라는 관용 표현을 발화한다. 'say (말하다)'는 'talk (말하다)'와 달리, 타동사이기 때문에 빈칸에 들어갈 말로 적절하지 않다.
② (A) A는 2년 전에 모나리자를 봤을 때 상상했던 것보다 훨씬 더 아름다웠다고 말한다. B는 A의 말에 공감하며 '정말 그래 (Tell me about it)'라고 말한다. 'say (말하다)'는 사람을 목적어로 하지 않는 타동사이기 때문에 빈칸에 들어갈 답으로 옳지 않다.
④ (A) 'Talk (말하다)'는 일방적인 전달보다는 주고받는 대화에 적절한 동사이므로 (A)의 빈칸에 적합하지 않다. (B) 'telling (말하는)'은 목적어를 필수로 하는 타동사이기 때문에 목적어가 없는 (B)의 빈칸에 올 답으로 알맞지 않다.

해석

A: 내가 2년 전에 파리를 방문했을 때 루브르 박물관을 갔어.
B: 모나리자 봤어?
A: 물론이지. 그것은 내가 상상했던 것보다 훨씬 더 아름다웠어.
B: (A) <u>그런 말을 듣지 않아도 알고 있어</u>. 사람들이 사진 찍으려고 줄 서는 이유가 있어.
A: (B) <u>드디어 이야기되네</u>. 내가 파리를 재방문할 기회가 있다면 나는 모나리자를 위해 루브르 박물관으로 직행할 거야.
B: 좋은 생각이야. 그것은 의심할 여지 없이 두 번 볼 가치가 있어.

	(A)	(B)
①	말하다	말하는
②	말하다	말하는
③	말하다	말하는
④	말하다	말하는

어휘

gorgeous 아름다운
worth 가치
doubtlessly 의심의 여지가 없는
Now you're talking 이제야 말이 되다

오답률 TOP 3
05 정답 ②

정답해설

② 출제 포인트: 혼동하기 쉬운 동사

해당 문장에서 'lay'는 완전타동사가 아닌 완전자동사 'lie'의 과거형으로 옳게 사용되었으며, 이때 'remained'는 완전자동사로 사용되었음에 유의해야 한다.

오답해설

① 출제 포인트: 불완전자동사의 주격 보어/so 원인+that 결과 부사절의 접속사

불완전자동사 'seem'은 부사를 주격 보어로 가질 수 없다. 해당 문장은 'seems'의 주격 보어로 부사구 'such attractively'를 사용하였으므로 틀린 문장이다. 이때 형용사로 쓰이는 'such'는 명사만 수식하므로 'such attractively'를 'so attractive'로 수정해야 한다. 또한 'it would be ridiculous to say no'는 접속사 'that'이 생략된 부사절임에 유의해야 한다.

③ 출제 포인트: 형용사 vs. 부사/number of vs. amount of

부사는 명사를 수식할 수 없다. 해당 문장은 부사 'certainly'가 명사 'amount'를 수식하므로 틀린 문장이다. 따라서 'certainly'를 형용사 'certain'으로 수정해야 한다. 또한 'a certain amount of' 뒤에 목적어로 불가산명사 'noise'가 옳게 사용되었다.

④ 출제 포인트: 원급 비교

「as+원급+as」는 원급 비교 구문으로 원급자리에 비교급을 사용할 수 없다. 해당 문장은 「as+원급+as」가 쓰인 문장으로 원급자리에 비교급 'drier'를 사용하였으므로 틀린 문장이다. 따라서 'drier'를 원급 'dry'로 수정해야 한다.

해석

① 그 거래는 매우 매력적으로 보여서 아니라고 말하는 것은 말도 안 된다.
② 그녀는 고통과 좌절감에 울부짖었고, 누워 있던 곳에 그대로 있었다.
③ 시가지에 산다면, 일정한 양의 소음을 예상해야 한다.
④ 땅이 뼈처럼 말라 있기 때문에 나는 그가 이 식물들에 물을 주었다고 생각하지 않는다.

오답률 TOP 1
06 정답 ①

정답해설

① 출제 포인트: 형용사 관용 표현

'acquainted'는 전치사 'from'과 결합할 수 없으며 전치사 'with'와 결합하여 '~을 알고 있는'을 나타낸다. 따라서 'from'을 'with'로 수정해야 한다.

오답해설

② 출제 포인트: a number of vs. an amount of/타동사구[완전타동사+목적어+전치사+목적어]

「provide+목적어[사물]+for+목적어[대상]」을 옳게 사용하였고 'a number of' 뒤에 복수 가산명사인 'publications'를 옳게 사용하였다.

③ 출제 포인트: 수여동사 gain

해당 문장에서 'gained'는 수여동사로 사용되어 간접목적어 'him'과 직접목적어 'many commissions'를 가진다.

④ 출제 포인트: 관계부사

관계부사 'where'가 이끄는 절은 완전한 형태이다. 해당 문장에서 'where'이 이끄는 절 'he eventually settled'는 완전한 문장으로 옳게 사용되었다. 또한 'settled'는 'settle'의 과거형으로 해당 문장에서는 완전자동사로 사용되었다.

해석

네덜란드에서 Ehret은 스웨덴의 박물학자인 Carl Linnaeus를 알게 되었다. Linnaeus와 다른 사람들과의 공동 작업을 통해 Ehret은 수많은 중요한 원예 출판물에 삽화들을 제공했다. 과학적 정확성에 대한 Ehret의 명성은 특히 영국에서 부유한 후원자들로부터 많은 그림 제작 의뢰를 받게 했고, 그는 결국 그곳에 정착했다.

어휘

Holland 네덜란드
illustration 삽화
collaboration 공동 작업
acquainted with ~을 알고 있는
horticultural 원예의
patron 후원자, 고객

오답률 TOP 2
07 정답 ②

정답해설

② 출제 포인트: 전치사+관계대명사/능동태 vs. 수동태

「전치사+관계대명사」가 쓰인 문장으로 관계대명사 'which'의 선행사는 'the local grammar school'이다. 또한 주어진 해석이 '교육을 받았다'이므로 수동태 'was educated'를 적절하게 사용하였다. 또한 'went on'은 '자동사+부사' 표현으로 '계속하다'의 의미에 해당된다. 해당 문장에서 'on'은 부사이므로 전치사와 혼동하지 말아야 한다.

오답해설

① 출제 포인트: 접속사의 역할/-thing류 명사 수식

접속사 없이 두 개의 절이 연결되어 있으므로 틀린 문장이다. 따라서 주어진 해석에 맞게 'I know' 앞에 접속사 'but'을 사용해야 한다. 또한 to부정사구 'to do with computers'는 부정대명사 'something'을 뒤에서 수식하고 있는 to부정사의 형용사적 용법으로 사용되었다.

③ 출제 포인트: not A until B / It ~ that 강조용법

해당 문장은 'John discovered they were going for two weeks to New York not until they had just left the Church.'에서 부사절에 해당되는 'not until they had just left the Church'를 강조하기 위해 'It ~ that 강조용법'을 사용하고 있다. 따라서 'which'를 'that'으로 수정해야 한다. 'It ~ that 강조 용법'의 경우 'that'이 문장에서 관계사를 대신하는 경우이기 때문에 부사절인 'not until 주어+동사~'를 강조하는 경우에는 'that'대신에 관계부사 'when'을 사용할 수도 있는 점에 유의하자.

④ 출제 포인트: enough의 위치

주어진 해석을 통해 'enough'가 형용사이며 명사 'families'를 수식해야 한다는 것을 알 수 있다. 따라서 'enough'를 'families' 앞으로 이동해야 한다.

08 정답 ③

정답해설

해당 지문은 '당장 눈앞의 걱정으로 인해 어떤 것을 미루게 되면 더 큰 걱정에 직면할 수 있다'고 설명하고 있다. 주어진 문장의 'procrastination or an inability to make a decision(미루는 버릇 또는 결정 장애)'을 (B)에서 'If you are putting something off ~ (당신이 무언가를 미룬다면)'를 이용해 가리키고 있으므로 주어진 문장 이후에는 (B)가 위치하는 것이 가장 적절하고, '미루는 것의 단기적인 효과'를 설명한 (B) 이후에는 '장기적인 측면(in the long run)'에서 미루는 것의 효과를 설명하고 있는 (A)가 와야 한다. 그리고 (A)를 근거로 하여, '미루지 말고 걱정거리를 받아들이고 처리하라'라고 조언해주는 (C)가 이어지는 것이 문맥상 가장 자연스럽다. 따라서 정답은 '③ (B) - (A) - (C)'이다.

오답해설

①, ② (A)의 'However(그러나)'로 보아 이전에 (A)의 내용과 대조되는 문장이 등장해야 한다는 것을 알 수 있다. 따라서 주어진 문장에 (A)가 바로 이어지는 것은 어색하다.
나머지 선지는 문맥상 어색하므로 오답이다.

해석

때때로 우리의 걱정거리는 미루는 버릇 또는 결정 장애로부터 야기된다.
(B) 당신이 무언가를 미룬다면, 걱정은 정면으로 맞닥뜨리는 것을 피하는 방법으로서 작용한다.
(A) 그러나, 장기적으로 걱정과 예상은 실제로 당신이 문제를 처리할 때보다 당신을 훨씬 더 불안하게 만들 수 있다.
(C) 그러므로 당신의 걱정거리를 받아들여라. 문제를 처리하기 위해 당신이 필요한 단계를 밟아감으로써 걱정을 멈추어라.

어휘

procrastination 미루는 버릇, 지연
anticipation 예상
put off 미루다, 연기하다
head-on 정면으로
inability 무능, 불능
anxious 불안한, 걱정하는
face 맞닥뜨리다, 부딪치다, 직면하다

09 정답 ③

정답해설

해당 지문은 '걱정이 건강에 미치는 영향'에 대해 설명하고 있다. 본문 초반 "People who worry are more likely to seek preventative care like yearly check-ups, mammograms, colonoscopies, and even wear more sunscreen, she says(걱정하는 사람들은 연간 건강검진, 유방 X선 사진 촬영, 대장 내시경 검사와 같은 예방적인 치료를 받을 가능성이 더 높고, 심지어 선크림을 더 많이 바른다고 그녀는 말한다)."와 "A little worry can also spur you to make a plan to help with current problems, like losing weight or cleaning up your diet(약간의 걱정은 또한 당신이 체중을 줄이는 것이나 식단을 정화하는 것과 같은 현재의 문제에 도움이 될 계획을 세우도록 자극할 수 있다)."를 통해 적당한 양의 걱정이 건강에 주는 긍정적인 측면을 언급한 후, 이후 "But there's a fine line between acting on your worries to prevent future problems and becoming a full-blown hypochondriac(그러나 미래의 문제를 예방하기 위해 걱정에 따라 행동하는 것과 완전한 심기증 환자가 되는 것은 종이 한 장 차이이다)."이라고 언급하며, '너무 많은 걱정이 부정적 영향을 미칠 수도 있다'라고 설명하고 있다. 따라서 글의 요지로 가장 적절한 것은 '③ A modest amount of worry can be helpful for your health(적당한 양의 걱정은 건강에 도움이 될 수 있다).'이다.

오답해설

① 글의 내용과 관련 없는 문장이므로 오답이다.
② 본문 후반에서 '너무 많은 걱정을 하면 병원에 가는 것에 대해 두려움을 느낄 수도 있다'라고 언급하고 있으나, 본문 초반에서 '적당한 걱정은 예방적인 치료를 받거나 현재의 문제에 도움이 될 계획을 세울 수 있는 자극제가 될 수 있다'고도 설명하고 있으므로, 걱정에는 긍정적인 영향과 부정적인 영향이 모두 있을 수 있다는 것을 알 수 있다. 따라서 글의 요지로 부적절하다.
④ 글의 내용과 관련 없는 문장이므로 오답이다.

해석

가슴의 통증을 느끼거나 심하게 넘어졌는가? 당신 신체의 가장 최초의 반응 중 하나는 걱정하는 것이다. 그리고 Shelly Smith-Acuña 박사에 따르면 그것은 좋은 것이다. 걱정하는 사람들은 연간 건강검진, 유방 X선 사진 촬영, 대장 내시경 검사와 같은 예방적인 치료를 받을 가능성이 더 높고, 심지어 선크림을 더 많이 바른다고 그녀는 말한다. 약간의 걱정은 또한 당신이 체중을 줄이는 것이나 식단을 정화하는 것과 같은 현재의 문제에 도움이 될 계획을 세우도록 자극할 수 있다. 그러나 미래의 문제를 예방하기 위해 걱정에 따라 행동하는 것과 완전한 심기증 환자가 되는 것은 종이 한 장 차이이다. 그녀는 "'Dr. Google'"을 지속적으로 확인하지 말고, 대신에 당신의 주치의와 같이 당신을 도울 수 있는 사람들에게 연락하라."라고 말한다. "그리고 너무 많이 걱정을 하여 반대의 효과를 초래하고, 이에 따라 당신이 병원에 가는 것을 두려워하게 만들지 말라."

① 당신은 병원에 가는 것을 두려워해서는 안 된다.
② 걱정은 삶의 질에 부정적인 영향을 미칠 수 있다.
③ 적당한 양의 걱정은 건강에 도움이 될 수 있다.
④ 발생하지 않은 일에 대해 걱정하는 것은 불필요하다.

어휘

twinge 찌릿한 통증
take a fall 넘어지다, 떨어지다
mammogram 유방조영상(유방암 검진용 X선 촬영)
colonoscopy 대장내시경검사, 결장경 검사(법)
spur 원동력[자극제]이 되다, 자극하다
act on …에 따라 행동하다[조치를 취하다]
full-blown …의 모든 특성을 갖춘, 완전히 발달한[진행된]
hypochondriac 심기증 환자
follow up with someone …에게 연락을 취하다
opposite 반대의
nasty 끔찍한
preventative 예방적인
constantly 지속적으로, 계속하여
modest 적당한

10 정답 ③

정답해설

본문 전반적으로 '미국의 주택 시장의 붕괴'에 대해 설명하며, 그에 대한 여파를 서술하고 있다. 본문 마지막에서 'the housing collapse in the United States is commonly considered as the trigger for the global financial crisis(미국의 주택가격 붕괴는 보통 세계 금융위기의 계기로 여겨진다)'라고 언급하고 있으므로, '세계 금융위기를 일으킨 원인'에 대한 글이라는 것을 알 수 있다. 따라서 정답은 '③ Global Financial Crisis: What May Have Caused It?(세계 금융위기: 무엇이 그것을 야기했을까?)'이다.

오답해설

①, ② 본문과 관련 없는 내용이므로 오답이다.
④ 세계 금융위기가 발생하기 이전의 상황을 설명하는 글이므로, 본문의 제목으로 적절하지 않다.

해석

서브프라임 론을 받은 많은 주택 소유자들이 자신들의 모기지 대출금을 상환하지 못한다는 것을 깨닫게 됨에 따라 미국 주택 시장은 크게 타격을 받았다. 주택의 가치가 폭락함에 따라 수많은 대출자들이 자신들이 역자산 상태에 있다는 것을 깨달았다. 수많은 대출자들이 채무를 불이행했고 은행들은 압류한 주택과 토지가 그들이 대출을 승인해줄 그 당시보다 시장에서 가치가 더 낮게 떨어진 상황에 직면하게 되었다. 은행들은 유동성 위기라는 부담을 지게 되었고, 서브프라임 대출 거품이 붕괴됨에 따라 주택 대출을 승인하고 획득하는 것이 점점 더 어렵게 되었다. 이것은 일반적으로 2007-08년 신용경색이라 칭해지며, 미국의 주택가격 붕괴는 보통 세계 금융위기의 계기로 여겨진다.

① 서브프라임 론은 어떻게 작동하는가?
② 주택 시장을 규제하는 것의 중요성
③ 세계 금융위기: 무엇이 그것을 야기했을까?
④ 세계 금융위기의 여파는 무엇인가?

어휘

- repayment 상환(금)
- default on …의 이행을 게을리하다
- liquidity 유동성
- on one's hands …의 책임[부담]이 되어
- collapse 붕괴
- regulate 규제하다
- plummet 수직으로 떨어지다
- repossess 압류하다
- trigger 계기, 도화선
- aftereffect 여파

결국엔 성정혜 영어 하프모의고사
기적사 복습 모의고사 6회

01	②	02	②	03	①	04	④	05	①
06	①	07	①	08	①	09	①	10	④
11	②	12	①	13	②	14	④	15	③
16	②	17	②	18	①	19	③	20	②

01 정답 ② Day 55-01

정답해설

밑줄 친 단어는 '악명이 높은'의 의미로 사용되었고, 유의어로는 ② disreputable이 적절하다.

해석

"인간은 큰 수로 모여 있는 동물의 수를 추정하는 것에 형편없고 서두르기로 **악명이 높다**," Perryman은 설명한다.
① 조화시킬 수 있는
② 평판이 안 좋은
③ 기이한, 이국풍의
④ 가난한, 가지지 않은

02 정답 ② Day 60-01

정답해설

밑줄 친 단어는 '악의적인'의 의미이고, 유의어로는 ② malignant가 적절하다.

해석

그 중국인들은 대부분 석탄 연소와 **악의적인** 산업의 덤핑 관행으로부터 고통받는다.
① 보통의
② 악의가 있는
③ 옳은
④ 솔직한, 똑바른

03 정답 ① Day 51-02

정답해설

'at the drop of a hat'은 '즉시'라는 뜻을 가지며, 이와 유사한 의미를 가지는 것은 ① immediately이다.

해석

그 회사는 내가 집과 가족을 **즉시** 이사시키는 것을 기대할 수 없다.
① 즉시
② 시간대로, 늦지 않게
③ 주저하면서, 말을 더듬으며
④ 정기적으로

04 정답 ④ Day 54-02

정답해설

주어진 빈칸에는 문맥상 '이용하다'가 적절하다. 따라서 정답은 ④ draws on이다.

해석
일본의 구 관할 경찰서는 사람들에게 모르는 번호로 걸려 오는 전화를 즉시 받지 말라고 주의를 주기 위해 만화 캐릭터들을 **이용한다**.
① 폭로하다, 자백하다, ~인 체하다
② 보상하다
③ 고용하다, 떠맡다
④ 이용하다

05 정답 ① — Day 52-06

정답해설
① 출제 포인트: It ~ that 강조용법
해당 문장은 「It ~ that」 강조 구문과 주격 관계대명사절 두 가지 경우로 볼 수 있다.
1. 「It ~ that」 강조 구문
   Jane's car got broken into last Friday night. (Jane's car를 강조)
   It was Jane's car that got broken into last Friday night. (이때 that은 which로 바꾸어 사용할 수 있다.)
2. 주격 관계대명사절
   It was Jane's car. + Jane's car got broken into last Friday night. (Jane's car를 선행사)
   It was Jane's car that got broken into last Friday night. (이때 that은 which로 바꾸어 사용할 수 있다.)

따라서 해당 문장은 「It ~ that」 강조 구문으로 보아도 옳은 문장이고 주격 관계대명사절로 보아도 옳은 문장이다.

해석
① 지난 금요일 밤에 망가진 것은 Jane의 차이다.
② 그녀는 오늘날 건축가들이 지적이고 공간 효율적인 건물을 설계하는 것을 본다.
③ 그것이 아무리 가치가 있다고 해도 그녀가 그 법안을 의회에서 통과시키는 데 성공할 것 같지 않다.
④ 이전 종업원들에 따르면, 투자 부족은 여러 해 동안 계속되고 있다.

06 정답 ① — Day 57-05

정답해설
① 출제 포인트: 혼동하기 쉬운 동사
'laying'은 완전타동사 'lay(~을 놓다)'의 현재분사이며 뒤에 목적어 'an arm'을 사용하였으므로 옳은 문장이다. 또한 'sighed'는 'sigh'의 과거형으로 '한숨 쉬다'의 의미를 가지고 있으며 해당 문장에서는 완전자동사로 쓰였다.

해석
① John은 내 어깨에 팔을 살며시 올려놓고 한숨을 쉬었다.
② 음악은 많은 사람들에게 엄청난 양의 즐거움을 준다.
③ 왜 이것이 오리지널만큼 좋은 영화일 수 없는지 분명한 이유가 없다.
④ 모든 것이 너무 빠르게 발생해서 그녀는 모든 정보를 좀처럼 받아들일 수 없었다.

07 정답 ① — Day 53-05

정답해설
① 출제 포인트: 최상급 대용표현
「비교급+than+any other 단수 가산명사」는 최상급 대용표현에 해당한다. 해당 문장은 최상급 대용표현을 사용하였으나 'any other' 뒤에 복수 가산명사 'countries'를 사용하였으므로 틀린 문장이다. 따라서 'countries'를 단수형태 'country'로 수정해야 한다. 또한 'any other countries'를 'the other countries'로 사용하는 것도 옳다.

08 정답 ② — Day 56-07

정답해설
② 출제 포인트: not A until B/It ~ that 강조용법
「It is ~ that」 강조 구문의 형태로, 'not until ~ math test'를 강조한 구문이다. 원래 문장은 'He did not decide to study hard until when he failed the math test.'이다.

09 정답 ① — Day 52-04

정답해설
A는 B에게 어젯밤에 무슨 꿈을 꾸었는지 묻는다. B는 A의 질문에 자기의 꿈은 승무원이 되는 것이었다고 답변한다. B가 말한 '꿈(dream)'은 장래희망의 의미로 사용한 것이므로 A가 한 질문 의도에 어긋난다.

해석
① A: 너 어젯밤에 무슨 꿈 꿨어?
   B: 내 꿈은 미래에 승무원이 되는 것이야.
② A: 네 팔꿈치에 상처 났어.
   B: 어쩐지 많이 아프더라.
③ A: 너 동물원 가본 적 있어?
   B: 나 되게 어렸을 적에 가봤어.
④ A: 가장 가까운 우체국이 어디 있는지 알아?
   B: 두 구역 직진하고 첫 번째 모퉁이에서 왼쪽으로 가.

10 정답 ④ — Day 57-04

정답해설
A는 B에게 쇼핑을 가야 한다며 대화를 시작한다. B는 A에게 살 것이 있는지 묻는다. A는 자신이 어제 옷장을 살펴보다가 '귀향 파티(homecoming party)'에 입고 갈 것이 없다는 것을 깨달았다고 한다. B는 귀향 파티에 대해 완전히 잊고 있었다며, 베스트 드레서로 선정되고 싶다고 한다. 그러자 A는 자신도 마찬가지라고 B의 말에 동의하면서, 그러면 둘은 그날 '④ 최상의 옷을 차려입어야(be dressed up to the nines)' 한다고 말한다.

해석
A: 나는 이번 주말에 쇼핑을 가야 해.
B: 너 뭐 좀 사야 해?
A: 내가 어제 내 옷장을 살펴봤는데, 내가 귀향 파티에 입고 갈 옷이 아무것도 없다는 것을 깨달았어.
B: 오, 나는 귀향 파티에 대해 완전히 잊고 있었어. 나는 베스트 드레서로 선정되고 싶어.
A: 나도. 그러면 우린 그날 최상의 옷을 차려입어야 해.
B: 우리 같이 쇼핑가야겠다.
① 평화를 구하다, 무기를 거두다, 화해하다
② 허풍을 떨다
③ 목이 쉬다
④ 최상의 옷을 차려입다

11 정답 ② Day 55-10

정답해설

본문에서 세 번째 문장 "Back in 1782, when cotton mills were powered by water, Richard Arkwright opened the innovative – and the world's first – steam-driven textile mill in Manchester(면직 공장이 물로부터 동력을 얻던 시절인 1782년 Richard Arkwright가 혁신적이고 세계 최초의 증기로 동력을 얻는 직물 공장을 Manchester에 열었다)."를 통해 '물로 동력을 얻는 면직 공장은 1782년 이전에도 있었고, Arkwright가 Manchester에 최초로 세운 공장은 증기 동력 직물 공장인 것을 알 수 있으므로, 글의 내용과 일치하지 않는 것은 "② Arkwright established Manchester's first cotton mill driven by water(Arkwright는 Manchester 최초의 물로 움직이는 면직 공장을 설립했다)."이다.

해석

19세기 Manchester는 면 무역과 직물 산업의 국제 중심이라는 지위를 지녔다. 그곳은 면의 도시라는 것이 매우 잘 알려져 있어서 'Cottonopolis'라는 별칭이 붙었다. 면직 공장이 물로부터 동력을 얻던 시절인 1782년 Richard Arkwright가 혁신이고 세계 최초의 증기로 동력을 얻는 직물 공장을 Manchester에 열었다. 직물 제조업이 가정으로부터 대규모의 공장으로 옮겨 감에 따라 Manchester와 주변 도시들은 세계에서 단연 가장 크고 가장 생산적인 면방적의 중심지가 되었다. 1871년 전 세계 면 생산의 32%가 Manchester에서 이루어졌다. Arkwright가 상징적인 공장을 세운지 200년 이상이 지난 후, 여전히 작동하는 공장은 없지만 Manchester는 여전히 면에 의해 형성된 도시이다. Great Manchester에는 여전히 면직 산업에 종사하는 약 5,000명의 사람들이 있다. Manchester의 방적의 도시로서의 과거는 건물에서 찾아볼 수 있다: 개조된 공장이 사무실, 호텔, 그리고 아파트로서 새 유리 같이 반짝거리는 고층 건물들과 나란히 하며 새 삶을 찾았다.
① Manchester는 1800년대에 면으로 알려져 있었다.
② Arkwright는 Manchester 최초의 물로 움직이는 면직 공장을 설립했다.
③ Manchester는 한때 세계 면 생산량의 30% 이상을 생산했다.
④ 오늘날 Manchester에 사는 사람들은 면직 공장에서 일하지 않는다.

12 정답 ① Day 52-10

정답해설

본문은 'St. Louis에서 매년 여름 실시하는 무료 급식 프로그램인 Schools Out Café'에 대해 소개하고 있다. 두 번째 문장 "Every summer, Schools Out Café provides free breakfast and lunch to daycare centers, recreation programs, churches, and other organizations which then serve those meals to young people(매년 여름 Schools Out Café는 음식을 젊은이들에게 배식할 어린이집, 레크리에이션 프로그램, 교회, 그리고 기타 기관들에 무료 아침과 점심을 제공한다)."에서 해당 프로그램이 '매년 여름(Every summer)'에 실시된다고 언급하고 있으므로, '정기적인(regular) 행사'라는 것을 유추할 수 있다. 따라서 글의 주제로 가장 적절한 것은 '① a regular meal program(정기 급식 프로그램)'이다.

해석

이번 주 Lyda Krewson 시장은 Schools Out Café라고 알려진 청소년을 위한 시의 여름 급식 프로그램의 시작을 발표했다. 매년 여름 Schools Out Café는 음식을 젊은이들에게 배식할 어린이집, 레크리에이션 프로그램, 교회, 그리고 기타 기관들에 무료 아침과 점심을 제공한다. St. Louis의 학생들 중 약 80~90%가 무료 또는 할인 급식에 등록되어 있는데, 이는 여름 동안 영양이 충분한 음식에의 규칙적인 접근 기회가 부족하다는 주요 지표이다. "배고픈 학교들이 여름 동안 문을 닫을 때도 쉬지 않습니다."라고 Krewson은 말했다. "저는 또한 음식 배급 장소가 되길 자원한 모든 단체와 기관에 매우 감사드립니다. 그러나 우리는 항상 더 많은 곳을 찾고 있습니다. 젊은이들에게 식사를 기꺼이 배급할 어느 기관이든지 우리에게 연락주시길 바랍니다. 우리가 음식을 제공할 것입니다."
① 정기 급식 프로그램
② 학교 급식의 중요성
③ St. Louis의 젊은이들을 위한 장소
④ 학교 급식 서비스의 문제점

13 정답 ② Day 53-09

정답해설

주어진 문장 "Science has defined the modern era in many ways ~(과학은 여러 방식으로 현대 시대를 정의했고)"를 통해 '현대 시대에서의 과학의 역할'에 대해 언급하고 있다. 이어서 이어질 문장으로는 '과학에 의해 정의된 현대성의 특징(The key features of modernity, specialization and technology ~)'에 대해 언급하는 (A)가 이어지는 것이 적절하며, 이후 'But (그러나)'을 이용해 앞서 언급된 내용과는 대조되는 논점을 제시하며, '과학이 현대 세계를 이끈 반면, 인간의 의미 추구를 위태롭게 만들기도 했다'라고 서술하는 (C)가 이어지는 것이 자연스럽다. 마지막으로 (B)의 "This is the case because ~"를 이용해, (C)에서 언급된 내용의 근거를 설명하고 있으므로 (C)에 (B)가 이어지는 것이 적절하다. 따라서 정답은 '② (A) – (C) – (B)'이다.

해석

과학은 여러 방식으로 현대 시대를 정의했고, 현대 시대에서 진정으로 우세한 지식 패러다임이다.
(A) 과학에 의해 정의된 현대성의 주요 특징인 전문화와 기술은 Galileo와 Kepler 시대 이래로 지난 400년 동안의 과학 기술과 지식의 놀라운 발전에 의해 가능해졌다.
(C) 그러나 과학이 매우 실제적이고 직접적인 방식으로 우리를 현대 세계로 데려다준 반면, 그것은 또한 우리를 인간의 끊임없는 의미 추구가 위태로워진 지점까지 데려왔다.
(B) 오늘날의 과학적 세계관이 우주에서 우리의 공간에 대한 질문, 의식의 본질, 그리고 신, 목적, 및 여러 다른 심오한 주제에 관한 질문들을 포함해 인간이 지속적으로 중요하다고 생각했던 많은 탐구들의 중요성을 부인하는 것처럼 보이기 때문에 이것은 사실이다.

14 정답 ④ Day 55-08

정답해설

해당 지문은 '선지자들은 비즈니스 분야에서 종종 찾아볼 수 있다'라고 주장하며, 그러한 선지자의 대표적인 예로 영국 사업가 James Dyson을 제시하고 있다. 주어진 문장의 'them'이 가리키는 대상을 ④ 이전 문장 "We call them prophets, visionaries, or oracles(우리는 그들은 예언자, 선지자 또는 현인이라 부른다)."에서 찾을 수 있으며, 또한 주어진 문장에서 'in the realm of business(비즈니스계에서)'에서 '선지자(them)'를 찾을 수 있다고 언급하고 있는데, 이에 해당하는 인물의 예(James Dyson)를 ④ 이후 문장에서 최초로 언급하고 있다. 따라서 주어진 문장이 들어가기에 가장 적절한 곳은 ④이다.

해석

우리들 중 실용주의자들은 미래를 들여다보는 것을 불가능하다고 말할 것이다. (①) 그들은 능글맞게 웃으며 수정 구슬과 우리의 운명을 예언하는 인간의 손바닥의 지워지지 않는 선은 없다고 말할 것이다. (②) 우리들 중 나머지는 실제로 내일 무엇이 일어날지를 예언할 수 있는 사람들이 있다고 믿는다. (③) 우리는 그들을 예언자, 선지자 또는 현인이라 부른다. (④ **그리고**

우리는 종종 인간이 실제로 그들이 상상하는 미래를 창조해 낼 수 있는 얼마 되지 않는 분야 중 하나인 비즈니스계에서 그들을 발견한다.) 이러한 예언자들 중 가장 놀라운 사람 중 하나는 영국인 사업가 James Dyson이다. Dyson이 그것들을 생각해내기 이전에는 모두 *Jetsons*과 같은 시대의 허구였던 Dyson의 기발한 먼지봉투 없는 청소기, 불가능한 것 같은 날 없는 선풍기, 그리고 초고속 헤어드라이어는 대부분의 국가에서 그의 이름을 문자 그대로 가정용 브랜드로 만들었고, 72세 영국인을 억만장자로 변화시켰다.

15 정답 ③ Day 58-09

정답해설

본문 첫 문장 "Negative news will normally cause individuals to sell stocks(부정적인 뉴스는 보통 개인이 주식을 매각하도록 만들 것이다)."에서 '부정적인 뉴스가 주식 투자자들에게 미치는 영향'에 대해 언급한 후 '부정적인 뉴스가 주식 가격 하락으로 이어질 것이다'라고 설명하고 있다. 이어서 "Positive news, on the other hand, will normally cause individuals to buy stocks(반면, 긍정적인 뉴스는 보통 개인이 주식을 구매하도록 만들 것이다)."를 통해 '긍정적인 뉴스가 주식 투자자들에게 미치는 영향'에 대해 언급한 후, '긍정적인 뉴스가 주식 가격 상승으로 이어질 것이다'라고 설명하고 있다. 이후, 실제로 '자연재해'라는 부정적인 뉴스가 주가에 미치는 영향을 예로 들어 '뉴스가 주식 가격에 미치는 영향'에 대해 설명하고 있으므로, 글의 제목으로 가장 적절한 것은 '③ How Does News Affect Stock Prices? (뉴스가 주가에 어떻게 영향을 미치는가?)'이다.

해석

부정적인 뉴스는 보통 개인이 주식을 매각하도록 만들 것이다. 예상치 못한 불행한 사건들뿐만 아니라 좋지 않은 수익 보고서, 빈약한 기업 지배구조, 경제적 그리고 정치적 불확실성이 매각 압박과 주식 가격 하락으로 이어질 것이다. 반면 긍정적인 뉴스는 보통 개인이 주식을 구매하도록 만들 것이다. 긍정적인 경제 그리고 정치의 전반적 지표뿐만 아니라 좋은 수익 보고서, 발전된 기업 지배구조, 신제품 및 인수는 구매 압력과 주식 가격 상승으로 이어질 것이다. 예를 들어, 산사태를 일으키는 허리케인은 공공사업의 주가의 하락을 야기할 것이다. 한편, 폭풍의 강도에 따라 뉴스에 의해 보험사의 주가 또한 타격을 입거나, 또는 예상된 피해가 크지 않을 것이라고 추정된다면 주가가 더 높게 올라갈 것이다.
① 주식 투자 성공법
② 자연재해들과 주식시장
③ 뉴스가 주가에 어떻게 영향을 미치는가?
④ 주가 상승을 야기하는 것은 무엇인가?

16 정답 ② Day 54-10

정답해설

본문은 어느 교구의 급식 정책의 변화에 대해 설명하는 글이다. 세 번째 문장 "Previously in the majority of schools we have been providing more food than the average elementary child could eat, and much of the food was wasted(과거에 대부분의 학교에서 우리는 보통의 초등학생이 먹을 수 있는 것보다 더 많은 음식을 제공해왔고, 많은 음식이 낭비되었다)."에서 '기존의 급식 체제에서는 필요보다 많은 음식을 제공하여 낭비되는 음식이 많았다'라고 설명하고 있다. 그리고 두 번째 문장 "In lieu of a price increase for elementary students, we have removed one item from the menu and are using the dessert to meet the type A requirements(초등학생들을 대상으로 한 가격 인상 대신에 우리는 메뉴에서 한 가지 품목을 제외시켰고 A유형의 요건에 맞추기 위해 디저트를 이용하고 있다)."에서 '기존의 메뉴에서 한 가지 품목이 제외되었으며', 기존보다 적은 양의 음식이 제공될 것임을 유추할 수 있다. 따라서 변화된 정책에 따라 낭비되는 음식이 줄어들 것을 기대할 수 있으므로, 글의 내용과 일치하는 보기는 '② The amount of wasted food in elementary schools is expected to decrease(초등학교에서 낭비되는 음식의 양이 줄어들 것이라 기대된다)'이다.

해석

1959년 이래 최초로 우리는 메뉴와 가격을 크게 변화시켰다. 초등학생들을 대상으로 한 가격 인상 대신에 우리는 메뉴에서 한 가지 품목을 제외시켰고 A유형의 요건에 맞추기 위해 디저트를 이용하고 있다. 과거에, 대부분의 학교에서 우리는 보통의 초등학생이 먹을 수 있는 것보다 더 많은 음식을 제공해 왔고, 많은 음식이 낭비되었다. 우유를 포함하는 A유형의 초등학생 점심의 가격은 35센트이다. 중학교에서 우리는 채소의 선택을 제외시켰고, 특별 주문 서비스를 아이스크림과 신선한 과일로 제한시켰다. 수많은 학생들이 짧은 시간에 중학교 급식실을 이용해야 하며, 메뉴를 간소화하고 특별 주문 품목을 제한함으로써 우리는 더 빠른 서비스를 제공할 수 있을 것이다. 중학교의 완전한 점심 식사의 가격은 40센트이다.
① 초등학생을 위한 학교 급식의 가격은 증가해왔다.
② 초등학교에서 낭비되는 음식의 양이 줄어들 것이라 기대된다.
③ 우유는 모든 학교의 점심 급식에 포함되어 있다.
④ 중학생들은 아이스크림 또는 신선한 과일을 더 이상 선택할 수 없다.

17 정답 ② Day 59-09

정답해설

빈칸에는 '주가 변동(stock fluctuations)'의 영향이 제한적인 이유를 설명하는 내용이 들어가야 한다. 빈칸 이후에서 '대공황 이전 65% 이상의 미국인들이 주식을 보유하였으나, 몇 차례의 주식시장 붕괴를 경험한 후인 현재는 55%만이 주식을 보유하고 있고, 일부 조사에서는 그보다 더 낮은 주식 보유 비율을 나타내고 있다'라는 내용을 설명하고 있으므로, '과거에 비해 주식을 보유한 인구의 비율이 낮으므로 주가 변동이 직접적인 영향을 미치는 대상도 상대적으로 축소되었다'라는 것을 유추할 수 있다. 따라서 빈칸에는 '② stocks are not an important form of saving for most households(대부분의 가정에서 주식은 주요한 저축 형태가 아니다)'가 들어가는 것이 가장 자연스럽다.

해석

주가 변동이 제한된 직접적 영향을 미치는 한 가지 이유는 대부분의 가정에서 주식은 주요한 저축 형태가 아니기 때문이다. 최근 갤럽 여론 조사에 따르면 미국인 중 오직 55퍼센트만이 그들 또는 가정의 구성원들이 주식을 보유하고 있다고 말한다. 다른 설문 조사들은 훨씬 더 낮은 주식시장 참여율을 보여준다. 만일 당신이 주식을 보유하고 있지 않다면, 월스트리트가 심각한 실패를 겪는다는 이유로 당신의 소비, 저축 또는 업무 계획을 변경할 이유가 거의 없다. 갤럽 여론 조사는 지난 10년간 주식 보유가 줄어들었다는 것을 나타낸다. 대공황 직전, 미국인 중 65퍼센트 이상이 주식을 보유하고 있다고 답했다. 분명, 2000~2002년 그리고 2008년의 두 번의 주식시장 붕괴가 위험성에 대한 저축자들의 기호를 위축시킨 것이다.
① 미국에서 극심한 주식시장 위기가 현재 진행 중이다
② 대부분의 가정에서 주식은 주요한 저축 형태가 아니다
③ 주식시장에 대한 정부의 규제가 더 엄격해졌다
④ 주식시장에 투자하는 사람들의 수가 증가했다

18 정답 ② Day 54-09

정답해설

본문은 '현대에서의 의미 추구'에 관한 글이며, 빈칸에는 '현대 세계에서 추구되는 의미의 특성'을 묘사할 수 있는 표현이 들어가야 한다. 과거에는 "a coherent life-conduct based on religion and set within the parameters of meaningful cosmos(종교와 의미가 가득한 우주의 범위 내의 사회에 기반을 둔 일관성 있는 생활 방식)"에 근거하여 '통합적인 의미 추구'를 했지만, '현대 세계에서는 5가지의 독립된 가치 영역 내에서 개별적인 의미 추구가 이루어진다(the modern world is structured as a series of five competing, separate value-spheres).'라고 설명한다. 즉, 각 영역 내에서만 유효한 의미이기 때문에, 현대 세계에서의 의미는 '제한적이고 조건적인 것'이라고 볼 수 있다. 따라서 빈칸에 가장 적절한 표현은 '② limited and conditional(제한적이고 조건적인)'이다.

해석

서양 역사상에서 의미 추구의 모순적인 결과는 현대성을 무의미하게 만드는 데 커다란 역할을 해왔다. 그러나 이상적인 이해관계와 문화와 같은 Weber의 연구에서 발견된 개념들이 더 이상 적용되지 않는 것은 아니다. 오히려 Weber는 현대적인 의미 추구에서 발견되는 지속적인 모순적 결과에 기초한 현대성의 이해를 제공해준다. 매혹적이고 장대한 의미의 통합 효과 없이 현대 세계는 5가지의 경쟁적이고 독립된 가치 영역으로서 구성되어 있다: 경제, 지성, 정치, 미학, 그리고 성애. 바로 이 가치 영역 이론을 통해 Weber는 현대에서 지속적인 의미 추구를 이해하려고 노력할 것이다. 본질적으로, 종교와 의미가 가득한 질서 내의 사회에 기반을 둔 일관성 있는 생활 방식 대신에, 사회 전체의 다른 분야, 즉 가치 영역은, 제한적이고 조건적이긴 하지만, 새로운 의미를 제공해 준다.
① 효과적이지 못하고 쓸모없는
② 제한적이고 조건적인
③ 텅 비어 있고 무의미한
④ 한정되고 구식의

19 정답 ③
Day 57-09

정답해설

(A) 빈칸 이전에서 'Some degree of risk aversion in investing is perfectly rational(투자에 있어서 어느 정도의 위험 회피는 매우 합리적이다).'라고 언급한 후, 빈칸 이후에서 '위험을 회피하는 상황'에 대해 예를 들어 설명하고 있으므로, 빈칸에는 '예시'를 나타내는 'For example(예를 들어)' 또는 '재서술'을 나타내는 'In other words(다시 말해)'가 들어갈 수 있다.

(B) 본문 초중반에서는 '사람들이 투자를 할 때 어느 정도 위험 회피적(risk averse) 또는 위험 지향적(to expect higher returns for taking on more risk)이 되는 것은 모두 합리적인 성향이다'라고 설명하고 있다. 이후에는 '손실 회피(loss aversion)'의 경우에 대해 언급하며 'loss aversion holds that all else being equal, losses fundamentally loom larger than gains(위험 회피는 모든 상황이 동일할 때에도 수익보다는 손실을 더 크게 받아들인다).'라고 설명한다. "This includes cases where, win or lose, the outcome will have little material effect on someone's life circumstances(이것은 이기든 지든 그 결과가 누군가의 생활 환경에 물질적 영향을 거의 미치지 않는 경우를 포함하며)"의 상황, 즉 수익과 손실이 인생에 큰 영향을 미치지 않는 경우에도 위험 회피적이라는 것은 '사람들이 과도하게 위험 회피적'이라는 것을 보여주는 근거이므로, 빈칸에는 '인과관계'를 나타내는 'thus(따라서)' 또는 'therefore(그러므로)'가 들어가는 것이 적절하다. 따라서 정답은 ③이다.

해석

투자에 있어서 어느 정도의 위험 회피는 매우 합리적이다. (A) 예를 들어, 만일 당신의 투자 계좌에서 1만 달러를 잃는 것이 당신이 월세를 마련하지 못할 것이라는 것을 의미하고, 반면 추가적인 1만 달러를 획득하는 것이 당신이 추가 휴가를 보낼 수 있다는 것을 의미한다면, 당신의 거처를 잃을 위험을 무릅쓰기보다 안전책을 강구하는 것이 완전히 합리적이다. 이와 같이, 투자자들이 더 많은 위험을 무릅쓰는 것에 대해 더 높은 수익을 기대하는 것 또한 비합리적이지 않다. 그러나 손실 회피는 모든 상황이 동일할 때, 수익보다 손실이 근본적으로 더 크게 다가온다고 간주한다. 이것은 이기든 지든 그 결과가 누군가의 생활 환경에 물질적 영향을 거의 미치지 않는 경우를 포함하며, (B) 따라서 사람들이 과도하게 위험 회피적이라는 것을 암시한다.
① 결과적으로 - 반면에
② 다시 말해 - 그렇지 않으면
③ 예를 들어 - 따라서
④ 그럼에도 불구하고 - 게다가

20 정답 ②
Day 59-08

정답해설

본문은 '북한의 인터넷 시스템'에 관한 글로써, 북한에는 두 가지 버전의 통신망이 있는데 '첫 번째는 고위층을 위한 상대적으로 자유로운 통신망이며, 두 번째는 일반 대중이 이용할 수 있는 다이얼 접속 방식의 구식 통신망'이라고 설명한다. 그 중 '광명'이라 불리는 두 번째 통신망은 "The latter is heavily curated and mostly consists of state propaganda(후자는 과도하게 관리되며 대부분 국가에 대한 선전으로 구성되어 있다)."라고 언급하고 있다. 즉, 일반 대중이 접속할 수 있는 인터넷망을 대부분 '국가 선전(state propaganda)'을 위해 이용하고 있다는 것을 알 수 있으므로, 글의 내용과 일치하는 것은 '② North Korea uses the Internet as an instrument of conveying positive messages about the nation(북한은 국가에 대한 긍정적인 메시지를 전달하는 수단으로 인터넷을 이용한다).'이다.

해석

북한은 두 가지 버전의 월드 와이드 웹을 자랑한다: 고위 관료들과 상류 산업에 종사하는 사람들을 위한 배타적이고 통제가 없는 모델과 나머지 모든 사람들을 위한 빈약한 대안이다. 후자는 과도하게 관리되며 대부분 국가에 대한 선전으로 구성되어 있다. 설상가상으로, ("광명"이라 불리는) 구식의 서비스는 90년대의 AOL과 별반 다르지 않은 다이얼 접속을 통해서만 접근이 가능하다. 그러나 어쨌든 대부분의 북한 사람들이 그것의 비용을 감당할 수 없을 가능성이 있기 때문에 그것의 노후한 환경은 별로 중요하지 않을 수도 있다. 결과적으로, 웹 사용 수치는 깜짝 놀랄 만큼 낮다: 북한 전체가 단지 1,024개의 IP주소를 보유하고 있다. 남한에서는 1억 1,232만 개의 IPv4 주소가 사용 중이며, 심지어 인구가 18,000명인 태평양의 팔라우섬에서 북한보다 더 많은 IP주소를 사용한다.
① 북한의 고위 관료만이 사용할 수 있는 통신망 또한 극심히 통제가 된다.
② 북한은 국가에 대한 긍정적인 메시지를 전달하는 수단으로 인터넷을 이용한다.
③ 모든 북한 사람들은 다이얼 접속을 통해서만 인터넷에 접근할 수 있다.
④ 일반 북한 사람들은 주로 질이 낮은 서비스 때문에 인터넷을 거의 이용하지 않는다.

결국엔 성정혜 영어 하프모의고사
기적사 DAY 01 핵심어휘

01

☐ itinerant	떠돌아다니는, 순회하는
☐ impoverished	빈곤한, 결핍된
☐ ravenous	배가 고파 죽을 지경인, 엄청난
☐ native	토박이의
☐ legendary	전설적인
☐ filmmaker	영화제작자, 감독
☐ indigenous	토종의, 토착의
☐ gather	모으다

02

☐ on a par with	~와 동등한(같은)
☐ a far cry from	~와는 거리가 먼 (전혀 다른)
☐ contingent upon	~여하에 달린
☐ a prelude to	~의 서막
☐ talent	재주, 재능, 장기

03

☐ crime	범죄
☐ determine	알아내다, 밝히다
☐ identity	신원
☐ malefactor	범죄자
☐ culprit	범인
☐ dilettante	예술 애호가
☐ pariah	(사회에서) 버림받은 사람
☐ demagogue	선동 정치가

04

☐ learner's permit	임시 운전면허증
☐ be behind the steering wheel	운전하다
☐ get my feet wet	참가하다, 시작하다
☐ take a rain check	다음을 기약하다

07

☐ domesticated	가축화된
☐ effective	효과적인
☐ strain	부담
☐ utilize	사용하다
☐ considerably	상당하게
☐ supplementary	보충적인
☐ foodstuff	음식 재료
☐ burden	짐
☐ obviously	명확하게

08

☐ document	기록하다, 서류로 만들다
☐ abuse	유린, 학대, 남용
☐ corruption	부패
☐ endure	견디다, 인내하다
☐ term	형기
☐ penal	형벌의
☐ proper	적절한, 알맞은
☐ laureate	수상자
☐ in danger	위험에 처한
☐ free	풀어주다, 석방하다
☐ roll	명단, 명부
☐ dissident	반체제 인사
☐ expire	죽다, 기한이 다하다
☐ jail cell	감방

09

☐ stereotype	고정관념
☐ define	규정하다, 정의하다
☐ classify	분류하다
☐ infinite	무한한
☐ handful	한 줌, 적은 수
☐ stereotyped	판에 박은, 진부한
☐ fashion	방식
☐ wearing	몹시 지치게 하는
☐ economize	절약하다, 아끼다
☐ blooming	만발한, 엄청난
☐ buzzing	웅성대는

☐ cut-out	잘린 것
☐ trouble	수고
☐ accustomed	익숙한
☐ look	모습
☐ stick to	~를 고수하다
☐ prejudge	예단(속단)하다
☐ lay eyes on	~을 보다 [발견하다, 만나다]
☐ from scratch	맨 처음부터

10

☐ PhD	박사학위(학생)
☐ academic position	교수 자리
☐ closely	밀접하게, 면밀하게
☐ current	현재의
☐ caregiver	돌보미, 간호사
☐ absent	부재중인
☐ miss a beat	순간적으로 주저하다
☐ classified ad	(구인, 구직, 매매 등을 위한) 3행 광고, 안내 광고
☐ ordinance	법령, 조례
☐ obituary	부고, 사망 기사

결국엔 성정해 영어 하프모의고사
기적사 DAY 02 핵심어휘

01

☐ inhabitant	거주자
☐ vagabond	방랑하는
☐ ravenous	탐욕스러운
☐ aboriginal	고유의, 토착의, 원주민의
☐ unprivileged	가난한, 특권이 없는

02

☐ starvation	굶주림

☐ contingent	조건으로 하는
☐ cursory	피상적인, 겉핥기의
☐ irate	격노한
☐ natant	떠도는, 헤엄치는, 물에 떠 있는

03

☐ dilettante	아마추어의
☐ necessitous	가난한
☐ faultless	정확한, 결점이 없는
☐ astounding	몹시 놀라운

04

☐ suffer from~	~로 고통을 겪다
☐ on medicine	복용 중인
☐ over-the-counter	처방전 없이 파는 약
☐ get one's feet wet	경험하다
☐ prescribe	처방하다

07

☐ particular	특정한
☐ organization	조직, 단체, 기구
☐ define A as B	A를 B로 정의하다
☐ design+목적어 +to+동사원형	~이 …하도록 꾀하다
☐ distinguish A from B	A와 B를 구분하다
☐ nature	특성, 본성, 자연

08

☐ authority	당국
☐ put ~ on trial	~를 재판에 회부하다
☐ human rights	인권
☐ defender	(주의, 사상 등의) 옹호자, 수호자
☐ on charges of	~혐의로, ~죄로
☐ state	국가의
☐ entity	독립체, 실체
☐ intentionally	고의적으로, 의도적으로

☐ leak	유출하다
☐ court	법원, 법정
☐ verdict	판결, 평결
☐ allow	허락하다, 허용하다
☐ attend	참석하다, 참가하다
☐ make public	공표하다, 알리다
☐ closed-door	비공개의
☐ hearing	심문, 심리, 청문회
☐ violate	위배하다, 위반하다
☐ fair	공정한
☐ independent	독립한
☐ unconditionally	무조건적으로
☐ release	석방하다
☐ persecution	박해
☐ exercise	(권력·권리·역량 등을) 행사하다
☐ association	결사, 연계, 유대

09

☐ stereotype	고정관념; 고정관념을 형성하다
☐ circulate	퍼뜨리다
☐ oversimplication	지나친 단순화
☐ whereas	~에 반하여
☐ generalization	일반화
☐ widely-accepted	널리[일반적으로] 받아들여지는[인정된]
☐ factor	요인, 인자
☐ racial	인종의
☐ well-known	잘 알려진, 유명한
☐ average	평균의
☐ hesitate	망설이다
☐ identify	확인하다, 식별하다
☐ excel	뛰어나다
☐ that is	즉, 다시 말하면
☐ repeat	되풀이하다
☐ mythology	(많은 사람들의) 근거 없는 믿음, 신화
☐ perpetuate	영속시키다, 불멸하게 하다
☐ to be brief	간단히 말해, 요컨대

☐ be rooted in	~에 뿌리박고 있다
☐ unlike	~와 달리
☐ debate	논쟁, 논란
☐ A as well as B	B뿐만 아니라 A도
☐ enable	~할 수 있게 하다
☐ respond	대응하다, 응답하다
☐ rapidly	빨리
☐ necessarily	반드시, 필연적으로

10

☐ synthetic rubber	합성 고무
☐ give life	살리다
☐ organ donor	장기 기증자
☐ be willing to	기꺼이 ~하다
☐ guardian	후견인, 보호자
☐ mean	못된, 심술궂은
☐ spiteful	악의에 찬, 앙심을 품은
☐ reference letter	추천서
☐ autobiography	전기, 자서전
☐ obituary	부고, 사망 기사
☐ journal	일기, 일지

결국엔 성정혜 영어 하프모의고사
기적사 DAY 03 핵심어휘

01

☐ inadvertent	우연한, 우발적인, 예상 못한
☐ allusive	암시하는, 냄새가 나는
☐ insatiable	탐욕스러운, 만족할 줄 모르는
☐ uneven	이상한, 고르지 않은

02

☐ a far cry from	~와는 거리가 먼
☐ common	보통의, 공통의, 흔한

☐ naive	순진한, 생각이 얕은, 소박한
☐ indigenous	고유의, 토착의
☐ candid	솔직한, 공정한

03

☐ classify	분류하다
☐ specimen	표본
☐ far removed from	아주 거리가 먼
☐ on equal terms with	동등하게, 완전히 부합하여
☐ on the spot	당장
☐ bombard with	비난을 받다

04

☐ faucet	수도꼭지
☐ drip	물이 떨어지다
☐ washer	와셔
☐ replace	교체하다
☐ had better	~하는 편이 낫다
☐ plumber	배관공
☐ cut corners	절차를 무시하다
☐ come to terms with it	합의를 보다
☐ drop one a line	편지를 쓰다

07

☐ goods	상품
☐ reliably	확실하게, 믿음직하게
☐ lifeline	생명선
☐ infrastructure	인프라, 기반 시설
☐ hazard	위험

08

☐ social contract theory	사회계약설
☐ in every respect	모든 면에서
☐ sovereign	통치자, 주권자
☐ consent	동의

☐ will	의지, (강한) 의견
☐ so long as	~하는 한, ~이기만 하면
☐ govern	통치하다, 다스리다
☐ in accordance with	~에 따라
☐ sovereignty	통치권
☐ constitutional government	입헌정치
☐ property	재산
☐ appoint	임명하다, 정하다
☐ besides	게다가, 뿐만 아니라
☐ desirable	바람직한
☐ circumstance	상황

09

☐ empiricist	경험주의자
☐ claim	주장하다
☐ ultimate	궁극적인, 최후의
☐ maintain	주장하다
☐ raw	가공하지 않은, 원료 그대로의, 날것의
☐ material	재료, 자료
☐ perception	지각
☐ process	절차, 과정
☐ hold	생각하다, 간주하다
☐ classic	대표적인, 전형적인
☐ on the contrary	반대로, 반면에
☐ rationalist	이성주의자, 합리주의자
☐ reason	이성

10

☐ vice versa	거꾸로, 역으로, 반대로; 역 또한 같다
☐ thrive	번영하다
☐ alternative	대안의
☐ invest	투자하다
☐ assumption	전제, 가정, 추정
☐ underlie	기저[기초]를 이루다
☐ investment	투자
☐ return	수익, 이윤

☐ eventually	결국
☐ equal	(수, 양, 가치 등이) 같다, 맞먹다, 필적하다
☐ decline	감소하다, 줄다
☐ restriction	제한
☐ neither A nor B	A와 B 어느 것도 아닌
☐ will	의지

결국엔 성정혜 영어 하프모의고사
기적사 DAY 04 핵심어휘

01

☐ be subject to	조건으로 하는, 당하기 쉬운, 따라야 하는
☐ itinerant	떠돌아다니는
☐ juratory	선서한
☐ vehement	열정적인

02

☐ distress	고민
☐ delegate	대리인, 대표자, 하원 의원
☐ austerity	근엄, 엄격
☐ omen	전조, 예언, 징조

03

☐ perpetrator	범인, 가해자, 하수인
☐ deputy	대리인, 대표자
☐ anonymousness	익명, 개성(특색)이 없음
☐ principal	(단체의) 장, 주요한, 원금의

04

☐ give me a break	휴식 시간을 주다
☐ understand	이해하다
☐ get cold feet	무서워하다, 주눅 들다

☐ come out of one's shell	소심함의 틀을 깨다 (너의 세상 밖으로 나오다)

07

☐ pediatrics	소아과
☐ advise + 목적어 + to	~에게 ~하도록 + 동사원형 권고하다
☐ timeout	일시적 중단
☐ discipline	훈육, 훈련, 징계, 징벌
☐ corporal	육체의, 신체의
☐ deleterious	해로운, 유독한

08

☐ performance	성능
☐ on a regular basis	정기적으로, 규칙적으로
☐ free	해방시키다, 석방하다
☐ prevent	예방하다, 막다
☐ crash	(시스템의) 고장, 충돌
☐ sufficient	충분한
☐ invasion	침해, 침입
☐ thwart	좌절시키다, 방해하다
☐ attempt	시도
☐ breach	침해, 위반
☐ threat	위협
☐ invade	침입하다, 침해하다
☐ pros and cons	장단점

09

☐ generate	생성하다, 발생시키다
☐ store	저장하다
☐ access	접근, 접속; 접근하다, 접속하다
☐ batch	묶음, 무리, 다발
☐ cook up	만들다
☐ go through	겪다, 경험하다
☐ lengthy	긴, 지루한
☐ process	과정, 절차
☐ identify	확인하다, 식별하다
☐ given	특정한, 정해진

reveal	밝히다, 드러내다
require	요구하다, 필요하다
gain	얻다, 획득하다
contain	포함하다
place	위치[배치]시키다
determine	결정하다, 알아내다
authorization	권한

10

claim	주장
activist	운동가, 활동가
potential	가능성
operator	운영자
spy on	염탐하다, 감시하다
bulletin	회람, 고시
issue	발행하다
allegedly	주장한[전해진, 알려진] 바에 의하면, 이른바
find out	알아내다
inaccurate	부정확한
widespread	널리 퍼진

결국엔 성정혜 영어 하프모의고사
기적사 DAY 05 핵심어휘

01

allegedly	주장한(전해진) 바에 의하면, 이른바
purgee	망명자
fatality	사망자, 치사성, 숙명
criminal	범인
fledgling	미숙한, 풋내기

02

existence	존재, 현존, 생존
refugee	난민, 이탈자, 망명자
villain	악당, 악한, 악역

casualty	사상자, 희생자, 피해자
par	동등, 기준타수

03

ranch	목장
indignation	분노
apprehension	불안감
appreciation	이해, 감사, 상승, 강세
demagogue	선동 연설가

04

yet	아직
step out	나가다
make up with~	~와 화해하다
burn one's bridge	배수진을 치다
burn the candle at both ends	몹시 지치다

07

borderline	경계선
receive	받다, 수용하다
contemporary	현대의, 동시대의

08

metaphysics	형이상학
involve	포함하다, 수반하다
principle	원리, 원칙
being	존재, 생명체
abstract	추상적인
existence	존재
Theory of Forms	이데아론
material object	사물
in oneself	그 자체로는, 본질적으로, 원래
rather	오히려, 차라리
correspond	조화하다, 일치하다, 부합하다
eternal	영원한
immutable	불변의

□ form	[철학] 이데아; 형상(形相)
□ perceive	인식하다, 지각하다, 이해하다
□ intellect	지성
□ manifestation	현시, (유령, 영혼 등이) 나타남
□ ultimately	궁극적으로
□ deny	거부하다, 부인하다
□ poetic	낭만적인, 시적인
□ empiricist	경험주의자
□ rejection	거부, 거절
□ detestation	혐오
□ admiration	찬양, 감탄

09

□ be made up of	~로 구성되다
□ cornerstone	기초, 초석
□ describe	묘사하다
□ temperament	기질
□ humor	체액(고대 생리에서 인간의 체질, 기질을 정한다고 생각되었던 4액)
□ aether	에테르, 하늘, 창공, (옛사람들이 상상한) 대기 밖의 정기(精氣), 영기(靈氣)
□ earthly	지구의, 이 세상의
□ align	나란히 하다, 일렬로 서다, 일치하다
□ plasma	플라스마 (고도로 이온화된 기체)

10

□ revolution	혁명
□ foundation	토대, 근거, 기초
□ the Enlightenment	계몽주의 (시대)
□ come to	~하게 되다
□ leading	가장 중요한, 선두적인
□ discourse	담화, 담론, 논설
□ background	배경, 경력, 학력, 경험

□ associate A with B	A를 B와 관련시켜 생각하다
□ overthrow	전복, 타도
□ authority	권위
□ in favor of	…에 찬성[지지]하여
□ broadly	대략적으로, 넓게
□ empiricism	경험주의
□ rational	합리적인, 이성적인
□ embed	깊숙이 박다
□ dominate	지배하다
□ society	-회, 단체, 협회
□ academy	협회, 학회
□ replace A as B	A를 대신하여 B가 되다
□ backbone	중추, 근간
□ maturation	성숙
□ profession	-계, 종사자들
□ popularization	대중화
□ literate	글을 읽고 쓸 줄 아는, 교양 있는
□ population	주민, 시민, 사람들
□ regard	존중하다, 중요시하다
□ curb	억제하다, 억압하다
□ dominance	지배, 우세, 권세

결국엔 성정혜 영어 하프모의고사
기적사 DAY 06 핵심어휘

01

□ subscriber	구독자
□ reliable	믿을 수 있는
□ figure	수치
□ industry	산업
□ discern	구별하다
□ concern	관계되다
□ distinguish	구별하다
□ strengthen	강화하다
□ undermine	약화시키다
□ abandon	버리다, 포기하다

02

☐ stand out	돋보이다
☐ overwhelm	압도하다
☐ impressive	인상적인
☐ depressed	우울한
☐ optimistic	긍정적인

03

☐ schooling	학교 교육
☐ compulsory	강제적인, 의무적인
☐ vary	다르다, 다양하다
☐ complementary	보완적인
☐ systematic	체계적인
☐ mandatory	의무적인
☐ innovative	혁신적인

04

☐ delicious	맛있는
☐ chopped	다진
☐ vegetable	채소
☐ dip	찍다

05

☐ richness	풍부함, 풍성함
☐ take ~ for granted	~을 당연한 것으로 여기다
☐ deforestation	삼림 벌채
☐ temperate	온난한
☐ wilderness	황야, 황무지

06

☐ entrepreneur	기업가
☐ ingenuity	독창성
☐ execute	실행하다
☐ dichotomy	양분, 이분

08

☐ risk-averse	위험을 회피하려는
☐ consequence	결과

☐ outweigh	~보다 더 크다/대단하다
☐ reward	보상
☐ look down on	~을 경시하다/얕보다
☐ likely	가능성 있는, 있음직한
☐ risk one's neck	위험을 무릅쓰다
☐ progress	진보
☐ inextricably	불가분하게
☐ entwine	얽히다
☐ underestimate	과소평가하다
☐ take risks	위험을 감수하다
☐ turbulent	격동의, 격변의
☐ suffer from	~로 고통스러워하다
☐ anorexia (nervosa)	거식증
☐ enterprising	진취적인, 기획력 있는
☐ transition	과도, 이행, 이동
☐ combinatoric	결합의, 조합의

09

☐ nature	본성, 천성
☐ trait	특성, 특징
☐ motor car	자동차
☐ perpetually	영속적으로
☐ out of order	고장 난
☐ boast	자랑(하다)
☐ skillful	숙련된, 능숙한
☐ mechanic	정비공
☐ put right	고치다, 바로 잡다
☐ uninteresting	재미없는, 시시한
☐ plebeian	천한, 보통의
☐ delicate	허약한, 섬세한
☐ digestion	소화
☐ indispensable	필수적인, 없어서는 안 되는
☐ equipment	갖추고 있어야 하는 것, 준비, 기술, 능력
☐ impulse	충동, 자극
☐ vexed	화난
☐ come across	우연히 만나다
☐ phobia	공포증

10

☐ open land	평야
☐ herd	몰다, 모아서 몰다
☐ cattle	소떼
☐ make a living	생계를 꾸리다
☐ ranch	목장
☐ rope	밧줄을 던져 잡다
☐ steer	거세한 수소
☐ rancher	목장에서 일하는 사람
☐ property	재산
☐ sport	장난, 재미, 스포츠
☐ brutal	잔인한
☐ to take an example = for example	예를 들면
☐ to be brief	간단히 말해서, 요컨대
☐ on the other hand	반면에, 다른 한편으로는
☐ by the same token	같은 이유로, 마찬가지로

결국엔 성정혜 영어 하프모의고사
기적사 DAY 07 핵심어휘

01

☐ mainstay	주역
☐ defector	탈주자, 망명자, 탈당자
☐ offender	범죄자, 위반자
☐ agitator	정치운동가, 선동자
☐ subscriber	구독자

02

☐ discern	구별하다
☐ estimate	평가하다, 추정하다
☐ allocate	분배하다, 배치하다
☐ abominate	혐오하다

03

☐ despise	혐오하다, 멸시하다
☐ unravel	해결하다, 해명하다
☐ give up	포기하다
☐ convey	양도하다, 운반하다, 전달하다

04

☐ lose track of	~의 소식이 끊어지다, ~을 놓치다
☐ remark	발언
☐ bygone	과거의, 지나간
☐ Let bygones be bygones.	[속담] 과거사는 물에 흘려보내라, 과거는 잊어버려라
☐ keep close tabs on	~을 엄중히 감시하다
☐ shed light on~	~에 빛을 비추다
☐ come down with a cold	감기에 걸리다
☐ make fun of~	~을 놀리다
☐ used to v	~하곤 했었다
☐ suppose	가정하다

05

☐ fruitful	유익한, 열매가 많이 열리는
☐ distribute	배포하다, 분배하다
☐ virtual	가상의
☐ emulate	모방하다
☐ extensive	광범위한, 넓은

06

☐ focus on	~에 초점을 맞추다, 주력하다
☐ separate	분리하다, 나누다
☐ prioritize	우선순위를 결정하다
☐ task	과제, 일, 직무
☐ underestimate	과소평가하다

08

reward	보상하다
defeat	패배
prospect	가능성, 가망
success-driven	성공 지향적인
non-option	비(非) 선택지
deem	생각하다
deficiency	결함, 부족
inferiority	열등
hardly	거의 ~않다
attempt	시도하다
misstep	실수, 과실
gloss over	얼버무리고 넘어가다, 둘러대다
selectively	선택적으로
edit out	삭제하다, 잘라내다
miscalculation	계산 착오, 오판
resume	이력서
top the list	목록의 제일 위에 있다, 가장 위에 있다
meta-	자신과 관계되는, 복합의, 더 높은, 초월의
far from	전혀 ~이 아닌, ~이 아니라 오히려
as...as any	무엇에도 못지않게...한
intellectual	지적인, 지성의
capacity	능력
err	실수하다, 잘못하다
crucial	중대한
cognition	인지, 인식, 지식
only if	~해야만, ~할 경우에 한해
embrace	기꺼이 받아들이다
challenge	도전, 도전 과제
face	직면하다
be aware that	알다, 인식하다
achieve	달성하다, 이루다
either A or B	A 이거나 B(둘 중 하나)
stepping stone	디딤돌, 발판
stumbling block	장애물

aim for	~를 겨냥하다, 목표로 하다
settle for	~로 만족하다, 받아들이다
mediocrity	평범

09

weird	이상한, 기묘한
compulsion	충동
nibble	조금씩 물어뜯다
from time to time	때때로
bizarre	기괴한
typical	전형적인
nature	특징, 본성, 본질
factor	요인
at work	작용하여
adorable	귀여운, 사랑스러운
huggable	껴안고 싶은
activate	작동시키다, 활성화시키다
pleasure center	쾌락 중추
response	반응, 응답
stimuli	stimulus(자극)의 복수형
theory	이론, 학설
seemingly	겉으로 보기에
note	언급하다, 주목하다
occurrence	발생
mammal	포유동물
primate	영장류
non-threatening	위협적이지 않은
demonstrate	보여주다, 입증하다
even if	~에도 불구하고
instinct	본능
characteristic	특징

10

attraction	명물, 명소
draw	(손님 등을) 끌다
spectacle	구경거리, 행사

☐ take it for granted ~	~을 당연한 일로 여기다, 대수롭지 않게 여기다
☐ compete	경쟁하다
☐ ranch	목장, 농장
☐ rope	밧줄을 던져 잡다
☐ herd	(짐승을) 몰다
☐ take part in	참여하다
☐ bronc	야생마
☐ legitimate	정통의, 진짜의, 합법의

결국엔 성정혜 영어 하프모의고사
기적사 DAY 08 핵심어휘

01

☐ approve	확인하다, 인정하다
☐ undermine	약화시키다
☐ accelerate	서두르다, 가속하다, 촉진시키다
☐ renounce	포기하다, 부인하다

02

☐ laziness	게으름
☐ overwhelm	압도하다
☐ despise	경멸하다
☐ revise	변경하다, 개정하다
☐ scan	자세히 살펴보다, 조사하다, 훑어보다

03

☐ reprimand	질책하다, 비난하다
☐ loathe	혐오하다, 싫어하다
☐ deceive	속이다, 기만하다, 현혹시키다, 거짓말을 하다.
☐ protect	보호하다
☐ evade	피하다, 빠져나가다, 얼버무려 넘기다

04

☐ stomachache	복통
☐ dizzy	어지러운
☐ pig out	게걸스럽게 먹다
☐ hardly	거의 ~하지 않다
☐ serious	심각한
☐ have butterflies in one's stomach	긴장하다, 안달하다

05

☐ perceive A as B	A를 B로 인식하다
☐ spend+시간+-ing	~하는데 시간을 보내다
☐ verbal	말의, 구두의
☐ take+목적어+for granted	~을 당연시하다
☐ toolbox	도구상자
☐ enhance	강화하다, 향상시키다

06

☐ encourage+목적어+to 동사원형	~에게 ~하도록 격려하다
☐ consider+목적어+(to be)+명사	~을 …이라고 여기다, 생각하다
☐ let+목적어+동사원형	~에게 ~하도록 시키다
☐ literacy	읽고 쓰는 능력
☐ effortless	노력이 필요 없는, 쉬운
☐ fluency	유창함

08

☐ massacre	(대량)학살
☐ expressionistic	표현주의적인
☐ criticism	비판, 비난
☐ intervention	개입
☐ in question	문제의, 논의가 되고 있는
☐ depict	묘사하다
☐ civilian	민간인

☐ communist	공산주의자
☐ force	세력, 집단, 군대
☐ critic	비평가
☐ inspire	영감을 주다
☐ atrocity	잔학행위, 포악한 행위
☐ draw from	(결론, 생각 등을) ~에서 끌어내다, 얻다
☐ execute	처형하다, 사형을 집행하다
☐ mass	대량의, 집단의
☐ province	(행정 구역으로서의) 도(道), 주(州), 성(省)

09

☐ statement	표현
☐ reaction	반응
☐ devastating	엄청나게 파괴적인
☐ practice	실행
☐ tragedy	비극
☐ suffering	고통
☐ inflict	가하다, 주다
☐ civilian	민간인, 일반 시민
☐ status	신분, 지위, 신망
☐ perpetual	끊임없는, 영속하는
☐ embodiment	구현, 구체화, 실체
☐ acclaimed	찬사를 받은, 호평을 받은
☐ monumental	기념비적인, 역사적 의미가 있는
☐ apathy	무관심, 냉담
☐ paltry	하찮은, 보잘것없는
☐ reproach	비난
☐ recognition	인식, 인지, 인정

10

☐ pick up on	알아차리다, 이해하다
☐ academic	학자, 학구적인 사람, 교수
☐ plaster cast	석고 모형
☐ admit	(단체·학교 등에서) 받아들이다, 가입[입학]을 허락하다

☐ fine art	미술
☐ incredibly	믿기 힘들게도, 놀랍게도
☐ rigorous	엄격한, 엄밀한
☐ reproduce	모조하다, 복사하다
☐ entrance exam	입학시험

결국엔 성정혜 영어 하프모의고사
기적사 DAY 09 핵심어휘

01

☐ uncanny	기묘한
☐ complementary	보완적인
☐ pertinent	적절한, 관계가 있는
☐ impractical	비현실적인, 비실용적인
☐ inerrant	과오를 범하지 않는
☐ odd	이상한, 특이한, 홀수의, 별난

02

☐ evaluate	평가하다
☐ frail	약한
☐ compensate	보상하다
☐ inflame	악화시키다, 격분하게 하다
☐ reckon	평가하다, 생각하다
☐ swear	욕하다, 맹세하다, 단언하다

03

☐ culminate	최고점에 달하다
☐ incessant	진행 중인, 끊임없는
☐ ponderous	다루기 어려운, 크고 무거운, 황황한, 지루한
☐ chronic	상습적인, 만성의
☐ imperious	오만한

04

☐ trust	믿다, 신뢰하다
☐ get rid of	없애다
☐ vouch for	보증을 하다
☐ wet blanket	흥을 깨는 사람
☐ tip of the iceberg	빙산의 일각

05

☐ short story	단편소설
☐ take place	발생하다
☐ come up with	~을 생각해내다
☐ last	계속되다, 지속되다
☐ downtown	시내에

06

☐ spread A with B	A에 B를 바르다
☐ homemade	집에서 만든, 손으로 만든
☐ little	어린, 작은, 거의 없는
☐ cover A with B	A를 B로 덮다
☐ giggle	낄낄 웃다
☐ cabin	오두막집

08

☐ attach	붙이다, 부착하다
☐ skull	두개골
☐ versatility	융통성, 다재, 다능
☐ provide A with B	A에게 B를 제공하다
☐ pull	끌기, 끌어[잡아]당기기
☐ latch	걸쇠, 잠금장치
☐ fiercely	사납게
☐ row	열, 줄
☐ rip	찢다
☐ flesh	살
☐ struggle	투쟁, 몸부림
☐ replace	대체하다, 대신하다
☐ gear	(장비 등을) 설치하다, 준비하다
☐ army	집단, 무리

09

☐ pluck	(잡아 당겨) 빼내다 [뽑아내다]
☐ reproduce	번식하다
☐ demand	수요
☐ fin	지느러미
☐ decline	감소하다
☐ prey	먹이
☐ species	종
☐ ray	가오리
☐ in turn	결국, 결과적으로
☐ scallop	가리비
☐ mollusk	연체동물
☐ ripple effect	파급효과
☐ dramatic	극적인, 급격한
☐ grouper	그루퍼 (농엇과(科)의 식용어)
☐ parrotfish	비늘돔
☐ algae	조류, 해조
☐ coral reef	산호초
☐ result in	(결과적으로) ~을 낳다[야기하다]
☐ ecological system	생태계
☐ resource	자원
☐ habitat	서식지
☐ predator	포식 동물
☐ alter	변화시키다

10

☐ determine	결정하다
☐ precisely	정확하게
☐ species	종
☐ mature	성숙한; 성숙하다
☐ i.e.	즉
☐ contender	경쟁자, 도전자
☐ measure	길이(높이, 폭, 넓이 등)가 ~이다

결국엔 성정혜 영어 하프모의고사
기적사 DAY 10 핵심어휘

01

ostensible	표면상의
imperious	오만한, 긴급한
strange	이상한
adventitious	우연한

02

depression	우울증
stealthy	은밀한
manifest	명백한, 분명한
grudging	마지못해 하는
imprecise	모호한, 부정확한

03

offensive	공격적인
impeccable	결점이 없는, 죄를 범하지 않는
insulting	무례한, 모욕적인
mandatory	의무적인
impermanent	순간적인, 덧없는

04

vanish into thin air	완전히 사라지다, 흔적도 없어지다
get the picture	이해하다
break a leg	행운을 빌다
neck and neck	막상막하
hit the nail on the head	맞는 말만 하다
be at the end of one's rope	인내의 한계에 다다르다

05

specialize	전문화하다, 특수화하다
stool	의자

have no difficulty (in) ~ing	~하는 데 어려움이 없다, ~하는 데 지장이 없다

06

isolate	고립시키다, 격리하다
go on	일어나다, 벌어지다
have got to + 동사원형	~해야 한다
share A with B	A를 B와 공유하다
battle	싸우다

08

debate	논쟁
relative	상대적인
contribution	기여
inheritance	유전(되는 것)
refer to	지칭하다
nurture	양성, 양육
inborn	타고난, 선천적인
argue for	~에 찬성 의견을 말하다
slate	석판
determine	결정하다
interaction	상호작용
biological	생물학적인
puberty	사춘기
onset	(특히 불쾌한 일의) 시작, 발병
nutrition	영양
on the contrary	그와는 반대로
consequently	그 결과
nevertheless	그럼에도 불구하고
in summary	요컨대, 요약하면

09

heredity	유전적 형질, 유전
nurture	양성, 양육
interaction	상호작용
perfect pitch	절대음감
detect	간파하다, 감지하다

pitch	음의 높이
musical tone	악음
reference	참조, 대조, 비교
run in family	집안 내력이다, 유전되다
be tied to	~와 관련되다
gene	유전자
possess	소유하다
proper	적절한, 알맞은
inherit	(육체적·정신적 성질 등을) 물려받다, 유전하다
manifest oneself	나타나다, 드러내다, 분명해지다
comprehensively	포괄적으로
discretely	따로따로, 별개로
separately	따로따로, 개별적으로, 단독으로

10

prior to	~이전에
social learning theory	사회학습이론
apply	적용시키다
gender reassignment	성 전환
rebel	저항하다, 반항하다
assign	할당하다, 지정하다
anatomy	해부학
reproductive	생식의, 번식의
application	적용
inadequate	부적당한
inherent	유전적인, 내재하는, 타고난
have little to do with	~와 거의 관련이 없다
appearance	외관
genital	성기, 생식기

결국엔 성정혜 영어 하프모의고사
기적사 DAY 11 핵심어휘

01

turmoil	소란, 혼란
disclose	밝히다, 공개하다
let on	말하다, 털어놓다
let off	봐주다, 터뜨리다
let up	누그러지다, 약해지다
let down	실망시키다

02

drift	떠가다, 이동하다, ~하게 되다
root	근원, 기원, 뿌리
pagan	이교도
Catholic	가톨릭의
spirit	정신, 영혼
replace	교체하다, 대체하다

03

make light of	~을 가볍게 여기다, 얕보다, 경시하다
treat	취급하다, 대우하다
make an effort	노력하다
seek	찾다, 추구하다
acceptable	용인 가능한, 허용할 수 있는

04

be used to N	~에 익숙하다
get accustomed to N	~에 익숙하다
prize	상
keep one's fingers crossed	행운을 빌다
mind	꺼려하다
never mind	걱정하지 마

08

☐ commonly	흔히, 통상적으로
☐ exploration	탐험
☐ liberty of thought	생각의 자유
☐ complacency	안일함
☐ absence	부재
☐ challenge	도전
☐ flabby	축 늘어진
☐ oppose	반대하다
☐ rarely	거의 ~하지 않다
☐ erroneous	잘못된
☐ supplement	보완
☐ alternative	대안
☐ replication	복제
☐ defense	방어
☐ partiality	편중성
☐ incompleteness	불완전성
☐ constraint	제약

09

☐ conventional	기존의, 관습적인
☐ mortgage	주택담보대출
☐ net	최종의
☐ disposable income	가처분 소득
☐ affordability	비용
☐ policy maker	정책 입안자
☐ differentiate	구별하다
☐ median	중위
☐ unaffordability	감당할 수 없는 비용
☐ inversely	반비례하여
☐ tendency	경향
☐ infer	추론하다
☐ tenant	세입자

10

☐ expenditure	지출, 소비, 경비
☐ operational cost	업무비
☐ telecommunications	전기통신
☐ rather than	~보다는 (오히려)

☐ specialize in	~를 전문으로 하다
☐ expand	확장하다
☐ specific	특정한, 구체적인
☐ integrate	통합시키다
☐ scrutinize	조사하다, 검토하다
☐ elaborate	정교한
☐ split	분열시키다, 나누다
☐ universal	보편적인

결국엔 성정혜 영어 하프모의고사
기적사 DAY 12 핵심어휘

01

☐ affront	모욕, 무례한 언동
☐ concoct	만들어내다, 꾸며내다, 꾀하다
☐ withstand	참다, 이겨내다
☐ roam	돌아다니다
☐ disclose	밝히다, 공개하다

02

☐ register	기록하다, 등록하다
☐ examine	살펴보다, 조사하다, 검토하다
☐ disclose	밝히다
☐ appease	달래다

03

☐ seek	추구하다
☐ repress	진압하다
☐ rectify	변경하다, 바로잡다
☐ provoke	자극하다, 도발하다

04

☐ no sweat	별거 아냐
☐ wet behind the ears	미숙한

☐ a piece of cake	쉬운 일, 유쾌한 일
☐ keep one's finger crossed	행운을 빌다

08

☐ recognize	인정하다, 알아주다
☐ philosophy	철학
☐ chiefly	주로
☐ refine	개선하다, 세련되게 하다
☐ Utilitarian	공리주의의
☐ establish	수립하다, 정립하다
☐ reemphasize	다시 강조하다
☐ primacy	최고, 제일
☐ liberty	자유
☐ self-determination	자기 결정
☐ inroad	침해, 침략, 침입
☐ majority	다수, 대부분
☐ democratic	민주주의의
☐ legal	법적인, 합법의
☐ equality	평등
☐ subordination	복종, 종속 관계
☐ in itself	그 자체로, 본질적으로
☐ chief	최고의, 주요한
☐ hindrance	방해물
☐ improvement	향상, 진보
☐ in a nutshell	간단히 말해, 간결하게
☐ advocate	옹호하다
☐ liberation	해방
☐ subordinate	하위의, 지배된, 열등한
☐ de facto	사실상의, 실제로
☐ opposition	반대
☐ slavery	노예, 노예제
☐ race	인종
☐ call for	(~에 대한) 요구, 요청
☐ emphasis	강조
☐ democracy	민주주의
☐ influential	영향력이 있는
☐ advocate	옹호자, 지지자

09

☐ urbanization	도시화
☐ squat	불법 거주하다, 쪼그리고 앉다
☐ settlement	정착지, 거주지
☐ authority	당국
☐ face	직면하다
☐ housing problem	주거 문제
☐ undertake	착수하다
☐ policy	정책
☐ reveal	드러내다, 밝히다
☐ unit	(한 개) 단위
☐ require	요구하다, 필요로 하다
☐ annually	매년
☐ up to	~까지
☐ clear	(재고 등을) 처분하다, (빚 등을) 청산하다
☐ backlog	재고, 잔무, 밀린 일
☐ average	평균의
☐ stand	(수준, 양 등이) ~이다
☐ sector	부문
☐ meanwhile	한편
☐ low income	저소득
☐ household	가구, 가족
☐ access	접근; 접근하다
☐ loan	대출, 대부
☐ mortgage	융자, 저당, 주택담보대출
☐ financial institution	금융 기관
☐ be engaged in	~에 종사하다
☐ secure	확보하다, 획득하다
☐ livelihood	생계
☐ capture	확보하다, 점유하다
☐ micro-financing	소액금융
☐ flexible	탄력적인, 유연한
☐ as such	그렇기 때문에, 그러함에 따라
☐ resort to	~에 의지하다, 기대다
☐ incremental	점진적인
☐ house	거처를 제공하다, 살 곳을 주다

☐ registration	등록
☐ approval	허가, 승인
☐ process	과정, 절차
☐ rigid	엄격한
☐ cumbersome	복잡하고 느린, 번거로운
☐ thus	그래서, 그러므로
☐ hindrance	방해물
☐ affordable	(가격이) 알맞은, 감당할 수 있는
☐ unauthorized	무허가의, 권한이 없는
☐ gap	차이, 격차
☐ supply and demand	수요와 공급
☐ bracket	계층
☐ heavily	몹시, 크게
☐ unofficial	무허가인, 비공식적인
☐ income-generating	소득을 창출하는
☐ take advantage of	(기회로 삼아) 이용하다

10

☐ term	용어, 말
☐ telecommunications	통신
☐ whole	(정도에 대하여) 큰, 어마어마한
☐ complex	복합체
☐ means	수단, 방법
☐ be intended to	~할 의도이다
☐ distance	거리, 간격
☐ process	처리하다
☐ equipment	장비
☐ contain	포함하다
☐ allow	허용하다, 허가하다
☐ transfer	옮기다, 전송하다
☐ via	통하여
☐ optical fiber	광섬유
☐ radio	무선 통신, 무전
☐ electromagnetic	전자기의
☐ supplement	보충하다
☐ build up	강화하다, 증진하다
☐ transmit	전송하다, 송신하다

☐ carry out	수행하다
☐ facilitate	용이하게 하다
☐ bring together	~을 합치다, 결합시키다
☐ encrypt	암호화하다

결국엔 성정혜 영어 하프모의고사
기적사 DAY 13 핵심어휘

01

☐ let on	털어놓다
☐ duteous	순종하는, 충실한
☐ vain	헛된, 시시한, 허영심이 강한
☐ incandescent	열렬한, 백열광의, 훌륭한
☐ clandestine	비밀의

02

☐ fortuitous	우연한, 우발성의
☐ provoking	자극하는, 유발하는
☐ scattered	산발적인, 뿌려진
☐ seductive	매력적인, 유혹적인

03

☐ make light of	가볍게 여기다
☐ acquitted	무죄인
☐ hoaxed	속은
☐ indisposed	마음이 내키지 않는, 불쾌한
☐ consolidated	강화된, 통합된, 연결된

04

☐ guess	추측하다
☐ raise	올리다; 승급
☐ should have p.p.	진작에 했어야 했다
☐ get accustomed to~	~에 익숙해지다

☐ chicken out	겁이 많다
☐ poke your nose into~	~에 참견하다
☐ your head against the wall	쇠귀에 경 읽기

08

☐ Pastafarianism	파스타파리아니즘, 날아다니는 스파게티 괴물교
☐ mock	가짜의, 조롱의, 풍자의
☐ demand	요구하다
☐ evolution	진화론
☐ Pastafarian	파스타파리안, 날아다니는 스파게티 괴물 신도
☐ worship	숭배하다
☐ privilege	특권
☐ jurisdiction	사법권, 관할권
☐ seek	추구하다, 얻으려고 (노력)하다
☐ recognition	인정
☐ varying	다양한
☐ colander	(음식 재료의 물을 빼는 데 쓰는) 여과기, 체
☐ permit	허가하다, 허락하다
☐ headgear	머리 장식물, (머리에 쓰는 모자 등의) 쓸 것
☐ recognize	인정하다, 인식하다

09

☐ existence	존재
☐ poll	여론 조사, 투표
☐ somewhat	어느 정도, 다소
☐ fairly	매우, 아주, 꽤
☐ debate	논쟁
☐ scholar	학자
☐ claim	주장하다
☐ facilitate	촉진하다, 용이하게 하다
☐ well-being	(건강과) 행복, 웰빙

☐ lead to	초래하다, 일으키다, 이어지다
☐ neurosis	신경증
☐ pseudo-religion	사이비종교
☐ obvious	명확한, 분명한

10

☐ identify as	~라고 밝히다
☐ Protestant	개신교도
☐ Mormon	모르몬교도
☐ represent	대표하다
☐ bloc	세력권, 진영, 연합
☐ Judaism	유대교
☐ practitioner	(특정 생활·종교 양식을) 실천하는 사람
☐ Baha'i faith	바하이교 (신앙)
☐ various	다양한

결국엔 성정혜 영어 하프모의고사
기적사 DAY 14 핵심어휘

01

☐ magnificent	훌륭한, 멋진, 아름다운
☐ let down	실망시키다
☐ fructuous	비옥한, 열매가 많은, 다산의
☐ hollow	실속이 없는, 표면이 우묵한, 공허한
☐ luxurious	낭비하는, 일류의, 화려한
☐ rampant	(병, 범죄, 소문 등이) 만연한, 무성한, 덤벼들 것 같은

02

☐ comply	준수하다
☐ apprehend	체포하다, 이해하다
☐ haste	서두르다

☐ adhere	고집하다, 충실하다, 달라붙다

03

☐ encumber	간섭하다, (책임을) 지우다
☐ seclude	고립시키다, 은퇴시키다
☐ mitigate	완화하다, 경감하다
☐ discern	구별하다, 알아보다

04

☐ hire	고용하다
☐ temporary staff	임시직원
☐ budget	예산
☐ pay for	지불하다
☐ human resources	인사부
☐ right away	당장
☐ handle	다루다, 처리하다
☐ play it by ear	임기응변하다
☐ turn a blind eye to	못 본 체 하다
☐ bite off more than one can chew	분에 넘치는 일을 하려고 하다
☐ work overtime	초과 근무를 하다

08

☐ referee	심판
☐ officiate	심판을 맡아 보다
☐ athletic	운동(육상) 경기의
☐ impose	부과하다
☐ penalty	벌칙, 패널티
☐ official	(운동 경기의) 경기 임원 (심판원·기록원 등)
☐ diploma	졸업 증서
☐ equivalent	동등한, 상당하는
☐ umpire	심판
☐ possess	보유하다, 소유하다
☐ occur	생기다, 발생하다
☐ requirement	요건, 필요조건

09

☐ home plate	본루, 홈베이스
☐ umpire	심판
☐ call	판정
☐ threat	위협하다
☐ comeback	만회, 역전
☐ closer	마무리투수
☐ slugger	강타자
☐ pitch	투구
☐ mph	시속 …마일
☐ cutter	커터(컷패스트볼 (cut fastball))
☐ batter's box	배터박스, 타자석
☐ significantly	상당히, 중대하게
☐ disbelief	불신
☐ stray	빗나간, 길 잃은
☐ seldom	거의 ~않는
☐ rectify	바로잡다, 정정하다
☐ harshly	가혹하게, 심하게
☐ berate	비난하다, 몹시 꾸짖다

10

☐ referee	심판
☐ umpire	심판
☐ terminology	용어
☐ sports official	스포츠 심판
☐ be riddled with	(특히 나쁜 것이) 가득하다[-투성이다]
☐ case	사실, 실상
☐ dizzying	어지럽게 만드는, 현기증을 일으키는
☐ an array of	다수의, 다양한
☐ unifying	통일[통합]하는, 통일적인
☐ structure	구조, 구성
☐ as to	~에 관한
☐ trap	(사람을 속이는) 함정 [덫]
☐ interchangeable	교환할 수 있는
☐ established	확립된

☐ lead official	주심
☐ lacrosse	라크로스(양 팀 10명씩 하는 하키 비슷한 구기)
☐ a variety of	다양한

기적사 DAY 15 핵심어휘

01

☐ turmoil	소란
☐ stink	악취가 나다, 평판이 나쁘다, 악취로 가득 차게 하다
☐ snuff	킁킁 냄새 맡다
☐ convert	전환하다, 바꾸다, 개조하다, 개종하다
☐ covert	비밀의, 은밀한, 암암리의

02

☐ assign	할당하다
☐ step out	은퇴하다, 잠깐 떠나다
☐ flash on	떠올리다
☐ hop off	이륙하다
☐ take up	차지하다, 걸리다, 시작하다

03

☐ unsurpassed	전례 없는, 뛰어난, 비길 데 없는
☐ verbose	말이 많은
☐ unadulterated	순수한, 완전한
☐ ordinary	일상의, 평범한

04

☐ up to sb	~에게 달려있다
☐ cannot agree more	전적으로 동의하다

☐ Speak for yourself	너만 그렇다
☐ It's no big deal	별거 아니다

08

☐ inflation	인플레이션, 통화 팽창, 물가 상승
☐ consistent	지속적인
☐ currency	통화
☐ widget	(가공의 것으로써 말해지는) 이런저런 제품
☐ worth	…의 가치가 있는[되는]
☐ opposite	반대
☐ deflation	디플레이션, 통화 수축, 물가 하락
☐ deflationary	디플레이션의

09

☐ inflation	인플레이션, 통화 팽창, 물가 상승
☐ upside	(나쁜 상황 속의) 좋은 면
☐ anticipate	예상하다, 기대하다
☐ worth	…의 가치가 있는[되는]
☐ prevent	예방하다, 막다
☐ deflation	디플레이션, 통화 수축, 물가 하락
☐ inverse	역의, 반대의
☐ cut back	축소하다, 삭감하다
☐ workforce	노동자, 노동력
☐ at all costs	무슨 수를 써서라도, 어떻게 해서든, 반드시
☐ critical	결정적인, 대단히 중요한
☐ stabilize	안정시키다

10

☐ in stock	재고가 있는
☐ underpin	근거가 되다
☐ head	이끌다
☐ preside	지배하다, 통솔하다
☐ declare	선언하다
☐ inflation rate	물가 상승률, 인플레이션율

☐ flee(fled-fled)	떠나다, 벗어나다	
☐ regime	정권	
☐ oppressive	강압적인, 억압하는	
☐ dissent	반대 의견, 반대	
☐ estimated	추정의, 추측의	

결국엔 성정혜 영어 하프모의고사
기적사 DAY 16 핵심어휘

01
☐ promotional	선전용의, 홍보의

02
☐ disappoint	실망시키다
☐ eventually	결국

03
☐ Jew	유대인
☐ ethnically	민족적으로
☐ decisive	결정적인, 단호한
☐ permissible	허용되는, 무방한
☐ lest	~하지 않도록
☐ stigma	치욕, 오명, 낙인
☐ stuck up	우쭐대는, 건방진

04
☐ cup of tea	(보통 부정문에 사용) 기호에 맞는 사람(물건)
☐ ride	놀이기구

08
☐ law enforcement	법 집행
☐ detective	수사관
☐ crime lab	범죄 수사 연구소
☐ body fluid	체액
☐ saliva	타액, 침
☐ fingerprint	지문
☐ match	일치하다
☐ convicted	유죄 판결을 받은
☐ permanently	영구적으로
☐ reveal	드러내다, 밝히다
☐ medication	약, 물약
☐ identify	신분을 확인하다
☐ as a result	결과적으로

09
☐ juvenile	청소년의
☐ undergo	겪다, 거치다
☐ cling to	~에 매달리다, ~을 고수하다
☐ corporal	신체의
☐ reclaim	갱생시키다, 교정하다
☐ rehabilitate	재활시키다
☐ orthodox	정통의
☐ passing	(법안 등의) 통과
☐ draw upon[on]	~을 이용하다, ~에 의지하다
☐ delinquency	비행, 범죄
☐ parenting	육아
☐ reformation	개혁, 개선
☐ magistrate	치안판사
☐ overhaul	점검하다
☐ curb	억누르다
☐ proponent	옹호자, 지지자
☐ accentuate	강조하다

10
☐ definite	분명한, 뚜렷한, 확실한, 확고한
☐ hierarchy	계급, 계층
☐ elaborate	정교한, 정성을 들인
☐ banquet	연회, 만찬
☐ in charge of	~을 맡아서, 담당해서
☐ steward	호텔종사원
☐ supervise	감독하다, 지휘하다, 지도하다

☐ butler	집사(대저택의 남자 하인 중 책임자)
☐ silverware	은식기류
☐ confection	과자, 당과 제품
☐ undercook	요리사의 조수

결국엔 성정혜 영어 하프모의고사
기적사 DAY 17 핵심어휘

01

☐ capable	유능한
☐ informal	비공식적인
☐ bothersome	귀찮은, 성가신
☐ ordinary	보통의, 일반적인, 평범한

02

☐ pre-monarchical	군주제 이전의
☐ narratives	이야기
☐ get over	극복하다
☐ outspoken	솔직한
☐ principal	주요한, 원금의, 우두머리, 장, 주연 배우
☐ connotative	암시하는
☐ improvised	즉흥적인

03

☐ abortive	쓸모없는
☐ furious	격노한, 격렬한
☐ intellectual	지적인
☐ unparalleled	전례 없는

04

☐ immediately	즉시, 바로
☐ the lost and found	분실물 보관소
☐ Even Homer sometimes nods.	원숭이도 나무에서 떨어질 때가 있다.

08

☐ burden of proof	입증 책임
☐ claim	주장하다
☐ welfare state	사회 복지
☐ strangle	억제하다, 억누르다
☐ productivity	생산성
☐ besides	~외에
☐ social welfare	사회 복지
☐ relative to	~에 비례하여
☐ industrialized	산업화된
☐ expenditure	지출
☐ adverse effect	역효과
☐ crude	있는 그대로의, 날것의, 미가공의
☐ ill effect	부작용

09

☐ ammunition	자신의 주장에 유리한 정보[조언], 공격[방어] 수단
☐ desirability	바람직함
☐ feasibility	가능성, 실행할 수 있음
☐ backward country	후진국
☐ object	목표, 목적
☐ distribution	분배
☐ wisdom	타당성
☐ prediction	예측, 예상
☐ regarding	~에 관한

10

☐ contradiction	모순
☐ paradox	역설
☐ income inequality	소득 불평등
☐ macro	거시적인
☐ illusion	환상, 환각
☐ Gini ratio	지니계수(소득분배의 불균형 수치)
☐ income gap	소득 격차
☐ reserve	확보하다
☐ make it	가다, 도달하다

☐ social welfare	사회 복지
☐ poverty	빈곤
☐ ultimately	궁극적으로

기적사 DAY 18 핵심어휘

01

☐ enigmatic	불가사의한, 수수께끼의
☐ momentous	중요한
☐ affordable	입수 가능한, (가격 등이) 알맞은
☐ incomparable	비길 데 없는, 비교할 수 없는

02

☐ get away	도망가다
☐ confident	건방진, 확신 있는
☐ reserved	냉담한, 남겨 둔, 예약되어 있는
☐ integrative	불가결한, 통합적인
☐ plentiful	풍부한

03

☐ unprejudiced	편견 없는
☐ secluded	고독한, 격리된
☐ hospitable	친절한, 환대하는; (기후, 환경이) 쾌적한
☐ unlabored	자연스러운, 노력하지 않은, 불로 소득의

04

☐ cup of tea	(보통 부정문에 사용) 기호에 맞는 사람(물건)
☐ The 비교급, the 비교급	~할수록 ...하다

☐ meet the deadline	마감시한을 맞추다
☐ work against the clock	(마감을 맞추려) 시간을 다투며 일하다
☐ turn night into day	밤늦게까지 일하거나 놀다
☐ touch-and-go	아슬아슬한
☐ odds	확률
☐ from scratch	처음부터
☐ call sb on the carpet	~을 불러 혼내다

08

☐ lobotomy	뇌엽절리술, 로보토미
☐ obsolete	쓸모없게 된, 구식의
☐ physiology	생리학
☐ disorder	장애, 이상
☐ disrupt	파열시키다, 잡아 찢다
☐ circuit	회로, 순환로
☐ controversial	논쟁을 불러일으키는
☐ prescribe	처방하다
☐ psychiatric	정신 의학의
☐ deem	간주하다, 여기다
☐ surgically	외과적으로
☐ prefrontal cortex	전두엽 피질
☐ frontal lobe	전두엽
☐ procedure	수술, 절차, 방식
☐ symptom	증상
☐ at the cost of	~라는 희생을 치르고 [대가로]
☐ impairment	장애
☐ largely	주로, 대부분
☐ discontinue	중단하다, 중지하다
☐ conduct	실시하다
☐ operative	수술의
☐ side effect	부작용

09

☐ neurotransmitter	신경전달물질
☐ circuit	순환(로), 순회(노선)

결국엔 성정혜 영어 하프모의고사
기적사 DAY 19 핵심어휘

☐ biology	(생물의 특유한) 생활 현상, 생활사
☐ involve	관련시키다, 포함하다
☐ run in family	집안 내력이다, 유전되다
☐ trigger	촉발시키다
☐ worsen	악화시키다
☐ psychological	심리적인
☐ abuse	학대
☐ divorce	이혼
☐ aggravate	악화시키다

10

☐ evidence	증거
☐ abound	풍부하다, 많이 있다
☐ inhumane	비인간적인, 비인도적인, 잔인한
☐ evolve	(서서히) 발전하다, 진화하다
☐ practitioner	(개업) 의사
☐ seizure	발작, 경련
☐ epilepsy	간질
☐ schizophrenia	조현병
☐ intentionally	의도적으로, 고의적으로
☐ induce	유도하다
☐ medication	약물, 투약
☐ stimulant	흥분제
☐ metrazol	중추 신경 흥분제, 메트라졸
☐ effective	효과적인
☐ outcome	결과
☐ realize	깨닫다, 알아차리다
☐ mutually	상호적으로, 서로
☐ inclusive	포괄적인, 포함하는
☐ therapy	치료(법)
☐ lead to	~로 이어지다, 초래하다
☐ electric shock	전기충격
☐ electroconvulsive therapy	전기 경련 요법

01

☐ typical	전형적인
☐ humble	수수한
☐ subtle	미묘한
☐ delectable	맛있는, 기분 좋은

02

☐ converse	이야기하다
☐ get down	내려가다
☐ refrain	억제하다
☐ assign	분배하다

03

☐ interior	안의/내부
☐ experienced	경험 있는
☐ prudently	신중하게
☐ inextricably	밀접하게
☐ irrespectively	관계없이
☐ fastidiously	꼼꼼하게, 세심하게, 까다롭게

04

☐ cry wolf	(도와달라고) 거짓으로 소란 피우다
☐ package	택배
☐ I am at your command.	시키는 대로 하겠다.
☐ stack	쌓다
☐ for the birds	필요 없는
☐ get cold feet	겁을 먹다

08

☐ evolve	진화하다
☐ former	전자
☐ invertebrate	무척추동물

☐ arthropod	절지동물
☐ emerge	나타나다, 등장하다, 나오다
☐ vibration	진동
☐ trilobite	삼엽충
☐ compound eye	(곤충 등의) 겹눈, 복안
☐ eyespot	안점 (하등 동물의 시각 기관)
☐ lens	수정체
☐ multicellular	다세포의

09

☐ interact	상호작용하다
☐ blindness	시각상실
☐ disability	(신체) 장애
☐ deafness	청각상실
☐ retinal cancer	망막모세포종
☐ navigate	방향을 찾다, 돌아다니다
☐ sign language	수화
☐ lip reading	구화, 독순술
☐ clicking sound	혀 차는 소리, 흡착음, 딸깍 하는 소리
☐ three-dimensional	3차원의

10

☐ insert	삽입하다, 끼워 넣다
☐ saccade	단속성 운동, 도약 안구 운동 (안구가 한 응시점에서 다른 응시점으로 신속하게 이동하는 운동)
☐ occur	발생하다, 일어나다
☐ take in	받아들이다
☐ detect	탐지하다, 간파하다, 감지하다
☐ ear canal	외이도
☐ middle-ear muscles	중이근
☐ tug	잡아당기다, 끌어당기다
☐ eardrum	고막
☐ indicate	나타내다, 가리키다

☐ interact	상호작용하다
☐ perceive	지각하다, 감지하다

결국엔 성정혜 영어 하프모의고사
기적사 DAY 20 핵심어휘

01

☐ leverage	지렛대
☐ deliberately	신중하게, 의도적으로
☐ typically	전형적으로
☐ fleshly	신체의, 속세의, 관능적인
☐ promptly	즉시, 급히, 신속히

02

☐ get ahead	성공하다
☐ termly	정기적으로
☐ minutely	세심하게
☐ permanently	영구적으로
☐ promptly	즉시, 급히, 신속히

03

☐ athletic	건강한, 운동선수의
☐ eco-friendly	친환경적인
☐ precisely	세심하게, 정확하게
☐ promptly	즉시, 급히, 신속히
☐ pleasantly	매우 기쁘게
☐ independently	관계없이

04

☐ depressed	우울한
☐ hopeless	절망적인
☐ disheartened	낙담한
☐ it serves you right	꼴 좋다
☐ that's the way cookie crumbles	세상사가 그런 거야

□ every dog has its day	쥐구멍에도 볕들 날이 있다
□ let the cat out of the bag	비밀을 누설하다

08

□ leading	대표적인, 선두적인
□ singularity	특이점
□ inflate	팽창하다
□ instrument	기구, 장치
□ astronomer	천문학자
□ peer at	~을 응시하다, 살펴보다
□ mathematical	수학적인
□ formula	공식
□ echo	흔적, 자취, 반향, 메아리
□ expansion	확장
□ phenomenon	현상
□ cosmic microwave background	우주배경복사

09

□ expand	확장하다
□ accelerate	속도를 늘리다, 가속하다
□ redshift	적색이동하다
□ detectable	찾아낼[탐지할] 수 있는
□ astronomer	천문학자
□ microwave background radiation	마이크로파 배경복사
□ existence	존재
□ radiation	방사선
□ cosmological	우주 철학의
□ cease	중지하다, 멈추다
□ reverse	거꾸로[반대로] 하다
□ culminate in	드디어[결국] …이 되다
□ collapse	붕괴, 무너짐
□ crunch	부서짐
□ rip	찢어짐

□ eventually	결국, 마침내
□ lead to	~로 이어지다
□ tear apart	갈가리 찢어[뜯어] 버리다
□ overtake	추월하다, 따라잡다
□ take place	발생하다

10

□ civil engineer	토목기사
□ artillery officer	포병장교
□ seminary	(가톨릭의) 신학교[대학]
□ ordain	(성직자로) 임명하다
□ priest	신부, 사제
□ solar physics	태양 물리학
□ laboratory	연구실, 실험실
□ acquainted with	~를 알고 있는, ~을 알게 되어
□ finding	발견
□ astronomer	천문학자
□ expand	확장하다, 팽창하다
□ astrophysics	천체 물리학
□ recession	후퇴, 침체
□ framework	틀, 뼈대
□ theory of general relativity	일반 상대성 이론
□ notably	특히
□ Dutch	네덜란드의
□ modify	수정하다, 변형하다
□ leading	매우 중요한, 이끄는, 선두의
□ cosmology	우주론
□ be engaged in	~에 종사하다
□ warfare	전쟁
□ clergyman	성직자

결국엔 성정혜 영어 하프모의고사
기적사 DAY 21 핵심어휘

01

☐ relic	유물, 유적
☐ sensibility	감성, 감수성
☐ bury	매장하다
☐ excavate	발굴하다, 파내다
☐ exhume	파내다, 발굴하다
☐ pack	짐을 싸다(꾸리다)

02

☐ joy ride	폭주 드라이브, 재미있는 드라이브
☐ strap	끈으로 묶다
☐ questioning	의문, 의심
☐ sheer	완전한, 순전한
☐ rush	급증
☐ utter	완전한
☐ scary	무서운
☐ occasional	가끔의
☐ manageable	관리(감당)할 수 있는

03

☐ slow to a trickle	아주 느려지다, 아주 소량으로 줄다
☐ race	급히 뛰다, 빨리 달리다
☐ be engrossed in	~에 열중하다
☐ apathetic	무관심한
☐ stabilize	안정시키다
☐ be preoccupied with	~에 사로잡히다

04

☐ exchange	교환하다
☐ currency	통화, 돈
☐ convert	전환하다, 변환하다
☐ exchange rate	환율
☐ commission	수수료

☐ receipt	영수증
☐ buy-back	역 구매, 되사기

05

☐ pedestrian	보행자
☐ globally	전 세계적으로
☐ constitute	구성하다
☐ fatality	사망자
☐ proportion	비율
☐ injure	부상을 입히다
☐ be left with	~를 계속 지니다
☐ permanent	영구적인
☐ disability	장애
☐ suffering	고통
☐ grief	비탄
☐ hardship	어려움, 곤란

08

☐ haunt	떠나지 않다, 계속 출몰하다
☐ make sense of	이해하다
☐ weigh down	짓누르다
☐ make progress	전진하다, 진행하다
☐ discipline	학문 분야, 훈련, 훈육
☐ be familiar with	~에 익숙하다
☐ deliberately	의도적으로, 고의적으로, 신중하게
☐ strip down	분해하다, 분해되다, 벗겨내다, 벗겨지다
☐ representation	묘사, 표현
☐ phenomenon	현상
☐ thus	이와 같이, 따라서
☐ in terms of	~라는 면에서
☐ join to	~로 잇다
☐ relevant	관련된
☐ contemporary	현대의, 동시대의
☐ causal	원인이 되는, 원인의
☐ enable	가능하게 해주다
☐ aspect	측면, 양상
☐ interact	상호작용하다

09

☐ prehistoric	선사 시대의
☐ distinguish	구별하다
☐ physical	신체적인, 물리적인
☐ disorder	장애
☐ abnormal	비정상적인
☐ convulsive	경련의
☐ convulsive attack	경련 발작
☐ attribute A to B	A를 B의 탓/덕분으로 돌리다
☐ evil spirit	악령
☐ inhabit	거주하다
☐ afflicted	병에 걸린
☐ demonic possession	악령의 빙의
☐ sorcery	마법
☐ behest	명령, 간청
☐ offended	화가 난
☐ ancestral	조상의
☐ demonology	귀신론
☐ be (held) responsible for	~에 책임이 있다
☐ partly	부분적으로
☐ misfortune	불행(한 일), 불운
☐ cave dweller	동굴 거주자
☐ treat	치료하다
☐ surgical	수술의, 외과의
☐ skull	두개골
☐ chip away	깎다, 쪼다
☐ opening	구멍, 틈
☐ escape	빠져나가다, 탈출하다
☐ state	상태
☐ heal over	아물다, 낫다
☐ indicate	암시하다, 보여주다, 언급하다
☐ patient	환자
☐ crude	조잡한, 거친, 날것의
☐ operation	수술
☐ differentiate	구별하다
☐ result from	~에서 비롯되다

10

☐ upend	뒤집다, 충격을 주다
☐ transformation	변신, 변형
☐ frequency	빈도
☐ make up	지어내다
☐ go along	계속하다, 진행하다
☐ show up	나타나다, 등장하다
☐ immigration	이민
☐ at the top of the hour	매 정시에
☐ at the bottom of the hour	매시 30분에
☐ presidential convention	대선 후보 선정을 위한 전당대회
☐ script	대본

결국엔 성정혜 영어 하프모의고사
기적사 DAY 22 핵심어휘

01

☐ wall painting	벽화
☐ expunge	지우다, 파괴하다, 멸종시키다
☐ shovel	~을 파다, ~을 삽으로 뜨다.
☐ reinforce	강화하다
☐ immerse	몰두시키다

02

☐ absolute	완전한, 순수한, 확고한
☐ essential	필수의, 본질적인
☐ bullish	낙관적인, 완고한, 어리석은
☐ obligatory	강제적인, 필수의, 평소의

03

☐ loom	어렴풋이 나타나다, 솟아오르다, 우뚝 서다
☐ immerse	몰두시키다
☐ ruin	망가뜨리다, 파산시키다, ~을 타락시키다
☐ discriminate	식별하다, 차별하다

04

☐ in a while	최근에
☐ get better	나아지다
☐ stress out	스트레스를 받다
☐ properly	제대로

05

☐ look through	~을 자세히 살펴보다
☐ relevant	관계가 있는
☐ appear	생기다, 나타나다
☐ attempt	시도하다, 애써 해보다
☐ attach	붙이다, 첨부하다
☐ compare	비교하다

08

☐ simplify	단순화하다
☐ description	설명, 묘사
☐ yield	산출하다, 만들어내다
☐ hypothesis	가설 (pl. hypotheses)
☐ consist of	~로 구성되다
☐ equation	방정식
☐ describe	설명하다, 묘사하다
☐ clue	단서, 실마리
☐ rational	합리적인
☐ agent	행위자
☐ feature	특징
☐ necessarily	필연적으로, 반드시
☐ subjective	주관적인
☐ objective	객관적인
☐ measure	기준, 척도
☐ outcome	결과물

☐ judgement	판단
☐ explain	설명하다
☐ interpretation	해석

09

☐ prior to	이전에
☐ ether	에테르
☐ anesthesia	마취
☐ absolutely	극도로, 굉장히
☐ radical	극단적인, 과격한
☐ wide-awake	완전히 깨어있는
☐ oftentimes	종종, 자주(= often)
☐ hold down	억제하다, 제압하다
☐ operating	수술의
☐ plea	간청
☐ sob	흐느낌, 흐느껴 울기
☐ standardized	표준화된
☐ guarantee	보장하다, 보증하다
☐ quality	품질, 질
☐ when it comes to	…에 관한 한
☐ overjoy	매우 기쁘게 하다
☐ embrace	수용하다, 받아들이다
☐ transformative	변화시키는, 변화시키는 힘이 있는
☐ innovation	혁신
☐ immediacy	긴박, 즉시(성)
☐ surgeon	(외과) 의사
☐ consciousness	의식
☐ horrifically	끔찍하게, 무시무시하게
☐ regain	회복하다, 되찾다
☐ overdose	과잉 투여, 과다 복용

10

☐ neutral	중립적인
☐ debate	토론
☐ complicated	복잡한
☐ detached	사심 없는, 공정한, 거리를 두는
☐ observer	관찰자

☐ process	과정
☐ participate in	…에 참여하다
☐ neutrality	중립성
☐ detachment	공정성, 분리
☐ primary debate	예비선거 토론회
☐ authority	권위자
☐ declare	선언하다
☐ determination	결정
☐ B-roll	특징적인 소리가 빠진 영상, 리포터가 묘사와 해설을 할 때 쓰이는 영상
☐ consensus	(의견) 일치
☐ organically	조직적으로
☐ mainstream	주류의
☐ objective	객관적인
☐ forum	(공개) 토론
☐ coverage	보도, 취재

결국엔 성정혜 영어 하프모의고사
기적사 DAY 23 핵심어휘

01

☐ disclose	공개하다, 폭로하다
☐ ebb	쇠퇴하다
☐ bundle	싸다, 재촉하여 몰아내다
☐ preserve	보존하다

02

☐ inertia	무력감
☐ hideous	끔찍한, 무시무시한
☐ extend	확장하다
☐ daunt	기죽게 하다, ~을 위협하다
☐ dissatisfy	언짢게 하다
☐ say	말하다
☐ railing	욕설
☐ rail	욕하다

☐ panegyric	칭찬, 찬사
☐ fellow	같은 처지에 있는

03

☐ component	구성 요소
☐ suicidal	자살의
☐ disinhibition	탈억제
☐ slacken	줄이다, 느슨하게 되다
☐ intensify	~을 강하게 하다, ~을 증대하다
☐ stow	채워 넣다, 수용할 수 있다
☐ unearth	발굴하다, 폭로하다, ~을 발견하다

04

☐ impress	감명을 주다
☐ starring	주연의

05

☐ communicate A to B	A를 B에게 전달하다
☐ organization	조직, 단체, 기구
☐ organizationwide	조직 전체에
☐ executive	간부, 임원
☐ attention	관심, 주의, 주목
☐ cathedral	대성당

08

☐ simulate	시뮬레이션하다, 모의실험 하다
☐ forecast	예측하다; 예측
☐ given	~을 고려하면
☐ behavioral	행동의, 행동에 관한
☐ working	작용
☐ take ~ as given	~을 기정사실로 하다
☐ respond to	~에 반응하다
☐ spike	급등, 급증
☐ effective	효과적인
☐ precisely	정확하게

☐ not least	특히
☐ structural	구조적인
☐ uncertainty	불확실성
☐ projection	예상, 추정
☐ at best	기껏해야
☐ illustrative	설명적인, 예증하는
☐ marginal	미미한, 중요하지 않은, 주변부의
☐ impulse	충격
☐ transformation	변형, 변화
☐ vague	모호한, 애매한
☐ theoretical	이론적인

09

☐ ailment	(그렇게 심각하지 않은) 질병
☐ involve	포함하다, 수반하다
☐ supernatural	초자연적인
☐ element	요소
☐ priest	승려, 사제
☐ call on	요청하다, 요구하다
☐ physician	(내과) 의사
☐ incantation	주문, 마법
☐ ingredient	재료
☐ emphasis	강조
☐ remedy	치료(약)
☐ seemingly	외견상으로, 겉보기에는
☐ derive	끌어내다, 얻다
☐ substance	물질
☐ in some way	어떤 점에서는
☐ correspond to	…에[와] 일치하다, 들어맞다
☐ symptom	증상
☐ ostrich	타조
☐ amulet	부적
☐ portray	그리다, 묘사하다
☐ hedgehog	고슴도치
☐ baldness	대머리, 탈모
☐ due to	…때문에
☐ being	존재

☐ process	절차, 과정
☐ perform	행하다

10

☐ drastic	과감한, 강렬한
☐ partake	참여하다
☐ process	과정, 절차
☐ ordinary	평범한, 보통의
☐ source	공급자, 근원
☐ define	정의하다
☐ required	필수의
☐ gain expertise (in)	전문적 식견을 쌓다
☐ prospective	장래의, 미래의
☐ savvy	소식에 밝은, (사정에) 정통해 있는
☐ influencer	인플루언서(많은 SNS 팔로워를 보유한 유명인)
☐ emergence	등장, 출현
☐ consume	소비하다
☐ positive	긍정적인
☐ have no choice but to	~할 수밖에 없다
☐ be engaged in	…에 몰두하다, 종사하다

결국엔 성정혜 영어 하프모의고사
기적사 DAY 24 핵심어휘

01

☐ complimentary	찬사의, 무료의
☐ captivate	마음을 사로잡다
☐ differentiate	~을 식별하다, 차이를 만들다, ~을 분화시키다
☐ commemorate	축하하다, 기념하다
☐ discontinue	그만두다, 포기하다, 중단되다

02

☐ ingenious	독창적인
☐ frightening	무서운
☐ splendid	화려한, 훌륭한
☐ efficient	능률적인

03

☐ sedulous	근면한, 부지런한
☐ sporadic	산발적인
☐ absolute	완전한, 순수한, 확고한
☐ reciprocal	상호 간의, 보답의
☐ indifferent	무관심한, 공평한

04

☐ head to~ be headed to be heading to	~로 향하다, ~로 가다 ~로 향하다(상태에 초점) ~로 향하다(진행에 초점)
☐ cafeteria	카페테리아, (기업, 학교의) 구내식당
☐ have company	일행이 있다
☐ gain weight	살이 찌다

05

☐ non-agricultural employment	비 농업직
☐ Pacific	태평양의
☐ percentage	비율

08

☐ existing	기존의
☐ unable	~할 수 없는
☐ either A or B	A 또는 B 둘 중 하나
☐ explain	설명하다
☐ cause	원인
☐ severe	극심한, 심한
☐ collapse	붕괴, 무너짐
☐ adequate	알맞은, 충분한
☐ jump-start	활성화하다, 재생시키다
☐ spearhead	선봉에 서다

☐ revolution	혁명
☐ overturn	뒤집다
☐ prevailing	우세한, 지배적인
☐ as long as	~하는 한
☐ flexible	융통성 있는
☐ demand	요구
☐ assert	주장하다, 단언하다
☐ lead to	~로 이어지다
☐ justify	정당화하다
☐ intervention	개입
☐ achieve	달성하다, 도달하다
☐ stability	안정
☐ recession	불황, 침체
☐ up until	…까지
☐ predominating	우세한, 주된, 지배적인
☐ deny	부정하다, 거부하다

09

☐ process	과정, 절차
☐ edible	먹을 수 있는
☐ identify	확인하다, 식별하다
☐ ailment	(그렇게 심각하지 않은) 질병
☐ soothe	진정시키다
☐ physician	(내과) 의사
☐ stumble on	우연히 발견하다
☐ substance	물질
☐ tonic	강장제[음료], 보약
☐ orthodox medicine	전통 의학
☐ extract	추출물
☐ dropsy	수종, 부종
☐ constituent	구성 성분[요소]
☐ standard	일반적인, 보통의
☐ stimulant	각성제, 흥분제
☐ various	다양한
☐ culinary	요리의
☐ purpose	목적
☐ practice	실행하다, 실천하다
☐ as well	또한, 역시

10

☐ admit	인정하다, 시인하다
☐ archive	(데이터 등의) 보관(소)
☐ previous	이전의
☐ prediction	예측
☐ establish	확립하다, 설립하다
☐ continuing	지속적인
☐ presence	존재(함), 있음
☐ draw	(사람의 마음을) 끌다, 끌어들이다
☐ seek (sought – sought)	추구하다
☐ legitimacy	정당성, 합법성, 타당성
☐ credential	자격을 부여하다
☐ presidential	대통령의
☐ convention	(전문직 종사자들이나 정당 등의 대규모) 대회[협의회]
☐ call on	초빙하다, 초청하다
☐ press conference	기자회견
☐ wary	경계하는, 조심하는
☐ entrant	갓 들어온[합류한] 사람
☐ institutional	제도상의, 규격화된
☐ reputation	평판, 명성, 신망
☐ at stake	…에 달려있는, 위기에 처한
☐ prone to	~을 잘하는, ~하는 경향이 있는
☐ accusation	혐의 [제기], 고발, 비난
☐ disseminate	퍼뜨리다
☐ deplore	비탄하다
☐ casual	격식 없는, 가벼운
☐ accuracy	정확성
☐ constant	꾸준한, 지속적인
☐ scrutiny	감시
☐ blogosphere	블로그 세상

기적사 DAY 25 핵심어휘

01

☐ sensibility	민감성
☐ revival	부활, 재생, 회복, 신앙 부흥 운동
☐ enlightenment	깨달음, 계발, 계몽
☐ achievement	업적, 성취
☐ discouragement	좌절

02

☐ additional	부가된, 추가의
☐ alarming	놀라운
☐ intermittent	간헐적인, 주기적인
☐ feasible	편리한, 실현 가능한

03

☐ sustain	지지하다, 유지하다, 견디다
☐ engulf	포로가 되다, 휩쓸리게 하다, ~을 침몰시키다
☐ intensify	~을 강하게 하다, ~을 증대하다
☐ identify	식별하다, 동일시하다

04

☐ mistake	실수
☐ suggest	제안하다, 추천하다
☐ apologize	사과하다
☐ political issue	정치적 문제
☐ donate	기부하다, 기증하다
☐ earnings	소득, 수입
☐ charity	자선단체

05

☐ promote	조장하다, 홍보하다, 승진시키다
☐ disagreement	의견 차이, 다툼

☐ consensus	의견 일치, 합의
☐ coercion	강압, 강제

08

☐ burning	(문제 따위) 의견이 분분한
☐ substitute	대체(물), 대용품
☐ connected	결합된
☐ encourage	장려하다
☐ plenty of	많은
☐ empowerment	권한[기능] 부여, 권한[기능] 분산
☐ lower	낮추다
☐ expense	비용, 경비
☐ replace	대신하다, 대체하다
☐ existing	현존하는, 현재 있는
☐ value	가치
☐ continuum	연속체, 군집 연속
☐ mounting	(흔히 우려스러울 정도로) 증가하는[커지는]
☐ pressure	압력, 압박
☐ in many ways	여러모로
☐ capacity	수용력
☐ face-to-face	마주 보는, 대면하는
☐ intervention	개입, 간섭

09

☐ lolly	사탕
☐ mildly	약간
☐ genetically	유전적으로
☐ averse	싫어하는
☐ response	반응, 응답
☐ hunter-gatherer	수렵·채집인
☐ poisonous	유독한
☐ toxic	유독한
☐ make sense	이해하다, 타당하다
☐ prevent A from B	A가 B하는 것을 막다[예방하다]
☐ potentially	잠재적으로

☐ explain	설명하다
☐ taste bud	미뢰[맛봉오리]
☐ ever so	매우, 몹시, 굉장히
☐ challenging	도전적인, 힘든
☐ genetic	유전의

10

☐ density	밀도, 농도
☐ make up	구성하다
☐ stroke	뇌졸중
☐ absorb	흡수하다
☐ flush	내보내다, (물을) 내리다
☐ lower	낮추다
☐ blood vessel	혈관
☐ plaque	플라크
☐ narrow	좁아지다
☐ blood flow	혈류
☐ organ	기관, 장기
☐ heart attack	심장 발작, 심장마비, 심근경색

결국엔 성정혜 영어 하프모의고사
기적사 DAY 26 핵심어휘

01

☐ justification	정당화
☐ account	설명
☐ deny	부정하다
☐ pejorative	경멸적인
☐ derogatory	경멸적인
☐ extrovert	외향적인
☐ mandatory	의무적인
☐ redundant	불필요한

02

☐ rule out	제외하다

☐ sanitation	위생
☐ cause	원인
☐ yellow fever	황열병
☐ carrier	매개체
☐ suspected	의심되는
☐ uncivilized	문명화되지 않은
☐ volunteered	자진해서

03

☐ concrete	구체적인
☐ project	투사하다
☐ certainty	확실성
☐ fulfill	이행하다, 완수하다
☐ hallucination	환각
☐ template	견본
☐ inquiry	질문, 문의
☐ commotion	소동

04

☐ pressed	다림질한
☐ take	시간이 걸리다

05

☐ inventor	발명가
☐ attribute A to B	A는 B의 덕분이다
☐ capture	잡다
☐ cannibal	식인종
☐ spear	창
☐ sewing machine	재봉틀
☐ feature	특징

06

☐ emerge	드러나다
☐ successor	후계자
☐ embark	착수하다
☐ policy	정책
☐ peaceful coexistence	평화 공존
☐ whereby	~하는

☐ competition	경쟁
☐ confrontational	대립하는
☐ manner	방법

07

☐ cuttlefish	갑오징어
☐ cephalopod	두족류
☐ contain	포함하다
☐ pigment	색소
☐ appearance	외모, 외향

08

☐ throughout	~전반에 걸쳐, ~전역에, ~하는 내내
☐ wilderness	황무지
☐ field	들판
☐ term	용어
☐ vacant	비어 있는
☐ refer to	~를 의미하다
☐ gather	모이다, 모으다
☐ spontaneous	즉흥(자발)적인
☐ vacate	비우다, 떠나다
☐ texting	문자 전송
☐ rural	시골의
☐ roam	돌아다니다, 배회하다
☐ free-ranging	마음대로 돌아다니는
☐ unaccompanied	동반되지 않는, 함께 하지 않는
☐ fort	진지, 요새
☐ terrain	지형
☐ creek	개울, 시내
☐ urban	도시의
☐ counterpart	비교 대상, 상대방
☐ turn to	~에 의지하다
☐ sedentary	앉아서 지내는, 몸을 움직이지 않는
☐ entertainment	오락

09

☐ famine	기근

☐ die of	~로 죽다
☐ rest	나머지
☐ shortage	부족
☐ dehydration	탈수
☐ deport	강제 추방하다
☐ trauma	충격적 경험, 외상
☐ immigrate	이주하다
☐ starvation	기아
☐ emigrate	이주하다
☐ fatigue	피로
☐ detain	억류하다

10

☐ component	요소
☐ virtual - reality	가상현실
☐ on one's way to	~로 가는 도중에
☐ accessible	이용(출입/접근) 가능한
☐ affordable	(가격이) 알맞은
☐ convincingly	설득력 있게
☐ break apart	부서지다, 쪼개지다
☐ midcourt	코트 가운데
☐ may as well V	~하는 편이 낫다
☐ get a sense	감을 잡다
☐ inadequate	부적절한
☐ battlefield	전장, 전쟁터
☐ distant	먼
☐ row	줄, 열

결국엔 성정혜 영어 하프모의고사
기적사 DAY 27 핵심어휘

01

☐ pejorative	경멸적인, 비난하는 의미의
☐ pertinacious	끈질긴, 집요한, 고수하는

☐ controversial	논란의 여지가 있는, 갈등을 빚고 있는
☐ guileless	순진한, 성실한

02

☐ sanitation	공중위생
☐ drastic	강렬한, 급격한
☐ detrimental	불리한, 해로운
☐ impressionable	예민한
☐ incongruous	앞뒤가 맞지 않는, 조화되지 않는

03

☐ corresponding	상응하는, 통신의
☐ avaricious	탐욕스러운, 갈망하는
☐ hallucinated	환각이 느껴진
☐ peremptory	결정적인, 위압적인, 거만한

04

☐ arrive	도착하다
☐ plan on~	~을 계획하다
☐ traffic jam	교통 체증
☐ decide	결정하다
☐ trip	여행, 여정
☐ manage to~	~을 가까스로 해내다

05

☐ lend A B	A에게 B를 빌려주다
☐ turn A into B	A를 B로 바꾸다
☐ publication	출판, 발행
☐ version	판, 형태
☐ copy	사본

06

☐ relevant	관련 있는, 적절한
☐ self - definition	자기 인식
☐ engage in	~에 관여하다, 참여하다
☐ reflection	반영, 반사

□ whereby	(그것에 의하여) …하는
□ accomplishment	성취, 업적, 공적

07

□ cognitive	인지의, 인식의
□ sort	종류, 부류, 유형
□ analyze	분석하다, 분해하다
□ extensive	아주 넓은, 광범위한
□ factual	사실에 기반을 둔

08

□ emergency	응급
□ treat	치료하다
□ equipment	기구, 설비
□ prevent	예방하다
□ make sure	확실히 하다
□ surface	표면
□ underneath	아래에
□ absorb	흡수하다
□ soften	약화시키다, 부드럽게 하다
□ impact	충격
□ land	(땅에) 떨어지다
□ steer clear of	…에 가까이 가지 않다, …을 비키다
□ material	재료
□ wood chip	우드칩, 목재칩(목재를 잘게 절삭한 목재 조각)
□ mulch	피복(포장 토양의 표면을 여러 가지 재료로 덮는 것)
□ extend	(거리가 어떤 점까지) 달하다
□ avoid	피하다

09

□ famine	기근
□ catastrophic	파멸의, 비극적인
□ turbulent	격동의
□ regard	간주하다
□ context	맥락, 상황

□ controversial	논쟁의
□ for	왜냐하면 …이므로, 그 까닭은
□ empire	제국
□ sufficient	충분한
□ starvation	기아, 굶주림
□ flee	달아나다, 피난 가다, 도망치다
□ describe	설명하다, 묘사하다
□ mass	대량의, 집단의

10

□ Augmented Reality	(AR) 증강현실
□ Virtual Reality	(VR) 가상현실
□ variation	다양성
□ immerse	~에 몰입시키다
□ whether it be~	~이든지 아니든지 간에(성경이나 법조문에 주로 쓰이는 가정법 현재 표현, 현대영어에서는 주로 be 대신에 is를 사용함)
□ haptic	촉각에 관한, 촉각의
□ sensation	감각, 느낌, 감동
□ enhance	~을 강화하다
□ superimpose	첨가하다, 포개 놓다
□ composite	혼합하다
□ application	응용, 지원, 적용

결국엔 성정해 영어 하프모의고사
기적사 DAY 28 핵심어휘

01

□ conjunction	결합, 연결함
□ futile	무익한, 시시한
□ acute	결정적인, 격렬한
□ redundant	불필요한
□ increscent	증가하는

02

☐ suspected	의심되는
☐ contentious	논쟁적인
☐ spiritous	순수한, 알코올성의, 원기 있는, 정신적인
☐ corresponsive	상응하는, 노력에 반응하는

03

☐ conjecture	추측, ~을 추측하다
☐ refine on	~을 개량하다, ~을 갈고 닦다, ~보다 우수하다
☐ at a charge of	~의 비용으로
☐ pertaining to	~에 관하여
☐ notwithstanding	~에도 불구하고

04

☐ scholarship	장학금
☐ materials	직물, 재료, 자료
☐ grocery	식료품 잡화점, 식료품
☐ investment	투자

05

☐ prospect	가망, 예상, 전망
☐ overwhelm	압도하다
☐ provide A with B	A에게 B를 제공하다
☐ assistance	도움, 원조, 지원
☐ extra	추가의, 가외의, 여분의

06

☐ traditional	전통의
☐ consumption	소비, 소모
☐ thrift	절약, 검약, 검소
☐ affluent	부유한
☐ scarce	부족한, 드문
☐ communally	공동으로

07

☐ space	공간

☐ post	게시하다, 발송하다
☐ organize	체계화하다, 조직하다
☐ corrupt	오염시키다, 타락시키다
☐ junk	쓰레기, 폐물
☐ filter	여과장치, 필터

08

☐ mindful	염두에 두는
☐ depending on	~에 따라
☐ minefield	지뢰밭(보이지 않는 위험들이 도사리는 곳)
☐ arrangement	배열
☐ communicate	전달하다, 의사를 소통하다
☐ specific	특정한
☐ intend	의도하다
☐ convey	전하다, 전달하다
☐ safe bet	확실한 것[일]
☐ local	(특정 지역에 사는) 주민, 현지인, 지역 사람
☐ attractively	보기 좋게
☐ just about	모든, 거의
☐ context	상황

09

☐ famine	기근
☐ watershed	분수령
☐ demographic	인구(통계)학의
☐ consequence	결과
☐ agricultural	농업의
☐ smallholder	소규모 자작농[소작농]
☐ undergo	겪다, 경험하다
☐ drastic	급격한
☐ decline	감소
☐ aftereffect	여파
☐ clearing	제거, 청산
☐ concentration	집중
☐ landownership	토지소유권
☐ thereafter	그에 따라, 그 후
☐ graze	방목하다

☐ export	수출
☐ following	다음의, …에 이은

10

☐ immersive	몰입형의
☐ destination	목적지
☐ claustrophobic	밀실 공포증
☐ stateroom	특등실, 특별실, 개인실
☐ test the waters	(행동을 하거나 결정을 내리기 전에) 미리 상황을 살피다 [조심스럽게 알아보다]
☐ explore	답사하다, 탐험하다
☐ A as well as B	B뿐만 아니라 A도
☐ prior to	…에 앞서, 먼저
☐ book	예약하다
☐ aside from	…외에
☐ venue	장소, 현장, 건물
☐ budget	예산, 경비
☐ relive	다시 체험하다

결국엔 성정혜 영어 하프모의고사
기적사 DAY 29 핵심어휘

01

☐ justification	정당화
☐ on behalf of	~을 대신하여, 위해서
☐ in a person's stead	~을 대신하여
☐ in the matter of	~에 관하여
☐ in a class with	~와 동등하게
☐ at a cost of	~의 비용으로

02

☐ clonish	독창성이 없는
☐ callow	미숙한

☐ cumbersome	다루기 어려운, 거추장스러운, 성가신
☐ timid	내성적인, 겁이 많은

03

☐ well-worn	진부한, 오래 써서 낡은
☐ inquiring	탐구심이 있는
☐ offenseless	거슬리지 않는, 악의가 없는
☐ not in the least	조금도 ~가 아니다
☐ not in conclusion	결론이 안 나는

04

☐ mid-term	중간고사
☐ Mathematics	수학
☐ fault	잘못
☐ semester	학기
☐ grade	성적
☐ actually	사실
☐ give up	포기하다

05

☐ competition	경쟁, 대회, 시합
☐ zero sum game	제로섬 게임
☐ organization	조직, 기구
☐ intense	극심한, 강렬한
☐ face A with B	A를 B에 직면시키다
☐ cost	비용

06

☐ interfere	방해하다, 간섭하다
☐ inferior	열등한
☐ superior	우수한, 우월한
☐ species	종
☐ lose out	지다
☐ take over	장악하다

07

☐ aisle	통로

☐ temptation	유혹
☐ exclaim	소리치다, 외치다
☐ row	줄, 열

08

☐ introduce	도입하다
☐ essentially	기본적으로, 본질적으로
☐ platform	기반, 플랫폼
☐ standard	기준
☐ definitely	명확히
☐ comply with	~을 따르다, 준수하다, 지키다
☐ regulation	규정
☐ emerge	나타나다, 생기다
☐ consist of	~로 구성되다
☐ roughly	대충
☐ structure	구조(물)
☐ edge	모서리, 가장자리
☐ do damage	해를 끼치다
☐ crude	조잡한, 거친
☐ properly	제대로, 잘, 올바르게
☐ humble	초라한, 보잘것없는
☐ exclusively	배타적으로, 독점적으로
☐ primitive	원시적인
☐ constantly	지속적으로
☐ sophisticated	정교한, 복잡한, 고도로 발달한
☐ appropriately	알맞게, 적당하게

09

☐ strain	(동, 식물 질병 등의) 종류[유형]
☐ Phytophthora infestans	감자역병균
☐ widespread	널리 퍼진, 광범위한
☐ devastation	황폐, 폐허, 참해
☐ lead to	초래하다, 일으키다
☐ famine	기근
☐ sequence	(유전자 분자의) 배열 순서를 밝히다

☐ genome	게놈
☐ blight	병충해, 마름병
☐ conclude	~을 결론짓다
☐ previously	이전에
☐ molecular biologist	분자 생물학자
☐ extract	~에서 추출하다
☐ botanical	식물의
☐ specimen	견본, 표본
☐ culprit	원인, 범인

10

☐ start-up	신생 회사, 스타트업
☐ spin out	만들다, 스핀아웃 (기업의 일부 사업부 또는 신규 사업을 분리하여 전문 회사를 만드는 것)
☐ team up	협력하다
☐ showcase	공개하다, 소개하다, 선보이다
☐ navigation	운행, 조종
☐ route	경로
☐ steering	(차량의) 조종 장치
☐ g-force	관성력
☐ acceleration	가속도
☐ translate	옮기다
☐ enable	가능하게 하다
☐ correspond to	…에[와] 일치하다, 들어맞다
☐ real-time	실시간의
☐ immerse	몰입시키다

결국엔 성정해 영어 하프모의고사
기적사 DAY 30 핵심어휘

01

☐ monopolistic	독점적인, 전매의
☐ ingenuous	솔직한, 순진한

☐ extrovert	외향적인
☐ humdrum	평범한, 단조로운

02

☐ unreadable	이해하기 어려운, 읽기 어려운
☐ unexampled	전례가 없는
☐ volunteered	자진해서
☐ unballasted	모호한, 불확실한

03

☐ distinguish oneself	두각을 나타내다
☐ blunt	솔직한, 퉁명스러운, 둔화시키다
☐ concrete	구체적인
☐ baffling	당황하게 만드는, 좌절시키는
☐ numerous	다양한, 수많은

04

☐ noticeably	눈에 띄게
☐ indeed	(긍정적인 진술·대답을 강조하여) 정말
☐ surprising	놀라운

05

☐ corporation	회사, 기업
☐ complication	복잡성, 복잡한 상태
☐ set something up	~을 세우다
☐ assign A to B	A를 B에게 부여하다
☐ bring about	~을 야기하다, 초래하다

06

☐ colony	식민지
☐ rigid	경직된, 엄격한
☐ dominance	지배, 우세
☐ hierarchy	계급, 체계
☐ innovation	혁신

07

☐ would like to + 동사원형	~하고 싶다
☐ formation	형성
☐ determine	알아내다, 밝히다
☐ topsoil	표토, 표층토
☐ erosion	부식, 침식
☐ clue	단서, 실마리

08

☐ describe	묘사하다
☐ internal	내적인, 내면의
☐ confidence	자신감
☐ intelligence	지능, 지성
☐ natural-born	타고난, 천부적인
☐ great man theory	위인설
☐ assume	가정하다, 생각하다
☐ capacity	능력
☐ inherent	고유의, 본래부터의
☐ portray	그리다, 묘사하다
☐ mythic	신화의
☐ destined	…할 운명인
☐ rooted	~에 뿌리[근원]를 둔
☐ behaviorism	행동주의
☐ mental	정신의, 마음의
☐ opposed	반대된
☐ nurture	양성하다, 양육하다
☐ approach	접근법, 접근
☐ explain	설명하다

09

☐ dementia	치매
☐ treatment	치료, 치료법
☐ progression	진행
☐ hypertension	고혈압
☐ vascular	(혈관 등의) 관의
☐ affect	영향을 미치다
☐ journal	학술지
☐ finding	발견

☐ indicate	가리키다, 나타내다
☐ cerebral blood flow	대뇌 혈류
☐ translate	바꾸다
☐ note	(중요하거나 흥미로운 것을) 언급하다

10

☐ linguist	언어학자
☐ predict	예언하다, 예상하다
☐ extinct	멸종된
☐ endangered	멸종 위기에 처한
☐ mammal	포유동물
☐ dominate	지배하다
☐ replace A with B	A를 B로 교체[대체]하다
☐ minor	소수의
☐ widespread	널리 퍼진
☐ allow	허용하다, 가능하게 하다
☐ diversity	다양성
☐ not less ~ than	…못지않게 ~한
☐ in its way	그 나름대로
☐ biological	생물학의
☐ extinction	멸종, 사라짐
☐ species	종(種: 생물 분류의 기초 단위)
☐ cause	원인이 되다, 야기하다
☐ ecosystem	생태계
☐ collapse	붕괴하다, 무너지다
☐ in the sense that	~라는 점에서
☐ community	공동 사회, 일반 사회, 공동체
☐ typically	일반적으로, 전형적으로
☐ vehicle	수단, 매개물
☐ abandon	버리다

기적사 DAY 31 핵심어휘

01

☐ paramount	다른 무엇보다 중요한, 최고의
☐ chief	가장 중요한, 주된, 최고의
☐ sworn	맹세한, 선서한
☐ successful	성공한, 성공적인
☐ mysterious	불가사의한, 신비한

02

☐ unusual	특이한, 흔치 않은, 드문, 이상한
☐ ambitious	야심 있는, 포부에 찬
☐ exhausted	지친
☐ saddened	슬픈

03

☐ state-of-the-art	최첨단의, 최신식의
☐ intimidating	겁을 주는, 위협하는

04

☐ shut down	멈추다, 정지하다
☐ charge	충전하다
☐ technician	기술자, 기사

05

☐ in response to	~에 응하여
☐ reference	추천서
☐ requirement	필요조건
☐ job description	직무 기술서
☐ indeed	(강조하여) 정말
☐ integrity	진실성, 무결함

08

☐ apply to	~에 적용하다

☐ performance	실적, 수행 능력
☐ tend to R	~하는 경향이 있다
☐ short term	단기
☐ that being the case	그렇다면, 사정이 그러하다면
☐ eventually	결국, 끝내
☐ associate	연관 짓다
☐ increment	증가, 인상
☐ reward	보상해주다
☐ incremental	서서히 증가하는
☐ overwhelm	압도하다
☐ enormity	엄청남, 막대함
☐ profession	직종, 분야

09

☐ expert	전문가
☐ insist	주장하다
☐ miasma	나쁜 공기(분위기)
☐ fancy	화려한
☐ term	용어
☐ assumption	가정
☐ pass along	넘기다, 전달하다
☐ inhabit	살다, 거주하다
☐ quarter	처소, 숙소
☐ germ	균
☐ come along	나타나다, 생기다
☐ overnight	하룻밤 새
☐ microbe	미생물
☐ sweeping	전면적인, 광범위한
☐ surgeon	외과 의사
☐ adopt	채택하다
☐ antiseptic	소독약
☐ antibiotic	항생제
☐ momentously	중대하게
☐ ordinary	평범한
☐ thoroughly	철저하게, 완전히
☐ cuts and scrapes	찰과상
☐ iodine	요오드
☐ irrelevant	무관한
☐ density	농도, 밀도

10

☐ follower	추종자
☐ critical	중대한, 비판적인
☐ equation	방정식, 상황
☐ appreciate	감사하다, (진가를) 인정해주다
☐ subordinate	하급자, 종속된 사람
☐ passively	수동적으로
☐ obediently	고분고분하게
☐ over time	시간이 지남에 따라
☐ theory	이론
☐ gradually	점차
☐ worth ~ing	~할 가치가 있는
☐ note	주목하다
☐ regard	점, 사항
☐ restrict	제한하다
☐ exert	가하다, 행사하다
☐ for a length of time	상당 시간 동안
☐ deny	부인하다, 부정하다
☐ participate in	~에 참여하다

결국엔 성정해 영어 하프모의고사
기적사 DAY 32 핵심어휘

01

☐ overt	공공연한, 명백한
☐ fictitious	허구의, 가상의
☐ prosperous	성공한, 번영한
☐ arguable	논란의 여지가 있는

02

☐ reserved	[사람·기질이] 쌀쌀한, 마음을 털어놓지 않는; [언행이] 조심스러운, 주저하는, 말이 없는
☐ garrulous	말이 많은
☐ impromptu	즉흥적인

☐ taciturn	말수가 없는	
☐ dubious	의지할 수 없는, 의심스러운	

03

☐ enervate	무기력한
☐ indifferent	냉담한, 무관심한
☐ talkative	말이 많은
☐ ambitious	야망의

04

☐ shake a leg	서둘러 하다
☐ drop the ball	실수하다
☐ talk through one's hat	비현실적인 이야기를 하다
☐ call a spade a spade	터놓고 이야기하다

05

☐ entrepreneur	사업가, 기업가
☐ internship	인턴직, 인턴사원 근무
☐ tailor	조정하다, 맞추다
☐ mastery	숙달, 통달
☐ keep up with	~을 따라잡다
☐ evolving	발전하는

08

☐ unrelated	관계가 없는
☐ knock down	때려눕히다, 쓰러뜨리다
☐ reasoning	논거, 추론
☐ momentum	추진력, 탄력
☐ get[have] ··· under your belt	···을 달성하다, 차지하다
☐ come to	달하다, 다다르다, 이르다
☐ precise	정확한, 명확한
☐ manageable	처리할 수 있는, 감당할 수 있는
☐ accomplish	달성하다, 이루다
☐ achieve	이루다

☐ skill	능력, 역량, 솜씨
☐ belief	확신, 믿음

09

☐ theorize	이론을 세우다
☐ germ	세균
☐ rigorous	혹독한, 가혹한
☐ debate	논쟁
☐ exhalation	날숨, 숨을 내쉼
☐ vapor	(수)증기
☐ hold	지속[계속]되다
☐ well-ventilated	환기가 잘 되는
☐ ward	병동
☐ accepted	일반적으로 인정된
☐ founder	창시자, 창설자
☐ epidemiology	역학(疫學), 전염병학
☐ claim	주장하다
☐ cholera	콜레라
☐ water borne	수인성의, 물로 전파되는
☐ microorganism	미생물
☐ epidemic	유행병, (유행성) 전염병
☐ argument	주장, 논거
☐ manufacturing	제조의
☐ blame	···을 탓하다, ··· 책임[때문]으로 보다
☐ noxious	유독한, 유해한
☐ exhaust	배기가스
☐ skeptical	회의적인, 의심하는
☐ point of view	관점, 견해
☐ in line with	···와 비슷한, ···에 따르는
☐ ventilation	환기, 통풍

10

☐ authoritative	권위의, 강압적인
☐ induce	초래하다, 야기하다
☐ spur	···을 자극하다, 격려하다, 고무하다
☐ misunderstanding	불화, 오해
☐ exaggerated	과장된

☐ comprehend	이해하다
☐ require	필요로 하다, 요구하다
☐ instruction	지시, 명령, 설명
☐ conduct	수행하다, 처리하다
☐ delegate	위임하다
☐ inquisitive	탐구적인, 호기심 있는
☐ make an inquiry	질문하다
☐ supporting	지지하는
☐ body	주요부, 중심, 본체
☐ effectively	효율적으로
☐ hence	따라서
☐ essential	중요한, 필수의
☐ quality	자질, 자격
☐ possess	보유하다, 소유하다
☐ followership	추종, (지도자를) 따르는 것, (지도자에 대한) 지지, 충성
☐ complementary	보완적인, 보충적인

결국엔 성정혜 영어 하프모의고사
기적사 DAY 33 핵심어휘

01

☐ defy	거부하다
☐ sovereign	최고의, 주권의
☐ bogus	가짜의
☐ enigmatic	불가사의한, 수수께끼의
☐ pompous	자만하는, 화려한, 허풍 떠는

02

☐ ecstatic	무아지경의
☐ material	물질의, 물질, 육체의, 중요한
☐ systematic	조직적인, 체계적인
☐ reminiscent	회고의, 연상시키는

03

☐ frank	솔직한
☐ down-to-earth	현실적인, 견실한
☐ fave	인기 있는
☐ intimidating	위협적인

04

☐ dress up	옷을 차려입다
☐ dinner out	외식을 하다
☐ convenience store	편의점
☐ take ~ off	~(동안)을 쉬다
☐ twelve midnight	밤 열두 시

05

☐ competent	능숙한
☐ encounter	맞닥뜨리다, 마주치다
☐ insurmountable	대처할 수 없는
☐ cope with	~에 대처하다, 대응하다
☐ step-by-step	단계적인, 점진적인
☐ symbolic	상징적인, 상징하는

08

☐ work with	…을 연구[작업] 대상으로 하다
☐ complete	완료하다
☐ session	세션, 회기, 기간
☐ distal	(중심에서) 먼
☐ subgoal	하위 목표
☐ lead to	~로 이어지다, 이끌다
☐ completion	완수, 완료
☐ accurate	정확한
☐ turn out	…인 것으로 드러나다 [밝혀지다]
☐ proximal	(중심에서) 가까운, 인접하는
☐ intervention	개입
☐ self-efficacy	자기효능감(자신이 어떤 일을 성공적으로 수행할 수 있는 능력이 있다고 믿는 기대와 신념)

☐ deplete	대폭 감소시키다 [격감시키다]
☐ eliminate	제거하다, 없애다
☐ ameliorate	향상시키다, 개선하다
☐ disperse	…을 흩어지게 하다, 분산시키다

09

☐ sanitation	위생
☐ existing	기존의, 현존의
☐ lend weight to	…을 뒷받침[입증] 하다
☐ miasma	(지저분한·불쾌한) 공기 [기운/냄새]
☐ presence	존재, 있음
☐ poisonous	유독한
☐ vapor	증기
☐ suspend	〈먼지·미립자 등을〉 (공중·수중에) 떠 있게 하다, 부유(浮遊)시키다
☐ particle	입자
☐ decay	부식하다, 썩다
☐ characterize	특징짓다
☐ foul	(냄새가) 더러운, 악취 나는
☐ endure	오래가다[지속되다]
☐ make sense	타당하다, 말이 되다
☐ sanitary	위생의
☐ reformer	개혁가
☐ industrialization	산업화
☐ urbanization	도시화
☐ filthy	불결한, 지저분한
☐ tend to	~하는 경향이 있다
☐ focal point	(관심·활동의) 초점[중심]
☐ epidemic	전염병, 유행병
☐ disprove	틀렸음을 입증하다, 반박[반증]하다
☐ reject	거부하다
☐ merit	가치, 장점
☐ inadvertently	우연히, 의도치 않게

10

☐ process	과정, 절차
☐ emerge	생기다, 나타나다
☐ bind (bound – bound)	결속시키다, 묶다
☐ indicate	나타내다, 가리키다
☐ look to	~을 생각해[고려해] 보다
☐ advance	증진시키다, 개선하다
☐ perspective	관점
☐ identify	확인하다
☐ flaw	결함, 흠
☐ aspiring	포부[야심]를 가진
☐ seek to	~하도록 시도[추구]하다
☐ stand out from	…중에 두드러지다
☐ peer	동료, (법적·사회적으로) 동등한 사람
☐ serve	(사람을) 섬기다, 봉사하다, 모시다
☐ ensure	확실히 하다
☐ be willing to	기꺼이 ~하다
☐ on one's behalf	…의 이익을 위해, …을 대신하여

결국엔 성정해 영어 하프모의고사
기적사 DAY 34 핵심어휘

01

☐ conduct	수행하다, 운영하다, 안내하다
☐ convince	납득시키다, 설득하다
☐ plunge	급격히 감소하다, 추락하다, (물, 구멍 등에) 뛰어들다
☐ oppress	억압하다, (권력 등으로) 압박하다

02

☐ acquire	인수하다, 취득하다
☐ assert	주장하다
☐ transfer	양도하다, 옮기다, 바꾸다
☐ gratify	만족시키다

03

☐ tend	돌보다, ~하는 경향이 있다
☐ daunt	(기력을) 꺾다
☐ comprehend	이해하다, 포함하다
☐ frighten	놀라게 하다

04

☐ mention	언급하다
☐ subway station	지하철역
☐ monthly rent	월세
☐ afford	감당하다
☐ invitation	초대

05

☐ developing country	개발도상국
☐ globalization	세계화
☐ the Iron Curtain	철의 장막
☐ compete	경쟁하다, 겨루다
☐ problematic	문제가 있는
☐ obstacle	장애, 장애물

08

☐ flexible	유연한, 융통성 있는
☐ adapt to	…에 적응하다
☐ circumstance	상황
☐ leave	…을 (어떤 상태가) 되게 하다, …을 (어떤 상태) 그대로 두다
☐ make sense	이치에 맞다, 말이 되다, 타당하다
☐ priority	우선순위
☐ roll around	다가오다

☐ fit	건강한
☐ sleep-deprived	수면 부족의
☐ unproductive	비생산적인
☐ establish	확립하다
☐ inefficient	비효율적인
☐ accomplish	달성하다, 이루다

09

☐ infectious	전염성의
☐ chickenpox	수두
☐ pneumonia	폐렴
☐ microscopic organism	미생물
☐ prevent	예방하다
☐ infection	감염
☐ remarkably	몹시, 매우
☐ discovery	발견
☐ millennium	천년(pl. millennia)
☐ physician	내과 의사
☐ swampy	늪 같은, 습지가 있는
☐ blame	…을 탓하다, … 책임[때문]으로 보다
☐ microscope	현미경
☐ enable	가능하게 하다
☐ generation	세대
☐ microbiologist	미생물학자
☐ investigate	조사하다, 연구하다
☐ previously	이전에
☐ unseen	본 적이 없는, 미지의
☐ organism	유기체
☐ carry out	시행하다, 수행하다
☐ contribute towards	…에 기여하다[공헌하다]
☐ formation	형성
☐ proof	증거
☐ achievement	성과, 성취

10

| ☐ be capable of | ~할 수 있다 |

☐ cut out for	적합한, 알맞은
☐ contribution	기여, 공헌
☐ bring … to the table	(단체 등의 이익을 위해) …을 제공하다[기여하다]
☐ trick	비결, 요령
☐ qualified	자격 있는, 적합한
☐ fill	(지위 등을) 차지하다, (직무를) 맡아 하다
☐ desire	욕망, 욕구
☐ distinction	차이
☐ element	요소
☐ forefront	선두, 맨 앞
☐ be in charge	담당하다, 책임지다
☐ influential	영향력이 있는
☐ contribute	기여하다, 공헌하다

결국엔 성정혜 영어 하프모의고사
기적사 DAY 35 핵심어휘

01

☐ govern	지배하다, 관리하다
☐ settle	해결하다, 정착하다, 타협을 보다
☐ scrutinize	살펴보다, 조사하다, 검토하다
☐ adulate	아첨하다

02

☐ dissolve	분해하다
☐ triturate	갈다
☐ complete	끝나다, 완성하다
☐ abridge	축소하다

03

☐ occur	일어나다
☐ investigate	조사하다
☐ disjoint	해체하다
☐ remove	없애다

04

☐ paperwork	서류작업
☐ advice	조언
☐ spare time	여가
☐ encounter	맞닥뜨리다
☐ unexpected	예상치 못한

05

☐ well-dressed	(옷을) 잘 차려입은
☐ fancy	화려한, 값비싼, 일류의
☐ contagious	전염되는, 전염성의
☐ recall	상기하다, 생각나게 하다
☐ freshman	신입생

08

☐ dominate	지배하다
☐ discourse	논설, 담론
☐ evolution	진화, 발달
☐ kinship	혈족 관계, 친족 관계
☐ overlook	간과하다
☐ contribution	기여
☐ vegetal	식물의
☐ merely	단지
☐ in terms of	~측면에서
☐ caloric	칼로리의
☐ complementary	보완적인, 보충적인
☐ array	집합체, 무리, 모음
☐ acquire	획득하다
☐ persist	지속하다
☐ component	구성 요소
☐ requirement	요건, 필요조건, 필요
☐ process	가공하다, 처리하다
☐ consumption	섭취, 소비
☐ apportionment	배분, 할당
☐ fall to	~에게 책임이 주어지다
☐ represent	대표하다
☐ dynamic	역학

09

☐ sociologist	사회학자
☐ principal	주요한
☐ founder	창설자
☐ sociology	사회학
☐ approach	접근
☐ conflict	갈등
☐ academic system	교육 제도
☐ curriculum	교과 과정
☐ humanistic	인문학의, 인간성 연구의
☐ attention	관심, 주의
☐ psychology	심리학
☐ philosophy	철학
☐ ethics	윤리학
☐ eventually	결국
☐ academic appointment	교수직
☐ provincial	지방의
☐ result in	야기하다
☐ publication	출판, 발표
☐ gain	얻다
☐ recognition	인식, 인정
☐ earn	획득하다
☐ teaching appointment	교사직
☐ position	위치, 직책
☐ reform	개정하다
☐ introduce	도입하다

10

☐ collaborator	합작자, 협력자
☐ settle	정착하다
☐ guidance	지도, 안내
☐ vivid	선명한, 생생한
☐ medieval	중세의
☐ chivalry	기사도
☐ stylistically	양식상으로
☐ inspiration	영감
☐ melancholy	우울, 비애
☐ attenuated	매우 마른, 야윈

☐ exhibition	전시회
☐ influence	영향, 영향력
☐ decorative	장식의
☐ ecclesiastical	교회 조직의
☐ stained glass	스테인드글라스, 착색유리

결국엔 성정혜 영어 하프모의고사
기적사 DAY 36 핵심어휘

01

☐ make a face	얼굴을 찌푸리다, 침울한 표정을 짓다
☐ glance	흘끗 보다
☐ rejoice	크게 기뻐하다
☐ grimace	얼굴을 찡그리다

02

☐ guffaw	큰 웃음; 크게 웃다
☐ reflective	사색적인, 반영/반사하는
☐ chuckle	낄낄 웃음; 낄낄 웃다
☐ greet	반응을 보이다
☐ sarcastic	빈정대는, 비꼬는
☐ remark	발언, 말, 언급
☐ laughter	웃음
☐ means	수단
☐ ratify	비준/인가하다, 승인하다
☐ smirk	히죽 웃음; 히죽거리며 웃다
☐ tittle	작은 점
☐ giggle	낄낄 웃음; 낄낄거리다
☐ belly laugh	큰 웃음

03

☐ pearl	진주
☐ wink	깜박거리다, 반짝이다
☐ glimmer	희미하게 빛나다, 깜박이다

☐ cozen	속이다, 기만하다
☐ deceive	속이다, 기만하다
☐ brighten	밝히다

04

☐ so far	지금까지
☐ at all	조금도, 전혀
☐ rude	무례한
☐ slack off	빈둥대다
☐ initiate	시작하다
☐ haste	서두름, 급함
☐ keep one's chin up	용기를 잃지 않다

06

☐ severe	극심한
☐ acute	급성의
☐ respiratory	호흡(기)의
☐ SARS	중급 급성 호흡 증후군
☐ pneumonia	폐렴
☐ identify	확인하다
☐ infection	감염
☐ distress	고통
☐ respiratory distress	호흡곤란
☐ coronavirus	코로나바이러스
☐ epidemic	전염(병); 유행성의
☐ mammal	포유류

07

☐ figure out	생각해내다, 이해하다
☐ detective	수사관
☐ ordinary	평범한
☐ search for	찾다
☐ reveal	드러내다, 밝히다
☐ investigate	조사하다
☐ prehistoric	선사 시대의, 유사 이전의
☐ remain	잔해, 유물
☐ long-extinct	멸종된

☐ speculate about	추측하다, 짐작하다
☐ fascinating	흥미로운, 매력적인

08

☐ proper	(명사 뒤에 사용되어) 엄밀한 의미의
☐ double-layered	두 겹의
☐ occasionally	이따금
☐ convey	전달하다
☐ coherent	조리 있는, 일관성 있는
☐ one another	서로
☐ sequence	연속, 순서
☐ matter	중요하다
☐ specialized	전문화된
☐ exercise	행사하다, 발휘하다, 작용시키다
☐ relatively	상대적으로
☐ dialect	방언
☐ species	종
☐ white-crowned sparrow	노랑턱멧새
☐ from area to area	지역마다
☐ supposedly	아마, 추정상
☐ tell	구별하다
☐ note	음, 음표
☐ critical	중대한, 비판적인
☐ exist	존재하다

09

☐ psychologist	심리학자
☐ economics	경제(학)
☐ upend	뒤집다
☐ rational	이성적인
☐ along the way	그 과정에서
☐ discipline-crossing	여러 분야를 넘나드는, 여러 분야를 통합하는
☐ alter	바꾸다
☐ physician	(내과) 의사
☐ paper	논문
☐ outline	개요를 설명하다[짜다]

☐ strategic	전략적인, 전략상의
☐ label	부르다, 분류하다, 식별하다
☐ mediate	중재하다, 조정하다
☐ assessment	평가
☐ protocol	규약, 의례, 의식
☐ put off	미루다, 연기하다
☐ gut-based	감에 기반을 둔
☐ a number of	많은
☐ separate	분리된, 개별적인
☐ intuition	직감, 직관력
☐ structured	조직된
☐ call for	~를 필요로 하다
☐ analyze	분석하다
☐ attribute	특성, 속성
☐ assign	할당하다, 배정하다
☐ relative	상대적인
☐ holistic	전체론의
☐ percentile	백분위의
☐ possess	소지하다
☐ facilitate	용이하게 만들어주다

10

☐ fear	두려움
☐ threat	위협
☐ measure	방법, 수단
☐ perspective	관점
☐ stock trader	주식투자자
☐ approach	접근
☐ outcome	결과
☐ embrace	받아들이다

결국엔 성정혜 영어 하프모의고사
기적사 DAY 37 핵심어휘

01

☐ rejoice	기뻐하다
☐ augment	증가시키다
☐ occur	발생하다
☐ revise	개정하다, 수정하다, 조정하다, 바꾸다

02

☐ withdraw	~에서...을 빼다
☐ yoke	멍에, 속박
☐ sarcastic	빈정대는
☐ lethal	치명적인
☐ unwonted	드문
☐ bankrupt	파산한, 부도
☐ prevalent	만연한, 유행하는

03

☐ occurrent	우연한
☐ glimmering	희미하게 비치는
☐ mischievous	말썽부리는
☐ superlative	최고의, 최상급의, 과장된

04

☐ driver's license	운전면허
☐ summer vacation	여름 방학

06

☐ methodologies	방법론
☐ gravity	중력, 심각성, 중대성
☐ genome	게놈
☐ incidental	부수적인

07

☐ paper	논문, 서류, 종이
☐ review	검토하다
☐ literature	문학
☐ via	~을 통하여, ~을 거쳐

08

☐ universal	보편적인
☐ hallmark	특징
☐ humanity	인류
☐ vowel	모음
☐ consonant	자음
☐ syllable	음절
☐ string together	연결하다, 결합시키다
☐ cluster	자음군 (string에서의 str처럼 연이어 나타나는 자음들)
☐ surrounding	환경, 주변
☐ varied	다양한
☐ linguist	언어학자
☐ landscape	지형, 풍경
☐ evolve	진화하다
☐ race	인종

09

☐ attempt	시도하다
☐ figure out	알아내다, 파악하다
☐ psychological	심리학의
☐ perspective	관점
☐ draw on	의지하다
☐ cognitive psychology	인지 심리학
☐ manage to	~해내다
☐ team up	협력하다
☐ formulate	만들다
☐ prospect theory	전망 이론
☐ alternative	대안
☐ involve	포함하다, 수반하다
☐ in terms of	…에 관하여, … 면에서

☐ utility	효용, 실리, 유익
☐ relative to	…에 비례하여, …에 관하여
☐ reference point	(판단, 비교용) (참고) 기준
☐ absolute	절대적인
☐ outcome	결과
☐ frame	표현하다, 말하다
☐ indicate	나타내다, 가리키다
☐ loss-averse	손실을 회피하려 하는
☐ equivalent	동등한, 상당하는
☐ be willing to	기꺼이 ~하다

10

☐ achieve	달성하다, 성취하다
☐ irrespective of	…와 관계[상관]없이
☐ diversify	분산시키다
☐ anecdotal	일화적인
☐ wisdom	명언
☐ allocate	할당하다
☐ security	(증권·회사채 등의) 유가증권
☐ diversification	분산
☐ downside risk	(투자 예측시의) 가능 손실액, 가격 하락 리스크
☐ necessarily	반드시, 필연적으로
☐ return	수익
☐ leap	도약하다, 껑충 뛰다

결국엔 성정혜 영어 하프모의고사
기적사 DAY 38 핵심어휘

01

☐ preeminent	우세한, 출중한
☐ grimacing	얼굴을 찡그리는
☐ mandatory	필수의, 의무적인
☐ reversed	거꾸로의, 파기된

02

☐ disinter	발굴하다, 세상에 내놓다, 빛을 보게 하다
☐ subside	진정되다, 가라앉다, 드러눕다
☐ occupy	점령하다
☐ rejoice	기뻐하다

03

☐ controllable	지배할 수 있는
☐ insolvent	파산한
☐ outright	완전한, 솔직한, 무조건의
☐ convivial	친목적인, 우호적인

04

☐ valuable	귀중한
☐ moment	순간
☐ depressed	우울한
☐ language barrier	언어 장벽
☐ uneasy	불편한
☐ manage to	~간신히 ~하다
☐ classmate	학급 친구

06

☐ well-groomed	단정한, 말쑥한
☐ trimly	정돈하여, 손질하여
☐ refinement	세련, 고상함, 개선, 정제
☐ delicacy	섬세함, 사려 깊음, 연약함
☐ bearing	태도, 자세, 영향, 관련
☐ fierce	사나운, 격렬한, 맹렬한

07

☐ dentist	치과 의사, 치과
☐ preventative maintenance	예방 관리
☐ hear of	~에 대해 듣다
☐ ignore	무시하다

08

☐ linguist	언어학자
☐ examine	조사하다
☐ laboratory	실험실
☐ setting	환경
☐ contrasting	대조적인
☐ deliver	전하다, 전달하다
☐ analyze	분석하다
☐ consistently	일관하여, 지속적으로
☐ vocalization	발성
☐ acoustic	청각의, 음향의
☐ label	표식, 표시

09

☐ acronym	두문자어, 약어, 줄임말
☐ cognitive	인지적인
☐ bias	편향, 편견
☐ describe	묘사하다, 설명하다
☐ rational	합리적인
☐ refer to	표현하다, 말하다, 언급하다
☐ assert	주장하다
☐ take into consideration	고려하다, 참작하다
☐ regardless of	…에 관계없이
☐ coherent	앞뒤가 맞는, 조리 있는, 일관성 있는
☐ accurate	정확한
☐ reliable	신뢰할 수 있는
☐ incomplete	불완전한
☐ non-representative	대표적이지 않은

10

☐ absolutely	전혀
☐ intention	의도
☐ window(-)shop	쇼윈도 속을 보며 걷다
☐ out of the corner of one's eye	곁눈질로, 흘깃 보고
☐ customer service representative	고객 서비스 담당자

☐ take advantage of	…을 이용하다, …을 기회로 활용하다
☐ miss out (on something)	(참여하지 않음으로써 유익하거나 즐거운 것을) 놓치다
☐ unspecified	불특정한, 명시되지 않은
☐ involved with	…와 연관된
☐ be convinced	확신하다
☐ encourage	조장하다, 부추기다
☐ impulsive	충동적인
☐ trigger	촉발하다

결국엔 성정혜 영어 하프모의고사
기적사 DAY 39 핵심어휘

01

☐ adept	능숙한
☐ imprecise	모호한, 부정확한
☐ pragmatic	실용적인, 분주한
☐ hesitant	우유부단한, 주저하는
☐ perfervid	열정적인

02

☐ irresolute	우유부단한
☐ vulnerable	취약한, 민감한
☐ impassioned	열정적인, 인상적인
☐ cozen	속이다, 기만하다

03

☐ smirk	히죽거리며 웃다
☐ intervene	간섭하다, 화해시키다, 사이에 있다
☐ expound	설명하다, 해석하다
☐ undertake	떠맡다, 착수하다

04

☐ order	주문하다
☐ decide	결정하다

☐ suggestion	추천

06

☐ Iranian	이란 사람
☐ matter	중요하다
☐ civil war	내전
☐ kinship	친족
☐ lobby	영향력을 행사하다, 로비를 하다
☐ humanitarian	인도주의적인

07

☐ obstacle	장애, 장애물
☐ overcome	극복하다
☐ commitment	전념, 약속
☐ rejoice	크게 기뻐하다
☐ embrace	받아들이다, 수용하다, 포옹하다

08

☐ vary	다르다
☐ regionally	지역적으로
☐ avian	조류의, 새의
☐ species	종
☐ geographic	지리적인
☐ variation	차이, 변화
☐ vocal	음성의, 목소리의, 발성의
☐ dialect	방언
☐ natal	출생의
☐ territory	구역
☐ acquire	습득하다, 얻다
☐ peculiarity	특색
☐ rendition	(노래·음악의) 연주[공연]
☐ functional	기능적인
☐ significance	중요성, 의의, 의미
☐ elusive	붙잡기[파악하기] 어려운, 이해하기 어려운
☐ arise	생기다, 발생하다

ornithologist	조류학자
assume	추정하다
indicator	지표, 나타내는 것
genetic	유전적인
adaptation	적응
condition	환경
enable	가능하게 하다
presumably	아마
carry	(특질·특징을) 지니다
gene	유전자
adapt	적응시키다, 조정하다, 맞추다
breeding	번식
occur	발생하다
function	기능하다
promote	촉진시키다, 활성화하다
positive assortative mating	동종 교배
innate	타고난, 선천적인

09

investor	투자자
pitch	(물건을 팔거나 사람을 설득하기 위해 하는) 권유[주장], 홍보
present	(특히 손윗사람에게 …을 정식으로) 소개하다
highlight	강조하다
return	수익
decline	하락하다, 감소하다
prospect theory	전망 이론
assume	추측하다, 가정하다
gain	수익
loss	손실
averse	싫어하는, 꺼리는

10

neurotransmitter	신경 전달 물질
norepinephrine	노르에피네프린
response	반응

transporter	운반체
crucial	주요한
arouse	자극하다, 각성하다
loss aversion	손실 회피 성향
pronounced	명백한, 단호한
compared to	…와 비교하여
vary	다양하다, 각기 다르다
outcome	결과
impaired	손상된, 제 기능을 못 하는
addict	중독자
occur	발생하다
odds	(노름에서) 승률, 배당률
regulate	조절하다, 규제하다

기적사 DAY 40 핵심어휘

01

martyrdom	순교, 고난
obstinacy	완고함, 고집셈, 집요한 끈기
confidential	은밀한, 신용 있는
stimulating	도발적인, 자극적인, 격려가 되는
overt	명백한
concentrate	집중시키다, 전념하다

02

leverage	지렛대
deliberately	신중하게, 의도적으로
lightly	가볍게
fleshly	신체의, 속세의, 관능적인
promptly	즉시

03

☐ suicide	자살
☐ evidence	증거
☐ exclude	배제하다, 불가능하게 하다
☐ redeem	보상하다, 상환하다
☐ glimmer	희미하게 빛나다
☐ scatter	분배하다, 뿌리다, 쫓아 버리다

04

☐ interesting	흥미로운
☐ political protest	정치적 시위
☐ demonstration	시위
☐ peacefully	평화롭게
☐ nonviolent	비폭력의
☐ nonresistant	무저항의
☐ movement	운동
☐ similarity	유사성
☐ purpose	목적
☐ implement	시행하다
☐ affirmative action	차별 철폐 조처
☐ alleviate	완화하다
☐ sex discrimination	성차별
☐ contemporary society	현대 사회

06

☐ first impression	첫인상
☐ faulty	결함이 있는, 불완전한
☐ unconscious	무의식; 의식이 없는
☐ have no idea	전혀 모르다
☐ principal	교장; 주요한

07

☐ moral	도덕적인
☐ code	규칙, 암호
☐ conduct	행동, 처리
☐ disapprove of	~을 못마땅해하다
☐ conflict with	~와 충돌하다, 상충하다
☐ hold 목적어 in esteem	~을 존경하다

08

☐ perceptual	지각의, 지각에 의한
☐ schema	스키마, 도식, 개요
☐ impression	인상
☐ appearance	외모
☐ interaction	상호작용
☐ trait	특징, 특성
☐ perception	지각, 인식
☐ heuristic	휴리스틱, 발견적[경험적] 방법
☐ shortcut	지름길
☐ computation	계산
☐ symmetrical	대칭적인
☐ symmetry	대칭
☐ tendency	경향
☐ assumption	추정, 생각
☐ blessing	축복
☐ curse	저주
☐ make sense	이해하다
☐ complex	복잡한
☐ inaccurate	부정확한
☐ insufficient	부족한, 불충분한
☐ complicated	복잡한

09

☐ attempt	시도하다
☐ reduce	줄이다, 감소시키다
☐ optimism bias	낙관주의 편향
☐ particularly	특히
☐ promote	촉진시키다
☐ risky	위험한
☐ eliminate	제거하다, 없애다
☐ incredibly	믿을 수 없을 정도로, 엄청나게
☐ involve	포함하다, 수반하다
☐ participant	참가자

□ risk factor	위험 요소
□ encourage	장려하다
□ subject	연구[실험] 대상, 피험자
□ lead to	~로 이어지다
□ instance	사례, 경우
□ negatively	부정적으로
□ affect	영향을 미치다

10

□ oligarchic	과두정치의, 소수 독재 정치의
□ i.e.	즉
□ emerge	나타나다, 생기다
□ regain	되찾다, 회복하다
□ ultimate	최후의, 궁극적인
□ presidency	대통령의 지위[임기]
□ phenomenon	현상
□ representative	대표자
□ refer to	칭하다, 언급하다
□ oligarch	과두제 집권층의 일원
□ undergo	겪다
□ as a consequence	그 결과, 결과적으로
□ presidential election	대선, 대통령 선거
□ reshuffle	조직개혁
□ take place	발생하다
□ expand	확장하다
□ durable	견고한, 영속성 있는
□ efficient	효율적인
□ flaw	결점, 결함

결국엔 성정혜 영어 하프모의고사
기적사 DAY 41 핵심어휘

01

□ eliminate	제거하다, 없애다
□ cooperation	협조

□ enticing	유혹적인, 마음을 홀리는
□ enhanced	향상된, 강화한
□ fertile	풍부한, 비옥한
□ futile	무용지물의, 무효인

02

□ scratch the surface of	~을 수박 겉핥기식으로 다루다
□ superficially deal with	~을 피상적[표면적]으로 다루다
□ hit the nail on the head of	~에 대해 적절한 말을 하다, 요점을 찌르다
□ seize hold of	~을 붙잡다, 잡다
□ positively follow up on	~을 긍정적으로 끝까지 하다, ~을 긍정적으로 추적보도 하다

03

□ personal	개인적인
□ stick	내밀다, 붙이다, 찔리다
□ hurry	서두르다
□ interfere	참견하다, 간섭하다
□ sniff	코를 훌쩍거리다
□ resign	물러나다

04

□ tablecloth	식탁보
□ fit	맞다, 적합하다, 어울리다

07

□ saying	속담, 격언
□ affect	영향을 미치다
□ handle	다루다
□ stable	안정된, 안정적인
□ prevent A from B	A가 B하는 것을 막다

08

□ mapping	지도 제작

☐ application	응용(분야)
☐ molecular	분자의
☐ geophysicist	지구물리학자
☐ core	핵
☐ oceanographer	해양학자
☐ ocean floor	대양저, 해저
☐ imaginary	상상의, 허구의
☐ hazard	위험(요소)
☐ computerization	전산화
☐ virtual reality	가상현실
☐ artificial	인공의
☐ stimulate	자극하다
☐ entertainment	오락
☐ realm	영역
☐ general	전반적인, 일반적인
☐ related	관련된
☐ definition	정의, 규정
☐ cartography	지도 제작
☐ employ	이용하다, 고용하다
☐ resemble	닮다
☐ frontier	경계, 새로운 분야

09

☐ performance	수행(능력)
☐ recipient	수신자
☐ past	지난, 과거의
☐ estimate	추정(치)
☐ frequency	빈도
☐ content	내용(물)
☐ prod	자극하다, 찌르다
☐ corrective	교정의
☐ sap	약화시키다
☐ initiative	진취성, 계획
☐ adequate	적절한, 중간의
☐ settle into	~에 자리 잡다
☐ advancement	발전, 진전
☐ specific	구체적인
☐ sanction	제재; 승인
☐ lay off	해고하다

☐ explicit	분명한
☐ time	시간을 맞추다[조절하다]
☐ customize	맞춰주다, 주문 제작하다
☐ tailor	맞추다, 조정하다
☐ avoid	피하다
☐ goal-oriented	목표 지향적인

10

☐ pursue	추구하다
☐ discipline	교육, 훈련, 훈육
☐ poem	시
☐ experimental	실험적인
☐ incorporate	통합시키다
☐ authentic	진짜의
☐ dialect	지역 언어
☐ adapt	변형시키다, 적응시키다
☐ embrace	수용하다
☐ cadence	리듬, 억양
☐ fuse	결합(융합)시키다
☐ prejudice	편견
☐ witty	재치 있는

결국엔 성정혜 영어 하프모의고사
기적사 DAY 42 핵심어휘

01

☐ ambivalent	상반하는 감정을 품은, 애증이 엇갈리는
☐ itinerant	순회하는, 떠도는, 순회자, 편력자
☐ fertile	풍부한, 비옥한
☐ singular	전례 없는, 뛰어난, 유일한

02

☐ ostensibly	표면상으로
☐ seize	~을 붙잡다, 잡다

☐ abhor	혐오하다
☐ loathe	혐오하다
☐ dislike	싫어하다

03

☐ erode	손상시키다, 침식하다, 부식하다
☐ sniff	코를 훌쩍거리다
☐ modify	변경하다
☐ assemble	모이다
☐ (the) authorities	정부 당국

04

☐ audition	오디션; 춤, 연기, 노래 등을 테스트 하다(받다)
☐ organize	개최하다
☐ apply	지원하다
☐ lend a hand	도움을 주다
☐ cross	꼬다
☐ keep a straight face	웃음을 참고 무표정한 얼굴을 하다
☐ keep one's fingers crossed	행운을 빌다

07

☐ be proud of	~을 자랑스러워하다
☐ precaution	예방조치
☐ conventional	관습적인, 관례적인
☐ snap	쉬운, 수월한
☐ life work	평생의 일

08

☐ identify	발견하다, 확인하다
☐ chromosome	염색체
☐ transmit	전송하다, 전달하다, 전염시키다
☐ relatively	상대적으로
☐ inherited	유전의

09

☐ fortnightly	2주일마다, 격주로
☐ make sense	타당하다, 말이 되다
☐ milestone	중요한 시점[단계]
☐ commitment	약속, 의무, 책임
☐ postpone	미루다, 연기하다

10

☐ privileged	특권[특전]을 가진
☐ complexion	피부색, 안색
☐ colorism	색 차별주의
☐ off-limits	출입[사용] 금지의
☐ upper-crust	상류층의
☐ routinely	일상적으로
☐ administer	시행하다, 실시하다
☐ social circle	사교계
☐ admit	받아들이다, 가입[입학]을 허락하다

결국엔 성정혜 영어 하프모의고사
기적사 DAY 43 핵심어휘

01

☐ interfere	간섭하다, 방해하다, 지장을 주다
☐ acquire	인수하다
☐ surmise	추측하다, 짐작하다
☐ entice	유혹하다

02

☐ sniff	코를 킁킁거리다
☐ revoke	폐지하다
☐ abolish	폐지하다
☐ annul	무효로 하다

03

☐ scornful	경멸하는
☐ valiant	용맹한
☐ hurry	서두르는
☐ terrifying	무서운

04

☐ anxiety	근심
☐ exchange student	교환학생
☐ once-in-a-lifetime	일생일대의
☐ attend	다니다
☐ abroad	해외에
☐ accompany	수반하다
☐ responsibility	책임
☐ recommend	추천하다
☐ path	길
☐ under the table	남몰래
☐ out of the blue sky	예기치 못하게
☐ to one's heart's content	원하는 대로, 흡족하게
☐ at the top of one's lungs	목소리를 높여

07

☐ wrapper	포장지
☐ disposable	일회용의
☐ drink container	음료 용기
☐ generate	만들어 내다, 발생시키다
☐ cut down on	~을 줄이다
☐ reusable	재사용할 수 있는

08

☐ illustration	도해, 삽화
☐ arrange	배열시키다
☐ hierarchical	계층적인
☐ represent	표현하다, 나타내다
☐ descriptive	기술적인, 서술적인
☐ define	정의하다
☐ mutual	상호의, 서로의

☐ applicable	적절한
☐ acknowledge	인지하다, 확인하다, 인정하다
☐ discipline	지식 분야, 학과목
☐ portray	묘사하다
☐ consequently	결과적으로
☐ broaden	넓히다, 확장시키다
☐ existing	기존의

09

☐ misconception	오해
☐ give a raise	급여를 인상하다
☐ reveal	밝히다
☐ recognition	인정, 표창
☐ contribution	기여, 공헌
☐ fulfilling	성취감을 주는
☐ contribute to	…에 기여하다, 공헌하다
☐ neglect	등한시하다, 무시하다
☐ when it comes to	…에 관한 한
☐ take A for granted	A를 당연시하다

10

☐ earn one's living	생계를 꾸리다
☐ phenomenal	놀라운, 경이로운
☐ acceptance	수용, 받아들임
☐ prerogative	특권
☐ apex	꼭대기, 정점
☐ relevance	관련(성)
☐ precisely	바로, 꼭, 정확히
☐ reservoir	저장소
☐ artistry	예술적 재능
☐ reflect	반영하다
☐ count	넣어 생각하다, 포함시키다
☐ controversial	논란을 일으키는
☐ gauge	(평가, 판단 등의) 기준

결국엔 성정혜 영어 하프모의고사
기적사 DAY 44 핵심어휘

01

☐ pundit	권위자, 전문가
☐ brag	자랑하다
☐ enhanced	향상된, 강화한
☐ ingenuous	순진한, 천진난만한
☐ problematic	논란의 여지가 있는, 미해결의
☐ sneering	조롱하는, 비웃는

02

☐ sneak out	몰래 빠져나가다
☐ vigilant	조금도 방심하지 않는, 조심성 있는
☐ cautious	조심하는, 신중한
☐ circumspect	신중한
☐ tremendous	거대한
☐ prudent	신중한, 검약하는

03

☐ cordial	다정한
☐ personal	개인적인
☐ methodical	조직적인, 꼼꼼한, 공들인
☐ genial	상냥한, 다정한
☐ gutless	무기력한

04

☐ apply	지원하다
☐ hands-on experience	실전 경험
☐ overwhelming	압도적인, 대항할 수 없는
☐ play it by ear	임기응변으로 대처하다
☐ bite the bullet	어떻게든 견뎌내다
☐ keep one's nose clean	나쁜 일에서부터 멀어지다

☐ bite off more than one can chew	과욕을 보인다

07

☐ primitive	원시적인, 원초적인
☐ match	맞수, 호적수
☐ encounter	만남, 직면
☐ slay	죽이다, 살해하다
☐ bring+목적어+down	~을 쓰러뜨리다
☐ clothe	~에게 옷을 입히다

08

☐ cartography	작도, 지도 제작
☐ essentially	본질적으로
☐ geographical	지리학의
☐ allied	관련된, 동종의
☐ occupation	직업
☐ evolve	진화하다
☐ surveying	측량
☐ satellite	인공위성
☐ remote	원격의, 먼
☐ sensing	감지, 탐지
☐ aerial	공중의, 항공의
☐ photogrammetry	(항공사진에 의한) 사진 측량[제도]법
☐ hydrography	수로 측량
☐ geodesy	측지학
☐ geomatics	지리정보학[연구]
☐ geoscience	지구 과학, 지학
☐ boundary	경계, 한계
☐ integrate	통합시키다
☐ applied	응용의
☐ geography	지리학
☐ essential	필수적인, 극히 중요한
☐ visualization	시각화, 구체화
☐ spatial	공간의

09

constructive	건설적인
underused	충분히 이용[활용]되지 않는
well-rounded	(문제·프로그램 따위가) 균형이 잡힌
implication	(행동·결정이 초래할 수 있는) 영향[결과]
consistently	지속적으로
typo	오타
reiterate	반복하여 말하다, 반복하다
rectify	(잘못된 것을) 바로잡다
come up with	(해답·아이디어 등을) 찾아내다[내놓다]
timeframe	(어떤 일에 쓰이는) 시간[기간]

10

narrative	서술, 기술
evolve	(점진적으로) 발달[진전]하다
consequence	결과
era	시대
inspiration	영감, 고취
destination point	목표[목적] 지점
discipline	(지식, 학문 등) 분야
address	(문제·상황 등에 대해) 고심하다[다루다]
heritage	(국가·사회의) 유산

결국엔 성정혜 영어 하프모의고사
기적사 DAY 45 핵심어휘

01

sunset years	황혼기
agreeable	알맞은, 동의할 만한, 상냥한
uncanny	불가사의한, 신비로운
sanguinary	피를 흘리는, 포악한
futile	무용지물인, 무효인

02

Epistemologist	인식론자
inquisitive	탐구적인, 캐묻기 좋아하는
combative	전투적인
analytical	분석적인
nosy	꼬치꼬치 캐묻는
meddlesome	참견하기 좋아하는
superficial	피상적인

03

obliterate	없애다
divulge	폭로하다, 파헤치다
let off	발사하다, 내리게 하다
annihilate	전멸시키다
stick	고수하다

04

aurora	오로라
look forward to	~를 기대하다
vegetarian	채식주의자
suffer from	~을(를) 앓다
chronic disease	만성 질병
contemporary society	현대 사회
exhausted	피곤한, 지친
time-off	일을 쉰 시간(수)

07

rush	급히 움직이다, 서두르다
efficiency	효율성, 능률성
suffer	악화되다, 고통 받다, 시달리다, 겪다
mindful	~을 의식하는, ~에 유념하는

□ steal+목적어[사물]+from+목적어[대상]	~을 ~에게서 빼앗다

08

□ add to	…을 늘리다[증가시키다]
□ buoyancy	부력
□ relatively	상대적으로
□ bulk	부피, 크기
□ shallow	얕은
□ comparatively	비교적
□ negatively	반대 방향으로, 부정적으로
□ buoyant	부력이 있는, 물에 뜨는
□ pectoral fin	가슴지느러미
□ lift	상승력, 양력
□ energy-efficient	에너지 효율적인, 연비가 좋은
□ blimp	비행선
□ make sense	이치에 맞다
□ ecosystem	생태계
□ beware	조심하다
□ efficiently	효율적으로

09

□ various	다양한
□ vast	거대한
□ inefficient	비효율적인
□ seldom	좀처럼[거의] ~않는
□ acquire	습득하다, 획득하다
□ what is called	소위, 이른바
□ accurate	정확한
□ spouse	배우자
□ lack	…이 없다[부족하다]

10

□ tuition	학비, 등록금
□ in-state	주내(州内)의
□ portion	부분
□ waive	[규칙 등을] 적용하지 않다
□ out-of-state	주외(州外)의, 다른 주의
□ room and board	식사비를 포함한 숙박 요금, 식사를 제공하는 하숙
□ waiver	면제
□ commute	통학하다, 통근하다
□ graduate study	대학원 과정
□ scholarship	장학금
□ be entitled to	…를 받을 자격이 있다
□ apply for	신청하다
□ financial aid	학자금 융자
□ inclusive of	…를 포함한
□ postgraduate student	대학원생

기적사 DAY 46 핵심어휘

01

□ mathematics	수학
□ optics	광학
□ mechanical physics	역학 물리학
□ unprecedented	전례 없는, 엄청난
□ mediocre	보통의
□ suggestive	시사하는, 암시적인, 도발적인
□ unsurpassed	유례없는, 매우 뛰어난
□ provocative	도발적인, 자극하는

02

□ charge forward	돌진하다
□ aloof	초연한, 냉담한
□ incensed	분개한, 격노한
□ unbiased	공정한, 편견 없는
□ unpretentious	순수한, 겉을 꾸미지 않는

03

☐ take on	고용하다, 떠맡다
☐ get on	타다, 오르다
☐ put upon	속이다, 부당하게 이용하다
☐ hit upon	불현듯 떠올리다 [생각하다]

08

☐ staggering	충격적인, 믿기 힘든
☐ financial	금융의, 재정의
☐ rational	이성적인
☐ aware of	~을 인식하는
☐ status	지위, 상태
☐ excessively	과도하게
☐ make a bet on	~에 돈을 걸다
☐ complicated	복잡한
☐ derivative	파생상품
☐ virtual	가상의
☐ currency	통화
☐ radically	근본적으로, 극단적으로
☐ crisis	위기
☐ breakdown	붕괴
☐ progress	진전, 진척, 진행
☐ address	다루다
☐ capitalize	자본화하다
☐ regulator	규제 기관
☐ conduct	수행하다
☐ stress test	부하 검사

09

☐ complex	복잡한
☐ over the course of	~동안
☐ rise up	올라가다
☐ hierarchy	계층, 계급
☐ attain	얻다, 달성하다
☐ partnership	동업자 관계
☐ striking	눈에 띄는, 현저한
☐ eliminate	제거하다

☐ alternative	대안(의)
☐ in-group	내집단
☐ outcome	결과

10

☐ visionary	선지자
☐ segment	분야, 부분
☐ fundamentally	근본적으로
☐ opposite number	상대방
☐ leverage	~에게 영향을 주다; ~에 지레를 사용하다
☐ competitive advantage	경쟁 상의 우위
☐ come about	발생하다, 생기다
☐ well-tested	입증된
☐ extensive	광범위한
☐ reference	참조, 언급
☐ indicate	암시하다
☐ at any rate	아무튼
☐ pragmatist	실용주의자
☐ value	가치 있게 여기다

결국엔 성정혜 영어 하프모의고사
기적사 DAY 47 핵심어휘

01

☐ perspective	관점
☐ contingent	의존적인, 일어나기 쉬운, 우발적인, 조건으로 하는
☐ cardinal	가장 중요한, 진홍색의; 추기경
☐ suggestive	시사하는, 암시적인, 도발적인
☐ mandatory	강제적인, 명령을 받은

02

☐ decently	깔끔하게, 상당히

☐ hit upon	불현듯 떠올리다 [생각하다]
☐ peculate	횡령하다
☐ misappropriate	(남의 돈, 재산을) 유용하다
☐ usurp	빼앗다

03

☐ on the ground of	~라는 까닭으로
☐ procrastinate	미루다, 연기하다
☐ card	결정적 수단, 카드, 표, 명함
☐ peel	벗기다
☐ meddle	간섭하다
☐ distribute	분배하다
☐ dawdle	꾸물거리다

04

☐ impossible	불가능한
☐ despite	~에도 불구하고
☐ a copycat	모방하는 인간
☐ under fire	공격을 받다
☐ blue blood	명문, 귀족 가문
☐ talk through one's hat	비현실적인 이야기를 하다

08

☐ boast	자랑하다, 뽐내다
☐ destruction	파괴
☐ wrought	만들어진, 초래된
☐ flourish	번영하다
☐ succeed to	…를 잇다, 계승하다
☐ eliminate	없애다, 제거하다
☐ apparent	외견상의, 겉보기의
☐ touch off	촉발하다, 야기하다
☐ plunge	밀어 넣다, 쑤셔 박다
☐ simplistic	지나치게 단순화된
☐ contraction	침체, 불황
☐ underlying	근본적인, 기저의
☐ spiral	소용돌이, 나선형

☐ despair	절망
☐ multiple	복수의, 다수의
☐ recession	불황, 침체

09

☐ juvenile	청소년의; 청소년
☐ engage in	…에 관여하다
☐ finding	결과, 결론
☐ adolescent	청소년
☐ prone to	…하기 쉬운
☐ peer	또래
☐ delinquency	비행, 범죄

10

☐ pragmatic	실용적인
☐ factual	사실의
☐ occurrence	사건, 일어난 일
☐ visionary	선지적인, 예언적인
☐ utopian	이상향의
☐ manner	방식
☐ path	(목표에 이르는) 길, 방향
☐ weigh	(결정을 내리기 전에) 따져 보다, 저울질하다
☐ obstacle	장애물

결국엔 성정혜 영어 하프모의고사
기적사 DAY 48 핵심어휘

01

☐ head off	막다, 회피하다
☐ prevent	막다
☐ review	평가하다, 재검토하다
☐ correct	수정하다
☐ flatter	아첨하다

02

☐ provocation	도발, 자극

☐ regime	정권
☐ charge with	~으로 가득 채우다
☐ make over	양도하다, ~을 고치다
☐ come down with	~ (병 등에) 걸리다
☐ put up with	~을 참다

03

☐ eulogize	칭송하다, ~을 칭송하다
☐ venerate	숭배하다
☐ glorify	찬미하다
☐ discard	버리다
☐ idolize	숭배하다

04

☐ movie theatre	영화관
☐ on screen	상영하는
☐ recommendation	추천
☐ pop up	튀어나오다
☐ nuts about	~에 빠지다
☐ a wildcard	만능의 패
☐ goose bumps	소름
☐ in the wake of	~의 영향을 받아
☐ sour grapes	지기 싫어함, 오기
☐ in the heyday of	한창 시절에

08

☐ intervene	개입하다, 끼어들다
☐ ingrained	깊이 배어든, 뿌리 깊은
☐ disastrous	처참한
☐ at large	전반적으로
☐ catastrophic	비극적인, 파멸의
☐ ripple effect	파급효과
☐ conceptually	개념적으로
☐ bailout	긴급 구제
☐ in comparison to	…와 비교하여
☐ allocate	할당하다

09

☐ pronounceable	발음할 수 있는

☐ unreliable	믿을 수 없는, 신뢰할 수 없는
☐ trivia	퀴즈, 상식
☐ undesirable	바람직하지 않은
☐ untrustworthy	믿을 수 없는, 신뢰할 수 없는

10

☐ debate	논쟁
☐ entertain	(생각·희망·감정 등을) 품다
☐ viability	생존 능력, 실행 가능성
☐ traction	끄는 힘, 매력
☐ pragmatism	실용주의
☐ fire	해고하다
☐ withdraw	중단[취소/철회]하다
☐ destitute	빈곤한, 결핍한
☐ cost	희생하게 하다, 잃게 하다
☐ pursue	추구하다

결국엔 성정혜 영어 하프모의고사
기적사 DAY 49 핵심어휘

01

☐ undocumented	증거가 없는, 증명서를 가지지 않은
☐ anecdotal	일화의, 일화적인, 입증되지 않은
☐ unsubstantiated	입증되지 않은
☐ unsurpassed	유례없는, 매우 뛰어난
☐ enraged	격노한
☐ perplexed	이해하기 어려운, 당혹한, 복잡한

02

☐ Ministry of Justice	법무부
☐ National Intelligence Service	국가정보원

☐ aloof	초연한, 냉담한
☐ adjuvant	보조의
☐ auxiliary	보조의
☐ accessory	부수적인

03

☐ hit upon	불현듯 떠오르다
☐ snapping turtle	무는 힘이 강해 한번 물면 잘 떨어지지 않는 거북류의 동물을 총칭. 한국식으로는 자라, 미국식으로는 악어거북
☐ augmentative	증가적인, 증대하는
☐ tenacious	강인한, 완강한
☐ precise	정확한, 꼼꼼한
☐ supplementary	보충의, 임시의

04

☐ upcoming	다가오는
☐ feedback	피드백
☐ crowd	군중
☐ black out	깜깜해지다
☐ confident	자신감 있는
☐ comfortable	편안한
☐ advice	조언
☐ roll out the red carpet	각별히 환영하다
☐ keep an ear to the ground	새로운 것을 주의 깊게 지켜보다
☐ have a chip on one's shoulder	안 좋은 감정을 갖다
☐ have butterflies in one's stomach	가슴이 철렁철렁하다, 걱정을 하다

08

☐ asset	자산
☐ five-fold	5배의
☐ soar	급증하다, 치솟다
☐ disbursement	지출, 지불
☐ go under	도산하다, 파산하다

☐ trigger	촉발시키다
☐ meltdown	붕괴, 폭락
☐ unpredictable	예측할 수 없는
☐ inevitable	불가피한

09

☐ stereotypically	전형적으로, 진부하게
☐ be labeled as	…로 분류되다
☐ applicant	지원자
☐ counterpart	상대방
☐ call in	부르다, 요구하다
☐ compendium	목록, 개론, 개요
☐ disturbing	충격적인
☐ bias	편견

10

☐ pragmatism	실용주의
☐ pragmatist	실용주의자
☐ on one's (own) merits	시비곡직에 따라
☐ hesitant	주저하는, 망설이는
☐ messy	골치 아픈, 성가신, 지저분한
☐ prone to	…을 잘하는
☐ ideologue	이론적 공론가
☐ indecisive	결단력 없는, 우유부단한
☐ decisive	결단력 있는
☐ reference	인용, 언급
☐ mission statement	강령
☐ irrelevant	관계없는, 무의미한
☐ endure	참다, 견디다
☐ rigmarole	복잡한 절차
☐ seeming	…하게 보이는

결국엔 성정혜 영어 하프모의고사
기적사 DAY 50 핵심어휘

01

☐ tyrant	독재자, 폭군
☐ inhibit	억제하다
☐ talk out of	설득해서 그만두게 하다
☐ obstruct	막다
☐ put upon	속이다, 부당하게 이용하다
☐ crony	친구, 측근자

02

☐ float over	떠다니다
☐ concede	인정하다, 허용하다
☐ collude	공모하다
☐ deal with	대하다, 처리하다

03

☐ masculine	남자다운
☐ restraint	억제, 규제
☐ impair	손상시키다
☐ emulate	따라 하다, 모방하다
☐ brush up on	복습하다
☐ hit upon	불현듯 떠올리다 [생각하다]

04

☐ check-up	건강검진
☐ regular	정기적인
☐ backbone	척추
☐ posture	자세
☐ exercise	운동하다
☐ effective	효과적인
☐ spinal issues	척추 문제
☐ progress	진전, 성과
☐ a big bug	대단한 인물
☐ fit as a fiddle	건강한

☐ on the water wagon	금주하고 있는
☐ a needle in a haystack	발견하기 힘든 것

08

☐ represent	보여주다, 기술하다, 표현하다
☐ specific to	…에 한정된, … 고유의
☐ genuine	진짜의
☐ Cockney	런던 토박이, 런던 내기; 런던 사투리; 런던 사투리의
☐ well-to-do	부유한
☐ effective	효과적인

09

☐ confer	부여[수여]하다
☐ make sense	이해되다, 의미가 통하다, 타당하다
☐ territory	영토
☐ ordnance	군수품, 육지 측량
☐ trigonometrical	삼각법의
☐ survey	측량
☐ shift	변화
☐ routing	여정의 설정
☐ descriptive	도형 묘사의
☐ grid	격자, (지도의) 경선·위선
☐ triangulation	삼각측량
☐ notion	개념
☐ reference point	기준
☐ scalability	확장성
☐ cartography	지도 제작
☐ advancement	발전

10

☐ adopt	채택하다, 택하다
☐ process	과정, 절차
☐ performance	성과, 수행, 업무

☐ potentially	어쩌면, 잠재적으로, 가능성 있게
☐ awkward	어색한
☐ on the go	끊임없이 일하는, 계속 일하는
☐ praise	칭찬
☐ matter	중요하다, 문제되다

결국엔 성정혜 영어 하프모의고사
기적사 DAY 51 핵심어휘

01

☐ reverence	존경심
☐ kerchief	스카프
☐ meticulously	조심스럽게
☐ carefully	조심스럽게
☐ hurriedly	급히
☐ decisively	결정적으로
☐ delightfully	즐겁게, 유쾌하게

02

☐ at the drop of a hat	즉시
☐ immediately	즉시
☐ punctually	시간대로, 늦지 않게
☐ hesitantly	주저하면서, 말을 더듬으며
☐ periodically	정기적으로

03

☐ make up to	아첨하다, 친해지려고 하다
☐ brush up on	복습하다
☐ shun away from	~로부터 떠나다
☐ come down with	(병에) 걸리다, 몸져눕다

04

☐ mentally	정신적으로

☐ financially	재정적으로
☐ strategic	전략적인, 중요한
☐ segment	부문, 부분, 영역

07

☐ up-to-the-minute	가장 최근의, 최첨단의
☐ externally	외적으로, 외부에서
☐ attract	마음을 끌다, 끌어들이다, 불러일으키다
☐ cover	다루다, 덮다, 걸치다
☐ celebrity	유명 인사, 연예인

08

☐ ailment	질병
☐ short-lived	오래가지 못하는
☐ long-lasting	오래 지속되는
☐ exist	존재하다
☐ realm	영역
☐ ancient	고대의
☐ astronomer	천문학자
☐ examine	조사하다, 점검하다
☐ sustain	지속시키다, 유지하다
☐ extraterrestrial	외계의
☐ physiological	생리학적인
☐ psychological	심리적인
☐ suffer from	~로 고통을 겪다
☐ motion sickness	멀미
☐ gravity	중력
☐ differentiate	구별하다
☐ internal	내부의
☐ confusing	혼란스러운
☐ result in	~를 초래하다
☐ nausea	매스꺼움

09

☐ bother	애쓰다, 괴롭히다
☐ literature	문학
☐ gene	유전자
☐ physics	물리학

☐ disorientation	혼미, 혼란, 방향 감각 상실
☐ anomie	사회적 무질서
☐ despair	절망
☐ disenchantment	각성, 환멸
☐ unified	통합된
☐ origin story	기원 설화
☐ enchantment	황홀감, 현혹
☐ argue	주장하다
☐ inevitable	불가피한, 필연적인
☐ rationality	이성, 합리성
☐ modernity	현대성
☐ fragment	조각, 파편

결국엔 성정혜 영어 하프모의고사
기적사 DAY 52 핵심어휘

01

☐ executive	경영자, 행정부의
☐ make up to	~에게 아첨하다
☐ reciprocate	앙갚음하다, 보답하다
☐ get even with	복수하다
☐ retort	응수하다

02

☐ intuitive	직관력 있는, 통찰력이 있는
☐ knowing	빈틈없는, 박식한 체하는
☐ sly	교활한, 은밀한
☐ eerie	괴상한
☐ retrospective	회고의
☐ punctual	시간을 잘 지키는
☐ abrupt	가파른, 갑작스러운, 퉁명스러운

10

☐ date from	~부터 시작되다
☐ Great Depression	대공황
☐ surplus	잉여의
☐ agricultural	농업의
☐ commodity	상품
☐ explosion	폭발
☐ fuel	연료를 공급하다, 자극하다
☐ shift	이동시키다
☐ federally	연방 차원에서
☐ fund	자금을 지원하다
☐ steadily	꾸준히
☐ nutritious	영양가 높은
☐ underprivileged	혜택을 받지 못한, 소외계층의
☐ if anything	말하자면
☐ boost	신장시키다
☐ shortage	부족

03

☐ make up to	아첨하다, 친해지려고 하다
☐ candid	솔직한
☐ egotistic	자기중심인, 독선적인
☐ heedless	부주의한, 경솔한
☐ haphazard	우연의, 우연히

04

☐ flight attendant	승무원
☐ elbow	팔꿈치
☐ zoo	동물원
☐ post office	우체국

07

☐ a good deal of	다량의, 많은
☐ encode	암호화하다, 부호화하다

☐ auditory	청각의
☐ interval	간격, 사이, 중간 휴식 시간
☐ recall	기억해 내다, 상기하다

08

☐ devastating	엄청나게 충격적인
☐ malfunction	기능 불량, 고장
☐ seal	밀봉[밀폐] 부분[물질]
☐ destabilize	불안정하게 만들다
☐ astronaut	우주 비행사
☐ civilian	민간인, 일반 시민
☐ fatality	사망자

09

☐ sociologist	사회학자
☐ aspiring	출세 지향적인
☐ liberal	진보의
☐ Calvinist	아주 엄격한, 칼뱅파의
☐ orthodoxy	정통[정교적] 신앙
☐ tolerant	관대한, 너그러운
☐ theology	신학
☐ Puritan	청교도의
☐ morality	도덕
☐ diminish	줄어들다, 감소하다
☐ distance	멀어지게[거리를 두게] 하다
☐ spurn	냉대하다, 퇴짜 놓다, 일축하다
☐ prolonged	오래 끄는, 장기의
☐ grief	슬픔
☐ in turn	결국, 그 결과
☐ authoritarian	권위주의적인
☐ obedience	복종
☐ bleak	암울한, 어두운, 황량한
☐ mark	상처를 남기다, 자국을 남기다, 오점을 남기다
☐ contribute to	…의 원인이 되다
☐ agony	고통, 고뇌
☐ haunt	(오랫동안) 계속 문제가 되다[괴롭히다]

10

☐ estimated	추측의, 예상의
☐ be enrolled in	…에 등록하다
☐ indicator	지표, 표시
☐ access	접근, 접촉[접근] 기회
☐ nutritionally	영양적으로
☐ adequate	충분한, 적절한

결국엔 성정혜 영어 하프모의고사
기적사 DAY 53 핵심어휘

01

☐ suffocate	숨차다, 억압하다
☐ asphyxiate	질식시키다
☐ smother	질식시켜 죽이다
☐ stifle	질식시키다
☐ place	~에 두다

02

☐ surreptitious	비밀의
☐ faultless	결점이 없는
☐ clandestine	비밀리에 하는, 은밀한
☐ superb	훌륭한, 웅장한
☐ interdependent	상호 의존의

03

☐ perpetuate	영속하게 하다
☐ make up to	아첨하다, 친해지려고 하다
☐ disentangle	얽힘을 풀다, 해방되다
☐ eternize	영원성을 부여하다
☐ reexamine	재시험하다, 재검토하다, 재심문하다

04

☐ come across~	~을 우연히 마주치다
☐ sincere	진실된

☐ apology	사과
☐ forgive	용서하다
☐ hold one's tongue	묵묵부답하다
☐ be caught red-handed	현장에서 발각되다
☐ live from hand to mouth	겨우 삶을 연명하다
☐ put one's foot in one's mouth	실언하다

07

☐ launch	착수하다, 출시하다
☐ article	기사
☐ investigation	조사, 연구
☐ enhance	높이다, 향상시키다
☐ coincidentally	(우연히) 일치하여, 동시적으로
☐ supplement	부록, 보충

08

☐ orientation	방향
☐ gravitational force	중력
☐ transition	변환, 이동
☐ voyage	여정, 여행
☐ adaptation	적응
☐ physiological	생리학적인
☐ couple to	…에 연결하다
☐ motion sickness	멀미
☐ nausea	메스꺼움
☐ illusion	환상, 환각
☐ disorientation	방향 감각 상실, 혼미
☐ astronaut	우주 비행사
☐ exposure	노출
☐ centrifuge	원심 분리기

09

☐ define	정의하다
☐ reigning	단연 우세한, 지배적인
☐ primarily	주로

☐ remarkable	놀라운
☐ case	사실, 실정
☐ consciousness	의식, 자각
☐ perennially	지속적으로, 영속적으로
☐ imperil	위태롭게 하다, 위험에 빠뜨리다

10

☐ mandate	명령하다
☐ be entitled to	~할 자격이 있다, 권리가 주어지다
☐ district	구역
☐ humiliation	수치심, 창피함, 굴욕
☐ outstanding	아직 처리되지 않은, 미지불된
☐ debt	빚
☐ forster care	위탁 가정[시설]
☐ accrue	모으다, 축적하다
☐ intimidate	위협하다, 겁을 주다
☐ embarrassment	무안함, 당혹감
☐ obedience	복종
☐ subject	받게 하다
☐ nutrient	영양분

결국엔 성정혜 영어 하프모의고사
기적사 DAY 54 핵심어휘

01

☐ persecute	박해하다, 처벌하다
☐ conscience	양심의 가책, 뉘우침, 회한
☐ compunction	죄책감, 거리낌
☐ complacency	자기만족
☐ qualm	꺼림직함, 양심의 가책, 불안
☐ scruple	양심

02

☐ let on	폭로하다, 자백하다, ~인 체하다
☐ make up for	보상하다
☐ take on	고용하다, 떠맡다
☐ draw on	이용하다

03

☐ morose	우울한
☐ refuge	쉼터, 피난처
☐ cranky	짜증을 내는
☐ dour	시무룩한, 음침한
☐ melancholy	구슬픈
☐ enticing	유혹적인

04

☐ frustrated	짜증 난
☐ report	보고서
☐ useless	소용없는, 쓸모없는
☐ square one	원점
☐ bread and butter	생계 수단
☐ go on a wild goose chase	헛된 노력을 하다
☐ have ants in one's pants	초조하다
☐ hit the bull's eye	목표를 달성하다
☐ teach an old dog new tricks	노인에게 새로운 것을 가르쳐 주다 (오래된 사고방식은 고치게 하기 힘들다)

07

☐ sufficient	충분한
☐ conclude	끝내다, 결론을 내리다
☐ authoritative	권위적인, 권위 있는
☐ variable	변수; 가변적인, 변동이 심한
☐ lasting	지속적인, 영속적인

08

☐ adapt to	…에 적응하다

☐ subside	가라앉다, 진정되다
☐ astronaut	우주 비행사
☐ contribution	공헌, 기여
☐ payload specialist	(우주선에 탑승하여 실험하는) 탑승 과학 기술자
☐ be subjected to	…을 받다[당하다]
☐ adopt	채택하다
☐ devise	창안[고안]하다
☐ scale	척도, 등급
☐ incapable	몸을 제대로 가누지 [정신을 차리지] 못하는
☐ be dubbed	…로 불리다
☐ apparently	보기에, 외견상으로
☐ no more than	고작, 겨우
☐ underestimated	과소 평가되는
☐ unintentional	의도하지 않은, 고의가 아닌
☐ trivial	사소한, 하찮은
☐ unwitting	자신도 모르는, 본의 아닌
☐ abrupt	갑작스러운, 돌연한

09

☐ paradoxical	모순적인, 역설적인
☐ outcome	결과
☐ significant	커다란, 주요한
☐ render	(어떤 상태가 되게) 만들다
☐ rather	오히려
☐ unify	통합시키다
☐ enchanted	매혹된, 황홀한
☐ cosmic	장대한, 우주의
☐ aesthetic	미의, 심미의
☐ coherent	일관적인
☐ conduct	경영, 운영, 처리
☐ set	(특수) 사회, 집단
☐ parameter	한계, 제한(범위)
☐ cosmos	질서, 우주
☐ whole	전체, 완전체
☐ if	…더라도[…이긴 하지만]
☐ old fashioned	구식의

10

☐ significant	커다란, 주요한
☐ in lieu of	… 대신에
☐ meet	(필요, 요구 등을) 충족시키다
☐ eliminate	제거하다, 없애다
☐ restrict	제한하다
☐ a la carte	특별 주문의, 따로따로 시키는

결국엔 성정혜 영어 하프모의고사
기적사 DAY 55 핵심어휘

01

☐ notorious	악명이 높은
☐ lousy	형편없는, 볼품없는
☐ reconcilable	조화시킬 수 있는
☐ disreputable	평판이 안 좋은
☐ outlandish	기이한, 이국풍의
☐ destitute	가난한, 가지지 않은

02

☐ unreliable	의지할 수 없는
☐ impeccable	결점이 없는, 죄를 범하지 않는
☐ instrumental	주된 역할을 하는, 악기로 연주되는
☐ innocent	결백한

03

☐ equitable	공정한, 정당한
☐ provocative	도발적인
☐ reasonable	합리적인
☐ impartial	공정한
☐ unbiased	편견에 치우치지 않은

04

☐ ultimate	최종적인
☐ promising	유망한
☐ salary	월급, 급여
☐ first priority	최우선
☐ capitalist society	자본주의 사회
☐ realistic	현실적인
☐ perspective	관점
☐ devastating	파괴적인, 비탄스러운
☐ money talks	돈으로 다 된다
☐ pigs may fly	말도 안 되는 일
☐ dead broke	완전히 파산하여
☐ on the house	무료로
☐ a couch potato	TV를 보며 소파에 앉아 감자를 먹는 게으른 유형의 사람

07

☐ frame	표현하다, 틀에 넣다
☐ leave+목적어+목적격 보어	~을 ~한 상태가 되게 하다
☐ appropriately	적절하게
☐ as opposed to	~와는 정반대로, ~와는 대조적으로
☐ disclose	밝히다, 폭로하다, 드러내다
☐ associate A with B	A를 B와 연관 짓다

08

☐ realm	영역, 분야
☐ rare	드문
☐ mortal being	인간, 죽는 존재
☐ envision	상상하다, 마음에 그리다
☐ pragmatist	실용주의자
☐ peer into	자세히 들여다보다
☐ smirk	능글맞은 웃음
☐ indelible	지워지지 않는
☐ destiny	운명
☐ prophet	예언자

☐ visionary	선지자
☐ oracle	현인
☐ remarkable	놀라운, 주목할 만한
☐ improbable	일어나지 않을 듯한, 기발한
☐ figment	허구, 꾸며낸 것
☐ Jetsons	젯슨 가족(우주의 자동화된 주택에 사는 젯슨 가족을 중심으로 벌어지는 일상 이야기를 담은 애니메이션)
☐ dream up	생각해 내다

09

☐ mandate	명령, 칙령, 지령
☐ federal	연방의
☐ subsidy	보조금
☐ district	구역, 지구
☐ scramble to R	(앞을 다투어) ~하려고 애쓰다
☐ cover	(무엇을 하기에 충분한 돈을[이]) 대다[되다]
☐ turn to	의지하다, 의존하다
☐ consist of	…로 구성되다
☐ restrict	제한하다
☐ declare	선언하다, 공표하다
☐ outcry	강력한 항의
☐ indicate	나타내다, 보여주다, 가리키다
☐ innutritious	영양 불량의, 영양분이 없는

10

☐ textile	직물, 섬유
☐ industry	산업
☐ nickname	~에게 별명을 붙이다
☐ cottonopolis	방적의 도시
☐ innovative	혁신적인
☐ steam-driven	증기로 움직이는
☐ manufacturing	제조
☐ large-scale	대규모의
☐ surrounding	주변의

☐ productive	생산적인
☐ cotton spinning	면방적
☐ take place	발생하다
☐ iconic	상징이 되는
☐ convert	변하게 하다, 개조하나
☐ flat	(연립주택, 다세대 주택 등을 포함하는) 아파트식 주거지
☐ sparkling	반짝이는, 생기 넘치는
☐ glassy	유리 같은
☐ high-rise	고층 건물

결국엔 성정해 영어 하프모의고사
기적사 DAY 56 핵심어휘

01

☐ pore over	살펴보다, 세세히 보다
☐ examine	살펴보다, 조사하다, 검토하다
☐ distribute	나눠주다, 배포하다
☐ discard	버리다
☐ correct	수정하다

02

☐ celestial	하늘의, 천체의
☐ vastness	광대함
☐ employ	이용하다, 고용하다
☐ unerring	정확한
☐ voyage	항해, 여행, 탐험
☐ planetary	행성의, 지구의
☐ travail	노고, 진통; 산고를 겪다
☐ faultless	정확한, 결점 없는
☐ unreliable	의지할 수 없는
☐ gutless	무기력한
☐ unscientific	비과학적인

03

☐ issuance	발급, 발행, 배포

☐ minimize	최소화하다, 과소평가하다
☐ appreciating	(가치를) 정당하게 평가하기
☐ aggravating	악화시키기
☐ meditating	숙고하기
☐ facilitating	쉽게 하기, 용이하게 하기

04

☐ sound	적절한, 건강한
☐ mechanic	수리공, 정비사
☐ appointment	약속, 임명, 예약

06

☐ transient	일시적인, 순간적인
☐ be free of	~에서 자유롭다
☐ whereas	~이지만, ~임에 반하여
☐ monitor	측정하다, 감시하다, 관찰하다
☐ cumulative	누적되는

08

☐ boast of	자랑하다, 뽐내다
☐ wired	컴퓨터 시스템에 연결된
☐ addiction	중독
☐ drop dead	급사하다
☐ exhaustion	탈진
☐ skip	건너뛰다
☐ self-destructive	자기 파괴적인
☐ intensely	강렬하게
☐ embrace	수용하다
☐ ready	손쉬운, 준비된
☐ come at a price	상당한 대가를 치르다

09

☐ ease	완화하다
☐ regulation	규제
☐ revise	개정하다, 수정하다
☐ draw up	만들다, 작성하다

☐ strategy	전략
☐ curfew	출입제한 시간
☐ impose	적용하다, 부과하다
☐ access	접속하다, 접근하다
☐ enact	제정하다
☐ addiction	중독
☐ permit	허가하다, 허용하다
☐ adolescent	청소년
☐ lift	해제하다, 폐지하다
☐ curb	(특히 좋지 않은 것을) 억제하다
☐ loosen	약화시키다, 느슨하게 하다
☐ aggravate	악화시키다
☐ reinforce	강화하다
☐ tackle	(힘든 문제 상황과[을]) 씨름하다, 부딪치다, 다루다
☐ implement	시행하다, 실시하다
☐ intensify	심화시키다, 강화하다

10

☐ observe	관찰하다
☐ constantly	끊임없이, 거듭
☐ the minute	...하자마자
☐ manifested	명시된, 분명한
☐ surrounding	인근 환경, 주변 환경
☐ environment	환경
☐ architecture	건축, 건축물
☐ construct	건설, 구성
☐ collective	집단의, 공동의
☐ consciousness	자각, 의식
☐ relevant	관련 있는, 적절한
☐ conceive	계획하다
☐ reflection	반영
☐ surround	둘러싸다, 에워싸다
☐ presence	존재
☐ participation	참여
☐ legacy	유산
☐ manifestation	징후, 표명
☐ futuristic	초현대적인

기적사 DAY 57 핵심어휘

01

☐ sleek	매끈한, 유선형의
☐ ring a bell	반응을 불러일으키다, 생각나게 하다
☐ discard	버리다
☐ divulge	폭로하다, 파헤치다
☐ dismay	겁먹게 하다, 당황하게 하다

02

☐ convert	~을 변하게 하다, 변형시키다
☐ proliferate	증식하다, 급증하다
☐ reproduce	번식하다
☐ pore over	탐독하다, 살펴보다
☐ revise	복습하다, 개정하다, 변경하다
☐ resemble	닮다, 같다

03

☐ reserved	말을 잘 하지 않는
☐ introspective	자기 성찰적인
☐ mediating	조정하는
☐ restrained	자제하는, 차분한

04

☐ go through	뒤지다
☐ homecoming party	귀향 파티
☐ closet	옷장
☐ select	선정하다
☐ bury the hatchet	평화를 구하다, 무기를 거두다, 화해하다
☐ blow one's own trumpets	허풍을 떨다
☐ have a frog in one's throats	목이 쉬다
☐ be dressed up to the nines	최상의 옷을 차려입다

06

☐ effect	효과, 영향, 결과
☐ others	다른 사람들
☐ accomplished	기량이 뛰어난, 재주가 많은
☐ so as to+ 동사원형	~하기 위해서
☐ as to+목적어	~에 관해

08

☐ compulsive	강박적인, 강제적인
☐ addict	중독자
☐ deprivation	부족, 결핍
☐ immerse	몰두하게 하다, 몰입시키다
☐ comprised of	…로 구성된
☐ dehydrated	탈수 상태의
☐ malnourished	영양 부족의
☐ agoraphobia	광장 공포증
☐ identify A with B	A를 B와 동일시하다
☐ popularize	대중화하다
☐ reclusive	은둔한, 세상을 버린
☐ adolescent	청소년
☐ withdraw from	…에서 철수하다, 끊다, 중단하다

09

☐ aversion	싫어함, 혐오
☐ rational	합리적인
☐ roof over one's head	거처
☐ as such	이와 같이, 그러한 것처럼
☐ irrational	비합리적인
☐ return	수익
☐ hold	간주하다, 생각하다
☐ fundamentally	근본적으로
☐ loom large	(걱정·위기 등이) 크게 다가오다
☐ averse	싫어하는

10

☐ cultivate	배양하다, 양성하다, 계발하다
☐ bestow	주다, 부여하다
☐ a host of	많은
☐ mindfulness	마음 챙김(현재 순간을 있는 그대로 수용적인 태도로 자각하는 것)
☐ intentional	의도적인
☐ mindful	집중하는, 유념하는, 마음에 새기는
☐ involve	포함하다, 수반하다
☐ grasp	쥐다, 잡다
☐ immune functioning	면역 기능
☐ cope with	대항하다, 대처하다, 극복하다
☐ exuberant	원기 왕성한
☐ empathetic	공감적인
☐ secure	불안이 없는, 안정된

결국엔 성정해 영어 하프모의고사
기적사 DAY 58 핵심어휘

01

☐ unpretentious	수수한
☐ profane	모독적인, 불경한
☐ eccentric	비정상적인
☐ adventitious	우발적인, 부정의, 외래의

02

☐ gutless	무기력한
☐ partisanship	당파심
☐ preliminary	서두의, 준비의, 예비의
☐ aberrant	비정상인, 엉뚱한
☐ contradictory	모순되는
☐ principal	주요한

03

☐ clandestine	비밀의, 은밀한
☐ diplomatic	외교적인
☐ avenue	방법, 수단
☐ dub	~이라고 부르다, 찌르다
☐ facilitating	용이하게 하는
☐ covert	비밀의, 은밀한
☐ furtive	은밀한
☐ surreptitious	비밀리의
☐ condescending	생색내는 듯한, 잘난척하는

04

☐ prepare	준비하다
☐ platform	타는 곳, 승강장
☐ global warming	지구 온난화
☐ aggravate	악화하다
☐ speed bump	방지턱

06

☐ entirely	전적으로, 완전히, 전부
☐ vibration	진동, 흔들림
☐ auditory	청각의
☐ stimulus	자극
☐ transfer	전하다, 옮기다, 바꾸다
☐ overall	전반적인, 전체의

08

☐ famed	아주 유명한
☐ skyscraper	고층 건물, 마천루
☐ reside	거주하다
☐ urban	도시의
☐ ratio	비율
☐ hold	유효하다, 적용되다, 들어맞다
☐ essentially	근본적으로, 본질적으로
☐ equivalent	맞먹는, 동등한, 상당하는
☐ density	밀도, 밀집

claustrophobic	폐쇄 공포증의
infrastructure	기반 시설
put it	말하다
fiber optic	광섬유의
steep	급격한, 가파른
remoteness	멀리 떨어짐
seldom	좀처럼 ~않는
proximity	근접, 가까움
barely	거의 ~않는

09

corporate governance	기업 지배구조
as well as	…뿐만 아니라 ~도
occurrence	사건, 일어난 일
translate	(다른 형태로) 바뀌다
acquisition	인수
indicator	지표
landfall	산사태
utility	공익[공공]사업
take a hit	타격을 입다
project	예상[추정]하다
moderate	보통의, 중간의, 적당한

10

habitually	습관적으로
become[be] used to	…에 익숙해지다
daydream	공상, 백일몽
identify	확인하다
impending	다가오는
association	관련, 연관, 연상
self-preservation	자기 보호
dictate	…을 좌우하다, …에 영향을 주다
attached to	…에 소속된, …에 연관된
outcome	결과

결국엔 성정혜 영어 하프모의고사
기적사 DAY 59 핵심어휘

01

separate	구별하다
reinforce	강화하다
head off	~을 피하다, ~의 앞을 가로막아 진로를 방해하다
distribute	나눠주다, 배포하다

02

gasp	숨이 차다, 헐떡거리다
evoke	불러일으키다
shun away from	피하다
inspect	자세히 살펴보다, 조사하다
desert	버리다, 탈주하다

03

ingenuous	솔직한, 순진한
innocent	순진한, 결백한
childlike	순진한
inconclusive	결론에 이르지 못하는

04

relieve	해소하다, 완화하다
tremendous	어마어마한, 엄청난
sweets	단 음식들
tension	긴장
alleviate	완화하다
strain	짓누르다
desire	욕망
lose heart	실망하다
lose one's head	자제심을 잃다
paint the town red	신명 나게 놀다
beat one's head against the wall	달걀로 바위 치다

06

☐ response	응답, 반응
☐ visualization	시각화, 구상화
☐ hypothesis	가설
☐ state	진술하다, 말하다
☐ restrict	제한하다, 방해하다

08

☐ boast	자랑하다, 뽐내다
☐ exclusive	배타적인, 독점적인
☐ restriction-free	통제가 없는
☐ select	상류 사회의, 고급의
☐ threadbare	빈약한, 초라한, 케케묵은
☐ alternative	대안
☐ latter	후자
☐ curate	관리하다, 조직하다
☐ propaganda	선전
☐ dated	구식의
☐ dub	별명을 붙이다
☐ decrepit	노후한, 낡은
☐ afford	(금전적) 여유가 되다
☐ figure	수치
☐ entirety	전체
☐ restrict	제한하다, 통제하다
☐ instrument	수단, 도구
☐ convey	전달하다, 전하다

09

☐ fluctuation	변동, 오르내림
☐ equity	주식
☐ reverse	실패, 좌절, 후퇴
☐ shrink	줄다, 감소하다
☐ appetite	기호, 좋아함

10

☐ the here and now	현시점, 현재
☐ occur	일어나다, 발생하다
☐ dwell on	…을 곱씹다 [깊게 생각하다]

☐ identify	확인하다, 발견하다
☐ implement	실행하다
☐ mull over	…에 대해 곰곰이 생각하다
☐ cling on to	…에 매달리다, 달라붙다

결국엔 성정혜 영어 하프모의고사
기적사 DAY 60 핵심어휘

01

☐ mediocre	보통의
☐ malignant	악의가 있는
☐ correct	옳은
☐ forthright	솔직한, 똑바른

02

☐ take over	인수하다
☐ collude	공모하다
☐ recognize	분간하다, 인정하다
☐ swamp	물에 잠기게 하다, 압도하다, 쇄도하다

03

☐ turbulent	사나운, 동요한
☐ daunt	기가 죽다
☐ submerge	물에 잠기게 하다, 매몰시키다
☐ moderate	누그러지다, 완화되다
☐ deviate	벗어나다, 일탈하다

04

☐ gorgeous	아름다운
☐ doubtlessly	의심의 여지가 없는
☐ worth	가치
☐ Now you're talking	이제야 말이 되다

06

☐ Holland	네덜란드
☐ acquainted with	~을 알고 있는
☐ illustration	삽화
☐ horticultural	원예의
☐ collaboration	공동 작업
☐ patron	후원자, 고객

08

☐ procrastination	미루는 버릇, 지연
☐ inability	무능, 불능
☐ anticipation	예상
☐ anxious	불안한, 걱정하는
☐ put off	미루다, 연기하다
☐ face	맞닥뜨리다, 부딪치다, 직면하다
☐ head-on	정면으로

09

☐ twinge	찌릿한 통증
☐ nasty	끔찍한
☐ take a fall	넘어지다, 떨어지다
☐ preventative	예방적인
☐ mammogram	유방조영상(유방암 검진용 X선 촬영)
☐ colonoscopy	대장내시경검사, 결장경 검사(법)
☐ spur	원동력[자극제]이 되다, 자극하다
☐ act on	…에 따라 행동하다 [조치를 취하다]
☐ full-blown	…의 모든 특성을 갖춘, 완전히 발달한[진행된]
☐ hypochondriac	심기증 환자
☐ constantly	지속적으로, 계속하여
☐ follow up with someone	…에게 연락을 취하다
☐ opposite	반대의
☐ modest	적당한

10

☐ repayment	상환(금)
☐ plummet	수직으로 떨어지다
☐ default on	…의 이행을 게을리하다
☐ repossess	압류하다
☐ liquidity	유동성
☐ on one's hands	…의 책임[부담]이 되어
☐ collapse	붕괴
☐ trigger	계기, 도화선
☐ regulate	규제하다
☐ aftereffect	여파